D0572167

$20 New User Discount

Valid to September 30, 1996

The **Canadian Internet Handbook** is pleased to announce that new users of the Internet can obtain a discount on their sign-up to the Internet. The Internet Service Providers listed on the reverse will provide a discount of $20 off your first month's usage, sign-up fee or some combination of both.

Coupon Participants

Accès au Noeud Internet Québec (A.N.I.Q.)
Accès-Cible
Access Route Canada Online Systems
Achilles Internet
AEI Internet Services
Alberta Supernet
ANSA Internet
Astra Network
Atlantic Connect
Atréide Communications
Axess Communications
Axion Internet Communications
Babillard Synapse
Barrie Connex
Barrie Internet
BC TEL Advanced Communications
Binatech Information Services
British Columbia Business Connections
Burlington Network Services
Cable Island
cafe.net
Canada Connect Corporation/ XCITE Technology
Chatham Internet Access
CIMtegration
CitéNet Telecom
ClicNet Télécommunications
CoastNet Designs
Communications Accesssibles Montréal
Les Communications DANIA
Communications Inter-Accès
Communications Vir
Connection MMIC
ConsuLan
Cosmos Network Access
Cyberlink Online
Cyberlink Systems
CyberPlus Technologies
Cyberspace Online Information Systems
Cybersurf Internet Access
Cyberus Online
Cycor Communications
Data Link Canada West (DLC-West)
Debug Computer Services
Deep Cove Online
Digital Ark Internet Services
DOCUSystems InterNet Services
Dtronix Internet Services
Durham Internet Services
Easy Internet
eConnect
E-Design
Electro-Byte Technologies
Elgin and St. Thomas Community Centre for Information Access
Enterprise Online
Escape Communications
EZENET
the FIX
Fleximation Systems
Foxnet Communications
Gate West Communications
Generation Net Services
Glen-Net Communications
Globalserve Communications
Global-X-Change Communications
Go! Online Communications
Grant Internet Communications

headwaters network
Helix Internet
HEXonX Internet Services Providers
HMT Internet
HookUp Communications
Horizon Net
ICE Online
iCOM Internet Services
Ilink Communications/Waterloo Internet Cooperative
Inasec
Infobahn Online Services
InfoHighway OnRamp Centre
Infomatch Communications
InfoRamp
Information Gateway Services Belville
Information Gateway Services Cornwall
Information Gateway Services Hawkesbury
Information Gateway Services Kingston
Information Gateway Services Kitchener-Waterloo
Information Gateway Services Oshawa
Information Gateway Services Peterborough
Information Gateway Services Renfrew County
Infostream Services
InfoTeck Centre de l'Ordinateur
Inline Information Services
Innovative Online
Intégration en Technologie de l'Information (ITI)
InterActions
Interactive Telecom
Inter*Com Information Services
Interhop Network Services
InterLinx
InterLog Internet Services
Internet Access-Worldwide
The Internet Café
Internet Connect Niagara
Internet Connectivity Services
Internet Express
Internet Front
Internet Global Info-Access
Internet Innovations
Internet JRV
InterNet Kingston
Internet Laurentides
Internet Light and Power™
Internet Montréal
Internet North
Internet Passport Services
Internet Saguenay Lac St-Jean
Internet Services and Information Systems (isis)
The InterNet Shop
Internet Solutions
Internet Sorel-Tracy
Internet Trois-Rivières
InternetXpress
Internex Online
InterNode Networks
Intertek Internet Technology Services, Inc., o/a ITSI
Intervider Communications
INTRANET Technologies
Island Internet
Island Net

Island Services Network
iSTAR Internet
Kingston Online Services
Kneehill Internet Services
Kootenay Network Systems
LANZEN
Lethbridge Internet Services
Lexicom
Lien Internet du Nord-Ouest (L.I.N.O.)
Local GlobalAccess
Logical Solutions Computer Systems
Magic Online Services Winnipeg
Magnett Internet Gateway
Managed Network Systems
Manitoba Telephone System
MapleNet Regina
MapleNet Technologies
Maritime Internet Services
Matrox SphereNet
MCD*Net-Mindemoya Computing and Design
MEG@Toon Station
Metrix Interlink
MGL Systems Computer Technologies
MicroAge Internet Access
MicroAge Internet Services
Millennia Net
MIND LINK! Communications
Montreal Internet
Mortimer Online
Multi-Médias Québec
MultiNet Media Solutions
Muskoka.com
Myna Communications
Navnet Communications
NBTel
Neocom Communications
NetAxis
Net Communications
NetCore
NetReach International
Network Enterprise Technology (NET)
Network North Communications
Networx Internet System
NirvCentre/Web Networks
Nisa Communications Group
Norfolk Internet Services
Norlink Communications & Consulting
North Okanagan Information Freeway
North Shore Internet Services
Northumbria Associates
NovaTech Computer Careers
Nucleus Information Service
Nunanet Circumpolar Communications
Nunavut Communications
o://info.web
OA Internet
Odyssée Internet
Odyssey Network
Okanagan Internet Junction
Online Internet Services
ONLink
ONRAMP Network Services
Osiris
Pacific Interconnect Enterprises
Passport Online
Pathway Communications
PCS Internet

PEINet
PG DataNet
Planet Internet Communications
Point Net Communication
Portage Internet Connection
Praline
ProNET Communications
Pronet Internet Services
PubNIX Montreal
Qnetix Computer Consultants
Resudox Online Services
Rocler: Les Services Télématiques Rocler
SaskTel
SeaFare Access
Sentex Communications
SERiX Technologies
Services Internet ABACOM
Services Internet de l'Estuaire
Silk Internet
SmartNet Internet Services
SooNet
Span Information Technology
SpectraNet Connections
SSI Micro
Stargate Connections
STAR-NET
St-Jean InterNet
Sunset Communications
Systems Knowledge Link
T-8000 Information Systems
Tamarack Computers
Technology Plus
Telnet Canada Enterprises
TELOS Online/TELOS Communications
TeQ Works
TerraPort Online
Ticnet—The Internet Companion
Times.net
TKM Software
TransData Communications
Travel-Net Communications
Trytel Internet
TST Consulting
ULTRAtech.net
UPC Communications Internet
UUNET Canada
UUNorth International
Vaxxine Computer Systems
V(DL)2
ViaNet
WBM Office Systems
Weslink DataLink
Whistler Networks
Wimsey Information Services
WINCOM (Windsor Information Network Company)
-the-Wire-
WorldCHAT™
WorldGate
WorldLink Internet Services
WorldLinx Telecommunications
World Online
World Tel
World Web Technologies
Worldwide Data Communications
World Wide Wave
XBASE Technologies
Xenon Laboratories
Xyberlynx Canada
Zerocom Technologies

1996 CANADIAN Internet HANDBOOK

Jim Carroll

Rick Broadhead

Prentice Hall Canada Inc.
Scarborough, Ontario

Canadian Cataloguing in Publication Data

Carroll, Jim, 1959-
  Canadian Internet handbook

1996 ed.
ISBN 0-13-505017-0

1. Internet (Computer network) — Handbooks, manuals, etc.
I. Broadhead, Rick. II. Title.

TK5105.875.I57C37   1996   004.6'7   C95-931897-6

Prentice Hall, Inc., Englewood Cliffs, New Jersey
Prentice-Hall International (UK) Limited, London
Prentice-Hall of Australia, Pty., Limited, Sydney
Prentice-Hall Hispanoamericana, S.A., Mexico
Prentice-Hall of India Pvt., Limited, New Delhi
Prentice-Hall of Japan, Inc., Tokyo
Simon & Schuster of Southeast Asia (Pte.) Ltd., Singapore
Editora Prentice-Hall do Brasil Ltda., Rio de Janeiro

ISBN: 0-13-505017-0

Acquisitions Editor: David Jolliffe
Production Editor: Avivah Wargon
Copy Editor: Betty Robinson
Production Coordinator: Anita Boyle-Evans
Cover/Interior Design: Olena Serbyn
Cover Image: Imtek Imagineering/Masterfile
Page Layout: Hermia Chung/Steve Lewis
Manuscript Processing: Deanne Walle

1 2 3 4 5   99 98 97 96

Printed and bound in U.S.A.

For Canadians, or for anyone who needs access to Canadian Internet resources, this book is a goldmine.

Matrix News, April 1994

…[The Canadian Internet Handbook] is quickly becoming the bible of Internet users.

The Evening Telegram, St. John's, April 4, 1994

One must-read is the Canadian Internet Handbook. Written in everyday language, it's a uniquely Canadian treatment of the on-line world.

Toronto Computes! April 1, 1994

If you are into using your computer for information, this book is for you. Bravo to its authors!

Allan Gould, Books Today column, Thomson News Service

…an invaluable resource for the half million Canadians already linked up to the Internet, as well as the millions more who are likely to get wired in the coming years.

Robert Wright, The Toronto Star, May 5, 1994

…tells you step by step exactly what you have to do to start surfing the Internet. And it does it in a language that even the rawest of computer users can understand. It not only tells you what the Internet is and how rapidly it's growing but takes you by the hand and leads you there.

Connie Woodstock, The Toronto Sun, April 3, 1994

This is a good book: well written, nicely organized and attractively illustrated. The Canadian Internet Handbook is for newbies and 'Net vets alike, and the appendices are a mother lode of 'Net information.

Paul Williams, The Chronicle-Herald/The Mail-Star, February 8, 1995

…a comprehensive, near-invaluable guide for Canadian cybernauts.

Kevin O'Connor, The Regina Leader Post, February 11, 1995

…THE book for Canadian Internet users.

Terry Taylor, The Province (Vancouver), December 11, 1994

The Canadian Internet Handbook calls itself the "Definitive Guide to the Internet in Canada." It is. For most people who are using or planning to use the Internet, this is probably the only book they'll ever need.

Keith Schengili-Roberts, The Computer Paper, December 1994

An exhaustive compendium of WWW services, software information and common-sense advice makes this book so important it should be placed right next to the monitor.

Jack Kapica, *The Globe and Mail*, June 30, 1995

An essential guide for Canadian users...

Gerry Blackwell, *Chatelaine*, April 1995

If you're wondering what the Net is really all about, pick up a copy of the Canadian Internet Handbook by Jim Carroll and Rick Broadhead. It's a good introduction to how the Internet evolved, what you need to get on the network, and what you can do once you're logged on.

Marketing Magazine, April 4, 1994

This widely available, national best-seller is quickly becoming the definitive text on Canadian Internetting.

Robb Cribb, *London Free Press*, August 21, 1995

...it's refreshing to read a balanced review of the Internet from knowledgeable veterans who admit it's no magical solution to all of Canada's problems.

Quill & Quire, May 1994

The handbook is bursting with Canadian content...

The Financial Post, March 26, 1994

I highly recommend this book to both new and experienced Internet users. The Canadian Internet Handbook has joined Newton's Telecom Dictionary as a key reference which I keep right beside my computer.

Ian Angus, editor, *TELEMANAGEMENT* magazine, The Angus Report on Communications Systems, Services, and Strategies, February 1995

This is one of the best books for helping anybody planning to get on the Internet and navigate around it once there.

Keith Schengili-Roberts, *The Computer Paper*, March 1995

The real value of this book lies in its pure business sense. Carroll and Broadhead have done their homework.

Sandra Mingail, *Toronto Computes!* September 1995

...it's the most comprehensive roadmap for the electronic highway I've seen for Canadians. I highly recommend it.

Richard Morochove, March 7, 1994

Contents

Foreword

by the Prime Minister of Canada, Jean Chrétien

Canada has always been a leader in the field of communications.

Think about it. Alexander Graham Bell's telephone. Marconi's historic wireless telegraph message from Newfoundland. Marshall McLuhan of the University of Toronto was regarded as the world's leading communications theorist. Vancouver author William Gibson is recognized as the world's leading author of fiction related to "cyberspace" — a term he coined. Canadian companies such as Northern Telecom are world leaders in telecommunications.

Considering our unique circumstances in Canada, our fascination with communications systems is easy to understand. With a small population thinly scattered across one of the world's largest countries, spanning six time zones, surrounded by three oceans, and including incredibly diverse and often difficult terrain, our communications systems have served the critical role of bringing Canadians together and preserving our culture and identity.

A century ago, it was the railroad that linked Canadians together. Today, the information highway is playing a similarly important role. It is vital to Canada's future prosperity.

In his observations on communications technology, Marshall McLuhan spoke of the "global village." Modern technology allows us to communicate with people around the world as easily as if they were just around the corner.

It's been said that in the electronic global village, the Internet is the main street.

It's a street that's becoming increasingly popular. I'm told that the *Canadian Internet Handbook* has been a number-one Canadian bestseller. I think that gives us some indication of how many Canadians are becoming involved.

My government believes that Canada's success in developing this technology will have profound implications for our country's future. Our communications technology can give Canada a crucial competitive edge in the global marketplace of the future. And that means jobs for Canadians. That's why the federal government is adopting a number of policies and programs to encourage the builders and users of the information highway.

In April 1994 we announced the formation of an Information Highway Advisory Council comprising experts and leaders representing a cross-section of Canadian society. The Council advises the government on the challenging issues that need to be resolved in order for Canadians to make the most of this exciting technology. If you are interested, the discussion papers of the Council's recommendations are available on the Internet.[1]

1 **http://info.ic.gc.ca/info-highway/ih.html**

With our SchoolNet initiative, the federal government is working with provincial ministries of education to encourage them to connect all of Canada's 20,000 schools and libraries to the information highway by 1998. We've already made a lot of progress.

Our government has also joined with businesspeople, educators, and researchers to develop the Canadian Network for the Advancement of Research, Industry and Education (CANARIE). We will support CANARIE's business plan to speed the development of key parts of the information highway in Canada by investing $80 million over four years, matched with an estimated $396 million from the private sector and the provinces. CANARIE provides funding for CA*net, one of the backbones of the Internet in Canada.

Our government also recognizes that the information highway offers exciting opportunities to deliver many government services more efficiently. Many federal departments are actively exploring how the Internet can be used most effectively.

Already, there are many different kinds of federal government information accessible on the Internet. For example, businesses can access information on opportunities for government procurement contracts with our open bidding system. We will be seeing a lot more of this in the future.

There is no doubt that computer networks such as the Internet will have a profound impact on the lives of Canadians — how we communicate, how we work, how we do business, how we learn, how we entertain ourselves.

I think that the Information Highway Advisory Council put it eloquently in their report to the government:

> The Information Highway is not a cold and barren highway with exits and entrances that carry traffic, but a series of rich and dynamic intersecting communities, large and small, north and south, east and west, populated by creative thinking people who reach out and enrich one another.

For Canadians who are intrigued by the Internet, the Canadian Internet Handbook is a very useful tool — even for those of a certain age, like me, who are sometimes daunted by the rapidly changing technologies we see all around us.

In these pages, you will learn more about a whole new world of exciting discoveries.

Jean Chrétien

Preface

This is the third edition of the *Canadian Internet Handbook*.

Our first 1994 edition was a small, 4 1/2 × 9–inch book with a little over 400 pages.

The second, 1995 edition expanded to a size of 7 × 9 inches, with just over 900 pages, thus reflecting growth in the Internet between editions.

And now this, the 1996 edition, is really *almost a brand new book*.

And the Internet has grown so quickly that we have had to split our efforts into two books — this Handbook, and a companion product, the *Canadian Internet Directory*.

If you bought either our 1994 or 1995 editions, you won't go wrong having purchased this edition, since it is really a very different, and we must say, very new edition.

There are a significant number of completely new chapters. We have updated and modified extensively other, older material. And we have combined many of the Canadian Internet resources into one comprehensive index found in our *Canadian Internet Directory*.

Why have we changed the book so much? Four words: *World Wide Web* and *Netscape*. Quite simply, the Web and the software from Netscape have come to significantly alter the landscape of the Internet.

What's new in this book? Almost everything — let's take a look, chapter by chapter.

The **Foreword** by the Prime Minister of Canada, Jean Chrétien.

Chapter summaries at the beginning of each chapter that highlight important facts and lessons from the chapter.

Chapter 1, What Is the Internet?, is *mostly new*, reflecting many of the changes which have occurred in the Internet through the last year. And, in particular, we've introduced new sections which focus on the future impact of the Internet as the technology that drives it continues to move forward at a blinding speed.

Chapter 2, What Can I Do on the Internet?, is a *brand new* section that describes in a summary form the four main activities to be found on the Internet — e-mail, USENET, the Web, and information publishing on the Internet. It serves as an introduction for those who are new to the Web.

Chapter 3, The Internet in Canada, contains *brand new* case studies of how various organizations and people in Canada are using the Internet.

Chapter 4, Internet Service Providers in Canada, is a *brand new* chapter that takes apart the Internet industry in Canada, to help you understand what organizations sell or provide access to the Internet. It examines how the Internet industry in Canada is changing as the result of the entry of so many different participants.

Chapter 5, How Does the Internet Work? is a chapter that describes how the Internet works, and takes a look at TCP/IP and the Domain Name System of the Internet. It includes *many new sections*, plus some material from previous editions.

Chapter 6, Direct versus Indirect Internet Connections, is a *brand new* chapter that will help you to understand the difference between a direct and indirect connection to the Internet, and the impact that this will have on the way you use the Internet.

Chapter 7, Internet Electronic Mail, and **Chapter 8, Knowledge Networking**, are updated versions of prior material, with *substantial reworking and new additions*.

Chapter 9, The World Wide Web, is a *brand new* chapter that focuses on perhaps the most important area of the Internet.

Chapter 10, You Ain't Seen Nothing Yet, is a *brand new* chapter that takes a look at where the Internet is headed in the future, by examining several new applications: "telephone calls" through the Internet, 3-dimensional Web technology, and the HotJava technology from Sun Microsystems, as well as many other new developments.

Chapter 11, Older Internet Applications, focuses on FTP, Telnet, Gopher and other applications.

Chapter 12, Connecting to the Internet, has been *dramatically restructured* from the prior year's edition to reflect the growing importance of SLIP/PPP accounts.

Chapter 13, Internet Software, is a *brand new* chapter that takes a look at some of the "all-in-one" software programs or suites available from organizations such as Quarterdeck, Wollongong, OpenText, CompuServe/SPRY, and Netscape. It will help you understand how the Internet is becoming an even easier place to access and use.

Chapter 14, Microsoft and the Internet, is a *brand new* chapter that takes a look at the involvement of this company in the Internet, and which examines how you can use Windows 95 to connect to the Internet.

Chapter 15, Why the Internet? is a revised and updated version of Chapter 9 from the prior year's edition, that looks at the strategic importance of the Internet.

Chapter 16, How to Get a World Wide Web Site, is a *brand new* chapter that looks at methods by which you can get a presence on the World Wide Web. It includes a brief look at some Web editing software now available on the market.

Chapter 17, The Internet in Canada: From Niche to Mainstream, is a *brand new* chapter that examines the results of an Angus Reid survey of Internet usage in Canada.

Chapter 18, Fraud and Deception, is a *brand new* chapter that examines the role of the media in its coverage of the Internet.

And finally, **Chapter 19, Is the Internet Real?** is a *brand new* chapter that offers some of our closing comments on whether the Internet is hype, or whether something really is going on here.

We have undertaken substantial revisions and updates to our Appendices as well, specifically:

Canadian Internet Milestones (formerly the Canadian Internet Timeline) has been *revised and updated* to reflect important Internet events in this country over the past year. In this edition, we're awarding ribbons to Canadian "firsts" on the World Wide Web. Check it out!

The **Directory of Canadian Internet Access Providers** now includes *over 300* organizations that sell Internet access in Canada.

Canadian Organizations with Registered Internet Domains now includes over *9,000* Canadian domain names.

Canadian Government Subdomains is a *new* appendix that includes a list of domains allocated by the Government of Canada Internet Subdomain Registrar.

Places to Start Surfing is a *new* appendix that provides some useful Canadian and non-Canadian starting points on the World Wide Web.

Canadian USENET Newsgroups has been *revised and updated* for 1995–1996.

Community Networking Organizations in Canada has been *revised and updated* for 1995–1996.

Staying Current includes *new* material on Internet organizations in Canada.

Identifying Countries on the Internet is a *new* appendix that provides a handy list of two-letter country codes used on the Internet.

Canadian IRC Servers has been *revised and updated* for 1995–1996.

Internet Forms has been *revised and updated* and includes a new form for Canadian Government Subdomains.

Mailing List Software Commands has been updated for 1995–1996.

Sample Windows 95 Configuration is a *new* appendix with sample configuration instructions for configuring Windows 95 for use with the Internet.

We've added a **Glossary** at the end of the book that contains definitions for many Internet terms and concepts.

Conventions Used in This Book

This book is sprinkled with the names of particular Internet applications and programs, including e-mail, FTP, Telnet, Gopher, World Wide Web (or WWW), Mosaic, Netscape, Archie, and IRC.

Each of these applications is described in some depth in Chapters 7–12, and several are introduced in Chapter 2. Until you get to those chapters, the following short reference might be useful as you browse through the next chapters.

E-mail	The ability to send a message from your system to someone else on the Internet.
Mailing lists	Systems which combine the e-mail addresses of two to several thousand Internet users. These are often used to discuss and debate topics, to publish newsletters, or for any other purpose imaginable. A message sent to a mailing list reaches every individual that belongs to that mailing list. There are mailing lists on thousands and thousands of topics.
USENET	An area of the Internet that is organized into several thousand topics. Similar to mailing lists, but usually accessed with different software.
Telnet	The ability to use the Internet to reach a computer located somewhere else on the Internet, in order to run a program on that computer.
FTP	File Transfer Protocol, the ability to retrieve files from computers located on the Internet. This is often used to retrieve documents or computer programs made available by individuals or companies from throughout the Internet.
Archie	A program used to locate other programs or files located on the Internet.

Gopher	Gopher is both a database of information as well as a program used to access that information. There are several thousand Gopher databases available from around the world.
World Wide Web (WWW)	A database or "server" application that contains information that can be accessed with special "browser" software. A WWW server can include text, sound, image, voice and even moving pictures.
Netscape/Mosaic	The software most often used to access WWW servers.
IRC	An interactive "chat" program used through the Internet.

Information Pointers

Throughout this book, we provide pointers to documents, files or programs that might be useful to you or might help you to access particular information sources on the Internet.

Tips on e-mail etiquette (and other general "netiquette" issues) can be found at the following URLs:

http://www.webfoot.com/advice/email.top.html
http://www.fau.edu/rinaldi/netiquette.html
http://www.screen.com/understand/Netiquette.html

Instructions like these are found throughout our book. We've standardized all our instructions using what is known as the URL — Uniform Resource Locator — method, since URL addresses are found throughout the Internet today.

Keep in mind that the Internet is in a state of flux. All of these locations were verified at the time of printing of this book, but inevitably some locations will change, move or disappear forever. The authors cannot guarantee that the listings as provided in this book will stay consistent.

Acknowledgments

This is the third edition of the *Canadian Internet Handbook.*

We've been working for over two years now with the folks at Prentice Hall, and it seems to be getting easier every year. First and foremost, we appreciate the continued ongoing involvement and guidance of John Isley, President of Prentice Hall Canada. Hart Hillman deserves praise for putting up with us when our short fuses flare; Karen Hammond for marketing support; David Jolliffe and Avivah Wargon for production coordination; Jan Coughtrey for continuing to talk to us even after we missed many deadlines; Cedric Hefkie for his effort in whipping the book into shape; Erich Volk for technical support; Sharon Sawyer and Judy Bunting for administrative support.

We'd like to extend a special thank-you to Prime Minister Jean Chrétien for contributing the foreword to this edition. The serious role that the Internet is beginning to play is evidenced by the fact that the Prime Minister of our country would find the time to participate in our project, and we truly appreciate his efforts. We hope to see him browsing the Internet one day soon!

There are numerous other people to thank. First and foremost, Betty Robinson, our editor, who first helped us on our other book, *The Canadian Internet Advantage*, did an absolutely marvelous job, and was once again a joy to work with.

Mike Martineau of NSTN Inc. has now undertaken a technical review of the 1994, 1995 and 1996 editions of this book, as well as the *Canadian Internet Advantage*, and we are happy to have him around.

James Saunders of NSTN Inc. played an invaluable role by using his technical genius to assist in pulling together our updated domain listing. We are grateful to Armand Saintonge of Rochester, New Brunswick who took the time to send us his detailed thoughts on a glossary for the book — we've added one!

Additional thanks go to John Demco, the CA Domain Registrar, for answering our questions and for granting us permission to publish his CA Domain documents; James Milles of the Saint Louis University Law Library (and owner of the NETTRAIN discussion list) for permission to reproduce his reference document on mailing list commands; Canadian IRC experts Yves Lepage, Christopher Oates, Dwight Spencer, and Andrew Dick for their help compiling IRC information for this book; Rocco Lallone at WorldLinx and Ed Placenis at Sprint Canada for their assistance with the Directory of Canadian Internet Access Providers; Joyce Leblanc at GTIS (Government Telecommunications and Informatics Services) for supplying information about the Government of Canada Domain Name System; and Chris Portman for sharing his brilliant programming talent with us.

For contributions to Appendix A, Canadian Internet Milestones, we'd like to acknowledge the following individuals and organizations: Lewis S. Eisen (Ottawa, Ontario), Keith W. Kerr (AGT Limited), Bob Fillmore (Natural Resources Canada), Roger Taylor (ONet Networking), Gary Cleveland (National Library of Canada), Terry Jones (Toronto, Ontario), Yves Lord (Emergency Preparedness Canada), Ross Morrissey (Ashbridges Bay Yacht Club), Clive Keen (University of Northern British Columbia Caving Club), John Demco (CA Domain Registrar), Brian McLean (Thunder Bay, Ontario), Bill Reid (University of Manitoba), Andrew Barss (Government of Nova Scotia), Stephen E. Dearth (Government of Manitoba), Peter McAuslan (McAuslan Brewing), Michael Thoen (Statistics Canada), Roger McKenzie (Canadore College), Ron Dallmeier (MBnet), Shebah Tatz (Government Works and Public Services Canada), Rob Moore (Floradale Boardheards Windsurfing Club), Bill Fernihough (BC Hydro), Darrel Brown (Government of New Brunswick), Mike Plante (Camosun College), R. Eric Sutherland (University of Waterloo Bridge Club), Victor Desroches (Agriculture and Agri-Food Canada), Elise Chodat (Indian and Northern Affairs Canada), Digdo Digdoyo (Embassy of Indonesia), Louis Aube (Atlantic Lottery Corporation), Fedor Steer (Avalon Masters Swim Club), Maritime Internet Services, Paul A. Canniff (Canniff and Company), Eric Carroll (fONOROLA), Alan Emtage (Bunyip Information Systems), Ken Fockler (CA*net), Berni Gardiner (Cycor), Jim Hancock (University of Prince Edward Island), Richard Lawrence (Arcticomp), Jack Leigh (University of British Columbia), David Macneil (University of New Brunswick), Michael Martineau (iSTAR Internet), Rory O'Brien (Web), Tim Symchych (Department of Defence), Vincent Taylor (Department of Defence), Mario Vachon (CRIM), and Roger Watt (University of Waterloo).

Special thanks to Kyle Trainor who assisted us with research and also to InfoRamp Inc. of Toronto and iSTAR Internet Inc. of Ottawa for furnishing us with accounts to "surf" the Internet. InfoRamp also implemented our mail robot. Osama Arafat, Stuart Lombard, Adam Deaves and the rest of the gang at InfoRamp deserve credit for their ongoing assistance with the book. Dave Little and the rest of the folks at E-Commerce, an Internet presence provider, helped us with technical questions. Thanks also to NETCOM in San Jose, California, and in particular Stephen Connors, for their support.

Cybersmith Inc. of New Brunswick, specifically Tim Smith and Ian Allen, have generously sponsored the World Wide Web site for this book. We would also like to thank InfoRamp Inc. and E-Commerce for sponsoring Web sites for the authors.

To the Internet software vendors who rushed about to satisfy our often impossible deadlines — we owe a word of thanks.

And finally, the authors must thank their families. Jim would like to thank his wife Christa — for someone who professes not to be much of a writer, we now find that she is taking on an increasing role with the book and is becoming a bit of a Net expert in her own right. Willie, who loves to surf the *Thomas the Tank Engine* Web site. And Thomas, for not spitting up on the keyboard too much when visiting Daddy at his desk. To the Carroll and Steube parents for the support and encouragement they provided during the project. And finally, to Dot and Chris for their (questionable) help in dreaming up book titles. Rick would thank his family for their continued support and assistance.

Finally, we'd like to thank the many people out on the Internet in Canada, who have been kind enough to send us letters and e-mail us with words of thanks and encourage-

About the Authors

Jim Carroll, C.A., is principal owner of J.A. Carroll Consulting, a Mississauga-based firm which assists organizations with the strategic use of telecommunications technology. Through J.A. Carroll Consulting, Mr. Carroll has assisted many organizations with the strategic use of the Internet to support global marketing, support, or customer-based activities. Mr. Carroll is a prolific writer with a regular monthly column on electronic mail in *Computing Canada* and the *Toronto Star*, as well as a number of other publications. Mr. Carroll is a popular speaker and seminar leader with respect to the Internet, and is in particular demand by companies and organizations seeking advice and strategies with respect to the global information highway and the Internet. Mr. Carroll is represented nationally and internationally by the National Speakers Bureau of Vancouver, B.C., which can be reached at 1-800-661-4110 or 1-604-224-2384, or by sending a message to **jcarroll@jacc.com** or **speakers@nsb.com.**

Rick Broadhead, B.B.A., is the principal of Intervex Consulting, a Toronto-based Internet consulting firm. He is an authority on the Internet in Canada and is recognized as a clear articulator of the Internet's benefits for organizations. Mr. Broadhead has been a speaker on the Internet at conferences and seminars across Canada. He has counselled the senior management of several Canadian organizations to help them understand the strategic opportunities available on the Internet and the emerging information highway. Mr. Broadhead is a contributing author to "DoubleClick," a nationally syndicated newspaper column on the Internet. He can be reached on the Internet at **rickb@inforamp.net** or by visiting his World Wide Web home page at **http://www.handbook.com/intervex.**

Contacting Us

We want to hear from you about this book — we welcome comments, criticisms, and suggestions. We do try to respond directly to all e-mail sent to us.

We are very interested in tracking Canadian Internet "success stories." If you are aware of new or significant initiatives by a Canadian organization related to the Internet, please let us know. We are also interested in hearing what's on your mind. Drop us a line and let us know how you are using the Internet. If you have developed a Canadian Internet resource or home page that you think other Canadians should know about, please tell us about it. Our e-mail address is **handbook@uunet.ca.**

Contacting the Authors Directly

Here's how to reach us on the Internet:

To Reach	Send e-mail To:
Both of us	**handbook@uunet.ca**

Use this address to send us feedback and general comments and questions about the book.

Jim Carroll	**jcarroll@jacc.com**
Rick Broadhead	**rickb@inforamp.net**

Our Mail Robot

We have established an automated mail response system (or 'mail robot') which provides information about our books by e-mail.

To obtain current information about this book or our other books, the *Canadian Internet Directory* and the *Canadian Internet Advantage: Opportunities for Business and Other Organizations*, send a message to **info@handbook.com**. You will be sent back a message that will provide information on how you can find out more about our Internet books and our on-line resources.

Our World Wide Web Sites

You can access our World Wide Web home page at **http://lydian.csi.nb.ca/handbook/handbook.html**. There, you will find information about this book and our other Canadian Internet books. We have placed selected chapters of our 1995 and 1994 Canadian Internet Handbooks on-line, and so we would encourage you to visit our home page.

Jim Carroll maintains a World Wide Web site at **http://www.e-commerce.com/jacc.html**. He posts to this site, on a regular basis, articles that he writes about the Internet and the "information superhighway" for *Computing Canada*, the *Toronto Star*, and other publications. Rick Broadhead maintains a World Wide Web site at **http://www.handbook.com/intervex** that includes pointers to major corporations and businesses that have a presence on the World Wide Web.

What Is the Internet?

If nothing else, the growing public awareness of the Internet has made it a household word. While people may not know exactly what information is available on "the Net," they do know it exists.

Weaving a Web to Catch a Dollar
Globe and Mail, March 14, 1995

PCs put computing power in the hands of ordinary people; the Internet gives them something compelling to do with that power.

The Accidental Superhighway
Economist, July 7, 1995

The Internet will one day plug together every computer chip in the world. The computer chip — that small piece of sand, glass, and metal containing the logic and hence the capability of processing information — is a device that has already reshaped and changed our world. You will find computer chips everywhere — not just inside computers, but inside your car, your telephone, in some cases even your microwave and toaster ovens. The computer chip has become ubiquitous.

And so far, for the most part, all these little computer chips have lived in splendid isolation. They have existed mostly by themselves, doing what they are supposed to do, and usually doing that quite well. That is about to change because of the Internet.

What is the Internet? It is a trend that is making all these little computer chips aware of each other and providing them the ability to link together.

The Internet and Evolution

Computers have had a short history compared to the overall history of man. Even so, they have gone through several distinct phases. The 1960s saw the arrival of the mainframe. Big, complex machines that required entire rooms, air conditioning, and, it seemed, people in white jackets with plastic pocket protectors.

The 1970s saw the arrival of the minicomputer, machines that expanded computing power to companies around the world. Suddenly, all kinds of business organizations could take advantage of computers, and folding, spindling, and mutilating became catch phrases.

The 1980s saw the arrival and proliferation of personal computers, relatively small machines that could be used by a single person to do any number of new tasks. "Computers for the rest of us," they were called, allowing anyone to work with these magical devices.

And the early 1990s saw the arrival of the network — local area networks, which linked together computers located within a particular building, and wide area networks, which linked together all the computers owned by a particular company or organization around the world.

Four discrete phases: mainframes, minicomputers, PCs, and networks. The next step? The GAN, or global area network. That is the Internet.

The Internet is the next significant step in the ongoing proliferation of computers in our world, for it has become the leading candidate, of all technology trends in the world, to link together all the computers, and all the computer chips, in the world.

The Reality of the Internet

The Internet, stripped down to its fundamentals, is simply the world's largest computer network, linking together some 20, 30, 40, or 50 million people, depending on who you talk to. The Internet has become the *information highway* for many people.

People are discovering that using the Internet leads to personal enrichment, to new business opportunities, and to new friendships that are global in nature. And indeed, the Internet happens to be many things to many people. It is:

◆ The world's largest computer network. One of the most difficult things about the network called the Internet is that no one really knows how big it is. Its nature means that it is impossible to measure accurately; the best anyone can hope to do is to estimate its size.

    The survey above puts Canada into perspective. Worldwide estimates have ranged from a low of 3 million people to perhaps 60 or 70 million people. The best estimates now indicate that some 40 million people are participating worldwide.

◆ A unique global revolution. The Internet is shaping Canadian and global history.

    In Canada, the technology of the Internet, along with fax

WHAT IS THE INTERNET

1 The Internet is part of a trend that is linking computers all over the world and is the next logical step in the evolution of computer technology.

2 On the Internet, you can send and receive electronic-mail, discuss, debate and track topics, undertake research, access news and information, "surf," entertain yourself, "talk on the phone," put out a newsletter or establish an Internet information resource.

3 Every area of our economy is being touched by the Internet, from government, banking and finance, and telecommunications and computing firms to the investment community and corporations.

4 Some believe the "information highway" has arrived in the form of the Internet, while others still believe it is yet to come as a result of the merger of television, computer, and telephone technologies.

5 The future will see us "plugged" into the Internet all the time through high-speed links, in essence, giving us a universe of a million channels in which everyone is a publisher of information.

machines and cellular phones, has shown how difficult it can be
to prevent the free flow of information. The Internet has had an
effect on the evolution of democracy in the former Soviet
Union. It has become a global force that is affecting the world in
much the way that CNN has. The Internet is a completely new
and different information distribution system. Do you think TV
and radio changed our world? Just watch what the Internet does
in the next decade!

◆ The world's largest pen-pal system. Daily, the Internet is used
around the world by people who enjoy simple interaction with others around the globe through computer networks. Using electronic
mail and other tools, people are reaching out so that someone in
Moose Jaw is as close electronically as someone in Hong Kong.
Through the Internet, it is as easy to communicate with someone in Estonia as in
Metro Toronto.

The Internet is bringing cultures together around the world and is probably
doing more to provide a greater understanding between different peoples than any
other human invention.

◆ A massive global information service. The Internet is chock full of information —
some of it useful, some of it useless, and some of it of questionable taste. Governments worldwide are making public information available to everyone. The United
Nations views the Internet as a powerful tool to "free" information. Corporations
have realized the Internet is a powerful corporate public relations tool. Individuals
have realized that the Internet provides them the opportunity to become editors of
newly established "electronic newsletters." Quite simply, the Internet is rapidly
becoming the storehouse of all of human knowledge.

◆ A technology platform, a common method to link networks between companies.
The Internet has, in many ways, become the standard for interenterprise computing.
A computer networking protocol known as TCP/IP has become the *de facto* standard method through which you might link a computer from your company to that
of another company.

The Internet offers an unprecedented degree of connectivity from one business
to another, from one organization to another, from customers to business and from
business to customers. Its massive growth means that a link into it offers an organization a unique opportunity to participate in global commerce, a way of business
that has not previously been seen on our planet. The mere growth of such a network
within a business world will change the way that business is conducted.

Organizations that learn how to internetwork, that is, support communications
and activities between themselves, their customers, their suppliers, their business
associates, and others, will be the ones that survive and prosper in the future.

◆ A set of standards for data communications, based on TCP/IP, that allow companies
to develop software without having to worry about how to develop links to other
types of computers. In this book we will take a look at some of those applications.
We will look at how you can make a "telephone call" through the Internet, how

videoconferencing is emerging on the network, and how radio stations and "just plain folks" are starting to broadcast "radio shows" through the Internet.

The Internet allows computers around the world to link together, which means that people can focus on developing neat, nifty computer applications, rather than having to worry about how to plug things together.

◆ A marketplace without boundaries. The Internet is emerging as a place where people are shopping, obtaining product literature, looking at advertisements, and interacting with companies and organizations.

There can be no doubt that we are entering an era in which business will be conducted, on a regular basis, between companies and customers through computer networks. There is even a buzzword for it: "disintermediation"! As the world's largest computer network, the Internet represents a substantial global marketplace with significant new business opportunities. An interesting point is that only those people and organizations that take time to learn the unique Internet culture are learning how to prosper on the network.

◆ A brand new information distribution system. The Internet is not TV, it is not radio, it is not a newspaper or a magazine. But through it, you can access radio, newspapers, and magazines. You can retrieve video through it (if you have a fast enough link), and one day, perhaps, you will even be able to watch TV of some sort through it.

Yet, it is a completely separate system. Perhaps the best thing about the Internet is that it is not controlled by what we know as "media." Big companies are not (yet) in charge of the Internet; anyone can be a publisher through it. And the Canadian Radio & Telecommunications Commission (CRTC) thankfully has little to do with the Internet.

For some, the Internet is a sociological revolution, a system that is helping to return "power to the people" from the "media and government elites." It is a system that cuts through today's power and information structures and a system that is changing society in dramatic ways by doing so. To others, the Internet is a global nation that transcends national borders.

Simply put, it is a big network of computers. The biggest.

What Can You Do on the Internet?

Everything and anything. We will take a longer look at this question in the next chapter, but for now, we will put into perspective how the Internet is many things to many people. Take a look around, and you will find that people use it for

◆ Sending and receiving global electronic mail (e-mail). Across Canada, people are using the Internet to send and to receive Internet electronic mail. E-mail, as it is known, is fast and effective, very inexpensive, and is quickly becoming a common method of communicating across Canada and around the world.

E-mail is used in business to support communications between companies. Students are learning to communicate with other students around the world via e-mail to find information for class projects; they are also contacting their parents via e-mail. Researchers located in different parts of the world collaborate on projects through e-mail.

Friends are discovering and, in some cases, rediscovering each other across the country and communicate on a regular basis through the network. E-mail is a technology that is reshaping the way people interact and is making the world a smaller place.

◆ Discussing, debating, and tracking topics. Through areas of the Internet known as USENET and through what are known as electronic mailing lists, people are participating in discussions on tens of thousands of topics. Through USENET newsgroups and e-mail, people post questions to others from around the world who share an interest in a topic. The unique spirit and cooperative nature of the Internet means that complete strangers often spend a few minutes keying an answer to your question. People are gaining a brand new capability by learning to use the Internet to globally "knowledge network" in this way, and by doing so are generally improving their skills, an important fact as we continue to wake up to the reality of global competition.

The Internet, particularly within USENET, is really thousands of small global communities, in which people around the world with an interest in a common topic are linked together through their computers.

◆ Undertaking research. There is a lot of information on the Internet. But one of the often-repeated phrases is that "it's too difficult to find stuff on the Internet." This used to be the case, but really isn't today. As long as the information exists somewhere on the area of the Internet known as the World Wide Web, there is a good chance you will be able to find it.

There are a number of "tools" emerging on the Internet that help you to search for information from throughout the world. Spend a little bit of time, and you can find yourself traveling through documents around the world related to a topic. Learn a little bit about the various search systems available throughout the Internet, and you can soon become a master of electronic research.

Some have said that the Internet is the world's largest library, an on-line database of such scope and reach that it contains the ability to access more information than the human race has ever had at its disposal. Certainly as the Internet continues to grow, the opportunities to undertake such electronic research are increasing and becoming truly astounding.

◆ Accessing news and information. Need up-to-date information? Want an additional source of news? Missed the television news last night and want to catch up? You can retrieve the transcript of the CBC *National News* from the prior evening's newscast or take a look at hourly news headlines from CBC Radio. You can pick up today's top news stories from the *Halifax Daily News*, or access detailed news from countless other sources right around the world. It's not news you are after? Voyage over to *Canadian Biker*, or *Frank Magazine*, the *Hill Times*, or *Shift Magazine*, all various Canadian magazines with some type of content on-line. Don't want information from an established organization? Find one of the many thousands of informal publications available on the Internet. The Internet is an absolutely massive source of information, with up-to-date information from around the world.

◆ "Surfing." Exploring the Internet has become a leisure-time activity for many. Traveling from location to location and from country to country by modem, you can review details about upcoming concerts in Canada, take a look at a detailed sports report, and then examine tomorrow's weather.

The World Wide Web, an enormous system of interlinked computer systems, provides information that includes sound, graphics, and images and permits you to travel from site to site simply by clicking your mouse. Information about entertainment, news, reference sources, weather reports, computer support, health care, business, investments, the economy, literature, music, videos, government, biology — the list is extensive and endless.

Since everything is linked together through the Web (hence its name), you can find yourself starting out somewhere and quickly find yourself traveling right around the world from site to site. For those tired of the banality of television, "surfing" the Web has become a leisure activity and a type of entertainment of sorts. It is a fascinating place to go and visit.

◆ Getting a laugh. Zip off to the Dilbert comic strip on-line. Visit the world's largest database of lightbulb jokes, or the Official David Letterman Top Ten List. Run a "roulette" wheel that will take you to some totally random place on the Internet.

Visit unofficial lists of the most useless things on the Internet, for some really bizarre humor, such as a fellow who has linked his CD player into the Internet to tell you what he is playing right now. Visit a place where you can go and talk to a real live cat by keying some words into a keyboard.

Weird? Sure. Silly? Yes. Stupid? Perhaps. Fun? Well, it has caught the imagination of many people around the world. The Internet is a new form of entertainment, a new type of system very different from TV and radio, which is unleashing the humorous and bizarre aspects of human nature around the world.

◆ Talking on the "phone." There are a few programs available that permit you to have a conversation through your computer with someone else on the Internet, across the street or right around the world. To do this, you need a computer that has a sound card and a microphone. The interesting thing is that such a conversation is billed to you not at long distance rates, but at the rates you pay for Internet access, which might be as low as $0.50 an hour, depending on how you access the Internet.

◆ Putting out a newsletter or establishing an Internet resource. Anyone can be a publisher on the Internet. Anyone can contribute. Do you think there should be a site that provides information about the Canadian dairy industry? Establish one. Do you think we need a site that includes information about Canadian attitudes on wine? Put one up. Do we need a newsletter about the Toronto Raptors NBA team? Write one, and make it available to anyone on the Internet who chooses to subscribe to it. The thing about the Internet is that anyone, anywhere, can be a publisher on any topic.

What can you do on the Internet? In a nutshell, participate in something that is very unique, very different, and very, very fascinating.

1995 Was a Watershed Year

There is a lot of talk about the Internet and a lot of media coverage. It has entered popular culture. Canadians seem to be hearing about it everywhere. Examine, however, what people have to say about the Internet. On the one hand, people clearly *awed* by the interactive nature of the Internet write breathless articles that predict that the Internet is the greatest thing since the invention of the automatic hand dryer. On the other hand, skeptics write that the Internet is really all just a waste of time and that it would do us well to ignore it.

The most fascinating thing about the debate is that each side draws a "definitive conclusion" about the Internet. But for all intents and purposes, the Internet has only been around for about a year or two. Aside from the fact that the Internet had a twenty-fifth birthday in 1995, for most of us, the Internet is something that we only began to become aware of around 1993 or later. So being a relatively new system, its technology, its impact, its use, and its pervasiveness in our society are still evolving. The jury is still out on the Internet regarding what it will really mean.

In this book, we try to put into perspective what the Internet really is today and what it might be tomorrow. Some people think that the Internet is a fad — it's hype, it's a fad, and it will soon go the way of CB radio. It is hyped. It is a fad. But it is not going to go away. Read on:

◆ There is no doubt that a significant trend is underway with the Internet: slowly and inevitably it is plugging together all the computers in the world. This fact cannot be denied: it is the only technology that has the capability of linking computing devices worldwide. The network itself has undeniable and relentless growth, a momentum that shows no sign of slowing down. Companies, individuals, governments, organizations right around the world are scrambling to get on board. There is simply too much momentum behind the Internet, and the momentum is not slowing down. *The Internet does not have an off switch.*

◆ There is a significant amount of venture capital and investment money pouring into the Internet. Companies involved in the business of providing access to the Internet are seeing their initial share price double within hours of their stock offering. Money solves problems (for the most part) and capitalism moves industries forward at breathtaking speeds. *The Internet industry, one might say, has legs.*

◆ The technology that drives the Internet is moving forward at an amazing pace. Computer companies are making the Internet central to anything they do. It is already possible to listen to real time "radio shows" through the Internet using a new program called RealAudio. By next year, many will be able to watch real time multimedia "shows" through the Internet given the arrival of cable network access to the Internet, a technology that will provide blindingly fast Internet access. *Six months in Internet years is like 20 human years.*

◆ The Internet is "driving" the "information highway" agenda. Telephone, communication, and cable companies got excited about "video on demand," "the 500-channel universe," home shopping and other interactive television-based applications. As they now rush to get involved with the Internet, they are sheepishly indicating that once again, they had the future all wrong. Interactive TV seems to be going the way of polyester leisure suits. *Oops!*

◆ Young people in particular are enthusiastic about the Internet. We are seeing an entire generation grow up not with just a television in their home, but an interactive computer plugged into the world. The older generation thought the information highway was all about more TV (something they understand), while the younger generation is saying, "nope, we don't want more TV, we want the Internet." *The Internet is a generation gap, and many baby boomers do not understand what it means to young people.*

◆ As people plug in and learn the Internet, they are slowly becoming electronic consumers. They are becoming familiar and comfortable with the technology. They are undergoing a mindset change. Gradually, they will come to expect an electronic relationship with the companies with whom they do business. Their *behavior* will have changed, which is really what this is all about, isn't it? *If you doubt it is happening, talk to your kids.*

The Internet is here today, and it is not going to go away.

In 1995, it became evident to many people that something significant was happening with the Internet. Let's take a look at some of the trends above in more depth.

Government and the Internet

Around the world, political leaders realized the impact, potential, and promise of the Internet. National, local, and world government bodies scrambled to become involved. There can be no better example of the importance of the Internet to Canada than the fact that the Prime Minister of Canada, Jean Chrétien, wrote the foreword to this book. Carefully read what he has to say about it.

In Ottawa and elsewhere, we are seeing federal government departments and agencies explore how they can use the Internet in the delivery of government services. Entire projects dedicated to the "re-engineering" of the delivery of government services often now include the question, "how can the Internet help us in our quest?"

Elsewhere, we are seeing provincial and municipal governments get involved in the same way. We are seeing political parties and politicians explore how to use the Internet to interact with constituents. We are seeing a cyber-electorate begin to demand electronic information through the network. We are seeing the early stages of a society — its government and its constituents — slowly being transformed by the arrival of the Internet.

Computer users can now tour Parliament on line through the computer network. They can also learn about parliamentary procedure and read transcripts from committee meetings.

Parliament has Signed on to the Internet
Globe and Mail, June 20, 1995

In a message recently posted on the Internet, a world-wide "network of networks," the United Nations invites young people to advise world leaders on how to reduce poverty, unemployment and social conflict.

UN Invites Children into Cyberspace
Globe and Mail, February 13, 1995

Bank of Montreal and several large U.S. banks and technology companies have teamed up to develop a way for consumers to send personal cheques electronically over the Internet, the companies said yesterday.

B of M Eyes Internet for Electronic Cheques
Globe and Mail, August 24, 1995

A Kentucky thrift is the first company to be granted authority from the U.S. Office of Thrift Supervision to offer banking services on the Internet. The regulatory agency said yesterday that customers of Cardinal Bancshares Inc. of Lexington will be able to transfer money between accounts, pay bills and check bank statements using the computerized service. The services are akin to telephone banking, OTS said.

Thrift to go on Internet
Globe and Mail, May 11, 1995

Canada's largest phone company wants to cash in on the world's single fastest-growing market — the Internet. Plans are afoot at Bell Canada to set up an Internet access service so customers can dial into the international computer network of 40 million users.

Bell to Offer Access to Internet
Globe and Mail, January 19, 1995

Forget neo-Marxist, postmodern or gender-based theories — the real reason the Internet is infested with geeks is because you have to be one just to get the software to work. But this month, all that starts to change.

Painless Ways to Get Hooked into the Net
Globe and Mail, August 21, 1995

Banking and Finance

In 1995 the financial sector realized that the Internet represents a significant communication pipeline through which financial institutions can offer computer-based banking, investment, and "electronic commerce" services.

Throughout Canada, we saw a flurry of activity in the financial sector. Most of the major banks in Canada established World Wide Web sites and began to explore and experiment how they could integrate the Internet into their service offerings. Mutual fund companies established sites through which you could find out information about various mutual funds as well as market values and other up-to-date information. Various investment firms such as Merrill Lynch established locations on the Internet. Companies like Visa and MasterCard established initiatives to provide credit card authentication through the Internet.

Everywhere you turn, you can find examples of a financial sector that has realized that the Internet is a significant and important technology.

Major Providers

In 1995 the Internet finally gained the serious attention of large telecommunication and computing firms. Right across the country, telephone companies signaled their intention to enter the Internet business, if they were not already involved. Mighty Microsoft introduced the Microsoft Network with their Windows 95 operating system, bringing the Internet to the masses. Major cable companies like Rogers Cable and Shaw Communications announced plans to provide access to the network.

This was not just a Canadian trend — around the world major companies got involved in the Internet in a big way. As the *Economist* so eloquently put it, "…the telephone companies are fighting to regain the pipes. The explosive growth of the Internet may have caught them off-guard, but they are now believers."

Quite simply, the Internet became a serious business, and it shows no signs of slowing down. As noted in the World Wide Web site of Simba Media Daily (**http://www.iw.com/simba/**), "the growth in sales of personal computers combined with increasing interest in the Internet will help worldwide on-line sales grow 75% to $24.1 billion in 1999, according to a new report from SIMBA Information Inc.…The average annual growth for the 1995–1999 period is estimated to be about 11.9%, SIMBA said."

The Computer Industry

The Internet has become a multi-billion-dollar industry. It used to be tough to get on the Internet. Indeed, it used to be tough to do anything with the Internet. All that changed dramatically in the last year or two, 1995 in particular, with the arrival of a lot of sophisticated Internet software.

Many software companies began to release all kinds of software to help individuals and companies join the Internet. Products such as Wollongong's

Emissary, Quarterdeck Internet Suite, and Netscape's Personal Navigator consist of everything you need to get on and start using the Internet immediately. These packages, which we look at in Chapter 13, are making the Internet straightforward to access and to navigate.

It doesn't stop there. Several Canadian companies released software used by individuals to create World Wide Web sites and gained international acclaim for their products. In terms of hardware, Sun MicroSystems revealed that a good chunk of its revenue came from Internet-related hardware sales and that it was the hardware system most used throughout the network. IBM announced strategies to begin incorporating the Internet into everything that it offers. Other computer hardware companies continued to make the Internet central to much of what they do.

Quite simply, the Internet has come to dominate the agenda of many hardware and software firms, a trend that began earlier than 1995, but certainly gained a heck of a lot of steam that year.

Serious Money

Wall Street and Bay Street discovered the Internet in 1995. If you are going to have a multi-billion-dollar industry, you need to have equity money to finance it. So the world's money managers discovered the Internet as a potential place to invest. Anything "Internet-related" became a hot target of their interest, resulting in a flurry of activity on public stock markets and a number of private deals. No doubt some of this interest is due to hype, but you cannot deny the fact that the Internet has become a serious place to invest. Such investment simply continues to drive the Internet forward at a relentless pace.

Netscape Communications Corp. stunned investors last week with a hot initial public offering. The California-based firm that makes software to help navigate the Internet jumped 108 per cent in its first day on the Nasdaq Stock Market.

Funds Join High-Tech Parade
Globe and Mail, August 17, 1995

Corporate Involvement

In 1995 corporate Canada finally rushed into the Internet. From Air Canada to the Vancouver Real Estate Board, organizations across the land became involved. What happened? Companies began to realize the possibilities that might arise from "interactive marketing" through the Internet. The World Wide Web provided a vehicle through which organizations could publish product catalogues and product descriptions, through which they could seek customer feedback, and through which they could take sales orders.

No doubt, one day, there will be a lot of business conducted on-line. For corporate Canada, rushing in to stake out its territory on the Internet, the concept of on-line marketing on the Internet remains a bit of an enigma. It is a period of experimentation, observation, and careful thought. The success or failure of the Internet as a marketing tool is not going to be decided in the next minute, the next hour, the next week, or even the next year. But there is no doubt that a transformation to business — what we call networked business — is underway.

Molson Breweries hopes to win the hearts and pocketbooks of young well-heeled drinkers by serving up "leading edge" information on the Internet. Molson unveiled yesterday what it says are the most interactive commercial sites available on the World Wide Web, with seven main areas focusing on entertainment and sports.

Marketing Reporter
Globe and Mail, July 19, 1995

As Canada's largest travel agencies grope their way toward the brave new world of electronic sales and marketing, Uniglobe Travel (International) Inc. is claiming an early lead on the Internet.

Travel Agencies Going Electronic to Avoid Squeeze-Play
Globe and Mail, July 19, 1995

> *What do pedophiles, academics, hate-mongers, many Canadian public schools, potential terrorists and suicidal teen-agers all have in common? Access to the Internet and the information highway. Nowhere else on the open market can information be found ranging from vile hate-mongering to the advocating of child sex, from details on making pipe bombs to instructions on how to commit suicide.*
>
> Something Wicked This Way Comes, and It's on the Internet
> *Globe and Mail*, March 16, 1995

> *Netsurfers are constantly being told that they swim in a swamp of sexual depravity. They console themselves by noting that their critics — religious conservatives, censorious feminists and parents who mistake the Internet for a playground for children — usually have little knowledge of the Internet and a lot of experience in social pressure.*
>
> A Gross Distortion of the Porn Picture
> *Globe and Mail*
> July 14, 1995

> *As the masses plug into the Internet, some of its original inhabitants are fleeing — including scientists and scholars who made it such a valuable resource in the first place.*
>
> An Advantage and a Curse
> *Globe and Mail*, August 17, 1995

Controversy

In 1995, many older people in the "establishment," unfamiliar with the Internet and certainly not users of the network, issued a call for a clampdown on the Internet. We have seen middle-aged politicians, who have not even taken a minute to look at the World Wide Web, stand up in the House of Commons and issue grandiose "calls for action" involving "control" of the Internet. Naive spokesmen for various national groups display an amazing technical ignorance state by indicating we need some type of "CB radio style regulation" to deal with the Internet. Quite frankly, we have representatives of an entire generation — baby boomers — condemning a system about which they actually know very little.

And lost in all the horror-babble is the simple reality that the Internet cannot be controlled on a technical level. There is no doubt that the Internet poses many difficult issues to society. But such issues are not dealt with through sensationalism, ignorance, and the need to get on the evening news. They can only be dealt with through maturity, understanding, and knowledge.

In 1995, the Internet laid bare the generation gap that exists in society today. While these "old folks" scream and rant their outrage, young people who actually use the Internet day by day, who live within its unique culture and understand its technical foundation, react with complete and utter disdain to these calls for "censorship" and "control." They react with disgust to the opportunistic statements by politicians. They lose faith in the ability of the older generation to even comprehend what the Internet is all about.

Baby boomers — that idealistic generation of the 1960s, once so full of passion and enthusiasm for issues of democracy and freedom — are calling for censorship. It is a strange state of affairs.

An Internet Backlash

And not unexpected, a backlash began to occur about the Internet throughout 1995. It is not surprising. You simply cannot have something like the Internet emerge and not introduce many, many concerns.

Many people react with fear to the concept of the Internet, and others with horror. Some are concerned that we will become a world of cyber-zombies, attempting to live our lives through the vacuousness of our computer keyboards. Others express concern that if everyone can become a publisher, then we are becoming a world full of junk information. Some media "elites" bemoan the fact that, oh, they are the *only* ones qualified to write prose worthy to be read by other members of society. In other cases, many Internet veterans have thrown their hands up in disgust as the common man begins to invade the network.

Elsewhere in this book we comment that some areas of the Internet known as USENET are coming to resemble a men's washroom, in terms of the profanity, the insaneness, the idiocy of the discussions that occur. We note in another section that visiting another area of the Internet known as IRC is like visiting a Grade 5 locker room — maturity is certainly not the strong suit of this particular application.

There is no doubt that the Internet is changing as it grows larger. It will continue to change and to evolve. Who knows what it will become? Many of the concerns being expressed are real, and many are not. Whatever the case may be, there is a debate occurring in society on just what the Internet *means* to all of us and to our society. It is a good, healthy, and useful debate, and it is important that everyone keep an open mind to both sides of the story. But even as the debate occurs, the Internet grows larger and more pervasive. The Internet in 1995 has become a part of all of us.

What about the "Information Highway?"

Probably some time in 1995 (or even before then) the phrase "information highway" obtained the dubious status in Canada and elsewhere of perhaps being one of the most disliked phrases in popular culture. Certainly it is an overused phrase. But, in understanding the Internet, it is important to know how the "information highway" relates to it.

What does the information highway really mean?

♦ For some people, it is here today in the form of the Internet. The information highway is simply a system that we will access through computers and a system that will link together all the computers on the planet. The Internet is the network that permits this.

♦ For others, the information highway does not yet exist. It is a system that we will access through television, and will result from a forthcoming merger (or "convergence") of television, computer, and telephone technologies.

There are still many who believe the second point. Mostly they are senior executives in Canada's telephone, cable, and other telecommunication companies. Many people on the Internet believe this to be the entirely wrong track, for it would appear that they believe that the information highway is simply about *more television*.

Let's start at square one. Starting in mid-1993, excitement within the telecommunication industries about the information highway began to reach a feverish pitch. We had the unique situation in which all kinds of senior executives within the telecommunication industry began to talk of "convergence," a future world that would provide home banking and home shopping through the television. In this world, you would be able to sit back and click on your TV remote control to order a video. You would be able to travel through your television to your local restaurant to order some junk food. You would have not 20, not 30, but 500 TV channels! The information highway — why, it is simply more TV!

Much of the talk by these senior telecommunication companies focused on the need for some type of device that sits on top of a television with a credit card reader attached to it. This "set-top box" would let

Despite all of the current reportage and rhetoric about the Internet and the electronic information highway, I, like the late, great Canadian author George Woodcock, still manage to get along with my trusty Olympia manual typewriter and a bottle of white-out. When one stops to think about it, the quill pen produced some of the world's greatest literature, and the writers of that era didn't have to worry about losing their body of work due to power outages or gremlins in their CD-ROM or DOS. Life is complex enough without getting lost in cyberspace.

John Grimshaw
Campbellville, Ont.
Letter to the Editor
Globe and Mail, February 16, 1995

For the past few years the titans of media and communications have waged a war for the digital future. With great fanfare, telephone and cable TV companies have launched dozens of trials to demonstrate their vision of speedy electronic networks, connecting homes to a boundless trove of information, communication, education and fun. Shambling towards their distant goal of a wired world, they have been too busy to notice the unruly bunch of computer hackers, engineers and students scurrying about at their feet. They should have paid more attention. For while the giants have just been talking about an information superhighway, the ants have actually been building one: the Internet.

The Accidental Superhighway
Economist, July 7, 1995

consumers buy products from some fancy home shopping network, let consumers pay for video-on-demand or allow access to a 500-channel universe.

Your TV would become interactive and would become the key for you to interact with the world in the future. You would interact with the world with your TV remote control.

In this vision, the telecommunication companies would control the infrastructure. They would run the wires. They would publish content. They would become not just cable and telephone companies, but "information companies" and "multimedia conglomerates." They would become rich simply by running the world's information infrastructure. They would control the information highway and hence have repositioned themselves to profit well into the twenty-first century.

And we consumers? We would sit on our couch, enter the world through the "boob tube" and spend money. We would become consumer zombies in an information highway world gone mad. We would become passive participants in the ultimate home shopping network. We would master the world with our TV remote control.

For a long time, so much of the talk in Canada focused on this television-based vision. Government, industry, media, politicians all seemed to think that interactive TV was what the future was all about. But, to many people, such applications seemed limited and even silly. As we put it in our 1995 edition, in a burst of frustration, "Canada seems intent on building an information highway that will let us order fried chicken through our TVs." We bemoaned the state of affairs. And on the Internet, people who had mastered the intricacies of the global Internet and who had discovered a world in which everyone is a publisher of information just *snickered* at these old folks and their focus on the television.

What Went Wrong?

By 1995, it had become apparent to everyone that the Internet *is* the information highway. But it took some time. What has become evident is that we have had a huge generation gap when it comes to the Internet, with many senior executives in major telecommunication companies and other middle-aged folks originally failing to understand how the future was evolving.

What happened? These folks — executives well into and beyond middle age — grew up in a world in which the television was the centre of the universe. Because of their age and their lack of familiarity with computers, they thought the information highway was all about more TV. "The information highway?" they said, "Sure, we'll give you one. Look, it has got 500 channels, and video-on-demand, and you can buy fried chicken with it. You can run your credit card though it. You can buy stuff. All through your television!" These folks had mastered their TV remote control, but didn't know their way around a computer keyboard.

Meanwhile, in Canada as elsewhere around the world, computers were beginning to outsell televisions for the first time (as they did in the Christmas season in Canada in 1994). People began to work with computers at the office and decided to buy one for home. The Internet began to explode, and the user-friendly World Wide Web came into being.

The result? Children and teens were growing up with two information appliances in their home — a television, which all they could do was watch, and computers, which they could control, program, and through which they could interact.

The younger generation grabbed onto the Internet in a major way. And many people in society — clearly not impressed or enthused with the increasingly slim offerings on TV regardless of the growth in the number of channels — looked to the Internet as a form of entertainment, knowledge, and fun.

Now this older generation is waking up to the fact that the rest of the world, particularly youth, is into something different than just television: the Internet and on-line computer services.

Sadly, these cable and telecommunications executives originally missed the fact that the youth of today do not want more TV junk, but want the interactivity as found through computers and the global Internet. They do not want video-on-demand, they want access to knowledge and information. They do not want to be couch potatoes in front of the "boob tube," but want to lose themselves in the mystery of the World Wide Web. They do not want home banking through their TV sets, they want it through the Internet. They do not want to interact with a TV remote, they want to interact with their computer keyboard.

These executives are waking up to the fact that the highway is not about more TV, it is about connectivity between computers. And that connectivity is occurring, for the most part, through the Internet.

What is happening here is an admission by telephone and cable companies that the much-hyped television-based information highway will not be here for some time (if ever) and a recognition of the growing significance of the Internet. And perhaps a recognition that it does not make sense to try to stuff computer intelligence into a television, when we have all these computers with intelligence lying around in our homes and offices in the first place.

Control of the Highway

If anything, the Internet is changing the global information paradigm, and it is giving control of the information highway back to the people. In the television-based information highway described above, everything would have been controlled by the same people who control our television world. Big corporate conglomerates, the government, the CRTC. The CRTC! Everyone remembers early 1995 when the CRTC tried to dictate to average Canadians what they should watch on their televisions.

Quite frankly, the continuing disillusionment in Canadian society has meant that many people have lost faith in large institutions. Many people in Canadian society have no faith in a television-based information highway that is run by the same old folks, who control the content, and who extract their revenue by virtue of controlling the means of "publishing." That is one reason why the Internet has exploded. Anyone can be a publisher in this system. Anyone can be an information contributor. Anyone can become an information source.

> *...the information superhighway will arrive sooner, but it will be a very different kind of road from the one the giants intended. Cable and telephone companies will still build their high-speed networks to people's homes, but what will pour through them will be the Internet, not just the network providers' canned content.*
>
> The Accidental Superhighway
> *Economist*, July 7, 1995

The control of the highway has been decentralized with the arrival of the Internet, which promises to revolutionize the flow of information around the world by wresting control away from the "elite." And it is for this reason that the Internet is a very different model from the highway first imagined by big telecommunication companies.

The real impact of the Internet? It is that the entire global information "paradigm" that we know is in the very early stages of a radical and fundamental shift. No longer will information come just from magazines, newspapers, television, and radio sources. No longer will the means of publishing be controlled by the elites, by the mega-corporations, by government regulatory bodies. Instead, information will originate from anyone, from anywhere, on any topic imaginable.

The Internet has become the world's largest publishing system and, indeed, the world's largest on-line library service. For example, one fellow on the Internet runs what he believes is the world's largest database of lightbulb jokes. No one pays him to do this, and no one has asked him to. In fact, many of us might wonder why he would bother to spend his time on such a bizarre undertaking. But because he can be a global publisher through the Internet, his database is available to anyone in the world who might be in need of some comic relief. He has become a global publisher, one of millions around the world. He is an information producer. He is an important entity on the information highway. Such is the reality of the Internet. Anyone, everywhere, is a publisher.

We sincerely doubt we might ever find a database of lightbulb jokes on the television information highway of the future. If we do, we imagine that the jokes will have been approved by some CRTC bureaucrat somewhere to ensure that they have an adequate level of Canadian content. It would be funny if the thought of it weren't so sad.

The Future

When you hear about the Internet, you hear a lot about technology. Techno phrases such as Gopher, FTP, IP addressing, Telnet, Mosaic, and World Wide Web can dominate a conversation about the Internet. But such techno bits and bytes often fail to convey the global information revolution that is occurring through the Internet.

In this book, we will take a look at a lot of this technology. But before we do, we should spend some time describing to you what the Internet means for the future. There is a lot that you can do on the Internet today, but the Internet is changing and evolving on a continuous basis. To understand why you should want to read this book to learn about the Internet, we thought we would describe to you how the Internet will become even more significant and all-encompassing in the future. In many ways, the Internet has only just begun. So let's look at where the Internet is going, before we begin to outline where it is today.

We Will Be Plugged in All the Time

> The world has never seen a technology like this before. "Data dialtone" — networking as widespread as the telephone — suddenly seems not only possible, but likely.
>
> The Accidental Superhighway
> Economist, July 7, 1995

Over time, most computers in the world will be plugged into the Internet all the time. Today, many of us "dial in" to the Internet from our home or office using our personal computers via devices known as "modems." We make a conscious decision to "go on to the Internet" and then do what is necessary to get on.

But in the near future (from one to five years) the Internet will become so pervasive and all-encompassing throughout the computer world that most of us will have a direct high-speed link to the Internet *at all times*. We will not even have to think about "logging on" to the Internet; we will simply be linked to it automatically as soon as we turn on our personal computers. In fact, the Internet will be a basic part of our computer and part of the "operating system" of our PC.

The early signs of this trend can be seen now. Microsoft includes access to something called the Microsoft Network as part of its Windows 95 operating system, which is a convenient route into the Internet. More importantly, it has included within the system the "computer protocol" known as TCP/IP, the fundamental technology or language of the Internet. IBM and Apple have also included the Internet and TCP/IP within their OS/2 and Macintosh operating system software. Most other computer vendors have done the same.

It is as if we are all being given an automatic transmission instead of having to use a standard: we do not have to think about changing gears, and we will not have to think about getting on to the Internet.

We Will Have High-Speed Links to the Internet

All of us will be stunned by the communication speeds to become available to our homes and offices in the next decade. And we will be stunned by what these fast communication links will let us do with the Internet.

"Bandwidth" is simply a term often used to describe how much information we can get into our computing devices. Most people who access the Internet today using modems do so at speeds of "14,400" and "28,800 baud," a pretty small amount of "bandwidth." While these modems are on the leading edge, they are essentially an old, slow, and frustrating technology.

However, recent announcements indicate that the future promises to get very interesting, very quickly. At the 1995 annual meeting in Halifax of the Canadian Cable TV Association, several major cable companies announced that they would provide high-speed access to the Internet via devices known as "cable modems." The significance of this announcement cannot be overstated. Plans are to make available such technology sometime in 1996.

Once the cable companies iron out the wrinkles, it is said, individuals will be able to access the Internet at speeds up to 1,000 times faster than the modems we use today. This will dramatically change how the average person uses the Internet because today, even accessing the Internet at speeds of 14.4 or 28.8 Kbps, it is often too impractical for people to spend the minutes or hours downloading a small bit of video data or retrieving a song through the Internet. It can take time to browse through graphics-rich pages of information. It is almost impossible to have a real time videoconference call.

The cable company announcement means that in the coming years it will be possible to retrieve full motion video files or other large computer files through the Internet.

The cable announcement is but one announcement: the telephone companies have a technology called ATM, a blindingly fast communications technology that permits so much data to be sent and received that none of today's personal computers could possibly keep up with it. It is being implemented now in Canada by major telephone companies in various parts of the country, and when they get around to putting an optical fibre link into your home, you will be able to participate in some pretty amazing developments on the Internet.

As a result of these faster speeds, the Internet will change from being a place where we can retrieve text and pictures, to a place where we can also retrieve sounds and video.

> *If you are amazed by the fast drop in the cost of computing power over the last decade, just wait till you see what is happening to the cost of bandwidth.*
>
> Andy Groves
> Chairman of Intel
> The Bandwidth Tidal Wave,
> *Forbes Magazine,*
> December 5, 1994

We Will Have a Million-Channel Universe

As we indicated, our entire global information paradigm is changing because of the Internet. One result of the availability of inexpensive, fast communication speeds to the home and office when combined with the Internet is that we won't have the much talked about 500-channel universe. Instead, we will have a *million-channel* universe, or even a *500-million channel* universe. Soon, everyone in the world will be able to have his/her own "TV station" and his/her own "radio station."

The real impact of the Internet is that we will no longer be just a world of "information consumers" (you and me) and "information producers" (newspapers, magazines, radio, TV). We will be a world of "information consumer/producers," any of us able to publish and broadcast on a global basis.

How is this so? In the future, anyone in the world will be able to put up a computer file on their site on the Internet. This file could contain a TV show, movie, recording, or some other type of interactive media program *that they created*. Why? Because any type of movie or voice recording can be turned into a computer file.

Take a home movie that you have filmed on your camcorder. With a few hundred dollars of equipment, anyone can take such a home video and turn it into the ones and zeroes of computer language — they can *digitize* it. In essence, any type of movie video can be turned into a computer file. And the Internet is simply a tool that permits you to retrieve computer files from anywhere in the world. Put your video file up on the Internet. Anyone can come and get it when they want to. And watch it at their leisure. Presto! You are a TV station!

The limitation today is that because of the massive size of these files, only individuals with really fast links to the Internet (such as those found in universities and research organizations) can take advantage of this capability. But, extend fast links to everyone else through cable-based Internet technology, and everyone can participate.

We Will See Internet "Iceberg" Applications

The concept of wired software is real, and it is coming faster than you think. One reason many people believe Microsoft jumped into the on-line world in 1995 with the Microsoft Network is due to the incredible potential that occurs from linking personal computers around the world to systems at Microsoft.

Many future computer programs will be what we call "iceberg" applications, in that they will operate below the surface, unknown to you, interacting with some other computer somewhere, more often than not through the Internet.

Your accounting software might dial up your bank through the Internet on a regular basis to get cheque information. Your word processor might go out on to the Internet to provide some data to a mainframe computer in Germany to do an automatic language translation. Your home inventory program might automatically notify your insurance company that you have purchased a new stereo, by querying your bank for details about the latest Visa bill.

The concept of wired software is tantalizing, fascinating, and a bit scary all at the same time. It is a new type of software, one that uses the Internet to enhance and change its capabilities. And it is destined to arrive before you even have a chance to think about it.

We Will See Other "Things" Plugged into the Internet

Soon, all kinds of devices from around the planet will plug into the Internet. As we describe in Chapter 10, people are experimenting with plugging all kinds of things into the Internet. Many of these efforts seem silly, but are, in essence, a form of leading-edge research.

Imagine a point five years from now when your vacuum cleaner breaks down. You zip into the Internet, access the World Wide Web archive for the manufacturer of your model, and read information on where to go for help. You review some electronic pages about the likely cause of your particular problem. You figure out what you need to do. Seems easy enough, doesn't it?

But now imagine that when it breaks down, your vacuum cleaner — plugged into the wall outlet — and the computer chip inside it begin to communicate with the manufacturer, providing some diagnostic and other information. It does this automatically, since your household electrical system has become part of the Internet. Later in the day, you receive an e-mail from the manufacturer, diagnosing the problem and notifying you what to do.

Imagine that your pool heater contacts your gas company through the Internet to compare gas consumption this summer against last year. Observing that it is up 20% this year, the gas company creates an e-mail message to let you know, offering some helpful tips on how to manage your energy usage.

Far-fetched? Many people do not believe so. Such is the reality of the future of the Internet, a network that is quickly becoming the *de facto* method of linking all kinds of computing devices, not just computers.

> *Internet surfers trip across many oddities in the World Wide Web, put there for no apparent reason other than their curiosity value. The original silliness was a photograph, updated every 10 minutes, of the coffee pot in a computer laboratory in a British university. Today, it's Lou Montulli's Amazing Fishcam.*
>
> Curious Byways Off the Superhighway
> *Globe and Mail,* June 16, 1995

The Internet

Who knows what the Internet really means? None of us do. Things are moving so quickly in so many places all at once that it is often difficult to keep up. All we can do, at any given time, is take a look around and see where it is and where it is going. So in this book we will try to help you understand where it is. And we will talk a bit about where it is going. We will help you understand what it is you can do with it today, and what you might do with it tomorrow. We will try to help you understand this thing called the Internet.

What Can I Do on the Internet?

What Can I get from the Internet?

The Internet is all about connectivity. Quite simply, the Internet is the leading edge of a trend in which computers and computer networks around the world are linking together, resulting in one massive, large-scale global network that brings together individuals, businesses, governments, educational institutions, science and research bodies, and other organizations in ways not previously seen in human history.

Through the Internet you can send electronic mail to family, friends, business associates, and other people around the world. You can participate in on-line "discussions" about various topics and automatically receive newsletters on particular subjects. You can browse information from around the world as easily as you might go to the library; you can retrieve pictures, images, and, in some cases, video. You can publish information worldwide for a very low cost. What you might use the Internet for is only limited by your imagination.

The Internet is Changing the Role of Computers

The Internet is a significant development for *you*, because what it really represents is a complete change in the way in which you use your personal computer. It is a significant development for business, since it is changing the way business is conducted.

For people, the Internet changes the role of personal computers. By linking computer users together around the world, *personal computers* (PCs) become *information appliances*. Change the role of the PC, and people discover that they can use their PCs for more than just simple spreadsheets, word processing, and family finance programs. Through the Internet people discover that their PCs become a window to the world, a world full of information.

For organizations, the Internet represents a new method to reach existing and potential customers, shareholders, stakeholders, the general public, government bodies, and other third-party groups. The reality of the Internet for many organizations is that it is changing business such that an organization can have an "information relationship" with those people and organizations with which it already has a business relationship.

This chapter puts into perspective some of the things that you can do with the Internet to demonstrate what is possible. We do not describe how to do these things here; we will reserve that for later chapters. This chapter is simply an introduction to the universe of the Internet.

Be Real About Your Expectations

There is an incredible amount of hype about the Internet, and its real impact is sometimes oversold. You should be cautious in your expectations of how long it will take you to "master" the Internet. It might take you no time at all to get "on" to the Internet, but it will take time to learn to use it effectively. Because the Internet is a brand new means of communication, very different from paper, the telephone, and fax machines, what you are really doing when you encounter the Internet for the first time is learning all over again — learning how to communicate, how to interact, how to perform research, how to publish information.

The Internet is also a new technology on the computer scene. Because it is happening so quickly, some joke that the technology that supports the Internet is evolving so fast that 6 months in Internet years is similar to 20 human years. And indeed, the Internet of today will be completely different from that of tomorrow. Hence, when you learn about the Internet, you must understand that you will be learning about something that is continually changing and expanding.

The Internet is a massive network with all kinds of people, information, and organizations — it can be a wonderful place to

WHAT CAN I DO ON THE INTERNET

1 People are discovering that through the Internet their PCs have become a window to the world.

2 Main uses of the Internet:

- Electronic mail, which has quickly become the fax machine of the 1990s;

- Discussion groups, in areas of the Internet known as USENET newsgroups /and electronic mailing lists, through which people can "knowledge network";

- Information access through the World Wide Web, which allows people to access information in the form of text, sound, pictures, images or video, from computers around the world;

- Information research, by using various "search tools" on the Internet in order to undertake sophisticated on-line research;

- Information publishing, in which anyone can publish information on the Internet.

explore. It is also a frustrating, disorganized, anarchic network that sometimes will cause you to shake your head in anger. Sometimes you will wonder why you ever chose to become involved. *The Internet is not a magic solution.* Sometimes you will look for information on the Internet and you will not find it. You will hope to use the Internet for one purpose, only to discover that it cannot be done. Sometimes you will encounter people and information on the Internet that you will not like.

Yet, you will also discover on the Internet something that you have never seen before: a global sense of community; information riches of untold depth; fascinating and ongoing developments in business activities; people who share your interests; knowledge about topics that you never knew existed. Over time, you will be stunned by what you discover. We are willing to bet that you will not be able to walk away from it.

Electronic Mail

One of the most popular uses of the Internet is electronic mail (e-mail). The Internet has quickly become the world's largest global e-mail system. Anyone joining the Internet from home or work is provided with an Internet e-mail address. In addition, many organizations are providing employees with Internet e-mail capabilities by linking their corporate e-mail networks to the Internet.

The result is an ever-increasing exchange of e-mail through the network. Many have adopted this way of communication, as evidenced by the number of e-mail addresses appearing on business cards, corporate stationery, in advertisements, and in television shows, newspapers, and magazines. People now exchange Internet e-mail addresses like they exchange fax numbers, and so in some way, e-mail is becoming the fax machine of the 1990s.

Why are so many people adopting Internet e-mail? Because it is fast, efficient, and cost-effective. As we will explain in Chapter 7, it is also the application on the Internet with the furthest reach and the greatest number of participants.

One result of its far-ranging reach is that there are literally hundreds of different methods by which people access their Internet mailbox — there is a lot of different e-mail software out there. Thus everyone might see something completely different when creating and sending e-mail messages, depending on the software and the company used to access the Internet. Regardless of what people see, they do share some things in common. Everyone has an "inbox" of new messages, for example:

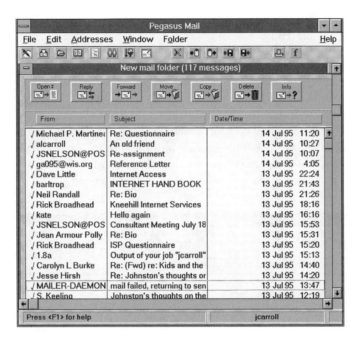

Everyone can create a new message (or "envelope") to send a message to someone:

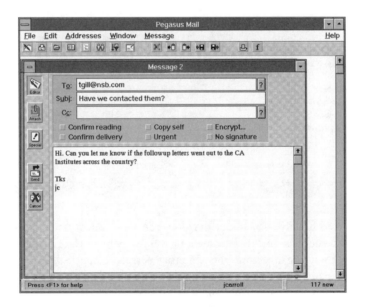

In Chapter 7 we will take an in-depth look at Internet e-mail and issues such as e-mail etiquette, the nature of e-mail "addresses" and how to find them, special features of Internet e-mail, and security issues.

Discussion Groups

Although the Internet is a large and massive global system, it is also a place that consists of thousands of small "communities" (known as USENET newsgroups and electronic mailing lists) where people with a common interest exchange information and ideas. For example, there is a place on the Internet where people who are interested in the art of bonsai trees "hang out." They have their own spot (or "community") on the Internet where they exchange information about the topic. They go on their way and do their own thing, without bothering anyone. On any given day you might see discussions on any number of topics related to bonsai trees, as can be seen in the following screen (**rec.art.bonsai**):

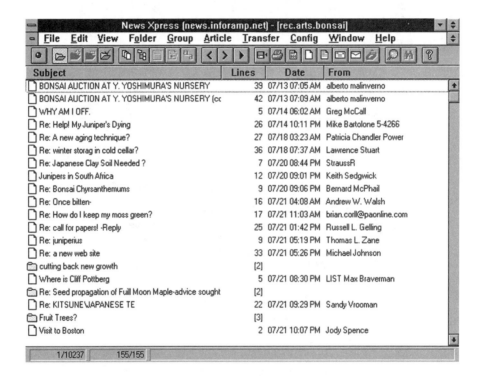

The Internet is used heavily throughout the global business, scientific, and research communities, and the Internet has quickly become a method by which leading-edge public research is shared among these organizations. The Internet permits global collaboration on research projects between many disparate organizations to an extent not previously possible, a development that many believe to be fundamentally reshaping the manner in which public and private research is conducted. Since anyone can participate in these research groups, the Internet opens up a new wealth of information to its users.

Elsewhere, on a less serious note, Internet discussion groups are used by people to discuss and debate all kinds of topics, such as popular TV shows and soaps; musical bands and entertainers; sports, recreation, or leisure activities; and thousands of other topics. The range of topics available is extensive, serious, and bizarre all at the same time; you can exchange information about leading biological research or track the postings by people who sincerely believe they were abducted by aliens.

For what purpose can you use Internet "discussion groups"? You can "knowledge network," that is, use the discussion groups to gain information on a particular topic, to bring yourself up-to-date on a certain issue, or to find an answer to a question.

"Knowledge networking" is the term used to describe the ability to harness on-line information, either by regularly tracking information on a particular topic by receiving information on that topic or by seeking information or answers to questions by discussing a topic with others on-line. Since the Internet has broken itself down into so many thousands of topics, you can quickly narrow in on a particular topic that interests you.

For example, let's say you are a parent, and like many parents, are wondering what the Internet can do for you. One of the most active USENET newsgroups on the Internet is **misc.kids**, a place where parents "hang out." A sample of some of the activity within this group on a particular day shows topics that are being discussed on the right-hand side of the screen, while the left side of the screen shows a list of various USENET newsgroups. The bottom of the screen shows a message that one individual has posted about getting gum out of her child's hair (**misc.kids**):

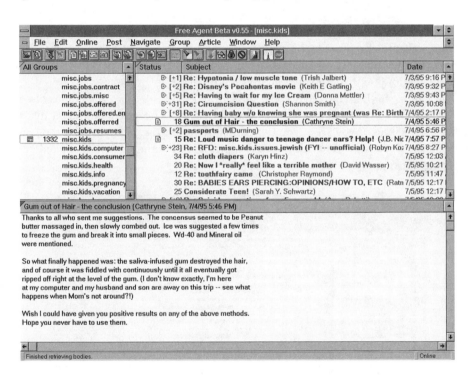

On this particular day there were all kinds of other topics in the group, from discussion about the movie *Pocahontas*, to the benefits of cloth diapers, to recovery after pregnancy, to the need for passports for kids. It's as if we put thousands of parents in a room and then listened in on their discussion.

The power of USENET is that anyone can participate and post a question. In the next example, someone named Chris Kouba has asked the group a question about baby formula (**misc.kids**):

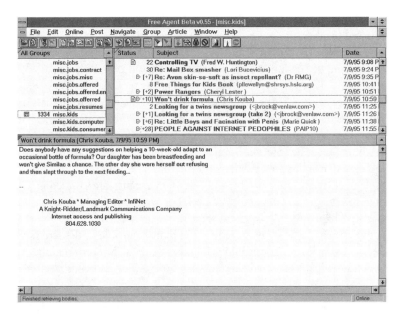

The unique nature of the Internet is such that other parents will probably spend a few minutes answering her question, by sending her an e-mail, or, hopefully, by posting a message to the **misc.kids** group so that everyone can see their thoughts.

Through USENET you can see the questions that people post and, quite often, the answers. You can track a topic that is being debated, or you can access a newsletter that someone has posted. And, if you wish, you can participate too. **Misc.kids** is one of thousands of USENET newsgroups — the available list of topics is truly stunning. Another good example is the group **alt.support.asthma**:

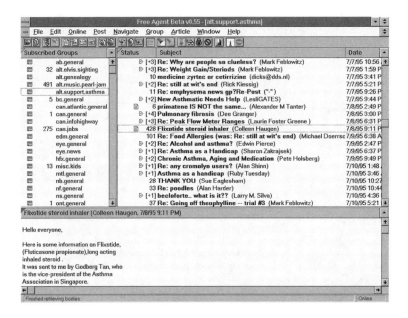

Within this group asthma sufferers around the world share information about how to cope with the medical condition. They provide pointers to other information resources around the Internet related to asthma. They report on new research developments in the field. They offer tips, hints, advice, and warnings. It has become sort of a giant self-help group, and many people with asthma participate.

USENET is also used for serious scientific pursuit. Given its roots in the academic and research community, there are still many areas on the Internet used for this purpose. For example, here is a posting from the group **bionet.organisms.zebrafish** (obviously for discussing scientific research about zebra fish), from someone at the University of California School of Medicine:

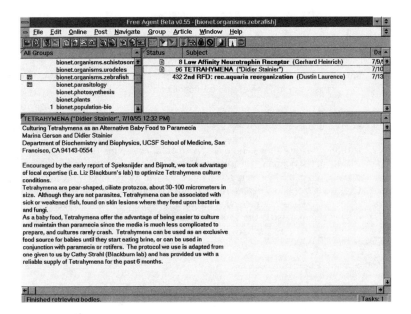

Through these USENET "communities" people around the world often collaborate to put together definitive documents about a particular topic. Consider the group **alt.folklore.urban**, which is certainly one of the most interesting groups for many on the network. Within this group people work at putting into perspective the real truth about popular "urban legends." The research is often very detailed, with much debate occurring on-line as the group works toward getting a definitive answer to a particular question. Their efforts over the years have resulted in a large archive of summaries about popular myths; for example, here is the one about alligators in sewers:

From: twcaps@tennyson.lbl.gov (Terry Chan)

Subject: Re: alligators in sewers?

In article <3080@keele.keele.ac.uk> cla04@seq1.keele.ac.uk (A.T. Fear) writes:

+> In article <1992Jun27.235945.4406@dartvax.dartmouth.edu>

zk@coos.dartmouth.edu

+> (Generator) writes:

+>> Hey, I was wondering … Anyone know why people claim there are

+>> alligators in sewers?

+

+I don't know, maybe it's the fear of the nearby unknown. In Victorian London there was a scare about savage black pigs living in the sewers. Are there any present day reports of subterranean porcine horrors?

Sounds like a great story. I'd like to hear of some details/updates.

Well, it's been a while since I've written a long post, so here goes.

A wealth of detail on the "alligators in the sewers of New York City" legend is detailed in The Vanishing Hitchhiker by Jan Harold Brunvand (more abbreviated versions are in More of the Straight Dope and Rumor!).

While I won't recount the details of the legend this time around, I will share some details on what may have been the origins of this story in The Vanishing Hitchhiker.

Anthropologist Loren Coleman checked out "unusual phenomena and events" and especially animal lore in the United States. He found over 70 such reports from 1843-1973 but only one pertaining to sewers.

In the February 10, 1935 New York Times, there was a report of kids in the East 123rd Street area who were dumping snow into an open manhole. Salvatore Condulucci, 16 yrs old was watching near the rim of the manhole and would direct his friends to dump more slush in as the level went down to ensure that the sewer wouldn't be overly clogged. Then there were signs of clogging 10 feet down where the sewer connects to the Harlem river. He saw something black moving and then shouts to everyone, "Honest, it's an alligator." The story is summarized in the Times' headlines as:

ALLIGATOR FOUND IN UPTOWN SEWER

Youths Shoveling Snow into Manhole

See the Animal Churning in Icy Water

SNARE IT AND DRAG IT OUT

Reptile Slain by Rescuers

When It Gets Vicious--

Whence It Came is Mystery

The reporter speculated that the alligator came from a passing boat from "the mysterious Everglades."

Separately, Robert Daley in The World Beneath the City writes that there was apparently a problem with alligators in the sewers in the 1930s. Former Commissioner of Sewers Teddy May personally inspected the sewers and told Daley that he found alligators with an average length of 2 feet. He then commenced on an eradication campaign and announced that all were exterminated by 1937.

These two points then seem to form a pretty good basis for the enduring legend.

Daley's writeup of his talk with May was published in 1959. Brunvand includes a fantasy-parody of the alligator story in the 1974 New Yorker and also mentions that Thomas Pynchon's 1963 sci-fi V contains one of the most detailed treatments of the legend. Brunvand speculates that Pynchon may have been influenced by hearing of Daley's discussion with May.

> If the accounts are true, then perhaps the "alligators in the sewers" legend may be similar to the Shergold stories. I think there is some debate as to whether one would say that the alligators were indeed living in the sewers or were they dumped and found there or whatever.
>
> Terry "tastes like chicken" Chan

USENET also reflects the sometimes silly and bizarre sides of human life. For example, there is a place on USENET where you can post your very own sighting of Elvis (**alt.elvis.sighting**). This is a busy group with a lot of postings, such as this one from a fellow who spotted Elvis in a Pacer in Arizona:

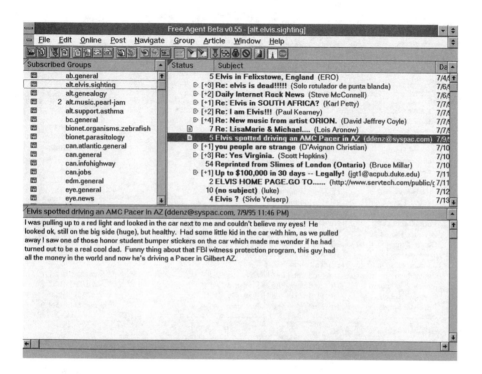

Thanks to the Internet, it is apparent that Elvis is alive and well and is such an awesome fellow that he can sometimes appear on four different continents around the world on the same day!

Seriously though, USENET is one of the most fascinating (and sometimes frustrating and controversial) places on the Internet. The unique cooperative spirit of the Internet, and the fact that it permits people to participate in only those areas in which they are interested, has led to a stunning diversity in topics, information, and debate.

USENET isn't the only place where you will find such communities. As we will discuss later in this book, you can also join electronic mailing lists on any one of several thousand topics. These mailing lists are yet another method by which to exchange information with your peers around the world and are gaining in popularity because they are often more specialized and restricted to smaller groups of people. (One of the hazards of the Internet is that often a group will be visited by people who do not stay on topic or who just post garbage in an effort to provoke people.)

There are public mailing lists that anyone can join, and there are private, "invitation only" mailing lists. As an example of the latter, the authors of this book belong to a mailing list called "Netscribes," which consists of some 150 authors of Internet books from around the world as well as writers who focus on the Internet for the *New York Times, Washington Post*, and *San Jose Mercury News*. The mailing list is used to discuss popular issues of the day, to discuss royalty and contract negotiation issues, and to share information and ideas on other general issues related to the Internet. (We won't give you the address, since it is a private list.)

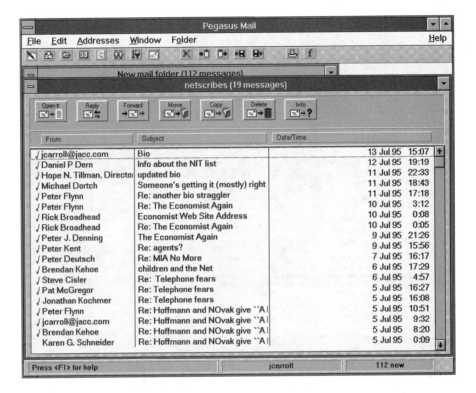

Information in USENET and within mailing lists does not consist solely of discussions between people; you can obtain other information as well. For example, you can

◆ subscribe to formal or informal electronic journals and newsletters, published by individuals or organizations from around the world;

◆ join mailing lists that will send you announcements of concerts, events, new publications or new products, or information about new initiatives by various organizations and governments.

The world has never seen anything like the information exchange that has become possible on a global basis through USENET and electronic mailing lists. In Chapter 8 we'll take an in-depth look at how you can use these powerful resources.

Information Access

In addition to e-mail and discussion groups, the Internet has become an absolutely massive system of interconnected information resources from all over the world. Since anyone in the world can become a publisher on the network, there is an overwhelming variety of information available.

One area on the Internet in particular has captured the imagination of the world. The World Wide Web (or the Web), estimated to be doubling in size every 53 days through 1995, has become *the* place to be on the Internet. Through the Web you can access thousands of "sites," each containing page upon page of information. These pages can contain text, sound, pictures, images, and even video (if you have a fast enough link to the network).

The magic of the Web is that any page can be linked to any other page on the planet, hence the name "Web." Experiencing this for the first time is something that most people never forget. You can start out on the Web in Paris, France, one minute and then the next minute be in Halifax, Nova Scotia, Australia, Russia, or the United States; with a click of the mouse you travel the globe from location to location, from information site to information site. Since everything is interconnected, you suddenly find yourself in a location completely unrelated to what you were looking at two minutes ago.

Where can you go on the Web, and what can you do? It's barely possible to describe the breadth and diversity of information in this area of the Internet, and so we will just try to whet your appetite. Through the Web you can find yourself accessing information about new movies from Alliance Releasing one minute (**http://alliance.idirect.com/**):

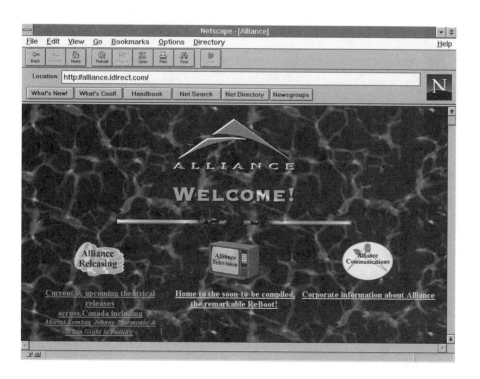

to Track Canada the next (**http://home.cc.umanitoba.ca/~csghoy/index.html**):

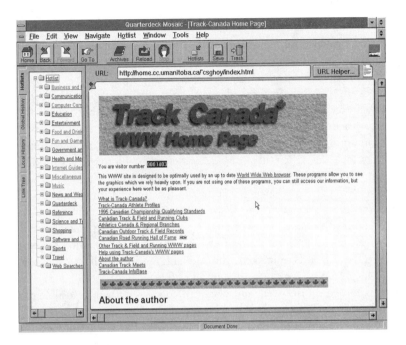

and accessing information about the Canadian band Tea Party (**http://www.teaparty. com/tp/**) the next:

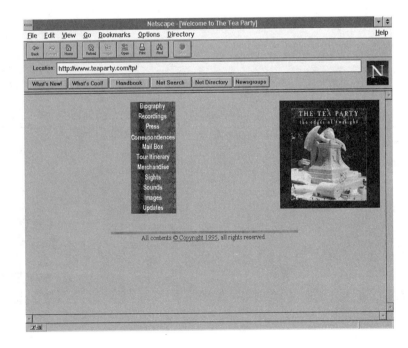

You can travel to the Blind Childrens Center (**http://www.blindcntr.org/bcc/**), which has compiled and points to information from around the Internet concerning blind children:

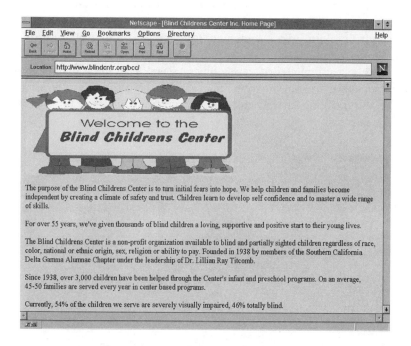

or you can visit the site for the TD Bank (**http://www.tdbank.ca/tdbank**):

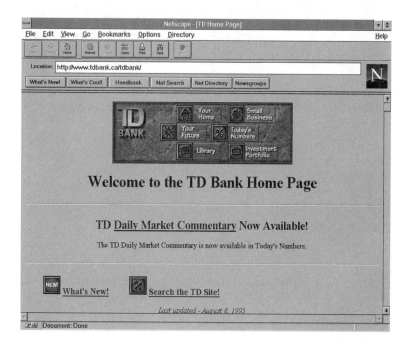

The World Wide Web is truly an amazing application and is the area of the Internet that is gaining the most attention. Through the World Wide Web our world is becoming wired, and since almost anyone can put up a Web site (if he/she can pay for it or convince someone to "host" it), all kinds of information is available.

The diversity of information is sometimes stunning. There are many situations in which an organization puts up "official" information, and yet there are several "unofficial" sites, established by people also interested in the topic. An unofficial site is one that has been created and is maintained by someone not affiliated with the organization or particular topic. Consider the Toronto Blue Jays. There is an official site established by the team (**http://www.bluejays.ca/bluejays/**):

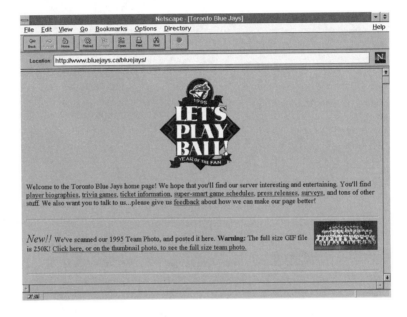

There are also a number of unofficial sites, including this one maintained by a graduate student (**http://fas.sfu.ca/cs/people/GradStudents/niguma/personal/jays.html**):

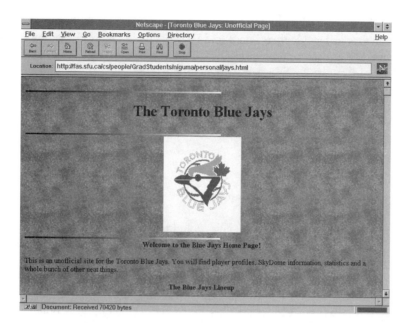

The technology that supports the Internet is evolving at a breathtaking pace, particularly on the World Wide Web. If you have the RealAudio program, a new program that lets you listen to sound on the Internet as it is received, you can visit Web sites and listen to "radio shows" and other sound sources in real time through your computer speakers. (We discuss RealAudio in greater depth in Chapter 10.)

Below is a visit to the CBC Radio Show *Quirks and Quarks* (**http://radioworks.cbc.ca/ radio/programs/currents/quirks/june17.95.html**). When this picture was taken, we were listening to the show through our computer:

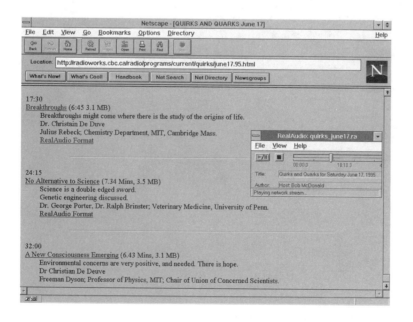

The World Wide Web is but one information retrieval application on the Internet. You will hear of other applications such as Gopher, Telnet, and FTP. But quite simply, these days, the only one that really seems to matter to most people is the Web. In Chapter 9 we'll take an in-depth look at the Web; in Chapter 10 we'll take a look at some of the leading-edge developments in software on the Internet, and in Chapter 11 we'll take a look at some of the older Internet applications.

Information Research

Given the information resources to be found in USENET, electronic mailing lists, the Web, and other sources, many people are learning to use the Internet to perform simple research on particular topics, companies, or issues.

One impact of the continuous, ongoing evolution of Internet technology has been the arrival of a number of "tools" that help you to perform a search among the millions of pages that make up the Web or to perform a search of the "archives" of particular mailing lists. We will look at a few examples of Web search tools to put this into perspective.

Let's say you are looking for information concerning Canadian politics. A Waterloo, Ont., company (OpenText Corporation) has developed a program that builds an index of information found in Web sites from all over the world. You can try it out by going to the Web site **http://www.opentext.com**. Once there, simply choose to do a search and then key "Canadian politics" into the search box:

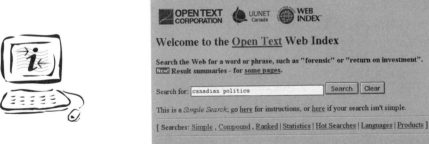

Within seconds, OpenText returns with a listing of Web sites that contain some type of information relating to Canadian politics:

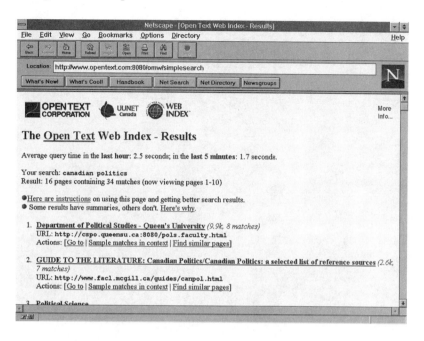

We can travel to these sites simply by selecting them with the mouse.

There are a growing number of similar search tools found throughout the Internet, such as WebCrawler (**http://webcrawler.com**). If we are looking for information on the import/export business as it applies to Estonia, we can key in such a search:

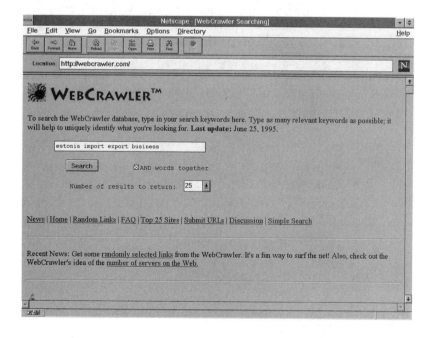

Once again, in seconds the WebCrawler system returns with a list of Web sites that might have such information:

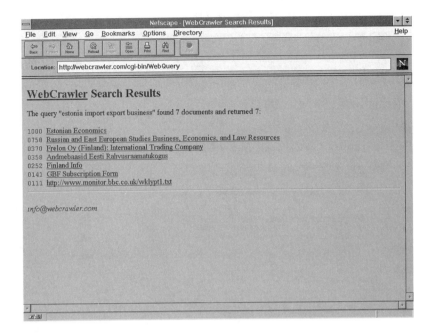

Choosing the first item takes us to the site of The Institute of Baltic Studies, which looks like a promising location for information on this topic:

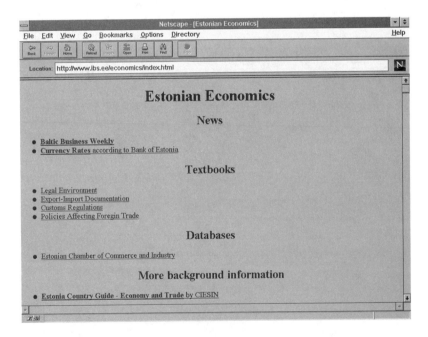

Such search tools are useful but are sometimes limited, since you can only find the information you are looking for if you come up with an effective search strategy, and only if the type of information you are looking for *is really on the Internet*. It might not be there.

While there is a lot of free information on the Internet, we are also seeing the arrival of fee-based information services, which let you do a search for free but charge you a fee to retrieve particular documents. Related to this trend is the arrival on the Internet of information from the publishing and business worlds, such as newswires, magazines, and newspapers. Such organizations are trying to determine how they can use their information as a component of their for-profit business. They do not give their information for free in the "real world" and hence do not want to give it away in the Internet world. Hence they place a charge on it.

An example of such a service is Canada NewsWire, which has established an up-to-the-minute database of news and press releases (**http://newswire.flexnet.com/cdnews.htm**). You can perform a search of the Canada NewsWire system by date, subject, company, or, in this case, industry category:

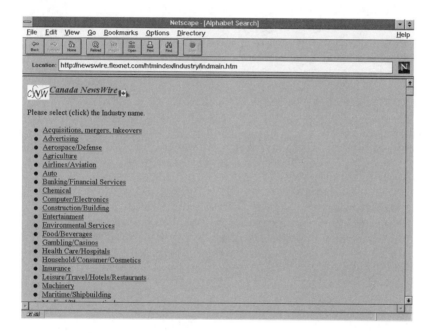

If we perform a search on the Royal Bank, we are presented with a list of the most recent press releases concerning the company:

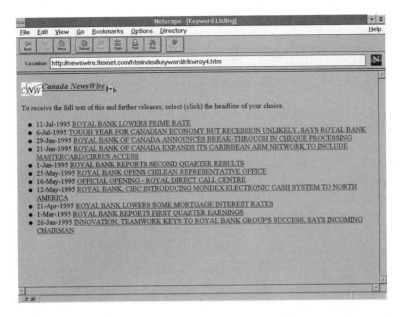

At this point, if we want to access an actual article, we are asked to identify our subscription number. If we are not subscribers, we can fill out a form to have a salesperson contact us to arrange for an account:

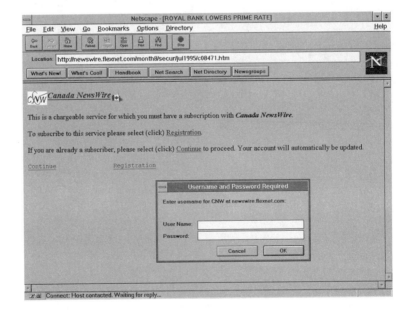

The result? You end up paying for the information that you want. If you find the information that you need, then your expenditure is worth it.

Learning how to undertake research on the Internet is becoming easier, but it is still not a simple task. In this book we outline search strategies on the Internet and some of the ways that you can undertake research on the Internet.

Publishing Information

You can also choose to publish your own information on the Internet and make it available to people through electronic mailing lists or through the World Wide Web. In some circumstances you can also make it available in USENET.[1]

Any individual or company can establish a "Web site" on the Internet and can place on the site text, graphs, sound, or motion video images — information that can be accessed by people around the world. Some publish information about themselves, simply for the fun of it. This fellow, David Woodsworth, has done so (**http://mindlink.bc.ca/David_Woodsworth/**):

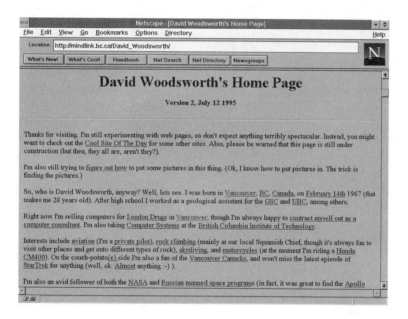

Others establish Web sites on their own initiative about topics in which they are interested. These sites might include pointers to information related to that topic elsewhere around the Internet, which is one reason why the Web can become such a complicated place: there are so many places to start that have an index of information about a particular topic! Here is a fellow in Nova Scotia who has created his own page about the passion in his life, violin repairs (**http://emporium.turnpike.net/A/AAllen/violin.html**). (In this case, we are using another Web browser, called Quarterdeck Mosaic, to show that there are many different programs that can be used to access the Internet.)

---

1. One of the significant aspects of USENET is that it is noncommercial in nature. Therefore, commercial postings are frowned upon.

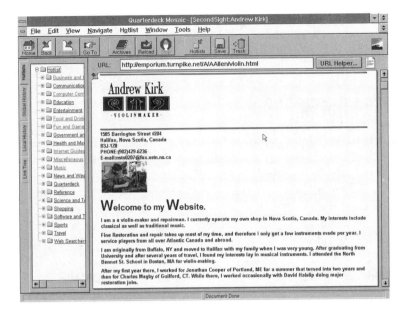

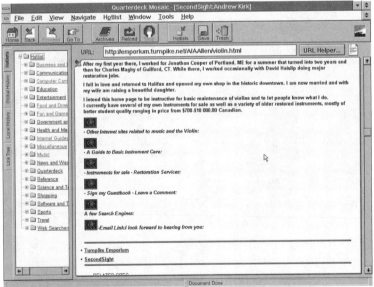

Anyone can establish his/her own Web site. Companies that sell you access to the Internet will "rent" you space on their systems so that you can create one of your own. With a little bit of skill and patience, you can learn to create your own "pages" of information on the Web. And there are a number of programs available on the market that make it even easier for you to create your own page. Consider this index about Canada, built by a graduate student at Carnegie Mellon University (**http://www.cs.cmu.edu/Web/Unofficial/Canadiana/README.html**).

The site provides a comprehensive index of all things Canadian on the Internet. Choosing something from the list leads you to a computer somewhere else in Canada or around the world that provides details on that topic:

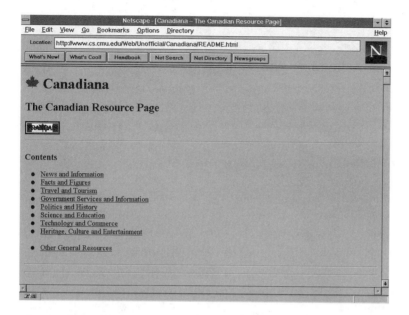

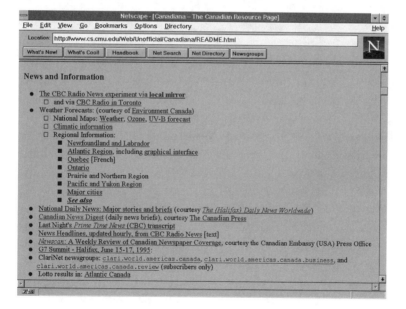

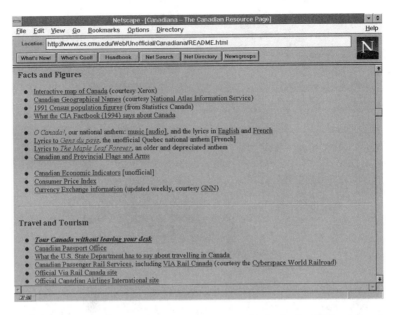

Others have established newsletters that you can access through the Web. A good example of an Internet-related publication is *Netsurfer Digest*, which summarizes on a weekly basis new events, sites, and other information appearing on the network (**http://www.netsurf.com/ nsd/index.html**):

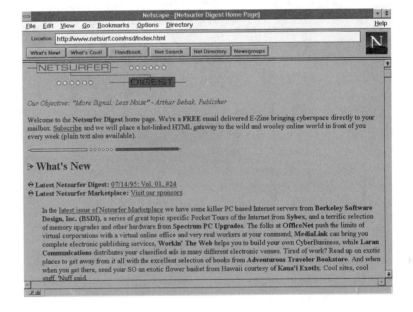

You can also choose to receive new issues of *Netsurfer Digest* automatically by e-mail, simply by filling in a form:

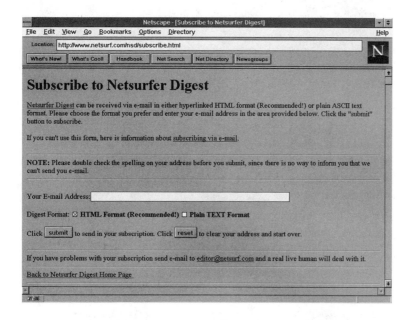

The Web is catching the attention of the business world, since it makes clear the strategic possibilities to be found in the Internet. We refer in-depth to many of these strategic opportunities in our book about Internet business strategy, *The Canadian Internet Advantage: Opportunities for Business and Other Organizations.*

The World Wide Web represents to an organization the opportunity by which it can electronically publish information for access by customers, suppliers, business associates, government bodies, stockholders, stakeholders, the general public, and other individuals and organizations. Used intelligently, the World Wide Web can be used as a strategic business tool and can help an organization enhance its capabilities to market its products and services.

A good example of a sophisticated marketing initiative can be found at Molson's site at **http://www.molson.com**. In this case, Molson has built a site that contains national information about Canadian concerts, a unique hockey pool, and other information:

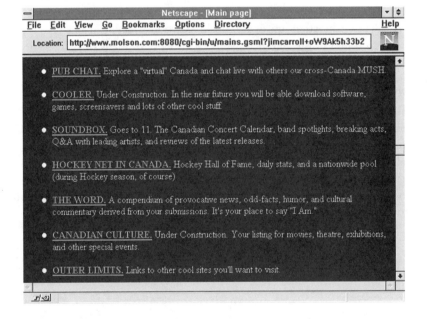

What are People Doing with the Internet?

It is obvious that there is a lot you can do on the Internet. In the next chapter we will take a look at what everyday, average Canadians have been doing with the Internet.

CHAPTER 3

The Internet in Canada

Who surfs the Internet? Conventional wisdom says it's young white men. But according to a recent survey, that profile is changing quickly.

Cyberia
Globe and Mail, August 4, 1995

Indeed it is. Speak to those unfamiliar with the Internet, and their idea of someone using the Internet will probably be the typical Hollywood image of a strange little geeky teenager with greasy hair and plastic pocket protectors, poking away at the keyboard, never seeing the light of day, as he tries to figure out the best way to hack computers at the Pentagon. Either that, or ultracool, beautiful, intelligent *beings* with perfect teeth, great hair, and IQs that are well over 200 — masters of the Internet. Right.

Let's forget Hollywood for a moment and come back to reality. In this chapter, we take a look at some of the individuals and organizations who are using the Internet on a day-to-day basis across Canada. We have tried to choose a broad range of people, organizations, and applications to show how the Internet is being used in many different situations. Have a look around, and you will discover that it is being used by your friends, neighbors, co-workers, parents, children, and grandparents. Basically, the Internet is becoming mainstream.

If you want to read a few more case studies like the ones that follow, take a voyage to our Web site, where we have posted many of the case studies from the 1994 and 1995 editions of the *Canadian Internet Handbook*. You will find them at **http://www.csi.nb.ca/handbook**.

Evelyn Perdue, Mother of Two

Evelyn Perdue (**evelyn.perdue@canrem.com**) is the mother of two young children. "I quit the corporate world to stay at home to raise my kids. I do part-time contract work writing policy manuals from home. My husband and I both enjoy working with computers but have little time to pursue this interest at this point in our lives."

How did we first come across Evelyn Perdue, and how did she come to be featured in this book? She has been on the Internet since November 1994 and sent her first e-mail in January 1995 after reading an earlier edition of *The Canadian Internet Handbook*. As is sometimes the case, she took us up on our offer to hear reader feedback and sent us a message at **handbook@uunet.ca**.

When writing this year's edition, we decided to follow up on a few of the people who had sent messages. Given Evelyn's unique situation (two young kids, remote community, no time), we decided to explore a little more what the Internet meant to her. So far, Evelyn has been using the Internet to send e-mail, to browse USENET, and to obtain some files. Has it been worth it? Perdue is blunt. "So far, I have not found any of it particularly fruitful." Intrigued, we decided to dig deeper.

Given that her early experience with the Internet has not brought any real benefit, we asked if she was going to walk away from it. Not quite. "I did renew my subscription already," she notes, indicating that she believes something is going on with the Internet. "I am reminded of a TV report one night that commented that when the telephone was introduced, everyone needed instructions and a learning curve to use it. The same was true of the car. Now we go from home to home and use the phone or drive a car with virtually no instructions. As a home office worker, mother of two young kids, I am obviously not the target techie who will turn this Internet into the household device I need. But my interest is definitely there." So, like many people, Perdue is willing to take the time to learn about the system, convinced that something will come of it.

It was not really her plan to be the Internet user in the household. "I actually gave the subscription to my husband for Christmas last year but absentmindedly put my own name on the sign-up form; as it turns out he hasn't had a chance to use it at all yet." Curious, she decided to venture in. "I had hoped to learn enough about the Internet to teach my 7-year-old to access libraries and other information around the world, as a sort of alternative to buying encyclopedias. I had hoped that he could get pen pals from other cultures different from our rural Ontario perspective."

Once she ventured in, she discovered a lot of things that were useful to her. "Being an avid CBC listener, especially while I work on the computer, I have found that it is great to be able to sign on the Internet and dash off a comment to Gzowski, RadioNoon, etc. The Internet allows me to respond with my

THE INTERNET IN CANADA

1 This chapter examines how various Canadians and Canadian organizations are making use of the Internet. These case studies include such people as Evelyn Perdue, the mother of two young children, Dr. Hor Yak D. Zung, a dentist from rural Alberta, Rob Washburn, a reporter with the *Cobourg Daily Star*, Mark Jeftovic, who created "The Primordial Schmooze" site, Phil Morrow, a lighting consultant located in Winnipeg, Manitoba, Judge Irv Goldenberg, a member of the Court of Queen's Bench for Saskatchewan, and Jean Johnston, a 75 year old grandmother

2 Organizations using the Internet in Canada that we profile are Molsons, Hastings Park Racecourse, Emergency Preparedness Canada, and the Canadian Parliamentary Channel, Halifax Police Department, the Regina Duplicate Bridge Club, the University of Northern British Columbia Caving Club, St. Paul's Anglican Church, and the town of Birtle, Manitoba.

two cents without leaving the office or being placed on hold." She is also discovering that even though she is in isolation working at home, the Internet does link her into the world.

But there are frustrations. "I have attempted to get answers to work-related questions through conferences, USENET and miscellaneous files and bulletin boards, but have found that very frustrating. Discussions seem to be either too superficial or too in-depth, or maybe that's just me." And e-mail is a challenge. "Finding addresses is the biggest problem. I have wasted a lot of time trying to track people or organizations. I haven't got the time to spend on this but I think if I had a better handle on the tools I would send much more e-mail." Certainly with two young children, we can understand the time limitations.

Even though she is experiencing some frustration with the Internet, she believes it important that the government do something to ensure that local communities can join it. "Rural areas that are not serviced by cable, although not in the majority by population, must be allowed access to the Internet. The old Bell monopoly for phones may not have had a lot of redeeming qualities, but their mandate to provide service when requested in any location was important and valuable in setting up the current telephone network. The same mentality must be applied to Internet access."

Being the mother of two children, we asked if she was concerned about the issue of pornography on the Internet. "I have not gone looking for it, and given my track record of finding sources of information for work I doubt if I would find it if I wanted it! I do feel that it is probably exaggerated, but I have some concerns because the access will probably eventually become as easy as flipping TV channels." Yet she believes strongly in the parental role when it comes to the Internet. "As with everything violent or perverted in today's world, though, I believe that if you do all you can to instill in your kids some values you cherish, you can only hope that they will exercise judgement when confronted with trash."

We chatted further with Perdue about what she might use the Internet for, such as the USENET newsgroup **misc.kids**, a place where parents exchange tips about the challenges of raising children, and **misc.kids.health**, where they exchange health and safety information. She expressed some excitement at the thought of these topics and indicated she would look for them the next time she went on-line. Through our discussion with her, it became apparent to us that while she has a lot of enthusiasm for the network, she simply needs a bit of guidance on how to find some of the more relevant areas on the network. That guidance is best found on the Web.

But she is not yet a user of the World Wide Web. "I've seen it and want to get on, but simply don't have the time," she notes. In this regard, Perdue is like many early pioneers of the Internet — people are using the network without discovering the information retrieval power that the Web provides.

Of course, others like Perdue are frustrated. Since she is not using the Web, it is as if she has been thrown into a library where all the lights have been turned off, and each and every book has been scattered on the floor! It is difficult for her to find something, but once she gets on the Web, she will discover a place where people have turned on the lights and are taking the time to put the books on the shelf.

Molson

The arrival of Molson to the Internet in the summer of 1995 is indicative of the extent to which corporate Canada is beginning to invest in the network. With press reports of an investment of upwards of $1 million in the Molson Web site, it is obvious that the Internet is becoming a mainstream corporate promotion and marketing tool.

Many throughout the corporate world are working with the Internet in order to figure out how it can be used for a strategic benefit. Given that this is so, Molson's entrance into the Internet caused a stir in the media. Consider the headlines:

◆ Marketing & Advertising — Molson on the Internet, *Globe and Mail*, July 20, 1995;

◆ Suds marketers look to future and dive into the Internet —Molson invests in cyberspace, *Vancouver Sun,* July 22, 1995;

◆ Brewer offers tickets on Internet, *Calgary Herald*, July 21, 1995;

◆ Something's brewing on the Internet; Molson spreads its web site with a selection aimed squarely at the beer-drinking crowd, *The Edmonton Journal*, July 21, 1995;

◆ Molson uncaps Internet site aimed at young adults, *The Toronto Star*, July 20, 1995;

◆ Molson entertains with guide on 'Net, *Vancouver Province*, July 19, 1995.

We noted in Chapter 2 the types of information that Molson was making available in its site.

An interesting feature is that Molson is encouraging a level of interactivity with its customers as part of its marketing effort on the Internet. In order to encourage a regular stream of visitors to its "place" on the Internet (known as "I Am Online," based on the "I am" phrase used in Molson marketing campaigns), Molson has built a number of innovative features increasingly found throughout the Web.

For example, it includes a registration process. You can visit the Molson site (**http://www.molson.com**), but in order to access all areas, you must register. This gives Molson an idea of the background of people visiting it on the Web. This registration process also permits the organization to provide for new, exciting uses of the Web. For example, on the welcome screen below, you can see that the Web site is not just about graphics and pictures; through it you can send and receive e-mail as well as participate in on-line "chats" with other people at the site:

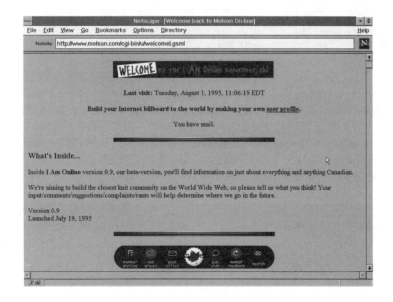

The theme of interacting with other users is found throughout the site. For example, you can search or browse through the profiles of various people who have registered with the site:

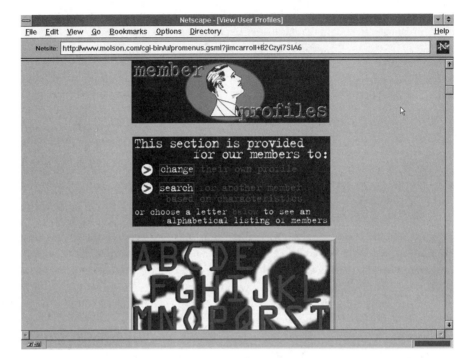

Clearly, Molson is investing in the Web as a new means of reaching and dealing with its customers and others.

To find out how the site was performing, we contacted Diana Rose, Brand Manager for the Molson Canadian product, and Brian Flanagan, Supervisor, Internet Projects at Molson (**bmflanag@molson.com**). Their reaction was that the site was beginning to exceed expectations. Within two months of opening, the site was drawing a steady stream of visitors each and every day. The vast majority were males under 40, reflecting the fact that not only are men the main beer drinkers, but are the predominant users of the Internet.

Another interesting fact is that most visitors were from Ontario and British Columbia, yet in proportion to population, British Columbia was certainly drawing a much higher percentage. Why? In British Columbia, at the time the statistics were calculated, Molson was including its Web address in its regular advertising and on its beer label, while it was prohibited at that time by the Liquor Control Board of Ontario from doing so. (Government authorities are sometimes slow to recognize that the world is changing around them at a furious pace, so sometimes bureaucracies move at a slow pace when it comes to the Internet.)

The most active areas on the Molson Web site would appear to be the summaries of up and coming concerts, with a lot of interest by users, the bands themselves, and certainly by record companies. In addition, the area in which people can send questions directly to the brewmaster, Walker Hoag, has generated a lot of interest, with detailed questions coming from, for example, a few microbiologists from around the world.

And the most exciting area of the Molson site reflects its Canadian heritage. Its on-line hockey pool has been officially sanctioned by the National Hockey League, which provides Molson with immediate, up-to-date statistics each and every day. Through the pool (which anyone over legal drinking age can join), people can draft together a team of hockey players from the NHL and play against other players. Each day the statistics are used to update the win/loss status for each "fantasy team," and at the end, the winner wins a trip to the Stanley Cup. Clearly, Molson has launched onto a new form of interactive marketing with individuals across Canada and around the world with its "I Am Online" site.

Birtle, Manitoba

You do not need to be an organization the size of Molson to enjoy success on the Internet. Birtle, Manitoba, is a small town located in southwestern Manitoba. Where in Manitoba? Well, they tell you on their home page on the Internet (**http://www.docker.com/~birtle/birtle.htm**):

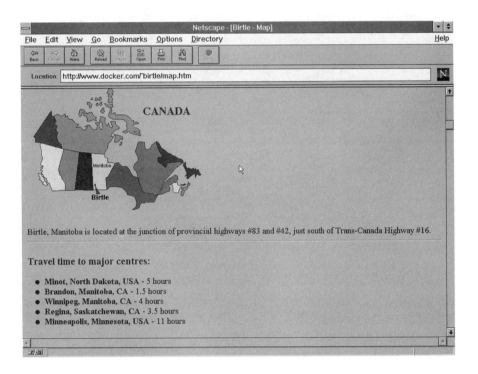

Like many rural towns, Birtle saw its local economy undergo a substantial change during the 1970s and 1980s due to increasing urbanization. With a population of about 800, and so many residents in the past moving to larger cities and towns, Birtle found that it needed some economic revitalization, and to accomplish that it had to encourage some new people to move to the town. Residents of Birtle did not sit around and bemoan their lot in life. In fact, several of them got together in 1995 and decided it was time to do something.

These residents, including folks like Ron Bell (a farmer) and his wife, Brenda Evans (a teacher), established a program called "Birtle into the Future," the objective of which was to encourage people to relocate to Birtle. With the backing of the town council, they launched in 1995 a comprehensive publicity campaign extolling the benefits of Birtle. The campaign, advertised in several major Canadian newspapers, noted the availability of residential building lots for $1 (yes, that's right, $1). And if you are interested in establishing a business, noted the ads, the town will provide you a building along Main Street. If you are still in business in five years and have paid all your taxes, the building is yours. *Free.*

Quite often in Canada, people in large cities tend to think that they are at the centre of the electronic universe. There is a little bit of snobbishness about big cities, but the beauty of the Internet is that it reaches everywhere. In the case of Birtle, these folks did not restrict themselves to the traditional media — they took to the Internet. Jeremy Geras, a Grade 9 student in the local school, was enlisted to build a Web site that provided details about Birtle, the benefits of relocating there, and the relocation program. In addition, an electronic mail ID (**birtle@docker.com**) was created to receive any potential queries:

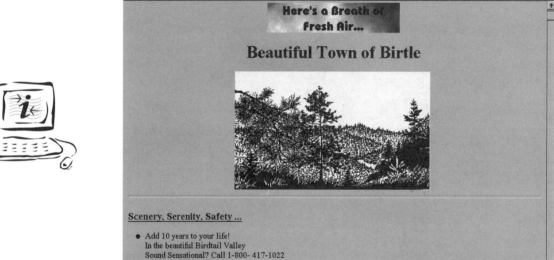

The folks at Birtle are uncanny marketers. Notice that the first item on the Web site is something entitled "Scenery, serenity, and safety." Choosing that item, you are told the benefits of relocating to Birtle; the town is clearly appealing to those fed up with the urban life.

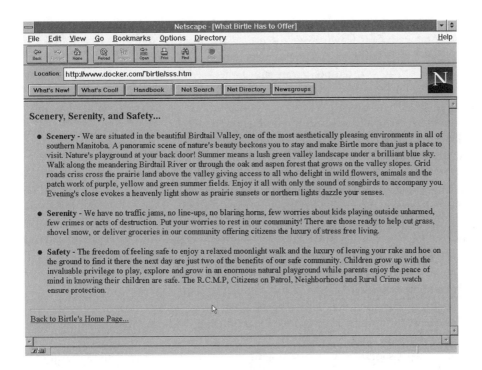

Has the campaign worked? Certainly they have drawn a lot of inquiries as a result of their newspaper advertisements. And as for the Internet, they have received from 30 to 60 queries for more information. That might not sound like a big number for those companies with Web sites that draw hundreds of thousands of visitors a week, but then again, Birtle is not Molson.

"It's the quality, not the quantity," notes Bell, when asked if the Internet part of the campaign has been a success. "The enquiries we received through the Internet have been good, solid ones that might lead to something." In one case, a chap from Toronto who found and contacted them through the Internet has come to town and has put in an offer on a building. Nothing is confirmed yet, but it looks like something could happen. It is this type of thing that makes the Internet a worthwhile investment for a community like Birtle. And it is not a huge investment. When asked what it cost so far, Bell just chuckles: "The Internet side of things cost us about $300 so far."

Halifax Police Department

In August 1995, while vacationing in Nova Scotia and trying to ignore all things related to the Internet, one of the authors noticed that a crime story in *The Halifax Daily News* noted that the "wanted poster" for a crime that had just been committed had been "posted to cyberspace."

You really cannot get away from the Internet if you want to. Curious, we decided to follow this up and find out what was going on (once the vacation was over). We immediately discovered a police department that was rapidly becoming involved with the Internet and one that was gaining global attention for its innovative use of the Internet. Behind the scenes, we found Sgt. William S. (Bill) Cowper (**sarge@loki.atcon.com**), the NCO (non-commissioned officer) in charge of the #1 Watch Communications for the Halifax Police Department (HPD). And with Sgt. Cowper, we discovered the story of someone who found that the Internet led to a dynamic and exciting career change.

Cowper is a 46-year-old police sergeant, father of three boys (14, 18, and 21), and husband of, as he puts it, "a very patient wife, Claudia, who puts up with a webaholic/career cop for a husband." Sgt. Cowper has been a police officer for 23 years, with stints in regular patrol, undercover narcotics work, and homicide.

He now carries the title Communications Sergeant and is responsible for the World Wide Web site for the Halifax Police Department (soon to be the "Metro Police Department" as several municipalities in the area merge). As such, he is responsible for maintaining, enhancing, and expanding use of the Internet by the HPD.

How does an ex-homicide detective become involved with the Web? As is often the case with many people, a career change comes about as the result of something unexpected. In October 1994, Sgt. Cowper broke his ankle and leg in three places while on the job (actually chasing a 13-year-old female car thief). He soon found himself with his leg in a cast. Not one to sit about ruminating about his condition, he used all his newly found spare time to sit in front of a home computer 12 hours a day, in order to learn about the Internet.

He quickly dove into the topic. "I spent a fortune on books," he notes. "I've been a computer hobbyist for ten years…and once I started using Netscape and the World Wide Web there was no turning back."

Sgt. Cowper soon felt himself getting further into the Internet. With a dream of always having his own business, he decided to focus on the Internet. "I started a business called Sarge Computer Consultants and developed seminars to teach the Internet. I had two goals. One was to realize my dream of starting a business, but the other was to get the Halifax Police Department on the World Wide Web." Eventually, through the business, he began to do a number of local computer seminars about the Internet and continues to this day.

Returning to work in April 1995, he made a pitch to establish a site on the Web. "I presented a written proposal to management upon my return to active duty but had to wait until May '95 to actually demo the Internet for the Chief and his senior officers." The Chief, at the time the President of the Canadian Association of Chiefs of Police, gave the go-ahead to delve into the Internet a bit further. Sgt. Cowper quickly set a deadline for completion. "I wanted to have it up and running before the G7 Summit being held in Halifax in June of '95 so we could showcase ourselves to the world." With the assistance of friends, volunteers and the corporate community, he managed to achieve that goal, despite the lack of a budget and funds.

Once the site was established, it began to draw some notice and caught the eye of the media. "On June 7/95 we unveiled the home page at a well-attended news conference and went live. We got TV, newspaper and radio coverage. We wanted to be unique on the Web, and so we became the first police home page worldwide to profile all our unsolved murders."

Since then, the site has continued to attract the attention of people worldwide. "In the first month we made it on an internationally ranked 'Cool Site of the Day' list, and broke more than half a million 'hits' on the page. E-mail started to flood in worldwide. Because of this exposure, Sgt. Cowper now finds himself in contact with police departments around the world, seeking his guidance and comments as they create their own Web sites.

Sgt. Cowper is quick to note that the success of the Web site is not strictly because of his efforts. He notes the involvement of Atlantic Connect, a local Internet service provider, and the involvement of Shawn Preston from that organization, as well as Sandy Gillis of the Halifax Police Department, and Multimedia House International, which helped out with some graphic and design work. He also convinced a local computer company, Vtech Computers/ Capitol Business to provide computers, and the local telephone company, MT&T, to provide the phone hook up as a community service.

His involvement with the Internet has not been limited to building a Web site. He has been involved in real police work through the Internet on occasion. "On the Saturday night of the G7 summit, I intervened on IRC to prevent a suicide in Oshawa, Ont. A 19-year-old boy was threatening to slash his wrists. Other people on the channel included persons from Texas, Oregon, California and Halifax. I went on the channel after a call to our emergency phone line from the Halifax individual who was on-line. I talked on-line to persons who fed me information about this kid. We soon discovered this youth's address and as a result I called Durham Regional Police and they dispatched a car and ambulance. They found the kid with a knife and prevented the suicide."

He also uses the Internet as a tool to keep in touch with law enforcement officials world-wide. "I have joined several listservs that are police-related, such as police-l for the discussion of general policing issues and foren-l for the discussion of forensic issues, and others." Hence the Internet has become his own knowledge network.

Sgt. Cowper is clearly enthusiastic about the possibilities for this technology. "I'm very excited about the Internet and how the police and community can use it to interact. I know that the Halifax Police Department can be a leader in this area. We consider ourselves on the vanguard of community-based policing worldwide and we wanted our home page to reflect that image."

The Primordial Schmooze

Where else could you buy a book that lists something called the "Primordial Schmooze" coming so closely after the Halifax Police Department? One thing about the Internet is that you will find anything on-line — from serious police organizations such as the Halifax Police Department to an entertainment-based site called the Primordial Schmooze.

The Primordial Schmooze is a follow-up to an item that was briefly mentioned in the 1995 edition of this book. In that edition we mentioned a chap named Mark Jeftovic (**markjr@schmooze.net**), a guitarist with the Toronto band LANDSLIDE. At the time, Jeftovic indicated that he had "grandiose plans for the system, including plans to put sound-bites from bands on the server." Back then, Jeftovic was experimenting with using the Internet as a means through which independent bands could promote themselves. His real goal was to include the capability for those bands to put their actual music on-line, so that people could try them out, so to speak.

As you begin to use the Internet, you will quickly discover that things move forward at an often amazing pace. In early 1995, the Internet was still an experiment for many musical acts, but by the end of the year, it was almost a necessity. Indeed, a look around would seem to indicate that being on the Internet is a critical activity for any Canadian act, large or small. You will find all kinds of bands on-line, ranging from independent bands like LANDSLIDE to large established acts like Tea Party and Brian Adams.

In Jeftovic's case, his dream has come true. He has built the Primordial Schmooze, a site where independent bands, record labels, comic artists, and music magazines can promote themselves. Where can you find it? One Web address is **http://www.shmooze.net/pwcasual**, the first name Jeftovic registered on the Internet. When a co-band member noted that "shmooze" usually included a "c," Jeftovic registered the name **schmooze.net** on the Internet as well, so the address **http://www.schmooze.net** will work too.

And Jeftovic's "grandiose" plans have come true — and quite common. Traveling into the Schmooze or any on-line musical site, you can sample all kinds of music from various artists. In the case of the Schmooze, you can access information about a number of Canadian bands that market themselves through the service:

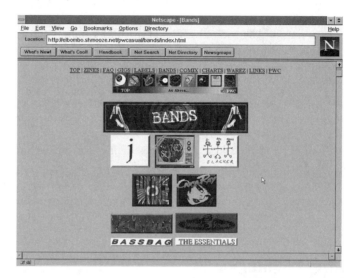

If you have configured your Web software correctly, it is a piece of cake to listen to sound clips. Looking at Jeftovic's band, you simply move to the "Multi-Media" song at the bottom, double click, and depending on the speed of your link, you will hear a clip from the song in a few seconds or minutes:

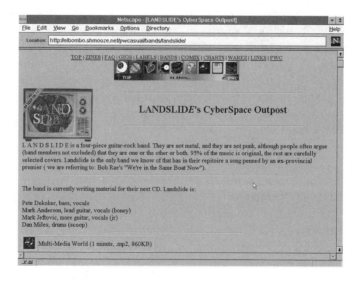

One impact of the Internet and sites like the Primordial Schmooze is that the network has now become a vehicle through which up-and-coming artists can directly reach fans and potential fans, and thus bypass the traditional route of having to "schmooze" with established music industry organizations. From that perspective, it plays right into the "alternative" music scene, which is flourishing across Canada.

Has it worked? One band listed on the site, The Essentials, has had a number of contacts through the Internet and has been invited to participate in a few concerts in the United States. And a magazine on the site has seen an increase in circulation since it began to publicize itself and publish through the Internet. Hence there is some benefit to be found in involvement with the Internet.

As for LANDSLIDE, unfortunately, they broke up in 1995. Jeftovic is not deterred, however. He believes it is only a matter of time before sites like the Schmooze provide bands with significant opportunities to reach potential fans. Perhaps it was too early for LANDSLIDE in this case.

Regina Duplicate Bridge Club

Do you think that you have to be someone special to have a Web page? Or that you need all kinds of special computer programming talent? Or that you need to have a million-dollar budget? Think again. The Regina Duplicate Bridge Club has a page (**http://regina.ism.ca/orgs/rdbc.htm**):

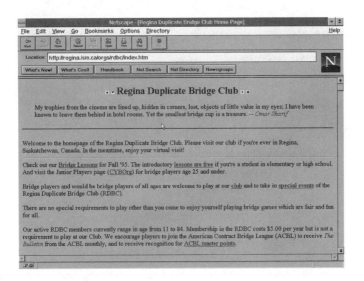

"We use it to publicize schedules for our members. As well, we've got information about our bridge camps and upcoming tournaments," notes Arnie Lind, one of the club members (**arnie.lind@dlcwest.com**). A retired employee of IBM, he is now a "business process reengineering" consultant. The page was created with his guidance by John Cornell, a computer specialist with ISM, a computer consulting firm.

Why a Web page for a bridge club? Lind cites: "Communication. We're having a major regional tournament, with people coming from across North America including Texas. It's a way that they can find out details without necessarily having to phone." Lind believes that there is some real potential for use of the Internet within the global bridge community. "We should, for example, ensure that we get the ACB League on-line, and all the other clubs." He indicates that there is already quite a bit of e-mail between bridge club members throughout North America.

Lind was not deterred by thoughts of complexity in putting up such a site and certainly believes that it helps to keep the club involved with high technology. "It also involves, I suppose, a bit of prestige — it's a bit of an honor to have a Web page," notes Lind.

Interview with a Dentist (A Future Novel by Anne Rice?)

We were browsing on-line one day for information about a certain virus that affects children. And as often happens when you are looking for something on the Internet, some information found in your travels will catch your attention. In this case, we came across a posting by a Dr. Hor Tak D. Zung of Alberta (**zung@freenet.calgary.ab.ca**). In the posting, he was responding to a question that had been posted to the USENET newsgroup **sci.med.dentistry**, by someone named Otter.

Re: Teeth Cleaning

From: "Hor Tak D. Zung" <zung@freenet.calgary.ab.ca>

Date: 1995/04/15

MessageID:

Pine.A32.3.90.950415002452.22070A-100000@srv1.freenet.calgary.ab.ca#1/1

organization: The University of Calgary

content-type: TEXT/PLAIN; charset=US-ASCII

mime-version: 1.0

newsgroups: sci.med.dentistry

> I had my gum pockets measured the other day followed up by a cleaning,

> and when I left the dental office my mouth was bleeding like I've never

> done before. In fact, my gums were bleeding before they even got to the

> cleaning!

Hi Otter,

Gums usually will tend to bleed a bit after a dental cleaning. If they are not bleeding, the hygienist is probably not doing a thorough enough job. It might seem strange, but it is because the instruments which are used must enter the gum pocket area which can be very tight so bleeding can be illicited. The more severe the gum disease, the more hemorrhaging will occur. When the gums are in trouble, they are inflamed and can bleed easily!

> Normally, I don't get any bleeding when I brush or floss, nor do my gums

> hurt. When I floss I go in as far as I can go and I wrap around each tooth.

Well, the early stages of gum disease are pretty painless. I don't think people can generally feel a 5 mm pocket coming on until it gets to 7 or 8 or 9 or 10 and abscessy. Brushing and flossing aren't placed into the gum pockets quite the same as a hardened steel scaler instrument.

> question: Does height have anything to do with gum pocket depth? I'm six

> foot one inches tall.

Heh, I've never heard that one before! :) Is that like how some people believe that shoe size relates to ..... size?

> I've heard from a friend of mine who said that their dentist says that

> anyone worth his or her salt should never make anyone bleed. Is that

> true? Any comments or suggestions about my situation?

Bloodless dentistry. An interesting concept. It'd be nice to be able to do it, but it's like looking for a surgeon that never makes a person bleed. Must be some real powerful homeopathic dentistry if no bleeding is ever caused by that dentist! I could pop out some wisdoms without a drop. Boy, it'd be nice not to get that red stuff on my nice, clean latex gloves too. :)

On the other hand, there are some over aggressive hygienists who sometimes will overdo it a bit, but these are probably rare. I've had a small piece of my interdental papilla lopped off by the swoosh of a not so carefully pivoted sickle scaler, and let me tell you, that stings! And it doesn't grow back too well either. :) Still, gums will be sore after a cleaning for about 1 to 2 weeks if you haven't had one for a long time and depending on how severe your gums are.

Don't be scared by a little blood or soreness!

It's usually worth it. Just tell your practitioner your concerns.

Hor Tak D. Zung, D.D.S., B.Sc.

Calgary, Alberta, Canada.

What possesses a dentist to spend time in the **sci.med.dentistry** USENET newsgroup answering questions from people he doesn't even know? When those people might be anywhere in the world? And when he isn't getting paid for it?

Curious, we contacted Dr. Zung by e-mail. His reply was instructive. "Well, I don't know," he said. But digging a little deeper, he said: "I sure get enough questions asked at work that only God knows why I pursue it on the Internet. Maybe it's because what it means to me to be a health care practitioner includes helping people even in my spare time. I like talking to people on the Internet because you just never know where in the whole wide world they may be living. That reward of maybe providing a different, perhaps helpful answer to someone also might be the answer."

Dr. Zung is a 26-year-old dentist in the town of Strathmore, a small town 30 minutes east of Calgary. "I've been in general practice for a bit over 3 years now, and I find it nice to work in a smaller community because the people here are friendly and the workload is pretty steady." And given the remoteness of the community, the Internet is a natural draw for him. He has been involved in the on-line world for some time. "I've always dabbled in local bulletin board systems, so I guess it was a natural transition to try out the Internet areas. I read about the Free-Net in the *Calgary Herald* and decided to join out of curiosity. It was a nice way to e-mail my brother who lives in Toronto without paying long distance charges."

How does he spend most of his time on-line? "I used to read the **Alt.pets.cats**, Star Trek Voyager, Ford Probe, and CD ROM review newsgroups, but lately I stick to the **sci.med.dentistry** base area. It's nice to help people on the Internet with their dental problems. I'm sure that there are plenty of more experienced and knowledgeable dentists out there, but I feel that I can contribute my opinions too. It's more of a hobby, I suppose."

But Dr. Zung has also discovered that the Internet is a powerful tool to help him keep in touch with other dentists, an important issue given his location in a small community. "It gives me a view on other dentist's techniques and ideas. I belong to a private dental message area for dental professionals only called **dentistry@stat.com**. And I do talk to other dentists through the Internet on occasion," he notes. "I find that members of my profession generally don't have that much of an opportunity to interact with one another so the Internet helps in this way. I've discussed some techniques with more experienced practitioners in the States, which has come in handy. I feel that there is good opportunity to get advice or consult other people more easily through the Internet."

In communicating with Dr. Zung, you discover someone who is more interested in what he can use the Internet for than what the Internet really is. "I have no idea what USENET is," he commented, when asked whether he had other uses for USENET. "In fact, even after modeming for years, I was totally lost as to the terminology used on the Internet. Eudora, FTP, HTTP, WWW, Archie, etc. are still foggy terms to me."

Clearly, here is an individual who has found that it is what the Internet can be used for, and not its exciting razzle-dazzle technology, that is the most fascinating thing. A refreshing individual to meet, given that so much of the focus on the Internet so often is on the technical side.

Hastings Park Racecourse

The horse racing industry has come to the Internet. If you will pardon our pun, we feel compelled to say that "they're off and running." Hastings Park Racecourse is one of Canada's largest thoroughbred racing courses and is located in Vancouver, British Columbia. With a lengthy, respected history, they now have the distinction of being Canada's first racecourse on the Internet. Through their Web site (**http://www.hastingspark.com/**), they publish a wide variety of local race information, including daily race summaries and race results, images of each race "card," and jockey and trainer information. In addition, they provide links to other racetracks and race-related information around the world:

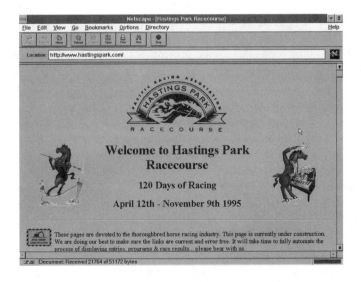

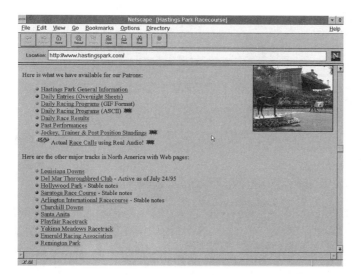

Perhaps the most exciting and innovative application — and one that portends the future of racetracks on the Internet — is the fact that they make available the audio of actual race "calls" soon after a race is run. For example, on the following screen, we are listening to the announcer as he "calls" the $150,000 British Columbia Derby:

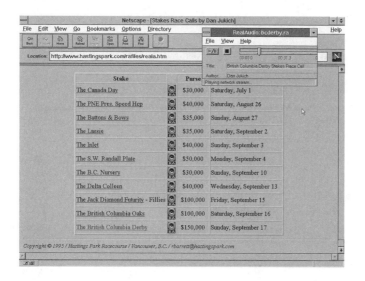

The Web site for the raceway was created primarily through the efforts of Ray Barrett III (**rbarrett@hastingspark.com**), the Desktop Publishing Coordinator for the organization. He is primarily responsible for putting together the daily programs and race cards, which are sold in the form of paper programs. But with his involvement in the desktop publishing field, he could not help but hear everyone talking about the Internet, and worked to convince the General Manager of the raceway, Bill Taylor, to go ahead with establishing the site. Through the summer of 1995, he began to figure out what would be involved in getting this information onto the Internet and wrote the pages containing the information.

The result is an impressive and quite complete site. For example, each daily race card is available on the Internet both in text form and in the form of an image taken directly from that day's program:

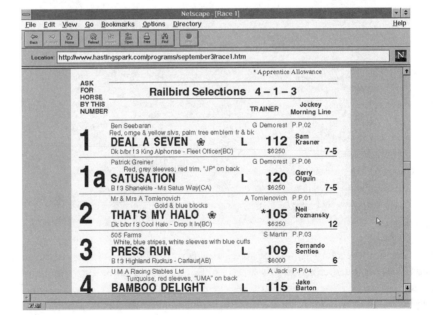

The raceway is now thinking about the strategic potential of the Internet. "The racing market has traditionally been isolated to individual communities," notes Taylor. "Yet there are racing fans throughout the world who have an interest in what is going on at various tracks. We can use the Internet to reach everyone who has an interest in our track, horses, and jockeys and provide information and services to a broader audience."

Taylor notes that some people might be interested in tracking a particular jockey, while in other cases there might be some interest by someone in Kentucky in a particular horse at Hastings. "This is a first step to communicating with customers and potential customers electronically," notes Taylor, "wherever they might be."

Where might the site go in the future? While the folks at Hastings are reluctant to talk about what the Internet might mean to the industry, those familiar with the fast pace of change in Internet technology can see the day, not too far off in the future, when such a Web site could include the "tote board" (i.e., the board that shows the odds and amount bet before each race) and the ability to place electronic bets. And with the trend for real-time broadcasting through the Internet, a racetrack Web site could provide a race in "real time." And even — one day — live video. The result? A virtual raceway, available to racing fans right around the world.

Taylor is quite cognizant that technology on the Internet is moving forward at an amazing pace and believes that Hastings Park Racecourse must keep up for reasons of international pressure if nothing else. "There are some challenges that we have in Canada when it comes to government and the Canadian Pari-Mutuel Agency," he cautiously observes when asked about how the Internet might affect the industry. And when he is asked about the scenario of real-time wagering and broadcast through the Internet — the virtual raceway concept — he comments wryly that one thing is certain: "Our U.S. counterparts will do it at some point."

The Internet often makes national borders irrelevant and has the potential to reshape and change entire industries. Certainly the Hastings Park Racecourse is in the early stages of discovering just how the Internet can be used within its own industry, while keeping a wary eye on what the future might bring.

Community Newspapers

Rob Washburn (**rwash@eagle.ca**) is a reporter with the *Cobourg Daily Star*. In this role, he has become quite involved with the Internet. You might think that someone with a newspaper might feel threatened by the concept of the Internet. After all, some people believe that the Internet will make newspapers irrelevant, because we will one day get all our news through our computer screens.

That is not likely. Many doubt that at the end of the day we are going to curl up with our computer and keyboard to read the newspaper. And individuals like Washburn are realizing that by embracing the Internet, they can bring positive and beneficial change to the role of the community newspaper. In Washburn's case, he uses the Internet as a tool to help him with his job as a reporter. But he has not stopped there; he has become proactively involved in helping to bring the Internet into his local community.

For Washburn, the Internet is a powerful tool that helps him to access information that was not previously easily obtained. Washburn gives one example, a recent release of budget information from the Ontario government. Traditionally, news organizations put a person in the "lockup," a secured media room in Toronto where reporters can browse through budget information for the day and then release their stories as soon as the budget is released in the legislature.

For many community newspapers such as the *Cobourg Daily Star*, the resources and funds do not exist to dedicate a person for the day to such an event. But this makes it difficult to get accurate information quickly enough to put together a story.

The Internet has opened the door for a community newspaper like the *Cobourg Daily Star* to once again participate in an event like a budget release. Notes Washburn, "When the Ontario budget was released, I was able to go to the Ontario government Web site and immediately pick up some of the relevant budget summaries. If I had to wait for a fax, it wouldn't have come till later that night since smaller newspapers are usually at the bottom of a fax distribution list. And if it was sent in the mail, it would have taken a week or more."

The benefits of the Internet go beyond speed of delivery, says Washburn. "Not only that, but it's in electronic form, so I can cut and paste sections directly into the relevant parts of my article."

Washburn sees that his use of the Internet is an example of how the role of the PC is changing the job of the reporter. Instead of simply being a fancy typewriter, the computer is becoming a tool used in gathering and analyzing information. The industry calls it "computer-assisted reporting," and the Internet is beginning to play a major role in this type of activity.

A good example of this changing role is found within Washburn's involvement with the Canadian Association of Journalists. "We are in the process of setting up a database of information useful to Canadian journalists, which will be available through the Internet. It's the one place that Canadian journalists can come to in order to start their search for resources. There's a lot of stuff on-line, but hopefully we'll help narrow it down to some of the things that are good for Canadian journalists in particular."

He also takes part in an electronic mailing list in which over 100 journalists discuss issues of computer-assisted reporting in Canada; they share tips, ideas, strategies, and observations. Through these activities, Washburn is one of many journalists who are beginning to discover how the Internet is a useful tool to gather and analyze news information.

Yet, even given his use of the network, the role of the Internet extends beyond its use in computer-assisted reporting. Washburn believes that the community newspaper has an important role in shaping what a community uses the Internet for. Recently, he has been working on a community-wide project that is looking to coordinate Internet activities related to the local Northumberland community; he calls it an "electronic village." Part of the effort involves helping to make the community aware of what is possible with the Internet.

To accomplish this goal, Washburn is one of the founding members of the "Northumberland Networked Communities Council," a group of local citizens with the plan of ensuring that people in the community learn to benefit from the Internet. Its ambitious goals include

- helping to ensure that local schools have access to the Internet;

- ensuring that there are public access terminals in libraries with which patrons can access the Internet, so that no one is prevented from getting on to the Internet;

- helping all citizens have access to Internet training;

- creating a climate that will encourage local businesses to market themselves through the Internet to a local, national, and global audience;

- encouraging local citizens to participate in on-line discussions of local issues;

- ensuring that local politicians and public servants are accessible by e-mail;

- ensuring that leading-edge communications technology related to the Internet and on-line communications is available in the community.

The council will act as a facilitator to encourage many of the activities described above. Their original plan was to create a Free-Net, a community organization that provides free access to the Internet. But once they looked around the community, they realized that there were many commercial organizations that already provided on-line services. Hence they decided not to compete with established services, but to concentrate on encouraging the widespread use of Internet services throughout the community.

The Committee has managed to obtain federal funding to hire three people for 44 weeks to begin some of the activities related to the project. In the short term, their efforts will go to creating a regional Web site providing information on all local Internet activities, as well as laying the groundwork for some of the ambitious plans described above.

What will the role of the community newspaper be in ten years? Washburn feels that it will be one in which the newspaper delivers information in both paper and electronic forms. He also believes that it will be an organization that will provide much of the on-line information for a community in terms of events, announcements, schedules, and notices. He believes that the newspaper will become more involved in the type of community-networking initiative seen with the Northumberland Networked Communities Council and will thus be an active player in encouraging local involvement with global networks.

"Community newspapers have the credibility in many communities to help see that such initiatives are successful," he notes. "They have the credibility in the community to help pull together an electronic community."

There are many small communities across Canada that complain about the fact that they do not have easy access to the Internet. They should look to individuals like Rob Washburn and to initiatives such as the Northumberland Networked Communities Council for inspiration on how to put a positive, proactive project in place that will encourage the community to become more involved in the global Internet.

Lighting in Canada

One of the greatest benefits of the Internet is the fact that people can use it to build an "on-line community" of their peers. A community does not necessarily have to be a physical place like Cobourg, Ontario; it can be a collection of people who share an interest in a common topic. Once such a "community" has been built, members can then use the Internet to share knowledge, tips, pointers, ideas, and other information.

Anyone venturing into the Internet should keep in mind that it is a system that is in many ways still new and growing. One result is that when some new users first encounter the Internet, they become frustrated by the inability to find companies or information — a "community" — related to their particular industry or area of interest. In other cases, they discover such information but all too often find that it is too focused on American issues, not Canadian.

Discouraged by their inability to use the network to find relevant information, or because they cannot find methods to network with their peers in the industry, they lose some of their enthusiasm for the Internet.

But rather than bemoaning the fact that the Internet might not be fully developed in their area of interest, some people take a different approach. Rather than complaining about the fact that "something has not been done," they take the "I might as well do something" approach.

A good example of an individual with the latter type of attitude is Phil Morrow, a lighting consultant located in Winnipeg, Manitoba. (**pmconsult@mbnet.mb.ca**). Morrow has created "Lighting in Canada" (**http://www.mbnet.mb.ca/pmconsult/corner.html**), a

Web site dedicated to information about, well, lighting in Canada. "I was looking for information on the Web about the lighting industry and could only find American information," he says. "So I decided to fix that problem, and created a place where we can educate people that there is a lighting industry in Canada."

Through Lighting in Canada you can find a variety of information, including selected information from industry publications, a "guest author" section, information on new products, pointers to designers and consultants in the lighting industry in Canada, links to other lighting resources around the world, and a pointer to the Illuminating Engineering Society of North America. Not to mention the fact that you can find a pointer to what must be the world's largest on-line database of lightbulb jokes. If you are going to work in an industry, you really should have a sense of humor about the industry.

Morrow has been involved with the Internet "for a couple of years. I used e-mail, USENET and several other things. It wasn't until I saw the Web with Netscape that I saw the opportunity." Working on his own, he figured out HTML, the language of the Web, and set about creating the Lighting in Canada site.

It is a good source of information to find information about the industry. For example, it has quickly become the best place to find out about new lighting companies joining the Internet by establishing their own Web sites:

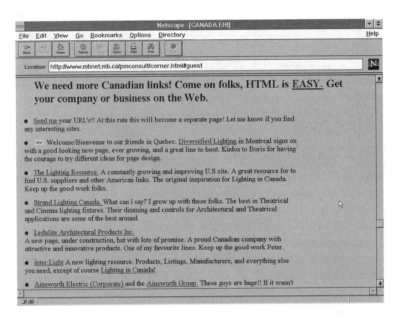

"I'd like it to become a focal point of the lighting industry in Canada. I've been talking to a few industry publications to see if there is some information they can bring on-line, and I'd like to make it a central resource for the industry, so that people could quickly find, for example, lighting designers." It is this type of attitude that is quickly making the Internet such a useful resource. Folks like Morrow see that an index of information does not exist about a particular topic, so they go off and create one.

Morrow is the first to agree that the site is by no means comprehensive and reflects the fact that many within the lighting industry in Canada are still trying to determine just what the heck the Internet is and what it is good for. "It's much like any industry," observes Morrow. "Many people are just sitting back and waiting."

But Morrow also believes it is only a matter of time before the lighting industry wakes up to the strategic business potential of the Internet. "What I find fascinating is that in most cases in the industry, corporate Web sites are being built by 'propeller heads' in the backroom on their own time. They then take it to management to show them that there is an incredible advertising and marketing vehicle emerging."

It is with this type of "bottom-up" pressure in industry, and through efforts of individuals like Morrow, that the Internet will quickly become prevalent throughout the lighting industry, as it will through all industries in Canada.

Judges on the Internet

If you were asked to define the characteristics of a typical judge, you might typically respond that it is most likely an older male with white hair and a white beard. Asked what he might have on the bench with him, you would probably suggest a legal pad and pen, and not much else. Judge Irv Goldenberg (**gold@eagle.wbm.ca**) chuckles at the image. "Well, I've got the white hair and beard. But I've just returned from court," he notes, "with my Ascentia 910 laptop. I use it in the court to take down the evidence that I hear."

It is important that when it comes to Canadian judges we dispel our perceptions; many of them have been high-tech for quite some time. And certainly, like any other industry and profession, Canadian judges, both male and female, are discovering the value of the Internet.

To find out what Canadian judges are doing with the Internet, we sought out Judge Goldenberg, a chap involved in one of the main "unofficial" and "informal" projects on the Internet involving the legal profession — maintaining the Web site "Judges on the Internet" (**http://www.law.ubc.ca/jurist/judges.html**). He is a member of the Court of Queen's Bench for Saskatchewan.

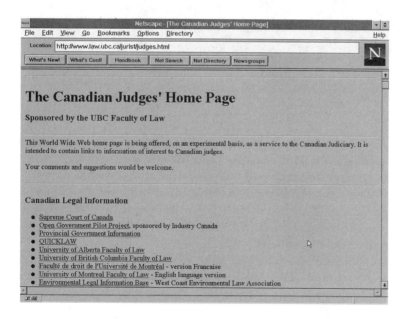

The site, sponsored by the law faculty at the University of British Columbia, provides pointers to information of interest to Canadian judges, ranging from Supreme Court decisions to information from various law faculties, as well as pointers to information of special interest to judges. It stemmed from the efforts and encouragement of a recently retired law professor at the university, Robert Franson. In essence, "The Canadian Judges' Home Page" is a place that can help a Canadian judge discover information on the Internet of special interest and relevance to him/her.

Certainly there is a growing number of Canadian judges on the Internet. And like many professions, many are just beginning to discover how the Internet can be used in a legal context.

But it is also important to note that this is a profession that long ago made the leap into "cyberspace." In fact, many judges across Canada were exposed to concepts of on-line electronic searching in the late 1980s, and many have been using such technology for quite some time. One estimate, for example, indicates that perhaps 60% to 70% of federally appointed judges have at one time or another used QuickLaw (**http://www.qlsys.ca/quicklaw.html**), a comprehensive pay-per-use database service that provides access to over 1,000 Canadian legal databases. These databases contain, for example, the full text of millions of court cases from across the country.

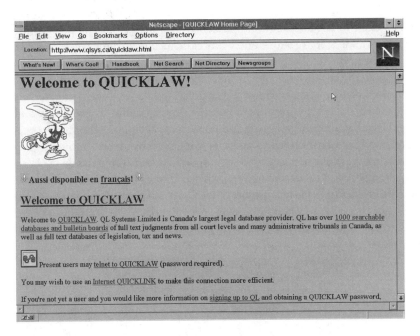

Through such a database, a judge can quickly search for legal precedents or research difficult questions involving case law. An entire legal database industry can be found in Canada, separate and apart from the Internet.

Federal judges either perform such research within QuickLaw themselves or know what type of electronic research is possible and direct their assistants to undertake the research. Hence this is a profession that has learned to deal with electronic information long, long before the hype of the Internet began.

But, with the arrival of the Internet, some new vehicles for accessing legal information are emerging. For example, Judge Goldenberg notes that the federal Department of Justice has linked a CD ROM containing federal statutes to the Internet, so that it can be searched by anyone (**http://canada.justice.gc.ca/folio.pgi/ESTATS.NFO?**). He finds this to be an invaluable tool and an innovative and powerful use of the Internet.

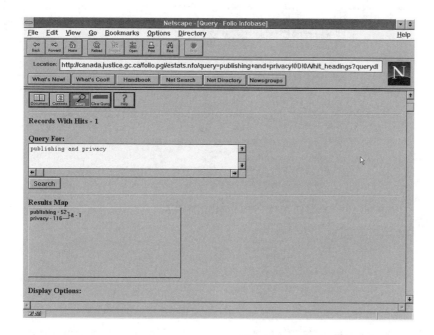

Even given such advances, the Internet remains a mystery and a challenge for many professions, including judges. To help those encountering the Internet for the first time, Judge Goldenberg also maintains a listing of "Suggested Sites for Judges Who Are New to the Net," which can be found directly from The Canadian Judges' Home Page.

He also participates in a closed Canadian judges' mailing list, along with a growing number of other Canadian judges. The purpose of the list? At this time, it is mostly used for sharing tips and information related to use of the Internet, such as the discovery of new sites containing legal information. But there are certain security issues that must be resolved before such lists are used for the discussion of sensitive legal topics.

Judges and the Internet? Look around, and you will discover a number of computer-literate, high-tech judges who are trying to keep up with technology in an effort to provide "good judging." One more example of how the Internet is transforming entire professions.

St. Paul's Church

St. Paul's Anglican Church is one of the oldest churches in Canada, established in 1750. But it is also one of the newest Canadian churches — that is, out in cyberspace — since it is one of the first churches in Canada to establish a presence on the Internet. You can access St. Paul's on the World Wide Web at **http://ccn.cs.dal.ca/Religion/StPauls/**. Once there, you will discover all kinds of local church information, including the schedule of services and upcoming events, historical information, and a staff list. Other information on-line includes baptism and wedding policies, as well as copies of the parish newsletter:

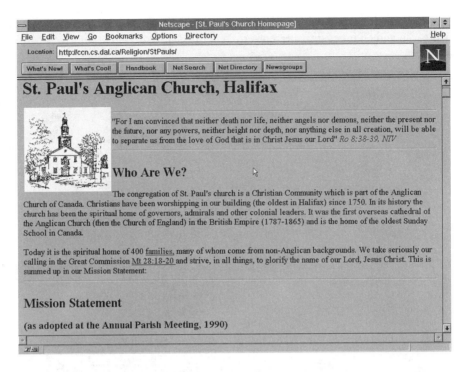

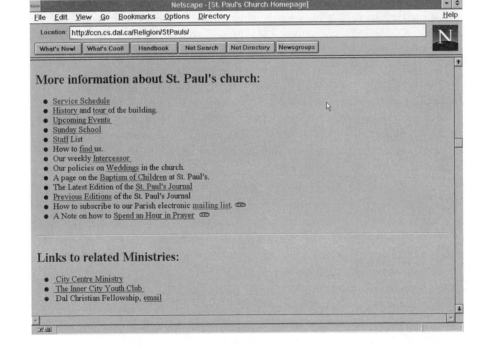

And in a very interesting move, the parish has set up an electronic mailing list that parishioners and others can join. "We use the Internet as a communications tool within our own parish. There are about 30 people on the mailing list, but I think over time we will have much more than that."

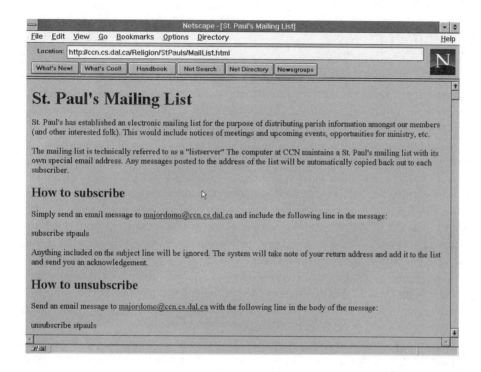

The site was built by a parishioner, Dave Hazen (**dave.hazen@dal.ca**), who works at keeping it up-to-date. The other driving force behind the site is the Rev. Stephen Peake (**speake@ra.isisnet.com**), the associate rector of St. Paul's. Why bring the church onto the Internet? "It's a neat thing to do," jokes Rev. Peake. "But seriously, as Christians, we believe that we should be where the people are, and it is obvious that many people, including our parishioners, are on the Internet."

Rev. Peake sees the Internet as a new method by which the church can reach people. "We are a university city, and with the number of university students on the Internet, this is a good way to appeal to them." He notes the involvement of a number of university students in the local parish and comments: "I think that with the number of people — particularly younger people — on the Internet, we need to be there."

They are also discovering the benefit to be had in reaching other churches around the world. "We get a lot of messages from other churches and people around the world — perhaps one to two messages a day," he notes. "We find ourselves sharing information with other churches worldwide."

Where will the site go in the future? Rev. Peake believes that there are all kinds of opportunities, including more use of electronic mailing lists both locally and globally on specialized topics. "On-line bible studies, for example," he indicates. "I think the real benefit of the Internet is as a tool to keep in contact with people and as a means of keeping them informed."

St. Paul's is but one of many, many churches and religious organizations around the world discovering the benefits and reach of the Internet. As one of Canada's oldest established churches, it is fascinating to find it taking a lead role as we move toward the twenty-first century.

Jean Johnston

Jean Johnston (**jj@mbnet.mb.ca**) is a 75-year-old grandmother. She is also an Internet expert in her own right. "I first got onto the Internet about a year ago," says Johnston, when reached at her home in Winnipeg, Manitoba. "I access it using a 486 DX-100 with a 14,400 baud modem," she proudly notes, listing the specifications of the computer that she uses.

For Johnston, it is not the magic of the World Wide Web and other areas of the Internet that are the most exciting; instead, it is the electronic mail component. "I use e-mail to communicate with my children and grandchildren." This includes her eldest son in Victoria who, since he works for the B.C. government, has an e-mail account that is linked into the Internet. She also reaches electronically across the generations: she is in touch with her grandson who is an engineer in Victoria, and a granddaughter who just graduated from the University of Victoria (and who has an e-mail account there as a student). She is also in regular touch by e-mail with her brother in Ottawa, who uses CompuServe.

Although new to the Internet, Johnston is not new to computers. "I've been using computers for about 11 to 12 years," she says. "I was taking some political science courses at the university, since I had to get out and do something." It was at this point that she found herself drawn to the world of computer technology.

Today, she is involved with "Creative Retirement" and spends some of her days teaching word processing to senior citizens. "I think it is important that we help each other," she says. "I show them the Internet and help them to use it. And in most cases, they can then go off on their own to explore."

Not only that, but the group undertook a more fascinating project recently. "We just finished refurbishing 12 dinosaurs," notes Johnston. "We took 12 old IBM AT computers and cleaned them, took them apart, upgraded the hard drives, so that they could be used again." One can just picture Jean and four of her friends tackling the innards of these computers. "My family thinks I'm crazy," she notes.

These days, Johnston lives a very busy and hectic life, teaching at least two days a week and assisting with all kinds of other activities the rest of the week. When asked if she plans to get onto the Web or explore more fully other areas of the Internet, she ruefully says, "Right now, I just don't have the time, so for now it's just e-mail."

But it is clear that even though she does not have a lot of time to explore, she is certainly someone who has plans to get more involved in the Internet. "There is just so much to learn everyday." Johnston's attitude to life and learning is one that so many of us should share.

Emergency Preparedness Information Exchange (EPIX)

A very interesting point with the recent Los Angeles, California and Kobe, Japan earthquakes was that most telephone lines were clogged, but significant components of the Internet still worked. The result was that the Internet emerged as a tool with which emergency groups could send and receive important information with respect to emergency response and disaster relief.

The Internet has gained global recognition as a critical and important tool in emergency management and in the field of emergency preparedness. Around the world there is a buzz of activity as national government bodies and organizations such as the Red Cross begin to explore how the network can be used for emergency management and preparedness.

In Canada, we have seen the arrival of EPIX, developed by the Centre for Policy Research on Science and Technology at Simon Fraser University, "to facilitate the exchange of ideas and information among Canadian and international public and private sector organizations about the prevention of, preparation for, recovery from and/or mitigation of risk associated with natural and socio-technological disasters" (**http://hoshi.cic.sfu.ca/~anderson/index.html**):

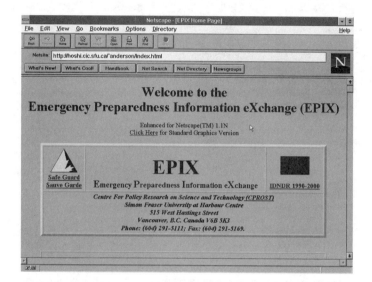

Through this site the Centre makes available an impressive number of documents and pointers to information about emergency prevention and management. The effort has also led to a heightened awareness of use of the Internet within the field, so it now provides pointers to federal, provincial, and other initiatives related to emergency issues:

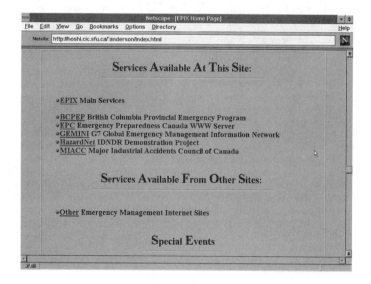

One federal government department that has become involved is Emergency Preparedness Canada, which developed a Web site in collaboration with EPIX. Notes Yves Lord, Coordinator, Evaluation and Analysis, with Emergency Preparedness Canada, who first became attracted to the concept of emergency preparedness on the Internet through the efforts of EPIX: "We have two mandates. The first is to provide information to the public on how to deal with an emergency." Thus the organization is beginning to provide public information on its Web site:

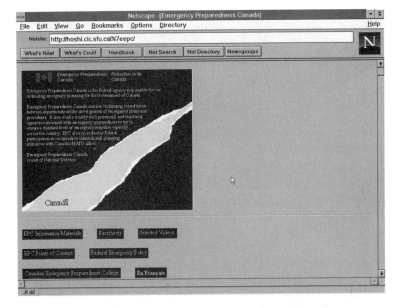

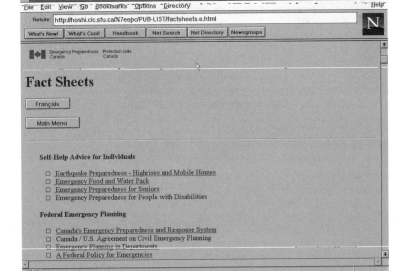

"The secondary goal is to get our partners in emergency management to work together," using discussion groups, e-mail, and the Web. "For example, other federal departments and emergency groups for other provinces. There is usually an emergency team in each federal department — Transport Canada has one, for example, dealing with dangerous goods." Lord believes, as many do in the field, that there is a tremendous opportunity to use the Internet for such information sharing, and such activities are being actively explored.

"For example, we have a new initiative called Safeguard," he notes. "The objective there is to establish partnerships with all kinds of other organizations dealing with emergency management, such as the Red Cross, industrial groups, and municipalities. We want to get some type of emergency networking group together." The department views the Internet as a powerful tool to help achieve these goals.

Lord believes that the field of emergency management and preparedness is only just emerging on the Internet. "What we see here is an emerging library of emergency preparedness for Canada. People can have a link to our page, or we will host a page of some information if we need to on their behalf."

He also acknowledges the global impact. "It's important to note that using the Internet as an emergency information tool isn't limited to Canada — it's happening globally. In particular, there is now an international initiative to expand electronic networking as a result of discussions which occurred at the G7 meeting."

Another one who has undertaken an initiative to build a sophisticated emergency preparedness site is David Gronbeck-Jones, a municipal/provincial planner with the British Columbia Provincial Emergency Program (PEP) (**dgronbec@sfu.ca**). "I discovered the Internet on my own," he notes, "saw an application in my field and decided to run with it." Hence the B.C. PEP site (**http://hoshi.cic.sfu.ca/~pep/index.html**):

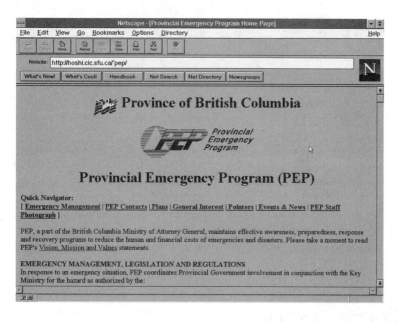

The Department, a part of the B.C. Ministry of Attorney General, has established a comprehensive source of information for awareness and preparedness emergency information largely as a result of Gronbeck-Jones' efforts. The site includes information on emergency management, how to contact provincial emergency staff, information of general interest, links to other sites, and events and news.

There is some information on-line perhaps unique to British Columbia, including the 100-page document "British Columbia Earthquake Response Plan," a "shortened version of the British Columbia Tsunami Warning and Alerting Plan," a family-oriented guide called "Prepare Now for an Earthquake in British Columbia" and an "Emergency Preparedness Checklist." And in a unique area, the site makes available a weekly log of emergency rescues and efforts undertaken by provincial emergency groups:

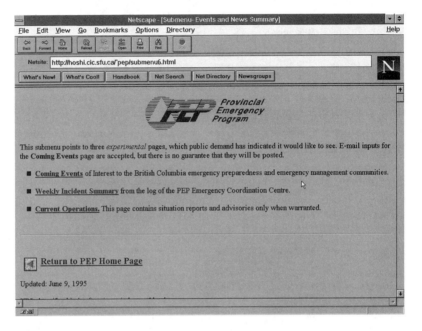

"I'm normally a planner — I'm not a systems guy," Gronbeck-Jones is quick to comment. "It didn't take me all that long to create the site though, since we had the documents in electronic form. It probably took me three months to create it, on a part-time basis." What about the maintenance time? "It takes me about 15 minutes a week to update the site," he says. As for the weekly operations report, that information is updated by the amateur radio community.

What is now becoming evident is that through the efforts of EPIX, and with the involvement of people like Gronbeck-Jones and Yves Lord, the concept of use of the Internet as an emergency preparedness tool is attracting senior level management attention throughout Canada. There is finally a realization that a significant, local, national, and global communications tool that can help government and industrial emergency preparedness groups meet their many objectives is emerging on the Internet. "What we are really talking about here is an emergency lane on the information highway," notes Lord.

Canadian Parliamentary Channel (CPAC)

Many Canadians would believe that the only thing CPAC ever broadcasts are the proceedings from the House of Commons. Through CPAC you can certainly witness the goings-on in Ottawa and the inanities of some of our elected representatives. But many Canadians are coming to realize that beyond its mandate of carrying broadcasts of Parliament, CPAC has become a world leader in the broadcasting of information related to public policy issues and that it has made the Internet an integral part of this effort. Tune in any day — and when Parliament is not in session — you will find live broadcasts of all kinds of public affairs programming (some taped and some live broadcasts), as seen on the following screen:

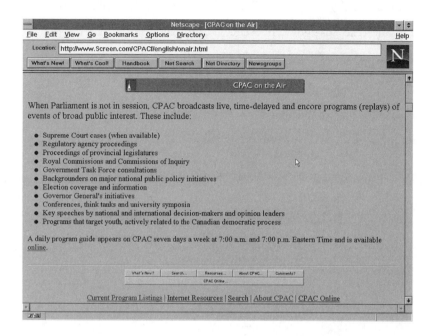

As can be seen, CPAC has established an impressive World Wide Web site (**http://www.screen. com/cpac**) that it uses to interactively deal with its viewers:

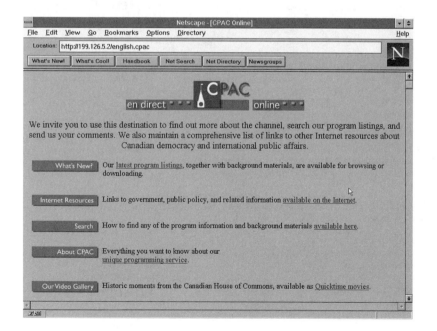

Through this resource, you can access all kinds of information related to CPAC and the information it broadcasts, including

♦ an excellent series of pointers to government-related Internet resources;

♦ information about CPAC itself: its mandate, mission, and objectives;

♦ a movie archive of significant events in Canadian history;

♦ archives of historical Canadian documents (including Consumer Price Index information from 1985, the Meech Lake and Charlottetown accords, and the Canadian Charter of Rights and Freedoms);

♦ pointers to other public policy documents;

♦ information on how to submit proposals to CPAC for it to cover a particular event or conference;

♦ information on how to reach CPAC, including the e-mail addresses of many staff.

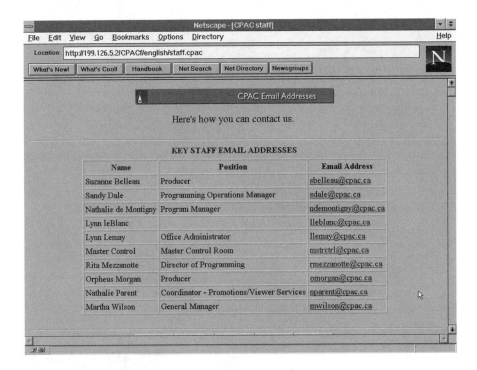

KEY STAFF EMAIL ADDRESSES

Name	Position	Email Address
Suzanne Belleau	Producer	sbelleau@cpac.ca
Sandy Dale	Programming Operations Manager	sdale@cpac.ca
Nathalie de Montigny	Program Manager	ndemontigny@cpac.ca
Lynn leBlanc		lleblanc@cpac.ca
Lynn Lemay	Office Administrator	llemay@cpac.ca
Master Control	Master Control Room	mstrctrl@cpac.ca
Rita Mezzanotte	Director of Programming	rmezzanotte@cpac.ca
Orpheus Morgan	Producer	omorgan@cpac.ca
Nathalie Parent	Coordinator - Promotions/Viewer Services	nparent@cpac.ca
Martha Wilson	General Manager	mwilson@cpac.ca

Martha Wilson, the General Manager for CPAC (**mwilson@cpac.ca**), indicates that there are a number of reasons why CPAC became involved with the Internet. "First off, the nature of our programming is such that we can't get listings in publications like *TV Guide*, who need to know program schedules three weeks in advance. We might not know until the day before that we are covering an event. So a problem for our viewers is that they haven't had easy access to our schedule. They now do through the Internet." The Web site provides viewers with the ability to quickly obtain the CPAC schedule for the coming week:

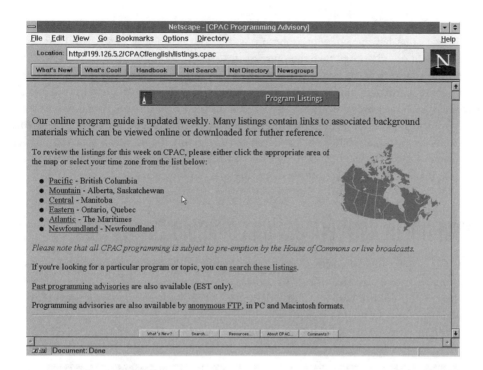

But Wilson passionately believes that there is a more fundamental issue at work here than just using the Internet to provide program schedules or promotional information about CPAC. "We believe that the people who watch CPAC are the same people as those who use the Internet. People who want news information without media filters, uninterrupted, unedited, and with no commentary, much like the information they get on the Internet." Hence the CPAC effort with the Internet is a natural tie-in to CPAC's mission. "We want to get the stories behind the news — all the raw materials of public affairs," notes Wilson.

In essence, CPAC appeals to those people who are tired of the 30-second news clips on the nightly news. There are many people who want more in-depth news information without the bias introduced by many national media outlets. CPAC helps these people by providing such "raw" information in its broadcasts. It also recognizes that most of the people who want such "raw" information are those who use the Internet. Hence, as Wilson puts it, "the Internet and CPAC is a marriage made in heaven."

Wilson also believes that the Internet permits CPAC to go beyond its role of simply broadcasting information. "We broadcast many conferences. Our goal is to actually try to recreate the experience of attending the event. We can tie in what we broadcast to the Internet by making companion documents available in electronic form."

Hence, CPAC is creating a broadcast system that combines television and computer-based information access. "We are trying to develop a Web site that pulls together everything on a topic that we might broadcast and make it as easy as possible for people to get information on that topic." Hence you will find that the Web site provides a number of excellent pointers to other public policy documents found throughout the Internet. You will also find that the particular item you are watching on TV will include references to how you can obtain particular documents through the CPAC Web site.

Wilson strongly believes that the Internet offers broadcasts opportunities for viewer feedback in ways that have not previously been possible. But, for her, it goes beyond viewer feedback. "We can use the site to take the pulse of the Canadian public," she observes. She cites a number of examples where individuals across the country have used the Internet to contact CPAC about particular public policy issues. And it is obvious that their Internet effort is proving to be a success. For example, she is aware of a number of cases where university professors are using the combined CPAC/Internet approach in such courses as political science.

For Wilson, the Internet is not just a tool for marketing the network. "It's beyond simple promotion of the channel — the Internet has quickly become integral to what we do. There's this incredible connection between broadcasting and the Internet."

University of Northern British Columbia Caving Club

When Clive Keen (**keen@unbc.edu**) is not teaching at the University of Northern British Columbia in Prince George, British Columbia, he is hanging around in the underground. Not the counter-culture underground, but under the ground. He likes to go caving (or spelunking, the proper term) and is involved with the UNBC Caving Club. He also created their site on the Internet (**http://quarles.unbc.edu/keen/netcave.htm**):

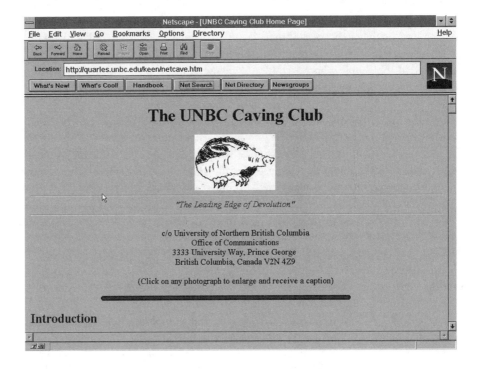

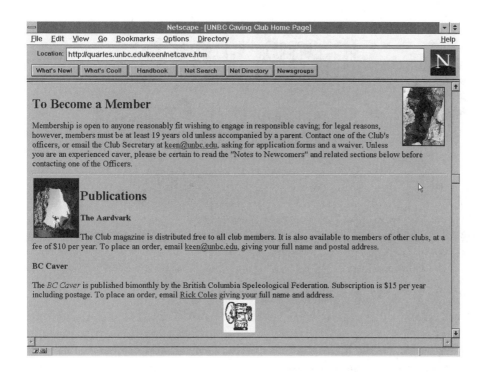

It is a site that contains local membership information as well as listings of "cavers" from across Canada. "For the number of members that we have, getting in touch isn't that easy. We've got 50 or 60 people in the Prince George and Fort St. John region, and we can reach a lot of them via electronic mail," notes Keen. "We also encourage them to use the Web site." He also notes that the number of people that he can reach through e-mail and the Web is steadily increasing, which makes it easier to get information out.

"We also use it for new people who are interested in caving," says Keen. "Through our Web site, they can get some introductory information about caving. They can get a good idea of what is going on and understand it's a serious sport. This helps to weed out some potential cavers, and certainly saves time for us in answering questions, since there's a huge amount of information that we usually have to tell new people about."

Like many people, Keen took the time to figure out how to create the Web site on his own. "It was incredibly easy," he notes. "It was astonishing how quickly I was able to figure it out. It took me only the better part of a weekend." He thinks it is important that people realize it is not too difficult to do a lot of basic stuff on the Web. "I started with the simple stuff, and expanded from there. I figured it out merely by examining the HTML code from other people's pages," a method used by many people who set up their own pages. "You can get more sophisticated, but you don't have to."

And that, in a nutshell, is perhaps the best way to draw our case studies to a close. *You can get more sophisticated, but you don't have to.* Let's start to dig into the basics.

Internet Service Providers in Canada

Created by the Defense Department in the 1960s to link government labs, contractors, and military installations, the Net is designed to operate without central authority so that it can survive a nuclear war. Now it is setting the world on fire in a way its designers never foresaw. By establishing open standards that let computers all over the world link files and relay messages, it has sparked an explosion of innovation and entrepreneurship reminiscent of the epoch-making boom that launched the personal computer.... The online industry has grown so complex that even its leaders have difficulty comprehending what's going on.

As the Internet sizzles: Online services battle for stakes
Fortune, May 1, 1995

Providing Internet access may soon become a tough commodity business. The companies that will continue to make money are those who offer more.

The shape of nets to come
Economist, July 7, 1995

To join the Internet, you need an Internet service provider. This is the company or organization that will provide you with an account by which you can dial into the Internet or will provide your organization with a link to the network via some type of permanent connection.

In this chapter we will take a look at the Canadian Internet industry to help you understand which companies are providing Internet services. We will describe some of the other organizations in Canada and around the world that help to exchange information through the Internet. Then in Chapter 5 we will describe the way Internet service providers route you through the network, because like many people, you will want to know how the Internet "works."

The Role of the Internet Service Provider

The first question many ask about the Internet is, "OK, so how do I get on?" This is the role of an "Internet service provider" (ISP), a company that sells access to the Internet.[1] ISPs range in size from small systems that might be managed by one or two people, to medium-sized organizations that provide service in one or more cities or towns in Canada, to large multinational organizations like IBM that provide service across

---

1. As you deal further with the Internet, you will come to realize that there are even more subtle categorizations of ISPs: there are Internet access providers, who actually sell access to the Internet, and Internet presence providers, who do not sell access to the network but will allow you to put your "Web site" on their computer system to gain a "presence" on the Internet.

Canada and around the world to major on-line services such as CompuServe and America Online.

For our purposes, the definition of an ISP is simple: it is a company or organization that provides, for a fee or for free, access to all or part of the Internet. An ISP sells either individual accounts for use by people with modems or higher-speed "bulk access" via direct connections for use by individuals, companies, and other organizations. An ISP sells connectivity to the Internet. Consider what an ISP has put in place to "get into" the Internet business:

◆ it has bought the hardware and software necessary to support access to the Internet;

◆ it has purchased phone lines to accept inbound modem connections from people and companies;

◆ it has (hopefully) put in place a support system to take calls from customers;

◆ it has a billing and administrative system, used to charge customers for access to the system;

◆ it has hired staff to manage its services and has spent money to promote its services.

In other words, it has become a full-fledged business organization.

Most importantly, an ISP has purchased one or more high-speed communication links to some other Internet service provider to support its connection to the rest of the world.[2] Having done so, it has configured its computer system to access the rest of the Internet through use of what is known as the Domain Name Service and TCP/IP addressing.[3] It has plugged itself into the world. Don't worry about *how* all these ISPs plug together. That is the subject

INTERNET SERVICE PROVIDERS IN CANADA

1. Internet service providers (ISPs) are organizations that provide access to the Internet for a fee or for free. Categories of ISPs include for-profit organizations, cooperative (not-for-profit) networks, community networks (also known as FreeNets), and many bulletin board systems.

2. Many people who live in rural areas of Canada find that access to the Internet is very expensive, because most ISPs are located in major urban centres.

3. There are many things that make the Internet marketplace very dynamic, including the fact that new ISPs will continue to be established across Canada.

4. A number of smaller ISPs will begin to disappear as larger companies (particularly computer, telephone, and cable companies) enter the marketplace, but these large companies will not come to dominate the marketplace.

5. High-speed networks are inevitable in Canada.

---

2. The most fascinating thing about the Internet is that much of it runs through global telephone data networks. For example, when an ISP buys a high-speed link to another ISP as described above, it is buying not only the right to link to that other ISP; it is really purchasing a high-speed communication line from a telephone company or some other type of communication company.

3. This is an important issue and will be examined in depth later in Chapter 5.

of the next chapter. Right now, we just want to give you an idea of where you can get access to the Internet.

Expertise is What is Sold

Everyone always asks, when confronted with the Internet, "where does the money go?" It goes to your ISP. In effect, what you are paying for when you buy your Internet account or high-speed Internet link is access to the equipment, knowledge, expertise, and support that the ISP has put in place. You are paying for the fact that your ISP has the brilliant technical staff who know how to configure their computers, routers, and software to support connectivity to every other Internet computer on the planet. Thus you are buying connectivity to every other individual and computer that make up the global Internet.

Appendix A includes a detailed listing of ISPs in Canada. As you can see, there are quite a few of them right across the country.

What You Need to Buy

Before we describe the Internet in Canada, you should understand the two main types of Internet access that are available: casual (or temporary) dial-up access and dedicated (or full-time) access.

With casual (or temporary) dial-up access, you access the Internet using a "modem," a device that lets your PC "talk" to another computer. You join the Internet by purchasing a dial-up account with an ISP. The modem calls your ISP and establishes a connection; you are only connected to the Internet when you choose to be. The dial-up accounts are either SLIP/PPP accounts or shell accounts. We will examine the difference between these types of accounts in the next chapter. Dial-up accounts are what most people use to access the Internet from home. They are also used by people in companies and organizations that do not have a full-time link to the Internet.

With dedicated (or full-time) access, you put in place a connection between your corporate network and the Internet so that everyone is "plugged into" the Internet at all times. You purchase what is called a "dedicated connection" to the Internet. The connection is usually open all the time. It can consist of a "dedicated high-speed line" or can simply be a SLIP/PPP account that is "on" all the time. Dedicated access is used by companies and organizations that have chosen to provide staff members with full-time access to the Internet or in cases where business organizations have chosen to use dedicated Internet connections to provide for wide-scale connectivity of corporate local area networks. Normally, individuals do not require (nor can they afford) dedicated access.

Some ISPs sell only temporary dial-up accounts, others sell only dedicated access, and many sell both. Other ISPs (such as CA*Net) only sell Internet access to other ISPs, thus restricting their role to a particular segment of the industry.

We will examine the issues of what you purchase and what you ask for in setting up an account in Chapter 12. For now, we will concentrate on describing who these ISPs are.

The "Old Days" on the Internet

The "old days" of the Internet were as recent as 1994. Back then, the Internet "industry" in Canada was straightforward: we had what were known as "regional networks," and we had "commercial Internet service providers." It was somewhat easy to tell the basic difference between the two, and in earlier editions of our book we had categorized the differences as follows.

"Regional networks" were organizations, often government-funded, that provided Internet access to educational institutions and research organizations. There was one regional network per province. Most regional networks operated on a not-for-profit basis and had "acceptable use policies" forbidding business use of the Internet. (Some of the regional networks never had such policies and never restricted business use.)

"Commercial providers" were for-profit companies in the business of selling access to anyone who wanted to get onto the Internet. There were no restrictions on use of the Internet for business purposes (other than respecting Internet cultural norms).

Some of the regional providers could be categorized as commercial providers; it just so happened that their primary mandate was to provide Internet access to the educational institutions and research organizations. Hence the lines were blurry very early on.

History Was Important

This breakdown between regional providers and commercial providers reflected the earlier history of the network. The Internet emerged in the 1980s in the academic/research community, and "acceptable use policies" (AUPs) were, at the time, predominant throughout the global Internet. The AUPs arose because many of the networks that made up the Internet at that time, in Canada, the United States and elsewhere, were funded by government to support research and education.

AUPs specified that the Internet could not be used for non-research-related business purposes; it could be used only to further education and research activities. Given the growth that the Internet began to encounter, however, AUPs were under assault almost from day one. Gradually, people on the Internet used it increasingly for commercial purposes, and eventually a number of commercial providers arrived on the scene, organizations that did not try to restrict use of the Internet by purpose (but encouraged people not to violate the academic AUPs if communicating with people or organizations found on those systems).

The growth in the number of commercial providers meant that many more people began to use the Internet for business purposes, with the result that more and more people on the academic/research networks began to use the Internet for business purposes. Business activity gained a momentum on the Internet that just would not slow down.

Soon AUPs began to have about as much effect as trying to dam the Amazon River with chicken wire — not very effective. Eventually, they were scrapped, since most of the networks that make up the Internet became commercialized or evolved into cooperatives (described below).

Describing the history of the Internet was an important part of earlier editions of the *Canadian Internet Handbook*; so the earlier editions spent much time describing these AUPs. The reason was that the existence of AUPs often led to confusing situations in which people had to know whether they could use the Internet for business purposes through the particular network that they used to access the Internet.[4]

The history of the Internet is less important today in knowing what you can use the network for, given that by and large AUPs do not exist. Over the last year there has been a flood of venture capital and investment money rushing into anything Internet-related, with one result being a literal explosion in the number of small and large Internet service providers.[5] The result? An ever-increasing number of options by which you can choose to get on the Internet in major cities and towns.[6]

One result of the change in the network is that we can no longer categorize the Internet industry in Canada as consisting of regional networks and commercial providers, since that distinction had begun to blur by late 1994. The reality is that through 1995 the Internet industry began to mature, with an amazing number of opportunities available to the consumer or company by which they could join the Internet. Thus this chapter focuses less on the history of the Internet and more on putting into perspective the companies and organizations that make up the Internet industry in Canada today.[7]

Everyone is Becoming a Provider

The Internet in Canada and around the world has become a growth industry. Many people and organizations caught the Internet "bug" in 1995 and rushed to become ISPs. Consider these quotes from an article that appeared in the June 5, 1995 edition of *Business Week* ("Everyone's rushing the Net: Snaring subscribers with Internet access is now the big play"):

◆ "... the Internet access market will grow from $123 million this year to more than $4 billion in 2000, according to Forrester Research Inc., a market researcher in Cambridge, Mass. Maloff Co., another researcher, based in Dexter, Mich., estimates that the number of so-called SLIP connections, a particularly popular way of plugging PCs into the Net, is growing by 38% every month."

◆ "not since the cellular-telephone boom of the late 1980s has there been such a mad scramble to win subscribers to a new communications service. Local and long-distance phone companies as well as cable-TV operators are all looking to grab a portion of this market. Commercial online services such as America Online, CompuServe, GEnie, and Prodigy Services are increasingly emphasizing their improved Internet connections...."

◆ "more competition is coming. Microsoft Corp. plans to make Internet access a major component of its forthcoming network service."

Canadian cable companies, telephone companies, and other communication firms are staking their claims to the Internet frontier. Major international computer hardware and software

---

4. Previous editions of the Directory of Internet Service Providers in this book included a category on whether an ISP had an AUP. Such a category is no longer necessary or relevant.
5. The Internet industry in Canada is evolving at a rapid rate. Our 1994 edition counted just 41 suppliers of Internet services in Canada, and by 1995, there were 163 major providers of services.
6. Unfortunately, it is still difficult or impossible to get onto the Internet in many small towns or rural areas without making a long distance call. This is a topic that we explore in further depth later on in this chapter.
7. For those with a historical interest in the Internet, we have included on our Web site, at **http://lydian.csi.nb.ca/handbook/handbook.html**, some information from our previous books about the history of the Internet in Canada.

firms are getting into the business. And just to ensure that the Internet marketplace will never become a monopoly marketplace, we have seen all kinds of people — business professionals, technical specialists, venture capitalists, retired business executives — invest their own money to set up their own ISP companies in Canada. It is said that anyone with about $250,000 can establish him/herself as a serious provider of Internet services, although at this stage, with the competition that is occurring, one wonders if this is fool's money.

One result of all this activity is that consumers and potential purchasers of Internet services must shop carefully so that they clearly understand what it is they are buying and from whom they are buying it. As *Business Week* concluded in its article, "Internet access has turned into one of the hottest markets around. So if you're shopping for a connection, you would do well to avoid signing any long-term contracts. The competition is sure to bring new services and better prices for months, if not years, to come."[8] Later in this book we will discuss some of the things you should look for in an ISP.

Categories of ISPs

In this section we take a look at who provides Internet access in Canada to help you understand where to start. The providers are categorized as follows:

- ◆ for-profit ISPs;
- ◆ cooperative ISPs;
- ◆ community networks;
- ◆ bulletin board systems.

There can be some overlap between these categories; for example, a bulletin board could also be a for-profit company. However, for our purposes, we'll work within these categories.

For-Profit ISPs

This category includes

- ◆ primary Internet service providers, including those whose sole business is the provision of Internet services (e.g., InfoRamp in Toronto) and small- to medium-sized system integrators who also sell Internet access as part of their business (e.g., Western Business Machines in Saskatchewan);
- ◆ major computer companies such as IBM and Microsoft;
- ◆ major telephone and cable companies, such as BCTel, SaskTel, NBTel, Bell Canada, and cable companies, such as Rogers Communications and Shaw Communications;

---

8. "Everyone's rushing the Net: Snaring subscribers with Internet access is now the big play," *Business Week*, June 5, 1995.

◆ major on-line information systems such as CompuServe, America Online, and Prodigy who provide access to the Internet as well as access to other on-line information services.

We will examine each type of provider in greater depth.

Primary Internet Service Providers

There continues to be strong growth in the number of ISPs across Canada, particularly companies strictly in the business of selling access to the Internet and those who have supplemented their core business activity with involvement in the Internet. In fact, it seems that a week doesn't go by without the authors of this book being advised of some new Internet service somewhere in the country. The number, range, size, and diversity of these providers is truly stunning.

A number of these organizations, in existence for several years or brand new to the Internet business, are dedicated to the Internet business, that is, they derive most of their revenue from the sale of access to the Internet or from the provision of other related Internet services.

InfoRamp in Toronto, for example, was started by two project managers who had worked together at CAE Ltd. Faced with a desire to get out and do something entrepreneurial, they identified the Internet as a good opportunity in early 1994. They quit their jobs on June 17, 1994, incorporated on June 22, and were in operation with a full Internet service by August 1. They now have some 4,200 customers in the Toronto area and have gained an excellent reputation for their service and support and their "no busy signal" policy. In the future they plan to focus on the rapidly evolving field of integration of internal corporate information systems to the Internet to support strategic customer activities. InfoRamp is typical of many of the new ISPs arriving in the industry in Canada — small, innovative, quick to move, and quick to establish itself.

Many of these providers are now attempting to establish a national presence by offering cross-Canada Internet services. For example, Cycor, based in Prince Edward Island, offers access in major cities across Canada. With many other providers following Cycor's steps, it seems that there is a trend underway, in which every provider is trying to become a national provider, as if it is the next step in avoiding the rigors of competition in the local marketplace. One must wonder how successful they all will be.

Inevitably, the growth in the ISP business means that a process of consolidation of some Internet providers will begin to occur in Canada. Two large organizations, NSTN and i*internet, recently merged to establish one of Canada's largest ISPs. The two companies are complementary: NSTN has established a strong base in Toronto and points east, while i*internet (previously operating under the name of its affiliate, *f*onorola) operates from Ottawa to the west. NSTN brought to the merger extensive experience with dial-up customers and low-speed connectivity, while i*internet's focus has been on the large corporate market (Fortune 2000 organizations) by providing mostly full-time dedicated access. This type of consolidation will inevitably occur across the country.

We are also seeing the arrival of a number of ISPs in smaller communities across Canada, for example, in Acme, Alberta.[9] Where's that, you ask? Well, they tell you, on-line (**http://www. kneehill.com**):

---

9. These folks forever endeared themselves to our hearts: when we called them to talk about their Internet service, we were greeted by an answering machine which stated they were not available because they had gone fishing.

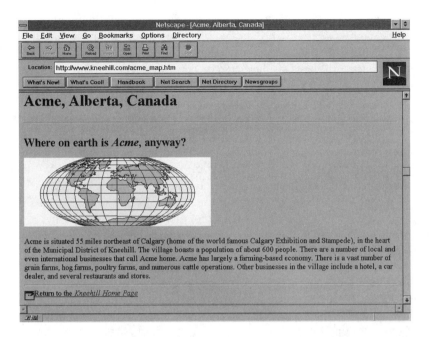

Terry Esau of Kneehill Internet Services has been a computer consultant for seven years in the community and saw a need to establish a local Internet service provider. His partner is Dann St-Pierre, the manager of the body shop at a local car dealership. St-Pierre's company had bought computers and services from Esau's company for a number of years, and eventually they began to talk about establishing an Internet service. "It took about two weeks worth of work to get the system established," noted Esau, who says that they established the service on a Windows NT system. Interest in the Internet is growing in the three communities that they service.

What should be apparent is that there are many ISPs and that more are announced every week. The entry cost to establish a basic Internet service is not that high. But what does cost money is support, customer service, and all the other overhead that goes with a serious business organization. Hence, while we see a lot of ISPs arrive, we also see a number of them go.

Major Computer Companies

Another recent trend has been the arrival of major computer companies to the Internet industry. It's no wonder, for the Internet is quickly becoming a fundamental part of everything that computer companies do. *Business Week*, in an article in April 1995 ("Planet Internet: How the center of the computing universe has shifted"), noted that "the strategic shift — and opportunity — that the Internet represents is far more important than the short-term revenues. The big names such as IBM, DEC, Apple, Sun, and Microsoft are all building Net-centered strategies — not because they want to fight over a few billion dollars, but because they need to stake out their futures in the $300 billion computer business."

In other words, major computer companies are entering the Internet business because they believe it will become pivotal to much of what we do with computers in the next 10 to 20 years. It has become so important that it can no longer be ignored. IBM is an example of a company that got involved in a big way. In fact, the significance of the Internet to IBM cannot be overstated. As *Business Week* indicated, "at IBM, every computer line from PCs to mainframes, is being readied to create information for viewing over the Web. Plus, Big Blue is counting on the Net as the basis of a new class of 'networked' applications."

IBM jumped into the Internet "dial-up" business in a major way in late 1994 with the release of its OS/2 Warp software, an operating system that competes with Microsoft Windows. OS/2 Warp included tools to access and navigate the Internet through the IBM network (or, if you wanted to, through any other ISP). By routing Internet traffic through its global communications network (Advantis), IBM was able to provide worldwide dial-up access to the Internet in over 175 cities around the globe — a first for any ISP, with access provided in over 440 cities by the end of 1995, making it the first truly global ISP.

One of the most interesting things about the Warp software is its new user sign-up feature. IBM showed the way to the future in terms of easy sign-up to the Internet by providing within Warp one of the easiest "instant sign-up" methods to get on to the Internet. Fill in a form, provide a credit card number:

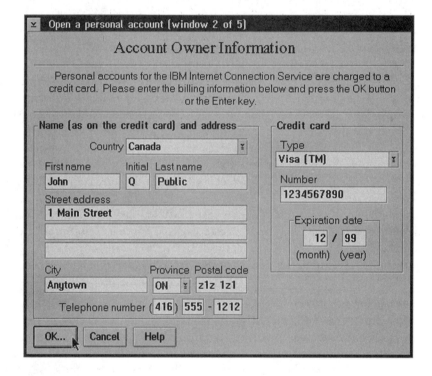

and wait a few seconds for the system to dial IBM, and before you could say Internet, you were signed up to the service.

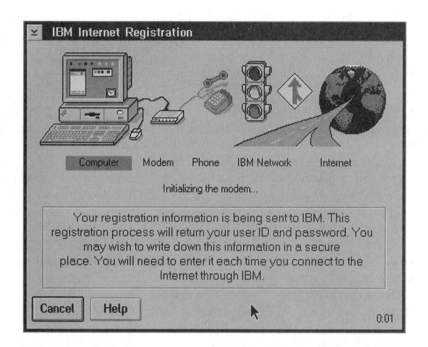

In addition to its efforts to become a full-fledged provider of dial-up Internet services for the individual accessing the Internet from home or the office, IBM has also become involved in the business of assisting business organizations in using the Internet for strategic purposes. Through Advantis, IBM began to provide a number of consulting, management, and advisory services related to the Internet, including

◆ providing dedicated high-speed connections to those organizations wishing to connect their corporate networks directly to the Internet;

◆ security consulting, to help those organizations that wish to link directly to the Internet properly to secure their corporate network;

◆ assisting companies in developing Internet-based marketing and public relations strategies;

◆ hosting Web sites on behalf of organizations. For example, IBM Canada "hosts" and manages the World Wide Web sites for Canadian organizations such as Air Canada and Insurance Canada.

IBM is but one computer vendor getting involved with the Internet in such a significant way; it has become big business to other computer companies. A tour of Web sites for major computer hardware companies, such as Apple, Digital Equipment, Sun Microsystems, or Hewlett Packard, indicates that all have a belief that something powerful is happening through the Internet. (Only IBM, Apple (with eWorld), and MicroSoft (with the MicroSoft Network) have become ISPs in Canada; the rest are involved in terms of their hardware and software products and through services offered by their systems integration and consulting divisions.) A good starting point to explore the initiatives of each of these computer companies is **http:// www.yahoo.com/Business/Corporations/Computers/Systems/**.

In addition to these companies, the Microsoft Network, which is easily accessible from within Windows 95, includes Internet access. In effect, Microsoft has become an ISP, and given its dominant role in the software industry, its participation will have a significant impact on the Internet industry in Canada.

Telephone and Cable Companies

For several years, telephone and cable companies have talked about the "information highway" that they would build. They believed that "we the consumer" would access this "highway" using something called interactive television. We would drive the "highway" with our TV remote controls. Video on demand, home shopping, interactive television, and the "500 channel universe" were the buzz-phrases emanating from the mouths of Canada's leading telecommunication executives.[10]

Yet, like most companies caught up in the hype about the highway, telephone and cable companies are now waking up to the fact that the rest of the world, particularly the younger generation, isn't that excited by their vision of a television-based information highway, but are into something different — the Internet. The result is that these companies now realize that the information highway isn't about more TV, it is about connectivity between computers, and that much of that connectivity is happening through the global Internet. What is happening here is an admission by telephone and cable companies that the much-hyped television-based information highway will not be here for some time (if ever) — and recognition of the growing significance of the Internet.

Throughout 1994 and 1995, we saw a rush of telephone companies getting into the ISP business. SaskTel, BCTel, and NBTel have already become major players in their respective provinces. Elsewhere, companies such as Bell Canada, Newfoundland Telephone, and AGT in Alberta staked their claims by announcing plans to get into the business in 1995.

It's not just the telephone companies waking up to this fact. In May 1995, Rogers Communications, Shaw Cablesystems, and several other cable companies announced that they would get into the business of selling high-speed access to the Internet through "cable modems," an announcement greeted with excitement by many Internet users. Plans as stated in their press releases announced introduction "sometime in early 1996."

Some of these companies are enjoying great success as they become involved with the Internet. SaskTel and NBTel, for example, are the major providers of Internet services in their respective provinces and have fairly solid reputations among their subscriber base. Yet, some of the telephone companies have stumbled with their plans to get into the Internet marketplace. AGT, for example, found itself in hot water with other Internet service providers in Alberta when it announced plans to enter the business. Other, smaller ISPs charged that given the scope and size of AGT, it would be able to compete unfairly against them. The ISPs went so far as to request a government hearing into the matter, which we will look at shortly.

On-Line Information Systems

The category of "on-line information systems" consists of major U.S.-based computer services such as CompuServe, America OnLine, and Prodigy. Smaller players include GE's GEnie and Apple's eWorld.

---

10. Previous editions of the *Canadian Internet Handbook* ridiculed these efforts. For historical purposes, we have placed these chapters on our World Wide Web site.

As reported in EDUPAGE, an on-line publication (new issues are available at **http://www.educom.edu/edupage.new**), "a survey by the Information & Interactive Services Report indicates the number of subscribers to commercial online information services increased 17% in the past three months, for a total of about 8-1/2 million, 3 million of which belong to America OnLine, 3.2 million to CompuServe, and 1.6 million to Prodigy — Atlanta Journal-Constitution 7/14/95 H3."

On-line systems have been around for quite some time, in the case of CompuServe, since 1982. These services have offered access to a wealth of information, such as up-to-the-minute news, weather, stock quotes, computer support forums, on-line shopping, information research databases, and other services. For many years these companies enjoyed a marketplace in which their only competition was each other. Each had its own special software or proprietary "look," and a visit to each of them was like visiting a different country.

You can buy an account on one of these services and access all kinds of information. Since these services have been around such a long time, they have helped to introduce many to the on-line world and are still useful services today. However, depending on what you are using them for, they can be pricey.

For a while, these on-line services were the only game in town when it came to large, global information services. *Thud!* In mid-1994, the rapid growth and interest in the Internet hit these companies like a freight train, and all of them have been scrambling to react ever since. Each has invested millions of dollars to participate in the Internet industry.

The impact of the Internet on these on-line services has been undeniable. Consider, for example, the fact that these services were once the only place that many companies would turn to for customer-focused on-line services. We saw travel companies, stock brokerages, airlines, and other companies set up shop on CompuServe, America OnLine, and elsewhere. An on-line industry involving consumer interaction was born.

Some companies still turn to these services to try to reach their customers. Yet there is a growing realization that there is less of a need to do so, given the massive growth and acceptance of the World Wide Web. Consider this report, taken from an Internet news report called Simba Media Daily, which reports on the fact that America OnLine is now beginning to stumble in attracting new companies to establish information sites on its service:

America Online Marketing Program Meets Resistance

America Online Inc. is running into some difficulty luring marketers and their ad agencies into its new interactive marketing program, according to Electronic Marketplace Report. Widespread fascination with the Internet's World Wide Web is part of the problem.

AOL initiated the program in April, asking agencies and their advertisers to pay $240,000 annually for AOL to develop and maintain an interactive marketing area on its service. For an additional $60,000 annually, AOL said it would also create and maintain a Web home page for the client.

AOL said it expected to sign about 24 marketers in the first year. And while it is still early in the game, the only announced taker so far is Oldsmobile—and Oldsmobile actually signed up 18 months ago, before the new pricing plan was announced.

Anastasia Betts, account executive at Leo Burnett in Chicago, Oldsmobile's ad agency, would not disclose financial details of its deal with AOL.

Jonathan Bulkeley, VP of business development at AOL, blamed the slow pace of the program on the Internet. "It started happening about three or four months ago," he said. "It's called Web mania."

Apparently, ad agencies, which play an important role in convincing advertisers to go online, are having an easier time selling the concept of marketing on the Web than on consumer online services.

When advertisers see the large number of Web browsers—estimated to be in the 8 to 10 million range, and the "low cost" of setting up show on the Web—they jump to it. Web sites can be created for as little as $1,000—though sophisticated, commerce-capable sites can cost up to $1 million.

Still, AOL is committed to its pricing strategy, and Bulkeley said the company plans to announce new interactive marketing partners in the next three to four weeks. They will come from the automobile, financial and travel industries, he said.

Also, AOL is developing a sponsorship program for its Web browser home page, which already features Saturn as a sponsor. A rate card has not been finalized, but it is expected to be less expensive than Netscape Communication Corp.'s home page, which starts at $30,000 per month.

Also under consideration is the sale of pointers to marketers' Web sites with AOL taking a 5%-20% cut of those marketers' Web transactions.

Electronic Marketplace Report is published by SIMBA Information, publisher of this newswire.

=Cowles/SIMBA Media Daily 7/7/95=

=Copyright 1995 SIMBA Information Inc. All rights reserved.=

The impact of the Internet on CompuServe, America OnLine, and other services has been that many people have signed onto the Internet, rather than signing on to them. The result? These companies are becoming significant ISPs in a hurry and will thus compete with all the other companies involved in the Internet. They are investing significantly to get this to happen. Consider what CompuServe did in 1995:

◆ Early in the year it permitted its users to access USENET as well as some other basic Internet services (it had already provided access to Internet e-mail for some time).

◆ Later it announced that it was buying Spry, a software company that makes the popular Internet in a Box software, for over $100 million.[11] Spry has since released version 2.0 of the product, which permits instant access to all Internet services via CompuServe.

◆ It announced that it would provide "PPP access" (discussed in the next chapter). Hence anyone can access the Internet via CompuServe via a local number in major Canadian cities or via an 800 number in the rest of the country (albeit at a steep price for the latter — $20 per hour). You can purchase the full Internet in a Box product from CompuServe in order to get on-line, or if you are already a subscriber, you can download CompuServe NetLauncher, a software product that combines elements of Spry's product with a simple dial-up program.

◆ It also modified its CompuServe Information Manager so that people can access certain Internet services without needing a full Internet account:

---

11. We take a look at this software in Chapter 13.

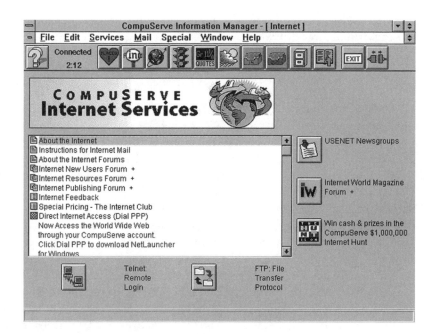

♦ Like IBM, it too established a systems integration service, which helps companies and organizations use the Internet for business purposes.

CompuServe boasts some 90,000 users in Canada as of July 1995.

Organizations like CompuServe are responding aggressively to the arrival of the Internet and will be major players on the Internet scene. However, as we will examine in Chapter 12, in some ways these services are still not an attractive option by which to access the Internet in Canada, since they have so far been unable to compete in price against some of the dedicated Internet service providers around. However, things change quickly on the Internet scene, and we shouldn't count out their potential impact in Canada.

Cooperative [Not-For-Profit] Networks

CA*Net and ONet are two of the largest cooperative not-for-profit networks in Canada.

ONet

ONet is the organization that was originally responsible for providing Internet access to academic and research institutions throughout the province of Ontario. Now, it is rapidly evolving to become a provider of Internet services to any organization that wants it. It is doing so not as a profit-oriented enterprise but as a cooperative organization. Its members pay a base level of funding to establish, operate, and manage the ONet infrastructure, and any surplus funds are returned at the end of the year.

ONet's members include most of the universities and academic institutions in Ontario as well as organizations like the Ontario government, the National Capital FreeNet in Ottawa, and the Ontario Science Centre. ONet has also begun to sell connectivity to companies that want to become ISPs. One of its first customers in this regard was Internet Access Worldwide, a Niagara area ISP. ONet sees its mission as being a high quality provider of dedicated Internet access to any organization that wants it. It will do so on a cost-recovery, "cooperative" basis rather than as a for-profit institution.

CA*Net

CA*Net is a different case altogether. It is an ISP, but it is a very special type of ISP. As one of the major Internet systems in Canada today, CA*Net operates a large, high-speed Internet network across the country and sells access to this network to other organizations. CA*Net does not sell Internet access to individuals, and it does not sell access to companies seeking a direct link to the Internet. It does, however, provide connectivity to its high-speed network to many of the major Internet service providers across Canada.

CA*Net was originally established in the late 1980s as a coordinating body with the objective of providing connectivity between what were known as Canada's regional networks, most of which were established with the primary objective of providing Internet access to academic and research organizations. Originally, a few of the regional networks (primarily ONet, BCNet, and RISQ) were the only way to get onto the Internet in Canada. Each had links to the U.S.-based NSFNet and exchanged traffic among themselves via the United States.

By mid-1995, CA*Net was operating a high-speed communication network (on what are known as T1 lines, which operate at "1.544 megabits per second") across Canada that connected the original 12 regional networks (now a mix of for-profit and not-for-profit organizations) and one federal government network. Thus it is the source of Internet connectivity for much of the Canadian Internet community. If you access the Internet using services such as NSTN, NBNet, SaskNet, MBNet, BCNet, you are taking advantage of the CA*Net "backbone."

ORGANIZATIONS THAT ARE LINKED TO CA*NET	
Alberta	ARNET
British Columbia	BCNET
Federal Government	GTIS (Government Telecommunications Informatic System)
Manitoba	MBNet
New Brunswick	NB*Net
Newfoundland	NInet
Northwest Territories	NTnet
Nova Scotia	NSTN (Nova Scotia Technology Network)
Ontario	ONet
Prince Edward Island	PEINet
Quebec	RISQ (Reseau Interordinateurs Scientifique Quebecois)
Saskatchewan	SASK#net
Yukon	YukonNet

In the summer of 1995, CA*Net signed a contract with Bell Advanced Communications Inc. (BACI), a division of Bell Canada, for BACI to take over the CA*Net infrastructure. Over time, BACI will become responsible for management and operations of the CA*Net network, with the participation of its partners Bell Sygma, UUNet Canada, and the University of Toronto Computing Centre.

As part of the change, CA*Net has changed from running a network consisting of fixed communication links using T1 lines: in September 1995, as part of its contract with Bell, the network was upgraded to use Bell's much larger communication facilities. Specifically, efforts began that month to upgrade CA*Net from a basic size of 1.544 Mbps to an eventual 10 Mbps, an increase of five to six times capacity. Because an advanced technology known as ATM (asynchronous transfer mode) has been deployed by Bell to support the network, this increase in capacity was actually put in place for a cost lower than what CA*Net was paying for its older 1.544 Mbps lines.

CA*Net is an organization clearly in transition. By 1995, 75% of CA*Net's funding was from government organizations, yet that level of funding is scheduled to disappear by the end of 1996. The organization is undergoing a transition to a cooperative that will be fully member-funded and is evolving from an organization that was managed in the academic community to one that is managed in the commercial sector.

To ensure that the transition is smooth, CA*Net is seeking to sell Internet access to other ISPs, to cable companies, and to other communication companies seeking to resell Internet services. To ensure that it adheres to a mandate of being a "provider to providers," it is cautiously defining the criteria by which organizations can purchase Internet access. In fact, it looks to member organizations like ONet to sell access to companies and individuals.

Community Networks

Other services that are helping people across Canada enjoy certain aspects of the Internet are community initiatives. Most often known as FreeNets, they are in some cases also known as community networks. These initiatives have arisen because of a belief by many that access to the Internet should not be restricted to those who can afford to pay for it.

It is clear that the Internet will have a profound impact on our personal and business lives in the future, particularly as our world and the economy that drives it become wired together through the network. However, because people have to pay to join, there is a belief that a large number of people will not be able to participate. The concern has arisen that those who can afford to access the network will have an automatic advantage over "non-wired people" when it comes to job and career opportunities in the future.

This concern began to arise almost as soon as computers were invented and became more alarming once electronic communication networks exploded into public consciousness in the mid-1980s. It led to a number of initiatives around the world to provide for community access to networked resources, with the largest and most successful effort being the establishment of the Cleveland FreeNet in 1986.

The objective of the Cleveland FreeNet and most other FreeNets that have followed since is simple: to provide free or low-cost access to on-line information resources such as local community information and global information through the Internet to anyone who wants it. It is important to note that due to limited resources, most FreeNets do not let you access all Internet capabilities, particularly the World Wide Web.

In Canada, we now see many FreeNets in operation across the country, with many more in a planning phase. The size and scope vary, with some of the most successful initiatives being the Ottawa-based National Capital FreeNet (boasting over 20,000 members), the Toronto FreeNet (15,000 members), and the Chebucto FreeNet in Halifax.

FreeNets exist because of the hard work and dedication of volunteers throughout the community. FreeNets, which are mostly free to their users, are funded through government grants and by donations from corporate organizations. For example, the Toronto FreeNet has obtained significant funding from Rogers Communications, and Sun Microsystems has donated several hundred thousand dollars worth of Sun computer equipment to the National Capital and Toronto FreeNets (in addition to others).

FreeNets have helped in furthering use of the Internet in Canada by drawing many people to the network for the first time. They are enjoying some success in achieving their goal of providing "equitable access" to the Internet across the country.

Yet, observing some of the people who make use of FreeNets, it is obvious that there are also many who are merely taking advantage of them for a "free ride." Given the rapidly decreasing cost of Internet access across the country (as low as $1 an hour or less in many cases), one must wonder whether FreeNets are giving birth to a new generation of wired "freeloaders."

In addition, some FreeNets have also caused a fair degree of frustration in various cities. If you consider use of a FreeNet to explore the Internet, keep in mind the caveat "you get what you pay for." In Chapter 12, in which we discuss how to go about selecting an Internet service provider, we will talk about some of the problems that you might encounter using a FreeNet to access the Internet. Appendix G lists a number of FreeNet organizations in Canada.

Bulletin Board Systems

Anyone with a personal computer, a modem, a phone line, and the right software can create a "bulletin board system" (BBS). Long before the Internet existed, and long before commercial on-line systems such as CompuServe arrived, BBSs were used by many for computer-based communications.[12] A bulletin board is a system that permits people to exchange e-mail, discuss topics within "discussion groups," or download computer files or software. Some BBS systems also permit people to play computer games with other people or participate in live chats with other users, while others permit access to research information on CD ROM systems. BBSs range in size from one PC with one dial-in phone line to systems that involve several hundred PCs with several hundred dial-in lines.

Today, there are literally thousands of BBSs across Canada, with new ones arriving on a daily basis and others disappearing just as quickly. A peek into a popular computer industry newspaper such as *Toronto Computes*, the *Computer Paper*, or Ottawa's *Monitor* reveals a wealth of local services. Some consist of only one or two phone lines, while others, such as Canada Remote Systems, boast several hundred phone lines and several thousand users.

---

12. Technically, the Internet is over 25 years old. However, for most purposes, it has really only been used to any great extent in Canada and around the world for 10 years or so.

Many BBSs provide partial access to two of the most popular Internet features: e-mail and USENET. People who dial into these BBSs can exchange e-mail with Internet users around the world and can join and participate in any number of USENET conferences. They might be charged a small fee for doing so, or might find that the BBS owner provides these services for free. Some BBSs have evolved into full-fledged ISPs (such as Canada Remote) and can no longer be considered mere BBSs. Others are content to stay in their role as "special outposts on the information highway."

BBS software is maturing. Originally, dialing into a BBS was like dialing into an old 1980s style PC running the MSDOS operating system: you were faced with a clunky menu and chose what to do by pressing a key. Today, sophisticated BBS software like Galaticomm and FirstClass offer simple, easy-to-use, mouse-driven interfaces. And some, like FirstClass, are going the next step, by promising to introduce World Wide Web access, thus becoming full-fledged Internet software.

Regardless of who they are, often a BBS is an inexpensive and easy way to introduce yourself to the on-line world.

The Rural Problem

It is easy to get onto the Internet in Canada — if you are in a major city or town. Indeed, we have seen massive growth in the number of ISPs in Canada over the last three years such that there are now well over 300 across the country. Most major cities have 20 or more providers. Mid-sized cities have a fair degree of competition, and, increasingly, small providers are establishing themselves in smaller towns.

Yet, the sad reality is that many Canadians outside of these areas cannot reach an Internet service provider through a local phone call; hence the Internet is much too expensive for them. To solve this problem, we need to create a telecommunications environment that encourages national Internet access, and to do that, we need a government that is in tune with the significant opportunity that the Internet represents to all Canadians.

If you live in a rural area, you can dial into CompuServe's 800 number at $20 per hour or access via an 800 number through some other large provider, or make a long distance call to some other Internet provider. (In some provinces, New Brunswick and Saskatchewan in particular, the local provincial telephone company provides province-wide access, but with a surcharge of several dollars per hour.) Given the popularity (and addictiveness) of the Web, access from a rural community can be a wonderful way to spend a lot of money. Unfortunately, in Canada, this is a barrier for many trying to get onto the Internet.

The Nature of the Problem

There are people who desperately want to get onto the Internet. Examples abound. In May 1995 one of the authors gave a keynote address to a conference sponsored by the Ontario Hospital Association concerning use of the Internet within the health care industry. The address focused on the role that the Internet is already playing in health care services today, for example, by providing patients with access to support networks and by permitting the exchange of leading-edge medical research among medical professionals.

At the end of the speech a young doctor spoke up and basically said, "I'm convinced that there are good and valid reasons why I should be on the Internet. My problem is that I live in a small, northern Ontario town and I can't get on this thing. What's wrong?"

Indeed, what is wrong? The day before, the Canadian Radio-television and Telecommunications Commission released its "information highway report." The report says all the right things and certainly sounds important. Unfortunately, it demonstrates that the CRTC really does not have a clue that the real information highway is emerging in the Internet in Canada and around the world. The CRTC has failed to make the leap from television to this new media world as found in the Internet.

A careful reading of the CRTC report (available, incidentally, at their Web site at **http://www.crtc.gc.ca**) and a review of subsequent press clippings reveal that the main conclusion drawn by the CRTC (after many weeks of public hearings) is that telephone companies should be able to compete against cable companies in the delivery of video movies to the home.

A lot of people, many familiar with the role that the Internet is playing in business, education, and health care, tried to get the point across at the CRTC information highway hearings that the highway is not all about interactive television and video on demand; it is about access to knowledge and information through computer networks. They tried to stress that we should create a telecommunications and investment climate in Canada that encourages the creation of Internet access services accessible by all Canadians.

It is obvious their pleas fell on deaf ears. What became apparent is that the CRTC, like many old-time government regulatory bodies, has missed the increasing scope and relevance of the Internet to the whole concept of the information highway. What has gone wrong is that the CRTC is so dominated by a generation of people — broadcast executives — who grew up thinking that television is the centre of the universe, that it hasn't realized that we have an entire generation growing up with computers, not TVs.

The CRTC could have done much more in its information highway report. It could have addressed, for example, how we can create a telecommunications environment that would encourage expansion of the Internet to all communities in Canada. It didn't, and it should be condemned for not doing so.

There is Hope

Fortunately, other government bodies place a little more relevance on the ongoing development of the Internet and understand that a significant new information distribution system is emerging in Canada and around the world. For example, on February 17, 1995, Industry Canada announced the "Community Access Project," an effort to help 1,000 rural communities across Canada join the Internet. The initiative provides assistance and guidance to rural communities seeking to link to the network and a level of cash funding to establish the link. Keeping in mind the reduced involvement of the government in the economy, the press release noted that "communities will be expected to raise most of the needed cash and in-kind contributions themselves with other partners, including public sector agencies, community organizations and the private sector." (The press release can be found at **http://info.ic.gc.ca/ic-data/announcements/news-releases/1995/02-17-95.e**)

Through the program, "a national network of community access sites will be established to help create new and exciting opportunities for growth and jobs. Through a competitive process, communities will be selected to establish and operate public access sites in low cost public locations, such as schools and libraries, to serve as Information Highway 'on ramps'. The aim of the project is to establish up to 300 centres across Canada annually for three years. The actual number of sites will depend on the availability of resources."

A project called "Community ACCESS" has been established to assist Industry Canada in its goal of helping to "provide rural communities with affordable public access to the Internet, as well as the skills to use it effectively...." Based in New Brunswick but with national responsibilities, the project includes the involvement of the University of New Brunswick and the New Brunswick Department of Education. Their Web site notes the specific rural objectives of the project and is a good starting point for those interested in the potential of the project for their own rural community (**http://cnet.unb.ca/cac/cac.html**):

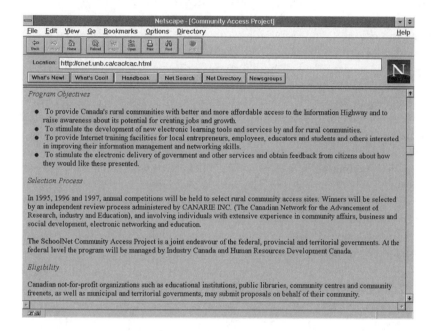

According to Community ACCESS, there has been tremendous interest in the program from across the country. Hopefully this initiative will help many rural communities across Canada get onto the Internet in the next three to five years.

The Maturing Internet Marketplace

The ISP industry in Canada is in a constant state of evolution. Currently there are many ISPs from which to choose to get onto the Internet, and the market will only continue to grow. Many wonder if the entry of larger companies to the ISP business will mean that many of the small ISPs will disappear. While no one can predict the future, we believe in one simple fact: competition is a reality of the Internet and will be for a long time.

The Canadian Internet marketplace is also very competitive: with over 300 full Internet service providers across Canada, the potential customer in major metropolitan cities is faced with a dazzling number of choices and opportunities to get on the Internet. Service levels, price, support, and technology vary wildly, with the result that there is much "churn" within the marketplace, in which consumers leave one particular service for another. There appears to be little brand or company loyalty.

In some ways, the Internet marketplace is becoming too crowded, with too many people becoming ISPs without any real appreciation for what the business is all about, or without any real business background necessary to manage a complex business. The ISP business is an industry of rabbits — they are appearing everywhere. It can't go on. Hence any ISP will have to work hard to position itself or maintain an edge in the marketplace, and service, support, and "one-stop shopping" rather than price will become the keys to success.

Another factor to keep in mind about the Internet is that, given its roots in the academic world, there is a cultural mindset among many Internet users that is anti-establishment, anti-big-business, anti-monopoly. The Internet is both a wild and wonderful place to do business — nothing is predictable, and everything is subject to change at any time. By the very nature of this mindset (which is changing as the Internet becomes more mainstream and commercialized), larger organizations will find entry into the marketplace attacked and subject to debate.

This has already happened. Rumors run rampant on occasion on the Internet in Canada that "the telephone companies are out to take over and control the Internet." Paranoia and concern are the rule of the day. AGT, the primary Alberta telephone company, stumbled badly when it found that its announcement of an Internet service put it immediately on the defensive with some Internet service providers. These providers charged that AGT, because of its size, scope, and ability to access telephone records, would be able to compete unfairly against smaller, established Internet service providers. By May 1995, these providers had filed a "Statutory Declaration" with the federal Director of Investigation and Research of the Bureau of Competition Policy to undertake an inquiry into AGT's actions (**http://www.canuck.com/Agt/statdec.html**):

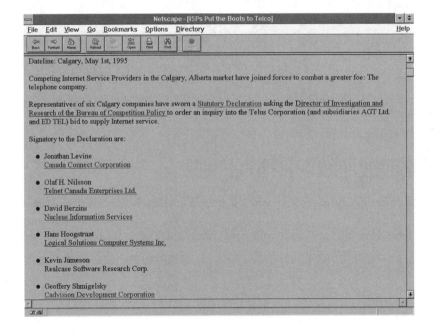

The position of these smaller Internet service providers, in their request to the Director, indicated the following (taken directly from a Web page at **http://www.canuck.com/Agt/statdec.html**):

Telus Corporation, through AGT Limited and ED TEL, completely controls the supply of local subscriber telephone service in the province of Alberta. Independent commercial Internet Service Providers (ISPs) must buy this service from AGT in order to supply Internet services to their customers. The large numbers of these telephone lines required makes telephone service the largest single expense incurred by ISPs in the course of their business. The price of this service is fixed by regulatory tariff and as such is not negotiable or subject to discount. AGT/Telus, as a profitable entity, thus can effectively supply to itself this necessary service at a rate unavailable to ISPs.

AGT/Telus has, in financing the installation of the equipment required to support this service, provided a capital subsidy to its Internet operation. Additionally, the use of the company's existing billing mechanisms, et. al., will comprise operating subsidies, as may the use of "800" toll-free long distance service.

Further, AGT/Telus has stated an intention to withdraw from ISPs the "Centrex" class of telephone service. This relatively inexpensive service is presently, in a low-margin business, one of the few advantages available in the struggle toward profitability. Withdrawal of Centrex service and its replacement by conventional "business" service will result in a dramatic increase in telephone service costs to the ISPs, guaranteeing their failure. AGT claims that they are withdrawing Centrex service on technical grounds, yet have stated that they intend to use Centrex in the delivery of their own Internet service.

The threatened AGT/Telus entry into competition against independent commercial ISPs within the Internet market is, by its nature, a margin squeeze by a supplier holding a total monopoly over a service required by its competitors. Additionally, the increase in operating expense to ISPs attendant in withdrawal of Centrex service will assure the destruction of these competitors.

Finally, by virtue of their position as a monopoly common carrier, AGT/Telus is uniquely privy to confidential and proprietary information regarding the independent ISPs with which it wishes to compete. As all of an ISP's business consists of telephone communications with customers, the ISPs' customer lists and detailed information on their usage are in AGT/Telus's possession. AGT/Telus would thus have an unfair competitive advantage by virtue of having access to this information, and the potential exists for abuse of this confidential and proprietary information.

In the circumstances, the above-noted acts of AGT/Telus constitute an abuse of dominant position in the telecommunications industry and will substantially lessen competition in the Internet market.

AGT eventually entered the Internet marketplace in August 1995; it was inevitable that all major Canadian telephone companies would jump into the business. Yet, the situation is indicative of the concern shared by small ISPs at the entry of giants into the marketplace, and with so many companies getting into the ISP business, it is inevitable that conflicts will occur. (At press time, the issue above was still unresolved.)

Clearly, many of the smaller ISPs are concerned that the giants will "squeeze them out" of the industry. But let's put some things into perspective. There are several certainties about the Internet business in Canada:

◆ We will continue to see the establishment of new ISPs. The entry level investment to get going in a small community, for example, might be in the range of $250,000. Hence becoming an ISP is not difficult from a financial perspective, but staying in the business for the long run will be. The low entry level price means that Internet access will never become a monopoly like so many other telecommunication services are in Canada (unless the government makes some thoughtless moves with respect to regulation of the Internet, which we discuss in later chapters).

◆ We will see a number of smaller ISPs disappear. There will be an inevitable shakeout in the marketplace as larger companies continue to get involved. Some of the smaller ISPs are undercapitalized, do not have a business track record, and will not be able to weather the perils of competition in the marketplace. Some have lousy service reputations and overburdened systems. Customers will migrate to those systems that work well and provide good support.

◆ We will see mergers in the marketplace of small- and medium-sized ISPs. *fonorola* and NSTN have already merged to become one of Canada's largest ISPs. Such moves help to ensure the presence of these smaller/medium-sized companies in the marketplace in the face of competition from organizations like Bell Canada and IBM.

◆ We should not take for granted the idea that organizations like the phone companies will enjoy instant success in the marketplace. Bell, for example, has long enjoyed a monopoly, and it is only now learning to compete against other companies. It will find participating in the Internet industry to be a wild experience, unlike anything it has done before.

◆ Things are becoming even more interesting in the Internet marketplace as Microsoft begins to muscle its way in with Windows 95, which includes built-in access to the Internet. Many predict that Microsoft will quickly begin to dominate the ISP business in Canada and elsewhere, while others predict that the Internet will prove to be Microsoft's "Vietnam" — it will find itself in a competitive war that it cannot hope to win. In fact, its price for Internet access is in excess of what many ISPs across Canada charge, so it certainly isn't competing on price. Things will be interesting even for mighty Microsoft.

◆ The cable companies entering the business of providing access to the Internet have a leg up on the telephone companies, since they can offer economical, extremely high-speed access to the Internet through the cable wire to come into the home and office. Without having the customer invest in expensive equipment or by laying fiber into the home, telephone companies will find themselves at a severe competitive disadvantage against the cable companies.

Hence we should not expect that small providers are doomed and that large companies (in particular the telephone companies) will necessarily overwhelm the market. Indeed, many of the smaller providers will continue to thrive and grow.

Some Good Sources to Track Issues in the ISP Industry

Good sources pertaining to ISPs can be found in these sites. Most are heavily U.S.-focused, but give a good idea of the industry overall.

Edupage

URL: **http://www.educom.edu/edupage.new**

    (current issues)

    http://www.educom.edu/edupage.old/.index.html

    (back issues)

To subscribe: Send a message to **listproc@educom.edu** and in the body of the message place the following command:

subscribe edupage YourFirstName YourLastName

Edupage promotes itself as "a summary of news items on information technology." It is published three times a week by Educom, a Washington, D.C.-based consortium of colleges and universities. Edupage provides concise summaries of articles in the mainstream press about the Internet, the information highway, telecommunications, and other technology issues. It is an excellent source of news and information for any one with an interest in current information technology trends.

In, Around, and Online

URL: **http://www.clark.net/pub/robert/home.html**

To subscribe: Send a message to **listserv@clark.net** and in the body of the message place the following command:

subscribe online-1 YourFirstName YourLastName

You can also subscribe through the Web site listed above.

This publication promotes itself as "a weekly survey of events in the consumer online services industry" and includes reports on industry initiatives related to electronic commerce, significant new Internet initiatives by major Fortune 500 companies, and other Internet-related events. Very well written and up-to-date.

Cowles/SIMBA Media Daily: Internet Information

URL: **http://www.mecklerweb.com/simba/internet.htm**

A good daily source of information for what is going on in the on-line industry; similar to a news wire. Reports can be found on the evolution of electronic commerce and other business activities on the Internet.

Interactive Age

An electronic version of some articles from the newspaper of the same name. The publication reports on many Internet developments, including those related to ISPs.

URL: **http://techweb.cmp.com/ia**

Netsurf

URL: **http://www.netsurf.com/nsd/index.html**

To subscribe: Send a message to **nsdigest-request@netsurf.com**

Include the following command in the body of the message: **subscribe nsdigest-text**

Netsurf is an upbeat, interesting newsletter summarizing new World Wide Web sites established on the Internet: a "guide to interesting news, places and resources on-line …" with "… short crisp newsbytes, notices, and reviews designed to provide informative and entertaining snapshots of the vast wired world." A good way to keep in touch with new Internet initiatives and appreciate the diversity of the Internet.

Where Do We Go Next?

As you saw in this chapter, there are many ISPs through which you can join the Internet in Canada. In the next chapter we will take a look at how the Internet "works" and examine some of the technology and standards that make it work. We will look at how all these providers cooperate in order to route your use of the Internet across Canada and around the world. And in Chapter 12 we will take a look at that all important question, how do I choose an Internet service provider?

CHAPTER 5

How Does the Internet Work?

When confronted with the concept of the Internet, most people first ask the question, "OK, so how does it work?"

Getting from Point A to Point B

It is funny that many people feel compelled to understand how the Internet works. Yet few of us have a strong desire to know how a telephone system works, or how our cable television network works, or how our can opener manages to open a can. We have come to take for granted the reliability of our telephone, electrical, and gas systems and other infrastructures across the land. And you should not have to worry about how the Internet works; you only need to be aware that it does (in most cases). It is truly a curious state of affairs; most of us are not interested in other *systems* that are part of our lives, but we do want to know how the Internet works. So, in this chapter, we will try to answer that question.

Telephone Protocols are the Heart of the Phone System

To begin explaining how the Internet works, consider the telephone system. You probably do not even give a second thought to telephone numbers. You simply pick up the telephone, punch in a number (unless you have an older rotary phone), and it connects to a telephone somewhere else in the world.

It is a massive system, the global telephone network. Today, you can pick up your telephone and dial any one of several hundred million telephones around the world. And when you call someone in Sydney, Australia, you do not think or worry about how the telephone system manages to figure out how to get from your telephone in Canada down to the one in Australia. You do not lose sleep wondering how the call is routed. In fact, you do not worry about whether the call goes via an undersea wire or an overhead satellite. All you care about is the fact that you can pick up the phone, dial a number, and the call is established within seconds.

Behind the scenes there is a system of amazing complexity. And what makes this global telephone network function correctly is agreement between many people and organizations on how this complex telephone system should function. The global telephone network works because of a common *protocol* and an accepted set of *standards*. These protocols and standards involve many things. They define, for example, the structure of telephone numbers, how telephone switches should connect, what the red wire and the green wire should do in your telephone handset, and how telephone systems can best figure out how to route a call anywhere in the world.

But we only see these standards in their simplest form. A North American telephone number, for example, of the form xxx-xxx-xxxx; the fact that you can call 604-555-1212 and get a long distance operator in British Columbia, and call 905-555-1212 and get a long distance operator in Ontario; the fact that 911 is being adopted as a standard emergency number and that 411 is directory assistance; the fact that England has the international code 44 and Canada and the United States share the code 1.

What makes the global telephone system work? Telephone companies around the world have agreed on standard methods on how they will interact. Conferences are held on a regular basis that deal with emerging technology issues. Special international committees and organizations such as the International Telecommunications Union deal with special technical standards. Technical specifications are agreed upon and are published for wide distribution. Telephone companies sign written contracts in which they agree to link to other telecommunications companies around the world.

HOW DOES THE INTERNET WORK?

1 Computer protocols (accepted standards and interorganization agreements), primarily something known as TCP/IP (transmission control protocol/Internet protocol), are at the heart of the Internet.

2 The Domain Name Service (DNS) and IP figure out how to route you from your computer to another location/computer on the Internet.

3 Your seemingly simple link from your computer to another location on the Internet might actually take a long and convoluted route through the Internet.

4 Every computer directly linked to the global Internet has a unique "IP" address.

5 The Domain Name System provides names to Internet computers and resources.

6 You can register your own corporate domain name either with a Canadian authority in the Canadian domain or with an international authority based in the United States, in a more general domain.

7 Your choice of where to register will depend on many issues.

All these activities provide the foundation for the global telephone network. Protocols, standards, and agreements are the foundation of the simple telephone number that we have come to know. And somehow, telephones just "work."

Computer Protocols are the Heart of the Internet

A computer protocol is simply an agreed upon definition on how a particular piece of computer hardware or software should work. By having common protocols, hardware and software from different companies can still "talk" to each other. The Internet industry is no different than the global telephone industry: common protocols, accepted standards, and interorganization agreements determine how the Internet all fits together. These protocols define many things, including:

- ◆ how you link to a World Wide Web site in Australia from your dial-up connection in Iqaluit;

- ◆ how your e-mail message to the United Kingdom is routed from your dedicated Internet link in Halifax;

- ◆ how your USENET posting travels to most USENET sites around the world from your cable company connection in Kelowna;

- ◆ how you can be a unique name in the global Internet world.

There are many Internet protocols; we will take a look at a few of them here in this chapter. We can by no means be comprehensive, nor can we cover these standards in a great deal of technical depth. Our objectives are to give you an idea of how the Internet works, and to raise some of the important issues related to your use of the Internet.

In this section we will take a step-by-step voyage, describing what it takes to get onto the Internet and how we can find ourselves traveling around the world. We will describe what happens in the background, within the Internet system, to make the Internet work.

TCP/IP

At the heart of the Internet is a common computer networking protocol called TCP/IP, which has quickly become the protocol used to link together millions of people and computers around the world through the Internet. *If TCP/IP is anything, it is the protocol that is defining how all the computers and computer-related devices in the world can eventually plug together. It is very, very significant for this reason.*

TCP/IP networking, and thus the technology and protocols that drive the Internet, involves many different components. TCP/IP in and of itself defines how computers can share information by turning that information into small, discrete chunks of information known as "packets." It essentially defines how different computers can share information through a wire.

There are many components that complement TCP/IP in addition to its basic hardware role of sharing information through a wire. For example, domain name servers exist throughout the Internet and know how to find and provide a route to computers and resources throughout the Internet. SMTP is the messaging, or electronic mail protocol, at the heart of many of the e-mail transfers that occur through the Internet. NNTP is a protocol that supports the distribution of information through USENET, a popular area of the Internet used for global "discussions." HTTP is a protocol that supports the exchange of information through the World Wide Web. There are many other such protocols that support some aspect of the Internet.

And these protocols are used regardless of how you might access the Internet. Today, most of us in Canada access the Internet using relatively slow modems, devices that permit our computer to link to other computers through the phone line. Some people in business, research, and educational organizations in Canada have what is known as "direct access" to the Internet, in that they have a full-time, "high-speed" link to the network from their corporate or organizational computer network to the Internet. And a very fortunate minority access the Internet at high speeds through the cable television wire that comes into their home. Regardless of how people are linked to the Internet, they are sharing the use of a common computer technology, or protocol.

What is happening through the global Internet is a quick adoption, by business, education, and government, of commonly accepted methods by which computers around the world can link together and by which information can be exchanged. Internet protocols are being adopted by computer hardware and software vendors around the world; developments in the computer industry are occurring at such speed that some people joke that six months in Internet years is like 20 human years.

An important thing to note about TCP/IP is that organizations are adopting it not only to link to the Internet, but as the foundation to their internal computer networks. As we wrote in our business strategy guide to the Internet, the *Canadian Internet Advantage*, "the Internet is important to anyone in business, government, or education, because it is the leading technology candidate to link all the computers in the world." In effect, we are seeing in the Internet the emergence of the first true standard to support global connectivity of computers.

Who Writes the Standards?

Any global cooperative effort of the size and scope of the Internet requires a high degree of coordination, standardization, and registration. The issue of the evolution of Internet standards is a complex one. There are many hundreds of organizations (including computing companies, research and educational organizations, government bodies, and corporations) and individuals involved around the world who debate, discuss, design, test, and implement the standards. The process is far beyond the scope of this book.

Suffice it to say that much of the design, debate, and discussion occurs through the Internet itself. For example, check the USENET newsgroup **comp.protocols.tcp-ip** for an ongoing discussion of issues related to the TCP/IP protocol.

There are also a number of organizations responsible for these activities, including the following:

◆ Internet Society, an organization dedicated to promoting the growth of the Internet. The key mission of the Society is "to provide assistance and support to groups involved in the use, operation and evolution of the Internet." Anyone can join the Internet Society. For a small fee you will receive a quarterly newsletter reporting on Internet issues; you can also participate in an on-line mailing list to which Internet news and developments are posted.

- ◆ Internet Architecture Board (IAB), an organization that coordinates research and development in Internet-related issues and standard setting for Internet activities. The IAB is responsible for the technical evolution of the network.

- ◆ Internet Engineering Task Force. A component of the IAB, this Task Force develops Internet standards for review by the IAB.

- ◆ The Internet Network Information Centre (InterNIC), run by AT&T and Network Solutions, Inc. InterNIC serves as a registrar for Internet domain names and network numbers and provides information and directory services concerning the Internet. If you want to register a domain name outside of the Canadian domain (as described below), you can do so through the InterNIC. The InterNIC has established a number of extremely useful Internet services, including several that provide pointers to useful Internet resources from around the world.

A good place to start exploring the world of Internet standards is the InterNIC at **http://www.internic.net** and the Internet Engineering Task Force at **http://www.ietf.cnri.reston.va.us**. A good source of information about Internet protocols and standards can be found at **http://netlab.itd.nrl.navy.mil/Internet.html**.

In Canada, organizations such as CA*Net and the Canadian Domain Registry (which we discuss below) are very involved in the standard-setting process as it might affect Canada. In addition, many Internet veterans within the Canadian academic community (many of whom have now migrated to commercial Internet service providers) remain very involved in all activities related to the Internet.

Internet Software

When you link to the Internet, you are using, in some way, TCP/IP and all the standards and protocols that make up the Internet. The extent to which you use these protocols depends on the method used to link into the Internet. In most cases, these protocols work silently in the background, just as protocols work within the global telephone network, to route your requests for information and to move your e-mail around the world.

The next step in our voyage in understanding how the Internet works is to take a look at the software that you need to access the network. There are various technical methods through which you can establish a link to the Internet, each involving different types of communication software. We will go into those options in greater depth in a subsequent chapter. But basically, once you have an Internet account from an Internet service provider (ISP), to get onto the Internet you need, obviously, a computer, a modem (the faster the better), and communications software.

For now, since we want to concentrate on how the Internet works rather than how to get connected, we will make use of the most common type of Internet connection, a dial-up SLIP/PPP account.[1] This is a special type of TCP/IP connection that lets you link directly to the Internet using a dial-up modem. Hence your computer starts to talk TCP/IP and can *talk* to all the other computers in the world talking TCP/IP that are linked into the Internet. To use such an account, you will need communications software that supports a SLIP/PPP con-

---

1. SLIP and PPP are two different but very similar methods to establish a link to the Internet using a modem. We describe in the next chapter what is involved in using such an account.

nection and software to support popular Internet services such as e-mail, the World Wide Web, and USENET.

You can buy such software in computer stores; products such as Internet in a Box, Quarterdecks' Internet Suite, Netscape's Personal Edition, and many others are available.[2] For our example, we will use the services of InfoRamp, an ISP that sells access in the Metropolitan Toronto area, and the software that they provide.[3]

Many providers provide "shareware," or "public domain," programs to establish your SLIP/PPP connection to the Internet. InfoRamp, like many ISPs across Canada, provides new users with a shareware software product known as Trumpet Winsock. They also provide some of the more popular shareware Internet programs to let you use electronic mail (Eudora), an early version of a popular browser to access the World Wide Web (Netscape), and other software to access other Internet services from within Microsoft Windows. (They also provide appropriate Macintosh software.) Individuals who are adept with modems can download this software directly from InfoRamp, while novices will be sent, on request, a disk containing the required software.

Establishing a Connection

Now that you have software to link you into the Internet, you need to access a provider. To establish our link to the Internet, we run a program that establishes the modem connection to the InfoRamp Internet service. In our example, we are using a PPP program called Trumpet Winsock, which has been configured to connect to the provider we are using, InfoRamp. Once the connection has been established, our screen looks like this:

```
┌─────────────────────────────────────────────────────────────────┐
│ ─                        Trumpet Winsock                    ▼  ▲ │
├─────────────────────────────────────────────────────────────────┤
│  File  Edit  Special  Trace  Dialler  Help                       │
├─────────────────────────────────────────────────────────────────┤
│ Trumpet Winsock Version 2.0 Revision B                        ↑  │
│ Copyright (c) 1993,1994 by Peter R. Tattam                       │
│ All Rights Reserved.                                             │
│ THIS IS AN UNREGISTERED SHAREWARE VERSION FOR EVALUATION ONLY.   │
│ PPP ENABLED                                                     │
│ Internal SLIP driver COM2 Baud rate = 115200 Hardware handshaking│
│ IP buffers = 32                                                 │
│ My IP = 0.0.0.0 netmask = 0.0.0.0 gateway = 0.0.0.0             │
│ Executing script c:\ppp\socket\login.cmd.  Type <esc> to abort  │
│ PPP DISABLED                                                    │
│ atz                                                            │
│ OK                                                             │
│ atz                                                            │
│ OK                                                             │
│ atm1dt4163632815                                               │
│ CONNECT 28800/ARQ/V34/LAPM/V42BIS                              │
│                                                                │
│                                                                │
│ User Access Verification                                       │
│                                                                │
│ Username: jcarroll                                             │
│ Password:                                                      │
│ ts5>ppp default                                                │
│ PPP mode selected.  Will try to negotiate IP address.          │
│                                                                │
│ Script completed                                               │
│ PPP ENABLED                                                    │
│ My IP address = 198.53.144.212                              ↓  │
└─────────────────────────────────────────────────────────────────┘
```

---

2. We take a comprehensive look at some of these software packages in Chapter 13.

3. At this time, there are over 50 such providers who sell some type of access in Metro Toronto, compared to only 10 a few years ago, an indication of the rapid rate at which the Internet is growing.

In effect, our personal computer dialed InfoRamp through our modem and established a connection to a modem at InfoRamp. Once it had done so, it provided our user name and password and then told InfoRamp it wanted a "ppp default" account. Finally, InfoRamp provided us with an "IP address," which establishes us as a computer that is directly attached to the Internet.

At this point, we are connected to the Internet, we are running the TCP/IP protocol on our own computer, and we can begin to use other software to access popular Internet services. We could choose to use electronic mail, USENET, the World Wide Web, or any other Internet service using the software that InfoRamp has provided to us.

Traveling Through the Web

Now that we have our SLIP/PPP connection to the Internet, we will access one of the areas on the Internet, the World Wide Web, using a "browser," in our case with the popular software program Netscape, to help you understand how the Internet works.

Say we want to use Netscape to get to the World Wide Web site of the Royal Bank of Canada. We load the Netscape software into our PC, and since we know the address is **http:www.royalbank.com**, we key this into the location box of the Netscape software.[4] Within seconds we are taken to the introductory page (or "home page") of the Royal Bank Web site:

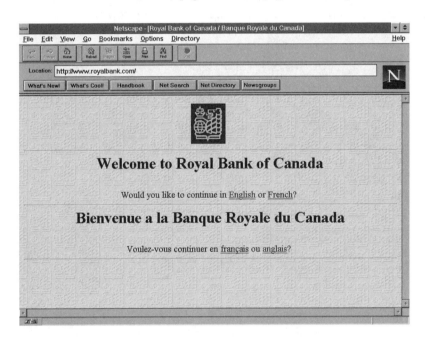

Voilà! The magic of the Internet, and the TCP/IP and other protocols that drive it, permitted us to connect directly from our PC to the Royal Bank.

---

4. Later in this book, we will talk about some of the methods to use to locate particular companies and information resources on the Internet.

How did the InfoRamp system know how to get us there? What route did it take through the Internet? Who and what was involved? These are the types of questions that many new users want to know, so to put the Internet into perspective, we will take apart our journey to the Royal Bank.

Domain Name Service

The Domain Name Service (DNS), part of the Internet protocol, determines how to establish a link from one computer to another on the Internet. Individuals do not interact with the DNS; it is the Internet software that interacts with it. We describe it here simply to help you in your quest to understand how the Internet works.

Essentially, in its simplest form, the DNS is a large, globally distributed database found throughout the Internet that provides a "route" to each company or organization on the Internet. When we indicate to our software that we want to go somewhere, it is the DNS that figures out how to get there.

To find out what happens when we indicate we want to use Netscape to go to the Royal Bank World Wide Web site, we can turn on the "trace" command within Trumpet Winsock so that it shows us the query that it makes of the domain name server at InfoRamp:

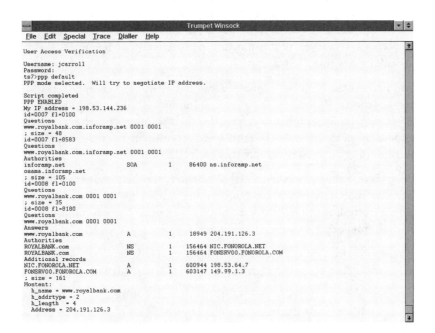

On the screen above we can see the Trumpet Winsock software asking the DNS "where is **www.royalbank.com**?" The DNS responds that the bank can be found at the "IP address" **204.191.126.3**, which is itself found via the **NIC.FONOROLA.NET** system. It also tells us that the **NIC.FONOROLA.NET** system can be found at the address **198.53.64.7**. (Notice that a second set of addresses is provided, in case the first route is not working. Thus the Internet provides for automatic redundancy.)

In effect, the DNS has told our system how to get to the system at the Royal Bank from our account at InfoRamp. It has told our system the route that we will take. Many voyages through the Internet are not direct, but take a number of steps to get from point A to point B. We can now take a look at the exact route it took to get there.

Traceroute

We do so using a UNIX command, "traceroute"[5] or by using a program that can access the traceroute command. We are provided with the following detail from the traceroute command:

```
jcarroll@cliff:[jcarroll] 21>traceroute www.royalbank.com
traceroute to www.royalbank.com (204.191.126.3), 30 hops max, 40 byte packets
1 cheers (198.53.144.25) 6 ms 2 ms 3 ms
2 inforamp-fonorola (198.53.144.1) 3 ms 3 ms 3 ms
3 S3-0-6.C7-1.tor.fonorola.net (198.53.32.29) 7 ms 9 ms 7 ms
4 C7-1-ott.fONOROLA.net (198.53.254.10) 21 ms 21 ms 29 ms
5 www.royalbank.com (204.191.126.3) 19 ms 31 ms 15 ms
jcarroll@cliff:[jcarroll] 22>
```

What does this tell us? Quite a bit. The information shows us the computers and hardware devices known as "routers" that we traveled through in order to get from InfoRamp to the Royal Bank. (Each step is counted as a hop, and as a general rule of thumb, the fewer hops the better, since it means the route is shorter and will happen quicker.)

Using the example above, we can put into perspective what happened when we keyed **www.royalbank.com** within Netscape:

◆ Our traceroute command showed that we started out at a computer at InfoRamp named "cheers" (InfoRamp has a sense of humor and like most providers, uses an interesting, funny, or humorous name for their computer systems). It took 6 milliseconds to get to "cheers." (The other two columns are the time it took for a second and a third try, that is, traceroute tries each step three times.)

◆ From there, a connection was made to *fonorola*, another Internet service provider in Canada. InfoRamp, in fact, has bought a high-speed link to *fonorola* and thus uses the company as its primary link to the outside world. There is nothing to prevent one ISP from being a customer of another ISP.

◆ We then traveled through a few systems at *fonorola* (a few milliseconds in all) and then went directly to a computer at the Royal Bank of Canada (another 19 milliseconds).

The time on the right of each "hop" represents the time that it took to get from the previous hop to that hop and is measured in milliseconds. Thus it took us less than 60 milliseconds to travel to the Royal Bank.

What is also apparent to us from this example is that the Royal Bank has purchased its link to the Internet from the ISP *fonorola* and that InfoRamp has done the same. This means

---

5. Traceroute is a UNIX command that tells us the route that we take when traveling from the InfoRamp Internet service to another location on the Internet and thus helps us understand where we are traveling in order to get there. Most users do not need to know how to use traceroute (and many will not have access to the command), but it is a fun way to take a look at how the Internet works. At a UNIX prompt in our InfoRamp account, we can simply key **traceroute www.royalbank.com** to get a snapshot of the route that we took from InfoRamp to get to the Royal Bank.

that we have made a very straightforward link from our computer, through InfoRamp to *f*onorola, and from there directly to the bank.

We can also take a look at the traceroute detail using a program called Trumpet Hop Check. In this case, the times are about 100 times higher than when we used the traceroute command above:

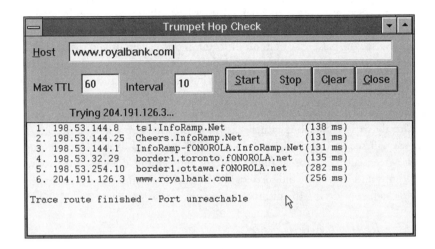

The reason it takes longer in this case is technically complex, but in a nutshell,

◆ When we used the traceroute command directly above, we were "closer" to the Internet, since we were using a computer at InfoRamp as the starting point.

◆ When we were using Trumpet Hop Check, we were a little farther away from the Internet, since we were using our own PC as the starting point.

Our modem link has slowed us down just a touch (i.e., 100 milliseconds, which is really not a big deal in the Internet).

Things Get Complicated

There are many ISPs in Canada, and thus our route is often not as direct as in the example above. For example, say we want to travel from our InfoRamp account over to the Canadian Airlines Web site (**http://www.cdnair.ca**). Once again, the DNS is queried, and a path is provided from InfoRamp over to Canadian Airlines in Vancouver. Taking a look at our traceroute results, we can see that the route was a little bit more complex :

```
traceroute to www.cdnair.ca (142.147.1.8), 30 hops max, 40 byte packets
1 cheers (198.53.144.25) 10 ms 2 ms 2 ms
2 inforamp-fonorola (198.53.144.1) 5 ms 4 ms 3 ms
3 S3-0-6.C7-1.tor.fonorola.net (198.53.32.29) 8 ms 7 ms 11 ms
4 ix-iinternet.on.canet.ca (204.138.26.41) 14 ms 9 ms 10 ms
5 psp-ix.on.canet.ca (204.138.26.14) 13 ms 34 ms 11 ms
6 psp.bc.canet.ca (192.70.164.101) 51 ms 56 ms 52 ms
```

```
7 regional2.bc.canet.ca (192.68.61.102) 50 ms 57 ms 56 ms
8 nb40-2.hc.BC.net (134.87.108.35) 65 ms 53 ms 50 ms
9 yvrrout2.CdnAir.CA (142.147.231.1) 304 ms 283 ms 375 ms
10 yvrrout2.CdnAir.CA (142.147.231.1) 299 ms !H * 144 ms !H
jcarroll@cliff:[jcarroll] 23>
```

Interpreting this, we can see that Canadian Airlines has linked a computer located in Vancouver to the Internet through BC*Net, a major provider of Internet services in British Columbia. We can also see the path that we took: InfoRamp once again linked to *fonorola*. But from there, *fonorola* performed a direct link to CA*Net, which is the major Internet backbone in Canada today. CA*Net routed us to one of its member organizations, BC*Net, and from there to Canadian Airlines.

Had we done a traceroute earlier in 1995, we would have seen *fonorola* make a connection not directly to CA*Net, but rather a connection through a serious of U.S.-based networks, as we will see in the next example below. But in mid-1995, *fonorola* and CA*Net came to an agreement to exchange traffic directly, resulting in the shortened route above. It took us 10 hops and over 800 milliseconds to get from our InfoRamp account to Canadian Airlines. Not bad, considering the number of systems it went through.

Things Get Really Complicated

So far, both of our examples have involved some fairly straightforward connections from our account at InfoRamp over to another company, through one or more Canadian ISPs. But sometimes the route gets quite complicated, and you might not even be aware of it. Often, you might link from your Canadian Internet account to another organization in Canada and, unbeknownst to you, travel all over the United States on your way there. We will see this in our next example.

Why is this so? The answer is simple: the Internet is in the final stages of undergoing a transition from being a government-funded academic/research network to one that is almost completely commercially driven. Since the Internet in Canada is still in this state of transition, as it is elsewhere in the world, there are often some weird routings in place as a result of older network policies.

As recently as 1994, certain ISPs in Canada restricted use to those organizations that agreed to abide by what were known as "acceptable use policies" (AUPs). These policies stipulated that the network could be used only for research or academic purposes and could not be used for business purposes. These ISPs (which are still known as regional networks) refused to establish a direct link to some of the new commercial ISPs that were being established in Canada, since that would imply "business use." In other cases, two commercial ISPs in Canada might not have agreed (and might still not have agreed today) to exchange traffic directly. In both cases, the funny thing was that a link could still occur, often via the United States, regardless of the refusal in Canada to support a direct connection.

AUPs resulted in long, complicated routing for many Internet activities. We will see some complicated routes as a result of Internet service providers still arranging for more direct routing within Canada. For example, say we want to travel from our InfoRamp account over to the World Wide Web site of the Canadian Broadcasting Corporation. It seems simple enough. We run Netscape, key in **http://www.cbc.ca**, and it seems that we are almost instantly connected to the CBC.

But running traceroute shows an almost completely different story:

```
carroll@cliff:[jcarroll] 21>traceroute www.cbc.ca
traceroute to www.cbc.ca (159.33.1.51), 30 hops max, 40 byte packets
1 cheers (198.53.144.25) 9 ms 2 ms 2 ms
2 inforamp-fonorola (198.53.144.1) 6 ms 6 ms 5 ms
3 S3-0-6.C7-1.tor.fonorola.net (198.53.32.29) 9 ms 7 ms 11 ms
4 C2-nyk.fONOROLA.net (198.53.254.13) 87 ms 63 ms 67 ms
5 en-0.cnss35.New-York.t3.ans.net (192.103.63.5) 47 ms 33 ms 34 ms
6 mf-0.cnss32.New-York.t3.ans.net (140.222.32.222) 127 ms 61 ms 51 ms
7 t3-0.cnss48.Hartford.t3.ans.net (140.222.48.1) 58 ms 82 ms 67 ms
8 t3-2.cnss43.Cleveland.t3.ans.net (140.222.43.3) 73 ms 101 ms 60 ms
9 t3-2.cnss25.Chicago.t3.ans.net (140.222.25.3) 157 ms 84 ms 91 ms
10 t3-1.cnss96.Denver.t3.ans.net (140.222.96.2) 93 ms 123 ms 105 ms
11 t3-1.cnss8.San-Francisco.t3.ans.net (140.222.8.2) 111 ms 112 ms 121 ms
12 t3-0.enss144.t3.ans.net (140.222.144.1) 142 ms 159 ms 149 ms
13 ICM-FIX-W.ICP.NET (192.203.230.16) 190 ms 114 ms 119 ms
14 sl-stk-5-H2/0-T3.sprintlink.net (144.228.10.21) 114 ms 133 ms 157 ms
15 sl-dc-6-H1/0-T3.sprintlink.net (144.228.10.1) 111 ms 153 ms 116 ms
16 sl-dc-4-F0/0.sprintlink.net (144.228.20.4) 111 ms 118 ms 117 ms
17 sl-hookup-1-S0-T1.sprintlink.net (144.228.78.66) 171 ms 145 ms 148 ms
18 hu-isdn-2.tor.hookup.net (165.154.1.14) 216 ms 286 ms 150 ms
19 159.33.1.73 (159.33.1.73) 497 ms 1091 ms 941 ms
20 www.cbc.ca (159.33.1.49) 1682 ms * 2018 ms
```

In this case, InfoRamp made the same link out through *fonorola* as it did in our previous two examples. But something different then happened: our link went south to the United States!

What the traceroute command shows is that *fonorola* linked to a system known as ANS (Advanced Network Services) in New York, a very large provider of high-speed Internet services in the United States. We then traveled via the ANS Internet network through Hartford, Cleveland, Chicago, Denver, and San Francisco. There, we hopped from the ANS network to the Sprintlink network, run by the large U.S. telecommunications company Sprint Communications. This eventually brought us back to HookUp Communications, an Oakville, Ont. ISP that provides Internet access to the CBC.

What is happening here? Why such a bizarre route to get from one downtown Toronto company (InfoRamp) to another downtown Toronto location (the CBC)? Simply, *fonorola* and HookUp have not yet agreed that they should exchange traffic directly with each other in Canada. As a result, our simple connection travels a long and seemingly bizarre route throughout the United States, and it takes longer, with some 20 hops now involved and seconds instead of milliseconds. Very different from our earlier examples.

And the key in this case is that two of the major U.S. ISPs — ANS and Sprint — are agreeing to exchange traffic. All InfoRamp has to do is plug into a company that has an agreement with ANS (*fonorola*, in this case). HookUp has plugged into Sprint, and since Sprint and ANS have agreed to interlink, then a route can be established from InfoRamp to Sprint.

Behind the scenes, the DNS is operating as a massively distributed database, defining the route that should be taken in this case.

The Internet is so full of such wild and wonderful routing that sometimes it never makes sense but it is this type of routing that makes the Internet work. And in fact, the impact of such routing on the dial-up Internet user is often marginal. Most people would not notice that it seems to take a few milliseconds more to get to the CBC than it does to other locations in Canada.

The routing is constantly in a state of flux, as well. Perhaps by the time you read this, *f*onorola and HookUp will have agreed to directly exchange traffic, so that a one-kilometre physical difference in downtown Toronto will not translate into a 16,000-kilometre trip through the networks that make up the Internet.

What to Keep in Mind

As a user of the Internet, you do not have to worry about such routing details. Your Internet software and the Internet service provider take care of the routing for you. All you need to know is the Internet address that you are trying to reach.

What is significant about the Internet is that the many thousands of organizations and millions of individuals involved have all agreed to use the TCP/IP and related protocols. Hence InfoRamp has agreed to exchange information with *f*onorola, ANS, and the many other Internet service providers involved in the routing of your simple World Wide Web request. It really is no different from the global telephone companies agreeing to route telephone calls.

Many people ask, "who owns the Internet?" This is like asking "who owns the global telephone system?" No one does. There is no big, global, giant telephone company. Instead, there are several thousand telephone companies, all of which have agreed to work together to exchange telephone calls according to common protocols and standards. The Internet is no different. There is no big, global, giant Internet company. Instead, there are several thousand Internet companies, all of which have agreed to work together to exchange Internet connections according to common protocols and standards.

And the fascinating thing is that much of this Internet information is routed through the telecommunication networks of the telephone companies in the first place. As noted by *Economist* magazine, "The Internet's builders laid no cables and dug no trenches; they simply leased existing telephone lines."[6] Later in the article, the publication notes that "equally, it was not the telephone companies that built the Internet, although it uses their networks. They carry its data for a fee, just as they carry data from thousands of other sources. The companies that lease this capacity to bring the Internet to users around the world (see map) are mostly newcomers: Performance Systems International, Netcom, Pipeline, UUNet, Demon, Pipex. America alone has more than 600 of them. Almost all of them are under five years old." And as we noted in our previous chapter about ISPs in Canada, there are now well over 300 of them.

---

6. The Accidental Superhighway, *Economist Magazine*, July 7, 1995.

In other words, the Internet runs through global telecommunication networks, mostly those of telephone companies, but really is a *separate system within that telephone system.*

What Is Next?

You do have some learning to do. Going back to our telephone analogy: you have learned to talk on the telephone, you have learned how to use voice mail, and you have learned how to call directory assistance on occasion. But you have not had to learn how telephone companies program their telephone switches. You trust it — it works.

In the same way, you will have to learn how to use your Internet software, how to obtain the addresses of companies on the Internet (i.e., **http://www.cbc.ca**), and how to navigate your way around an absolutely massive information network. But you will not have to learn how the ISPs program their systems or keep their domain name servers up-to-date, nor do you have to worry about how Netscape knows how to get from your computer to the CBC. Trust it — it works.

In the next two sections, we will take a look at the basics of TCP/IP addressing and the Domain Name System, since you will need some familiarity with these standards as you begin to use the Internet.

TCP/IP BASICS

TCP/IP stands for transmission control protocol/Internet protocol. Every computer that is directly attached to the Internet has an IP address associated with it. IP addresses consist of four sets of numbers separated by periods. For example, the particular computer that has the Royal Bank's World Wide Web site has the IP address **204.191.126.3**. The address is unique throughout the Internet world and is used by individuals and by Internet applications to reach particular Internet applications on that computer at Acadia University. Think of an IP address as being the Internet equivalent to a telephone number, since it refers to the address of a specific computer on the Internet.

However, you do not normally need to use IP addresses, since you can use domain names instead. Since people often remember names better than numbers, the people involved in the Internet came up with the Domain Name System. This permits each computer (referred to as a "host") on the Internet to be reached by a simple name rather than just by IP addresses. It is like using 1-800-GO-FEDEX instead of using 1-800-463-3339.

Internet applications such as the World Wide Web or FTP can be used with either an IP address or Domain Name System to reach a particular computer. Only in rare cases, however, is an IP address used instead of a domain name. In fact, you should always use the domain name to avoid any problems that might occur in case a particular Internet resource is moved from one computer to another, which results in a change to an IP address but not a domain name.

An example of a name under the domain name system is **royalbank.com**, and to reach the World Wide Web site for the Royal Bank you would use **www.royalbank.com**.

Let's put this into perspective. To reach the Royal Bank on the Web, you could use the address **http://204.191.126.3**, or you could use the address **http://www.royalbank.com**. Try it! It is no wonder that people prefer to use the domain name system over IP addresses. The IP address and Domain Name System form the heart of the global Internet.

IP Addresses

The current IP numbering scheme allows for what are known as Class A, B, and C addresses. There is an upper limit on the number of potential A, B, and C addresses. Class A addresses (of which there are only 128) are allocated only to the largest organizations or networks in the world and are virtually impossible to get. Class B addresses are used by most large networks or organizations around the world, but new ones are not available to Canadian organizations due to a shortage of remaining available Class B addresses. Class C addresses are used by smaller or medium-sized organizations or networks and are the only addresses available to Canadian organizations that have not already obtained a TCP/IP address. In many cases, multiple Class C addresses are used by one organization.

How Do I Know If I Need an IP Address?

The decision whether you need your own IP address depends on how you plan to access the Internet:

◆ If you plan on linking the computer networks in your organization "directly" to the Internet at some time, you will need an IP address. An IP address is fundamental to establishing this direct link, since it provides a unique identity for your network in the global Internet.

◆ If you plan on accessing the Internet through what is known as a SLIP/PPP account, you will need an IP address. However, this will usually be assigned to you automatically by your Internet service provider, and the software you use to access the Internet determines the TCP/IP address on your behalf. You do not need to obtain one on your own from the CA*Net IP Registry.

◆ If you access the Internet in any other way (i.e., through a bulletin board, through what is known as a "shell account," or through an "e-mail gateway"), you do not need an IP address. In this case, IP addresses will not be terribly important to you other than as a means of reaching certain Internet resources.

How Do I Get an IP Address If I Need One?

Organizations in Canada desiring an IP address must obtain it from the CA*Net IP Registry (detailed below), which has been allocated a set of numbers by the InterNIC for use within Canada. At this time, only Class C addresses are available for use in Canada. Appendix K contains the form "Canadian Internet Protocol Network Number Application for Class C Network Number(s)," which should be used by Canadian organizations wishing to obtain an IP address.

> Obtaining this application form by FTP:
>
> URL: **ftp://ftp.canet.ca/canet-templates/ip-req.txt**
>
> Obtaining this application form by e-mail:
>
> Send message to: **ipregist@canet.ca**
>
> Request information on obtaining the application form.

Keep in mind that since there is a limited number of available IP addresses as mentioned above, and although solutions are in the works, the best advice is to plan ahead.

Indeed, at one time you could contact the Canadian IP Registrar and obtain sufficient Class C addresses for your organization in advance. Now, you must establish that you have a real need for such addresses. As noted by the Registrar, "on requests for the assignment of multiple Class C IP numbers, the InterNIC now requires the Canadian IP Registrar to verify need."

You must verify your need by providing information on the number of sites you intend to link to the Internet, the "minimum, average and maximum number of networks per site," and the "minimum, average and maximum number of hosts per network." Details on the information required by the CA*Net IP Registry are in the document mentioned above.

INTERNET DOMAIN NAMES

Figures 5.1 and 5.2 give some examples of the registered names for several Canadian organizations. As we can see in Figure 5.1, several Canadian organizations have registered in what is known as the Canadian domain and have **.ca** at the end of their domain name. In Figure 5.2 we can see that a number of other Canadian organizations have domains ending in **.com**, **.org**, **.net**, **.edu**, and **.gov**.

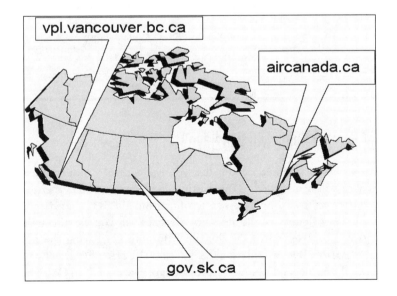

FIGURE 5.1

Organizations in the "Canadian .Ca Domain"

FIGURE 5.2

Organizations in the Top Level "Zone Names"

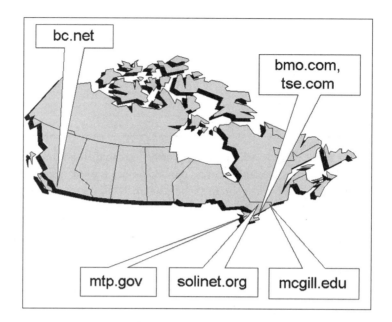

These organizations are listed in the table below:

DOMAIN NAME	ORGANIZATION
aircanada.ca	Air Canada
gov.sk.ca	Government of Saskatchewan
vpl.vancouver.bc.ca	Vancouver Public Library
bmo.com	Bank of Montreal
mtp.gov	Metropolitan Toronto Police
solinet.org	Canadian Union of Public Employees
mcgill.edu	McGill University, Montreal
tse.com	Toronto Stock Exchange

What Type of Domain Name Will You Have?

If you purchase a dial-up Internet account that you will access by modem for your own use, often your account will be assigned to the existing domain of your Internet service provider. For example, if you get a dial-up Internet account from the B.C.-based provider Internet Direct, you will be assigned to the domain **direct.ca**. If you obtain an account from InfoRamp, you will be assigned to the domain **inforamp.net**. Using the examples above, your Internet e-mail ID would look like **YOUR-NAME@direct.ca** or **YOUR-NAME@inforamp.net**, depending on the provider you were using. **YOUR-NAME** will, of course, be replaced by your personal account name.

Your Own Domain Name

If you plan on linking your organization to the Internet, you can obtain an Internet domain name for your organization, usually for a small fee. This involves registering in either the Canadian domain or in one of the "descriptive zone names." You register for such a domain name through your Internet service provider.

You might want to have your own Internet domain name, primarily as a means of establishing to your customers, trading partners, business associates, or others that you are serious about the role you plan to have the Internet play in your organization. In general, your own domain name helps to reinforce your corporate identity. It is easier for those doing business with you to remember how to reach you if you have your own domain name than if you simply exist under the domain name of an ISP. It also helps to protect your intellectual property.

Another good reason to have a domain name is that it is portable. For example, if you are **jsmith@provider.net** and decide to move to another Internet service provider, your e-mail address will change. If you are **jsmith@yourcompany.com**, you can take your domain name with you to your new provider, and hence your e-mail address and Web addresses will not change.

The directory of Internet Providers in *The Canadian Internet Directory*, a companion to this book, provides information on which ISPs offer domain name registration service and what fee applies, if any.

Top Level Domains

As seen in Figures 5.1 and 5.2, at the extreme right of every Internet domain name is a top level domain, which is either: a country code or a descriptive zone name. Country codes are two-character codes, as defined by the International Standards Organization. The country code for Canada is **.ca**. A list of country codes is included in Appendix I. Descriptive zone names include the categories shown in the table below:

ZONE NAMES	CATEGORIES
.com	Commercial, for-profit organizations.
.edu	Educational institutions or sites. New registrations are limited to colleges and universities with 4-year programs.
.gov	Government institutions or sites. New registrations are limited to U.S. Federal Government departments.
.int	International organizations (e.g., NATO), established by international treaty or law.
.mil	U.S. military sites.
.net	Network organizations; most often used by organizations reselling Internet services.
.org	Other organizations, primarily not-for-profit.

Choosing Where to Register

The choice of whether your organization should register in the Canadian (**.ca**) domain or within one of the descriptive zone names as outlined above depends on several factors, mostly having to do with the image your organization wishes to create with respect to its Internet domain name. If you wish to create an international image and do not necessarily wish to create an image of being a strictly Canadian organization, you would choose to register in one of the descriptive zone names. If, on the other hand, you mostly do business in Canada, you might choose to register in the Canadian domain. A few examples will help illustrate this:

- ◆ Delrina Corporation is a Toronto-based software company known internationally for its award-winning products, including WinFax Pro. Because of the fact that it has an international image as opposed to a strictly Canadian image, it chose to register as **delrina.com**.

- ◆ Air Canada does business around the world, but it wants to create an image that it is closely linked to its home base, Canada. As a result, it registered in the Canadian domain as **aircanada.ca**.

It is not just an issue of national or international image when it comes to registration. Looking at Figure 5.2, we can see that some organizations have registered outside of the **.ca** domain, when we might think they should have registered in the Canadian domain (e.g., McGill University, in the **.edu** domain).

Several Canadian organizations have chosen to register in the descriptive zone names for several reasons:

- ◆ Historical reasons. For example, several educational institutions registered in the **.edu** domain prior to the establishment of a Canadian (**.ca**) domain and have kept that domain name.

- ◆ It indicates the organization type. Some choose to register in the **.org** or **.gov** descriptive zone names instead of the Canadian domain name, because they believe it helps them indicate to the Internet community the type of organization they are. A commonly used zone name, **.net**, is used by many Internet service providers in Canada (e.g., **hookup.net**, **inforamp.net**).

- ◆ They cannot register the name they wanted in the **.ca** domain. Some organizations choose to register in the descriptive zones because their proposed name was not accepted by the Canadian authorities. For example, the Addiction Research Foundation registered as **arf.org**, because the Canadian Domain Committee did not believe **arf.ca** to be an acceptable name.

- ◆ Frustration with the current Canadian domain name system. In particular, smaller organizations that are required to use provincial and municipal subdomains as described below often do not like the complex names that might arise, for example, **company.prince-rupert.bc.ca** versus **company.com**. As a result, some organizations turn to the InterNIC to register directly within a **.com** or **.org** domain.

When it comes to registration of a domain name on the Internet, diversity is certainly the watchword.

Registering Under the Canadian (.ca) Domain

Your organization is permitted only one registration under the **.ca** domain.[7] If your organization registers in the Canadian domain, your domain name might include provincial and municipal subdomains, depending on the size and scope of your organization.

A company or organization name is also included. If the legal name of your organization includes both an English form and a French form, you may apply for a domain name for each form. As noted by the CA Domain Registrar, "this change is intended to benefit those organizations which do business in both languages, but whose French and English names are different." For example, Consumers Distributing, the national chain of retail stores, has registered both **consumers.ca** and **dac.ca** (which stands for Distribution Aux Consommateurs Inc.). Similarly, the National Film Board of Canada has registered **nsb.ca** and **onf.ca** (the latter standing for Office National du Film du Canada).

Figure 5.1 shows examples of some organizations that have registered in the Canadian (or **.ca**) domain. The names used by two of the organizations use subdomains. In Canada, under the **.ca** domain, a geographically oriented subdomain hierarchy is used. This means the domain name that you can obtain will be determined by the scope or presence of your organization within Canada. Subdomains, when used, include

- a provincial code, for example, **.sk** for Saskatchewan in the example in Figure 5.1;

- a city or municipality name, for example, **.vancouver** in the example in Figure 5.1.

The Canadian Domain Registrar provides the following rules for guidance in determining what type of subdomain name an organization can obtain in Canada:

- If the organization is national in scope, that is, has presence in more than one province or is incorporated or chartered nationally, the name of the company is used with the **.ca** domain name. For example, Air Canada has the domain name **aircanada.ca**.

- If the organization owns a trademark that is registered with the Canadian Registrar of Trademarks and is being put forward in full as the organizational part of the subdomain name, the name of the trademark within the domain name. For example, Teledirect Publications has registered **yellowpages.ca**.

- If the organization is based in only one province, but has multiple locations in the province, or is incorporated or registered provincially or territorially, the two-letter provincial or territorial abbreviation in the domain name is included (i.e., provincial or territorial governments, colleges, or universities). For example, the Government of Saskatchewan domain name is **gov.sk.ca**.

- If the organization is small and based in only one jurisdiction, the municipality name is included in the subdomain name. (Examples include local hospitals, libraries, municipal governments, small or local businesses, and schools.) For example, the Vancouver Public Library domain name is **vpl.vancouver.bc.ca**.

---

7. This is effective in 1995.

The codes in the table below are used within Canadian subdomains for provinces and territories in Canada.

CODE	FOR ORGANIZATIONS REGISTERED IN
.ab	Alberta
.bc	British Columbia
.gc	Government of Canada
.mb	Manitoba
.nb	New Brunswick
.nf	Newfoundland
.ns	Nova Scotia
.nt	Northwest Territories
.nu	Nunavut (possible)
.on	Ontario
.pe	Prince Edward Island
.qc	Quebec
.sk	Saskatchewan
.yk	Yukon

Two changes occurred in the table above in 1995. Once Nunavut is created as a new territory from the Northwest Territories, it may be allocated the code **.nu**. In addition, there is now a new government domain, **gc.ca**, and there is now a Canadian Government Domain Registrar that handles all requests for Internet domains from Canadian government departments and agencies. [8]

Registration under the Canadian (**.ca**) domain is coordinated by the CA Domain Registrar, currently John Demco at the Department of Computer Science at the University of British Columbia, except for registration requests from within the Government of Canada (**.gc**) domain, which is currently coordinated by Joyce LeBlanc in the Government Telecommunications and Informatics Service in Ottawa.

Appendix F includes the document "Internet Forms," which provides full details for registering with the Canadian **.ca** domain and the **gc.ca** domain. You can obtain this document by using FTP or e-mail.

---

8. The reason **gc.ca** was chosen is because **gov.ca** does not translate well into French. "Government" in French is "gouvernement." Thus **gc.ca** was chosen because it can stand for Government of Canada and gouvernement du Canada.

Obtaining the CA domain application form:

Using anonymous FTP:

URL: **ftp://ftp.cdnnet.ca/ca-domain/application-form**

Using e-mail:

Send message to:

archive-server@relay.cdnnet.ca

In text of message, type:

send ca-domain application-form

Obtaining the **gc.ca** application form:

URL: **http://www.gc.ca**

Most Internet service providers in Canada offer domain name registration services and will fill out and submit the form for you for a nominal fee. Filling out the form on your own can be difficult, particularly if you are not familiar with the nuances of the Internet. Even if you retrieve either of these forms and fill it out yourself, you should not send a registration application directly to the CA Domain Registrar or the Government of Canada Domain Registrar. Instead, you should submit the form to your Internet service provider.

Once an application is submitted to either the CA Domain Registrar or the **gc.ca** Domain Registrar, the application is reviewed and scrutinized by a domain name committee to ensure its compliance with the domain name policies and procedures. Both the CA Domain Registrar and the **gc.ca** Domain Registrar maintain a committee for this purpose. The CA Domain Committee consists of representatives from several of the large Canadian Internet access providers. You can obtain a current list of CA Domain Committee members at the following site:

Using FTP:

URL: **ftp://ftp.cdnnet.ca/ca-domain/committee-members**

Keep in mind that you should seek guidance from your Internet service provider about the name you plan on choosing, since they will be best able to let you know whether the name you have selected will be acceptable to the committee. If you want to see examples of current domain names that have been registered, see Appendix C.

Registrations Under a Descriptive Zone Name

You follow a different process if you choose to register within one of the descriptive domain names (e.g., **.com**, **.edu**). In this case, you register directly with InterNIC Registration Services, a component of the Internet Network Information Center in the United States. You would usually do this through your Internet service provider. Much more flexibility in your domain name is possible, since it can consist of a domain name of up to 24 characters, followed by the 3-character descriptive zone name, for example, **.com**, **.edu**. If you would like to understand how to register directly in one of these descriptive zone names, you can obtain the document **domain-template.txt**, by using FTP or Gopher.

Using Gopher:

URL: **gopher://rs.internic.net**

Using FTP:

URL: **ftp://rs.internic.net/templates/domain-template.txt**

Completion of these forms requires some technical knowledge about the Internet. We recommend once again that you get your Internet service provider to complete and submit the forms on your behalf.

Trademarks and Domain Names

For some time it was possible for anyone registering with the InterNIC to obtain a domain name that may infringe upon the trademark of another organization. This was not so in Canada, where, as mentioned previously, a Canadian Domain Name Committee exists with the responsibility of scrutinizing domain name applications. For example, where it might have been easy to obtain **bmw.com** through the InterNIC, it would have been extremely difficult to obtain **bmw.ca**, if you were not the proper owner of the BMW trademark in Canada.

The InterNIC's loose policies on this matter first gained the attention of corporate management throughout Canada with the publication of an article in the *Globe and Mail*:

Guess who owns the right to use the name McDonald's on the Internet. If you said a major international hamburger chain, you guessed wrong. As of two weeks ago, it was an enterprising New York reporter, who registered the name just to show he could do it. A number of major North American companies are about to find out just how important — and valuable — it is to have a highly visible address on the "information highway." The rights to use business and product names as registered addresses on the Internet are being staked out in an electronic equivalent of the Yukon gold rush."[a]

---

a. Playing the Name Game on the Internet, *Globe and Mail*, October 25, 1994.

But the issue really came out into the open earlier in 1994, when an enterprising young writer for *Wired* magazine, on finding that McDonalds had not yet bothered to register on the Internet, obtained the domain name **mcdonalds.com**. The InterNIC, at the time, did not have a policy with respect to registration of a corporate name or trademark by someone other than the respective organization or holder of the trademark, so this fellow was able to obtain **mcdonalds.com**, much to the chagrin of the hamburger chain. (He has since worked out a deal that reverted the name back to McDonalds, after the organization donated a sum of money to a school in Brooklyn.)

The InterNIC took the viewpoint that due to limited resources, they could not take the time to ensure that every potential registrant was the proper owner of a corporate or trademark name. Thus, they basically registered each and every name that came their way. But, legal pressure began to build. From mid-1994 to mid-1995, many individuals and organizations rushed to obtain as many domain names as possible, reserving trademark names, corporate names, and even the names of competitors. Lawyers started to get involved, as difficult trademark and copyright issues began to emerge around the globe. Clearly, something had to give.

Finally, in 1995, the InterNIC introduced rules that, in effect, prohibit someone from obtaining a domain registration for a corporate name to which they do not have rights, or to register as a domain name a phrase, word or brand name for which they are not the proper registered trademark owner. The press release from Network Solutions Inc., the organization that is the part of the InterNIC responsible for domain registrations, issued the following press release:

NETWORK SOLUTIONS ANNOUNCES INTERNET DOMAIN NAME POLICY

(HERNDON, VA) July 28, 1995 -- A new policy that deals with disputed Internet domain names until ownership issues are resolved by the courts was announced today by Network Solutions, Inc., a subsidiary of Science Applications International Corp. (SAIC).

The new policy recognizes that an Internet domain name may conflict with an existing trademark or service mark, but that the trademark or service mark holder may not have the exclusive right to use that name on the Internet.

NSI serves as the InterNIC domain name registrar under a cooperative agreement sponsored by the National Science Foundation.

Domain names are assigned to organizations that want to be accessible on the Internet. The Internet's growing popularity has led to an explosion of requests for domain names, with NSI currently processing more than 600 per day.

Domain names will continue to be assigned on a first-come, first-serve basis, with NSI checking to ensure that a requested domain name has not already been given to another user. Like a telephone book publisher, NSI presumes that an applicant for a domain name has the legal right to use that name. Applicants now will be asked to confirm this on their registration forms.

NSI has found that Internet users occasionally select domain names which may be identical to the registered trademarks or service marks of other organizations. While NSI cannot resolve such legal disputes, the company is concerned that domain names not cause confusion or interfere with the legal rights of third parties. Although ownership of a trademark or service mark does not automatically include rights to domain name ownership, the new policy recognizes trademarks as quantifiable evidence relevant to domain name disputes.

If the holder of a trademark provides evidence to NSI that a domain name already assigned to an Internet user is identical to that trademark, NSI will ask the Internet user to submit proof that the user also has a trademark for that name (for example, the trademark Acme may have been issued to many different entities for different types of products or services). If the Internet user cannot provide such proof of trademark, the holder of the domain name will be allowed a reasonable period of time to transition to a different domain name.

Then the disputed name will be placed in a hold status and not used by anyone until a proper court resolves the dispute. This policy is intended to be neutral as to the respective rights of the registrant and trademark holder to the disputed domain name.

If the user does provide proof of its trademark, that user can continue to use the name as long as the user agrees to protect NSI from the costs of defending lawsuits brought against NSI by the other trademark holder. Otherwise, the domain name will again go on hold.

NSI will also apply these procedures in dealing with foreign trademark holders who have their trademarks certified by the U.S. Patent and Trademark Office.

"We want to emphasize that Internet users don't need to have a trademark to get a domain name", said NSI attorney Grant Clark. "The problem is that NSI doesn't have the authority or expertise to adjudicate trademark disputes. Some have even suggested that NSI should pre-screen domain names to check for possible infringement. That would turn us into a mini-trademark office with costs going through the roof and processing times in months rather than days."

Clark said NSI will evaluate its policy on an ongoing basis, and will remain sensitive to the opinions of the hundreds of thousands of diverse Internet users.

Note:

The complete agreement for receiving a domain is available in URL: **ftp://rs.internic.net/policy/internic/internic-domain-1.txt**

The InterNIC Domain Registration form now contains this note:

The party requesting registration of this name certifies that, to her/his knowledge, the use of this name does not violate trademark or other statutes.

Registering a domain name does not confer any legal rights to that name and any disputes between parties over the rights to use a particular name are to be settled between the contending parties using normal legal methods.

In Canada registrations in the **.ca** domain never really were a problem, since the CA Domain Commitee scrutinized each application so carefully. However, in 1995 the Committee did make one change: the registration form was changed to permit companies to register trademarks as a domain name within the **.ca** domain. Important changes are highlighted in the text below:

Here are requirements and guidelines to help determine the appropriate level of subdomain name for your organization:

(1) second (national) level — To qualify for a second level domain, your organization must have offices or other points of presence (such as computer hosts or dial-up facilities wholly owned by your organization) in more than one province or territory, or be incorporated or chartered nationally, *or own a trademark which is registered with the Canadian Registrar of Trade-marks and which is being put forward in full as the organizational part of the subdomain name.*

Organization:

The full name of your organization. For a for-profit corporation, the full name includes its legal element, e.g. Limited, Limitee, Incorporated, Incorporee, Corporation, or Societe par actions de regime federal, or an abbreviation such as Ltd, Ltee, Inc, Corp, or S.A.R.F. For a non-profit organization, depending on where it is incorporated, the name may be required to include one of the legal elements specified above, or a word such as Society, Association, or Club.

If a trademark is being proposed as the organizational part of the subdomain name, please include both the trademark and the full organization name in the Organization field as shown in this example for the subdomain coke.ca:

Organization: Coke (TM), Coca Cola Ltd.

You may register just one CA subdomain name, so please be very careful when proposing to use a trademark which does not cover all of your organization's activities.

Overall, it is your responsibility to ensure that you have the right to use the name you have chosen. Registering a domain name does not confer any legal rights to that name; you should consider registering a trademark if you have not already done so. Any disputes between parties over the rights to use a particular name are to be settled between the contending parties using normal legal methods.

Hence, at this point, you are only able to register as domain names those names to which you have a legal right. What is not clear are your remedies should your corporate name have already been registered by some other organization.

Other Issues Related to Domain Names

There are two other issues related to the Domain Name System:

◆ There are many organizations not yet directly on the Internet; that is, they do not have a computer that directly connects to the Internet, and hence cannot be directly reached via the Internet. However, these organizations might desire to link their internal e-mail system into the Internet using their own domain name. In order to do this, they must have a name registered on the Internet.

To get around this dilemma, the concept of an MX (mail exchange) record was introduced; this allows an organization to obtain and use a name for purposes of e-mail. Accordingly, as we examine the domain name scheme, keep in mind that any organization, even if it is not directly linked to the Internet, can have an Internet domain name.

◆ There is nothing to prevent an organization from registering within multiple domains. For example, the University of Toronto has the subdomain names **utoronto.ca** and **toronto.edu**. The media company Southam has registered **southam.ca** and **southam.com**.

The continued rapid growth of the Internet means that many domain names are being claimed very quickly. As a general rule, you should plan on reserving a name for your organization as quickly as possible, even if you do not have plans to link your organization to the Internet in the near future. This will prevent some other organization with a similar name from reserving the name you might want.

You might even consider reserving the name with both the Canadian Domain Registrar and with the InterNIC so that both options are available to you in the future. For example, if your company name is BIGTOOLS, and you are national in scope, you might consider registering both as **bigtools.com** and **bigtools.ca**, for two reasons. First, potential customers might try to find you on the Internet by using your company name within the **.com** and **.ca** extensions. Second, obtaining both will help prevent a circumstance in which some organization with the same corporate name registers and gets the name before you do.

You can register your domain name, in advance of getting on the Internet. It is advisable to do so, to obtain your desired domain name before someone else does. Appendix C, the "Canadian Organizations with Registered Internet Domains," contains a complete listing of the domain names used by Canadian organizations.

Chapter 7, which is about electronic mail, describes different methods to find domain names registered on the Internet. You can use these procedures to determine if your desired domain name has already been taken.

The Next Step

We opened this book by commenting that "the Internet is, in some ways, nothing less than a trend that is making all of these little computer chips aware of each other and providing them the ability to link together." So far, the Internet has succeeded at linking together some computers around the world. However, it is still in its infancy; it has a long way to go before most computers around the world are linked. Some people believe that one day this will be the case.

Connectivity to the Internet need not be restricted to computers that have a keyboard and a screen. Some believe that one day your home burglar alarm system, house monitoring system, office lighting system, and indeed your toaster oven will be wired into the Internet.

Some also believe that it will be possible to query the microprocessor in your automobile via the Internet to download data about your trip yesterday. Or use the Internet to see if you turned the lights off in the house in the morning. Or other day-to-day routines.

Quite simply, these people believe that the Internet is rapidly becoming the protocol and network that will link all devices of computing intelligence. Will it happen? Maybe yes, maybe no. The key thing is that there is no similar commonly accepted protocol like TCP/IP and the Internet.

One challenge, however, is that TCP/IP has an upper limit in terms of the number of computers that it can reach. Simply, we run the risk of running out of Class A, B, and C TCP/IP addresses. Some estimates have said that we will hit this limit globally as early as 1997, while others predict that it might still be some time off.

There is a solution in the works. The various groups and standards bodies involved in Internet protocols have designed IPng, which stands for *IP* addresses, *next generation*. The standard provides for many billions more possible computer chips, addressing the future potential of the Internet as one giant network of all computing intelligence on the planet.

What's Next

In the next chapter, we will take a look at what it takes to actually get "connected" to the Internet along with a few sample applications. In subsequent chapters we will take a look at these individual Internet applications to describe them in more depth.

But hopefully, by now, you feel a little bit better in knowing a little more about how the Internet works.

CHAPTER 6

Direct Versus Indirect Internet Connections

It just may be a computer maker's dream come true—the Internet. Suddenly, computer-industry executives have grasped that the Net is a lot more than just the world's biggest E-mail system or a place where computer jocks can get their jollies. The Net, they've come to realize, could very well be the IBM Personal Computer all over again—a powerful, low-cost, open, standards-based technology "platform" upon which to build all sorts of new products, strategies, companies, markets, and even a few fortunes. Like the PC, this global network stands to reshape the business model of the entire industry. "This is a rocket that has been launched," says Eric E. Schmidt, chief technology officer at workstation maker Sun MicroSystems Inc. "There's no one who can stop it. The future of computing is defined by the Net."

Planet Internet: How the Center of the Computing Universe has Shifted
Business Week, April 3, 1995

What does this *Business Week* quote really say? In essence, the arrival of the Internet has resulted in a technology for which all kinds of new software, applications, and programs can be made available. In this chapter we will take a look at why it is better to have a direct Internet connection than an indirect one, an issue that is directly related to the *Business Week* quote. In the chapters that follow we will take a look at several major Internet applications:

◆ Chapter 7: "Internet Electronic Mail" (e-mail);

◆ Chapter 8: "Knowledge Networking," using applications such as USENET and Internet mailing lists;

◆ Chapter 9: "The World Wide Web," perhaps the most exciting application to be found on the Internet;

◆ Chapter 10: "You Ain't Seen Nothing Yet," a review of future applications on the Internet;

◆ Chapter 11: "Older Internet Applications," which takes a look at applications such as Telnet and FTP.

In Chapter 12 we take a look at, "Connecting to the Internet." In that chapter we go into more depth about the concepts we introduce in this chapter. And in Chapter 13, "Internet Software," we take a look at some of the software you can use to actually get onto the Internet.

But before we start our journey of describing to you various Internet applications, it is important for you to have a basic understanding how you might interact with the Internet. You might access the Internet through what is known as a "shell account" or through a "direct connection" using a SLIP, PPP, or dedicated TCP/IP connection.

This might sound like technical mumbo jumbo, and indeed it is if you are new to the whole world of the Internet. That is why in this chapter we will put these two types of access methods into perspective. To do so, we first explain the concept of "client/server" computing. Then we explain how each of these access methods uses client/server computing just a little differently, but with a dramatic impact on the way that you might use the Internet.

Client/Server Computing and the Internet

If you read computer magazines or work in the industry, you will be inundated with articles that mention client/server computing. It sounds like one of those scary, technical terms, but it really is quite straightforward. And understanding the concept of client/server computing will help you to understand what is involved in using and accessing the Internet.

A Technical Definition of Client/Server Computing

In the client/server computing model, a "client" computer runs a program that acts on behalf of a user to access data located on a "server" computer. It is really that straightforward.

DIRECT VERSUS INDIRECT INTERNET CONNECTIONS

1 You can connect to the Internet through an indirect connection (or "shell" account) or through a TCP/IP connection.

2 A TCP/IP connection can be made through a SLIP/PPP account or by establishing a full-time link to the Internet from a corporate network.

3 The client/server model of computing is the concept that is at the heart of the Internet.

4 In most cases a relatively powerful computer is required for SLIP/PPP accounts; however, the Internet is easiest to use through such an account.

5 Virtually any type of computer can be used to access a shell account, since you do not need a lot of computer "horsepower"; however, the Internet is more difficult to use through such an account.

FIGURE 6.1

Client/Server Model

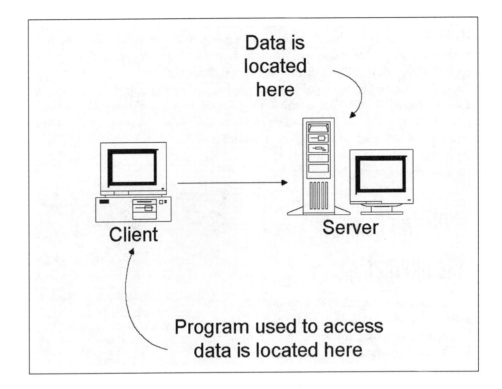

The client computer contains the program that formulates a query or runs a program, while the server contains the horsepower and capability of accessing the data it stores. A good example of a client/server system is the World Wide Web on the Internet. When using the Web, you run "client" software (such as Netscape or Mosaic) to access all kinds of Web "servers" scattered throughout the Internet all over the globe.

The benefit of the client/server model is that a client can be used to access any number of server applications. On the Internet, this means that your World Wide Web "client" software can access all kinds of Internet Web "servers" around the world. You do not need a separate program to access data in different computers around the world — you only need one.

Likewise, a single World Wide Web server can service a number of clients, regardless of what type of computer they might be coming from. Hence a Web server can cater to Netscape clients, Mosaic clients, HotJava clients — any type of Web browser. This tremendous flexibility is the reason the client/server model of computing is at the heart of the Internet:

◆ Each participant in the Internet is a client.

◆ Each resource on the Internet is located on a server somewhere in the world.

An important point is that when you are on the Internet, you are somehow using client/server computing. But a key fact is that when you use various Internet applications, the location of the client that you use will often have a direct effect on:

◆ how an Internet application is used;

◆ how easy it is to use;

◆   what the application looks like as you use it;

◆   the speed with which the application runs.

The location of the client that you use will for the most part be in one of two places:

◆   on your own computer, in the case of a direct connection to the Internet, in the form of a SLIP connection, PPP connection, or a dedicated TCP/IP connection; or

◆   on a computer located at your Internet service provider, when you have an indirect connection to the Internet, in which case you are using what is known as a shell account.

Although it is not a hard-and-fast rule, it can be said that those who are considered to be directly connected to the Internet can use a far greater number of sophisticated Internet clients and hence will enjoy much easier use of the Internet than those who are not directly connected to the Internet.

Methods of Accessing the Internet

In reality, there are more than just direct and indirect types of connections to the Internet. In Chapter 12 we take an in-depth look at the ways you can link yourself or your organization to the Internet. This will include examination of five basic methods of establishing Internet connectivity, as seen in the following diagram:

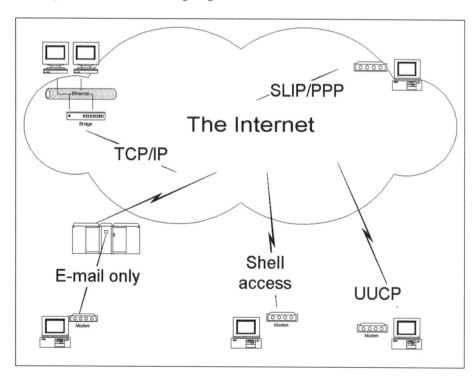

FIGURE 6.2

Methods of Linking to the Internet

◆   Those who only send and receive e-mail to and from the Internet are not "directly connected" to the Internet and can do little else besides sending and receiving e-mail.

◆ Users of UUCP are not "directly connected" to the Internet and can do no more than Internet e-mail and participate in USENET newsgroups.

◆ Individuals with a shell account are not "directly connected" to the Internet. If you have such a connection, the "client" software that you will use is usually located on your Internet service provider, resulting in limitations in the sophistication of the programs that you can use. If your Internet service provider does not provide a client for a particular Internet application, you can use the Internet capability known as Telnet to link to a site that does have a client you can use, again limiting the sophistication and ease of use in what you can do.

◆ Individuals on networks that have a "hardwired" (i.e., permanent) TCP/IP network connection to the Internet are considered to be "directly" on the Internet. In addition, individuals or networks with SLIP or PPP access through a dial-up modem are also considered to be "directly" on the Internet.

  Individuals with such direct connectivity can use many of the more sophisticated and useful versions of client software when interacting with the Internet and hence will enjoy greater ease of use with the network. In particular, it is only these individuals who can use Netscape and Mosaic to browse the World Wide Web, which is the client application certainly gaining the most attention on the Internet.

  If you have such a connection, you are running the "client" software directly on your own computer. This has a dramatic impact on the ease of use of the Internet.

In most cases, if you are an individual and you want to access the Internet with a modem:

◆ You should always choose to purchase an Internet account that is a direct connection instead of an indirect connection. If you use a modem and want to access the Internet, this means that your preference is to have a SLIP or a PPP account, instead of a shell account.

◆ You should only use a shell account to access the Internet if you cannot purchase a SLIP/PPP account in your area, or if one is not available to you. (Many university students are provided with shell accounts to access the Internet, due to hardware or resource/funding limitations, for example.)

◆ If you have a technical bent and would prefer to receive your Internet e-mail and USENET news on a "batch-oriented basis," then you might choose a UUCP account. If you do not know what "batch-oriented" means, then a UUCP account is definitely not for you.

Let's take a more in-depth look at why a SLIP/PPP account is preferable. (SLIP and PPP accounts are somewhat similar in the way they operate, and so in this book we use the term SLIP/PPP.)

Shell Accounts Versus SLIP/PPP Accounts

Because the "communications software" used to dial into a shell account does not involve using TCP/IP, a shell account user will often find that the Internet is difficult to deal with and to learn. Although most major Internet applications, including Gopher, FTP, and Archie, can be used from a shell account, they are accessed using a client located at the Internet service provider or elsewhere on the Internet. Since the client is not on the PC of the user, it is less sophisticated and more difficult to use.

On the other hand, individuals with dial-up SLIP or PPP access to the Internet or those who have a direct network link can run most clients directly on their own PC, since they are using TCP/IP. This means that they can use many of the easy-to-use Windows and Macintosh-based Internet applications, including Netscape and Mosaic, making their use of the Internet much more straightforward. The result of this is that when it comes to dial-up access to the Internet, SLIP accounts are in great demand, with a lessening of demand for shell account access.

Keep in mind that as a general rule you need a relatively powerful computer (in the DOS/Windows world, an 80386 or better) to access a SLIP/PPP account, while any computer can be used to access a shell account. Hence shell account access is still very important and very worthwhile and is certainly used by people who do not have sophisticated computing horsepower.

Let's look at this by comparing the Internet through a PPP account and through a shell account.

A Sample Internet Session: PPP

When you use a PPP account (or a SLIP account), the first thing you need to do is dial into your Internet service provider (ISP). You usually do this by running a program, such as Trumpet Winsock or Quarterdeck Winsock for Windows, or MacPPP for a Macintosh, which has the capability of dialing the ISP. Once it connects to the ISP, it provides a user ID and password and perhaps some other information. We call this "logging on." Once it has logged on, it obtains a TCP/IP address from the ISP. You are now "directly" connected to the Internet.

Your SLIP/PPP program must be configured to work with the particular ISP that you use. It must be provided details, for example, about the phone number to dial at the ISP, your user ID and password, as well as the TCP/IP address of the domain name server it is expected to use. Quite often, additional information will be required.

Your ISP will either preconfigure the software for you or will provide instructions to you on how to configure it yourself. And as we will see in Chapter 13, newly emerging software onto the Internet marketplace is making the process of configuring such software to work with a particular ISP easier and more straightforward.

Within the Windows environment, the software used to establish a SLIP/PPP account is referred to as Winsock. In Chapter 5, while explaining how the Internet "works," we showed a screen from the program Trumpet Winsock; this was the program that we were using to dial into establish a PPP connection with the Internet service provider InfoRamp.

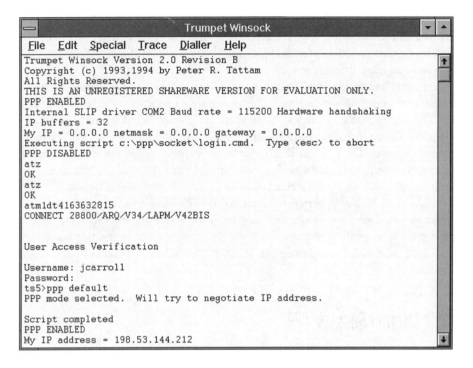

```
                        Trumpet Winsock                    ▼ ▲
  File  Edit  Special  Trace  Dialler  Help
Trumpet Winsock Version 2.0 Revision B                        ↑
Copyright (c) 1993,1994 by Peter R. Tattam
All Rights Reserved.
THIS IS AN UNREGISTERED SHAREWARE VERSION FOR EVALUATION ONLY.
PPP ENABLED
Internal SLIP driver COM2 Baud rate = 115200 Hardware handshaking
IP buffers = 32
My IP = 0.0.0.0 netmask = 0.0.0.0 gateway = 0.0.0.0
Executing script c:\ppp\socket\login.cmd.  Type <esc> to abort
PPP DISABLED
atz
OK
atz
OK
atm1dt4163632815
CONNECT 28800/ARQ/V34/LAPM/V42BIS


User Access Verification

Username: jcarroll
Password:
ts5>ppp default
PPP mode selected.  Will try to negotiate IP address.

Script completed
PPP ENABLED
My IP address = 198.53.144.212                               ↓
```

Trumpet Winsock is but one program that can be used within Windows to establish such a connection. There are a number of commercial software programs that have come to the market that allow us to do the same thing. For example, here is the dial-in procedure from the Internet in a Box program:

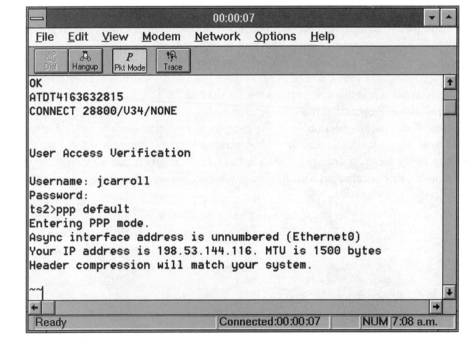

```
                        00:00:07                          ▼ ▲
  File  Edit  View  Modem  Network  Options  Help
  ┌────┐ ┌────┐ ┌────┐ ┌────┐
  │ Dial│ │Hangup│ │ P  │ │Trace│
  └────┘ └────┘ │Pkt Mode│ └────┘
OK                                                            ↑
ATDT4163632815
CONNECT 28800/V34/NONE


User Access Verification

Username: jcarroll
Password:
ts2>ppp default
Entering PPP mode.
Async interface address is unnumbered (Ethernet0)
Your IP address is 198.53.144.116. MTU is 1500 bytes
Header compression will match your system.

~~                                                           ↓
←                                                            →
Ready                  Connected:00:00:07      NUM 7:08 a.m.
```

Here is the same type of thing, except through the Quarterdeck Winsock program, which handles the dial-up for the Quarterdeck Internet Suite product:

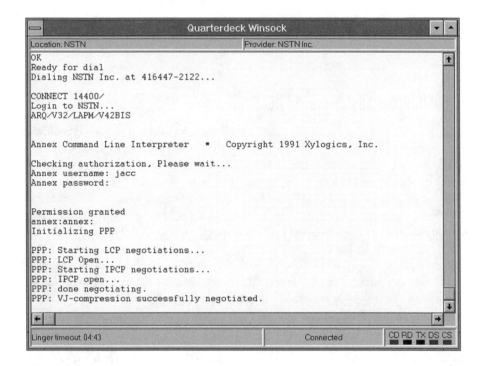

In all these cases, we have dialed into the Internet and have established a PPP connection. This means that we are "directly" on the Internet: the software above has obtained from our ISP a unique TCP/IP address (which could be different each time we dial in).

Now that we have a SLIP/PPP connection to the Internet, we can run any number of Internet clients, such as Netscape to access the World Wide Web, Eudora to read e-mail, or, as we will see in Chapter 10, Internet Phone to make a "phone call." It is this flexibility that demonstrates the real power of the Internet; once we have our TCP/IP connection to the Internet, we can run any type of TCP/IP-compatible Internet client software to access any number of servers out of the Internet. It is the client/server model of computing in its truest form.

In this book, we will detail the many types of software available on the Internet. To get a real idea of the flexibility available to you, visit The Consummate Winsock Apps List at **http://cwsapps.texas.net/cwsa.html**. This site contains an extensive listing of all kinds of Windows programs that you can retrieve or purchase once you have a direct connection to the Internet. Or, if you are a Macintosh user, visit Macs and the Internet at **http://www.iquest.com/mac-ppp.html**, a site that details all kinds of similar software for the Macintosh environment. Keeping track of these two sites is a useful thing to do, since you will discover all kinds of new and innovative Internet applications over time.

Take a look once again at the quote that opened this chapter. The key part of the quote is that the Internet is "a powerful, low-cost, open, standards-based technology 'platform' upon which to build all sorts of new products, strategies, companies, markets, and even a few fortunes." Anyone with a direct Internet connection, regardless of whether it is a SLIP, PPP, or full-time TCP/IP link, and regardless of whether they are on a PC, Macintosh, or

UNIX system, are running a common computer protocol and can plug any type of TCP/IP-compliant software into that protocol.

It is analogous to the electrical system in your house: you can plug in a toaster, a stereo, a TV, an iron, a dishwasher, and perhaps a few things not even yet invented. And with your TCP/IP connection, you can plug in a Web client, a USENET client, an e-mail client, and in the future, a few applications not even yet invented.

A Sample Internet Session: Shell Account

Contrast this with a shell account. To access a shell account, you can use any type of communications software. You dial into your ISP using this software and provide a user ID and a password. You are then left at either a UNIX command prompt, a menu, or a listing of choices of things that you can do.

You are not allocated a TCP/IP number, since you are not running software that uses TCP/IP. You cannot run Netscape, Mosaic, or any other TCP/IP-based applications on your own computer. Instead, you run them off a computer at your ISP. This makes the Internet more difficult to learn and to use.

For example, in the screen below, we have dialed into a shell account at InfoRamp (in fact, using the same user ID and password that we use for our PPP account; most let you dial in as a shell user as well). We are left at a prompt "ts8>." Not terribly friendly, since we have to figure out from here what we can do.

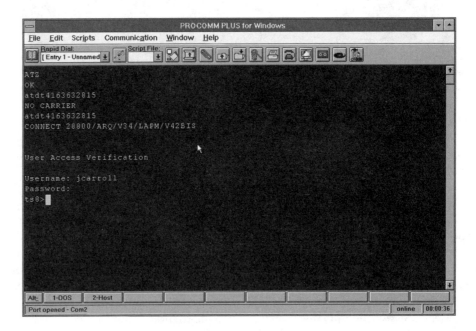

From here, we can begin to use various clients located on the InfoRamp computers. For example, in the screen below we are using Lynx, a program located on the InfoRamp system that lets us access World Wide Web sites. We accessed this by keying "lynx" at the prompt above.

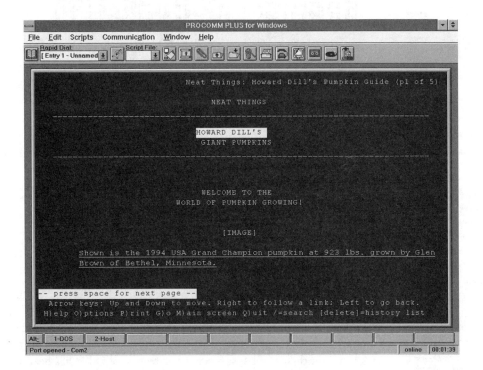

As you can see, it is a text application; it does not involve the graphical interface that we might see through a program used on our PPP account such as Netscape.

The difference between a direct Internet connection and a shell account should be quite obvious at this stage.

Summary

Today, there are many people who still use the Internet through a shell account, and there will be for quite some time to come. That is why it is important for us to strike a careful balance by ensuring that we point out important differences in the way a particular application might operate within a shell account.

In the chapters that follow we will look at various Internet applications. We will first examine them from the perspective of an individual with a direct connection to the Internet, using a SLIP, PPP, or full-time TCP/IP connection. We then offer a few comments about the particular application if it is being accessed through a shell account.

Internet Electronic Mail

I am glad that the Record has an e-mail address and I do not worry that it does not have a World Wide Web home page. The reason? As of now, accessibility and speed are the needs of ordinary users and they are perfectly filled by a simple e-mail address.

E-mail will do
Kitchener–Waterloo Record,
March 31, 1995

Electronic mail will be the next great frontier for software developers, says the founder of one of the world's most successful word processing programs.

E-mail called field of future
The Edmonton Journal, March 24, 1995

In an age of information highways, multimedia, CD -ROMs, and other exciting technologies, electronic mail (e-mail) can seem decidedly dull. Although it might be new to you, there are many people in Canada and around the world who have used e-mail for several years to send messages within their company. Since it is a technology that has been with us for some 15 years or more, many people just cannot get excited about it.

Yet, establish a personal mailbox on the Internet and something magical happens — you discover that you can reach out to the world. Link a corporate e-mail network to the Internet, and an organization discovers that many of its business activities can be made more straightforward through the sheer efficiency of global Internet e-mail. Internet e-mail has established a new method for people and organizations to communicate around the globe. And as more and more people sign up to Internet e-mail, its use and value increase at an ever-spiralling rate.

Why Is Use of Internet E-Mail Exploding?

Many organizations have discovered that a link to Internet e-mail is the most useful application of all Internet capabilities. The reason for this is that e-mail is the only application that extends well beyond the boundaries of the real Internet and involves many other e-mail systems and many different technologies. With a simple Internet e-mail address, it is said that you can reach an estimated 60 million people around the globe.

E-mail has entered the Canadian public consciousness. E-mail addresses appear on TV shows, from the CBC *National News* to the *Dini Petty Show*. They appear in newspapers ranging from the national *Globe and Mail* to local community weeklies. They are appearing in advertisements, on product labels, on business cards, and on stationery. There is even a truck in Toronto that has its e-mail address painted on the side in big 2-foot-high letters: **umb@passport.ca**.

Many people recognize them, and more people are ensuring that they get one. One thing is for sure: the use of Internet e-mail across Canada is growing by leaps and bounds, with an ever-increasing use for all kinds of business, social, personal, and organizational communication. The trend is not slowing down.

It Has Gained Acceptance

In some ways, Internet e-mail has become the fax machine of the 1990s and has become an accepted means of communication between people, business, and government. As more and more people sign onto the Internet, there is a growing expectation that they should be able to expect e-mail communications with business associates and friends. The practical impact of the rapid adoption of Internet e-mail is that those individuals without an Internet e-mail address are feeling a little left out — and feeling compelled to get one. It is a self-feeding kind of growth that shows no signs of slowing down — as more and more people use Internet e-mail, more and more people want to get on.

It Saves Money

Cost savings are a big reason why many are so enthusiastic about Internet e-mail. Using it is dramatically less expensive than courier, fax, and telephone costs. And with more and more people putting Internet addresses on their business cards, and with more and more people joining the Internet at home, there are *tremendous* opportunities for cost savings.

Most Internet connections are based upon either a flat hourly fee or purchase of a certain amount of Internet access for a flat monthly fee. This fee includes the use

INTERNET ELECTRONIC MAIL

1. Many organizations have discovered that a link to Internet e-mail is the one of the most useful applications of all Internet capabilities.

2. Internet e-mail has gained acceptance throughout many organizations as an accepted means of communication, offering cost savings, time savings, and strategic benefits

3. Internet e-mail can be many things and is generally considered to be any e-mail system in the world that can send and receive e-mail to and from the Internet.

4. Internet e-mail addresses have become easily recognizable.

5. You should be cognizant of important e-mail etiquette issues.

6. There are a few methods to locate an e-mail address for someone else, but a "big database" of all e-mail addresses in the world does not exist.

7. There are some potential security problems with Internet e-mail.

of Internet e-mail. This means that the incremental cost to send a message from one location to another is practically nil. The cost to send a message to several hundred people is, in most cases, the same as sending a message to one person.

Consider this example: let's say you had to send a two-page letter to someone in Halifax, Vancouver, and Winnipeg. If you sent a fax to those three cities, it would probably cost at least a couple of dollars. Sending paper mail will cost $1.32 each or more. Sending three courier packages might cost $15 or $20 each.

Sending that same information via the Internet will cost, at most, *a penny*, and in most cases, even less. And since you can send a message to many people all at once, you'll face the same cost whether you send a message to one person or to 200 people. The cost savings are tremendous and are a very good argument for why you want to be on the Internet.

It is Easy to Use

Once people get on to the Internet, they discover that it is not all that difficult to send a message, nor is it difficult to read messages that have been sent to them. E-mail software is becoming more sophisticated all the time, and with the increasing dominance of software like Microsoft Windows, IBM's OS/2, and Macintosh computers, simple "point-and-click" e-mail software is becoming the rule rather than the exception.

Want to create a new message to send to someone? Click on the little envelope. Want to see if there is any new mail? Click on the post office icon. Want to attach a file? Click on the icon of the paper clip. Regardless of what you are doing, e-mail is becoming something that is easier and easier to use with each passing year, thus helping to encourage more people to try it out.

It is a Time Saver

Once people get on to the Internet and discover e-mail, they realize the tremendous efficiencies in its use. Consider the "old-fashioned method" by which a company might communicate with a number of people at different companies. Someone

- types the letter;
- prints the letter;
- copies the required numbers by taking it to the photocopy machine;
- stuffs the letters into envelopes;
- runs the envelopes through the postage meter or completes multiple courier waybills;
- gets the messages to the post box or courier.

All in all, a time-intensive and, in effect, expensive process, particularly when there are many recipients of the letter.

A company might save a bit of time by sending the paper through a fax machine instead of sending it through the post or by courier, but in doing so runs up substantial telephone bills. In addition, lineups form at the fax machine — they have become the "water cooler" of the 1990s. All in all, a very inefficient process. (Some organizations are reducing some of the inefficiencies found with paper-based fax machines by using fax softwares, which lets them send faxes directly from their computers.)

Many organizations expend vast human resources in shuffling paper, when technology exists that can result in significant time and efficiency savings. The Internet represents a significant opportunity for substantial improvement in the efficiency of regular communications by a business. Compare the process above with electronic mail. Someone

- keys the memo into a computer;
- selects an e-mail address, which could be for one individual or could be an electronic "mailing list" of several hundred people;
- presses a button to send the message.

Messages through e-mail are sent within seconds of completion; there is no paper shuffling. They are sent instantaneously and often simultaneously to a large number of recipients combined in mailing lists. There is simply no comparison in terms of efficiency between paper/fax mail and e-mail.

Individuals at home using the Internet for non-business purposes discover that they can enjoy the same efficiencies. Indeed, we are seeing more and more people discover that they can reach friends, families, and other people around the world using Internet e-mail. Since it is easier to send someone a message via e-mail than it is via the post, in many instances people end up communicating through e-mail more than they might ever have using more traditional methods.

It Transcends Time Zones and Eliminates Telephone Tag

Those who use Internet e-mail discover that it is a particularly useful tool to use when communicating with people in other time zones. You can send a message to someone at the other end of the country while they are still sleeping. They will receive it when they get into the office in the morning. Or, if you are communicating with people in Australia, you do not have to coordinate a time to call when you are both available. You can just jot off a message to them at any time and send it. In addition, people find e-mail to be a particularly convenient method of communicating with someone without the annoyance of voice mail or the frustrations in "telephone tag."

It Is Strategic

Many companies are gradually discovering the benefits of an internal e-mail system as an alternative to traditional phone, fax, and paper communication. E-mail is thus used to support communications between employees at many different locations throughout the company. Yet, if your company only has an internal e-mail system, it's like having a telephone that cannot be used to call anyone in the outside world, hence the trend where Internet e-mail is becoming a critical business application for many organizations, as companies discover that the ability to establish an e-mail link with customers, business associates, and other third parties is an invaluable and strategic business use of technology.

Clearly, there is an increasing trend throughout the corporate world to adopt Internet e-mail as a means of providing intercompany communications. This in itself has helped to fuel the growth in Internet e-mail.

It Has No Alternative

There is a so-called "global standard" for e-mail. It is called X.400. Fortunately, Internet e-mail has nothing to do with it. X.400 is a standard adopted by an international standards body (CCITT) defining how e-mail should be exchanged between different e-mail systems.

X.400 works well at a technical level, but fails miserably as a simple, easy-to-use method of sending and receiving e-mail. It requires the user to know too much about X.400 to be able to use it.

For example, one of the authors of this book has had, at various points in time, the following X.400 addresses on three different commercial e-mail systems:

```
C=CA;A=TELECOM.CANADA;DD=ID=JA.CARROLL;F=JIM;S=CARROLL

C=US;A=MCIMAIL;DD=ID=JCARROLL;F=JIM;S=CARROLL

/C=CA/AD=ATTMAIL/O=JACC/PN=JIM.CARROLL
```

His Internet address is **jcarroll@jacc.com**. Which would you prefer?

You will find a lot of business cards with Internet addresses appearing on them. You will not find many listing X.400 addresses. The world is quickly accepting the use of Internet e-mail addresses because they are easy to understand and easy to use. It would appear that X.400 addresses are being rejected because they are confusing, complex, and not easy to use or to remember.

Yet, there are some who believe that X.400 has a role to play. Alan Guilbault, Director, Office Information Systems, BC Systems Corporation, is responsible for e-mail strategy of the BC Government (**aguilbault@galaxy.gov.bc.ca**). He notes that "X.400 is important as a standard for the commercial networks that must guarantee reliable delivery and security for their customers." There is a ring of truth in this, as we will see in the final section of this chapter, Problems with Internet E-mail.

As a result, X.400 is being used in Canada, particularly as a system to support the exchange of formal business transaction documents between those companies participating in a form of commerce known as EDI (electronic data interchange). However, it would seem that its use is not extending beyond that population.

There are some people who are still convinced that X.400 is the right way to go when it comes to interorganization e-mail. However, this group is dwindling in the face of overwhelming use of the Internet. Their arguments tend to dissolve once you get involved in pointing out the sheer incomprehensibility of X.400 e-mail addresses.

It Works

To understand the real potential of Internet e-mail, you only need to talk to those who use it. Paul Berger (**pberger@nic.wat.hookup.net**) is with a small Ontario computer consulting firm. In a note to the authors, he indicated that "once you have been using Internet e-mail for awhile you kind of take it for granted. You forget about just how powerful it is to be able to correspond with your peers half way around the world or down the street at minimal cost."

For Derek Wyatt (**dwyatt@uoguelph.ca**), a computer science student at the University of Guelph, it's the global aspect of e-mail that is important. "Not only can you communicate with people you know personally and see every day but you can keep in touch with friends all over the world that you have met at one time or another. I keep in touch with people that I haven't even met. We exchange programming code, and work together on programming projects."

Alec Grynspan (**CNB10704@nt.com**), who runs a service that provides Internet e-mail access to many hundreds of bulletin board systems, notes that "e-mail is terrific! I was using other e-mail systems, but the Internet is faster and more reliable. There are children and parents now keeping contact via e-mail, which is far more immediate than the old paper mail and far less expensive than long distance. Families and friends communicate more than ever. My own service has reached a point where it is processing several THOUSAND messages a day — yet this is a small service compared to most. The size stuns me!"

What Is Internet E-Mail?

A strict definition of Internet e-mail is that it consists of e-mail sent and received from computers directly connected to the Internet. Strictly speaking, it is e-mail based on SMTP (simple mail transfer protocol), the software that defines how messages should be sent between different computers on the Internet. However, that definition is unworkable today, given the number of other systems connecting to the Internet.

Quite simply, Internet e-mail, because of its easily recognized address, is increasingly used for interorganizational communications and is rapidly emerging as the backbone of a globally linked e-mail network.

Basically, all kinds of e-mail systems around the world are plugging together, by linking into the Internet as seen in the diagram below. They do so through software that translates the e-mail format into the SMTP format used throughout the Internet. The software that does this is known as a "gateway."

FIGURE 7.1

E-Mail Systems Connected to the Internet.

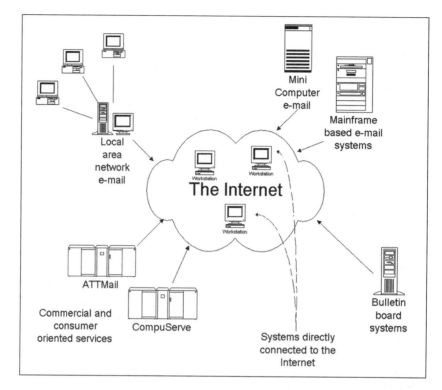

Internet e-mail addresses are based on the Internet Domain Name System described in Chapter 5, which provides standard format addresses to be used throughout the network. It is easy to recognize an Internet e-mail address: it is usually of the form **someone@somewhere**, for example, **jcarroll@jacc.com**. For our purposes, we define Internet e-mail as any type of e-mail system that is connected into the Internet.

And indeed, there are now many different types of e-mail systems being linked to the Internet. These systems include local area network-based systems, in-house mainframe and minicomputer systems, many bulletin board systems, and commercial e-mail systems.

Local Area Network (LAN)-Based E-Mail Systems

Many organizations are actively implementing LAN-based e-mail systems, such as Microsoft MSMail, Lotus cc:Mail, Lotus Notes, and WordPerfect Office, to support exchange of e-mail within the organization. These systems permit people within a company to send e-mail to each other, that is, from staff member to staff member, or from management to all staff. LAN e-mail is booming in the marketplace.

Organizations with advanced LAN e-mail strategies involving these technologies are actively implementing software that permits people to send and receive messages from the Internet. As a result, many people within organizations implementing cc:Mail, MSMail, or other similar LAN e-mail systems are finding that they have the capability to reach individuals on the Internet.

McCarthy Tetrault, a Toronto-based Canadian law firm with offices across Canada, linked its corporate LAN e-mail system (based on WordPerfect Office) to the Internet. Reports Cheri Turner, the systems administrator in the firm's Vancouver office, "Our users didn't have to learn a different mail system and the world of the Internet opened up at our desktop! We pursued the Internet gateway so we could provide better service and access to our clients. It has proved quite successful." Today, some 1,400 employees can send and receive Internet e-mail.

In-House Mainframe and Minicomputer Systems, Such as IBM PROFS or Digital All-in-1

These systems, the predecessors to LAN-based e-mail, are still in wide use throughout many organizations, particularly Fortune 1000 companies and major government bodies and allow companies to link their mainframe and minicomputer e-mail systems to the Internet. For example, the Ontario government, which uses a number of these systems as well as LAN-based e-mail systems, is linked to the Internet through the sub-domain **epo.gov.on.ca**. Individuals on an e-mail system in the provincial government can choose to register a user code with the EPO (electronic post office) and have an Internet e-mail ID of the form of **usercode@epo.gov.on.ca**. Any messages sent to that ID are automatically routed into the internal e-mail system.

The Ontario government is not alone. Alan Guilbault, in charge of e-mail strategy for the BC Government (**aguilbault@galaxy.gov.bc.ca**), notes that "we have a central electronic post office called 'GEMS' (Government Electronic Messaging Service) which currently delivers some 3 million notes a month between Government departments. GEMS handles all traffic to and from the Internet, routing messages to any of 40,000 Government staff using 12 different e-mail systems through the sub-domain **gems.gov.bc.ca**."

Bulletin Board Systems

Many bulletin board systems (BBSs), which range in size from a couple dozen people to thousands of subscribers, provide their members with access to Internet e-mail. Thus, while people on these BBSs might not be able to access some of the more sophisticated Internet services (such as the World Wide Web), they can use Internet e-mail, as seen with the example with Alec Grynspan above.

Commercial E-Mail Systems

Commercial e-mail systems, such as AT&TMail and MCIMail, and in Canada, TheNet:Mail (formerly Envoy 100) and Immedia, are used by some organizations that do not run e-mail on their own LANs, minicomputers, or mainframes. In addition, some Fortune 500 companies have adopted commercial e-mail systems for their communications to external companies.

Although these systems encountered growth in the 1980s, they now find their business base under attack due to the attractiveness and low cost of Internet e-mail. These systems have responded by providing direct links to Internet e-mail. For example, users of the Bell WorldLinx The:Net e-mail system can send and receive messages from the Internet.

Everyone Sees Something Different

When dealing with Internet e-mail, you must realize that everyone you deal with might read, send, and work with Internet e-mail in a way that is completely different from the way that you work with it. With so many different systems linked to Internet e-mail, it should come as no surprise that there is a wide variety of Internet e-mail software in use.

Some will find it easy to send and receive e-mail because they have access to simple, straightforward client software; for others, e-mail will be difficult because the client software they use is less straightforward. According to Mike Martineau of NSTN, Inc., "I think we need to remember that people's view of the Internet is significantly coloured by the client software they use."

Given the wide number of possible methods by which people can access and use the Internet, it is not possible within this book to detail all the steps involved in dealing with your own Internet e-mail. For that, we suggest you refer to the manual of the particular e-mail software you use and discuss with your Internet service provider any special technical considerations that it might involve.

The Structure of an Internet E-Mail Message

An Internet e-mail message has several distinct parts. Although any particular message might be more or less complex, a sample Internet message looks like this in plain text:

```
Date sent:Tue, 18 Jul 1995 17:42:07 -0400
To:   handbook@uunet.ca
From:   berzins@nucleus.com (Dave Berzins)
Subject:   book Update


Hi Guys. I was wondering how we would go about an update to a listing in
your book. Since submitting the form, we have made changes. Anything
would be appreciated.


Dave Berzins...


                              _ \\ \ / / _
                             ( - 0 - 0 - )
/-------------------------------------------------ooO- (_) -Ooo--------------------------------------------------\
| Dave Berzins, President Nucleus Inc. 1835B 10 Ave. S.W. Calgary, AB, T3C 0K2      |
|    403-541-9470 Voice, 403-541-9400 Modem, 403-541-9473 Fax                         |
| e-mail: berzins@nucleus.com www: http://www.nucleus.com finger:nis.nucleus.com  |
\-------------------------------------------------------------------------------------------------------------/
                                 | | | |
                                ooO Ooo
```

Take a moment and examine the message. You will note that it includes the following components, or fields:

- Date sent:

  The date/time the message was created by the sender.

- To:

  The intended recipient of the message.
  In this case, the message is being sent to the Internet ID **handbook@uunet.ca**. This is actually a "mailing list" that reaches both authors of this book.

- From:

  The name of the sender and the full Internet address of the sender. In this case, the sender is **berzins@nuclear.com**. The software has also included the sender's full name (Dave Berzins).

- Subject:

  Details the subject line entered by the sender. In some cases, if the message is in response to an earlier message, the e-mail software used might place a "Re:" in front of the original subject, and if the message has been "forwarded" by someone else, the software might place a "Fwd:" or similar indicator in front of the subject.

Depending on the e-mail software you use, you might also see other fields, including

- cc:

  Messages can also include a cc:, or carbon copy field. This indicates that the message has also been copied to other people.

- In-reply-to:

  A field used by many e-mail systems to uniquely identify messages.

- Message-ID:

  A unique message address, generated by the e-mail system of the sender.

- Mime-Version: and Content-Type:

  This appears or is used if the sender of this message is working with the newest evolution of Internet e-mail, known as MIME (multipurpose Internet multimedia extensions), which provides interesting new e-mail capabilities. MIME significantly extends the capabilities of simple Internet e-mail and is discussed in greater depth later in this chapter.

- X-mailer:

  Internet messages also often include an X-mailer: field, which indicates the e-mail client software used to create the message.

Other fields might appear in the message, again depending on the particular software that is in use. You might be using e-mail software that automatically shows you all kinds of other detail, known as the "headers."

Finally, the e-mail message above includes a "signature," or standard piece of information added to every message by the sender. Many e-mail software packages let you create a signature in which you can include your name, address, phone number, e-mail and World Wide Web addresses, and other information. Many messages do not include a signature.

In this case, the signature used by Dave Berzins is simple and straightforward, and actually quite humorous, since the sender has included a little bit of artwork. We talk about the signature further below.

It should also be noted that much of the software for the Internet strips an Internet message down to its fundamentals, by showing only To:, From: and Subject: fields. For example, this message, when viewed with Pegasus Mail for Windows,[1] appears as follows:

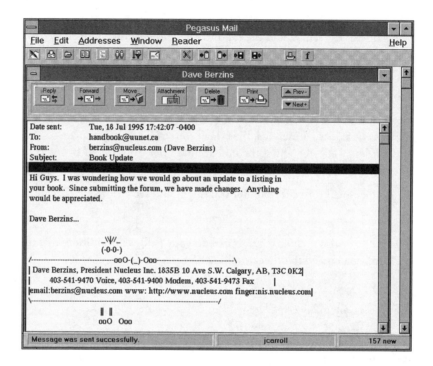

How Did This Message Get Here?

Since you are likely curious, we will explain how the message got from Dave to the two authors of this book. First and foremost, Dave sent the message to **handbook@uunet.ca**. This is a mailing list, kindly sponsored by UUnet Canada. When a message is sent to this mailing list, it is automatically forwarded to the ID of each author (**jcarroll@jacc.com** and **rickb@hookup.net**, located on the Internet service providers NSTN and HookUp, respectively).

Some e-mail software hides certain details of e-mail known as the "full headers," so that you do not have to see all the information about how the message got from point A to point

---

1. A shareware program, Pegasus Mail for Windows, is available from the URL **ftp://risc.ua.edu/network/pegasus**. Macintosh and DOS versions are available at the same location.

B. Some e-mail programs automatically show you these "full headers," while other software packages provide an option to view the headers. Using Pegasus, we can take a look at the full headers. The message now looks like this:

> From <@mail.uunet.ca,@cicerone.uunet.ca:berzins@nucleus.com> Tue Jul 18 18:47:22 1995
>
> Received: from Waffle on jacc.com by WafPeg 0.25, 93.04.04
>
> for JCARROLL on standalone PMail ; Wed, 19 Jul 1995 05:53:36 EST5EDT
>
> Received: by jacc.com (1.65/waf)
>
> via UUCP; Wed, 19 Jul 95 05:53:29 EDT
>
> for jcarroll
>
> Received: from seraph.uunet.ca (uunet.ca [142.77.1.254]) by yak.nstn.ns.ca (8.6.12/8.6.9) with ESMTP id SAA04281 for <jcarroll@jacc.com>; Tue, 18 Jul 1995 18:47:19 -0300
>
> Received: from cicerone.uunet.ca ([142.77.1.11]) by mail.uunet.ca with SMTP id <188701-1>; Tue, 18 Jul 1995 17:49:01 -0400
>
> Received: from nucleus.com ([199.45.65.129]) by cicerone.uunet.ca with SMTP id <206584-3>; Tue, 18 Jul 1995 17:47:05 -0400
>
> Received: from beavis.nucleus.com (beavis.nucleus.com [199.45.65.131]) by nucleus.com (8.6.12/8.6.5) with SMTP id PAA23042 for <handbook@uunet.ca>; Tue, 18 Jul 1995 15:42:07 -0600
>
> Date: Tue, 18 Jul 1995 17:42:07 -0400
>
> Message-Id: <199507182142.PAA23042@nucleus.com>
>
> X-Sender: berzins@nucleus.com
>
> X-Mailer: Windows Eudora Version 2.0.3
>
> Mime-Version: 1.0
>
> Content-Type: text/plain; charset="us-ascii"
>
> To: handbook@uunet.ca
>
> From: berzins@nucleus.com (Dave Berzins)
>
> Subject: Book Update
>
>
> Hi Guys. I was wondering how we would go about an update to a listing in
> your book. Since submitting the form, we have made changes. Anything
> would be appreciated.
>
>
> Dave Berzins...
> ```
>                            _ \\ I / / _
>                            ( - 0 - 0 - )
> /-------------------------------------------------ooO- (_) -Ooo-----------------------------------------------\
> I Dave Berzins, President Nucleus Inc. 1835B 10 Ave. S.W. Calgary, AB, T3C 0K2      I
> I    403-541-9470 Voice, 403-541-9400 Modem, 403-541-9473 Fax                       I
> I e-mail: berzins@nucleus.com www: http://www.nucleus.com finger:nis.nucleus.com   I
> \-------------------------------------------------------------------------------------------------------------/
>                            || ||
>                            ooO Ooo
> ```

The first few lines show the path that the message took as it went from Dave in Calgary to Jim Carroll. Interpreting this information tells us that

- Dave used the e-mail software Eudora 2.0.3 to prepare his message; he then sent it to the computer system **nucleus.com** (incidentally, the ISP that he manages);

- within seconds, **nucleus.com** opened a connection to UUNet Canada (**uunet.ca**) and transmitted the message there;

- UUNet Canada figured out that the message was to a mailing list and that it should be reforwarded to the two authors of this book (the two members of the list);

- UUNet opened a direct connection to NSTN and HookUp and sent the message, where it was eventually picked up by Jim Carroll and Rick Broadhead.

All of this occurred within minutes of Dave having sent the message, thus demonstrating the efficiency of Internet e-mail. The route was rather direct (as it often is today on the Internet), as computer systems at each ISP linked directly to each other to pass the message along. For example, the e-mail system at UUNet Canada opened a "direct" link to the e-mail system at HookUp Communications to send the message to the ISP used by Rick.

Yet, behind this simplicity, and even given that the message went "directly" from one ISP to another where it was then retransmitted to two others, is the fact that in one case the message really took a long and circuitous route across North America as it made its way to its destination, since, as we described in Chapter 5, messages to Rick Broadhead take a long route through the United States on their way to their destination.

Even though UUNet Canada opened a "direct" link of its e-mail system to the e-mail system at HookUp, this direct link actually traveled from Toronto through New York, Hartford, Cleveland, Chicago, Denver, and San Francisco before coming back to Oakville, Ontario, thus meaning the message traveled several thousand kilometres to really go only about 30 kilometres.

Internet routes change on a constant and frequent basis, so it is possible that a more direct route is in place by the time you read this. The key point is that the technology that makes up the Internet knows how to route e-mail messages around the globe, even if it uses a sometimes lengthy and seemingly illogical route.

What Can You Do with E-Mail?

Since there are so many different types of e-mail software that people might be using, the way that people create, read, and send messages will be different depending on the software used. Regardless of what software is used, however, there are certain basic things that you will want to do with Internet e-mail.

Create a Message

Obviously, you will want to create a message to send it to someone. To do so, you will need to know the e-mail address, which is the subject of a separate section below. Once you know the address, there is usually some type of function in your e-mail software that lets you create a new message. For example, using the software Eudora, a Windows application, you can choose to create a new message. When you do so, you see a screen that looks like this:

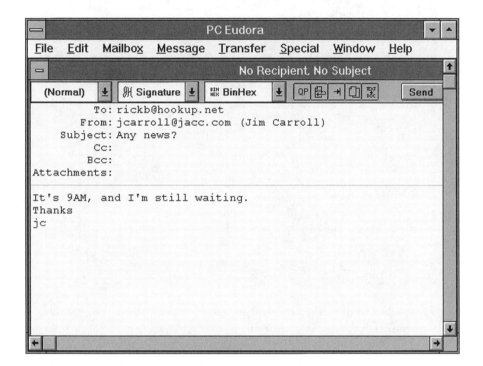

You can choose to do many different things with your message, depending on the e-mail software that you are using, such as sending a computer file to someone, inserting text from a document from within your word processor, making an automatic copy of the message for yourself, sending the message with a receipt request so that you are told when the recipient reads the message, or "encrypting" the message to protect against prying eyes.

Read a Message

Your e-mail software will have an "inbox," or "new mail folder," a place where new messages are listed. You can usually choose to read any particular message, or you can read all messages. A new mail folder might look like the one in the screen below. In this case, the √ symbol indicates that a message has already been read. Here is the inbox for one of the authors:

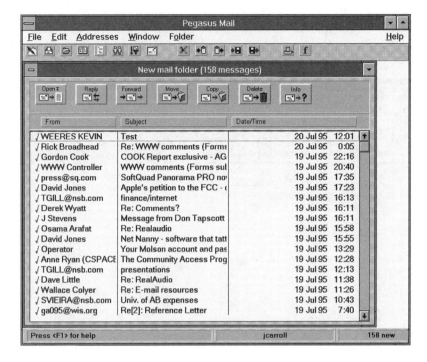

And here is the inbox for the other author. You can see some similarities in the way they are structured, even though there are two different programs in use:

Reply to a Message

When you read an e-mail message, you can usually choose to reply to a message sent to you by someone else. When you reply, to help that person remember what the message was about, many e-mail software programs will "quote" the original message within the body of the reply. For example, let's assume we are replying to our example message. When we do so, a new message box is opened up. The reply contains both the original text and our reply:

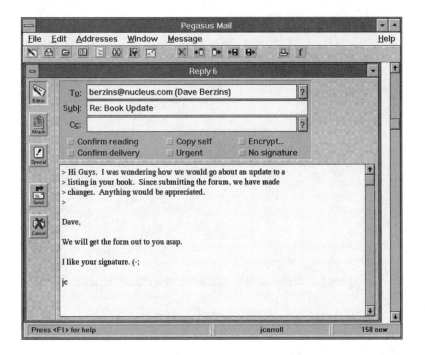

In the sample message a special marker has been placed by the software in front of the text of Dave's original message, a > symbol. (Many different types of markers are used.) This feature helps the recipient easily and quickly identify the original message in the message that he/she received from you and is a courtesy that is much appreciated by the Internet community. You will often see your original message quoted to you when you get replies to your message.

Delete, Print, or Save the Message

When reading a message, you can also usually choose to delete the message, print it to your printer, or save the text of the message to your computer so that you can view it later. Many e-mail programs also support the use of folders, so that you can file your messages within the e-mail program according to folders that you define. These folders have proven to be very effective tools by which people manage their information; for example, people have subject folders, project folders, "to do" folders. It's an easy way to organize your e-mail according to your particular needs. One of the authors organizes his e-mail into the following folders:

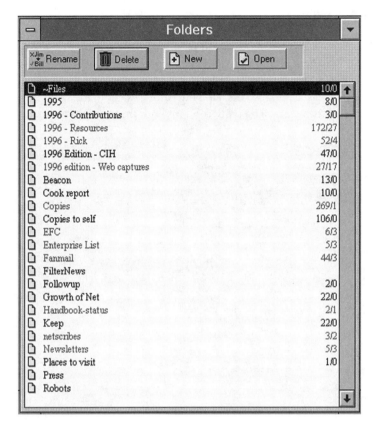

Send or Receive a Computer File

On occasion, you will receive a message that contains a "binary enclosure" or file. This means that someone has sent you an e-mail message that contains a program, a document or spreadsheet, or some other type of computer file. The enclosure or file is "encoded," that is, it is converted to a special format of text so that it can be sent through e-mail. On the Internet, binary files and enclosures are usually included in the message in one of three types: binhex, uuencode, or MIME. People usually find the issues of binary files/enclosures to be the most complicated issue related to Internet e-mail.

Why Does It Get So Complicated?

Computer programs and document files (such as Microsoft Word or WordPerfect documents) contain special codes that cannot be represented in the "plain text" that you normally see in an e-mail message. To be sent through e-mail, they must be "encoded" in some way and are therefore "attached" to a regular e-mail message. This means that when you receive such an e-mail message, it will be necessary for you to "extract" the file from your message and sometimes "decode" it. It is confusing, but once you do it a few times, you will get the hang of it.

You can deal with all three types if your e-mail software supports all types, and you might find that not to be the case. The result will be that your first encounters with trying to "extract" file attachments will be frustrating, until you and the sender can agree on a type of enclosure that you can both "extract."

When a computer file is turned into an attachment of one of these types, it is often turned into simple "text" that looks like gibberish. For example, if the file is "uuencoded," the binary file has been turned into rows and rows of text and is included in the body of the message that looks like this:

```
begin   644   config.sysM1$5624-%/4,Z7$$1/4UQ(24U%32Y365,-"D1%5DE#13U#.EQ$3U-
<14U-,S@VM+D5812!.3T5-4PPT*0E5&1D524STS,"PP#0I&24Q%S%TX,`T*1$]3/550@T*
```

The exact method that you will use to "extract" the file from the message, "decode" it, and save it to your computer will vary depending on the e-mail software that you might be using. Some e-mail software automatically "decodes" enclosures when you read the message, while with others you will need to save the mail message in a file and then use a separate program to decode it. For example, Pegasus Mail lets you automatically "extract" most enclosures in order to save them on your computer:

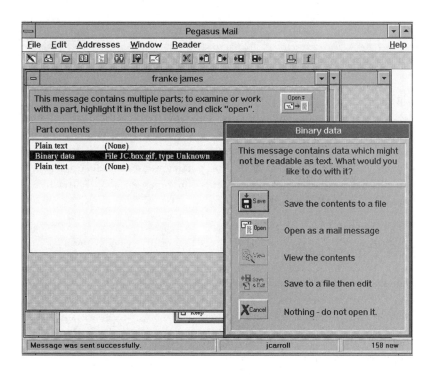

Older versions of Eudora recognize attachments in the binhex and MIME formats, but does not recognize uuencoded files. Hence the result is that if you read a message that contains a file attachment in uuencoded format, Eudora will not know what to do with it and will show you the gibberish within the text of the message:

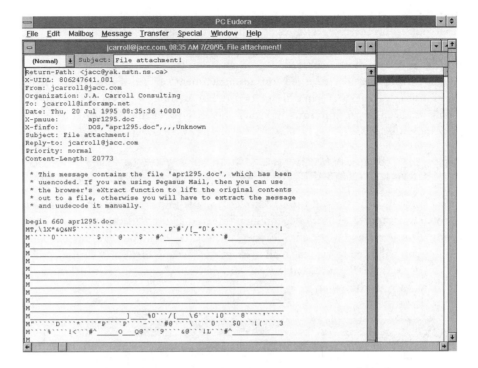

Is there any hope on the horizon of making this complexity go away? Eventually. That is what MIME is all about.

MIME is a rapidly emerging Internet standard to permit a more straightforward exchange of binary files and enclosures. MIME messages also look like uuencoded files if you receive them and do not have MIME-capable software. However, if the software you are using (and more and more e-mail software is supporting the standard) supports MIME, your software will automatically recognize the contents of the message as a file attachment. We talk more about MIME near the end of this chapter.

Attach an E-Mail Signature

Many e-mail software programs support the use of a signature. Other systems connected to the Internet, such as CompuServe, do not. Accordingly, you should not always expect to see them in every Internet message. (Indeed, the inability to have automatic signatures is often a great source of frustration for users of particular e-mail systems.)

Our sample message above from Dave Berzins included an e-mail signature which provided further information concerning the sender. In this case, his signature includes his name, e-mail, Web and paper addresses, as well as a humorous cartoon character.

If your software supports signatures, you can automatically append or add one to the end of a message. Some software allows you to choose the signature that you wish to use from a list of several. If the software does not support signatures, you can still type one in manually.

In general, signatures should be concise and should not be overdone. In a document released on USENET called "A Primer on How to Work With the USENET Community," by Chuq Von Rospac, guidance is given with respect to how to structure signatures. Although the document is specific to the use of the USENET news system, the guidance is equally applicable to e-mail signatures.

> Signatures are nice.... Don't overdo it. Signatures can tell the world something about you, but keep them short. A signature that is longer than the message itself is considered to be in bad taste. The main purpose of a signature is to help people locate you, not to tell your life story. Every signature should include at least your return address relative to a major, known site on the network and a proper domain-format address. Your system administrator can give this to you. Some news posters attempt to enforce a 4 line limit on signature files -- an amount that should be more than sufficient to provide a return address and attribution.

Filter Your Mail

With the growth in the use of Internet e-mail has come the inability for some people to deal with massive volumes of messages. One practical way to deal with this is through the use of e-mail filters, a feature found in a growing number of e-mail software packages.

You can think of a filter as an electronic program on your e-mail system or a computer that reads your e-mail before you do. It then acts upon those messages, depending on a set of rules that you have defined beforehand. For example, you might belong to an Internet service that regularly sends you, via e-mail, a newsletter. You notice that the message always arrives with the subject "Newsletter- (YY/MM/DD)." Using a filter, you could specify that any messages that you receive containing the subject "Newsletter" should automatically be moved to a folder in your e-mail system called "newsletters." You can then choose to go to this folder at any time to read the messages stored there, rather than seeing this particular newsletter arrive with your regular messages.

Using filters, you can specify that certain actions should be performed on incoming messages based upon the contents of the To:, From:, Subject:, or other fields. These actions include

- automatically moving or copying the messages to a particular file folder or automatically deleting certain messages;

- replying to every message with an automatic response, for example, "I am a little behind on my e-mail, and it will take me about three days to respond — don't fret";

- automatically adding a person to an e-mail list within your e-mail system.

E-Mail Addresses

Internet e-mail uses the domain name style of addressing, based upon the Domain Name System. An Internet e-mail address usually consists of a name or some identifier, followed by an @ symbol, followed by the domain name. For example, **jcarroll@jacc.com** contains the user name (**jcarroll**) and the domain name (**jacc.com**, which stands for J.A. Carroll Consulting, and which is listed in the commercial, or **.com**, domain).

As seen in Chapter 5, the Internet Domain Name System results in e-mail addresses in Canada that use a **.ca** extension, if registered within the Canadian domain. The address might include a city/jurisdiction name and province, depending on the size of the organization, and the location of that organization within Canada. Within the Canadian domain, some Internet addresses in Canada would appear with names such as **Pete_Smith@mediumcorp.ab.ca** for an organization in Alberta, **Tjones@smallco.ns.ca** for a company in Nova Scotia, or **Al_Stevens@bigcompany.ca** if the company is national in scope.

Other Internet addresses, within organizations that are not part of the Canadian domain but are registered directly with the Internet InterNIC, might have Internet addresses that end in **.com**, **.edu**, **.gov**, or other extensions. Such an address will usually include the name of the organization next to the extension, for example **TJones@Bigco.com**.

E-Mail Styles

It is important to note that the information that appears in front of the @ symbol in an e-mail address will vary depending on the particular e-mail system used, the Internet vendor, and the way that names are used within the organizational e-mail system:

◆ Some addresses will use some combination of the first name and last name, for example, **Pete_Smith** or **Psmith** or **pete.smith**. Since spaces are not allowed, the first and last name are separated, usually by a _ character or a dot.

◆ Other addresses might use alpha-numerical characters, for example, **76467.3502** for someone on CompuServe, or **aa123** for an address on a FreeNet.

◆ Other addresses might use nicknames or nonsense names.

In other words, there are no rules on what must be used in front of the @ symbol. Some sites will let you choose your own address. The result is an incredible diversity of addresses throughout the Internet.

Rejected Messages

On occasion, you will receive notification that a message sent to someone has been rejected or not delivered. A rejected message looks like this:

```
>Return-Path: MAILER-DAEMON

>Date: Sun, 23 Jul 1995 23:52:48 -0400

>From: Mail Delivery Subsystem <MAILER-DAEMON@hookup.net>

>Subject: Returned mail: User unknown

>To: <rickb@hookup.net>

>

>The original message was received at Sun, 23 Jul 1995 23:52:31 -0400
```

```
>from ts7-12.inforamp.net [198.53.144.232]

>

>Please contact postmaster@hookup.net for assistance.

>

>----- The following addresses had delivery problems -----

><kanata1@resudox.net> (unrecoverable error)

>

>----- Transcript of session follows -----

>... while talking to gabriel.resudox.net.:

>>>> RCPT To:<kanata1@resudox.net>

><<< 550 <kanata1@resudox.net>... User unknown

>550 <kanata1@resudox.net>... User unknown

>

>----- Original message follows -----

>Return-Path: rickb@hookup.net

>Received: from ts1-05.inforamp.net (ts7-12.inforamp.net [198.53.144.232])

by nic.wat.hookup.net (8.6.12/1.14) with SMTP id XAA23549; Sun, 23 Jul 1995

23:52:31 -0400

>Date: Sun, 23 Jul 1995 23:52:31 -0400

>Message-Id: <199507240352.XAA23549@nic.wat.hookup.net>

>X-Sender: rickb@noc.tor.hookup.net

>Mime-Version: 1.0

>Content-Type: text/plain; charset="us-ascii"

>To: kanata1@resudox.net

>From: rickb@hookup.net (Rick Broadhead)

>Subject: Re: MISA Conference

>X-Mailer: <Windows Eudora Version 2.0.2>

>

>[...]
```

The message usually includes the original message you sent.

Rejection messages come in all kinds of flavors and often look different depending on where they originated. If you get a rejected message, carefully check the e-mail address to which you sent the original message. Quite often, a simple spelling mistake in the address will have been made. Other times, you should check with the person (by phone or otherwise, of course) to verify the address. When you have a rejected message, you can usually forward it to the correct ID, but be sure to edit out all the details in the rejected message header.

E-Mail Etiquette

When sending and receiving e-mail on the Internet, you should keep in mind this simple rule:

> What you type and what you say in your e-mail messages could one day come back to haunt you. Be careful.

The use of Internet e-mail (or any e-mail system) requires an on-line etiquette, or a set of manners, that you should keep in mind.

E-Mail is Different

There are several characteristics about e-mail that should make you cautious in the way you use it.

◆ E-mail is fast. In the "good old days," before the arrival of computer technology, people were careful with paper letters. A response took time to prepare, was well thought out, and was probably reviewed a few times before being sent. There was no room for error on paper correspondence. That is not the case with e-mail. Within seconds of receiving a message, you can respond, often without thinking about what you have typed. Do you really want people to receive messages that you have not carefully thought about?

◆ E-mail is wide-reaching. Within seconds, you can create a message or response to a message that will reach one person, 20 people, or thousands of people (particularly if you are responding to a mailing list posting; if the mailing list is linked to a USENET newsgroup, your message will reach an even larger audience). If you write an e-mail message in anger, you might say something that you regret. Do you really want to send copies of your message to a lot of people?

◆ E-mail is easily saved. Computer technology permits people to easily store the e-mail messages they send or receive.[2] What this means is that any e-mail message you send to someone could end up in his/her personal data archive or even in an organizational archive. If you are posting to an Internet mailing list, your message could end up in several archives around the world that are open to public viewing. If you write

---

2. One of the authors has on file about 100 megabytes of messages, representing e-mail messages sent/received since October 1985.

something controversial or stupid, do you want to risk having your words come back to haunt you?

◆ E-mail is easily forwarded. E-mail technology promotes the easy distribution of information. What you write and send to someone can easily be forwarded by him/her to someone else or posted to a global mailing list or USENET newsgroup. The recipient of your message might not realize that you intended the message for limited distribution. Before you know it, your message could be sent all over the world. Do you really want a message that you intended for just one person to be forwarded to a number of people?

◆ E-mail is easily misinterpreted. The person reading your e-mail message cannot see your body language. He/she cannot see if you are smiling, frowning, or crying as you write. It is more difficult to interpret what you have written. Often this leads to misinterpretation. What the recipient thinks you mean is often not what you really mean. Do you want to run the risk of having someone misunderstand your message?

Flaming

The on-line world has come up with a term to describe what happens to people who ignore these risks and who write an e-mail message while their emotions are not in check. It is called flaming. Flaming is the tendency for someone to quickly key an e-mail message in anger without thinking the message through. As noted in a study entitled "The Human, Social, and Organizational Impact of Electronic Mail" from California Polytechnical University, "some laboratory and university research demonstrates that electronic mail can encourage overly emotional and negative messages."

It is all too easy to go overboard with e-mail. You might find that suddenly your emotions bubble over, and you start to send a really nasty message. Or that you feel you just have to straighten something out by being blunt. Yet, such anger and bluntness do not work well with Internet e-mail due to the lack of body language. People might read the wrong thing into what you are sending. Remember this warning. At some time, you will regret sending an e-mail message. You will regret it a lot. You should always, always think before sending a message to someone in anger.

E-Mail Guidance

A few simple suggestions might make it easier for you to avoid problems sending e-mail messages:

◆ Do not use just capitals in your messages. This is called shouting. Imagine receiving a message that looks like this:

GREG. WE NEED TO UNDERSTAND HOW TO REORGANIZE FOR THE JUNE 5TH MEETING. IT'S IMPORTANT THAT WE GET TOGETHER NOW. CALL ME SOON.

Messages like this are difficult to read and cause others frustration with the messages you send them. Always be careful to use upper- and lowercase.

◆ Use a meaningful subject line. Remember that the person you are sending the message to might receive tens or hundreds of messages each day. To make it easier to deal with your message, provide a subject line that is meaningful and to the point.

◆ Take your time thinking about a response to a message, especially if the message makes you angry. The best advice is to get up, go for a glass of water, or have a cup of coffee. Or take a walk. Or go shopping, watch TV, or read a book. Never respond to a message when you are angry!

◆ Do not send a carbon copy of your message to the rest of the world, unless you have to. When sending an e-mail message, it is easy to send copies to a lot of people, including some who may have no interest in your message. Be judicious about the people who get a copy of the message.

◆ Summarize the message to which you are responding. If you are lucky, you are using an Internet e-mail software package that quotes the original message text in your response, as we discussed earlier in "Reply to a Message." Be sure to use this feature to make it easier for the recipient to remember what the message was about. Edit the message so that only the relevant text is kept. There is nothing worse than getting three pages of an original message with a few words in response at the end.

◆ Use special characters to label your emotion. For example, to *highlight* a point, consider using >>>>>special<<<<<< characters. For example, rather than keying a message that looks like this:

It is important that we meet as soon as possible.

you might key

It is !!!!!!important!!!!!! that we meet as soon as possible.

This will help portray the urgency of the situation.

◆ Be careful when responding to messages received from a mail list (we discuss e-mail lists in the next chapter). With some mail lists the default is that any reply is sent to everyone on the list, while with others the reply is to the original message author only. You should check the reply address before sending the message to ensure that you are sending the reply to the intended recipient.

As you use the Internet, you will discover that people use all kinds of tricks to emphasize points within their messages. Carefully observe, and in time you will come up with your own distinctive Internet writing style.

Tips on E-mail etiquette (and other general "netiquette" issues) can be found at the following URLs:

http://www.webfoot.com/advice/email.top.html

http://www.fau.edu/rinaldi/netiquette.html

http://www.screen.com/understand/Netiquette.html

Smileys

The e-mail world has come up with an ingenious way of expressing emotion within a message by using special characters that some call "emoticons." Others call them "smileys." A smiley is a set of symbols that, when turned on its side, represents some type of character. For example, a (-: is a sideways smiley face; a (-; is a sideways smiley face winking, while)-: is a face with a frown.

A :-) is often used in a message to indicate that the preceding remark was made in jest. Smileys are important so that people do not misinterpret what you type. These characters can be used within e-mail messages to add additional emphasis. For example,

>   Pete, Your summary was interesting(-;.   Have a good day.   John

or

>   Pete, I didn't get the report finished.)-:   Call me. John

There are so many possible smileys that a book has been written about them.

As you use the Internet, you will see a lot of smileys in messages. Accumulate your own special list. If you are looking for more, you can find a number of sites on the Internet that keep lists of smileys, for example, an on-line database of smileys at the Web site for the Electronic Freedom Foundation (**http://www.eff.org/papers/eegtti/eeg_286.html**):

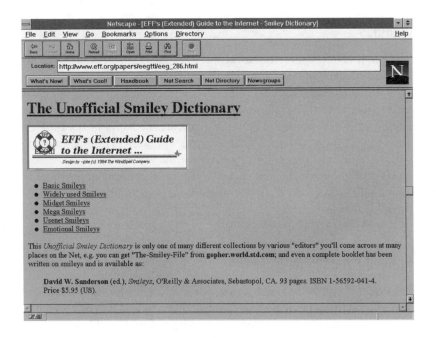

Listings of "smiley's/emoticons" can be found online at the following URLs:

http://www.emoticon.com

http://www.eff.org/papers/eegtti/eeg_286.html

http://olympe.polytechnique.fr/~violet/Smileys/

How Do I Locate an Internet E-Mail Address?

At some point you will want to determine how to obtain the e-mail address of a particular person or organization. Invariably, as you use various parts of the Internet, you will come across a message from someone that reads as follows:

> I am looking for Bob Smith in Toronto. Does anyone know his Internet address?

The question is silly, since there is no easy answer. Obviously, there are many Bob Smiths in Toronto, many of whom do not use the Internet.

The Internet does not have a central storage location that lists all possible users of the network, and such a directory will never exist, given the massive scope of the Internet. However, there do exist a number of smaller directories and query systems that you can use to try to locate the e-mail address of someone. However, such services are certainly not very comprehensive and are not really a good solution to your dilemma.

Fortunately, many people are starting to list their Internet addresses on their business cards, and addresses are beginning to gain as much acceptance on business cards and correspondence as fax numbers did in the mid-1980s. Hence sometimes the answer to the question is the obvious one.

Simple Solutions

The easiest way to find out the Internet address of someone is probably simply to ask. Pick up the phone and call. Maybe the person knows. If he/she knows he/she is on the Internet and knows how to send a message, but does not know the address, ask the person to send a message to your Internet address. You will see what the address is and can respond in the future.

If this does not work, and you must begin exploring the world of the Internet to try to locate an address, take a deep breath. There are a lot of resources on-line to look into. The first step is to try to find the person directly in one of the various directories available on the Internet. If that does not work, the next step is to see if the company or organization the person works for is on the Internet. If so, you might be able to contact the company to determine the e-mail address for the person.

Step 1: Try to Find the Person

There are a variety of sources on the Internet that might help you find the person you are looking for. A good starting point is the document "How to find people's E-mail addresses," originally written by Jonathon Kames and now maintained by David Lamb at Queens University in Kingston. It can be accessed via the Web at Queen's University in Canada (**http://www.qucis.queensu.ca/FAQs/email/finding.html**):

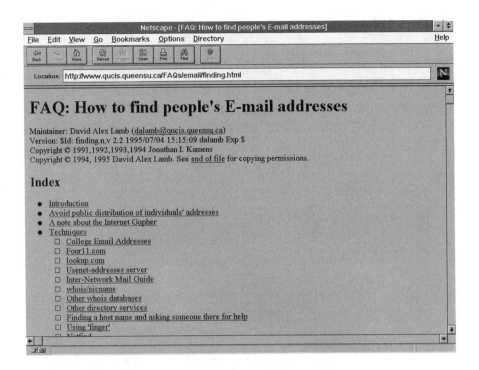

The document is posted on a regular basis to several USENET newsgroups, such as **news.answers**. You can also retrieve it on-line or through e-mail.

How to Obtain the "How to find people's E-mail addresses" summary

URL: **ftp://rtfm.mit.edu/pub/usenet-by-group/news.answers/finding-addresses**

or **http://www.qucis.queensu.ca/FAQs/email/finding.html**

By e-mail: Send a message to **mail-server@rtfm.mit.edu.**

In the text of message, type (on one line): **sendusenet/news.answers/finding-addresses**

WHOIS

One of the first places to look is a "WHOIS server," which is a simple program that lets you query for the name of an organization or individual. WHOIS servers are found throughout the Internet, but primarily within the academic and university communities. WHOIS servers are not a comprehensive source of information about e-mail users around the world, but do help you if you want to find someone in academic and research communities.

One of the most popular is the WHOIS database, located at the resource services department of the Internet Network Information Centre (InterNIC). (InterNIC, as we discussed in Chapter 5, is the organization that manages the **.com**, **.edu**, and other top level domains.) Although the database is not comprehensive, it is a useful starting point. To access the database, you can use Telnet to **rs.internic.net**, and key **whois** at the InterNIC prompt. You will then be prompted to enter a personal or company name to search for; here are the results of an example of a search for individuals with the surname Adamson (**gopher://ds.internic. net:4320/7whois%20ds.internic.net?adamson**) (Gopher is discussed in Chapter 11):

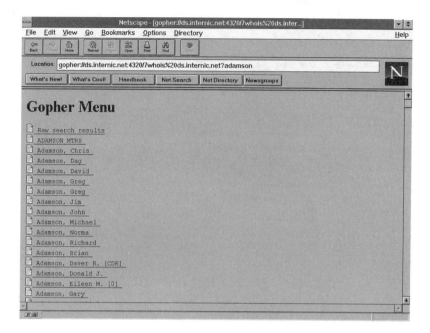

A search of WHOIS and related databases can be useful; however, 99% of the individuals on the Internet are not listed on WHOIS, which is what makes it such a limited tool.

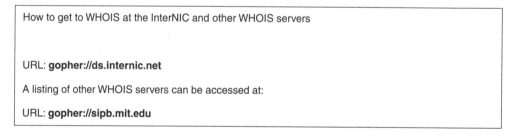

How to get to WHOIS at the InterNIC and other WHOIS servers

URL: **gopher://ds.internic.net**

A listing of other WHOIS servers can be accessed at:

URL: **gopher://sipb.mit.edu**

Other Resources

There are many other on-line resources that you can search to try to find a particular person. One strategy is to find the Web site of the company or organization where the person works or goes to school and see if an on-line telephone/e-mail directory is available there. A recent and significant trend is that some organizations are using the Web to list "phone books" of people within their organization, including their e-mail addresses. For example, here is the faculty and staff directory for the University of British Columbia (**http://www.ucs.ubc.ca:780/cgi-bin/ph.pl**):

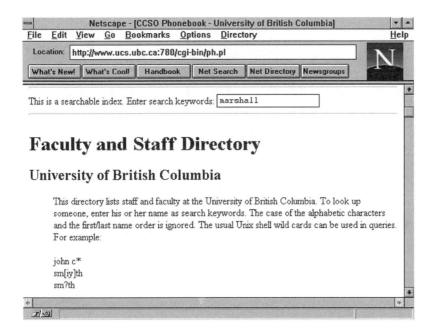

The Prince Edward Island Government also permits you to search for the e-mail addresses and phone numbers of provincial government employees (**http://www.gov.pe.ca/info/phone.html**). Here is a search for people with the name Smith:

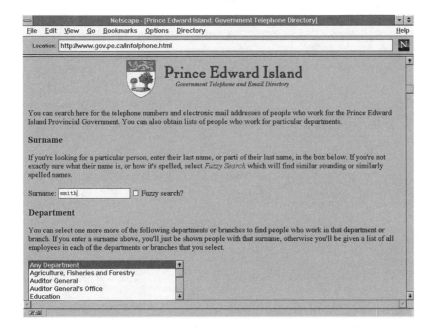

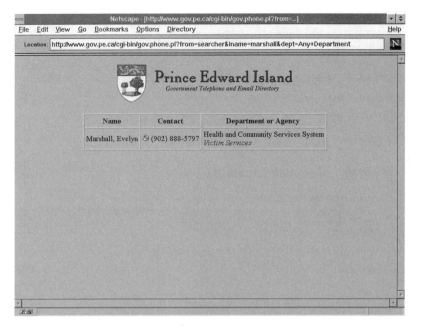

There are other systems that provide large databases of e-mail addressees from around the globe. For example, a system called Four11 is a comprehensive database of over 1.5 million Internet users (**http://www.four11.com**). You can add yourself to the Four11 database to make it easy for people to find you; it is easy to do and it is free.

The "How to find people's E-mail addresses" document previously mentioned includes pointers to a few sites similar to Four11.

The Massachusetts Institute of Technology has built a system that builds an index of user IDs of people posting information to USENET. The document describing the database notes that it "contains one-line entries consisting of names and E-mail addresses culled from the Reply-To or From lines of USENET postings." If you only have electronic mail, you can query the system through e-mail:

> Send message to: **mail-server@rtfm.mit.edu**
>
> In text of message, type: **send usenet-addresses/keyword**.
>
> Special instructions: Replace "keyword" with the surname of the person you are looking for.

Finally, various Internet service providers are trying to establish new and innovative methods to help you identify users of the Internet. As a result, you should always check with your Internet provider to see if there is a new method of looking up people on the Internet.

Step 2: Find the Company or Organization

If you cannot find the person you are looking for in one of these areas, look for the company or organization to which that person might belong. This might help you to locate the individual, since you might be able to write the postmaster or the name listed as the contact for the organization. The first step is to find the company, and once you know that, you then contact the postmaster or contact name to find a particular individual.

Finding a Company

The Directory of "Canadian Organizations with Registered Internet Domains" in Appendix C is a comprehensive listing of most companies and organizations in Canada with registered Internet domain names. The listing is current as of August 1995. Because of the massive growth of the Internet, new organizations are added all the time.

The Canadian registrations (i.e., for the **.ca** domain) are maintained in Canada, while all other registrations (**.com**, **.edu**, etc.) are maintained by the InterNIC in the United States. Hence, to find an organization on-line or to obtain further contact information about a registered organization, you can search databases maintained by these organizations. You can perform such searches on-line at a variety of locations, one of which is through Cybersmith in New Brunswick (**http://www.csi.nb.ca**); at this location you can search for details in the Canadian (**.ca**) domain:

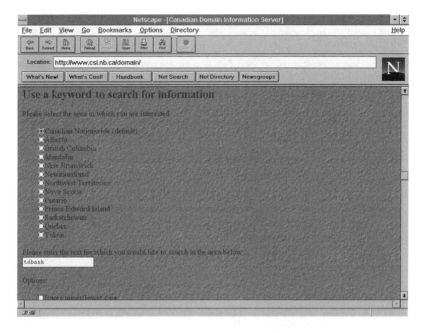

For example, if you search for the TD Bank, you are provided with a record for the domain **tdbank.ca**:

```
Subdomain:      tdbank.ca
Date-Received:  1994/05/17
Date-Approved:  1994/06/27
Date-Modified:  1995/01/12
Organization:   Toronto-Dominion Bank
Type:           Class A Canadian Chartered Bank
Description:    Large Banking Institution with over 1800 branches across
                Canada.
Admin-Name:     Rick Kwasnicki
Admin-Title:    Manager, Network Gateway Services
Admin-Postal:   Toronto Dominion Bank
                Central Computing Facility
                PO Box 1, Toronto Dominion Centre
                Toronto, Ontario
                M5K 1A2
Admin-Phone:    +1 (416) 982-5385
Admin-Fax:      +1 (416) 982-4527
Admin-Mailbox:  kwasnr@tdbank.ca
Tech-Name:      Osama Arafat
Tech-Title:     System Administrator
Tech-Postal:    InfoRamp Inc.
                134 Adelaide St. East
                Suite 207
                Toronto, Ontario
                M5C 1K9
Tech-Phone:     +1 (416) 393-9100
Tech-Fax:       +1 (416) 393-3551
Tech-Mailbox:   osama@inforamp.net
Location:       52 04 05 N / 97 37 46 W
```

You can access the entire Canadian domain directory at the URL **ftp://ftp.cdnnet.ca/ ca-domain**. From the choices presented once there, retrieve the document **index-by-organi zation** or **index-by-subdomain** for a complete, up-to-date list. You can also choose **directories-**

flat or **directories-hierarchical** to take a look at individual company listings. (This CA Domain information is also available at **gopher://owl.nstn.ns.ca /11/White%20Pages** and **gopher://gopher.fonorola.net/11/ca-domain**.)

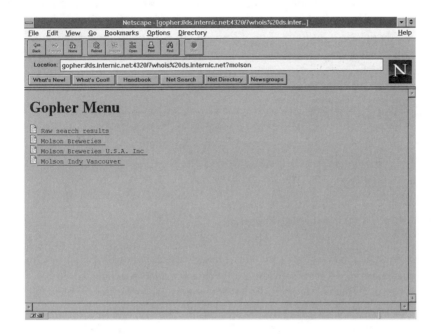

You can also search the InterNIC in the same way, at **gopher://internic.net** or **http:// www.internic.net**.

Contacting the Postmaster or Contact Name

Once you know the details about the company, you could try sending your message to the person by "guessing" the e-mail ID, based on the domain name. For example, if you are trying to reach John Smith at XYZ company, and you know the domain registration for XYZ is **xyz.com**, you could try sending a message to

- ◆ jsmith@xyz.com,
- ◆ john_smith@xyz.com,
- ◆ j.smith@xyz.com,
- ◆ smithj@xyz.com,

or any other derivation thereof. However, such a method is obviously hit and miss and is just as likely to upset a number of people as it is to enjoy any success.

When it is really important, you can usually send a message to the postmaster or contact name at a particular location to ask how you might get in touch with someone at their organization. Most locations on the Internet have a postmaster account for their organization, for example, **postmaster@epo.gov.on.ca**, which is the postmaster for the Province of Ontario.

Obviously, this will not work if you try to ask the question of a postmaster at an extremely large organization or commercial on-line e-mail system, for example, **postmaster@ibm.com** or **postmaster@compuserve.com**.

Use such queries with discretion, since you should remember that there is an individual at the other end of the system who might be swamped with requests. Do not be surprised, or angry, if you do not get a response. And if someone does respond, remember common courtesy and send a thank you.

Useful E-Mail Tools

With the emergence of the Internet, e-mail has become increasingly sophisticated, and there are a number of tools that you might consider useful if you are joining the network or expanding the capabilities that you already have.

Mail Robots

Often, the Internet solves unique problems through the simplest of methods. One problem on the Internet has to do with providing only those people who have an e-mail link to the Internet with the ability to retrieve files or documents. To solve the problem, the Internet came up with the concept of the "mail robot." E-mail filters can be used to implement a simple and effective mail robot, so that messages sent to a certain ID are automatically replied to with certain text.

A mail robot is a program that runs at the receiving e-mail location, takes apart an incoming message, and mails back some type of response automatically. Organizations are using e-mail robots to permit individuals throughout the Internet to easily request information from a company. Try one out: for an up-to-date message concerning the *Canadian Internet Handbook*, send a message to **info@handbook.com**. You will receive an automatic response via e-mail, usually within hours. Or send a message to the corporate mail robot **managingpartner@mccarthy.ca**.

Mail robots can be implemented quite easily with many popular e-mail systems and by many Internet service providers as well. Mail robots are close cousins to "listservs," which are discussed in Chapter 8.

MIME

As organizations began to exchange Internet e-mail with each other around the globe, they soon realized that there was no standard method to exchange computer files. Today, e-mail on the Internet is still very much a technology that simply permits people to exchange plain text. Standards like uuencode discussed previously are used here and there, but are by no means universal. MIME, the emerging multimedia Internet mail extensions standard, intends to change that.

Begun as a grassroots initiative on the Internet, it is poised to emerge as a global standard for the exchange of e-mail between different systems and platforms in which messages can contain voice, sound, video, binary files, images, or any other type of item. Imagine receiving an e-mail message containing digitized video with the text "Here's a video of the conference proceedings; in particular, check out what happened to Dan when the podium collapsed on him!" It is possible today for those with high-speed links to the Internet to send and to receive such e-mail messages.

Even though the sender and recipient are on completely different computer platforms, MIME will permit the easy exchange of such a message with all information about the particular file format remaining intact. This is a huge advance over current technology, since it would let the recipient immediately view the video file, if that particular video application were supported on the recipient PC system, simply by clicking on the attachment with a mouse.

Imagine receiving an e-mail message with the text "Hey, here's a document that I thought you should look at." With MIME, the message does not contain the actual document, but simply a pointer back to the document. By clicking on the pointer in the message, a program is invoked that goes to retrieve the file. MIME does this by supporting such items as Telnet and FTP commands within the body of an e-mail message. If you really want the document, your MIME mail reader will go off and get it; but only when and if you want it.

MIME will also enable the emergence of "hypertext" e-mail messages, messages that may contain, for example, a questionnaire, with the questions changing depending on the answers that you provide. The arrival of MIME will cause a massive change in the role of e-mail and will permit the development of many new applications that people are only just beginning to discover.

Problems with Internet E-Mail

Finally, if you plan on using Internet e-mail in your organization, there are a number of important considerations that you should think of:

◆ Internet e-mail is not necessarily secure nor is it private. The Internet is a cooperative global network, built upon a protocol (TCP/IP) that involves the routing of information through different paths in the network. This means that mail is sometimes routed through various systems on the network; at any point your e-mail message could be compromised. An Internet e-mail message is subject not only to possible access by third parties somewhere in its travels, but its contents could also be changed.

◆ Internet e-mail does not necessarily guarantee delivery nor is it necessarily fast. There is nothing to ensure that an Internet message is received. Sometimes systems disappear, and sometimes they go down. The result is that your message might not be sent. In some cases, you will be told of the failed delivery, and in other cases you might not. With some Internet e-mail systems you can request a "receipt" for messages that you have sent; however, you are not guaranteed that you will get such a receipt back. The result is that if you need a business application that guarantees delivery of e-mail with proof of delivery, the Internet is not the system for you.

◆ Internet e-mail can be forged. It is relatively easy for a person familiar with Internet e-mail protocols to forge e-mail. An experienced user could send you a message from **president@whitehouse.gov**, and you might be thrilled to receive such a message, but it is unlikely that Bill Clinton would decide to send you a message. There is no mechanism in Internet e-mail to prove the authenticity of the sender. However, the use of "digital signatures" is becoming increasingly commonplace on the Internet and will make forgery much more difficult in the future. With a digital signature it is possible to determine if the message has been tampered with and verify that the author is who says he is. Some predict that digital signatures will become much more widespread in the next 12 to 18 months on the Internet.

These issues result in the reluctance by some organizations to use Internet e-mail for anything more than casual messaging.

To solve the security problem, some organizations on the Internet use software that encrypts inbound and outbound messages, both to protect their contents and to ensure their authenticity. Such a capability does exist, but does involve some extra expense.

Mike Martineau of NSTN thinks the security issue is overblown. "It is quite possible for an organization to use a package like Pegasus (with built-in encryption) and delivery confirmation to build a secure e-mail system over the Internet. As well, encryption and authentication standards are in development and will be used by companies such as NSTN, who are aiming their services at small- and medium-sized businesses, businesses which cannot afford to set up their own private networks and for whom the Internet offers a cost-effective alternative."

The reality is that, despite the shortcomings, the use of Internet e-mail continues to explode. In the same way that people continue to use cellular phones, people continue to use Internet e-mail. In your case, if you have a great deal of sensitive e-mail, you should encrypt it. If you do not, you should always be cognizant of some of these fundamental concerns.

Knowledge Networking

Internet mailing lists and USENET are the two primary methods by which you can "knowledge network" through the Internet.

The Benefit of Knowledge Networking

If you have the need to be an expert on a particular topic, or wish to bring yourself up-to-date on a certain issue, or wish to find an answer to a question, you can often use the Internet as a means of "knowledge networking." Knowledge networking is the term used to describe the ability to harness on-line information, either by regularly tracking information on a particular topic by receiving information on that topic or by seeking information or answers to questions by discussing a topic with others on-line.

By participating in Internet knowledge networks found in mailing lists and USENET newsgroups, you can receive information on specific topics on a regular basis and can join discussion topics with others. The unique cooperative nature of the Internet means that information is available to you on thousands of topics and from thousands of sources. For example, you can

- ◆ subscribe to formal or informal electronic journals and newsletters published by individuals or organizations from around the world;

- ◆ join mailing lists that will send you announcements of concerts, events, new publications or new products, or information about new initiatives by various organizations and governments;

◆ participate in discussions with thousands of others from around the world on a variety of topics, ranging from the serious to the ridiculous.

Mailing Lists versus USENET

A mailing list is a collection of e-mail addresses. Any message sent to the address of the mailing list is automatically sent to the address of every member of the mailing list. There are thousands of mailing lists on all kinds of topics, and you can join practically any list by sending a specially formatted e-mail message to a system that manages the list. Mailing lists are a quick and easy method of distributing information, whether it is a newsletter or a question from a member of the list. Information that you receive from mailing lists comes in with your regular Internet e-mail; no special software is required to read a message sent to a mailing list, although special software is used to manage the mailing list itself.

USENET, on the other hand, is a global system for the exchange of information on thousands of topics, referred to as "newsgroups." Individuals can subscribe to any particular newsgroup, read information sent to the newsgroup, and add or "post" information to the newsgroup. Each posting is referred to as a "news article." There are also "follow-ups" and "replies" in USENET. A "follow-up" is a comment made to a previous posting, while a "reply" is an e-mail message that you send to someone directly. USENET is like a massive global bulletin board with thousands of different information resources. You read the USENET newsgroups that you belong to with "newsreader" software, which also permits you to post messages to USENET.

What Is the Difference?

Although the mechanics of a mailing list and USENET differ, both permit you to

KNOWLEDGE NETWORKING

1. You can "knowledge network" on the Internet either by regularly tracking information on a particular topic or by seeking information or answers to questions by discussing a topic with others on-line.

2. Knowledge networking is undertaken through two areas of the Internet known as USENET and electronic mailing lists.

3. USENET is a global system used for the exchange of information on thousands of topics called newsgroups.

4. Electronic mailing lists are collections of e-mail addresses organized into a list used to communicate about a particular topic.

5. There are extensive resources throughout the Internet to help you find particular USENET newsgroups and mailing lists.

join a particular group and receive information or converse with people concerning a topic within the group. Anyone with an Internet e-mail address can join any number of mailing lists; your only constraint will be the volume of information that you can read each day.

USENET newsgroups are not much different in concept from mailing lists. Since you can obtain USENET news through most Internet service providers, you can choose to subscribe to the newsgroups that interest you. Given current estimates that some 100 megabytes of information are posted to USENET each day, you will have to be selective with respect to which newsgroups you subscribe. The major differences between USENET newsgroups and mailing lists are the following:

◆ USENET information is more structured, with individual postings filed into particular newsgroups. In contrast, e-mail messages from mailing lists are part of your general e-mailbox, unless you have some type of special filtering software. (This is the benefit of e-mail filtering software, as discussed in Chapter 7.)

◆ Most USENET newsgroups undergo a series of steps of approval before they become widely distributed through the USENET system. On the other hand, anyone can start a mailing list on any topic if he/she has the right software.

◆ USENET has a culture that frowns upon networking for commercial purposes. Mailing lists can be used for anything, as long as you do not abuse the primary purpose for which a particular mailing list was established.

◆ USENET news articles have a limited life span. Because of the large number of USENET messages, many sites will delete messages beyond a certain date (usually two weeks, and sometimes much less). Messages sent to mailing lists will last as long as messages last in your mailbox.

◆ USENET news articles are not sent to personal mailboxes, but are received in batches of postings, which are then made available for reading through newsreader software.

◆ USENET was designed as a mechanism to permit the rebroadcasting of information on a very wide basis. Any USENET article goes out to all the Internet hosts on the planet that wish to receive that specific newsgroup or that do not refuse that newsgroup. E-mail, on the other hand, was designed as a point-to-point method of communicating, and even with mailing lists, suffers from some problems when trying to be a broadcast tool.

Other than these points, USENET is very similar in concept to mailing lists, since it permits people to participate in knowledge networking with others from around the globe on a variety of topics.

To make matters more complex, there are also some "bidirectionally gated newsgroups" within USENET. Any news article sent to such a USENET newsgroup is also distributed automatically to others via a mailing list, meaning that even if you do not have access to USENET, you might be able to receive copies of postings to a particular newsgroup through your e-mail account.

USENET

USENET is described by many as the "world's largest bulletin board system," even though it is definitely not a bulletin board system. USENET consists of several thousand topic areas known as "newsgroups," with topics ranging from locksmithing to pyrotechnics to religion to C++ computer programming. Within these newsgroups people discuss, debate, and share information concerning the topic at hand. Given the global nature of the Internet, and the fact that there are thousands of topics available, there is a wealth of information that you can obtain through USENET.

What Can I Do with USENET?

Before we describe how USENET works and what it is made up of, we should give you an idea of what you can do in this area of the Internet. Through USENET you can

- ◆ join newsgroups (topics) that are of interest;
- ◆ discuss, debate, keep current or ask questions about these newsgroups;
- ◆ receive newsletters or other information through some of these newsgroups;
- ◆ retrieve documents known as "frequently asked questions" (FAQs) related to these newsgroups.

Unmoderated Newsgroups

Many USENET newsgroups are used for interactive discussion between people interested in a common topic. There are thousands of topics, ranging from the serious to the bizarre, from mainstream to controversial, from conservative to silly. Many of the newsgroups are "unmoderated," that is, anyone can post information as long as they stick to the topic. (If they do not, they will get flamed, a topic discussed in Chapter 7.) For example, **alt.architecture** is used for the exchange of information between people involved in or interested in architectural issues. Here is a listing of just some of the topics discussed on a certain date:

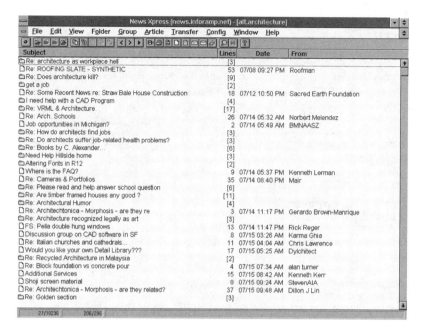

The power of USENET is that anyone can join a general discussion newsgroup like **alt.architecture** and post a question to people who belong to that newsgroup. Because of the unique cooperative spirit of the Internet, you will more often than not get answers from several people. In this case, we can see a question that has been asked, and the answer someone offered in response:

"Discussions" through USENET occur over a period of days and weeks (and often months) rather than in real time. Hence you can check every once in a while to see what is new. (However, keep in mind articles "expire"; due to the overwhelming volume of information that flows through USENET, most ISPs only keep articles for a week or two.)

Moderated Newsgroups

Of course, one of the problems with USENET is directly related to the massive growth of the Internet; as more and more people join the network, several things have begun to happen to USENET:

◆ The volume of information has increased substantially, such that you often cannot keep up-to-date on your chosen newsgroups.

◆ Expanding use of the network means that you might have to pay attention to a lot of other opinions that might not have existed in the newsgroup before. People who have a different point of view sometimes strenuously stress that point of view, causing you discomfort. Battles erupt and rage on topics unrelated to the newsgroup, causing you to leave the group until things return to normal.

◆ Cranks, kooks, nuts — people whose mental state might seriously be in doubt — post to many areas of USENET, causing you great frustration.[1]

One result of these problems has been a steady increase in the number of "moderated" groups. Within such groups, a volunteer or series of volunteers takes the time to "preread" postings to a particular group. Only those that fit the spirit (or "charter") of the newsgroup are posted. This helps to ensure that the group is focused on the topic at hand and helps to weed out a lot of the crank or useless postings that you might find in other unmoderated groups.

A very good example of a moderated group is **comp.dcom.telecom**, where people share information concerning telecommunication-related issues. In the case below, a moderator has "approved" all postings:

---

1. USENET is a wild and wonderful place and often responds to problems with a sense of humor. There is a newsgroup, **alt.kook.of.month**, in which people vote for whom they believe is the individual on USENET most obviously not in tune with their mental faculties. There must be something about Canada — Canadians have won the award many times.

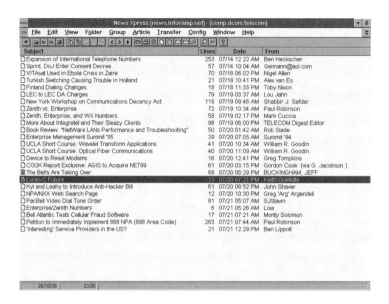

Some do not agree with the concept of moderated groups, while others think they are a good solution to a serious and growing problem on USENET. Whatever your opinion, keep in mind that USENET is a big place, and that often there are solutions for people who are on either side of the fence. For example, there is a similar telecommunications group, **alt.dcom.telecom**, which is not moderated, and which permits people to post anything related to the telecommunications topic. If you don't like the moderated aspect of **comp.dcom.telecom**, join the unmoderated **alt.dcom.telecom**.

USENET is used for many lighthearted purposes, but has a scientific side as well. Many moderated groups are used for reporting scientific information and other research; **sci.astro.hubble** is a group used by many space-related organizations for the posting of information directly related to the Hubble Space Telescope, for example:

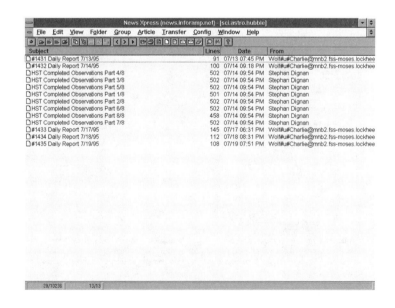

Lockheed posts a daily report of scheduled Hubble activities to the newsgroup, and thus **sci.astro.hubble** has become one of the primary methods by which space scientists worldwide keep in tune with projects and experiments involving the telescope.

ClariNews Newsgroups

A special type of USENET newsgroup can be found in the ClariNews topic, a special service offered by a few Internet service providers in Canada. ClariNews is a commercial newsgroup for which you or your provider must pay a subscription fee. ClariNews redistributes news stories from various global newswires. With approximately 300 topics covered, it is a good source of up-to-date news information. An example newsgroup in the ClariNews section is **clari.biz.industry.tourism**, where news articles concerning the tourism industry are accessible:

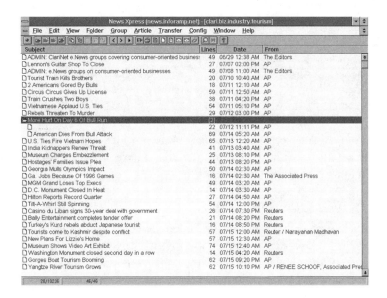

There are a number of Canadian ClariNews topics, such as this item from a Canadian business group:

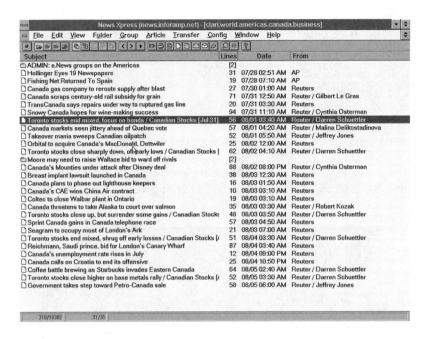

You might want to check to see if your Internet service provider provides access to ClariNews. If not, and you are interested in it, you can subscribe directly at **http://www.clarinews.com** or by sending a message to **info@clarinews.com**.

Frequently Asked Questions (FAQs)

Many newsgroups put together a FAQ, a document designed to answer the most frequently asked questions that new participants might ask within a newsgroup. FAQs are a good source of information about a particular topic, and if you plan to join a newsgroup, you should read its FAQ so that you do not ask questions that the group has talked about many times before, and so that you understand what types of discussions are appropriate (should one exist; they do not exist for all USENET newsgroups). FAQs are often used to detail the etiquette of the particular group, the "charter" of the group (which we discuss below). They are also often used to describe other sources of information related to the topic.

For example, here is the introductory page of the FAQ for the **rec.music.reggae** newsgroup, available at **http://www.cis.ohio-state.edu/hypertext/faq/usenet/music/reggae/top.html**:

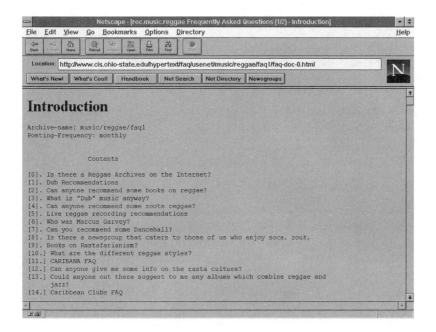

Many USENET FAQs can be found on-line at the following locations: **http://www.cis.ohio-state.edu/hypertext/faq/usenet/** and **ftp://rtfm.mit.edu/pub/usenet/**. You can also find a lot of FAQs in the newsgroups **news.answers** and **rec.answers**.

Newsgroup Archives

Finally, although it is useful to be able to participate on an ongoing basis in some USENET newsgroups, sometimes you might want to search postings that were made in the past to a particular USENET newsgroup. Some USENET newsgroups are automatically archived and are stored on various computers around the Internet. A comprehensive list of archived newsgroups can be found at **http://starbase.neosoft.com/~claird/news.lists/rootnewsgroup_archives.html** and **http://www.pitt.edu/~grouprev/Usenet/Archive-List/newsgroup_archives.html**.

The document "USENET Moderated Archive List" is a good, comprehensive summary of USENET archives. To obtain this listing using e-mail, send a blank message to **send-mod-archives@ftp.sterling.com**. To obtain this document on-line, contact **ftp://ftp.sterling.com/moderators/Archives.html** or **ftp://ftp.sterling.com/moderators/Archives.txt**.

There are also systems emerging that let you search thousands of USENET newsgroups. For example, DejaNews (**http://www.dejanews.com**) lets you undertake a search for words or phrases appearing in newsgroups:

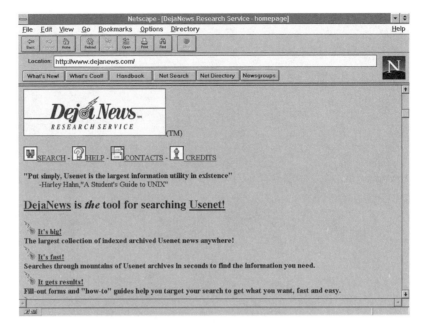

You can specify the sophistication of your search in several ways:

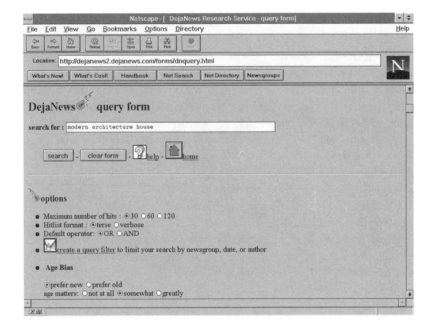

Here is the result of a search for USENET postings that contain the words "modern architecture" and "house":

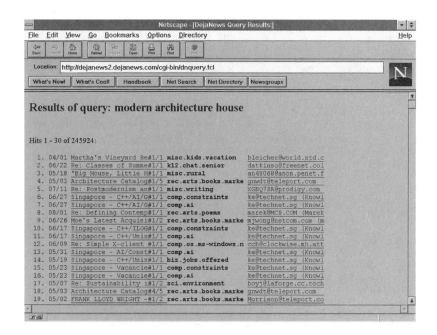

Another similar service is Infoseek, available at **http://www.infoseek.com**.

You can also try Stanford University Netnews (**http://woodstock.stanford.edu** or by e-mail, **info@netnews.stanford.edu**), which allows you to set a search profile of items/topics you wish to track within USENET. On a daily basis you are sent, via e-mail, the first few lines of any postings that match your search profile. You can then quickly retrieve the full text of any item by sending back the unique number for that posting.

Newsgroup Categories

Newsgroups within USENET belong to a series of categories. The major (global) newsgroup categories are listed in the following table:

CATEGORY	TOPIC
biz.	Business-oriented topics
comp.	Computer-oriented topics
misc.	Topics that do not fit elsewhere
news.	News and information concerning the Internet or USENET
rec.	Recreational activities, such as bowling, skiing, chess
sci.	Scientific topics
soc.	Sociological issues
talk.	Debate-oriented topics

There is also an **alt.** group. What can you find in **alt.** groups? You name it, **alt.** groups likely discuss it. Anyone can start an **alt.** group without approval, but not all Internet service providers carry all **alt.** groups. The result is a somewhat freewheeling atmosphere, with some of the most controversial newsgroups being located in the **alt.** category.

Subtopics

Each category consists of several hundred or thousands of topics, organized in subcategories. For example, the newsgroup category **rec.** (recreation topics) includes the subcategories

◆ **rec.arts**;

◆ **rec.audio**;

◆ **rec.music**;

and from this, a further categorization exists, for example

◆ **rec.arts.poems**;

◆ **rec.arts.misc**;

◆ **rec.arts.bonsai**.

For very popular topics, another level of categorization might be found. For example, because of the popularity of science fiction within the Internet, there are several science fiction newsgroups within the **rec.arts.sf** category, including

◆ **rec.arts.sf.misc**;

◆ **rec.arts.sf.movies**;

◆ **rec.arts.sf.science**.

An individual could choose to subscribe to all the **rec.arts.sf** groups (getting all three above as well as others) or could choose to subscribe to only the **rec.arts.sf.movies** group.

Canadian Newsgroup Categories

A separate set of newsgroup categories exists for Canadian USENET topics, consisting of a **can.** hierarchy as well as separate hierarchies for some provinces and some major cities in Canada. The categories include the following (excluding specific university categories found in Canada):

CATEGORY	TOPIC	CATEGORY	TOPIC
ab.	Alberta	**mtl.**	Montreal
atl.	Atlantic	**nf.**	Newfoundland
bc.	British Columbia	**niagara.**	Niagara
calgary.	Calgary	**ns.**	Nova Scotia
can.	Canadian	**ont.**	Ontario
edm.	Edmonton	**ott.**	Ottawa
hfx.	Halifax	**pei.**	Prince Edward Island
kingston.	Kingston	**qc.**	Quebec
kw.	Kitchener/Waterloo	**sj.**	St. John's
man.	Manitoba	**tor.**	Toronto
nt.	Northwest Territories	**van.**	Vancouver
yk.	Yukon	**wpg.**	Winnipeg

Some of the more popular Canadian newsgroups in the **can.** hierarchy include

♦ **can.general**. In this discussion of general Canadian issues, there is a wide-ranging number of topics, with debates, arguments, discussion, and announcements. A little bit of everything.

♦ **can.jobs**. A *lot* of job postings are made to this group. Many are for people with computer expertise, with a large number of postings by personnel agencies. However, we also see postings for other types of jobs and professional positions.

♦ **can.politics**. Deficits, governments, and all the related topics are discussed here. A very busy newsgroup. Be prepared to argue.

♦ **can.domain**. Announcements of organizations newly registered in the Canadian Internet domain are made in this newsgroup: a good way to track who is getting involved in the Internet in Canada. Some discussion of policies and procedures relevant to registration under the **ca.** domain also occurs.

There are many provincial discussion groups; in addition, several communities in Canada are very active with their local Internet newsgroups, including those within the **kw.** (Kitchener–Waterloo), **ott.** (Ottawa), and **tor.** (Toronto) newsgroups. A list of significant Canadian USENET newsgroups is found in Appendix F.

A Sample USENET Message

A USENET message looks like an e-mail message, with some subtle differences. The primary difference is that a newsgroup message includes a reference to the newsgroups to which the information was posted. Here is an example of a new posting:

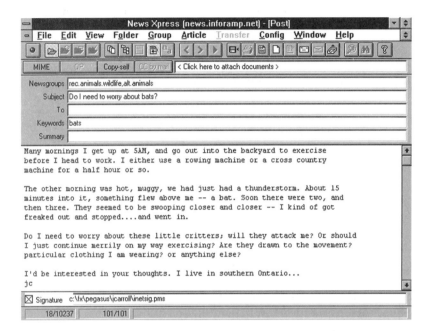

If we save the message to a file, we can see the structure that it has when it is sent through USENET:

Path: inforamp.net!ts1-06
From: jcarroll@jacc.com (Jim Carroll)
Newsgroups: rec.animals.wildlife,alt.animals
Subject: Do I need to worry about bats?
Date: Sat, 22 Jul 95 00:22:51 GMT
Organization: J.A. Carroll Consulting
Lines: 21
Message-ID: <3uqn65$4c6@inforamp.net>
NNTP-Posting-Host: ts1-06.inforamp.net
Keywords: bats
X-Newsreader: News Xpress Version 1.0 Beta #4
Xref: inforamp.net rec.animals.wildlife:3663 alt.animals:127
Status: N
Many mornings I get up at 5AM, and go out into the backyard to exercise
before I head to work. I either use a rowing machine or a cross country
machine for a half hour or so.

The other morning was hot, muggy, we had just had a thunderstorm. About 15
minutes into it, something flew above me -- a bat. Soon there were two, and
then three. They seemed to be swooping closer and closer -- I kind of got
freaked out and stopped....and went in.
Do I need to worry about these little critters; will they attack me? Or should
I just continue merrily on my way exercising? Are they drawn to the movement?
particular clothing I am wearing? or anything else?
I'd be interested in your thoughts. I live in southern Ontario...
jc
Jim Carroll, C.A. 905.855.2950 jcarroll@jacc.com
www.e-commerce.com/jacc.html
Co-Author, Canadian Internet Handbook/Canadian Internet Advantage

There are several components to the posting:

- The posting has been made to the **rec.animals.wildlife** and **alt.animals** news-groups.

- Each posting has a subject, date, and organization (should you list one in your software).

- Most newsreader software lets you list key words. This helps people quickly determine whether they want to read a particular posting. You can also key in a summary.

- The text of the message also contains other information that uniquely identifies the message to USENET.

When this message is "posted," it is sent to the news system at the Internet service provider. From there, the unique replication or duplication method found in USENET transmits the message to all other Internet service providers and Internet servers which carry that particular newsgroup within minutes, hours, and in some cases, days. The message will soon be available around the world and will be viewed by people who "subscribe" to the **rec.animals.wildlife** and **alt.animals** newsgroups.[2]

How Does USENET Work?

To understand what USENET is and how it works, consider the newsgroup **rec.sport.football.canadian**. Formed a number of years ago, it was established to provide a convenient discussion forum for the Canadian version of the sport.

Creating a Newsgroup

The process through which **rec.sport.football.canadian** was created sheds some light on how USENET currently operates. Note that this process applies for the "big-7 hierarchy," that is,

---

2. Subsequent postings from people who read the note confirmed that we do not need to worry about bats in Southern Ontario.

for the **comp.**, **rec.**, **sci.**, **news.**, **soc.**, **talk.**, and **misc.** newsgroups. Procedures for other hierarchies might vary.

♦ The individual who wanted to start the newsgroup sent a message to the moderator of the USENET newsgroup **news.announce.newgroups** as well as to several other newsgroups, indicating why such a newsgroup should be formed. The message contained a "charter" for the group, that is, the reasons for the group, and an overview of the purposes for which the group would be used (the discussion of Canadian football). The message was posted to **news.announce.newgroups** by the moderator of that group.

♦ A period of discussion concerning the merits of having a special group devoted to Canadian football took place within the newsgroup **news.groups** for a month or so. Anyone could have participated in this discussion.

♦ Once the period of discussion was complete, a "call for votes" went out for people to vote on whether the group should be created. A designated period of time was set aside for voting, and an individual volunteered to be the official vote-taker. Everyone was permitted to vote.

♦ Once the period of time was up (usually 21–30 days), the votes were tabulated, and the group was found to have met the standard USENET acceptance criteria (the standard rules are that there are at least 100 more "yes" votes than "no" votes and at least two-thirds of the votes must be "yes").

♦ Since the group "passed," a "newsgroup control message" was sent out by David Lawrence,[3] the moderator of the **news.announce.newgroups** newsgroup, advising all USENET sites that **rec.sport.football.canadian** was now considered to be on the "official" USENET list. The "newsgroup control message" provides the group with "official status." Everyone was advised of the results of the vote. Here is the original message pertaining to **rec.sport.football.canadian**:

>From 2893684@qucdn.queensu.ca Thu Jul 8 17:13:59 1993

Path: uunet!bounce-back

From: Andy <2893684@qucdn.queensu.ca>

Newsgroups:news.announce.newgroups,news.groups,soc.culture.canada,can.general,rec.sport.football
.pro,rec.sport.hockey,rec.sport.football.misc Subject: RESULT:rec.sport.football.canadian passes
175:27

Followup-To: news.groups Date: 8 Jul1993 11:10:15 -0400

Organization: Queen's University at Kingston Lines: 232

Sender: tale@rodan.UU.NET

Approved: tale@uunet.uu.net

---

3. In this role, David Lawrence comes the closest to being a central authority for USENET. He maintains his position as the result of having built up a large amount of trust and respect from all members of the USENET community through the years.

Message-ID:<21hdcnINNfd7@rodan.UU.NET>

NNTP-Posting-Host: rodan.uu.net

Xref: uunetnews.announce.newgroups:3775 news.groups:75889 soc.culture.canada:21106can.general:17008 rec.sport.football.pro:55872 rec.sport.hockey:63082rec.sport.football.misc:1835

As of 23:59 5 July 1993 (last moment votes can be accepted), the resolution to create rec.sport.football.canadian has PASSED by a margin of 175 YES votes (87%) to 27 NO votes (13%). As the number of YES votes outnumber that of NO votes by a margin of more than 2:1 and as there are at least 100 more YES votes than NO votes, both conditions for the creation of r.s.f.c have been met. There was one spoiled vote which would not have changed the outcome had it been counted. The voters' list is as follows [not reproduced here].

◆ Had **rec.sport.football.canadian** not passed the vote, a newsgroup control message to create the group would not have been sent out by David Lawrence, and the group would not be an official group. The result would have been that most USENET locations would refuse to carry the group, since it had not passed the vote. (In fact, it could even end up on a list of invalid newsgroups.) Everyone is advised of the results of the vote in a message like the one above. Those who ignore the guidance over how to establish a new newsgroup will almost certainly fail in their attempt.

◆ A list of new newsgroups is regularly posted to **news.announce.newsgroups**. When **rec.sport.football.canadian** was created, it would have been included in an announcement of "New USENET Groups." If **rec.sport.football.canadian** had *not* passed, a notice to this effect would be included in the "New USENET Groups" message. This is another method by which system operators around the world decide to carry a message, or exclude it.

◆ Another factor is that even though it is now an official newsgroup, any USENET site has the choice of whether or not it carries the **rec.sport.football.canadian** newsgroup

Here is the original charter for the **rec.sport.football.canadian** newsgroup:

>From 2893684@qucdn.queensu.ca Thu May 6 15:00:55 1993

Path: uunet!bounce-back

From: Andy <2893684@qucdn.queensu.ca>

Newsgroups:news.announce.newgroups,news.groups,soc.culture.canada,rec.sport.football.pro,rec.sport.football.misc Subject: RFD: rec.sport.football.canadian

Followup-To: news.groups

Date: 4 May 1993 19:42:56 -0400

Organization: Queen's University at Kingston

Lines: 28 Sender: tale@rodan.UU.NET

Approved: tale@uunet.uu.net

Message-ID: <1s6v20INN99p@rodan.UU.NET>

Xref: uunet.news.announce.newgroups:3542 news.groups:71409 soc.culture.canada:18619
rec.sport.football.pro:52567 rec.sport.football.misc:1743

RFD: Formation of Canadian Football newsgroup.

Time for discussion: 30 days starting May 4, 1993

NAME: rec.sport.football.canadian

STATUS: unmoderated

RATIONALE: There is currently no appropriate group in which to discuss

Canadian football and specifically the Canadian Football League. Canadian football is one of the oldest professional sports in North America with a long and honourable tradition and deserves discussion space. Reasons for r.a.f.c include the number of Canadians both in Canada and abroad who are CFL fans; the expansion of the CFL to the United States and the need to answer questions, provide a forum for discussion for Americans who are new to the game; discussion of the advantages and disadvantages of 3-down football and the effect that the larger field has on the game; the fact that many leading NFL coaches and players spent their early career in the CFL, r.a.f.c could thus give NFL fans a chance to familiarise themselves on possible NFL stars of tomorrow

CHARTER: Discussion topics open to anything of interest to participants particularly the CFL and CIAU (university football in Canada) Canadian rules and style, players and coaches, reviews of games, future of the league in Canada and the U.S., desirability or undesirability of the NFL adopting some Canadian rules, etc.

It is this global cooperative effort concerning the establishment of new newsgroups that is at the heart of USENET.

There are many documents around the Internet that pertain to the creation of a USENET newsgroup, including the following, which you can obtain on-line:

- "How to create a new USENET newsgroup" (**http://scwww.ucs.indiana.edu/ NetRsc/usenet.html**);

- "USENET newsgroup creation companion" (**http://www.cis.ohio-state.edu/ hypertext/faq/usenet/creating-newsgroups/part1/faq.html**);

- "So you want to create an alt newsgroup" (**http://www.math.psu.edu/barr/alt-creation-guide.html**);

- "Archives of USENET newsgroup charters and proposals" (1989 to current date) (this is an excellent resource if you want to create a new newsgroup and want to see what a charter looks like) (**ftp://ftp.uu.net/usenet/news.announce.newgroups**).

You can also check the USENET newsgroups **news.groups**, **alt.config**, **news.admin.misc**. A good pointer to all kinds of on-line information about USENET can be found at **http:// scwww.ucs.indiana.edu/NetRsc/usenet.html**.

Creating Newsgroups in the Canadian Hierarchy

The process above applies to the main USENET newsgroups, that is, **comp.**, **news.**, **soc.**, **rec.**, etc. The process does not apply to newsgroups in the Canadian hierarchy (i.e., **can.**, **ont.**, and others). In fact, there is no *formal* process for the creation of newsgroups in Canada. However, keep in mind that USENET exists because of the cooperation of many individuals, whether they be computer system administrators at universities, businesses and organizations or at Internet service providers or people who volunteer their own time to USENET administration. Because of this cooperative spirit, there is more or less an informal process in place involving creation of groups in some of the Canadian hierarchies.

For example, within the Canadian hierarchy (**can.**) a method has evolved in which proposals for new topics are posted and discussed in the newsgroup **can.config**. If there are no major objections, and if the consensus is that the group should be created, then a control message is propagated by a volunteer, and the group is created at Internet service providers across the country and in some others around the world (depending on who wants to carry Canadian newsgroups).

The process, as it currently exists, is summarized quite nicely in an FAQ maintained by Dawn Whiteside (**dawn@ca.dynix.com**). The document is posted on a regular basis to **can.config** and is also available at **ftp://ca.dynix.com/usenet/can.config**. The following comments, taken directly from the FAQ, put into perspective the role of **can.config**:

Subject: So this is **can.config.** What's it for?

It's a newsgroup for the discussion and evolution of the **can.*** hierarchy. Discussion of and requests for the charters of existing **can.*** groups and discussions related to the creation, removal or modification of **can.*** newsgroups are welcome here.

The document also addresses how new groups should be proposed:

New **can.*** newsgroups are proposed in **can.config**, similar to the procedure for creating new **alt.*** groups. The RFD is followed by a short (typically two weeks or less) discussion period which results in a general concensus as to whether or not the group will be created.

Is **can.config** the formal process for creation of new USENET newsgroups in the **can.** hierarchy? Certainly not. The FAQ addresses the fact that no real consensus has yet emerged:

While there have been many ideas and suggestions about newsgroup creation procedures here, no real consensus appears to have been reached at this point in time. What you want to do is convince the majority of Canadian news administrators to create the new newsgroup so it is propagated well across the country.

Yet, a tour on-line reveals that the **can.config** process is working remarkably well and seems to be the closest thing to a formal process for newsgroup creation in Canada.

What about provincial groups? In that case, no formal process exists, so it would seem you would have to sell your idea for a new discussion group within the general discussion group for a particular province or city.

Our advice? Since USENET succeeds based on its cooperative spirit, you must learn to work within the unique culture that it presents. If you want to see a new group created in the **can.** hierarchy, retrieve the document mentioned above, study it carefully, retrieve the other FAQs that it mentions, study them carefully, and then talk to an experienced Internet user about how to make your pitch for a new USENET newsgroup. Do not try to do it without knowing what you are doing, since you will more than likely be doomed to failure.

Finally, the informal process of creation of newsgroups in Canada is strengthened through the circulation of periodic "checkgroup messages," which detail the Canadian newsgroups that have more or less been accepted by the Canadian USENET community. This has lead to a high degree of consistency in what are accepted as the "official" Canadian USENET newsgroups.

Reading News

Once the newsgroup **rec.sport.football.canadian** was approved, people could subscribe to the newsgroup and could begin posting information to it. Hence, upon approval,

◆ Messages posted to **rec.sport.football.canadian** are now transmitted throughout the USENET system.

◆ Individual users of USENET choose which newsgroups they wish to join. Those with an interest in the CFL choose to belong to the **rec.sport.football.canadian** list.

◆ People throughout the world then read that newsgroup using their newsreader software.

Newsreader Software

Newsreader software is the computer program that lets you access USENET news. Just like electronic mail, many people on USENET will not be using the same "newsreader software." And some individuals will use USENET "on-line," that is, while linked to the computer of their Internet service provider by modem or some other link. Others use it "off-line," that is, all USENET articles for groups they belong to are transferred to their computer or local network and are read locally while not linked to another computer.

There are many different newsreader programs available; for example, tin, nn, Emacs and gnus are found on UNIX systems; Trumpet, Agent and News Xpress are used within the Windows environment; and a variety of programs are used on Macintosh computers. Obviously, each program operates and looks different, but all share certain basic functions. For example, let's take a look at accessing USENET news using tin, a popular UNIX newsreader. As can be seen, tin is a character-based system:

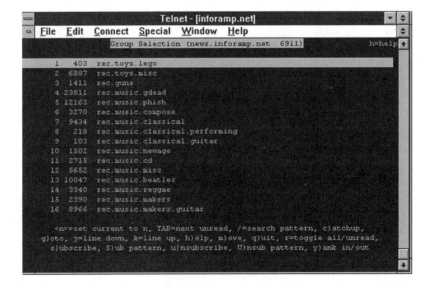

Looking at a similar listing through News Xpress in Microsoft Windows shows a completely different type of screen:

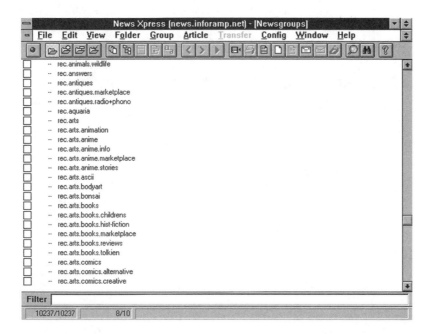

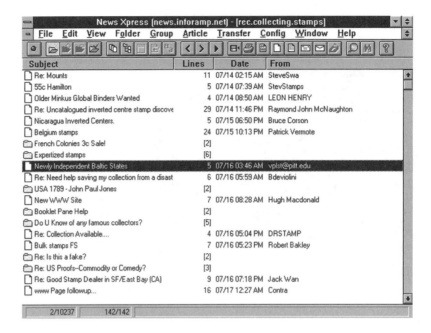

A new trend is the integration of USENET access into World Wide Web browser software (which is discussed in the next chapter). For example, consider the popular Netscape program, which in this case is being used to look at a particular newsgroup:

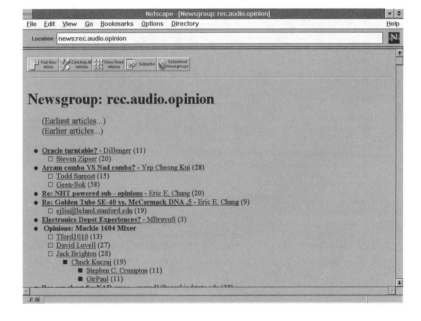

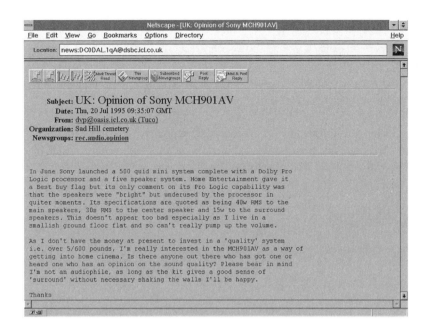

Millions of people access USENET news through character-based systems like tin, and millions use Microsoft Windows or Macintosh systems (which we call GUIs, or systems that have a graphical user interface) and thus use graphical software like News Xpress. The software that you will use depends upon the type of computer that you have. If you do not have a Macintosh or cannot run Microsoft Windows, then you will likely have to access the Internet through a "shell account" and will thus use some type of character-based newsreader such as tin. If you have Windows or a Macintosh, you can use a SLIP or PPP account and can thus use graphical newsreaders like News Xpress.

Where to Find Newsreader Software

For Windows:

FreeAgent: **http://www.forteinc.com** or **ftp://ftp.forteinc.com/pub/forte**. You will find directories containing Agent and FreeAgent.

Trumpet News: **ftp://ftp.cyberspace.com/pub/ppp/windows/utils/**. Retrieve the file **wt_wsk.zip**.

Software can be retrieved at **ftp://ftp.trumpet.com.au**

News Xpress: **ftp://ftp.microserve.net/pub/msdos/winsock/**. File name begins with NX. There may be several files starting with NX, retrieve the most recent one for the latest version of the software.

For Macintosh:

InterNews: **ftp://ftp.dartmouth.edu/pub/mac/InterNews_1.0.8.sea.hqx**

(version number might be different)

Newsview: **ftp://ftp://iraun1.ira.uka.de/pub/systems/mac/**

> Newswatcher: **ftp://ftp.acns.nwu.edu/pub/newswatcher/**
>
> A version of Newswatcher that works over dialup connections, i.e., no MacTCP required: **ftp://ftp.sfu.ca/pub/mac/newswatcher/**
>
> A version of Newswatcher that supports filtering and binary posting, also known as "Value Added Newswatcher": **ftp://grocne.enc.org/pub/V.A.NewsWatcher**

There is also a lot of sophisticated commercial software arriving for the Internet. In Chapter 13 we take a look at packages like Emissary, Internet in a Box, Quarterdeck Internet Suite and show some of the USENET newsreaders available within those programs.

Newsreader Features

Regardless of whether you access USENET through a character-based system or with graphical software, your newsreader will have a set of features that will let you do various things with USENET. Some of these features are described below. The particular software that you use may or may not have all these functions and may even support additional functions not listed here. You should be able to:

◆ Easily join USENET newsgroups. The term used for joining a newsgroup is "subscribe." Obviously, your newsreader software should let you join, or subscribe, to newsgroups, quickly and easily. FreeAgent lets you subscribe to a newsgroup, or, before doing so, you can "sample" a few of the entries within the newsgroup:

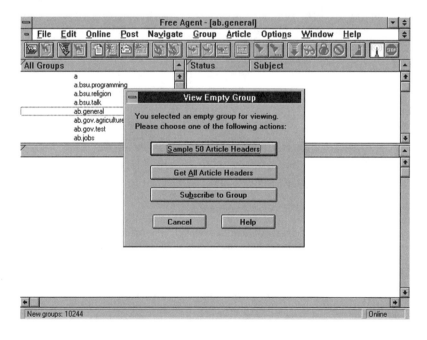

◆ Obtain a listing of all newsgroups and be able to search for newsgroups by "key word." One of the challenges of USENET is that new newsgroups are added to the system at a furious pace. And with several thousand newsgroups, finding the ones that might interest you can be a challenge. Your software will automatically update for any new USENET newsgroups each time you sign in. Hence your newsreader software should let you browse through a list of all USENET newsgroups; however, you should also be able to quickly see a listing of those newsgroups to which you have subscribed. In addition, you should be able to perform a quick search of all USENET newsgroups to identify only those that contain a certain word.

In the example below, News Xpress has been used to list only those newsgroups containing the word "research." News Xpress permits you to do this by keying a "search term" at the bottom of the screen:

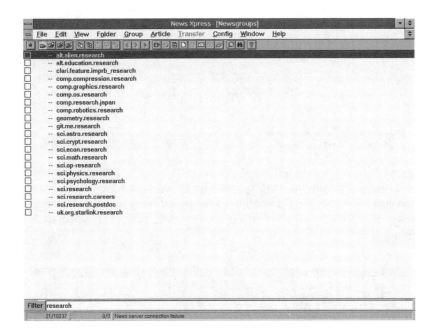

◆ Post an article or a follow-up to a previously posted message. Obviously, the whole point of USENET is that it allows you to participate in the discussions, so all newsreader applications support the capability for you to put up an item or respond to a previous item. A "post" or an "article" is the term used to describe an item in a USENET newsgroup. A "follow-up" is a posting made in reference to a previous posting. Be aware that when you send a follow-up, everyone in the newsgroup can see your response, so you should be certain that you want to respond in public. Your newsreader software usually inserts a "RE:" in the subject line of a follow-up. In addition, the software should "quote" the original message (similar to how e-mail responses are quoted, as described in the previous chapter).

As seen below, we are posting a follow-up to a USENET posting within the newsgroup **rec.travel.usa-canada**. In this case, the software has quoted the original message so that other readers will know what your follow-up is in reference to:

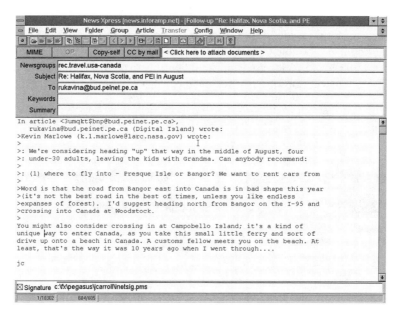

◆ Send e-mail to the author of an article or forward the message to someone else. Sometimes, you will not want to send a follow-up USENET post to everyone; you may just want to contact the author of the post directly via e-mail. Hence your newsreader software usually provides a way for you to send an e-mail to the author of any post.

In other cases, you might want to forward the posting on to someone else, so your newsreader should provide this capability.

◆ Sort articles in a newsgroup. Some of the newsgroups that you will join will have a lot of postings; some see upwards of several hundred per day. Obviously, sometimes you will want to scan the list of unread articles in various ways — looking at them by date, by subject, or by author.

◆ View articles by "thread." Discussions within USENET can go on, sometimes for a long, long time. Certain messages generate a fast and furious response from many people. One topic might break down into discussions about many related subtopics. It can be difficult keeping track of what everyone is communicating about! Newsreader software that organizes postings by subject is very useful. Then you can follow the "thread," or topic, at hand. A "thread" is the term used to describe the original posting and all the follow-up responses to that posting.

For example, the screen below is from the newsgroup **misc.immigration.canada**, a spot where many ask questions or share information about Canadian immigration issues. As can be seen, there were multiple postings about the topics "re: looking for a Canadian newsgroup with Job advertisements" and "The address of the Canadian Embassy in Australia." The newsreader software in this case (News Xpress) has organized the postings for us by topic, making it easier to track only those postings in which we are interested. Multiple postings related to one topic are listed under the subject:

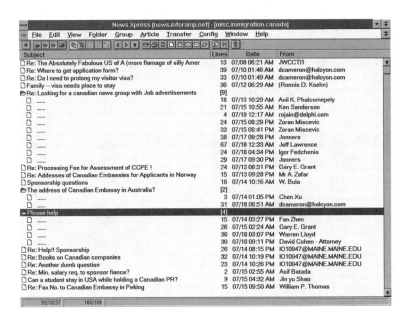

For another example of how threading works, take a look at the following view of the **misc.immigration.canada** topic through Netscape. In this case, the topics are underlined, with follow-ups to original postings indented:

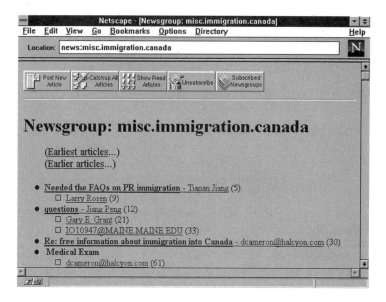

Threading is a particularly useful feature to have and is increasingly supported in newsreader software.

◆ Use "killfiles" or "bozo filters." Given the growth of the Internet and the number of kooks who seem to be joining it, killfiles are becoming absolute necessities. (They are often called bozo filters, since that is what they do — they filter bozos out of your USENET information. A bozo is whomever you would like it to be. You will meet lots of them on-line.) Killfiles "delete" articles sent to you that contain certain subjects or are sent from certain people, thus letting you screen out particular messages.

Here is a simple killfile that is being used to filter out messages related to gun control and any messages from Elvis:

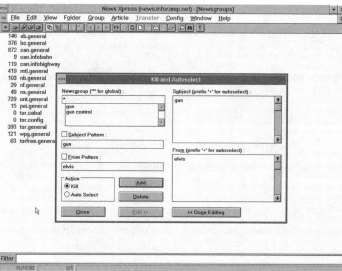

◆ Decode graphics. There are many USENET newsgroups to which people post graphic images, usually in uuencoded format. (Some of the more controversial newsgroups, for example, but many serious groups as well.) Remember from Chapter 7 that uuencoding is a technique that enables non-text computer files to be sent through the Internet.

Some newsreader software lets you quickly decode such images and will even go so far as to show you the image immediately. Consider this posting, from **sci.astro**, which contains images from space. Retrieving an article containing an image shows the gibberish of a uuencoded file; however, the newsreader software lets you easily automatically "decode" the image, and even run a program to immediately view it once it is decoded:

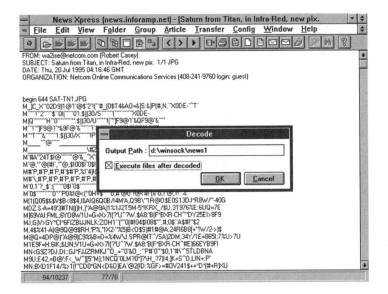

◆ Rotate postings (ROT-13). **rec.humor.funny** is the most popular USENET newsgroup. Within it, you can usually find all kinds of new humorous postings each and every day. This includes the occasional posting of politically incorrect or offensive information. To keep you from seeing such items without warning, they are "rotated," a very simple method of changing characters in a message; for example, A turns into N, B turns into O. If you want to read the posting, you choose to ROT-13 it, then you can see the politically incorrect or offensive item.

◆ Alert you to interesting stuff. Another way to deal with large volumes of information on USENET is to use the reverse of a bozo filter — an "interesting filter." Some newsreader software will let you set up a profile so that you are "alerted" if certain people post an item, or if there is a posting about a particular subject that interests you.

◆ See old articles. Sometimes, you may wish to look at older USENET postings, and some newsreader software will let you do so. However, keep in mind that due to the overwhelming volume of information sent through USENET, most providers do not keep more than a week or two of information.

◆ Crosspost to multiple groups. A newsreader should let you post to several groups at once (referred to as "crossposting"). However, this feature should be used with extreme caution, since it is easy to offend people on the Internet by crossposting.

USENET: What it is Not

There are some things that you should know about USENET:

◆ It is not the Internet. USENET happens to be carried over the Internet as well as other networks. However, it has come to be so closely identified as an "Internet resource" that most people think of USENET as being a fundamental part of the Internet.

◆ It is not owned by anyone, nor is there one central authority that runs it. USENET exists because of the cooperative efforts of thousands of people: first and foremost, the thousands of UNIX systems and news administrators of subscribing systems around the world, and second, through the efforts of a large number of volunteers who catalogue USENET resources, conduct votes, post information, and participate in countless other ways.

The result is an on-line system that is managed through the cooperative effort of literally thousands of people from around the globe. Some call it organized or cooperative anarchy. However, it does have a "culture" and it does have "rules," which have more or less been accepted throughout the community. This is referred to as network etiquette, or "netiquette," which is discussed in greater depth below.

◆ It is not for commercial use. There is no surer way to receive streams of on-line abuse than by using USENET for blatant advertising. USENET was formed by volunteers who wanted to exchange information on topics. Its entire history and culture hold the concept of advertising within USENET in extreme contempt. You do not do well by violating one of the cultural foundations of USENET.

USENET was developed to support the exchange of knowledge and information. There are thousands of topics; yet with all the millions of news articles posted to USENET, it maintains its culture. Even as the Internet becomes more commercialized, USENET seems to be maintaining its status as a system not to be blatantly used for commercial purposes, even though there are some buy-and-sell newsgroups.

◆ It is used to a limited extent for commercial purposes. Even though USENET is not for commercial use, there are some newsgroups that exist for distribution of information concerning certain products and for service announcements from system vendors. For example, **rec.comics.marketplace** is used by people to exchange information about the sale of rare comics. USENET is a study in contradictions.

What does this mean? You might use USENET with regard to your business: "I am trying to get my computer to do this; does anyone have any hints?" But you certainly should not use USENET to try to drum up business: "Hey, I've started a consulting firm. Call me if you need help — my rates are $120 an hour."

Network Etiquette

The most important thing you can learn about USENET is that it has a unique on-line culture, and those who do not respect this culture do so at their own peril. The culture includes procedures and guidance concerning topics such as newsgroup creation (as described above); what the network can be used for (e.g., non-commercial activity); how to post news articles; newsgroup names; official versus non-official newsgroups; chain letters; inappropriate postings; and hundreds of other issues of etiquette.

The easiest ways to learn about USENET culture are to join several newsgroups and to obtain documents on rules and netiquette. By joining several newsgroups, you can watch how they work for some time. In particular, if you are interested in how USENET newsgroups are established, subscribe to the groups **news.announce.newgroups** and **news.groups**. In **news.announce.newgroups** proposals for new groups are posted. **News.groups** is where these proposals are debated.

Be prepared to be shocked by what you might see in a debate involving a new proposed topic: sometimes simple proposals for a new newsgroup degenerate into raging debates, with emotions getting out of hand and insults and accusations flying with fury. Why? This is the culture of USENET. There is no better way to understand the culture of USENET than to belong to **news.groups** for a few months.

Documents such as "A Primer on How to Work with the USENET Community" and "Rules for Posting to USENET" are posted regularly to the groups **news.newusers.questions** and **news.answers** and can also be retrieved from a number of FTP locations. The following screen shows them as listed in **news.newusers.questions** and within **ftp://rtfm.mit.edu/pub/usenet/news.announce.newusers**:

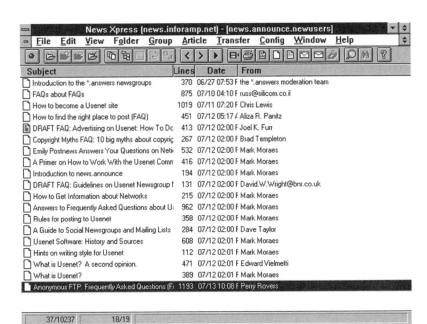

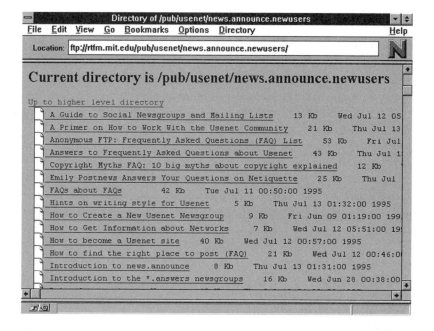

Retrieving documents about "Netiquette"

The Net: User guidelines and netiquette **http://www.fau.edu/rinaldi/netiquette.html**

A Primer on How to Work with the USENET Community

http://www.cis.ohio-state.edu/hypertext/faq/usenet/usenet-primer/part1/faq.html

and **ftp://rtfm.mit.edu/pub/usenet/news.announce.newusers**

What is USENET? A second opinion

http://www.cis.ohio-state.edu/hypertext/faq/usenet/what-is-usenet/part2/faq.html

The granddaddies of all documents about Netiquette can found in the series of documents noted below:

**ftp://rtfm.mit.edu/pub/usenet/news.announce.newusers/
A_Primer_on_How_to_Work_With_the_Usenet_Community**

**ftp://rtfm.mit.edu/pub/usenet/news.announce.newusers/
Answers_to_Frequently_Asked_Questions_about_Usenet**

**ftp://rtfm.mit.edu/pub/usenet/news.announce.newusers/
Emily_Postnews_Answers_Your_Questions_on_Netiquette**

ftp://rtfm.mit.edu/pub/usenet/news.announce.newusers/Hints_on_writing_style_for_Usenet

**ftp://rtfm.mit.edu/pub/usenet/news.announce.newusers/
Introduction_to_the_*.answers_newsgroups**

ftp://rtfm.mit.edu/pub/usenet/news.announce.newusers/Rules_for_posting_to_Usenet

ftp://rtfm.mit.edu/pub/usenet/news.announce.newusers/What_is_Usenet?

ftp://rtfm.mit.edu/pub/usenet/news.announce.newusers/

Lists of Newsgroups

Hopefully, your newsreader software will let you obtain a listing of all USENET newsgroups and perform a search of the list. However, if you want a list of USENET newsgroups in the major USENET categories, look for the document "List of Active Newsgroups," which is also posted to the group **news.announce.newgroups** on a frequent basis. It can also be found in the areas noted below:

To obtain the document "List of Active Newsgroups"

ftp://rtfm.mit.edu/pub/usenet/news.lists/List_of_Active_Newsgroups%2C_Part_I

ftp://rtfm.mit.edu/pub/usenet/news.lists/List_of_Active_Newsgroups%2C_Part_II

ftp://rtfm.mit.edu/pub/usenet/news.lists/Alternative_Newsgroup_Hierarchies%2C_Part_I

ftp://rtfm.mit.edu/pub/usenet/news.lists/Alternative_Newsgroup_Hierarchies%2C_Part_II
ftp://rtfm.mit.edu/pub/usenet/news.lists/Alternative_Newsgroup_Hierarchies%2C_Part_III

You can also access lists of newsgroups on the World Wide Web and through FTP. For example, here is the USENET Info Center Launch Pad at **http://sunsite.unc.edu/usenet-i/**:

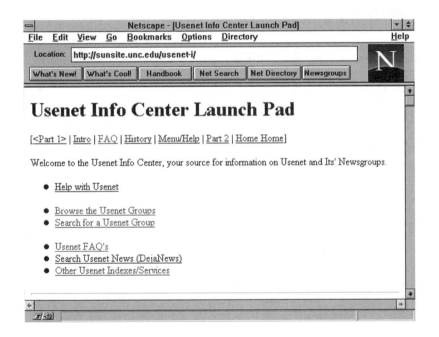

Other sites for USENET newsgroups:

For a list of newsgroups in the main USENET hierarchies:

http://www.cis.ohio-state.edu/hypertext/faq/usenet/active-newsgroups/part1/faq.html

ftp://rtfm.mit.edu/pub/usenet/news.answers/active-newsgroups

For a list of newsgroups in the **alt**. USENET hierarchy:

http://www.cis.ohio-state.edu/hypertext/faq/usenet/alt-hierarchies/top.html

ftp://rtfm.mit.edu/pub/usenet/news.answers/alt-hierarchies

You should check the document "How to find the right place to post (FAQ)" available at the URL **ftp://rtfm.mit.edu:/pub/usenet/news.answers/finding-groups/general**.

You should also check with your Internet service provider to obtain a list of the newsgroups provided. Not all providers distribute all newsgroups. If your ISP does not carry a newsgroup that interests you, you can ask the provider to do so; often the ISP will comply, although there is no obligation on the part of the ISP.

USENET Controversy

Many people new to the Internet venture into USENET, eager to participate in the promise that it brings. Unfortunately, many of these people are probably experiencing discomfort in certain areas of the Internet, and in particular, in many of the Canadian general discussion groups. Some have made the following observations about USENET.

Visiting USENET Is Often Like Visiting a Men's Bathroom

You might find your visit to particular areas of USENET to be a rather uncomfortable experience. You will meet all kinds of people, some of whom you will not like. Elsewhere, you will find that the language leaves much to be desired or that people "flame" too easily. In other cases, people will argue incessantly about the most obscure point. Elsewhere, you will encounter what USENET calls "kooks," people who just seem to have a chip on their shoulder or who seem to be not quite in control of their mental faculties.

It seems that more and more, going into a USENET newsgroup is sometimes like returning to the rough and tumble school yard of your youth. There are bullies about who will make you uncomfortable and who will throw sand and spit in your face without thinking. There are more crazies around the Internet who will babble about anything they like on-line, with total disregard to the pleas by others to *just go away*. There are others who have spent no time learning or trying to understand net culture, who will do whatever they please.

Many of the Canadian USENET newsgroups — **can.general**, **ont.general**, and others — suffer from these problems.

USENET has become an increasingly uncomfortable and unfriendly neighborhood, and you must have a thick skin to hang out there. Plain and simple — you might not like certain areas of USENET.

David Jones (**djones@insight.dcss.mcmaster.ca**), one of the leading figures with Electronic Frontier Canada, a group involved in electronic freedom of speech issues, has this to say about the changing nature of USENET: "I think it is fair to say that the Internet demographics are continuing to shift. It used to be techie nerds and academics. Largely male, mostly affluent, and generally well-mannered and educated. In those days, the 'public places', like USENET newsgroups, were fine hangouts. Now, just like lots of neighborhoods in the real world, some of these 'public places' are inhabited by kooks, kids, bullies, and so on. What do reasonable people do in the real world? They withdraw and move to a new hangout. Maybe it's a pub, or a club, or maybe it's the faculty lounge on campus. It's a bit more exclusive, but it's inhabited by the kind of company you wish to hang out with. I think the exact same thing applies in cyberspace. Almost everyone I know who is plugged in is starting to favour mailing lists."

In essence, if you cannot hack USENET, you might want to investigate mailing lists, which are detailed in the next section.

Another solution to the problem with USENET is the use of filters. Notes Jones: "It's been popular for some time now to talk about 'intelligent agents' that filter the gush of information flowing through the net, based on your own personalized set of interest parameters. I think this is becoming more and more important. What do you see when you look in a 'general' newsgroup? You see a lot of chatter. With tens of millions of people on the net, there's going to be more and more of it. We need filters."

USENET is often not fun. Filters might help, but you might just not want to participate in certain areas.

USENET is Hypocritical

One of the long-stated "rules" of etiquette with respect to USENET is that commercial use is frowned upon. Advertisements are a no-no. Junk mail is forbidden. Send it, and you will find people sending you streams of complaint and abuse. Yet, such "rules" seem to be selectively applied, to the great frustration of many people. What has become evident is that people on USENET are very selective, and indeed, hypocritical, about whom they choose to abuse. If you look at the Canadian general discussion group (**can.general**) for a representative two weeks, you can see all kinds of "commercial postings" that crossed the line: two postings advertising an Arizona reservations service; an advertisement extolling a new Canadian Internet service provider; a posting entitled "the easiest and quickest way to acquire real estate," with the text reading like some type of bad Amway ad; a posting — sorry, advertisement — from an organization announcing a big rock concert in Alberta; an ad for a bed and breakfast in Vancouver and another selling an apartment in Ottawa; a press release for the new Web site for the Adult Super Store chain. All clearly commercial postings, all violating "net etiquette" such as it is, all crossing the line in some way. Any protest? Not a word. Any huge debate on-line? Nope.

USENET is often contradictory. You should not advertise in USENET — and you will not succeed if you try. But do expect to get frustrated as you see it occur all around you, as other people attempt to do it.

Pornography and Other Information of an Illegal or Questionable Nature are Found in USENET

The Internet, when it comes to pornography and other questionable information, does present society with some difficult challenges. Join certain USENET newsgroups and you can find pornography. Pornography is a fact of life in our real society, and it is a fact of life in our virtual society. But USENET is used for the distribution of information that is of questionable taste, is in violation of the laws of Canada, or runs against current accepted "community standards," for example, for the distribution of material related to pedophilia. USENET is often in violation of the law. *The reality is, there is no way to control it.*

Yet, we often see politicians stand up and make grandiose statements about how the Internet should be regulated or censored. We see media organizations hype it. We see some enterprising young reporter somewhere write an exposé that the Internet contains pornography. Most often, these people are reacting with concern to some of the information that flows through USENET. Unfortunately, in making their call for technical regulation, or by hyping the topic, they are displaying an ignorance and lack of knowledge that causes most people within the USENET community to snicker at them and treat them with disdain.

The unfortunate thing is that few of these politicians and reporters seem to take the time to understand what is really going on. They are too interested in getting onto a 10-second sound clip on the national news, and display their shallowness by doing so. Or they are too interested in furthering their journalist careers by writing pathetic "scaremonger" stories. Such people gain little respect in the Internet community and do themselves a disservice.

There is no doubt that some of the information found in USENET represents some extremely challenging issues to society on the issue of information access and freedom of information and that it presents all of us with some difficult moral and legal issues. Somehow, we as a society have to learn to deal with technologies such as the Internet, which transcend national borders.

In essence, we need some diligent politicians to come forth in Canada to participate in a dialogue about some of the more uncomfortable aspects of USENET. We need politicians willing to become involved in the issue and willing to research and understand the nature of the problem and the technical challenges that it presents. We need more journalists who are willing to write with intelligence rather than satisfying some primal need for the lurid headline of the week. We need intelligence, not grandstanding.[4]

Many people become frustrated with USENET. It is true that the nature of USENET is changing. USENET is increasingly difficult to put up with because of its hypocrisy and because of the bullies and kooks who are on it. You will have to decide whether participating in USENET is worth it, and find the groups that have some value to you. The thing to keep in mind about USENET is that it is not life, so you cannot let it bug you.

---

4. If you are a politician or some other person reading this and want to understand the issue of censorship and regulation of the Internet, we invite you to contact Electronic Frontier Canada at **efc@graceland.waterloo.ca** or on the Web at **http://insight.mcmaster.ca/org/efc/efc.html**. The authors of this book would love to talk to you on an intelligent level about the topic without the hype and the media sensationalism that so often occurs. Send a message to **handbook@uunet.ca** to contact us.

Internet Mailing Lists

Sometimes you will not find a topic that you are looking for within USENET newsgroups. In other cases, you might tire of the freewheeling atmosphere of an unmoderated USENET newsgroup, but still want to keep up-to-date on a particular topic. In this case, you might prefer joining an Internet electronic mailing list instead.

Internet mailing lists are another convenient method by which people on different computer systems can discuss particular topics or share information concerning specific issues. A mailing list might consist of as few as two people, or it might contain several thousand. With thousands of different mailing lists on the Internet, you can choose to join any particular one that interests you, as long as it is a public, or open, list. Once you have joined, you will receive any messages sent to the list. An Internet mailing list operates as shown in Figure 8.1.

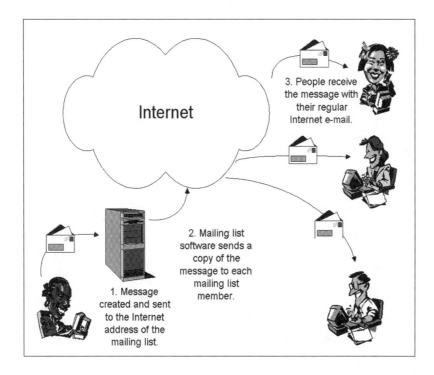

Internet

3. People receive the message with their regular Internet e-mail.

2. Mailing list software sends a copy of the message to each mailing list member.

1. Message created and sent to the Internet address of the mailing list.

FIGURE 8.1

Internet Mailing Lists

With the growing number of e-mail systems that have the capability of sending messages to and receiving messages from the Internet, it is no surprise that there are thousands of Internet mailing lists on virtually every topic imaginable.

Types of Lists

Mailing lists on the Internet differ by their purpose: some are used for discussion, while others are used for newsletters or announcements, and yet others are used to summarize information that has appeared in other lists or in USENET newsgroups.

Mailing lists have emerged as a new method of publishing, with a number of journals, newsletters, and other information summaries available to anyone with Internet e-mail access. In other cases, companies are establishing customer mailing lists that customers can choose to join in order to receive new product announcements or other information. The types of mailing lists available throughout the Internet are moderated, unmoderated, and closed.

Moderated

Lists are moderated to ensure that messages sent to the list are tightly focused on the list topic. In a moderated list, any message sent by you goes to the "moderator," who determines if it should be redistributed to the list. This helps to keep the list on topic. The moderator, who manages the list, is an individual who takes on responsibility for sending messages to the list. The moderator takes an active role in determining what should be sent to the list, ensuring that only those messages relevant to the topic of the list are received by subscribers.

Moderated lists are most often used for newsletters and journals. For example, you can join "Elements," a list to which the "Keplarian elements" of space shuttle flights are sent on a regular basis. Both professional scientists and amateurs input these numerical elements into space object tracking software to plot the track of the shuttle currently in orbit. (Send a message to **elements-request@thomsoft.com** for more information.)

Another example of a moderated list is Barley-L, a list run by Alberta Agricultural, Food and Development for the Alberta Government. A Web page details its purpose (**http://www.gov.ab.ca/~agric/disuss.html**):

Unmoderated

In an unmoderated list any message sent by you immediately goes to everyone on the list. An unmoderated list might permit anyone to send to it, or it might be restricted, permitting only members to send to it. A good example is the Track-Canada mailing list, which is used by those involved in Canadian track and field, road racing, and triathlons. Details about the list can be found at **http://home.cc.umanitoba.ca/~csghoy/WhatisTC.html**:

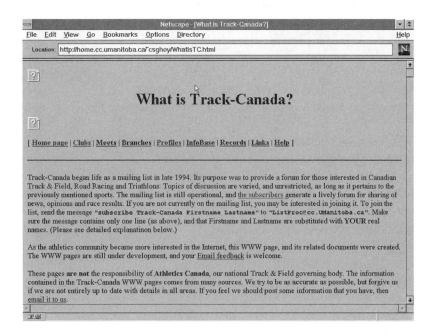

Closed

The Internet is a very diverse place; this results in some lists that simply are not open to everyone, "closed" lists. You must meet some type of qualification to join these lists — even to receive messages sent to the list. These lists are often used to restrict access to members of a particular organization. The Canadian Bar Association, for example, runs a number of mailing lists that only members can join.

List Information

Often, you can quickly obtain information about a list or series of lists by sending a message to the list itself. For example, if you send a message to **listserv@fait.gc.ca** with the word "help" in the text, you will get a message similar to this one:

> To: rickb@hookup.net
>
> Subject: Help on NetXpress's LISTSERV feature
>
> From: listserv@fait.gc.ca (NetXpress Listserv)
>
> Date: Mon, 31 Jul 1995 16:05:37 -0500
>
> Organization: Foreign Affairs & International Trade
>
> Content-Length: 4605
>
> Department of Foreign Affairs and International Trade
>
> InfoCentre BBS, Mailing List Service

16 January 95

This service is currently under construction, so please be patient if we have problems. Feedback would be appreciated via email to one of the following: ardeth.boyd@fait.gc.ca (Ardeth Boyd-Kirkham)

marc@tanda.on.ca (Marc Thibault)

Mailing Lists

ibbs-newsWhat's happening with the Infocentre BBS. Moderated.

CanadExportA newsletter published twice monthly in both English and French by DFAIT/BCT.

infotechSan Jose's informative Advanced Technology newsletter. Moderated.

communiqueDFAIT Press releases and Speeches. Moderated.

NABNorth Asia Bulletin. Moderated

AMEBAfrica-Middle East Bulletin. Moderated

EventsNotices of upcoming trade events

OpportunitiesInternational Market Opportunities

Subscribing and Un-subscribing

Send an email message addressed to "listserv@fait.gc.ca" with one of the following commands as the body text.

HELPThis message

SUBSCRIBE <mailing-list> <user-name>

Subscribes the sending address to the mailing list

UNSUBSCRIBE <mailing-list>

Unsubscribes sending address from the mailing list

CONFIRM <mailing-list>

Confirms that the sending address is subscribed to that mailing list

Where:

<mailing-list> is the name of the mailing list,

<user-name> is the user's name (the From: address of the message is used to send mail list messages)

Example:

To: listserv@fait.gc.ca

From: marc@tanda.on.ca (Marc Thibault)

Subject:

subscribe infotech Marc Thibault

Using Lists: The Mechanics

The mechanics of Internet mailing lists are quite straightforward. Normally, you join a list through electronic mail, although in some cases you can join one through the World Wide Web.

By E-Mail

In most cases, you subscribe or join an Internet mailing list by sending an e-mail message to an Internet address established for the purposes of list maintenance. Your e-mail message contains a special line of text indicating that you wish to join the list. For example, we can join a list called CANADA-L by sending a message to the e-mail address **listserv@vm1.mcgill.ca** and then we type into the text of the message **subscribe canada-l yourname**. The actual command you use will depend on the list software in use at the remote location.

Once your message has been received at the destination, your request to be added to or deleted from a list is processed manually by the list owner or processed by a specialized piece of software (called a "list manager," but also regularly referred to as a "listserver"), which automatically makes the change to the appropriate list. In the case of Canada-L, your request is processed by software known as a "listserv."

The following message is a copy of an original request to subscribe to the mailing list called Canada-L:

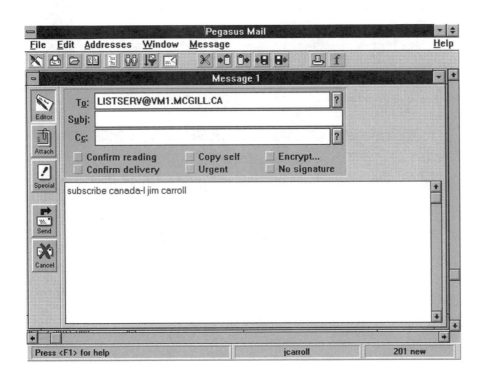

When this message was received at McGill University (at the e-mail address **listserv@vm1.mcgill.ca**), the program called listserv processed the details of the message, and the Internet e-mail address **jcarroll@jacc.com** was added to the list. Confirmation of this was sent back in the form of an e-mail message, which provided details about the list as well as all-important information about how to leave the list in the future. Never lose such instructions. Most lists return such a message as soon as you subscribe.

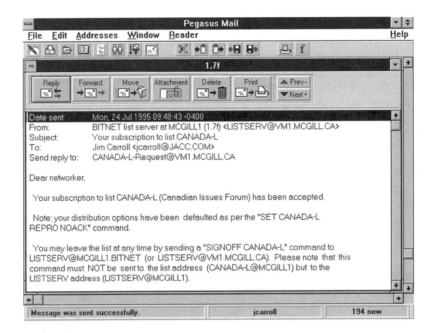

To leave this list, you simply send a message containing the sign-off instructions:

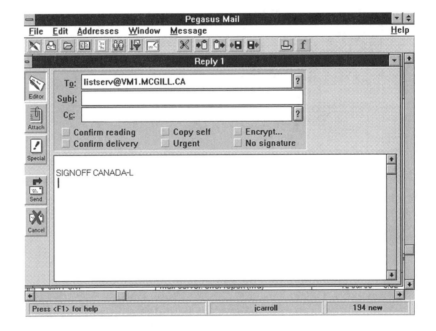

There are several automatic list managers throughout the Internet, including the programs majordomo, listserv, and mailserv, all of which have their own unique methods for joining and leaving a list.

We have reprinted, in Appendix L, a document by James Milles of the Saint Louis University Law Library (**millesjg@sluvca.slu.edu**), which summarizes most of the popular mail servers and the commands to use with each of them to join or leave a list.

To obtain this document using e-mail:

send a message to: **listserv@ubvm.cc.buffalo.edu**.

In text of message, type: **get mailser cmd nettrain**

To obtain this document on-line:

URL: **http://lawlib.slu.edu/training/mailser.htm**

Through the Web

An increasing number of mailing lists are supporting a feature that allows you to subscribe by filling out a form on the World Wide Web. For example, this form (at **http://www2.advan tage.com/Lists/Lists.html**) permits you to join various Vancouver Canucks mailing lists or permits you to easily request more information about a particular list before joining:

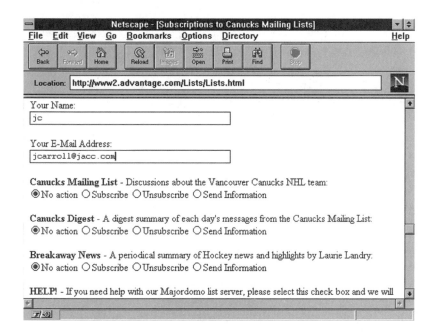

Starting Your Own List

One of the greatest benefits of the Internet is that anyone can establish an Internet mailing list. Your Internet service provider might be able to provide you with your own Internet mailing lists. If so, you can establish a mailing list on a particular topic and invite your friends and peers to join the list. Over time, you might find that the list begins to gain recognition throughout the Internet.

In addition, establishing automatic list servers through e-mail software is becoming more and more popular. Pegasus Mail for DOS and Windows, for example, includes this feature.

Many Internet lists began informally, yet some have emerged to become the global "home" for a particular topic. Given the power of global knowledge networking, establishing your own mailing list on a topic of importance to you could become one of your most useful Internet resources.

Finding Lists

The obvious question is, "How do I find a particular list?" You may hear about a mailing list by word of mouth or mentioned in some Internet resource that you track. Some USENET newsgroups, for instance, are often used to announce new lists (discussed in next section). However, there are also a number of resources on the Internet that provide details on thousands of mailing lists. These resources usually provide some background information concerning the list as well as instructions on how to join.

Let's take a look at a few examples. Later in this chapter we will detail some of the places you can go to access these "lists of lists."

Canada-L is a list used for the discussion of Canadian political, social, and other issues. It is listed in the "E-Mail Discussion Groups" archive (described below) as follows (**http://www.nova.edu/inter-Links/cgi-bin/lists?canada-1**):

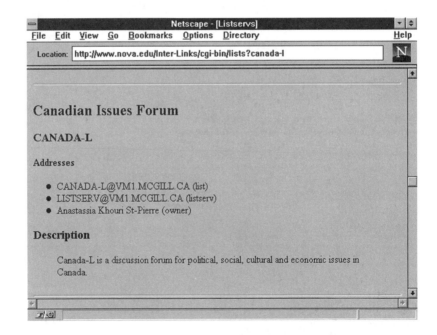

The same list is described in the Tile.Net listserv Database (described below) as follows (**http://www.tile.net/tile/listserv/canadal.html**):

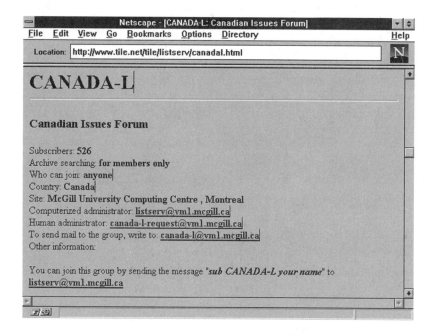

Yet, it is not listed in the "Publicly Accessible Mailing Lists" database (described below), which is one of the largest summaries available. Hence, if you are looking for a list about a particular topic, it is usually worthwhile to check several sources.

Whatever the case may be, it is now quite simple to find lists by topic. The level of detail that each Internet resource provides varies, and not all lists are included in all resources. Many of the resources also include information on lists that have become defunct or that have been superseded by some newer list. Some of the more popular sources are detailed below.[5]

If retrieving these documents by e-mail, keep in mind that these documents are quite large; for example, the List of Interest Groups described below is over 1.2 megabytes in size. If you are using a commercial e-mail provider that charges on a per character basis, be prepared for a rather hefty bill!

None of these sources are comprehensive. But since new lists are being added throughout the Internet on a regular basis, these summaries are a good starting point to get an idea of the lists that are out there. For each summary of lists, we describe how to obtain it by e-mail and also provide the uniform resource locators so that you can access them using FTP or through the World Wide Web.

---

5. This being the Internet, you might find that some of the instructions below do not work. The Internet is constantly changing, and we often find that sometimes we print a pointer to a list, only to have the pointer change the month after we go to print. We have had some readers complain about this, but keep in mind that the Internet is a massive global network with millions of people. Things go out of date, change, and disappear.

USENET

A good starting point to get many documents about lists on the Internet is through the USENET newsgroup **news.lists**. Here, you will find many of the following summaries posted on a regular basis, as well as other information concerning Internet lists.

BITNET Lists

BITNET is a global network that is separate from the Internet, yet it links academic institutions and research organizations worldwide. It is fair to say that although BITNET has not disappeared, it is rapidly merging into and becoming part of the Internet. BITNET provides global electronic mail and mailing list capabilities (and in fact, is where the listserv program originated). It is home to some of the most diverse and interesting mailing lists available. Internet users can join any of these mailing lists.

The document "List of all LISTSERV lists known to LISTSERV@LISTSERV.NET" (a summary of all BITNET mailing lists) provides a comprehensive summary of over 4,000 special interest lists.

To obtain this listing using e-mail:

Send message to: **listserv@listserv.net**

In text of message, type: **list global**

Publicly Accessible Mailing Lists

This is the definitive summary of Internet lists. Revised monthly, the list contains a detailed description of each list as well as information on how to subscribe.

To obtain this listing using e-mail:

Send message to: **mail-server@rtfm.mit.edu**

In text of message, type:

send /pub/usenet/news.answers/mail/mailing-lists/part01

send /pub/usenet/news.answers/mail/mailing-lists/part02

send /pub/usenet/news.answers/mail/mailing-lists/part03

send /pub/usenet/news.answers/mail/mailing-lists/part04

send /pub/usenet/news.answers/mail/mailing-lists/part05

send /pub/usenet/news.answers/mail/mailing-lists/part06

send /pub/usenet/news.answers/mail/mailing-lists/part07

send /pub/usenet/news.answers/mail/mailing-lists/part08

send /pub/usenet/news.answers/mail/mailing-lists/part09

send /pub/usenet/news.answers/mail/mailing-lists/part10

send /pub/usenet/news.answers/mail/mailing-lists/part11

send /pub/usenet/news.answers/mail/mailing-lists/part12

send /pub/usenet/news.answers/mail/mailing-lists/part13

send /pub/usenet/news.answers/mail/mailing-lists/part14

send /pub/usenet/news.answers/mail/mailing-lists/part15

send /pub/usenet/news.answers/mail/mailing-lists/part16

send /pub/usenet/news.answers/mail/mailing-lists/part17

To obtain the document on-line:

URL: **ftp://rtfm.mit.edu/ pub/usenet/news.answers/mail/mailing-lists/partxx**,

substituting the proper file name for partxx

URL: **http://www.neosoft.com/internet/paml/**

Viewing the document on-line through the World Wide Web is particularly useful, since you can quickly browse through the names of various lists or review list types by category:

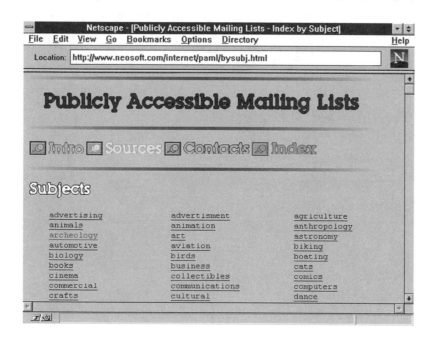

List of Interest Groups

This document refers to itself as the "List of lists," a listing of special interest group mailing lists available on the Internet.

To obtain this listing using e-mail:

Send message to: **mail-server@sri.com**

In text of message, type: **send netinfo/interest-groups.txt**

To obtain this listing on-line:

URL: **ftp://sri.com/netinfo/interest-groups.txt**

Note: this file is over 1 Mb in size.

E-Mail Discussion Groups

A comprehensive database of lists that can be searched by topic can be found at **http://www.nova.edu/Inter-Links/listserv.html**. A search for lists mentioning Canada found over 29 references:

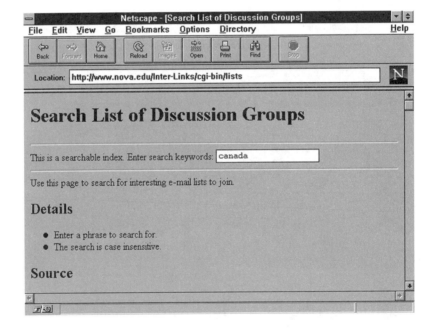

Tile.Net listserv Database

A comprehensive database of listserv lists from around the world that you can list by category or that you can search for a particular topic is found at **http://www.tile.net/tile/listserv/**:

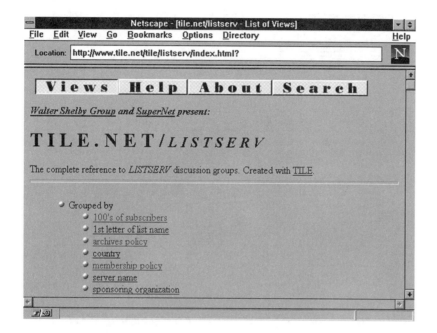

A search for Canada returned 41 results.

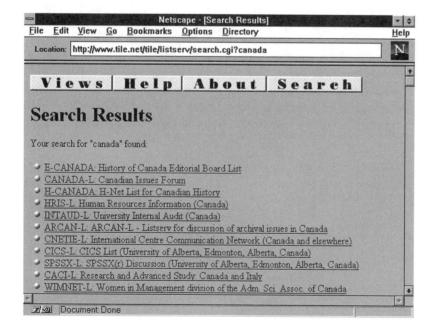

A very innovative feature of this Web site is that you can view lists by the number of subscribers and thus get an idea of some of the more popular lists around the world. The most subscribed to listserv list, with 66,000 subscribers, is a David Letterman Top Ten List:

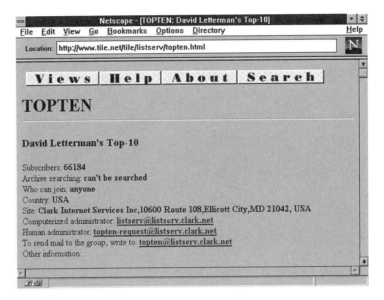

Clearinghouse for Subject-Oriented Internet Resource Guides

This is one of the first places to look when looking for a mailing list on a specific topic. The Clearinghouse for Subject-Oriented Internet Resource Guides (**http://www.lib.umich.edu/chouse/chhome.html**), based at the University of Michigan, contains dozens of topical guides to Internet mailing lists and other Internet resources. The guides have been prepared by countless volunteers and subject experts from all over globe. Categories include arts and entertainment, business and employment, education, engineering and technology, environment, government and law, health and medicine, the humanities, news and publishing, regional information, science, and social sciences and social issues. If you cannot find an Internet guide for your particular area of interest, consider compiling one and submitting it to the Clearinghouse.

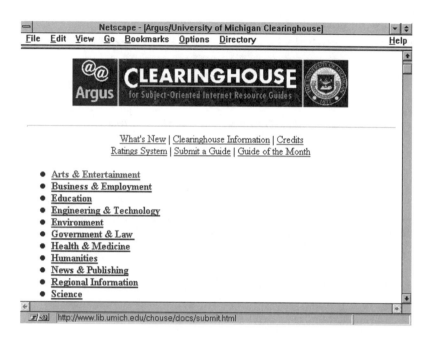

World Wide Web Virtual Library

A system distributed throughout the Internet, the World Wide Web Virtual Library covers over 150 different topics. Within each category you can find a comprehensive listing of mailing lists related to that category (**http://www.w3.org/hypertext/DataSources/bySubject/Overview.html**).

University of Indiana Mailing List Archives

This system contains over 12,000 mailing lists from around the world (**http://scwww.ucs.indiana.edu/mlarchive/**).

New-List Mailing List

This is a mailing list for announcements of new mailing lists. You might want to join this so that you can see if any new topics of interest to you have started up.

> To join this list using e-mail:
>
> Send message to: **listserv@vm1.nodak.edu**
>
> In text of message, type: **subscribe new-list firstname lastname**
>
> Special instructions: Replace firstname lastname above with your own firstname and lastname.

The Directory of Scholarly Electronic Conferences

The Directory of Scholarly Electronic Conferences contains descriptions of electronic mailing lists on topics of interest to scholars. The Directory is organized by academic subject area.

Files are available by subject type and use a file name that indicates the topic, for example, **acadlist.activist** for activist resources, **acadlist.anthro** for anthropology.

To obtain this listing using e-mail:

Send message to: **listserv@kentvm.kent.edu**

In text of message, type: **GET ACADLIST INDEX** f=mail for an index of available files

To obtain this document on-line:

URL: **ftp://ksuvxa.kent.edu/library/acadlist/**

URL: **gopher://gopher.usask.ca:70/11/Computing/Internet%20Information/Directory% 20of%20Scholarly%20Electronic%20Conferences**. (Through this site you can perform a search of the entire listing to find particular lists by topic.)

List of USENET Groups that are Available as Mailing Lists

This is a list of USENET newsgroups that are also available as mailing lists.

To obtain this listing using e-mail:

Send message to: **mail-server@rtfm.mit.edu**

In text of message, type: **send/pub/usenet/news.answers/mail/news-gateways/part1**

To obtain this listing online:

URL: **ftp://rtfm.mit.edu/pub/usenet/news.answers/mail/news-gateways/part1**

Net-Happenings List

If you really want to track what is going on with the Internet, you should join the net-happenings list.

To access this resource:

USENET: **comp.internet.net-happenings**

To review on-line:

URL: **http://www.mid.net/NET/**

This list has about 15 to 20 messages per day. Announcements concerning new mailing lists and other Internet resources are sent to this list on a regular basis throughout the day. In addition, information that even remotely impacts the Internet, such as initiatives relating to the "information highway" or "national information infrastructure," are often sent to the list.

The result is a continuous stream of messages that are wide-ranging and varied, but somehow relate to the Internet.

You should only join this list if you have a desire to receive a lot of e-mail and you want to track what is going on with the Internet. This list is for hard-core Internet junkies only. You can also search archives of this list at **http://www.mid.net/NET/**, so that you can quickly narrow in on announcements of new mailing lists, an example of which is seen below:

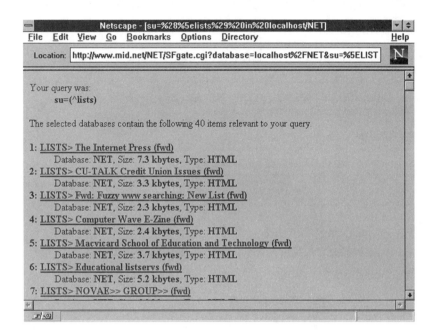

USENET FAQs
You can also search USENET FAQs to see if they refer to e-mail lists.

> To search USENET FAQs:
>
> URL: **http://www.cis.ohio-state.edu/hypertext/faq/usenet/top.html**

Searching BITNET Lists
It is possible to search several of these lists of lists. For example, you can search the BITNET lists database by sending a specially formatted e-mail message.

> To search the BITNET list database using e-mail:
>
> Send message to: **listserv@bitnic.cren.net**
>
> In text of message, type: **list global/keyword**
>
> Special instructions: Replace keyword above with the word you wish to do a search on.

For example, if you are looking for a list on Canada, you could send the command list global/canada to **listserv@bitnic.cren.net**. A search will be performed on the BITNET lists database, and an automatic reply will be mailed back to you containing the names of all the BITNET mailing lists that contain the word "canada." The automatic reply will look like this:

```
Date sent:   Sat, 5 Aug 1995 20:00:31 -0400
From:   BITNET list server at BITNIC (1.8a)
<LISTSERV@BITNIC.cren.net>
Subject: File:   "LISTSERV LISTS"
To:   Jim Carroll <jcarroll@JACC.COM>
Excerpt from the LISTSERV lists known to LISTSERV@BITNIC on 5 Aug 1995 20:00
Search string: CANADA
**********************************************************************
* To subscribe, send mail to LISTSERV@LISTSERV.NET with the following *
* command in the text (not the subject) of your message:*
*                                                        *
*SUBSCRIBE listname*
*                                                        *
* Replace 'listname' with the name in the first column of the table. *
**********************************************************************
Network-wide ID Full address and list description
--------------- ----------------------------------

ACMBSBBS        ACMBSBBS@MCGILL1.BITNET

                ACMBSBBS ACMBS Network of Canada Bulletin Board Service

ANCANACH        ANCANACH@UABDPO.BITNET

                Clan Henderson Society of US/Canada

ARCAN-L         ARCAN-L@UALTAVM.BITNET

                ARCAN-L — Listserv for discussion of archival issues in Canada

ASACNET         ASACNET@PDOMAIN.UWINDSOR.CA

                ASACNET- Administrative Sciences Association of Canada

ATLANT-L        ATLANT-L@UNBVM1.BITNET

                Atlantic Canada Region Computing Centre Staff

BIBSOCAN        BIBSOCAN@UTORONTO.BITNET

                Bibliographical Society of Canada

C-NET           C-NET@UNBVM1.BITNET

                C-NET: Community Access Net * Canada

CA-SPEED        CA-SPEED@ASUACAD.BITNET

                EDI topics among post-secondary institutions in Canada

CACI-L          CACI-L@UALTAVM.BITNET

                Research and Advanced Study: Canada and Italy
```

CANADA-L	CANADA-L@MCGILL1.BITNET
	Canadian Issues Forum
CASTOR	CASTOR@YORKVM1.BITNET
	American Schools of Oriental Research in Canada
CNC-L	CNC-L@UVVM.BITNET
	China News (Canada)
CNETIE-L	CNETIE-L@UALTAVM.BITNET
	International Centre Communication Network (Canada and elsewhe+
E-CANADA	E-CANADA@UICVM.BITNET
	History of Canada Editorial Board List
EIS	EIS@MORGAN.UCS.MUN.CA
	Humanities Canada Electronic Information Services Directors
FRANCO-L	FRANCO-L@UALTAVM.BITNET
	FRANCO-L Recherche & discussion entre francophones, surtout du+
GACGIS	GACGIS@MORGAN.UCS.MUN.CA
	Geological Association of Canada GIS List
H-CANADA	H-CANADA@MSU.EDU
	H-Net List for Canadian History
HELWA-L	HELWA-L@PSUVM.BITNET
	Malaysian Women in U.S. and Canada
HRIS-L	HRIS-L@UALTAVM.BITNET
	Human Resources Information (Canada)
INTAUD-L	INTAUD-L@UALTAVM.BITNET
	University Internal Audit (Canada)
PGS-S	PGS-S@UTORONTO.BITNET
	Physicians for Global Survival (Canada) — Students
SSFC-L	SSFC-L@UOTTAWA.BITNET
	Social Sciences Federation of Canada Discussion List
UBCREV-L	UBCREV-L@UALTAVM.BITNET
	UBCREV-L is a forum for Deans of Universities in Canada.
WIMNET-L	WIMNET-L@UALTAVM.BITNET
	Women in Management division of the Adm. Sci. Assoc. of Canada

WMCIC-L	WMCIC-L@QUCDN.BITNET
	Women's Committee of the Chemical Institute of Canada
YESCAMP	YESCAMP@UNBVM1.BITNET
	Youth Engineering and Science Camps of Canada

Any list description that contains the term "Canada" will be sent to you.

List Archives

A recent trend on the Internet is the emergence of searchable list archives. Automatic programs take all the information posted to a list and archive it in a database so that it can be searched by anyone at any time. Using such an archive is sometimes an attractive alternative to actually subscribing to a list, particularly lists that are very active. If the archive lets you list postings by date, you can quickly scan recent postings to determine which ones might be relevant to you; and, in some cases, you can also perform a search by key word.

Consider inet-marketing, the list in which people discuss Internet marketing-related issues. At the site **http://www.popco.com/hyper/internet-marketing/** you can perform a search of all postings; in this case, we are looking for items related to credit card security:

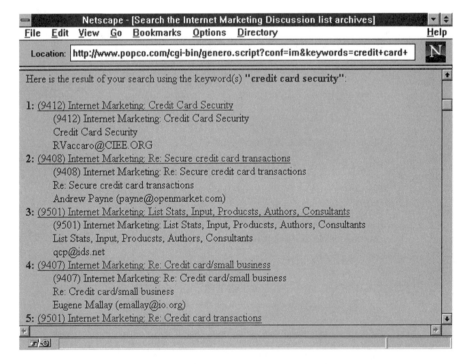

A listing of postings is provided, with the date of each posting detailed in brackets.

Another example is the archive for the Internet Vet column (which you can join by sending a message to **listserv@netcom.com** with **subscribe internetvet-column** in the text of the message). Archives of the list can be found at **http://www.io.com/~tittle/ivc/homepage.html**:

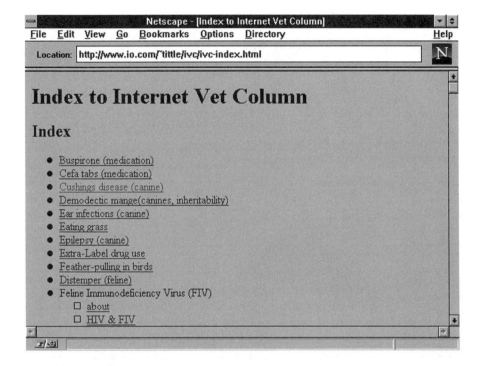

Not all lists are archived; in fact, at this time very few are. However, as with anything on the Internet, we should see a growth in the number of archived lists and increasing sophistication in the search capabilities that these archives provide.

Knowledge Networking and the Internet

Internet mailing lists and USENET newsgroups are a tremendous asset to any individual or organization in that they provide new methods and new capabilities to obtain answers to questions, to seek knowledge, or to track topics. With the explosion in use of the Internet in Canada and around the world, the number of topics available will certainly continue to increase. As you learn how to use the Internet, always keep in mind that if a topic you would like to track does not exist today, it could very easily exist tomorrow.

The World Wide Web

On the Web you can find a little bit of anything and everything. You can find information about fly fishing or deep-sea fishing, grain prices or stock prices, comics or cartoons. You can find information about movies or books, records or videos, economic policies or frat-house policies, and calculators and computers and toaster ovens. You can even find people's pets. You name it, it is probably on the Web somewhere.

In fact, if you are an aficionado of air guitar and want to impress your friends with some leading-edge skills at a party, you can find what you need in Volume 1 of the Air Guitar Guide, a publication specifically designed for use with the Philson Stratoblaster Air Guitar (**http:// www.wing.net/mirror/air/air.html**):

The Guide contains detailed instructions on playing air guitar as well as a picture of the components of the Philson Stratoblaster:

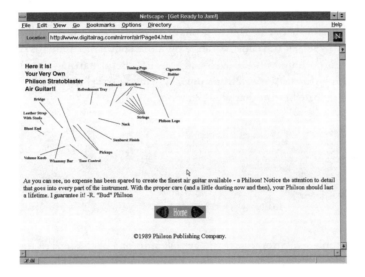

Now where else can you get information like that?

The Nature of the Web

Millions of individuals and organizations around the world are participating in the Web, since anyone can be a publisher there; a visit to the World Wide Web is a visit to the world. So how do we describe the World Wide Web? How do we portray the absolutely amazing place that the World Wide Web is? How do we describe the explosion of information that is occurring on-line?

We have to start somewhere, but the thing about the Web is that we can start anywhere and end up everywhere. The Web does not really have a starting point and it does not have a finish line. And it changes on a daily, minute-by-minute, and even millisecond-by-millisecond basis. The Web of right now is different from the Web of a moment ago. It is kind of a fascinating place. And that is an understatement.

THE WORLD WIDE WEB

1. A visit to the Web is a visit to the world.

2. The Web supports graphics, images, text, sound, and video.

3. Any Web page can link to any other Web page, hence you can start out anywhere and end up anywhere.

4. You use software known as a Web browser to view information on the Web, the most popular of which are Netscape and Mosaic.

5. There are many Web indices, such as Yahoo, OpenText, and others, which help you navigate through the Web.

A Random View of the Web

If we could only randomly select a few sites to give you an idea of what you could do on the Web, we would have a starting point. No problem! That is easy enough to do on the Web; there are lots of places that send you to a totally random location. As you begin to use the Web, you will find yourself traveling to Yahoo on a frequent basis. Yahoo is one of the largest indices to information found on the Web and thus is a useful starting place to find information about anything (**http://www.yahoo.com**). When you travel to Yahoo, look at the top of its screen: there is a little button that says "Random."

This is a fun button — by pressing it, you are taken to one of the tens of thousands of locations listed on Yahoo. It could be a Web site anywhere in the world. The first time we pressed it while writing this chapter, we were whisked off to the Nightmare Factory in Austin, Texas (**http://www.io.com/~nightime/**):

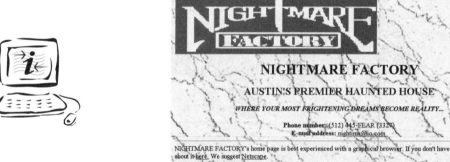

For the fun of it, we then tried it 10 more times and went to

◆ a "page" (or screen) with information from Apple Computer about the Newton personal digital assistant;

◆ an announcement for a play in Abingdon, Virginia;

- a site pointing to news articles about the 1994 race for the Senate in Virginia (the one that Oliver North lost);

- a page detailing information about classical music conductor James Levine, hosted on the Sony Music Web site;

- the Regional Planetary Image Facility, a site run by the Center of Earth and Planetary Sciences (a division of NASA), a site that has over 300,000 photographs of planets and satellites;

- a page that provided pointers to businesses in Arizona with a Web site;

- a page of information related to "Biodiversity Resources" maintained at Cornell University;

- "Shibumi's home page": information all about the board game GO;

- the welcome screen for a company called DEI Technical Information Consultants;

- "Indie Front": a page of information about independent Canadian bands[1];

- "Schrödinger's Cat Play Exchange," a site that "acts as a depository and distribution center for plays by new and unpublished playwrights with the purpose of exposing the theater world to works that would otherwise go unproduced and/or unread."

Is that 10? No? Eleven? We were having so much fun playing with the "Random" button that we quickly lost count. It is a wonderful way to get an idea of what is going on in the World Wide Web.

You're 404!

A few times when we pressed the "Random" button at Yahoo, we got a page that read "Error 404: The requested URL was not found on this server." This means that the information previously on that page has either moved, has been deleted, or that some type of error occurred. In other words, what was once there is not there anymore. This is not unusual on the Web. Some people use the term as a bit of an insult. "He/she is 404!" meaning, of course, that he/she is not all there.

HTTP What?

Aside from the fact that terms like "404" are entering our lexicon, the World Wide Web is also entering our world in a major way:

- Many advertisements for movies in newspapers now list Web addresses so that we can get more information about the film.

---

1. The Web can be as small as a neighborhood too. For example, it turns out that this site is maintained by Malibu Stacey, a band that we profiled in the 1995 edition of the *Canadian Internet Handbook*.

- Two-sided business cards are all the rage now. The first side details the old information about how to reach someone, such as a fax number, address, and telephone number. The flip side contains the World Wide Web address for the person or company.

- It is likely now that we will see a Web address listed in an advertisement or in the credits for a show.

- By reading the e-mail signature from a message received on the Internet, we are likely to see a Web address.

- Watch your cereal box, your beer bottle, your medicine labels. Sooner or later, they will all include Web addresses, right next to the 800 number.

The World Wide Web is entering the public consciousness because it is probably the most significant thing to happen on the Internet. The world is becoming wired through the Internet. And most people are learning how to use this wired world through the World Wide Web, because it is the easiest, funniest, and most exciting area of the Internet.

What Is Going on with the Web?

Our entire global information paradigm is changing because of the Internet. Everyone in the world can become a publisher through the Web. Anyone can put information on-line about any topic; there is no central authority, there are no rules, and there are no boundaries. Anyone can make his/her Web site "point" to any other Web site. Anyone can build an index of Web information, and anyone can list their favorite sites. The result is that through the Web, there is an amazing amount of information available, which consists of text, sound, images, pictures, and even "movies." Tomorrow, it will consist of much more (as we discuss in Chapter 13).

The Web is moving forward at an amazing pace; a chief scientist at Sun Microsystems estimates that it *is doubling in size every 53 days*. By the time this book is printed, we may be able to browse electronically the full catalogues of major Canadian stores while at the same time examine catalogues from small Canadian manufacturers. We will be able to confirm if a particular product is in stock, and if it is, we will be able to place an order for it on-line using a credit card. We will be able to then look at the transactions on our credit card this month, and if we want, travel to the bank to pay off the balance.

Using the World Wide Web by business to reach customers will become as common as the use of 800 numbers. Many businesses are now starting to take advantage of the incredible opportunities that can be found by making consumer education, product, and support information available on-line.

Governments are catching Web mania, too. Currently we can retrieve some government information on-line and soon will be able to immediately access some new government services through the network before being able to access it in person. We will be able to register our displeasure directly with the Premier of the province concerning some new legislative initiative and take part in an on-line electronic poll. We will be able to visit and join new initiatives lobbying for support on some type of environmental activity. We will be electronic citizens of a network that is the ultimate form of democracy.

Use of the Web presents government with tremendous opportunities for the "reengineering" of services and hence offers efficiencies and cost savings in the way that governments deal with their citizens. It also presents a significant change to the political landscape by permitting citizens to band together in ways that have not previously been possible.

You are able to research a topic for a classroom assignment by traveling through databases of information from around the world. You can publish the results of your research report online so that others can access it. You can even find classroom assignments for use within your Grade 6 geography class. And on the Internet you can find some of the friends with whom you went to university.

The Internet is reshaping education and is presenting new opportunities for use of up-to-date information within the classroom. It is changing the way educational research is conducted by providing a global audience for research reports. It is bringing excitement into the classroom.

Does all this sound far-fetched? It shouldn't. All the things mentioned above are already happening, or are about to, on the World Wide Web.

The History of the Web

The Web is little more than six years old. Viewing its history is a good indication of how quickly the Internet moves when it comes to the development and implementation of new technology.

◆ In March 1989, a project proposal to build an Internet "hypertext" system was made at CERN, the European Laboratory for Particle Physics, an organization involved in the fledgling Internet in Europe. The proposal envisioned a system on the emerging Internet that would permit "interlinked documents" located anywhere in the world to permit the exchange of information and to allow the cross-linking of reference and research papers by different institutions. Discussions and research into the concept took place through the next year. The proposal was resubmitted in October 1990, and a prototype of the World Wide Web was built the following month.

◆ In August 1991, details of the Web server software and preliminary "browser software" (i.e., the tools you use to travel through the Web) were posted to various USENET newsgroups on the Internet, so that anyone in the world could begin experimenting with World Wide Web technology. Global mailing lists to support online discussion of the Web protocols started two months later, so that people could share their research results instantly. Web development began at a breakneck pace.

◆ Through 1992, more browser software was released and more refinements to the server software took place. The Web began to gain a foothold in academic and research communities around the world, who realized that they had something significant on their hands.

◆ In February 1993, the first version of Mosaic was released for UNIX systems from NCSA, the U.S. National Center for SuperComputing Applications. Unlike previous Web browsers, Mosaic supports automatic display of images and pictures found in Web documents, supports multiple fonts, and many other enhancements that make the Web a dramatically different place.

◆ The next month, Web traffic took up 0.1% of the total traffic on the main Internet backbone network in the United States (NSFNet). Within six months it grew to 1% of total traffic, as use of Mosaic opened up the Web to many people.

◆ NCSA released versions of Mosaic for Windows and Macintosh systems in September 1993. Interest in the Internet began to hit the mainstream, as many discovered its magic for the first time.

◆ Some 500 global Web servers were in existence around the world by October 1993. Growth increased, as the Web gained attention in the *Globe and Mail, New York Times*, and other leading media organizations.

◆ In March 1994, the original developers of Mosaic left the NCSA to form Netscape Communications Corp. They released Netscape in September 1994 for Windows, UNIX, and Macintosh systems. Netscape solved many of the technical problems encountered by users of Mosaic who access the Internet using dial-up modems. The result was a tidal wave in growth of use of the Web by people at home.

◆ The Web exceeded all other types of Internet traffic in March 1994. It has not slowed down since.

◆ By June 1994, 1,500 Web servers were known.

◆ Netscape went public in August 1995, almost tripling its share price in a matter of days. Web mania seemed to envelop the world.

◆ By October 1995, a popular index of Web sites listed over 40,000 Web servers.

Why Is the Web Exploding?

There are many reasons why the Web gained so much interest and grew so quickly. And indeed, almost every individual or organization could give you a different reason why they think the Web is such an important development. Some of these reasons are:

It Supports Many Types of Information

With the arrival of the Web, the Internet was no longer restricted to dull, boring text. A Web page was something attractive to see and pleasing to the eye. When you look at a Web "page," a page of information located somewhere on the global Internet, you see text in different layouts and different fonts, and you can see logos, images, buttons, and pictures. You can hear sound, and if you have a fast enough link, rudimentary video. All kinds of data and information can be incorporated into a Web page.

For example, here is the introductory screen from the Web site for the Halifax Police Department. It incorporates pictures, text, and graphics (**http://www.atcon.com/HPD/hpd.htm**):

It Is Easy to Use

Before the Web came along, the Internet was a fascinating but sometimes technically challenging place. Systems like Telnet, FTP, and Gopher (which we review in Chapter 11) were used to discover information, but were sometimes difficult to use and not all that intuitive. Some people joked that the Internet was really "the revenge of the nerds."

Want to see what the chief of the Halifax Police Department has to say? Simply move your mouse to that line on their Web site, double click, and you will see a new page of information:

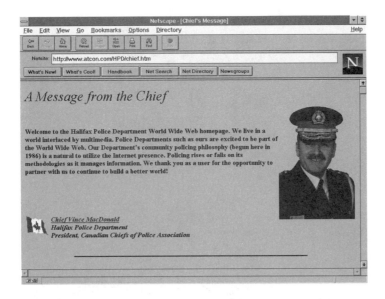

Click on the sound image, and if your Web browser is configured "correctly," you will hear him speak.

The Web made the Internet easy to use. Suddenly, everyone with a computer, modem, and an Internet connection could travel the world through the Web with just a click of the mouse.

It is no longer necessary to learn arcane computer codes or UNIX file directories or other technically challenging instructions to discover information on the Internet. Instead, using the "hypertext" features of the Web, when you see a word highlighted, you can double click on it with your mouse and be whisked away to another page of information. Images, buttons — anything on a Web page — can be made "clickable." The result is that you travel through the Web simply by pointing and clicking with your mouse.

You are not limited to pointing and clicking on text. You can point at images to go somewhere. And using "clickable maps" means that often you can click on various places within an image to choose another page of information.

It Supports Interlinking between Sites

When you click on an item on a Web page, you are, in most cases, taken to another page of information, which could be on the same computer to which you are linked. Or, it could be another computer somewhere else in the world. You might not even know where in the world you are.

Every page on the global Web can be linked to any other page on earth. Many individuals build pages that are linked to other pages. Follow a "link," and you will find yourself in New Zealand. Click again, and you are on a page in Timmins, Ontario. Click again, and you are in Madrid.

As soon as someone establishes a Web site on the Internet containing pages, any other Web site in the World can link to it; hence it is a massive "web" of interlinked sites.

If you look further down the Halifax Police Department page, you can see references to other types of information:

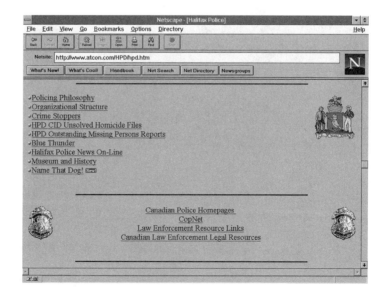

If you click your mouse on "Crime Stoppers," you will see a page of information about the crime stoppers program in Halifax. If you click on "Canadian Police Homepages," you are taken to a listing of other police departments on the Internet in Canada. Choosing "CopNet" takes you to a site at the University of Wyoming that has a massive index of police and legal resources from around the world. Choosing "Law Enforcement Resource Links" provides a summary of Canadian law enforcement information, as seen in the following screen:

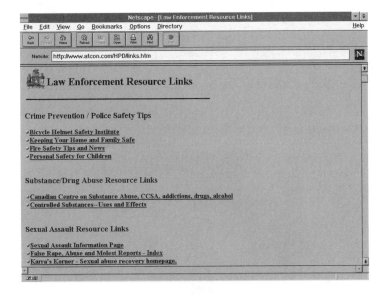

From here, you could choose the first item, at which point you will be taken off to the Bicycle Helmet Safety Institute. The result of this interlinking is that you will often find yourself on a fascinating journey ("surfing") through the Web, from site to site, from location to location.

Sometimes this interlinking leads to controversy. For example, Robert Toupes, Jr., established a site known as "Babes of the Web," which provided pointers to the Web sites of various women around the Internet (**http://www.tyrell.net/~robtoups/BABE.html**). Many people around the world recoiled in horror at such a sexist development on the Internet. Newspaper editorials were written. Some women listed in the "Babes of the Web" site demanded that the link to their site be removed. Others applauded the fact they were listed.

How did the Internet deal with the issue? Like it deals with most controversy — nothing was done (nor could anything be done). Yet, in the ultimate form of freedom of expression, a young lady named Blake Kritzberg established the site "Babes of the Web II," which provided pointers to attractive men throughout the Internet (**http://ucsub.colorado.edu/~kritzber/new/babes.html**). Now, both Toupes and Kritzberg cross reference each other's page, offending some, and causing many others to just laugh at the bizarre nature of it all. The Internet and political correctness? Don't count on it.

It Has Massive Participation

The Web is the ultimate form of democracy in which anyone, anywhere can publish information on any topic. Publishing on the future television-based "information highway" that we discussed in Chapter 1 will probably be restricted to the media elites, or to those who can afford to pay for it.

On the Web there are no such restrictions. Anyone can become a Web publisher by "renting" space on a Web server at an Internet service provider or some other type of company. On that space they can put up their own Web site, containing their own information, for access by the world. Consequently, on the Web you will find anything and everything — from the serious to the bizarre, from the useful to the useless, from the tasteful to the tasteless. Here is Beatrice. She is a bulldog belonging to Wilf LeBlanc, a senior research scientist at Carleton University (**http://nowaksg.chem.nd.edu/pub/pictures/beatrice**):

Many people have put their pets on the Web and many other peculiar bits of information. And why not? The nature of the Web is that it gives everyone in the world his/her own "printing press," a revolutionary development in history rivaled only by the invention of the original printing press. Since everyone is a publisher, venturing into the Web is a fascinating journey into the human psyche.

It Can Use Existing Data

There is a lot of information around the world that exists in digital, computer form. Organizations and individuals have learned to use word processors to prepare reports or to publish brochures. Massive databases of information on mainframe computers drive entire businesses. Movies are edited on computer, and radio shows are compiled on disk rather than tape. Even before the arrival of the Internet, our world was becoming wired by information becoming digital.

This digital information can become part of the Web; in fact, it is often easy to do so. Software tools are now available, for example, that convert information prepared in popular word processing programs into a format that can be used by the Web. Scanners can take pictures and convert them into digital form. Movies can be turned into digital bits and bytes so that they are accessible through Web site.

Organizations are suddenly discovering that the information they generate on a day-to-day basis in digital form can easily be converted so that it is accessible on the Web. Below is the site for the *Kamloops Daily News*, which is updated daily. The information is taken directly from their newspaper production system and converted so that it can be put up on the Web (**http://www.netshop.bc.ca/dailynews/daily_news.html**):

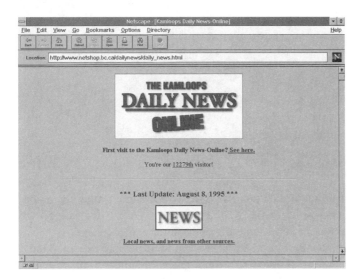

As a result, we have become a world in which digital information is turned into paper form for distribution in print, but which is also used to make available in digital, electronic form through the Web.

It Is Easy to Find Information

Before the Web, you had to learn the vagaries of FTP and Telnet to discover information on the Internet. Then along came a program called Gopher, which was a slight improvement, since it made navigating the data in the Internet a little easier.[2] Yet, it was often difficult to find information using these tools, let alone navigate your way around the network. Now, with the arrival of the easy-to-use Web, it is easier to find information on the Internet than it was before.

The fact that any Web site can link to any other Web site has meant that individuals and companies are spending time building indices of information found on the Web. These indices range from a large-scale category index like Yahoo ("list for me all construction companies in the World who are on the Web") to full-text systems like OpenText ("find me anything from anywhere in the world that mentions French Fries") to smaller, specialized indexes ("show me anything about the information highway in Canada").

---

2. All three applications are discussed in Chapter 11.

For example, here is an index built by a lawyer about Canadian lawyers and law firms on the Internet (**http://www.io.org/~lawdir/**):

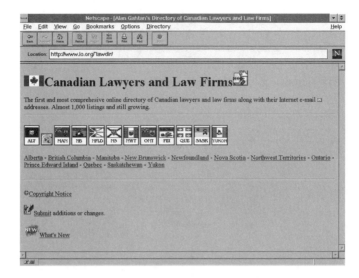

There is a proliferation of such indices on the Web because people are taking the time to catalogue, index, and cross-index the Web. The result is an ever-increasing number of guides to help you in your quest to find something out on the Web.

Here is an index developed by Dean Tudor, a member of the Wine Writers Circle of Canada. It is an index that points to alcohol-related resources from around the global Internet (**http://www.interlog.com/eye/Food-drink/Drinks/tudor.htm**):

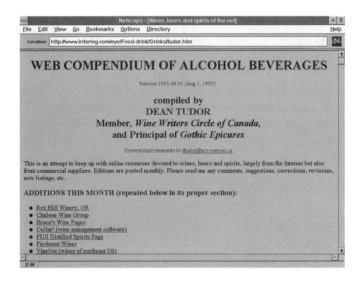

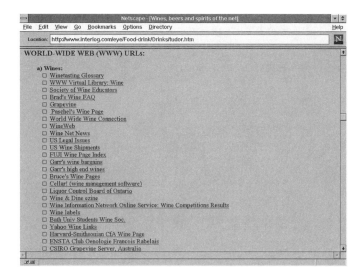

It Provides Interactivity and Customizability

Because of the many technologies coming together in the Web, there is now a type of business-customer interaction that has not previously been possible. For example, the technology behind the Web supports the use of forms. Through these forms you can answer questions, provide information, fill out surveys, or any number of other things. When you finish with the form, it is sent to the "owner" of the Web site. Here is a fairly sophisticated form, found at the site of Greenberg, Trister & Turner, a law firm. When the form is completed, it is sent to the law firm, where your responses are analyzed and you are advised of the likelihood of success of immigrating to Canada (**http://www.inforamp.net/gttlaw/assessment.html#top_of_assessment.html**):

The companies or organizations that receive the information coming from your form can integrate the data into their own computer systems. They can interface it to an order-entry system or have it perform an inquiry of an electronic catalogue. They can build sophisticated customer-based information systems in which the Web acts as a "front end."

The Web offers business a level of interactivity and customizability that is fascinating. Programmers are getting involved with the Web to integrate Web sites with corporate information systems. Software is emerging to make the whole process that much easier. Analysts are spending time clearly outlining the "architecture" of a complete customer interaction system. Corporate computer strategies are being changed to encompass the Web.

The Web is quickly becoming the window into the world of business. Sophisticated and not-so-sophisticated electronic catalogues are springing up to support on-line shopping. Credit card companies and mainframe computer system vendors are becoming involved and providing the tools of "electronic commerce." Elsewhere, small business organizations are establishing outposts on the Internet through which they can sell their products and services. Other business organizations are establishing sophisticated product information and customer support sites. The possibilities are intriguing — and endless.

The Internet is reshaping business and will have a profound impact on our daily lives as we head into the twenty-first century. Business is not the only area affected, but government, education, not-for-profit organizations, charities, and activist organizations too. (See our book, *The Canadian Internet Advantage: Opportunities for Business and Other Organizations*.) The Web is becoming a significant *strategic tool*. Certainly business and other organizations are discovering the strategic potential of the Web, yet involvement is not restricted to those who can afford to pay to establish a Web site. Many ISPs allow their members a few Web pages at no charge, and since it can be relatively easy to learn how to create a Web page (which we discuss in Chapter 16), personal pages abound on the network.

Personal pages can also be interactive. Lee Chen is a computer science student at the University of Calgary. He has developed an innovative guest book at his home page where visitors can leave their comments. All the comments left in the guest book are available for others to see (**http://www.cpsc.ucalgary.ca/~lchen/form-guest.html**):

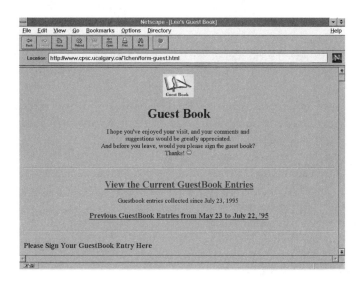

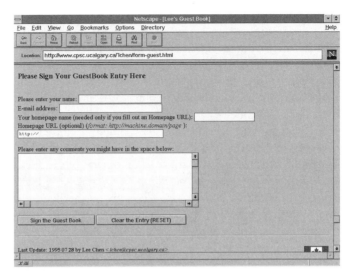

It Is Drawing Significant Investment Money

Perhaps the most significant development is that the Web has caught the attention of Bay Street and Wall Street. Fascinating sums of money are pouring into anything Web-related. The popular software company Netscape saw its stock price double within hours of issue. OpenText, a Canadian software company with very powerful Web-indexing software, went public in 1995 and enjoyed great market success. SoftQuad and InConText, Canadian companies that make software to help people build Web sites, enjoyed a rocket ride in their stock price within weeks of issue.

The result of all this venture capital is that the Web is no longer an experiment. It is a serious system being funded by some serious research and development dollars — the Web is running on the fuel of capitalism.

Consequently, the technology is maturing faster and faster. New Web software is released on a monthly, and in some cases, weekly basis. Indeed, it was a challenge for the authors of this book to keep up with the amazing pace at which this network is maturing, and it is inevitable that some of our predictions for the future of the Web that we make in the next chapter will be true by the time you read it.

In many ways the Web represents so many things to so many people that it is really becoming the one universal information system, applicable to business, government, education, science, health care, and people in general.

Surfing the Web

It is almost impossible to describe the Web on paper. You can find yourself traveling to so many places and doing so many different things that you will often forget where you started. You might sometimes forget what you were looking for, because you found something else that was just so … interesting.

You may start off at one site and find an interesting link pointing somewhere else. You may travel there, read a bit and see a pointer to another spot. Choosing that, you end up at a site located on the other side of the world, and you are fascinated by what you have discovered. And oh, this place points somewhere else ... Before you know it, you are surfing the Web.[3]

Let's Go Surfing

We started out writing this chapter by trying to present an overview of surfing. But we feel that our example lacked the spontaneity of what really happens on the Web. While pondering this dilemma, a client called looking for information about the "information highway" in Canada. We went to have a look. An hour or so later, we had a good chunk of information about the topic.

Yet, during that time, we ended up doing a bit of surfing. It is too easy to do; sometimes, there is something that is just so fascinating that you have to explore it. To get our information highway material, we started out at a few places on the Web — we will describe a few of the common starting points later in this chapter — one of which was the Canadiana page, an index maintained by a Canadian student at Carnegie Mellon University. It is an excellent site to find information about Canadian resources on the Internet (**http://www.cs.cmu.edu/Web/ Unofficial/Canadiana/README**):

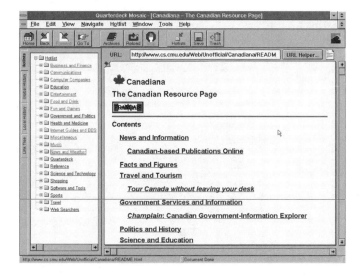

---

3. There is a lot of debate about when the phrase "surfing the Internet" first came into vogue. Most indications are that it arose around October 1991, after a pamphlet published by an organization called CERFNet showed "Captain Internet" on a surf board. You may hear different stories; no one is sure.

Browsing through the list, we found a listing for "The Information Highway in Canada":

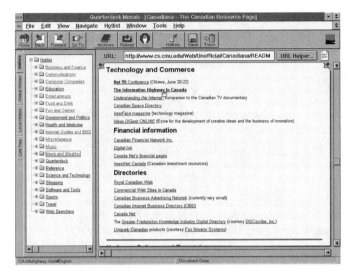

Choosing that, we traveled to a number of items, including something called the "Canadian Information Highway Shopping List":

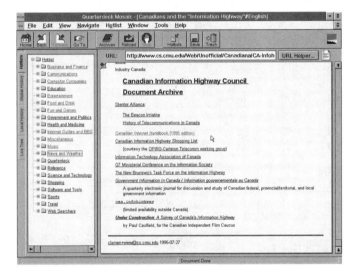

This turned out to be a site unknown to us; it contains a summary of some discussions that occur in the USENET newsgroup **can.infohighway**, a good source of information about the topic:

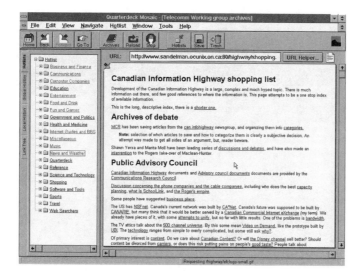

Intrigued, we were curious to know who took the time to prepare such an overview of the discussions that occur in this popular newsgroup, so we took a look at the biography of the fellow who created the site:

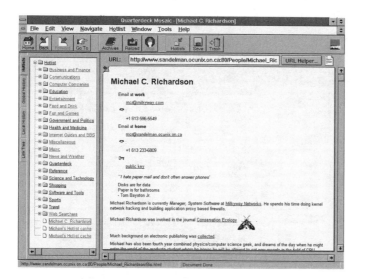

Within his biography, he includes a pointer to a listing of a few of his favorite places on-line:

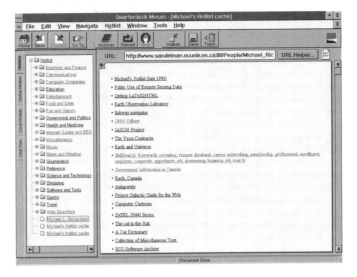

Using that, we found ourselves going off to take a look at a fascinating government document describing how the Tasmanian government in Australia is reacting to publishing government information on the World Wide Web:

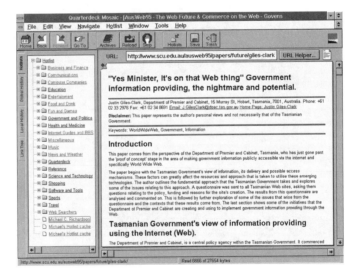

There was also a pointer to a site that lets you determine routes through various world subway systems:

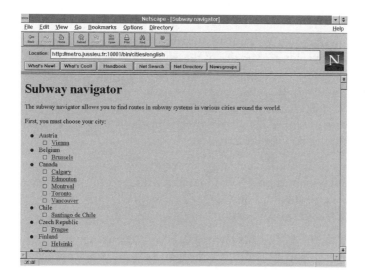

and a pointer to a site that features a daily cartoon about computers, with the cartoon text in either English or Spanish:

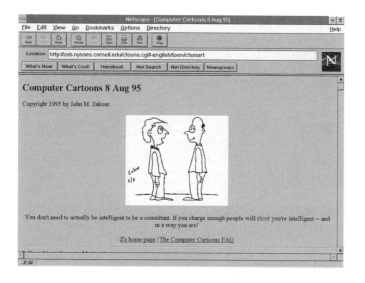

The thing about Internet surfing is that you can find yourself anywhere, at any moment in time. You can find yourself diverted, looking at information that you did not know existed, or viewing something completely unrelated to what you were originally looking for. It is a heck of a lot of fun.

Searching the Web

If looking for a specific piece of information, rather than just going surfing, you start out with a few of the good Web indices. And one of the reasons for the success of the Web is that there are so many good indices through which you can find information about a topic.

All kinds of individuals and organizations are establishing indices about topics on the Web. The indices range from the very large to the very small, from the serious to the silly. Some are voluntary efforts, while others have become fairly sophisticated businesses. Most of these indices are free; they exist because of the following:

◆ Individuals or organizations spend their time compiling the index and "give it away" for free. They might do this simply because they are interested in the topic and want to ensure a good index exists. Or they might provide the index as a means of drawing people to their Web site.

◆ If it is a commercial business, it might be an "advertising-sponsored index." When you use the index, you might see the logo for a company or product appear in addition to the index information. Click on the logo and you are whisked away to the Web site of the advertiser. The advertising money helps to pay for the cost of maintaining the index and permits people to use it for free. This advertising-supported model is one that is increasingly being adopted throughout the Internet. Yahoo, for example, is advertising-supported.

Say you are planning a trip to Prince Edward Island and want to get some tourism information. There are a few ways that you might find this information using the indices that exist on the Web.

Yahoo

A starting point for many is the Yahoo directory, perhaps one of the largest listings of Internet sites in the world. We will talk more about Yahoo later, but suffice it to say, if you are looking for something, you have to start here (**http://www.yahoo.com**). Through Yahoo, you can key in a simple search phrase:

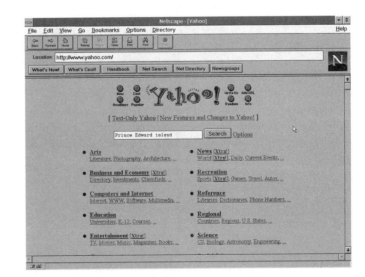

This returns a listing of all items in Yahoo that contain the phrase "Prince Edward Island":

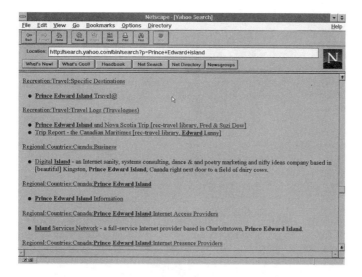

Browsing the list, you see an item for "Prince Edward Island Travel"; choosing that item, you see a listing of three items within the category:

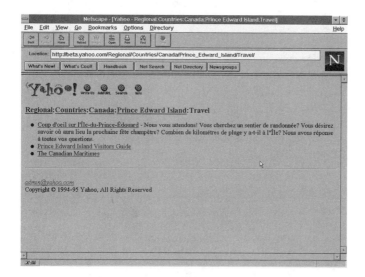

You finally choose the "Prince Edward Island Visitors Guide" and are taken directly to the guide run by the Department of Tourism in PEI:

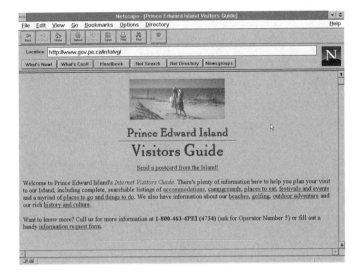

Simple enough to find. Once you get the hang of it, you will find that you can look something up in an index like Yahoo, and if it is listed, get there within just a few seconds.

Full-Text Indices

Elsewhere, leading-edge companies are building "software robots" that travel throughout the World Wide Web on a regular basis to discover information sites, topics, etc. They then build a big index of that material, and you can query that index to find companies, people, or topics. A good example is the OpenText search system, based on software from the Canadian company OpenText Corporation. You can use the OpenText search system at their search site (**http://www.opentext.com**) and specify that you are looking for any Web information that includes the words "Prince Edward Island tourism":

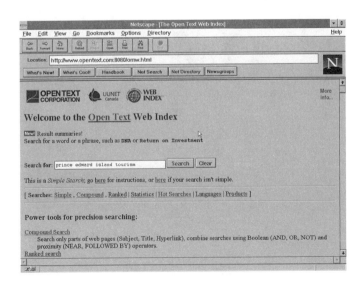

Within a second or two, OpenText returns with a list of "26 pages containing 29 matches." You can try each of these to see if they have the information you need. The first item listed might work: a listing of "WWW Sites in Prince Edward Island":

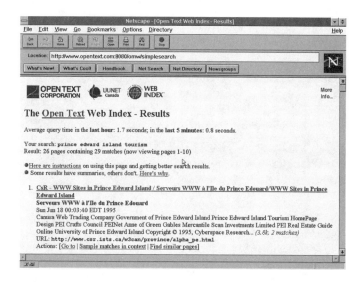

Choosing that item, you are whisked to a site that does indeed list some of the World Wide Web sites in PEI. (Interestingly enough, this site is itself an index like Yahoo, entitled "The Central Index of Canadian WWW Servers." You could have just started out right here to look for PEI tourism information.)

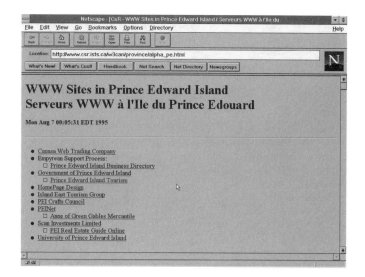

From there, you choose the "Prince Edward Island tourism" item and are taken to the guide as seen above.

Topical Indices

As you work with the Internet, you will also discover that there are all kinds of indices that focus on particular topics. For example, you might end up using City.Net when you are looking for a specific place, for it is probably the best index to focus on country/region/city information on the Internet (**http://www.city.net**). Traveling to City.Net, you can search for a place by specifying the location you are looking for (as seen below):

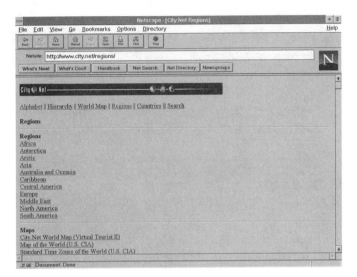

or by pointing and clicking on a map:

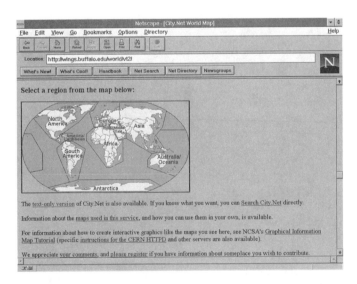

You can search by city, town, province, state, country, and with thousands of listings, you can pretty well find information on every country in the world. At the time of our visit, City.Net had information about 251 countries/territories and 837 cities on-line, ranging from Aachen,

Germany to Zvolen, Slovakia. City.Net also helped us to quickly narrow in on PEI information in this case:

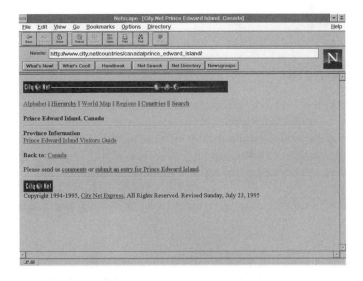

(Not only that, but City.Net also has a random button, should you just want to explore or go surfing.)

Going There Directly

Finally, many organizations are realizing the strategic benefits that can be found if they include their World Wide Web address directly within their marketing, promotional, and advertising literature. For example, PEI includes its Web address in all its tourism information, including brochures and advertisements. Here is a clip from the credits of a PEI tourism video. Note how it includes the Web address for the Visitors Guide site:

Hence over time, you will discover many Web sites simply by seeing them listed in newspapers, on TV, in brochures, and on product labels.

What Is Next?

So far, we have given you an idea of what you can do on the Web. Now, let's spend some time putting into perspective how it works and how you can use it.

How Does It Work?

When you connect to a Web site, you are actually using software known as a "Web browser" to travel to a Web server somewhere. But the magic of the Internet is that even though it might be a long and circuitous route from your browser to the site containing the information, you really do not have to know how the Web works in order to use it. Simply key in the address of the place you want to go to, and you should arrive there (at least most of the time).

However, like many you probably do want to know how the Web works. Basically, there are three things that happen on the Web that permit you to see a "page" of information anywhere in the world:

◆ You use software known as a Web browser to view information on the World Wide Web. The location you travel to is known as a URL, or uniform resource locator. The URL consists of the Web server that your browser should travel to and the specific "page" of information that should be viewed at that site. Your Web browser is told how to get to a particular site and page in one of two ways: either you tell it where to go, or it is told to go somewhere by a "hypertext" link that you choose from a page. In effect, your browser interprets the URL to figure out where to go on the Internet.

◆ Your browser establishes a link to the Web server containing the information specified in the URL. The information at the place you travel to is in what is known as HTML format — hyper text markup language — a type of computer code.

◆ Your Web browser interprets the HTML information being sent to you by the remote Web server and presents it to you in a friendly, simple fashion.

In general, at a very simplified level, the process works like this:

FIGURE 9.1

How the Web works

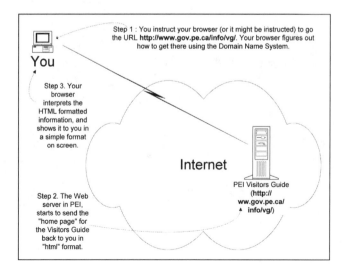

In this section we will put into perspective

◆   the types of browsers that you can use;

◆   the components of a URL;

◆   what makes up HTML;

◆   the types of information you can see in a Web browser.

Different Browsers, Different Views

You travel through the World Wide Web using a browser. This is software that is designed to interpret the HTML code sent to you by a remote Web server. The browser, in most cases, can show images and pictures, as well as text in many different formats. If you have configured your browser correctly (or if it is preconfigured), you can also listen to sound files and video files as well as other types of information. More on that later.

There are many Web browsers available. Netscape, for example, is the most popular, with versions available in Windows, Windows 95, Macintosh, and various UNIX formats. Here is a site about Howard Dill, the famous Canadian who grows big pumpkins, as seen through Netscape (**http://www.ips.ca/ibp/neat_things/dills_pumpkins/index.html**):

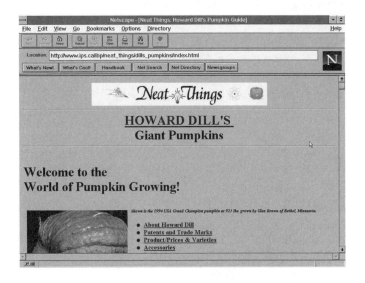

Here is the same thing as seen through Quarterdeck Mosaic:

and the same thing through Wollongong's Emissary product:

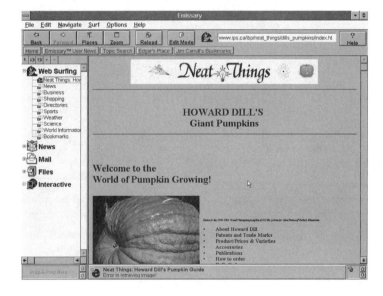

All three Web browsers are very different in the way they operate and in the way you use them, but they more or less show the information in Dill's site in the same format. The slight difference that does occur is a result of how each program interprets the HTML code sent to them and the fonts and text styles that they are configured to use.

Most people access the World Wide Web using browsers on computers that work in "windowing systems" such as Microsoft Windows and Macintosh computers, and thus they see the text in different fonts and can view the images, as seen above. Yet, there are many who do not have computers with the power to run windowing software; they can only view plain text information. One popular software package available for basic MSDOS PCs is Lynx. When it is used, Dill's site looks like the following screen:

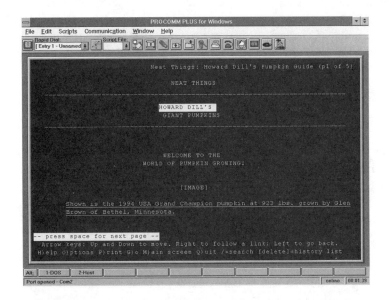

Like everything else you have encountered with the Internet, it is important to keep in mind that individuals accessing the Web are using all kinds of different computers and all kinds of different software. Thus everyone sees something a little different.

Caching

An important feature in Web browser software is support for "caching." When you travel to a Web site, your software "pulls down" information: text, graphics, images, etc. It takes time to bring this information through your Internet connection, and it can take some time if you are using a modem.

A lot of Web software supports "caching." This means that it keeps a copy on your PC of the pages of sites that you have visited on the Web. When you go back to that site, your Web software first checks the cache to see if a copy of that page is stored on your hard disk. If so, it uses that file, rather than getting the information through the modem again. Caching greatly speeds up your use of the Internet.

How Does a URL Work?

We have been using the word "site" to indicate a place on the Web that contains information. A site is located on a Web server somewhere, a computer that has a full-time connection to the Internet. The Web server runs "Web server software," which interprets incoming requests from Web browsers around the globe, and sends back the appropriate page of information in HTML format.

The vast majority of Web servers are actually Sun Microsystems computers running the UNIX operating system, running a server program known as http, hyptertext transfer protocol. There are many other types of UNIX systems in use on the Internet, including systems from IBM, Digital, Silicon Graphics, Hewlett Packard, and others. There are also many servers running Windows 95, Windows NT, or Macintosh Web server software.

The Web server might be a computer actually located at the company to which you are linking. For example, Canadian Airlines has its own Web server located on its premises in Vancouver. In other cases, the Web server might be a computer located at an Internet service provider or Internet presence provider — the company or person whose Web pages you are accessing might be renting space at that provider. For example, *Shift Magazine*, a Toronto-based arts publication, "rents" Web space on a server located at the Internet presence provider E-Commerce (**http://www.e-commerce.com**).

On the Web server is a collection of "pages of information" in HTML format. Each page has a unique identity known as the URL (URL is most often pronounced "you are el," but is also pronounced "earl"). We describe HTML format below. The URL is, in effect, the address of a particular page on the Web.

Say you want to examine a picture of Fort Beausejour, located at Barbara Safran Studios in New Brunswick:

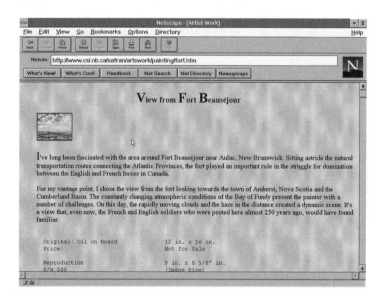

The URL of this particular painting is **http://www.csi.nb.ca/safran/artswork/painting/fort.htm**. Let's take it apart to see what it means.

◆ The first part is the URL "service type." The most common type of service you will access is **http://**, which means a server running the *h*yper*t*ext *t*ransmission *p*rotocol. This is the protocol run by Web servers and is the protocol that supports the inter-linking of documents (the interlinking is known as hypertext). Whenever you see an address starting with **http://**, you can assume that it is a Web address. As you will see later, there are other service types, so that you can access Gopher, FTP, and other resources through your Web browser. For purposes of our example in this section, we will concentrate on **http://** servers. "Service type" is required information.

◆ The next part is the "server name." In our example, the Web server for the studio is located at **www.csi.nb.ca**, which is actually Cybersmith Inc. in Sackville, New Brunswick, a company that hosts and builds Web sites on behalf of people and companies. "Server name" is required information.

◆ Next is the "directory path." In this case, the directory where the HTML files for paintings by the studio will be found is **safran/artswork/painting/**. This is optional information.

◆ The last part is the file name containing the HTML information for this particular page, in this case, **fort.htm**. This is optional information. If a filename is not specified, the server will usually show a default file found in the directory specified, or a file directory listing will be shown.

Pulling all the parts together, it means that you are looking at the file **fort.htm**, in the directory **safran/artswork/painting**, at the Web server at Cybersmith (**www.csi.nb.ca**). The actual file **fort.htm** contains instructions in HTML format to show a picture stored at that site.

There can be even more components to a URL. Sometimes you might see a "port number," which is extra information required by the server you are accessing. Or in other cases, particularly when using Web servers that perform a search of information, you might see a lot of other text or symbols in the URL, including text with **?** or **#** throughout. Sometimes URLs can be very simple, and other times they can be very complex. However, the URL above is typical of many of the URLs that you will encounter throughout the Internet.

Home Pages

Closely related to URLs is the concept of the "home page." You will often see people refer to their home page: it is the first page that you access on a Web site or within the directory for a particular person or company. For example, if you key in the URL of Cybersmith (the company that hosts the studio above) without any directory and file information (i.e., **http://www.csi.nb.ca/**), you get the "home page" for Cybersmith:

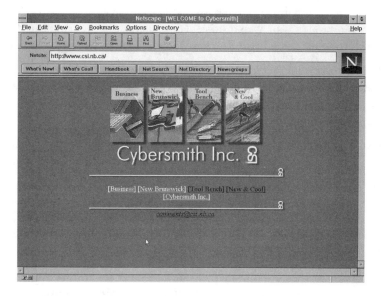

If you key in the URL of Cybersmith with the directory for the Safran Gallery (i.e., **http://www.csi.nb.ca/safran/**), you get the home page for the Gallery. URLs are sometimes specified with the exact file name of the home page (i.e., **http://www.csi.nb.ca/safran/xxxx**) or without (**http://www.csi.nb.ca/safran/**). It really does not matter which you use.

HTML

Most Web browsers let you look at the "source," or HTML code, that makes up a site. For example, you can look at the HTML code for the Safran Gallery site with the Netscape software simply by choosing "View" from the Netscape menu and then choosing "Source":

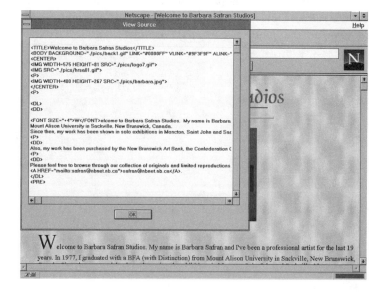

This is what HTML code looks like: some plain text, but a lot of funny codes and other symbols. Why would you want to look at the HTML code? You might just be naturally curious, or, if you wish to create your own Web pages, looking at other Web pages is often a useful starting point to learn what is involved in HTML coding.

The HTML codes tell your browser how to show certain information; they are called "tags." They surround text or other information, in effect telling your Web browser to do something special with that information. For example, notice in the diagram below the "tag" **<center>**. This tells your browser that everything from that point should be centered until the tag **</center>** is encountered; then it should stop. We describe a few of the components of HTML in the diagram below:

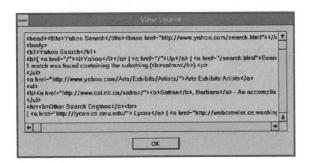

A few of the most common tags are the following:

◆ **<h1>** to **<h6>** headings, each showing a different font size;

◆ **<p>** signifies a new paragraph;

◆ **
** inserts a line break;

◆ **<hr>** draws a horizontal line;

◆ **<i>** shows text in italics;

◆ **<b>** shows text in bold;

◆ **<li>** indicates a list item (i.e., bullets);

◆ **<A>** "anchor hyperlink," that is, includes a reference to another Web page or other resource somewhere, by including the URL. Usually of the form **<A HREF=URL>**, although sometimes you might see one **<A NAME=something>**, which simply points to another section on the same URL.

There are all kinds of HTML tags, and obviously there is a lot of complexity to some of them. This book cannot hope to put into perspective the "science" of HTML. After all, our objective is just to give you an idea of what is going on. We can, however, point you to a few sites that contain beginners' guides to HTML.

A Beginners Guide to HTML (from NASA):

URL: **http://www.ncsa.uiuc.edu/General/Internet/WWW/HTMLPrimer.html**

The Bare Bones Guide to HTML:

URL: **http://www.access.digex.net/~werbach/barebone.html**

How to Publish on the Web:

URL: **http://www.thegiim.org/**

Also check out Yahoo:

URL: **http://www.yahoo.com/Computers_and_Internet/Internet/World_Wide_Web/Beginner_s_Guides/**

Types of Information You Can Access

You can consider the types of information that you can access through the Web from two perspectives: the type of server you can access and the type of data you can obtain.

Type of Server

You are not restricted to accessing information supported by hypertext transfer protocol servers (i.e., those with an **http://** in the URL). As mentioned earlier, you can also access information from Gopher sites, FTP, and Telnet sites, and other information types. Most Web browsers can access several different types of servers. The basic ones are:

◆　**http://** for Web sites;

◆　**https://** for secure Web sites;

◆　**ftp://** for FTP locations;

◆　**gopher://** for Gopher servers;

◆　**telnet://** for Telnet locations;

◆　**netnews://** to access USENET news.

This means that you can often use your Web browser to do many different things instead of having to use separate programs to accomplish separate tasks.

For example, as you saw in Chapter 8, Netscape can be used to access USENET news-groups using the URL format **netnews://newsgroup.name**. In Chapter 11, we will see how the same program can be used to access FTP sites using the format **ftp://ftpdirectory/filename**. Hence the typical Web browser is quickly becoming one of the only pieces of software that you need next to an e-mail program. And as we will see in Chapter 13, at least one program has combined everything, including e-mail, into one all-purpose program.

Type of data

The World Wide Web lets you access several types of information, including text, graphics, pictures, sound, and video. Sometimes this information is shown to you as soon as you see a page, and in other cases, you have to "download," or retrieve, the information from that page.

In the first case when you see information on the screen as soon as you enter a site, you immediately see text (in multiple formats and fonts) and can, with most browsers, immediately see some images or pictures. However, there are certain other "data types" that you cannot "view" immediately. You must first "download" them, that is, transfer them from the Web server to your computer, before you can "view" them. By "view" we mean listen to, view, or watch, depending on the type of information it is.

Why do you have to download them? Because there can be all kinds of data in all kinds of format. Sounds can come in "**.au**" format or "**.wav**" format. Video can come in MPEG files or QuickTime format. Images can come in "**.tif**" or "**.gif**" or "**.jpeg**" or other formats. It is difficult for the programmers of a Web browser to ensure that their program can deal with all kinds of different formats, particularly since new file types are emerging all the time. Hence with many browsers today, you have to download the file first, and then use a separate program to view it. You download the file by "clicking" on it. If your browser is configured correctly, once the file has finished downloading, the "viewer" program will be loaded automatically to work with the file.

For example, here is a page from Canadian Music Express (**http://www.io.org/~cme/**), a site that profiles many independent Canadian bands. The page for Hip Club Groove (**http://www.io.org/~cme/NXNE/ARTISTS/hcg.html**), a hip-hop band from Truro, Nova Scotia, includes some text and images, which are shown immediately. It also has a reference to two sounds clip that play in "MPEG sound format." The sound is not automatically played; we must first download it.

To do this, we double click on the sound link on the document. Once it has finished transferring to our PC, our "MPEG Sound player" starts to play the song. On this screen, we can look at their site and listen to a clip of one of their songs:

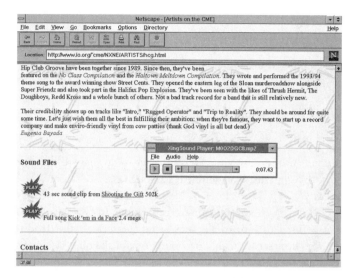

In this case, we had specifically configured our Netscape software in advance, telling it what to do with any MPEG files it encounters. As can be seen on the screen below, we have instructed Netscape to run the program XING_PLY.EXE whenever it encounters an MPEG file. (Xing_ply is the software that we use in this case to listen to the MPEG file. The next paragraph describes how we got it.) This is called "configuring a viewer."

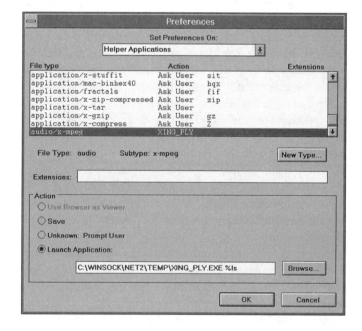

Where did we get the software to play MPEG sound files? The Canadian Music Express home page provided us with a simple pointer that we clicked on to get the necessary program to listen to "MPEG sound":

Another example is with Citizenship and Immigration Canada, which has a Web site in which are published various documents. You can view these documents on the screen, or if you want, download them in WordPerfect 5.1 format. The latter files are in a "compressed" format, "zip," so that they do not take long to retrieve.

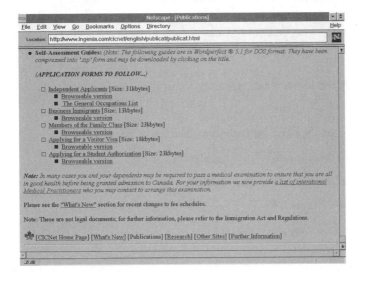

In this case, you can configure your Netscape browser with a "viewer" that will automatically "unzip" (i.e., decompress) any zip files that it encounters:

The next time we encounter a zip file, our version of Netscape will automatically know what to do with it.

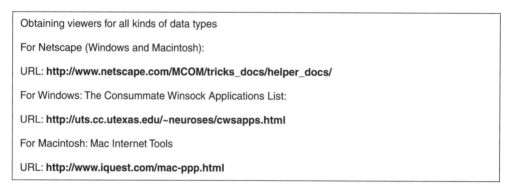

Obtaining viewers for all kinds of data types

For Netscape (Windows and Macintosh):

URL: **http://www.netscape.com/MCOM/tricks_docs/helper_docs/**

For Windows: The Consummate Winsock Applications List:

URL: **http://uts.cc.utexas.edu/~neuroses/cwsapps.html**

For Macintosh: Mac Internet Tools

URL: **http://www.iquest.com/mac-ppp.html**

Today, you have to customize most Web software to handle special data types, in particular "movie" files, in some cases "sound files," and in other cases "special image files." It can be a complicated and intimidating task, but with a little experience you can get it right the first time. But since Web software is constantly evolving, over time the major programs will include automatic support for many different data types.

Where to Obtain Web Software

The Internet is a place in which a lot of the software has been available for free, or is available on a "shareware" or "public domain" basis. It is a place where you can download software, try it out, and if you use it, may be required to send in a payment. In other cases, you are not actually required to send in a payment, but can do so if you wish. The spirit of sharing and community has dominated much of the development of software for the Internet. Until now.

There is no doubt that the Internet is evolving quickly into a commercial marketplace with commercial software. And in Chapter 13 we take a look at a lot of this software, including programs through which you can access the Web. However, there is still a lot of Web browser software out there that you obtain for free or for a minor fee. We provide details on this software below.

Note that the listings below are subject to change as new versions come out and as companies reexamine their distribution policies. Software that is free today may not be tomorrow. As a result, the following list provides guidance on where you can locate Web browser software, but obviously conditions might change by the time you read this section. If a file name is not provided for an FTP site, look in the directory mentioned for the most recent file. FTP is discussed in Chapter 11.

Windows:

Cello

Browser from Cornell LII:

URL: **ftp.law.cornell.edu/pub/LII/cello**

    http://www.w3.org/hypertext/WWW/Windows/Status.html

    ftp://ftp.law.cornell.edu/pub/LII/cello

Mosaic for Windows:

From NCSA

URL: **ftp://ftp.ncsa.uiuc.eduPC/Windows/Mosaic**

    http://www.w3.org/hypertext/WWW/MosaicForWindows/Status.html

    ftp://ftp.ncsa.uiuc.edu/PC/Windows/Mosaic

WinWeb

From EINet

URL: **ftp://ftp.einet.net/einet/pc/winweb/winweb.zip.**

    http://www.einet.net/EINet/WinWeb/WinWebHome.html

Netscape

Netscape is a commercial product but can be evaluated free of charge for an unlimited period of time by individuals.

URL: **http://home.netscape.com/info/index.html**

Quarterdeck Mosaic

A commercial product

URL: **http://www.qdeck.com/beta/** for a beta version.

Spry Mosaic

A commercial product. A demo is available on-line.

URL: **ftp://ftp.spry.com/AirMosaicDemo/AMOSDEMO.EXE.**

     http://www.spry.com/airmos.html

SlipKnot

SlipKnot is the only graphical WWW browser that operates entirely without SLIP or PPP connection.

URL: **ftp://oak.oakland.eduSimTel/win3/internet**

     http://www.interport.net/slipknot/slipknot.html

Emissary

Emissary, from Wollongong, is a commercial browser for Windows

URL: **http://www.twg.com**

Pythia

A Canadian product with a focus on security

URL: **http://www.pythia.com**

Mac Browsers:

NCSA Mosaic for Macintosh

URL: **ftp://ftp.ncsa.uiuc.edu in the directory Mac/Mosaic.**

     http://www.ncsa.uiuc.edu/SDG/Software/MacMosaic/MacMosaicHome.html

     ftp://ftp.ncsa.uiuc.edu/Mac/Mosaic/

Netscape

URL: **http://home.netscape.com/info/index.html**

MacWeb

URL: **ftp://ftp.einet.neteinet/mac/macweb**

     http://galaxy.einet.net/EINet/MacWeb/MacWebHome.html

Where to Find Information on the Web Indices

There are so many places to start looking for information on the Web that we cannot possibly hope to list them all. A few of the major items that you might consider are listed below:

◆ The most popular index on the Web is one that we have discussed throughout this book, Yahoo (**http://www.yahoo.com**). If you are looking for anything on the Web, start here.

◆ There are several "search systems" through the Internet, such as the OpenText system, which we outlined earlier in this chapter. These systems are often referred to as "spiders," for they are programmed to automatically travel through the Web, discovering and indexing new information sources. Aside from OpenText (**http://www.opentext.com**), try Lycos (**http://lycos.cs.cmu.edu**), WebCrawler (**http://www.webcrawler.com**), and Infoseek (**http://www.infoseek.com**).

◆ Much of the new software that we examine in Chapter 13 is arriving on the market with preconfigured hot lists, some of which include pointers to Canadian resources.

◆ One excellent place to start looking for Web-based information is the World Wide Web Virtual Library, which contains subject-oriented guides on everything from aboriginal studies and accelerator physics to yeasts and zoos (**http://www.w3.org/hypertext/DataSources/bySubject/Overview.html**):

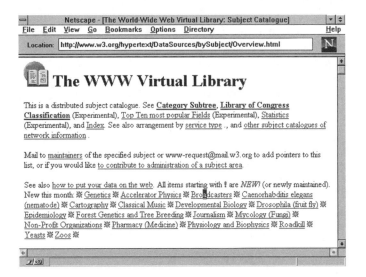

◆ To find out what is new on the Web, check out the NCSA What's New site (**http://www.ncsa.uiuc.edu/SDG/Software/Mosaic/Docs/whats-new.html**):

You can also monitor the **comp.infosystems.www.announce** USENET newsgroup. Here is a sample posting. There is a lot of traffic within this newsgroup.

From: mah@cs.ualberta.ca (Dean S. Mah)

Newsgroups: comp.infosystems.www.announce,rec.games.chess.misc

Subject: Alberta Chess [Canada]

Followup-To: comp.infosystems.www.misc

Date: 6 Aug 1995 06:19:35 GMT

Organization: Computing Science, U of Alberta, Edmonton, Canada

Lines: 20

Approved: www-announce@boutell.com

Message-ID: <401mtn$lsk@big.aa.net>

NNTP-Posting-Host: boutell.com

Originator: announce@Linux

Xref: newshub.ccs.yorku.ca comp.infosystems.www.announce:7119

rec.games.chess.misc:986

For anyone interested in Chess in Alberta, Canada come to:

<URL:http://www.cs.ualberta.ca/~mah/ACA/>

There's a listing of clubs, tournaments, and membership info. There's also a

searchable ratings list that will be updated bi-monthly.

There's also a list of WWW sites for chess clubs and federations in Canada, the US, and around the world.

Dean

--

Dean S. Mah (email: mah@cs.ualberta.ca) | — Give a monkey a brain and he will swear that he is the center of the universe. Edmonton, Alberta, http://www.cs.ualberta.ca/~mah

Department of Computer Science

the University of Alberta

Canada

◆ The *Canadian Internet Directory* provides a detailed listing of Web resources and other information available throughout the Canadian Internet.

Appendix E includes a listing of useful resources that will help you on your journey into the World Wide Web.

Problems with the Web

As fascinating as the Web is, you will encounter frustrations with it as you use it.

◆ Links become outdated. Web pages can disappear as easily as they appear. Individuals or companies can decide to stop publishing on the Web or may find that circumstances beyond their control do not make it possible for them to participate any longer. In other cases, page names change, the name of the server hosting the page changes, or the directories change. Whatever the case may be, cross references (or links) within the Web are constantly changing. This means that sometimes you will click on a link and get the infamous "Error 404!"

◆ Sites often get busy. When a popular movie comes out, there is often a lineup to get into the theatre. What do you do? You wait a few weeks and try again when its popularity has eased. It's the same with the Web. When a new, innovative, or interesting Web site comes up, there will often be a rush of people trying to access it. The result? You can't get in. Or, when you do, it is terribly slow. Just wait a few weeks and try again.

◆ You might have speed limitations. Some individuals design pages full of wonderful graphics, so many, in fact, that it can take many seconds or minutes to view a page. You might become frustrated with the fact that you only have a dial-up connection to the Internet. This problem is being solved in two ways. First, as we will see in the next chapter, higher access speeds are slowly coming to the Internet. Second, many Web designers, conscious that many access their sites with modems, minimize the use of graphics so that pages "load" as fast as possible.

◆ You might find it too big and too difficult to keep up. The Web is just too darn big. You can spend hours in it. Many experience frustration with the Web, simply because it seems to have become too all-encompassing and too large, with too much information. In a general sense, the Web is overwhelming. In other cases, you will become frustrated because you will feel that the Web is moving so quickly that you can never keep up with it. A feeling of helplessness descends. You will experience both feelings at some point or other. But then you will sign on again. And again. And again.

◆ The Web wastes time. Some feel that the Web is just a big waste of time. It has become trendy for the "elite" in the press and scientific fields to knock the Internet by suggesting that people are not getting value out of it, and that valuable knowledge and time are being wasted as people surf the mindlessness of the Web. Maybe it is a waste of time. Maybe it isn't. But one thing is certain: many find that a session surfing the Web is far more entertaining than watching some of the drivel on TV every night.

◆ It is too difficult to find information. Learning how to search for information on the Internet is not a skill that can be picked up in a few minutes or a few days or even a few weeks. Learning to undertake research on the Internet is a skill that is developed.

◆ There are too many indices. With any topic you may find 30 indices of information related to that topic. Some are up-to-date and excellent. Others are outdated and useless — few of the links work, or when they do, they take you to old and outdated sites. Hence you can become frustrated as you begin to use some of the seemingly useful indices that people have built.

◆ Too many ill-fated attempts dissolve to nothingness. In some cases, you might travel the Web and discover a resource that looks promising — its home page promises to be the "definitive guide to" whatever. Yet, when you look through it, you discover that it is more or less an empty shell and does not contain the information you were hoping for. Many can get involved with the Web, and many become excited about building some type of resource that others can use, whether an index or other information. Yet they discover that maintaining such a resource takes an increasing amount of time. They become busy on other things, or their interest tails off. Whatever the case, you cannot get angry at such things; you just have to accept that some of the things that you encounter on the Web will not be quite the thing that you were hoping for.

◆ People go silly with Web features. You will encounter Web features that over time will make your blood boil. For example, one of the most overused HTML tags is the **<blink>** feature: it causes the text that follows it to blink. People have gone silly with use of this feature. You will begin to wish that some people took HTML design courses.

◆ Sites exist that really and truly do not serve a useful purpose, consist of a bad design, or somehow are just plain "bad." Of course, given that this is the Web, you can check out "Mirsky's Worst of the Web" (**http://mirsky.turnpike.net/wow/Worst.html**) for a daily pointer to a site that is just plain lousy.

◆ The Web server protocol (http) is inefficient. If you want a good technical explanation why, you can view a document by Venkata N. Padmanabhan at the University of California–Berkeley, who notes that "the HTTP protocol, as currently used in the World Wide Web, uses a separate TCP connection for each file requested. This adds significant and unnecessary overhead, especially in the number of network round trips required" (**http://www.ncsa.uiuc.edu/SDG/IT94/Proceedings/DDay/ mogul/HTTPLatency.html**).

As a result, sometimes the Web is slow. It can take forever to pull down a page. This inherent inefficiency of the Web server protocol means that you will have to learn to be patient.

◆ The Web is exceeding its capabilities. As we will see in the next chapter, companies are exploring how the Web can be used for sound and video transmission. The Web and the Internet were not developed to support such capabilities, which is another reason why in some cases it seems to be slow.

You will encounter frustration with the Web. You will also be in awe of it, and constantly fascinated by what it represents. The best way to deal with the Web is to develop an open mind and, most importantly, keep a sense of humor.

You Ain't Seen Nothing Yet

Cable modems are anywhere from 15 times to 400 times faster than conventional telephone modems, making it possible to view live video clips, for example, or download pictures and software programs in seconds rather than minutes.

Alacazam! Welcome to the Magical World of Cable Modems
Los Angeles Times, May 3, 1995

The Internet will soon be so ubiquitous, or "transparent," as experts say, that we'll take it for granted, as we do electrical power or the phone system today. The grand vision now sparking imaginations and business plans throughout the computer industry is that by 2000, all major software programs will be "aware" of the Net and depend on it for a continuous stream of new data and updated functions. Less and less will you have to make a conscious decision to "get on the Internet," as you do today. Whenever it needs to, your PC will reach into the Web for a piece of data, a movie clip, or even a new program.

PLANET INTERNET: How the center of the computing universe has shifted
Business Week, April 3, 1995

Many people have joined the Internet since 1994, and many of them use the World Wide Web.

The Web is a stunning application; it seems amazing to be able to zip from site to site, around the world in a matter of seconds. The type of information that is accessible is astounding, and the number of new sites… Superlatives and adjectives are just not enough to describe the World Wide Web.

But, the Web is an early development in the universe of the Internet. Around the world, developments are taking place at a breathtaking pace, developments that will once again change your view of the Internet. Computer software firms, ranging from powerhouses like Sun Microsystems to small independent outfits, are releasing new products that serve notice to the world that the Internet can be used for anything — from telephone calls, to movies, to interactive three-dimensional games.

In this chapter, we will take a look at some of these tantalizing and fascinating new technologies to show where the Internet is headed in the next month, next year, and next decade.

Complex Documents

There has been an explosion in electronic publishing on the Web, as organizations try to capitalize on the growing use of the Internet. The result has been that within the last year or two, the World Wide Web has become a very exciting and interesting technology: it supports graphics, text, and other information, and is accessible in a friendly format.

Many organizations are trying to use the World Wide Web for electronic publishing, but become frustrated that they cannot transfer the layout principles inherent in print publications over to the Internet. This is due to some basic limitations in HTML, the language that supports the Web, as well as the difficulty of getting across the specific fonts used in printed publications. Since everyone is using different computers, everyone has a different configuration of fonts.

Magazines, for instance, are loaded with graphics: pictures are placed in strategic locations to catch your eye; advertisements jump out at you from the page; complex blends of colors, fonts, and graphics are used to produce a page layout that is pleasing to the eye. A hundred years of typesetting skills has led to the science of page layout.

Enter Adobe Acrobat. First released in 1992 to slow sales and mediocre reviews, the product has since gained a new foothold in the Internet as *the* method by which publications can be distributed in the exact format in which they appear in print. Acrobat lets you view a document on your computer screen exactly as it would have appeared had it been printed, regardless of the type of computer you are using. This might sound like a trivial undertaking, but it is actually a significant technical advance.

Some organizations now place publications on their Web sites in Adobe Acrobat format. Since Adobe makes the "viewer" program (or, as they call it, a "reader" program) available for free, you can download both the software and a document at the same time. (The viewer is available for free at **http://www.adobe.com**. It can also be easily obtained from many of the sites that publish in Acrobat format.) For example, the Canadian office of Ernst & Young, an international accounting firm, makes various books and publications available in Acrobat format at its site (**http://tax.ey.ca/ey/**):

YOU AIN'T SEEN NOTHING YET

1 The Internet is moving forward at a rapid pace. This chapter examines those developments.

2 A data format supported by a program known as Adobe Acrobat permits the distribution of documents through the Internet in a form that is identical to how they appear in print.

3 Corporate databases are being linked to the Web in order to support some type of strategic customer activity.

4 Software companies are rapidly releasing software for secure electronic transactions on the Internet.

5 HotJava, a technology from Sun Microsystems, allows Web pages to automatically display information as it changes without having to reload the Web page.

6 New software allows you to hear sound and audio through the Internet in real time; there is now also software that permits you to place "telephone calls" and to watch "multimedia shows" through the Internet.

7 Videoconferencing is now starting to occur through the Internet with software such as CU-SeeMe.

8 Virtual reality promises to change the way we navigate through the Internet, turning a flat, two-dimensional Web space into a fascinating three-dimensional world.

9 People are investigating how the Internet can be used in remote monitoring applications and other activities.

10 The limitation in many of the above applications is the speed of the access to the Internet, but this limitation will disappear in the near term.

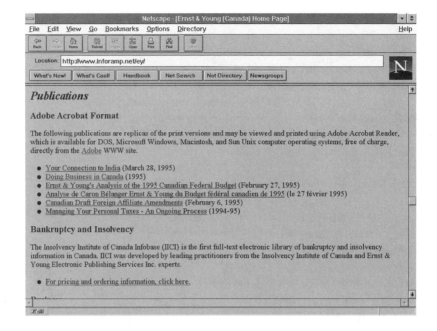

Once you retrieve a publication, you can view it with Acrobat in its actual printed form:

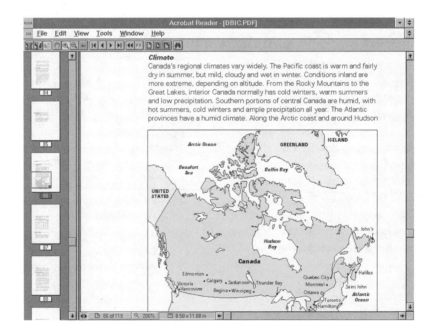

The *New York Times* places on-line an Acrobat version of its special fax edition each day:

Rogers Communications puts it 75th annual report on its Web site, available in Adobe format (**http://www.rogers.com**):

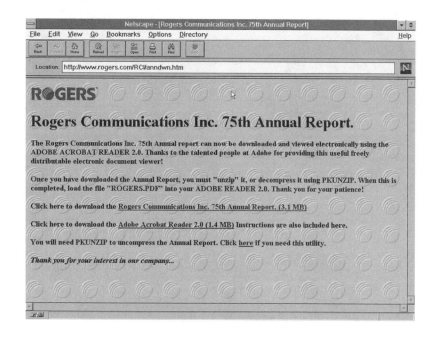

And Time Life has put on-line *Landscaping*, a book from its Home Repair and Improvement series:

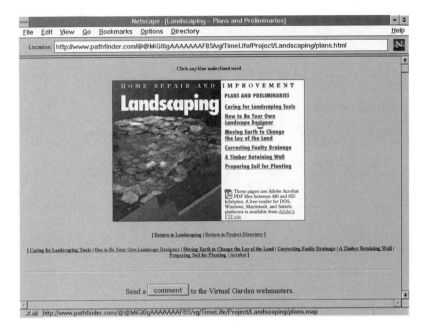

You can obtain an Acrobat version of any particular chapter simply by clicking on it:

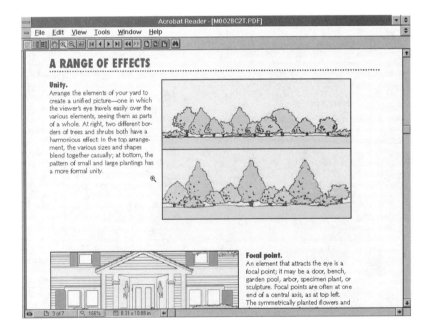

As you travel through the Web, you will find more and more sites placing publications in Adobe format. And since Netscape has incorporated the Adobe "reader" directly into its version 2.0, the process of viewing such a document is automatic, meaning that a whole new dimension of electronic publishing is now possible.

Real Database Information

While some sites go to great effort to update their Web pages on a frequent basis, many contain information that does not change regularly. In many cases, this is because companies have built sites just to have a "presence" on the Web. Their initiative has been pursued because of a "me too" syndrome, rather than a desire to meet any strategic business purpose. The result is a Web site that is created, never maintained, and never updated.

Many business organizations are now realizing that there are strategic opportunities to be found through involvement with the World Wide Web and that customers are seeking real content and real information on-line. As management becomes involved in strategic planning involving use of the Internet, decision makers are discovering the opportunities and benefits in making selected information from a corporate database available to customers or other parties. Thus one of the more significant recent trends on the Internet has been the linking of internal corporate information databases to the World Wide Web, thus permitting visitors to interact with large volumes of information.

The high profile pioneer of this line of thinking is Federal Express, which linked its worldwide package tracking system to the Web in 1995. Through the site you can determine the status of a package that has been shipped with the courier company. Simply travel to the FedEx Web site and key in a waybill number (**http://www.fedex.com**):

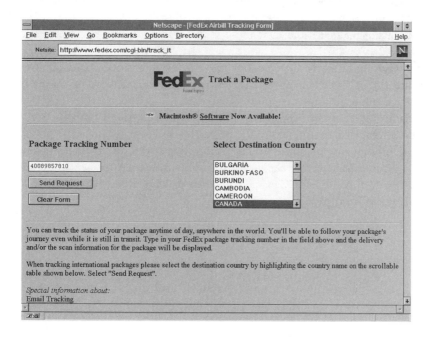

Within a second or two, detailed information, such as when your package was delivered and who had signed for it, is presented on your screen:

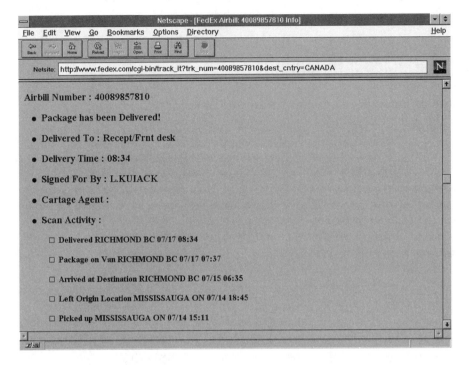

What happens is this: the Web server at FedEx takes your request and submits that request as a query to the mainframe computer that serves as the FedEx package tracking system. It then takes the results of the query and dynamically turns it into a new Web page that it immediately shows to you.

The integration of database technology into the Internet is opening up all kinds of new opportunities through which companies can establish strategic applications on the Internet or through which an organization can fulfill its mandate.

For example, here is the National Pollutant Release Inventory, available from Environment Canada. One of the mandates of the organization is to ensure that the public can find out about significant environmental events. An opening screen on the Web site describes the purpose: any company releasing significant quantities of certain substances or wastes must provide details to Environment Canada, who then make it available to the public (**http://www.geod.emr.ca/html-public**):

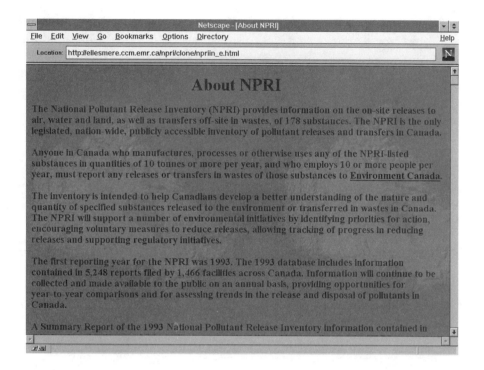

Through this site anyone can query the Environment Canada database about the release of a particular substance anywhere in Canada:

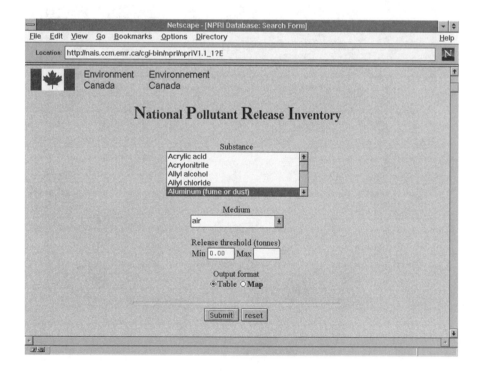

The results of the query can be displayed in text form:

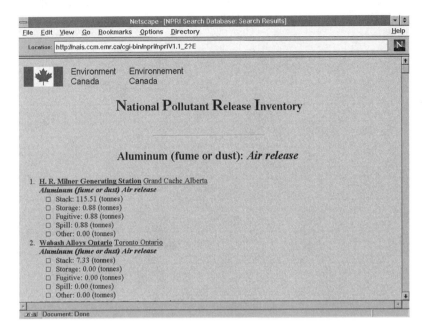

or can be displayed in the form of a map. For example, this screen indicates that a large quantity of aluminum dust was released into the air at a site in Alberta:

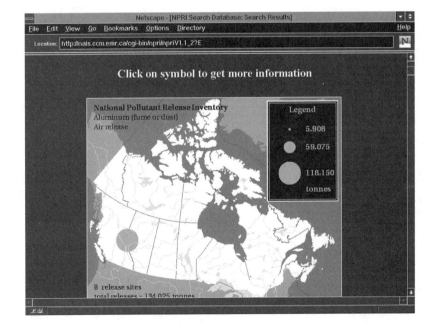

Similar sophisticated sites are now appearing around the Internet. For example, Molson's "I Am Online" site (**http://www.molson.com**) permits users to query a cross-Canada database detailing concerts in their particular area. In this case, we are searching for information about concerts in the Toronto area:

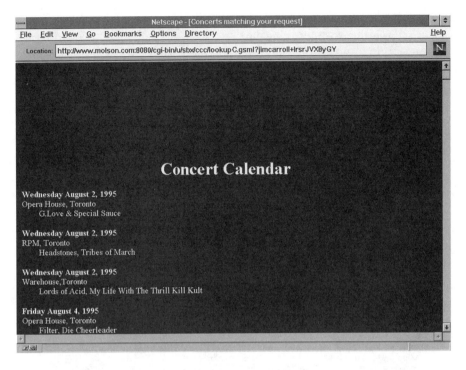

The linking of corporate and other databases is an important trend and provides a teasing glimpse into the real future of the Internet. We are already seeing signs of where this might lead in the future. For example, one day it might be possible to do some of the things that we list below, and in certain cases, we note where it has already become possible:

♦ query your bank balances or the balance on your mortgage after properly identifying yourself to your banking institution (this is currently possible; the first bank to do this was Wells Fargo in the United States, in mid-1995);

♦ examine the value of your investment holdings at the current moment by querying the information maintained by your investment representative;

♦ run a program that will compare your natural gas usage this summer compared to last so that you can understand the impact of use of a pool heater all summer;

♦ examine an up-to-date status report on your frequent flyer miles or some other type of frequent shopper program;

♦ obtain a listing of long distance telephone calls or charge card items so that you can analyze them in a spreadsheet;

♦ browse electronic catalogues that contain up-to-the-minute prices, product descriptions, and quantities in stock.

Spurring this area on are technical developments enhancing the sophistication of the types of forms that can be built within the World Wide Web and the release of tools from major database software companies (such as IBM, Oracle, and Sybase) that permit a straightforward integration of a Web site into a corporate database.

Oracle, for example, is one of the world's largest database companies and has released a kit that permits corporate organizations to develop such links (**http://www.oracle.com**):

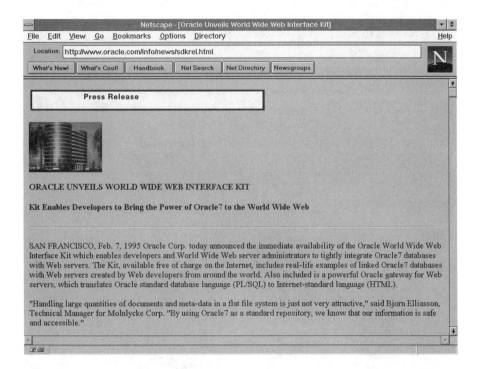

Related to this trend is the emergence of new consulting companies that combine marketing skills with database technical talent; these consultants can merge corporate information sources into World Wide Web sites.

Through such technologies emerge a whole new type of Web application, applications that go beyond static, unchanging pages of information to sites that let you do something really useful, by retrieving information of particular relevance to you, from companies and individuals around the world. The integration of the World Wide Web into corporate information systems is perhaps one of the most significant developments of all the issues we review in this chapter.

Electronic Commerce Capabilities

One of the oft-repeated refrains about the Internet is that it is not ready to support real business; for example, it is not safe to send credit card orders through the Internet. Don't believe it. Companies involved in the Internet are rapidly releasing software tools that permit real electronic commerce to take place on the Internet. These tools provide the basis for secure on-line credit card orders and credit card authentication. Elsewhere, we are seeing the emergence of new forms of electronic payment and conceptual ideas of cyberspace currencies. Security problems are rapidly being solved through the development of sophisticated new hardware and software solutions.

We are entering an era in which business is increasingly being conducted through the Internet, and thus there is a rush to ensure that the infrastructure of the network can support such activities on a secure and efficient basis. Netscape is in the forefront of such efforts with its Commerce Server, Netscape Istore, and the Netscape Merchant system. Details about each are available on its Web site (**http://www.netscape.com**):

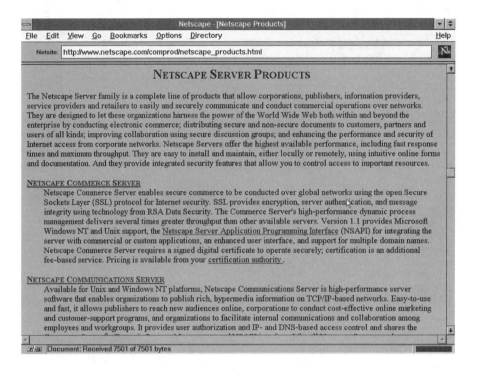

The Commerce Server provides organizations with secure Web sites in which information between the customer and seller can be provided on a secure, encrypted basis. The Merchant system provides the seller with the capability of establishing a Web site that supports order capturing and processing, statistical reporting on sales and orders, the ability to display product information — basically, everything a company might need to get into the business of establishing an electronic catalogue. The Istore is a similar initiative.

Related to the Netscape family of commerce products is the emergence of Secure HTTP, a form of Web access that provides a secure encrypted link between your version of Netscape and the Web server at the other end. In the screen below we have chosen to go to Cybersmith (**https://www.csi.nb.ca/**), the company that hosts the Web site for the *Canadian Internet Handbook*. Notice how the Web address is **https**. This means we are accessing a secure server. Upon linking there, Netscape advises us we are entering a secure site where anything we do will be protected, at least as it is in transit through the Internet. Over time we will see more https sites:

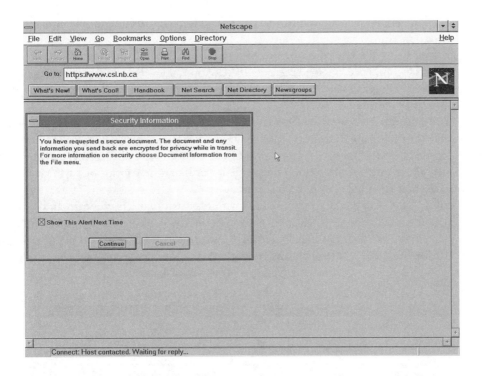

Once we are linked to the site, we see a normal Web page. However, Netscape lets us know it is a secure site by locking the normally unlocked key located in the bottom left of the screen:

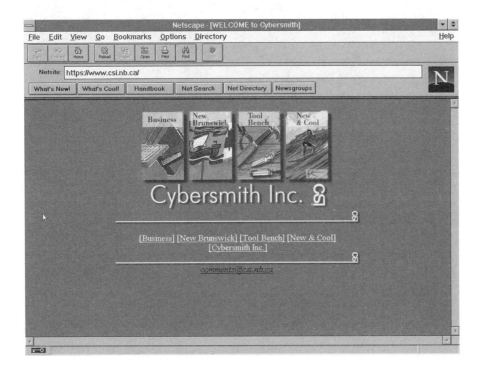

Major and minor Internet service providers across Canada are rushing to put in place such secure electronic commerce tools.

Netscape is not the only company involved in the forefront of releasing products to support electronic commerce on the Internet. IBM, Apple, Hewlett Packard — virtually all major computer companies are scrambling to ensure they can provide "electronic commerce" solutions to their customers.

Major banks are becoming involved, as they see the emergence of a new transaction market. Credit card companies including MasterCard and Visa are participating in the development of methods for credit card authentication on-line with the software companies mentioned above. And we are seeing the emergence of brand new forms of payment on the Internet, in some cases not even using real currency.

DigiCash, for example, has experimented with a system that lets you earn and spend a brand new form of "money" (DigiCash) not based on any currency in the world. You can travel through the Internet and spend your DigiCash, and if you have something to sell, you can sell it for DigiCash credits. DigiCash is nothing less than some software and some bits and bytes on a computer in Amsterdam (**http://www.digicash.com**):

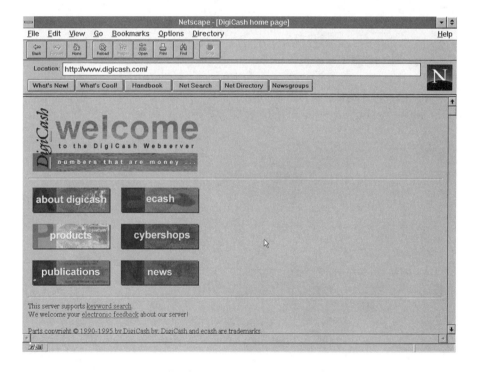

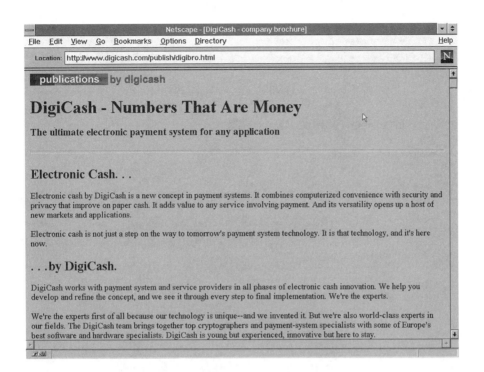

The DigiCash system is more experimental and conceptual than real at this point, but offers a glimpse into some of the future directions that the Internet might take. Ulcers and stress at national taxation bodies might be the rule of the day in the future!

The concept of electronic commerce on the Internet is an extremely hot topic and is one in which there are almost daily developments. When it comes to business on the Internet, technology will not be the limitation.

Real Time Data

A very real limitation of the Web is that the information you see is always "old." Whether it is one second old, two days old, or a year old, information on a Web page is from the past. And the biggest limitation is that the information on the page does not change as you watch it.

We see many Web sites try to get around this problem by suggesting that you "click here to load this page again." When you do that, the page loads itself again, and manages to grab more recent information in doing so. A cumbersome process. For example, the United States government runs a "census page" that estimates the population of the country at the particular moment in time that you look at the page (**http://www.census.gov/cgi-bin/popclock**):

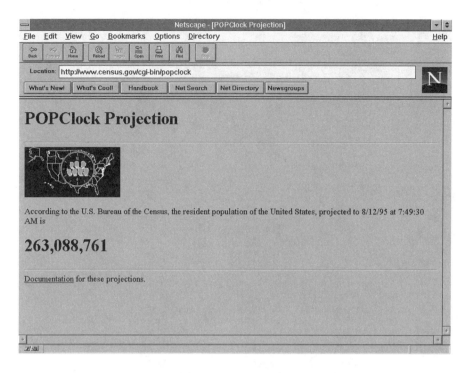

The data are not updated in real time. If you want to see the population estimate five minutes later, you have to load the page again. A crude example, but it helps to get the point across that Web pages are not automatically updated.

This limitation on the Web is quickly being removed through the release of perhaps one of the most significant technologies to hit the Web since its introduction a few years ago. In fact, Sun Microsystems' "HotJava" technology promises to redefine the Web in ways that we are only beginning to comprehend, for it introduces to the Web the concept of real time information. HotJava allows Web pages to incorporate:

- real time information updates that you can see without having to reload the page;

- animation, in which objects on the page might do something in response to your command;

- three-dimensional viewing of objects on the page.

It does this by downloading within the Web page small computer programs (called "applets") that do something. The applet might reserve a section of the Web page to put up a special information section and then constantly update that section of the page with real time information that comes through the Web, for example, stock quotes or sports scores. Or it might cause a certain area of the page to do something when the mouse moves over it, such as talk to you or have a little cartoon character jump out to say hello.

It is very difficult to describe what HotJava can do; we are limited by the confines of the printed page. A few examples will portray the significance of the technology. In the screen below, a Web page has been set up that uses HotJava code. When you view the page, you see three stock items in addition to the plain text and graphics on the page: a stock ticker, a chart of stock prices, and a section of a spreadsheet containing stock values:

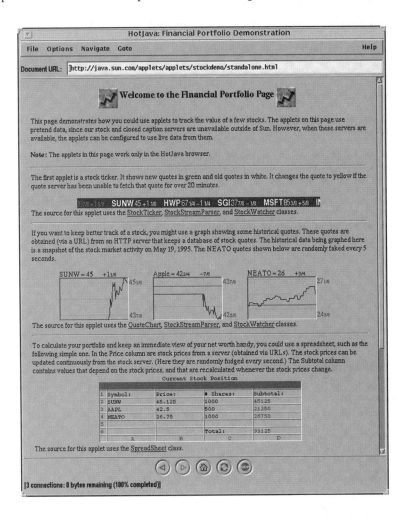

The key thing to keep in mind is that these three elements are constantly changing as you watch the page. The stock ticker travels across the screen on a regular basis; the chart dynamically updates itself every five seconds, and the spreadsheet recalculates automatically every moment there is a change. There is no need to reload the page to see new data; there is no need to click a button or do anything to see the updated information. You load the page once, and the page dynamically updates itself by using the HotJava code.

In this second example we see models of chemical data. It does not look very exciting and for many of us might rank as one of the most boring Web pages of all time (unless, of course, you are a chemist):

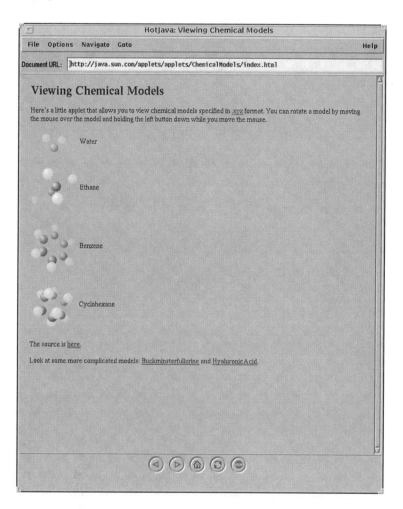

Yet this is perhaps one of the most revolutionary Web pages on the Internet. Using your mouse, you can move to any of these models and rotate them; the image will actually rotate in real time on your command. HotJava introduces to the Web the concept of three-dimensional viewing and three-dimensional modeling. This capability in itself will lead to entirely new forms of electronic publishing and completely new methods by which leading-edge scientific research can be shared worldwide. It will lead to "virtual reality" on the Internet (which we discuss later).

A third example concerns sound and animation. Consider the home page for the developers of HotJava, Sun Microsystems. It looks like any other serious home page — well-designed with an attractive layout, and it helps you to quickly narrow in on the information you are looking for:

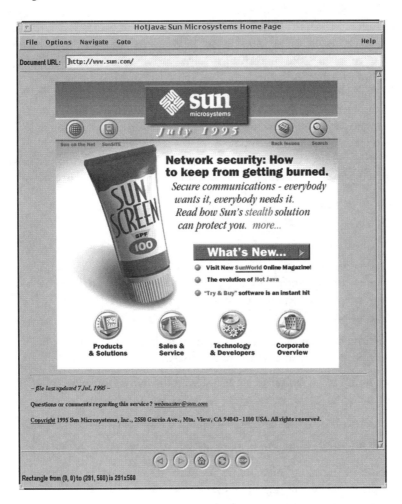

Yet, Aaron Kumove, a systems engineer at Sun Microsystems in Toronto, notes that "this page has an audio message that is automatically delivered when the page is loaded. This page also delivers audio messages and animation as the mouse is moved around the page. For example, when the mouse is moved over the icon for Technology and Developers the gears start to turn and an audio description of the type of information found on the page is delivered."

In the next section we will talk about how real time sound is being delivered through Web sites using RealAudio. Sun Microsystems is already doing it today through its HotJava programming language, a very significant development.

But the most interesting thing about the example above is the introduction of animation into the Web site. Animation will permit Web sites to include cartoons, which will help to emphasize a particular point (imagine going to the Disney site and seeing Mickey run up the screen to point out the What's New item); a financial page in which a spinning graphic is used to highlight important new financial trends, or even an O.J. Web page in which O.J. walks up to the witness stand.

HotJava promises to recreate for everyone what the Web really is and is providing computer programmers around the world with the foundation upon which exciting new Web pages can be built that feature animation. Who knows where this will lead us. HotJava is such a significant development that we really cannot do it justice here. To understand its significance, you really need to talk to companies and individuals involved in building sophisticated Web sites. They speak of HotJava with awe and respect, for they appreciate that it is a new foundation or building block that fundamentally changes our perceptions of the World Wide Web.

And things are moving so quickly on the Internet that you can likely experience HotJava on your own, since it has been introduced into Netscape version 2.0. It will quickly become a foundation to much of what we see and do on the World Wide Web, and within a year or two, it will have provided yet another important shift in the role that the World Wide Web plays in our business and personal lives. For more information on HotJava, visit **http://www.sun.com**.

Sound

There are also significant developments on the Internet related to the distribution of sound. Many companies and organizations are placing "sound files" on their Web sites. These "sounds" are usually in the form of a computer file that you can download. For example, you can retrieve such sounds as

- ◆ clips from the CDs of popular artists from major record labels and in other cases, small independent bands (e.g., from Sony Records);

- ◆ clips from new movie releases directly from the movie distributor (e.g., Disney Studios and MGM);

- ◆ complete radio shows or clips from TV news shows from organizations such as the CBC;

- ◆ all kinds of other sounds from all kinds of people on thousands of topics and subjects.

You will often see these sound files around the Web; they are in what are known as ".**au**" or ".**wav**" file formats. These are simply computer files that contain the sound in a computer form. To listen to one, you have to download the file containing the sound data and then play it with a "sound player," a program that plays a sound file. There are three obstacles that prevent people from actively listening to sound through the Internet.

- ◆ Not all computers have a sound card. Gradually, more new computers are shipping with multimedia capability built right in. However, if you do not have a sound card, then you cannot participate in this capability of the Internet.

- ◆ Some Web browsers require you to configure your software properly to support sound files. For example, older versions of Netscape and Mosaic require you to configure the software to use an external program to play the sound. If such a program was not sent to you by your provider, you have to go out and find one and then learn how to configure your software. This problem is gradually being eliminated;

for example, Netscape now automatically ships with a sound player as does the version of Mosaic found with the Quarterdeck InternetSuite product.

◆ Cumbersome processes to listen to sound files. You have to first download a sound file before you can hear it, meaning that you tie your computer up for some time while it retrieves the sound file.

This has meant that not many people regularly download sound files from the Internet. The last point is best illustrated by example: here is the Web site for popular Canadian artist Sarah MacLachlan. Through her site at Vancouver's Nettwerk Records (**http://www.nettwerk.com**), you can read information about her albums and download sound clips of various songs that she has recorded. We discussed in the previous chapter how you can configure a "viewer" to listen to such sound clips:

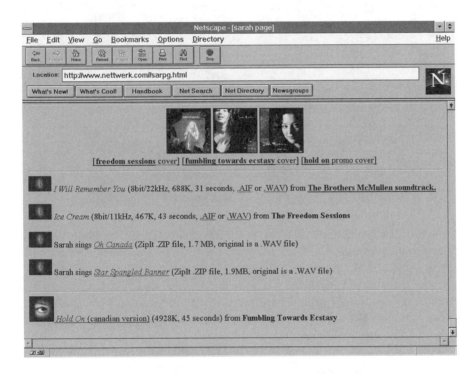

To listen to these songs you must first download them by double clicking with your mouse, and since sound files are usually quite large, you must wait a few minutes to retrieve them. Then, assuming that your Web browser is configured correctly, you can listen to them.

Obviously, the Web would make more sense if you could just choose a sound item from a Web page and hear it automatically *as it was being downloaded*. However, the Internet was not really designed to support such a capability — until the folks at RealAudio came along.

Using the RealAudio program, you hear a sound file as soon as it starts being retrieved. Upon installation, RealAudio links itself to your Netscape or Mosaic browser so that it will run automatically as soon as it sees a RealAudio sound file being obtained from a Web site. (A version of the RealAudio player can be obtained at **http://www.realaudio.com**.)

Travel to a Web site that supports RealAudio, double click with your mouse, and within a few seconds, you will hear the sounds through the speakers on your PC. For example, here is the site for Stony Plain Records (**http://www.axionet.com/stonyplain**), a Vancouver-based record label. Not only can you view information about various artists represented by this label, you can also listen to clips from those artists in real time as you browse the Web site. At the time this screen was taken, we were listening to a song from the songwriter Bobby Charles:

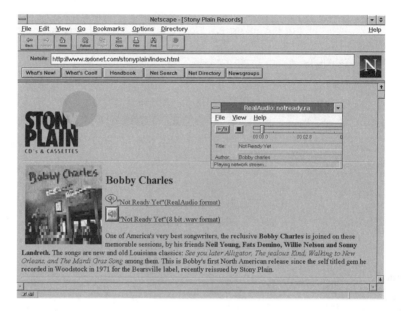

RealAudio provides its sound player program for free. The revenue comes from selling a program that permits companies or organizations with a Web site to convert digital sound files to the format required by RealAudio.

The sound quality of a RealAudio file through a 14,400 baud modem obviously is not of compact disc quality, nor is it completely unintelligible. And it works better with voice than with songs. But most likely, the technology that supports instant sound through the Internet will mature and become more sophisticated over time.

RealAudio is pointing the way to the future, rather than being the definitive answer. The important thing about RealAudio is that it shows that the Web can support the instant playing of sound information, taking the Internet one step closer towards being a true multimedia system.

The Effect of RealAudio

The real result of the path trailblazed by RealAudio was the establishment of real time audio information as a regular application through the Internet. A number of Web browsers now support the direct, immediate playing of sound files from a Web site, and it is only a matter of time before most automatically include this capability as a standard feature.

The impact will be seen over time, and your use of the World Wide Web will change as sites begin to incorporate sounds as a regular part of their content. You will likely see little "welcome" messages play when you arrive at a site and special sound effects once you begin to leave. Images on the Web will be accompanied by voice descriptions, annotating what you view. You will have the choice of viewing the text or listening to a narrative of some document. The applications are really only limited by one's imagination.

Consider some of the things you can do on the Internet today with an automatic sound player such as RealAudio:

◆ visit ABC News on the Web and listen to recent newscasts that are less than an hour old (**http://www.abc.com**):

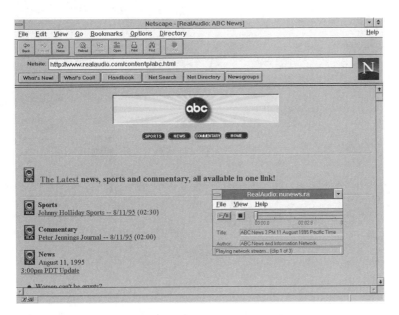

◆ travel to the CBC and listen to various radio programs broadcast in the past, such as recent *As It Happens* radio shows (**http://www.radiocbc.ca**):

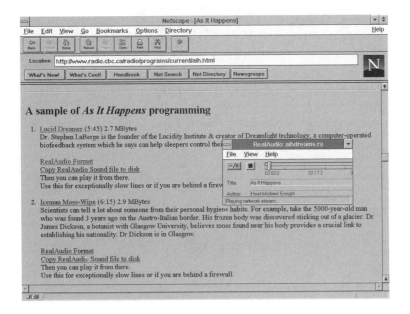

◆ travel to the ESPN sports network site and listen to sound clips from various recent sporting events (**http://ESPNet.sportzone.com**):

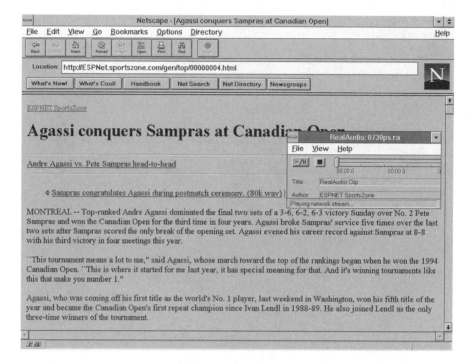

The Internet has emerged as an information archive, with most of the information consisting of text, graphics, and images. Sound has not previously played a big role, since it was such a cumbersome process to retrieve sound files. But with the emergence of tools like RealAudio, a whole new dimension of Internet "publishing" is emerging, in which you will be able to access "radio shows" from all kinds of organizations and people around the planet. You will be able to visit Web sites and retrieve "broadcasts" or other sounds from sites that are days, weeks, and months old.

Over time, we will see "radio archives" emerge on the Internet, containing historical broadcasts or the favorite radio show that you missed last week. You will be able to selectively retrieve which "shows" you want to listen to, when you want to listen to them. Many institutions and organizations will become involved with Internet broadcasting. But one of the most fascinating aspects of RealAudio is that eventually anyone will be able to create a real time sound file.

We are seeing some early signs of this already: Adam Miller, for example, is a young chap somewhere in the world who plays the French horn. He has put on his Web site (**http://www.cyberspace.com/~adamm/fhorn.html**) a few of the tunes that he has learned to play:

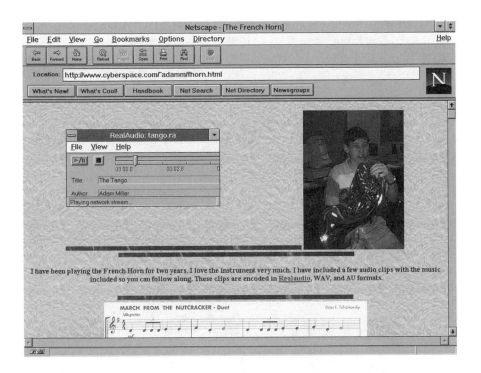

He has become a global "broadcaster," able to publish his "skills" for a potential worldwide audience.

What do RealAudio and products like it represent? The reality that the Internet is on the leading edge, establishing a brand new type of information distribution system not previously seen in the world, one in which anyone in the world will soon be able to establish his/her own "radio station." Anyone can obtain RealAudio from **http://www.realaudio.com**.

Telephone Calls

The Internet has caught the imagination of many a bright computer software developer, particularly since it offers such low-cost global connectivity. Keep in mind, for example, that when you link from Canada to a Web site in Hong Kong, you are paying a rate of anywhere from $0.35/$1 or $2 *per hour* for that link (or maybe less, if you have a full-time dedicated connection to the network). Imagine if you could make a long distance phone call anywhere in the world for such a low cost.

Sound capabilities are quickly becoming a regular part of the Internet through developments such as RealAudio as discussed above. If you can listen to "radio shows" and other sounds through the Internet, you should be able to talk through the Internet, too, right? And if you can talk through the Internet, well, you should be able to make phone calls, right?

No problem. A number of programs have now emerged on the Internet that permit you to talk to people across the street or around the world through your Internet connection. All you need is a link to the network, the proper software, and a microphone that plugs into your sound card. Internet Phone is a product that lets you place "phone calls" through the Internet and is one of several products that began to arrive throughout 1995.

You can obtain a sample copy of Internet Phone at the Web site of Vocaltec, the company that produced the software (**http://www.vocaltec.com**). Their promotional literature promises that "with Internet Phone you can use the Internet to speak with any user all over the world! Yes, real-time voice conversations over the Internet, at the price of a local phone call or even less. All you need is Internet Phone, a TCP\IP Internet connection and a Windows-compatible audio device. Plug in a microphone and speaker, run Internet Phone, and, by clicking a button, get in touch with Internet users all over the world."

In effect, Internet Phone allows you to make inexpensive "phone calls" around the world at Internet rates. It is not like a real phone call — on a dial-up modem the sound is a little scratchy; you can only connect to those who have similar software; talking through a microphone and listening through speakers certainly are not exactly like a telephone handset; and, finally, with many of the sound cards found in PCs, only one person can talk at a time, so you cannot have a real two-way conversation. Yet, even given these problems, when the Internet Phone product first came out in 1995, it took off like a rocket within the Internet community.

How it works is really quite straightforward. After you install it, it runs a little test to see if it will work on your computer. You then choose to connect to an Internet Phone "server" from a list of available ones, and you are connected and ready to go:

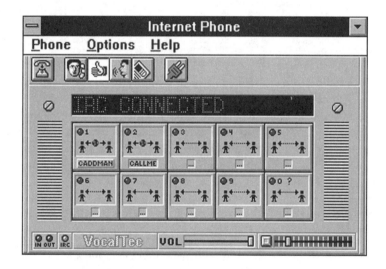

You can choose to make a "call" to someone by clicking on the telephone icon. You see a list of people connected to this particular server — choose one, and it will contact them to see if they want a call from you. Internet Phone makes sounds like a telephone while connecting to heighten the effect:

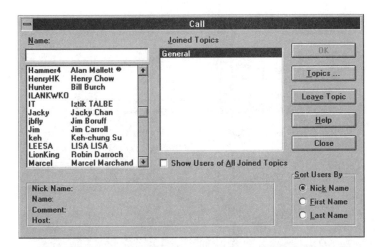

If you have set the software to accept calls, you will automatically be notified when someone wants to talk to you. When this happens, your computer "rings":

Internet Phone is kind of an eerie product: although it is normal to exchange e-mail with people you do not know around the world, and although it is an everyday thing to participate in USENET discussion groups or electronic mailing lists, there is something odd about opening up a "phone call" with someone you do not know. The conversations tend to be forced (until you get the hang of it) and concentrate on basic things, like asking the other person where he/she is and what the weather is like there.

Yet, if you do line up a time to talk with someone whom you know, you can meet on a particular Internet Phone server and have regular, day-to-day conversations. Your conversation can be with anyone in the world, which is perhaps the most attractive thing about it.

Where to get Internet Phone

Internet Phone

URL: **ftp://ftp.vocaltec.com/pub/iphone*.zip** (where * represents the version number). This is a demo version that you can try. It permits calls only 2 minutes in length. You can order a full version on-line.

Video

The Internet does not stop at conquering the worlds of radio and telephone; it is taking on the concept of television, too. As you travel the Internet, you will notice that many sites not only let you download sounds, they let you retrieve video or "multimedia" presentations. The process is just like that for sound files. In most cases, to obtain a video file or multimedia presentation, you travel to a site that contains a video file (the most popular formats being MPEG and Apple's QuickTime format), download the video, and then play it back with a player. If you have configured your browser software correctly, you can watch the "video" as soon as it has finished downloading.

There are numerous sites supporting such files. For example, the Ministry of Small Business, Tourism & Culture for the British Columbia Government (**http://www.tbc.gov.bc.ca/ tourism/tourismhome.html**) makes available a few short clips of tourism promotion videos available on its site. Here is a brave chap about to jump off a cliff:

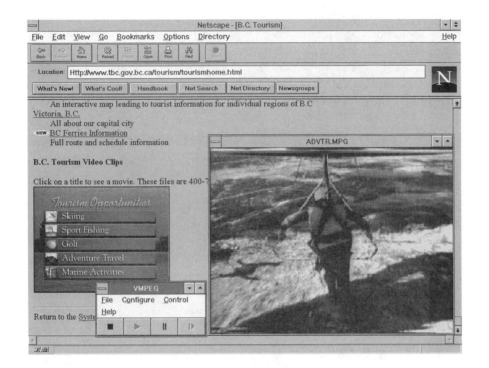

and here he is once in flight:

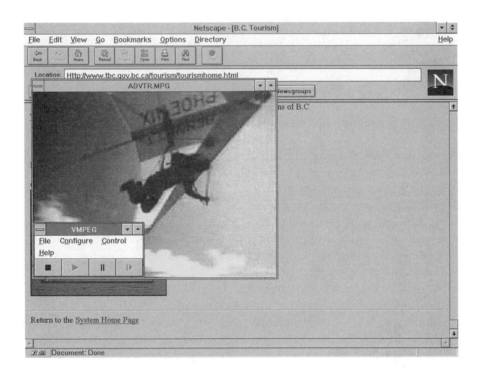

These are from a video that is about 15 seconds in length; this 15-second video took a few minutes to download using a relatively fast 28,800 baud modem. Video files today are simply too large to be easily distributed through the Internet.

There are many organizations experimenting with the idea of putting video on-line. Here is a section from the Web site of the Royal Bank, in which short clips about business banking are made available (**http://www.royalbank.com**):

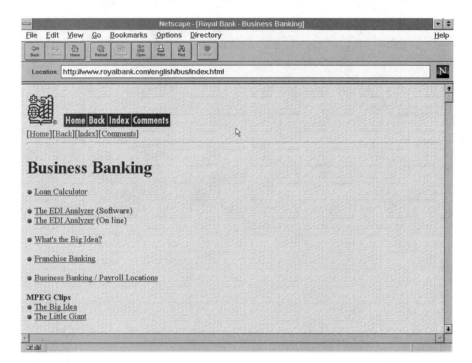

The Importance of Video and Multimedia

Development of video and multimedia programs is accelerating throughout the computer industry, driven primarily by the explosion in CD ROM. Throughout the computer industry we are seeing the emergence of an entirely new type of multimedia "show," computer files that contain video, moving graphics, and sounds.

Companies have begun to distribute their annual reports on CD ROM. Magazines distribute special multimedia advertisements on diskettes bundled into this month's issue. Kiosks appear in stores that run high-tech multimedia catalogues. Multimedia seems to be everywhere, except for the Internet.

Indeed, multimedia has become a large part of the global computer industry. You need a program to put together a multimedia show, and a good example of a leading-edge and high-profile multimedia program is Macromedia's Director program. It permits anyone to develop sophisticated "multimedia shows" containing video, graphics, sound, and other information. These "shows" can be saved in QuickTime movie format so that they can be distributed to anyone.

Here is an example of a short Director show. *Freakshow and Wired* is a promotional item put together by Ludke Design of San Francisco, California. You can retrieve it from Macromedia's Web site at **http://www.macromedia.com/Gallery/Movies/Graphics/freaks.html**. Macromedia has a number of similar "best-of" presentations available at its site. This particular "show" is about 30 seconds in length:

In this case, we had to go to the Macromedia site and retrieve the file containing *Freakshow and Wired*. The file is 2.4 Mb in size and took almost 35 minutes to retrieve during normal business hours.[1] That is a lot of time to get a simple 30-second video. Clearly, for all the excitement generated by the Internet, it obviously has some real limitations when it comes to video and multimedia.

---

1. The benefits of using the Internet at odd hours really became apparent. Retrieving the file one night at 6:00 p.m., a busy period on the Internet, took about 35 minutes. Retrieving it again the next morning at 5:00 a.m., when the Internet isn't so busy, took only about 15 minutes.

But there are many potential video applications for those with a high-speed link to the network. For example, various organizations are using video technology on the Internet for promotional purposes. Here is a clip from a promotional video about *101 Dalmatians*, available on the Disney site (**http://www.disney.com**):

Elsewhere, *Popular Mechanics* makes clips of various videos available for promotional purposes; training courses are made available in multimedia form; samples of medical videos are put on-line so that doctors and medical students can access up-to-date medical research. Clearly, there are many potential applications for information distribution via multimedia and video through the Internet, if only the speed problem could be solved.

Speed Limitations Are for the Medium Term

The real limitation with video on the Internet is that most of us access the Internet using dial-up modems at speeds of 14,400 or 28,800 baud (or even less in many cases).[2] Yet video and multimedia files are often huge as we saw above. We do not as yet have enough "bandwidth" (capacity) to support such large files. Simply put, using a modem takes too long to make downloading any type of video file practical for many people.

---

2. Individuals who work for companies that have direct, high-speed links to the Internet do not face such barriers in their use of the network. They are still limited, however, by the fact that video and multimedia on the Internet are still evolving, and clearly, are not of a quality comparable to television.

There is a solution in sight to the bandwidth dilemma, however. Through the next decade, we will see the emergence of high-speed communication links into the home and office. Cable companies are examining how they can use the cable network to deliver Internet data to the home, while telephone companies are coming to realize that the long-planned "fibre into the home" investment might be supported through deployment of the Internet.

One of the most exciting potential developments in store for the Internet industry is that cable companies around the world are working with "cable modems," devices that permit a direct link of a computer to the Internet via the cable television wires that come into the home and office. Cable companies are testing these devices to see how much information they might be able to send and receive through the network. And it could be quite a bit. (We take a look at the cable modem idea at the end of this chapter.)

Conservatively, we might expect that cable modems can send and receive at rates of 1.544 Mbps, compared to the 14,400 baud modems and 56 Kbps lines used by many individuals and companies today. Graphically, the difference is stunning; there really is no comparison in the speed (or capacity):

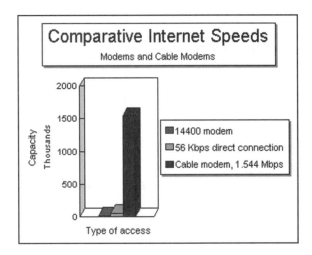

Macromedia puts the capacity increases into perspective in a document on its Web site, comparing the time it would take to retrieve certain types of files.

SPEED LIMITATIONS ON THE INTERNET			
SPEED	**TYPE OF FILE**	**SIZE OF FILE**	**TIME TO RETRIEVE**
14.4 Kbps	Small graphics and animation	30 K	20 seconds
14.4 Kbps	Small complete title	100–200 K	1–2 minutes
28.8 Kbps	Small graphics and animation	30 K	10 seconds
28.8 Kbps	Small complete title	100–200 K	30–60 seconds
28.8 Kbps	Short video clip	500 K	2–3 minutes
56 Kbps	Small graphics and animation	30 K	5 seconds
56 Kbps	Small complete title	100–200k	15–30 seconds
56 Kbps	Short video clip	500 K	1 minute
56 Kbps	Full-size title	1 M	2 minutes
1.5 Mbps	Small graphics and animation	30 K	under 1 second
1.5 Mbps	Small complete title	100–200 K	1 second
1.5 Mbps	Short video clip	500 K	3 seconds
1.5 Mbps	Full-size title	1 M	6 seconds
1.5 Mbps	Title with full video and sound	2 M	12 seconds
1.5 Mbps	MPEG video stream	—	continuous

Courtesy of Macromedia.
From their *"Director-on-the-Internet Technology White Paper"* (**http://www.macromedia.com/Tools/Director/Shockwave/index.html**).

Examining the table above makes it apparent that once high-speed cable modems become accessible, more people will be able to take advantage of the multimedia and video information available on the Internet. The last line of the table is the most intriguing, however. Just what does "MPEG video stream" mean, and why does the "Size of file" column say "continuous"?

Real Time Video

Remember what the RealAudio program that we discussed above accomplishes: it permits you to play sound files instantly as soon as you begin to retrieve them from the Web, rather than having to wait for them to download. You will soon be able to do the same thing with video and multimedia: play a video file continuously as soon as you begin to retrieve it, rather than waiting for it to download.

You cannot have a computer industry that is literally bursting at the seams with new developments in multimedia almost every day and an emerging global network like the Internet and have these two developments ignore each other. Indeed, companies that develop Internet software are quickly implementing video features as a core part of their offering. Add cable modems into the mix, and soon almost everyone will be able to participate in a new type of multimedia network.

Netscape's version 2.0, for example, incorporates technology that permits direct viewing of Macromedia multimedia files in a "continuous stream." If your link to the Internet is fast enough, you can travel to a Web site containing a video or multimedia file, double click with your mouse, and immediately begin "watching the show" in real time.

Once video and multimedia are integrated into the Internet, it will become clear that what we are really seeing in the Internet is a whole new information distribution system. It is not radio, it is not television, it is something different altogether. Since anyone can buy a program like Macromedia's Director and thus prepare his/her own multimedia files that can incorporate full motion video and other information, it is apparent that the Internet is becoming a system in which anyone in the world can soon establish his/her own "television station."

WHERE TO GET VIDEO VIEWERS	
Windows:	
MPEGPlay (Shareware)	**ftp://ftp.netcom.com/pub/ms/msimmons**
VMPEG Lite	**ftp://papa.indstate.edu/winsock-l/ Windows95/Graphics/vmpeg*.exe** (where * represents latest version)
QuickTime Video viewer	**ftp://ftp.ncsa.uiuc.edu/Mosaic/Windows/ viewers/qtw11.zip** Also check out the Consummate Winsock Applications list at **http://cwsapps.texas.net/**
Macintosh:	
QuickTime Video viewer	**http://quicktime.apple.com** Also check out the list of Macintosh Internet applications at **http://www.astro.nwu.edu/lentz/mac/ software/mac-internet.html**

The effort by Macromedia and Netscape is but one announcement. Other companies are looking at the opportunity of providing real time video through the Internet. Expect a lot of development in this area in the next few years.

Videoconferencing and Television

If you can do sound and video through the Internet, why not broadcast in real time? In fact, videoconferencing and broadcasting are not far behind on the Internet. Consider the software development known as CU-SeeMe.

Originally developed at Carnegie Mellon University, the product permits a rudimentary form of videoconferencing and broadcasting through the Internet. Recently commercialized, details about the product and copies of the program are available at the Web site for White Pine Software (**http://www.wpine.com/cuprodinfo.html**).

Notes the product information: "CU-SeeMe can be used over the Internet to make connections to any other desktop using CU-SeeMe in the same fashion as e-mail, except that with CU-SeeMe you can have a real-time meeting with video, audio and written messages. With its unique 'Reflector' technology, CU-SeeMe can be used for group conferencing or 'TV' type broadcasting. CU-SeeMe is targeted at low bandwidth connections, requires no special hardware and supports inexpensive video cameras. A software only solution for both Windows and Macintosh, CU-SeeMe will affordably bring Videoconferencing to offices, educational institutions and homes worldwide."

A tall order for any product. And certainly those who access the Internet with a modem cannot really take advantage of the product. Yet, the promise afforded by high-speed cable modems and other forms of high-speed access means that one day, products like CU-SeeMe will be a mainstream, everyday application on the Internet.

If you have a SLIP or PPP dial-up connection to the Internet, you can try out CU-SeeMe. At the end of this section we let you know where to get it. But you will find it almost impossible to use with a dial-up connection, since you really need a faster link to the network.

To use the product simply to view other CU-SeeMe sites, you do not need any special equipment. If you want to set your site up to send pictures and sound, however, you will need a digital camera and a PC that can support it as well as a microphone.

It is all mostly experimental at this time, but the possibilities are intriguing. Taking a look at how it is being used today offers a tantalizing glimpse of the future of "broadcasting" through the Internet. For example, here is a snippet of a video from the band Kiss, taken from a CU-SeeMe broadcast of the Canadian MuchMusic television channel, available from KVR TV in Austin, Texas:

Notes a press release available on the KVR Web site (**http://www.utexas.edu/depts/output/www/pr.html**): "this pilot project was conceived by students to merge cutting-edge technology…computer-literate students will be on their Macintosh computers watching MuchMusic while they work." Certainly experimental, possibly controversial, but imagine how such a broadcast technology could be used in a real educational or research setting.

The scientific aspects are already making themselves known. NASA is the first organization to regularly broadcast through the Internet, using CU-SeeMe to transmit full-day coverage of shuttle missions and other endeavors. Here is NASA's program schedule as posted early in the day, announcing what will be shown through its "station" later in the day:

The limitations in the CU-SeeMe concept are obvious: even for those with a high-speed link to the Internet the screens are jerky, it is only in black and white, and it is obviously not broadcast quality.

Another hot technology on the Internet is MBONE, or multicast backbone, which provides another sort of TV through the Internet. It is a complex technology; leading-edge researchers are figuring out with MBONE another method of providing video distribution through the Internet. You can find the FAQs about it at **http://www.research.att.com/mbone-faq.html**.

Both Cu-SeeMe and MBONE are still experimental technologies. However, these experiments have involved many things, including

♦ the broadcast of a concert by the Rolling Stones, soon followed by regular concerts by numerous other bands being "simulcast" through the Internet;

♦ the premiere of the movie *Tank Girl* on the Internet at the same time it was premiered at the Seattle Film Festival, and the premiere of the movie *Cyberstalkers;*

♦ live broadcasts from the Winter Olympics in Lillehammer, Norway;

♦ the broadcast of various Internet conferences.

Technology on the Internet evolves at a rapid pace. What starts as an experiment often ends up as a commercial product. Combine the concept of high-speed Internet access with the CU-SeeMe concept and you can see where the Internet is headed. Examine MBONE and you can see the makings of a new type of video network.

Soon, anyone with a high-speed link to the Internet and a PC equipped with a sound card and digital video camera can become a "broadcaster" on the Internet. In fact, anyone will soon be able to establish his/her own live, global television station. How long will it take? Two years? Five years, 10 or 20? No one knows, but keep your eyes and ears tuned, for there are some fascinating developments underway. We are not going to have a 500-channel universe, we will have a million-channel universe one day in the future.

WHERE TO GET CU-SEEME

Windows:

ftp://gated.cornell.edu/pub/video/PC.CU-SeeMeW0.66b1/cuseeme.zip
Also check out the Consummate Winsock Applications list at **http://cwsapps.texas.net/**

Macintosh:

ftp://ftp.gated.cornell.edu/pub/video/macxxxx, where xxxx is the latest file version.
Also check out the list of Macintosh Internet applications at **http://www.astro.nwu.edu/lentz/mac/software/mac-internet.html**

Virtual Reality

So far, we have looked at how sound and video can be sent through the Internet. The next step for the Internet is virtual reality. Think of what you encounter on the Web. You discover a vacation resort that is marketing itself on the Internet. You travel through the site and discover pictures of the resort, the pool, the rooms, the casino. Somehow, it seems interesting, yet it also seems so limiting. Right now, the Web is mostly a two-dimensional experience. You can see pictures and graphics. It certainly isn't three-dimensional. It soon will be.

Imagine visiting the same resort on the Web, except that you do not just view some pictures. You start at the front door and enter. You observe the sweeping expanse of the lobby and decide to turn right to look into the casino. You come back out and get into an elevator. In a few seconds the doors open, and you "travel" down the hall to view a model suite. You look around the room… .

Far-fetched? No. A newly emerging technology on the Internet known as VRML (virtual reality modeling language) promises to change the way we navigate through the Internet, turning a flat two-dimensional Web space into a fascinating three-dimensional world.

Silicon Graphics, a leading computer hardware/software company, is leading the trend towards three-dimensions on the Internet. They have released a browser called "WebSpace" that permits you to travel through interactive three-dimensional sites on the Internet. The program can be run separately or can be set to run from within popular Web browsers such as Netscape and Mosaic. (Information about WebSpace and VRML is available from Silicon Graphics at **http://www.sgi.com/Products/WebFORCE/WebSpace/**. Another good site for information about VRML in general is **http://www.lightside.com/3dsite/cgi/VRML-index.html**.)

Virtual reality has long been talked about within the computer industry, and much experimentation and many products have come to market. Anyone who has attended a computer trade show has seen someone in a "virtual world," wearing one of those funny helmets. Virtual reality is now coming to the Internet, and you do not have to wear a funny helmet. The potential applications are enormous:

- ◆ interactive tours of cities and towns, used in a geography classroom;

- ◆ the opportunity to view the seating layout of a theatre before you buy your ticket — try out a few chairs to see what the view of the stage is like;

- ◆ medical professionals discussing possible treatments while viewing a three-dimensional image of a collapsed lung.

You might think that it will take a long time for virtual reality to emerge on the Internet. Not so. Some people have said that they expect it to become fairly common and mainstream throughout 1996. You might be concerned that you do not have a fast enough link to the Internet to support it. Not so. A key thing about VRML is that it does not necessarily send large graphic files of a "virtual" something; instead, it might send mathematical formulas and other information that describes that world. The Silicon Graphics Web site says that to send a VRML of a ball on a flat space takes less than 100 bytes of information!

Here is an example of a virtual reality site using a VRML browser, WebSite, from Silicon Graphics:

You can navigate your way down this hallway, look up, down, to the left and to the right, and enter various rooms, such as this electronic classroom:

The three items at the bottom of the screen are the navigation tools; you use these to indicate where you want to travel within the room.

In the following view a number of Silicon Graphics computers are included in the room. You can move your way to any one of them, and when you click on one, a Web page is loaded that contains information about that computer:

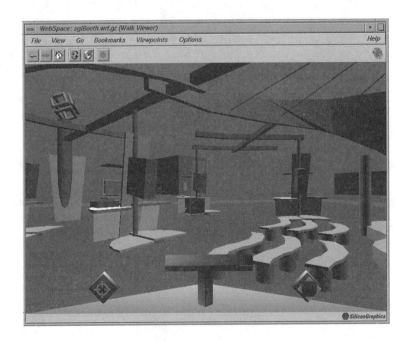

Obviously, we are limited in terms of what we can show about virtual reality on the Internet, and the field is still in its early state. However, one executive with a popular Web browser company recently indicated that he expected most Web browsers to support full VRML by the end of 1996. Silicon Graphics does have Macintosh and Windows versions of its Web site software available at **http://www.sgi.com**.

Remote Control of Devices

Read a magazine or newspaper about the Internet, and you are bound to hear about some of its sillier aspects, such as

◆ the fellow who has linked his telephone into the Internet so that you can see the last time it rang;

◆ the Amazing Fish Cam, a fish tank located at Netscape Communications Corporation with a camera that takes a picture once a minute, and the picture is available on the Internet;

◆ a hot tub in California: you can find out how hot it is and whether the cover is on or off;

◆ innumerable soda machines that tell you how many cans of certain types of soda are left, and coffee machines that tell you if they are on or off;

◆ CD players in dormitory rooms that tell you what song is currently playing;

◆ Christmas trees that would tell you if their lights were on or off, and doors that would tell you if they were open or closed.

There is a fellow who has set up a Web site in which you key a message, and speech synthesizer takes what you have keyed and turns your message into speech in his office. You can say anything you like to him:

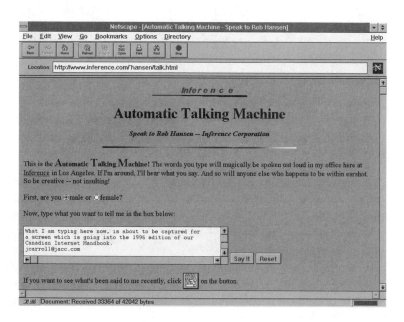

There is even a model railroad in Germany that you can watch and control:

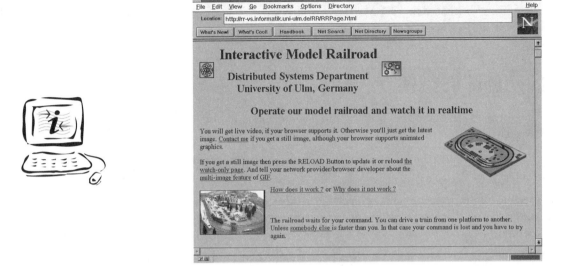

Throughout the world, there is an amazing number of devices and various technologies that are linked into the Internet. A tour reveals a fascinating number of silly, inane, serious, amusing, and amazing things that are plugged into the Internet. You can spend hours and hours exploring this fascinating and bizarre side of the network.

Of course, given that indexing the Web is a popular pastime, you can find lists and summaries of some of the most interesting "useless sites" on the Internet. For example, Yahoo points to a number of these "useless" lists:

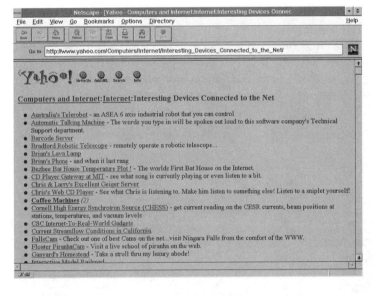

It all seems like a waste of resources. In fact, many people who are not Internet users and who encounter these devices for the first time come to the conclusion that much of the Internet is all a waste of time. But it really is not. All these efforts to connect devices to the Internet represent leading-edge research, which is providing insight into the computer protocols and technology that will drive our wired world into the future. Individuals working with these devices — brilliant computer techies — are discovering what is involved in linking mechanical devices to the all-important TCP/IP computer protocol that supports the Internet. They are determining how remote control via the Internet is possible. They are determining how to turn analogue experimentation results into the digital bits necessary for transmission through the Internet.

In effect, these "silly" folks are like so many Thomas Edisons around the world, discovering what it takes to establish a new type of computer network-machine interaction. Their efforts are already paying off. For example, consider devices that remotely monitor the water level and flow at various key locations in California. Members of the U.S. Geological Survey can remotely monitor sensor data on water flow to determine if there are any potential floods:

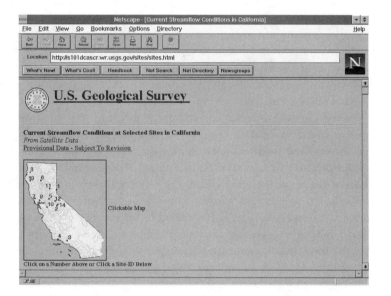

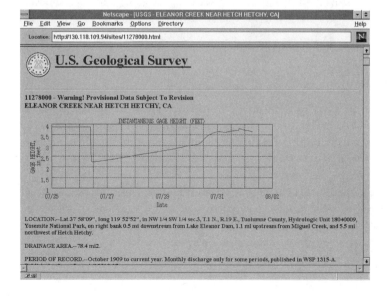

The use of such a technology in this case is helping a government department perform a unique and valuable service by providing early warnings about potentially dangerous conditions.

In the scientific field "device" concepts are used by scientists to remotely monitor and manipulate their experiments through the Internet. In other cases, devices that monitor local traffic patterns in various cities are being linked to the Internet; people in these cities can check in before they leave work for the day to see the best route home. Seismographs in earthquake-prone areas are linked into the Internet to provide scientists and the general population with ongoing information about tremors and potential quakes.

What is really happening as people around the world link "silly" devices into the Internet is another step forward in technological evolution. What is happening on the Internet, believe it or not, is research into the methods by which other technologies can be monitored, supported, manipulated, and accessed on a remote basis through the Internet. These silly experiments — granted, many are very silly — are in many ways helping researchers discover how computer technology can be used for remote purposes in many aspects of our day-to-day lives.

Keep in mind that many of the everyday devices that we take for granted also contain computer chips: televisions, radios, refrigerators, stoves, stereos, alarm systems, automobiles, factory devices all contain increasing amounts of computer intelligence, all of which can be linked into the Internet. The Internet is plugging together all the computers in the world, but the computers do not necessarily have to be full-fledged computers to be part of it all.

Where is this leading? The Internet is defining the future of our wired world. One day you will be able to check your home heating, air conditioning, and alarm system from a remote location through the Internet. You will be able to program your tape deck at home and record a radio program from afar. Doctors and health care staff will be able to access medical monitoring devices at the other end of the country through the Internet. Staff at a mining company in Toronto might actually control an excavator in Northern Ontario through an Internet connection. It is not far-fetched to believe that at some point in time a farmer will be able to direct an overhead satellite to take an infrared picture of the farm, after providing longitude and latitude coordinates through a Web site, with the picture being sent back after credit card information was validated by the satellite company.

There is nothing wrong with the fact that this leading-edge research is fun and interesting — and silly. In fact, maybe it helps to move the technology along a little bit quicker. Whatever the case, this is another area of the Internet that is providing a tantalizing glimpse into the future.

Cable Access

The limitation in many of these applications is the speed of the access that we have to the Internet. Certainly, staff at organizations with full-time high-speed links to the Internet will be able to participate in these exciting developments, but many others accessing the Internet from home using modems are restricted. It is as if we have been let into the candy store, but we cannot get to the shelf that we like.

As noted earlier in this chapter, we are in for a change in the way we access the Internet with the arrival of cable modem technology and with the arrival of higher speed telephone access. It is already happening in some locations in Canada: Fairview Technology Centre Ltd. provides Internet access in the Okanagan Valley area of British Columbia, and has been providing cable modem access to the Internet in cooperation with the local cable company.

Notes Bernard Klatt, the President: "We have a working arrangement with OTV Cablevision, the local cable company. OTV has full reverse channel capability throughout their service area with a population of about 12,000." What this means is that the local cable network has been upgraded so that it is a two-way system: it can send and receive data. Some cable systems in Canada are only one-way, so cable companies have been upgrading them to support two-way capability, a necessity for access to the Internet.

If you are interested in the technology that is used, Bernard explains: "We are using Zenith Data Systems CATV products. We use the Zenith HomeWorks 500 Kb/s cablemodems, Zenith ChannelMizer bridge to connect the CATV LAN to the Ethernet LAN where our servers and router are located. A Zenith frequency translator is also located at the cable company headend." What this means is that in essence, the cable network has been turned into a large, local area network.

The cost is quite reasonable: "OTV Cablevision adds $9.95 a month to the residential subscriber's cable service bill. We charge a flat rate of $49 a month for unlimited Internet access via cablemodem. Subscribers can purchase the Zenith cablemodem from OTV Cablevision for $645, or they can rent it from OTV Cablevision for $24.50 a month." So overall, about $75 a month gets you unlimited, high-speed access to the Internet through a cable modem. Many people in Canada would jump at the opportunity.

So far, users of the cable modems in the Okanagan Valley can only go out and use Internet applications such as e-mail, USENET newsgroups, and the Web; they cannot establish their own Web server. "Cablemodem access is more costly than dial-up for occasional users, but it's a bargain for heavy users that want excellent performance. No dialing delay, never a busy signal, instant access from Windows." So cablemodem access is a reality in at least one community in Canada today. We will quickly see it expand to others.

But there are challenges. There is a rumor in the industry that while cable companies have proved that Internet access through the cable wire works within the lab, it is a different story once they get out in the real world. It seems in some cases there are significant technical and logistical challenges. Although you might have high-speed access through the cable wire, you might end up sharing that access with several people, meaning that your access might not be as fast as you hoped. Time will tell how the cablemodem situation will develop.

Another promising technology is ISDN, now in widescale deployment by many Internet service providers. It is a telephone system technology that offers a tripling or quadrupling of the speed offered by the highest speed dial-up modem and thus offers an attractive alternative to cablemodem access. Many people report perfectly satisfactory results in accessing the Internet using an ISDN link. ISDN still remains somewhat pricey for home use, but its cost is expected to fall. Our directory of Canadian Internet service providers in Appendix B denotes those who offer ISDN services. If you are serious about use of the Internet, it might be worthwhile investigating.

Limitations of the Internet

There are many limitations to all these applications, technologies, and potential opportunities:

◆ There is not enough capacity on the Internet to support sound, video, three-dimensional images, and conferencing. In fact, many experts throughout the Internet community express alarm at the demands that such applications place on the system.

This school of thought takes the view that these new applications will cause more problems than solutions and will help to see the collapse of the Internet as it begins to overburden its capabilities. Simply put, there is not enough communications capacity on the Internet to support these new technologies.

◆ The Web, USENET, and e-mail are easy technologies. Solving the problems associated with virtual reality on the Internet or getting rid of the jerky screens and other limitations found in videoconferencing on the Internet will take much longer to solve. Solutions will come, but progress will become much slower than in the past. This school of thought presents honest skepticism in that so far, all the Internet has dealt with are the easy technologies.

◆ Certainly the threat that products like Internet Phone presents to telephone companies and other similar technologies will lead to a regulatory clampdown on the Internet in countries around the world. This line of thought indicates that the Internet is a technology threat that should be controlled, rather than one that should be encouraged and expanded.

All these criticisms and concerns are valid. There are some serious challenges ahead with regard to the Internet. The authors of this book happen to believe that something profound is occurring here. We also believe that there are three theories about the future Internet: the engineering theory, the capitalism theory, and the political theory.

The engineering theory would agree with many of the points and observations made above. There are limitations, there are problems, and many of them are not easily solved. Progress will be slower.

The capitalism theory? Huge amounts of money are pouring into anything Internet-related. Money drives technology forward at a relentless pace. Money will render most of the above arguments invalid. Money solves problems.

The political theory? Given its global nature, perhaps the best thing about the Internet is that politicians around the world are really and truly impotent with regard to its present and future role in our wired world.

We happen to believe in the capitalism theory and thank God that the political theory is true.

Where Is It All Going?

Trying to predict where the Internet is headed is really an impossible task. But we can observe some of the developments that are mentioned in this chapter and look around at the computer industry. We can watch the investments being made and the products being developed. We can observe the collective discussions held around the world about some interesting new Internet development. We can see that things are moving so fast on the Internet that six months in Internet years is like 20 years in human terms.

The Internet presents opportunities to everyone, to every software program, to every industry. The real key to the Internet is that it provides a common platform upon which all kinds of computer applications can be built. Software programs do not have to know how to link to other computers on the Internet — the Internet does that for them. The Internet is leading to a world in which we will see an entirely new type of computer software program, the globally connected program.

We opened this chapter with a quote from *Business Week*. In that article of April 3, 1995, they also noted that "the Net, it now seems, will take computing to a new plane — where information and computing resources from all over the world will be at your fingertips. If what's needed isn't in the disk on your desktop machine or the server down the hall, the next place your PC will look is on the Web… .The boundary between your computer's contents and the rest of cyberspace will be almost imperceptible."

This fact is the heart of the developments that we will see on the Internet in coming years. The entire role of our personal computers and workstations will change as they become plugged into everything and anything.

Imagine that the accounting software you use to manage your business has an automatic link to your bank via your Internet connection. Consider that a future version of Lotus 1-2-3 might have a connection via the Internet to a database of commodity prices or that your CD ROM game might have an automatic link to a database containing new game updates. Imagine that your personal scheduler keeps in touch with that of your consulting partner, located some 3,000 km away. Imagine having an "electronic whiteboard": as soon as you "write" on it, your information appears on other "electronic whiteboards" on 2,000 other computers around the world. All these ideas are within the realm of the possible on the Internet and in some cases are being actively tested and developed.

All you have to do to understand the power of the Internet is take a look at Internet applications as they emerge. Have a look at sites that we referenced earlier in this chapter: the Consummate Winsock Applications list at **http://cwsapps.texas.net/** and the Macintosh Internet applications list at **http://www.astro.nwu.edu/lentz/mac/software/mac-internet.html**. In both cases, you can see a stunning diversity of Internet application software. As long as you have a SLIP, PPP, or direct TCP/IP connection to the Internet, you can run any of these programs. And there will be many more to come. That is the real potential of the Internet.

The Internet provides the common communications pipeline through which any computer can communicate with any other computer on earth and through which any program can communicate with any other program.

The real potential of the Internet is only just beginning. We close this chapter with an excerpt from an article that appeared in the *Forbes ASAP* publication on December 5, 1994. It was written by George Gilder and is entitled "The BandWidth Tidal Wave." In it Gilder comments: "Let us paraphrase a 1988 speech by John Moussouris, chairman and chief executive of the amazing Silicon Valley startup MicroUnity, which gains a portentous heft from being financed heavily by Gates and Malone: If the leading sage of computer design, in his last deathbed gasp, wanted to impart in one word all of his accumulated wisdom about the coming era to a prodigal son rushing home to inherit the business, that one word would be 'bandwidth.' Andy Grove knows it well. Early this year he memorably declaimed: 'If you are amazed by the fast drop in the cost of computing power over the last decade, just wait till you see what is happening to the cost of bandwidth."

In the article, which is available on-line at **http://sunsite.unc.edu/horizon/gems/gemlong.html**, Gilder puts into perspective the tremendous advances that are going to occur in the next decade in terms of the data capabilities that will be available to our humble little personal computers. He also puts into perspective that much of this capability already exists: "During the very period of apparent bandwidth doldrums during the 1980s, phone companies installed some 10 million kilometers of optical fiber. So far only an infinitesimal portion of its potential bandwidth has been delivered to customers."

If you have any doubt whatsoever that the developments outlined in this chapter are going to happen, you *must* read this article.

CHAPTER 11

Older Internet Applications

Just as the home-oriented dial-up services have moved e-mail from the realm of high-level Internet sites into the public domain, so URLs promise to bring the rest of the Net to the masses. The key is that URL technology transforms what have been enormously complex commands in the computer language used by AT&T's UNIX operating system into the same sort of drag-and-drop on-screen techniques that computer users employ with Microsoft Corp.'s Windows or Apple Computer Inc.'s Macintosh.

For nearly a decade, those UNIX commands have served as the key to the information in the Internet when it was the sole domain of computer scientists and the more sophisticated hobbyists. These commands have names like File Transfer Protocol (FTP), Gopher, Veronica, Usenet, Finger, Archie and Internet Relay Chat.

The Internet Business
Chicago Tribune , March 26, 1995

What a difference a year can make. In our 1995 edition we spent much time describing such Internet applications as Gopher, Telnet, FTP, and Archie. Anyone getting involved with the Internet had to become quite familiar with these applications, since they were the main tools used to access information from around the Internet. Even today, these older applications continue to provide access to a wealth of information. Using Telnet, you might link to other computers on the Internet, such as a mainframe at a public library, to review and search information on that remote computer (such as a catalogue of books). You might use FTP to retrieve a computer program or document from somewhere on the Internet. You might use Archie to find a particular computer file by searching for it by name. And you might use Gopher to access all kinds of information from around the world using a simple "menu" of choices.

However, you might also find that you have no need for most of these applications or if you need to access an FTP site or look at a Gopher site, you can do so through your World Wide Web browser, rather than having to run a separate program. Sometimes you might find yourself retrieving a file using FTP from within the Web, without even realizing that you are using FTP.

These applications have become, in a way, superseded by the sophistication, reach, and power of the Web. Reflecting this fact, in this 1996 edition of the *Canadian Internet Handbook* we have moved these applications to this chapter under the title "Older Internet Applications." You still need to learn about them (in particular, FTP), but you will find them to be less important and useful than simple e-mail, USENET, and the World Wide Web.

The Changing Internet

Until late 1994, you had to learn how to use separate programs such as Gopher and FTP if you wanted to know how to use the Internet; thus they were an important part of previous editions of this book. Then, in the fall of 1994, Netscape was released, a program of such sophistication and power that it helped to fuel an explosion in growth and use of the World Wide Web. The arrival of the Web changed the Internet forever, by resulting in a concentration on the Web as the tool of choice for the publishing of information by individuals and companies.

Until 1994, companies and individuals establishing information sites on the Internet might have chosen to establish them on a Gopher server or might have made documents available in an FTP site, but now they largely ignore Gopher and FTP and use the Web instead. In other cases, companies might have linked internal computers to the Internet so that they could be accessed via Telnet, but now link those systems to the Web.

Whatever the case may be, these "older" technologies are used less and less throughout the Internet. (FTP and IRC are perhaps the only real "survivors" of these early Internet applications, as we will see below.)

The Role of the Web Browser

The Internet is a system that is constantly evolving. One result is that there are still many FTP, Gopher, and Telnet sites throughout the Internet. And if you want, you can access these sites with separate FTP, Gopher, and Telnet client software. In this chapter, we will take a look at examples of how this is done.

But, in most cases you can also access Gopher and FTP sites using your Web browser (such as Netscape and Mosaic), using the standard URL (uniform resource locator) method of addressing. Hence for many of these applications your Web

OLDER INTERNET APPLICATIONS

1 There are several Internet applications, such as Telnet, FTP, Gopher and Archie, that have in some ways become superseded by the sophistication, reach, and power of the Web.

2 Even as their usage decreases, Gopher, FTP, and Telnet sites still exist and can be accessed with separate client software or by Web browser software such as Netscape and Mosaic using the standard URL method of addressing.

3 Gopher is an information retrieval system that presents a text-oriented view of information.

4 FTP is a program used to retrieve files and information from around the Internet.

5 Telnet is an application that lets you travel from your Internet account to another computer somewhere else on the Internet in order to run a program at that computer.

6 Archie is a program that permits you to search file archives around the Internet by file name.

7 Finger is a utility that lists details about users located at another location on the Internet.

8 Internet relay chat allows you to participate in on-line discussions in real time with other Internet users.

browser can become the one and only information access tool in your life, rather than separate programs for separate purposes. More and more, these applications are being integrated into the Web. Why would you want to do this? It helps to avoid complexity; you can use one program to access many different types of information, rather than having to use separate programs to access different information sites.

In this chapter you will see each of these applications from the perspective of someone with a SLIP or PPP connection to the Internet. We will describe some of the special considerations for those who might access the Internet using a shell account. And in each case, we will show you how they are used via a separate client software program and how they are accessed through the World Wide Web.

Gopher

Gopher is an information retrieval system developed at the University of Minnesota to permit easier access to local university information. Like many developments within the Internet community, the authors of the Gopher software made it available on the Internet so that anyone could use it and set up their own Gopher server. Given that it was such an easy application to set up, there was an explosion of growth in the use of Gopher right around the world, with well over 7,000 "sites" accessible by 1994. But that year the World Wide Web arrived in full force, and the number of new Gopher sites being established began to decrease.

One key to Gopher's success is that it is not overly complicated. It is easy to use and, moreover, makes an orderly, logical presentation out of dissimilar and scattered "chunks" of information from all over the Internet (although the Web does a much better job of doing this). The other key feature of Gopher is that unlike the World Wide Web, its presentation of information is text-oriented, meaning that people with old character-based computers running a "shell account" still find Gopher easy to use. In other words, you do not need a powerful computer to access Gopher.

The result is that today there are still many Gopher resources around the Internet that are being constantly updated and maintained, particularly within academic institutions in Canada where it is used to provide a campus-wide information system.

Using Gopher

With a SLIP/PPP account or a direct Internet connection, you can access Gopher in one of two ways:

- ◆ using Gopher client software such as Winsock Gopher, or
- ◆ using a World Wide Web browser that supports access to Gopher resources, such as Netscape.

Gopher appears similar regardless of the software used, in that it presents a listing of items in the form of a menu from which you can choose.

For example, here is the Gopher site for Electronic Frontier Canada, an organization that gets involved in issues related to freedom for electronic communications in Canada. Their site can be found at the Gopher address **insight.mcmaster.ca**. Here is what it looks like using the program Winsock Gopher:

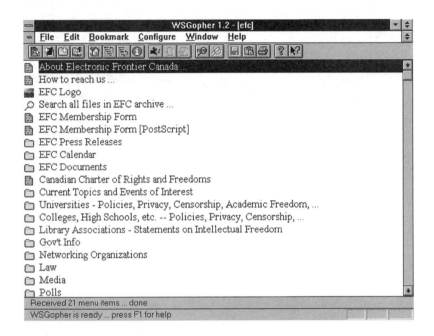

Here is the same thing as seen through Netscape, accessed using the URL **gopher://insight. mcmaster.ca**:

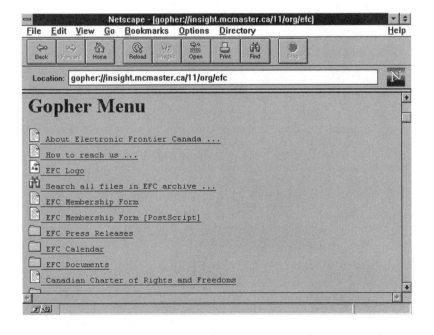

As you can see, accessing a Gopher resource is not that much different whether you are using a Gopher client (i.e., a software program used to access Gopher) or a World Wide Web browser.

Gopher is quite easy to use because of its menu system. For example, if you want to take a look at the item "'EFC documents" using the Winsock Gopher program, you move your computer mouse to the line "EFC Documents":

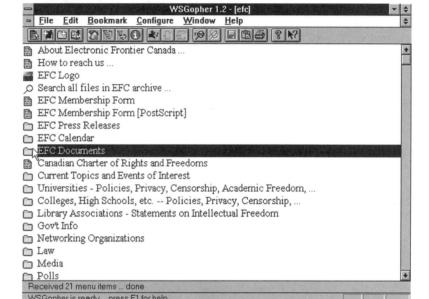

and double click. This presents the items underneath that menu:

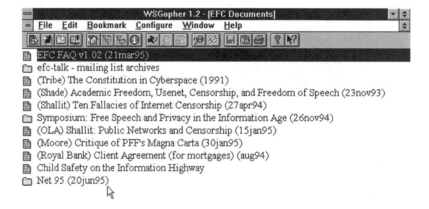

Winsock Gopher and other software packages used to access Gopher through a SLIP account present various icons beside each menu item to detail the type of information to which the menu item will lead. Binoculars, for example, signify that the item will perform a search for information when selected. A folder indicates that another menu is available under the item. A page indicates that some text will be shown for that particular item. Examples can be seen in the menus above.

Many Gopher sites are linked to other sites; in fact, the interlinking of Internet resources from around the world through Gopher predated the interlinked structure of the World Wide Web. For example, the Electronic Frontier Canada Gopher points to other related information sources around the world:

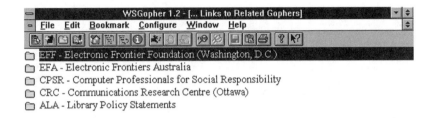

Many Gopher menus are linked to other Gopher menus, meaning that you can often start out in one location and quickly travel to another location somewhere else in Canada or around the world, similar to the way you do in the World Wide Web. This interlinking was often used to provide geographical-based access to information. For example, most Gopher sites include the category "Other Gophers and Information Servers," which leads to a listing of Gopher servers by country. For example, you can quickly obtain a listing of Gopher sites from across Canada:

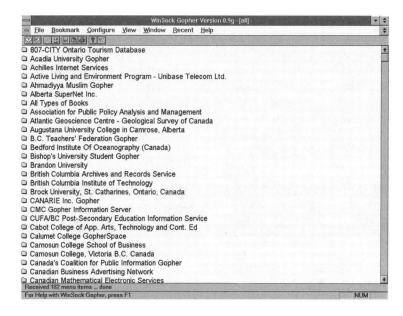

Useful Gopher Resources

There are still many Gopher sites around the Internet, and there are a number of ways in which Gopher can be an invaluable tool in discovering Internet information resources. There are many special capabilities that make the use of Gopher more convenient. These include

- ◆ Gopher Jewels, an initiative in which the "best" Gopher servers are categorized by information type;

- ◆ Veronica, a program that helps you search global "gopherspace" for particular words;

- ◆ the ability to search for documents in particular Gopher databases;

- ◆ the use of Gopher bookmarks so that you can easily find your way back to a location that you have visited.

Keep in mind that not all Gopher software or Gopher servers will support all capabilities that we review here.

Gopher Jewels

Originally, the massive growth in the number of Gopher sites and services brought together a group of people who believed that they should index some of the more interesting Gopher sites on the Internet. The result was Gopher Jewels, a service that categorizes some of the best Gopher sites. You can go directly to the main Gopher Jewels site with your Web browser using the URL **gopher://cwis.usc.edu:70/11/Other_Gophers_and_Information_Resources/Gopher-Jewels**.

You can go there using your Gopher client software by choosing to "open" a new Gopher site and by keying in the address **cwis.usc.edu** (the main "home" for the Gopher Jewels project). Then choose the menu item "Other Gophers and Information Resources" and from that one, "Gopher Jewels." You will see this screen:

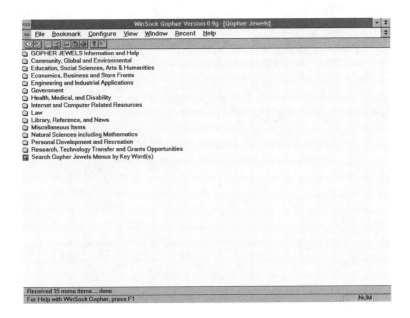

You can choose to search all the menu names in the Gopher Jewels listing by choosing the last item. In this case, we want to find Gopher menus that mention medicine:

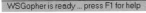

Gopher immediately returns a list of sites that include that word in their name:

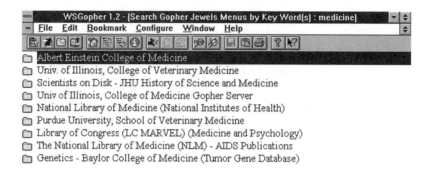

By simply choosing with the mouse we are immediately taken to the National Institutes of Health:

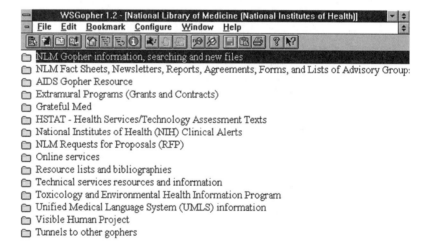

Using Gopher Jewels is an interesting and useful way to navigate your way through the information to be found in Gopher sites around the world. This benefit is the result of many individuals having taken the time to categorize Gopher sites from around the world by topic, with some 2,200 sites in all. For example, the "Anthropology and Archaeology" item provides a summary of resources found in this listing:

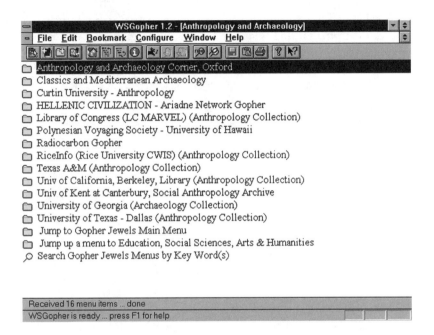

You can join a mailing list for new Gopher Jewels by e-mail, as follows:

Using e-mail:

Send message to **listproc@einet.net**

In the text of the message, input: **subscribe gopherjewels firstname lastname**

e.g., subscribe gopherjewels john smith

This will put you on a mailing list that will keep you up-to-date on new Gopher sites established around the world.

Searching for Information in "Gopherspace"

Another way to search various Gopher sites for information is to use Veronica, a program that lets you search global Gopher menus for particular topics or phrases, thus searching a wider number of sites than found through a search of Gopher Jewels. People refer to this as a search through all of "gopherspace."

Veronica is available on many Gopher servers. You can connect to the main one at the Gopher address **gopher.tmc.umn.edu** (URL: **gopher://gopher.tmc.umn.edu**), and then by choosing "Other Gopher and Information Servers" and then "Search Titles in Gopherspace" using Veronica. You are presented with a number of locations in which you can perform the Veronica search. After choosing one, you can input the text that you wish to search. You are then presented with a list of Gopher menus that matches your search phrase.

In the following screen, for example, we have chosen to search for information on genealogy and are presented with a listing of sites from around "gopherspace" that mention genealogy. You can look at any one of these sites quite easily by clicking with your mouse:

Searching for Information within Gopher Sites

In addition to the ability to search menus throughout Gopher, a number of Gopher servers also support the ability for you to search for information within a particular Gopher site based on a term that you specify. For example, when accessing the Industry & Science Canada Gopher (at **debra.dgbt.doc.ca**), you can choose the menu item "Search Industry Canada Documents."

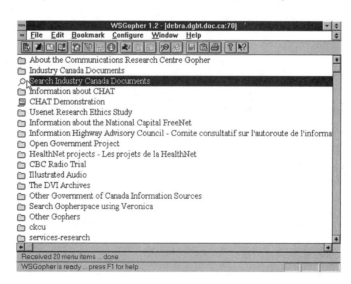

When you do so, you are presented with a dialog box in which you specify your search term. Once you run the search, you will be presented with a list of documents that mention the term.

Gopher Bookmarks

Finally, another useful aspect of Gopher is the ability to use bookmarks. When you have used Gopher to locate a particular Internet resource, and you want to access it again, you might find that you have a difficult time locating it. Remembering which menus you worked your way through is not the easiest thing to do.

Gopher bookmarks permit you to keep track of particular Gopher resources and to access them through your own personal Gopher menu or summary. You can easily add favorite sites to your Gopher bookmark list simply by clicking on the bookmark icon within your software. Doing so presents you with a box in which you can change the name for your bookmark or modify other details. You can then click on the "bookmark" within your Gopher software at any time to travel to one of your "bookmarked" locations. They are very similar to the concept of bookmarks that you will find within your Web software.

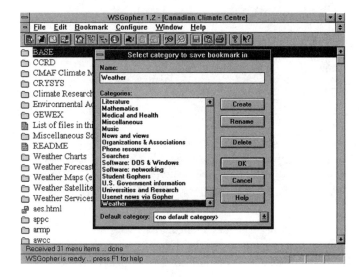

Gopher through a Shell Account

If you are accessing Gopher through a shell account, there are a few special considerations.

How Can I Access Gopher through a Shell Account?

If you are using a shell account, you can run a Gopher session in one of two ways:

◆ by using a Gopher program on your Internet service provider if it provides such a client (or software), or

◆ by using Telnet to access a site at which you can run a Gopher client. In this case, you are in effect using Telnet to get to a site where you can run a Gopher client (or program).

Most shell accounts provide direct access to a Gopher client. Using a shell account, you can access Gopher by keying "gopher" at your shell account prompt. This will usually present you with the main Gopher menu for your Internet service provider.

Gopher through a shell account looks similar to that through Windows; it just isn't as fancy. For example, here is the same Gopher site for Electronic Frontier Canada that we looked at above, as seen through a shell account:

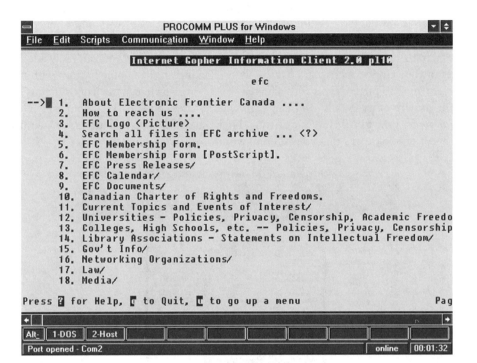

If your Internet service provider has not installed a local Gopher client, keying in "gopher" at your shell account prompt will not work. In this case, you must access a Gopher client by using Telnet to link to a location that offers a public Gopher client.

Gopher Tools in a Shell Account

Notice in the screen above that the prompt --> is placed at the first entry on the screen. To choose an item, you key in its corresponding number or move the prompt with your cursor keys. In a shell account, the symbols on a Gopher menu include "?" for an item that will lead you to a search prompt, "/" to indicate that the menu is followed by another menu, and "<TEL>" to indicate that the menu item will link you to another site via a Telnet session (discussed later in this chapter).

A useful feature of Gopher within a shell account is the ability to send yourself a copy of your document by e-mail. This is done by moving the arrow to the desired document and typing "m" for "mail" and then keying in the Internet e-mail address to which you want to send the document:

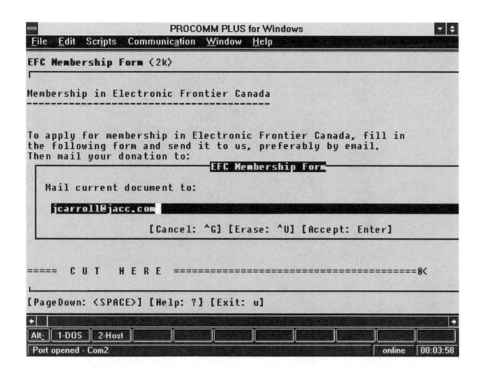

Shell accounts also support the use of bookmarks as discussed above. There are four basic bookmark commands that you might use:

a	Add an item to your bookmark list.
A	Add the current search to the bookmark list. For example, you might have run a search within Gopher and retrieved a list of documents. Keying "A" will save the search to your personal Gopher menu so that you can quickly return there.
v	View your current bookmark list.
d	Delete a bookmark.

The Demise of Gopher

During 1993 and 1994, by one estimate, the number of Gopher servers on the Internet was increasing at an annual rate of 997%. But, by March 1994, use of the World Wide Web had surpassed use of Gopher on the Internet,[1] and growth of the World Wide Web has not slowed down since. Why? Most new Internet sites are based on the Web, not Gopher, because the World Wide Web provides an easier, richer, and more sophisticated environment to present information in electronic form. Most new information sites on the Internet are established on the Web. For example, here is the Web site for the popular Toronto weekly newspaper, *Eye*:

---

1. As discussed on the Web site found at **http://www.rpi.edu/~decemj/cmc/mag/1994/oct/webip.html**

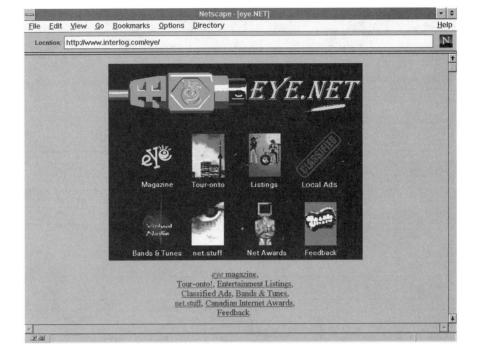

and here is a Gopher site at the University of Toronto:

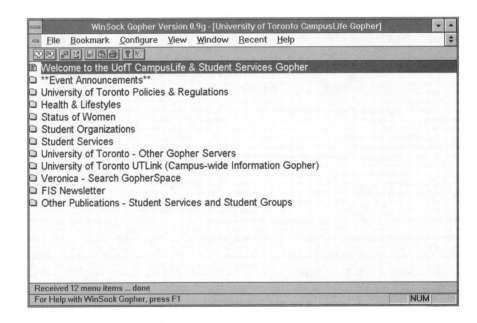

There really is no comparison in terms of presentation, organization, and ease of use.

Will Gopher disappear? Not likely. Many organizations on the Internet are actively encouraging the use of Gopher, particularly universities. There are many computers out there that do not have the power to access the graphical sophistication of sites found on the World Wide Web. The simple text-based structure of Gopher provides a neat solution to this problem, such that you should still see a lot of Gopher servers scattered around the Internet for a long time to come. And given that more and more of us will use a program like Netscape, which allows us to easily reach Gopher sites, it really is all quite irrelevant to us, isn't it?

Obtaining Gopher Software:

Keep in mind that most popular Web browser software lets you access Gopher sites, using URLs of the format **gopher://address**. Thus you do not need a separate Gopher client software. However, if you must have it, try the following:

For Windows:

WSGopher	**ftp://dewey.tis.inel.gov/pub/wsgopher/wsg-12.exe**
Hgopher	**ftp://ftp.ccs.queensu.ca/pub/msdos/tcpip/winsock/hgoph24.zip**

For Macintosh:

Turbo Gopher	**ftp://ftp.wustl.edu/systems/mac/info-mac/comm/tcp/turbo-gopher-20b8.hqx**
GopherApp++	**ftp://ftp.wustl.edu/systems/mac/info-mac/comm/tcp/gopher-app-22b43.hqx**
PNL Info Browser	**ftp://ftp.wustl.edu/systems/mac/info-mac/comm/tcp/pnl-info-browser.hqx**

As in all cases, check for the proper version numbers.

FTP

You could describe FTP as one of the granddaddies of all Internet applications, right beside Telnet (which we describe next). Before the World Wide Web began to dominate information retrieval through the Internet, people needed a way to retrieve documents, files, and computer programs from throughout the Internet. That's where FTP came in.

FTP, which stands for file transfer protocol, was the program used most often to retrieve files and information from around the Internet. In fact, until early 1995, FTP was the application that saw the highest volume of information transferred through the Internet. And, of course, all that changed with the arrival of the World Wide Web.

But FTP is still used quite heavily throughout the Internet community. In fact, of all the "older" Internet applications, it is likely the one you might use the most. You might even find yourself using FTP while in a World Wide Web session without even knowing it.

The reason for this is that in many cases it is still convenient for organizations to put actual computer programs or fully formatted word processing documents (or other types of computer files) up on FTP sites. These FTP sites can then be accessed directly with FTP software to retrieve a file, or they can be linked to a Web site so that you can retrieve the file with your Web browser. Thus throughout the global Internet you can find "FTP servers" that contain

◆ Public domain and shareware software, that is, software written by people and released for general use by anybody. In some cases, a fee or donation is required in order to comply with the terms provided with the software.

◆ Documents discussing the Internet or virtually any topic imaginable, in text form or specialized word processor form. In other cases, documents are available in "Postscript" format, which requires a printer with Postscript capability.

◆ Images from NASA and other organizations in a variety of formats. You will need a file viewer compatible with the particular file type in order to view the image.

◆ Sound files, for example, CBC radio programs, which are now available via the Internet. You will need sound capability on your system to deal with the file.

Many of these FTP sites have now been linked into World Wide Web pages so that when you go to retrieve a particular document from the World Wide Web, you are actually using an FTP session to do so!

Hence people no longer think of FTP as being a separate program that you run on the Internet to access a file, but, rather, think of it as a different type of Internet resource to access with your World Wide Web browser.

Using FTP

FTP sites are referred to in two ways: by their older address and file directory instructions and by the newer URL (uniform resource locator) method. As you start to use the Internet, you might still see references to documents or other information available by FTP. For example, you might come across the phrase "To obtain a document about 'Opportunities in Selected Ethnic Markets in Canada', use anonymous FTP to access **foodnet.fic.ca** and get **ethnic1.exe** in the directory **Documents/trends**." This is the "older method" by which people describe how to obtain a file using FTP.

You might also see the phrase "You can obtain the document about 'Opportunities in Selected Ethnic Markets in Canada', using the URL **ftp://foodnet.fic.ca/Documents/trends/ethnic1.exe**." This is the newer way of describing how to find information in an FTP site, based on the URL method of addressing. You would use this address to retrieve the document using your Web browser.

The key thing to keep in mind is that you can retrieve this document using FTP software or by using a World Wide browser like Netscape. Let's look at both cases.

Retrieving Files Using FTP Software

First, we retrieve the document described above using FTP client software, in this case, the program WS_FTP.

An FTP document reference usually contains three pieces of information that will help you retrieve the information mentioned:

◆ the domain address or domain name of the FTP site;

◆ the file location, in terms of the directory location;

◆ the file name.

In our example above **foodnet.fic.ca** is the FTP site, **Documents/trends** is the directory location, and **ethnic1.exe** is the file name that you want to get.

Using WS_FTP, you can choose to open up an FTP session to this site, and key in the directory information directly. Note that our session is based on an "anonymous log-in," which is described below:

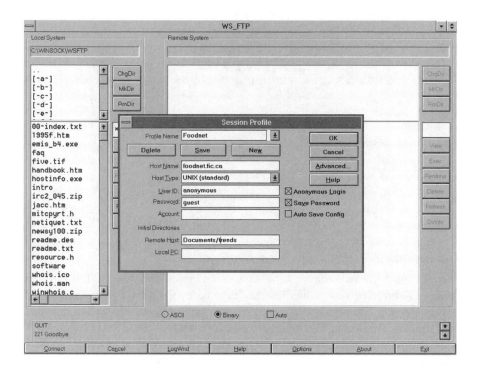

When you are logged into an FTP site with software such as WS_FTP, you will see your local hard disk files on the left and the files on the remote FTP site on the right. In this case, once the FTP software connects with the **foodnet.fic.ca** FTP server, you are presented with a listing of files in the directory **Documents/trends**.

To retrieve the document you want, point to the file (**ethnic1.exe**) and press the **<---** key to transfer it back to your computer:

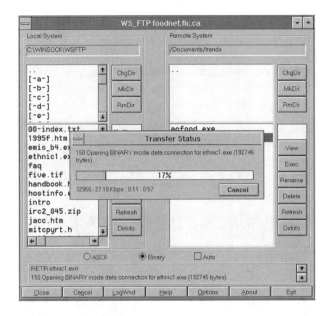

Thus you can use a separate FTP client to perform an FTP transfer.

Retrieving Files Using Your Web Browser

Most people wonder, why bother to use a separate FTP program? The need to run a separate FTP program to retrieve such a file has been negated by the arrival of sophisticated World Wide Web browsers. Netscape, for example, lets you easily access FTP sites, in this case using the URL **ftp://foodnet.fic.ca/Documents/trends/ethnic1.exe.** Simply keying in this address into your Web browser will result in the file being transferred to your system.

You can also view FTP directories with a program such as Netscape. If you want to view the directory that contains the file for our example, use the URL **ftp://foodnet.fic.ca/Documents/trends/**, and you will see the following:

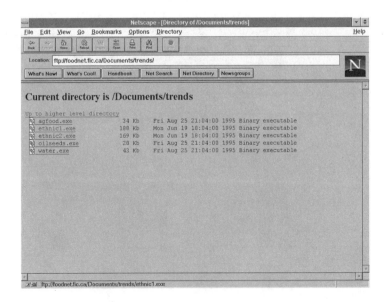

From here, you can easily retrieve the specific file that you want, simply by double clicking on it within the listing.

FTP Basics

There are a few things to remember when using FTP on the Internet:

◆ Many services permit "anonymous" log-ins; that is, they allow anyone on the Internet to access them by providing a user ID of "anonymous." If you access an FTP site using a Web browser, you do not need to worry about "anonymous" log-ins.

However, if you are using a separate FTP client, you are asked for a password along with the user ID "anonymous." As a courtesy, you should use your own e-mail address as the password. In some cases, the FTP server will only permit a connection if you do identify yourself in this way. Some even validate what you supply.

Most graphical FTP software supports simple anonymous log-ins; for example, in WS_FTP, you can choose an anonymous log-in simply by clicking on the "Anonymous Login" button:

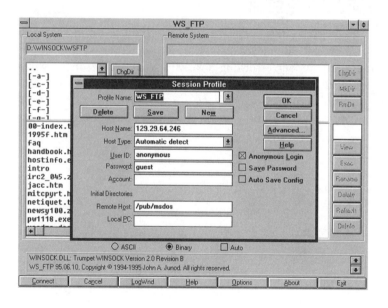

◆ In order to speed up the file transfer process, many of the files throughout the Internet have been compressed or combined. Files with the extensions **.zip**, **.arc**, **.Z** or **.z**, **.tar**, **.lzh**, **.sit** or **.cpt** are compressed or combined or both. The most common type of file extension is **.Z**, indicating a file that has been compressed using the UNIX program "compress." You will need appropriate software to uncompress or uncombine the file that you retrieve. Many FTP sites on the Internet include an uncompress program. If you do not have an uncompress program available, obtain one from your Internet service provider.

Make sure that you have appropriate tools to uncompress or uncombine files that you might retrieve. The following table lists some of the more popular compression programs, the file extension used, and the probable computer environment that the file is from.

EXTENSION	PROGRAM	PLATFORM
.zip	Pkzip/Pkunzip	DOS/Windows
.arc	Arc	DOS/Windows
.sit	Stuffit	Macintosh
.cpt	CompressIt	Macintosh
.z	Compress	UNIX
.lzh	LZH	DOS/Windows

Using FTP from a Shell Account

As seen above, if you have a direct connection or SLIP/PPP link to the Internet, file retrieval will be a one-step process: simply access an FTP site with your FTP client software or Web browser, choose a file by double clicking on it with your mouse, and it will be transferred from the remote FTP archive directly to your computer. However, if you are accessing the Internet using a "shell account" (i.e., you are not directly connected to the Internet), your retrieval of any file by FTP might be a two-step process, as seen in Figure 11.1.

FIGURE 11.1

Two-Step File Retrieval

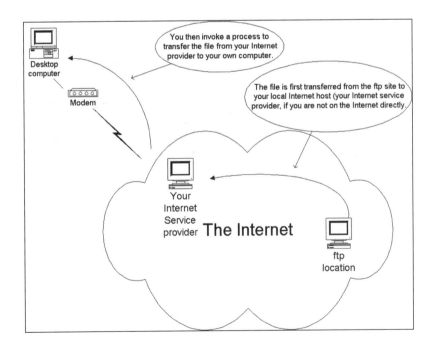

In the first step, you use FTP to retrieve a particular file from a remote system on the Internet. This transfers the file back to the system of your Internet service provider.

In the second step, you invoke a process to transfer the file from your Internet service provider to your own computer. What you do in this step will vary by service provider; hence it is important for you to check with your Internet service provider to make sure that you understand what is involved.

Finally, it should also be noted that this second step might not be required with the shell accounts of some Internet service providers: the file transfer might occur directly to your own computer when you input the "get" command.

A Sample FTP Session: Shell Account

When using FTP through a shell account, you must become familiar with some of the commands used to navigate through an FTP archive and to retrieve files. You must then become familar with how to retrieve a file. It is really not that difficult; once you are linked to another computer, you can use the "get" command to retrieve particular files, the "dir" command to look at file directories, and the "cd" command to change directories. Other commands are available, as detailed below.

Here is how you would go and get the ethnic foods document previously described in this chapter:

◆ You link to the site **foodnet.fic.ca**. Once there, a log-in name of "anonymous" is used, and a password is entered (matching the e-mail address of the user). The password is usually not echoed (i.e., shown on the screen) as it is keyed.

◆ Once we have "logged in" and are at the "ftp" prompt, we key in the command "cd Documents/trends" to move to the directory containing the file. Once there, a directory is obtained by keying "dir", as seen below:

```
                        PROCOMM PLUS for Windows
 File  Edit  Scripts  Communication  Window  Help
 Rapid Dial:              Script File:
 [ Entry 1 - Unnamed ]

 Terminal type is unknown
 $ ftp foodnet.fic.ca
 Connected to foodnet.fic.ca.
 220 foodnet.fic.ca FTP server (Version 2.1aWU(1) Mon Feb 27 09:24:23 GMT-0500 19
 95) ready.
 Name (foodnet.fic.ca:jcarroll): anonymous
 331 Guest login ok, send your complete e-mail address as password.
 Password:
 230 Guest login ok, access restrictions apply.
 Remote system type is UNIX.
 Using binary mode to transfer files.
 ftp> cd Documents/trends
 250 CWD command successful.
 ftp> dir
 200 PORT command successful.
 150 Opening ASCII mode data connection for /bin/ls.
 total 492
 -rw-r--r--  1 joan      html      35751 Aug 25 21:04 agfood.exe
 -rw-r--r--  1 joan      html     192746 Jun 19 18:04 ethnic1.exe
 -rw-r--r--  1 joan      html     173470 Jun 19 18:04 ethnic2.exe
 -rw-r--r--  1 joan      html      29294 Aug 25 21:04 oilseeds.exe
 -rw-r--r--  1 joan      html      45022 Aug 25 21:04 water.exe
 226 Transfer complete.
 ftp>
 Alt   1-DOS   2-Host
 Port opened - Com2                                        online   00:01:51
```

◆ The command **"get ethnic1.exe"** is then keyed to retrieve the particular file.

◆ Upon completion, the FTP session indicates that the file was successfully transferred. (If you are directly on the Internet, this will have transferred the file to your own computer system; if not, this indicates that the file has been copied to the file of your Internet service provider.)

◆ Once the file is successfully transferred, the "quit" command is entered to return to the computer of your local Internet host.

◆ Since the session occurred in a shell account, one more procedure is necessary to finally transfer the file. The command "sz ethnic1.exe" is then keyed to transfer the file from the system of the Internet service provider to a local PC, using the Zmodem protocol.[2]

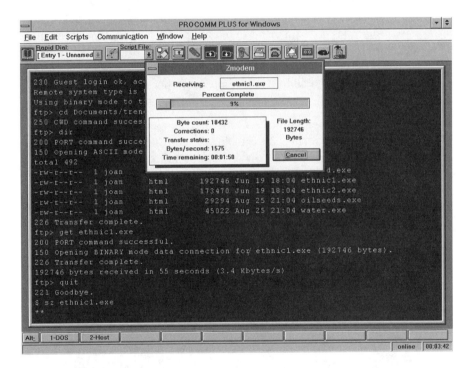

There are two other special considerations when it comes to using FTP with a shell account.

◆ Most of the services you will access with FTP on the Internet are UNIX-based and will be running software that is case-sensitive. For other services, you might be retrieving files from a non-UNIX machine, with file names that are not case-sensitive, in uppercase. File names must usually match the case exactly as seen within the directory or as specified in the note that you read about the file. If you are using a Web browser or a

---

2. These two steps, and the commands used, are specific to the Internet service provider used in this example. The procedure used on your particular provider will vary.

graphical FTP client such as WS_FTP, you do not have to worry about case; you retrieve a file simply by clicking on it. However, if you are using a shell account, and key in the file name that you want to retrieve, you must use the proper case.

If you are retrieving anything other than a text file, and you are using a shell account, you must use the binary command to ensure that the file is sent to you in the proper format. This is usually done by clicking the binary item within your client software, or by keying "binary" if you are using a shell account. (If you are using your Web browser, it does not matter.)

More people get frustrated by fetching a file in the wrong format when using FTP. If the file does not have **.TXT** or **.PS** in its name, or if it is not named **README**, it is likely a binary file.

FTP Directories

When using FTP, you are most often interacting with a computer that is based upon UNIX, and hence you are working with the UNIX file directory structure. Although these directories can seem simple when using FTP through an account directly linked to the Internet, it is still important to have a good grasp of how they work. Although they are similar to DOS directories, there are some subtle differences.

For example, as seen above, you can see that UNIX directories have a lot of extra information, which happens to be information on the type of file, the status of the file, and the "owner" of the file. For the uninitiated, these directories can seem overwhelming at first, unless you remember a couple of key points:

◆ Entries that begin with a "d" are directories. The DOS user can think of them as subdirectories beneath the directory currently shown.

◆ Entries beginning with anything else are usually files.

As with any resource on the Internet, there are several commands that you can use at the FTP prompt when in a shell account. The most often used commands to retrieve files and view directories are as follows:

COMMAND	MEANING	EXAMPLES
cd	Change directory.	cd public to switch to the directory public. **cd /** to return to the top directory. **cd ..** to go up one directory level.
dir	List the directory.	**dir** for a basic directory listing. Can also use ls on most systems.
get	Retrieve a file.	**get filename** to retrieve a particular file.
mget	Get multiple files.	**mget new*.*** to get any files beginning with the letters new.
quit	Leave the FTP site	

If you have the right to leave files at a particular Internet site (i.e., HTML files, if you have your own Web site), you can use the "put" and "mput" commands to transfer files to that site. More information on the above and other FTP commands can be obtained by keying "help" at the FTP prompt.

Retrieval of Files by E-Mail

It is possible to retrieve many of the files that are available via FTP via e-mail instead, through a few FTP archives. This is done by sending an e-mail message containing the file name that you want, including the directory details, to a specific e-mail address at the FTP archive site. At the FTP archive, a "mail robot" takes apart your request, obtains the selected file, and sends it back to you via e-mail. The requests are handled on a very low priority basis, so you might not receive the file for several hours or even several days.

One of the most popular of these sites is a server at the Massachusetts Institute of Technology, which has an FTP site containing information about the Internet. For example, to retrieve a document from this site that details how to use the ftp-by-mail service:

◆ Create a message to **mail-server@rtfm.mit.edu**.

◆ In the text of the message, you input a command that will send a help file or will retrieve specific files that might otherwise have been available via FTP. For example, to obtain help, send an e-mail message to **mail-server@rtfm.mit.edu** that contains the word "help" in the text of the message.

To obtain actual files, use the send command within the body of the message, that is,

---

Date: Thu, 30 Dec 1996 08:43:06 est

Reply-To: jcarroll@jacc.com

From: jcarroll@jacc.com (Jim Carroll)

To: mail-server@rtfm.mit.edu

Cc:

send /pub/usenet/news.answers/mail/mailing-lists/part01

send /pub/usenet/news.answers/mail/mailing-lists/part02

send /pub/usenet/news.answers/mail/mailing-lists/part03

send /pub/usenet/news.answers/mail/mailing-lists/part04

send /pub/usenet/news.answers/mail/mailing-lists/part05

send /pub/usenet/news.answers/mail/mailing-lists/part06

This will result in e-mail messages being sent to you that summarize some of the mailing lists available on the Internet.

There are several sites throughout the Internet that permit file retrieval by e-mail. Although there might be minor variations in the method, the concept is consistent from location to location. If in doubt, obtain the help file from a particular site first.

Obtaining FTP software:

For Windows:

CuteFTP	**http://papa.indstate.edu:8888/CuteFTP**
WSFTP	**http://www.csra.net/junodj/ws_ftp.htm**

For Macintosh:

Fetch:	**ftp://ftp.wustl.edu/systems/mac/info-mac/comm/tcp/fetch-212.hqx**

The Slow Demise of FTP?

Like Gopher, the use of FTP was finally surpassed by World Wide Web traffic in 1994. One reason has been an increased tendency to publish a document on the World Wide Web for viewing, rather than simply making the document available on an FTP site for people to come and get it. Using the World Wide Web, people can view a formatted document with images, sound, and other information immediately on the screen. Using FTP, you would have to go and retrieve a file first, and then do something to view the file. There is simply no comparison in terms of ease of use.

Even as electronic publishing migrates to the World Wide Web, there will still be a big need for FTP servers. There will always be a lot of information in FTP sites — computer files, programs, and other information that you do not view on-line, but that you do need to retrieve. But, over time you will likely find that most of your FTP file retrieval occurs automatically from within a World Wide Web session, rather than by using separate FTP client software.

Telnet

Telnet is an application that lets you travel from your Internet account to another computer somewhere else on the Internet in order to run a program (such as an electronic catalogue) at that computer. As recently as one or two years ago, it was a major Internet application in use throughout the Internet. Telnet was the primary method, next to Gopher, through which you might access library catalogues or browse on-line "stores" of books and records.

Telnet still exists and is in use throughout the Internet — it is just not used or implemented as widely as it was in the past, since it is an older, character-based application. In Canada, these locations include

◆ Links to the on-line catalogues of various libraries, such as the Vancouver Public Library, to search for particular books or other materials.

◆ Access to pay-per-use database services such as Dialog and Nexis, if you have an account already set up with these services.[3]

Using Telnet today is a little like time travel, if you are currently using the World Wide Web with software like Netscape or Mosaic. With Telnet, you leave the comfortable, 1990s world of point-and-click information access and retreat back to a computer screen based on characters, menus, numbers, an application that looks like it was designed (and often was) in the 1970s and 1980s.

A Sample Telnet Session

Once you reach a location by Telnet, you will be able

◆ to directly access the resource, if no "log-in" or "sign-in" ID is required;

◆ to access the resource by providing a public user ID;

◆ to access the resource by providing a valid user ID and password for a system that has generally restricted its access.

There is not much of a difference in using a shell or SLIP/PPP account to use Telnet. In our example, we will use a Windows program, Trumpet Telnet.

The following session details the steps taken to Telnet to the Alberta Wheat Pool (AWP). In this case, the AWP has set up a system through which farmers can obtain up-to-date livestock and grain prices, as well as other information, on-line. Within Trumpet Telnet, we choose to "open" a new session and key in the Telnet address for the AWP, **fis.awp.com**:

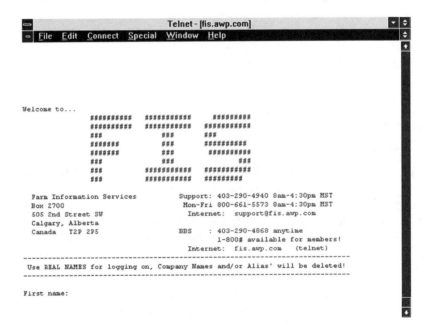

---

3. Often, accessing these services through the Internet is less expensive than accessing them through regular data services like Datapac or Tymnet.

Trumpet Telnet opens a connection to this site and displays the welcoming screen. (Anyone can obtain a user ID and password at this site by filling out the forms that follow this welcome screen.)

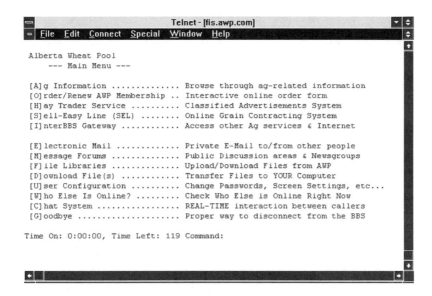

Once you are signed in, you can access the "main menu" of information:

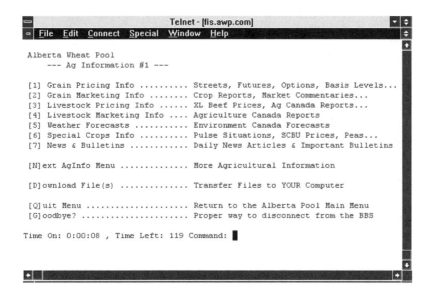

From here, you can access several types of information, including a wealth of livestock and commodity marketing information:

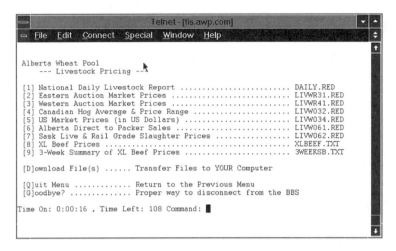

Using Telnet through a shell account is not that different from what was seen above; at your shell account prompt, simply key **telnet fis.awp.com** to access the service above. The screens you see will be virtually identical to what was shown above. The benefits of a graphical user interface such as found with Windows have virtually no effect on a Telnet session, which is why Telnet is considered by many to be one of the least friendly Internet applications.

One final thing about Telnet: such sites are often linked into the World Wide Web. If you have configured your Web browser properly, when you choose such an item from the Web, your browser will load your Telnet software and take you to the site. The AWP has established a Web site, and the Telnet site above is accessible through it:

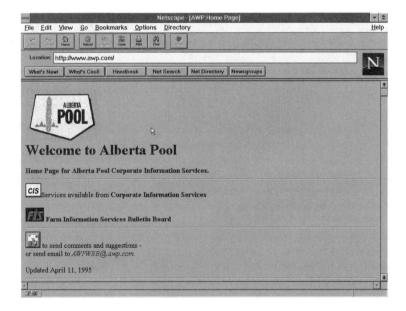

Special Things about Telnet

There are some special things that you should keep in mind as you use Telnet:

- On occasion, you will be advised to use the domain name with a particular "port" number. This is required when you are accessing a system on the Internet in which the port directs you to a particular application. You are usually told when a particular port address is required. Type the port number after the Telnet address when a port number is required. For example, access to the University of Michigan Weather Underground system, which includes Canadian weather details, requires a port number. In this case, you are advised to telnet to the address **downwind.sprl.umich.edu 3000**, where 3000 is the port number used for this particular application.

- When using Telnet, you should always keep in mind that you are accessing other computers on the Internet, and as a result you are "pretending" to be directly linked to them through "terminal emulation." "Terminal emulation" when using Telnet is one of the necessary evils of the Internet. When using Telnet, you could be linking into all kinds of different computers around the globe, each of which might run differently. Your computer has to pretend to be the proper type of "terminal" for each system that it might access, and given the different types of systems out there, it cannot pretend to be everything to everyone.

   What does this mean? Likely that you will experience some frustration with Telnet due to the use of "terminal emulation" and due to the fact that every system that you Telnet to could operate differently and present you with a completely different way of doing things. The result of this is that Telnet is not, nor can it ever be, a completely friendly, mouse-driven application.

- Some applications that you access will ask you to specify the terminal type that you are using. Be sure that you understand the various types of terminals that your communications software supports, and how to switch to any particular terminal type when you are on-line. Most services will support, at a bare minimum, the popular terminal type VT-100.

- Be aware of any special instructions that might apply to certain Internet resources. For example, if you review some of the Internet resources described in our resource directory that are accessible using Telnet, you will see that some libraries require you to use an access method known as TN3270, which is a variation of Telnet modified for special terminal types. The Directory includes the special instructions that you should use when accessing these locations.

- Remember the "escape character" for the particular Telnet client that you are using. There is nothing worse than traveling somewhere on the Internet without understanding how to get back to where you started.

   In our link to the Alberta Wheat Pool, you were told once you had signed in that "escape character" is "^]". This means that you press the ctrl key and] together on your computer when you are ready to leave this particular Telnet site. The escape character permits you to exit from a particular Telnet session in case the service you have linked to does not make it obvious how to exit, or if your current session seems to "hang" or "freeze."

The Evolution of Telnet

Telnet was most often used by companies or organizations to permit people to run a program located on their computer. This program would let the person query some type of database for information at that remote computer. The Alberta Wheat Pool example used above permits people to retrieve on-line market prices, which are actually stored on a computer system at the Wheat Pool.

But, we are seeing many such applications spring up on the World Wide Web, instead of being implemented as a Telnet application. This permits people to query a database somewhere, yet do it through the friendliness and simplicity of a World Wide Web browser. We discuss this trend in greater depth in Chapter 13.

Obtaining Telnet clients:

For Windows:

CommNet   **ftp://ftp.radiant.com/cmnet*.exe**
EWAN   **http://www.lysator.liu.se/~zander/ewan.html**

For Macintosh:

NCSA Telnet 2.6 **ftp://ftp.wustl.edu/systems/mac/info-mac/comm/tcp/ncsa-telnet-26.hqx**

As in all cases, check for the proper version numbers on-line.

Archie: The Tool to Find Files

The Internet contains many millions of computer programs, files, documents, sound files, images, and other information that you can access using FTP. Part of the challenge, however, is finding a particular program or document. Most times, you will read about a specific document or file in a document that mentions the actual FTP archive, including the directory location and file name. You can easily travel there to retrieve the file.

Certainly, the World Wide Web and popular search indices such as Yahoo and Opentext can help you to locate particular files around the network. In many cases, even these search tools might not help you locate a particular file that you are looking for. However, in other cases, you might know of a program but have no idea where to go to find it.

Archie, a program developed in Canada at McGill University and now marketed and supported worldwide by a Canadian company, Bunyip Information Systems, permits you to search file archives around the Internet by file name. Once again, the process is completely different using Windows software on an account that has a direct link to the Internet.

In this case, we have used the WinSock Archie program. We are looking for the program **pmail301.zip** (a recent version of Pegasus Mail) and have chosen the Canadian Archie archive at **archie.uqam.ca**:

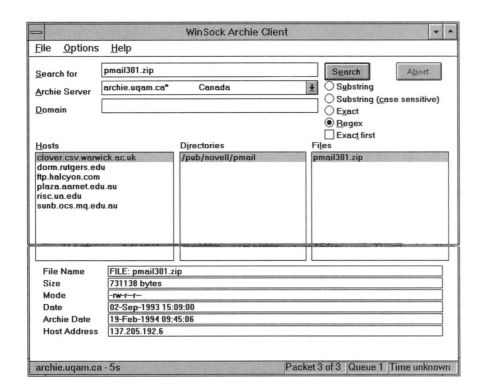

After a moment or two, Archie returns with a list of hosts that have the software, details the directory location and the file name, as seen above. At this point, if you click on the file name in the right column, you will invoke an FTP session to grab the file for you.

Archie is a useful tool if you know the name of the computer file that you are looking for, since it will help you to find it among multiple FTP sites around the world. It is of limited use, however, if you do not know the file name. In that case, you are best to start your search using the World Wide Web through an index like Yahoo or OpenText.

Finding Archie Clients:

For Windows:

WS_Archie: **ftp://ftp.coast.net/SimTel/win3/winsock/wsarch08.zip**

For Macintosh:

Anarchie **ftp://ftp.wustl.edu/systems/mac/info-mac/comm/tcp/anarchie-14.hqx**

Archie **ftp://ftp.wustl.edu/systems/mac/info-mac/comm/tcp/archie-10.hqx**

Finger

Finger is a utility originally used in the UNIX world to list users on a local system or to list users located at another location on the Internet. In some cases, you can use Finger to determine the last time that someone logged into their Internet account.

Other locations on the Internet are now using Finger as a simple method of making information available. For example, if you are in a shell account that has a Finger client, you can obtain recent information on auroral (Northern Lights) activity in Canada by keying: **finger aurora@xi.uleth.ca**. If you have a direct connection to the Internet, you can use Winsock Finger, a public domain Finger client. Accessing the site above, for example, shows you the following:

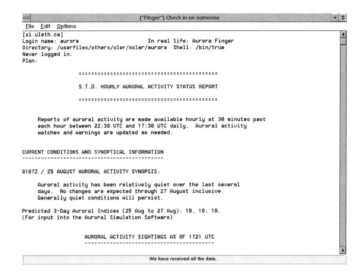

You can "finger" **seisme@seismo.emr.ca** to get information on recent earthquake activity in Canada:

Like most older applications, Finger is being eclipsed by the World Wide Web. For example, the same information above is available directly through a Web site (**http://www.seismo.emr.ca**):

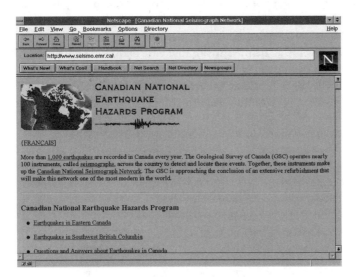

Obtaining Finger Software:

For Windows:

WS-Finger

ftp://sparky.umd.edu/pub/winsock/wsfngr*.zip (where * is the latest version number)

IRC

IRC is best described as a CB radio for the Internet. Often forgotten or overlooked by many Internet users, it is also an application that has a large number of very enthusiastic fans. Using IRC, you can participate in on-line discussions in real time with other Internet users. Discussions are either open or private. To use IRC, you must either

◆ have a direct connection to the Internet and have the IRC client software on your own system, or

◆ use a version located on your Internet service provider.

In both cases, you will also need an IRC server location to access. Your Internet service provider might automatically link to a site. A listing of IRC servers in Canada can be found in Appendix J.

When you are in an IRC "session," you join a "channel," or topic, that interests you. If you key something, all other members of that channel will see what you keyed within seconds, and you will see what they have input. This permits you to have an "interactive," or "real time," discussion through the Internet.

IRC is used for serious purposes, for example, as a communications channel during several major world events, including the Oklahoma bombing crisis in April 1995. You can find the IRC archives related to the crisis at **http://www.procyon.com/~pda/disaster.html**. It was also heavily used during the 1994 California earthquake, the 1993 Russian revolt and 1992 revolution, and the 1991 Persian Gulf War. You can find archives/logs of IRC communications during these events at **http://sunsite.unc.edu/dbarberi/chats.html#chat-links**. Both archives will provide you a good glimpse into the serious side of IRC.

To access an IRC session, the first thing you must do is access a server that will link you into IRC. In the following screen, we are using the program WSIRC to link to an IRC server at York University:

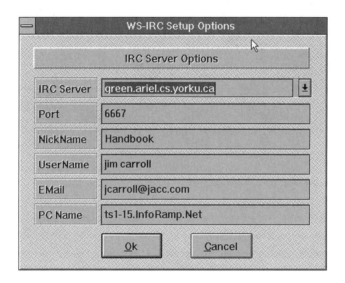

Once we are linked into the IRC server, we can choose a "channel" to join. You can request a list of channels from the server you are linked to by clicking on an icon.

In the following screen, we have joined the **#riskybus** channel, which permits us to participate in a Jeopardy-style game. The interesting thing about IRC is that it is populated by what are known as "bots" (or "robots"), programs that automate some of the interaction within various IRC channels. In this case, the **#riskybus** channel is managed (i.e., the questions are asked and the answers are checked) by a "bot" named RobBot:

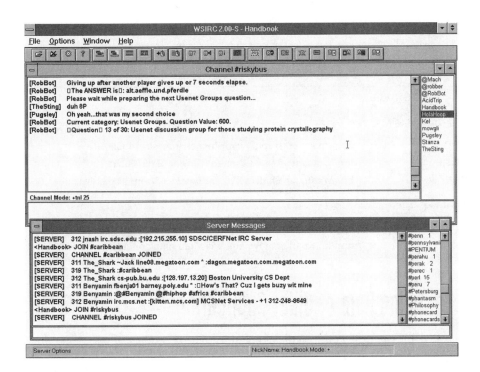

IRC is an interesting place to visit, but it is a little weird. More often than not, a venture into IRC is a voyage to the weirdness of the human psyche. For example, an IRC "channel" known as **#hottub** is a place where people pretend to be in a hot tub and talk back and forth; the discussions that take place in **#netsex** should be obvious. Other channels carry more lurid titles.

You will truly discover the global character of the Internet in an IRC session. More often than not, someone will ask "where's everybody from?" Responses will come from locations right around the world.

The discussions that occur in some IRC channels are in some cases off the wall, zany, and in other cases appear to be of the mentality found in a Grade 5 boys locker room. IRC has a no-holds-barred, anything-goes mentality, so if you plan to visit, you should be prepared for anything. There are many "fans" of IRC who participate in IRC sessions on a regular basis. In fact, some might be considered "IRC junkies," in need of a daily fix.

But there are many real IRC applications as well. Aside from its use as a disaster recovery tool, IRC is used as a support tool by some companies and is also used for training courses.

IRC also provides a fascinating glimpse into the future: new software is being released that permits you to view pictures of those with whom you are conversing. It does not take a huge leap of the imagination to picture the day when we will have live, real time, video-based IRC.

The application is also becoming more mainstream as it becomes integrated into the Web. For example, Netscape has released a "Chat" program, integrated with the Web, which allows you to take part in IRC discussions.

Obtaining IRC Software	
For Windows:	
WSIRC	ftp://ftp.eznet.net/pub/win/winsock/irc/wsirc14g.zip
mIRC	ftp://papa.indstate.edu/winsock-l/winirc/mirc36.zip
IRC4Windows	ftp://winftp.cica.indiana.edu/pub/pc/win3/winsock/irc4win.zip
For Macintosh:	
Ircle	ftp://ftp.wustl.edu/systems/mac/info-mac/comm/tcp/ircle-151.hqx
Homer	ftp://ftp.wustl.edu/systems/mac/info-mac/comm/tcp/homer-0934.hqx

The Declining Role of Older Applications

Telnet and FTP could be considered the granddaddies of Internet applications, since they have been used for many years, and there still are a number of resources throughout the global Internet that you can Telnet to, and there are many FTP sites available. But, the trend in Canada and elsewhere is that most organizations setting up new Internet information resources are using the increasing sophistication of the World Wide Web. The result is that Telnet and FTP and applications like Finger and Archie are falling into disfavor as general, day-to-day applications for most Internet users.

However, it is important that you learn about them, because there are still a number of resources throughout the Internet that you can access through these two capabilities. We can expect to see many FTP sites throughout the Internet, particularly as methods to retrieve files from these sites using the World Wide Web become common.

CHAPTER 12

Connecting to the Internet

With locutions like Internet, E-mail, and World Wide Web becoming household words, more and more people are beyond wondering why they should get connected to information networks and are beginning to wonder how. What can some-one new to the on-line realms expect to find on-line? Which approach is best—a "true" Internet account, an account with a for-profit on-line service, or signing up with a homegrown bulletin-board system?

How to Get Connected, and What's On-line to See
Globe and Mail, March 14, 1995

My mother told me recently that she was afraid of the Internet. She's never been on-line in her life and doesn't want to be, but even from a distance cyberspace seems to her a scary place. I suspect that part of what spooks her and many others is the vagueness of the word. Cyberspace, from all you'd glean from a typical usage, is the name of an energetic nowhere, popu-lated by ghosts.

Plenty of Ordinary Folk are Stak-ing Out Territory in Cyberspace
Globe and Mail, May 4, 1995

So far, most of our exploration of the Internet has been from the per-spective of someone who has a direct connection to the Internet. As we discussed in Chapter 6, if you are directly connected to the Internet, your use of the system will differ from those who are not, because you will be able to take advantage of many of the more sophisticated soft-ware programs available for various applications on the Internet, such as Netscape and Mosaic. So again, the way that you access the Internet will have an effect on what you can do with it and how easy it will be for you to use. In this chapter, we look at some of the technical meth-ods to connect to the Internet.

Internet Service Providers

Appendix B includes a list of Canadian Internet service providers which details the range of services offered by these companies. As you review the listings, you will appreciate that there are many methods to link into the Internet in Canada. However, keep in mind that providers come and go. Obviously, some might not be here later, and new ones will appear. At least a few ISPs listed in prior editions of this book have disappeared within a few months of the book hitting the bookstores. With the massive growth in the number of ISPs in Canada, it is inevitable that some will not be able to survive the rigors of competition.

As you review the listings of providers in Appendix B, keep in mind that the list is current as of September 1995. Since then, new providers may have appeared on the local or national scene, or existing providers may have gone out of business.

Types of Connections to the Internet

In our look at the many technical options to connect to the Internet, we first offer a novice guide for those who want a simple answer to the question, "what type of account should I buy?" We then provide a more comprehensive guide for those who require a more in-depth answer. In order to clarify your options, we examine what you can do with the Internet as an individual with a modem and then what you can do as an organization with a direct network link.

Connecting, for Novices

This is, by necessity, a rather technical chapter. If you do not want to understand all the technical issues related to a link to the Internet, this novice section is for you. We have tried to keep it simple and straightforward.

Your questions are probably simple. What do you need to buy, and from whom do you buy it? We offer the following general rules of guidance:

◆ As we indicated in Chapter 6, if you are a user of Microsoft Windows or a Macintosh, and just want to get connected to the Internet, our advice to you is to obtain a SLIP/PPP account from an Internet service provider. SLIP (Serial Line Interface Protocol) and PPP (Point to Point Protocol) are two different but similar protocols. Most providers are moving towards adopting PPP as the protocol of choice. For our purposes, we refer to them in a combined form, SLIP/PPP.

To run a SLIP/PPP connection, you need a fairly powerful computer (i.e., Windows on an 80386 computer or better with at least 4 to 8 Mb of RAM), a fast modem (9,600, 14,400 or 28,800), and a substantial amount of disk storage (at least 100–200 Mb, since you might find yourself

CONNECTING TO THE INTERNET

1 There are several levels of Internet connectivity, ranging from access as an individual to full-time corporate access.

2 Many people choose a SLIP/PPP connection, which provides the best possible type of Internet access for a dial-up user.

3 You can also use a shell or menu account, use computer services that are not part of the Internet but that provide Internet e-mail, or use UUCP, which permits batch-oriented collection and sending of Internet e-mail and USENET news.

4 Many organizations have become convinced of the strategic benefit of a full-time link of a corporate network to the Internet.

5 Some organizations link only their e-mail system to the Internet, while others establish a full-time link of their network to the Internet, so that employees are always "on" the Internet.

6 New technologies that provide higher-speed links to the Internet are rapidly emerging.

7 There are many issues that you should consider when choosing an Internet service provider.

8 Anyone can become an ISP with the proper amount of investment capital and time, but there are many complex business and support issues in doing so.

running a lot of different Internet client software, all of which is stored on your PC, as described in Chapter 6).[1]

If you are buying a new modem, consider purchasing a 28,800 modem. Prices are falling to less than $250, and since many ISPs charge on the basis of time on-line, you could quickly earn back some of that money in the form of cost savings.

◆ If you do not have adequate computer power as described above, you will likely have to use a shell account (as described in Chapter 6) and will find the Internet to be more difficult to use. Keep in mind that accessing the Internet through a Free-Net uses an account similar to a shell account; therefore, you can only do certain things on the Internet, and it is more difficult to use than a SLIP/PPP account.

◆ Examine your information needs; there are alternatives to the Internet. Systems such as CompuServe and America Online offer "menu accounts," which provide access to a wealth of information often not found on the Internet, such as airline schedules, computer support forums, official software sites, magazines and newspapers, and other information sources. You might find an account on one of these services to be perfectly adequate, while letting you enjoy some aspects of the Internet such as Internet e-mail.

◆ One of the most common questions we get is, "can I not just continue using my CompuServe account?" As we describe in the next section, unless you have arranged to access SLIP/PPP using CompuServe as an ISP, you are not really on the Internet when you use CompuServe. You can do a lot, much of which you will find to be quite worthwhile. But you cannot use your everyday CompuServe account to access the World Wide Web using software such as Netscape. To do that, you need a SLIP/PPP account, which you can arrange through CompuServe or one of the many ISPs mentioned in this book.

Should you use CompuServe as your SLIP/PPP connection? It depends. Keep in mind that even as CompuServe makes a push into being a major ISP across Canada, its rates are often higher than those with a local Internet service provider. But, in some cases it might offer better support and reliability. The question really comes down to one of service, support, reliability, and cost, and for that there is no easy answer.

If you are interested in any of the following issues, then you should read the remainder of this chapter:

◆ You want to know methods of obtaining an e-mail only link to the Internet for yourself or your corporate organization.

◆ You want to know about methods of linking your corporate network to the Internet.

◆ You simply want to know the various ways of linking into various parts of the Internet.

---

1. We offer these comments as suggestions. We often get mail from people regarding these types of statements, saying "You are wrong, because I am running SLIP/PPP on my computer which is...." These are general rules of guidance. What works and does not work in any particular circumstance will depend on many, many factors.

Individual Access

Many people in organizations first choose to access the Internet as individuals in order to explore it and understand it better. More often than not, they do this from a PC at home or, in other cases, through their office. Some of these providers provide UUCP, shell, permanent, and temporary SLIP/PPP access to the network; others provide only one or two of these options, while several others provide only e-mail access to the Internet.

Part of the art for you is to figure out what type of connectivity you need and for what purpose. What is appropriate in your circumstances depends upon

◆ your particular communication needs;

◆ the technical effort you are willing to make to participate in the network;

◆ the amount of money that you are willing or have available to spend;

◆ the hardware and operating system platform in which you operate, that is, the power of the computer that you have.

This section details methods to access the Internet on your own, usually through a dial-up modem connection. This includes examination of how to get on the Internet through a SLIP/PPP account for access to most Internet services, shell and menu accounts, which let you access only some areas of the Internet, proprietary software solutions, simple e-mail only access to the Internet, and the use of UUCP-based programs to use Internet e-mail and USENET news.

SLIP/PPP Connections

Direct connections for use by individuals to the Internet are most often supported by the use of the SLIP or PPP protocols. This is the recommended type of access for an individual accessing the Internet. SLIP and PPP provide full TCP/IP capabilities to the casual dial-up user and hence allow you to be directly connected to the Internet.

Networks directly linked to the Internet have a registered Internet IP address and are able to link directly to any other computer on the Internet. When using a SLIP or PPP connection, you are using a registered Internet IP address, albeit on a temporary basis.

If you purchase a SLIP/PPP connection to the Internet, you are usually provided some type of SLIP/PPP software by your ISP. In other cases, you must find or purchase such software. In this chapter, we describe some of the public domain software you can use for this purpose and in the next chapter describe some of the commercial software now available in the marketplace.

Benefits of a Direct Connection

More and more people across Canada are buying SLIP/PPP connections to the Internet rather than shell accounts (which we discuss next), because you can run more Internet software (such as Netscape) in a much friendlier environment. As we saw in Chapter 6, a direct connection lets you use all Internet services, most often with a point-and-click interface. This results in a substantial lessening in complexity of the Internet and a significant increase in the usefulness of the network.

SLIP/PPP *for a Casual Modem Connection*

Dial-up modem connections via SLIP/PPP usually involve a speed of 9,600 or 14,400 bits per second (9.6 Kb or 14.4 Kb). And with the arrival of 28,800 bps modems, more are accessing at 28.8 Kb. To use SLIP or PPP, you will require software that supports SLIP or PPP. There are a number of implementations of SLIP and PPP available for most operating system platforms in the public domain.

As we will see in Chapter 13, there are a number of commercial programs available that provide such a connection. In Chapter 14 we discuss how Microsoft Windows 95 provides you with the software necessary to support a PPP connection to your Internet service provider directly without any special programs. Trumpet Winsock is the most popular public domain/shareware SLIP/PPP alternative within the Windows environment. It has rapidly gained favor throughout the Internet as a method of providing PPP access from Microsoft Windows systems. You can download Trumpet Winsock from many locations throughout the Internet, including the one detailed below. Similarly, MacPPP is the most popular alternative for the Macintosh environment.

Obtaining SLIP/PPP connection software:

Windows:

Trumpet Winsock	**ftp://ftp.trumpet.com.au/winsock/twsk .zip**
	(= version number)
	http://www.trumpet.com.au/

Macintosh:

InterSLIP	**ftp://ftp.intercon.com/InterCon/sales/InterSLIP**
File:	**InterSLIPInstaller**
	InterSLIPInstaller 1.0.1.hqx
MacPPP	**ftp://merit.edu/pub/ppp/macppp2.0.1.hqx**

You can find pointers to additional SLIP or PPP programs for Windows at "The Consummate Winsock Apps List" (**http://cwsapps.texas.net/cwsa.html**) and for Macintosh systems at "Mac Internet Tools" at **http://www.iquest.com/macppp.html**. To use such a package, you will usually need the guidance of your Internet service provider for entering the proper information, possibly including an IP address, domain name, name server, and other tidbits.

Access through a Shell or Menu Account

If you cannot use a SLIP/PPP account, you can consider using a "shell account" or a menu account. Strictly speaking, a shell account has a specific definition within the Internet community: it is an account that leaves you, once you have identified yourself with a user ID and password, at a UNIX prompt. You can then run various UNIX client programs to do various things on the Internet, and you have to learn your way around UNIX to use the account.

If you are using a shell account, the Internet will sometimes prove to be a difficult and mysterious place. Simply put, a SLIP/PPP account opens up the entire Internet world to you with simple, easy-to-use software, while a shell account makes that world sometimes very tough to deal with. Take a look at Chapter 6 again to understand why this is so.

You would only choose a shell account instead of a SLIP/PPP account if

♦ you do not have a computer powerful enough to run SLIP/PPP software in a graphical environment;

♦ your modem is less than 9,600 baud, in which case a SLIP/PPP account is likely impractical for you;

♦ SLIP/PPP access is not available in your area, but a shell account is;

♦ you cannot afford a SLIP/PPP account. In some cases, shell accounts are less expensive than a SLIP/PPP account.

Closely related to shell accounts are menu accounts. These are accounts that do not leave you at a menu prompt, but put up on the screen a series of text menus that you use to navigate your way through Internet services.

Accessing a Shell Account

You access a shell account like you would any other on-line computer service. Using communications software, you dial your Internet service provider and sign in to an account with your user ID and password. You are then presented with a menu from which to choose Internet services, or you are presented directly with a prompt from which you can access various Internet services.

You access a shell account most often through a Canadian Internet service provider. Many of the Internet service providers in Canada offer shell access. Quite often, you can dial in as a shell user or as a SLIP/PPP user on your ISP account, that is, the account serves a dual purpose.

Accessing a Menu Account

A menu account is, strictly speaking, not a shell account, since you are left at a menu or series of choices through which you can interact with the Internet, rather than at a UNIX command. However, the concept of a menu account is similar to that of a shell account—you are left at a text prompt at which point you can begin to do certain things on the Internet. In the case of a menu account, you can choose to access USENET news or an FTP session by choosing a letter or number from the menu.

Like real shell accounts, menu accounts are difficult and sometimes frustrating to use. There are two ways that you can get a menu account to access the Internet: through a commercial on-line service and through a Free-Net.

Through a Commercial On-line Service

Several major commercial on-line services such as Delphi, BIX, and Genie that provide on-line conferences, games, research libraries, and other services also provide full or partial access to the Internet through a menu account. Other systems, like CompuServe and America Online, let you access parts of the Internet through a basic menu account; they also offer direct SLIP/PPP access. For example, through a regular (non-SLIP/PPP) CompuServe account, you can use FTP and Telnet. You do so with a series of graphical commands (or by using a graphical program such as CompuServe Information Manager). You are not really part of the Internet in this case.

But access to some Internet services through systems like CompuServe or America Online is often an easy way of accessing parts of the Internet and works well for those who do not have inexpensive access through a local Internet service provider. In addition, the range of other on-line services available, such as forums, games, and on-line research libraries, makes them an attractive alternative for your communication needs.

However, since you are using services based in the United States, you do end up paying a premium to use the Internet this way. With the growing number of Canadian Internet providers providing 1-800 access, there is even less incentive to use a U.S.-based service.

Through a Free-Net

Most Free-Nets in Canada provide a menu that lets you access a few areas on the Internet. Free-Nets are sometimes a good option people can use to explore the Internet. But there are limitations. Most Free-Nets in Canada only provide access to a few Internet services, such as electronic mail, USENET, and Gopher, due to the limitations of a menu account. Most do not provide access to the most exciting area of the Internet, the World Wide Web, because use of such an application could quickly overwhelm their link to the outside world.

You might find that you never succeed in linking to a Free-Net or that you cannot get support. Free-Nets operate on limited budgets and succeed because of the efforts of volunteer members. Quite often there are only a limited number of phone lines available to access the service, and support capabilities are sometimes few and far between. The result is that many people who try to access various Internet services through a Free-Net become frustrated.

Users might rarely get a connection, particularly during busy periods in the evening, since there are so many people trying to access the service at once. Support questions are sometimes left unanswered for days. Reliability of the service is sometimes subject to question. Inevitable fund-raising drives take place on-line to try to shore up meager finances.

What is fascinating is that given that Free-Nets are volunteer efforts, some individuals have the audacity to complain about service levels or the limited technology. If you want a free service but also want to complain, you will find that you get little sympathy. Our suggestion? Volunteer some of your own time to help solve the problems, or go out and buy a real account. Hence, while Free-Nets are a good way to begin exploring the concept of on-line information and the Internet, they will provide you a limited picture at best.

If you would like some information on Free-Net activities in your area, take a look at Appendix G, "Community Networking Organizations in Canada," which includes a listing of most operating Free-Nets in Canada, as well as contacts for the organizing committees for other Free-Nets.

Proprietary Software

Prior to the widespread adoption of SLIP/PPP accounts for dial-up access to the Internet, a number of organizations provided proprietary software solutions to make it easier for people to use the Internet. One of the most exciting proprietary systems is Pipeline, a U.S. package that is provided by a few Canadian ISPs. The software uses a proprietary computer protocol that is not SLIP/PPP, but provides many of the benefits of a SLIP/PPP connection.

The protocol, which the Pipeline folks call "Pink Slip," provides a very effective, very easy-to-use interface into most Internet services through what is really a dial-up shell account. It does this by performing a number of nifty background tricks while it is on-line.

The Pipeline software provides one-program access to pretty well every Internet feature. When you load the Pipeline software, you see a single screen that provides simple access to news, e-mail, and other services. Clicking on Connect!, you are linked through a dial-up call into Passport, an ISP in Toronto that provides the Pipeline software.

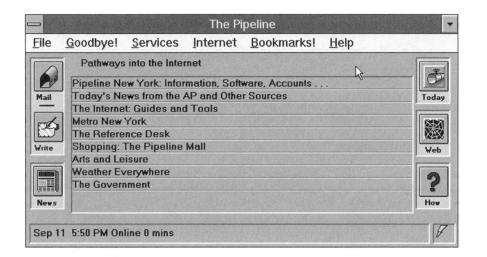

The Services menu item lists additional services that you can reach, such as IRC, the Web and FTP:

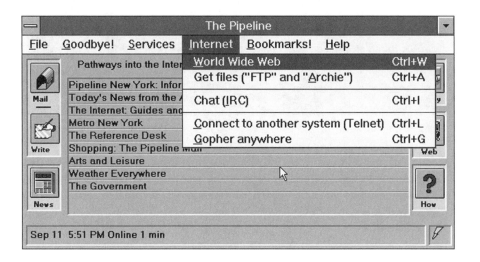

The centre of the screen is an entry point to Gopher resources. Choosing any one of the menu items by double clicking on it presents a Gopher menu, albeit in a very straightforward graphical environment. The product also comes with a simple, proprietary Web browser so that you can access the World Wide Web.

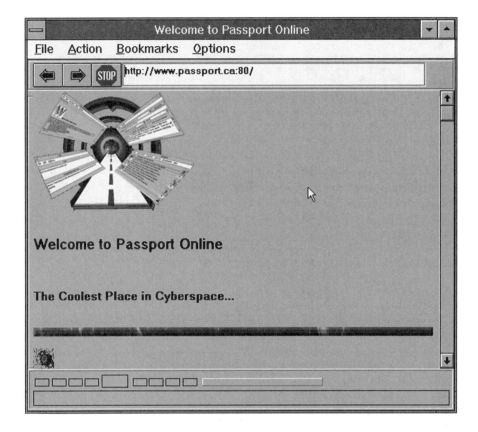

The Pipeline software is a highly effective tool for new users of the Internet, given that it wraps together many of the Internet applications discussed in this book into a simple package that can be used with any modem. There are limitations to the product, one being that it is only available with a few ISPs in Canada (for example, Passport Online in Toronto and Sask-Tel in Saskatchewan).

Another is that by adopting Pipeline, you lose one of the key benefits of a SLIP/PPP connection, that is, the ability to use any of the TCP/IP clients that are being developed for the Internet (such as Internet Phone). You pay a price for using a proprietary product, in that you are restricted to use of that product only.

Pipeline is a good piece of software for novices who would like to get onto the Internet and is highly recommended in that regard. However, experience has shown that many users of the Pipeline software soon migrate to a SLIP/PPP account, in order to be able to use some of the more sophisticated client software to be found on the Internet such as Netscape.

Electronic Mail Access Only

With the growing popularity of Internet e-mail, it is evident that many individuals want to have an Internet e-mail address. But some may not wish to take the step of establishing a full connection to the Internet. To establish e-mail only access to the Internet, you can subscribe on your own to a commercial electronic mail or on-line service.

The list of Canadian Internet service providers in Appendix B includes references to a number of commercial e-mail and on-line services that have established links to Internet e-mail. These systems include U.S. commercial e-mail services such as ATTMail and MCIMail, on-line services such as CompuServe and Genie, and the Canadian TheNet:Mail system (formerly known as Envoy 100/iNet 2000) and Mpact Immedia.

If you just want to have an Internet e-mail address and do not want or need access to other Internet services, you might consider joining a service such as CompuServe[2] or one of the commercial e-mail providers mentioned above, such as MCIMail. Many of these services come with, or make available, special communications software that makes it easy to send and receive e-mail messages.

When you use a software package such as CompuServe Information Manager, available for both Windows and Macintosh, sending and receiving Internet e-mail is made much easier. The following screen shows a message being created destined for someone on the Internet:

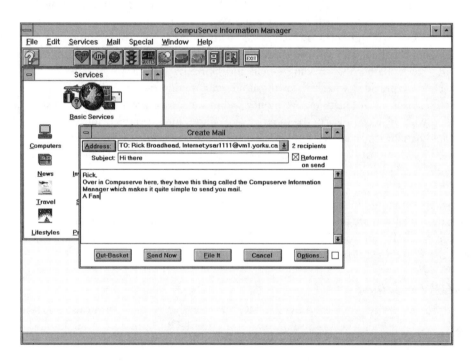

Using a service such as CompuServe or MCIMail provides you with your own unique Internet address that can be used to receive Internet messages and provides you with the capability of sending e-mail to anyone with an Internet e-mail address.

---

2. We include CompuServe in this section, because many CompuServe users find it to be a convenient method of sending and receiving messages through Internet e-mail, without actually having to be on the Internet. In 1995, however, as we discussed in Chapter 4, CompuServe became a major Internet service provider and now offers full SLIP/PPP access in addition to its basic services as described in this chapter. The same holds true for America OnLine.

There is one main concern with this approach, and that is cost. Some commercial e-mail services charge for messages sent to and received from the Internet on a per-kilocharacter basis, that is, for every 1,000 characters sent or received. With rates reaching as high as $0.25 per kilocharacter, you might find yourself spending a lot of money very quickly. At that rate, a simple one-page note might cost you $0.50; to do the same thing on a real Internet account would cost you less than a penny.

As a result, if you take this approach, it is suggested that you closely examine and fully understand the cost of the alternative. In particular, be very careful about joining any mailing lists, since the volume of e-mail you might receive as a result could easily end up costing you a lot of money.

E-Mail and USENET through UUCP

The second method of establishing your own personal link to the Internet is to use the "UUCP" protocol and to purchase or find software that uses this protocol. By using UUCP, you can participate in Internet e-mail and USENET newsgroups, but you cannot use any other Internet services such as the World Wide Web or FTP.

UUCP is an older protocol that has existed within the Internet community for many years. It is designed for those who wish to speed up the process of receiving and sending e-mail and USENET news. Rather than reading e-mail and USENET news while you are on-line to an Internet service provider, you first download all your waiting e-mail and USENET news and then read it off-line. This helps to save money and in some ways provides a more flexible means of dealing with these two areas of the Internet. (Of course, Internet rates being as low as they are, you would have to send and receive a lot of e-mail to really save any appreciable sum of money.)

Is UUCP for you? If you have a technical bent and want some flexibility in the way you deal with your e-mail and news, perhaps. You might consider exploring it to see how it might benefit you.

Strictly speaking, since you are not directly connected to the Internet and do not have an IP address when you are using UUCP, you are not "on" the Internet. Note that using UUCP does not preclude you from having a SLIP/PPP account on the Internet so that you can also access the Web on a dial-up basis.

UUCP Explained

Some Internet service providers provide UUCP service, that is, they permit users to send and receive Internet e-mail and USENET news using the UUCP protocol. You should keep in mind that not all ISPs offer UUCP; in fact, some are not even aware of what it is. UUCP is an older technology used less and less in the computing mainstream, even though there is a large and dedicated number of people around the world who use it on a regular basis (and who will probably continue to do so for some time).

UUCP stands for UNIX-to-UNIX copy protocol, which is a "store-and-forward" file transfer utility found within most UNIX systems. UUCP takes on responsibility for copying e-mail and USENET postings to and from your Internet service provider. Using UUCP, you are only intermittently connected to your Internet service provider. To use UUCP, you will need a UUCP program for your system and an e-mail program and newsreader software that work with your version of UUCP. This often comes with the UUCP program you are using. There are commercial and public domain versions of UUCP available for both DOS/Windows and Macintosh systems.

How Does UUCP Work?

UUCP is a batch-oriented system, that is,

◆ any messages you create are not sent to your Internet service provider immediately, but are sent the next time you make a UUCP call to your provider;

◆ any messages sent to you are only received by you when you make a UUCP call to the provider;

◆ USENET news is delivered to you, for the groups to which you belong, when you make a UUCP call to your provider.

UUCP Public Domain Software

There are many implementations of UUCP for popular operating systems available in the public domain, which means that you can use the program for free as shareware (you are requested to pay a fee to use the software). It is often necessary to mix and match the following components to get a full working system in place:

◆ A basic UUCP system to send and receive e-mail and news to and from your Internet service provider. The basic UUCP system sometimes includes rudimentary e-mail and news programs.

◆ More full-featured e-mail and/or newsreader software.

For example, UUPC for MSDOS (do not confuse UUPC with UUCP) comes with a simple program that permits you to send and receive Internet e-mail and has the capability of receiving USENET news. However, it does not have a newsreader, a program that permits you to read the USENET news you receive. In this case, you need newsreader software such as SNEWS in addition to your UUPC software. SNEWS and UUPC have been modified by their authors to work closely together.

You should only explore the use of public domain or shareware software if you have a technical bent and want the maximum degree of flexibility in your use of Internet e-mail and USENET news, because it can take a little bit of playing to get a full configuration working correctly. However, once you do get it working, you might find it to be a tremendously valuable way to use the Internet.

One of the authors of this book now uses a combination package for stand-alone purposes that consists of

◆ FXUUCP, a UUCP program for DOS computers that dials up his Internet service provider and sends/receives e-mail and USENET news;

◆ Pegasus Mail for Windows, a full-featured, local area network-based e-mail system (used on a stand-alone basis);

◆ Helldiver, a simple, effective Windows newsreader program.

Pegasus Mail for Windows provides a very straightforward means of sending and receiving Internet e-mail.

Another very popular DOS/Windows-based UUCP combination consists of Waffle, a program that handles the UUCP connection, combined with Helldiver, a Windows-based program that provides an excellent front end to e-mail and USENET news collected by Waffle.

In the Macintosh world, you can look for Mac/GNUUCP or UUPC 3.0 for the Macintosh to send and receive your UUCP batches, and for ToadNews, rnMac or TheNews-UUCP to read your USENET news.

In addition, some shareware packages have bundled both the UUCP and e-mail/USENET news components into one simple, straightforward package. An interesting piece of software is WinNet, a Windows program available for U.S. $99 that combines e-mail and news software into one friendly, easy-to-configure package. Originally programmed to work with a particular Internet provider in the United States, it will also work with any other UUCP provider as long as the shareware fee is paid.

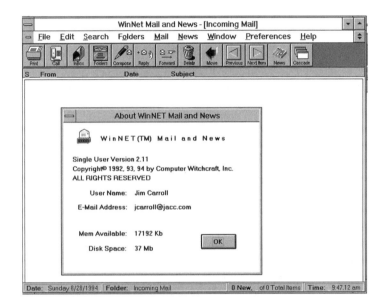

You can obtain a listing of various public domain UUCP alternatives from one of the main "Frequently Asked Questions" FTP archives on the Internet, as follows. Also check the USENET newsgroup **comp.mail.uucp**.

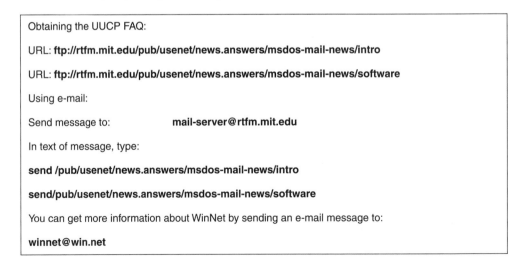

Obtaining the UUCP FAQ:

URL: **ftp://rtfm.mit.edu/pub/usenet/news.answers/msdos-mail-news/intro**

URL: **ftp://rtfm.mit.edu/pub/usenet/news.answers/msdos-mail-news/software**

Using e-mail:

Send message to: **mail-server@rtfm.mit.edu**

In text of message, type:

send /pub/usenet/news.answers/msdos-mail-news/intro

send/pub/usenet/news.answers/msdos-mail-news/software

You can get more information about WinNet by sending an e-mail message to:

winnet@win.net

There are also some commercial UUCP packages with sophisticated e-mail and USENET newsreader software available on the market. In the Macintosh world, look for UUCP/Connect, a full-featured UUCP package.

Questions to Ask Your Provider

You should shop around when looking for a dial-up account. Be sure you understand what you are buying and spend a little time determining what type of support, service, and help you might get. Be sure you know what type of interface you are buying with a shell account or a SLIP account. Also keep in mind that the Internet is growing quickly, and sometimes service providers and telephone lines get very busy. There is nothing more frustrating than trying to dial into your Internet account and continually encountering busy signals or trying to reach your service provider and being placed on hold.

If you are considering a certain Internet provider, do not hesitate to ask around for references—friends, counterparts, or others who might be willing to share their experiences with you. If you already have access to the Internet and are looking for another provider, consider posting your question to some of the USENET newsgroups that discuss Internet providers (in particular, **alt.internet.services** or a regional group, e.g., **ont.general** or **bc.general**). The questions you should be trying to answer include the following:

- How many phone lines does your provider provide? When choosing a provider, determine if they guarantee a maximum number of accounts per phone line. Determine what kind of guarantee it is: is it a service promise, or is it a contract item? Another way to check performance is to ask about "consecutive busy minutes," which provides a direct measure of what you might actually encounter. Do they offer a no-busy signal policy? Your best choice is a provider that has a large number of phone lines that are never busy.

- How do they link to the outside world of the Internet? What type of through-put do they support to the outside world: do the links get congested and slow? Do they have any acceptable use policies in place? Are there any restrictions on your use? Do they spell out your rights and responsibilities as a customer? Your best choice is a provider that has a high-speed link to the outside world.

- Is the service busy or unreliable? Ask around. Does the Internet service provider have a reputation for being a slow server, with lousy support, system crashes, being unreliable? How often are they down for maintenance? Your best choice is a provider that tends to have a good name in the community.

- How much help will you get from them? Do they have a good support team? Are their staff knowledgeable? Do they have an on-line group that you can read to determine if people are complaining about their service? Do they have manuals or other documents to make your access easier? Your best choice is a provider that acts, appears, and is professional at all times.

- What is the cost of the connection? Are there any hidden extras? Keep in mind that your best choice is not necessarily the least expensive, taking into account the other factors outlined in this section.

◆ Will they allow you to set up your own World Wide Web site? Is there a fee for doing this? Some ISPs let you have a World Wide Web site for free (i.e., a few pages only), while others charge for this capability. Your best choice depends on your expertise in working with HTML, the language used to develop Web sites.

◆ Does the ISP have a "roaming" service, that is, with dial-up phone numbers in several cities in Canada? This choice depends on whether you travel a lot.

Taking the time to understand some of these issues will help you select the best possible vendor.

Corporate or Organization Access

Beyond simple dial-up access for an individual, there is a link to the Internet for an entire corporation or organization. There are a number of business benefits that result from a direct Internet link, which are discussed in greater depth in Chapter 15. In a nutshell, it has become clear to many people that a direct link to the Internet is quickly becoming as necessary for a company or organization as telephones and fax machines.

As the business and organizational benefits of a link to the Internet become clearer, many organizations will want to move beyond a few simple dial-up accounts used by individuals and establish a more direct link to the network so that employees in effect always have a direct link to the Internet.

This section examines the methods of providing access to the Internet for many people within a company or an organization, most often from a local area network. These include

◆ Linking the corporate e-mail network to the Internet, so that employees can send and receive messages to and from the Internet. This may or may not include the ability to receive and read USENET news.

◆ A permanent TCP/IP network link to the Internet, either through a permanent dial-up SLIP/PPP link to an Internet service provider or through more direct network links involving leased lines or other methods. This provides the ability to use all Internet services, not just e-mail and USENET news.

E-Mail Only

A direct e-mail or network link to the Internet will support communications to trading partners, business associates, computer system vendors, suppliers, and customers. Many organizations would like to link their internal corporate e-mail system to the Internet without having to establish a full, dedicated Internet connection. In this case, there is no perceived need or benefit from the ability to use the World Wide Web or other Internet tools.[3]

---

3. Organizations that do not understand the Internet from a strategic perspective are encouraged to read our business strategy guide to the Internet, *The Canadian Internet Advantage: Opportunities for Business and Other Organizations*. The book provides a management perspective on the role and potential of the Internet from a non-technical perspective.

There are several types of e-mail *gateways*—special software packages that link together different e-mail systems—which can be put in place from a corporate e-mail system so that the organization has the ability to send and receive Internet messages. These include

◆ a gateway to a commercial e-mail service or some other type of on-line service that has e-mail connectivity to the Internet;

◆ a UUCP gateway directly from the e-mail system in use within the company to an Internet service provider;

◆ an SMTP-based gateway (described below), directly from the corporate e-mail system to an Internet service provider.

Through a Commercial or On-line Service

It is possible to link a local area network-based e-mail system or other e-mail system in your organization to a commercial e-mail system or on-line service, and from there communicate with people on the Internet. This is usually done by implementing an e-mail gateway, purchased or provided directly by the e-mail service or purchased from a third party. The method of establishing such a link ranges from the technically simple to the technically complex.

For example, it is possible to link a corporate local area network e-mail system, cc:Mail, to a commercial e-mail service, MCIMail, using a cc:Mail gateway provided by MCIMail. Since MCIMail has connectivity to and from Internet e-mail, individuals on the cc:Mail network are effectively linked to Internet e-mail. Many organizations already linked to a major commercial e-mail service such as GEQuickcomm, MCIMail, ATTMail, The:Net Mail, Immedia, or other systems might be pleased to discover that they already have access to and from Internet e-mail.

What Is Involved

There are several things you need to put in place:

◆ Gateway software. Mpact Immedia will, for example, provide you with gateways at no charge for many popular local area network-based e-mail systems, such as cc:Mail, MSMail, and MHS, to their service.

◆ An account or registration on the commercial e-mail provider into which the gateway links.

◆ A connection to the commercial e-mail provider, either via a dial-up modem or via some type of leased line or other connection.

Things to Watch for

If you link your corporate e-mail system to the Internet, there are several important things to keep in mind. These include ensuring that you have a good understanding of what you will pay for such a link and ensuring that you select a service with straightforward, simple addressing.

◆ Several of the commercial e-mail vendors charge for e-mail sent and received based on the number of kilocharacters. With rates as high as $0.25 for every thousand characters, you could quickly find yourself spending a fortune for your e-mail link to the Internet. Be sure you understand the definition of what constitutes a kilocharacter. Is it charged for just the message sent through the Internet or for every person on the Internet to whom that message is sent?

For example, at the rate of $0.25 per thousand characters, what would happen if you sent a message via the Internet that was 30,000 characters in size? If you sent the message to one person, the charge would be $7.50. If you sent it to 10 people on the Internet, the charge could be $7.50 or $75.00, depending on whether the service charges you for each Internet message recipient or not. The numbers add up quickly!

Also, determine if you are responsible for paying a fee for each inbound Internet message, and if so, how the fee is calculated. If you plan to use the account to receive mailing lists, for example, you could find yourself spending a fortune as the volume of inbound e-mail increases.

Some commercial e-mail services charge on the basis of time spent on-line as opposed to the number of characters sent. CompuServe is an excellent choice as a service to link your e-mail network to, since it charges on the basis of a flat hourly fee. The bottom line is: carefully examine the costs of the alternatives.

◆ Clearly understand what you will be faced with in terms of inbound and outbound Internet addressing. For example, if you have Microsoft Mail on your local area network, you will find that it comes with a gateway to the commercial e-mail service ATTMail, and that this is promoted as a method to reach the Internet. But people who receive messages from you will get a message from an ID that looks like **org!org!name@attmail.com**.

On the other hand, if you link your internal local area network e-mail system to CompuServe, your Internet address might be in the straightforward form **name@company.compuserve.com**, which is recognizable to the Internet community. The bottom line is: be clear on how you will send messages to and receive messages from the Internet, to ensure that it is straightforward both ways.

◆ If the link from the commercial e-mail service to the Internet involves X.400, stay away. Your Internet address will likely consist of a combination of X.400 and Internet addressing. Since few people on the Internet accept X.400 style addressing, you will likely find that this is not a workable solution. For example, if you have a gateway to the Sprintmail service, messages received from you by people on the Internet will appear as an ugly mixture of X.400 and Internet addressing. Imagine receiving a message on the Internet from an organization that has linked its e-mail network to Sprint, which has a link to the Internet:

/G=Michael/S=Nettleton/O=EDS/ADMD=TELEMAIL/PRMD=DIAMONDNET/ C=US/DD.ID=osipc1d.mnettl01/@SPRINT.COM

This ID is rather incomprehensible to mere mortals! In fact, the organization that this fellow works for has put in a nice, simple Internet gateway recently, so that he is now addressable as **michael_nettleton.mcs@mcs.eds.com**. He need no longer be ashamed of his X.400-based address.

With this type of alphabet soup address, you can see why it is important to carefully consider your options.

Through an Internet Service Provider

The second method of establishing a link to Internet e-mail from a corporate e-mail system is to establish an e-mail link directly to an Internet service provider. There are several methods to do this, including gateways based on the UUCP protocol or SMTP. If neither of these alternatives work for your current internal e-mail system, you might consider adopting one that does work with the Internet.

UUCP Method

As outlined earlier in this chapter, UUCP is a protocol that permits the batching of e-mail to and from an Internet service provider. Some local area network-based e-mail systems provide a UUCP gateway that allows a quick, effective link to Internet e-mail. Such gateways are available from the LAN e-mail vendor or third parties, and include

♦ UUCPLINK, a product sold by Lotus for use with the popular Lotus cc:Mail e-mail system. Information concerning this product can be obtained through Lotus Canada; the product itself is available through many software resellers for as little as $500.

♦ TFS Gateways, a product written by TenFour Sweden AB. The product provides simple, UUCP-based gateways to Lotus cc:Mail, Lotus Notes, Microsoft Mail, and Word Perfect Office 4.0a. TenFour Sweden AB can be reached by sending a message to **info@tenfour.se**.

When examining a UUCP solution like these, keep in mind that the product might provide you with e-mail only; that is, UUCPLINK does not provide for your organization to receive USENET news.

SMTP Method

You can put in place a gateway from your e-mail system to an Internet service provider by using an SMTP gateway. SMTP stands for simple mail transport protocol and is the e-mail system at the heart of many UNIX operating systems. It is also the e-mail system that is at the heart of the transfer of e-mail throughout the Internet.

There are a variety of gateways to SMTP-based e-mail from many other e-mail systems. For example, you can purchase a cc:Mail to SMTP gateway or an MSMail to SMTP gateway, either directly from Lotus and Microsoft or from various third parties. There are ways of linking minicomputer and mainframe-based e-mail systems to Internet e-mail through SMTP gateways as well. Although these gateways are readily available, you should be aware of a number of complexities in implementing them:

♦ To implement such a gateway, you must have a working SMTP-based e-mail system. Unless you already have a direct network connection to the Internet and a fully functioning UNIX server running SMTP, you will be out of luck. An alternative, if you have neither, is to convince an Internet service provider to act as your SMTP server and to accept a modem-based SLIP/PPP call to link to that SMTP server.

♦ It seems that few technical people on the Internet have anything pleasant to say about some of the available SMTP gateways. For example, although Microsoft has an SMTP gateway for MSMail, people in the USENET newsgroup **comp.misc.mail** can rarely say anything nice about it. It would seem that some of these gateways are not yet reliable, stable systems, and you could expect some frustration in implementation and ongoing maintenance.

Organizations desiring to link systems such as MSMail or cc:Mail to SMTP must appreciate the complexity of the undertaking. SMTP is recognized throughout the Internet world as one of the most demanding software programs ever developed. Accordingly, should you wish to establish this type of e-mail connectivity, be sure that you obtain adequate technical advice or resources, either internally or from external organizations.

Implementing Other E-Mail Software

The final option is to implement some other type of LAN e-mail software that has a direct or indirect link to Internet e-mail. If you do not have a LAN-based e-mail system but would like to put one in place that has a link to the Internet, you could consider Pegasus Mail or other alternatives.

Pegasus, which works primarily on Novell networks, has a number of available UUCP gateways and an SMTP gateway called Mercury that runs directly on a Novell File Server. It enjoys substantial use throughout the global college and university community. You can find out more about Pegasus by locating it in the FTP archive detailed below, or you can retrieve a FAQ (frequently asked question summary), which details other locations where you can find it.

To obtain Pegasus:

URL: **ftp://risc.ua.edu/pub/network/pegasus/pmail*.zip** (DOS version)

URL: **ftp://risc.ua.edu/pub/network/pegasus/winpm*.zip** (Windows version), where * is current version number. Check the file name; new versions are regularly released. Pegasus Mail can also be found on other file servers around the world.

Using e-mail:

Send message to: **maiser@pmail.gen.nz**

In text of message, type: **send version.faq**

A good technical resource with respect to e-mail gateways can be found at **http://andrew2. andrew.cmu.edu/cyrus/email/**. You might also check the e-mail category within the Yahoo index, at **http://www.yahoo.com/Business_and_Economy/Companies/Computers/Software/ Electronic_Mail/**.

A Full Network Connection

The final or ultimate state of Internet connectivity is a direct link from the network in use at your organization to the Internet. In this case, your network is linked directly to the Internet through some type of low- or high-speed part-time or dedicated link. Everyone on your network is attached to the Internet all the time; it is not necessary for employees to dial out to the Internet with a modem since they are always part of the Internet. Your computers are considered to be "hard-wired" to the Internet.

Why might you want to do this? First and foremost, as an organization you have determined that there are good business strategies that can be met by establishing a full-time link to the Internet. You have decided that you no longer want the inefficiencies or slow speeds involving modems. Or you have determined that you need high-speed access to the Internet, faster than you can get through a modem, in order to participate in some of the more innovative emerging technologies. Or you want to establish your own World Wide Web site on your own computer networks, rather than "renting" space on someone else's site (as we will discuss in Chapter 15).

There are many organizations in Canada with a full-time link to the Internet. Most of Canada's colleges, universities, and research organizations have had such a link in place for several years.

In corporate Canada, there are some organizations with a full-time link in place, but not an extensive number. For example, the corporate office of George Weston Limited, one of Canada's largest conglomerates, has what is known as a 56 Kb link to the Internet, in effect making the PCs and local area network in the office directly part of the Internet. Staff can access the Internet simply by clicking a button; they are permanently part of the network.

However, this type of connectivity is more the exception than the rule in corporate Canada. Potential concern about security (often misguided, as we will see below), the resources involved, or the lack of understanding of the Internet from a strategic perspective has meant that this is an area still to see a lot of growth in the years to come.

In the estimation of the authors, however, it is inevitable that most organizations in Canada will one day find themselves with a permanent connection to the Internet—the tools of electronic commerce that are emerging on the Internet will see to that. As more and more companies begin to learn what is involved in "networked business"—in effect, as our economy becomes more and more wired into the Internet—it is inevitable that a direct connection to the Internet will one day be as common and necessary as fax machines and telephones.

What Is Involved?

Establishing a hard-wired connection to the Internet is not necessarily a trivial undertaking. At the risk of greatly simplifying a complex matter, connectivity in the DOS/Windows environment would involve several components:

◆ Each PC on the network must load software that provides the PC with the ability to "talk TCP/IP" (referred to as the TCP/IP protocol stack), the main protocol of the Internet.

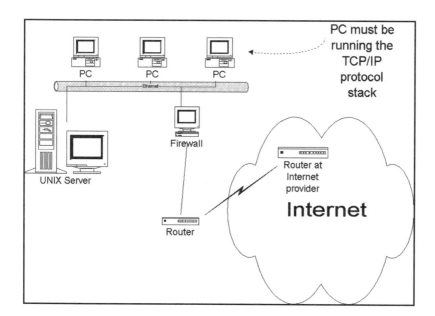

There are many TCP/IP software packages available for most computer platforms. For DOS/Windows, for example, you can purchase many different packages: Beame & Whiteside's BW-NFS, Frontier Technologies' Super TCP/NFS for Windows, FTP Software's PC/TCP, IBM's TCP/IP for DOS/Windows, NetManage Chameleon NFS for Windows, and Walker, Richer & Quinn's Reflection/TCP Connection. There are a number of alternatives for Macintosh systems, including MacTCP from Apple and TCP/Connect II, as well as some public domain and shareware programs.

In addition to these, you can use some of the public domain versions, including some of the TCP/IP PPP programs described earlier in this chapter. But it may not be necessary to use any of these programs.

One of the key benefits of Windows 95 is that it provides the TCP/IP protocol stack directly within the operating system. Load Windows 95 and your computers can "talk TCP/IP." We take a look at this system in greater depth in Chapter 14. Other operating systems, such as IBM's OS/2 Warp, also provide the necessary TCP/IP software as a fundamental part of the computer operating system. Hence it is becoming less necessary to purchase a separate TCP/IP software program for each PC.

◆ Your network must be linked into an Internet service provider, usually through a device known as a router or network bridge.

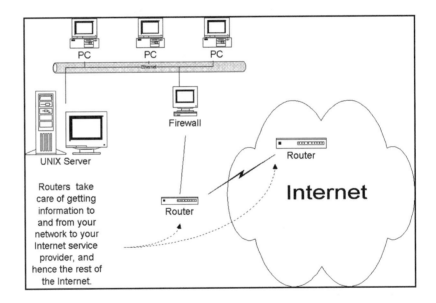

The router at your location links to the router at your Internet service provider and does what it suggests: it routes traffic from your network to your Internet provider and then to the global Internet and vice versa. It routes this traffic according to the TCP/IP protocol and Domain Name System, using your IP address and domain name as your fundamental link to the outside world. There are many router products available in the marketplace; in fact, an entire industry is involved in router hardware and software.

◆ Dedicated communication lines must be brought into the organization to support the network connection to your Internet service provider.

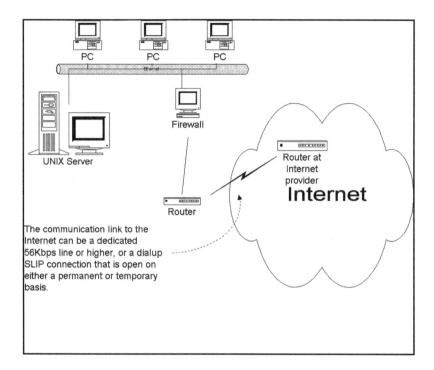

You arrange to purchase these lines from an ISP, who, quite often, will arrange for the actual line itself to come from your local telephone company or other type of telecommunication organization. The ISP provides the necessary infrastructure so that the line can "talk TCP/IP." Most often, this will involve a 56 Kb leased line or higher-speed connections up to what is known as a T1 (1.1544 Mbps).

How fast is such a line? Since these connections usually operate at speeds of 56 Kb to 1,544 Kb, they are significantly faster than your 14.4 or 28.8 Kb modem. In addition, there are many other possible and emerging technologies. Later in this chapter we will talk about one such technology, ISDN.

In the "Directory of Canadian Internet Service Providers," we provide details on the type of high-speed connectivity offered by ISPs. Keep in mind that many ISPs are equipped to deal only with the dial-up marketplace and may not be able to help you, should you want to establish a direct permanent connection.

As an alternative to connectivity via a permanent line, you can also put in place a dedicated link through a dial-up SLIP or PPP modem connection and permit people on your network to access the Internet that way, but this slow speed will certainly impact on how they can use the Internet.

◆ A server or servers, usually UNIX-based, must be located at your site to support the Internet applications you plan to implement within your organization.[4]

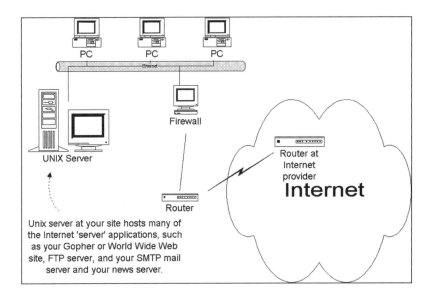

This might include an SMTP server to support e-mail to the Internet (as discussed earlier), an NNTP server to support the receipt and posting of USENET news directly through your Internet link, and a Gopher, Archie, FTP, or a World Wide Web server to support Internet applications.

◆ If you link your network directly to the Internet, you must consider security, because once you connect your network to the Internet, anything on your network is accessible to anyone on the Internet if you do not properly prevent access to it. To properly understand the risk that you might face, you should engage the services of someone who is thoroughly familiar with Internet security issues. If you put in place a direct connection to the Internet and ignore security, you will probably discover yourself an open target of the mischievous and malicious from around the world.

---

4. The days of needing a UNIX server are slowly coming to an end. There is an increasing number of servers (Gopher, WWW, FTP, etc.) that run under Windows, OS/2, and Windows NT, as well as modules that load onto Novell file servers. As the Internet gains prominence as a serious wide area network alternative, major software companies such as Novell and Microsoft are including Internet support in their software.

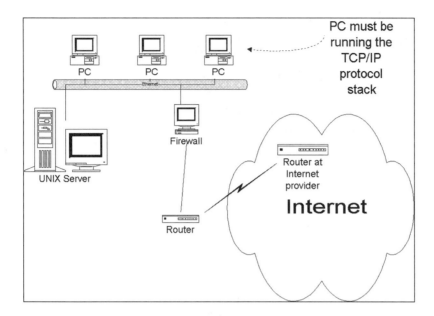

To handle security, you should consider implementing a "firewall," a system that protects your network from access by people on the Internet. A firewall is either hardware, software, or both. You should also keep in mind that while firewalls are certainly valuable, they are still quite expensive, require very specialized knowledge to implement, and often end up inhibiting your use of the Internet. Alternatives to firewalls are available. Internet security is just like office security, in that you need to properly assess the risk and the cost to protect against the risk.

◆ Client software to access the applications above, and to access other Internet services, must be implemented on your PCs.

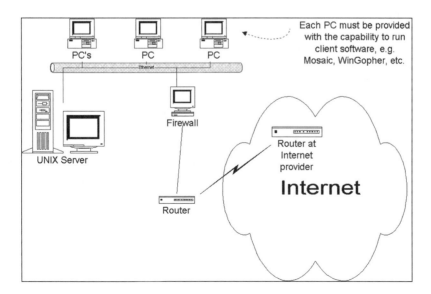

This includes client software to access the World Wide Web servers on the Internet (such as Netscape), and client software for your e-mail system (e.g., MSMail if you are linked through an SMTP gateway or Eudora if you are using SMTP directly).

In addition to the technical components, there are many other non-technical issues related to establishing a full-time Internet link. For example, you cannot ignore training, support and implementation, productivity issues, administration efforts, ongoing security monitoring, and a host of other issues. Bundle it all together, and you can see that you have a project on your hands. The scope of establishing TCP/IP connectivity directly to the Internet is far beyond the capabilities of this book. Many excellent sources and reference guides exist, both in print and on the Internet.

A number of Internet service providers take an active role in assisting an organization to establish a direct, hard-wired or permanent connection to the Internet. In addition, across Canada there are a number of excellent consultants who have implemented dedicated connectivity for many organizations. Ask around, and you can probably quickly discover who they are.

Evolving Technology

One thing about communication technology holds true: it is becoming more sophisticated at a lower cost. This trend has a direct impact on organizations seeking dedicated connectivity to the Internet. Most organizations that start out with a direct link into the Internet do so with a 56 Kb line, a connection that is about two to four times faster than the average high-speed modem. As their needs increase, they might move up to a 128 Kb connection or multiples thereof, and eventually up to a T1 line, which provides 1,544 Kbs.

These lines usually come from the local telephone company in combination with the ISP (which these days could very well be the same telephone company). In effect, you purchase a high-speed link and dedicate it to link to the Internet.

There are many new (and old) communication technologies that are being adopted throughout the Internet community today, however, that are providing higher-speed connections to the Internet or speeds similar to today's technology but with less complexity. An example of the latter is ISDN, which stands for Integrated Services Digital Network. A technology that has been around for some 10 to 15 years with few users, ISDN has found a home in the Internet community as a technology that can provide moderate-speed, full-time Internet access without a lot of technical complexity.

In major centres in Canada, such as Toronto and Vancouver, it is possible to purchase an ISDN connection from an ISP to link your network into the Internet on a full-time basis. Often, the cost of establishing this type of link is less than other traditional alternatives (such as a 56 Kb line), but provides about the same amount of bandwidth (64 or 128 Kbs). The beauty of it is that the technical implementation can be less challenging.

Most ISPs that offer ISDN make information about their service available online. UUNET Canada, one of Canada's largest ISPs, provides information about its ISDN services on its Web site (**http://www.uunet.ca**). As you browse the directory of ISPs, you will notice those who offer ISDN. You can usually check their Web site for pricing and other details.

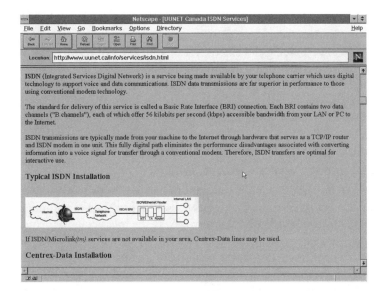

As you get involved with the Internet, you will also hear phrases like ATM (asynchronous transfer mode) and frame relay. ATM is the next generation of high-speed communication links that will affect not only the Internet but any possible television-based information highway in the future. It is an amazingly fast technology compared to most other communication technologies around the world today.

Several organizations are already working with ATM, using it as a method of providing high-speed connectivity. BCTel provides details of its ATM services on its World Wide Web site (**http://www.bctel.net**). In this case, ATM provides links of 10 Mbs (10,000 Kbs) compared to a T1 (1.544 Mbs or 1,544 Kbps).

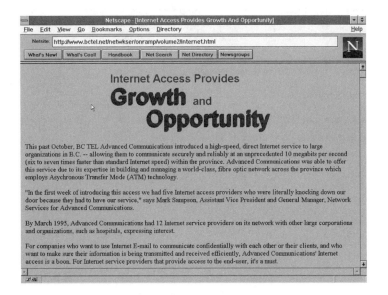

And as we mentioned earlier in this book, high-speed connections through cable will one day be a reality across Canada.

Consequently, we are seeing the emergence of a plethora of methods by which you can establish a high-speed direct network link to the Internet.

For a technical overview of ATM and related technologies, read the "High Speed Networking" page at **http://www.cs.purdue.edu/homes/saydjari/high-speed.html**. To understand the implications of ATM from a non-technical perspective, read articles from the popular communications guru, George Gilder, at **http://homepage.seas.upenn.edu/~gaj1/ggindex.html**.

Information about Direct Connections

Where else can you find information if you want to pursue direct connectivity to the Internet? Our first suggestion is to go out and hire someone to help you. Talk to an Internet service provider to find such a person, or talk to people involved in the Internet in your community. There are a lot of people throughout the Internet community involved in establishing such connectivity, and it is such a specialized area that it might make sense for you to take advantage of the knowledge of an expert rather than trying to master such knowledge yourself.

If you must know what it is all about, you can certainly find a lot of reference information on the Internet. If you are in the DOS environment, a good source for information is the "The PC-Mac TCP/IP & NFS FAQ List" at **http://www.rtd.com/pcnfsfaq/faq.html**. Another good site is the Web site for Trusted Information Systems, a company involved in Internet networking and security issues, at **http://www.tis.com/**. Another good site can be found at **http://web.syr.edu/~jmwobus/lans/**.

You can also try the PC TCP/IP FAQ, which provides a good overview of TCP/IP networking issues.

To obtain the PC TCP/IP FAQ:

URL: **ftp://rtfm.mit.edu/pub/usenet/news.answers/ibmpc-tcp-ip-faq/part1**
(and part2, part3)

Using e-mail:

Send message to: **mail-server@rtfm.mit.edu**

In text of message, type:

send /pub/usenet/news.answers/ibmpc-tcp-ip-faq/part1
send /pub/usenet/news.answers/ibmpc-tcp-ip-faq/part2
send /pub/usenet/news.answers/ibmpc-tcp-ip-faq/part3

Although no comparable document exists for Macintosh networks, a document about communications in the Mac environment does address TCP/IP connectivity issues.

Obtaining the Macintosh communications document:

Using anonymous FTP:

ftp://rtfm.mit.edu/pub/usenet/comp.sys.mac.comm

Retrieve the documents:

comp.sys.mac.comm_Frequently_Asked_Questions_[1_4]
comp.sys.mac.comm_Frequently_Asked_Questions_[2_4]
comp.sys.mac.comm_Frequently_Asked_Questions_[3_4]
comp.sys.mac.comm_Frequently_Asked_Questions_[4_4]

Using e-mail:

Send message to: **mail-server@rtfm.mit.edu**

In text of message, type:

send /pub/usenet/news.answers/macintosh/comm-faq/part1
send /pub/usenet/news.answers/macintosh/comm-faq/part2
send /pub/usenet/news.answers/macintosh/comm-faq/part3
send /pub/usenet/news.answers/macintosh/comm-faq/part4

Questions to Ask Your Internet Service Provider

Finally, when looking at a dedicated link to the Internet for your organization, there are some things you should keep in mind when talking to various service providers:

- What is the true "through-put" (i.e., a measure of how much information is really sent through the link that you have purchased), and will you encounter congestion as you try to link to various sites on the Internet through your service provider because of limitations at your service provider?[5] If you put a dedicated 56 Kbps line in place to your network, are you getting 56 Kbps through-put or 56 Kbps access? There can be a difference; make sure you know what you are buying.

- How much support do they provide? How is troubleshooting handled should there be a problem with your network link to the Internet? Do they provide 24-hours-a-day, 7-days-a-week support?

- What is involved in upgrading your network link to faster speeds in the future, and how much will it cost? Are there less expensive upgrade paths available?

- Do they help with security issues, implementation, and other matters?

---

5. Keep in mind that certain locations on the Internet will always experience some congestion, regardless of what type of through-put you have.

◆ Will they assist you in the establishment of a World Wide Web site, or will they host your site on your behalf?

◆ Will they undertake domain name registration on your behalf?

◆ Do they have a good track record? Will they provide references of other companies that have purchased dedicated connectivity through them?

Keep in mind that establishing a direct link to the Internet is a project, not a purchase, and hence involves more time, more effort, and definitely more research in advance. Take time to understand your options, particularly when it comes to selecting an Internet service provider.

How Do I Become an ISP?

Finally, many people wonder if they too can get into the Internet service provider business. And certainly many have: our Canadian ISP list this year includes well over 300 entries.

Becoming an ISP is not necessarily a difficult thing to do. In many ways, the technical efforts are similar to those above for establishing a direct Internet connection. You then link into your local area network a number of modems that people can dial into to access the Internet. But it is obviously far more complicated than that. You have to deal with support and customer queries, marketing and billing issues, administration issues, lawyers, accountants, government, tax authorities and rules and regulations—and all the other complexities involved in running a small business.

And even before you begin to deal with those issues, you should ask yourself whether the effort is worth it. The Internet has become a hot and competitive market. In some major cities in Canada, there are over 50 local ISPs. Add in Microsoft, IBM, the phone companies, cable companies and who knows who else, and you have a business that is very competitive and one where low prices are often becoming the rule of the day. Your chance of success might be doomed even before you start.

Obviously, this book cannot hope to go into the issues of what is involved in establishing yourself as an ISP. Be aware it is a complex undertaking and that you first need to learn quite a bit about the Internet, and quite a bit about the Internet business.

The best on-line document that describes some of the many issues related to becoming an ISP is "The Inet-Access Frequently Asked Questions List" (**http://www.amazing.com/internet/ faq.html**). To browse through all kinds of existing ISPs around the world to understand their strategies and efforts, take a look at **http://www.yahoo.com/Business_and_Economy/Companies/ Internet_Access_Providers/**.

Finally, many people within the Internet community (including the authors of this book) and several of the larger ISPs, will assist you in your quest on a consulting, for-fee basis.

Summary

Each method discussed in this chapter differs in complexity, cost, functionality, and ease of use. What is appropriate for you depends on your own circumstances. If you just want the ability to send and receive Internet e-mail messages, examine the alternatives for establishing e-mail only access, either as an individual or by linking the e-mail system of your organization to the network. If you are interested in exploring the Internet, our recommendation is a dial-up SLIP/PPP account. You should only go with a shell account if SLIP/PPP is not available or not possible on your computer, due to the limitations that such an account introduces.

Finally, if you discover that the Internet is right for you, establishing a permanent or hard-wired connection for your organization could be the next step. Related to this will be the need to convince management of your organization of the need for a dedicated Internet connection. In the next chapter we talk about some of the strategic applications of the Internet.

Keep in mind as you explore your options that Canada continues to see substantial growth in the number of Internet service providers, as detailed in Appendix B, and even more comprehensively in *The Canadian Internet Directory*.

Internet Software

Only someone immured in a cave for the last year could be unaware of the explosion of interest in and activity on the Internet.

Browser wars fallout to benefit all Web users
Computer Technology Review,
May 8, 1995

As the above quote suggests, only someone living in a cave for the last year could have missed the explosion of new Internet software packages emerging in the marketplace. Visit a computer store, and you are likely to see "shrink-wrapped" versions of Internet in a Box from SPRY, Netscape Navigator Personal Edition, Quarterdeck's Internet Suite, OpenText Internet Anywhere, and Emissary from Wollongong, and many other software packages. Look at the advertisements of some new ISPs, and you will see some of these packages included in their service. Read the computer trade press, and you will see product reviews focusing on these and many other similar programs.

Certainly the Internet has gained the attention of the computer industry, with the consequent release of an ever-increasing number of "packages" like those listed above. Most of these packages include everything you need to dial into the Internet and software to help you use most of the popular Internet services, such as e-mail, USENET news, and the World Wide Web. They essentially contain everything you need to take full advantage of the Internet.

In this chapter, we will limit ourselves to taking a look at just a few of these Internet software packages; we hope to give you an idea of the flexibility available to you as you begin to access and use the Internet. Because of the nature of the Internet, we cannot provide a comprehensive overview of *all* the programs that are available. And for purposes of describing to you what is possible with this software, we are concentrating on packages available for the Windows environment. Many of these packages are also available for Macintosh computers: Netscape Navigator Personal Edition, for example.

Whatever the case may be, we hope that this brief look will help you gain an appreciation of some of the software options available to you, so that if you are shopping for an Internet program, you will have an idea of what to look for.

From Shareware to RealWare

For a long time, many ISPs in Canada provided their customers with disks containing some of the public domain and shareware programs that we have described in this book. In other cases, you had to go out and find the Internet programs that you wanted to use from the Internet itself. You could end up spending a lot of time "shopping" on the Internet for the software you need. And you were usually using a separate program for each Internet application, that is,

♦ Telnet required a Telnet client;

♦ Web required a Web client;

♦ USENET required a news client.

Most of this software was not commercially developed so quality was not always that great and support was not always easily available.

But there are exceptions: some of the shareware and public domain software out there is absolutely excellent. In the Windows environment, for example, the most popular program for dialing into the Internet has been Trumpet Winsock. It is associated with Trumpet FTP, Telnet, and Gopher programs that have been used by people to navigate throughout the network. Indeed, the full range of Trumpet programs has a large and loyal following; it is a perfectly fine set of programs and for many years has satisfied the needs of millions of people around the world.

However, the Internet industry is turning serious, and with that change comes a move away from use of public domain and shareware programs to real commercial "shrink-wrapped" software programs and packages. Many of these programs fill a real need, for they make it easier for new users to join the Internet and include tools that are in many ways friendlier and easier to use than the shareware programs previously available.

The programs are designed to make it easy for people to get onto the Internet by including programs that permit instant

INTERNET SOFTWARE

1 The Internet is now seeing the release of a lot of commercial shrink-wrapped software.

2 Such software often includes instant sign-up to providers, a dialer program necessary to sign onto a SLIP or PPP account, and software for purposes of accessing e-mail, USENET. and the World Wide Web.

3 The software reviewed in this chapter is Netscape Personal Navigator, Quarterdeck Internet Suite, CompuServe Internet in a Box, OpenText Internet Anywhere, and Wollongong's Emissary. All are impressive packages and deserve a look.

4 An important issue to examine should be the extent to which these software companies have worked with Canadian ISPs in order to customize the sign-up process and to minimize the effort that you must put in to getting the software to work with your existing provider.

sign-up to various Internet service providers.[1] And the programs are highly customizable: should you already have an Internet account, you can quickly set up the software to use it rather than having to get another account somewhere. (Even if you do not think you have the technical knowledge to do this, you might find it to be a pleasantly simple experience.)

In some cases, you do not even have to buy the program, or it may be available to you at a discounted price. Given the proliferation of Internet service providers across Canada and the fierce competition within the ISP marketplace, many of the larger ISPs have decided to include a customized version of some of these software packages as part of their basic service.

There are some real benefits to commercial Internet software:

◆ Comprehensive technical support. Many of the organizations in the marketplace, such as Quarterdeck, have been in the business of providing their customers with excellent support for many years. Their move into the Internet marketplace can only result in a major improvement in service and support.

◆ Value-added features. For example, many of the programs permit you to easily customize the software to work with your existing ISP account.

◆ Accessibility in computer stores with other similar software. This means that you will find it easier not only to obtain the software, but easier to get product reviews and advice.

◆ Better quality. Although there is excellent shareware and public domain software, some of the products available on the Internet are just plain terrible. Overall, the quality of the commercial product is better.

And finally, just because you buy a commercial package does not mean you cannot use a shareware product that is available on the Internet (e.g. you can still use Pegasus Mail even if you are using Quarterdeck's Internet Suite).

Major Software Programs

In this chapter we take a look at five basic "packages" used to access and travel around the Internet. All have been selected because they provide the basic components to join the Internet: a program that offers instant sign-up to providers, a dialer program necessary to sign on to a SLIP or PPP account, and software for purposes of accessing e-mail, USENET, and the World Wide Web:

◆ Netscape Navigator Personal Edition;

◆ SPRY's Internet in a Box;

◆ Quarterdeck's Internet Suite;

---

1. Most of these developers are not ignoring the uniqueness of the Canadian Internet scene as they bring their product to the marketplace. Many of them permit you to instantly sign up as a new user to particular Canadian ISPs or provide you with pointers to Canadian Internet resources.

- ◆ OpenText Internet Anywhere;

- ◆ Wollongong's Emissary.

There are many other similar packages: NCD Mariner, Chameleon, TCP/Connect II. Undoubtedly, many new ones will emerge on the marketplace throughout 1996. To keep up-to-date, you might consider tracking such software in an Internet or PC/Macintosh computer magazine.[2]

At the end of this chapter we offer a few suggestions and comments on what to watch for as you consider which package might be right for you. However, our purpose here is not to present a detailed product review, nor do we offer criticism of each individual package. That, we believe, is best left to the many computer magazines available.

Finally, we provide contact information for each company. Note that some of these companies make available a demo version from their Web site.

Netscape Navigator Personal Edition

It is no secret that Netscape commands a majority of the market for World Wide Web browser software. This package is their entrant into the market of providing a complete kit for access to the Internet. Given Netscape's dominant position in the market, this package is bundled in with the Internet services offered by many major ISPs, including those of Canadian telephone companies. It is also sold throughout computer and retail stores across Canada. The package combines all the Internet applications into one program and includes a program to dial into a PPP account:

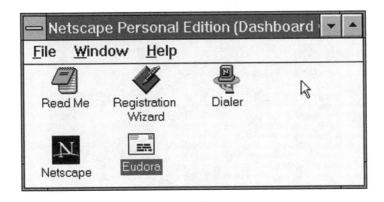

The product comes with the Netscape Registration Wizard, a program that helps you set up the software for your computer and through which you can instantly obtain an Internet account. Netscape is working with various large-scale Canadian ISPs to provide instant account sign-up:

---

2. If you are a software developer with such an all-inclusive program, please contact the authors at **hand book@uunet.ca** so that you can be included in future updates and editions of this book.

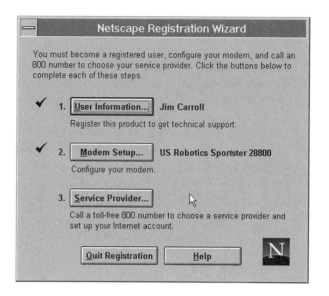

Once you install the software, you must register your software. You provide the necessary information within the Registration Wizard, and once the software figures out the type of modem you are using, the registration takes place automatically via an 800 number.

Once the registration is complete, you are left within the Netscape registration system. At this point you can create an Internet account automatically with one of several Internet service providers, or you can obtain information on how to customize the Netscape program for use with your existing ISP:

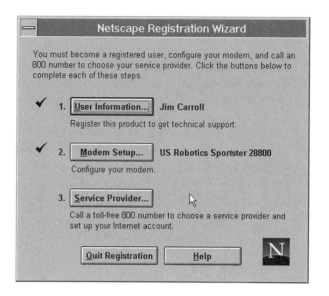

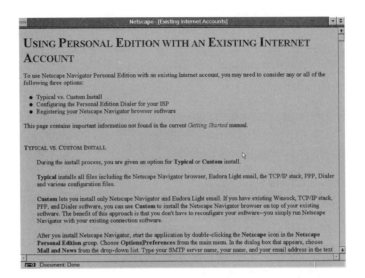

If you choose to subscribe immediately to an ISP, you are taken to a screen that provides details about that ISP, including the cost to sign up:

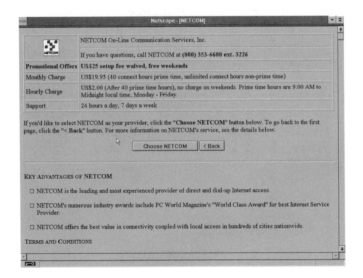

Your account is created immediately. Since Netscape is using its secure Commerce Server for the registration, you do not need to worry about your credit card. Once you have an account with an ISP and are set up and ready to go, you use the Netscape dialer program to link into your ISP. It is a simple, straightforward, uncomplicated program that establishes your PPP connection to the Internet:

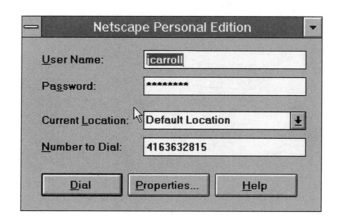

Netscape 2.0 includes all the tools you need in one package: a Web browser and USENET newsreader as well as an e-mail client. The Web browser can be used to access FTP, Telnet, and Gopher sites.

The e-mail program is a model of simplicity:

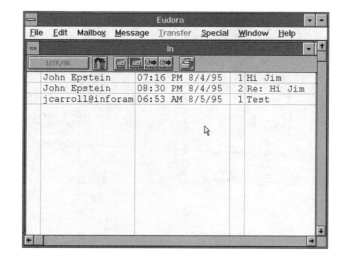

Creating a message within Netscape is easy to do; simply key in the address of the recipient, a subject, and the text of the message. You can attach files, modify your signature, and a number of other things that you would expect to find in an e-mail program:

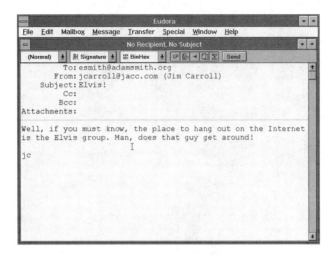

Netscape Navigator is, of course, the *raison d'être* of Netscape. It integrates USENET news and FTP into the same package as is used for access to the Web and hence gives you everything you need for these three services (as well as the ability to access Gopher and other Internet resources).

Accessing an FTP site is as easy as keying in the FTP URL. In this case, we are logged into the FTP site at Netscape:

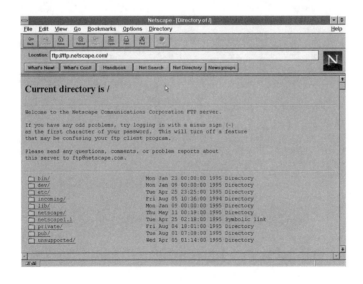

To retrieve a particular file, you simply click on it.

Similarly, USENET newsgroups are accessed from within Netscape. Most features (with the exception of "killfiles") are supported through the software:

You can post to a newsgroup at any time: a dialog box is placed on the screen in which you key your new message or your follow-up message:

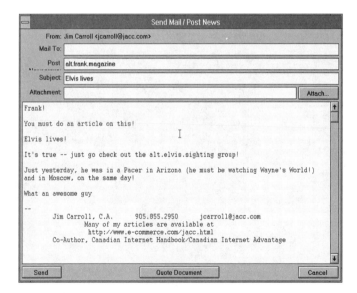

Finally, Netscape excels in providing access to the World Wide Web, and as discussed earlier in this chapter, is certainly in the forefront of many leading-edge developments with respect to business and commerce on the Internet. Given that Netscape is very aggressive in its development and support for HTML, you will often see features of the Web that you do not see in other Web browsers.

One of the keys to Netscape's success is the link between the software program and information at the Netscape site in California. For example, clicking on the "Handbook" button takes you directly to a help screen at Netscape:

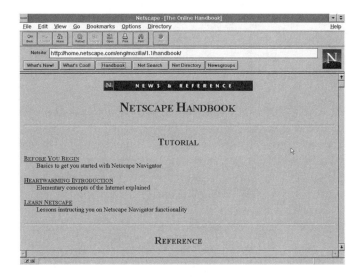

Clicking on "Net Search" takes you to a site of Internet search engines:

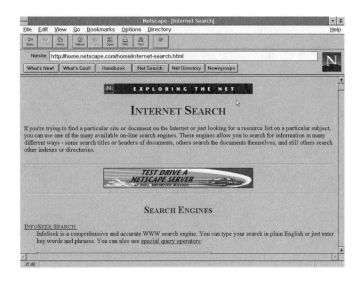

By having the program buttons automatically take you to the Netscape Web server, they can continually update the pages that these buttons are linked to and thus provide you with the most up-to-date sites, information, help, and assistance related to the Internet and the World

Wide Web. Netscape has been discussed extensively elsewhere in this book; hence we do not go into further detail here.

Contacting Netscape:	
Web:	**http://www.netscape.com**
Phone:	(415) 528-2555
E-mail:	**info@netscape.com**

SPRY's Internet in a Box

SPRY's Internet in a Box ranks as perhaps one of the most anticipated products in the Internet industry. Announced in early 1994, the product was the first to capitalize on the need for a real, "shrink-wrapped" Internet software product. It finally shipped in early 1995, a year behind schedule. It was worth the wait: Internet in a Box is an impressive product. Impressive enough that the large, global online information service CompuServe bought its developer, SPRY Inc., for a price of U.S. $100 million as one of the key foundations in CompuServe's effort to become a significant Internet service provider.

Internet in a Box is certainly a full-featured program. It includes a simple dial-up program (which can be used with CompuServe or configured for use with another Internet service provider) and includes a number of separate programs to use Internet mail, USENET news, FTP, Telnet, Gopher, and the World Wide Web (using Mosaic):

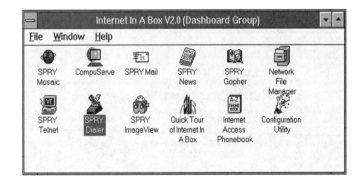

Installing the program and configuring it for your PC and modem is a very straightforward process. You can change your setup at any time through the configuration screen below:

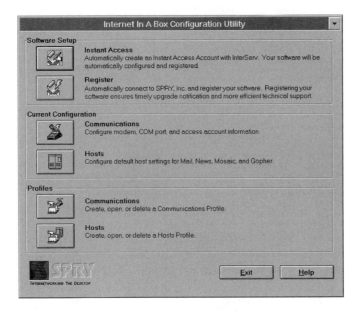

When you install the program, the configuration utility is run for the fist time, and you are given the option of immediately signing up for a CompuServe Internet account (which they call InterServ). If you choose to do so, you must provide your credit card information:

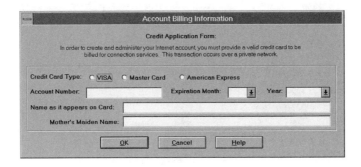

The program then dials in to CompuServe and gives you a number of choices regarding the type of Internet "plan" you want to sign up for:

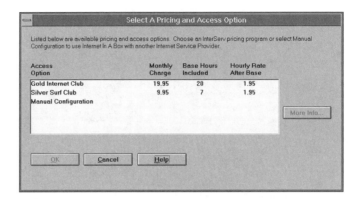

As part of the sign-up process for Internet access through CompuServe, the program will advise you of the local CompuServe dial-in number (available in most major Canadian cities) or an 800 number if you live outside a major metropolitan area. All in all, Internet in a Box makes it easy for you to establish your Internet account with CompuServe.

But you might not necessarily want to join the Internet through CompuServe. You might want to obtain a new account or use an existing account on another ISP. In that case, you can choose to instruct Internet in a Box to access the Internet via that other ISP; you will need to provide the phone number, domain name server addresses, and some other information, as seen in the following screen:

You will also be required to set up the "scripting information" in order to instruct Internet in a Box how to navigate through the log-in sequence for your ISP. You should not be intimidated by this type of screen; you might find that a quick phone call to your ISP will quickly result in the exact configuration information that you need:

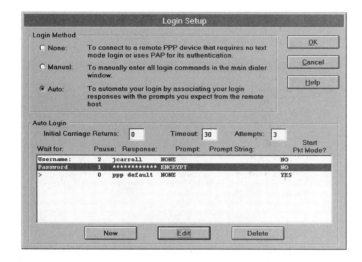

Once you have your CompuServe account set-up or have configured Internet in a Box to dial your own ISP, connecting to the Internet is easy enough: simply load the SPRY dialer and click on the "dial" icon. Within seconds, you should have a link to the Internet. You can now begin accessing various Internet services using the software that SPRY has provided:

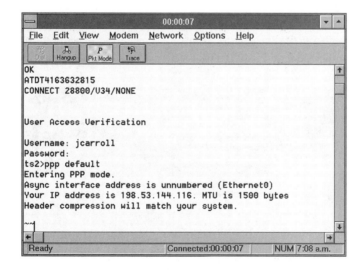

The dialer does feature an automatic hang-up mode. You can specify that your link to the Internet should be terminated if you do not do anything for a certain period of time. This will help avoid a situation in which you forget that you are on-line and begin to run up a bill.

There are several software components to the SPRY Internet in a Box package. You load each one separately, although there is a link between some of them.

SPRY Mail is a basic, straightforward e-mail system. The organization of the program is very "neat" and straightforward, without any of the "clutter" found in some other e-mail programs. Creating a message is simple: key in the user ID, subject, and message, and you are on your way. You can attach files to the message using MIME or binhex (protocols discussed in Chapter 7):

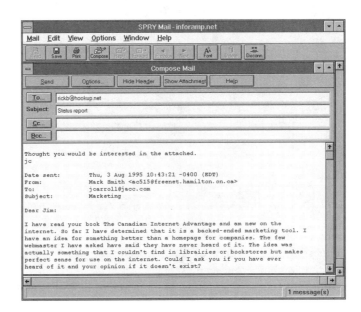

Similarly, the e-mail inbox is simple and straightforward. You read a message simply by double clicking on it. If the file contains an attachment in a form recognized by your computer, clicking on the attachment will load the program and then load the file attachment:

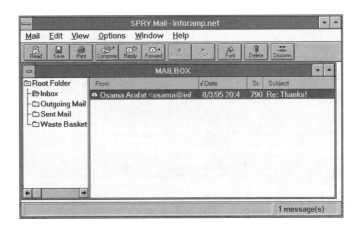

The USENET newsreader shares the simplicity found in the mail program: uncomplicated, simple to use, and easy to navigate around. It has most of the features you might want in a news program; for example, you can choose to examine articles within USENET newsgroups by date, thread, or a number of other methods:

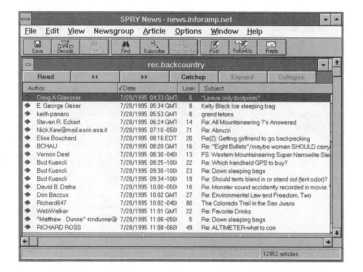

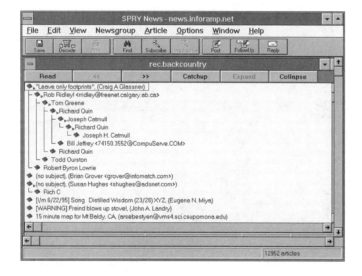

SPRY's "Network File Manager" program lets you access an FTP site and easily navigate your way through directories to retrieve a specific file. One interesting feature is that it also loads your Windows File Manager program, so that when you want to retrieve a file from your FTP site, you just "drag" it over to your File Manager program:

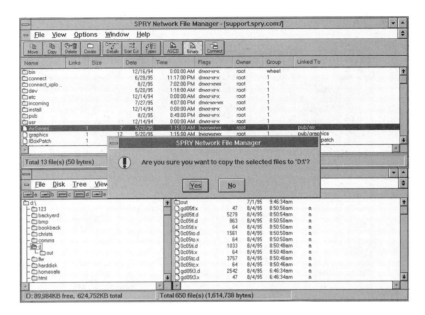

To browse the World Wide Web, SPRY has licensed the Mosaic program code from the original developers at NCSA and has improved upon it dramatically. The result is a full-featured, impressive Web browser that supports most of what you would need to do while on the World Wide Web:

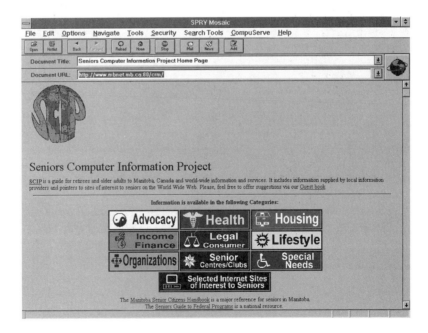

The browser includes many important and useful features, including

◆ A comprehensive hot list of interesting sites to visit on the Internet. You can add your own items to the list. The hot lists can be "nested," that is, you can have categories by type of hot list item (e.g., business, entertainment) and sites within those categories:

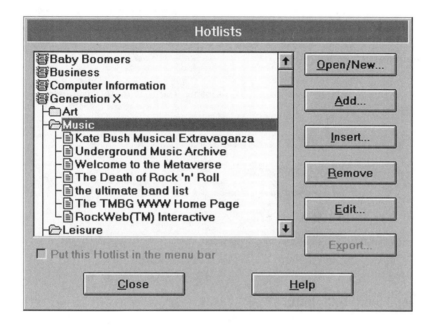

The only complaint is that like many Internet programs, the hot list is a little too specific to the United States, with not enough emphasis given to Canadian sites.

◆ A complete history of where you have been during your session. This allows you to easily return to a specific location.

◆ An intriguing security section. This allows a number of options by which you can securely provide credit card and other information through the Internet.

◆ Caching. This capability allows you to keep copies of information on sites that you visit on your hard disk, so that the next time you go, the site will load from your hard disk rather than through the Internet. This speeds performance dramatically over time. The cache is not as extensive as that supported by Netscape.

◆ The ability to use Mosaic to access FTP sites, Gopher resources, and USENET newsgroups (such as is found within Netscape), even though Internet in a Box ships with separate programs to access these information sources.

All in all, SPRY Mosaic is a very impressive Web browser. If this is the only browser that you might choose to use, you will be perfectly satisfied. The only concern would be for SPRY to support the Netscape extensions as discussed in Chapter 12, since there are some sites that are "Netscape-specific."

Finally, the Mosaic browser has one unique feature not yet seen in other Web browsers: a "kiosk" mode, which removes the regular Windows menus, as seen below. This feature will be very useful to organizations that want to establish a "kiosk" of information accessible to the public. In this case, SPRY Mosaic could actually be used by itself on a PC without a keyboard, located in a shopping mall or bank, to allow people to access information without even being plugged into the Internet!

Internet in a Box would be a worthwhile investment and is definitely one package worth looking into.

Contacting SPRY:	
Web:	**http://support.spry.com**
Phone:	(206) 515-2998
E-mail:	**iboxtalk@spry.com**
You can also contact CompuServe for more information.	

Quarterdeck's Internet Suite

Quarterdeck is a company best known for some of its computer utilities; QEMM, for example, a well-known and popular memory management program for Windows. Quarterdeck released Internet Suite in August 1995 as part of an overall push to build a significant presence in the Internet. It also released WebAuthor, a program that can be used to create the HTML code within a Web site.

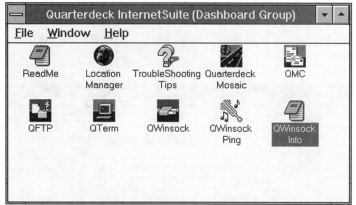

Like Internet in a Box, Internet Suite consists of separate software programs: Quarterdeck Message Center for e-mail and USENET news, Mosaic for accessing the Web, QFTP and QTerm for accessing FTP and Telnet, and Qwinsock for dialing into the Internet.

The program also comes with a "Location Manager" program, which allows you to customize your access, so that you can easily use the software from home (without having to dial 9, for example) and from the office (where you do have to dial 9 for an outside line). You can also use the Location Manager to support the use of several ISPs.

When you first install the program, you are presented with a screen that gives you several options:

You can sign onto the Internet by establishing a new account with an ISP. This uses Quarterdeck's "Connect and Play" option. Quarterdeck has gone to great lengths to include in the software many Canadian ISPs, so that you can instantly get an account in various locations across the country:

Or you can use a "preconfigured" ISP with which you already have an account. In this case, Quarterdeck has programmed the software so that it is configured automatically to work with a particular ISP. All you have to do is choose that ISP from a list of ISPs. Quarterdeck has included many Canadian ISPs on its list:

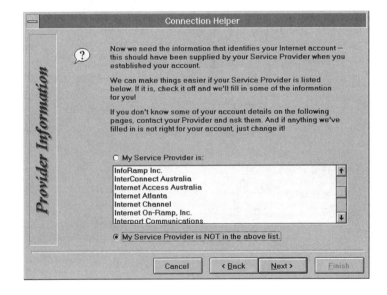

Or, finally, you can customize the product to work with any other ISP, but you figure out how to set it up. It is not that difficult, and you might find that your ISP can provide you specific instructions on what to do:

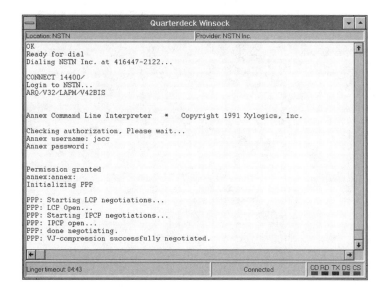

Internet Suite comes with Quarterdeck Winsock, the program that dials up your Internet service provider and establishes a PPP connection:

Quarterdeck has taken an innovative approach to e-mail and USENET news by combining both into one program, Quarterdeck Message Center. Notice that the left side of the Message Center lists your mail folders as well as the USENET newsgroups to which you belong. You can have folders of newsgroups, so that you can selectively review only those newsgroups that interest you at a particular time. Thus you can choose to view your "inbox" for new messages:

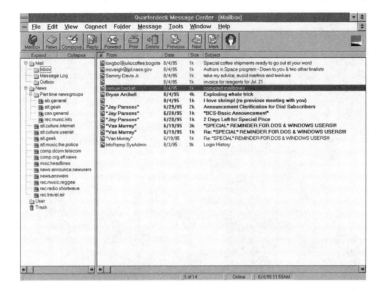

or choose to examine the new postings in a particular newsgroup that you have chosen to join:

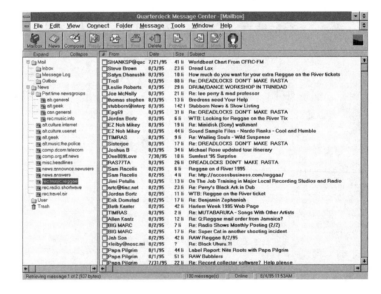

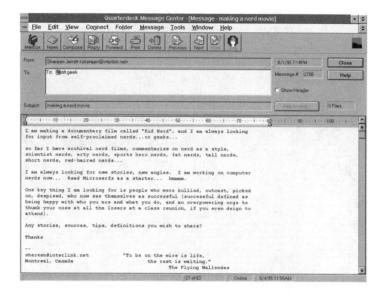

However, e-mail messages and USENET postings look so much alike that you will have to be careful not to reply to a USENET posting as if it were an e-mail message; you might end up saying something in public that you didn't intend!

Creating a new message is straightforward; Message Center supports all the features that you might need, including the ability to attach files. Message Center encodes the files using the uuencode format and will even compress those messages so they take less time to transmit:

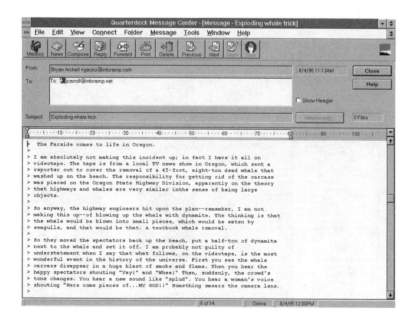

QFTP is Quarterdeck's FTP program and is one of the nicer FTP programs around. Sites that you have visited in the past are listed on the left-hand side of the screen; to travel to one, simply move your cursor to it and double click. Or you can connect to a new site just by clicking on the lightning bolt and inputting its FTP address. Once you are in a site, to retrieve a file, highlight it and click on the "Get a file" icon:

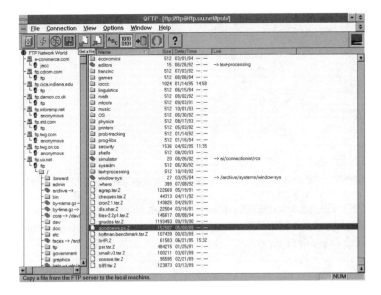

Finally, Quarterdeck's Mosaic program is a fascinating Web browser with a number of interesting features:

◆ When you first load the software, it puts up a few Web pages that have been stored on your hard disk. This helps you to discover some of the information available on the Web and is a good place to start surfing:

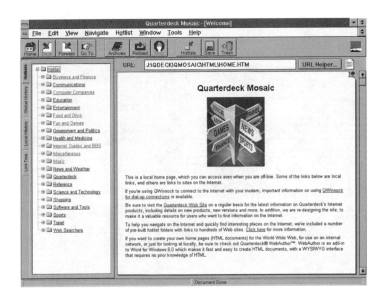

◆ The left side of the screen lists four tabs: hot lists, global history, local history, and link tree. The hot list is a summary, by category, of interesting Internet Web sites to visit. Thoughtfully, Quarterdeck has put together a listing of Canadian sites:

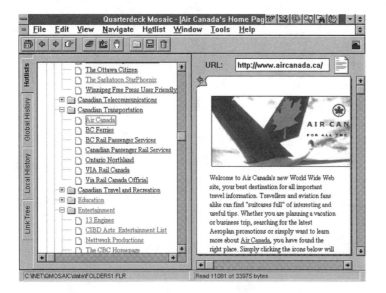

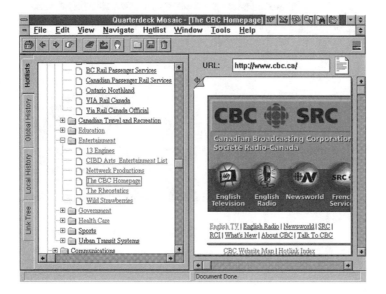

◆ The global history is a summary of the last 500 sites visited in the last seven days, while the local history lists the sites visited this session:

◆ The "link tree" is a summary of all the pointers found on the current Web pages that you have visited. It can be useful to quickly locate key information on other sites to visit, particularly useful if you are doing research.

This version of Mosaic has extensive support through which you can manage your hot list; for example, to add a new item to your hot list, you can drag an entry from your global or local history list to the hot list category that you would like it saved in or drag the little icon found at the top right of the screen to the hot list. For example, in the screen below, the cursor is moved to the little icon at the top right, which is then dragged over to a hot list item on the left:

Quarterdeck's Internet Suite product is an impressive package: simple and straightforward for novice users, while powerful enough to meet the needs of Internet veterans. The Web browser is sophisticated, and its hot list aspect is extremely useful.

In addition, Quarterdeck deserves kudos for paying attention to the Canadian marketplace through its customized access via Canadian ISPs and through preparation of a Canadian version of a hot list folder. You won't go wrong with this package.

Contacting Quarterdeck:	
Web:	**http://www.qdeck.com**
Phone:	(310) 392-9851
E-mail:	**info@qdeck.com**

OpenText Internet Anywhere

Version 1.0 of OpenText Internet Anywhere was released in 1994. It is a program that supports Internet e-mail and USENET newsgroups via the UUCP protocol. It was then upgraded to version 2.0, which introduced PPP connectivity, and FTP and Web support, using the Mosaic Web browser.

The program has been configured to provide for automatic sign-up with Portal, a large U.S.-based provider; they are also planning on providing automatic sign-up with several Canadian ISPs. However, it is easy enough to configure the software to work with any Canadian Internet provider that supports SLIP or PPP access. For example, you can quickly navigate your way through the set-up of your account, modem and other details related to your provider through the configuration screen. The only tricky part might come from "scripting" the log-in to your provider. But the documentation is clear enough that even a novice should be able to figure this step out — and do not forget, you can always ask for help from your ISP.

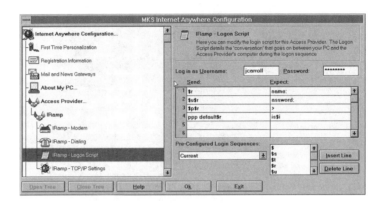

Once loaded, you see the "OpenText Internet Anywhere Desktop," which provides access to programs for e-mail, USENET news, FTP, Telnet, Finger, and Mosaic for the World Wide Web. The latter is actually based on code licensed from SPRY.

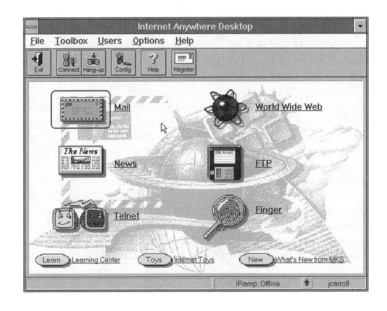

You link to your ISP by clicking on "Dial." OpenText Internet Anywhere provides a handy status screen to let you know how your connection is doing:

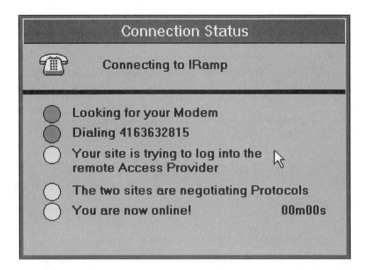

Like the other software looked at in this chapter, the mail program provides most of the features that you would want:

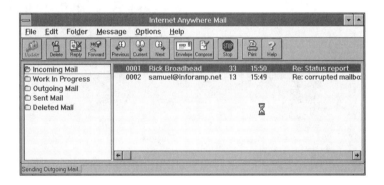

The program is easy to use; the only complaint is that the program splits the process of creating or replying to a message into two parts: a part for addressing the message and a part for the text of the message:

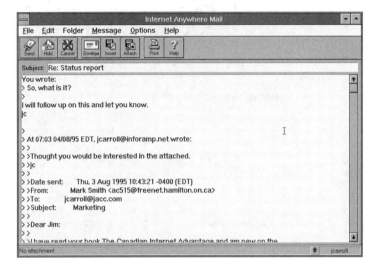

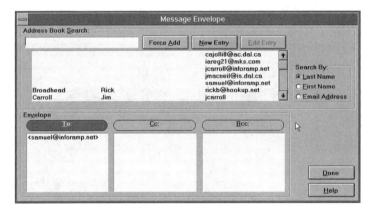

The newsreader is like the mail program and allows you to get a quick listing of the items in your favorite newsgroups:

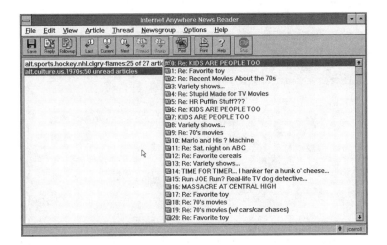

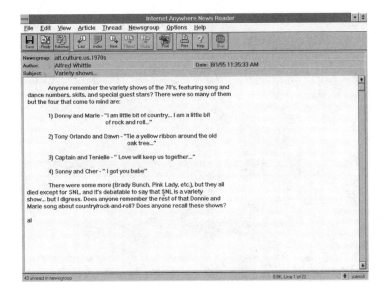

One interesting feature is that it puts a line through those articles that you have read. It also supports killfiles, so that you can easily set up your system so that you never see any postings from particular people or about particular topics:

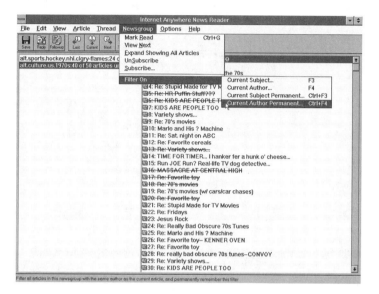

The Internet Anywhere FTP program actually seems more straightforward than some of the other packages looked at in this chapter; a novice should be able to learn how to do FTP with relative ease with this one. Once again, you transfer a file merely by clicking and dragging with your mouse:

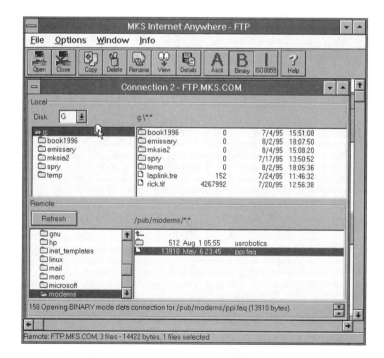

Finally, Internet Anywhere has also licensed the code from the original NCSA Mosaic program and improved it. The result is a Web browser that does most of what you need it to do:

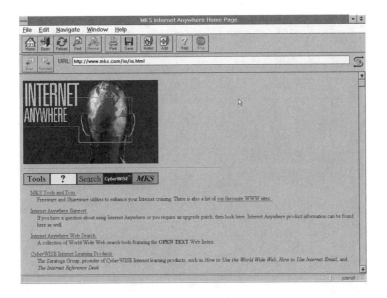

The Web browser supports hot lists, but the preconfigured list is not as extensive as found in other packages. However, it does get you to Yahoo and some of the other popular sites, so it is fine in terms of getting you going:

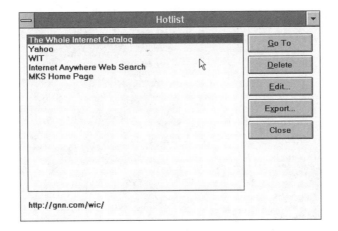

Internet Anywhere makes up for the lack of an extensive hot list by providing a direct link to the OpenText site, an index of World Wide Web information. Through this site, you can quickly narrow in on information from around the world, through a simple search form:

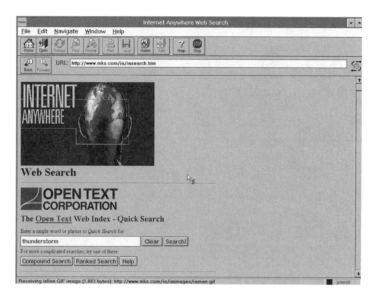

The OpenText system returns comprehensive pointers to information from around the world; for example, here is a snippet from our search for information about thunderstorms:

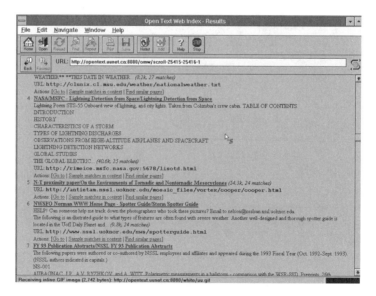

The OpenText Internet Anywhere software is an impressive package. Although it does not share some of the innovative features seen in some of the other software packages outlined in this chapter, it does most of what you need such a program to do. Perhaps its greatest strength is the fact that it is so easily customizable to other ISPs, allowing you to quickly use it with any Internet service provider in the country that supports SLIP or PPP access.

Contacting OpenText:

Web: **http://www.opentext.com**

Phone: (800) 507-5777 or (519) 883-3242

E-mail: **iasales@opentext.com**

Wollongong's Emissary

Emissary, from Wollongong, is gaining a lot of attention as a particularly inventive and dramatically different Internet program. The product abandons the approach taken by most of the preceding packages by incorporating everything into one software program: mail, USENET news, FTP, the World Wide Web are all accessible from one simple screen:

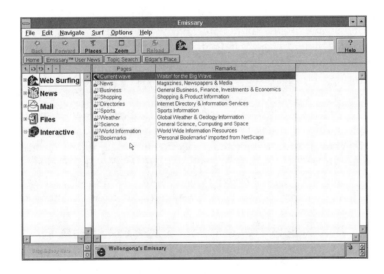

And in an interesting departure from the other programs, you do not have to load a separate "dialer" program to sign onto the Internet. Instead, you load Emissary, and when it realizes that you want to do something on-line on the Internet it dials in on its own.

Say you want to create a few e-mail messages. You can load Emissary and key them. All your messages are saved to your hard disk when you finish them. Finally, you might tell Emissary to send your e-mail so you can check for new mail. At this point, Emissary will dial out to your Internet service provider.

Emissary is easy enough to configure with existing ISPs, and Wollongong is working on a program of instant sign-up throughout Canada.

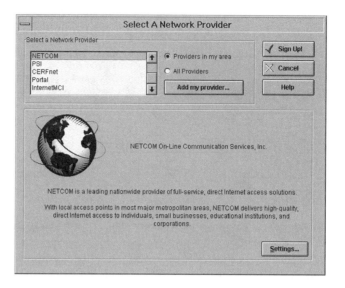

Emissary supports the concept of "drag and drop" throughout the software. Indeed, it seems to be the underlying "philosophy" of the program. Wollongong notes at its on-line Web site: "There's no reason I shouldn't be able to drag anything anywhere. If I can think of it, it should just work." This concept is found throughout the Emissary program. For example, rather than choosing a file in an FTP session and then clicking on a "download" icon, simply drag the file from the Internet site to your local file site.

This style of thinking has led to a package that is innovative, amusing, and sometimes downright awe-inspiring. Learning to use it is very straightforward; after all, with the "drag and drop" concept you end up trying to do something just to see if it will work.

Once you are connected, you can use all its features. The mail program is simple yet sophisticated. Its simplicity can be demonstrated by the "Composing a Message" window, where you only have to fill out a "To:" field, the subject, and key in the message:

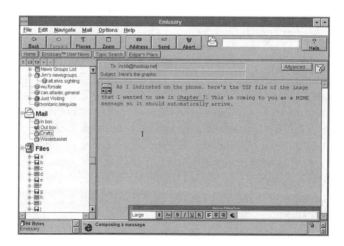

But this simplicity hides a sophistication not seen in other packages. For example, notice the "Paint" icon in the text of the message. This indicates that an image file has been attached to the message. But unlike the other software packages, you do not key in the name of the file—

you simply drag one from the "Files" item to the "Mail" item, and a new message is immediately created with the file attached:

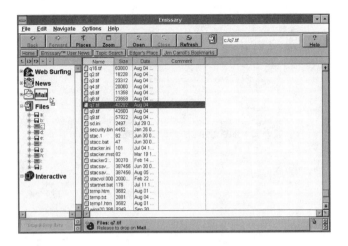

Emissary embeds information about the file attachment within the message using the e-mail protocol MIME. This means that if you send the message to someone who has a MIME-capable e-mail program that is configured correctly, he/she can immediately view the image upon receiving it. Likewise, if you receive a message from someone with a MIME attachment in a recognized file format, you only need to double click on the item to see the image, listen to the sound file, or view the video.

Switching over to USENET news is easy enough, since it works just like the mail program does. The first thing that you will notice is that the line of buttons on top has switched to icons that are relevant to USENET. You will find this occurring as you move from place to place in Emissary. In addition, you can see the USENET newsgroup to which you belong, a summary of postings in a particular group, and a specific message all at one time. (We are quickly learning that, of course, some people like to cause stress for the believers that hang out in the I-saw-Elvis group):

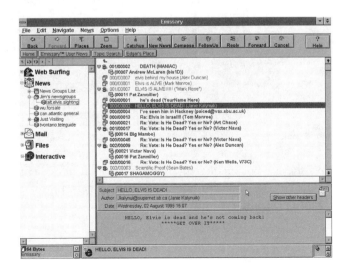

FTP is as straightforward as mail and news. Need a file? Just travel to an FTP site, pick out a file, and drag it to one of your local drives listed on the left-hand side of the screen:

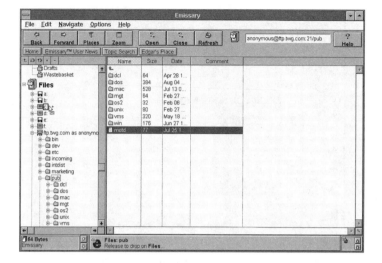

Finally, Emissary's Web browser shares the approach taken by the other applications: the layout is neat and straightforward, with your applications on the left and your Web screen on the right. The current Web site that you are visiting is found at the top of the list:

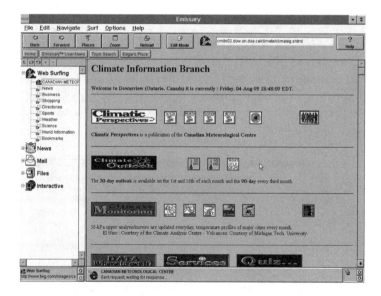

If you want to save a site as a bookmark item or want to store it in one of the folders on the left, drag the item from the top of the list into one of your folders. In this case, we are saving the location for Toronto's *eye* magazine into our bookmark list:

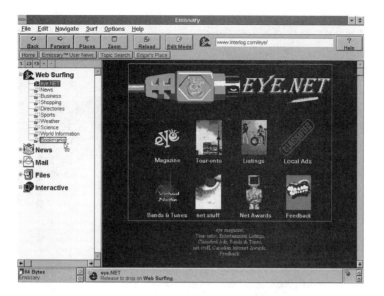

Emissary uses some of the niftiest graphic concepts you are likely to see in an Internet software package. It has the often-used "surfer-on-a-wave" metaphor found in so many other Internet packages, but it does some things that are just downright funny. For example, rather than a spinning "globe" or "icon" that you see in other Web browsers to indicate that you are traveling somewhere, Emissary gives you a bouncing earth.

The documentation both within the packages and on the Wollongong Web site is nothing less than hilarious, often taking the approach of poking fun at Edgar the "geek." Wollongong is trying to win over people intimidated by the Internet and by computer experts by trying to make the experience whimsical and fun. And if you want to know more, you can visit Edgar's place for more technical information and tips:

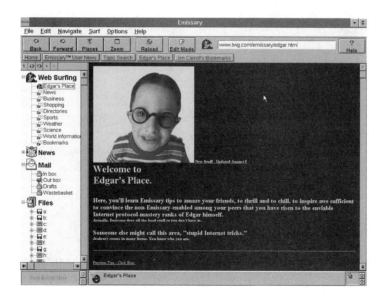

Emissary also has a "Places" button that you can choose at any time, which provides you with a list of every site visited during this particular session. Not just Web sites, but FTP sites, USENET newsgroups, everything you have done during this session. It can be useful as you navigate your way around the software:

It is this type of simplicity and attention to detail that causes Emissary to shine. Certainly, the product is straightforward enough that it will make it easy for an Internet novice to get used to traveling throughout the Internet. Overall, Emissary is a fascinating program and an important development on the Internet software scene. It starts out with the mission of insulating you from many of the complexities of the Internet, and it succeeds admirably.

Contacting Wollongong:	
Web:	**http://www.twg.com** and **http://www.twg.on.ca** (for Canadian Web site)
Phone:	(519) 747-9900
E-mail:	**posales@twg.com**

Issues to Think about

In this chapter, we hope that we have given you an idea of how the Internet software marketplace is shaping up. We have not provided detailed software reviews, nor have we undertaken critical analyses of the programs' features. We leave that to the computer magazines. However, we do have a few general comments:

◆ All the programs mentioned varied in the speed with which they handled USENET news, e-mail, or the Web. Some were very fast at one thing, only to be slow at another. And there were frustrations with the way that some operated, particularly when it came to USENET news. The first time you access USENET with any of these packages, they all retrieve a listing of all the newsgroups for your provider. That's fine—you can just go and get a coffee while it takes the 5 to 15 minutes to obtain such a list. But even after the listing was obtained, some of the packages were frustrating. For example, some packages took a minute or two just to access USENET news because of some obvious inefficiencies in the way they processed the list. Others accessed USENET news in a second or two.

◆ Perhaps one of the fascinating findings was that some packages required a double click to choose to do something, while others only required one click. If you end up using multiple packages, you will find this to be most frustrating!

◆ Microsoft Windows 95 includes built-in access to the Internet, and its impact on the Internet and the Internet software industry cannot be ignored. We take a separate look at this software in the next chapter.

The choice of a package depends on many factors. In this chapter it was our intent to provide you with a summary of some of the features of these leading packages. If you need a detailed review to help you make your decision, you should consider one of several Internet magazines that are available or track reviews that are starting to appear in personal computer publications. We list various Internet publications in Appendix H of this book.

Microsoft and the Internet

Microsoft released Windows 95 in a blaze of publicity in August 1995. Certainly the world had never seen a computer product launch like it — in Canada, Microsoft even went so far as to hang a banner promoting Windows 95 down the side of the CN Tower. People everywhere — even those who know little about computers — knew about Windows 95. The advertising, marketing and high technology industries will be talking about it for a long time to come.

There are many who believe that Windows 95 offers significant improvements in the use of personal computers, and there are many who believe that the product is largely a marketing sham. There are those who believe that it is a significant advance in computing, and others who believe that it does not even offer the power and sophistication found on Macintosh computers and in IBM's OS/2 software. There are those who love Microsoft, and there are those who hate it.

This chapter does not examine issues related to Windows 95 and its role in the computer world. Nor does it offer an assessment on Windows 95. Instead, this chapter will take a look at Windows 95 as it affects the Internet, and we will examine how individuals can use the product to access, use, and take part in the Internet.

Why Windows 95?

You might ask why we devote a special chapter to Windows 95 in this book. What about IBM's OS/2 and Apple's Macintosh System 7? IBM and Apple have both made significant investments in the Internet and have already done many of the things that are now found in Windows 95 within their own operating systems. Why not a separate chapter about their products as well?

It is a good question. The answer is this: we devote a separate chapter to Microsoft and the Internet because of Microsoft's scope and size in the personal computer industry.

The authors believe, as many do, that Windows 95 will have a far more significant impact on the Internet in the years to come than OS/2 and Macintosh systems. It is simply a matter of numbers. Over time, it is expected that far more people will install Windows 95 than those other two systems.

This does not overlook the fact that IBM is doing some important work with the Internet. It is, for example, working with some of the world's largest organizations to integrate their internal information systems into the Internet. It is developing some of the most sophisticated Internet sites on the planet by linking corporate information to the World Wide Web. It is working intensely with the Internet throughout all its activities and is making the Internet central to everything that it does. It, too, is having a profound impact on the Internet.

As for Apple, it, too, has recognized the role of the Internet in the computing industry. It has developed eWorld, an on-line service, which includes access to most Internet services including the World Wide Web. It has readied software that allows organizations to set up World Wide Web software on their Macintosh systems. It is at the forefront of many multimedia development efforts related to the Internet. Apple is a significant player in the market.

But, even given IBM's efforts with OS/2 and Apple's own efforts, most industry analysts agree that Windows 95 will outsell OS/2 and Macintosh systems by a wide margin. Simply put, Windows 95 will find its way onto a heck of a lot of computers in the years to come. And given what Microsoft has done with Windows 95 to help people get onto the Internet, it is bound to have a significant and profound impact on the future evolution of the Internet.

Microsoft and the Internet

With the announcement, development, and release of Windows 95, Microsoft

---

MICROSOFT AND THE INTERNET

1 Windows 95 will have a significant impact on the Internet in the future if for no other reason than the dominance of Microsoft within the personal computing industry.

2 In August 1995 Microsoft became a major player in various aspects of the Internet by providing access within Windows 95 to the Microsoft Network (MSN), an on-line computer system providing access to entertainment, technology, news, weather, and other information.

3 Microsoft also announced the intention of becoming one of the world's largest providers of Internet access, by establishing a global dial-in Internet network as part of the MSN initiative.

4 Microsoft became actively involved in developing Internet client software, such as the release of Internet Explorer, a sophisticated Web browser.

5 Mircosoft included, directly within the Windows 95 operating system, the TCP/IP protocol, the foundation of the global Internet.

6 Individuals who use Windows 95 can use the software to access MSN or to access an existing account with an ISP, a somewhat complicated process.

undertook many initiatives related to the Internet. For this chapter, we focus on four of those initiatives:

◆ Microsoft established the Microsoft Network, a system intended to compete with services like America Online, CompuServe, and, in fact, the Internet itself. Related to this system, Microsoft established a global dial-in TCP/IP network with the intent of becoming one of the world's largest providers of SLIP/PPP connections to the Internet.

◆ Microsoft has taken on the role of an Internet service provider.

◆ Microsoft has become actively involved in developing Internet client software as part of its efforts in the two first areas above.

◆ Microsoft included the TCP/IP protocol directly within the Windows 95 operating system, perhaps the most significant development within Windows 95 as it affects the Internet.

We will take a look at each of these issues in greater depth.

The Microsoft Network

The Microsoft Network (MSN) is the result of Microsoft's effort to get involved in the business of providing people something to do with their modems. Bill Gates, the Chairman and Chief Executive Officer of Microsoft, has indicated many times his belief that existing on-line services and the Internet are too difficult for many people (although some may disagree with him). His stated intention with the development and delivery of MSN was to provide a tool with which new, average, non-technical users could begin to discover the on-line world.

MSN is similar in concept to systems such as CompuServe and America Online, which we discussed in Chapter 4. MSN provides access to a wealth of information, much of which is not found on the Internet — news, sports, weather, computer support sites, forums, on-line "chats," games, and all kinds of other information. Many of these services are above the basic rate that you pay to access something on MSN. As we described in Chapter 4, there is an entire on-line world found in systems like CompuServe, America Online, and now MSN that is not available on the Internet.

Microsoft hosts the information for MSN services on computers at its location in Seattle; hence, when you are accessing MSN, you are in essence traveling to systems located there. From Seattle, you are taken to other information sources (i.e., out on the Internet) as might be required.

Of course, you do need to get to Seattle, and to accomplish that, Microsoft provides access through 1-800 numbers, X.25 data networks (X.25 being an older protocol similar in concept to TCP/IP, one of the advantages of which is that there are a lot of cities across North America that have X.25 access), and its own private data network. Microsoft is establishing the latter with the assistance of UUNet, one of the largest U.S. Internet service providers (not to be confused with UUNet Canada). Microsoft has plans to provide access through its own data network through local telephone numbers in 70 cities in Canada.

Joining MSN is a model of simplicity. When you install Windows 95, you will find on your "desktop" (i.e., the main screen you see when you load Windows 95) an icon for the Microsoft network. If you click on it, you will be led through a series of screens through which you can sign up for the network. At one point, you will be provided information on rate plans, which includes the opportunity for a free trial account:

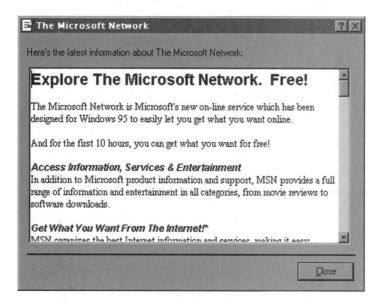

You will also be asked to provide information necessary for billing. If you do not cancel your free trial account at the end of 10 hours, you will be automatically billed for any future usage.

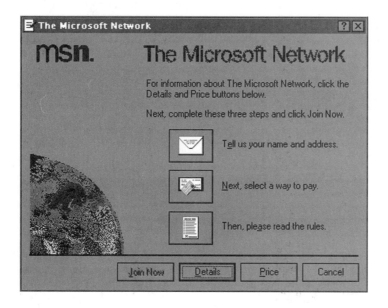

You will also be provided with phone numbers that you can use locally to access MSN.

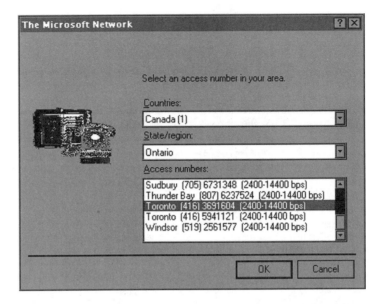

Microsoft has done an excellent job building and providing the tools to ease new users into the process of establishing an account, which is perhaps one reason why organizations like CompuServe and America OnLine complained so loudly to the U.S. Department of Justice that Microsoft had an unfair competitive advantage.

Once you are on-line, you will discover that MSN is very tightly integrated into Windows 95, so tightly, in fact, that sometimes it is difficult to know if you are on-line. For example, you might find yourself clicking on an icon with MSN that goes off and loads your copy of Word for Windows, in order to show a document. You spend time reading your document and forget that your modem is still on-line, and the clock is ticking.

One complaint that many users of MSN have is that it seems every time you do something, it opens up a window. You can find yourself opening up window after window after window and ending up quite confused over just what the heck it is you are trying to do.

Significance

Certainly MSN is an important development in the computer industry; to have a software company enter the on-line business is a significant event. And Microsoft has certainly done a good job making it easy for people to get on-line. But they were not the first to do so. Apple established eWorld two years ago, a network similar in concept to MSN. It, too, provides easy sign-up and features a tight integration of the on-line world to the operating system. Even though it does not boast a large number of users (perhaps a few hundred thousand worldwide), it was a trailblazing system, identifying the potential for the link between the operating system and the on-line service.

Microsoft, Windows 95, and the Internet

The purpose of this book is to review the Internet, not general information services like CompuServe, America Online, and MSN; hence we do not go into further detail here on what you can do in various areas of MSN. We do not want to concentrate on whether MSN has better computer support forums than CompuServe; nor do we want to indicate that it has more on-line "chats" with celebrities (something you will find on all these services); nor do we want to know who has more comprehensive weather reports. Instead, we concentrate on what you can do with the Internet from within MSN. As we noted above, there are four areas we want to examine:

◆ MSN access and what it provides;

◆ Microsoft's role as an Internet service provider;

◆ Microsoft's involvement in the development of Internet software;

◆ the introduction of the TCP/IP protocol into Windows 95.

We will look at each of those four areas in the sections that follow.

Types of Access to MSN

You can be one of two types of a MSN user:

◆ MSN without Internet. You are a MSN user who is accessing MSN through a non-SLIP/PPP account. You are not directly connected to the Internet, but are using a "menu-type" account as we described in Chapter 13.

◆ MSN with Internet. You are a MSN user who is accessing MSN with a SLIP/PPP connection. In this case, you are directly connected to the Internet (so that you can use the World Wide Web as well as access the menu-type MSN system).

MSN *without Internet*

Until Microsoft completes establishing its Canadian TCP/IP network, most users of MSN in Canada will fit into this category. In this case, you are accessing MSN with a non-SLIP/PPP connection. You can do a lot with MSN related to the Internet, but you cannot access the World Wide Web through your MSN account. For example, you can send and receive Internet e-mail and participate in USENET newsgroups from within MSN.

When you first access MSN, you see a main "menu" that includes a "Categories" item:

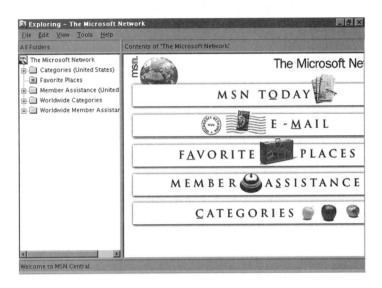

From Categories, you can choose to go to the MSN Internet Center, the primary place where you can begin accessing various Internet applications from within MSN:

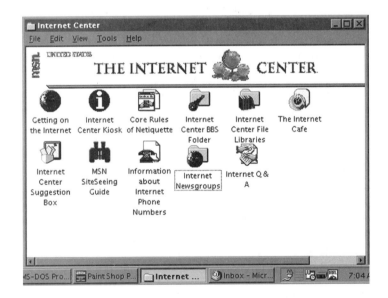

This area includes a lot of good information for the novice, describing the Internet, etiquette issues, and other information. You can also access USENET newsgroups from here or obtain a document that updates you on the status of direct SLIP/PPP access to the Internet through MSN.

If you choose Internet newsgroups, you can browse through a listing of groups by category and eventually select the ones to which you wish to belong:

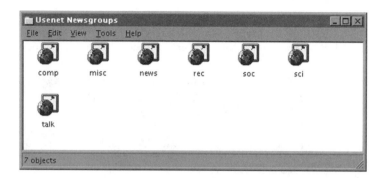

Microsoft has prepared a full-featured newsreader that provides a simple and straightforward interface to USENET, similar to some of the other newsreaders we have examined in this book:

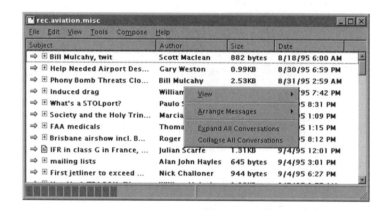

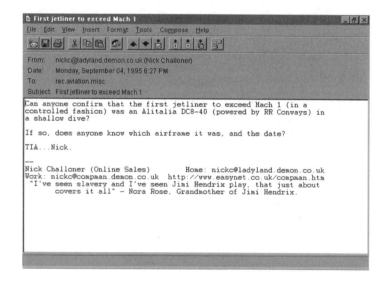

Sending e-mail to the Internet from MSN is done through the "universal mailbox" feature of Windows 95. It is an e-mail program that not only handles e-mail from MSN and the Internet, but can also receive faxes and can send and receive mail through the Microsoft MSMail program, software used throughout many corporations. The program itself is a model of simplicity:

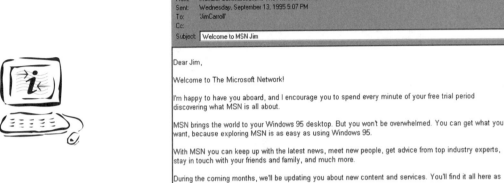

In summary, should you decide to use MSN, you can find yourself participating in Internet e-mail and USENET news quite quickly, given the interface that has been built. And given the work that Microsoft has done integrating MSN into Windows 95, it is a very slick, easy, and fun interface to these parts of the Internet.

Microsoft as an Internet Service Provider

Coincident with the announcement of the Microsoft Network, Microsoft announced that it was going to provide for global access to the Internet via PPP connections. In effect, it would become an Internet service provider. Through this type of connection, Microsoft permits users to take part in the hottest area of the Internet, the World Wide Web, in addition to other areas of MSN as outlined above. Through one phone number, you have access to both MSN and the Internet.

In Canada, you will only be able to access the Internet through Microsoft once it establishes a dial-up PPP number in your community. Plans in Canada are to provide local dial-up capabilities in 70 locations, providing fairly extensive coverage across the country. Microsoft is also setting up access throughout the United States and indeed right around the world. One convenient aspect is that, like the IBM global Internet network that precedes it, you can travel around the world and still access the Internet from major cities and towns.

When you use the Microsoft Network for a PPP connection, you can use any type of TCP/IP client software such as Netscape or Mosaic or Microsoft's own Web browser.

In essence, Microsoft plans to become a significant player in the business of providing access to the Internet and will be competing against not only small and medium-sized ISPs in Canada, but heavyweight organizations such as IBM and Bell Canada. Their involvement is yet another indication of the growing importance of the Internet across Canada and around the world.

Microsoft has perhaps one thing going against it in the ISP business. At the time this book was prepared, Microsoft was charging $3.50 per hour to access the Internet via a PPP connection. Should you choose to use a local ISP in many of the cities and towns across Canada, you will find yourself paying rates of $0.50, to $1.00, to $1.50 an hour (in most cases). Certainly, Microsoft is not entirely cost-competitive in the ISP marketplace.

Is the extra money worth it? That is for you to decide. As we discussed in Chapter 12, there are many more considerations in choosing an ISP than just price, such as service, support, features, capabilities, and coverage. Certainly Microsoft provides other intangibles over and above price; hence you should not discount it strictly on price alone.

Significance

Microsoft's success in the ISP business is not guaranteed. And it should be noted that Microsoft is not the only company to break this ground. Indeed, IBM established the IBM Global Information Network in 1994 with the aim of providing global Internet access. IBM provides phone numbers in cities around the world, for prices comparable to that of Microsoft. They feature 24-hour support, strong marketing, and excellent service. They, too, are worthy of consideration as an ISP; in fact, they pioneered many of the ideas now being pursued by Microsoft. Given IBM's global scope and the fact that its revenues still dwarf those of Microsoft, it remains a mighty and powerful player in the global ISP business.

Microsoft as an Internet Client Developer

Coincident with its efforts with the Internet and MSN, Microsoft has become very involved in the development of Internet software. As we saw above, Microsoft has developed a sophisticated USENET newsreader that permits you to access, browse, and read particular topics. In addition, Microsoft has released the Microsoft Internet Explorer, a full-featured World Wide Web browser modeled on the original NCSA Mosaic program:

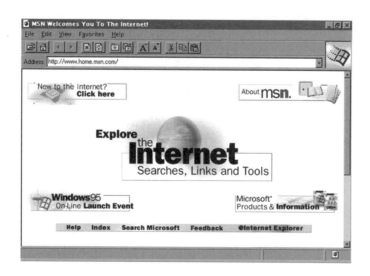

The browser has most of the capabilities found in the other Web browsers reviewed in this book. And we can certainly expect that Microsoft will continue to enhance and to develop the product.

These are but two examples and are early indications that Microsoft plans to play a key role in the ongoing development of software to access and use the Internet.

Significance

From the perspective of Apple and IBM, Microsoft is joining a business that has already seen the involvement of many other companies. OS/2 Warp, when released, provided a news-reader, World Wide Web browser, mail software — many of the components found in Windows 95 today. Apple's push with eWorld saw the same level of development. For both companies, their development efforts are not slowing down. Microsoft is, by rights, just one more competitor in an increasingly crowded market. And given the dominance of Netscape in the browser software industry, one wonders if any of these organizations have a role to play at all. The cover of *Forbes ASAP* for August 1995 showed a picture of the smiling Marc Andreessen, the 24-year-old cofounder of Netscape, with the title "George Gilder Thinks This Kid Can Topple Bill Gates."

TCP/IP and Windows 95

Perhaps the most important thing about Windows 95 is the fact Microsoft has included the TCP/IP protocol directly within the operating system. This more than anything has given notice to the rest of the world that TCP/IP really and truly is becoming the overriding protocol that will link together different computers around the world.

By making TCP/IP a part of Windows 95, Microsoft is providing computers with the basic capability to "talk TCP/IP" to other computers. Since the Internet is built on top of the TCP/IP protocol, this provides each computer running Windows 95 with the basic building blocks to link that computer to the Internet. There are several impacts:

◆ Before Windows 95, individuals seeking to get onto the Internet had to find or purchase PPP or SLIP software in order to establish the connection to the Internet. But, with the introduction of Windows 95, PPP access is built right in as part of the TCP/IP software in Windows 95, so it is not necessary to install or to purchase separate PPP software (although, as we describe below, you might still want to).

◆ Before Windows 95, corporations seeking to provide employees with a full-time link to the Internet through a dedicated connection had to install TCP/IP software on each PC that is connected to the Internet. But the TCP/IP protocol software is now included within Windows 95. Configuring a particular PC in the organization to work with the Internet in this case does not involve buying and installing a separate TCP/IP program for each PC. Instead, it involves configuring Windows 95 for the proper domain name server, IP address, and other configuration details.

The inclusion of TCP/IP (and its component, PPP) within Windows 95 is very significant, because it will permit more and more people to use the product as a fundamental tool to link into the Internet.

Using Windows 95 with Another ISP

Many existing users of the Internet who are upgrading to Windows 95 might want to use these built-in PPP capabilities to establish a connection to their current ISP, rather than signing up with Microsoft in order to get on the Internet. And in some cases, new users of the Internet might not necessarily want to use Microsoft as an Internet service provider, but might want to use some other Canadian ISP. The reasons for this chore are varied:

◆ Cost. Internet access is available from many ISPs in Canada at rates of $0.50 to $1.00 an hour, and sometimes less and sometimes more, compared to Microsoft's $3.50 an hour. You might certainly find it to be less expensive to go through an ISP other than Microsoft in order to access the Internet, particularly if you have no interest in MSN itself.

◆ Location. You might be in a location in which Microsoft does not provide access via a local number.

◆ Preference. You may simply prefer to deal with a company other than Microsoft as your ISP. In this case, you need to customize the Windows 95 PPP program to work with your ISP.

As we noted earlier, Microsoft has included the basic components of the TCP/IP computer protocol within Windows 95. This includes a dial-out version of PPP, which you can use to access any ISP offering PPP access.

Setting up Windows 95 to use your existing ISP can be done, but before you commence, be aware that it is evident that Microsoft has not gone out of its way to make the process of using Windows 95 with providers other than Microsoft easy or straightforward. As you will see below, there are a lot of buttons to push and a lot of "stuff" to configure. Quite clearly, it is evident that they would prefer you to access the Internet using them as an ISP.

High-quality Canadian ISPs with good support and service will be able to provide you the necessary information and instructions on how to configure Windows 95 to dial into their service. In other cases, you may have to figure out how to do it on your own, seeking help from others who may have already done it.

Here is an example of what is involved. InfoRamp is one of Toronto's largest ISPs, providing SLIP/PPP access to several thousand people. In order to help their customers with Windows 95, they have published a document (available on-line **http://www.inforamp.net/iramp/inforamp/help/win95.html**), which provides step-by-step instructions on configuring Windows 95 to access InfoRamp. You will find this document in Appendix M.

The instructions they provide — seven pages in length — give you an idea of what is involved in getting Windows 95 to work with an ISP other than Microsoft. (The instructions are specific to InfoRamp and will not work with your own ISP, since the domain address, domain name server, and other details will be different.)

Complexity versus Simplicity

We certainly must compare the instructions necessary to getting Windows 95 to work with an ISP other than Microsoft to the simplicity of installation that is found in other Internet software that we have looked at in this book. For example, if you want to use the Quarterdeck

Internet Suite product with the InfoRamp service, you choose InfoRamp from a list of ISPs provided in the product:

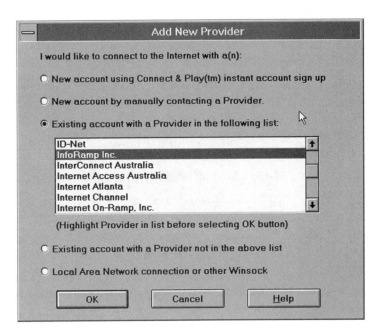

If you are trying to set up the Quarterdeck Internet Suite product for a provider for which Quarterdeck has not yet customized its product, you must spend a little more time configuring the software. But as we saw in the last chapter there are only a few screens that you have to fill out — Quarterdeck has spent a lot of time preparing a software interface that makes it easy to customize their PPP program to work with any Internet service provider.

We are seeing many other Internet software packages come to the market that are also a model of simplicity. One must wonder why Microsoft has not done the same. One must wonder if Microsoft has made it particularly difficult for Windows 95 to work with any Internet service provider other than MSN as part of its strategy. They certainly have not applied the often amazing Microsoft programming prowess to make it easy to use Windows 95 with another ISP; hence its users and customers should demand that Microsoft fix this obvious deficiency.

Simply put, there are many people who will prefer to use Windows 95 with an ISP other than Microsoft, particularly given the differences in access charges that can be found when comparing MSN to local providers. Microsoft should recognize this fact and upgrade the software accordingly. Not everyone wants to use MSN.

Once It Works, It Works Very Well

One final comment. Even though the steps of getting Windows 95 to work with another ISP are complicated, once you have it working, it works very well. You will also find that you can have multiple Windows 95 "shortcuts" that provide direct access to different dialing instructions, and indeed, different ISPs, so that you can move about with ease. All in all, it is a good product and is worthy of the little bit of extra time that it will take to get it working with your own ISP.

Significance

IBM integrated the TCP/IP protocols into its OS/2 Warp system when it came out in 1994. It enhanced those capabilities with the release of OS/2 Warp Connect in 1995. Apple, too, has been a leader in integration of TCP/IP into its operating system. Microsoft is not the first, nor is it the last, software company to realize the importance of TCP/IP by introducing it into the basic operating system of a computer.

Summary

From one perspective, the entrance of Microsoft into so many different aspects of the Internet, through its Windows 95 release and other activities, is a positive step. It will help to introduce many people to the Internet and will in some ways make it easier for them to use it. The introduction of TCP/IP and PPP directly into the operating system solidifies the role of the Internet around the world. Its efforts with Internet software are bound to lead to some fascinating programs in the years to come.

But, given the mostly positive impact, there are many who are concerned that Microsoft's involvement is not good for the Internet. They believe that its track record of the past indicates that it will bully its way around the Internet, doing things that are not good for the Internet as a whole but that are good only for Microsoft. They believe that Microsoft will show no respect for the ideals that led to the creation of the Internet in the first place. They believe that Microsoft will come to dominate much of the Internet in the future, and hence its involvement in the Internet is an extremely ominous development for the entire network.

Are these concerns well-founded? How will the future unfold? Is Microsoft good or bad? Should we love it or should we hate it? No one really knows, but one thing is for sure: the involvement of Microsoft in the Internet does change the network in many, many ways, and we will see some interesting developments in the future.

CHAPTER 15

Why the Internet?

Business is jumping onto the Internet in a big way but can't explain why, a new study shows. "Internet usage today resembles a typical highway on a Sunday afternoon — lots of people driving around aimlessly with no particular place to go," says a report by the Yankee Group, an international consulting firm in telecommunications strategy. "Many are confused or lost, but most are having a grand old time just the same," the report says.

Businesses Can't Say Why
They're on Internet
Globe and Mail, July 4, 1995

If the buzz on the floor of Canada's largest government and technology trade show Tuesday is any indication, then bureaucrats are quickly joining the global rush on to the Internet. In the past year, the Canadian government has become a major user of the Internet, the global community of about 30 million computers...Government downsizing is forcing civil servants to be more creative, and the Internet is a cheap way to not only circulate information but also complete government transactions such as filling out forms.

Surf's Up for Government on Internet; By Getting on the Information Highway, Governments Make it Easier to do Business
The Ottawa Citizen, September 13, 1995

In 1995 the Internet entered the mainstream of business and government. We saw corporate Canada — small, large and medium-sized organizations — embrace the strategic potential of the Internet, and we saw government departments realize that the Internet could be used to reengineer some government services.[1] But there remain many more people and organizations — perhaps including you — who are not quite sure just what the strategic potential of the Internet is or are not convinced that there is any real benefit to the network.

In other cases, there are many people who become involved with the Internet who have become too lost in the technology. They do not focus on the strategy, benefit, or purpose of an Internet initiative. They get wrapped up in the excitement of the World Wide Web and forget that any technology should be driven first by strategy and not by technology "wow factors."

In the 1995 edition of this book, we wrote this chapter, "Why the Internet?" We did so to provide guidance to people on how to think about the Internet from a strategic perspective. The response was so overwhelming that we soon expanded the chapter into an entire book, our second book, entitled *The Canadian Internet Advantage: Opportunities for Business and Other Organizations*. We invite you to read more about that book at our Web site at **http://www.csi.nb.ca/handbook/** or by sending a message to **info@handbook.com**. In that book you will find a lengthy and detailed examination of the potential of the Internet from a strategic perspective for business, government, education, health care, and not-for-profit organizations.

---

1. We saw Finance Minister Paul Martin holding up a copy of the *Canadian Internet Handbook* as he announced an Internet initiative with respect to the release of the 1995 federal budget, a picture that was run in *Maclean's* magazine and newspapers across the country.

However, we think it important that this handbook continues to provide some concise observations on some of the strategic aspects of the Internet. Hence in this chapter we take a look at the question "Why the Internet?"

Learning to Think Strategically

If you plan to use the Internet for more than entertainment, you must learn to think about it strategically. It is easy to get carried away with the Internet and to become excited with its possibilities. There is certainly a lot of hype about its potential impact on business, education, and the government. But how much of the hype is real?

Many wonder if there are real opportunities on the Internet. There certainly seem to be. Certainly it will reshape the way that organizations do business with each other. It will help reshape government by letting them reach their citizens in new and innovative ways. It will change everything that it touches. But in many ways it will take some time for this change to occur and for the opportunities to become real.

Computer Trends and the Internet

In one way, the organizations in which we work have spent many years learning how to take advantage of information technology and computers effectively. Our investment in personal computers, local area networks, and software such as electronic mail, groupware and other systems has taught us to make internal knowledge available throughout our organizations, and has provided a high degree of efficiency in our internal communications.

Information, knowledge, and ideas traverse from one end of the organization to the other through sophisticated networking technologies. Many organizations have

WHY THE INTERNET?

1 Learning to do business on the Internet means that you must learn to think strategically about technology.

2 We are entering an era of "interorganization" networking, which will somehow transform the way that organizations reach and interact with the customers, suppliers, trading partners, and other people and organizations.

3 There are some organizations and industries that do not appreciate the profound change that the Internet represents; thus they seem to be sleepwalking into the future.

4 There are many issues having to do with methods of doing business on the Internet that you must be aware of, including Internet culture and the tools available to you.

5 It is surprising that Canadian organizations still find it necessary to justify an investment in the Internet, since it is quickly becoming a ubiquitous business tool.

6 In order to justify its use, you must be prepared to take a real, honest look at the potential strategic opportunities within your own particular organization.

become truly "networked" and are able to support themselves through the intelligent use of computer technology.

We have learned how to use computers to support our internal activities and have become quite good at it. But that is all we have learned. Most of us have learned *absolutely nothing* about how business can be transformed through links to our customers, trading partners, business associates, and others. We have learned nothing about how to use computer technology to deliver government services.

We Need to Communicate

An organization does not just communicate internally. On any given day, an organization receives any number of telephone calls, faxes, letters, parcels, cellular phone calls, and other types of communications. Day-to-day activity involves communications with trading partners, customers, business associates, regulatory and government authorities, consumer watchdog agencies, business advisors, and any number of other people. We do this today with telephones and fax machines and couriers and letters.

But what is happening all around us today is that many of these day-to-day communications are now being supported through the Internet. Somewhere, strategic advantage can be found if we channel our energies to the way that we use it for these communications.

Internet Organization Networking

With the arrival of the Internet, we are entering an era of interorganizational networking, that is, networking from one organization to another. It is because of interorganization networking that business, government, and education will be forever transformed.

You have a computer. Your customer has a computer. They are linked together through the Internet. Somehow, you will discover that this will change your relationship, and it will change the way that you reach and deal with that customer. Somehow, it will present an opportunity for you to increase sales to that customer. Somehow, if you plug together all the computers in the world, the way that business is conducted will be transformed. Somehow, you will find ways to reach new, potential customers.

To understand how your organization will be transformed, you must learn to think strategically about the impact of the Internet on your particular industry or area of interest.

Strategic Questions

Doing business through computer networks is going to be very different than business over the phone and fax. It involves asking strategic questions:

- ◆ What are the benefits of customer support with e-mail?

- ◆ How can we link the data in our mainframe application to the World Wide Web so that our suppliers can automatically monitor stock volume?

- ◆ Can we really build this custom data module so that our industry associates can pull custom market data from us through the Internet?

- ◆ Can we use the Internet to reduce these 25 steps of paperwork between myself and the customer to two electronic forms?

- ◆ Can I let the customer access my corporate information system through the Internet to find out certain information in order to provide them with better service?

- ◆ Can we get more communication happening between federal and provincial government departments through the Internet?

- ◆ Can we do something strategically with the Internet that gives us an edge over our competition?

- ◆ Can we use it to help us change, for the better, something that we already do?

- ◆ Can we use it to save money?

- ◆ Can we use it to make it easier for the customer to do business with us?

If you start with questions like these, you will find that you will start to think about the Internet strategically, not technically.

It Is about More Than a Web Site!

With the hype of the Internet the authors now see many people blindly rushing to set up a Web site to "advertise on the Internet." We see people rushing, with unreal expectations, to create the site. We see people in the Internet industry making some unreal promises about "business on the Internet." As a result, people create a site, sit back, wait for the customers, and become disappointed when opportunities do not arise.

In may ways, executives — management and information technology professionals — are going to have to learn what business is all about all over again. Networked business is a new frontier, and things promise to change pretty fast. Learning about the Internet is about more than just putting up a Web site. It is about more than dealing with cool, fun technology. It is about thinking of what this network might do to your organization. You need to avoid sleepwalking into the future.

Sleepwalking into the Future

There are many organizations and industries that fail to recognize the strategic impact of the Internet. As such, there remain entire industries that do *not* seem to be waking up to the fact that the Internet is a system that will, over time, cause profound change to them or to their belief in how the future might unfold. You can find examples almost anywhere.

One example is the Canadian newspaper industry. One of the participants in the 1995 CRTC "information highway" hearings in Ottawa was the Canadian Newspaper Association. Apparently, they are concerned that telephone and cable companies will soon be able to offer direct competition in the form of classified advertisements and other "content" along the "information highway." They want to make sure that the "rules of the road" ensure they are full participants.

Obviously, by talking like this it is evident that the industry is missing the point that the Internet will quickly begin to marginalize its role in the emerging wired world. Industry believes that the "highway" is a television-based system controlled by cable and telephone companies and would appear to be quite clueless regarding the existence of the computer-based Internet. How can this be so?

It is the fundamental assumption that is wrong; it would appear that industry executives believe the world of the future will be the same as the world of today. They naively assume that in the future wired world there will still be *traditional* information producers (i.e., newspapers and magazines, TV, and radio) and information consumers (i.e., you and me). This assumption means that they think they only need to whine to the appropriate "information gods" (the CRTC), to ensure their future role (and riches) on the information highway. They believe that all they need to do is get their content (newspapers) on the distribution system (a television-based information highway controlled by telephone and cable companies) and their future is assured.

How wrong they are, for it would appear that they fail to understand that the Internet makes everyone a producer and that the Internet is a completely new information distribution system. Newspapers now have some new competition, because the Internet represents the most substantial shift to the information industry since the invention of the printing press. In essence, the Internet completely changes the dynamics and cost of information publishing, by giving everyone a "printing press."

It used to be that you had to have a lot of money to become a publisher; after all, the capital cost of a physical printing plant is quite high, and the cost to establish a distribution system is significant. These significant barriers to entry are ripped apart by the Internet, for with it, everyone in the world gets his/her own printing press and distribution system for an extremely low cost. Internet e-mail is so inexpensive it is almost free, and anyone can put up a World Wide Web site on the Internet for less than $100 a month through an Internet service provider. In effect, the cost to become a global publisher is quickly becoming *next to nothing*.

The Internet rips apart, blatantly and with no apologies, the assumption of the newspaper industry that the information world of today will be the same in the future. The real impact of the Internet is that the competition for the *Globe and Mail* is not just the *Toronto Star* or *Toronto Sun* or telephone and cable companies; it is every newspaper and magazine in the world. More importantly, it also happens to be anyone in the world with a PC, a modem, and a few dollars to spare.

The Internet permits anyone to be a publisher and a journalist. The result is an incredible diversity of new publications and news sources from around the world. Granted, early experience has shown that a lot of this information is completely useless and some is just plain dumb. But in the ore body that is the Internet, one can find a lot of diamonds.

Ten years from now, most of us will likely still sit down with our morning paper. Newspapers in paper form will not disappear. However, we will have extensive electronic news sources that we will then review on-line, much of which will come from people and median organizations around the world. In this wired world the *San Jose Mercury News* will be as close to you as the *Globe and Mail*. To track news about high technology, would it make sense to pay for an electronic version of the *Globe* or get such news from a newspaper right in the heart of Silicon Valley? The answer should be obvious.

Through such submissions to the CRTC, Canadian newspapers are showing that they fail to understand that their competition is not now, nor will it ever be again, the newspapers and magazines in their geographic locale; it is every other median organization on this planet and every individual with a PC and a modem. They must realize that they will have to do something pretty compelling to come up with a product that the wired consumer will want to buy. They have to do more than whine to various regulatory bodies about the information superhighway.

What became apparent is that they failed to appreciate the fundamental change that the Internet is causing to their industry. They must learn to think about the Internet strategically, as must you. In this chapter, we will try to look at the Internet from that perspective.

Doing Business on the Internet

Growth of the Internet is exploding because it is directly linked to many of the trends that are shaping our economy today. Many of these trends have a direct impact on the usefulness of the Internet to a business:

- ◆ Canadian organizations must learn to compete globally. Read any number of articles, and you are told that the forces of globalization are causing Canadian organizations to rethink their traditional place in the world. Not only do we have to compete with our mighty neighbors to the south, but we must be able to compete with the economic powerhouses emerging in Asia.

- ◆ Canadian organizations are trying to seek out new markets and new opportunities in a world that is increasingly competitive. The Internet directly helps an organization faced with the trend to globalization because it helps to make the world a smaller place. A presence on the Internet is global in scope and extends the reach of any organization well beyond Canada for an extremely low cost. The Internet eliminates global time barriers to doing business abroad and makes people and organizations on five continents as accessible as someone down the hall.

  The simple fact is that Canadian organizations participating in the Internet can learn to sell products and services worldwide as a result of their presence on the Internet, can learn to collaborate globally, and can learn how to leverage the knowledge and information they find on the Internet into business strategy. The Internet is quickly becoming a fundamental requirement for an organization seeking to do business around the world.

- ◆ The 1990s have become the "decade of the customer." Terms like "total quality," the "customer is king," and "customer responsiveness" have become paramount to the mission of an organization. Clearly, organizations are scrambling to ensure that the highest possible degree of customer support is available.

  Leading-edge organizations are discovering that a link to the Internet is an extremely powerful and invaluable customer service tool. An organization can encourage direct customer feedback through Internet e-mail and thus ensure that it will hear directly from customers about quality or other concerns. Organizations can monitor particular USENET newsgroups that might relate to the products and services they sell, in order to gauge customer reaction and attitudes. Organizations can establish Web resources that encourage customer feedback.

  Organizations that have learned to make effective use of Internet e-mail realize that this is a tool that permits direct communications to and from their customer base. A direct e-mail link is a vehicle for establishing a continuing relationship with a customer and over the long term can be used to enhance and develop that customer relationship, with a direct impact on future sales opportunities.

By establishing on-line information resources using such tools as the Web, an organization can make available help manuals, support information, and any number of documents helpful to the customer. Making this information readily available makes it easier for the customer to get answers to questions, resulting directly in a much more satisfied customer.

Simply put, by linking itself to the Internet, an organization can make a statement to customers in the Internet community. Organizations should also realize that the lack of Internet accessibility will increasingly become a hindrance in today's high technology, networked world, in which an ever greater number of current and potential customers are "Internet citizens." The Internet is a fundamental tool for an organization seeking to provide the highest possible degree of customer service.

◆ Organizations are finding it necessary to establish joint ventures, partnerships, and new methods of working with other organizations. The Internet directly supports these interorganizational partnerships. Whether an organization is involved in a joint product development project or is working with another organization in order to have access to skills it does not currently have available in-house, the sheer efficiency of Internet communications makes sense. The Internet has become one of the key tools to support such intercompany and interorganization networking.

◆ The demand for interorganization networked communications will increase. It is not only joint ventures and projects that are supported by Internet communications; many believe we are entering an era in which "doing business" through computer networks will become a necessity as opposed to an opportunity. Over time, organizations will discover that all kinds of intercompany communications can be supported through the Internet, whether it is access to price lists, general day-to-day correspondence, project reports, knowledge exchange, or the exchange of transactional information. The Internet offers a common electronic mail link between organizations, and provides standard methods to access corporate information through the Web and other information services.

◆ Canadian organizations are finding it necessary to establish new methods of marketing products and services in an increasingly competitive environment. The Internet has become a new marketing resource, permitting not only local but global marketing efforts.

There is a lot of misconception when it comes to the Internet and marketing. While it is not acceptable to send unsolicited information to people on the Internet, it has become perfectly acceptable to put up information resources that are available to anyone. By establishing an Internet resource, you can make it easier for an existing or potential customer to obtain information about the products and services offered by your organization.

Establishing an on-line information resource on the Internet with such technologies as the Web allows an organization to establish an on-line "store front" that current and potential customers can access through the Internet at their leisure. We will see an explosion of new, marketing-oriented Internet resources based on the Web in the years to come. The Internet has become an invaluable global marketing resource.

◆ Organizations are increasingly sensitive to telecommunications costs and are looking for cost savings. As Canada enters a deregulated telecommunications environment, there are any number of opportunities for cost savings. One of the most significant is a simple Internet link, since it offers substantial reductions in communication costs.

The Internet is having a profound impact on the pricing of information services around the world for the reason that organizations or individuals can often buy access to the Internet for a flat fee. Once you have paid for your basic link to the Internet, you can use it for whatever you want — electronic mail, access to Internet databases, information servers, or other services.

With high-speed dedicated Internet access costing as little as $600 a month in major metropolitan areas, you could, if you wanted, send e-mail all day long, with no additional charge for any particular message.

People are becoming used to a communications environment in which there are no incremental charges for each additional minute spent doing something on the Internet. Purchasing access to the Internet for a flat fee is resulting in a communications market in which the costs for national and global communications are being completely rewritten.

Clearly, the Internet is becoming as fundamental to a business as a telephone and fax machine. Indeed, given the fact that the Internet links you to the world, many organizations are discovering that the Internet has quickly become an integral part of their day-to-day operations.

Strategic Uses of the Internet

When thinking about what you can use the Internet for within your business, you must toss aside any thoughts about how neat or cool the technology is. Instead, you must think about it from a business strategy perspective. This includes examining how you can use the Internet.

◆ As a tool to sell goods and services on-line. Is there some type of business opportunity here? Is yours an industry in which customers might purchase on-line? Keep in mind, as we reviewed in Chapter 10, the tools to support "electronic commerce" on the Internet largely exist already, so technology is not a barrier to selling on-line; customer attitudes are.

◆ As a marketing tool. Organizations working with the Internet are discovering how it can be used as an integral part of their marketing plan. This includes using it to find and educate potential customers and making available detailed product and other marketing literature.

◆ For customer relations. This includes using the Web and e-mail for purposes of customer feedback and customer support. The concept of interactive marketing with direct contact with the customer is one that is gaining increasing attention in the business community.

◆ For "intelligence" and information gathering. This includes using USENET as a tool to monitor customer discussions and attitudes and using the Web to research particular topics that might relate to your marketing mission or other activities.

◆ For corporate communications. This includes using the Internet as a public relations tool as well as regular corporate communications including press releases.

◆ For new business ventures. This might include the development of new electronic publishing vehicles and new information services, which could become new revenue sources.

◆ Saving money. This includes examination of how the Internet can be used to achieve cost savings and efficiencies as well as reducing the cost of distributing information.

Before you rush off to do something on the Internet, take the time to ask these questions and identify your strategy. From that will flow what you should be trying to do on-line.

Be Real!

There are many people out there who oversell the Internet and create unrealistic expectations about its potential impact on your business. It is important to be real, and to keep your expectations in check.

Keep in mind that the Internet is still relatively new. It will take some time for the Internet to change the *behavior* of the consumer. An explosion of successful marketing on the Internet must await the emergence of the "electronic consumer"; people who are used to spending time on-line looking for product or service information. There are a few of these people around today, but they certainly are not an overwhelming majority of the population. There are many people who are actively exploring the Internet, just like you. We are still dealing with an infant. Hence take your time, and do not get carried away.

Internet Culture

Another key point is that to successfully do business on the Internet, you must take the time to learn about the unique culture of the Internet. Doing business on the Internet without understanding its culture and unique ways is like trying to do business in another country without understanding its language, culture, rules, and regulations. You can try, but you are likely destined to fail.

The Culture of the Internet

There is a clear and simple rule when it comes to doing business on the Internet: advertising and junk mail do not work, but marketing might. This is perhaps the most fundamental aspect of the unique Internet culture. The important thing is to recognize that there are distinct differences between advertising and marketing. The best thing that you can do if you decide you want to do business through the Internet is to work with the Internet for at least six months in order to learn about, and respect, its unique on-line culture. Once you understand the unique culture, you can then learn how to work within the culture in a subtle way to successfully market your product or service.

Advertising Does Not Work on the Internet

Many organizations, when they think about the potential of business on the Internet, wonder why they cannot just send out an advertising flyer. If it works in the real world, why can it not work on the Internet? There is one key cultural rule related to marketing on the Internet that you must respect: no one wants information they have not asked for. Unsolicited information does not work. It will never work. The Internet considers this to be junk mail. Organizations that try to use junk mail on the Internet are spectacularly unsuccessful.

There are several reasons why you will not be successful if you abuse the culture of the Internet and send junk mail out on the system. The Internet culture is a strong, global force, and really cannot be fooled with. You abuse it at your own risk.

◆ The Internet can shut you down if you play with it, and the Internet will fight back. If you send out an advertisement on the Internet, either through e-mail or through USENET, you will guarantee yourself an extremely negative reaction from your potential customers. So negative, in fact, that you might discover that the Internet has reacted by effectively shutting down access to your account by sending you several million e-mail messages of protest, or by posting your home telephone number with suggestions that people call you to voice their displeasure at 3:00 a.m. Such is the penalty for real abuse of the Internet.

Even if you post a single message to a USENET newsgroup or mailing list that is considered to be "advertising" in nature, you might find that you have unleashed a storm of protest. You have to keep in mind that people on the Internet refuse to gracefully accept information that they have not asked for.

◆ Unlike the fact that we receive regular mail for free in the real world, you have to recognize that many people receiving e-mail and USENET news are paying to do so. People get particularly upset when they have to pay to get junk mail. They react differently, often with anger.

◆ By abusing the culture of the Internet, you upset your potential customer rather than getting their attention. This is a fundamental breach of the first rule of Marketing 101: never, never upset your customer. Why expend the energy, if you are doomed to fail in your approach in the first place?

If you plan to use the Internet to send junk mail, the authors of this book and the balance of the Internet community will have no respect or sympathy for your actions. You deserve whatever the Internet community might throw at you. A strong statement, but such is the reality of the Internet.

How to Market on the Internet

Marketing is different from advertising. Marketing implies a subtle campaign to make information available to the potential customer in an unobtrusive fashion. It implies a carefully thought-out strategy on how to get the attention of the customer while respecting the feelings of the customer on certain issues. It is quite different than simply sending out junk mail haphazardly.

Marketing on the Internet involves choice and respects the fact that people on the Internet should have the choice whether or nor they want to receive your information.

Since the Internet has continued to evolve in the last two years from an academic network to a commercial network, it has become completely acceptable to put up information resources that people can choose to access. In particular, there has been an explosion of interest in the commercial potential use of the World Wide Web in order to market products and services. We looked at many examples in Chapter 9.

When it comes to marketing on the Internet, it really is quite simple: unsolicited information will not work. Establishing information resources will. We will see what this means when we look at marketing tools below.

Tools for Marketing on the Internet

There are a number of Internet tools that can be used to effectively market products or services. These tools include the World Wide Web, electronic mailing lists, and "mail robots" (also known as listservs). Each can be used in a different way. For example, through the use of simple "mail robots," individuals from around the world can contact your organization for information. Through Internet mailing lists, you can establish an area where customers can choose to receive regular product and service information from you.

Through a Web server you can establish an Internet site containing price lists, product information, press releases, and other background information. You can make available detailed information about your organization, your products, and your mission. Order forms can be placed on-line. Sounds, graphics, and images can be used to add pizzazz to your on-line presentation. Individuals "surfing the Web" can access this site from anywhere in the world. Clearly, these Internet tools can be used to great advantage in a new type of marketing campaign, the "cybermarket."

Using Internet Tools for Marketing Purposes

Let's consider how you can use these tools to implicitly market through the Internet:

◆ You can permit individuals to automatically retrieve an order form through an Internet e-mail message, with a mail robot. For example, it is quite straightforward to create a mail robot using your existing e-mail software so that a message sent to **order@yourdomain.com** returns a simple text-based order form that can be returned by fax or e-mail. Voilà: anyone from around the world can easily obtain an order form from you. Most Internet service providers will set you up with a mail robot for a small fee.

◆ You can permit individuals to request more information about your product, service, or organization through a mail robot. For example, using a mail robot, you can set up your system such that a message sent to the ID **info@yourdomain.com** returns a message that contains an index of information that you make available through the Internet, including price lists, product information, and ordering information. The potential customer can then retrieve any of these documents by sending a message to your mail robot and by including the name of the document from the index in their message.

You can easily add additional information postings to the mail robot at any time, making this a very flexible and attractive option for marketing through the Internet. We have done this with the *Canadian Internet Handbook*; send a message to **info@handbook.com** to give it a try.

◆ You can establish a mailing list that anyone can join so that customers and others can receive product, support, and other updates directly from you as well as other information postings. In doing so, you can effectively build a captive audience that is receptive to receiving information from you. Individuals can join and leave this list on a selective basis, and since only those who choose to belong to your list receive postings to it, you are not violating the unique Internet culture of sending unsolicited information.

You can use this list to post announcements concerning new releases of your products, information about product updates or other significant announcements, or information of interest to the participants. The mailing list can be archived on a periodic basis, such as once each month, so that the full text of past postings can be retrieved by e-mail.

◆ You can provide a place to visit on the Web for those individuals "surfing the Internet" and allow them to request additional information about your products and services. In effect, you can establish an Internet "store front" in order to market your products and services through the Internet, while respecting the unique culture of the Internet. We discuss in Chapter 16 what is involved in creating your own Web site.

For example, you could establish a World Wide Web site that could contain the following information: an overview of your organization; a description of products or services available; press releases; a listing of major customers; a price list; testimonials from several customers; information on how to order products through e-mail and fax; information on how to contact you through e-mail and fax.

You can take it one step further and provide on-line forms to provide interactive communications directly to the potential customer. For example, you could include on your Web server an order form that is automatically sent to you through Internet e-mail when completed or a form to request more information from your organizations. The form, when completed, would be sent to you by e-mail and would permit you to directly contact the potential customer.

Make People Aware of Your Resource

Once you establish your on-line presence on the Internet, it will be important for you to get word out on the Internet to attract "visitors" without attracting charges that you are advertising. A key thing to keep in mind is that there are many individuals and many organizations who spend their time "indexing" the Internet, whether in magazines, books, or on-line. It is to your benefit to have your Internet resource added to one of these indices, hence you want to try to get the attention of these people. This can be done in several ways:

◆ Information about your new World Wide Web site should be posted to **comp.info systems.www**. Check these USENET newsgroups to see what an acceptable posting should be like; it should be succinct. Posting to these groups will draw people to your location and might help you to get indexed in other locations.

◆ Consider sending your press release to **sackman@plains.nodak.edu** (Gleason Sackman) to see if he is interested in posting information about it to the **net-happenings** list. If he does decide to post it, this will go to one of the premier announcement lists on the Internet, and news of your new Internet resources will travel the globe in a flash.

◆ Get listed in Yahoo. Details are available at **http://www.yahoo.com**. It is the primary place on the Internet where you should list yourself. There are many other sites like Yahoo. Make sure you get listed in as many as possible.

◆ See if you can get your World Wide Web site cross-indexed at other locations. There is a tendency wherein many people or organizations who run World Wide Web servers like to offer additional sophistication by offering "links" or pointers to other Web servers, which could include a pointer to your server.

◆ Consider a press release for distribution to the general media concerning this new Internet initiative. For a period of time, there will be an interest in new, significant Internet initiatives, although this time might be running out. The key point to play up in the press release is that your new Internet resource is a product that is being carefully marketed on the Internet without upsetting the unique culture of the Internet that forbids advertising. The press release should include information concerning the resources that you have brought on-line.

◆ Consider a brief announcement of your new resource in your e-mail signature. Just list the address. People will use it to visit your site when they have to.

◆ Consider adding your Internet resource information to your regular marketing information. List Internet e-mail addresses, or even your WWW server address, on your business cards. Consider how you can make customers aware through your traditional media campaigns about your Internet resources. A T-shirt company has gone so far as to print their e-mail address in their advertisements!

Integrate

It is perhaps this last area that will provide the greatest benefit. You can build a fairly impressive Web site that contains useful customer and marketing information. But you have to tell your customers that it exists. You must integrate it into your newspaper and magazine advertisements. You must list it next to your 800 number. It must be a regular part of all of your corporate communications.

Rule number one is this: Let the customer know how to reach you on the Web. This involves a very strong integration of print and other media campaigns to your Internet site. Consider a regular newspaper or magazine advertisement. You might have a 4 × 4-inch space on a piece of paper in which you try to attract a potential customer. Such an advertisement is a powerful tool, but you are limited by the fact that you only have 16 square inches with which to work.

Now, link those 16 inches to an infinite space where you can make available to the consumer any information that you want — your Web site. What you need to do is attempt to draw the potential customer from a flat, one-dimensional piece of paper in an advertisement to a site that contains unlimited customer education information and marketing literature. Product support information. Customer loyalty information. Brand trial sample information or brand launch information. Feedback forms, complaint forms, and places where the customer can request more information. Interactive contests. Training videos, voice files, and other information. You are limited only by your imagination.

In your newspaper, magazine, and other advertisements you must tell the customer how to get to your Web site. Put the Web address on your letterhead, on business cards, on product labels, and on inserts.

Summary

The Internet is changing business in slow and subtle ways. There are opportunities for marketing on the Internet, opportunities to sell your products and services globally, and opportunities for efficiencies in your operations. Clearly, this chapter provides only a hint of what is possible on-line. The only real way to discover what works best for you is to get on-line, learn about the Internet, and use it and understand it in order to determine how it might best fit your particular circumstances.

Justifying the Internet

Patricia Seybold, a leading U.S. information technology consultant, has stated that "if you're not an active Internet citizen by the mid-1990s, you're likely to be out of business by the year 2000." Although this might overstate the facts, there is no doubt that the impact of the Internet is such that the world of business, education, and government is changing rapidly and dramatically before our eyes.

But many organizations in Canada still find it necessary to educate senior management about the need for an Internet connection and to justify the costs for a link to the network. This is a strange state of affairs. After all, how many organizations found it necessary to justify those other fundamental business tools, the telephone and fax machine?

Moving from Simplicity to Complexity

In the last three years, many individuals have signed up with one of the Internet service providers listed in this book and have spent time on the network using a dial-up modem in order to try to understand the opportunities related to the Internet. It is easy to go out and buy an individual dial-up account to access the Internet. Linking your organizational network to the Internet is a challenging task, however.

Part of the challenging task many people in Canada now face is the need to convince senior management that it is important for the organization to have a direct link to the Internet. And as we discussed, it is much more complex to have a direct link to the Internet than simple dial-up access.

In order to develop the strategic case for a direct link to the Internet, you need to think about several things:

◆ Approach the issue of the Internet not from a technology perspective, but from a strategic perspective. Examine the key strategy objectives for your organization. Relate how those objectives can be met through practical implementation of the Internet. Translate organizational goals into Internet activities. Speak the language that management understands.

Nothing will turn management off more than technical solutions to strategic problems. What management wants are strategic solutions to strategic problems, so ensure that you are speaking the right language!

◆ Understand what the Internet opportunities are for your organization. How are other, similar organizations using the Internet? What is your business competition doing? What are other schools doing? What are similar government bodies doing? This requires a fundamental, critical look at your organization in light of the opportunities presented by the Internet and means that you must determine which of your activities, such as working with your customers, could be supported through a link to the Internet.

If you work for a business, think about whether you sell your product internationally. If not, why not? Has the high cost of selling internationally prevented you from marketing in this way? Is there an opportunity to provide better customer service through the Internet? How might making customer support information available through the Internet improve business opportunities?

If you work for a school, are your students learning about computers, or are they using computers to learn? If you work for a government, do you have plans to use communications technology to reach your "customers," the citizens of this country?

◆ Determine if you are "internetwork" capable, or determine what you need to do to get there. Are you running or utilizing TCP/IP networking in your organization? If not, why not? What technology investments could you begin making to start on the road to Internet connectivity?

◆ Do not overhype the Internet. When it comes to the Internet and business, you should be realistic about the opportunities it presents, particularly when dealing with management. The Internet is changing the world of business, education, and government. However, in many ways, it is a slow and subtle change, and will not happen overnight.

◆ Be realistic about expectations. Do not promise sudden riches or expect revolutionary results. Instead, help the organization recognize that the Internet is a long-term investment as opposed to a short-term initiative. Plugging into the Internet will start you on the long road to discovering how to do business through networked systems in the years to come.

◆ Understand its limitations. The Internet is but one technology tool to help your organization. Understand the role of all communications technologies in your organization — not just the Internet — from a strategic, business perspective.

If you are looking for a lot of case studies on organizations successfully doing business on the global Internet, don't hold your breath. There are many organizations on the Internet experimenting, establishing resources, and putting up mail robots, mailing lists, and Web sites. Some are discovering what works, while others are discovering what doesn't work. There is no magic formula with respect to how to do business on the Internet, and there likely will not be for some time. What the Internet represents is nothing less than a completely new method of doing business, which means that it will be some time before we see major, significant success stories.

◆ Not everyone has Internet tools available. Many of the individuals linked to the Internet have simple e-mail access to Internet services. Many of these people have never signed onto a Web site. Fewer still have the high-speed access necessary to run the graphically oriented Netscape and Mosaic programs. The simple reality is that we are still in a period of transition and that it will be a long time before the Web is ubiquitous.

◆ Not everyone will adapt to the Internet. To be fair, the Internet remains, even with tools such as Mosaic, a little "geeky." Basic Internet tools need to mature before they are usable by the "rest of us."

All indications are that the Internet is a fundamental revolution in the way business is conducted around the world. When it comes to the Internet and your organization, keep in mind that even if you are not there, your competition and counterparts in the rest of the country and around the world will be. The most important thing to think about is that in order to avoid falling into a state of competitive disadvantage, it is important for you to determine how you should participate now.

CHAPTER 16

How to Get a World Wide Web Site

It's probably fair to say that no publishing medium has ever seen faster growth than the World Wide Web on the Internet. Spanning a mere handful of sites two years ago, the Web now stretches across thousands of systems around the world.

New Programs Untangle the Web Producing Documents for the Internet No Longer Needs to be a Laborious Process
Globe and Mail, May 16, 1995

How can I set up my own World Wide Web site? This is perhaps one of the most frequently asked questions in Canada from those who are dealing with the Internet. One of the key reasons the Internet is growing at such a furious pace is because anyone can have a Web page. In this chapter, we will take a look at what is involved. There are two basic issues: finding a home for your Web site and preparing the Web pages. We look at both issues as well as the cost of establishing a site.

A Home for Your Web Site

The first thing you need is a place to locate your Web site — a computer somewhere on the Internet that acts as an HTTP server. There are two options:

◆ You "rent" space on the computer of a company that will "host" the site on your behalf. This company runs an HTTP server program that is accessible through the Internet. (We discussed HTTP in Chapter 9 on the World Wide Web.) Most often, this company is an Internet service provider (which we talked about in a previous chapter). In addition to selling access to the Internet, these companies will rent space to you on their computer to host your Web site.

You could also look for an Internet presence provider, a company in the business of hosting (and developing) Web sites for individuals and organizations (as well as helping them establish such sites) on its own computer system. These companies focus on helping organizations develop an Internet *presence* on the Web and do not sell Internet *access* services to the general public. Thus they are sometimes a little more focused on their mission than Internet service providers.

Renting space is by far the easiest option. There are many Internet service and presence providers across Canada who would love to host your Web site for you. Just browse through the Canadian directory of Internet service providers in Appendix B to get an idea of which providers host Web sites. Talk to people within the Internet community to find out about Internet presence providers, or ask your Internet service provider.

You can also check out Yahoo at **http://www.yahoo.com/Business_and_Economy/ Companies/Internet_Presence_Providers/** for a comprehensive listing of Internet presence providers from around the world, including Canada. A review of some of the companies in this listing will give you an idea of the range of services offered.

◆ You "host" the site yourself by setting up a computer that has a full-time link to the Internet to act as an HTTP server. In this case, you have created or need to create a full-time link of your corporate network to the Internet so that one of your computers can be the HTTP server. Or you provide a full-time link from a dedicated personal computer or a multitasking computer (such as a Windows NT or UNIX system) to the Internet and run an HTTP server program on this computer. This is the more complicated route.

You would only establish your own Web site if it is related to your plans to establish a full-time link of your corporate network to the Internet, or if you have the technical expertise to establish a full-time link to the Internet from your own PC or multitasking system. Most such servers are based on UNIX systems, although as we will see at the end of the chapter, this is changing.

Let's look at an example wherein you would rent space. There are three Web sites associated with this book. The authors chose not to establish their own Web

HOW TO GET A WORLD WIDE WEB SITE

1 Many people who become familiar with the Internet want to know how they can establish their own World Wide Web site.

2 There are two options: you can host the Web site on your own computers, which are directly attached to the Internet, or rent space from a company that will host the site on your behalf.

3 You can undertake to design your own Web site or contract it out to an organization that specializes in Web site design.

4 There are a number of sophisticated and easy-to-use software programs available that permit you to create your own Web pages.

5 There are many, many third-party organizations that have jumped into the business of helping companies establish Web sites.

6 The cost to develop and support your Web site will depend on many factors, including the sophistication and design of the site, whether you do it yourself or whether you contract it out, and how frequently it is updated.

7 Soon it will become much easier for individuals to host their own Web sites.

server, but instead use the servers of two different Internet presence providers and that of one Internet service provider, who host these three Web sites. (Why three Web sites? No particular reason.)

The sites and the companies that host them can be found at

◆ **http://www.csi.nb.ca/handbook/**. This is our main book site and is hosted on the computers of Cybersmith Inc., an Internet presence provider located in Sackville, New Brunswick;

◆ **http://www.e-commerce.com/jacc.html**. This is Jim Carroll's Web site and is hosted on the computers of E-Commerce Inc., an Internet presence provider located in Mississauga, Ontario;

◆ **http://www.handbook.com/intervex**. This is Rick Broadhead's Web site and is hosted on the computers of InfoRamp, an Internet service provider located in Toronto.

It is very easy to find a location to host your Web site; there are literally hundreds of organizations across Canada that can help you.

An example of someone with his/her own Web site would be the folks behind the Primordial Schmooze site, which we discussed in Chapter 3; they have their own personal computer running the "Linux operating system" (a type of UNIX for Intel PCs), with an ISDN communication link into the Internet service provider InfoRamp. Hence they have their own computer on the Internet on a full-time basis on which they host their Web site. Obviously, they have the technical expertise to figure out what is involved in doing this.

Things to Ask

If you use an Internet service or presence provider to host your Web site, there are a few important questions you should ask:

◆ What is the speed of their link to the outside world, and how reliable is their service? You do not want to create a fantastic Web site only to discover that no one can access it because the communication link of your provider is too busy or the service is unreliable. Speed and reliability are important.

◆ Will they support use of your own domain name? Will they help you obtain and use your own domain name for a Web address, or will you be forced to be part of their domain name with some long, complicated directory structure. For example, you would likely prefer to have a Web address of **http://www.yourco.com**, rather than one of the form **http://provider.ca/homepages/companies/yourco.com**.

◆ Will they help you to promote the site? Do they have marketing and strategic expertise? Will they know all the areas and indices where your site should be indexed?

◆ What features do they offer on their Web server? For example, can they support **https**, the secure HTTP transfer protocol? Do they offer other features, such as Real Audio?

◆ Do they schedule maintenance for off-hours, or do they bring down the server to accomplish it whenever they feel like it?

◆ Will they permit you to directly control your site by allowing you to use FTP to upload your HTML files?

◆ Do they provide some type of statistical monitoring or allow you to obtain the "access logs" so that you can review detailed information about traffic at your site?

◆ What is their technical depth and attitude? You need a professional organization to provide your Web site, since reliability of service will be key.

Should you decide to host your own site, you will have to deal with many of these issues on your own.

Preparing the Web Pages

When it comes to creating the content for your Web site, there are once again two choices:

◆ You can create it yourself, by learning HTML or by learning to use an HTML editor;

◆ You can contract the design of your site to a third-party organization (i.e., hire a "Web company").

Create It Yourself

To create your own Web site, you can learn HTML, the language of the Web, and create your pages in any text editor or language in HTML format. As we described in Chapter 9, you can use the "View Source" command in Netscape or similar commands in other Web browsers to learn more about HTML coding. But today it makes more sense to use an HTML editor, a program specifically designed to help you create Web pages. And to find an HTML editor, you need look no further than Canada itself.

There must be something about Canadian winters. Canada has emerged as the country with some of the best leading-edge Windows-based HTML editors available. Reviews in various PC magazines show several of the products listed below as the top-ranked HTML editors in the world:

◆ HoTMetaL PRO 2.0 from SoftQuad (**http://www.sq.com/**);

◆ HTMLed from Internet Software Technologies (**http://www.ist.ca**);

◆ HTMLed from Internet Software Technologies (**ftp://tenb.mta.ca/pub/HTMLed/**);

◆ HTML Assistant (**http://fox.nstn.ca/~harawitz/index.html**);

◆ InContext Spider (**http://www.incontext.com**).

In many cases, you can retrieve evaluation or limited versions of the editors above on-line in order to try them out before purchasing. In this way, you can try the editors out to see what is involved in creating your own home pages. We strongly recommend this approach.

The sophistication of these packages is in many ways amazing. For example, in Chapter 9, we looked at the components of HTML and saw that it consisted of many special "tags" that define how information should be presented when it is accessed through the Web. Let's look at an example of two of these editors and how they handle these tags. Here is a section from the home page for this book as seen through Netscape:

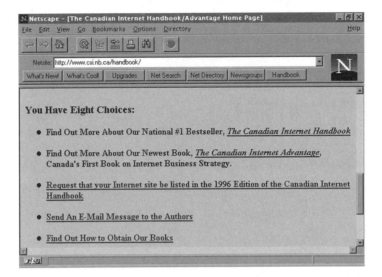

We can edit this HTML page in SoftQuad's HoTMetaL PRO 2.0, one of the most full-featured packages available:

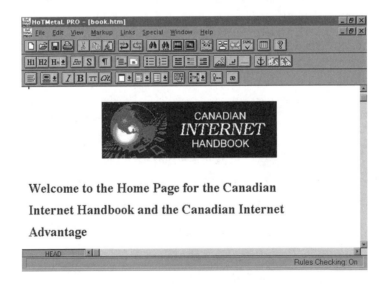

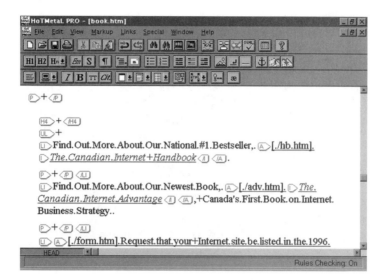

With this program, you have all kinds of flexibility in your creation of Web pages. Looking above, you will see that the editor includes

- ◆ the ability to italicize, bold, and bullet items;

- ◆ various hyptertext links (i.e., hb.htm), which are used to identify where this page should be linked to other pages;

- ◆ the ability to view images directly within the HTML document as you prepare it;

- ◆ special symbols for HTML tags (i.e., for paragraphs, list items, and "anchors," as described in Chapter 9).

The InContext program provides a somewhat similar yet different view, in which you can use a series of items on the left side of the screen to build your page:

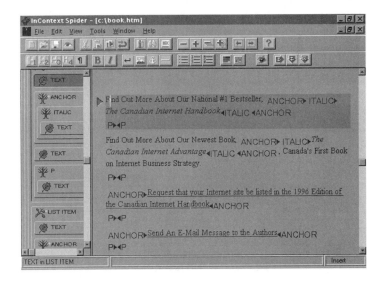

An important point is that with both of these programs, you can turn off "tag viewing" so that you can create your HTML pages without necessarily having to view all the tags. This permits you to prepare and edit your Web pages seeing only the items that you would see when viewing them on-line.

All five of the Web editor programs listed above are excellent alternatives and are highly recommended. You should try them out if you are interested in creating your own HTML pages. Since they are all Canadian, you would be supporting some important Canadian software innovators. You can find reviews of these and other HTML editors on-line as well as information about HTML editors for a variety of other computer platforms such as Macintosh at various sites on the Internet:

HTML editor reviews (Windows)

URL: **http://homepage.interaccess.com/~cdavis/edit_rev.html**

Macintosh WWW Development Resources

URL: **http://www.uwtc.washington.edu/Computing/WWW/Macintosh.html**

W3 and HTML Tools (comprehensive list for all platforms)

URL: **http://www.w3.org/hypertext/WWW/Tools/**

Also keep in mind that there are *extensive* resources on the Web itself to help you in your quest of learning how to create your own pages. Try **http://www.yahoo.com/Computers_and_Internet/Internet/World_Wide_Web/** to begin your exploration.

Hire a "Web Company"

If you do not want to take the time to learn how to create your own Web pages, you can hire someone to create them for you. In this case, you hire an individual or a company to create the Web pages on your behalf. There are many options that you can pursue. some days it seems that everyone and his/her dog is becoming an Internet presence provider. Consider some of the organizations that can help you in this regard:

◆ Advertising and marketing firms. Major Canadian advertising companies such as Padulo Advertising in Toronto have divisions that specialize in developing Web sites. Check with any major or minor advertising firm, and you will probably find they have some type of resource upon which you can draw.

◆ Internet service providers, that is, companies in the business of selling access to the Internet, are also very heavily involved in helping companies to establish Web sites.

◆ Internet presence providers, as discussed earlier. Not only will they host the Web site on your behalf, but they almost always design and maintain your site for you.

◆ Computer companies, ranging in size from mighty IBM to smaller computer consulting firms have jumped into the business of "creating Web sites."

◆ Other companies, including consulting companies, independent contractors, desktop publishers, graphic artists, graphic design firms, printing firms — the list goes on, with every type of organization imaginable getting involved.

◆ Just plain individuals — people who work at home, university students, high school kids, just about anyone.

As a result, there are all kinds of people and organizations who can help you to create and maintain a Web site.

Issues to Think about

When hiring an individual or organization to create and maintain your home page, there are several important things that you should think about:

◆ Track record, track record, track record. Have they developed other sites? Go and have a look. Get references. There is perhaps no more significant criterion.

◆ Business background. Anyone can create Web pages. The strategy behind the Web site is important. Look for someone with a good grasp of Internet strategy issues.

◆ Graphic design skills. Do they have a sense of graphic design? Are they artistic? Putting together a Web site is a bit more involved than just throwing together some information. Issues related to graphic design become very important, because the result must be visually pleasing to the eye.

◆ Marketing skills. Do they have skills in marketing through the Internet? Building a Web site is one thing. It is rather useless if no one comes to visit you. Hence you have to think of how to attract people to your site. They should be able to help in this regard.

◆ Programming skills. Do they have skills in "CGI-scripting" and UNIX program-ming? These are the skills used most often in the creation of Web sites; for example, these skills are used to create sites that promote a high level of interactivity and that allow the user to create sophisticated information forms. Anyone can learn to create basic HTML code, but the ability to create a site that permits visitors to complete comprehensive forms and the ability to process the data in those forms can be a spe-cialized skill.

What Does It Cost?

The next most popular question is "what does it cost to host/develop a Web site/home page?" The answer is, of course, "it depends."

Hosting Your Site

Internet presence and service providers charge wildly different rates to host Web sites. We suggest you shop around, compare rates, and clearly understand what you are getting for your investment. The directory of Canadian Internet service providers in Appendix B is a good place to start.

Developing Your Site

Asking what it costs to develop your Web site is as wide open a question as "what does it cost to prepare a brochure?" That depends, of course, on whether you do it yourself or whether you contract it out. Or whether you go black and white or full color, or two-sided or two-sided with a fold. Whether you design it yourself or you have someone design it on your behalf. Whether it has just text or a lot of graphics. Obviously, you can prepare a brochure quite inexpensively, or you can spend a fair chunk of money on it. The Web is not any differ-ent, and the money you pay for your Web site will depend on how far you go with it.

Keeping with our theme, you can create your brochure by learning desktop publishing software, by hiring a graphics desktop publishing effort to do it for you, or by hiring a profes-sional marketing company to do it. The same is true with the Web; you can create the pages for your Web site yourself using one of the editors above, or hire professionals to do it on your behalf. The cost of your site will vary accordingly, and the result will depend upon your own creative skills.

Hence answering what it costs to develop a Web site is wide open. We have seen situa-tions in which it costs less than a $100 (i.e., the cost of one of the HTML editors reviewed below) up to million-dollar Web campaigns involving major *Fortune 500* companies and large-scale national advertising firms, with the participation of specialized Internet presence providers. Obviously, what is right depends on your own circumstances — and your budget.

The Future

The most common option today for most people involves a Web site that is hosted by an Internet presence or service provider. It is simply too difficult and complex for people to set up their own Web servers. This will change over time, due to two factors:

◆ The introduction of high-speed cable and telephone link access to the home, as discussed in Chapter 10;

◆ The arrival of inexpensive, full-featured Web server software.

It used to be you had to establish a Web server within a UNIX system, and certainly many of us do not have the technical brilliance necessary to master UNIX. However, we are now seeing the arrival of Web server software for Windows NT (both shareware and commercial versions), Macintosh systems, and even Windows 3.1/95. A good example is WebSite. Originally available as a shareware program for the Windows NT platform, it is now a commercial product sold by O'Reilly & Associates, one of the most respected publishers of books for UNIX systems. WebSite turns a simple Windows NT or Windows 95 workstation into a Web server able to handle multiple Web requests. You can obtain a 60-day evaluation copy at **http://website.ora.com/**.

What does this mean? If you get a full-time link into the Internet, you can bring in a high-end PC, load it up with Windows NT or Windows 95, configure WebSite (which costs around U.S. $600), and you have got your own Web server. It really is a world in which anyone, anywhere, can be a publisher on the Internet at any time.

CHAPTER 17

The Internet in Canada: From Niche to Mainstream

More than one million Canadi-ans are connected to the Internet from their homes, according to an Angus Reid Group poll. In total, 17 per cent of adults — or 3.4 million people — have access to the globe-spanning web of computer networks from home, work, school or a public facility, such as a library.

Internet a Million Strong
Globe and Mail, July 5, 1995

Throughout 1995 it seemed that we could not pick up our telephone without hearing the question "Do you know of any demographic infor-mation about the Internet in Canada?" That is exaggerating a little, but with so many people and businesses seeking to understand how they can use the Internet, there has been a cry across the land for some type of statistical informa-tion with respect to Internet usage in Canada. We thought it was an appropriate issue to tackle, so we approached Canada's leading and most respected polling organization, the Angus Reid Group. They were pleased to share with readers of the *Canadian Internet Hand-book* the results of one of their most recent detailed surveys about use of the Internet in Canada.

Angus Reid is truly a household name in Canada. And given their advances in polling Canadians about their activities in cyberspace, the Angus Reid Group has come to be recog-nized as the Canadian polling organization most in tune with the needs, wants, desires, and activities of the emerging wired world.

Through sophisticated telephone interviews, focus groups, and other methods of collect-ing information, the Angus Reid Group regularly captures and summarizes information con-cerning consumer behavior, attitudes, and perceptions about users of the Internet in Canada. Their efforts provide a stunning and often fascinating view into what is driving the Internet forward in this country. And given the scientific polling methodology used, they certainly help to make some of the hype that surrounds the Internet real or, in other cases, provide concrete evidence to dispel certain myths.

The Angus Reid Group conducts such surveys on a regular basis. Detailed reports and analysis are available on a fee/subscription basis from Angus Reid. Such information is not inexpensive; the science of polling is a complex and expensive one and hence is the bread and butter of an organization like the Angus Reid Group. We would strongly encourage you to contact Angus Reid should you need more in-depth information than what we provide here.

Finally, we must note that much of the information provided in this chapter has been contributed to the *Canadian Internet Handbook* by the Angus Reid Group, but remains the copyright and property of the company and as such, may not be reproduced or reused without permission.

Survey Methodology

Angus Reid undertook an extensive series of interviews with 4,504 Canadians from the period August 21 to September 6, 1995, in order to come up with a sample of Internet users in Canada. From this sample group, they came up with 600 current users of the Internet, as well as 415 others who had definite plans to join the Internet within the next 12 months. The survey results are assumed to be accurate 19 times out of 20 and hence are assumed to be representative of all Internet users in Canada. It is important to note that these users are weighted regionally across Canada and thus give a true cross-Canada perspective.

The Internet: From Niche to Mainstream

Do you think that the Internet isn't a mainstream system, pervasive throughout Canadian society? Think again. Perhaps the most dramatic result of the Angus Reid survey is that almost one in five — 18% — Canadian adults in Canada have accessed the Internet from home or work. Another 12% plan to subscribe before September 1996.

The survey also indicated a substantial increase in the number of Internet users in Canada from a similar survey conducted three months earlier. We spoke to the founder of the Angus Reid Group, Angus Reid himself, about the survey: "In 1995

THE INTERNET IN CANADA: FROM NICHE TO MAINSTREAM

1. The Angus Reid Group, one of Canada's most widely respected polling groups, has undertaken intensive studies of Internet users in Canada and has been kind enough to share this information with readers of the *Canadian Internet Handbook*.

2. The number of Internet users in Canada is continuing to grow.

3. Over 41% of Canadian homes have personal computers, and 44% of Canadians use computers at work.

4. The typical Canadian Internet user is well educated, well paid, motivated, and very, very active on the Internet.

5. Internet e-mail and the World Wide Web are the most widely used applications, with continued strong growth in use of the Web.

6. Canadians on the Internet are not "cyberzombies" and still have a life.

7. Canadians on the Internet are concerned about sexual information, hate literature and gambling on the Internet, but most users of the Internet believe that self-regulation and industry regulation are the only solutions to these difficult issues.

8. The majority of Canadian users of the Internet believe that there should be some type of restriction on advertising on the Internet.

9. It will be some time before consumer behavior is clearly altered through the arrival of the Internet.

10. Most users of the Internet in Canada are extremely concerned about security and privacy issues on the Internet.

11. Few Canadians not on the Internet know where to turn to purchase Internet services.

12. Angus Reid believes that the Internet is in the early stages of a substantial shift with the arrival of many new users, comparable to the settling of the wild west by "city folk."

the world woke up to the Internet. The hype and media attention that the Internet received pushed this network of networks from the vocabulary of technophiles into the common vernacular. In Canada, the Angus Reid Group measured Internet usage at 17% in June and 18% in August." Such growth is indicative of the massive interest that one can find about the Internet right across Canada.

Why so much interest, and why such phenomenal growth? Reid believes one reason has to do with the high level of penetration of computers into the workplace and home. "The personal computer has almost completely saturated the Canadian workplace, with over 44% of Canadians using one to do their daily tasks. At the same time, increasing functionality at decreasing price points has moved 41% of Canadian households to purchase a computer."

The impact of such figures is stunning. Contrary to popular perception, the Internet is not a haven of cyberpunks, dweebs, geeks, and other assorted weirdos. In fact, quite the opposite is true. Users of the Internet in Canada are your friends, neighbors, co-workers — all kinds of normal, everyday, average people. Or are they average? Who are these people, and what is driving them to use the Internet? We take a look at them in a little more depth.

Who Are They?

A detailed review of the Angus Reid survey provides fascinating insight into the types of people you will find on the Internet:

◆ Sixty-eight percent were male and 32% female. The image that most of the Internet users in Canada are male is quickly dispelled, but it is still undeniably male-dominated. However, a further examination shows that more women plan to come on-line, indicating that women are starting to catch up to men on the Internet.

◆ Eighty-seven percent of them had a personal computer at home, and 76% of them use a computer at work in the performance of their jobs. Internet users in Canada and those who plan to join the network are a group of highly computer-literate individuals.

◆ Over 73% of those PCs had modems, of which 60% were of a speed of 14,400 Kb or faster. This would indicate that there is still a fairly large market for the sale of high-speed modems in Canada.

◆ Fifty-two percent of them use the Internet both for business and personal reasons, while only 11% use it strictly for business. Obviously, people are finding the Internet both as a business tool and as a source of entertainment and personal interest.

◆ Of those Canadian individuals on the Internet, 63% access the Internet more than four times a week, and 17% of them access it more than 14 times a week. Canadians who access the Internet do so fairly frequently. Ninety-eight percent of Canadians on the Internet access it at least once a week.

◆ Average use of the Internet by users in Canada is 7 hours per week, compared to 10 hours per week for television, 12 hours per week listening to the radio, and four hours reading the newspaper. The Internet has become a mainstream day-to-day activity for many Canadians.

- Seventy-nine percent have been using the Internet for less than two years. Clearly, the Internet in Canada is still very, very new to many Canadians; it is still in its infancy.

- Contrary to popular perception, rural areas are well represented in Internet usage, 26% of the existing users being in rural locations and 35% of planned users found in rural locations. This is due in many ways to the massive growth in the number of Internet service providers in rural locations in Canada as well as the result of local community efforts to bring Internet access to rural areas.

- Eighty-seven percent are paying less than $30 a month for their Internet connection. Clearly, a price point has been reached that has made the Internet acceptable to a broad cross section of society.

- Fifty-one percent of users of the Internet in Canada have children at home, of which only one in four uses the Internet. Surfing the Net would not yet appear to be a family activity. This will likely change as more Canadian schools link into the Internet.

- Almost half the Internet users in Canada access the Internet most often during the six hours between 6:00 p.m. and midnight compared to the other 18 hours during the day. This would imply that the vast majority access the Internet from their home PCs.

- A variety of different accounts are used in Canada by those accessing the Internet. Ninety-one percent of those who are on the Internet are satisfied with their Internet provider.

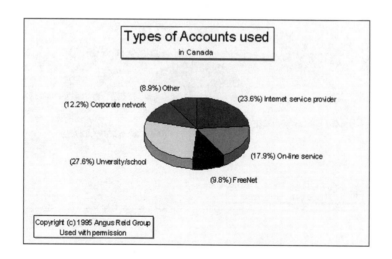

Types of Accounts used
in Canada

(8.9%) Other
(12.2%) Corporate network
(23.6%) Internet service provider
(27.6%) Unversity/school
(17.9%) On-line service
(9.8%) FreeNet

Copyright (c) 1995 Angus Reid Group
Used with permission

- Almost half the Internet users in Canada are under the age of 34, but there are quite a few between the ages of 35 and 44; the Internet has attracted the attention and interest of baby boomers, but is still very much a youth culture.

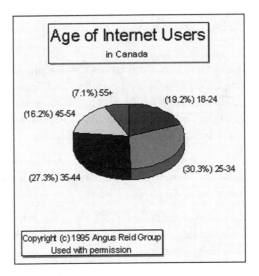

◆ Internet users in Canada are very well educated, with the majority having some level of university education.

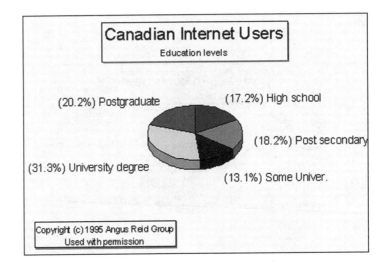

◆ Users of the Internet in Canada are an extremely affluent group of people. They have a healthy income, with almost half earning more than $60,000 per year, even though only one-quarter of the Canadian population falls into this income bracket.

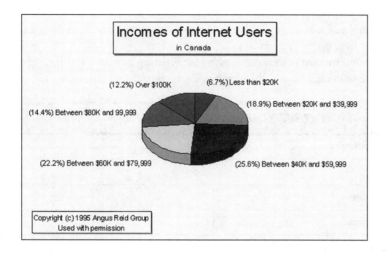

◆ Why is this so? Twenty-four percent of the users of the Internet in Canada are professionals, while the balance tend to be in executive, clerical, service, and retail businesses. There is little representation from blue collar and unskilled labor categories.

◆ Perhaps a more important point is that 36% of the Internet users in Canada report that they own a business, half of which are based in the home. Clearly, the Internet is a system that is permitting more and more Canadians to support business activities out of their homes. This is a fact that has stunning implications for the Canadian economy.

The typical Canadian Internet user is well educated, well paid, motivated, and *very, very active on the Internet.*

Why Do They Use It?

Of those individuals already on the Internet, a basic human trait — curiosity — led them to the network.

WHY DID THEY JOIN THE INTERNET?	
Curiosity	34%
Access to information	29
Conduct business	16
Job or school requirement	6
Personal entertainment	3

This is not that surprising. With the incredible amount of hype generated about the Internet in the last several years, it is inevitable that many Canadians have been drawn to the network to find out if it lives up to its promises.

Of even more interest is that the reasons for wanting to access the Internet are quite different for those who plan to join the network in the next 12 months:

WHY DO YOU WANT TO JOIN THE INTERNET?	
Access to information	54%
Curiosity	16
Conduct business	10
Social interaction	7
Personal entertainment	5

This would indicate that the motivation to join the Internet is now changing from simple curiosity to more practical reasons. Clearly, people who adopt technology early (and who needed to satisfy their curiosity) are now mostly on the network. But we are now seeing people who are slower to adapt to new technology move onto the network for a more practical reason: access to information. This indicates that the Internet is becoming more mainstream and will continue to spread through Canadian society. Clearly, many more people now see the Internet as a useful tool.

Are They Staying On-Line?

Does the Internet live up to people's expectations? From one perspective, no. Of those on-line, a little more than half think that the impact of the information highway and the Internet on society has been overstated. Perhaps people are tired of hype and want reality.

But clearly people are finding reasons to be on-line. *Ninety-six percent of existing users of the Internet in Canada access it at least once a week.* Digging even deeper, the Angus Reid survey indicates that the Internet *met or exceeded the expectations of over 85% of people who use it in Canada.* Fifty-nine percent of the users of the Internet in Canada use it "frequently" or "fairly often."

Are People Scared of the Internet?

Most users of the Internet in Canada think that they are pretty good navigators of the network, with four of five users indicating that they would rank themselves in the "expert/skilled" category of Internet user, rather than the "not skilled" category. This is an interesting finding, since it helps new users of the Internet realize that maybe it is not all that difficult.

Many do not venture near the Internet because they think it is going to be too difficult to use. But look to the experience of these "cyberpioneers" — 87% of those who use the Internet in Canada are satisfied with its general ease of use, and 78% are satisfied that it is "easy to navigate." And 81% indicate that they are not scared of the complexity of the Internet.

Even given that most find it easy to use, there are some frustrations. For example, if you look deeper, you will find that one of the major frustrations that Internet users in Canada have is the ability to find information; more than one-third indicate that it is too difficult to find what they want on the Internet.

Thus there is a paradox at work here: the Internet is easy to use, but it is difficult to find specific information. This is one reason why we are seeing systems like Yahoo, OpenText, and other search systems on the Internet gain such a high degree of attention.

In summary, when it comes to the Internet in Canada, the Angus Reid survey indicates that you should not be scared of getting on-line. Clearly, those who are venturing into the Internet are discovering something of value once there, and they are not finding it too difficult to "drive the information highway."

What Do They Use It for?

In this book we have looked at many Internet applications and have commented on the usefulness of those applications. For example, in Chapter 7 we noted that "many organizations have discovered that a link to Internet e-mail is the most useful application of all Internet capabilities." In Chapter 9 we commented that "most people are learning how to use this wired world through the World Wide Web, because it is the easiest, funniest, and most exciting area of the Internet." Certainly the Angus Reid study reflects these statements:

APPLICATION	HAVE USED AT ONE POINT	MOST FREQUENTLY USED
E-mail	89%	46%
World Wide Web	79	32
USENET	66	8
Gopher	64	4
FTP	59	5
IRC	33	3

Most Internet users in Canada have experience with the majority of the Internet applications outlined in this book, but the vast majority clearly indicate that e-mail and the Web are the applications most often used.

What is quite surprising is that while many have tried USENET, few use it on a regular basis. Many people have difficulty in discovering the value of USENET, while others stay away because of its wild, anarchic nature. USENET is not representative of the Internet mainstream.

Use of the World Wide Web and E-Mail

Almost half the Internet users in Canada indicated that their level of usage of the Web had increased in the last six months. It is a system that is growing and will continue to grow as the number of sites increases at a frenetic pace. Clearly, the Web is "where it's at." However, an important point to keep in mind is that many companies in Canada interested in pursuing business strategies on the Internet often focus solely on the World Wide Web. This is likely a mistake, for they should not ignore e-mail.

Organizations getting involved with business strategy on the Internet should ensure that they consider how they can take advantage of the widespread use of Internet electronic mail, such as through the use of voluntary e-mail lists, given that it is still the dominant application on the Internet.

Boredom On-Line?

Even given the result above, it is also interesting to note that 13% of users of the Internet in Canada report that they have decreased the amount of time that they spend on the World Wide Web. Most of them indicate that this was due to such factors as leaving school (and hence losing their accounts) or simply having less available time, reasons not having to do with the Web. But, looking further, we can see that 3% of Canadians reported that the novelty of the Web was beginning to wear off. This is a figure that should be watched closely in the years to come to determine the real impact of the Internet over time.

The Impact of the Internet on Our Lives

The myth is often perpetuated that people on the Internet are all a bunch of cyberzombies; all they do is stare into their screens and pound away at their keyboards all day long. Social scientists bemoan the idea that cyberculture is turning people away from regular social interaction and into a bunch of computer-focused droids, too lost in their monitors to have a real life. Hogwash. If the Angus Reid survey has a key message, it is that people on the Internet in Canada *have a life*. We need to keep in mind that the Internet is just a tool — albeit an extremely useful one — and that most people view it as such. As we will see below, the Internet does not necessarily draw people away from other activities in their regular everyday lives.

The Impact of the Internet on TV, Radio, and Newspapers

For example, the Angus Reid survey showed that most of the current users of the Internet in Canada were watching TV, reading newspapers, and listening to radio as often as they did before.

ACTIVITY	LESS	SAME	MORE
Watching television	39%	59%	2%
Listening to radio	12	82	6
Reading newspapers	17	76	7

So from one perspective, the Internet does not replace traditional activities; we need to keep in mind that it is simply another communications source in our lives and that it will not necessarily supplant other day-to-day activities. Or will it? Perhaps the most interesting point about the numbers above is that it is television that appears to suffer the most from the arrival of the Internet. Is the Internet an ominous sign for TV? Talk to anyone who has discovered the World Wide Web and you will find that for many it has become a source of entertainment. Factor into this the statistic that almost half of Internet access is between 6:00 p.m. and midnight. Clearly, people are spending less time watching TV in the evening and more time surfing the Web. And it is not surprising that this is the case. As the technology begins to emerge in which the Web becomes a "million-channel universe" (as we discussed in Chapter 10), we might see an even more dramatic impact on TV in the near future.

Think about what seems to be happening here. Even after the introduction of many more channels to the Canadian cable TV system, people find less of a reason to watch TV and more of a reason to be on the Internet. The people watching less TV are those who advertisers love to reach: wealthy, well-educated Canadians. This should be a telling sign for companies investing their advertising and marketing dollars in television.

As everyone in the world becomes a publisher and a producer of information, perhaps the future will see a shift away from traditional producers and publishers of information to the world of the Internet in which everyone is a producer and publisher of information.

The Impact of the Internet on the Way We Communicate

People on the Internet are all a bunch of cyberzombies, locked up in their room all day, who have forgotten how to communicate with the real world? Not quite. Take a look at the impact of the Internet on other, normal, everyday activities:

ACTIVITY	LESS	SAME	MORE
E-mailing correspondence	4%	16%	78%
Mailing letters/documents	48	43	9
Long distance	34	56	9
Faxing documents	23	53	24
Local telephone	12	79	9
Visiting friends/business associates	11	81	7

Clearly, the majority of Internet users in Canada still make phone calls, send faxes, and visit real people in real life as often as they did before.

As use of the Internet expands throughout Canadian society, it is obvious that it is just another communications tool. We are foolhardy if we believe that it will replace the other ways that we communicate (at least in the short term). We are foolish if we believe the "prophets of doom" and "media elites" who warn us that Internet users risk becoming a bunch of zombies without a life. Even so, there are two interesting observations that we can draw from the information above:

◆ Obviously with the large increase in use of e-mail that comes with the Internet (it is, after all, one of the main applications of the network) comes a corresponding decrease in sending letters and documents by regular mail. This is not surprising; many Canadians are discovering many of the efficiencies and dramatic cost savings of e-mail as discussed in Chapter 7. Perhaps the Internet will begin to have a real impact on Canada Post over time.

◆ A little over one-third of the Internet users in Canada reported they were spending less time on long distance calls. Obviously, people are sending more e-mail and spending less on long distance phone calls. The Internet is having a direct impact on long distance telephone revenue. What might happen in the future? With the release of software as discussed in Chapter 10 that permits people to make telephone calls through the Internet, this will certainly be a number and trend to watch.

The Impact of the Internet on Society

Netsurfers are constantly being told that they swim in a swamp of sexual depravity. They console themselves by noting that their critics — religious conservatives, censorious feminists and parents who mistake the Internet for a playground for children — usually have little knowledge of the Internet and a lot of experience in social pressure.

A Gross Distortion of the Porn Picture
Globe and Mail, July 14, 1995

If you become a user of the Internet, you might as well get used to the fact that many people will believe that all you do is use it to look at dirty pictures all day long. As we discuss in the next chapter, there is an often fraudulent and deceptive degree of reporting in the media about the issue of pornography on the Internet. The result of such reporting is that many Canadians are led to believe that the Internet is a "swamp of sexual depravity," as noted in the *Globe and Mail* article above.

No doubt there is controversial and illegal information on-line; we are not here to deny that fact. And indeed, the Angus Reid survey shows that typical users of the Internet in Canada are concerned enough that most believe that there should be restrictions on certain types of information on the Internet:

AVAILABILITY OF INFORMATION	SEXUAL IMAGES	HATE LITERATURE	GAMBLING
Should be available to anyone	12%	11%	12%
Should be available but with restrictions	50	19	30
Should not be available	38	69	57

Clearly, there is little tolerance on the Internet for hate literature and an attitude that there should be some form of restriction on the distribution of sexual imagery through the Internet. This is not surprising, since 51% of Internet users in Canada have children and are thus indicating concern about the exposure of children to inappropriate material through the network. Does this mean that the government should step in and police the Internet? No! According to Internet users in Canada, when it comes to policing the Internet, most believe that it is the actual Internet that should be responsible for policing itself, by the users of the Internet industry:

RESPONSIBILITY FOR SCREENING CONTENT	
Users of the Internet	27%
Internet service providers	21
CRTC	25
RCMP	9
CSIS (Canadian Security and Intelligence Service)	6

Fewer than half of those interviewed believe that there is any type of role for government in the screening of content on the network.

What is even more interesting is the finding that actual users of the Internet were more likely to call for screening by the Internet user. Those who plan on joining the Internet in the next 12 months believed otherwise; for example, that the CRTC should take on such a role.

Clearly, once people join the Internet, they gain an appreciation of the futility of law and regulation when it comes to content on the network. But before they join the network, they naively believe that technical solutions are possible.

We also believe that it is due to the fact that we are dealing with an intelligent, educated crowd of people who realize the futility of trying to control the Internet on a technical level. Clearly, users of the Internet in Canada are concerned about offensive content on the Internet, but also believe that the problem is best dealt with through self-regulation. Government and Internet critics in Canada would do well to take notice.

Business on the Internet

Another hot topic is business on the Internet. The Internet is becoming increasingly commercialized, particularly the World Wide Web. Today, there is widespread acceptance of the inevitability of advertising on the Internet and the likelihood that home shopping will be available.

AVAILABILITY OF INFORMATION	ADVERTISING	HOME SHOPPING
Should be available to anyone	40%	54%
Should be available but with restrictions	48	37
Should not be available	11	8

Over one-half of the users of the Internet in Canada believe that advertising on the Internet should have some restrictions. Companies need to be cognizant of the extreme sensitivity of the Internet to advertising on-line, as we discussed in Chapter 15. What is surprising are the ways that Canadians on the Internet say that it should be restricted:

RESTRICTIONS ON ADVERTISING	
Ads only for those who want them	17%
No alcohol/cigarette	13
Not to minors	12
Limit space and time of advertising	12
Should be same restrictions as for other media	10

The consensus is emerging that advertising and marketing through the Internet is acceptable, but there are restrictions.

Influence on Consumer Behavior

Has the Internet, and advertising through the network, influenced consumer behavior? Not to a great degree:

- ◆ Sixty-three percent of the users of the Internet in Canada have not requested more information about a product or service as the result of advertising on the Web or other areas of the Internet.

- ◆ Advertising on the Internet has had no impact on purchasing decisions for 82% of the users of the Internet in Canada.

Why is this so? We believe it is simply because the Internet is still in its infancy when it comes to consumer behavior. As we noted earlier, almost four of five users of the Internet in Canada have been on the network for less than two years. It should be obvious that it will take some time for the Internet to really begin influencing consumer behavior in this country. That is why we caution people to be realistic about the Internet opportunity; it will take some time to emerge.

Will the Opportunity Emerge?

What will it take before the Internet really begins to influence consumer behavior? The Angus Reid study examined this concept by taking a look at three questions:

- ◆ Do people know how to access information about particular topics on-line (i.e., skills)?

- ◆ Have they accessed that information on the Internet (i.e., action)?

- ◆ If that information were available, would they access it (i.e., intent)?

By examining consumer behavior from these three perspectives, Angus Reid wanted to determine what barriers existed to business on-line from the perspective of the consumer. The poll found that while people are very aware that they can access information about particular goods and services on the Internet, few have actually taken the time to access this information for personal use. If given the chance, however, they would look for such information.

In other words, most users of the Internet in Canada possess the *skills* necessary to find consumer-related information on the Internet, have the *intent* of finding and using such information, but few are undertaking the *actions* to get this information. This is clearly a paradox. What is going on?

We believe that this indicates that it is a behavioral issue. It has to be that people in Canada are still learning what it is like to be an "electronic consumer." They are still learning about the Internet and are taking some time to modify their behavior by virtue of what they have learned. So it is not surprising given that most have only been on the Internet for less than two years. Let's take a look at the specific results:

AVAILABILITY OF INFORMATION	AWARE THEY CAN ACCESS ON-LINE	HAVE ACCESSED ON-LINE	INTERESTED IN ACCESSING IF AVAILABLE
Current news information	92%	76%	91%
Home banking capabilities	28	4	68
Gaming, i.e., lotteries	24	3	13
Government services	44	22	90
Health care information	72	34	86
Automotive information	48	14	66
Education information or courses	59	21	87
Retail information or shopping on-line	67	21	63
Ticketing purchases for entertainment	41	6	76
Travel information and booking	63	19	78

One can assume from such figures that business on the Internet is impeded simply because most of the users of the Internet in Canada are still learning about what it is to *live and function* in this on-line world; they are interested in accessing certain information on-line, know how to find it, but few have done it. For example, 72% were aware that they can access health care information on the Internet, but fewer than 34% have actually done so. Sixty-seven per-cent are aware that you can purchase things on-line, but 21% have done so. But in both cases, the vast majority express an interest in getting such information on-line.

The Angus Reid survey confirms the opinion of many that it will take some time before we become "electronic consumers." As we wrote in our *Canadian Internet Advantage* book, "We are still a society of consumers learning how to shop electronically." That much is clear from a review of these numbers regarding the mindset of the Internet user today. Hence you should be realistic if you plan to use the Internet for business purposes and recognize that it will take some time for the Internet to change the *behavior* of the consumer.

Security and Privacy

Another barrier in the way of business on-line is the consumer concern about security and privacy. Quite clearly, existing users of the Internet in Canada are very concerned about the potential for misuse of sensitive information through the network. The Angus Reid survey provides a tantalizing glimpse into the minds of these users on this issue:

CONCERN ABOUT ACCESS TO:	PERSONAL INFOR- MATION	CREDIT CARD INFOR- MATION	SECURITY OF MONEY EXCHANGE	SECURITY OVER BANK INFOR- MATION
Very con-cerned	61%	75%	56%	72%
Somewhat concerned	25	17	28	18
Not very con-cerned	8	5	10	6
Not at all con-cerned	5	3	5	3

In addition, 90% of the users of the Internet in Canada agreed that each transaction on the Internet should be electronically safeguarded against interception. Furthermore, an over-whelming majority expressed concern over any collection of information about what they do on-line. Consequently, organizations seeking to do business on the Internet must be sure to address these security and privacy concerns in their approach to customer-based activities on the Internet; hence these issues should be in the forefront of any attempts to do business through the Internet.

The Internet Industry

Finally, a very interesting fact from the survey would indicate that the Canadian Internet industry has definitely done a *lousy job* of promoting itself. Of the 415 potential users of the Internet (those who plan to join within the year), fewer than half (42%) knew where to buy Internet access.[1] This for an industry that now boasts well over 300 service providers in Canada. Clearly, companies involved in the Canadian Internet industry should be considering ways of promoting themselves through a trade association or some other method.

What also becomes apparent is that almost one-third of those who use the Internet are opposed to Canadian cable and telephone companies entering the Internet industry. This is a telling figure, for it indicates that there is still some concern on the Internet over the involvement of larger companies. But if given a choice between the two, most users of the Internet in Canada would prefer to purchase Internet services from a telephone company instead of a cable company, one reason, perhaps, why we are seeing a rush of telephone companies into the Internet business.

What Do We Want from Internet Access?

One item comes through loud and clear in the Angus Reid survey: Canadians do not necessarily want less expensive access to the Internet; they simply want faster access.

DESIRED IMPROVEMENTS	
Faster access	44%
Easier access to information	36
Cheaper access	10

And secondary to that, they want easier methods of finding and accessing information. Hence the market spoils will clearly go to those organizations that can provide faster access to the Internet.

Why So Much Interest in the Internet?

The Angus Reid survey is but a first glimpse into the unique world of the Internet in Canada. When dealing with a survey, numbers and statistics provide fascinating insight into a topic. However, we should not lose sight of what the numbers really mean. We asked Reid to share his observations of what the survey tells us: why are so many people and organizations being driven to the Internet?

First off is an increasing emphasis on computerization. Notes Reid: "In the workplace the impetus is twofold. In the face of the corporate restructuring and re-engineering that has been forced upon corporate Canada by new global economics, the only path to maintaining our standard of living is through increased productivity from the front line to the executive suite. While this has occurred, our economy has shifted from a manufacturing or 'hard goods' base into a service oriented or 'soft goods' base. Canada is leading the way in developing the knowledge-based economy of the future, an economy that demands that individuals are able to access information quickly and easily. The personal computer has been the single most

---

1. In an ominous note for this book, less than 1% of them would plan to use a book to find an Internet access provider. Far more (56%) plan to use family, friends, or associates to guide them. We would like to ask you to tell your friends, families, and associates about this book!

active ingredient in Canada's renewed and growing productivity by increasing our productivity and allowing us to compete on a global scale."

There are many more fundamental reasons that have led to the fact that 41% of Canadian homes have a computer. "In the household, three forces have driven demand. First, many Canadians are finding that in order to keep pace with the demands that working in a competitive work environment place on their lives, they must be able to stretch their productivity outside of traditional office space and office hours. These busy individuals are looking to increase their personal productivity, yet still need to manage their personal and family lives. Canadians are coming home, spending precious time with their children until bedtime and then switching on their home PC or portable computers for one last assault against their ever-growing work loads."

The second reason has to do with concern for the future, notes Reid, which helps to lead parents to the Internet. "Canadian parents are seeing the wave of the future and insuring that their children will be familiar with the tools that will shape this future. Computer usage is just a start; many parents are insisting that their children are multi-media and Internet savvy as well. The home PC is the guilt purchase of the 90's, with more and more parents citing their children as their primary purchase motivation."

And perhaps one of the most significant trends has to do with the trend towards working at home and the rise of the home office. "Today, with advances in technology and telecommunications, the workplace has lost its need to be centralized. Many individuals are finding good reasons to avoid traffic and commuting, finding that they are much better off to work from home for either part or all of the week."

Examples are found throughout the corporate world, says Reid. "Chiat Day, a major international advertising agency, has decided that the investment in large amounts of expensive downtown office space does not result in better advertising. In fact, their bold initiative to have creative and account services work from home on projects for the bulk of their time, while banding together as necessary in teams within centralized locations, has increased creativity and boosted morale."

There is also a significant home office trend. "Many individuals who have been victims of down-sizing or have decided to abandon their corporate lives are starting up small and home offices. The SOHO (small office/home office) phenomenon has been made possible by the fact that individuals can create a highly productive office environment with all the functionality of a major corporation for less than $30,000."

Early Adopters of the Internet

The impact of all these trends is an increase in computer usage and literacy across Canada, a trend that lays the foundation for usage of the Internet. Angus Reid believes that from analysis of the survey we can extrapolate why there is now such heightened interest in and rapid growth of the Internet.

"To begin, current Internet users are the ultimate in early adopters. They have the latest in PC technology (CD ROM, high-speed modems, Pentium chips) and they have a burning passion to be on the cutting edge of new technologies. For these early adopters, the Internet has been a cyber-frontier, full of the same lawless behavior that typified the wild west of

North America. These pioneers have rushed into the open plain and have created a world that has a wealth of potential, with just enough anarchy thrown in to make things interesting."

So we see in the numbers above the mindset of the current Internet user, the cyberpioneer. But what of the Internet in the future? To answer that question, we must examine the perceptions of the new wave of people beginning to use the Internet.

A New Wave of Internet Users

Reid notes a warning, however, that one must dig deeper than just looking at existing users to understand the future of the Internet. "As the Internet moves from its niche roots to a more mainstream base, we can expect to see things change." In undertaking its survey, Angus Reid separately analyzed the responses to many of the questions by examining the responses of those who are already on the Internet against those who were planning to join the network. Clearly, the attitudes of those planning to join the Internet in the near future will be indicative of how the Internet might change.

Reid offers his thoughts on what the survey tells us: "Current Internet users are progressive, male urbanites who are young, well educated, and affluent, but clearly this is changing as the next wave of netizens immigrates to cyber-space."

Reid believes that the survey results show that a significant change will soon be coming to the Internet, part of which is due to the fact that its population is changing. "Rural and small town populations with less education and more representation from the female gender and the 35–54 age range are joining the ranks of the Internet user. These people are more likely to represent either grey, pink and blue collar occupations (sales, clerical and labor positions), or business owners and operators. They are more likely to come from middle income households earning between $20,000 and $40,000 with children."

Significantly, the reasons to join the Internet are different for this new wave of people. "While the demographics of the new breed of Internet user is much less young, male and upscale, the motivation for their wanting to access the Internet is the fundamental difference between the cyberpioneer and the cyberimmigrant. When we asked current Internet users why they were first interested in accessing the Internet, 34% of them responded 'curiosity' versus 28% who cited 'access to information.' Yet when we asked future or potential Internet users why they are interested in obtaining access to the Internet only 16% responded 'curiosity' versus 54% who cited 'access to information'."

What does this mean? New users are looking for practical Internet applications. "As in the wild west, the first wave of Internet users were adventurers, true early adopters and technophiles that saw the act of exploring new lands as reason enough to jump on board. The next wave of Internet users is not interested in adventure as much as in utility. They see the Internet as a valuable tool that will allow them to expand their productivity and value." What is really happening is that people now view the Internet as an important and useful tool, rather than a fascinating new "toy" to be explored.

What this portends for organizations seeking to do business on the Internet is that the mindset of the "electronic consumer" will begin to emerge. "The utility that is accrued to this new Internet user depends on the specific Internet tool that is used. From e-mail to the World Wide Web, the Internet has been increasing its usefulness. The new wave of Internet users has specific needs that they are matching with the capabilities of the Internet. The first tool that brought in these more utilitarian users was e-mail. Then, the potential for information retrieval on general topics — for example, world trade statistics — as well as very specific topics such as information on health management for cancer victims brought in more utilitarian minded users."

The result is that Reid believes the numbers show that the "electronic consumer" is imminent. "There are vast possibilities for entertainment and shopping to become new tools or utilities that will bring in new users who want to 'do something real' on the Internet."

These New Users Are Concerned

Earlier we commented that the majority of users of the Internet in Canada believe that the Internet should be self-regulating. But Angus Reid believes that by examining the attitudes of those who plan to join the Internet, compared to those already on the network, one can see the signs that the next wave of Internet immigrants believes that self-regulation might not be the answer. "The new wave of netizens is much less interested in a rough and tumble, anarchistic approach to life on the Net. With their utilitarian focus, they are much more concerned about the security of credit card and financial transactions on the Internet and they are wary of giving out personal information and are more fearful of lurking and stalking on the Net. Finally, and most importantly, they are looking for someone to play 'Sheriff' on the Internet. They are concerned about the lack of government enforcement of national, provincial or local laws. They are much more likely than current users to look to the C.R.T.C., the R.C.M.P. or C.S.I.S. to be responsible for screening content on the Internet."

It is because their motivations are different that they have different attitudes to regulation of the Internet. "They are moving to Internet City to take up a respectable place in society. They plan to become consumers of many different types of products and services, but want to make sure that they are living and doing business someplace safe."

What the survey confirms for us, notes Reid, is that the Internet is in a period of rapid and wrenching change. "The movement of the Internet from its anarchic and wild west roots to a place where a status quo is established and enforced may sadden or anger the pioneers. In the wild west, the cowboy and the farmer took to violence over the fencing in of open plains. Cowboys wanted to be able to move across the free range unhindered by legalities of property ownership and constricting social demands, while farmers wanted to make sure that they could count on law and order to keep themselves and their families safe and prosperous in the new world."

Reid thinks that history is about to repeat itself. "The trending on the Internet from niche to mainstream gives us another opportunity to observe that the more things change, the more they stay the same."

Fraud and Deception

If you are a user of the Internet or are about to become one, you are probably aware of the growing number of calls for censorship of the Internet. In 1995, the Internet came under attack like it has never before. Calls erupted for its control, its censorship, its regulation. Members of Parliament stood up calling for government action, while well-meaning organizations pleaded for regulation to stop a flow of hate literature on the Internet. Parents recoiled in horror at the concept of the Internet, given what they have heard about it. In Canada and elsewhere around the world, the clamor for regulation of the Internet reached a feverish pitch. And the average Canadian would likely believe that all most people with a connection to the Internet did was look at dirty pictures all day long.

It is no wonder. Many of these people, not familiar with the reality of the Internet, are relying on media coverage that in some cases is guilty of fraud and dishonesty in its reporting and coverage of the Internet.

The authors of this book are the first to agree that the Internet presents Canada and indeed the world with some very serious and difficult moral and legal issues. As we wrote in Chapter 8, "the Internet, when it comes to pornography and other questionable information, does present society with some difficult challenges. Join certain USENET newsgroups and you can find pornography. Pornography is a fact of life in our real society, and it is a fact of life in our virtual society. But USENET is used for the distribution of information that is of questionable taste, is in violation of the laws of Canada, or runs against current accepted 'community standards', for example, for the distribution of material related to pedophilia."

The problems that the Internet introduces are serious. Somehow society around the world must learn to deal with them. The authors of this book believe that in all practicality we cannot deal with these issues on a technical level, and that the only way to do so would be to unplug every single telephone in the country. This seems rather unlikely. We need to deal with the difficult issues with a level of intelligence and maturity. Sadly, quite often, this intelligence and maturity are lacking in our media.

The authors of this book, like many Internet users in Canada, are sometimes disgusted with the fraud and deception that often permeates coverage of these difficult Internet issues in the media. There is no doubt that the Internet presents us with difficult issues. We as Canadians have to learn how to deal with these issues. But we cannot hope to start dealing with them as long as we have media, politicians, and spokespeople for national organizations who find a need to sensationalize the Internet through the national media.

We Need Maturity in Our Media

As the Internet continues to enter the mainstream, inevitably its more unsavory aspects catch the attention of the media novice. A new reporter stumbles across the Internet, discovers it has dirty pictures, and writes an article that the Internet is full of dirty pictures! *Shock! Horror!*

Think about some of the coverage you have seen about the Internet. People are faced with an endless supply of news stories that "the Internet is full of pornography" or that "Nazis are using the Internet to get hate literature into the hands of our youth" or that "you can find information on how to build bombs on the Internet." The number of sensationalized news stories in Canada about the Internet has grown as general coverage of the Internet has grown.

The impact? If you become a user of the Internet, people are going to suspect that all you do is look at dirty pictures all day. Try explaining the Internet to your 78-year-old mother, and she will think it is an electronic type of *Playboy* magazine, or even worse. But a more real, sinister impact is that these sensational articles fuel the calls for censorship and control of the Internet.

The media has a need to sensationalize the news. After all, that is what sells newspapers. And it has found a perfect target with the Internet. But one of the challenges

FRAUD AND DECEPTION

1. The Internet presents Canada and indeed the world with some very serious and difficult moral and legal issues.

2. These issues need to be dealt with in an intelligent and mature way.

3. Unfortunately some in the media, certain politicians, and spokespeople for national organizations seem to lack these two qualities.

4. The story of DeathNET published in the *Calgary Sun* in March 1995 and picked up by many other Canadian newspapers is one example of how certain reporters find a way to sensationalize aspects of the Internet without paying attention to the facts.

5. The *Time* Magazine "cyberporn" article of July 1995 is another example where the need to have a sensational news story got in the way of honest, professional journalism.

6. Many have called for the Internet to be regulated and censored, but fail to recognize the technical impossibility of doing so.

7. We need responsible media coverage of the Internet in Canada, rather than stupid, dishonest, and fraudulent reporting.

of course is that sometimes the sensational media coverage of the Internet is simply not true. The authors acknowledge that there are many responsible, intelligent and ethical media reporters who take the time to report on the Internet from a balanced point of view. But there are also those who do not.

DeathNET

Consider this example of a story that went wrong. In 1995, the Canadian Right to Die Society established a site on the World Wide Web. The organization is involved in matters related to euthanasia and suicide for the terminally ill. There is no doubt that these are difficult and complex issues and that many people tend to find themselves on one extreme or another with respect to this issue. We live in a complex society, and we are faced with many complex issues such as euthanasia.

In March 1995, the *Calgary Sun* printed an article about the arrival of DeathNET on the Internet. The article was soon picked up and reprinted across the country. Here are some of the headlines that appeared:

"Suicide Advice Sold on Internet: Experts Worried Teens at Risk," *The Halifax Daily News*, March 13, 1995;

"Suicide Guru Using Internet to Tell Teens How To Die; Canadian Youth Experts Blast Service," *The Toronto Sun*, March 12, 1995;

"Suicide Manual Available on Internet: How-to Guide Threatens Teens and Other Vulnerable Groups, Mental-Health Advocate Warns," *Kitchener – Waterloo Record*, March 13, 1995;

"DeathNEt a How-to on Committing Suicide; 'It would be a good idea to ban this outright', Mental Health Official Says," *The Spectator*, March 13, 1995;

"DeathNEt Offers Graphic Advice on How Users Can Commit Suicide," *Montreal Gazette*, March 13, 1995.

Now, if you knew nothing about the Internet and read these headlines, you would probably believe that through DeathNET, anyone on the Internet could obtain detailed suicide instructions. With headlines like this, hysteria rules the day.

Understandably so, the reaction of many normal, everyday, non-Net-literate Canadians would be that the Internet is this terrible, terrible system, full of information that will assist our young people in killing themselves. The reality compared to what you read in the headlines above is quite different. But it seems that in this case, reality had little to do with the media coverage. After all, reality does not sell newspapers, does it?

Let's probe the story a little further:

◆ DeathNET does not provide information about suicide on-line and never has. If you want such information, the Canadian Right to Die Society will make it available to you; however, you have to be a member for three months; this prerequisite is to discourage impulsive people from obtaining such information.

◆ If you do need such information, you can go to a library or bookstore. Bookstores across the country do contain detailed suicide information. Explains John Hofsess, Executive Director, the Right to Die Society of Canada: "Anyone of any age can walk into a bookstore and buy or order a copy of Derek Humphry's *Final Exit*. It was on the international best-seller lists in both the *New York Times* and *Globe and Mail* in 1991–1992, selling some 500,000 copies in hardcover alone. It is now available in paperback."

◆ Libraries across the country carry the book *Final Exit*; the Edmonton Public Library, for example, has 16 copies.

◆ What does DeathNET contain? In one case, extensive federal government information. John Hofsess comments: "In September, after considerable effort, we were granted exclusive permission by the Senate of Canada to make available on-line the complete hearings of the Senate Special Committee on Euthanasia and Assisted Suicide. This marked the first time that the Senate had released information electronically. We are also the only on-line source of this material....So far, we have installed the first thirteen weeks of public hearings (in French and English interleaf format); another batch of diskettes is due in the coming week."

Visiting the World Wide Web site, you will read that "DeathNET offers the world's largest collection of 'right to die' materials and services on the Internet. It gathers together a wide array of information dealing with specific illnesses and severe disabilities — especially those of a life-threatening nature. It provides connecting links to medical libraries and other on-line services dealing with bereavement, caregiving, emotional support and counselling. DeathNET also provides expert advice on 'living wills', palliative care, and all aspects of assisted suicide and euthanasia. There are more than 650 individual files on DeathNET (as of August 20, 1995); and more than 125 links to other medical and health-related resources."

This is certainly far different from the media distortion reported in the press.

Suicide information is not available nor is it sold on DeathNET.

The issues of euthanasia and right-to-die/right-to-life are extremely complicated, emotional, and difficult topics. They are best dealt with maturity, sensitivity, knowledge, and information. They cannot be dealt with through sensationalism.

Does reality count when it comes to reporting about the Internet? Reading the press reports, apparently not. The entire DeathNET media event should become a classic case study of the downright fraud and deception that can occur in our national media through sensationalistic reporting.

Perhaps the best report of the sheer media irresponsibility in this case was written by Toronto's K.K. Campbell, in his *eye* magazine column (**http://www.interlog.com/eye/**). K.K. is known for his graphic writing style, and so we reprint his entire article with permission, unedited. Keep in mind, of course, that if some of the calls for censorship of the Internet succeed, this article would violate proposed laws, due to its use of certain words.

---

eye WEEKLY (Toronto)

May 11, 1995

THE LITTLE DEATHNET STORY THAT GREW

Why many people now believe that teens can login and learn how to off themselves

by

K.K. CAMPBELL

Last December, eyeNET presented readers that most irreplaceable of Internet resources, the "How To Kill Yourself" file. It gives detailed instructions on creative ways to end one's life. It has circulated the net for years, uploaded to newsgroups and found languishing in FTP sites such as Canadian universities, where it is particularly useful come exam time.

Of it, I wrote: "Some of the ways are serious, drawn from references like Derek Humphry, publisher of Hemlock — and some aren't. It's not hard to guess which is which ... One wonders how long before the Hard Copy-esque legions who staff mainstream media news outlets discover it: Suicide Tips On The Information Superhighway! Film at 11!"

Let's fast-forward: Sunday, March 12. Out at Bathurst and College St, enjoying the spring-like day, I spied a somewhat startling *Toronto Sun* front page headline — startling not only because it was actually more than one word, but because it read: SUICIDE GURU USING INTERNET TO TELL TEENS HOW TO DIE.

Looking around and not seeing eye staff snickering and spluttering in doorways, I deduced it was not one of those phony mock-up papers and dug out some coin to read it. (The article now proudly adorns wall space in eyeNET's luxurious HQ.)

This *Toronto Sun* "exclusive" was bylined Steve Chase of the *Calgary Sun*. It opens: "An American suicide advocate has teamed up with his Canadian counterpart to flog a how-to manual across the Internet, the *Sunday Sun* has learned."

Personally, I'm of the opinion that the *Toronto Sun* might better serve readers if, in its next net story, the phrase "the *Sunday Sun* has learned" is immediately followed by the phrase "how to login."

I immediately realized they were writing not about the How To Kill Yourself Guide but DeathNET. DeathNET is one of the many informational/research tools on the World Wide Web. It deals with the controversial "right to die" issue.

One might have just chalked this up to another sensationalistic pro-censorship *Sun* story, except this one would eventually be picked up around the world. Millions of people were told DeathNET is helping teens use the Internet to learn how to kill themselves.

THE UNBLINKING NEWS SYSTEM

DeathNET — http://www.islandnet.com/~deathnet — is maintained by Victoria, B.C., resident John Hofsess (jh@islandnet.com), executive director of the Right to Die Society of Canada. It's an info-rich site, even including the massive transcripts from the Senate Special Committee on Euthanasia and Assisted Suicide. (The American content is maintained by Oregon's Derek Humphry, founder of the National Hemlock Society and author of *Final Exit*.) It opened Jan. 10.

On March 5, *Calgary Sun* managing editor Chris Nelson — who admits he's net- illiterate — saw Hofsess on a TV show. Hofsess was discussing DeathNET. Somehow Nelson thought this meant DeathNET was openly distributing technical information on performing efficient suicide. Suicide kits.

Nelson immediately assigned someone to cover his exclusive and the *Calgary Sun* went into a full-court press on The Big Story: "Suicide tips on the information superhighway."

One *Sun* editor phoned Anne Mullens — the former *Vancouver Sun* science and medical reporter who won the 1993–94 Atkinson Foundation Award for Public Policy and wrote an eight-part series on euthanasia. The *Calgary Sun* correctly realized it would be hard to find a more expert source — especially as Mullens is also quite net.savvy.

"The *Sun* employee (I can't remember her name) asked if I knew anything about an Internet site in Victoria freely distributing tips to help teenagers die," Mullens told eyeNET. "I told her, 'If you mean DeathNET, you're way off base. DeathNET does nothing of the kind and is, in fact, a wonderful resource for writers and researchers.' "

Among the several "expert opinion" quotes in the final story, the *Calgary Sun* would somehow forget to include Mullens.

Nelson assigned *Sun* business reporter Steve Chase (chase@freenet.calgary.ab.ca) to actually find the site. Chase did so and started exploring it on March 7.

(Turns out I'd had contact with Chase before. On Feb. 14, he wrote eye email applauding our web site and asking for advice on books to learn about bringing newspapers onto the Internet. I never responded.)

Chase sent Hofsess no less than three pieces of email, pretending to be a teenager requesting information on how to kill himself, asking that his family not be told about his request. They were all signed Steve Chase. Hofsess replied that one cannot get such information on the Internet.

Chase had directly attempted to get "a suicide kit" while pretending to be a teenager. The *Calgary Sun* would somehow forget to include this.

Upon that failure, Chase dropped the charade and called Hofsess directly, leaving a message on Hofsess' machine. Hofsess, hearing the name Steve Chase again, suddenly realized what was happening. He wrote another piece of email to Chase, demanding the "troubled teen" never call him again.

As Chase would later admit to me in a phone conversation, he was (and remains) extremely ticked off Hofsess refused to grant him that interview. A few days later, the *Sun* story was released.

STICK IT WHERE THE SUN DON'T SHINE

In the story, the *Calgary Sun* had no choice but to admit one can't actually get "suicide kits" on the Internet after all — much to Nelson's dismay. So they cobbled together a paragraph as a sort of legal disclaimer, mentioning this fact.

However, the entire tone of the story is exactly as if DeathNET is giving away "suicide kits" to teens on the evil Internet. And it's clear all the aghast "experts" quoted are reacting to Chase's panic-mongering assertion that DeathNET is openly posting on the net suicide tips.

The "exclusive" came out simultaneously in the *Ottawa* and *Toronto Suns*. With a stunning flourish of editorial wizardry, the *Toronto Sun* actually cut the critical ass-covering paragraph from their story. Chase would later complain about this. The *Toronto Sun* editors either deliberately removed it because it took away from the impact of the story, or were too dense to understand its importance.

All this was pretty bad, but it got worse. The next day, CP rewrote the *Calgary Sun* copy and launched it across the wires. Newspapers across the country carried the CP story — the *Edmonton Journal*, *Hamilton Spectator* and *Vancouver Sun*, among others. Then the electronic news gang soon scooped. A couple of talk shows even called Hofsess, hoping to book the evil man who was giving suicide tips to troubled teens on the evil Internet.

The myth then hit the op-ed pages. For instance, on March 17, *The Globe and Mail* ran a piece coauthored by Bernie Farber of the Canadian Jewish Congress. Farber presented the myth as fact to further his own agenda of invoking government legislation to censor the net.

Then the Associated Press picked up the story and who knows where it went from there. Last sighting: England's London *Sunday Times*.

'GOD WILL PUNISH YOU!'

Hofsess was soon receiving harassing phone calls from "right to life" right-wing extremists. On the receiving end of this news media juggernaut, he found the only way to fight back at all was through the most powerful grassroots "broadcast" medium he could find: netnews. The newsgroups.

Hofsess wrote a two-part criticism ("Inventing Internet Hysteria") of the *Calgary Sun* story in can.info highway. In it, he made public copies of Chase's "troubled teen" emails. (He also transcribed Chase's answering machine message. In that message, Chase left his work and home phone numbers — which Hofsess included for all the world to read, a nasty trick, to be sure. Chase got a taste of harassment himself, discovering censorship is a dirty word on the net.)

> Chase directly responded to Hofsess' posts. The post remains an embarrassment to read. Besides being formatted a la raging newbie, it flames Hofsess in the lamest of manners. Chase ignored Hofsess' complaints about the story itself and attacked Hofsess personally. Not surprisingly, Chase was flamed in return by a few readers across Canada.
>
> Chase's intense personal dislike of Hofsess, as evidenced in his reply, might help explain why the *Calgary Sun* disregarded Anne Mullens; why it did not report Chase's complete failure to get "suicide tips on the Internet"; why it ignored the enormous wealth of research data on DeathNET while obsessing over the existence of a book called *Departing Drugs* in the mail-order section.
>
> But most disheartening is the way the story swept the entire country without anybody ever calling Hofsess to confirm. Considering the nature of the Internet, it is the easiest thing in the world to see DeathNET firsthand.
>
> My conversation with *Calgary Sun* editor Nelson got very heated when I suggested his story was bull. We started yelling at each other, I insistent the story was a gross misrepresentation designed to invoke censorship, he retorting angrily, "Oh ho! What's your interest in this?! What's your interest in this?!" — as if only some hidden motive could explain why anyone would think his story was a piece of shit.
>
> I realize now why Nelson was so defensive: he and Chase had experienced a strong backlash to their story, not from the newspaper-reading community but from the net.community. Netters implicitly understood what the *Sun* story was really about: hysteria intended to provoke censorship.
>
> "It's interesting that all positive feedback I got came through email or postings to newsgroups," Hofsess told eyeNET. "While anything negative — including crank calls telling me that 'God will punish you!' — came from people unfamiliar with the net — the gullible readers of the *Sun* and other newspapers."

You should, at this point, be appalled with the situation. Do the words fraud, deception, dishonesty, and duplicity cross your mind? These were words used on the Internet at the time to describe the situation.

People on the Internet cannot come up with sufficient adjectives to describe their disgust with the Canadian media with respect to the coverage afforded the DeathNET situation. Canadians clearly deserve better. One often wonders if we should place more faith in USENET newsgroups like **alt.elvis.sighting** instead of traditional news media.

Time and "Cyberporn"

The DeathNET example is not an isolated case. Such media irresponsibility is not limited to the Canadian press. Consider *Time*. In 1995, it published a cover story, "Cyberporn," that reported that 83.5% of the images on the Internet were pornographic. The cover read: "CYBERPORN EXCLUSIVE: A new study shows how pervasive and wild it really is. Can we protect our kids — and free speech." It is a shocking article when you read it in *Time*. And surely it has meant that those Canadians who read it are disgusted with this thing called the Internet. After all, 83.5%! Dig a bit deeper, and you will discover another case of media dishonesty. As reported by the respected publication *Wired* (**http://www.hotwired.com/special/pornscare/**): "According to *Time* magazine, pornography is pervasive in the online world. The national weekly magazine's 3 July cover story — with a cover illustration of a young boy staring into the blue glow of a computer screen — is billed as an evaluation of a pornography 'study.' There is a major problem with the *Time* story. It is not true."

Dig deeper. The truth? Reality? The following has since become evident:

◆ The study has no scientific credibility and is deeply flawed. As noted by researchers who have examined the so-called study in-depth: "these flaws and errors are sufficiently severe that neither the Rimm study nor the *Time* cover story should be taken seriously by policy makers considering issues involving the Internet and the so-called 'Information Superhighway'" (**http://www2000.ogsm.vanderbilt.edu/cyberporn.debate.cgi**).

The study upon which *Time* relied was done by an undergraduate and did not undergo normal university level peer review. The accuracy of the study has now become completely disproven by several leading U.S. researchers, who have clearly indicated how the methodology was deeply flawed. Full details of how such a deeply flawed study could form the basis of an article by a national magazine can be found at the World Wide Web site above, as well as many detailed analyses of the study methodology and the reasons why it is flawed.

◆ Analysis of the process that *Time* used to generate the article indicated several serious flaws in its editorial process, which some believe indicated that *Time* seemed to be purposely ignoring the truth in favor of a sensational headline. It became evident to many that *Time* studiously ignored experts familiar with the study, who were trying to wake it up to the fact that the study was flawed, in order to ensure that it could put out a sensational story. Details of this are also available on the Web site above and are fully documented. It is a rather disgusting story in itself.

◆ *Time* printed a "mea culpa" several weeks later. It buried its reporting of its error way at the back of the magazine. *Time* is not one to admit to mistakes loudly, in public. However, the average person probably still believes that the flawed article is true.

◆ The 83.5% figure is a make-believe number, *based on a review only of those USENET newsgroups known to carry pornography*. If you examine the newsgroups known to carry pornography, of course you will discover that the majority have dirty pictures! The real number? Further analysis has come up with numbers of less than 1/2 of 1% within USENET.

◆ But it is the 83.5% number that is now widely bandied about — a U.S. Congressman proudly held up the *Time* article in Congress yelling that 83.5% of the Internet was pornography and that it should be controlled and censored!

How easy is it for a responsible media outlet to fall into the trap of sensationalizing the Internet? If they are that stupid, should we not be able to convince them that 80% of magazines are full of pornography?

It should be easy. Say you go into your local corner store. You go to the top shelf, the one that holds *Playboy*, *Playgirl*, and other assorted pornographic magazines. You look at them all! Over 80% of them contain dirty pictures, you conclude! Well, of course they do. You went to the shelf with the dirty pictures, after all. But now, based on your review, you draw the amazing conclusion that 80% of *all* magazines consist of dirty pictures! You sell this conclusion to *Time*. After all, it is leading-edge research. And *Time* prints it. It becomes fact. Eighty percent of all magazines have dirty pictures, concludes *Time*!

This is the same type of study that *Time* magazine relied upon for its cyberporn cover story. Disgusted? *Wired* magazine was, so much so that it established a special "JournoPorn" site devoted to taking apart how a magazine like *Time* could make such a stupid mistake (**http://www.hotwired.com/special/pornscare/**):

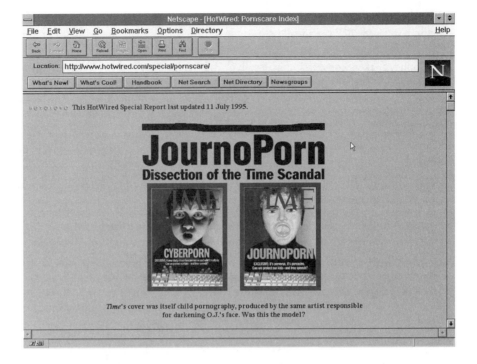

Time's cover was itself child pornography, produced by the same artist responsible for darkening O.J.'s face. Was this the model?

In it, *Wired* notes about the article: " 'Much of it may be bogus, error-ridden, or just plain wrong.' When *Time* magazine's Philip Elmer-DeWitt wrote those words more than a year ago, he was describing news on the Net. In retrospect, it seems he's found the perfect sentence to describe the news in *Time* magazine. 'Bogus,' 'error-ridden,' and 'just plain wrong' are only a few of the terms being used by journalists and Net experts to describe both the 'Cyberporn' cover story in the 3 July issue of *Time* and the study it used as a story hook. In this special section, HotWired destroys both story and study."

If it were not so sad, we would almost laugh. The unfortunate thing is that the general public does not see the reality. The amazing thing is that a publication like *Time*, in its quest to sensationalize the Internet, makes such a major mistake. As *Wired* magazine wrote, "should we be dismayed that the nation's largest newsweekly could fall for a 'scientific' study so shoddy that it seems hardly distinguishable from a hoax on the order of the Hitler Diaries?" Do you sense a pattern here?

We Need Media Reality

These are but two examples. We could go on with others. Clearly, something is lacking when it comes to media coverage of the difficult issues associated with the Internet. There is no doubt that the Internet poses challenging questions to society. There is pornography, child pornography, and illegal, disgusting, and revolting information on-line. We are not trying to deny that. One of the authors responded to a "hysteria" article within the *Globe and Mail*, in an article printed on March 21, 1995.

I know the Internet, and it's not a cauldron of evils

The *Globe and Mail* Commentary March 21, 1995

by Jim Carroll

FEEDBACK / *Yes, there's a small amount of disgusting stuff on the Internet, but to blow it out of proportion is to insult the network's users. And, given the impossibility of controlling digital bits in our wired world, those users are the ones who will have to deal with the hateful materials.*

In seeking support for a clamp-down on the Internet (Something Wicked This Way Comes, And It's On the Internet-March 16), Hal Joffe and Bernie Farber use a scare tactic: stories of pipe bombs and pornography and pedophilia, guaranteed to raise the ire of the average Canadian.

In many ways this is typical of the sensationalist media coverage of the Internet. One need look no further than any Canadian newspaper to believe that the 'Net consists of a bunch of teen-aged boys who, when they're not breaking into NORAD defence computers around the world, are staring at pictures of naked women on their Internet screens all day while they trade E-mail with tips on how to blow up the Pentagon. As the co-author of a best-selling book about the Internet, I get a lot of calls from members of the press, and their first question is often "Isn't the Internet full of pornography (or pedophiles or Nazis or hackers or dweebs or geeks)?"

C'mon! The reality is far different. Tens of millions of people sign on to the Internet every day to do research. Companies are discovering new ways to compete globally through the Internet. Global knowledge access throughout the Internet has become fundamental to the regular working lives of many millions of people. Science, business — our entire world — is transformed as the whole of human knowledge becomes available in electronic form. And yes, some fringe elements use the Internet too.

Often the level of Internet hysteria becomes, well, silly. The recent DeathNet nonsense in the press, repeated in the Joffe-Farber article, is a good example. The situation is this: The Right to Die Society of Canada recently established an Internet site. The press printed shocking stories that the Internet now "gives explicit instructions on how to commit suicide." Mr. Joffe and Mr. Farber repeated this line without any further research on their part, lending credibility to misreporting.

In fact, suicide information is *not* available on the Internet through DeathNet. What the media haven't bothered to report is that DeathNet contains mostly information that exists in libraries and bookstores across the land, and that visitors to DeathNet must wait three months before receiving "suicide information" from the organization. (Heck, if someone wants to commit suicide, all he or she has to do is pick up a copy of *Final Exit*, a book that has sold some 500,000 copies in North America.)

As for "details on making pipe bombs," sure: Someone posted such information to the Internet — and anyone with a library card can go to the Library of Congress in Washington or many other major libraries in the world and check out a book that instructs readers in the building of *atomic bombs*. Read *Soldier of Fortune* magazine and you'll find advertisements that enable anyone (including kids) to order all kinds of nasty stuff. Pornography on the Internet? Excuse me, but has anyone walked down Yonge Street in Toronto lately, or gone into a video store?

Am I missing something here? Much of this information seems to be available in our real world. Why should we expect to control it in our virtual world?

Let me say that I entirely sympathize with the author's concern about the distribution of hate literature on the Internet. On the other hand, I am a realist; I know, as *The Economist* recently put it, that "technological change will open new possibilities so fast that government efforts to regulate it and control it will seem ponderous."

Let's think about what is happening here. The Internet is simply the leading edge of a trend in which all the computers in the world are plugging together. These computers can exchange digital bits, the binary language of our wired world, through global telecommunication networks: television, satellites, cell phones, microwave dishes. I am a realist: In the same way that I understand it to be impossible for anyone to control what millions of people might say through their telephones at any given moment, I understand it to be impossible to control what digital bits people might choose to exchange at the same time.

I have been on the Internet for some six years, and I have never heard anyone tell me of a feasible technical solution to the challenge presented by these digital bits. (Well, there was one, but I don't think we want Canada to become a sort of North Korea by unplugging every single telephone in every home and office, for good.)

Brilliant computer "geeks" — the geniuses building the technology of the information highway — understand that digital 1's and 0's have no respect for national laws, national borders and national controls. They understand that these digital bits travel the world at breathtaking speeds, via billions and trillions of different routes on our global communication spine. Shut down one digital route, and digital bits discover another, instantly. If we accept the impossibility of controlling digital bits in our wired world (and I do), we need a lot more maturity in our discussions about the Internet's impact on our society.

I am the first to agree that the Internet — in fact, our entire digital society — presents some pretty challenging issues. No doubt the global exchange of digital bits results in the distribution of information that is of questionable taste, is in violation of the laws of Canada or runs against currently accepted community standards. There is some pretty disgusting stuff out there.

But folks must realize that they won't succeed in obtaining support in dealing with hate literature on the Internet if they insult the intelligence of the many members of the Internet community — average, hard-working, intelligent Canadians — by resorting to sensationalism. Hysteria breeds contempt.

The solution? The other day I encountered my first neo-Nazis on the 'Net, a madman spouting hate. You know what happened? A bunch of Internet citizens ran him out of town. Chased him away. Sent him packing. Gave him the big heave-ho. I saw Internet providers refuse to sell him an account. I saw a community galvanized into action.

What I saw was a community — a global nation called the Internet — that has learned to deal with the challenges presented by free-flowing literature on the Internet. It's staring you in the face, and its name is the Internet.

Yes, you can find information on bomb building in *Encyclopedia Britannica*, in your home or library. You can find disgusting pornography in corner stores, video stores, and in department stores. You can find suicide information faster in your local library than you can on the Internet.

How ridiculous does the situation get? In Canada, there is a mailing list sponsored by Electronic Frontier Canada in which people discuss some of the inanities in our press and issues related to electronic censorship. Details on joining can be found at their site, which is mentioned below. Consider the following note from that group:

From:	"Mike Robinson" <mrobinso@netaccess.on.ca>
To:	efc-talk@insight.dcss.McMaster.CA
Date sent:	Fri, 1 Sep 1995 00:37:41 +0000
Subject:	Re: cops can't stop cyberspace bomb recipes
Priority:	normal

Send reply to: "Mike Robinson" <mrobinso@netaccess.on.ca>

on Thu, 31 Aug 95 20:51:45 EDT

David Jones wrote...

> hot off the AP wire service, 31aug95

>

> Police Patrol "Lawless" Info Highway

> MONTREAL (AP) -- Police cruising the information highway are

> frustrated there aren't laws they can enforce against dangerous

> data such as recipes to make bombs, a convention on electronic

> security heard Thursday.

>

> "It's a lawless territory", said RCMP Cpl. Dominique Delage,

> an officer with the force's computer crime section in Montreal.

>

> -snip-
>

> "We as police are against bomb recipes but we can't do anything

> about it", added Sgt. John Norris, of the same RCMP department.

>

> "We're patrolling the highway but we don't have a ticket book."

Funny. Heavily armed military style police forces vs. information stream. It's

par for the course that domination is sought over new frontiers. Much of what

is available to the public on the Internet is available at a public library or

bookstore. The Book Villa in downtown Hamilton has copies of *The Anarchists'*

Cookbook available at about $20.00 a pop, and with another $10 in chemicals

available at IGA any jerk could put together a device large enough to blow a

storefront out.

You can't cure a sick tree by trimming the leaves.

Look there for the symptoms, then work on the roots.

The problem isn't the Internet or the people using it.

Mike Robinson

<mrobinso@netaccess.on.ca>

"The Police are the persons who can arrange for us to have less crime

news in the newspapers." ~Herbert V. Prochnow

We need to keep things in perspective. Ask yourself a question. Should the RCMP be able to control bomb information on the Internet, if it ignores information on how to build bombs as found in libraries and bookstores? Does any of this make sense?

We as a society have to learn to deal with all the difficult things that the Internet presents in addition to the wonderful opportunities it provides. We will not learn to deal with these things if the media coverage of it is stupid, dishonest, and fraudulent, and we will not do it if the average Canadian reads such fraudulent and dishonest information.

What we are pleading for, and what all Canadians need to be cognizant of, is a need for maturity, responsibility, honesty, and integrity in our media when it comes to coverage of the Internet. Sensationalism and all the other characteristics seen with the DeathNET and *Time* magazine situations should play no role in what our media does.

What can you do as a user of the Internet? Be vigilant. Fight back. When you see the sensational article, write a letter to the editor. Speak out. Help reporters understand both sides of the story. Become involved in Electronic Frontier Canada, by visiting their site at **gopher:// insight.mcmaster.ca:70/11/org/efc**.

Take the time to become acquainted with the issue. Understand the reality first, and not the hysteria. A good starting point can be found on-line at **http://www.yahoo.com/Government/ Politics/Censorship/Censorship_and_the_Net/**, which provides pointers to many sites of information about censorship and the Internet.

Notes John Hofsess of the Right to Die Society: "It's time for the Internet to strike back at unscrupulous journalists who exploit the general public's ignorance and fear of the new communications technology. We may not own newspapers, radio or television stations but we are not powerless in dealing with institutionalized forms of stupidity." In many ways, Canada is at a crossroads with the Internet, and it is important that you understand what is going on.

Is the Internet Real?

Is the Internet just like CB radio, a passing fad? In the 1994 edition of this book, we wrote that "in the final days leading up to the conclusion of writing this book, the level of Internet hype within the media seemed to reach a feverish pitch...." Wow, were we wrong! The hype then was nothing compared to the hype of today.

The problem with too much hype — certainly a problem from which the Internet suffers — is that hype causes skepticism. Sometimes such skepticism can be well-founded. It shouldn't be in this case. We do not believe that the Internet is a CB radio. We believe it is more like a telephone, and that it is here to stay. And we will explain why in this chapter.

An Incredible Rate of Change

If there is any type of trend with the Internet today, it is that its rate of change is accelerating rather than slowing down.

Part of the challenge in writing a book about the Internet is learning how to deal with this rate of change. For example, as we go to press, Netscape is about to release version 2.0 of its Netscape browser software. It is a significant software release and will set the standard for, and indeed change, the Internet for a long time to come. But most of the information in this book was prepared using version 1.2 of that software, all that was available to us in the summer of 1995. We will likely update this book soon after it is printed to reflect the change.

As we write about companies involved in the Internet industry, we discover in the week following that they have merged, have been bought out, or taken over. As we write about sites on the World Wide Web, we discover that they have changed overnight or in other cases have simply disappeared. Once we list e-mail addresses, people move on or establish new careers, invalidating the address. Once we complete the most comprehensive list of Internet resources in Canada, we discover a substantial number of brand-new sites in the week before we go to print. As soon as we write about a new piece of Internet software, we hear of announcements by 20 other software companies of something similar. The rate of change with the Internet is relentless.

When we released the 1994 edition of this book, many individuals and organizations were still thinking of the Internet as a "geek experiment." What is now evident is that the experiment conjured up by these brilliant geeks worked.

The Internet has a momentum that is unequaled in the computer industry. It shows no signs of slowing down. Talk to a computer executive, listen to others in the computer industry, and you will discover that the entire industry realizes that we are at the crest of a significant and fundamental change in the entire role of PCs. And it is not only the computer industry. Talk to any executive in any industry, and you will likely find a growing awareness of the importance of the Internet. Talk to a government official and you will hear the same. Talk to an average Canadian, and you will find an awareness that something "big" is happening.

For many, the Internet conjures up a sense of awe, much of which comes from how fast it is moving and evolving. But why is the Internet "happening" so quickly? Three trends have come together that are driving the Internet forward at an incredible pace:

- ◆ A computer industry being fueled by the realization that the Internet will forever change the role of computers and that this represents huge new opportunities;

- ◆ A communications industry that has now realized the Internet is a system that is fundamentally changing the rules of global telecommunications;

- ◆ Individuals and organizations who realize something important seems to be happening.

IS THE INTERNET REAL?

1 The Internet can no longer be called a passing fad; it is more like the telephone, here to stay.

2 The Internet is considered by many to be the most important development in the computer industry since the IBM PC was introduced in 1981.

3 With the Internet we see a computer industry that realizes the Internet will forever change the role of computers, a telecommunications industry that has realized that the Internet is changing the rules for global telecommunications, and individuals and organizations who are discovering that the Internet provides them with new activities and capabilities on their computers.

4 All these factors mean that the Internet is very real and is quickly becoming as ubiquitous as the telephone in our daily lives.

The Computer Industry

At first, many software companies were caught unaware by the Internet explosion. Most are now scrambling to catch up. Everywhere you turn, companies are releasing new Internet access software. Software to make it easier for you to access and browse the Internet. Or software that helps you build Web sites or provides security, or software for on-line credit card ordering. Or software to help you monitor your Web site. Or software that integrates corporate databases to the Internet. The list goes on and on.

Let's look at one example. In Chapter 13 we examined some of the Internet access software emerging in the marketplace, "suites" that provide everything you need to link into the Internet. The growth in the number of such "suites" is relentless. Delrina, for example, a company famous for its WinFax Pro software, has released CyberJack 7.0, a program that "gives you all the tools you'll need to make traveling the Net easy and fun," according to their press release. This from a company in which the President, Mark Skapinker, was stating as recently as March 1995 at a major Canadian computing conference that the Internet was full of holes, populated only by young male geeks, that there was no security and that hence people should not risk their time working their way around such a ridiculous system. Now they are embracing the Internet. How quickly things change, and how quickly people eat humble pie.

Far more important than the release of individual computing programs to browse the Internet is the fact that the Internet is really becoming integrated into the global economy. The companies that develop the tools that will drive the economy forward will become very significant, very quickly. Consider Netscape. When it went public in 1995, this company (with $16 million in sales) was valued by Wall Street at close to $2 billion. Why? Because of the belief by many that Netscape is the company that will largely define the future of the Internet and, hence, the future of our global business world for a long time to come.

Perhaps the most important development on the Internet is the release of HotJava by Sun Microsystems. HotJava will change the Internet in ways that many do not yet fully comprehend. As noted in *Forbes ASAP*, "Your computer will never be the same."[1] If you want to comprehend the future of computing on our planet, watch HotJava.

Wherever you look, you can see an industry that is galvanized into action by the arrival of the Internet. As Bill Gates observed, "The surging popularity of the communications network called the Internet is the most important single development in the computer industry since the IBM PC was introduced in 1981.... Like the PC, the Internet is a tidal wave. It will wash over the computer industry and many others, drowning those who don't learn to swim in its waves. The Internet has shortcomings, but they will be overcome."[2]

The Communications Industry

The communications industry worldwide was also caught unaware by the Internet, but it is now struggling to catch up. The Internet is clearly coming to dominate the agenda of many major telecommunication organizations. From the perspective of the telephone and cable

---

1.   Telecosm: The Coming Software Shift, *Forbes ASAP*, August 28, 1995.
2.   Bill Gates, Internet Gaining PC-like Momentum, *The Halifax Daily News*, August 18, 1995.

companies two or three years ago, the Internet was a bit of a joke. How might this world of "geeks" and "dweebs" and cyberidiots possibly affect their grand visions of an "information highway?" Of course it couldn't!

It was originally assumed that the information highway was all about television. As we wrote in Chapter 1, "In this vision, the telecommunication companies would control the infrastructure. They would run the wires. They would publish content. They would become not just cable and telephone companies, but 'information companies' and 'multimedia conglomerates.'"

Consider an article from 1994, about the merger of Canada's two largest cable companies: "Rogers Communications Inc. and Maclean Hunter Ltd. struck a surprise deal yesterday that clears the way for one of the biggest takeovers in Canadian history. The agreement means that Rogers will spend about $3 billion to buy Maclean Hunter and create a huge media conglomerate with holdings across Canada in cable television, telecommunications, broadcasting and publishing....Ted Rogers, the company's president and controlling shareholder, said the takeover will produce a company with the ability to build a Canadian 'information highway' and to create programming for it."[3]

In effect, they would control the printing press and the means of distribution, since they would control television. The information highway to them? A system with 500 TV channels, video on demand, and the ability to order fried-chicken through your TV remote control! How wrong they have been.

Listen to Ted Rogers now, in 1995: "Rogers told the merchants he expects little change in the way people use television and that it will not be the essence of the 'information highway'.... The information highway, he said, will develop only through the spread of personal computers. 'We expect a very sizeable demand for interactive services to personal computers. People will want to dial into databases containing multimedia programs, interactive games, electronic publishing and other new services' including shopping services, Rogers said....Rogers said his cable company expects within five years to get as much revenue from providing online interactive services to PC users as it does from television customers."[4]

Oops! We guess that Ted Rogers has realized that there are a heck of a lot of PCs out there and that people do not subscribe to his vision of being passive couch potatoes on some type of home-shopping television information highway.

Satellite companies are getting into the act, too. "Telesat Canada and Hughes Network Systems have created a high-speed Canadian satellite-personal computer hookup service — DirecPC — that will allow businesses fast access to the Internet and the ability to deliver digital video, audio and data to personal computers. 'We can deliver 90 megabytes per minute to the desktop....That's like using a firehose to fill up a coffee cup,' Telesat president Larry Boisvert said at a Vancouver press conference Tuesday."[5]

It is not just the cable and satellite companies that have realized the world has changed. Stentor, the consortium of major telephone companies in Canada, announced in 1994 the Beacon Initiative, a grand plan to provide video in Canadian homes, home shopping, home banking — all the typical television-based information highway services.

---

3. Maclean Hunter OKs Surprise Deal with Giant Rogers, *The Halifax Daily News*, March 9, 1994.
4. Home Shopping Loss for Rogers 5-year Try Shows TV Isn't Main Lane of Info Way, *The Toronto Star*, June 13, 1995.
5. Plug in to a Satellite; Telesat Offers High-speed Data Link to Computers, *The Edmonton Journal*, September 14, 1995.

At the time, they said of the information highway: "Stentor, an alliance of Bell Canada and eight other phone companies, said it plans to create a network that would carry television, telephone and other services to 80 to 90 per cent of businesses and homes by 2005. John McLennan, president of Bell Canada, agreed it would cost less if telephone and cable companies worked together to build one information highway that carried competitive services....Under the Stentor proposal, called the Beacon Initiative, the phone companies will upgrade their networks to provide two-way transmission of voice, video and data messages. That opens the door for a host of interactive services such as home shopping and banking."[6] Oops!

Listen to John McLennan, the President of Bell Canada, in 1995: "The Internet and wireless are indicators of the fundamental changes coming in the way we communicate, conduct business, entertain and live. The Internet explosion caught many by surprise. Not only does it give us a glimpse of the applications that will shape the future but it has caused a fundamental shift in how we think about networks."[7] Beacon still exists and indeed is moving forward at a rapid pace; but the Internet has become a significant component of what Beacon will eventually be.

Certainly the Internet has caused a major shift in how communication companies think about networks. Across Canada, telephone companies such as Bell scrambled to become involved in the delivery of Internet services.

Everywhere you turn, you see a communications industry galvanized into action by the growing dominance and reach of the Internet. What is significant is that in the next decade, it is expected that telecommunications technology will permit us to access vast volumes of information at incredibly high speeds.

Systems such as the Beacon Initiative and access to the Internet through cable wires and satellite will bring to bear many of the future possibilities to which we alluded in this book. Soon everyone in the world will be able to establish his/her own television station or radio station. Telephone calls and video conferencing will occur through the Internet. Multimedia of incredible proportions will flow around the network on a regular basis. We will have an information highway, and it will be found on the Internet.

Individuals and Organizations

Bill Gates observed in one of his computer columns recently that the Internet "has enough users now that it is benefiting from the positive feedback loop: The more users it gets, the more content it gets; and the more content it gets, the more users it gets."[8] This is certainly true. The Internet has reached a point that it has self-sustaining growth. The Internet is growing because of the number of people joining it, and the volume of information available is growing because every one of these individuals can be a publisher.

This type of self-sustaining growth does not usually slow down, particularly when people believe they are getting something of value. The Angus Reid survey previously referred to in this book showed that use of the Internet *met or exceeded the expectations of over 85% of people who use it.* Clearly, people are discovering the many ways that the Internet can benefit them. The majority of those who join it are not walking away from it.

---

6. Static Over Stentor $8.5b Upgrade Plan, *Business Information Wire*, April 5, 1994.
7. Industry Leaders Take the Long View, Report on Telecommunications, *Globe and Mail*, September 12, 1995.
8. Internet Gaining PC-like Momentum, *The Halifax Daily News*, August 18, 1995.

It is not just individuals who are involved in this self-sustaining growth. You can examine practically any industry on the planet and find significant Internet initiatives. You can look at any government and see signs of Internet activity, or review charitable organizations and find that they are wondering about the role the Internet can play. You can see educational bodies around the planet seeking to plug in. You can examine the religions of the world and observe that they, too, are either involved or plan on becoming involved. Across Canada and around the world, an ever-increasing number of individuals are finding a reason to link into the Internet.

Bringing It All Together

You cannot bring these three trends together — a computer industry, a telecommunications explosion, and a self-sustaining growth in a population — and not have a dramatic impact on our world. The explosion in CB radio died because you could only do one thing with it: talk to other people. The Internet will not die because you can do any number of things with it. It is simply a platform, a set of building blocks, upon which entire new industries, applications, activities, businesses, and opportunities will be built. Plug together all the computers in the world, and you simply discover something magical happens.

Is It Real?

Think of it this way: the number of telephones finally exploded in the early part of this century once a "magic number" of people had a telephone. As soon as that "magic number" was surpassed, it became necessary to have a telephone, and telephones became ubiquitous around the globe. The Internet is about to hit that magic number. The answer to the question of whether the Internet is real is simple: its incredible momentum means that it does not have an off switch.

Canadian Internet Milestones

Notable Dates and Events in Canadian Networking

This is a chronology of key dates and events in the evolution of the Internet in Canada. It is an attempt to permanently record important events and Canadian Internet "firsts" before they are lost to history, forever.

Thanks to Internet users across Canada for their contributions to this time line.

Help us Document Canada's Internet History!

↪ Have you created a home page that is the first of its kind in Canada?

↪ Are you the first club or organization in your interest area to launch a World Wide Web site in Canada?

↪ Has your organization achieved an important Internet milestone that the rest of Canada should know about?

↪ If Canadian Internet history is in the making, and you are involved, let us know about it!

Submissions can be e-mailed to Rick Broadhead and Jim Carroll at
handbook@uunet.ca

1970

October | New Brunswick Educational Computer Network is formed, and later renamed the New Brunswick/Prince Edward Island Educational Computer Network. It is still operating.

1971

August | Science Council of Canada Report 13 is titled "A Trans-Canada Computer Communications Network."

1972

May 17 | CANUNET, the Canadian Universities Network, is designed for the Federal Department of Communications, but the project is never funded.

1981

October | New Brunswick/Prince Edward Island Educational Computer Network establishes an electronic mail system called "Mercury."

1982

May 14 | The Canadian and U.S. Defence Departments agree on a project proposal which will link computer networks in the two countries. The Canadian Defence Department's network will be called DREnet.

1983

October | DREnet (Defence Research Establishment Network) is created, linking Defence Research Establishments in Ontario and Nova Scotia. The network consists of a 9600 bps link between the Communications Research Centre in Ottawa and the Defence Research Establishment Atlantic in Nova Scotia.

1984

William Gibson of Vancouver coins the term "cyberspace" in the novel *Neuromancer.*

March 1 | CDNnet officially starts as a test network. CDNnet's purpose is to provide network services to Canada's research and education communities.

April	OUNET, the Ontario Universities Network, is launched. Six Ontario universities plus Humber College and Ryerson Polytechnical Institute [now Ryerson Polytechnic University] participate in the network that links the central computers at each of the eight institutions.
June	OUNET is renamed NetNorth because several non-Ontario educational institutions have asked to join the OUNET network.
Fall	NetNorth establishes a connection to Cornell University in the U.S., linking NetNorth to BITNET (Because It's Time Network).
Fall	NetNorth organizes into three "regional" networks—one in Central Canada, one in Atlantic Canada, and one in Western Canada.
December 31	CDNnet [see March 1, 1984] has 14 hosts at 12 institutions.

1985

January	NetNorth's link to Atlantic Canada is established at the University of New Brunswick. IBM grants $60,000 per year for three years to help develop the network.
February	DREnet connects to ARPAnet in the U.S., a U.S. Defence Department network connecting several U.S. universities. The DREnet-ARPAnet link is a 56 Kbps line connecting the Communications Research Centre in Ottawa to the University of Rochester in New York. The University of Rochester was chosen because it was the closest ARPAnet site to Ottawa. This event is important for two reasons. First, the ARPAnet eventually evolved into the Internet. Second, this was the first Canadian connection to the ARPAnet. Use of the Canada-U.S. link was restricted to people involved in authorized research programs. This restriction was lifted in June 1987.
February 25	New Brunswick/Prince Edward Island electronic mail system is linked to NetNorth.
June	NetNorth's link to Western Canada is established at the University of Alberta.

1986

Mid-1986	The Canadian end of the DREnet link to ARPAnet is moved from the Communications Research Centre in Ottawa to the Defence Research Establishment in Ottawa.
October	CRIM (Computer Research Institute of Montreal) establishes a computer network linking five universities and two research centres with 56 Kbps lines **<http://www.crim.ca>**. The participating institutions are the University of Quebec (Montreal), University of Montréal, Concordia University, École Polytechnique de Montréal, McGill University, SIRICON, and the Computer Research Institute of Montreal.

October 4	BCnet (British Columbia Regional Network) receives start-up funding **<http://www.bc.net>**.
November	John Demco (now the Registrar of the CA Domain) organizes a group to oversee the creation of a CA Domain for Canada.

1987

May	Web, a Canadian computer network, is launched with $20,000 in start-up funding from Environment Canada. Web was created to link environmentalists and other social-change activists across the country who were interested in issues of peace, environment, human rights, social justice, and international development. Web continues to exist today **<http://www.web.apc.org>**.
May	The CA top-level domain (.ca) is registered.
June	As a result of a Defence Department policy change, anyone on the DREnet is now permitted to use the DREnet-ARPAnet link for communications. Prior to this date, use of the DREnet-ARPA-net connection was restricted to authorized individuals only.
June 16	The first Canadian Networking Conference is held at the University of Guelph **<http://www.uoguelph.ca>** in Guelph, Ontario. Approximately 80 people attend.
September	The CRIM Network (see October 1986) is linked to CSNET (Computer and Science Research Network) in Cambridge, Massachusetts. The speed of the link is 9600 bps.
October 26	The National Research Council **<http://www.nrc.ca>** hosts a meeting in Ottawa to plan a national research network for Canada. Representatives from Canadian research institutions, computer networks and universities attend.
October	BCnet (British Columbia Regional Network) activates its first interorganization connection (between Simon Fraser University and the University of British Columbia).
November 25	The University of Prince Edward Island **<http://www.upei.ca>** becomes the first Canadian organization to submit an application for a subdomain under the CA top-level domain.

1988

January 7	CDNnet requests a connection to the National Science Foundation **<http://www.nsf.gov>** Network [NSFnet] in Washington.

April – May	Representatives from two of Ontario's provincial centres of excellence [Information Technology Research Centre and the Institute for Space and Terrestrial Science] and from four Ontario universities [Queen's, University of Waterloo, University of Western Ontario, and the University of Toronto] begin to plan a computer network to interconnect their respective institutions. The network is initially called ORNet (Ontario Research Network), and later renamed ONet (Ontario Network) **<http://www.onet.on.ca>**.
May 26	BCnet and CDNnet establish a 19.2 Kbps link to the NSFnet in Washington. The link is shared between BCnet and CDNnet.
May 31	The second Canadian Networking Conference is held in Fredericton, New Brunswick, at the University of New Brunswick **<http://www.unb.ca>**. Over 100 people attend.
June 10	BCnet (British Columbia Regional Network) officially opens **<http://www.bc.net>**.
June 19	Roger Taylor and Allan Heyworth of the National Research Council deliver a paper at the 1988 Supercomputing Symposium entitled "NRCnet: A National Network for Canada's Research Community." This is the first "public" announcement of the plan to develop a Canada-wide computer network.
Summer	The National Research Council decides to change the name of Canada's national computer network from NRCnet (National Research Computer Network) to NRNet (National Research Network) **<http://www.nrc.ca>**.
August	CDNnet has 175 hosts at 32 institutions. CDNnet's busiest host is processing 5,000 messages per day.
August	Fifty-seven institutions are participating in NetNorth.
August	ONet (Ontario Regional Network) connects its first institutions. Connections were first installed between the University of Western Ontario, the University of Toronto, the University of Waterloo, and Queen's University. Connections were established at York University and McMaster University shortly thereafter.
October	The University of Toronto establishes a 56-Kbps link to the NSFnet at Cornell University.
October	The University of Toronto establishes a connection to the ARPAnet.
November	CRIM [Computer Research Institute of Montreal] establishes a 19.2 Kbps link to CSNET [Computer Science Network] in Cambridge, Massachusetts.
December 31	58 Canadian organizations have registered subdomains under the .ca top level domain.

1989

June	The third annual Canadian Networking Conference is held at Concordia University **<http://www.concordia.ca>** in Montreal. More than 150 people attend.
June 19	Roger Taylor and Allan Heyworth of the National Research Council **<http://www.nrc.ca>** present an update on NRNet at the1989 Supercomputing Symposium in Toronto.
June 20	*The Globe and Mail* publishes an article about NRNet.
September	The CRIM Network (see October 1986) is replaced by a Quebec regional network called RISQ **<http://www.risq.net>**. The founding members are McGill University, École des Hautes Études, Université Laval, Université de Sherbrooke, Université de Montréal, Concordia University, Hydro-Québec, Computer Research Institute of Montréal, Université du Québec à Montréal, École Polytechnique de Montréal, AES-Dorval, and Siège social de l'Université du Québec.
September	RISQ (Quebec regional network) is connected to NYSERnet (New York State Education and Research Network). The speed of the link is 56 Kbps.
October	A meeting is held to form NBNet, a regional computer network for New Brunswick. The meeting is held in Moncton, New Brunswick, and hosted by the New Brunswick/Prince Edward Island Educational Computer Network.
November	Nova Scotia Technology Network [NSTN] is incorporated to provide Internet access in Nova Scotia **<http://www.nstn.ca>**.
November	RISQ (Quebec regional network) is connected to ONet (Ontario regional network). The speed of the link is 56 Kbps.
November 23	A press release is issued, announcing plans for a high-speed national research network in Canada called the "National Research Network" (NRNet).
December 31	97 Canadian organizations have registered subdomains under the .ca top level domain, a 67% increase over the previous year.

1990

January	"CA*net" is chosen as the new name for Canada's soon-to-be launched high-speed national research network. The name was suggested by John Curley of the National Research Council at an NRNet Board meeting.
January	NetNorth reaches its peak in membership with 65 members.

January	ARnet [Alberta Regional Network] begins with three members.
March	RISQ (Quebec regional network) is connected to NSTN (Nova Scotia Technology Network). The speed of the link is 19,200 bps.
March	Alan Emtage places the first prototype of "archie" on the Internet, at McGill University in Montreal. Archie is an Internet tool that helps users locate files on the Internet. The name "archie" is derived from the word "archive."
May 15	The Atlantic Canada Opportunities Agency **<http://www.acoa.ca>** approves funding for a link between CA*net and Prince Edward Island.
June	Documents are signed to create CA*net (Victoria).
June	Representatives from Web and six other national and regional networks sharing the same vision [see May 1987], and serving similar communities, meet in San Francisco. The result is the formation of the Association for Progressive Communications — an international organization representing computer networks that link social change activists. Web is a founding member of the APC.
June 12	The fourth annual Canadian Networking Conference is held at the University of Victoria **<http://www.uvic.ca>** in Victoria, British Columbia.
June 15	New Brunswick/Prince Edward Island Educational Computer Network (Fredericton) establishes a link to CA*net.
July	Manitoba's provincial Internet network (MBnet) opens with four members **<http://www.mbnet.mb.ca>**.
July 30	The first international Internet Engineering Task Force meeting, hosted by John Demco, is held at the University of British Columbia.
August	Nova Scotia Technology Network **<http://www.nstn.ca>** starts to connect its first clients.
October 25 12:00 Noon	CA*net, Canada's high-speed national research network, is officially opened in Toronto by the University of Toronto and the National Research Council. It is announced that the network will connect regional computer networks in each Canadian province. It is also announced that CA*net users will have access to research networks in Canada and throughout the world through three links to the National Science Foundation Network [NSFNET] in the United States. The CA*net<==>NSFNET links will be from Toronto, Ontario to Ithaca, New York; Montreal, Quebec to Princeton, New Jersey; and Vancouver, British Columbia to Seattle, Washington. **<http://www.canet.ca>**
October	The Nova Scotia Technology Network (NSTN) is officially launched **<http://www.nstn.ca>**.

October 25	In Albuquerque, New Mexico, members of the Coordinating Committee for Intercontinental Research Networks (CCIRN) drink a champagne toast to celebrate the opening of CA*net.
November 20	The University of New Brunswick **<http:// www.unb.ca>** becomes the first university in Canada to establish a public on-line library catalogue on the Internet.
December 31	137 Canadian organizations have registered subdomains under the .ca top level domain, a 41% increase over the previous year.

1991

January	The first version of Hytelnet is released by Peter Scott **<scottp@herald.usask.ca>** at the University of Saskatchewan. Hytelnet is a program that provides links to dozens of Telnet-accessible sites on the Internet, including library catalogues, community computer networks, campus-wide information systems, and databases.
March	A second archie server [see March 1990] is established on Finland's national computer network (FUNET). The FUNET server is the first archie site outside of Canada. The number of archie servers on the Internet has since grown to over twenty.
April 23	A consortium is formed to operate NBNet (see October 1989).
June	NetNorth announces its intention to wind down its operations.
June	The fifth annual Canadian Networking Conference is held at Queen's University **<http://www.queensu.ca>** in Kingston, Ontario. More than 200 people attend.
September	The link from CA*net in Vancouver to the NSFNET in Seattle, Washington is upgraded from 56 Kbps to 112 Kbps.
September	CA*net is carrying 27 Gigabytes of traffic per week—10% of the load of the NSFNET T1 backbone at the time.
October	Toronto-based Web [see May 1987] begins to provide electronic communications to several computer networks in Cuba, giving Cubans Internet-based e-mail for the first time. The link is still maintained to the date of writing.
December 31	242 Canadian organizations have registered subdomains under the .ca top level domain, a 77% increase over the previous year.

1992

January 3	The link from CA*net in Vancouver to the NSFNET in Seattle, Washington is upgraded from 112 Kbps to 224 Kbps.
January 7	Peter Deutsch and Alan Emtage form Bunyip Information Systems Inc. to develop new versions of archie and other Internet tools. (See March 1990.)
January 28	NB*net (New Brunswick Regional Network) is formally launched to provide Internet access in New Brunswick **<http://www.nbnet.nb.ca>**.
January 31	Total traffic on CA*net for the month of January 1992 is 160.3 megabytes.
February 29	Average growth rate on CA*net since August 1991 is 14 gigabytes per month.
April	The first commercial version of archie is released.
May 5	The link from CA*net in Toronto to the NSFNET in Ithaca, New York is increased from 224 Kbps to 1.544 Mbps (T1 speed).
May 29	The link from CA*net in Montreal to the NSFNET in Princeton, New Jersey is increased from 112 Kbps to 224 Kbps.
June 2	The sixth annual Canadian Networking Conference is held at the Memorial University of Newfoundland **<http://www.mun.ca>** in St. John's.
July	MBnet becomes the first organization in Manitoba to sell public dial-up access to the Internet **<http://www.mbnet.mb.ca>**.
November	Canada's first Free-Net is launched in Victoria, British Columbia **<http://www.freenet.victoria.bc.ca>**.
November 16	The NeXT User Group in the Yukon Territory becomes the first site in the Yukon to receive a domain in the .yk subdomain.
December	The can.domain USENET newsgroup is created to discuss issues pertaining to the CA Domain.
December 31	The total traffic carried by CA*net in 1992 is 271.53 megabytes.
December 31	445 Canadian organizations have registered subdomains under the .ca top level domain, an 84% increase over the previous year.

1993

January 1	CA*net hires its first full-time staff member, an Executive Director.
January 14	The Polar Bear BBS in Rankin Inlet, Northwest Territories becomes the first site in the Northwest Territories to receive a domain in the .nt [Northwest Territories] subdomain.
March 5	CANARIE [The CAnadian Network for the Advancement of Research, Industry, and Education] is established as a not-for-profit corporation. Its goal is to assist in the development of a communications infrastructure in Canada that will improve Canada's competitiveness in the information age **<http://www.canarie.ca>**.
March 31	National Research Council funding for CA*net terminates.
March 31	The original CA*net agreements with the University of Toronto (to maintain and operate the network) and INSINC (to supply long-distance telephone service) terminate. These agreements are later renewed.
March 31	The link between DREnet and the U.S. is upgraded from 56 Kbps to 1.544 Mbps.
March 31	CDNnet terminates its activities.
April	NetNorth's membership is down to 41 members.
June 15	The seventh annual Canadian Networking Conference is held at McGill University **<http://www.mcgill.ca>** in Montreal.
June 21	CANARIE **<http://www.canarie.ca>** is officially launched. (See March 5, 1993.)
August	PEInet is officially incorporated to provide commercial Internet access in Prince Edward Island. Plans are initiated to transfer control of the regional network from the University of Prince Edward Island to PEInet, a joint venture between IslandTel (PEI's telephone company) and On-Line Support (PEI's largest consulting and development firm).
October	Camosun College in British Columbia becomes the first college in Canada to establish a World Wide Web site **<http://www.camosun.bc.ca>**.
October 15	SchoolNet, a cooperative initiative among federal, provincial, and territorial governments and the private sector, is launched. SchoolNet's mission is to connect elementary and secondary schools to the information highway.
November	Natural Resources Canada launches its World WideWeb site **<http://www.emr.ca>**.
December 31	The total amount of traffic carried by CA*net in 1993 is 680.16 megabytes. This is a growth of 250% in one year.
December 31	767 Canadian organizations have registered subdomains under the .ca top level domain, a 72% increase over the previous year.

1994	
January	The Nova Scotia Technology Network expands beyond provincial borders, the first CA*net regional network to do so. NSTN opens a Point-of-Presence in Ottawa.
January	The CA*net Board admits the Government of Canada (GTIS) as a member of CA*net.
January 4	PEInet officially opens in Charlottetown, Prince Edward Island.
January 13	The YukonNet Operating Society is incorporated in Whitehorse, Yukon Territory, to provide commercial Internet services to residents of the Yukon Territory.
January 20	Premier Frank McKenna of New Brunswick announces the appointment of a Minister responsible for the electronic highway. New Brunswick is the first province in Canada to appoint a cabinet minister responsible for the development of the electronic information highway.
January 20	Premier Frank McKenna of New Brunswick publicly announces his Internet address <premier@gov.nb.ca> in a speech given to the Fredericton Chamber of Commerce. Premier McKenna becomes the first Canadian Premier to have a public Internet address.
March 17	Federal Industry Minister John Manley announces the government's intention to create an Advisory Council to help implement a Canadian strategy for the Information Highway.
April 19	Federal Industry Minister John Manley announces the membership of the National Advisory Council on the Information Highway.
April 19	Federal Industry Minister John Manley releases a discussion paper called "The Canadian Information Highway — Building Canada's Information and Communications Infrastructure." This paper explains why it is essential for Canada to have an information highway, provides an overview of Canada's existing communications and network infrastructure, and identifies some key policy issues that need to be addressed.
April 19	Canadore College becomes the first college in Ontario to launch a World Wide Web site **<http://www.canadorec.on.ca>**.
April 19	An Internet Domain Registrar is created for the Government of Canada. The government registrar assumes responsibility for registering Internet domains for all Canadian government organizations. A new Canadian government subdomain (gc.ca) is established for this purpose. Previously, Canadian government organizations registered Canadian subdomains through the CA Domain Registrar in Vancouver.

May	CA*net completes its upgrade to T1 speeds.
May 7	The *Canadian Internet Handbook* reaches the #1 position on the *Toronto Star's* National Bestsellers List. It is the first Internet book to reach the #1 position on a general bestseller list.
May 31	ONet Networking **<http://www.onet.on.ca>** becomes incorporated as a non-profit corporation under the laws of Ontario.
June	The CA*net Board approves connections to the Yukon Territory and Northwest Territories.
June	The CA*net Board approves a 1994-1998 Strategic Plan for CA*net.
June	NetNorth's membership is down to 25 members: British Columbia Systems Corporation, TRIUMF, University of Alberta, University of Manitoba, Natural Resources Canada, Lakehead University, York University, University of Toronto, University of Waterloo, Concordia University, École Polytechnique de Montréal, University of Victoria, University of Ottawa, British Columbia Institute of Technology, University of Calgary, University of Regina, Humber College, Queen's University, École des Hautes Études Commerciales de Montréal, McGill University, Université Laval, Université de Sherbrooke, Mount Allison University, Université de Moncton, University of New Brunswick.
June 7	The Government of New Brunswick launches its World Wide Web site, the first official provincial government Web site in Canada **<http://www.gov.nb.ca>**.
June 20	The eighth annual Canadian Networking Conference is held at The University of Saskatchewan in Saskatoon.
July	Human Resources Development Canada launches its World Wide Web site **<http://www.hrdc-drhc.gc.ca>**.
July 2	The *Canadian Internet Handbook* reaches the #1 position on the *Financial Post's* Bestseller List.
July 7	The Prince Edward Island Crafts Council in Charlottetown, Prince Edward Island becomes the first institution on the island to officially launch a World Wide Web server.
July 20	The ONet Association is disbanded and replaced by the ONet Networking corporation, which assumes responsibility for ONet.
July 25	Internet is on the cover of Time magazine.
July 31	The NetNorth consortium ceases funding of its National Administrative Centre at the University of Toronto.
September 13	The University of Waterloo Bridge Club becomes the first Canadian bridge club to establish a World Wide Web site **<http://watserv1.uwaterloo.ca/~uwbc/uwbc.www.html>**.

October 14		SaskTel announces plans to provide province-wide Internet access, making it the second province in Canada to offer universal Internet access to everyone in the province (the first was New Brunswick).
November	1st	The Saint John Port Corporation becomes the first port authority in Canada to establish a World Wide Web site. It is also the first known port authority in the world to have an official presence on the World Wide Web **<http://www.sjport.com/port/port.html>**.
November	1st	The Canadian Consulate in San Jose, California, becomes the first Canadian Consulate to launch a site on the World Wide Web **<http://www.globalx.net/ccto>**.
November 8	1st	Terry Jones of Toronto creates the first Canadian World Wide Web page devoted to water skiing **<http://www.utoronto.ca:80/ski/water>**.
November 15		The Government of Manitoba launches its World Wide Web site **<http://www.gov.mb.ca>**.
December	1st	British Columbia Hydro becomes the first Canadian utility to establish a World Wide Web site **<http://www.bchydro.bc.ca/bchydro>**.
December 17		CA*net's connection to the rest of the Internet is cut over from ANS (Advanced Network and Services) to MCI. As of 0600 EST, CA*net is routing to the rest of the Internet via MCI.
December 18		SASKnet's connection to CA*net changes location from the University of Saskatchewan to SaskTel's Central Office in Regina.
December 31		Annual growth in the number of Canadian subdomains exceeds 100% for the first time. The number of Canadian organizations with registered subdomains under the .ca top level domain is now 1,632, a 113% increase over the previous year.

1995

January		Statistics Canada launches its World Wide Web site **<http://www.statcan.ca>**.
February	1st	The Floradale Boardheads Windsurfing Club in Ontario becomes the first Canadian windsurfing club on the Internet **<http://www.sentex.net/~remoore/fbh.html>**.
February	1st	Ashbridge's Bay Yacht club in Toronto becomes the first Canadian yacht club to launch an official World Wide Web site **<http://www.io.org/~sail/ABYC>**.
February 1		MBnet, Manitoba's provincial Internet network, discontinues selling dial-up Internet accounts in order to encourage the growth and success of private Internet providers in the province **<http://www.mbnet.mb.ca>**.

February 3	A federal government advisory committee meets for the first time to discuss Internet home page standards. The meeting is attended by representatives from a cross section of federal government departments.
February 20	The first Internet industry association in Canada — the British Columbia Internet Association — is incorporated in British Columbia **<http://www.bcia.bc.ca/bcia>**.
February 28	Agriculture and Agri-Food Canada launches its World Wide Web site **<http://aceis.agr.ca>**.
March	The New Brunswick Division of the Canadian Red Cross Society becomes the first Red Cross organization in Canada to establish a World Wide Web site **<http://www.mi.net/redcross/redcross.html>**.
March 8	The Ontario Easter Seal Society becomes the first Canadian charity to establish an official World Wide Web site **<http://www.easterseals.org/CyberPlex/ EasterSeals.html>**.
March 31	The Canadian Radio-television and Telecommunications Commission issues a press release announcing its intention to launch a World Wide Web site on April 3.
April	The Avalon Masters Swim Club in Newfoundland becomes the first Canadian swimming club on the World Wide Web **<http://www.infonet.st-johns.nf.ca/providers/ amsc>**.
April	The Government of Nova Scotia establishes a home page on the World Wide Web **<http://www.gov.ns.ca>**.
April 3 9:00 a.m.	The Canadian Radio-television and Communications Commission officially launches its World Wide Web site **<http://www.crtc.gc.ca>**.
April 3	The Vancouver Fire Department becomes the first fire department in Canada to establish a presence on the World Wide Web **<http://www.wimsey.com/ ~maddison/index.html>**.
April 7	The Canadian Embassy in Washington, D.C., becomes the first Canadian embassy to establish an official World Wide Web site **<http://www.nstn.ca/wshdc>**.
April 28	Indian and Northern Affairs Canada officially launches its World Wide Web site **<http://www.inac.ca>**.
May	A detailed draft of the federal government's standard for federal government World Wide Web pages is circulated to the Deputy Ministers of all government departments and agencies that are subject to the Government of Canada's federal identity program. The draft is sent out under the signature of the Chief Informatics Officer of the Government of Canada.

May	Five Alberta Internet service providers petition Canada's federal competition tribunal in an attempt to block AGT, Alberta's primary telephone company, from selling Internet access in the province.
May	Emergency Preparedness Canada launches its World Wide Web site **<http://hoshi.cic.sfu.ca/~epc>**.
May	Canada's Treasury Board Secretariat launches its World Wide Web site at **<http://www.tbs-sct.gc.ca>**.
May 1	McAuslan Brewing of Montreal becomes the first Canadian brewery to launch a World Wide Web site **<http://www.iisys.com/www/corp/mcauslan/mcauslan.htm>**.
May 24	Ken Polsson of British Columbia establishes the first World Wide Web page dedicated to Canadian numismatics **<http://www.islandnet.com/~kpolsson/cancoin.htm>**.
June	The Atlantic Lottery Corporation becomes the first lottery jurisdiction in Canada to launch its own World Wide Web site **<http://www.alc.ca>**.
June 1	Hastings Park Racecourse in Vancouver becomes the first race track in Canada to launch a World Wide Web site **<http://www.hastingspark.com>**.
June 7	The CA Domain Registrar changes its long-standing subdomain name policy and permits CA subdomain names to be based on an organization's trademark.
June 14	The National Library of Canada launches its World Wide Web site **<http://www.nlc-bnc.ca>**.
June 15	Brian McLean of Thunder Bay, Ontario, establishes Canada's first World Wide Web site devoted to bowling **<http://www.foxnet.net/users/bowling/foxbowl.html>**.
June 20	The ninth annual Canadian Networking Conference is held at Carleton University in Ottawa. Information on the conference can be found at **<http://enterprise.ic.gc.ca/~will/net95/Net95.html>**.
June 22	The first annual Canadian Internet awards are presented at the 1995 Canadian Networking Conference in Ottawa. The list of awards and nominees can be found at **<http://enterprise.ic.gc.ca/~will/net95/Net95.html>**.
June 22	The Canadian Internet Hall of Fame is created at the 1995 Canadian Networking Conference in Ottawa. The first five inductees are named.
July 4	The Vancouver Stock Exchange becomes the first Canadian stock exchange to launch an official World Wide Web site **<http://www.vse.ca>**.

July 9	The University of Northern British Columbia caving club establishes Canada's first World Wide Web site devoted to speleology **<http://quarles.unbc.edu/keen/ netcave.htm>**.
July 10	Government Works and Public Services Canada officially launches its World Wide Web site **<http://www.pwgsc.gc.ca>**.
July 13	ED TEL receives CRTC approval to launch its Internet access service. The product is named PLAnet—Public Live Access Network.
July 26 9:30 a.m.	The official World Wide Web site for the Department of Foreign Affairs and International Trade is officially inaugurated by Canada's Deputy Foreign Affairs Minister Gordon Smith. A ceremony is held in the lobby of the Lester B. Pearson Building in Ottawa **<http://www.dfait-maeci.gc.ca>**.
July 31	The Canadian Radio-television and Communications Commission grants approval to AGT, Alberta's primary telephone company, to launch an Internet access service in the Alberta.
August 1	A change is made to the CA subdomain registration procedures to allow Canadian organizations whose legal name includes both an English form and a French form to apply for one CA subdomain corresponding to each form.
August 2	The Treasury Board of Canada issues "The Internet — A Guide to Internet Use in the Federal Government," the first Internet guide for Canadian federal government employees **<http://www.tbs-sct.gc.ca/tb/pubs/in/ine.html>**.
August 14, 11:00 p.m.	580 CFRA in Ottawa becomes the first radio station in the world to continuously broadcast live over the Internet **<http://www.worldlink.ca/KOOLCFRA/ cfra.htm>**.
August 17	The Embassy of Indonesia in Ottawa becomes the first embassy in Canada to establish its own World Wide Web site **<http://www.prica.org>**. The launch takes place as part of ceremonies commemorating the fiftieth anniversary of Indonesia's independence.
August 21	The Department of Justice officially launches its World Wide Web site **<http://canada.justice.gc.ca>**.
September	The Consulate General of Pakistan becomes the first consulate in Canada to establish a World Wide Web site **<http://global.ca:80/~pakistan>**.
September 1	Approximately 9,450 Canadian organizations have registered Internet domains.
September 1	3,314 Canadian organizations have registered subdomains under the .ca top level domain.

September 10	The Government of Ontario officially launches its World Wide Web site **\<http://www.gov.on.ca\>**.
September 18	BMW Canada becomes the first automobile manufacturer in Canada to launch a World Wide Web site. It is the first official BMW site worldwide **\<http://www.bmc.ca\>**.
September 29	The Government of Nova Scotia officially launches its World Wide Web site **\<http://www.gov.ns.ca\>**.

Directory of Canadian Internet Access Providers

Your Guide to Getting on the Internet in Canada

Welcome to the directory of Canadian Internet Access Providers! This is a guide to organizations that sell access to the Internet in Canada. Whether you are looking for a personal Internet account or an Internet connection for your entire organization, you can use this directory to find Internet access providers that are operating in your city or town. For more detailed information on the same Internet access providers, see this book's companion volume, *The 1996 Canadian Internet Directory.*

A&W Internet Inc. (The AWINC Network)

Kelowna, British Columbia
awinc.com, awinc.net

21–1851 Kirschner Road
Kelowna, BC V1Y 4N7

Voice: 604-763-1176
Fax: 604-860-1654
E-mail: info@awinc.com
Web: http://www.awinc.com

Service Area: Satellite offices ("nodes"):
British Columbia: *Kelowna* A&W Internet Inc.:, 21-1851 Kirscher Road, Kelowna, BC, V1Y 4N7, Tel: 604-763-1176, Fax: 604-860-1654. *Williams Lake* Stardate Internet: 297A Borland Street, Williams Lake, BC, V2G 1R4, Tel: 604-392-7175, Fax: 604-392-7175.

Penticton Ashnola Internet Management Ltd., 456 Main Street, Penticton, BC, V2A 5C5, Tel: 604-492-7672, Fax: 604-492-4334. *Merritt* Valley Business & Computer Services Ltd.: Box 188, 204-2090 Coutlee Avenue, Merritt, BC, V0K 2B0, Tel: 604-378-9272, Fax: 604-378-5221. *Nelson* PACIFIC ONRAMP: 532 Baker Street, Nelson, BC, V1L 4H9, Tel: 604-352-9600, Fax: 604-352-9585. *Quesnel* ABC Internet: 248 Reid Street, Quesnel, BC, V2J 2M2, Tel: 604-992-1230, Fax: 604-992-3930. *Prince Rupert* Kaien Computer Solutions: 297-1st Avenue East, Prince Rupert, BC, V8J 1A7, Tel: 604-624-5424, Fax: 604-627-1093. *Trail* PACIFIC ONRAMP: 1265 Cedar Avenue, Trail, BC, V1R 4B9, Tel: 604-364-2099, Fax: 604-364-2296.

Fort St. John Computer World: 9912-97th Avenue, Fort St. John, BC, V1J 6L8, Tel: 604-787-7200, Fax: 604-787-0702. *Kamloops* CommPass Internet Services Inc.: 1314 McGill Road, Kamloops, BC, V2C 6N6, Tel: 604-851-0176, Fax: 604-851-0175. *Creston* Kootenay Internet Services: Box 398, 1815 Canyon Street, Creston, BC, V0B 1G0, Tel: 604-428-4492, Fax: 604-428-2840. *Cranbrook* Kootenay Internet Services: 32-11th Avenue South, Cranbrook, BC, V1C 2P1, Tel: 604-489-4228, Fax: 604-489-4272. *Vancouver* Bretham Communications Ltd. 5579–204th Street, Langley, BC, V3A 1Z4 Tel: 604-534-2534, Fax: 604-534-7028.

Alberta: *Banff* Bowest Computer Systems Ltd.: Box 1689, 210 Bear Street, Banff, AB, T0L 0C0, Tel: 403-762-5159, Fax: 403-762-2052. *Brooks* Eastern Irrigation District: P.O. Bag 8, 550 Industrial Road, Brooks, AB, T1R 1B2, Tel: 403-362-1400, Fax: 403-362-6206. *Edmonton* Access Internet: 9868 63rd Avenue, Edmonton, AB, T6E 0G6, Tel: 403-944-0745, Fax: 403-435-9989. *Lloydminster* MicroAge Computer Centres, 5009-50th Street, Lloydminster, AB, T9V 0L9 Tel: 403-875-8880, Fax: 403-875-8898. *Medicine Hat* Memory Lane Computer Electronics Ltd.: 1221 Kingsway Avenue S.E., Medicine Hat, AB, T1A 2Y2, Tel: 403-526-2288, Fax: 403-527-8780.

Manitoba: *Winnipeg* Teledisc Systems Ltd.: 1871 Portage Avenue, Winnipeg, MB, R3J 0H1, Tel: 204-885-1414, Fax: 204-888-0805.

Saskatchewan: *Estevan* Grill Computer Services Ltd.: 238A 4th Street, Estevan, SK, S4A 0T6, Tel: 306-634-7533, Fax: 306-634-8979. *Moose Jaw* Focal Point Computers: 138 Fairford Street West, Moose Jaw, SK, S6H 1V3, Tel: 306-692-2694, Fax: 306-692-6460.

Swift Current Double "T" Computer Services: 374 Powell Crescent, Swift Current, SK, S9H 4L7, Tel: 306-773-2054. *Yorkton* Harvest Moon Technologies: 36-2nd Avenue North, Yorkton, SK, S3N 1G2, Tel: 306-782-9150, Fax: 306-786-6160.

Ontario: *Kenora* TechNet of Kenora, Inc.: 205 Main Street South, Kenora, ON, P9N 1T3, Tel: 807-468-9696, Fax: 807-468-3738. *Thunder Bay* MicroAge Computer Centres: 871B Tungsten Street, Thunder Bay, ON, P7B 6H2, Tel: 807-343-4490, Fax: 807-346-4963.

Planning to expand to: British Columbia: Victoria, Abbotsford, Hope, Prince George, Princeton, Osoyoos, Burns Lake, Smithers. Alberta: Red Deer, Calgary, Grand Prairie, Pincher Creek. Saskatchewan: Regina, Saskatoon, North Battleford, Prince Albert, Weyburn. Manitoba: Brandon, Flin Flon, Thompson. Ontario: Toronto, Barrie, Kitchener, St. Catharines, Hamilton, London, Peterborough, Galt.

Services: Leased line, dedicated ISDN, dedicated SLIP/PPP, frame relay, dial-up ISDN, dial-up SLIP/PPP, shell access, UUCP service, domain registration, free Web home page with personal dial-up account, Web design, Web hosting.

World Wide Web: http://www.awinc.com

Accès au Noeud Internet Québec (A.N.I.Q.)

Québec, Québec
aniq.com, aniq.net

3930, boul. Hamel ouest, Suite 086
Québec, PQ G1P 2J2

Voice:	418-872-6008
Fax:	418-872-6750
E-mail:	info@aniq.com
Web:	http://www.aniq.com

Service Area:	Quebec City, Sainte-Foy, Lévis, Charlesbourg, Beauport and other cities in the province of Quebec.
Services:	Leased line, dedicated ISDN, dedicated SLIP/PPP, frame relay, dial-up ISDN, dial-up SLIP/PPP, shell access, UUCP service, domain registration, Web design, Web hosting.
World Wide Web:	http://www.aniq.com

Accès-Cible inc.

St-Luc, Québec
acces-cible.qc.ca

122, rue Rimbaud
St-Luc, PQ J2W 1Y8

Voice:	514-359-6632
Fax:	514-349-4972
E-mail:	info@acces-cible.qc.ca
Web:	http://www.acces-cible.qc.ca

Service Area:	Montreal, St-Jean-sur-Richelieu, Bedford, Venise-en-Québec, Lacolle, Saint-Blaise, Notre-Dame-de-Stanbridge, Henryville, St-Luc, Iberville, Saint-Bruno, Longueuil, Saint-Lambert, La Prairie, Beloeil, Chambly, Boucherville, Saint-Rémi, Marieville, Verchères, Saint-Marc, St-Denis, Saint-Constant, Sainte-Julie-de-Verchères, Varennes, Laval, St-Sauveur, Saint-Calixte-de-Kilkenny, Sainte-Julienne, Lavaltrie, L'Épiphanie-L'Assomption, Saint-Lin, Sainte-Anne-des-Plaines, Ste-Thérèse, Mirabel Aéroport, Mirabel St-Augustin, St-Eustache, Oka, Mascouche, Terrebonne, Le Gardeur, Sainte-Rose, Chomedey, Pont-Viau, Roxboro, Sainte-Geneviève, Pointe-Claire, Lachine, Île-Perrot, Rigaud, Hudson, Vaudreuil, Beauharnois, Sainte-Martine, Châteauguay, Napierville, Hemmingford, Clarenceville.
Services:	Dedicated SLIP/PPP, dial-up SLIP/PPP, UUCP service, domain registration, Web design, Web hosting.
World Wide Web:	http://www.acces-cible.qc.ca

Access Route Canada Online Systems

Toronto, Ontario
arcos.org, bbs.arcos.org, www.arcos.org

5415 Dundas Street West
Etobicoke, ON M9B 1B5

Voice:	416-337-5785
Fax:	416-234-5345
E-mail:	sysop@arcos.org
Web:	http://www.arcos.org

Service Area:	Toronto, Mississauga, Scarborough, Ajax, Oakville, Brampton, Pickering. Planning to expand to include all of southern Ontario.
Services:	Dedicated ISDN, dedicated SLIP/PPP, dial-up ISDN, dial-up SLIP/PPP, shell access, terminal accounts, domain registration, free Web home page with personal dial-up account, Web design, Web hosting.
World Wide Web:	http://www.arcos.org

Achilles Internet Ltd.

Nepean, Ontario
achilles.net

14 Colonnade Road, Suite 260
Nepean, ON K2E 7M6

Voice:	613-723-6624
Fax:	613-723-8583
E-mail:	office@achilles.net
Web:	http://www.achilles.net

Service Area:	Ottawa/Hull, Almonte, Carleton Place, Low, Embrun, Russell, Rockland, Luskville, Wakefield, St-Pierre-de-Wakefield, Quyon, North Gower, Kanata, Stittsville, Gatineau, Perkins, Aylmer, Manotick, Metcalfe, Gloucester, Jockvale, Orleans, Osgoode, Chelsea, Constance Bay, Cumberland, Navan, Richmond, Carp.

Services: Leased line, dedicated ISDN, dedicated SLIP/PPP, dial-up SLIP/PPP, shell access, terminal accounts, UUCP service, domain registration, free Web home page with personal dial-up account, Web design, Web hosting.

World Wide Web: http://www.achilles.net

Advantis Canada (IBM Global Network)

Markham, Ontario
ibm.net, ibm.com

3500 Steeles Avenue East
Markham, ON L3R 2Z1

Voice: 1-800-225-5426
Fax: 905-316-6967
E-mail: connect@vnet.ibm.com
Web: http://www.canada.ibm.net

Service Area: Vancouver, Victoria, Calgary, Edmonton, Regina, Winnipeg, London, Toronto, Ottawa, Quebec City, Montreal, Halifax. 1-800 service is also available and users who subscribe to the Canadian service can make a local call in 400 cities around the world at no additional surcharge. Planning to expand to Kitchener, Hamilton, Windsor, St. Catharines, Guelph.

Services: Leased line, dedicated SLIP/PPP, frame relay, dial-up SLIP/PPP, domain registration, Web design, Web hosting.

World Wide Web: http://www.canada.ibm.net

AEI Internet Services

Montréal, Québec
aei.ca, aei.net

3577 Atwater, Suite 320
Montréal, PQ H3H 2R2

Voice: 514-939-2488
Fax: 514-939-0677
E-mail: info@aei.ca
Web: http://www.aei.ca

Service Area: Greater Montreal area. Planning to expand to Quebec City and Toronto.

Services: Leased line, dedicated ISDN, dedicated SLIP/PPP, frame relay, dial-up ISDN, dial-up SLIP/PPP, UUCP service, domain registration, free Web home page with personal dial-up account, Web hosting.

World Wide Web: http://www.aei.ca

AGT Limited

Edmonton, Alberta
agt.net

10020–100 Street
Edmonton, AB T5J 0N5

Voice: 1-800-608-1155
E-mail: billing@agt.net, help@agt.net, webmaster@agt.net
Web: http://www.agt.net

Service Area: Calgary and Calgary Extended Flat-Rate Calling Areas, Edmonton Extended Flat-Rate Calling Areas. Planning to expand to most AGT phone lines in most cities, towns, and Extended Flat-Rate Calling Areas in Alberta.

Services: Leased line, dedicated SLIP/PPP, dial-up ISDN, dial-up SLIP/PPP, domain registration, free Web home page with personal dial-up account, Web design, Web hosting.

World Wide Web: http://www.agt.net

Alberta Supernet Inc.

Edmonton, Alberta
supernet.ab.ca

Pacific Plaza, Suite 325
10909 Jasper Avenue
Edmonton, AB T5J 3L9

Voice: 403-441-3663
Fax: 403-424-0743
E-mail: info@supernet.ab.ca
Web: http://www.supernet.ab.ca

Service Area:	Slave Lake, Edmonton, Red Deer, Calgary, Innisfail, Lacombe, Olds, Ponoka, Rocky Mountain House, Stettler. Planning to expand to Saskatchewan and Manitoba.
Services:	Leased line, dedicated ISDN, dedicated SLIP/PPP, frame relay, dial-up SLIP/PPP, shell access, terminal accounts, UUCP service, domain registration, free Web home page with personal dial-up account, Web design, Web hosting.
World Wide Web:	http://www.supernet.ab.ca

America Online Inc.

Vienna, Virginia
aol.com

8619 Westwood Center Drive
Vienna, VA 22182-2285

Voice: 1-800-827-6364
Web: http://www.aol.com

Service Area:	Alberta: Calgary, Edmonton. British Columbia: Vancouver, Victoria. Manitoba: Winnipeg. Nova Scotia: Halifax. Ontario: Hamilton, Kitchener-Waterloo, London, Ottawa, St. Catharines, Toronto, Windsor. Québec: Quebec City, Montreal. Saskatchewan: Regina, Saskatoon.
Services:	Terminal accounts.
World Wide Web:	http://www.aol.com

ANSA Internet

Burnaby, British Columbia
ansa.com

4720 Kingsway, Suite 1801
Burnaby, BC V5H 4N2

Voice: 604-435-9549
Fax: 604-435-9572
E-mail: info@ansa.com
Web: http://www.ansa.com

Service Area:	Burnaby, Vancouver, Richmond, North Vancouver, West Vancouver, Surrey, Delta, New Westminister, Maple Ridge, Matsqui, White Rock.
Services:	Leased line, dedicated ISDN, dedicated SLIP/PPP, frame relay, dial-up SLIP/PPP, UUCP service, domain registration, Web design, Web hosting.
World Wide Web:	http://www.ansa.com

ARnet

See the entry for iSTAR Internet Inc.

Astra Network, Inc.

Winnipeg, Manitoba
man.net

2633 Portage Avenue
Winnipeg, MB R3J 0P7

Voice: 204-987-7050
Fax: 204-987-7058
E-mail: info@man.net
Web: http://www.man.net

Service Area:	Winnipeg, Selkirk, Stonewall, Teulon, Altona. Planning to expand to Steinbach.
Services:	Leased line, dedicated ISDN, dedicated SLIP/PPP, frame relay, dial-up SLIP/PPP, domain registration, free Web home page with personal dial-up account, Web design, Web hosting.
World Wide Web:	http://www.man.net

Atlantic Connect Incorporated

Halifax, Nova Scotia
atcon.com

3845 Dutch Village Road, 4th Floor
Halifax, NS B3L 4H9

Voice: 902-429-0222, 1-800-661-0222
Fax: 902-429-0218
E-mail: info@atcon.com
Web: http://www.atcon.com

Service Area:	Nova Scotia: Halifax, Dartmouth, Sackville, Bedford, Bridgewater, Hubbards, Enfield, Shubenacadie, Liverpool, Milton, Brooklyn, Amherst, Springhill, Wentworth, Tatamagouche, Truro, New Glasgow, Stellarton, Antigonish, Pictou, Guysborough, Port Hawkesbury, Baddeck, Whycocomagh, Sydney. Prince Edward Island: Summerside, St. Eleanor's, Wilmot. Newfoundland: Stephenville, Corner Brook. Planning to expand to: Nova Scotia: Kentville, Wolfville, Windsor, Middleton, Kingston, Bridgetown, Annapolis Royal, Digby, Meteghan, Yarmouth, Barrington Passage, Shelburne, Mahone Bay, Lunenburg, Western Shore, New Ross, Canso, Glace Bay. Prince Edward Island: Charlottetown, Cavendish, Montague, Alberton. New Brunswick: Moncton, Riverview, Dieppe, Fredericton, Saint John and area. Newfoundland: St. John's.

Services:	Leased line, dedicated ISDN, dedicated SLIP/PPP, frame relay, dial-up SLIP/PPP, domain registration, free Web home page with personal dial-up account, Web design, Web hosting.

World Wide Web: http://www.atcon.com

Atréide Communications

Hull, Québec
atreide.net

195 Devault
Hull, PQ J8Z 1S7

Voice:	819-772-2854
Fax:	819-777-0428
E-mail:	tech@atreide.net
Web:	http://www.atreide.net

Service Area:	Ottawa, Gloucester, Nepean, Hull, Gatineau, Aylmer, Buckingham, Masson, Luskville.

Services:	Dedicated ISDN, dedicated SLIP/PPP, dial-up ISDN, dial-up SLIP/PPP, UUCP service, domain registration, free Web home page with personal dial-up account, Web design, Web hosting.

World Wide Web: http://www.atreide.net

auroraNET Inc.

Burnaby, British Columbia
aurora.net, aurora-net.com, disc-net.com

5065 Anola Drive
Burnaby, BC V5B 4V7

Voice:	604-294-4357
Fax:	604-294-0107
E-mail:	sales@aurora.net
Web:	http://www.aurora.net

Service Area:	British Columbia: Aldergrove, Bowen Island, Burnaby, Cloverdale, Fort Langley, Haney, Ladner/Beach Grove, Langley, Newton, New Westminster, North Vancouver, Pitt Meadows, Port Coquitlam, Port Moody, Richmond, Surrey, Vancouver, West Vancouver, Whalley, White Rock, Whonnock. Ontario: Toronto.

Services:	Leased line, dedicated ISDN, dedicated SLIP/PPP, frame relay, dial-up ISDN, dial-up SLIP/PPP, shell access, UUCP service, domain registration, free Web home page with personal dial-up account, Web design, Web hosting.

World Wide Web: http://www.aurora.net

Avalon InterConnect (Division of Avalon Software & Computers Inc.)

St. John's, Newfoundland
avalon.nf.ca

22 O'Leary Avenue
St. John's, NF A1B 2C7

Voice:	709-739-0739
Fax:	709-739-1739
E-mail:	info@avalon.nf.ca
Web:	http://www.avalon.nf.ca

Service Area:	St. John's, Mount Pearl, Paradise, Goulds, St. Philips, Torbay, Portugal Cove, Middle Cove, Outer Cove, Manuels, Long Pond.
Services:	Leased line, dedicated SLIP/PPP, dial-up SLIP/PPP, shell access, terminal accounts, domain registration, Web design, Web hosting.
World Wide Web:	http://www.avalon.nf.ca

Axess Communications

St-Laurent, Québec
axess.com

3700 Griffith, Suite 326
St-Laurent, PQ H4T 1A7

Voice:	514-731-0919
Fax:	514-731-8113
E-mail:	support@axess.com
Web:	http://www.axess.com

Service Area:	Montreal and all areas in the 514 area code.
Services:	Leased line, dedicated ISDN, dedicated SLIP/PPP, dial-up SLIP/PPP, shell access, terminal accounts, UUCP service, domain registration, free Web home page with personal dial-up account, Web design, Web hosting.
World Wide Web:	http://www.axess.com

Axion Internet Communications, Inc.

Vancouver, British Columbia
axionet.com

1380 Burrard Street, Suite 600
Vancouver, BC V6Z 2H3

Voice:	604-687-8030
Fax:	604-687-8130
E-mail:	info@axionet.com
Web:	http://www.axionet.com

Service Area:	Vancouver, Lower Mainland.
Services:	Leased line, dedicated ISDN, dedicated SLIP/PPP, dial-up ISDN, dial-up SLIP/PPP, domain registration, Web design, Web hosting.
World Wide Web:	http://www.axionet.com

Babillard Synapse Inc.

Gatineau, Québec
synapse.net

22 Beloeil
Gatineau, PQ J8T 7G3

Voice:	819-561-1697
Fax:	819-561-1697
E-mail:	dcoulomb@synapse.net
Web:	http://www.synapse.net

Service Area:	Gatineau, Hull, Aylmer, Masson-Angers, Ottawa, Gloucester, Nepean, Kanata, Orleans.
Services:	Dedicated ISDN, dedicated SLIP/PPP, dial-up ISDN, dial-up SLIP/PPP, terminal accounts, UUCP service, domain registration, free Web home page with personal dial-up account, Web design, Web hosting.
World Wide Web:	http://www.synapse.net

Barrie Connex Inc.

Barrie, Ontario
bconnex.net, connex.net

55 Cedar Pointe Drive, Unit 606
Barrie, ON L4N 5R7

Voice:	705-725-0819, 1-800-461-8883
Fax:	705-725-1287
E-mail:	info@bconnex.net
Web:	http://www.bconnex.net

Service Area:	Alliston, Barrie, Beeton, Borden-Angus, Cookstown, Creemore, Tottenham, Elmvale, Lefroy, Moonstone, Oro, Stayner, Stroud, Midland, Bluewater, Christian Island, Lafontaine, Penetanguishene, Port McNicoll-Victoria Harbour, Wabaushene, Coldwater, Orillia, Collingwood, Wasaga Beach.
Services:	Leased line, dedicated ISDN, dedicated SLIP/PPP, frame relay, dial-up ISDN, dial-up SLIP/PPP, shell access, UUCP service, domain registration, free Web home page with personal dial-up account, Web design, Web hosting.
World Wide Web:	http://www.bconnex.net

Barrie Internet

Barrie, Ontario
barint.on.ca, barint.net

48 Morrow Road
Barrie, ON L4N 3V8

Voice:	705-733-3630
Fax:	705-733-3637
E-mail:	info@barint.on.ca
Web:	http://www.barint.on.ca

Service Area:	Barrie, Orillia, Midland, Collingwood, Cookstown, Bradford, Newmarket, Alliston, Beeton, Lefroy, Wasaga Beach, Creemore, Borden, Angus, Elmvale, Port McNicoll, Victoria Harbour, Waubaushene, Coldwater, Oro, Schomberg. Planning to expand to Aurora, Keswick, Mount Albert, Oak Ridges, Queensville, Brechin, Severn, Bridge, Sebright, Christian Island, Bluewater, Lafontaine, Penetanguishene.
Services:	Leased line, dedicated ISDN, dedicated SLIP/PPP, dial-up ISDN, dial-up SLIP/PPP, shell access, domain registration, free Web home page with personal dial-up account, Web design, Web hosting.
World Wide Web:	http://www.barint.on.ca

BC TEL Advanced Communications

Burnaby, British Columbia
bctel.net

4270 Kingsway, Suite 2600
Burnaby, BC V5H 4N2

Voice:	1-800-268-3488
Fax:	604-454-5199
E-mail:	info@bctel.net
Web:	http://www.bctel.net

Service Area:	Nanaimo, Victoria, Vancouver, North Vancouver, Newton, Langley, Abbottsford, Kelowna, Vernon, Kamloops, Quesnel, 100 Mile House, Williams Lake, Prince George and the rest of British Columbia.
Services:	Leased line, dedicated ISDN, dedicated SLIP/PPP, frame relay, dial-up ISDN, dial-up SLIP/PPP, domain registration, Web design, Web hosting.
World Wide Web:	http://www.bctel.net

BCnet

Vancouver, British Columbia
bc.net

515 West Hastings Street
Vancouver, BC V6B 5K3

Voice:	604-822-1348
Fax:	604-291-5022
E-mail:	info@bc.net
Web:	http://www.bc.net

Service Area:	All of British Columbia.
Services:	Leased line, dedicated ISDN, dedicated SLIP/PPP, frame relay, dial-up ISDN, domain registration.
World Wide Web:	http://www.bc.net

Binatech Information Services Inc.

Hamilton, Ontario
binatech.on.ca, binatech.com

100 Main Street East, 40th Floor
Hamilton, ON L8N 3W6

Voice: 905-527-7007, 1-800-387-1073
Fax: 905-527-0585
E-mail: info@binatech.on.ca
Web: http://www.binatech.on.ca

Service Area:	Hamilton, Burlington, Oakville, Mississauga. Planning to expand to the Niagara peninsula.
Services:	Leased line, dedicated ISDN, dedicated SLIP/PPP, dial-up ISDN, dial-up SLIP/PPP, UUCP service, domain registration, Web design, Web hosting.
World Wide Web:	http://www.binatech.on.ca

British Columbia Business Connections Ltd.

Victoria, British Columbia
commercial.net, canlaw.com, golf-handicap.com

P.O. Box 2412
Sidney, BC V8L 3Y3

Voice: 604-652-4815
Fax: 604-652-4867
E-mail: bcbc@commercial.net
Web: http://www.commercial.net/vault/bcbc.html

Service Area:	Victoria, Vancouver. Planning to expand to Kelowna, Kamloops, Prince George, Penticton, Vernon, Cranbrook.
Services:	Frame relay, dial-up SLIP/PPP, UUCP service, domain registration, Web design, Web hosting.
World Wide Web:	http://www.commercial.net/vault/bcbc.html

Burlington Network Services

Burlington, Ontario
bserv.com

140 Plains Road East
Burlington, ON L7T 2C3

Voice: 905-632-3977
Fax: 905-632-3536
E-mail: d.cairney@bserv.com
Web: http://www.bserv.com

Service Area:	Hamilton, Burlington, Waterdown, Oakville, Mississauga, Metropolitan Toronto, Kitchener, Waterloo, Guelph, Cambridge (Hespeler, Preston, Galt), Stoney Creek, Ancaster, Grimsby, Port Credit, Milton, Cooksville.
Services:	Leased line, dedicated ISDN, dedicated SLIP/PPP, frame relay, dial-up SLIP/PPP, shell access, terminal accounts, UUCP service, domain registration, Web design, Web hosting.
World Wide Web:	http://www.bserv.com

Cable Atlantic Inc.

St. John's, Newfoundland
cableatlantic.nf.ca, cableatlantic.net

541 Kenmount Road
St. John's, NF A1B 3P2

Voice: 709-753-7760
Fax: 709-722-8384
E-mail: info@cableatlantic.nf.ca
Web: http://www.cableatlantic.nf.ca

Service Area:	St. John's, Mount Pearl.
Services:	Leased line, dedicated SLIP/PPP, domain registration, Web design, Web hosting.
World Wide Web:	http://www.cableatlantic.nf.ca

Cable Island Ltd.

Toronto, Ontario
cable.com, cable.on.ca

622 Mt. Pleasant Road
Toronto, ON M4S 2M8

Voice:	416-322-5339
Fax:	416-484-1599
E-mail:	info@cable.com
Web:	http://www.cable.com

Service Area:	Greater Toronto area. Planning to expand to Montreal, Calgary, Sudbury, Vancouver, Falls Church (Virginia), Los Angeles, Dallas, Chicago, Philadelphia.
Services:	Dedicated ISDN, dedicated SLIP/PPP, frame relay, dial-up ISDN, dial-up SLIP/PPP, shell access, UUCP service, domain registration, free Web home page with personal dial-up account, Web design, Web hosting.
World Wide Web:	http://www.cable.com

CADVision Development Corp.

Calgary, Alberta
cadvision.com

300–5th Avenue S.W., Suite 1590
Calgary, AB T2P 3C4

Voice:	403-777-1300
Fax:	403-777-1319
E-mail:	info@cadvision.com
Web:	http://www.cadvision.com

Service Area:	Calgary.
Services:	Leased line, dedicated ISDN, dial-up SLIP/PPP, shell access, UUCP service, domain registration, Web design, Web hosting.
World Wide Web:	http://www.cadvision.com

cafe.net

Richmond, British Columbia
cafe.net, in-sys.com

8171 Ackroyd Road, Suite 6080
Richmond, BC V6X 3K1

Voice:	604-681-6365
Fax:	604-681-9484
E-mail:	feedback@cafe.net
Web:	http://www.cafe.net

Service Area:	Vancouver, Richmond, Surrey, Burnaby, West Vancouver, North Vancouver, Delta, White Rock.
Services:	Leased line, dedicated ISDN, dedicated SLIP/PPP, dial-up SLIP/PPP, shell access, terminal accounts, UUCP service, domain registration, Web design, Web hosting.
World Wide Web:	http://www.cafe.net

Calgary UNIX Users' Group

Calgary, Alberta
cuug.ab.ca

300–5th Avenue S.W., Suite 1520
Calgary, AB T2P 3C4

Voice:	403-265-2289
Fax:	403-261-5633
E-mail:	postmaster@cuug.ab.ca
Web:	http://www.cuug.ab.ca:8001

Service Area:	Calgary local dial-in area.
Services:	Dial-up SLIP/PPP, UUCP service, free Web home page with personal dial-up account, Web hosting.
World Wide Web:	http://www.cuug.ab.ca:8001

Canada Connect Corporation/XCITE Technology

Calgary, Alberta
canuck.com, xcite.com

P.O. Box 2621
Station M
Calgary, AB T2B 3C1

Voice:	403-777-2025
Fax:	403-777-2026
E-mail:	info@canuck.com (Internet Access),
	info@xcite.com (Internet Presence)
Web:	http://www.xcite.com

Service Area:	Calgary. Planning to expand to Edmonton, Vancouver, Saskatchewan.
Services:	Leased line, dedicated ISDN, dedicated SLIP/PPP, frame relay, dial-up ISDN, dial-up SLIP/PPP, shell access, UUCP service, domain registration, Web design, Web hosting.
World Wide Web:	http://www.xcite.com

CCI Networks (Division of Corporate Computers Inc.)

Edmonton, Alberta
ccinet.ab.ca

4130–95 Street
Edmonton, AB T6E 6H5

Voice:	403-450-6787
Fax:	403-450-9143
E-mail:	info@ccinet.ab.ca
Web:	http://www.ccinet.ab.ca

Service Area:	CCINet Affiliates: *Edmonton:* CCI Networks, 4130-95 Street, Edmonton, Alberta, T6E 6H5 Tel: 403-450-6787, Fax: 403-450-9143. *Calgary:* CCI Networks, 1201-5 Street S.W., Suite 202, Calgary, Alberta, T2R 0Y8, Tel: 403-237-7737, Fax: 403-237-7734. *Fort McMurray:* Altech Communications, 10015 Centennial Drive, Bay 3, Fort McMurray, Alberta, T9H 1Y2, Tel: 403-743-1829, Fax: 403-791-7092.

Grande Prairie: Custom Communications, 10304-100 Street, Grande Prairie, Alberta, T8V 2M1, Tel: 403-538-2012, Fax: 403-539-5904. *Red Deer:* Real Time Technologies Inc. (RTT), 6831-52 Avenue, Red Deer, Alberta, T4N 4L2, Tel: 403-357-5930, Fax: 403-357-5932. *Wetaskiwin:* The Wetaskiwin Telephone Co., 5110-49 Street, Wetaskiwin, Alberta, T9A 1H7, Tel: 403-352-6029, Fax: 403-352-6034. *Drayton Valley:* Town of Drayton Valley, 5120-52 Street, Drayton Valley, Alberta, T0E 0M0, Tel: 403-542-5327 ext. 380, Fax: 403-542-5753. *Fort Vermilion:* Fort Vermilion School Division, P.O. Bay #1, Fort Vermilion, Alberta, T0H 1N0, Tel: 403-926-2537, Fax: 403-926-2726. *Cold Lake/Grand Centre:* Dynamic Systems Integration, 5026-40 Street, Grand Centre, Alberta, T0A 1T5, Tel: 403-594-0204. *Peace River/Grimshaw:* Arcacia Internet Services, 10011-102 Avenue, 2nd Floor, Peace River, Alberta, T8S 1N1, Tel: 403-624-8812, Fax: 403-332-1235. Planning to expand to Lethbridge, Hinton, Jasper, Edson, Lloydminster.

Services:	Leased line, dedicated ISDN, dedicated SLIP/PPP, frame relay, dial-up SLIP/PPP, UUCP service, domain registration, free Web home page with personal dial-up account, Web design, Web hosting.
World Wide Web:	http://www.ccinet.ab.ca

Chatham Internet Access

Chatham, Ontario
ciaccess.com

162 Queen Street
Chatham, ON N7M 5L1

Voice:	519-358-4638
Fax:	519-352-2095
E-mail:	kevin@ciaccess.com

Service Area:	Chatham, Wallaceburg, Dresden, Blenheim, Ridgetown, Tilbury, Wheatley.
Services:	Leased line, dedicated ISDN, dedicated SLIP/PPP, frame relay, dial-up ISDN, dial-up SLIP/PPP, terminal accounts, domain registration, Web design, Web hosting.
World Wide Web:	N/A

CIMtegration Ltd.

North York, Ontario
cimtegration.com, cimtegration.on.ca, interscape.net

2727 Steeles Avenue West, Suite 300
North York, ON M3J 3G9

Voice:	416-665-3566
Fax:	416-665-8285
E-mail:	info@cimtegration.com
Web:	http://www.cimtegration.com

Service Area:	Greater Toronto Area.
Services:	Leased line, dedicated SLIP/PPP, dial-up SLIP/PPP, UUCP service, domain registration, Web design.
World Wide Web:	http://www.cimtegration.com

CitéNet Telecom Inc

Montréal, Québec
citenet.net, citenet.com, citenet.ca

1155 René Lévesque West
Montréal, PQ H3B 3T6

Voice:	514-861-5050
Fax:	514-861-5953
E-mail:	info@citenet.net
Web:	http://www.citenet.net

Service Area:	Dedicated Connectivity: Anywhere in Canada. Quebec Dial-Up: Montreal, St-Jerome, Ste-Agathe, St-Sauveur, Joliette, Lachute, Valleyfield, Hemmingford, Granby, Ste-Hyacinthe, Drummondville, Sherbrooke, Quebec City, Trois-Rivières and more. Ontario Dial-Up: Ottawa, Toronto and suburbs. British Columbia dial-up: Vancouver and other major centres also served. Planning to expand to Hawkesbury and Cornwall, Ontario, plus many smaller urban centres.
Services:	Leased line, dedicated ISDN, dedicated SLIP/PPP, frame relay, dial-up ISDN, dial-up SLIP/PPP, shell access, terminal accounts, UUCP service, domain registration, Web design, Web hosting.
World Wide Web:	http://www.citenet.net

ClicNet Télécommunications, Inc.

Québec, Québec
qbc.clic.net

840, rue Ste-Thérèse
Québec, PQ G1N 1S7

Voice:	418-686-CLIC
Fax:	418-682-5594
E-mail:	info@qbc.clic.net
Web:	http://www.qbc.clic.net

Service Area:	Quebec City, Ste-Foy, Sillery, Charlesbourg, Beauport, Lévis, Loretteville. Planning to expand to Montreal, Trois Rivières, Drummondville, Chicoutimi.
Services:	Leased line, dedicated ISDN, dedicated SLIP/PPP, frame relay, dial-up SLIP/PPP, shell access, UUCP service, domain registration, free Web home page with personal dial-up account, Web design, Web hosting.
World Wide Web:	http://www.qbc.clic.net

Club Centra

Brossard, Québec
centra.ca, centra.com

8705, boulevard Taschereau
Brossard, PQ J4Y 1A4

Voice:	514-875-6615
Fax:	514-875-6617
E-mail:	info@centra.ca
Web:	http://www.centra.ca

Service Area: Montreal, Dorval, Verdun, Lachine, Lasalle, Dollard-des-Ormeaux, Beaconsfield, Ste-Anne-de-Bellevue, Pointe-Claire, Pierrefonds, Ste-Geneviève, Baie-d'Urfé, Senneville, Roxboro, Mount-Royal, St-Laurent, St-Léonard, Anjou, Westmount, Côte-St-Luc, Brossard, Longueuil, St-Lambert, Greenfield Park, St-Hubert, La Prairie, St-Bruno, Drummondville, Laval, St-Raphaël-de-l'Île Bizard. Planning to expand to Ottawa, Kingston, Toronto, Quebec City.

Services: Leased line, dedicated ISDN, dedicated SLIP/PPP, frame relay, dial-up ISDN, dial-up SLIP/PPP, domain registration, Web design, Web hosting.

World Wide Web: http://www.centra.ca

CoastNet Designs

Victoria, British Columbia
coastnet.com

1803 Douglas Street, Suite 304
Victoria, BC V8T 5C3

Voice:	604-384-6782
Fax:	604-384-3363
E-mail:	info@coastnet.com
Web:	http://coastnet.com

Service Area: Victoria. Planning to expand throughout B.C.

Services: Leased line, dedicated ISDN, dedicated SLIP/PPP, dial-up ISDN, dial-up SLIP/PPP, shell access, terminal accounts, domain registration, free Web home page with personal dial-up account, Web design, Web hosting.

World Wide Web: http://coastnet.com

Communications Accessibles Montréal

Montréal, Québec
cam.org, cam.net

2055 Peel, Suite 825
Montréal, PQ H3A 1V4

Voice:	514-288-2581
Fax:	514-288-3401
E-mail:	info@cam.org
Web:	http://www.cam.org

Service Area: Montreal area (includes Laval and the immediate South Shore: Longueuil, St. Lambert, Greenfield Park, St. Bruno, Boucherville, Brossard).

Services: Dedicated ISDN, dedicated SLIP/PPP, dial-up ISDN, dial-up SLIP/PPP, shell access, UUCP service, domain registration, free Web home page with personal dial-up account, Web hosting.

World Wide Web: http://www.cam.org

Les Communications DANIA

Laval, Québec
dania.com

4 Quintal
Laval, PQ H7N 4V4

Voice:	514-663-9131
Fax:	514-967-8537
E-mail:	sysop@dania.com
Web:	http://www.dania.com

Service Area:	Montreal, Laval, North Shore, South Shore, lower Laurentians.
Services:	Leased line, dedicated ISDN, dedicated SLIP/PPP, dial-up SLIP/PPP, domain registration, free Web home page with personal dial-up account, Web design, Web hosting.
World Wide Web:	http://www.dania.com

Communications Inter-Accès

Montréal, Québec
interax.net

5475 Paré, Suite 104
Montréal, PQ H4P 1R4

Voice: 514-367-0002
Fax: 514-368-3529
E-mail: info@interax.net
Web: http://www.interax.net

Service Area:	Montreal, Quebec City, Toronto. Planning to expand to Ottawa.
Services:	Leased line, dedicated ISDN, dedicated SLIP/PPP, frame relay, dial-up ISDN, dial-up SLIP/PPP, UUCP service, domain registration, Web hosting.
World Wide Web:	http://www.interax.net

Communications Vir

Montréal, Québec
vir.ca, vir.net, vir.com, montreal.com

C.P. 628, Succursale Victoria
Montréal, PQ H3Z 2Y7

Voice: 514-933-8886
Fax: 514-630-9047
E-mail: info@vir.ca
Web: http://www.vir.ca

Service Area:	St-Sauveur, Mirabel, St-Eustache, Ste-Thérèse, Oka, Rigaud, Hudson, Vaudreuil, Beauharnois, Ste-Martine, Châteauguay, St-Rémi, Hemmingford, Napierville, Clarenceville, St-Jean, La Prairie, St-Lambert, Chambly, Marieville, St-Bruno, Longueuil, Boucherville, Ste-Julie-de-Verchères, Beloeil, St-Marc, Varennes, St-Denis, Verchères, Le Gardeur, Lavaltrie, L'Épiphanie-L'Assomption, Terrebonne, Mascouche, St-Lin, Ste-Julienne, St-Calixte-de-Kilkenny, Ste-Anne-des-Plaines, Ste-Rose, St-Vincent-de-Paul, Pont-Viau, Chomedey, Laval, Ste-Geneviève, Île-Perrot, Pointe-Claire, Beaconsfield, Kirkland, Pierrefonds, Dorval, Roxboro, Baie-d'Urfé, Lachine, Ville-St-Pierre, St-Laurent, Notre-Dame-de-Grace, Montreal West, Montreal.
Services:	Leased line, dedicated ISDN, dedicated SLIP/PPP, frame relay, dial-up ISDN, dial-up SLIP/PPP, shell access, terminal accounts, domain registration, free Web home page with personal dial-up account, Web design, Web hosting.
World Wide Web:	http://www.vir.ca

Comnet

Brandon, Manitoba
common.net

P.O. Box 20116
Brandon, MB R7A 6Y8

Voice: 204-725-5750
Fax: 204-725-5751
E-mail: info@common.net
Web: http://www.common.net

Service Area:	Brandon, Shilo, Rivers, Kemney, Alexander, Forrest, Rapid City, Austin, Justice, Carberry, Douglas.
Services:	Leased line, dedicated SLIP/PPP, frame relay, dial-up SLIP/PPP, shell access, terminal accounts, UUCP service, domain registration, free Web home page with personal dial-up account, Web design, Web hosting.
World Wide Web:	http://www.common.net

Comnet Communications

Gloucester, Ontario
comnet.ca

5480 Canotek Road, Suite 14
Gloucester, ON K1J 9H6

Voice: 613-747-5555
Fax: 613-747-8796
E-mail: info@comnet.ca
Web: http://www.comnet.ca

Service Area:	Almonte, Alymer, Bourgette, Casselman, Carleton Place, Carp, Chelsea, Clarence Creek, Constance Bay, Crysler, Cumberland, Embrun, Gatineau, Gloucester, Hull, Jockvale, Kanata, Stittsville, Kemptville, Low, Luskville, Manotick, Merrickville, Metcalfe, Navan, North Gower, Orleans, Osgoode, Ottawa, Pakenham, Perkins, Plantagenet, Quyon, Richmond, Rockland, Russell, St-Pierre-de-Wakefield, Wakefield. Planning to expand to Montreal.
Services:	Dedicated ISDN, dedicated SLIP/PPP, dial-up ISDN, dial-up SLIP/PPP, shell access, UUCP service, domain registration, free Web home page with personal dial-up account, Web design, Web hosting.
World Wide Web:	http://www.comnet.ca

CompuServe Incorporated

Columbus, Ohio
compuserve.com

5000 Arlington Center Boulevard
P.O. Box 20212
Columbus, OH 43220

Voice: 1-800-848-8199
Web: http://www.compuserve.com

Service Area:	Vancouver, Victoria, Edmonton, Calgary, Regina, Saskatoon, Winnipeg, Toronto, London, Kitchener, Ottawa, Hamilton, Montreal, Quebec City, Halifax.
Services:	Dial-up SLIP/PPP, terminal accounts.
World Wide Web:	http://www.compuserve.com

Concepta Communications Inc.

Trois-Rivières, Québec
concepta.com, concepta.net, concepta.qc.ca

2425, boul. des Récollets
Trois-Rivières, PQ G8Z 4G1

Voice: 819-378-8362
Fax: 819-378-7335
E-mail: support@concepta.com
Web: http://www.concepta.com

Service Area:	Bécancour, Baie-de-Shawinigan, Baie-Jolie, Cap-de-la-Madeleine, Champlain, Gentilly, Lac Doucet, Louiseville, Maskinongé, Mont-Carmel, Nicolet, Pointe-du-Lac, Port-St-François, Red Mill, Shawinigan, Shawinigan-Nord, Shawinigan-Sud, St-Angèle-de-Laval, St-Barnabé, St-Boniface-de-Shawinigan, St-Célestin, St-Étienne-des-Grès, St-Grégoire, St-Justin, St-Louis-de-France, St-Luc-de-Vincennes, St-Mathieu, St-Maurice, St-Narcisse, St-Sylvère, St-Wenceslas, Ste-Gertrude, Ste-Marie-de-Blanford, Ste-Marthe-du-Cap-de-la-Madeleine, Ste-Monique-de-Nicolet, Trois-Rivières, Trois-Rivières-Ouest, Yamachiche. Planning to expand to Grandmère.
Services:	Leased line, dedicated ISDN, dedicated SLIP/PPP, dial-up SLIP/PPP, domain registration, Web design, Web hosting.
World Wide Web:	http://www.concepta.com

Connection MMIC Inc.

St-Laurent, Québec
connectmmic.net

5635, chemin St-François
St-Laurent, PQ H4S 1W6

Voice:	514-331-6642
Fax:	514-332-6642
E-mail:	info@connectmmic.net
Web:	http://www.connectmmic.net

Service Area:	Montreal, Valleyfield, Beauharnois, Ste-Martine, Châteauguay, Pierrefonds, Kirkand, Ste-Geneviève, Senneville, Hudson, St-Lazare, Vaudreuil, Dorion, Ste-Anne-de-Bellevue, Pointe-Claire, Dorval, Baie-d'Urfé, Beaconsfield, St-Jean-sur-Richelieu, St-Luc, Henryville, St-Laurent, Longueuil, Boucherville, Varennes, Verchères, Laval, St-Eustache, Ste-Marthe-sur-le-Lac, Deux-Montagnes, St-Joseph-sur-le-Lac, Oka, St-Sauveur, Ste-Anne-des-Plaines, Mascouche, Mirabel, Ste-Thérèse, Terrebonne, Île-Perrot, Roxboro, Lachine, St-Rémi, St-Constant, Ste-Catherine, Laprairie, St-Lambert, Chambly, St-Bruno, Ste-Julie, Beloeil, Pointe-aux-Trembles, Laval-Ouest, Chomedey, Pont-Viau, St-Vincent-de-Paul, Ste-Rose, Ste-Dorothée, Laval-Est, Le Gardeur, Repentigny, L'Épiphanie, L'Assomption. Planning to expand to Quebec City, Ottawa, Toronto.
Services:	Leased line, dedicated ISDN, dedicated SLIP/PPP, frame relay, dial-up ISDN, dial-up SLIP/PPP, UUCP service, domain registration, free Web home page with personal dial-up account, Web design, Web hosting.
World Wide Web:	http://www.connectmmic.net

ConsuLan

Montréal, Québec
consulan.com

5800, boul. Cavendish, Suite 402
Côte-St-Luc, PQ H4W 2T5

Voice:	514-482-4848
Fax:	514-482-5001
E-mail:	info@consulan.com
Web:	http://www.consulan.com

Service Area:	Greater Montreal area.
Services:	Dedicated SLIP/PPP, dial-up SLIP/PPP, domain registration, free Web home page with personal dial-up account, Web design, Web hosting.
World Wide Web:	http://www.consulan.com

CoreLAN Communications, Inc.

Mississauga, Ontario
corelan.com, infoshare.net

1299 Cermel Drive
Mississauga, ON L5H 3V3

Voice:	416-362-1700
Fax:	416-362-8772
E-mail:	webmaster@corelan.com
Web:	http://www.corelan.com

Service Area:	Toronto. Planning to expand to Montreal, Waterloo, Vancouver, Winnipeg.
Services:	Leased line, dedicated ISDN, dedicated SLIP/PPP, domain registration, Web design, Web hosting.
World Wide Web:	http://www.corelan.com

Cosmos Network Access Ltd.

Lethbridge, Alberta
cosmos.ab.ca

740–4th Avenue South, Suite 14
Lethbridge, AB T1J 0N9

Voice:	403-320-2253
Fax:	403-320-7044
E-mail:	sales@cosmos.ab.ca
Web:	http://www.cosmos.ab.ca

Service Area:	Taber, Vulcan, Claresholm, Warner, Fort Macleod. Planning to expand to Pincher Creek, Medicine Hat.
Services:	Leased line, dedicated ISDN, dedicated SLIP/PPP, dial-up ISDN, dial-up SLIP/PPP, shell access, UUCP service, domain registration, free Web home page with personal dial-up account, Web design, Web hosting.
World Wide Web:	http://www.cosmos.ab.ca

CRS Online Ltd.

Etobicoke, Ontario
canrem.com, crso.com

12 Steinway Boulevard, Unit 24
Etobicoke, ON M9W 6M5

Voice:	416-213-6000, 1-800-563-2529
Fax:	416-213-6038
E-mail:	info@frontier.canrem.com
Web:	http://www.canrem.com

Service Area:	Hamilton, Stoney Creek, Dundas, Lynden, Brantford, Burlington, Milton, Caledon East, Orangeville, Hespeler, Guelph, Kitchener-Waterloo, Brampton, Georgetown, Toronto and surrounding areas, Aurora, Newmarket, Barrie, Moonstone, Orillia, Midland, Ajax, Oshawa, Bowmanville.
Services:	Dial-up SLIP/PPP, terminal accounts.
World Wide Web:	http://www.canrem.com

Cyberlink Online

Toronto, Ontario
clo.com

464 Yonge Street, Suite 211
Toronto, ON M5G 1Y6

Voice:	416-410-0111
Fax:	416-921-7934
E-mail:	info@clo.com
Web:	http://www.clo.com

Service Area:	Toronto, Pickering, Whitby, Oakville, Mississauga, Thornhill, Bolton, Woodbridge. Planning to expand to Burlington, Milton, Oshawa.
Services:	Leased line, dedicated ISDN, dedicated SLIP/PPP, dial-up ISDN, dial-up SLIP/PPP, shell access, terminal accounts, UUCP service, domain registration, free Web home page with personal dial-up account, Web design, Web hosting.
World Wide Web:	http://www.clo.com

Cyberlink Systems Corp.

Cranbrook, British Columbia
cyberlink.bc.ca

44–12th Avenue South, Suite 102
Cranbrook, BC V1C 2R7

Voice:	604-426-5175
Fax:	604-489-5236
E-mail:	info@cyberlink.bc.ca
Web:	http://www.cyberlink.bc.ca

Service Area:	Cranbrook, Jaffray, Wardner, Moyie, Skookumchuck, Galloway, Canal Flats, Yahk, Elko. Planning to expand to Kimberley, Invermere, Fernie.
Services:	Dial-up ISDN, dial-up SLIP/PPP, shell access, terminal accounts, domain registration, free Web home page with personal dial-up account, Web design, Web hosting.
World Wide Web:	http://www.cyberlink.bc.ca

CyberPlus Technologies Inc.

Gloucester, Ontario
cyberplus.ca

5450 Canotek Road
P.O. Box 27011
Gloucester, ON K1J 9L9

Voice: 613-749-8598
Fax: 613-749-0285
E-mail: info@cyberplus.ca
Web: http://www.cyberplus.ca

Service Area:	Ottawa and local dial-in area, Gloucester, Nepean, Vanier, Kanata, Cumberland, Hull, Gatineau, Aylmer, Vancouver, Calgary, Edmonton, Winnipeg, Toronto, London, Windsor, Kitchener-Waterloo, Hamilton, Montreal, Quebec City, Halifax.
Services:	Dedicated ISDN, dedicated SLIP/PPP, dial-up ISDN, dial-up SLIP/PPP, shell access, UUCP service, domain registration, free Web home page with personal dial-up account, Web design, Web hosting.

World Wide Web: http://www.cyberplus.ca

Cyberspace Online Information Systems (Division of Group West Systems Ltd.)

Winnipeg, Manitoba
cyberspc.mb.ca

794 Sargent Avenue, Unit 18
Winnipeg, MB R3E 0B7

Voice: 204-775-3650
Fax: 204-775-3501
E-mail: info@cyberspc.mb.ca
Web: http:/www.cyberspc.mb.ca

Service Area:	Winnipeg. Planning to expand to rural Manitoba.

Services:	Leased line, dedicated ISDN, dedicated SLIP/PPP, frame relay, dial-up ISDN, dial-up SLIP/PPP, shell access, terminal accounts, UUCP service, domain registration, free Web home page with personal dial-up account, Web hosting.

World Wide Web: http:/www.cyberspc.mb.ca

Cyberstore Systems Inc.

Vancouver, British Columbia
Cyberstore.ca, Cyberstore.com, Cyberstore.net

601 West Broadway, Suite 201
Vancouver, BC V5Z 4C2

Voice: 604-482-3400
Fax: 604-482-3433
E-mail: info@cyberstore.ca
Web: http://www.cyberstore.ca

Service Area:	Vancouver, Victoria, Kelowna, Whistler.
Services:	Leased line, dedicated SLIP/PPP, dial-up SLIP/PPP, domain registration, Web design, Web hosting.

World Wide Web: http://www.cyberstore.ca

Cybersurf Internet Access

Calgary, Alberta
cia.com

1212–31 Avenue N.E., Suite 312
Calgary, AB T2E 7S8

Voice: 403-777-2000
Fax: 403-777-2003
E-mail: info@cia.com
Web: http://www.cia.com

Service Area:	Calgary, Lethbridge, Red Deer, Edmonton.
Services:	Leased line, dedicated ISDN, dedicated SLIP/PPP, dial-up ISDN, dial-up SLIP/PPP, domain registration, Web design, Web hosting.

World Wide Web: http://www.cia.com

Cyberus Online Inc.

Ottawa, Ontario
cyberus.ca, cyberus.com

99 Fifth Avenue, Suite 406
Ottawa, ON K1S 5P5

Voice:	613-233-1215, 1-800-809-9883
Fax:	613-233-0292
E-mail:	info@cyberus.ca
Web:	http://www.cyberus.ca

Service Area:	Ottawa, Carleton Place, Almonte, Kemptville, Merrickville, Buckingham, Low, Embrun, Russell, Rockland, Val-des-Bois, Luskville, Wakefield, St-Pierre-de-Wakefield, Quyon, Bourget, Clarence Creek, North Gower, Kanata/Stittsville, Pakenham, Gatineau, Shawville, Perkins, Plantagenet, Aylmer, Manotick, Casselman, Metcalfe, Gloucester, Jockvale, Orleans, Osgoode, Chelsea, Constance Bay, Cumberland, Navan, Richmond, Carp, Thurso and Crysler. Planning to expand to Toronto, Vancouver and Montreal.
Services:	Leased line, dedicated ISDN, dedicated SLIP/PPP, dial-up ISDN, dial-up SLIP/PPP, shell access, UUCP service, domain registration, free Web home page with personal dial-up account, Web design, Web hosting.
World Wide Web:	http:/www.cyberus.ca

Cycor Communications Inc.

Charlottetown, Prince Edward Island
cycor.ca

P.O. Box 454
Charlottetown, PE C1A 7K7

Voice:	902-629-2453, 1-800-282-9267
Fax:	902-629-2456
E-mail:	sign.me.up@cycor.ca
Web:	http://www.cycor.ca

Service Area:	Vancouver, Calgary, Saskatoon, Winnipeg, Toronto, Ottawa, Montreal, Moncton, Charlottetown, Halifax, Edmonton, Hamilton, Kitchener, London, St. John's, Oshawa, St. Catharines, Sudbury, Victoria, Regina, Windsor, Saint John, Thunder Bay.
Services:	Leased line, dedicated ISDN, dedicated SLIP/PPP, frame relay, dial-up ISDN, dial-up SLIP/PPP, domain registration, Web design, Web hosting.
World Wide Web:	http://www.cycor.ca

Data Link Canada West (DLC-West)

Regina, Saskatchewan
dlcwest.com

12 Gardiner Avenue
Regina, SK S4P 4P6

Voice:	306-585-0362
Fax:	306-352-6450
E-mail:	jim.nickel@dlcwest.com
Web:	http://www.dlcwest.com

Service Area:	Regina. Planning to expand to Saskatoon, Moose Jaw, Swift Current.
Services:	Leased line, dedicated ISDN, dedicated SLIP/PPP, frame relay, dial-up SLIP/PPP, shell access, terminal accounts, UUCP service, domain registration, free Web home page with personal dial-up account, Web design, Web hosting.
World Wide Web:	http://www.dlcwest.com

Debug Computer Services

Calgary, Alberta
debug.cuc.ab.ca, debug.ab.ca

Box 53096
Marlborough P.O.
Calgary, AB T2A 7P1

Voice:	403-248-5798
Fax:	403-248-5798
E-mail:	root@debug.cuc.ab.ca
Web:	http://198.53.165.200

Service Area:	Acme, Airdrie, Beiseker, Blackie, Bragg Creek, Calgary, Carstairs, Cochrane, Cremona, Crossfield, High River, Irricana, Langdon, Longview, Morley, Okotoks, Strathmore, Turner Valley.
Services:	Leased line, dedicated SLIP/PPP, dial-up SLIP/PPP, terminal accounts, UUCP service, domain registration, free Web home page with personal dial-up account, Web design, Web hosting.
World Wide Web:	http://198.53.165.200

Deep Cove Online Ltd.

White Rock, British Columbia
deepcove.com

Box 45504
Sunnyside P.O.
White Rock, BC V4A 9N3

Voice: 604-541-2025
Fax: 604-536-7418
E-mail: wayne@deepcove.com
Web: http://www.deepcove.com

Service Area:	Vancouver, Burnaby, New Westminster, North Vancouver, West Vancouver, Richmond, Delta, Surrey, White Rock, Coquitlam, Port Coquitlam, Port Moody, Maple Ridge, Cloverdale, Abbotsford, Clearbrook, Matsqui, Langley. Planning to expand to Chilliwack.
Services:	Leased line, dedicated SLIP/PPP, dial-up SLIP/PPP, shell access, terminal accounts, UUCP service, domain registration, Web design, Web hosting.
World Wide Web:	http://www.deepcove.com

Delphi Internet Services

Lowell, Massachusetts
delphi.com

Crosspoint Towers
900 Chelmsford Street
Lowell, MA 01951

Voice: 1-800-695-4005
E-mail: askdelphi@delphi.com
Web: http://www.delphi.com

Service Area:	Burnaby, Calgary, Dundas, Edmonton, Halifax, Hull, Kitchener, London, Ottawa, Toronto, Vancouver, Winnipeg, Windsor, Montreal, St-Laurent, Quebec City.
Services:	Terminal accounts.
World Wide Web:	http://www.delphi.com

Digital Ark Internet Services Inc.

Courtenay, British Columbia
ark.com

P.O. Box 3310
205–576 England Avenue
Courtenay, BC V9N 5N5

Voice: 604-334-9641
Fax: 604-334-2365
E-mail: info@mars.ark.com
Web: http://www.ark.com

Service Area:	Northern Vancouver Island (Irenyx Data Group Inc.): Courtenay, Comox, Cumberland, Oyster Bay, Union Bay, Willow Point, Campbell River, Black Creek, Denman Island, Quadra Island, Hornby Island, Merville. Central Vancouver Island (Zegna Electronic Inc.): Nanaimo, Parksville, Qualicum Beach, Bowser, Gabriola Island, Lantzville, Wellington, Nanoose, Cedar. Planning to expand to Toronto and Richmond.

Services: Leased line, dedicated SLIP/PPP, dial-up SLIP/PPP, shell access, domain registration, free Web home page with personal dial-up account, Web design, Web hosting.

World Wide Web: http://www.ark.com

Docker Services Ltd.

Brandon, Manitoba
docker.com

117–10th Street
Brandon, MB R7A 4E7

Voice: 204-727-7788
Fax: 204-726-4580
E-mail: info@docker.com
Web: http://www.docker.com

Service Area: Brandon, Rivers, Wawanesa, Souris, Rapid City, Minnedosa.

Services: Leased line, dedicated SLIP/PPP, frame relay, dial-up SLIP/PPP, UUCP service, domain registration, free Web home page with personal dial-up account, Web design, Web hosting.

World Wide Web: http://www.docker.com

DOCUSystems InterNet Services (Division of DOCUSystems Inc.)

Oshawa, Ontario
durham.net

306 King Street West
Oshawa, ON L1J 2J9

Voice: 905-725-1016
Fax: 905-728-7918
E-mail: sales@mail.durham.net
Web: http://www.durham.net

Service Area: Ajax, Blackstock, Bowmanville, Brooklin, Hampton, Newcastle, Newtonville, Oshawa, Pickering, Port Perry, Whitby, Wilmont Creek.

Services: Leased line, dedicated ISDN, dedicated SLIP/PPP, frame relay, dial-up ISDN, dial-up SLIP/PPP, shell access, UUCP service, domain registration, free Web home page with personal dial-up account, Web design, Web hosting.

World Wide Web: http://www.durham.net

Dtronix Internet Services

Mississauga, Ontario
dtronix.com

2857 Derry Road East, Suite 307
Mississauga, ON L4T 1A6

Voice: 416-410-2304
E-mail: info@dtronix.com
Web: http://www.dtronix.com

Service Area: Toronto, Mississauga.

Services: Dedicated SLIP/PPP, dial-up SLIP/PPP, shell access, UUCP service, domain registration, free Web home page with personal dial-up account, Web design, Web hosting.

World Wide Web: http://www.dtronix.com

Durham Internet Services Inc.

Ajax, Ontario
dis.on.ca

335 Bayly Street West, Suite 203
Ajax, ON L1S 6M2

Voice: 905-619-9863
Fax: 905-619-1686
E-mail: info@dis.on.ca
Web: http://www.dis.on.ca

Service Area:	Pickering, Oshawa, Whitby, Bowmanville, Newcastle, Port Perry, Orono, Newtonville, Blackstock, Hampton, Brooklin, Claremont, Ajax, part of Markham, Scarborough, Toronto and anywhere in the (416) area code. Planning to expand to Peterborough, Bailieboro, Lakefield, Bethany, Bridgenorth, Buckhorn, Burleigh Falls, Cavan, Hastings, Keene, Milbrook, Norwood and Omemee.
Services:	Leased line, dedicated ISDN, dedicated SLIP/PPP, dial-up SLIP/PPP, shell access, domain registration, free Web home page with personal dial-up account, Web design, Web hosting.
World Wide Web:	http://www.dis.on.ca

E-Design Inc.

Montréal, Québec
e-design.com, quebec.net

370 Guy Street, Suite 201
Montréal, PQ H3J 1S6

Voice:	514-933-9776
Fax:	514-931-5362
E-mail:	info@e-design.com
Web:	http://www.e-design.com, http://www.quebec.net

Service Area:	Greater Montreal area.
Services:	Leased line, dedicated ISDN, dedicated SLIP/PPP, dial-up ISDN, dial-up SLIP/PPP, domain registration, free Web home page with personal dial-up account, Web design, Web hosting.
World Wide Web:	http://www.e-design.com, http://www.quebec.net

Easy Internet

Nepean, Ontario
easyinternet.ca

39 Robertson Road, Suite 232
Nepean, ON K2H 8R2

Voice:	613-726-0473
Fax:	613-726-9577
E-mail:	information@easyinternet.ca
Web:	http://www.easyinternet.ca

Service Area:	Ontario: Ottawa, Orleans, Nepean, Kanata, Casselman, Constance Bay, Cumberland, Navan, Richmond, Carp, Crysler, Gloucester, Almonte, Carleton Place, Jockvale, Kemptville, Manotick, Merrickville, Metcalfe, Osgoode, Embrun, Russell, Rockland, Bourget, Clarence Creek, North Gower, Stittsville, Pakenham, Plantagenet. Quebec: Hull, Aylmer, Chelsea, Gatineau, Buckingham, Low, Val-des-Bois, Luskville, Wakefield, St-Pierre-de-Wakefield, Quyon, Shawville, Perkins, Thurso.
Services:	Leased line, dedicated SLIP/PPP, dial-up SLIP/PPP, shell access, domain registration, free Web home page with personal dial-up account, Web design, Web hosting.
World Wide Web:	http://www.easyinternet.ca

eConnect

Toronto, Ontario
econnect.com, econnect.ca, econnect.net

230 Richmond Street West, 7th Floor
Toronto, ON M5V 1V6

Voice:	416-585-2045
Fax:	416-585-1023
E-mail:	econnect@passport.ca
Web:	http://www.seneca.com/econnect

Service Area:	Montreal and surrounding suburbs, Toronto and surrounding suburbs, Calgary and surrounding suburbs. Planning to expand to Edmonton and surrounding suburbs, Vancouver and surrounding suburbs, Ottawa and surrounding suburbs.
Services:	Leased line, dedicated ISDN, dedicated SLIP/PPP, frame relay, dial-up ISDN, dial-up SLIP/PPP, shell access, UUCP service, domain registration, Web design, Web hosting.

World Wide Web: http://www.seneca.com/econnect

ED TEL PLAnet™ (Public Live Access Network) Internet Service

Edmonton, Alberta
planet.eon.net

44 Capital Boulevard
10044–108 Street
Edmonton, AB T5J 3S7

Voice:	403-423-4638
Fax:	403-428-0917
E-mail:	webmaster@planet.eon.net
Web:	http://planet.eon.net

Service Area:	Edmonton. Planning a provincial, possibly national, roaming service.
Services:	Leased line, dedicated ISDN, dedicated SLIP/PPP, dial-up ISDN, dial-up SLIP/PPP, domain registration.

World Wide Web: http://planet.eon.net

Electro-Byte Technologies

Sarnia, Ontario
ebtech.net, sarnia.com

559-B Exmouth Street
Sarnia, ON N7T 5P6

Voice:	519-332-8235
Fax:	519-332-8307
E-mail:	info@ebtech.net
Web:	http://www.ebtech.net

Service Area:	Sarnia, Petrolia, Brigden, Corunna, Bright's Cove, Point Edward, Oil Springs. Planning to expand to Grand Bend, Forest, Port Franks, Chatham, Alvinston, Tilbury, Riverside.
Services:	Leased line, dedicated ISDN, dedicated SLIP/PPP, frame relay, dial-up ISDN, dial-up SLIP/PPP, shell access, UUCP service, domain registration, free Web home page with personal dial-up account, Web design, Web hosting.

World Wide Web: http://www.ebtech.net

Elgin and St. Thomas Community Centre for Information Access

St. Thomas, Ontario
ccia.st-thomas.on.ca

153 Curtis Street
St. Thomas, ON N5P 3Z7

Voice:	519-633-1055
Fax:	519-631-1987
E-mail:	admin@ccia.st-thomas.on.ca
Web:	http://www.ccia.st-thomas.on.ca

Service Area:	St. Thomas, London, Port Stanley, Sparta, Belmont.
Services:	Dedicated SLIP/PPP, frame relay, dial-up SLIP/PPP, shell access, terminal accounts, domain registration, free Web home page with personal dial-up account, Web design, Web hosting.

World Wide Web: http://www.ccia.st-thomas.on.ca

Enterprise Online

Markham, Ontario
enterprise.ca

2820–14th Avenue
Markham, ON L3R 0S9

Voice:	416-932-3030
Fax:	416-626-8083
E-mail:	sales@enterprise.ca
Web:	http://www.enterprise.ca

Service Area:	Toronto, Markham.
Services:	Dedicated ISDN, dedicated SLIP/PPP, dial-up ISDN, dial-up SLIP/PPP, domain registration, free Web home page with personal dial-up account, Web design, Web hosting.
World Wide Web:	http://www.enterprise.ca

Escape Communications Corp.

Winnipeg, Manitoba
escape.ca

1383 Pembina Highway, Suite 206
Winnipeg, MB R3T 2B9

Voice:	204-925-4290
Fax:	204-925-4291
E-mail:	info@escape.ca
Web:	http://www.escape.ca

Service Area:	Winnipeg, Eriksdale, Ashern, St. Laurent, Poplarfield, Moosehorn, Lundar, Fisher Branch. Planning to expand to: Manitoba; Arborg, Beasejour, Fraserwood, Gimli, Hecla, Inwood, Libau, Lockport, Oakbank, Petersfield, Poplar Point, Riverton, Selkirk, Stonewall, Stony Mountain, Teulon, Warren, Winnipeg Beach, Woodlands. Ontario: Kenora.
Services:	Leased line, dedicated ISDN, dedicated SLIP/PPP, frame relay, dial-up ISDN, dial-up SLIP/PPP, shell access, UUCP service, domain registration, free Web home page with personal dial-up account, Web design, Web hosting.
World Wide Web:	http://www.escape.ca

eWorld (Apple Computer Inc.)

Cupertino, California
eworld.com

20525 Mariani Avenue
Cupertino, CA 95014

Voice:	1-800-775-4556
Web:	http://www.eworld.com

Service Area:	Calgary, Edmonton, Vancouver, Winnipeg, Halifax, Toronto, Kitchener, London, Windsor, Hull-Ottawa, Dundas, Quebec City, Montreal-St-Laurent.
Services:	Terminal accounts.
World Wide Web:	http://www.eworld.com

ExecuLink Internet Services Corporation

London, Ontario
execulink.com, suspects.com

P.O. Box 40004
London, ON N5W 3G3

Voice:	519-451-4288
Fax:	519-455-8805
E-mail:	info@execulink.com
Web:	http://www.execulink.com

Service Area:	London, Woodstock, Granton, Lucan, Centralia, Kirkton, Nairn, Crediton, Exeter, Strathroy, Kerwood, Mount Brydges, Dorchester, Harrietsville, Kintore, St. Marys, Thamesford, Glencoe, Melbourne, Ailsa Craig, Parkhill, Ingersoll, Thorndale, St. Thomas, Belmont, Lambeth, Ilderton, Dutton, Sheddan, Fingal, Sparta, Port Stanley, Alvinston, Watford.
Services:	Dial-up SLIP/PPP, terminal accounts, domain registration, free Web home page with personal dial-up account, Web design, Web hosting.
World Wide Web:	http://www.execulink.com

eXpress Lane Communications Corp.

Coquitlam, British Columbia
xpresslane.CA

571 Rochester Avenue, Suite 101
Coquitlam, BC V3K 2V3

Voice:	604-939-6995
Fax:	604-939-6445
E-mail:	info@xpresslane.ca
Web:	http://www.xpresslane.ca

Service Area: Vancouver, Victoria. Planning to expand to other major communities in British Columbia as well as Toronto, Montreal, Edmonton, Winnipeg, and Regina or Saskatoon.

Services: Leased line, dedicated ISDN, dedicated SLIP/PPP, dial-up ISDN, dial-up SLIP/PPP, domain registration, Web design, Web hosting.

World Wide Web: http://www.xpresslane.ca

EZENET Inc.

Toronto, Ontario
ezenet.com

1992 Yonge Street, Suite 300
Toronto, ON M4S 1Z7

Voice: 416-482-5250
E-mail: info@ezenet.com
Web: http://www.ezenet.com

Service Area: Toronto and anywhere in the 416 and 905 area codes.

Services: Leased line, dedicated ISDN, dedicated SLIP/PPP, dial-up ISDN, dial-up SLIP/PPP, shell access, terminal accounts, domain registration, Web design, Web hosting.

World Wide Web: http://www.ezenet.com

Fairview Technology Centre Ltd.

Oliver, British Columbia
ftcnet.com

Route 1, Site 24, Conc. 9
Oliver, BC V0H 1T0

Voice: 604-498-4316
Fax: 604-498-3214
E-mail: bwklatt@ftcnet.com
Web: http://www.ftcnet.com

Service Area: Oliver, Osoyoos. Planning to expand to Keremeos.

Services: Leased line, dedicated ISDN, dedicated SLIP/PPP, frame relay, dial-up SLIP/PPP, shell access, domain registration, Web design, Web hosting.

World Wide Web: http://www.ftcnet.com

Feldspar Networks

Sudbury, Ontario
feldspar.com

1901 LaSalle Boulevard
Sudbury, ON P3A 2A3

Voice: 705-525-2000
Web: http://www.feldspar.com

Service Area: Sudbury.

Services: Leased line, dial-up SLIP/PPP, free Web home page with personal dial-up account, Web hosting.

World Wide Web: http://www.feldspar.com

FIX, the (Steffen Open Systems Inc.)

Wingham, Ontario
sos.on.ca, wingham.com, huron.net

389 Josephine Street
Wingham, ON N0G 2W0

Voice: 519-357-4686, 1-800-603-5032
Fax: 519-357-4675
E-mail: support@sos.on.ca
Web: http://www.sos.on.ca

Service Area: Wingham, Hanover, Clinton, Owen Sound. Planning to expand to Hespeler, Cambridge, Kitchener-Waterloo, Guelph, St. Marys, Stratford, London.

Services: Leased line, dedicated SLIP/PPP, frame relay, dial-up SLIP/PPP, terminal accounts, domain registration, Web design, Web hosting.

World Wide Web: http://www.sos.on.ca

Fleximation Systems Inc.

Mississauga, Ontario
flexnet.com

1495 Bonhill Road, Units 1 and 2
Mississauga, ON L5T 1M2

Voice: 905-795-0300
Fax: 905-795-0310
E-mail: sales@flexnet.com
Web: http://www.flexnet.com

Service Area:	Halifax, Calgary, Montreal, Vancouver, Toronto, Winnipeg, Ottawa, Orangeville, Mississauga.
Services:	Leased line, dedicated ISDN, dedicated SLIP/PPP, frame relay, dial-up ISDN, dial-up SLIP/PPP, shell access, UUCP service, domain registration, Web design, Web hosting.
World Wide Web:	http://www.flexnet.com

Focus Technologies Networks

Mississauga, Ontario
ftn.net

5380 Timberlea Boulevard
Mississauga, ON L4W 2S6

Voice: 905-602-6266
Fax: 905-602-6272
E-mail: netadmin@ftn.net
Web: http://www.ftn.net

Service Area:	Toronto, Ottawa, Hamilton, Kitchener, London, Windsor. Planning to expand to St. Catharines, Montreal, Vancouver, Buffalo.
Services:	Leased line, dedicated ISDN, dedicated SLIP/PPP, frame relay, dial-up ISDN, dial-up SLIP/PPP, shell access, terminal accounts, UUCP service, domain registration, Web design, Web hosting.
World Wide Web:	http://www.ftn.net

ƒONOROLA i*internet

See the entry for iSTAR Internet Inc.

Foxnet Communications

Thunder Bay, Ontario
foxnet.net

28 South Cumberland
Thunder Bay, ON P7B 2T2

Voice: 807-343-0225
Fax: 807-343-0223
E-mail: root@foxnet.net, webmaster@foxnet.net
Web: http://www.foxnet.net

Service Area:	Thunder Bay, Pass Lake, Blake Township, Kakabeka, Shabaqua, Pearl, McKenzie, Dryden, Vermilion Bay, Oxdrift, Wabigoon. Planning to expand to Sioux Lookout, Kenora, Atikokan, Ignace, Nipigon, Dorion.
Services:	Leased line, dedicated SLIP/PPP, frame relay, dial-up SLIP/PPP, shell access, UUCP service, domain registration, Web design, Web hosting.
World Wide Web:	http://www.foxnet.net

Gate West Communications

Winnipeg, Manitoba
gatewest.net, gatewest.mb.ca

525 London Street
P.O. Box 64007
Winnipeg, MB R2K 2Z0

Voice: 204-663-2931
Fax: 204-667-1379
E-mail: info@gatewest.net
Web: http://www.gatewest.net

Service Area:	Winnipeg, Dugald, Lockport, Lorette, Oakbank, St. Adolphe, St. Andrews, St. François Xavier, Sanford, Starbuck, Stonewall, Stony Mountain.

Services: Leased line, dedicated ISDN, dedicated SLIP/PPP, frame relay, dial-up SLIP/PPP, UUCP service, domain registration, free Web home page with personal dial-up account, Web hosting.

World Wide Web: http://www.gatewest.net

Generation Net Services Inc.

Montréal, Québec
generation.net

1801 McGill College Avenue, Suite 555
Montréal, PQ H3A 2N4

Voice: 514-845-5555
Fax: 514-845-5004
E-mail: info@generation.net
Web: http://www.generation.net

Service Area: Montreal.

Services: Leased line, dedicated ISDN, dedicated SLIP/PPP, frame relay, dial-up ISDN, dial-up SLIP/PPP, UUCP service, domain registration, free Web home page with personal dial-up account, Web design, Web hosting.

World Wide Web: http://www.generation.net

GEnie (GE Information Services)

Mississauga, Ontario
genie.com

2300 Meadowvale Boulevard
Mississauga, ON L5N 5P9

Voice: 1-800-638-9636
E-mail: info@genie.com
Web: http://www.genie.com

Service Area: Calgary, Edmonton, Halifax, Hamilton, Kitchener, London, Mississauga, Montreal, Ottawa, Quebec City, Toronto, Vancouver, Victoria, Winnipeg.

Services: Terminal accounts.

World Wide Web: http://www.genie.com

Glen-Net Communications

Alexandria, Ontario
glen-net.ca, ecap.ca

39 Main Street North, Box 837
Alexandria, ON K0C 1A0

Voice: 613-525-3689
Fax: 613-525-3459
E-mail: sales@glen-net.ca
Web: http://www.glen-net.ca

Service Area: Alexandria, Cornwall, Maxville, Green Valley, Lancaster, Apple Hill, Glen Robertson, Dalkeith, Dunvegan, Ingleside, Martintown, Avonmore and all communities in Glengarry County.

Services: Leased line, dedicated SLIP/PPP, frame relay, dial-up SLIP/PPP, shell access, domain registration, Web design, Web hosting.

World Wide Web: http://www.glen-net.ca

Global-X-Change Communications Inc.

Ottawa, Ontario
globalx.net

170 Laurier Avenue West, Suite 709
Ottawa, ON K1P 5V5

Voice: 613-235-6865
Fax: 613-232-5285
E-mail: info@globalx.net
Web: http://www.globalx.net

Service Area: Ottawa.

Services: Dedicated ISDN, dedicated SLIP/PPP, dial-up SLIP/PPP, shell access, domain registration, Web design, Web hosting.

World Wide Web: http://www.globalx.net

Globalserve Communications Inc.

Oakville, Ontario
globalserve.on.ca, globalserve.net, globalserve.com

466 Speers Road, Suite 323
Oakville, ON L6K 3W9

Voice: 905-337-0152
Fax: 905-825-8046
E-mail: admin@globalserve.on.ca
Web: http://www.globalserve.on.ca

Service Area:	416 and 905 dial-in areas.
Services:	Dedicated ISDN, dedicated SLIP/PPP, dial-up ISDN, dial-up SLIP/PPP, shell access, UUCP service, domain registration, free Web home page with personal dial-up account, Web design, Web hosting.
World Wide Web:	http://www.globalserve.on.ca

GO! Online Communications

New Westminster, British Columbia
jumppoint.com

611 Belmont Street, Suite 636
New Westminster, BC V3M 5Z8

Voice: 604-540-0271
Fax: 604-540-0272
E-mail: info@jumppoint.com
Web: http://www.jumppoint.com

Service Area:	Vancouver, Abbotsford, Aldergrove, Burnaby, Coquitlam, Delta, Fort Langley, Langley, Maple Ridge, Mission, New Westminster, Port Coquitlam, Richmond, Surrey, White Rock. Planning to expand to Chilliwack.
Services:	Leased line, dedicated SLIP/PPP, dial-up SLIP/PPP, domain registration, Web design, Web hosting.
World Wide Web:	http://www.jumppoint.com

Golden Triangle On Line

Kitchener, Ontario
golden.org, golden.net

201 Bedford Road
Kitchener, ON N6G 3A5

Voice: 519-576-4649
Fax: 519-576-5567
E-mail: info@golden.org
Web: http://www.golden.org

Service Area:	Kitchener, Stratford, Cambridge, Guelph, Elmira, St. Jacobs, Conestogo, Brant, Branchton. Planning to expand to Toronto, Windsor, Ottawa, London, Kingston.
Services:	Leased line, dedicated ISDN, dedicated SLIP/PPP, frame relay, dial-up ISDN, dial-up SLIP/PPP, shell access, terminal accounts, UUCP service, domain registration, free Web home page with personal dial-up account, Web design, Web hosting.
World Wide Web:	http://www.golden.org

Grant Internet Communications Corporation

Collingwood, Ontario
georgian.net, grant.ca

243 Hurontario Street
Collingwood, ON L9Y 2M1

Voice: 705-446-2900
Fax: 705-446-2901
E-mail: info@grant.ca
Web: http://www.grant.ca

Service Area:	Creemore, Collingwood, Feversham, Stayner, Thornbury, Wasaga Beach. Planning to expand to surrounding areas.

Services: Leased line, dedicated SLIP/PPP, frame relay, dial-up SLIP/PPP, shell access, UUCP service, domain registration, free Web home page with personal dial-up account, Web design, Web hosting.

World Wide Web: http://www.grant.ca

Le groupe Médiom

Québec, Québec
mediom.qc.ca

74, rue Jacques Cartier
Québec, PQ G1L 3S1

Voice: 418-640-7474
Fax: 418-640-0515
E-mail: groupe@mediom.qc.ca
Web: http://www.mediom.qc.ca

Service Area: Quebec City.

Services: Leased line, dedicated ISDN, dedicated SLIP/PPP, frame relay, dial-up SLIP/PPP, domain registration, Web hosting.

World Wide Web: http://www.mediom.qc.ca

headwaters network

Orangeville, Ontario
headwaters.com

113 Broadway
Orangeville, ON L9W 1K2

Voice: 519-940-9252
Fax: 519-942-3776
E-mail: sales@headwaters.com
Web: http://www.headwaters.com

Service Area: Orangeville, Shelburne, Grand Valley, Caledon Village, Caledon East, Palgrave, Alton.

Services: Leased line, dedicated ISDN, dedicated SLIP/PPP, frame relay, dial-up ISDN, dial-up SLIP/PPP, shell access, UUCP service, domain registration, Web design, Web hosting.

World Wide Web: http://www.headwaters.com

Helix Internet

Vancouver, British Columbia
helix.net

1090 Homer Street, Suite 470
Vancouver, BC V6B 2W9

Voice: 604-689-8544
Fax: 604-689-8569
E-mail: info@helix.net
Web: http://www.helix.net

Service Area: Langley, Surrey, Delta, Burnaby, Coquitlam, Vancouver, White Rock, Yaletown. Planning to expand to most major British Columbia communities.

Services: Leased line, dedicated ISDN, dedicated SLIP/PPP, frame relay, dial-up SLIP/PPP, shell access, terminal accounts, UUCP service, domain registration, free Web home page with personal dial-up account, Web design, Web hosting.

World Wide Web: http://www.helix.net

HEXonX Internet Service Providers Inc.

St-Laurent, Québec
hexonx.com

3860 Côte-Vertu, Suite 210
St-Laurent, PQ H4R 1V4

Voice: 514-339-9704
Fax: 514-339-9869
E-mail: sales@hexonx.com
Web: http://www.hexonx.com

Service Area:	Montreal, Laval, South Shore, Rigaud, St-Lazare. Planning to expand to Ontario, Quebec City and outlying regions of Quebec.
Services:	Leased line, dedicated ISDN, dedicated SLIP/PPP, dial-up SLIP/PPP, shell access, UUCP service, domain registration, free Web home page with personal dial-up account, Web design, Web hosting.
World Wide Web:	http://www.hexonx.com

HMT Internet Inc.

Yorkton, Saskatchewan
hmtnet.com, awinc.com

36-2nd Avenue North
Yorkton, SK S3N 1G2

Voice: 306-782-9150
Fax: 306-786-6160
E-mail: info@hmtnet.com
Web: http://www.awinc.com/partners/sk/hmt

Service Area:	Yorkton, Springside, Dunleath, Gorlitz, Rokeby, Tonkin, White Spruce, Willowbrooke, Orcadia, Ebenezer.
Services:	Leased line, dedicated SLIP/PPP, frame relay, dial-up SLIP/PPP, shell access, domain registration, free Web home page with personal dial-up account, Web design, Web hosting.
World Wide Web:	http://www.awinc.com/partners/sk/hmt

HookUp Communications

Oakville, Ontario
hookup.net

1075 North Service Road, Suite 207
Oakville, ON L6M 2G2

Voice: 905-847-8000, 1-800-363-0400
Fax: 905-847-8420
E-mail: info@hookup.net, accounts@hookup.net
Web: http://www.hookup.net

Service Area:	Oakville, Mississauga, Milton, Ancaster, Dundas, Mount Hope, Grimsby, Hagersville, Stoney Creek, Winona, Millgrove, Thornhill, Maple, Markham, Pickering, Ajax, Aurora, Schomberg, Bolton, Caledonia, Cayuga, West Lincoln, Binbrook, Brampton, Lynden, Brantford, St. George, Burford, Cambridge, Preston, Breslau, Elora, Waterloo, Ayr, Petersburg, Wellesley, Heidelberg, Nepean, Kanata, Orleans, Almonte, Vanier, Gloucester, Kemptville, Aylmer, Gatineau, Guelph, Hull, Stittsville, Burlington, Hamilton, Mississauga, Toronto, Galt, Hespeler, Kitchener, Ottawa. Planning to expand to London.
Services:	Leased line, dedicated ISDN, dedicated SLIP/PPP, frame relay, dial-up SLIP/PPP, shell access, UUCP service, domain registration, free Web home page with personal dial-up account, Web design, Web hosting.
World Wide Web:	http://www.hookup.net

Horizon Net

Victoria, British Columbia
horizon.bc.ca

824 Fort Street
Victoria, BC V8W 1H8

Voice: 604-361-4410
Fax: 604-381-7129
E-mail: support@horizon.bc.ca
Web: http://www.horizon.bc.ca

Service Area:	Lower South Vancouver Island, Victoria, Langford, Cobble Hill, Sidney, Sooke. Planning to expand to Duncan, Nanaimo, Gulf Islands.
Services:	Dedicated SLIP/PPP, dial-up SLIP/PPP, shell access, terminal accounts, UUCP service, domain registration, free Web home page with personal dial-up account, Web design, Web hosting.
World Wide Web:	http://www.horizon.bc.ca

ICE Online

Vancouver, British Columbia
iceonline.com

2465 Beta Avenue, Suite 208
Burnaby, BC V5C 5N1

Voice: 604-482-7575
Fax: 604-482-7599
E-mail: krish@iceonline.com
Web: http://www.iceonline.com

Service Area:	Burnbay, West Vancouver, North Vancouver, Tsawwassen, Coquitlam, Surrey, Vancouver, New Westminster, Richmond, Victoria.
Services:	Leased line, dedicated ISDN, dedicated SLIP/PPP, dial-up SLIP/PPP, shell access, terminal accounts, UUCP service, domain registration, free Web home page with personal dial-up account, Web design, Web hosting.
World Wide Web:	http://www.iceonline.com

iCOM Internet Services

Hamilton, Ontario
icom.ca

7 Mary Street, Suite 201
Hamilton, ON L8R 1J6

Voice: 905-522-1220
Fax: 905-546-1996
E-mail: sales@icom.ca
Web: http://www.icom.ca

Service Area:	Hamilton, Burlington, Dundas, Stoney Creek, Ancaster, Winona, Grimsby, Smithville, Caledonia, Flamborough, Waterdown, Freelton, Carlisle, Binbrook. Planning to expand to St. Catharines and Niagara regions.
Services:	Leased line, dedicated ISDN, dedicated SLIP/PPP, dial-up SLIP/PPP, shell access, UUCP service, domain registration, free Web home page with personal dial-up account, Web design, Web hosting.
World Wide Web:	http://www.icom.ca

Ilink Communications/Waterloo Internet Cooperative

Waterloo, Ontario
waterloo.net

20 Mayfield Avenue, Suite 22
Waterloo, ON N2J 4M5

Voice: 519-886-0998
Fax: 519-886-6912
E-mail: info@waterloo.net
Web: http://www.waterloo.net

Service Area:	Waterloo, Kitchener, Cambridge, Ayr, Breslau, Baden, Bright, Drayton, Elmira, Elora, Galt, Hespeler, Linwood, New Dundee, New Hamburg, Plattsville, Preston, St. Clements, St. Jacobs, Wellesley.
Services:	Leased line, dedicated ISDN, dedicated SLIP/PPP, dial-up ISDN, dial-up SLIP/PPP, shell access, terminal accounts, UUCP service, domain registration, free Web home page with personal dial-up account, Web design, Web hosting.
World Wide Web:	http://www.waterloo.net

Inasec Inc.

Ottawa, Ontario
inasec.ca

29 Beechwood Avenue, Suite 320
Ottawa, ON K1M 1M2

Voice: 613-746-3200
Fax: 613-747-2046
E-mail: hcarter@inasec.ca
Web: http://www.inasec.ca

Service Area:	Ottawa, Arnprior, Richmond, Manotick, Kemptville, Russell, Embrun, Navan, Rockland, Gatineau, Hull, Aylmer.
Services:	Leased line, dedicated ISDN, dedicated SLIP/PPP, frame relay, dial-up ISDN, dial-up SLIP/PPP, shell access, UUCP service, domain registration, Web design, Web hosting.
World Wide Web:	http://www.inasec.ca

Infobahn Online Services

Montréal, Québec
infobahnos.com, ios.ca

5252 de Maisonneuve West, Suite 107
Montréal, PQ H4A 3S5

Voice:	514-481-2585
Fax:	514-481-2785
E-mail:	info@infobahnos.com
Web:	http://www.infobahnos.com

Service Area:	Montreal and surrounding area. Planning to expand to Toronto, Quebec City, Ottawa.
Services:	Leased line, dedicated ISDN, dedicated SLIP/PPP, frame relay, dial-up ISDN, dial-up SLIP/PPP, UUCP service, domain registration, free Web home page with personal dial-up account, Web design, Web hosting.
World Wide Web:	http://www.infobahnos.com

InfoHighway OnRamp Centre, Inc.

Winnipeg, Manitoba
wpg.ramp.net

375 York Avenue
Winnipeg, MB R3C 3J3

Voice:	204-925-7200
Fax:	204-925-7260
E-mail:	info@wpg.ramp.net
Web:	http://www.wpg.ramp.net

Service Area:	Winnipeg and local dial-in area.
Services:	Dedicated ISDN, dedicated SLIP/PPP, dial-up ISDN, dial-up SLIP/PPP, shell access, UUCP service, domain registration, free Web home page with personal dial-up account, Web design, Web hosting.
World Wide Web:	http://www.wpg.ramp.net

Infomatch Communications Incorporated

Burnaby, British Columbia
infomatch.com, thrill.com

9632 Cameron Street, Suite 143
Burnaby, BC V3J 7N3

Voice:	604-421-3230
Fax:	604-421-3230
E-mail:	accounts@infomatch.com
Web:	http://infomatch.com

Service Area:	Lower Mainland area, Burnaby, Vancouver, North Vancouver, Surrey.
Services:	Leased line, dedicated SLIP/PPP, dial-up SLIP/PPP, shell access, terminal accounts, domain registration, free Web home page with personal dial-up account, Web design, Web hosting.
World Wide Web:	http://infomatch.com

InfoRamp Inc.

Toronto, Ontario
inforamp.net, inforamp.com

134 Adelaide Street East, Suite 207
Toronto, ON M5C 1K9

Voice:	416-363-9100
Fax:	416-363-3551
E-mail:	staff@inforamp.net
Web:	http://www.inforamp.net

Service Area:	Toronto and surrounding local calling area. Planning to expand to Ottawa, Hamilton, London, Windsor, Oshawa, Calgary, Edmonton, Winnipeg, Montreal, Halifax with roam capabilities.
Services:	Leased line, dedicated ISDN, dedicated SLIP/PPP, dial-up SLIP/PPP, shell access, UUCP service, domain registration, free Web home page with personal dial-up account, Web hosting.
World Wide Web:	http://www.inforamp.net

Information Gateway Services Belleville

Belleville, Ontario
blvl.igs.net

Century Place
199 Front Street, Suite 209
Belleville, ON K8N 5H5

Voice:	613-962-9299
Fax:	613-962-0877
E-mail:	info@blvl.igs.net
Web:	http://www.blvl.igs.net

Service Area:	Belleville and the local dial-in area, Brighton, Bloomfield, Frankford, Madoc, Picton, Stirling, Thurlow, Trenton, Tweed, Wellington, Wooler. Planning to expand to Cobourg, Colbourne.
Services:	Dedicated ISDN, dedicated SLIP/PPP, dial-up SLIP/PPP, shell access, UUCP service, domain registration, free Web home page with personal dial-up account, Web design, Web hosting.
World Wide Web:	http://www.blvl.igs.net

Information Gateway Services Cornwall

Cornwall, Ontario
cnwl.igs.net

$11\frac{1}{2}$ Second Street West
Cornwall, ON K6J 1G3

Voice:	613-930-9942
E-mail:	info@cnwl.igs.net
Web:	http://www.cnwl.igs.net

Service Area:	Cornwall, Alexandria, Moose Creek, Long Sault, Ingleside, Monkland, Finch, Lancaster, Apple Hill, Williamstown, Martintown, Green Valley, Lunenburg, Vankleek Hill, Summerstown, Glen Walter, St. Andrews West, Bonville, St-Régis, Cornwall Island. Planning to expand to Morrisburg, Maxville, Curry Hill.
Services:	Leased line, dedicated SLIP/PPP, frame relay, dial-up SLIP/PPP, shell access, terminal accounts, UUCP service, domain registration, free Web home page with personal dial-up account, Web design, Web hosting.
World Wide Web:	http://www.cnwl.igs.net

Information Gateway Services Hawkesbury

Hawkesbury, Ontario
hawk.igs.net

186 Main Street East
Hawkesbury, ON K6A 1A5

Voice:	613-632-4075
Fax:	613-632-8137
E-mail:	info@hawk.igs.net
Web:	http://www.hawk.igs.net

Service Area:	Ontario: Hawkesbury, Vankleek Hill, Alfred, L'Orignal, St. Eugene. Quebec: Calumet, Grenville. Planning to expand to Lachute.
Services:	Leased line, dedicated SLIP/PPP, dial-up SLIP/PPP, shell access, UUCP service, domain registration, free Web home page with personal dial-up account, Web design, Web hosting.
World Wide Web:	http://www.hawk.igs.net

Information Gateway Services Kingston

Kingston, Ontario
king.igs.net

Canada Trust Building
181 Wellington Street, Suite 201
Kingston, ON K7L 3E3

Voice: 613-962-9299
E-mail: info@king.igs.net
Web: http://www.king.igs.net

Service Area:	Kingston and the local dial-in area, Gananoque, Odessa, Yarker.
Services:	Dedicated ISDN, dedicated SLIP/PPP, dial-up ISDN, dial-up SLIP/PPP, shell access, UUCP service, domain registration, free Web home page with personal dial-up account, Web design, Web hosting.
World Wide Web:	http://www.king.igs.net

Information Gateway Services Kitchener-Waterloo Inc.

Waterloo, Ontario
kw.igs.net

151 Frobisher Drive, Suite E-118
Waterloo, ON N2V 2C9

Voice: 519-884-7200
Fax: 519-884-7440
E-mail: info@kw.igs.net
Web: http://www.kw.igs.net

Service Area:	Ayr, Baden, Breslau, Bright, Drayton, Elmira, Elora, Galt, Guelph, Hespeler, Kitchener, Linwood, New Dundee, New Hamburg, Plattsville, Preston, St. Clements, St. Jacobs, Waterloo, Wellesley. Call for toll-free access.
Services:	Dedicated SLIP/PPP, dial-up SLIP/PPP, shell access, UUCP service, domain registration, free Web home page with personal dial-up account, Web design, Web hosting.
World Wide Web:	http://www.kw.igs.net

Information Gateway Services Oshawa

Oshawa, Ontario
osha.igs.net

57 Simcoe Street South, Suite 2N
Oshawa, ON L1H 4G4

Voice: 905-723-2750
Fax: 905-723-2199
E-mail: info@osha.igs.net
Web: http://www.osha.igs.net

Service Area:	Ajax, Bowmanville, Oshawa and the local dial-in area, Whitby, Port Perry, Orono, Newtonville, Ajax, Pickering. Planning to expand to Port Hope.
Services:	Dedicated ISDN, dedicated SLIP/PPP, dial-up ISDN, dial-up SLIP/PPP, shell access, UUCP service, domain registration, free Web home page with personal dial-up account, Web design, Web hosting.
World Wide Web:	http://www.osha.igs.net

Information Gateway Services Peterborough

Peterborough, Ontario
ptbo.igs.net

223 Aylmer Street, Suite 100
Peterborough, ON K9J 3K3

Voice: 705-876-9158
Fax: 705-876-9599
E-mail: info@ptbo.igs.net
Web: http://www.ptbo.igs.net

Service Area:	Peterborough, Lindsay, Bethany, Bridgenorth, Keene, Norwood, Lakefield, Buckhorn, Hastings, Omemee, Millbrook, Bailieboro, Cavan, Dunsford.
Services:	Dedicated ISDN, dedicated SLIP/PPP, dial-up ISDN, dial-up SLIP/PPP, shell access, UUCP service, domain registration, free Web home page with personal dial-up account, Web design, Web hosting.
World Wide Web:	http://www.ptbo.igs.net

Information Gateway Services Renfrew County

Renfrew, Ontario
renc.igs.net

255 Raglan Street South
Renfrew, ON K7V 1R3

Voice:	613-432-2372, 1-800-781-8070
Fax:	613-432-9242
E-mail:	info@renc.igs.net
Web:	http://www.renc.igs.net

Service Area:	Renfrew, Pembroke, Petawawa, Eganville, Cobden, Golden Lake, Beachburg, Westmeath, Douglas, Chapeau, Calabogie.
Services:	Dedicated SLIP/PPP, dial-up SLIP/PPP, shell access, UUCP service, domain registration, free Web home page with personal dial-up account, Web hosting.
World Wide Web:	http://www.renc.igs.net

Infoserve Technology Ltd.

Burnaby, British Columbia
infoserve.net

5438 Imperial Street, Suite 201
Burnaby, BC V5J 1E6

Voice:	604-482-8238
Fax:	604-482-8248
E-mail:	info@infoserve.net
Web:	http://www.infoserve.net

Service Area:	Vancouver, Burnaby, Richmond, New Westminster, Surrey, Coquitlam, Port Coquitlam, North Vancouver, Port Moody, Pitt Meadows, Whalley, White Rock, Whonnock, West Vancouver, Aldergrove, Cloverdale, Fort Langley, Haney, Ladner/Beach Grove, Langley, Newton. Planning to expand to Abbotsford, Mission.

Services:	Dial-up SLIP/PPP, terminal accounts, domain registration, free Web home page with personal dial-up account, Web design, Web hosting.
World Wide Web:	http://www.infoserve.net

InfoStream Services

Edmonton, Alberta
infostream.ab.ca

12120–106th Avenue, Suite 300
Edmonton, AB T5N 0Z2

Voice:	403-482-2850
Fax:	403-488-9674
E-mail:	admin@infostream.ab.ca
Web:	http://www.infostream.ab.ca

Service Area:	Edmonton, Sherwood Park, St. Albert, Spruce Grove, Leduc, Stony Plain, Fort Saskatchewan, Devon, Onoway, Bruderheim, Beaumont, Redwater, Nisku, Ellerslie, Morinville. Planning to expand to Calgary and area.
Services:	Leased line, dedicated ISDN, dedicated SLIP/PPP, dial-up ISDN, dial-up SLIP/PPP, shell access, domain registration, Web design, Web hosting.
World Wide Web:	http://www.infostream.ab.ca

InfoTeck Centre de l'Ordinateur

Trois-Rivières Ouest, Québec
infoteck.qc.ca, infoteck.net

5480, boul. Jean XXIII
Trois-Rivières Ouest, PQ G8Z 4A9

Voice:	819-370-3232, 1-800-861-3232
Fax:	819-370-3624
E-mail:	vente@infoteck.qc.ca
Web:	http://www.infoteck.qc.ca

Service Area:	Trois-Rivières, Cap-de-la-Madeleine, Shawinigan, Nicolet, Louiseville.

Services: Dedicated SLIP/PPP, dial-up SLIP/PPP, free Web home page with personal dial-up account, Web design, Web hosting.

World Wide Web: http://www.infoteck.qc.ca

Inline Information Services, Inc.

Mississauga, Ontario
inline.net

7305 Rapistan Court
Mississauga, ON L5N 5Z4

Voice: 905-813-8800
Fax: 905-542-9223
E-mail: info@inline.net
Web: http://www.inline.net

Service Area: Vancouver, Montreal, Quebec City, Southern Ontario. Planning to expand to Calgary and Edmonton. Frame relay service available in all cities throughout Canada.

Services: Leased line, dedicated ISDN, dedicated SLIP/PPP, frame relay, dial-up ISDN, dial-up SLIP/PPP, UUCP service, domain registration, Web design, Web hosting.

World Wide Web: http://www.inline.net

Innovative Online

New Minas, Nova Scotia
iol.ns.ca

9206 Commercial Street
New Minas, NS B4N 3E8

Voice: 902-681-1027
Fax: 902-681-6073
E-mail: swilsack@iol.ns.ca, isl@fox.nstn.ca
Web: http://www.iol.ns.ca

Service Area: Aylesford, Greenwood, Brooklyn, Hantsport, Berwick, Middleton, Cheverie, Walton, Kingston, Windsor, Clarksville, Wolfville, Canning, Kentville, New Minas.

Services: Leased line, dedicated SLIP/PPP, frame relay, dial-up SLIP/PPP, UUCP service, domain registration, Web design, Web hosting.

World Wide Web: http://www.iol.ns.ca

Instant Internet™ (Gyygnet Services, Inc.)

Pointe-Claire, Québec
gig.net

220 Brunswick Boulevard
Pointe-Claire, PQ H9R 1A6

Voice: 514-333-9480
Fax: 514-451-6477
E-mail: info@gig.net
Web: http://www.gig.net

Service Area: Montreal and area.

Services: Leased line, dedicated ISDN, dedicated SLIP/PPP, dial-up ISDN, dial-up SLIP/PPP, domain registration, free Web home page with personal dial-up account, Web design, Web hosting.

World Wide Web: http://www.gig.net

Intégration en Technologie de l'Information Inc. (ITI Inc.)

Boisbriand, Québec
iti.qc.ca

2816 Beriot
Boisbriand, PQ J7E 4H4

Voice: 514-895-3877
Fax: 514-437-4063
E-mail: info@iti.qc.ca
Web: http://www.iti.qc.ca/iti

Service Area: Montreal and suburban community, St-Jérôme, the Laurentians. Planning to expand to Joliette, Lanaudière.

Services: Leased line, dedicated ISDN, dedicated SLIP/PPP, frame relay, dial-up ISDN, dial-up SLIP/PPP, shell access, terminal accounts, domain registration, free Web home page with personal dial-up account, Web design, Web hosting.

World Wide Web: http://www.iti.qc.ca/iti

Inter*Com Information Services

London, Ontario
icis.on.ca, icis.net

1464 Adelaide Street North
London, ON N5X 1K4

Voice: 519-679-1620
Fax: 519-679-1583
E-mail: info@icis.on.ca
Web: http://www.icis.on.ca

Service Area: London, Woodstock, Sarnia, Tillsonburg, Stratford, Ingersol, St. Thomas. Planning to expand to Chatham, Windsor, Clinton, Kitchener/Waterloo.

Services: Leased line, dedicated ISDN, dedicated SLIP/PPP, frame relay, dial-up ISDN, dial-up SLIP/PPP, shell access, UUCP service, domain registration, Web design, Web hosting.

World Wide Web: http://www.icis.on.ca

InterActions (Division of Compusult Ltd.)

Mount Pearl, Newfoundland
compusult.nf.ca, nfld.com

40 Bannister Street, Box 1000
Mount Pearl, NF A1N 3C9

Voice: 709-745-4638
Fax: 709-745-7093
E-mail: connect@nfld.com
Web: http://www.nfld.com/InterActions

Service Area: St. John's, Mount Pearl, Bell Island, Long Pond, Portugal Cove, Torbay, Pouch Cove, Witless Bay and surrounding calling areas. Planning to expand to Holyrood, Avondale, Clarenville and surrounding calling areas.

Services: Leased line, dedicated SLIP/PPP, frame relay, dial-up SLIP/PPP, shell access, UUCP service, domain registration, Web design, Web hosting.

World Wide Web: http://www.nfld.com/InterActions

Interactive Telecom Inc.

Nepean, Ontario
intertel.net

190 Colonnade Road South, Suite 204
Nepean, ON K2E 7J5

Voice: 613-727-5258
Fax: 613-727-5438
E-mail: info@intertel.net
Web: http://www.intertel.net

Service Area: Ottawa, Hull, Aylmer, Gatineau. Planning to expand to Montreal.

Services: Dedicated ISDN, dedicated SLIP/PPP, dial-up SLIP/PPP, shell access, domain registration, free Web home page with personal dial-up account, Web design, Web hosting.

World Wide Web: http://www.intertel.net

Interhop Network Services Inc.

Newmarket, Ontario
interhop.net

171 Main Street South
Newmarket, ON L3Y 3Y9

Voice: 905-715-7600
Fax: 905-836-8324
E-mail: postmaster@interhop.net
Web: http://www.interhop.net

Service Area:	Newmarket, Keswick, Mount Albert, Sharon, Queensville, Bradford, Sutton, Shomberg, Beaton, Barrie, Bolton, Palgrave, Tottenham, Nobleton, Alliston, Oak Ridges, Aurora, Stayner, Moonstone, Elmvale, Innisfil. Planning to expand to Oshawa, Peterborough, Brampton, Burlington, Orangeville, Kitchener, St. Catharines, Niagara Falls, Welland, Cambridge, Midland, Orillia, Collingwood, Hamilton, Milton, Oakville, Mississauga, Toronto, Acton, Georgetown, Port Perry, Bowanville, Bramalea, Whitby, Pickering, Ajax, Newcastle, Kingston, Stouffville, Unionville, Markham, Vaughn.
Services:	Leased line, dedicated ISDN, dedicated SLIP/PPP, dial-up ISDN, dial-up SLIP/PPP, shell access, domain registration, Web design, Web hosting.
World Wide Web:	http://www.interhop.net

InterLinx

Sherbrooke, Québec
interlinx.qc.ca

1440 King Ouest
Sherbrooke, PQ J1J 2C2

Voice:	819-565-9779
Fax:	819-565-0374
E-mail:	info@interlinx.qc.ca
Web:	http://www.interlinx.qc.ca

Service Area:	Ascot, Ascot Corner, Bishopton, Bromptonville, Bury, Canton d'Ascot, Canton de Bromptonville, Canton de Hatley, Canton de Magog, Canton de Windsor, Chartierville, Coaticook, Compton, Cookshire, Deauville, East Angus, East Hereford, Fleurimont, Ayer's Cliff, La Patrie, Lennoxville, Magog, North Hatley, Omerville, Richmond, Rock Forest, St-Adolphe-de-Dudswell, St-Denis de Brampton, St-Élie d'Orford, St-François-Xavier de Brompton, St-Georges de Windsor, St-Isidore d'Auckland, St-Malo, Sawyerville, Scotstown, Sherbrooke, Ste-Christine, Stoke, Val-Jolie, Waterville, Watton, Windsor.

Services:	Leased line, dedicated ISDN, dedicated SLIP/PPP, frame relay, dial-up ISDN, dial-up SLIP/PPP, shell access, domain registration, free Web home page with personal dial-up account, Web design, Web hosting.
World Wide Web:	http://www.interlinx.qc.ca

InterLog Internet Services

Toronto, Ontario
interlog.com

1235 Bay Street, Suite 400
Toronto, ON M5R 3K4

Voice:	416-975-2655
Fax:	416-969-8916
E-mail:	sales@interlog.com
Web:	http://www.interlog.com

Service Area:	Toronto.
Services:	Leased line, dedicated ISDN, dedicated SLIP/PPP, dial-up ISDN, dial-up SLIP/PPP, shell access, domain registration, free Web home page with personal dial-up account, Web hosting.
World Wide Web:	http://www.interlog.com

Internet Access Inc.

Nepean, Ontario
ottawa.net, intacc.net

1916 Merivale Road
Nepean, ON K2G 1E8

Voice:	613-225-5595
Fax:	613-225-7733
E-mail:	info@ottawa.net
Web:	http://www.ottawa.net

Service Area:	Aylmer, Buckingham, Edwards, Embrun, Gatineau, Gloucester, Greeley, Hull, Kanata, Manotick, Metcalfe, Nepean, Notre-Dame-de-la-Salette, Orleans, Osgoode, Ottawa, Plantagenet, Rockland, Russell, Stittsville, Val-des-Bois, Vernon and surrounding areas.

Services: Leased line, dedicated ISDN, dedicated SLIP/PPP, frame relay, dial-up ISDN, dial-up SLIP/PPP, shell access, terminal accounts, UUCP service, domain registration, free Web home page with personal dial-up account, Web design, Web hosting.

World Wide Web: http://www.ottawa.net

Internet Access-Worldwide

Welland, Ontario
iaw.on.ca

15 Burgar Street, Second Floor
Welland, ON L3B 2S6

Voice:	905-714-1400, 1-800-560-4560
Fax:	905-732-0524
E-mail:	iaw@iaw.on.ca
Web:	http://www.iaw.on.ca

Service Area: Beamsville, Fort Erie, Grimsby, Niagara Falls, Niagara-on-the-Lake, Port Colborne, St. Catharines, Stevensville, Thorold, Vineland, Wainfleet, Welland, Hamilton, Burlington, Stoney Creek, Cayuga, Ancaster, Dundas, Mount Hope, Waterdown, Binbrook and surrounding areas.

Services: Leased line, dedicated SLIP/PPP, dial-up ISDN, dial-up SLIP/PPP, shell access, terminal accounts, UUCP service, domain registration, free Web home page with personal dial-up account, Web design, Web hosting.

World Wide Web: http://www.iaw.on.ca

Internet Café, The

Prince George, British Columbia
netbistro.com

1363–4th Avenue
Prince George, BC V2L 3J6

Voice:	604-563-8668
Fax:	604-563-4280
E-mail:	info@netbistro.com
Web:	http://www.netbistro.com

Service Area: Prince George. Planning to expand to Calgary.

Services: Leased line, dedicated ISDN, dedicated SLIP/PPP, frame relay, dial-up ISDN, dial-up SLIP/PPP, shell access, UUCP service, domain registration, Web design, Web hosting.

World Wide Web: http://www.netbistro.com

Internet Canada Corporation

Toronto, Ontario
ican.ca

150 York Street, Suite 1100
Toronto, ON M5H 3S5

Voice:	1-800-789-4226
Fax:	416-364-4790
E-mail:	webmaster@ican.ca
Web:	http://www.ican.ca

Service Area: Vancouver, Calgary, Edmonton, Winnipeg, Toronto, Ottawa, Hamilton, Montreal. Planning to expand to Halifax.

Services: Leased line, dedicated ISDN, dedicated SLIP/PPP, dial-up ISDN, dial-up SLIP/PPP, UUCP service, domain registration, Web design, Web hosting.

World Wide Web: http://www.ican.ca

Internet Connect Niagara

St. Catharines, Ontario
niagara.com

25 Church Street
St. Catharines, ON L2R 3B4

Voice:	905-988-9909
Fax:	905-988-1090
E-mail:	info@niagara.com, sales@niagara.com
Web:	http://www.niagara.com

Service Area: Ridgeway, St. Catharines, Crystal Beach, Fort Erie, Fonthill, Beamsville, Stevensville, Grimsby, Welland, West Lincoln, Niagara Falls, Lincoln, Thorold, Niagara-on-the-Lake. Planning to expand to the entire Niagara Region.

Services: Leased line, dedicated SLIP/PPP, dial-up SLIP/PPP, shell access, terminal accounts, UUCP service, domain registration, free Web home page with personal dial-up account, Web design, Web hosting.

World Wide Web: http://www.niagara.com

Internet Connectivity Services Inc.

Ottawa, Ontario
icons.net

2720 Queensview Drive, Suite 1148
Ottawa, ON K2B 1A5

Voice: 613-828-6221
Fax: 613-820-7135
E-mail: sales@icons.net
Web: http://www.icons.net

Service Area: Ottawa and the local dial-in area.

Services: Dedicated SLIP/PPP, dial-up SLIP/PPP, shell access, domain registration, free Web home page with personal dial-up account, Web design, Web hosting.

World Wide Web: http://www.icons.net

Internet Direct

Vancouver, British Columbia
direct.ca

555 West Hastings Street, Suite 1628
Vancouver, BC V6B 4N6

Voice: 604-488-1900
Fax: 604-691-1605
E-mail: helpme@direct.ca
Web: http://www.direct.ca

Service Area: Vancouver.

Services: Leased line, dial-up SLIP/PPP, shell access, domain registration, Web design, Web hosting.

World Wide Web: http://www.direct.ca

Internet Direct/ComputerLink

Etobicoke, Ontario
idirect.com, cml.com

5415 Dundas Street West, Suite 301
Etobicoke, ON M9B 1B4

Voice: 416-233-7150
Fax: 416-233-6970
E-mail: wolfmstr@idirect.com, sales@idirect.com
Web: http://idirect.com

Service Area: Etobicoke, Oshawa, Whitby, Georgetown, Halton Hills, Oakville, Burlington, Toronto, Hamilton. Planning to expand to Newmarket.

Services: Dedicated SLIP/PPP, dial-up SLIP/PPP, terminal accounts, domain registration, Web design, Web hosting.

World Wide Web: http://idirect.com

Internet Express

Vancouver, British Columbia
express.ca

1199 West Pender Street, Suite 610
Vancouver, BC V6E 2R1

Voice: 604-331-4638
Fax: 604-331-7057
E-mail: sales@express.ca
Web: http://www.express.ca

Service Area: Greater Vancouver area. Planning to expand to Calgary, Nanaimo, Kamloops, Edmonton, Vancouver Island, Kelowna.

Services: Leased line, dedicated ISDN, dedicated SLIP/PPP, frame relay, dial-up ISDN, dial-up SLIP/PPP, domain registration, free Web home page with personal dial-up account, Web design, Web hosting.

World Wide Web: http://www.express.ca

Internet Front Inc.

Scarborough, Ontario
internetfront.com, infront.on.ca

3300 McNicol Avenue, Suite 215
Scarborough, ON M1V 5K6

Voice: 416-293-8539
Fax: 416-814-5117
E-mail: support@internetfront.com
Web: http://www.internetfront.com

Service Area: Toronto, Mississauga, Brampton, North York, Markham, Unionville, Stouffville, Pickering, Scarborough.

Services: Dedicated SLIP/PPP, dial-up SLIP/PPP, domain registration, Web design, Web hosting.

World Wide Web: http://www.internetfront.com

Internet Global Info-Access

Montréal, Québec
globale.net, global.ca

2360, chemin Lucerne, Suite 2A
Ville-Mont-Royal, PQ H3R 2J8

Voice: 514-737-2091
Fax: 514-737-0133
E-mail: info@globale.net
Web: http://globale.net

Service Area: Greater Montreal area including St-Jérôme and the South Shore.

Services: Dedicated ISDN, dedicated SLIP/PPP, dial-up SLIP/PPP, domain registration, free Web home page with personal dial-up account, Web design, Web hosting.

World Wide Web: http://globale.net

Internet Innovations Inc.

Cambridge, Ontario
orchid.in.on.ca, orchid.innovations.net

320 Pinebush Road, Unit 8
Cambridge, ON N3C 2V3

Voice: 519-240-4740
Fax: 519-621-3350
E-mail: general@in.on.ca
Web: http://www.in.on.ca

Service Area: Cambridge, Kitchener, Waterloo, Guelph.

Services: Leased line, dedicated SLIP/PPP, dial-up SLIP/PPP, shell access, terminal accounts, domain registration, free Web home page with personal dial-up account, Web design, Web hosting.

World Wide Web: http://www.in.on.ca

Internet JRV Inc.

Granby, Québec
jrv.qc.ca, afiq.org, webmarket.com

184, rue Principale
Ste-Cécile-de-Milton, PQ J0E 2C0

Voice: 514-777-2983
Fax: 514-372-2984
E-mail: info@jrv.qc.ca
Web: http://www.jrv.qc.ca

Service Area: Granby, Bromont, Cowansville, Sutton/Bedford, Waterloo, St-Hyacinthe, Drummondville, Montreal, Quebec City, Sherbrooke, Joliette, Val-d'Or, Rouyn-Noranda, Rimouski, Victoriaville, the Laurentians, Gatineau/Hull.

Services: Leased line, dedicated ISDN, dedicated SLIP/PPP, frame relay, dial-up SLIP/PPP, shell access, UUCP service, domain registration, free Web home page with personal dial-up account, Web design, Web hosting.

World Wide Web: http://www.jrv.qc.ca

InterNet Kingston

Kingston, Ontario
kingston.net, ltd.com, losers.com

177 Wellington Street, Suite 302
Kingston, ON K7L 3E3

Voice: 613-547-6939
Fax: 613-547-5436
E-mail: info@adan.kingston.net
Web: http://www.kingston.net

Service Area: Kingston, Adolphustown, Bath, Enterprise, Gananoque, Harrowsmith, Inverary, Napanee, Newburgh, Odessa, Seeleys Bay, Selby, Sydenham, Tamworth, Verona, Wolfe Island, Yarker. Planning to expand to Smiths Falls and Belleville.

Services: Leased line, dedicated ISDN, dedicated SLIP/PPP, frame relay, dial-up SLIP/PPP, shell access, terminal accounts, UUCP service, domain registration, Web design, Web hosting.

World Wide Web: http://www.kingston.net

Internet Laurentides

St-Janvier, Québec
laurentides.mtl.net

18134 Lapointe
St-Janvier, PQ J7J 1K8

Voice: 514-433-8889
Fax: 514-979-7890
E-mail: info@laurentides.mtl.net
Web: http://www.laurentides.mtl.net

Service Area: Montreal, Laval, Ste-Thérèse, Boisbriand, St-Eustache, Bois-des-Filions, Lorraine, Rosemère, Blainville, Terrebonne, St-Janvier, Mirabel, St-Antoine, St-Jérôme, Bellefeuille, Ste-Sophie, Lafontaine, Lachute, St-Lin, St-Calixte, Ste-Anne-des-Plaines, St-Canut, St-Hippolyte, La Plaine, Mascouche, Dorval.

Services: Leased line, dedicated ISDN, dedicated SLIP/PPP, frame relay, dial-up ISDN, dial-up SLIP/PPP, shell access, terminal accounts, UUCP service, domain registration, free Web home page with personal dial-up account, Web design, Web hosting.

World Wide Web: http://www.laurentides.mtl.net

Internet Light and Power™

North York, Ontario
ilap.com

2235 Sheppard Avenue East, Suite 905
North York, ON M2J 5B5

Voice: 416-502-1512
Fax: 416-502-3333
E-mail: staff@ilap.com
Web: http://www.ilap.com

Service Area: Metropolitan Toronto, Agincourt, Ajax, Alderwood, Almira, Armadale, Aurora, Bay Ridges, Bethesda, Birch Cliff, Bolton, Bramalea, Brampton, Bronte, Brown's Corner, Buttonville, Caledon, Caledon East, Campbellville, Carrville, Cedar Grove, Cheltenham, Cherrywood, Claremont, Clarkson, Concord, Cooksville, Dixie, Don Mills, Downsview, East York, Ellesmere, Erin Mills, Erindale, Etobicoke, Fairport Beach, Georgetown, Glenorchy, Goodwood, Gormley, Hagerman's Corners, Highland Creek, Hornby, Huttonville, Inglewood, Islington, King City, Kleinburg, Lakeview, Langstaff, Lisgar, Locust Hill, Long Branch, Lorne Park, Malton, Malvern, Maple, Markham, Meadowvale, Milliken, Milton, Mimico, Mississauga,

New Toronto, Nobleton, Norval, Oakville, Orangeville, Oriole, O'Sullivan's Corners, Palermo, Palgrave, Park Royal, Pickering, Pine Grove, Port Credit, Port Union, Rexdale, Richmond Hill, Richvale, Rosebank, Rouge Hills, Scarborough, Schomberg, Sheridan Park, Snelgrove, South Pickering, Stouffville, Streetsville, Thistletown, Thornhill, Todmorden, Tottenham, Trafalgar, Unionville, Victoria, West Hill, Westmount, Weston, Whitevale, Wildfield, Willowdale, Woodbridge, York.

Services: Dial-up SLIP/PPP, shell access, UUCP service, domain registration, free Web home page with personal dial-up account, Web design, Web hosting.

World Wide Web: http://www.ilap.com

Internet Login (Division of Login Communications Inc.)

Montréal, Québec
login.net, login.qc.ca, newmarket.com, safe.org

8626, rue de Marseille
Montréal, PQ H1L 1R7

Voice: 514-493-8866
Fax: 514-493-1756
E-mail: info@login.net
Web: http://www.login.net

Service Area: Montreal, St-Jean, Drummondville, Sherbrooke, Trois-Rivières, St-Georges, Victoriaville. Planning to expand to Hull, Gatineau, Ottawa, Rouyn, Val d'Or, St-Jérôme, Ste-Adèle, Ste-Agathe, Valleyfield, Joliette, Sorel, Shawinigan, Grand-Mère, Granby, St-Hyacinthe, Thetford Mines, Ste-Marie, Quebec City, Alma, Chicoutimi, Rivière-du-Loup, Rimouski, Baie-Comeau, Sept-Îles.

Services: Leased line, dedicated ISDN, dedicated SLIP/PPP, frame relay, dial-up ISDN, dial-up SLIP/PPP, shell access, UUCP service, domain registration, Web design, Web hosting.

World Wide Web: http://www.login.net

Internet Montréal

Montréal, Québec
mtl.net, montreal.net, quebec.com

1 Place Ville Marie, Suite 2821
Montréal, PQ H3B 4R4

Voice: 514-393-1014
Fax: 514-527-4066
E-mail: info@mtl.net
Web: http://www.mtl.net

Service Area: Montreal, South Shore, North Shore. Planning to expand to the Laurentians, Sorel-Tracey, Quebec City, Joliette, Drummondville.

Services: Leased line, dedicated ISDN, dedicated SLIP/PPP, frame relay, dial-up ISDN, dial-up SLIP/PPP, shell access, terminal accounts, UUCP service, domain registration, free Web home page with personal dial-up account, Web design, Web hosting.

World Wide Web: http://www.mtl.net

Internet North

Yellowknife, Northwest Territories
internorth.com

4817–49th Street, Suite 27
Yellowknife, NT X1A 3S7

Voice: 403-873-5975
Fax: 403-873-2252
E-mail: info@internorth.com
Web: http://www.internorth.com

Service Area:	Yellowknife. Reduced long distance access also available from Inuvik, Hay River, Rae Lakes, Rankin Inlet, Baker Lake and Cambridge Bay. Planning to expand to Iqaluit, Hay River, Inuvik, Fort Smith, Cambridge Bay, Rankin Inlet.
Services:	Leased line, dedicated SLIP/PPP, dial-up SLIP/PPP, shell access, terminal accounts, UUCP service, domain registration, free Web home page with personal dial-up account, Web design, Web hosting.
World Wide Web:	http://www.internorth.com

Internet Passport Services Inc.

Dartmouth, Nova Scotia
ips.ca

Burnside Industrial Park
36 Topple Drive
Dartmouth, NS B3B 1L6

Voice: 902-468-3763
Fax: 902-468-9003
E-mail: sales@ips.ca, info@ips.ca (automated response)
Web: http://www.ips.ca

Service Area:	Halifax, Dartmouth, Bedford, Sackville, Chezzetcook, Elmsdale, French Village, Hubbards, Ketch Harbour, Mount Uniacke, Musquodoboit Harbour, Prospect Road, St. Margarets, Waverly.
Services:	Leased line, dedicated SLIP/PPP, dial-up SLIP/PPP, UUCP service, domain registration, Web design, Web hosting.
World Wide Web:	http://www.ips.ca

Internet Portal Services, Inc.

Vancouver, British Columbia
portal.ca

2525 Manitoba Street, Suite 201
Vancouver, BC V5Y 3A7

Voice: 604-257-9400
Fax: 604-257-9401
E-mail: info@portal.ca
Web: http://www.portal.ca

Service Area:	Aldergrove, Burnaby, Cloverdale, Coquitlam, Delta, Fort Langley, Haney, Ladner, Langley, Maple Ridge, New Westminster, Newton, North Vancouver, Pitt Meadows, Port Coquitlam, Port Moody, Richmond, Surrey, Tsawwassen, Vancouver, West Vancouver, Whalley, White Rock, Whonnock.
Services:	Leased line, dedicated ISDN, dedicated SLIP/PPP, frame relay, dial-up SLIP/PPP, shell access, UUCP service, domain registration, Web design, Web hosting.
World Wide Web:	http://www.portal.ca

Internet Saguenay Lac-St-Jean Inc.

Chicoutimi, Québec
saglac.qc.ca

930, Jacques-Cartier est
Chicoutimi, PQ G7H 2A9

Voice: 418-543-7777
Fax: 418-678-1129
E-mail: sysadm@saglac.qc.ca
Web: http://www.saglac.qc.ca

Service Area:	Chicoutimi, Jonquière, La Baie, Bagotville, Falardeau, Shipshaw, Laterrière, St-Ambroise, Bégin.
Services:	Leased line, dedicated ISDN, dedicated SLIP/PPP, frame relay, dial-up SLIP/PPP, shell access, free Web home page with personal dial-up account, Web hosting.
World Wide Web:	http://www.saglac.qc.ca

Internet Services and Information Systems (isis) Inc.

Halifax, Nova Scotia
isisnet.com

1505 Barrington Street, Suite 1501
Halifax, NS B3J 3K5

Voice:	902-429-1515
Fax:	902-429-9003
E-mail:	info@ra.isisnet.com
Web:	http://www.isisnet.com

Service Area:	Halifax, Dartmouth, Bedford, Sackville, and local dial-in areas. Planning to expand to Lunenburg, Bridgewater, Mahone Bay, Chester, Shelburne, Barrington, Windsor, Kentville.
Services:	Leased line, dedicated ISDN, dedicated SLIP/PPP, frame relay, dial-up SLIP/PPP, shell access, terminal accounts, UUCP service, domain registration, Web design, Web hosting.
World Wide Web:	http://www.isisnet.com

The InterNet Shop Inc.

Kamloops, British Columbia
netshop.net, netshop.bc.ca

1160-8th Street
Kamloops, BC V2B 2Y2

Voice:	604-376-3710
Fax:	604-376-5931
E-mail:	info@netshop.net
Web:	http://www.netshop.net

Service Area:	Kamloops, Logan Lake, Savona, Salmon Arm, Williams Lake, Quesnel, Kelowna, 100 Mile House, Grand Forks, Smithers, Lytton, Clinton, Cache Creek.
Services:	Leased line, dedicated SLIP/PPP, frame relay, dial-up SLIP/PPP, shell access, terminal accounts, UUCP service, domain registration, free Web home page with personal dial-up account, Web design, Web hosting.
World Wide Web:	http://www.netshop.net

Internet Solutions Inc.

Winnipeg, Manitoba
solutions.net, solutions.mb.ca, remcan.ca

Bridgeport Building
310 Nairn Avenue, 2nd Floor
Winnipeg, MB R2L 0W9

Voice:	204-982-1060
Fax:	204-982-1070
E-mail:	info@solutions.net
Web:	http://www.solutions.net

Service Area:	Winnipeg. Planning to expand to United Kingdom, Singapore, Thailand, Maryland, New Zealand.
Services:	Leased line, dedicated ISDN, dedicated SLIP/PPP, frame relay, dial-up ISDN, dial-up SLIP/PPP, UUCP service, domain registration, Web design, Web hosting.
World Wide Web:	http://www.solutions.net

Internet Sorel-Tracy

Tracy, Québec
sorel.mtl.net

807 Marie-Victorin
Tracy, PQ J3R 1L1

Voice:	514-746-1593
Fax:	514-746-1473
E-mail:	admin@sorel.mtl.net
Web:	http://sorel.mtl.net

Service Area:	Sorel, Tracy, St-Joseph-de-Sorel, St-Roch-sur-Richelieu, Ste-Victoire, St-Ours, Yamaska, St-David, St-Robert, St-Aimé, Contrecoeur, St-Laurent-du-Fleuve, Pierreville, St-François-du-Lac, Odanak, Notre-Dame-de-Pierreville. Planning to expand to Berthierville, St-Ignace-de-Loyola, Lanauraie.
Services:	Leased line, dedicated SLIP/PPP, dial-up ISDN, dial-up SLIP/PPP, shell access, UUCP service, domain registration, free Web home page with personal dial-up account, Web design, Web hosting.
World Wide Web:	http://sorel.mtl.net

Internet Trois-Rivières Inc.

Trois-Rivières, Québec
itr.qc.ca

400 Williams Street
Trois-Rivières, PQ G9A 3J2

Voice: 819-379-8649
Fax: 819-379-0343
E-mail: marc@itr.qc.ca (Marc Trudelle)
Web: http://www.itr.qc.ca

Service Area:	Trois-Rivières, Trois-Rivières-Ouest, Cap-de-la-Madeleine, Gentilly, Becancour, St-Célestin, Yamachiche, Louiseville, St-Barnabé, Charrette, St-Boniface, St-Étienne, Ste-Flore, St-Stanislas. Planning to expand to Granby, Bromont.
Services:	Leased line, dedicated ISDN, dedicated SLIP/PPP, frame relay, dial-up SLIP/PPP, shell access, domain registration, Web design, Web hosting.

World Wide Web: http://www.itr.qc.ca

InternetXpress

Winnipeg, Manitoba
kwanza.com, xpressnet.com

Bison Drive Professional Centre
1325 Markham Road, Unit 1
Winnipeg, MB R3T 4J6

Voice: 204-987-8380
Fax: 204-987-8382
E-mail: info@kwanza.com, info@Xpressnet.com
Web: http://www.kwanza.com,
            http://www.XpressNet.com

Service Area:	Winnipeg and all towns in local dial-in area.
Services:	Leased line, dedicated ISDN, dedicated SLIP/PPP, frame relay, dial-up ISDN, dial-up SLIP/PPP, UUCP service, domain registration, free Web home page with personal dial-up account, Web design, Web hosting.

World Wide Web: http://www.kwanza.com,
http://www.XpressNet.com

Internex Online Inc.

Toronto, Ontario
io.org

20 Bay Street, Suite 1625
Toronto, ON M5J 2N8

Voice: 416-363-8424
Fax: 416-363-8713
E-mail: info@io.org
Web: http://www.io.org

Service Area:	Toronto, Mississauga, Pickering, Brampton, Markham, Oakville. Planning to expand to Hamilton, Ottawa.
Services:	Dedicated ISDN, dedicated SLIP/PPP, dial-up ISDN, dial-up SLIP/PPP, shell access, terminal accounts, UUCP service, domain registration, free Web home page with personal dial-up account, Web design, Web hosting.

World Wide Web: http://www.io.org

InterNode Networks Inc.

Calgary, Alberta
internode.net

300–8120 Beddington Boulevard N.W., Suite 213
Calgary, AB T3K 2A8

Voice: 403-296-1190
Fax: 403-295-3276
E-mail: info@internode.net
Web: http://www.internode.net

Service Area:	Calgary.
Services:	Leased line, dedicated ISDN, dedicated SLIP/PPP, dial-up ISDN, dial-up SLIP/PPP, shell access, domain registration, free Web home page with personal dial-up account, Web design, Web hosting.

World Wide Web: http://www.internode.net

Intertek Internet Technology Services, Inc., o/a ITSI

Welland, Ontario
itsi.net

16 Steel Street
Welland, ON L3B 3L9

Voice:	905-734-1992, 1-800-567-4227
Fax:	905-732-0930
E-mail:	info@itsi.net
Web:	http://www.itsi.net

Service Area:	Welland, Pelham, Port Colborne, Port Robinson, St. Catharines, Thorold, Stevensville, Wainfleet. Planning to expand to Beamsville, Fort Erie, Grimsby, Niagara Falls, Niagara-on-the-Lake, Ridgeway, Vineland, Wainfleet, West Lincoln and Hamilton (local dialing); all points within Canada (1-800-dial-up); and all major Canadian centres (frame relay dial-up).
Services:	Leased line, dedicated SLIP/PPP, frame relay, dial-up SLIP/PPP, UUCP service, domain registration, Web design, Web hosting.
World Wide Web:	http://www.itsi.net

Intervider Communications Inc.

Oakville, Ontario
intervider.on.ca, intervider.net

466 Speers Road, Suite 311
Oakville, ON L6K 3W9

Voice:	905-337-5000
Fax:	905-842-8294
E-mail:	info@intervider.on.ca
Web:	http://www.intervider.on.ca

Service Area:	Oakville, Burlington, Mississauga, Milton, Etobicoke, Toronto. Planning to expand to North York, Brampton, Richmond Hill, Markham, Scarborough.

Services:	Dedicated ISDN, dedicated SLIP/PPP, dial-up ISDN, dial-up SLIP/PPP, shell access, domain registration, free Web home page with personal dial-up account, Web design, Web hosting.
World Wide Web:	http://www.intervider.on.ca

INTRANET Technologies Inc.

Ottawa, Ontario
intranet.on.ca

220 Laurier Avenue West, Suite 330
Ottawa, ON K1P 5Z9

Voice:	613-233-7455, 1-800-576-7704
Fax:	613-233-7535
E-mail:	info@intranet.on.ca
Web:	http://www.intranet.on.ca

Service Area:	Ottawa, Deep River, Belleville.
Services:	Leased line, dedicated ISDN, dedicated SLIP/PPP, frame relay, dial-up SLIP/PPP, shell access, domain registration, free Web home page with personal dial-up account, Web design, Web hosting.
World Wide Web:	http://www.intranet.on.ca

Island Internet Inc.

Nanaimo, British Columbia
island.net, islandnet.bc.ca

57 Skinner Street, Suite 3
Nanaimo, BC V9R 5G9

Voice:	604-753-1139, 1-800-811-4488
Fax:	604-753-8542
E-mail:	support@island.net
Web:	http://www.island.net

Service Area:	Nanaimo, Ladysmith, Crofton, Chemainus, Duncan, Lake Cowichan, Maple Bay Parksville, Qualicum, Bowser, Comox, Courtenay, Campbell River, Gold River, Port Hardy, Port McNeil, Port Alberni, Tofino, Queen Charlotte City, Massett. Planning to expand to Victoria.
Services:	Leased line, dedicated ISDN, dedicated SLIP/PPP, frame relay, dial-up SLIP/PPP, shell access, terminal accounts, UUCP service, domain registration, free Web home page with personal dial-up account, Web design, Web hosting.
World Wide Web:	http://www.island.net

Island Net (AMT Solutions Group Inc.)

Victoria, British Columbia
islandnet.com, amtsgi.bc.ca

824 Johnson Street, Suite 205
Victoria, BC V8W 1N3

Voice: 604-383-0096, 1-800-331-3055
Fax: 604-383-6698
E-mail: info@islandnet.com
Web: http://www.islandnet.com

Service Area:	Brentwood Bay, Chemainus, Cobble Hill, Colwood, Crofton, Duncan, Ladysmith, Langford, Lantzville, Metchosin, Mill Bay, Nanaimo, Nanoose Bay, Parksville, Qualicum, Shawnigan Lake, Sidney, Sooke, Victoria. Planning to expand to Salt Spring Island.
Services:	Dial-up SLIP/PPP, terminal accounts, UUCP service, domain registration, free Web home page with personal dial-up account, Web design, Web hosting.
World Wide Web:	http://www.islandnet.com

Island Services Network

Charlottetown, Prince Edward Island
isn.net, sellit.com, ecma.com

Home Building
129 Kent Street, Suite 303
Charlottetown, PE C1A 1N4

Voice: 902-892-4476
Fax: 902-566-3405
E-mail: info@isn.net
Web: http://www.isn.net

Service Area:	Charlottetown, Covehead, Crapaud, Eldon, Hunter-River, Morell-St. Peters, Mount Stewart, New Haven, Rusticoville, Vernon River. Planning to expand to Summerside and Montague.
Services:	Leased line, dedicated ISDN, dedicated SLIP/PPP, frame relay, dial-up SLIP/PPP, shell access, terminal accounts, UUCP service, domain registration, Web design, Web hosting.
World Wide Web:	http://www.isn.net

iSTAR Internet Inc.

Ottawa, Ontario
nstn.ca, fonorola.net

250 Albert Street, Suite 202
Ottawa, ON K1P 6M1

Voice: 613-780-2200
Fax: 613-468-3679
E-mail: info@nstn.ca, sales@nstn.ns.ca
Web: http://www.nstn.ca

Service Area:	Alberta: Edmonton. British Columbia: Vancouver, Victoria. Manitoba: Winnipeg. New Brunswick: Moncton. Nova Scotia: Amherst, Antigonish, Bridgewater, Halifax, Kentville, Middleton, New Glasgow, Port Hawkesbury, Shubenacadie, Sydney, Truro, Windsor, Yarmouth. Ontario: Kingston, London, Ottawa, Pembroke, Toronto. Québec: Montréal.

Service Area:	Planning to expand to Alberta: Calgary. New Brunswick: Bathurst, Belledune, Campbellton, Caraquet, Edmundston, Fredericton, Miramichi, Saint John, Shippegan. Ontario: Hamilton, Kitchener/Waterloo, St. Catharines, Windsor. Quebec: Quebec City.
Services:	Leased line, dedicated ISDN, dedicated SLIP/PPP, frame relay, dial-up SLIP/PPP, UUCP service, domain registration, Web design, Web hosting.
World Wide Web:	http://www.nstn.ca

KawarthaNET

Peterborough, Ontario
knet.flemingc.on.ca, news.flemingc.on.ca

526 McDonnel Street
Peterborough, ON K9J 7B1

Voice:	705-748-5638
Fax:	705-748-4849
E-mail:	admin@knet.flemingc.on.ca
Web:	http://www.knet.flemingc.on.ca

Service Area:	Peterborough, Lindsay, Millbrook, Pontypool, Cavan, Omemee, Hastings, Lakefield, Baillieboro. Planning to expand to Haliburton, Fenelon Falls, Minden.
Services:	Dedicated SLIP/PPP, dial-up SLIP/PPP, shell access, terminal accounts, free Web home page with personal dial-up account, Web design, Web hosting.
World Wide Web:	http://www.knet.flemingc.on.ca

Kingston Online Services

Kingston, Ontario
kosone.com

303 Bagot Street, Suite 309
Kingston, ON K7K 5W7

Voice:	613-549-8667, 1-800-208-0086
Fax:	613-549-0642
E-mail:	support@mail.kosone.com
Web:	http://www.kosone.com/kos/Welcome.html

Service Area:	Kingston, Gananoque, Trenton, Belleville, Picton, Bancroft, Brighton, Deseronto, Napanee, Verona, Sydenham, Amherstview, Wellington. Planning to expand to Ottawa, Toronto, Oshawa, Cobourg, Peterborough, Cornwall, Brockville.
Services:	Leased line, dedicated ISDN, dedicated SLIP/PPP, frame relay, dial-up ISDN, dial-up SLIP/PPP, shell access, terminal accounts, UUCP service, domain registration, Web design, Web hosting.
World Wide Web:	http://www.kosone.com/kos/Welcome.html

Kneehill Internet Services

Acme, Alberta
kneehill.com

Box 37
Linden, AB T0M 1J0

Voice:	403-546-3021
Fax:	403-546-2276
E-mail:	info@kneehill.com, dannstp@kneehill.com, terry@kneehill.com
Web:	http://www.kneehill.com

Service Area:	Acme, Linden, Beiseker, Three Hills, Swalwell, Calgary. Planning to expand to Olds, Didsbury, Trochu.
Services:	Dedicated SLIP/PPP, dial-up SLIP/PPP, domain registration, Web design, Web hosting.
World Wide Web:	http://www.kneehill.com

Kootenay Network Systems Inc.

Castlegar, British Columbia
kootenay.net

2313H–6th Avenue
Castlegar, BC V1N 2W1

Voice:	604-365-2323
Fax:	604-365-0151
E-mail:	info@knet.kootenay.net
Web:	http://www.kootenay.net

Service Area:	Castlegar, Nelson, Rossland, Trail. Planning to expand to south central British Columbia (East and West Kootenays).
Services:	Leased line, dedicated SLIP/PPP, frame relay, dial-up SLIP/PPP, shell access, terminal accounts, UUCP service, domain registration, Web design, Web hosting.
World Wide Web:	http://www.kootenay.net

LANZEN Corporation

Montréal, Québec
lanzen.net, lanzen.com

1751 Richardson, Suite 2525
Montréal, PQ H3K 1G6

Voice: 514-937-4422
Fax: 514-937-4317
E-mail: sales@lanzen.net
Web: http://www.lanzen.net

Service Area:	Montreal and the Laurentians. Planning to expand to Ottawa.
Services:	Leased line, dedicated ISDN, dedicated SLIP/PPP, frame relay, dial-up ISDN, dial-up SLIP/PPP, UUCP service, domain registration, free Web home page with personal dial-up account, Web design, Web hosting.
World Wide Web:	http://www.lanzen.net

Lethbridge Internet Services

Lethbridge, Alberta
lis.ab.ca

814–3rd Avenue South
Lethbridge, AB T1J 0H7

Voice: 403-381-4638
Fax: 403-320-0484
E-mail: info@lis.ab.ca
Web: http://www.lis.ab.ca

Service Area:	Barons, Cardston, Carmangay, Champion, Coaldale, Enchant, Fort Macleod, Glenwood, Iron Springs, Lethbridge, Magrath, New Dayton, Nobleford, Picture Buttle, Raymond, Standoff, Stirling, Taber, Wrentham.
Services:	Leased line, dedicated ISDN, dedicated SLIP/PPP, frame relay, dial-up ISDN, dial-up SLIP/PPP, UUCP service, domain registration, Web design, Web hosting.
World Wide Web:	http://www.lis.ab.ca

Lexicom Ltd.

Calgary, Alberta
lexicom.ab.ca

203 Lynnview Road S.E., Suite 60
Calgary, AB T2C 2C6

Voice: 403-255-3615
Fax: 403-640-2138
E-mail: rae@lexicom.ab.ca
Web: http://www.lexicom.ab.ca/lexicom

Service Area:	Calgary and local calling area.
Services:	Dedicated ISDN, dedicated SLIP/PPP, frame relay, dial-up ISDN, dial-up SLIP/PPP, shell access, terminal accounts, UUCP service, domain registration, free Web home page with personal dial-up account, Web design, Web hosting.
World Wide Web:	http://www.lexicom.ab.ca/lexicom

Lien Internet du Nord-Ouest (L.I.N.O.) Inc.

Val-d'Or, Québec
lino.com

1717–3rd Avenue
Val-d'Or, PQ J9P 1W3

Voice: 819-874-5665
Fax: 819-874-2077
E-mail: sjuteau@lino.com
Web: http://www.lino.com

Service Area: Val-d'Or, Amos, Rouyn-Noranda, Cadillac, Barraute, Senneterre, Granada, Belcourt, Vassan, Dubuisson, Rivière-Héva, Louvicourt, Malartic, La Corne, Beaudry, Bellecombe, Drolet. Planning to expand to La Sarre.

Services: Leased line, dedicated SLIP/PPP, frame relay, dial-up SLIP/PPP, domain registration, Web design, Web hosting.

World Wide Web: http://www.lino.com

Local GlobalAccess Inc.

Toronto, Ontario
lglobal.com

320½ Bloor Street West
Toronto, ON M5S 1W5

Voice: 416-515-7400
Fax: 416-515-1118
E-mail: info@lglobal.com
Web: http://www.lglobal.com

Service Area: Greater Toronto Area: Toronto, Markham, Brampton, Woodbridge, Oakville, Thornhill, North York, Scarborough.

Services: Dedicated SLIP/PPP, dial-up SLIP/PPP, shell access, domain registration, free Web home page with personal dial-up account, Web design, Web hosting.

World Wide Web: http://www.lglobal.com

Logical Solutions Computer Systems Inc.

Calgary, Alberta
logicnet.com

4624 Varsity Drive N.W.
Calgary, AB T3A 2L9

Voice: 403-299-9140
Fax: 403-299-9146
E-mail: sysop@bbs.logicnet.com
Web: http://www.logicnet.com

Service Area: Calgary.

Services: Dial-up SLIP/PPP, shell access, terminal accounts, domain registration, Web design, Web hosting.

World Wide Web: http://www.logicnet.com

Magic Online Services Toronto Inc.

Toronto, Ontario
magic.ca

260 Richmond Street West, Suite 206
Toronto, ON M5V 1W5

Voice: 416-591-6490
Fax: 416-591-6409
E-mail: info@magic.ca
Web: http://www.magic.ca

Service Area: Toronto.

Services: Leased line, dedicated ISDN, dial-up SLIP/PPP, shell access, domain registration, free Web home page with personal dial-up account, Web design, Web hosting.

World Wide Web: http://www.magic.ca

Magic Online Services Winnipeg

Winnipeg, Manitoba
magic.mb.ca

150–1483 Pembina Highway
Winnipeg, MB R3T 2C6

Voice: 204-949-7777
Fax: 204-949-7790
E-mail: info@magic.mb.ca
Web: http://www.magic.mb.ca

Service Area: Carmen, Winnipeg.

Services: Leased line, dedicated ISDN, dedicated SLIP/PPP, dial-up SLIP/PPP, shell access, UUCP service, domain registration, free Web home page with personal dial-up account, Web design, Web hosting.

World Wide Web: http://www.magic.mb.ca

Magma Communications Ltd.

Ottawa, Ontario
http://www.magmacom.com

52 Antares Drive, Unit 201
Nepean, ON K2E 7Z1

Voice:	613-228-3565
Fax:	613-228-8313
E-mail:	sales@magmacom.com
Web:	http://www.magmacom.com

Service Area:	Ottawa-Hull, Carleton Place, Almonte, Kemptville, Merrickville, Buckingham, Low, Embrun, Russell, Rockland, Val-des-Bois, Luskville, Wakefield, St-Pierre-de-Wakefield, Quyon, Bourget, Clarence Creek, North Gower, Kanata, Stittsville, Pakenham, Gatineau, Shawville, Perkins, Plantagenet, Aylmer, Manotick, Casselman, Metcalfe, Gloucester, Jockvale, Orleans, Osgoode, Chelsea, Constance Bay, Cumberland, Navan, Richmond, Carp, Thurso, Crysler.
Services:	Leased line, dedicated ISDN, dedicated SLIP/PPP, dial-up ISDN, dial-up SLIP/PPP, shell access, terminal accounts, UUCP service, domain registration, free Web home page with personal dial-up account, Web design, Web hosting.
World Wide Web:	http://www.magmacom.com

Magnett Internet Gateway

Montréal, Québec
magnet.ca

1425, boul. René Lévesque Ouest, Suite 1105
Montréal, PQ H3G 1T7

Voice:	514-861-8622
Fax:	514-861-8640
E-mail:	info@magnet.ca
Web:	http://www.magnet.ca

Service Area:	Montreal and the 514 dial-in area.
Services:	Leased line, dedicated ISDN, dedicated SLIP/PPP, frame relay, dial-up SLIP/PPP, domain registration, free Web home page with personal dial-up account, Web design, Web hosting.
World Wide Web:	http://www.magnet.ca

Managed Network Systems Inc.

Windsor, Ontario
mnsi.net

870 University Avenue West
Windsor, ON N9A 5R9

Voice:	519-258-1778
Fax:	519-258-3009
E-mail:	info@mnsi.net
Web:	http://www.mnsi.net

Service Area:	Windsor, Leamington, Comber, McGregor, Emeryville, Belle River, Kingsville, LaSalle, Tecumseh, Amherstburg, Maidstone, Harrow, Essex, Stoney Point (Point-aux-Roches), Wheatley, Cottam, Woodslee. Planning to expand to Chatham, Detroit.
Services:	Leased line, dedicated ISDN, dedicated SLIP/PPP, dial-up SLIP/PPP, domain registration, Web hosting.
World Wide Web:	http://www.mnsi.net

Manitoba Telephone System

Winnipeg, Manitoba
mts.net

Box 6666
489 Empress Street
Winnipeg, MB R3C 3V6

Voice:	1-800-280-7095
Fax:	1-800-317-6191
E-mail:	comments@mts.net
Web:	http://www.mts.net

Service Area:	Winnipeg, Altona, Brandon, Dauphin, Portgage La Prairie, Selkirk, The Pas, Thompson, Winkler. Toll-free access in areas with MTS Community Calling and Urban Unlimited calling services. Planning to expand to other areas in Manitoba.
Services:	Leased line, dedicated ISDN, dedicated SLIP/PPP, frame relay, dial-up ISDN, dial-up SLIP/PPP, domain registration, free Web home page with personal dial-up account, Web hosting.
World Wide Web:	http://www.mts.net

MapleNet Regina

Regina, Saskatchewan
maple.net

845 Broad Street
Regina, SK S4R 8G9

Voice:	306-569-4638
Fax:	306-569-1096
E-mail:	regina@maple.net
Web:	http://www.maple.net

Service Area:	Regina, Balgonie, Lumsden, Pense, Regina Beach, Riceton, Rouleau, Sedley, Vibank, Wilcox. Planning to expand to Moose Jaw, Saskatoon.
Services:	Leased line, dedicated ISDN, dedicated SLIP/PPP, frame relay, dial-up ISDN, dial-up SLIP/PPP, shell access, UUCP service, domain registration, Web design, Web hosting.
World Wide Web:	http://www.maple.net

MapleNet Technologies Inc.

North York, Ontario
maple.net

150 Consumers Road, Suite 500
North York, ON M2J 1P9

Voice:	416-756-2000
Fax:	416-756-2088
E-mail:	info@maple.net
Web:	http://www.maple.net

Service Area:	Toronto, Hamilton, Oshawa, Newmarket, Kincardine, Hanover, Collingwood, Calgary, Regina. Planning to expand nationally.
Services:	Leased line, dedicated ISDN, dedicated SLIP/PPP, frame relay, dial-up ISDN, dial-up SLIP/PPP, shell access, terminal accounts, UUCP service, domain registration, free Web home page with personal dial-up account, Web design, Web hosting.
World Wide Web:	http://www.maple.net

Maritime Internet Services Inc.

Saint John, New Brunswick
mi.net

28 King Street
P.O. Box 6477
Saint John, NB E2L 4R9

Voice:	506-652-3624
Fax:	506-635-3400
E-mail:	info@mi.net
Web:	http://www.mi.net

Service Area:	Saint John, Fredericton. Planning to expand to Moncton, Halifax, Sydney.
Services:	Leased line, dedicated ISDN, dedicated SLIP/PPP, frame relay, dial-up SLIP/PPP, shell access, UUCP service, domain registration, Web design, Web hosting.
World Wide Web:	http://www.mi.net

Matrox SphereNet

Dorval, Québec
spherenet.com

1120, St-Régis
Dorval, PQ H9P 2T5

Voice:	514-685-4442
Fax:	514-685-8780
E-mail:	info@spherenet.com
Web:	http://www.spherenet.com

Service Area:	Montreal, St-Sauveur, Mirabel, St-Calixte-de-Kilkenny, Ste-Julienne, Mirabel, St-Augustin, Ste-Thérèse, St-Eustache, Oka, Ste-Anne-des-Plaines, St-Lin, L'Épiphanie-L'Assomption, Lavaltrie, Mascouche, Le Gardeur, Terrebonne, Ste-Rose, Laval East, Laval West, Chomedey, Pont-Viau, St-Vincent-de-Paul, Rigaud, Hudson, Vaudreuil, Île-Perrot, Pointe-Claire, Ste-Geneviève, Roxboro, Lachine, Beauharnois, Châteauguay, Ste-Martine, St-Rémi, Hemmingford, St-Constant, Napierville, Clarenceville, La Prairie, St-Jean, Marieville, Chambly, St-Lambert, St-Bruno, Beloeil, Longueuil, Boucherville, Ste-Julie-de-Verchères, Varennes, St-Marc, Verchères, St-Denis.
Services:	Dedicated SLIP/PPP, dial-up SLIP/PPP, shell access, terminal accounts, domain registration, free Web home page with personal dial-up account, Web design, Web hosting.
World Wide Web:	http://www.spherenet.com

MBnet

Winnipeg, Manitoba
mbnet.mb.ca

c/o Computer Services
The University of Manitoba
603 Engineering Building
15 Gilson Street
Winnipeg, MB R3T 5V6

Voice:	204-474-7325
Fax:	204-275-5420
E-mail:	info@mbnet.mb.ca
Web:	http://www.mbnet.mb.ca

Service Area:	Manitoba.
Services:	Leased line, dedicated ISDN, dedicated SLIP/PPP, frame relay, domain registration.
World Wide Web:	http://www.mbnet.mb.ca

MCD*Net-Mindemoya Computing and Design

Sudbury, Ontario
mcd.on.ca

1935 Paris Street
P.O. Box 21013
Sudbury, ON P3E 6G6

Voice:	705-523-0243
E-mail:	info@mcd.on.ca
Web:	http://www.mcd.on.ca

Service Area:	Sudbury.
Services:	Dial-up SLIP/PPP, shell access, terminal accounts, UUCP service, domain registration, Web design, Web hosting.
World Wide Web:	http://www.mcd.on.ca

MEG@Toon Station

Québec, Québec
megatoon.com, lastation.com

750, côte de la Pente-Douce
Québec, PQ G1N 2M1

Voice:	418-527-7120
Fax:	418-527-4373
E-mail:	station@megatoon.com
Web:	http://www.megatoon.com, https://www.megatoon.com

Service Area:	Quebec City, Sillery, Ste-Foy, Cap-Rouge, St-Augustin, Lorretteville, Vanier, Charlesbourg, Beauport, Lévis, St-David, Charny, St-Romuald, Breakeyville, St-Jean-Chrysostome, St-Étienne, St-Lambert, St-Rédempteur, St-Nicolas, Stoneham, Valcartier, Ste-Catherine.
Services:	Dedicated ISDN, dedicated SLIP/PPP, dial-up ISDN, dial-up SLIP/PPP, shell access, UUCP service, domain registration, free Web home page with personal dial-up account, Web design, Web hosting.
World Wide Web:	http://www.megatoon.com, https://www.megatoon.com

Metrix Interlink Corporation

Montréal, Québec
interlink.net, interlink.ca

500, boul. René-Lévesque Ouest,
bureau 1004
Montréal, PQ H2Z 1W7

Voice: 514-875-0010
Fax: 514-875-5735
E-mail: info@interlink.net
Web: http://www.interlink.net

Service Area:	Montreal, Toronto, Quebec City. 130 cities across Canada for T1 frame relay access. Planning to expand to Ottawa, Calgary, Vancouver.
Services:	Leased line, dedicated ISDN, dedicated SLIP/PPP, frame relay, dial-up ISDN, dial-up SLIP/PPP, domain registration, Web design, Web hosting.

World Wide Web: http://www.interlink.net

MGL Systems Computer Technologies Inc.

Guelph, Ontario
mgl.ca

RR#1
Guelph, ON N1H 6H7

Voice: 519-822-2922
Fax: 519-836-1309
E-mail: sales@mgl.ca
Web: http://www.mgl.ca

Service Area:	St. Thomas, Belmont, Dutton, Shedden, Fingal, Sparta, Port Stanley, London, Breslau, Galt, Guelph, Hespeler, Cambridge, Kitchener, Waterloo, New Dundee, Acton, Elora, Erin, Fergus, Hillsburgh, Rockwood. Planning to expand to Mississauga, Hamilton, Windsor.

Services:	Leased line, dedicated ISDN, dedicated SLIP/PPP, frame relay, dial-up ISDN, dial-up SLIP/PPP, shell access, terminal accounts, UUCP service, domain registration, free Web home page with personal dial-up account, Web design, Web hosting.

World Wide Web: http://www.mgl.ca

MicroAge Internet Access

Thunder Bay, Ontario
microage-tb.com

871B Tungsten Street
Thunder Bay, ON P7B 6H2

Voice: 807-343-4490
Fax: 807-346-4963
E-mail: lhintikk@microage-tb.com
Web: http://www.microage-tb.com

Service Area:	Thunder Bay, Kakabeka Falls, Murillo. Planning to expand to northwestern Ontario.
Services:	Leased line, dedicated ISDN, dedicated SLIP/PPP, frame relay, dial-up SLIP/PPP, shell access, terminal accounts, domain registration, Web design, Web hosting.

World Wide Web: http://www.microage-tb.com

MicroAge Internet Services

Ville d'Anjou, Québec
microage.ca

9393 Louis-H. Lafontaine
Ville d'Anjou, PQ H1J 1Y8

Voice: 514-354-3810
Fax: 514-354-2299
E-mail: info@hartco.ca
Web: http://www.microage.ca

Service Area

Alberta: *Calgary* 403-234-7067 *Calgary* 403-263-5300 *Edmonton* 403-482-5605 *Lethbridge* 403-328-0555 *Lloydminster* 403-875-8880 *Red Deer* 403-340-8088
British Columbia: *Langley* 604-534-2534 *Richmond* 604-270-7261 *Richmond* 604-270-3555
Manitoba: *Brandon* 204-725-8500 *Thompson* 204-677-7800 *Winnipeg* 204-987-2700 *Winnipeg* 204-786-6466
New Brunswick: *Bathurst* 506-546-9943 *Moncton* 506-857-9422
Newfoundland: *St. John's* 709-576-1299
Northwest Territories: *Yellowknife* 403-873-5975
Nova Scotia: *Dartmouth* 902-468-7195
Ontario: *Barrie* 705-739-9191 *Belleville* 613-966-6201 *Brockville* 613-345-3861 *Chatham* 519-352-2112 *Cornwall* 613-938-8087 *Kingston* 613-546-3151 *Kitchener* 519-745-1190 *London* 519-673-6610 *Ottawa* 613-727-0386 *Owen Sound* 519-376-7735 *Pembroke* 613-735-2262 *Peterborough* 705-876-1177 *St. Catharines* 905-641-2500 *Sault Ste. Marie* 705-976-0876 *Sudbury* 705-523-3302 *Thunder Bay* 807-343-4490 *Toronto* 416-778-1300 *Toronto* 416-785-5022 *Windsor* 519-944-6600
Prince Edward Island: *Charlottetown* 902-566-4335
Quebec: *Drummondville* 819-477-8886 *Granby* 514-375-0052 *Greenfield Park* 514-672-0020 *Joliette* 514-752-6600 *Laval* 514-663-4429 *Montmagny* 418-248-2454 *Montreal* 514-397-9711 *Montreal* 514-483-6040 *Rimouski* 418-724-6448 *Ste-Foy* 418-681-1054 *St-Georges-de-Beauce* 418-227-2197 *St-Hyacinthe* 514-778-1122 *St-Jean-sur-Richelieu* 514-359-0113 *Sept-Îles* 418-962-6000 *Sherbrooke* 819-569-9663 *Tracy* 514-846-4636 *Trois-Rivières* 819-378-7910 *Valleyfield* 514-371-9771 *Victoriaville* 819-752-2511
Saskatchewan: *Regina* 306-525-0537 *Saskatoon* 306-934-8106

Services: Leased line, dedicated ISDN, dedicated SLIP/PPP, frame relay, dial-up ISDN, dial-up SLIP/PPP, domain registration, Web design, Web hosting.

World Wide Web: http://www.microage.ca

Microsoft Canada Inc.

Mississauga, Ontario
msn.com, microsoft.com

320 Matheson Boulevard West
Mississauga, ON L5R 3R1

Voice: 1-800-386-5550
E-mail: msninfo@microsoft.com
Web: http://www.msn.com

Service Area: Alberta: Calgary, Edmonton, Lethbridge, Red Deer. British Columbia: Kelowna, Prince George, Vancouver, Victoria. Manitoba: Brandon, Winnipeg. New Brunswick: Moncton, Saint John. Newfoundland: St. John's. Nova Scotia: Halifax. Ontario: Guelph, Hamilton, Kingston, Kitchener, London, Oshawa, Ottawa, St. Catharines, Sudbury, Thunder Bay, Toronto, Windsor. Quebec: Montreal, Quebec City, Sherbrooke.

Services: Dial-up ISDN, dial-up SLIP/PPP, UUCP service, Web hosting.

World Wide Web: http://www.msn.com

Millennia Net Inc.

Vancouver, British Columbia
millennia.net, millennia.com, mnis.com

555 West Hastings Street, Suite 800
Vancouver, BC V6B 4N5

Voice: 604-443-5053
Fax: 604-433-3053
E-mail: info@millennia.net
Web: http://www.millennia.net

Service Area:	Metropolitan Vancouver and surrounding areas. Planning to expand to Calgary, Edmonton, Victoria.
Services:	Leased line, dedicated ISDN, dedicated SLIP/PPP, frame relay, dial-up ISDN, terminal accounts, UUCP service, domain registration, Web design, Web hosting.
World Wide Web:	http://www.millennia.net

MIND LINK! Communications Corp.

New Westminster, British Columbia
mindlink.bc.ca, mindlink.net

435 Columbia Street, Suite 230
New Westminster, BC V3L 5N8

Voice:	604-668-5000
Fax:	604-668-5028
E-mail:	info@mindlink.net
Web:	http://www.mindlink.net

Service Area:	West Vancouver, North Vancouver, Vancouver, Burnaby, Richmond, New Westminister, Surrey, Coquitlam, Port Coquitlam, Port Moody, Langley, Fort Langley, Aldergrove, Abbotsford, Matsqui, Mission, Pitt Meadows, Clearbrook, White Rock, Kelowna, Rutland, Westbank, Vernon, Oyama, Winfield, Coldstream, Okanagan Centre, Prince George, Vanderhoof. Planning to expand to Victoria, Nanaimo.
Services:	Leased line, dedicated ISDN, dedicated SLIP/PPP, frame relay, dial-up SLIP/PPP, shell access, terminal accounts, UUCP service, domain registration, free Web home page with personal dial-up account, Web design, Web hosting.
World Wide Web:	http://www.mindlink.net

Montreal Internet Inc.

St-Laurent, Québec
montrealnet.ca

1070 Beaulac
St-Laurent, PQ H4R 1R7

Voice:	514-337-8185
Fax:	514-335-6949
E-mail:	admin@montrealnet.ca
Web:	http://www.montrealnet.ca

Service Area:	Montreal, Laval, South Shore, St-Jean-d'Iberville, St-Hyacinthe, Quebec City, Sorel, Mirabel, St-Jérôme, St-Sauveur.
Services:	Leased line, dedicated ISDN, dedicated SLIP/PPP, frame relay, dial-up ISDN, dial-up SLIP/PPP, UUCP service, domain registration, Web design, Web hosting.
World Wide Web:	http://www.montrealnet.ca

Mortimer Online (Division of Left Coast Systems Corp.)

Burnaby, British Columbia
mortimer.net, mortimer.com, kyle.com

2465 Beta Avenue, Suite 120
Burnaby, BC V5C 5N1

Voice:	604-294-2995
Fax:	604-294-8341
E-mail:	info@mortimer.com
Web:	http://www.mortimer.com

Service Area:	Vancouver and local dial-in area. Planning to expand to Abbotsford, Fraser Valley.
Services:	Leased line, dedicated ISDN, dedicated SLIP/PPP, frame relay, dial-up SLIP/PPP, terminal accounts, domain registration, free Web home page with personal dial-up account, Web design, Web hosting.
World Wide Web:	http://www.mortimer.com

Mountain Internet (Division of Tantalus Technologies Inc.)

Squamish, British Columbia
mountain-inter.net

38144 Cleveland Avenue
Squamish, BC V0N 3G0

Voice:	604-892-9556
Fax:	604-898-2643
E-mail:	admin@mountain-inter.net
Web:	http://www.mountain-inter.net

Service Area:	Squamish, Britannia Beach. Planning to expand to Whistler.
Services:	Leased line, dedicated SLIP/PPP, dial-up SLIP/PPP, shell access, UUCP service, domain registration, free Web home page with personal dial-up account, Web design.
World Wide Web:	http://www.mountain-inter.net

MPACT Immedia Corporation

Montréal, Québec
mpact.ca, immedia.ca

1155 René-Lévesque West, Suite 2250
Montréal, PQ H3B 4T3

Voice:	514-397-9747
Fax:	514-398-0764
E-mail:	service@immedia.ca
Web:	http://www.mpact.ca

Service Area:	Halifax, Moncton, Quebec City, Montreal, Ottawa, Toronto, London, Winnipeg, Calgary, Vancouver, Victoria.
Services:	Leased line, dedicated ISDN, dedicated SLIP/PPP, dial-up SLIP/PPP, shell access, UUCP service, domain registration, Web design, Web hosting.
World Wide Web:	http://www.mpact.ca

Multi-Médias Québec

Sherbrooke, Québec
multi-medias.ca

40, boul. Queen sud, bureau 200
Sherbrooke, PQ J1H 3P3

Voice:	819-563-4311
Fax:	819-563-5833
E-mail:	mike@multi-medias.ca
Web:	http://www.multi-medias.ca

Service Area:	Sherbrooke, Richmond, Asbestos, Magog, Bury, Waterville, Fleurimont, Ascot Corner, Danville. Planning to expand to Lac Mégantic, Beauce, Thetford Mines.
Services:	Leased line, dedicated ISDN, dedicated SLIP/PPP, frame relay, dial-up ISDN, dial-up SLIP/PPP, UUCP service, domain registration, free Web home page with personal dial-up account, Web design, Web hosting.
World Wide Web:	http://www.multi-medias.ca

MultiNet Media Solutions

Markham, Ontario
multinet.net

7050 Woodbine Avenue, Suite 201
Markham, ON L3R 4G8

Voice:	905-946-8033
Fax:	905-946-8019
E-mail:	sales@multinet.net
Web:	http://www.multinet.net

Service Area:	British Columbia: Burnaby, Coquitlam, North Vancouver, Port Coquitlam, Richmond, Surrey, Vancouver, West Vancouver. New Brunswick: Middleton. Nova Scotia: Amherst, Antigonish, Bridgewater, Halifax, Kentville, New Glasgow, Port Hawkesbury, Shubenacadie, Sydney, Truro, Windsor, Wolfville, Yarmouth. Ontario: Ajax, Aurora, King City, Kingston, Kleinberg, London, Maple, Markham, Metropolitan Toronto

Middleton, Nobelton, North York, Oak Ridges, Pembroke, Pickering, Richmond Hill, Schomberg, Stouffville, Thornhill, Unionville, Vaughan, Woodbridge. MultiNet has points of presence across Canada for dedicated connections.

Services:	Leased line, dedicated ISDN, frame relay, dial-up ISDN, dial-up SLIP/PPP, shell access, UUCP service, domain registration, Web design, Web hosting.

World Wide Web: http://www.multinet.net

Muskoka.com

Bracebridge, Ontario
muskoka.com, cottage.net

115 Manitoba Street
Bracebridge, ON P1L 1W5

Voice:	705-645-6097
Fax:	705-645-6632
E-mail:	info@muskoka.com
Web:	http://www.muskoka.com

Service Area:	Bracebridge, Huntsville, Gravenhurst, Bala, Port Carling, Dwight, Dorset.
Services:	Leased line, dedicated SLIP/PPP, frame relay, dial-up SLIP/PPP, shell access, terminal accounts, UUCP service, domain registration, free Web home page with personal dial-up account, Web design, Web hosting.

World Wide Web: http://www.muskoka.com

Myna Communications Inc.

Toronto, Ontario
myna.com

151 Front Street West, Suite 505
P.O. Box 14
Toronto, ON M5J 2N1

Voice:	416-362-7000
Fax:	416-362-7001
E-mail:	info@myna.com
Web:	http://www.myna.com

Service Area:	Metropolitan Toronto, Ajax, Brampton, Markham, Mississauga, Oakville, Pickering, Richmond Hill, Thornhill, Unionville.
Services:	Dedicated ISDN, dedicated SLIP/PPP, dial-up ISDN, dial-up SLIP/PPP, domain registration, free Web home page with personal dial-up account, Web design, Web hosting.

World Wide Web: http://www.myna.com

Navnet Communications

Halifax, Nova Scotia
navnet.net

106 Chain Lake Drive, Unit 20
Halifax, NS B3S 1A8

Voice:	902-450-1020
Fax:	902-450-1021
E-mail:	wmaster@www.navnet.net
Web:	http://www.navnet.net

Service Area:	Metropolitan Halifax/Dartmouth.
Services:	Leased line, dedicated SLIP/PPP, frame relay, dial-up SLIP/PPP, terminal accounts, domain registration, free Web home page with personal dial-up account, Web design, Web hosting.

World Wide Web: http://www.navnet.net

NBTel

Saint John, New Brunswick
nbnet.nb.ca, nbtel.nb.ca, nbi.nb.ca

One Brunswick Square
P.O. Box 1430
Saint John, NB E2L 4K2

Voice:	506-458-1690, 1-800-565-1690
Fax:	506-694-2168
E-mail:	info@nbnet.nb.ca
Web:	http://www.nbtel.nb.ca

Service Area:	New Brunswick.
Services:	Leased line, dedicated SLIP/PPP, frame relay, dial-up SLIP/PPP, domain registration.
World Wide Web:	http://www.nbtel.nb.ca

Neocom Communications

Scarborough, Ontario
neocom.ca, neocom.net

50 Tiffield Road, Unit 13
Scarborough, ON M1V 5B7

Voice:	416-321-8880
Fax:	416-754-4635
E-mail:	info@neocom.ca
Web:	http://www.neocom.ca

Service Area:	Toronto, Ajax, Pickering, Aurora, Bethesda, Bolton, Brampton, Castlemore, Claremont, Clarkson, Cooksville, Gormley, King City, Kleinburg, Malton, Maple, Markham, Mississauga, Nobleton, Oak Ridges, Oakville, Palgrave, Port Credit, Richmond Hill, Schomberg, South Pickering, Snelgrove, Stouffville, Streetsville, Thornhill, Unionville, Woodbridge. Planning to expand to Hamilton, Oshawa, Whitby, Montreal, Vancouver.
Services:	Leased line, dedicated ISDN, dedicated SLIP/PPP, dial-up ISDN, dial-up SLIP/PPP, shell access, domain registration, free Web home page with personal dial-up account, Web design, Web hosting.
World Wide Web:	http://www.neocom.ca

NetAccess Systems Inc.

Hamilton, Ontario
netaccess.on.ca, eidos.ca

231 Main Street West
Hamilton, ON L8P 1J4

Voice:	905-524-2544
Fax:	905-524-3010
E-mail:	info@netaccess.on.ca
Web:	http://www.netaccess.on.ca

Service Area:	Greater Hamilton region including Hamilton, Burlington, Stoney Creek, Ancaster, Dundas, Grimsby, Winona, Lynden, Freelton, Mount Hope, Waterdown, Binbrook, Caledonia, Hagersville, Cayuga, Selkirk, West Lincoln.
Services:	Leased line, dedicated ISDN, dedicated SLIP/PPP, dial-up ISDN, dial-up SLIP/PPP, shell access, domain registration, free Web home page with personal dial-up account, Web design, Web hosting.
World Wide Web:	http://www.netaccess.on.ca

NetAxis Inc.

Montréal, Québec
netaxis.qc.ca

5253 Decarie Boulevard, Suite 511
Montréal, PQ H3W 3C3

Voice:	514-482-8989
Fax:	514-483-6718
E-mail:	info@netaxis.qc.ca
Web:	http://www.netaxis.qc.ca

Service Area:	Greater Montreal area. Planning to expand across Canada.
Services:	Leased line, dedicated ISDN, dedicated SLIP/PPP, dial-up ISDN, dial-up SLIP/PPP, shell access, terminal accounts, UUCP service, domain registration, Web design, Web hosting.
World Wide Web:	http://www.netaxis.qc.ca

Net Communications Inc.

St-Jean-sur-Richelieu, Québec
netc.net

Aéroport municipal, bureau 1
St-Jean-sur-Richelieu, PQ J3B 7B5

Voice:	514-346-3401
Fax:	514-346-3587
E-mail:	netc.net
Web:	http://www.netc.net

Service Area:	Montreal, Verdun, Lasalle, Longueuil, Brossard, St-Lambert, Candiac, St-Bruno, St-Jean-sur-Richelieu, Iberville, St-Luc. Planning to expand to Sherbrooke, Drummondville.
Services:	Leased line, dedicated ISDN, dedicated SLIP/PPP, frame relay, domain registration, Web design, Web hosting.
World Wide Web:	http://www.netc.net

NetCore

Windsor, Ontario
netcore.ca

360 Victoria Avenue
Windsor, ON N9A 4M6

Voice:	519-258-0004
Fax:	519-258-9601
E-mail:	help@netcore.ca
Web:	http://www.netcore.ca

Service Area:	Windsor, Tecumseh, Lasalle, Essex, Puce, Belle River, Amherstberg, Kingsville, Leamington.
Services:	Leased line, dedicated ISDN, dedicated SLIP/PPP, dial-up SLIP/PPP, UUCP service, domain registration, free Web home page with personal dial-up account, Web design, Web hosting.
World Wide Web:	http://www.netcore.ca

NetCruiser On-Line Communication Services

San Jose, California
netcom.com, netcom.net

3031 Tisch Way
San Jose, CA 95128

Voice:	408-983-5950
Fax:	408-241-9145
E-mail:	info@netcom.com
Web:	http://www.netcom.com

Service Area:	Vancouver, Calgary, Toronto, Montreal.
Services:	Leased line, dedicated SLIP/PPP, frame relay, dial-up SLIP/PPP, shell access, domain registration.
World Wide Web:	http://www.netcom.com

NetLine 2000

Edmonton, Alberta
nl2k.edmonton.ab.ca

3328–138 Avenue
Edmonton, AB T5Y 1M4

Voice:	403-473-4587
E-mail:	root@nl2k.edmonton.ab.ca
Web:	http://www.nl2k.edmonton.ab.ca

Service Area:	Edmonton and area.
Services:	Dedicated SLIP/PPP, dial-up SLIP/PPP, shell access, terminal accounts, UUCP service, free Web home page with personal dial-up account, Web design, Web hosting.
World Wide Web:	http://www.nl2k.edmonton.ab.ca

NetReach International

Picton, Ontario
reach.net, workshop.net

29 Elizabeth Street
P.O. Box 2239
Picton, ON K0K 2T0

Voice: 613-962-6858
Fax: 613-476-1875
E-mail: rob@connect.reach.net
Web: http://www.reach.net

Service Area:	Brighton, Frankford, Trenton, Belleville, Deseronto, Picton, Madoc, Tweed, Sterling, Wellington.
Services:	Leased line, dedicated SLIP/PPP, frame relay, dial-up SLIP/PPP, shell access, domain registration, Web design, Web hosting.
World Wide Web:	http://www.reach.net

Network Enterprise Technology Inc. (NET)

Hamilton, Ontario
netinc.ca

20 Jackson Street West, Suite 206
Hamilton, ON L8P 3K9

Voice: 905-525-4555
Fax: 905-525-3222
E-mail: info@netinc.ca
Web: http://www.netinc.ca

Service Area:	Hamilton, Burlington, Brantford, Cambridge, Ancaster, Grimsby, Dundas, Winona, Lynden, Freelton, Stoney Creek, Mount Hope, Waterdown, Binbrook, Caledonia, Hagersville, Cayuga, Selkirk, West Lincoln, St. George. Planning to expand throughout southern Ontario, west of Toronto.

Services:	Leased line, dedicated ISDN, dedicated SLIP/PPP, frame relay, dial-up ISDN, dial-up SLIP/PPP, shell access, terminal accounts, UUCP service, domain registration, free Web home page with personal dial-up account, Web design, Web hosting.
World Wide Web:	http://www.netinc.ca

Network North Communications Ltd.

Yellowknife, Northwest Territories
netnorth.com, nnc.nt.ca

Box 2044
Graham Bromley Building
Yellowknife, NT X1A 2P5

Voice: 403-873-2059
Fax: 403-873-4996
E-mail: patg@netnorth.com
Web: http://www.nnc.nt.ca

Service Area:	Yellowknife. Planning to expand to Hay River, Inuvik, Norman Wells, Forth Smith, Fort Simpson, Fort Good Hope, Tuktoyaktuk, Fort Providence, Fort MacPherson.
Services:	Leased line, dedicated ISDN, dedicated SLIP/PPP, dial-up ISDN, dial-up SLIP/PPP, shell access, domain registration, Web design, Web hosting.
World Wide Web:	http://www.nnc.nt.ca

Networx Internet System

Hamilton, Ontario
networx.on.ca

154 Jackson Street East
Hamilton, ON L8N 1L4

Voice: 905-528-4638
Fax: 905-525-8473
E-mail: admin@networx.on.ca, sales@networx.on.ca
Web: http://www.networx.on.ca

Service Area:	Hamilton, Aldershot, Burlington, Dundas, Rockton, Greensville, Ancaster, Waterdown, Mount Hope, Burlington, Stoney Creek, Winona, Grimsby. Planning to expand to St. Catharines, Brantford.
Services:	Dedicated ISDN, dedicated SLIP/PPP, frame relay, dial-up SLIP/PPP, domain registration, Web design, Web hosting.
World Wide Web:	http://www.networx.on.ca

Newcomm

St. John's, Newfoundland
newcomm.net, newcomm.nf.ca

1 Anderson Avenue
P.O. Box 23205
St. John's, NF A1B 4J9

Voice: 709-738-7873
Fax: 709-726-1831
E-mail: surf@newcomm.net
Web: http://www.newcomm.net

Service Area:	St. John's metro area, Corner Brook. Planning to expand to Gander, Grand Falls.
Services:	Leased line, dedicated ISDN, dedicated SLIP/PPP, frame relay, dial-up SLIP/PPP, shell access, domain registration, Web hosting.
World Wide Web:	http://www.newcomm.net

NewEdge InterAccess

Halifax, Nova Scotia
newedge.net, newedge.ca

2441 Agricola Street
Halifax, NS B3K 4C1

Voice: 902-425-4222
Fax: 902-425-4433
E-mail: admin@newedge.net
Web: http://www.newedge.net

Service Area:	Halifax, Chezzetcook, Dartmouth, Elmsdale, Musquodoboit Harbour, Bedford, French Village, Prospect Road, Sackville, Hubbards, St. Margaret's, Mount Uniacke, Ketch Harbour, Waverley. Planning to expand to Digby, Truro, New Minas, Sydney.
Services:	Leased line, dedicated ISDN, dedicated SLIP/PPP, frame relay, dial-up SLIP/PPP, domain registration, Web design, Web hosting.
World Wide Web:	http://www.newedge.net

NirvCentre/Web Networks

Toronto, Ontario
web.net, web.apc.org

401 Richmond Street West, Suite 104
Toronto, ON M5V 3A8

Voice: 416-596-0212
Fax: 416-596-1374
E-mail: outreach@web.apc.org, outreach@web.net
Web: http://www.web.apc.org,
            http://www.web.net

Service Area:	Toronto, Ottawa, Guelph, Kitchener-Waterloo, North Bay, Thunder Bay, Montreal, Vancouver. Planning to expand to Edmonton, Victoria.
Services:	Dial-up SLIP/PPP, shell access, terminal accounts, UUCP service, domain registration, free Web home page with personal dial-up account, Web design, Web hosting.
World Wide Web:	http://www.web.apc.org, http://www.web.net

Nisa Communications Group

Nanaimo, British Columbia
nisa.net, nisa.nanaimo.bc.ca

9B–1150 N. Terminal Avenue, Suite 163
Nanaimo, BC V9S 5T8

Voice: 604-751-1111
Fax: 604-390-1624
E-mail: info@nisa.net
Web: N/A

Service Area:	Nanaimo and surrounding areas. Planning to expand to lower mainland of British Columbia.
Services:	Shell access, terminal accounts, UUCP service, domain registration, Web hosting.
World Wide Web:	N/A

NLnet (Newfoundland and Labrador Network)

St. John's, Newfoundland
nlnet.nf.ca

c/o Department of Computing and Communications
Memorial University of Newfoundland
St. John's, NF A1C 5S7

Voice: 709-737-4555
Fax: 709-737-3514
E-mail: support@nlnet.nf.ca
Web: http://www.nlnet.nf.ca

Service Area:	Labrador City, Happy Valley-Goose Bay, Stephenville, Port aux Basques, Corner Brook, Grand Falls-Windsor, Gander, Clarenville, Burin, Carbonear, Lewisporte, St. John's, Bonavista, Placentia, St. Anthony, Springdale.
Services:	Leased line, dial-up SLIP/PPP, shell access, domain registration, Web hosting.
World Wide Web:	http://www.nlnet.nf.ca

Norfolk Internet Services

Simcoe, Ontario
nornet.on.ca, nornet.com, gtp.com

395 Queensway West
Simcoe, ON N3Y 2M9

Voice: 519-426-5575
E-mail: info@nornet.on.ca
Web: http://www.nornet.on.ca,
http://www.gtp.com

Service Area:	Simcoe, Delhi, Waterford, Jarvis, Port Dover, Port Rowan and Langton areas. Planning to expand to Brantford, Paris, Mount Pleasant, Scotland, St. George.
Services:	Leased line, dedicated SLIP/PPP, dial-up SLIP/PPP, domain registration, free Web home page with personal dial-up account, Web design, Web hosting.
World Wide Web:	http://www.nornet.on.ca, http://www.gtp.com

Norlink Communications & Consulting

Thunder Bay, Ontario
norlink.net, norlink.com

176 Blucher Avenue
Thunder Bay, ON P7B 4Y9

Voice: 807-767-5055
Fax: 807-626-9663
E-mail: info@norlink.net
Web: http://www.norlink.net

Service Area:	Thunder Bay, Murillo, South Gillies, Kakabeka Falls. Planning to expand to Kenora, Dryden.
Services:	Leased line, dedicated SLIP/PPP, frame relay, dial-up SLIP/PPP, shell access, terminal accounts, UUCP service, domain registration, free Web home page with personal dial-up account, Web design, Web hosting.
World Wide Web:	http://www.norlink.net

North Okanagan Information Freeway

Vernon, British Columbia
noif.ncp.bc.ca

2179–11th Avenue
Vernon, BC V1T 8V7

Voice: 604-542-0112
Fax: 604-549-3751
E-mail: lspraggs@noif.ncp.bc.ca
Web: http://www.ncp.bc.ca

Service Area:	Vernon, Lumby, Enderby, Armstrong, Falkland, Salmon Arm, Sicamous, Oyama, Sorrento.
Services:	Leased line, dedicated SLIP/PPP, dial-up SLIP/PPP, terminal accounts, domain registration, Web design, Web hosting.
World Wide Web:	http://www.ncp.bc.ca

North Shore Internet Services

New Glasgow, Nova Scotia
nsis.com

169 Provost Street, Suite 407
New Glasgow, NS B2H 2P9

Voice: 902-928-0565
Fax: 902-755-3126
E-mail: sales@nsis.com
Web: http://www.nsis.com

Service Area:	New Glasgow, Pictou, Stellarton, Trenton, Westville, River John. Planning to expand to Halifax, Sydney, Bridgewater, Truro, Amherst.
Services:	Leased line, dedicated ISDN, dedicated SLIP/PPP, frame relay, dial-up ISDN, dial-up SLIP/PPP, UUCP service, domain registration, Web design, Web hosting.
World Wide Web:	http://www.nsis.com

Northumbria Associates

Cobourg, Ontario
eagle.ca

1011 William Street, Suite 26
Cobourg, ON K9A 5J4

Voice: 905-373-9313
Fax: 905-373-1801
E-mail: info@eagle.ca
Web: http://www.eagle.ca

Service Area:	Northumberland County. Planning to expand to Durham Region.
Services:	Leased line, dedicated SLIP/PPP, frame relay, dial-up SLIP/PPP, shell access, domain registration, free Web home page with personal dial-up account, Web design, Web hosting.
World Wide Web:	http://www.eagle.ca

Nova Scotia Technology Network (NSTN)

See the entry for iSTAR Internet Inc.

NovaTech Computer Careers

Kingston, Ontario
novatech.on.ca

857 Norwest Road
Kingston, ON K7P 2N2

Voice: 613-384-7959
Fax: 613-384-1358
E-mail: shawn@novatech.on.ca
Web: http://www.novatech.on.ca

Service Area:	Napanee, Kingston, Gananoque, Amherstview.
Services:	Leased line, dedicated ISDN, dedicated SLIP/PPP, dial-up SLIP/PPP, UUCP service, domain registration, Web design, Web hosting.
World Wide Web:	http://www.novatech.on.ca

NTnet Society

Yellowknife, Northwest Territories
ntnet.nt.ca

Box 1976
Yellowknife, NT X1A 2P5

Voice: 403-669-7284
Fax: 403-669-7286
E-mail: admin@ntnet.nt.ca
Web: N/A

Service Area:	Yellowknife, Iqaluit. Planning to expand to Fort Smith, Hay River, Inuvik, Rankin Inlet.
Services:	Leased line, dedicated SLIP/PPP, domain registration.
World Wide Web:	N/A

Nucleus Information Service

Calgary, Alberta
nucleus.com

1835B–10 Avenue S.W.
Calgary, AB T3C 0K2

Voice: 403-541-9470
Fax: 403-541-9474
E-mail: info@nucleus.com
Web: http://www.nucleus.com

Service Area:	Calgary and surrounding area.
Services:	Leased line, dedicated ISDN, dedicated SLIP/PPP, frame relay, dial-up ISDN, dial-up SLIP/PPP, shell access, terminal accounts, UUCP service, domain registration, free Web home page with personal dial-up account, Web design, Web hosting.
World Wide Web:	http://www.nucleus.com

Nunanet Circumpolar Communications

Iqaluit, Northwest Territories
nunanet.com

607A Ring Road, Box 87
Iqaluit, NT X0A 0H0

Voice: 819-979-0772
Fax: 819-979-0773
E-mail: admin@nunanet.com
Web: http://www.nunanet.com

Service Area:	Iqaluit. Regional phone service: Grise Fiord, Arctic Bay, Pond Inlet, Clyde River, Igloolik, Hall Beach, Broughton Island, Pangnirtung, Lake Harbour, Cape Dorset.
Services:	Leased line, dedicated SLIP/PPP, dial-up ISDN, dial-up SLIP/PPP, shell access, terminal accounts, domain registration, free Web home page with personal dial-up account, Web design, Web hosting.
World Wide Web:	http://www.nunanet.com

Nunavut Communications Ltd.

Iqaluit, Northwest Territories
ncl.nt.ca, netnorth.com, nnc.nc.ca

Box 670, Arctic Ventures Building
Iqaluit, NT X0E 0H0

Voice: 819-979-2740
Fax: 819-979-4594
E-mail: tammip@netnorth.com
Web: http://www.nnc.nt.ca

Service Area:	Iqaluit. Planning to expand to Arctic Bay, Broughton Island, Cape Dorset, Clyde River, Igloolik, Nanisvik, Pangnirtung, Pond Inlet, Lake Harbour, Resolute Bay, Grise Fiord, Sanikiluaq, Coppermine, Cambridge Bay, Rankin Inlet, Gjoa Haven, Baker Lake.

Services: Leased line, dedicated ISDN, dedicated SLIP/PPP, frame relay, dial-up ISDN, dial-up SLIP/PPP, shell access, domain registration, Web design, Web hosting.

World Wide Web: http://www.nnc.nt.ca

o://info.web (Division of Magi Data Consulting Inc.)

Nepean, Ontario
magi.com, can.org, infoweb.ottawa.on.ca

20 Colonnade Road North, Suite 100
Nepean, ON K2E 7M6

Voice: 613-225-3354
Fax: 613-225-2880
E-mail: info@magi.com
Web: http://infoweb.magi.com

Service Area: Ottawa, Hull, Nepean, Orleans, Gloucester, Rockcliffe, Kanata, Carleton Place, Stittsville, Oxford Mills, Kemptville, Gatineau, Chelsea, Old Chelsea, Wakefield, Masham, Aylmer, Arnprior, Manotick, Buckingham, Rockland, Cumberland, Pakenham.

Services: Dedicated ISDN, frame relay, dial-up ISDN, dial-up SLIP/PPP, shell access, domain registration, free Web home page with personal dial-up account, Web design, Web hosting.

World Wide Web: http://infoweb.magi.com

OA Internet Inc.

Edmonton, Alberta
oanet.com

4907–99 Street
Edmonton, AB T6E 4Y1

Voice: 403-430-0811, 1-800-910-3388
Fax: 403-436-9963
E-mail: info@oanet.com
Web: http://www.oanet.com

Service Area: Edmonton.

Services: Dedicated ISDN, dedicated SLIP/PPP, frame relay, dial-up SLIP/PPP, shell access, UUCP service, domain registration, Web design, Web hosting.

World Wide Web: http://www.oanet.com

Odyssée Internet

Montréal, Québec
odyssee.net, ody.net

85, de la Commune east, 3rd Floor
Montréal, PQ H2Y 1J1

Voice: 514-861-3432
Fax: 514-861-6599
E-mail: info@odyssee.net
Web: http://www.odyssee.net

Service Area: Montreal, Laval, South Shore. Planning to expand to Quebec City, Granby, Drummondville, Victoriaville, Sherbrooke, Trois-Rivières, St-Sauveur-des-Monts, St-Jérôme, Laurentides, Chicoutimi, Hull, Rimousky, Rouyn-Noranda, Lennoxville, Magog, Windsor, Bromont, Ste-Marie-de-Beauce, St-George-de-Beauce, Toronto, Ottawa.

Services: Leased line, dedicated ISDN, dedicated SLIP/PPP, frame relay, dial-up SLIP/PPP, domain registration, free Web home page with personal dial-up account, Web hosting.

World Wide Web: http://www.odyssee.net

Odyssey Network Inc.

London, Ontario
odyssey.on.ca

21 King Street, Suite 108
London, ON N6A 5H3

Voice: 519-660-8883
Fax: 519-660-6111
E-mail: info@odyssey.on.ca
Web: http://www.odyssey.on.ca

Service Area:	Ailsa Craig, Alvinston, Belmont, Centralia, Crediton, Dorchester, Dutton, Exeter, Fingal, Glencoe, Granton, Harrietsville, Ilderton, Ingersoll, Kerwood, Kintore, Kirkton, Lambeth, London, Lucan, Melbourne, Mount Bridges, Nairn, Parkhill, Port Stanley, Shedden, Sparta, St. Marys, St. Thomas, Strathroy, Thamesford, Thorndale, Watford. Planning to expand to Auburn, Bayfield, Blyth, Clinton, Dublin, Goderich, Hensall, Seaforth, Stratford, Woodstock.
Services:	Leased line, dedicated ISDN, dedicated SLIP/PPP, frame relay, dial-up ISDN, dial-up SLIP/PPP, domain registration, Web design, Web hosting.
World Wide Web:	http://www.odyssey.on.ca

Okanagan Internet Junction

Vernon, British Columbia
junction.net

4216–25th Avenue, Suite 1
Vernon, BC V1T 1P4

Voice:	604-549-1036
Fax:	604-542-4130
E-mail:	info@junction.net
Web:	http://www.junction.net

Service Area:	Lumby, Cherryville, Lavington, Vernon, Coldstream, Oyama, Armstrong, Enderby, Falkland, Grindrod, Mara, Revelstoke. Planning to expand to Salmon Arm, Sorrento, Sicamous, Kamloops, Kelowna, Westbank, Winfield, Peachland.
Services:	Leased line, dedicated SLIP/PPP, frame relay, dial-up SLIP/PPP, shell access, terminal accounts, UUCP service, domain registration, free Web home page with personal dial-up account, Web design, Web hosting.
World Wide Web:	http://www.junction.net

ONet Networking

Mississauga, Ontario
onet.on.ca

5925 Airport Road, Suite 200
Mississauga, ON L4V 1W1

Voice:	905-405-6263
Fax:	905-405-6271
E-mail:	info@onet.on.ca
Web:	http://www.onet.on.ca/onet

Service Area:	Barrie, Belleville, Brantford, Brockville, Chalk River, Guelph, Hamilton, Kingston, Kirkland Lake, Kitchener-Waterloo, London, North Bay, Oakville, Oshawa, Peterborough, St. Catharines, Sarnia, Sault Ste. Marie, Sudbury, Thunder Bay, Toronto, Welland, Windsor. Leased line facilities can be provided to any community within Ontario. Planning to expand to other centres.
Services:	Leased line, dedicated SLIP/PPP, dial-up SLIP/PPP, domain registration.
World Wide Web:	http://www.onet.on.ca/onet

Online Computer Distribution

Peterborough, Ontario
oncomdis.on.ca

194 Charlotte Street
Peterborough, ON K9J 2T8

Voice:	705-749-9225
Fax:	705-749-9226
E-mail:	sysop@oncomdis.on.ca
Web:	http://www.oncomdis.on.ca

Service Area:	Peterborough, Bailieboro, Bethany, Bridgenorth, Buckhorn, Burleigh Falls, Cavan, Hastings, Keene, Lakefield, Millbrook, Norwood, Omemee, Havelock, Campbellford, Blackstock, Lindsay, Oshawa, Roseneath, Hampton, Ajax, Pickering, Whitby, Bowmanville, Brooklin, Newtonville, Orono, Port Perry, Newcastle, Uxbridge, Warkworth.

Services: Leased line, dedicated SLIP/PPP, frame relay, dial-up SLIP/PPP, terminal accounts, UUCP service, domain registration, Web design, Web hosting.

World Wide Web: http://www.oncomdis.on.ca

Online Internet Services Corporation

Edmonton, Alberta
bol.net, olcorp.com, online.ab.ca

9650–20th Avenue, Suite 111
Edmonton, AB T6N 1G1

Voice: 403-466-2255
Fax: 403-466-5121
E-mail: info@online.ab.ca
Web: http://www.online.ab.ca

Service Area: Edmonton. Planning to expand to Calgary, Lethbridge, Red Deer, Grand Prairie.

Services: Leased line, dedicated ISDN, dedicated SLIP/PPP, dial-up ISDN, dial-up SLIP/PPP, domain registration, free Web home page with personal dial-up account, Web design, Web hosting.

World Wide Web: http://www.online.ab.ca

ONLink (Division of Ontario Northland Transportation Commission)

North Bay, Ontario
onlink.net

555 Oak Street East
North Bay, ON P1B 8L3

Voice: 705-495-2951, 1-800-667-0053
Fax: 705-495-2025
E-mail: info@onlink.net
Web: http://www.onlink.net

Service Area: North Bay, New Liskeard, Timmins, Temagami, Kirkland Lake, Kapuskasing. Planning to expand to Cochrane, Moosonee, Moose Factory, Englehart, Smooth Rock Falls, Iroquois Falls.

Services: Leased line, dedicated ISDN, dedicated SLIP/PPP, frame relay, dial-up SLIP/PPP, shell access, UUCP service, domain registration, free Web home page with personal dial-up account, Web design, Web hosting.

World Wide Web: http://www.onlink.net

ONRAMP Network Services Inc.

Markham, Ontario
onramp.ca

570 Hood Road, Unit 18
Markham, ON L3R 4G7

Voice: 905-470-4064, 1-800-613-0143
Fax: 905-470-6484
E-mail: sales@onramp.ca
Web: http://www.onramp.ca

Service Area: Toronto and the 416 dial-in area.

Services: Dedicated ISDN, dedicated SLIP/PPP, dial-up SLIP/PPP, domain registration, Web design, Web hosting.

World Wide Web: http://www.onramp.ca

Osiris (Software) Inc.

Montréal, Québec
osiris.com

2057 Papineau
Montréal, PQ H2K 4J5

Voice: 514-522-7475
Fax: 514-522-7937
E-mail: webmaster@osiris.com
Web: http://www.osiris.com

Service Area: Montreal, Toronto. Planning to expand to Quebec City.

Services: Leased line, dedicated ISDN, dedicated SLIP/PPP, frame relay, dial-up ISDN, dial-up SLIP/PPP, UUCP service, domain registration, Web design, Web hosting.

World Wide Web: http://www.osiris.com

Pacific Interconnect Enterprises Inc.

Victoria, British Columbia
pinc.com

4252 Commerce Circle
Victoria, BC V8Z 4M2

Voice: 604-953-2680
Fax: 604-953-2659
E-mail: info@pinc.com, sales@pinc.com
Web: http://vvv.com/pi

Service Area:	Vancouver, Duncan and surrounding area. Planning to expand to Nanaimo, Prince George.
Services:	Leased line, dedicated ISDN, dedicated SLIP/PPP, frame relay, dial-up ISDN, dial-up SLIP/PPP, shell access, UUCP service, domain registration, free Web home page with personal dial-up account, Web design, Web hosting.

World Wide Web: http://vvv.com/pi

Passport Online

Toronto, Ontario
passport.ca

230 Richmond Street West, 7th Floor
Toronto, ON M5V 3E5

Voice: 416-516-1616
Fax: 416-598-0480
E-mail: staff@passport.ca
Web: http://web.passport.ca

Service Area:	Metropolitan Toronto and surrounding dial-in areas. Planning to expand local dial-up access across Canada.
Services:	Leased line, dedicated ISDN, dedicated SLIP/PPP, frame relay, dial-up ISDN, dial-up SLIP/PPP, domain registration, free Web home page with personal dial-up account, Web design, Web hosting.

World Wide Web: http://web.passport.ca

Pathway Communications Inc.

Toronto, Ontario
pathcom.com

1 Yonge Street, Suite 2205
Toronto, ON M5E 1E5

Voice: 416-214-6363
Fax: 416-214-6238
E-mail: info@pathcom.com
Web: http://www.pathcom.com

Service Area:	Toronto and surrounding areas. Planning to expand to the eastern and northern suburbs of Toronto and all major metropolitan cities.
Services:	Leased line, dedicated ISDN, dedicated SLIP/PPP, dial-up ISDN, dial-up SLIP/PPP, domain registration, free Web home page with personal dial-up account, Web design, Web hosting.

World Wide Web: http://www.pathcom.com

PCS Internet

Winnipeg, Manitoba
pcs.mb.ca

1388 Spruce Street
Winnipeg, MB R3E 2V7

Voice: 204-988-3236
Fax: 204-783-3185
E-mail: info@pcs.mb.ca
Web: http://www.pcs.mb.ca

Service Area:	Winnipeg.
Services:	Dedicated ISDN, dedicated SLIP/PPP, dial-up ISDN, dial-up SLIP/PPP, shell access, domain registration, Web hosting.

World Wide Web: http://www.pcs.mb.ca

PEINet

Charlottetown, Prince Edward Island
peinet.pe.ca

94 Kent Street
Charlottetown, PE C1A 1M9

Voice: 902-892-7346
Fax: 902-629-2456
E-mail: signup@peinet.pe.ca
Web: http://www.peinet.pe.ca

Service Area:	Charlottetown, Summerside, O'Leary, Souris, Montague.
Services:	Leased line, dedicated SLIP/PPP, frame relay, dial-up SLIP/PPP, shell access, terminal accounts, domain registration, Web design, Web hosting.
World Wide Web:	http://www.peinet.pe.ca

PG DataNet Inc.

Edmonton, Alberta
datanet.ab.ca

4652–99 Street
Edmonton, AB T6E 5H5

Voice: 403-438-5897
Fax: 403-434-3957
E-mail: info@datanet.ab.ca
Web: http://www.datanet.ab.ca

Service Area:	Edmonton.
Services:	Dial-up SLIP/PPP, free Web home page with personal dial-up account, Web design, Web hosting.
World Wide Web:	http://www.datanet.ab.ca

Planet Internet Communications

St-Laurent, Québec
planete.com

2990 Brabant Marineau
St-Laurent, PQ H4S 1K7

Voice: 514-333-3371
Fax: 514-333-6005
E-mail: info@planete.com
Web: http://www.planete.com

Service Area:	Montreal, Laval, South Shore.
Services:	Leased line, dedicated ISDN, dedicated SLIP/PPP, frame relay, dial-up ISDN, dial-up SLIP/PPP, UUCP service, domain registration, free Web home page with personal dial-up account, Web design, Web hosting.
World Wide Web:	http://www.planete.com

Point Net Communication Inc.

Montréal, Québec
sim.qc.ca

1852, rue Rachel est
Montréal, PQ H2H 1P4

Voice: 514-524-3187
Fax: 514-524-2831
E-mail: info@sim.qc.ca
Web: http://www.sim.qc.ca

Service Area:	Montreal. Planning to expand to Quebec, Toronto.
Services:	Dedicated ISDN, dedicated SLIP/PPP, dial-up ISDN, dial-up SLIP/PPP, UUCP service, domain registration, Web design, Web hosting.
World Wide Web:	http://www.sim.qc.ca

Portage Internet Connection

Portage La Prairie, Manitoba
portage.net, portage.com

1820 Saskatchewan Avenue West
Portage La Prairie, MB R1N 0N9

Voice: 204-239-6342
Fax: 204-239-0106
E-mail: inform@portage.net
Web: http://www.portage.net

Service Area:	High Bluff, Portage, St. Claude, Gladstone, Amaranth, Delta.
Services:	Leased line, dedicated SLIP/PPP, frame relay, dial-up SLIP/PPP, shell access, terminal accounts, UUCP service, domain registration, free Web home page with personal dial-up account, Web design, Web hosting.
World Wide Web:	http://www.portage.net

Praline

Sherbrooke, Québec
praline.net

289 King Street West, P.O. Box 142
Sherbrooke, PQ J1H 5H8

Voice: 819-565-3666
Fax: 819-565-4195
E-mail: info@praline.net
Web: http://www.praline.net

Service Area:	Sherbrooke, Asbestos, Ascot, Coaticook, Compton, Bromptonville, East Angus, Fleurimont, Lennoxville, Magog, Richmond, Rock-Forest, Windsor. Planning to expand to Bromont, Drummondville, Granby, Lac Brome, Lac Megantic, Sutton.
Services:	Leased line, dedicated ISDN, dedicated SLIP/PPP, frame relay, dial-up ISDN, dial-up SLIP/PPP, shell access, terminal accounts, UUCP service, domain registration, free Web home page with personal dial-up account, Web design, Web hosting.
World Wide Web:	http://www.praline.net

Prodigy

White Plains, New York
prodigy.com

445 Hamilton Avenue
White Plains, NY 10601

Voice: 1-800-776-3449
Web: http://www.prodigy.com

Service Area:	Dial-up numbers in cities across Canada. Call Prodigy to determine if there is a local access number near you.
Services:	Terminal accounts, free Web home page with personal dial-up account, Web hosting.
World Wide Web:	http://www.prodigy.com

ProNET Communications Inc.

Vancouver, British Columbia
pro.net, pronet.bc.ca

120-890 West Pender Street
Suite 120
Vancouver, BC V6C 1J9

Voice: 604-688-9282
Fax: 604-688-9229
E-mail: info@pro.net
Web: http://www.pro.net

Service Area:	Greater Vancouver area.
Services:	Leased line, dedicated ISDN, dedicated SLIP/PPP, dial-up ISDN, dial-up SLIP/PPP, UUCP service, domain registration, Web design, Web hosting.
World Wide Web:	http://www.pro.net

Pronet Internet Services

Thunder Bay, Ontario
procom.net

1184 Roland Street
Thunder Bay, ON P7B 5M4

Voice: 807-622-5915
Fax: 807-622-2082
E-mail: info@mail.procom.net
Web: http://www.procom.net

Service Area:	Thunder Bay, Murillo, Kakabeka Falls, South Gilles and other smaller counties around Thunder Bay.
Services:	Leased line, dedicated SLIP/PPP, dial-up SLIP/PPP, shell access, terminal accounts, domain registration, free Web home page with personal dial-up account, Web design, Web hosting.
World Wide Web:	http://www.procom.net

PubNIX Montreal

Montréal, Québec
pubnix.net, pubnix.qc.ca

P.O. Box 147
Côte-St-Luc, PQ H4V 2Y3

Voice: 514-990-5911
E-mail: info@pubnix.net
Web: http://www.pubnix.net

Service Area:	Greater Montreal, Laval, South Shore.
Services:	Leased line, dedicated ISDN, dedicated SLIP/PPP, dial-up SLIP/PPP, shell access, UUCP service, domain registration, free Web home page with personal dial-up account, Web design, Web hosting.
World Wide Web:	http://www.pubnix.net

Qnetix Computer Consultants Inc.

Toronto, Ontario
qnetix.ca

95 King Street East, 4th Floor
Toronto, ON M5C 1G4

Voice: 416-861-0423
Fax: 416-861-1838
E-mail: paul@qnetix.ca (Paul Baron)
Web: http://www.qnetix.ca

Service Area:	North America.
Services:	Leased line, dedicated ISDN, dedicated SLIP/PPP, frame relay, dial-up ISDN, dial-up SLIP/PPP, shell access, terminal accounts, domain registration, Web design, Web hosting.
World Wide Web:	http://www.qnetix.ca

Réseau Interordinateurs Scientifique Québécois (RISQ)

Montréal, Québec
risq.qc.ca, risq.net

1801 McGill College, Suite 800
Montréal, PQ H3A 2N4

Voice: 514-398-1234
Fax: 514-398-1244
E-mail: info-cirisq@risq.qc.ca
Web: http://www.risq.qc.ca, http://w3.risq.qc.ca

Service Area:	Montreal, Quebec, Sherbrooke, Chicoutimi, Hull, Trois-Rivières. Planning to expand to Rimouski, Rouyn.
Services:	Leased line, dedicated ISDN, dedicated SLIP/PPP, frame relay, dial-up SLIP/PPP, domain registration, Web design, Web hosting.
World Wide Web:	http://www.risq.qc.ca, http://w3.risq.qc.ca

Resudox Online Services Inc.

Ottawa, Ontario
resudox.net

P.O. Box 33067
Nepean, ON K2C 3Y9

Voice: 613-567-6925
Fax: 613-567-8289
E-mail: admin@resudox.net
Web: http://www.resudox.net/resudox

Service Area:	Ottawa, Nepean, Hull, and surrounding areas.
Services:	Dedicated SLIP/PPP, dial-up SLIP/PPP, shell access, terminal accounts, UUCP service, domain registration, Web design, Web hosting.
World Wide Web:	http://www.resudox.net/resudox

Rocler: Les Services Télématiques Rocler

St-Timothée, Québec
rocler.qc.ca

6, Cléophas
St-Timothée, PQ J0S 1X0

Voice: 514-377-1898
Fax: 514-377-5139
E-mail: info@rocler.qc.ca
Web: http://www.rocler.qc.ca

Service Area:	Beauharnois, Coteau-Landing, Coteau-du-Lac, Franklin Centre, Howick, Huntingdon, Les Cèdres, Ormstown, Rivière-Beaudette, Saint-Clet, St-Polycarpe, St-Timothée, Ste-Justine-de-Newton, Ste-Marthe, Valleyfield.
Services:	Leased line, dedicated SLIP/PPP, dial-up SLIP/PPP, UUCP service, domain registration, Web design, Web hosting.
World Wide Web:	http://www.rocler.qc.ca

SaskTel

Regina, Saskatchewan
sasknet.sk.ca

2121 Saskatchewan Drive
Regina, SK S4P 3Y2

Voice: 1-800-644-9205
Fax: 306-359-0106
E-mail: feedback@sasknet.sk.ca
Web: http://www.sasknet.sk.ca

Service Area:	Saskatchewan.
Services:	Frame relay, dial-up SLIP/PPP, domain registration.
World Wide Web:	http://www.sasknet.sk.ca

SeaFare Access (Division of DataStore Inc.)

St. John's, Newfoundland
datastore.com, seascape.com

516 Topsail Road
St. John's, NF A1E 2C5

Voice: 709-745-8555
Fax: 709-745-8001
E-mail: support@seascape.com
Web: http://www.datastore.com,
            http://www.seascape.com

Service Area:	St. John's, Mount Pearl, Conception Bay South, Torbay, Logy Bay, Pouch Cove, Portugal Cove. Planning to expand to Grand Falls, Gander, Cuba.
Services:	Leased line, dedicated SLIP/PPP, frame relay, dial-up SLIP/PPP, shell access, domain registration, Web design, Web hosting.
World Wide Web:	http://www.datastore.com, http://www.seascape.com

Sentex Communications Corporation

Guelph, Ontario
sentex.net

727 Speedvale Avenue West, Unit 6
Guelph, ON N1K 1E6

Voice: 519-822-9970
Fax: 519-822-4775
E-mail: support@sentex.net
Web: http://www.sentex.net

Service Area:	Kitchener, Waterloo, Galt, Hespeler, Preston, Breslau, Guelph, Fergus, Elora, Acton, Rockwood, Cambridge, Toronto, Hamilton.
Services:	Leased line, dedicated ISDN, dial-up SLIP/PPP, shell access, UUCP service, domain registration, free Web home page with personal dial-up account, Web hosting.
World Wide Web:	http://www.sentex.net

SERiX Technologies

London, Ontario
serix.com

215 Piccadilly Street, Suite 306
London, ON N6A 1S2

Voice: 519-645-1532
Fax: 519-645-8930
E-mail: info@serix.com
Web: http://www.serix.com

Service Area:	London, St. Thomas, Strathroy, Dorchester, Ingersoll, Ilderton.
Services:	Dedicated ISDN, dedicated SLIP/PPP, dial-up ISDN, dial-up SLIP/PPP, shell access, terminal accounts, UUCP service, domain registration, Web design, Web hosting.
World Wide Web:	http://www.serix.com

Services Internet ABACOM

Sherbrooke, Québec
abacom.com

780 King Street West, Suite 240
Sherbrooke, PQ J1H 1R7

Voice: 819-820-2929
Fax: 819-820-8866
E-mail: info@abacom.com
Web: http://www.abacom.com

Service Area:	Sherbrooke, Magog, Rock-Forest, Lennoxville, Fleurimont, Ascot, Richmond, Windsor, Omerville, Deauville, East Angus, Compton, Waterville, North Hatley, Bromptonville, Coaticook, Bury, Cookshire, Stoke, Asbestos, Bishopton, La Patrie, Sawyerville. Planning to expand to Bromont, Granby.
Services:	Leased line, dedicated ISDN, dedicated SLIP/PPP, frame relay, dial-up SLIP/PPP, shell access, terminal accounts, domain registration, free Web home page with personal dial-up account, Web design, Web hosting.
World Wide Web:	http://www.abacom.com

Services Internet de l'Estuaire, inc.

Rimouski, Québec
sie.qc.ca, sie.net

165, rue Belzile, Suite 100
Rimouski, PQ G5L 8Y2

Voice: 418-723-7100
E-mail: info@sie.qc.ca
Web: http://www.sie.qc.ca

Service Area:	Rimouski, Bic, Rimouski-Est, Pointe-au-Père, Mont-Joli, Ste-Flavie, Luceville, Ste-Luce, St-Anaclet, St-Fabien, St-Simon, Trinité-de-Monts, St-Narcisse. Planning to expand to Rivière-du-Loup.

Services: Dedicated SLIP/PPP, dial-up SLIP/PPP, UUCP service, domain registration, free Web home page with personal dial-up account, Web design, Web hosting.

World Wide Web: http://www.sie.qc.ca

Silk Internet (Silk FM Broadcasting Ltd. and Silk.Net Media Ltd.)

Kelowna, British Columbia
silk.net

1598 Panosay Street
Kelowna, BC V1Y 1P4

Voice: 604-860-4202
Fax: 604-860-0505
E-mail: info@silk.net
Web: http://www.silk.net

Service Area: Kelowna, Winfield, Okanagan Centre, Westbank.

Services: Dedicated SLIP/PPP, dial-up SLIP/PPP, domain registration, Web hosting.

World Wide Web: http://www.silk.net

SmartNet Internet Services

Edmonton, Alberta
compusmart.ab.ca

16810–104A Avenue
Edmonton, AB T5P 4J6

Voice: 403-429-4388
Fax: 403-426-7110
E-mail: support@compusmart.ab.ca
Web: http://www.compusmart.ab.ca

Service Area: Edmonton and surrounding area.

Services: Dedicated ISDN, dedicated SLIP/PPP, dial-up ISDN, dial-up SLIP/PPP, domain registration, free Web home page with personal dial-up account, Web design, Web hosting.

World Wide Web: http://www.compusmart.ab.ca

SooNet Corp.

Sault Ste. Marie, Ontario
soonet.ca

477 Queen Street East
Sault Ste. Marie, ON P6A 1Z5

Voice: 705-253-4700
Fax: 705-253-4705
E-mail: service@soonet.ca
Web: http://www.soonet.ca

Service Area: Sault Ste. Marie, Echo Bay, St. Joseph's Island, Deborah, Thessalon, Heyden, Goulais, Searchmont. Planning to expand to Wawa, Chapleau.

Services: Dedicated SLIP/PPP, dial-up SLIP/PPP, shell access, UUCP service, domain registration, Web design, Web hosting.

World Wide Web: http://www.soonet.ca

South West Bruce Internet

Port Elgin, Ontario
swbi.net

722 Goderich Street
P.O. Box 2215
Port Elgin, ON N0H 2C0

Voice: 519-832-6260
Fax: 519-832-6291
E-mail: admin@swbi.net
Web: http://www.swbi.net/home.htm

Service Area: Port Elgin, Kincardine, Southampton, Paisley, Tiverton.

Services: Dedicated SLIP/PPP, dial-up SLIP/PPP, Web design, Web hosting.

World Wide Web: http://www.swbi.net/home.htm

Span Information Technology Inc.

Ajax, Ontario
spanit.com

110 Hunt Street
Ajax, ON L1S 1T5

Voice: 905-619-7726
Fax: 905-619-6819
E-mail: info@spanit.com
Web: http://www.spanit.com

Service Area:	Toronto, Oshawa, Whitby, Ajax, Pickering, Brooklin, Claremont, Markham.
Services:	Leased line, dedicated ISDN, dedicated SLIP/PPP, dial-up ISDN, dial-up SLIP/PPP, UUCP service, domain registration, free Web home page with personal dial-up account, Web design, Web hosting.
World Wide Web:	http://www.spanit.com

SpectraNet Connections Inc.

Oakville, Ontario
spectranet.ca

220 Wyecroft Road, Unit 46
Oakville, ON L6K 3V1

Voice: 905-338-3552
Fax: 905-338-7549
E-mail: mailbox@spectranet.ca
Web: http://www.spectranet.ca

Service Area:	Toronto and 416 dial-in area, Mississauga, Oakville, Burlington. Planning to expand to Chatham, Ottawa, Hull, Oshawa, Kitchener-Waterloo, Hamilton, London, Vancouver, Prince George.
Services:	Leased line, dedicated ISDN, dedicated SLIP/PPP, frame relay, dial-up SLIP/PPP, domain registration, free Web home page with personal dial-up account, Web design, Web hosting.
World Wide Web:	http://www.spectranet.ca

Spots InterConnect, Inc.

Calgary, Alberta
spots.ab.ca

100–4th Avenue. S.W., Suite 807
Calgary, AB T2P 3N2

Voice: 403-571-7768
Fax: 403-237-7380
E-mail: info@spots.ab.ca
Web: http://www.spots.ab.ca

Service Area:	Calgary and surrounding area. Planning to expand to Edmonton, Pincher Creek.
Services:	Leased line, dedicated ISDN, dedicated SLIP/PPP, dial-up SLIP/PPP, shell access, domain registration, free Web home page with personal dial-up account, Web design, Web hosting.
World Wide Web:	http://www.spots.ab.ca

SSI Micro

Yellowknife, Northwest Territories
ssimicro.com

Panda II Mall
4915–48th Street
Yellowknife, NT X1A 3F4

Voice: 403-669-7500
Fax: 403-669-7510
E-mail: sales@ssimicro.com
Web: http://www.ssimicro.com

Service Area:	Yellowknife. Planning to expand to Hay River, Fort Providence.
Services:	Leased line, dedicated SLIP/PPP, dial-up SLIP/PPP, shell access, domain registration, Web design, Web hosting.
World Wide Web:	http://www.ssimicro.com

St-Jean InterNet Inc.

Iberville, Québec
stjeannet.ca

18, rue Carmen
Iberville, PQ J2X 4J3

Voice:	514-358-5074
Fax:	514-346-7770
E-mail:	info@stjeannet.ca
Web:	http://www.stjeannet.ca

Service Area:	Baie Missisquoi, Blackpool, Cantic, Clarenceville, Henrysburg, Henryville, Iberville, Île-aux-Noix, Île-Ste-Thérèse, L'Acadie, Lacolle, Marieville, Napierville, Notre-Dame-de-Stanbridge, Notre-Dame-du-Mont-Carmel, Sabrevois, St-Alexandre-d'Iberville, Ste-Anne-de-Sabrevois, St-Athanase-d'Iberville, St-Bernard-de-Lacolle, St-Blaise, St-Cyprien, St-Grégoire, St-Jacques-le-Mineur, St-Jean-sur-Richelieu, St-Luc, St-Paul-de-l'Île-aux-Noix, St-Sébastien, St-Valentin, Venise-en-Québec. Planning to expand to St-Hyacinthe, Quebec City, Sorel.
Services:	Leased line, dedicated ISDN, dedicated SLIP/PPP, frame relay, dial-up ISDN, dial-up SLIP/PPP, UUCP service, domain registration, Web design, Web hosting.
World Wide Web:	http://www.stjeannet.ca

STAR-NET Inc.

Montréal, Québec
starnet.qc.ca

852 Decarie
St-Laurent, PQ H4L 3L9

Voice:	514-855-1515
Fax:	514-855-1010
E-mail:	info@starnet.qc.ca
Web:	http://www.starnet.qc.ca

Service Area:	Montreal, South Shore, Laval, North Shore, St-Sauveur.

Services:	Leased line, dedicated ISDN, dedicated SLIP/PPP, frame relay, dial-up ISDN, dial-up SLIP/PPP, UUCP service, domain registration, free Web home page with personal dial-up account, Web design, Web hosting.
World Wide Web:	http://www.starnet.qc.ca

Stargate Connections Inc.

Burnaby, British Columbia
starcon.com

6450 Roberts Street, Suite 347
Burnaby, BC V5G 4E1

Voice:	604-606-8999
Fax:	604-606-8998
E-mail:	Enquiries@Starcon.com
Web:	http://www.starcon.com

Service Area:	Burnaby, Vancouver, New Westminster, North Vancouver, West Vancouver, Richmond, Delta, Surrey, White Rock, Langley, Pitt Meadows, Maple Ridge, Port Moody, Port Coquitlam, Coquitlam.
Services:	Leased line, dedicated ISDN, dedicated SLIP/PPP, frame relay, dial-up ISDN, dial-up SLIP/PPP, shell access, domain registration, Web design, Web hosting.
World Wide Web:	http://www.starcon.com

STEM~Net

St. John's, Newfoundland
stemnet.nf.ca, k12.nf.ca

Memorial University of Newfoundland
St. John's, NF A1B 3X8

Voice:	709-737-8836
Fax:	709-737-2179
E-mail:	staff@calvin.stemnet.nf.ca
Web:	http://www.stemnet.nf.ca

Service Area: St. John's, Clarenville, Corner Brook, Grand Falls, Windsor, Stephenville, Labrador City, Wabush, Gander, Burin/Marystown, Happy Valley/ Goose Bay, Port aux Basques, Carbonear, Lewisporte. Planning to expand to Bay Roberts, Springdale, Deer Lake, Bonavista, St. Anthony, Grand Bank, Baie Verte, Freshwater/Placentia.

Services: Dedicated SLIP/PPP, frame relay, dial-up SLIP/PPP, shell access, domain registration, free Web home page with personal dial-up account, Web design, Web hosting.

World Wide Web: http://www.stemnet.nf.ca

Sunset Communications

Fort Frances, Ontario
sunsetcom.on.ca

279 Scott Street
Fort Frances, ON P9A 1G6

Voice: 807-274-5434
Fax: 807-274-5434
E-mail: info@sunsetcom.on.ca
Web: http://www.foxnet.net/mall/suncom/ suncom.html

Service Area: Fort Frances, Darwick, Bears Passage, Devlin, Emo, Mine Centre, Stratton. Planning to expand to International Falls (Minnesota), Nester Falls.

Services: Leased line, dedicated SLIP/PPP, dial-up SLIP/PPP, domain registration, Web design, Web hosting.

World Wide Web: http://www.foxnet.net/mall/suncom/suncom.html

Systems Knowledge Link

West Hill, Ontario
ski.com

91 Rylander Boulevard, Suite 7266
West Hill, ON M1B 5M5

Voice: 416-209-7005
Fax: 416-283-2281
E-mail: sales@ski.com
Web: http://www.ski.com

Service Area: Metropolitan Toronto.

Services: Dedicated SLIP/PPP, dial-up SLIP/ PPP, shell access, terminal accounts, UUCP service, domain registration, Web design, Web hosting.

World Wide Web: http://www.ski.com

T-8000 Information Systems

Calgary, Alberta
t8000.com

6449 Crowchild Trail S.W., Suite 36001
Calgary, AB T3E 3Y3

Voice: 403-686-1169
Fax: 403-686-1193
E-mail: brian.simpson@t8000.com (Brian Simpson)
Web: http://www.t8000.com

Service Area: Calgary, Cochrane, Turner Valley, Strathmore, Irricana, Langdon, Okotoks, Crossfield, Beiseker, Airdrie, Bragg Creek, Carstairs, Acme, Longview, High River, Blackie, Morley.

Services: Leased line, dedicated ISDN, dedicated SLIP/PPP, dial-up ISDN, dial-up SLIP/PPP, UUCP service, domain registration, free Web home page with personal dial-up account, Web design, Web hosting.

World Wide Web: http://www.t8000.com

Tamarack Computers Ltd.

Yellowknife, Northwest Territories
tamarack.nt.ca

Scotia Mall
5102–50th Avenue, Suite 24
Yellowknife, NT X1A 3S8

Voice:	403-920-4380
Fax:	403-920-4080
E-mail:	jimg@tamarack.nt.ca
Web:	http://www.tamarack.nt.ca

Service Area: Yellowknife.

Services: Leased line, dedicated SLIP/PPP, dial-up SLIP/PPP, domain registration, Web design, Web hosting.

World Wide Web: http://www.tamarack.nt.ca

Technology Plus Ltd.

Neepawa, Manitoba
techplus.com

244 Hamilton Street
Neepawa, MB R0J 1H0

Voice:	204-476-3389
Fax:	204-476-3479
E-mail:	mark_anderson@mail.techplus.com
Web:	http://www.techplus.com

Service Area: Neepawa, Carberry, Plumas, Minnedosa, Eden, Franklin, Arden, Kelwood, Riding Mountain, Brookdale, Glenella.

Services: Leased line, dedicated ISDN, dedicated SLIP/PPP, frame relay, dial-up ISDN, dial-up SLIP/PPP, UUCP service, free Web home page with personal dial-up account, Web design, Web hosting.

World Wide Web: http://www.techplus.com

Telnet Canada Enterprises, Ltd.

Calgary, Alberta
tcel.com

1812–4th Street S.W., Penthouse
Calgary, AB T2S 1W1

Voice:	403-245-1882
Fax:	403-228-9702
E-mail:	sales@tcel.com
Web:	http://www.tcel.com

Service Area: Calgary and extended flat-rate dial-in area.

Services: Leased line, dedicated ISDN, dedicated SLIP/PPP, frame relay, dial-up ISDN, dial-up SLIP/PPP, shell access, UUCP service, domain registration, free Web home page with personal dial-up account, Web design, Web hosting.

World Wide Web: http://www.tcel.com

TELOS Online/TELOS Communications Inc.

Belleville, Ontario
telos.ca, telos.org

100 Bell Boulevard, Suite 355
Belleville, ON K8P 4Y7

Voice:	613-962-5776, 1-800-898-3567
Fax:	613-962-5703
E-mail:	telos@telos.ca
Web:	http://www.telos.ca

Service Area: Belleville, Bloomfield, Brighton, Deseronto, Frankford, Madoc, Picton, Stirling, Thurlow, Trenton, Tweed, Wellington, Wooler. Planning to expand to Kingston.

Services: Dedicated SLIP/PPP, frame relay, dial-up SLIP/PPP, UUCP service, domain registration, free Web home page with personal dial-up account, Web design, Web hosting.

World Wide Web: http://www.telos.ca

TeQ Works Incorporated

Athabasca, Alberta

rrt.com

4903–49th Avenue
Athabasca, AB T9S 1C7

Voice: 403-675-5155
Fax: 403-675-9666
E-mail: sales@rrt.com
Web: http://www.rrt.com

Service Area:	Athabasca, Westlock, Edson, Valleyview and their extended flat-rate calling areas. Planning to expand to Peace River, Cold Lake/Grand Centre, St. Paul, Wainwright, Brooks, Vermillion, Whitecourt, High Prairie, Stettler.
Services:	Leased line, dedicated SLIP/PPP, frame relay, dial-up SLIP/PPP, shell access, domain registration, Web design, Web hosting.
World Wide Web:	http://www.rrt.com

TerraPort Online Inc.

North York, Ontario

terraport.net

191 Ravel Road
North York, ON M2H 1T1

Voice: 416-492-3050
Fax: 416-492-3255
E-mail: info@terraport.net
Web: http://www.terraport.net

Service Area:	Greater Toronto Area, Mississauga, Brampton, Concord, Markham, Richmond Hill, Thornhill, Pickering, Whitby, Ajax, Oakville. Planning to expand to Hamilton, Barrie, Vancouver, Ottawa, Montreal, Calgary.
Services:	Leased line, dedicated ISDN, dedicated SLIP/PPP, frame relay, dial-up ISDN, dial-up SLIP/PPP, UUCP service, domain registration, Web design, Web hosting.
World Wide Web:	http://www.terraport.net

Ticnet—The Internet Companion

Edmonton, Alberta

tic.ab.ca, webvertise.com

10712–176 Street, Suite 210
Edmonton, AB T5S 1G5

Voice: 403-489-5740
Fax: 403-487-0456
E-mail: info@tic.ab.ca
Web: http://www.tic.ab.ca

Service Area:	Edmonton and surrounding area.
Services:	Leased line, dedicated ISDN, dedicated SLIP/PPP, dial-up SLIP/PPP, shell access, terminal accounts, domain registration, free Web home page with personal dial-up account, Web design, Web hosting.
World Wide Web:	http://www.tic.ab.ca

Times.net

Bradford, Ontario

times.net

32 Holland Street East, Box 1570
Bradford, ON L3Z 2B8

Voice: 905-775-0372
Fax: 905-775-4489
E-mail: info@times.net
Web: http://www.times.net

Service Area:	Bradford, Newmarket, Sharon, Bond Head, Beeton, Cookstown, Lefroy, Schomberg, East Gwillimbury. Planning to expand to Aurora, Oak Ridges, Richmond Hill, Thornhill, Markham, Vaughn.
Services:	Leased line, dedicated ISDN, dedicated SLIP/PPP, dial-up ISDN, dial-up SLIP/PPP, shell access, domain registration, free Web home page with personal dial-up account, Web design, Web hosting.
World Wide Web:	http://www.times.net

TKM Software Limited

Brandon, Manitoba
tkm.mb.ca

839–18th Street
Brandon, MB R7A 5B8

Voice:	204-727-3873
Fax:	204-727-5219
E-mail:	iman@access.tkm.mb.ca
Web:	http://www.tkm.mb.ca

Service Area:	Alexander, Brandon, Douglas, Forrest, Rivers, Shilo. Planning to expand to Virden, Glenboro, Carberry.
Services:	Leased line, dedicated SLIP/PPP, frame relay, dial-up SLIP/PPP, shell access, terminal accounts, domain registration, free Web home page with personal dial-up account, Web design, Web hosting.
World Wide Web:	http://www.tkm.mb.ca

TNC The Network Centre Ltd.

Edmonton, Alberta
tnc.com

11211–76 Avenue S.W.
Edmonton, AB T6G 0K2

Voice:	403-955-7166
Fax:	403-436-6055
E-mail:	info@tnc.com
Web:	http://www.tnc.com

Service Area:	Edmonton, Calgary, Fort McMurray.
Services:	Leased line, dedicated ISDN, dedicated SLIP/PPP, frame relay, dial-up SLIP/PPP, domain registration, Web design, Web hosting.
World Wide Web:	http://www.tnc.com

TransData Communications

Barrie, Ontario
transdata.ca

128 Anne Street South
Barrie, ON L4N 6A2

Voice:	705-725-1070
Fax:	705-725-1065
E-mail:	sysop@mail.transdata.ca
Web:	http://www.transdata.ca

Service Area:	Barrie, Midland, Alliston, Moonstone/Orillia, Collingwood/Stayner. Planning to expand to Huntsville, Bracebridge, Owen Sound, Meaford.
Services:	Leased line, dedicated ISDN, dedicated SLIP/PPP, frame relay, dial-up SLIP/PPP, UUCP service, domain registration, Web design, Web hosting.
World Wide Web:	http://www.transdata.ca

Travel-Net Communications Inc.

Ottawa, Ontario
travel-net.com

292 Montreal Road
Ottawa, ON K1L 6B7

Voice:	613-744-3000
Fax:	613-744-2602
E-mail:	info@travel-net.com
Web:	http://www.travel-net.com

Service Area:	Ottawa, Gloucester, Vanier, Kanata, Orleans, Hull, Nepean, Carleton Place, Almonte, Kemptville, Merrickville, Buckingham, Low, Embrun, Russell, Rockland, Val-des-Bois, Luskville, Wakefield, Quyon, Bourget, Clarence Creek, North Gower, Stittsville, Pakenham, Shawville, Perkins, Aylmer, Manotick, Casselman, Metcalfe, Jockvale, Osgoode, Chelsea, Constance Bay, Cumberland, Navan, Richmond, Carp, Thurso, Crysler.

Services: Dedicated ISDN, dedicated SLIP/ PPP, dial-up SLIP/PPP, shell access, domain registration, free Web home page with personal dial-up account, Web design, Web hosting.

World Wide Web: http://www.travel-net.com

Trytel Internet Inc.

Ottawa, Ontario
trytel.com, trytel.on.ca

818 Boyd Avenue, Unit B
Ottawa, ON K2A 2C7

Voice: 613-722-6321
Fax: 613-722-6749
E-mail: info@trytel.com
Web: http://www.trytel.com

Service Area: Ottawa-Hull, Aylmer, Gatineau, Gloucester, Orleans, Manotick, Greeley, Kanata, Carleton Place.

Services: Leased line, dedicated ISDN, dedicated SLIP/PPP, dial-up ISDN, dial-up SLIP/PPP, shell access, domain registration, free Web home page with personal dial-up account, Web design, Web hosting.

World Wide Web: http://www.trytel.com

TST Consulting

Medicine Hat, Alberta
tst-medhat.com

877–17th Street S.W.
Box 1599 C153
Medicine Hat, AB T1A 7Y5

Voice: 403-529-1560
Fax: 403-526-1560
E-mail: tst@tst-medhat.com

Service Area: Bow Island, Elkwater, Irvine, Medicine Hat, Ralston, Redcliff, Schuler, Seven Persons, Walsh.

Services: Leased line, dedicated SLIP/PPP, frame relay, dial-up SLIP/PPP, shell access, UUCP service, domain registration.

World Wide Web: N/A

ULTRAtech.net Inc.

Markham, Ontario
ultratech.net

1211 Denison Street, Units 17 and 18
Markham, ON L3R 4B3

Voice: 905-946-1854
Fax: 905-946-1532
E-mail: sales@ultratech.net
Web: http://www.ultratech.net

Service Area: Metropolitan Toronto. Planning to expand to Ottawa.

Services: Dedicated ISDN, dedicated SLIP/ PPP, dial-up ISDN, dial-up SLIP/PPP, shell access, terminal accounts, domain registration, free Web home page with personal dial-up account, Web design, Web hosting.

World Wide Web: http://www.ultratech.net

UNIBASE Telecom Ltd.

Regina, Saskatchewan
unibase.com

3002 Harding Street
Regina, SK S4V 0Y4

Voice: 306-789-9007
Fax: 306-761-1831
E-mail: milton@unibase.unibase.com, leigh@unibase.com
Web: http://www.unibase.unibase.com

Service Area: Regina and local dial-in area, Saskatoon and local dial-in area, Prince Albert and local dial-in area. Planning to expand to Melville, Estevan, Moose Jaw.

| **Services:** | Leased line, dedicated SLIP/PPP, dial-up SLIP/PPP, terminal accounts, UUCP service, domain registration, free Web home page with personal dial-up account, Web design, Web hosting. |

| **World Wide Web:** | http://www.unibase.unibase.com |

UPC Communications Internet

Québec, Québec
upc.qc.ca

C.P. 9004
Ste-Foy, PQ G1V 4A8

Voice:	418-656-0090
Fax:	418-656-6981
E-mail:	info@upc.qc.ca
Web:	http://www.upc.qc.ca

| **Service Area:** | Quebec City, Ste-Foy, Lèvis, Boischa-tel, Charny, Château-Richer, Donna-cona, Loretteville, Notre-Dame-des-Laurentides, Neuville, Pont-Rouge, Ste-Anne-de-Beaupré, Ste-Brigitte-de-Laval, St-Agapit, St-Anselme, St-Anto-ine-de-Tilly, St-Apollinaire, St-Augus-tin, St-Basile, St-Bernard, Ste-Catherine, St-Charles-de-Belle-chasse, St-Férréol-les-Neiges, St-Fla-vien, St-Henri-de-Lèvis, St-Jean, St-Lambert, St-Michel-de-Bellechasse, St-Nicolas, St-Patrice-de-Beaurivage, St-Raymond, St-Tite-des-Caps. Planning to expand to St-Georges-de-Beauce, Chicoutimi. |

| **Services:** | Dedicated ISDN, dedicated SLIP/PPP, frame relay, dial-up ISDN, dial-up SLIP/PPP, UUCP service, Web design, Web hosting. |

| **World Wide Web:** | http://www.upc.qc.ca |

UUNET Canada, Inc.

Toronto, Ontario
uunet.ca, mail.net

20 Bay Street, Suite 1910
Toronto, ON M5J 2N8

Voice:	416-368-6621, 1-800-463-8123
Fax:	416-368-1350
E-mail:	info@uunet.ca
Web:	http://www.uunet.ca

| **Service Area:** | Calgary, Charlottetown, Edmonton, Halifax, Kitchener, London, Montreal, Ottawa, Quebec, Sudbury, Toronto, Vancouver. |
| **Services:** | Leased line, dedicated ISDN, dedicated SLIP/PPP, frame relay, dial-up ISDN, dial-up SLIP/PPP, UUCP service, domain registration, Web design, Web hosting. |

| **World Wide Web:** | http://www.uunet.ca |

UUNorth International Incorporated

Toronto, Ontario
north.net, north.on.ca

3555 Don Mills Road, Unit 6-304
Willowdale, ON M2H 3N3

Voice:	416-225-8649
Fax:	416-225-0525
E-mail:	info@uunorth.north.net
Web:	http://www.north.net

| **Service Area:** | Toronto. Affiliate offices: Oshawa, Thunder Bay, Barbados. Planning to expand to Vancouver, Montreal, central Ontario. |
| **Services:** | Leased line, dedicated ISDN, dedicated SLIP/PPP, frame relay, dial-up ISDN, dial-up SLIP/PPP, terminal accounts, UUCP service, domain registration, Web design, Web hosting. |

| **World Wide Web:** | http://www.north.net |

V(DL)2 Inc.

Montréal, Québec
vdl2.ca

Téléport de Montréal
1205 Papineau
Montréal, PQ H2K 4R2

Voice: 514-599-5712
Fax: 514-599-5729
E-mail: info@vdl2.ca
Web: http://www.vdl2.ca

Service Area:	Montreal, Quebec City, Toronto, Ottawa. Planning to expand to Chicoutimi, Trois-Rivières, Sherbrooke, Baie-Comeau.
Services:	Leased line, dedicated ISDN, dedicated SLIP/PPP, frame relay, domain registration, Web design, Web hosting.
World Wide Web:	http://www.vdl2.ca

Vaxxine Computer Systems Inc.

Jordan Station, Ontario
vaxxine.com, ontario.net, falls.net, niagara.net

4520 Jordan Road
Jordan Station, ON L0R 1S0

Voice: 905-562-3500
Fax: 905-562-3515
E-mail: admin@vaxxine.com
Web: http://www.vaxxine.com

Service Area:	St. Catharines, Thorold, Niagara Falls, Welland, Port Colborne, Fort Erie, Ridgeway, Niagara-on-the-Lake, Beamsville, Grimsby, Pelham, Vineland, Welland, Port Robinson.
Services:	Leased line, dedicated ISDN, dedicated SLIP/PPP, dial-up ISDN, dial-up SLIP/PPP, shell access, terminal accounts, UUCP service, domain registration, free Web home page with personal dial-up account, Web design, Web hosting.
World Wide Web:	http://www.vaxxine.com

ViaNet (Division of Via Computer and Communications)

Timmins, Ontario
vianet.on.ca

361 Algonquin Boulevard West
Timmins, ON P4N 2S3

Voice: 705-268-5021
Fax: 705-264-6277
E-mail: helpme@vianet.on.ca
Web: http://www.vianet.on.ca

Service Area:	Sudbury, Timmins, North Bay, Huntsville. Planning to expand to Sault Ste. Marie, Kirkland Lake.
Services:	Leased line, dedicated ISDN, dedicated SLIP/PPP, dial-up SLIP/PPP, shell access, domain registration, free Web home page with personal dial-up account, Web design, Web hosting.
World Wide Web:	http://www.vianet.on.ca

Vircom Inc.

Laval, Québec
vircom.com, gamemaster.qc.ca

1600, boul. Le Corbusier
C.P. 58009
Laval, PQ H7S 2M4

Voice: 514-990-2532
Fax: 514-681-3751
E-mail: sysop@vircom.com
Web: http://www.vircom.com

Service Area:	Montreal.
Services:	Dial-up SLIP/PPP, terminal accounts.
World Wide Web:	http://www.vircom.com

Voyageur.Net Inc.

Kenora, Ontario
voyageur.ca

109 1/2 Main Street
Kenora, ON P9N 1T1

Voice: 807-468-8658
Fax: 807-468-8638
E-mail: info@voyageur.ca
Web: http://www.voyageur.ca

Service Area: Kenora, Jaffray, Melick, Keewatin. Planning to expand to Red Lake, Sioux Lookout, Dryden.

Services: Leased line, dedicated SLIP/PPP, frame relay, dial-up SLIP/PPP, UUCP service, domain registration, free Web home page with personal dial-up account, Web design, Web hosting.

World Wide Web: http://www.voyageur.ca

WBM Office Systems

Regina, Saskatchewan
wbm.ca

421 McDonald Street
Regina, SK S4N 6E1

Voice: 306-721-2560
Fax: 306-721-2498
E-mail: webmaster@eagle.wbm.ca
Web: http://www.wbm.ca

Service Area: Saskatoon, Regina.

Services: Leased line, dedicated ISDN, dedicated SLIP/PPP, frame relay, dial-up ISDN, dial-up SLIP/PPP, UUCP service, domain registration, Web design, Web hosting.

World Wide Web: http://www.wbm.ca

Weslink Datalink Corporation

Hamilton, Ontario
weslink.ca

1603 Main Street West
Hamilton, ON L8S 1E6

Voice: 905-522-4101
Fax: 905-522-2123
E-mail: info@weslink.ca
Web: http://www.weslink.ca

Service Area: Hamilton, Dundas, Ancaster, Stoney Creek, Flamborough, Grimsby, Burlington. Planning to expand to Toronto, Oakville, Mississauga.

Services: Leased line, dedicated ISDN, dedicated SLIP/PPP, dial-up ISDN, dial-up SLIP/PPP, shell access, domain registration, Web design, Web hosting.

World Wide Web: http://www.weslink.ca

Westel Telecommunications Ltd.

North Vancouver, British Columbia
westel.com

949 West 3rd Street, Suite 121
North Vancouver, BC V6B 3T5

Voice: 604-990-2000
Fax: 604-689-9499
E-mail: info@westel.com
Web: http://www.westel.com

Service Area: Vancouver.

Services: Leased line, dedicated ISDN, dedicated SLIP/PPP, frame relay, dial-up ISDN, dial-up SLIP/PPP, domain registration.

World Wide Web: http://www.westel.com

Whistler Networks

Whistler, British Columbia
whistler.net

1200 Alpha Lake Road, Suite 204
Whistler, BC V0N 1B0

Voice: 604-932-0606
Fax: 604-932-0204
E-mail: webmaster@whistler.net
Web: http://www.whistler.net

Service Area:	Whistler, Pemberton. Planning to expand to Squamish.
Services:	Leased line, dedicated SLIP/PPP, dial-up SLIP/PPP, UUCP service, domain registration, free Web home page with personal dial-up account, Web design, Web hosting.
World Wide Web:	http://www.whistler.net

Wimsey Information Services Inc.

Vancouver, British Columbia
wimsey.com, wimsey.ca, wis.net

8523 Commerce Court
Burnaby, BC V5A 4N3

Voice: 604-257-1111, 1-800-670-6600
Fax: 604-257-1110
E-mail: info@wimsey.com (individual requests),
           sales@wimsey.com (commercial requests)
Web: http://www.wimsey.com

Service Area:	Vancouver, Burnaby, Bowen Island, Port Moody, Port Coquitlam, Coquitlam, Pitt Meadows, Maple Ridge, Anmore, Surrey, Aldergrove, Langley, Fort Langley, Tsawwassen, White Rock, Delta, Ladner, Richmond. Planning to expand to Calgary, Toronto.
Services:	Leased line, dedicated ISDN, dedicated SLIP/PPP, dial-up SLIP/PPP, shell access, terminal accounts, UUCP service, domain registration, free Web home page with personal dial-up account, Web design, Web hosting.
World Wide Web:	http://www.wimsey.com

WINCOM (Windsor Information Network Company)

Windsor, Ontario
wincom.net

4510 Rhodes Drive, Unit 700
Windsor, ON N8W 5K5

Voice: 519-734-7070
E-mail: mrw@pobox.wincom.net
Web: http://www.wincom.net

Service Area:	Leamington, Comber, Pleasant Park, McGregor, Emeryville, Belle River, Kingsville, La Salle, Tecumseh, Amherstburg, Maidstone, Harrow, Essex, Stoney Point, Cottam, Woodslee, Windsor
Services:	Leased line, dedicated ISDN, dedicated SLIP/PPP, frame relay, dial-up ISDN, dial-up SLIP/PPP, UUCP service, domain registration, Web design, Web hosting.
World Wide Web:	http://www.wincom.net

-the-Wire-

Toronto, Ontario
the-wire.com, toronto.com

12 Sheppard Street, Suite 419
Toronto, ON M5H 3A1

Voice: 416-214-9473
Fax: 416-862-9473
E-mail: sysadm@the-wire.com
Web: http://www.the-wire.com,
           http://www.toronto.com

Service Area:	Toronto and local 416/905 dial-in area.
Services:	Leased line, dedicated ISDN, dedicated SLIP/PPP, dial-up ISDN, dial-up SLIP/PPP, shell access, UUCP service, domain registration, free Web home page with personal dial-up account, Web design, Web hosting.
World Wide Web:	http://www.the-wire.com, http://www.toronto.com

WorldCHAT™

Burlington, Ontario
wchat.on.ca, wchat.com, infini.com,
brantford.com, kitchener.com

3018 New Street
Burlington, ON L7N 1M5

Voice:	905-637-9111
Fax:	905-637-0140
E-mail:	jhoskin@wchat.on.ca
Web:	http://www.wchat.on.ca

Service Area:	Burlington, Brantford, Hamilton, Mississauga, Kitchener, Oakville, Toronto, Milton, Stoney Creek, Grimsby, Dundas, Ancaster, Caledonia, St. George, Waterloo, Cambridge. Planning to expand to London, St. Catharines, Windsor, Belleville, Barrie.
Services:	Leased line, dedicated ISDN, dedicated SLIP/PPP, frame relay, dial-up ISDN, dial-up SLIP/PPP, shell access, terminal accounts, UUCP service, domain registration, free Web home page with personal dial-up account, Web design, Web hosting.
World Wide Web:	http://www.wchat.on.ca

WorldGate Inc.

Edmonton, Alberta
worldgate.com, worldgate.net,
worldgate.edmonton.ab.ca

16511–85 Avenue
Edmonton, AB T5R 4A2

Voice:	403-444-7720
Fax:	403-444-7720
E-mail:	admin@worldgate.com, info@worldgate.com (automated reply)
Web:	http://www.worldgate.com

Service Area:	Edmonton, Calgary.
Services:	Leased line, dedicated ISDN, dedicated SLIP/PPP, frame relay, dial-up ISDN, dial-up SLIP/PPP, shell access, terminal accounts, UUCP service, domain registration, free Web home page with personal dial-up account, Web design, Web hosting.
World Wide Web:	http://www.worldgate.com

WorldLink Internet Services, Inc.

Ottawa, Ontario
worldlink.ca

99 Bank Street, Suite 600
Ottawa, ON K1P 6B9

Voice:	613-233-7100
Fax:	613-233-9527
E-mail:	sales@worldlink.ca
Web:	http://www.worldlink.ca/welcome.html

Service Area:	Almonte, Aylmer, Carleton Place, Carp, Chelsea, Constance Bay, Cumberland, Embrun, Gatineau, Gloucester, Hull, Jockvale, Kanata/Stittsville, Low, Luskville, Manotick, Metcalfe, Navan, North Gower, Orleans, Osgoode, Ottawa, Perkins, Quyon, Richmond, Rockland, Russell, St-Pierre-de-Wakefield, Wakefield.
Services:	Dedicated ISDN, dedicated SLIP/PPP, dial-up ISDN, dial-up SLIP/PPP, shell access, domain registration, free Web home page with personal dial-up account, Web design, Web hosting.
World Wide Web:	http://www.worldlink.ca/welcome.html

WorldLinx Telecommunications Inc., a Bell Canada Company

Toronto, Ontario
worldlinx.com

BCE Place, Suite 350
181 Bay Street
P.O. Box 851
Toronto, ON M5J 2T3

Voice:	1-800-551-5638, 1-800-819-2638
E-mail:	worldlinx.com
Web:	http://www.worldlinx.com, http://www.bell.ca

Service Area:	Toronto, Montreal, Ottawa-Hull, Quebec City (dial-up service). Canada-wide (dedicated service).
World Wide Web:	http://www.worldlinx.com, http://www.bell.ca

World Online Inc.

Hamilton, Ontario
worldonline.ca

20 Jackson Street West, Suite 506
Hamilton, ON L8P 1L2

Voice:	905-529-5700
E-mail:	sysop@worldonline.ca
Web:	http://www.worldonline.ca

Service Area:	Hamilton and Burlington dial-in areas.
Services:	Leased line, dedicated ISDN, dedicated SLIP/PPP, frame relay, dial-up ISDN, dial-up SLIP/PPP, UUCP service, domain registration, Web design, Web hosting.
World Wide Web:	http://www.worldonline.ca

World Tel

Vancouver, British Columbia
worldtel.com

Royal Bank Building
675 West Hastings Street, Suite 810
Vancouver, BC V6B 1N2

Voice:	604-685-3877
Fax:	604-687-0688
E-mail:	info@worldtel.com
Web:	http://www.worldtel.com

Service Area:	Vancouver, Nelson, Toronto, Calgary, Edmonton, Manila (Philippines), Karachi (Pakistan). Planning to expand to Saskatoon, Winnipeg, Montreal, central and southeast Asia, South America.

Services:	Leased line, dedicated ISDN, dedicated SLIP/PPP, frame relay, dial-up ISDN, dial-up SLIP/PPP, shell access, terminal accounts, UUCP service, domain registration, Web design, Web hosting.
World Wide Web:	http://www.worldtel.com

World Web Technologies Inc. (formerly Vertex Communications Inc.)

Calgary, Alberta
worldweb.com, worldhost.com

410–1010 First Street S.W.
Calgary, AB T2R 1K4

Voice:	403-777-9300
Fax:	403-777-9304
E-mail:	sales@worldweb.com
Web:	http://www.worldweb.com

Service Area:	Calgary and surrounding area, Edmonton and surrounding area.
Services:	Dedicated SLIP/PPP, dial-up SLIP/PPP, domain registration, Web design, Web hosting.
World Wide Web:	http://www.worldweb.com

Worldwide Data Communications Inc.

London, Ontario
onlinesys.com, wwdc.com

383 Richmond Street, Suite 900
London, ON N6A 3C4

Voice:	519-642-0731
Fax:	519-642-0733
E-mail:	info@onlinesys.com, info@wwdc.com
Web:	http://www.wwdc.com

Service Area:	Sarnia, Woodstock, Stratford, Aylmer, London.

| Services: | Leased line, dedicated ISDN, dedicated SLIP/PPP, frame relay, dial-up ISDN, dial-up SLIP/PPP, shell access, terminal accounts, UUCP service, domain registration, Web design, Web hosting. |

World Wide Web: http://www.wwdc.com

World Wide Wave Inc.

Toronto, Ontario
wwwave.com

505 Consumers Road, Suite 506
North York, ON M2J 4V8

Voice: 416-499-7100
Fax: 416-499-7775
E-mail: info@wwwave.com
Web: http://www.wwwave.com

| Service Area: | Toronto, Mississauga, Oakville, Brampton, Markham. Planning to expand to Windsor, Oshawa, London, Hamilton. |
| Services: | Leased line, dedicated ISDN, dedicated SLIP/PPP, frame relay, dial-up ISDN, dial-up SLIP/PPP, shell access, UUCP service, domain registration, free Web home page with personal dial-up account, Web design, Web hosting. |

World Wide Web: http://www.wwwave.com

XBASE Technologies Corporation

Toronto, Ontario
xbase.com

119 Spadina Avenue, Suite 1101
Toronto, ON M5V 2L1

Voice: 416-340-1020
Fax: 416-340-1054
E-mail: mail@xbase.com
Web: http://www.xbase.com

| Service Area: | Greater Toronto Area. |
| Services: | Leased line, dedicated ISDN, dedicated SLIP/PPP, frame relay, dial-up ISDN, dial-up SLIP/PPP, UUCP service, domain registration, Web design, Web hosting. |

World Wide Web: http://www.xbase.com

Xenon Laboratories

Toronto, Ontario
xe.net, xemail.net

330 Bay Street, Suite 1109
Toronto, ON M5H 2S8

Voice: 416-214-5606
Fax: 416-214-5607
E-mail: info@xe.net
Web: http://www.xe.net

| Service Area: | Toronto, Ajax, Pickering, Aurora, Bethesda, Bolton, Brampton, Castlemore, Claremont, Clarkson, Cooksville, Gormley, King City, Kleinburg, Malton, Maple, Markham, Mississauga, Nobleton, Oak Ridges, Oakville, Palgrave, Port Credit, Richmond Hill, Schomberg, South Pickering, Snelgrove, Stouffville, Streetsville, Thornhill, Unionville, Woodbridge. |
| Services: | Leased line, dedicated ISDN, dedicated SLIP/PPP, dial-up ISDN, dial-up SLIP/PPP, shell access, UUCP service, domain registration, free Web home page with personal dial-up account, Web design, Web hosting. |

World Wide Web: http://www.xe.net

Xyberlynx Canada Inc.

Scarborough, Ontario
xyberlynx.net, xyberlinx.net

3640B McNicoll Avenue
Scarborough, ON M1X 1G5

Voice: 416-754-9432
Fax: 416-754-7701
E-mail: info@xyberlynx.net, corp@xyberlynx.net
            (corporate inquiries)
Web: http://www.xyberlynx.net

Service Area:	Greater Toronto Area. Planning to expand to the rest of Ontario, including most rural communities.
Services:	Leased line, dedicated ISDN, dedicated SLIP/PPP, frame relay, dial-up ISDN, dial-up SLIP/PPP, UUCP service, domain registration, Web design, Web hosting.
World Wide Web:	http://www.xyberlynx.net

Yellowhead Computer Services

Hinton, Alberta
ycs.ab.ca

114 Park Street, Suite 1
P.O. Box 6088
Hinton, AB T7V 1X5

Voice:	403-865-5933
Fax:	403-865-5937
E-mail:	info@ycs.ab.ca
Web:	http://www.ycs.ab.ca

Service Area:	Hinton, Jasper, Edson, Grand Cache.
Services:	Leased line, dedicated SLIP/PPP, frame relay, dial-up SLIP/PPP, domain registration, Web design, Web hosting.
World Wide Web:	http://www.ycs.ab.ca

YukonNet

Whitehorse, Yukon
yknet.yk.ca

YukonNet Operating Society
Box 4900
Whitehorse, YK Y1A 4N6

Voice:	403-668-8202
Fax:	403-668-4907
E-mail:	yknet@yknet.yk.ca
Web:	http://www.yknet.yk.ca

Service Area:	Whitehorse and Haines Junction. Planning to expand to Dawson City, Faro, Watson Lake.
Services:	Leased line, dedicated SLIP/PPP, dial-up SLIP/PPP, domain registration, Web hosting.
World Wide Web:	http://www.yknet.yk.ca

Zercom Technologies Inc.

St-Laurent, Québec
zercom.net

1594 Beaulac
St-Laurent, PQ H4R 1W8

Voice:	514-956-8337
Fax:	514-956-8329
E-mail:	info@zercom.net
Web:	http://www.zercom.net

Service Area:	Beloeil, Beauharnois, Boucherville, Chambly, Châteauguay, Chomedey, Clarenceville, Hemmingford, Hudson, Île-Perrot, Lachine, La Prairie, Laval-Est, Laval-Ouest, Lavaltrie, Le Gardeur, L'Épiphanie-L'Assomption, Longueuil, Marieville, Mascouche, Mirabel Aéroport, Mirabel Saint-Augustin, Montreal, Napierville, Oka, Pierrefonds, Ste-Geneviève, Pointe-Claire, Pont-Viau, Rigaud, Roxboro, Ste-Anne-des-Plaines, St-Bruno, St-Calixte-de-Kilkenny, St-Constant, St-Denis, St-Eustache, St-Jean, Ste-Julienne, Ste-Julie-de-Verchères, St-Lambert, St-Lin, St-Marc, Ste-Martine, St-Rémi, Ste-Rose, St-Sauveur, Ste-Thérèse, St-Vincent-de-Paul, Terrebonne, Varennes, Vaudreuil, Verchères. Planning to expand to Toronto, Quebec City.

Services:	Leased line, dedicated ISDN, dedicated SLIP/PPP, frame relay, dial-up ISDN, dial-up SLIP/PPP, shell access, terminal accounts, UUCP service, domain registration, free Web home page with personal dial-up account, Web design, Web hosting.
World Wide Web:	http://www.zercom.net

Canadian Organizations with Registered Internet Domains

As discussed in Chapter 5, when a Canadian organization wishes to register a domain on the Internet, it can apply to either the CA Domain Registrar in Canada (if it wishes to register in the **.ca** domain) or the InterNIC (Internet Network Information Center) in the United States (if it wishes to register a descriptive domain such as **.com**, **.edu**, **.gov**, **.net**, or **.org**). Some organizations choose to register both a geographical and a descriptive domain.

As of September 1, 1995, almost 9,500 Canadian organizations had registered Internet domains. A list of these organizations and their respective Internet domains is provided in the table below. The list is organized alphabetically by organization name. Before consulting the directory, there are a couple of things that you should be aware of:

(1) There is no guarantee that all the organizations listed in this directory are currently connected to the Internet. This directory is a list of Canadian organizations that have registered Internet domains. Registering an Internet domain and connecting to the Internet are two different things. Some organizations register an Internet domain weeks or months in advance of connecting to the Internet.

(2) A listing in this directory does not mean that all of the company's employees are connected to the Internet. Many of the organizations listed in the directory are experimenting with the Internet, and only one or two people within the organization may be using the Internet connection.

(3) If an organization does not appear in this directory, it does not necessarily mean that the organization is not using the Internet. This directory only lists Canadian organizations that have registered their own Internet domains. Keep in mind that an organization doesn't have to register its own Internet domain to use the Internet. Most organizations operate under the domain name of their Internet access provider and therefore will not appear in the directory below.

(4) There are two costs associated with registering a domain name. The first is the cost charged by your Internet access provider or Internet presence provider to fill out the paperwork and submit your domain name application. The cost ranges from free to up to several hundred dollars [a list of over 300 Internet access providers in Canada can be found in Appendix B]. The second cost is the fee charged by the organization that allocates your domain name. The InterNIC charges US$50.00 per year for each domain name you request. The CA Domain Registrar does not currently charge for domain names.

Obtaining an Up-To-Date List of Organizations Registered in the CA Domain

The list of organizations registered in the CA Domain is updated regularly by John Demco, the CA Domain Registrar. You can retrieve a current copy of the list by anonymous FTP, as follows:

Anonymous FTP Site:	ftp.cdnnet.ca
Directory:	ca-domain
File:	index-by-organization (Ordered alphabetically)
	index-by-subdomain (Ordered by subdomain)

The InterNIC does not keep track of U.S. and Canadian registrations separately, so it is not possible to obtain a list of Canadian registrations from the InterNIC. However, the entire InterNIC database is searchable, but only by domain name or organization name. If you're wondering whether a certain Canadian organization has registered an Internet domain name, and the organization isn't listed in John Demco's CA Domain list, try searching the InterNIC registration database. You can access the InterNIC database by telnet, as detailed below.

To Query the InterNIC Registration Database

Telnet:	rs.internic.net
At the **InterNIC>** prompt, type:	whois

The InterNIC database is easy to use once you get the hang of it. Once you've connected and logged in, enter your search word(s) at the **Whois:** prompt. Your search word(s) can either be an organization name, domain name, or any word(s) at all. For example, to find the domain name information for the Liquor Control Board of Ontario, type **Liquor Control Board of Ontario** at the **Whois:** prompt.

If your search produces multiple matches, you may need to enter the code that appears in brackets in your search output. For example, let's suppose you are looking for the Internet domain for Cott Corporation. If you enter the name **Cott Corporation** at the **Whois:** prompt, one of the lines you would get back is a line that looks like this:

Cott Corporation (COTT-DOM)	COTT.COM

This tells you that Cott Corporation has registered the domain **cott.com**. To receive information on this domain, you have to enter the code **COTT-DOM** (the code in brackets) at the **Whois:** prompt.

If you already know an organization's domain name, you don't need to look up the organization's name first. Simply type the domain name at the **Whois:** prompt. For example, you could have gone directly to the Cott Corporation entry by typing **cott.com** at the **Whois:** prompt.

This is a simplified look at the Whois database. The best way to become proficient with the **Whois:** database is to experiment with it. Use **quit** to exit the database when you are finished (you'll need to type "quit" twice, once to exit the **Whois:** database, and a second time to exit completely).

You can also query the **Whois:** database on the World Wide Web:

To Query the InterNIC Registration Database on the Web

http://www.rs.internic.net/rs-internic.html
Select: Whois Query Form

Name of Organization	Domain	Name of Organization	Domain
/Usr/Group/Edmonton	edm-unix.org	386324 B.C. Limited DBA Netcor Consulting	netcor.bc.ca
05968 New Brunswick Inc O/A Studio Staccato	staccato.nb.ca	390083 Alberta Ltd. O/A Mulvey Agency	mulvey.ab.ca
1048734 Ontario Inc.	ride.com	421554 Alberta Ltd.	o/alethbridgeinternet services
1061441 Ontario Inc.	laservision.com		
1085735 Ontario Inc.	oncology.com	433884 B.C. Ltd.	433884bc.com
1133332 Ontario Ltd. O/A Sunset Communications	sunsetcom.on.ca	469506 B.C. Ltd. DBA Intouch Cordless Communication	intouch.bc.ca
1141000 Ontario Inc. O/A Mobile Extensions	mobile.ca	4Comm Integrated Technologies, Inc.	4comm.com
123 Media Design	123md.com	4P Group	4p.com
13 Engines	13engines.com	4th & Vine Inc.	4th-vine.com
136864 Canada Inc O/A Ryan Associates	ryan.ca	507245 Alberta Ltd. O/A Internet Filters and Firewalls	iff.ab.ca
142792 Canada Inc. O/A Your News-Canada's Teaching Newspaper	yournews.ca	593765 Alberta Ltd.	latticetech.com
		5D Computer Systems and Supplies	5dcomputers.com
168486 Canada Inc.	ems.net	631776 Alberta Ltd.	kiosks.com
1st Choice Information Service	1choice.com	656085 Alberta Ltd. (Internet North)	inetnorth.ab.ca
20/20 Group Financial Inc.	ttgfi.ca		
20/20 Group Financial Ltd.	ttgfund.com	71280 British Columbia Inc. O/A Wolrige Mahon	wolrigemahon.bc.ca
2163818 Nova Scotia Limited O/A Busicomp Computers	busicomp.ns.ca	718135 Ontario Ltd.	worldofcatalogs.com
2331346 Nova Scotia Limited O/A Career Blazers Learning Center	cblazers.ns.ca	768812 Ontario Inc., O/A Vianet	vianet.on.ca
25506767 Quebec Inc. O/A Montreal Business Magazine	mbm.qc.ca	796112 Ontario Inc.	specnetwork.com
		800 Canada, Inc.	loancanada.com
2908018 Canada Inc.	resto.com	807-City	807-city.on.ca
2927497 Canada Inc. O/A Circle Air	circleair.ca	833321 Ontario, Ltd.	barcodenow.com
		9 To 5 Communications	9to5.com
2955768 Canada Inc. O/A Powersoft	powersoft.ca	9 To 5 Communications	cibd.com
3075796 Canada Inc.	hardbodies.com	9 To 5 Communications	electracity.com
3078337 Canada Limited	cmaonline.com	9014-2134 Quebec Inc. O/A Groupe Conseil I3	gci3.qc.ca
3096-3516 Quebec Inc. O/A Magazine Designers Inc.	designers.qc.ca	962101 Ontario Inc. O/A Heritage Institute	heritage.on.ca
3154017 Canada Inc.	at-net.com	992061 Ontario Inc. O/A Webworks	webworks.on.ca
365294 Alberta Incorporated O/A Abstract Consulting	abstract.ab.ca		
		9Bit Inc.	9bit.qc.ca
		@Darwin Incorporated	darwin.qc.ca
		@Dot.Dot	dot.on.ca

Name of Organization	Domain	Name of Organization	Domain
A & B Computer Systems Inc.	a-bcomputers.ca	Abitibi-Price	abitibi.com
A & B Computers	medical.org	ABL Canada Inc.	abl.ca
A & B Sound Ltd.	absound.ca	Able Crafters Ns Inc	able.pictou.ns.ca
A and W Food Services of Canada	awcda.com	ABM Systems Inc.	abmsystems.ns.ca
A Higher Vision Canada Ltd.	secretshopnet.com	Aboriginal Super-Information Hwy., Inc.	abinfohwy.ca
A La Carte Displays	portabledisplays.com	Aboriginal Youth Network (AYN)	ayn.ca
A M Productions Inc.	amproductions.com		
A S & R BBS	airsr.com	ABS Inc.	absinfo.com
A Sound Mind Production	soundmind.com	Absolu Technologies Inc.	absolu.com
A&W Internet Inc.	awinc.bc.ca	Absolu Technologies Inc.	absolu.qc.ca
A-Cubed, Inc	a-cubed.com	Absolu Technologies Inc.	telweb.com
A. B. Microtek Ltd	abmicrotek.com	Absolute Software	absolute.com
A. Dunn Systems Corporation	adscorp.on.ca	Absolute Solutions	absolutions.mb.ca
A. J. Clarke and Associates Ltd.	ajclarke.com	Abstract Arts Tattoo / Lower East Side Tattoo	tattoos.com
A. J. Lill Consultants	ajlc.waterloo.on.ca	Acadia University	acadiau.ca
A. J. P. Engineering Services	ajpeng.mb.ca	Acart Graphic Services, Inc.	acart.on.ca
A. R. Mani	armani.com	ACC TelEnterprises Ltd.	acc.ca
A.L. Info Services	alinfo.com	Accademia Qualitas Inc	accademia.com
A.L.I. Technologies Ltd.	ali.bc.ca	Accel Computer Solutions	accel.net
A.R.I. Management Services, Ltd.	expertscosmsurg.com	Accel Micro Systems	accel.ca
		Accent Internet	accent.net
A.W.A.R.D. Wholesale and Retail Distributors Ltd.	award.ca	Acces Internet Belin, Inc. (Ste-Justine)	belin.qc.ca
A.Z. Technologies	ntg-inter.com	Acces Public Llc Enr.	llc.org
A1- Vitamins	a1-vitamins.com	Acces-Cible Inc.	acces-cible.qc.ca
AAA Royal Motel	aaaaroyal.com	Acces-Domotique Inc.	domotique.com
Aaleye Acoustics	aaleye.com	Access 20/20 Inc.	access2020.com
Aardvark Consulting Ltd.	aardvark.com	Access Communications	pulseonline.com
Aastra Aerospace Inc.	aastra.com	Access Computer Systems, A Division of King-Cade Amusements Inc.	access.victoria.bc.ca
AAZ-Tech Computers	aaz-tech.com		
Abacus Computers	abacus.ca		
ABC	abc.net	Access Internet Mondial	fbicollege.com
ABC Internet Ltd.	acsabc.com	Access Internet Mondial	mercure.net
ABC Mall	abcmall.com	Access Media Systems	accmedia.com
Abel Computers, Ltd.	abelcomputers.com	Access Route Canada Online Systems	arcos.org
Ability Online Support Network	ablelink.org	Access Systems & Consulting	asconsult.com
Abisko Manufacturing Inc.	abisko.com	Access Technologies, Inc.	acctech.com

Name of Organization	Domain	Name of Organization	Domain
Access Web Marketing Services Ltd.	accessweb.com	Active Technologies Datasystems Ltd.	at-data.ns.ca
Accessory Concepts, Inc.	accessory.com	Acumen Computers Inc.	acumen.ca
Accident Investigation And Research, Inc.	airinc.com	Acura Technology Group Inc.	acura.com
		AD Enterprises Ltd.	bcauto.com
Accomodations Connectivity Service	hotel.net	AD OPT Technologies Inc.	adopt.qc.ca
		AD Technologies Inc.	adtech.ca
Accord	accord.on.ca	AD Technologies Inc.	adtech.com
Accord Real Estate	accord-group.com	ADA Computers Ltd.	adacom.com
Accubid Systems Ltd.	accubid.com	Adam Peripherals, Inc.	adamper.com
Acculogic Inc.	acculogic.com	Adanac Enterprises Corporation	adanacnet.com
Accumap Enerdata Corp	accumap.com		
Accumedia Multimedia	accumedia.com	Adapta Software	adapta.com
Accuware Business Solutions Ltd.	accuware.com	Adaptive Answers, Inc.	adaptive.mb.ca
		Adbusters Media Foundation	adbusters.org
Acdat System Services Ltd.	acdat.com	Adcognito Inc.	adcognito.ca
Ace Computer Services Ltd.	ace.bc.ca	Adcom Communications	adcomad.com
Aceldama Systems	aceldama.com	Adcom Technologies Inc.	adcomtech.com
Acheson Directories	toobig.com	Addiction Research Foundation	arf.org
Achilles	achilles.net		
Achilles Internet Ltd.	achilles.ca	Aden Systems Incorporated	vos.com
Achilles Online	achilles.org	Adeo Communicaton Corp.	adeo.com
ACI Computers	ial.com	ADI Limited	adi.ca
Acklands Ltd	acklands.ca	ADI Systems Ltd.	adisys.ca
Acme Analytical Laboratories Ltd.	acmelab.com	Adidas Canada Ltd.	adidascan.com
		Adin Group Inc.	adingroup.com
Acquired Intelligence Inc.	aiinc.bc.ca	Adlan Computer Services	adlan.com
Acres International Limited	acres.com	Adlon Publishing	adlon.com
Act III Design & Construction Ltd.	act3.com	Admax Regent International Management Limited	admaxregent.com
Act Informatique Inc.	act.qc.ca	Administrative Computer Technology	admincomp.mb.ca
Act-Com Consulting Inc.	act-com.ca		
ACTC Technologies Inc.	actc.ab.ca	ADN Quebec	smartdrink.com
Actiforme Inc.	actiforme.qc.ca	Adnois Research Inc.	adnoisresearch.com
Action Art Actuel Inc	action-art-actuel.qc.ca	Adonis Research Inc.	adonisresearch.com
		ADP Systems Partnership	adpsystems.mb.ca
Action Communications, Inc.	actioncom.com	Adrain Lee	dragonboat.com
Active Components Inc.	active.ca	Adria Impex Inc.	adr.com
Active Creative Technologies Inc.	actcorp.com	ADT Canada Inc.	adt.ca
Active Living Canada Ltd.	activeliving.ca	Adult Alliance Marketing	sexonthenet.com

Name of Organization	Domain	Name of Organization	Domain
Adult Superstore Corporation, O/A The Adult Superstore ™	superstore.ca	AED Internet Communications, Inc.	aed.net
Advance Electronics	advance.mb.ca	AEGO Consulting Inc	aego.ca
Advance Multimedia	advancemm.com	AEGO Consulting Inc	aego.com
Advanced Biological Products Inc.	abp.com	AEI Enterprises Ltd.	aei-enterprises.com
		Aerodat, Inc.	aerodat.com
Advanced Cultural Technologies Inc.	actinc.bc.ca	Aetna Life Insurance Company Of Canada	aetnacan.com
Advanced Datasystems Inc.	ads.ca	Aetna Trust Company	aetna-trust.com
Advanced Education Council of B.C.	aecbc.bc.ca	AFE Ltd.	afe.com
		Affinity Associates, Inc.	affinity.on.ca
Advanced Gravis Computer Technology Ltd.	gravis.com	Affinity Edge Inc.	affinityedge.ca
Advanced Image Communications	aic.com	Affinity Edge Inc.	affinityedge.com
		Affinity Systems	affsys.com
Advanced Information Technologies Corporation	ait.ca	AFG Industries Ltd.	afg.com
		AFI Communications	aficom.com
Advanced Internet Communications	addcom.com	Afternet	loom.com
		Afternet Inc.	afternet.ab.ca
Advanced Motion And Controls Ltd.	advm-c.com	Agassiz North Associates Ltd.	agaznrth.mb.ca
Advanced Multi-Point Conferencing Inc.	amc.ca	Agence Zone Communications	ERR
Advanced Radiodata Research Centre	arrc.ca	Agent's Equity Inc.	agentsequity.com
		AGF Management Ltd	agf.ca
Advanced Scientific Computing	asc.on.ca	Agfa Canada Inc.	agfa.ca
		Agile Systems Inc.	agilesys.com
Advanced Technology Centre	atc.edmonton.ab.ca	Agiss Power Technologies Corporation	agiss.com
Advanced Technology For Business	tourismniagara.com		
		Agoratech Canada Inc.	agoratech.ca
Advanced Trading Technology Group	collective.com	Agra Industries	agra.ca
		Agri-Smart Consulting	agrismart.on.ca
Advanet Technologies Inc.	advanet.com	Agriculture Canada	agr.ca
Advantage Computers Ltd.	advantage.com	Agriculture Canada, Policy Branch	fdpd-agcan.org
Advantedge Corp.	edge.ca		
Advantis Canada	advantis.ca	Agrivalu Technologies Corp.	agrivalu.ca
Adventure Drive Ltd.	adventuredrive.ca	Agronomix Software, Inc.	agronomix.mb.ca
Adventure Tours	advtours.com	Agropur	agropur.ca
Adventure Tours Limited	adventure.ca	AGT Advanced Communications Ltd.	agtac.net
Adventures En Excellence Inc.	aei.ca		
Adventures En Excellence Inc.	aei.net	AGT Directory Ltd.	agtdir.com
Adworld International Inc.	adworld.on.ca	AGT Limited	agt.ab.ca
AEC Infonet Inc.	aec-info.com	AGT Limited	agt.net

Name of Organization	Domain	Name of Organization	Domain
AGT Limited	alta.net	Alberta College	abcollege.ab.ca
Ahearn And Soper Inc.	ahearn.com	Alberta Educational Communications Corporation (Access Network)	accessnet.ab.ca
Ahlea Systems Corp.	ahlea.com		
Ahmadiyya Movement In Islam Ontario Inc.	ahmadiyya.org	Alberta Educational Technology & Research Foundation	educ.ab.ca
Al Axion Internet Communications Inc.	axion.net	Alberta Energy Company Ltd.	aec.ca
AIC Asia International Corporation	aicyvr.com	Alberta General Provincial Children's Hospital	child-hosp.ab.ca
AIM Systems	aim-systems.on.ca	Alberta Heritage Foundation for Medical Research, The	ahfmr.ab.ca
Ainsworth Technologies, Inc.	ainsworth.com	Alberta Hotels Association	aha.ab.ca
Aiolos Engineering Corporation	aiolos.com	Alberta Internet Communications Corp.	abcom.com
Air Canada	aircanada.ca	Alberta Legislative Assembly	assembly.ab.ca
Air Nova Inc.	airnova.ca	Alberta Medical Association	amda.ab.ca
Air Ontario Inc.	airontario.ca	Alberta Motor Association	ama.ab.ca
Air-Sea Research	as-res.com	Alberta Natural Gas	angnet.com
Air-Sea Research Ltd.	as-res.bc.ca	Alberta Newsprint Co.	altanewsprint.ca
AirBC	airbc.com	Alberta Packet Radio Network	ampr.ab.ca
Airline Crew Hotels Inc.	ac-hotels.com	Alberta Printed Circuits Ltd.	apcircuits.com
Airlink Software	airinfo.com	Alberta Provincial Government	gov.ab.ca
Airlink Software	airlink.org		
Airmiles	airmiles.com	Alberta Public Safety Services	apss.ab.ca
Airmiles Leisure Travel Inc	airmiles.ca	Alberta Regional Network	arnet.ab.ca
Airqual Consulting	airqual.mb.ca	Alberta Research Council	arc.ab.ca
AIS Advanced Information Systems Ltd.	ais.bc.ca	Alberta Stock Database Ltd.	altabase.com
		Alberta Stock Database Ltd.	altastock.com
AIS Advanced Information Systems Ltd.	aisnet.com	Alberta Supernet Incorporated	supernet.ab.ca
AIS Multiline	aismulti.com	Alberta Urban Municipalities Association	auma.ab.ca
Aislin Inc	aislin.qc.ca		
Aitken Johnson Associates Inc.	aitkenjohnson.com	Alberta Vocational College-- Calgary	avc.calgary.ab.ca
Ajax Shuttle BBS	ajaxshuttle.com		
AJDJ, Inc.	zeus.org	Alberta Weekly Newspapers Association	awna.ab.ca
Akran Systems Corp.	akran.ca	Alberta Wheat Pool	awp.com
Alacrity, Inc.	alacrity.com	Alcan Aluminium Ltd.	alcan.ca
Aladdin's Palace BBS Ltd.	aladdin.bc.ca	Alcan Smelters and Chemicals Ltd.	sno.net
Alan James	handshake.com		
Alan Mayhew Consulting	webvest.com	Alcatel Canada Wire, Inc.	alcatel.ca
Alan Shefsky	shefsky.com	Alchemedia Design Group	alchemedia.net
Alberta Cancer Board	cancerboard.ab.ca		

Name of Organization	Domain	Name of Organization	Domain
Alda Technologies	alda.com	Alpa Roof Trusses Inc.	alpart.com
Alert Music, Inc.	alertmusic.com	Alpha Designs	alphadsns.com
Alex Informatique Inc.	alex.qc.ca	Alpha Designs	stash.com
Alexander, Holburn, Beaudin & Lang Management Limited Partnership	ahbl.bc.ca	Alphabyte Inc.	alphabyte.qc.ca
		Alphacom Communications	alphacom.com
Alexandra Projects Limited, The	tap.bc.ca	Alphacom Enr.	alphcom.qc.ca
Algo Design Inc.	algodesign.qc.ca	Alphacom.Com	canadatravel.com
Algoma District Social Services Association	adss.on.ca	Alphacom.Com	travelcanada.com
		Alphanet Telecom, Inc.	interpost.com
Algoma Experts	algoma-exp.com	Alphen International Inc.	alphen.on.ca
Algoma University College	auc.on.ca	Alpine Computers Ltd.	alpine.ca
Algonquin College of Applied Arts and Technology	algonquinc.on.ca	Alroma Scientifique Inc.	alroma.com
		Alt Society, The	alt.ns.ca
Algonquin Travel	algotrav.com	Alta-Can Tours, Inc.	altacan.ab.ca
Algorithmics Inc.	algorithmics.com	Altagas Services Inc.	altagas.ca
Alias Research, Inc.	alias.com	Altair Electronics Ltd.	altair.on.ca
Alis Technologies Inc.	alis.ca	Altantic Connect Inc.	mysteries.com
Alis Technologies Inc.	alis.com	Altcom Business Data Inc.	altcom.on.ca
All Systems Go	asgo.net	Altel Canada Division of 1036084 Ontario Inc.	altel.com
All World Holdings, Ltd.	lagviole.com		
All-Tech Services	altec.com	Altera Systems Corporation	altera-systems.com
Allan Crawford Associates Ltd	aca.ca	Alteris Inc.	alteris.ca
Allante BBS	allante.net	Alternate Source Components, Ltd.	alternatesrc.com
Allard Communications Inc.	allard.com		
Alliance Action, Inc.	allianceaction.ca	Alternate Sources	alternate.com
Alliance Communications Incorporated	alliance.ca	Alternatives Information Systems	alternatives.com
		Altersys Inc.	altersys.com
Alliance Productions	reboot.org	Alumni Association of the University Of Manitoba, The	umalumni.mb.ca
Allied Canadian Corporation	allied.ca		
Allied Domeq Spirits & Wine	allieddomecq.com	Always An Adventure Enterprise Inc.	an-adventure.com
Allink Communications, Inc.	all-link.com		
Allinson-Ross Corporation	allross.com	Amaron Canada	amaron.com
Allo Stop Ltd	allostop.com	Amav Industries	amav.com
Allon, Morris, Garber and Fiss	allonpsych.com	AMB Inc.	amb.ca
		AMB Inc.	amb.com
Allsco Building Products Ltd.	allsco.ca	Ambassade de France	ambafrance.org
Allstate Insurance of Canada	allstate.ca	Ambassador Board BBS	ambassador.com
Almanac User's Group	almanac.bc.ca	Amberdon, Inc.	amberdon.com
Almerco, Inc.	almerco.ca	Amdahl Software Development Centre	amdahlcsdc.com
Almitra Consulting Inc.	almitra.mb.ca		

Name of Organization	Domain	Name of Organization	Domain
Amdica Capital Corporation	amdica.com	Andre Transport & Machinery Inc.	atm.qc.ca
American Killifish Association	aka.org	Andrew Chartwell & Company	chartwell.com
American Pacific Data Services	ampac.com	Andrew Cochran	adonai.org
American Sensors Electronics Inc.	asei.com	Andrew Cochran Associates	cochran.com
American Sightseeing Montreal	graylinemontreal.com	Andrew D. Morrow	packet.org
American Sightseeing Vancouver	vancouvertours.com	Andrew Haigh	haigh.com
		Andyne Computing Limited	andyne.on.ca
American Sightseeing Victoria, B.C.	graylinevictoria.com	Angiogenesis Technologies Inc.	angio.com
American Yard Products	paramount2.com	Anglican Church Of Canada, The	anglican.ca
Amerisys Inc.	amerisys.com	Angoss Software	angoss.com
Amex Canada Inc.	amex.ca	Angular Momentum Graphics	angular.com
Ami Microage Inc.	ami.qc.ca	Angus Reid Group	angusreid.com
Amico Corporation	amico.com	Angus Telemanagement Group Inc	angustel.ca
Amiga Mail Service BBS	amsbbs.bc.ca	Angus Telemangement Group Inc	angustel.com
Amiga Users Of Victoria	amusers.victoria.bc.ca	Aniq Ltd.	aniq.com
Amitrix Development	amitrix.com	Anitech Identification Systems	anitech.com
Amous I.D. Intelligence Database	amous.ca	Anitech Identification Systems Inc.	anitech.ca
AMT Solutions Group Inc (Island Net)	islandnet.com	Anne Black Communications	virtual-astrology.com
		Annex Inc.	annexpro.com
AMT Solutions Group Inc.	amtsgi.bc.ca	Annova Business Group Inc	annova.ca
Amtak Manufacturing, Inc.	amtak.com	ANO Office Automation	ano.com
Anachemia Solvents	anachemia.com	ANO Office Automation Ltd.	annova.com
Anaco Communications	windowontheworld.com	Another Roadside Attraction Touring Inc.	roadside.ca
Anadas Software Development	anadas.com	Ansatel Business Telephone and Voice Mail Systems	ansatel.com
Anais2	anais2.com	Ansco Information Systems Ltd.	ansco.ca
Analog Services Informatiques (1993) Inc.	analog.ca	Answer Plus Inc.	answer-plus.on.ca
Analysis Electronics Ltd.	ael.ca	Antares Alliance Group	toraag.com
Analysys Inc.	analysys.com	Antel Optronics Inc.	antel.on.ca
Anarchia Underground Society	aus.org	Anthon Pang	ocpnet.com
		Anthropy	anthropy.com
Anchises Investments Ltd.	anchises.com	Anza Travel Ltd	anza-travel.com
Anderson Associates Consulting Engineers Inc.	aace.ab.ca	AP Internet Services	apis.com
		Apak Systems, Inc.	apak.com
Anderson Sinclair	maccollect.com		

Name of Organization	Domain	Name of Organization	Domain
Apase	apase-equity.org	Arachnae Management Limited	arachnae.com
Apchq	apchq.com	Arafat Consulting	arafat.com
Apex Advanced Technologies Inc	apextor.com	Arakis Energy Corp.	arakis.com
Apex Advanced Technologies, Inc.	apex.ca	Aratar Management Corporation	aratar.mb.ca
APG Technologies Inc.	apg.ca	Arbor Vitae Inc.	arbor.ca
APG Technologies Inc.	apg.com	Arcane Computer Consulting	arcane.calgary.ab.ca
Aphelion Informatics Inc.	aphelion.com	Arch Systems	arch.org
Apollo Travel Inc.	apollo-travel.com	Archelon Inc.	archelon.com
Apotex Fermentation Inc.	apoferm.mb.ca	Archibald Clarke & Defieux Insurance	acd-insurance.com
Apotex Inc.	apotex.ca	Archinfo Incorporated	archinfo.com
Appland Microsystems	appland.com	Architech Microsystems Inc.	architech.on.ca
Apple Canada Inc.	apple.ca	Architectural Institute of British Columbia	aibc.bc.ca
Appleby College	appleby.on.ca	Arctic Co-Operatives Limited	arcticcoop.ca
Applewood Centre For Spirituality	applewood.com	Arena Communications Inc.	arena.com
Applican Marketing Systems, Inc.	applican.com	Arete Development Corporation Canada Inc.	adc.ca
Application Enhancements Inc.	aei.on.ca	Arete Software Inc.	arete.ca
Applied Analytics Corporation	aac.on.ca	Argus Control Systems Ltd	argus-controls.com
Applied Financial Systems Inc.	afsys.com	Argus Technologies	argusmap.com
Applied High Technology Aht Group Inc.	ahtgroup.com	Ariad Custom Publishing, 000865827 Ontario Ltd.	ariad.on.ca
Applied Information Management Services Inc.	aims.on.ca	Ark Global Networking, Inc.	globalark.com
		Arly Fashion Imports Inc.	arly.com
Applied Logic Systems Inc.	healthreach.com	Armchair Airlines Computer Services Inc.	armchair.mb.ca
Applied Microelectronics Institute	appliedmicro.ns.ca	Armstrong Electronic Communications	barmstrong.com
Applied Silicon Inc. (Canada)	asican.on.ca	Armstrong Funeral Home	armstrong-fnrl.com
Applied Terravision Systems	atsi.com	Armstrong Funeral Home	funeral.net
Appropriate Entertainment Ltd.	appropriate.com	Armstrong/Spallumcheen School District	schdist21.bc.ca
Appropriate Entertainment Ltd.	extraordinary.com	Armtec Construction Products	armtec.com
Aprotec Canada Ltd.	aprotec.com	Arnold Computers Ltd.	arnoldcomp.mb.ca
APT Innovations	aptinno.com	Around The Sun Travel	atstravel.com
Aquatic Sciences Inc.	aquatic.com	Arqana Technologies Inc.	arqana.com
Aquilini Investment Group	aquilini.com	Array Development	arraydev.com
Aquilium Software Corporation	aquilium.com	Array Systems Computing Inc.	array.ca
ARA Consulting Group	aragroup.ca		

Name of Organization	Domain	Name of Organization	Domain
Arraytech Systems Ltd.	atech.bc.ca	Assiniboine South School Division	assd.winnipeg.mb.ca
Arris Design And Development Limited	arris.on.ca	Associate Software Concepts	asc.net
Arrogant Worms	arrogant-worms.com	Associated Telephone Industries (ATI)	assoc-tel.com
ARS Technical Images	fotog.com	Association Canadienne-Francaise pour l'Avancement des Sciences (ACFAS)	acfas.ca
Artecon Canada Inc.	artecon.on.ca		
Artefact Informatique Inc.	artefact.qc.ca		
Artful Dodger Communications Inc.	artful.com	Association des Fournisseurs Internet du Quebec, Inc.	afiq.org
Arthur Gelgoot and Associates	ag.toronto.on.ca	Association for Community Living of Ontario, Inc.	acl.on.ca
Arts Alliance of British Columbia Ltd.	artsbc.bc.ca	Association Internationale des Loteries d'Etat Inc.	aile.qc.ca
Artsmarketing Service Inc.	artsmarketing.com	Association of BC Professional Foresters	rpf-bc.org
Artworld Ltd.	artworknet.com		
Arvic Search Services Inc.	arvic.com	Association of Canadian Community Colleges	www.accc.ca
Asa Consulting Ltd.	asa.ca		
Ascent Power Technology Inc.	ascent.ca	Association of Canadian Publishers	canbook.org
Ascii Binary Advertising Company	carnal.com	Association of Exploration Geochemists	aeg.org
Ascom Timeplex Canada	ascom-timeplex.ca	Association of Professional Engineers and Geoscientists of B.C.	apeg.bc.ca
Ascot Financial Services	ascot.com		
Ascot Financial Services Ltd.	ascot.bc.ca		
ASDN Incorporated	asdn.on.ca	Association of Professional Engineers of Manitoba (Apem), The	apem.mb.ca
Ashley Computer Systems Inc	ashley.com		
Ashlin Computer Corporation	ashlin.on.ca	Association of Professional Engineers of Nova Scotia, The	apens.ns.ca
Asia Pacific Foundation of Canada	apfnet.org		
Asimware Innovations Inc.	asimware.com	Association of Universities and Colleges of Canada	aucc.ca
ASL Analytical Service Laboratories Ltd.	asl-labs.bc.ca	Association Quebecoise Informaticiens Independants du Quebec	aqiii.org
Aspen Computing Solutions (Edmonton) Inc.	aspen.ab.ca		
Assemblee Nationale du Quebec / Quebec National Assembly	assnat.qc.ca	Association Québécoise des Utilisateurs de l'Ordinateur au Primaire et au Secondaire (AQUOPS)	aquops.qc.ca
Assertive Marketing Services Inc.	assertive.com	Astech Solutions Inc.	astech.com
		ASTI Consultants	t8000.com
Asset Computer Personnel Limited	asset.ca	Astoret Inc	astoret.qc.ca
		Astra Network	man.net
Assiniboine Community College	assiniboinec.mb.ca	Astra Pharma Inc.	astrapharma.on.ca
		Astral Communications Inc.	astral.com

Name of Organization	Domain	Name of Organization	Domain
Astrochild Software	astrospace.com	Atomic Broadcast Design	atomic-broadcast.com
Astroff Corkum Ross Associates, Inc.	acr.com	Atomic Energy Control Board	atomcon.ca
Async BBS	async.org	Atomic Energy Of Canada Limited	aecl.ca
AT Communications	atcomm.com	Atomic Ski Canada, Inc.	atoskican.com
AT Communications Inc.	aimcorp.com	Atreide Enr.	atreide.net
AT&T Canada Inc.	att.ca	ATS Aerospace Inc.	ats.qc.ca
ATCI	atci.com	ATS Automation, Inc.	atsauto.com
ATCI	econocall.com	Attache Data Link	airres.com
ATCI	maxcor.com	Attaina Information Services Inc.	attaina.com
ATD Ltd	hejira.com	Attic Enterprise	attic.bc.ca
Athabasca University	athabascau.ca	Attic Enterprise	attic.com
Athapap Canada	athapap.com	Attica Equipment Ltd.	attica-equip.com
ATI Aero Technology Inc.	atiaero.com	Attractions Ontario	attractions.on.ca
ATI Technologies Inc.	atitech.ca	Auctions	auctions.net
Atkinson-Dennis Technologies, Inc.	adtechno.com	Audio Online Inc.	audio-online.on.ca
Atlantic Business Connections Network Co. Ltd.	abcnet.nb.ca	Audio Online Incorporated	audio-online.com
Atlantic Canada Opportunity Agency	acoa.ca	Augustana University College	augustana.ab.ca
Atlantic Centre for Remote Sensing of the Oceans	acrso.ns.ca	Ault Foods Limited	aultfoods.ca
		Aupelf-Uref	refer.org
Atlantic Computer Institute	aci.ns.ca	Aupelf-Uref, Reseau Electronique Francophone pour l'Education et la Recherche	refer.qc.ca
Atlantic Connect Inc.	atcon.com		
Atlantic Geomatics Reasearch Incorporated	agri.ns.ca	Aurelius Software Corporation	aurelius.com
Atlantic Lottery Corporation	alc.ca	Aurigor Engineering Inc.	aurigor.com
Atlantic LRMI	lrmi.com	Aurora Cable Internet Ltd.	aci.on.ca
Atlantic Mercantile Company	amco.com	Aurora Communications Exchange	acemail.com
Atlantic Netcom Ltd.	netcom.ca	Aurora Microsystems Inc.	amsi.com
Atlantic Satellite Network Inc.	asn.ca	Austin Cara	investoffshore.com
Atlantic Systems Group (ASG (R))	atlsysgrp.nb.ca	Austin Knight Canada Inc.	akto.ca
Atlantic Television System Inc.	atv.ca	Australian Consulate	australian-con.com
Atlantic Universities Athletic Association	auaa.ca	Autobody Web Services	autobody.com
		Autobus Auger Inc	auger.ca
Atlantis Aerospace	atlantis.com	Autodata Marketing Systems, Inc.	adms.com
Atlantis Scientific Systems Group Inc.	atlsci.com		
Atlas Graham Industries Ltd.	atlasgraham.mb.ca	Autolab Systems	autolabsystems.com
Atlas Tube	atlastube.on.ca	Autolog Inc	autolog.com

Name of Organization	Domain	Name of Organization	Domain
Automated Software Design Systems	asds.com	Axion Internet Communications Inc.	axionet.com
Automated Systems Group	autosysgr.nb.ca	Axis Integration Inc.	axisint.com
Automation Systems Associates Ltd.	asa.bc.ca	Axys Group Services Ltd.	axys.com
Automation Works Inc.	automators.com	Ayotte Custom Drums	ayottedrums.com
Automotive Retailers Association	bcara.com	Azimuth Arts	azimutharts.com
Automotive Video Productions	automotivevideo.com	Aztec	aztec.ca
Autonet	autolinq.com	Aztec	aztec.net
Autoship Systems Corporation	autoship.com	Aztec	aztec.org
Autosystems Inc.	autosystems.ca	B&H Income Tax Service	bhits.mb.ca
Avaaz Innovations, Inc.	avaaz.com	B.A.R. Environmental Inc	barenviro.com
Avalon Software & Computers Inc.	avalon.nf.ca	B.C. Automotive Dealers Association	bcada.com
Avant Imaging and Information Management	aiim.com	B.C. Central Credit Union	bcccu.com
		B.C. Centre for International Education	bccie.bc.ca
Avant Management Consultants	avant.com	B.C. Children's Hospital	childhosp.bc.ca
Avant Management Consultants	insource.com	B.C. Filmnet	filmbc.com
Avantel Consulting, Inc.	avantel.com	B.C. Real Estate Services	bcrealestate.com
Avanti Inc.	avanti.ca	B.C. School District 22	sd22.bc.ca
Avcorp Industries	avcorp.com	B.C. School District 40	sd40.bc.ca
Avec Technical Services	avec.com	B.C. School District 45	sd45.bc.ca
Avenet Communications	avenet.com	B.C. School District 56 (Nechako)	sd56.bc.ca
Avenor Inc.	avenor.com	B.C. School District 62 (Sooke)	sd62.bc.ca
Avenue Park Entertainment	avenuepark.com		
Aver Media	aver.com	B.C. School District 69	sd69.bc.ca
Avesta Sheffield Inc.	avesta-canada.com	B.C. School District 71	sd71.bc.ca
Aviation Trader Magazine	aviationtrader.com	B.C. Silver Junior High School	bcsilver.halifax.ns.ca
Avita Technologies Corp.	avita.com	B.C. Transit	bctransit.com
Avon Glocal Network Limited	glocal.net	B.C. Women's Hospital And Health Centre	womenhosp.bc.ca
AVR Corporation	avrcorp.com	Babillard Com18	com18.com
Avtech Electrosystems, Ltd.	avtechpulse.com	Babillard Synapse Inc.	isis.org
Awear Clothing Inc.	awear.com	Babillard Synapse Inc.	synapse.net
Awnix Software	fortress.org	Babinszki Consulting Services	babinszki.ca
Axelco	axelco.ca	Babylon X BBS	babylonx.com
Axia International Inc.	axia.com	Bagh Technologies Inc.	architrion.com
Axiom Engineering Limited	axiom.nf.ca	Bahai Connect	bcon.com
Axiomatic Technologies Corporation	axiomatic.com	BAHD Enterprises	bahd.com

Name of Organization	Domain	Name of Organization	Domain
Bahn Interactive Technologies	bahn.com	Barrington Petroleum Ltd.	barrington.com
Baird and Associates	baird.com	Barrington Promotions	mopar.com
Bale Communications Inc.	adnews.com	Barry Swanson	esales.com
Ballard Battery Systems	bstar.com	Barter Business Exchange	barter-business.com
Ballard Power Inc.	ballard.com	Bartok Cruise Brokers	loveboat.com
Ballistic Energy Corporation	ballistic.ca	Barton & Company	law.org
Balron Systems	balron.com	Baseline Type and Graphics Cooperative	baseline-graphics.com
BAMF Corporation	bamf.com	Basics Office Products	basics.com
Bamfield Marine Research Station	bms.bc.ca	Bata Limited	bata.ca
Banff Centre for Continuing Education, The	banffcentre.ab.ca	Bata Limited	bata.com
		Baton Broadcasting Inc.	baton.com
Banff Publishing Workshop	bpw.org	Baxter Foods Limited	baxterfoods.nb.ca
Bangon Productions	bangon.com	Baydel North America Inc.	baydel.ca
Bank of Canada	bank-banque-canada.ca	Baydel North America Inc.	compusolve.com
		Bayleaf Software Inc.	bayleaf.com
Bank of Montreal	bmo.com	Bayleaf Software Inc.	bayleafsw.com
Bank of Montreal, The	bmo.ca	Bayne Systems	pcguitar.com
Bank of Nova Scotia, The	scotiabank.ca	Baynet Internet Services	baynet.net
Bannister Lake Software, Inc.	blsoft.com	Baynet Internet Services	baynet.thunder-bay.on.ca
Bansfield-Seguin	bsl.com		
Baran-Harper Group Inc.	baran-harper.com	Bayshore Trust Company	bayshoredirect.com
Barbican Properties Ltd	barbican.com	Bayside Consulting Services	canlaw.net
Barcode Applications Ltd.	barcode.bc.ca	Bayside Consulting Services Ltd.	commercial.net
Barcode Graphics	barcodegraphics.com		
		Baystreet Document Systems Inc.	baystreetdoc.com
Bare Metal Designs	baremetal.com		
Baremetal Designs	baremetal.bc.ca	Baystreet Manufacturing	healthguard.com
Bargonier & Associates, Inc.	bai.on.ca	Bayview Glen	bvg.on.ca
Barn ™, Applecroft Information Systems Inc., The	thebarn.ca	BBA Communications Link Ltd.	audiotex.com
		BBDO Canada, Inc.	bbdotor.com
Baron Insurance Services	baronins.com	BBM Bureau of Measurement	bbm.ca
Barr Business Systems	barrbusiness.com	BC Advanced Systems Institute	asi.bc.ca
Barrick Gold Inc.	barrick.ca	BC Adventures	bc-ad.bc.ca
Barrie and District Real Estate Board Inc.	barreb.on.ca	BC Alpine Ski Association	bc-alpine.bc.ca
		BC Alpine Ski Association	bcalpine.com
Barrie Computer Mart Inc.	bcmnet.com	BC Biotechnology Alliance	biotech.bc.ca
Barrie Connex Inc.	connex.net	BC Choral Federation	bcchoralfed.com
Barrie Connex, Inc.	bconnex.net	BC Courthouse Library Society	bccls.bc.ca
Barrie Internet Inc.	barint.on.ca	BC Dairy Foundation	bcdf.org
Barrigar & Moss	barrmoss.com		

Name of Organization	Domain	Name of Organization	Domain
BC Dairy Herd Improvement Services	bcdhis.com	Beakbane Marketing Inc.	beakbane.com
BC Federation of Agriculture Society	bcfa.bc.ca	Beame & Whiteside Software, Ltd.	bws.com
BC Ferry Corp.	bcferries.bc.ca	Beame and Whiteside Software, Ltd.	bw-software.on.ca
BC Government Employees' Union	bcgeu.bc.ca	Beamscope Canada Inc.	beamscope.com
BC Hot House	bchothouse.com	Bear Spots, Inc.	bearspots.com
BC Liquor Board	ade.com	Beatty, Franz & Associates, Ltd.	bfaltd.com
BC Medical Association	bcma.bc.ca	Beautiful British Columbia Magazine Corp.	bbcmag.bc.ca
BC Motion Picture Association	bcmpa.bc.ca	Beaver Lumber Company Limited	beaverlumber.ca
BC Pavilion Corporation	bcpavco.com	Beck Technologies	bectel.com
BC Provincial Government	gov.bc.ca	Beckett Technologies Corp.	becktech.ca
BC Realtor Net	bcrealtor.com	Bed and Breakfast Resource Centre	bednbreakfst.com
BC Rehab Society	bcrehab.vancouver.bc.ca	Bedford Institute of Oceanography	bio.ns.ca
BC Roadbuilders Assn.	roadbuilders.bc.ca	Bedlam Games Ltd.	bedlam-games.com
BC Sugar	sugar.com	Beehive Enterprises	beehive.mb.ca
BC Tel Advanced Communications	bctel.net	Beeman Inventions Ltd. (Manitoba)	beeminve.mb.ca
BC Telecom Inc.	bctel.com	Believer's On-Line Systems	beacom.com
BCAI Centre	bcai.org	Bell Advanced Communications Inc.	bac.ca
BCD Systems Inc.	bcds.com	Bell Advanced Communications, Div Of Bell Canada	bacomm.com
BCnet	bc.net		
BCnet	bcnet.bc.ca	Bell Advantage Business Centre	belltel.com
BCS Technology	bcs-tech.com	Bell Canada	accessbell.com
BCSL Inc.	bcsl.com	Bell Canada	bell.ca
BCtel Advanced Communications	bctel.bc.ca	Bell Canada - Communications	bellcan.com
BDM Information Systems Ltd.	bdm.ca	Bell Canada Employment	employabell.com
BDO Canada	bdo.ca	Bell Canada Enterprises Inc.	bce.ca
Be Considerate & Give A Share	bcgas.com	Bell Canada Inc.	bell.net
Be Crazy & Keen Society	becks.com	Bell Helicopter Textron	bhtc.com
Beachnet Association	beachnet.org	Bell Mobility Cellular	mobility.com
Beachweb Internet Services	beachweb.com	Bell Ontario	bellont.com
Beacon Communications	beacon.bridgetown.ns.ca	Bell Sygma	bellglobal.com
Beacon Communications Inc.	beaconcomm.com	Bell-Northern Research	bnr.ca
Beacon International Despatch Ltd.	beacon.ca	Bell/Mediatel	resonet.com
Beak Consultants Ltd.	beak.com		

Name of Organization	Domain	Name of Organization	Domain
Bellamy & Long	belong.com	BGI Systems Integration Ltd.	bgi.on.ca
Bellatrix Systems Corp.	belsys.com	BGW Multimedia Inc.	bgw.ca
Beltron, Information Technology Ltd.	beltron.com	BHN Construction Ltd	bhn-construction.com
Benchmark Reality Franchise Corp. O/A Homelife Realty Services	homelife.ca	BHP Diamonds Inc.	bhpdiamonds.com
		Bialik Hebrew Day School	bialik.on.ca
Benchmark Technologies Ltd.	ispw.com	Biblairie G.G.C Ltd.	biblairie.qc.ca
Benefits Interface	benefits.org	Biddenden Group Inc.	biddenden.com
Benjamin James Marketing and Advertising	benjames.com	Big V Pharmacies Co. Limited	bigv.com
		Biggs Industries, Inc.	biggs-ind.com
Bennett Gold Chartered Accountants Inc.	bennettgold.ca	Bilingual Plus Inc.	bplus.com
		Bimm Communications Group	bimm.com
Bennett Jones Verchere	bjv.ca	Bina Information Services, Inc.	bina.com
Benny's Bagels	bennys.com	Binary Workshop	reach.net
Bent Promotional Supply, Inc.	bent.com	Binary Workshop	workshop.net
Bentall Property Management Ltd.	bentall.com	Binatech Information Services Inc.	binatech.com
Benton Associates	benton.com	Binatech Information Services Inc.	binatech.on.ca
Berger and Associates	berger.ca		
Bergman Graphics	bergmans.com	Bingo Association of B.C.	bingo.org
Berkson Consulting	metaphone.com	Bingo Unlimited	bingonet.com
Bernard Podolski Design	bernie.com	Binnington Developement Corporation	binnington.com
Best Choice Hotels and Tours, Inc.	dynapro.com	Binomial Software	binomial.com
Bestway.Com, Bestway Tours & Safaris	bernini.com	Biokinetics & Associates Ltd.	biokinetics.com
		Biomira Inc.	biomira.com
Betacorp Technologies, Inc.	betacorp.com	Biopool Canada Inc.	biopool.on.ca
Betatron Sound & Signal Inc.	betatron.on.ca	Bioweb Incorporated	bioweb.org
Bethune Import-Export Ltd.	bethune.com	Birchmount Park Collegiate	bpci.org
Better Business Bureau of Mainland B.C.	bbbmbc.com	BIS Construction Select Ltd.	conselect.com
		Bishop Information Group Inc.	biginc.on.ca
Better Than Ever Tools	better-than-ever.com	Bishop's University	ubishops.ca
Between The Lines	btl.org	Bisnet BBS	bisnes.com
Beverage Recovery in Canada	brinc.org	Bitove Corporation	bitove.com
Bex Engineering Ltd.	bex.com	Bits & Bytes Computer Services	peeler.com
Bexx Design Inc.	bexx.com		
Beyen Corporation	beyen.com	Bizex Inc.	bizex.com
Beyond Words, Inc.	beyond-words.com	BKM Research & Development Inc.	bkm.ca
BFS Media Group Inc.	bfsmedia.regina.sk.ca		
		Black Board International	blackbd.com
BFS Media Group Inc.	bfsmedia.sk.ca	Black Gold Regional	blackgold.ab.ca

Name of Organization	Domain	Name of Organization	Domain
Black Sea Technologies Inc.	blacksea.com	Bob Henry	trbbs.org
Black's Photography	blackphoto.com	Bob's Nutbuster Inc.	busters.com
Black's Photography Corporation	blacks.ca	Boeing Canada	boeing.ca
Blake Coverett Development	bcdev.com	Bogomips Research Labs	bogomips.com
Blake, Cassels & Graydon	blakes.ca	Bohn & Associates	bohn.com
Blaney, Mcmurtry and Stapells	blaney.com	Boiler Inspection & Insurance Co.	biico.com
Blaneys Travel	blaneystravel.com	Bold Graghic Communication Ltd	boldgraphic.com
Blaupunkt Fan Club	blaupunkt.com	Bolduc Heritage Geneaology Corporation	bolduc.com
Blaze Telecommunications Inc.	blaze.bc.ca		
Bleumont Inc.	bleumont.com	Bombardier/Canadair	canadair.ca
Blizz Informatique Enr.	blizz.qc.ca	Bomem Inc.	bomem.qc.ca
Blizzard Publishing Inc.	blizzard.mb.ca	Bonder Bookstore	bonder.com
BLM Group Transportation	blmgrouptrans.com	Bondwatch Investments	bondwatch.com
BLMC Multimedia Services	blmc.com	Bonkers	bonkers.com
Bloc Quebecois	bloc.ca	Bonnechere Resources	bonnechere.on.ca
Blowhard Inflatable Sign Blanks Inc.	blowhard.com	Books For Business Inc.	booksforbusiness.on.ca
BLT Productions	reboot.com	Borden & Elliot	borden.com
Blue Bombers Winnipeg Footbal Club	bluebombers.com	Borden & Elliot	bordenelliot.com
Blue Cat Design	canadaonline.com	Borden & Elliot	businesscanada.com
Blue Globe Software	blueglobe.com	Border Network Technologies Inc.	border.com
Blue Mountain Resorts, Ltd.	bluemountain.on.ca	Boreal Laboratories Ltd	boreal.com
Blue Sky Freenet of Manitoba Inc.	freenet.mb.ca	Borealis Exploration Limited	borealis.com
Blue Water Media	stoked.com	Borealis Object Solutions, Inc.	borealis.ca
Blue World It Consulting Inc.	blue-world.net	Borland & Associates	chca.com
Bluesnorth	bluesnorth.com	Boss Systems Inc.	bossy.com
Bluesoft Systems Limited	bluesoft.ca	Bot Engineering Ltd.	botcorp.com
Bluesoft Systems Ltd.	bluesoftsys.com	Boulet Fermat Associates	bouletfermat.ab.ca
Blumer Le-Von Ltd.	blumer.com	Bourkas Corporation Systems Inc.	bcs.ca
BMC Health Associates Limited	pharm.com	Bouvry Bienvenu Castonguay & Associes Inc	bbcdesign.com
BMG Canada, Inc.	bmgcanada.com		
BMG Internet Resources	netresources.com	Boviteq Inc.	boviteq.com
BMR Communications	bmrc.com	Bow Software Inc.	bowsoft.com
BMW Canada Inc.	bmw.ca	Bowes Publishing Ltd.	bowes.com
Boart Longyear, Inc.	nmorissette.com	Bowest Computer Systems Ltd.	banff.net
Boart Longyear, Inc.	nmorrissette.com	Bowne de Montreal	bom.com
Boart Longyear, Inc.	sdsdrilling.com		

Name of Organization	Domain	Name of Organization	Domain
Boyle & Company Law Offices	boyleco.com	Bright Star Computer Services	bright-star.com
		Brincad Technologies, Inc.	brincad.com
Boyne Clark Incorporated	boyneclarke.ns.ca	Bristol Aerospace Ltd.	bristol.ca
BP Resources Canada Limited	bprc.ab.ca	British Columbia Association of Magazine Publishers, The	bcamp.bc.ca
BPI Business Planning and Instruction	bpiplan.com	British Columbia Automobile Association	bcaa.bc.ca
Brad's Cheap Network	raindogs.net	British Columbia Automobile Association	bcaa.com
Bradley Consulting	bradley.net		
Bradley Systems Incorporated	bradsys.com	British Columbia BBS Net	bcbbs.net
Bradson Personnel Services	bradson.com	British Columbia Drug and Poison Information Centre (Dpic)	dpic.bc.ca
Brak Systems Inc.	brak.com		
Branchez-Vous, Corpomedia Inc.	branchez-vous.qc.ca	British Columbia Hydro and Power Authority	bchydro.bc.ca
Brand Equities Marketing Consulting Group Inc.	brandequities.on.ca	British Columbia Institute of Technology	bcit.bc.ca
Brandon University	brandonu.ca	British Columbia Internet Association Inc.	bcia.bc.ca
Bravo Cable TV	bravo.ca		
Brazilian Plastics Corporation	plasticx.com	British Columbia Lotteries Corporation	ilid.org
Breakaway Tours	breakawaytours.com	British Columbia Research Corporation	bcr.bc.ca
Breakspear Consulting	breakspear.com		
Breakwater Resources, Ltd.	bwrbhk.com	British Columbia Systems Corporation	bcsystems.com
Brenrose Solutions	brenrose.com		
Brent Roberts Realty, Ltd.	rentown.com	British Columbia Teachers' Federation	bctf.bc.ca
Brentech Systems Ltd.	brensys.com	British Columbia Technology Industries Association	tia.bc.ca
Brentwood College Association	brentwood.bc.ca		
Bresver, Grossman, Scheininger & Davis	bgsdlawfirm.toronto.on.ca	British Virgin Islands Real Estate Services	brvirginislands.com
Bretech Engineering Ltd	bretech.com	Britton Jewellery Inc.	britton.com
Brewers Association Of Canada	brewers.ca	Brix Systems	brix.on.ca
		BRK Brands Canada, A Division of BRK Brands, Inc.	brkbrands.ca
Brewers Retail, Inc.	brewers.com		
Brian Dayes	no-load.com	Broadband Network Incorporated	bni.mb.ca
Brian Gerbrandt Reailty	rennie-realty.org		
Brian Gilhuly	kentrol.com	Brock University	brocku.ca
Bricolage Inc.	bricolage.com	Brockrust Ltd., O/A Candlewood Books	candlewood.mb.ca
Bridge City On-Line	saskatoon.com		
Bridge City Online	brcity.com	Brodie Morrice	bromo.com
Bridgetech Systems Inc.	bridgetech.com	Brompton Property Group Inc.	brompton.com
Brierley, Doucette & Simpson Consulting, Ltd.	bds.ca	Bronson Networks Inc.	bronson.ca
		Brooklyn North Software Works	brooknorth.bedford.ns.ca

Name of Organization	Domain	Name of Organization	Domain
Brother International Corporation (Canada) Ltd.	brother.ca	Burlington Public Library	bpl.on.ca
Brotherhood of Maintenance of Way Employees	bmwe.ca	Burlington Systems Integration	burlington.com
		Burmuda Real Estate Services	burmuda.com
Brouillette Charpentier Fournier	bcf.com	Burnaby Radio Communications Ltd.	burnabyradio.com
Brownlow, Thompson & Mckay	btmca.com	Burns Fry Limited	bfl.com
Bru*Net Inc.	brunet.nb.ca	Burnt Sand Solutions Inc,	burnt-sand.com
Brubacher Technologies Ltd	brutech.com	Burrowes Internet Marketing	businesses.com
Bruce Alan De Leenheer	gospel.net	Business Building Blocks	buildingblocks.com
Bruce Alan De Leenheer	gospel.org	Business Council on National Issues	bcni.com
Bruce Edmeades Sales, Ltd.	edmeades.on.ca	Business Data Systems	busdat.com
Bruce Grayson Consulting	quiz.com	Business Data Systems	webgate.net
Bruce Municipal Telephone Systems	bmts.com	Business Development Bank of Canada	bdc.ca
Bruins Juniors	bruins.com	Business Dimensions International Inc.	bdi-inc.com
Brunswick Micro Systems Inc.	brunswickmicro.nb.ca	Business Management Services Corp.	bmscorp.com
Bryan Adams	badman.com	Business Telecom Canada Inc.	business-telecom.com
Bryan, Fulton & Shee	bryantfs.com		
Bryant, Fulton, And Shee	bf-s.com	Busitech	busitech.com
Bryker Data Systems	bryker.com	Butchart Gardens Ltd., The	butchartgardens.bc.ca
Bsa Computer Services, Ltd.	bsa-ltd.com		
Bsoh Enterprises	bsoh.com	Butler Research Associates Inc.	butler.ca
Bubble Technology Industries Inc.	bubbletech.com	Butterfield And Robinson	bandr.com
Buck Consultants Ltd.	buck.ca	Butterfield And Robinson	butterfield.com
Buck Information Systems	bisinc.com	Butterfly Signal Processing Inc.	butterfly.com
Buckingham Press	buckingham-press.com	Butterfly Wings	bwings.com
Buff-Mar Cartage Limited O/A Speedy Transport	speedy.ca	Butterworths Canada, Ltd.	butterworths.ca
Bull HN Information Systems Limited	bull.ca	Buyers Choice Products Inc.	westland.com
		Buz Co Ltd	buz.com
Bull Housse & Tupper	bht.com	Buzz Image Group Inc.	buzzimage.ca
Bulldog Group, Inc., The	bulldog.ca	Buzz Image Group Inc.	buzzimage.com
Bunyip Information Systems Inc.	bunyip.com	Buzzeo and Wood Adjusters Ltd.	buzzeo.ab.ca
Burchell Macdougall Inc.	burmac.ns.ca	BWH Technologies Inc.	bwh.com
Burchill Communications Research Group	burchill.ns.ca	By The Fire Thornhill Ltd.	by-the-fire.on.ca
Burke Robertson	burke-robertson.com	Bydesign Computer Systems Ltd.	bydesign.com

Name of Organization	Domain	Name of Organization	Domain
Byers Casgrain	byers.ca	Cableshare Inc.	cableshare.com
Byrne, Crosby	byrncros.com	Cabo Condo Rentals	cabo-condo.com
Byte Computers	byteshop.com	Cabot Institute of Applied Arts and Technology	cabot.nf.ca
Byte Computers Ltd.	byte.bc.ca	Cad/Cam Solutions of Canada	cadcam-sol.com
Byte Designs Ltd.	byted.com		
Byte Size Media	bytesize.com	Cadabra Design Libraries Inc.	cadabra.ca
Byteback Technologies	byteback.com	Caddversion Graphics	caddversion.com
Bytecraft Limited	bytecraft.com	Cadence Management	cadence.mb.ca
Bytewide Marketing	bytewide.ca	Cadence Technologies Ltd.	cadence.bc.ca
C & L Multi Media Distributions Inc.	cnl.com	Cadex Electronics Inc.	cadex.com
C Cubed Computing	ccubed.com	Cadhamhayes Systems Inc.	cadhamhayes.ca
C&C Yachts	ccyachts.com	Cadillac Fairview Corporation	cadillacfairview.com
C-Mac Electronic Systems Inc.	cmac.ca	Cadlink Technologies	cadlink.com
C-Rel Technologies	creltech.com	Cadsoft International	cadsoft.com
C. Paul & Associates, Inc.	cpaulinc.mb.ca	Cadvision Development Corp.	cadvision.com
C. R. Mcguffin Consulting Services	crmcg.com	CAE Electronics Ltd	cae.ca
		Caeware Inc.	caeware.com
C. S. St-Hyacinthe-Val-Monts	csshv.qc.ca	Cail Systems Ltd	cail.com
C.A. Mcintosh & Associates	expatriate.com	Cairn Croft Best Western Motel	cairncroft.com
C.A. Project Development Corp.	canadian-agra.com		
		Caisse de Depot et Placement du Quebec	cdpq.qc.ca
C.A.N.S.Y.S. West Limited	cansys.mb.ca		
C.D. Howe Institute	cdhowe.org	Cal Consultants, Inc.	cal.ca
C.G Plastics Engineering Inc.	cgplastics.ca	Cal Corp	calcorp.com
C.M.Whittaker and Associates Ltd.	cmw.ca	Caledon Dot Org	caledon.org
		Caledon Laboratories Limited	caledonlabs.ca
C.O.R.E Digital Productions	coredp.com	Calexis	ault.com
C.O.S.E. Inc	cose.com	Calgary	calgary.com
C3I Precision Instruments	c3i.com	Calgary Airport Authority	airport.calgary.ab.ca
Ca Project Development Corporation	bruce.net	Calgary Board of Education	cbe.ab.ca
		Calgary Chamber of Commerce	chamber.calgary.ab.ca
CA*Net	canet.ca		
Caballero's Restaurant	caballeros.com	Calgary Economic Development Association	ceda.calgary.ab.ca
Cable Atlantic Inc.	cableatlantic.nf.ca		
Cable Atlantic, Inc.	cableatlantic.net	Calgary Exhibition and Stampede	calgary-stampede.ab.ca
Cable Island Limited	cableisland.on.ca		
Cable Island Ltd.	cable.com	Calgary Free-Net Association	freenet.calgary.ab.ca
Cable Island, Ltd.	cable.org	Calgary Health Services	health.calgary.ab.ca
Cable Parliament Affairs Channel	cpac.ca	Calgary Medical Laboratories, Inc.	cml.ab.ca

Name of Organization	Domain	Name of Organization	Domain
Calgary Real Estate Board Co-Operative Ltd.	creb.ab.ca	Camosun College	camosun.bc.ca
Calgary Regional Health Authority	crha-health.ab.ca	Campana Systems Inc.	campana.ca
		Campana Systems, Inc.	campana.com
Calgary Research and Development Association	crda.calgary.ab.ca	Campbell Helicopters	helicopters.com
		Campbell River Community Network	cn.camriv.bc.ca
Calgary Sun	calsun.com	Campfire Design	campfire.com
Calgary Television	cict.com	Campney & Murphy	campney-murphy.com
Calgary Transportation Authority	cta.calgary.ab.ca	Campney & Murphy	campneymurphy.com
Calgary UNIX Connect	cuc.ab.ca	Campus Crusade for Christ, Canada.	crusade.org
Calgary UNIX User Group	cuug.ab.ca		
Calgary Visitor Board	visitor.calgary.ab.ca	Can Sol Computer Corporation	ccc.on.ca
Calgary Zoological Society	zoo.calgary.ab.ca	Can-Am Surveys Ltd.	canam.com
Calian Technology Ltd.	calian.ca	Can-Dive Marine Services Ltd.	can-dive.com
California Systems Design, Inc.	csdi.com	Can-Pay Computer Software Ltd.	canpay.ca
Call Center Products	headset.com		
Calliari Import & Export Ltd.	gourmetcuisine.com	Can-Text Entertainment Company	cantex.com
Calling Centre	callingcentre.com		
Callstream Communications Inc.	callstream.com	Can-Van Property Investments Ltd.	can-van.com
Calpurnia Communication Corporation	watchit.com	Canac International Inc.	canac.com
		Canaccord Capital Corp.	canaccord.ca
Cals Edms Inc.	cals-edms.ca	Canada Centre For Inland Waters	cciw.ca
Camagazine Publishing Co. Inc.	camagazine.ca	Canada Colors & Chemicals Ltd.	cancol.com
Cambrian College of Applied Arts and Technology	cambrianc.on.ca	Canada Communication Group - Groupe Communciation Canada	ccg-gcc.ca
Cambridge House Internet Publishing Inc.	cambridgehouse.com		
		Canada Computer Paper Inc.	tcpon.com
Cambridge Memorial Hospital	cmh.org	Canada Computer Paper Inc., The	tcp.ca
Cambridge Shopping Centres, Ltd.	cscl.ca	Canada Connect	canuck.com
Camelford Graham Research Group Inc.	camelfordgraham.on.ca	Canada Employment Centre	cecstcath.com
		Canada Internet Direct, Inc.	idmail.com
Camelot-Info Inc	camelot.ca	Canada Life Assurance Company	canadalife.com
Cameo Magazine	cameomag.com		
Cameo Systems	cameosys.com	Canada Loan Administration Service Inc.	clas.ca
Camli Resources	camli.com		
Camlink Inc.	camlink.net	Canada Mortgage & Housing Corporation	cmhc.ca
Camms Consulting Corp.	camms.ca		

Name of Organization	Domain	Name of Organization	Domain
Canada Newswire Ltd.	newswire.ca	Canadian Association of Customs Brokers	cacb.ca
Canada Nova Scotia Business Service Centre	can-nsbsc.halifax.ns.ca	Canadian Association of Japanese Car Dealers	cajad.com
Canada On-Line	canada.com	Canadian Association of Paediatric Surgeons	caps.ca
Canada On-Line	col.net		
Canada Online Inc.	canada-online.com	Canadian Association of Petroleum Producers	capp.ca
Canada Overdrive On-Line, Inc.	cool.mb.ca	Canadian Association of Radiologists	car.ca
Canada Post Corporation	canpost.ca		
Canada Pro Marketing & Distribution	canadapro.com	Canadian Association of University Teachers	caut.ca
Canada Remote Systems Limited	canrem.com	Canadian Automobile Association	caa.ca
Canada Remote Systems Limited	crso.net	Canadian Bacterial Diseases Network	cbdn.ca
Canada Steamship Lines Inc.	cslchina.com	Canadian Bankers Association	cba.ca
Canada Steamship Lines Inc.	cslmtl.com		
Canada Swan Intl Travel	csit.com	Canadian Blue Cross Life Association	bluecross.ca
Canada Trust Company	canadatrust.com	Canadian Bridge Federation Inc.	cbf.ca
Canada Trust Company	ctfs.com		
Canada Trustco Mortgage Company	yourlife.com	Canadian Broadcasting Corporation	cbc.ca
Canada West R.V. Vacations Inc.	motorhome.com	Canadian Bureau For International Education	cbie.ca
Canada West Tours	canwst.com	Canadian Business Directory Listing	cbdl.com
Canada's Premier Business Club	incentive.com		
Canada-Nova Scotia Offshore Petroleum Board	cnsopb.ns.ca	Canadian Cancer Society	cancer.ca
		Canadian Center for Management Development	ccmd.org
Canadelle Incorporated	canadelle.com	Canadian Centre for Architecture	cca.qc.ca
Canadian Advisory Council on the Status of Women	cacsw.ca	Canadian Centre for Occupational Health and Safety	ccohs.ca
Canadian Aerospace History BBS	aerohost.org		
Canadian Aids Society	casinc.org	Canadian Centre for Swine Improvement, Inc.	ccsi.ca
Canadian Airlines International Ltd.	cdnair.ca	Canadian Centre on Substance Abuse	ccsa.ca
Canadian Almanac & Directory Publishing Co. Ltd	canadainfo.com	Canadian Charter Corporation	jetcharters.com
Canadian Association of Career Educators and Employers	cacee.com	Canadian Coast Guard College/College de la Garde Cotiere Canadienne	cgc.ns.ca

Name of Organization	Domain	Name of Organization	Domain
Canadian Connections	cancon.mb.ca	Canadian Health Reform Products Ltd.	aliv.com
Canadian Consulate Trade Office	canada-trade-san jose.org	Canadian Hearing Society, The	chs.ca
Canadian Coordinating Office for Health Technology Assessment	ccohta.ca	Canadian Helicopters Corporation	chc.ca
Canadian Council for Public Private Partnerships	pppcouncil.ca	Canadian Hemophilia Society, Manitoba Chapter Inc., The	hemophilia.mb.ca
Canadian Council of Ministers of the Environment Inc. (CCME)	ccme.ca	Canadian Home and Office Computing	homeoff.com
Canadian Council on Animal Care	ccac.ca	Canadian Horticultural Therapy Association	thegarden.org
Canadian Cyberlink Inc	cyberlink.com	Canadian Human Rights Commission	chrc.ca
Canadian Dairy Network	cdn.ca	Canadian Imperial Bank of Commerce	cibc.ca
Canadian Data Communications Corporation	canadata.net	Canadian Industrial Innovation Centre	innovationcentre.ca
Canadian Diabetes Association	cda-nat.org	Canadian Info Tech, Inc.	cit.com
Canadian Dimension Magazine	canadiandimension. mb.ca	Canadian Information Processing Society	cips.ca
Canadian Dispute Resolution Corporation	cdrc.com	Canadian Institute For Health Information	cihi.ca
Canadian Earthcare Society	earthcare.org	Canadian Institute for Native Training and Development - Institut Canadien pour la Formation et le Developpement Autochtones	cintad.ca
Canadian Earthday Coalition	earthday.ca		
Canadian Educational Standards Institute	cesi.edu		
Canadian Egg Marketing Agency Inc.	canadaegg.ca	Canadian Institute for Native Training and Development	cintad.org
Canadian Electricity Association (Formerly Canadian Electrical Association)	canelect.ca	Canadian Institute for Radiation Safety	cairs.ca
		Canadian Institute of Actuaries	actuaries.ca
Canadian Energy Pipelines Association	cepa.com	Canadian Institute of Biotechnology (CIB)	biotech.ca
Canadian Facts	canfacts.com	Canadian Institute of Chartered Accountants	cica.ca
Canadian Fishing Company	canfisco.com		
Canadian Football League	cfl.ca	Canadian Institute of the Arts for Young Audiences, The	youngarts.ca
Canadian Forest Products Ltd.	canfor.ca		
Canadian Fracmaster	fracmaster.ca	Canadian Interagency Forest Fire Center Inc.	ciffc.ca
Canadian Gas Association	cga.ca		
Canadian Genetic Diseases Network	generes.ca	Canadian International Development Agency	devcan.ca
Canadian Greeting Card Corp. Ltd.	cangreet.ca	Canadian International Group	cig.ca

Name of Organization	Domain	Name of Organization	Domain
Canadian International Group	cig.com	Canadian Niagara Power	cnpower.com
Canadian Interuniversity Athletic Union	ciau.ca	Canadian Northern Shield	cnsic.org
		Canadian Nurses Association	cna-nurses.ca
Canadian Investor Protection Fund	cipf.ca	Canadian Occidental Petroleum Ltd.	canoxy.ab.ca
Canadian Jewish Congress	cjc.ca	Canadian Offshore Financial Services S.A.	newpac.com
Canadian Kennel Club	ckc.ca		
Canadian Landmasters Resource Services Ltd.	cdn-landmasters.com	Canadian Online Systems	cos.org
		Canadian Pacific Hotels & Resorts Inc	cphotels.ca
Canadian Language Technology Institute - Institut Canadien de Technologie Linguistique	clti-ictl.nb.ca	Canadian Payroll Association, The	payroll.ca
		Canadian Personnel Services Inc.	personnel.ca
Canadian Lutheran World Relief	clwr.mb.ca	Canadian Petroleum Internet Consortium	canpic.ca
Canadian Machinery Vibration Association	cmva.com	Canadian Plastics Institute	plasticsinstitute.ca
Canadian Marconi Company	marconi.ca	Canadian Press, The	canpress.ca
Canadian Market Images	cmi.on.ca	Canadian Produce Marketing Association	cpma.ca
Canadian Mathematical Society / Societe Mathematique du Canada	math.ca	Canadian Psychological Association	psychologyassoc.ca
Canadian Medical Association	canmed.ca	Canadian Public Health Association	cpha.ca
Canadian Medical Laboratories Limited	canmedlab.com	Canadian Publishers	cpcomm.mb.ca
Canadian Mennonite Bible College	cmbiblecoll.mb.ca	Canadian Red Cross Society, The	redcross.ca
Canadian Micro Development	canmicro.com	Canadian Regional Airlines Ltd.	cral.ca
Canadian Microelectronics Corporation/Societe Canadienne de Micro-Electronique	cmc.ca	Canadian Research of Transmittable Cryogenic "H"	crotch.com
		Canadian Resources Marketing Group	d-destinies.com
Canadian Mortgage Listings	canlist.com		
Canadian Museum of Nature	mus-nature.ca	Canadian Satellite Communications Inc.	cancom.ca
Canadian Music Exchange Inc.	cme.ca	Canadian Scholars' Press Inc.	cspi.org
Canadian Musical Reproduction Rights Agency Ltd (CMRRA)	cmrra.ca	Canadian Ski Patrol System—Organisation de la Patrouille Canadienne de Ski	csps.org
Canadian National Railways - CN Rail	cn.ca	Canadian Society for Civil Engineering	csce.ca
Canadian Nazarene College	cnaz.com	Canadian Society of Cinematographers Inc.	csc.ca
Canadian Nazarene College	cnaz.mb.ca		

Name of Organization	Domain	Name of Organization	Domain
Canadian Society of Technical Analists	csta.org	Cando Transport Systems	can-do-transport. on.ca
Canadian Space Agency	sp-agency.ca	Canespa International Inc.	canespa.ab.ca
Canadian Sport and Fitness Administration Centre	cdnsport.ca	Cangene Corporation	cangene.com
Canadian Standards Association	csa.ca	Canjex. Ltd.	canada-stockwatch. com
Canadian Stock Reporter Inc	canstock.com	Canlin Import Export Inc	canlin.com
Canadian Strategic Software Consortium (C.S.S.C.)	cssc.ca	Canmark Print Ltd	plasticard.com
		Canron Inc.	canron-calg.com
Canadian Taiwanese Trade Association	ctta.com	Cansec Systems, Ltd.	cansec.com
Canadian Teachers Federation	canteachfed.ca	Canstar Aviation Ltd.	canstar.com
Canadian Teachers' Federation	ctf-fce.ca	Cantech International	cantech.com
Canadian Telecom Services	cdntelecom.mb.ca	Cantest Ltd.	cantest.com
Canadian Tennis Association	tenniscanada.com	Cantox Inc.	cantox.com
Canadian Thermal Dynamics	cantherm.mb.ca	Cantox Incorporated	cantox.ca
Canadian Tire Acceptance Limited	ctal.com	Cantrac	cantrac.com
		Canucks Trading Post	canucks.com
Canadian Tire Corporation	cantire.com	Canusa Trading Company	canusa.com
Canadian Turbo (1993) Inc.	turbo.ca	Canviro Analytical Library, Ltd.	canviro.com
Canadian Union College	cauc.ab.ca	Canway Home Plan Inc.	canway.com
Canadian Union of Public Employees	solinet.org	Canweb Internet Services Ltd.	canweb.ca
		Canwest Global Systems	canwest.com
Canadian Utilities Limited	cul.ca	Cape Breton Adult Vocational Training Campus	cbavtc.ns.ca
Canadian Vocational Association	cva.ca	Cape Breton Development Corporation	devco.ca
Canadian Wheat Board	canwheatbrd.ca	Cape Breton Freenet Society	cbnet.ns.ca
Canadian Wheat Board, The	cwb.ca	Capetown Computing	capetown.com
Canadian Wildlife Federation	cwf-fcf.org	Capilano College	capcollege.bc.ca
Canadiens Fan Club	canadiens.com	Capilano Computing Systems Ltd.	capilano.com
Canadore College of Applied Arts and Technology	canadorec.on.ca	Capintel, Inc.	capintel.com
Canapro Employment Trainers Ltd.	canapro.bc.ca	Capital Gains Forecaster	cgf.com
		Capital Health Authority	cha.ab.ca
CANARIE Inc.	canarie.ca	Capital Learning Systems	caplearn.ca
Canaska Racing Team	canaska-indy.com	Capital Offense BBS	capoff.on.ca
Canatom Inc.	canatom.ca	Capital Regional District	crd.bc.ca
Canbra Foods Ltd.	canola.com	Capital-Image Inc.	capitalimage.qc.ca
Cancom Technologies	can.com	Capitalnet	capitalnet.com
Cancopy	cancopy.com	Capitecq Management I Inc.	jrv.com
Candles Unlimited	flames.com		

Name of Organization	Domain	Name of Organization	Domain
Capitecq Management I Inc.	jrv.net	Carto Logix	cartologix.com
Cara Informatique	carainfo.com	Casas Communications Engineering	cce.com
Cara Operations, Ltd.	cara.com		
Caracao Real Estate Services	caracao.com	Cascade Communications	primestock.com
Caradon Lockwood A Division of Caradon Limited	lockwood.ca	Cascadia Geomatic Services	cascadia-geo.com
		Cascadia Interactive Solutions Ltd.	cascadia.bc.ca
Caravan Consultants	caravan-con. toronto.on.ca	Case-Tech Leather Inc.	case-tech.com
Cardinal Capital, Inc.	cardinal-capital.com	Caseware Inc.	caseware.ca
Cardinal Capital, Inc.	fundnet.com	Cashhandler Retail Systems Inc.	chrs.com
Cardinal Switching Systems	telephone.net		
Care Canada	care.ca	Casino Ware Ltd	casinoware.com
Career Connection	the-enterprise.net	Casinonet Unlimited	casinonet.com
Career Development Institutes Ltd.	cdivic.com	Cask Brewing Systems	cask.com
		Caspar Computer Services Inc.	caspar.on.ca
Careware Inc.	careware.mb.ca		
Caribbean Realty	caribbeanrealty.com	Cassels Brock & Blackwell	casselsbrock.com
Cariboo College	cariboo.bc.ca	Cast Lighting, Ltd.	castltg.com
Cariboolinks Web Services	cariboolinks.com	Castek Software Factory	castek.com
Caribou Ventures Limited	caribou.mb.ca	Casti Publishing Inc.	casti-publishing.com
Caritas Health Care Institute	caritas.ab.ca	Casting And Media Online Inc.	cameo.on.ca
Carleton Board Of Education	carletonbe.ottawa. on.ca		
		Cat's Eye Technologies	cats-eye.com
Carleton University	carleton.ca	Cata (Canadian Advanced Technology Association)	cata.ca
Carlson Marketing Group Ltd.	cardhotline.com		
Carlson Marketing Group Ltd.	carlson-marketing. ca	Catalyst Business Incubator Inc.	catalyst.ca
Carlson Training Group	carlson-training.com	Catel Communications Inc.	catel.ca
Carlton Cards Limited	carltoncards.ca	Cato Internetwork Solutions Ltd.	cato.net
Carlton Cards Ltd.	carltoncards.com	Caught In The Web Inc.	citw.ca
Carlynd Holdings Ltd	revnet.net	CB Media, Ltd.	cbmedia.ca
Carlynd Holdings Ltd	revres.com	CBC Radio Vancouver	cbcradio.com
Carolian Systems Corp.	carolian.com	CBC Stereo	cbcstereo.com
Carolyn Publishing	carolyn.org	CBM Metal Products	cbmetal.com
Carp Systems International CSI Inc.	csi.on.ca	CCD Inc.	inc500.com
		CCI Industries	masonry.com
Carrtech Consulting Inc.	carrtech.com	CCI Networks, A Division Of Corporate Computers Incorporated	ccinet.ab.ca
Carswell - Div of Thomson Canada	carswell.com		
Carswell Publishing	tppint.com	CCL Group Ltd.	cclgroup.ca
Carte International Inc.	carte.ca	CCL Industries, Inc.	cclind.com

Name of Organization	Domain	Name of Organization	Domain
CCMR Computers	ccmr.com	Central Newfoundland Regional College	cnrcoll.nf.ca
CD Publishing Corporation	cdpublishing.com	Central Plains Incorporated	centralplains.mb.ca
CD Publishing Corporation	netnewscd.com	Centre d'Expertise et de Services en Applications Multimedias	cesam.qc.ca
CD-Powermedia Productions Inc.	cdpower.com		
CDN BBS	cdn.org	Centre de Recherche Industrielle du Quebec	criq.qc.ca
CDNNet	cdnnet.ca		
CDSL	cdsl.ca	Centre de Recherche Informatique de Montreal	crim.ca
CDX Systems	cdx.net		
CDX Systems, Inc.	cdxsystems.com	Centre de Recherche Volvox Inc.	volvox.qc.ca
Ceco Integration	cecotech.com		
Cedrom-Sni Inc.	cedrom-sni.qc.ca	Centre Entreprendre Inc.	centreprendre.qc.ca
Cegep de Levis-Lauzon	clevislauzon.qc.ca	Centre for Image and Sound Research	cisr.bc.ca
Cegep de Saint-Hyacinthe	cegepsth.qc.ca		
Cegep de Saint-Jérôme	cegep-st-jerome.qc.ca	Centre for Indigenous Environmental Resources	cier.mb.ca
Cegep du Vieux Montreal	cvm.qc.ca	Centre for Industrial And Commercial Intelligence	logisticus.com
Cegep Vanier College	vaniercollege.qc.ca		
Cek Associates Inc.	cek.com	Centre for Professional Learning	cenpro.com
Celeris Aerospace Canada Inc.	celeris.ca		
		Centre Francophone de Recherche en Informatique des Organisation (CEFRIO)	cefrio.qc.ca
Celeris Arespace Canada Inc.	celaero.com		
Celeste Crystal Systems Inc.	celeste.com		
Celestica	celestica.on.ca	Centre Microtech Inc.	microtech.qc.ca
Cello Communications Ltd.	cello.com	Centre Regional de Services aux Bibliotheques Publiques de la Monteregie Inc.	crsbp.qc.ca
CEM Specialties	cemsi.on.ca		
Cemetary Memorial Design	memdesign.com		
Cenosis	cenosis.com	Centre Universitaire de Shippagan	cus.ca
Centennial College	bccc.com		
Centennial College of Applied Arts and Technology	cencol.on.ca	Centre Universitaire Saint-Louis-Maillet	cuslm.ca
		Centres Canadiens CAO/FAO	c3cam.com
Center for Frontier Engineering Research	cfer.ab.ca	Centtric Marketing Systems, Inc.	centtric.com
Centra Gas Manitoba Inc.	centragas.mb.ca		
Centragas Ltd.	centragas.com	CEO Systems Enhancements	ceo-systems.com
Central Alberta Freenet Exchange	cafe.ab.ca	Cepiq Inc	cepiq.com
		Cerberus Information Security Consulting Inc.	cerberus.com
Central Algoma Board of Education	cabe.edu		
		Cerebral Music Corporation	cerebral.com
		Cerf Call Centres Inc.	cerf.on.ca
Central Canadian Structures Ltd.	ccsl.ca	Certified General Accountants' Association of Canada	cga-canada.org

Name of Organization	Domain	Name of Organization	Domain
Certified General Accountants' Association of Alberta	cga-alberta.org	CGA Of Atlantic Region Educationassocation	cga-area.org
		CGI Inc.	cgi.ca
Certified General Accountants' Association of Barbados	cga-barbados.org	CGI Information Systems And Management Consulting	cgigroup.com
		Ch2m Hill Engineering, Ltd.	ch2mcan.com
Certified General Accountants' Association of British Columbia	cga-bc.org	Challenge Business Systems	challenge.com
		Challenger Motor Freight Inc.	challenger.com
Certified General Accountants' Association of N.W.T.	cga-nwt.org	Champagne, Parent & Associes Inc.	cpa.qc.ca
Certified General Accountants' Association of New Brunswick	cga-nb.org	Champlain Regional College	champlaincollege.qc.ca
		Chan, Carey	multimania.com
Certified General Accountants' Association of Newfoundland	cga-newfoundland.org	Channel E Co.	reonline.com
		Channel One	channelone.com
		Channel One Internet Services	channelone.net
Certified General Accountants' Association of Nova Scotia	cga-ns.org	Channel-23 Communications	channel23.com
		Chapman Software Design Inc.	csdi.on.ca
Certified General Accountants' Association of Ontario	cga-ontario.org	Chaps Group Inc	chaps.com
		Chaps Group Inc.	chapsgroup.com
Certified General Accountants' Association of P.E.I.	cga-pei.org	Charlebois Computer Services	charcom.com
		Charlene And Ben Dunk	thefalls.com
		Charles Fraser Computers Ltd.	cfraser.ns.ca
Certified General Accountants' Association of Quebec	cga-quebec.org	Charles Howard & Associates Ltd	chal.bc.ca
		Charon Systems, Inc.	charon.com
Certified General Accountants' Association of Saskatchewan	cga-saskatchewan.org	Chateau Cartier Sheraton Hotel & Golf Resort, Enr.	cchgr.qc.ca
Certified General Accountants' Association of the Yukon	cga-yukon.org	Chateau Virtuel Inc	chateau-virtuel.com
		Chatelaine Magazine	chatelaine.com
Cerulean Enterprises Inc.	cerulean.com	Chatham Internet Access Ltd.	ciaccess.com
Cez Inc.	cez.com	Chatsubo Design	chatsubo.com
CFAC 960 Radio	cfac.com	Chauvco Resources Ltd.	chauvco.ab.ca
CFAC 960 Radio	cfac960.com	Cheap Thrills Enterprises Inc.	thrills.ca
CFAX 1070 AM Radio	cfax1070.com	CHEC 6 Television	pop-cult.com
CFCF-12 Incorporated	cfcf12.ca	Chedoke-Mcmaster Hospitals	cmh.on.ca
CFOX	cfox.com	Cheetah's Gold Inc	cheetahs-gold.com
CFPL Radio	cfplradio.com	CHEK 6 Television Ltd.	chek6.bc.ca
CGA Atlantic Region Professional Services Directorate	cga-atldirectorate.org	Chem1Ware Systems Limited	chem1.com
		Chemex Labs Ltd.	chemex.ca

Name of Organization	Domain	Name of Organization	Domain
Chemex Labs Ltd.	chemex.com	CHUM Limited	muchmusic.com
Chen and Associates Ltd.	cz.com	CHUM Ltd.	mztv.com
Cherniak Giblon	cherniak.on.ca	Churchill Northern Studies Centre	cnsc.mb.ca
Chernoff Thompson Architects	cta.bc.ca	CI Investments	stockwatch.com
CHFM Lite 96 Radio	chfm.com	CIBC - Cash Management	cibc.org
CHFM Lite 96 Radio	chfm96.com	CIBC Investment Bank	cibcwg.com
CHI Systems, Inc.	chisystemsinc.ca	CIBC, Economics Division	cibc-econ.com
Children of Mothers Soc.	moms.com	CIBC-Finance Inc.	cibc-finance.ca
Children's Hospital of Eastern Ontario	cheo.on.ca	CIBL 101.5 Fm	cibl.org
Childrens Hospital of Western Ontario Foundation	chwo-foundation.org	Cibus Consulting Inc.	cibus.ca
		CIC Inc.	cic.qc.ca
Childtrack Identification Systems	childtrack.com	Cigam Entertainment Inc.	cigam.com
Chilean Wine Importers Inc.	chileanwine.com	Cima+ S.E.N.C.	cima.qc.ca
Chilliwack Information Systems	cissytems.com	Cimetrix Solutions Inc.	cimetrix.on.ca
		Cimtegration Inc.	cimtegration.on.ca
Chipperfield Unlimited	chipperfield.com	Cimtegration Inc.	interscape.net
Chipworks	chipworks.com	Cimtegration Ltd.	cimtegration.com
Chocolaterie Bernard Callebaut	bernard-c.com	Cimtek Automation Systems Inc.	cimtek.on.ca
Chocolaterie Bernard Callebaut - Canada	bernard-callebaut.com	Cinax Designs Inc.	cinax.com
		Cine-Byte Imaging, Inc.	2film.com
Choice Dental Supplies Inc.	pssnet.com	Cineflix, Inc.	cineflix.com
Choquette & Company Accounting Group	income.com	Cio Summit Inc.	ciosummit.com
		Circle Group	circlegroup.com
Choreo Systems Inc.	choreo.ca	Circuits Newspaper Services Inc.	circuits.net
Chown Cairns	chown-cairns.com		
Chris Boorman Consulting	cjb.com	Citenet Telecom Inc.	citenet.ca
Christal Enterprise Corp.	christalcec.com	Citenet Telecom Inc.	citenet.com
Christie Brown Co.	christie-brown.com	Citenet Telecom Inc.	citenet.net
Christopher Portway & Associates, Inc.	muskoka.net	Cithara Small Lately Users Group (S.L.U.G)	cithara.montreal.qc.ca
Christina Morwood	sputlink.com	Citibank Canada Inc.	citibank.ca
Chronofax Inc.	chronofax.com	Citizen Internet	citizeninternet.com
Chronologic Systems (Canada) Inc.	chronologic.ca	Citizens Trust	citizens.com
		Citizens Trust	citizenstrust.ca
Chrysalis Business Development, Strategic Focus, Synectic Advice, Inc., Joint Venture	cbdsfsai.com	City Entertainment Group	cityent.com
		City of Brampton	city.brampton.on.ca
CHUM Limited	chum.ca	City of Calgary, The	city.calgary.ab.ca
CHUM Limited	chumcity.com	City of Calgary, The	gov.calgary.ab.ca

Name of Organization	Domain	Name of Organization	Domain
City of Coquitlam, The	gov.coquitlam.bc.ca	CKMF 94.3 Energie	radioenergie.com
City of Dartmouth	city.dartmouth.ns.ca	CKVR Television	ckvr.com
City of Edmonton	gov.edmonton.ab.ca	CKVR Television	newvr.com
City of Fredericton	city.fredericton.nb.ca	Claremont Secondary School	claremont.victoria.bc.ca
City of Grande Prairie	city.grande-prairie.ab.ca		
City of Guelph	city.guelph.on.ca	Clark International Builders	cib.com
City of Halifax	city.halifax.ns.ca	Clark International Builders	clarkbuilders.com
City of Kamloops	city.kamloops.bc.ca	Clark Wilson	cwilson.com
City of Kitchener	city.kitchener.on.ca	Clarke Brown Associates	ohsnet.com
City of Lethbridge	city.lethbridge.ab.ca	Clarke Institute of Psychiatry	clarke-inst.on.ca
City of London	city.london.on.ca	Clarke Transport	clarke-transport.com
City of Mississauga	city.mississauga.on.ca	Classic Arms	classic.ns.ca
		Clear Thinking Technology	clearthink.com
City of Mississauga	comtw.org	Clearnet, Inc.	clearnet.com
City of Moncton	city.moncton.nb.ca	Clearwater Fine Foods Inc.	clrwater.ca
City of Nanaimo	city.nanaimo.bc.ca	Clickable Systems	clickable.com
City of Niagara Falls	city.niagara-falls.on.ca	Clientserv MSA	bluecross.com
		Clifford Elliot Database Consulting	cliffordelliot.com
City of North Bay	city.north-bay.on.ca		
City of Ottawa Corp.	city.ottawa.on.ca	Clifton Associates Ltd.	clifton.ca
City of Richmond	city.richmond.bc.ca	Clifton Associates Ltd.	clifton.sk.ca
City of Saint John	city.saint-john.nb.ca	Clone City Computers, Ltd. O/A R&H PC's	rhpcs.ca
City of Saskatoon	city.saskatoon.sk.ca		
City of Scarborough	city.scarborough.on.ca	Cloxt Corporation.	cloxt.com
		Club Culture	club-culture.com
City of Summerside, PEI	city.summerside.pe.ca	Club For People Who Make Revenue	revenue.com
City of Surrey	city.surrey.bc.ca	Club Internet Inc	club-inter.net
City of Toronto	gov.toronto.on.ca	Club Mac	cmac.org
City of Vancouver	city.vancouver.bc.ca	Club Macintosh de Quebec	cmq.qc.ca
City of Victoria	city.victoria.bc.ca	Club Net International	clubnet.org
City of Winnipeg	city.winnipeg.mb.ca	CMSI	powerwindows.com
Citylynx	citylynx.com	CNA Systems Group	jumppoint.com
CityTV/CHUM Limited	citytv.com	CNET Technology Inc.	cnetcan.com
Cityvu Inc.	cityvu.com	CNG Group Inc.	cng.on.ca
CJAY 92 Classic Rock	cjay.com	CNS Inc.	cns.bc.ca
CJAY 92 Classic Rock	cjay92.com	Co-Operators Insurance Company	cooperators.com
CJAY 92.1 FM "Classic Rock"	cjay921.com	Coast Forest Management Ltd.	cfm.bc.ca
CKIK FM	kikfm.com	Coast Masonry Supplies Ltd.	retaining-walls.com

Name of Organization	Domain	Name of Organization	Domain
Coast Paper	coastpaper.com	College de Bois-De-Boulogne	collegebdeb.qc.ca
Coast Peripherals and Systems Inc.	coast-peripherals. bc.ca	College de Jonquiere	cjonquiere.qc.ca
Coast Steel Fabricators Ltd.	coaststeel.com	College de L'Acadie (College Communautaire Francophone de Nouvelle Ecosse)	ccfne.ns.ca
Coastal Networks Inc.	cstlnet.com		
Coats Bell	coatscan.com	College de Limoilou	climoilou.qc.ca
Cobequid Life Sciences Inc.	cobequid.com	College Edouard-Montpetit	collegeem.qc.ca
Cochran Entertainment Incorporated	screen.com	College Francais	collegefrancais.ca
Cochran Interactive Incorporated	kidstv.com	College Institute Educator's Association of British Columbia	ciea.bc.ca
Codville Company, The	codville.mb.ca	College Jean Eudes	jeaneudes.qc.ca
Cody Montana Integrated	codymontana.com	College Jean-Guy Leboeuf Inc.	cedep.com
Coffeehaus, Inc.	coffeehaus.com	College Jean-Guy Leboeuf Inc.	collegeleboeuf.qc.ca
Coffyn Communications	ccom.mb.ca	College Lasalle	clasalle.qc.ca
Cogeco Cable Canada Inc.	cgocable.ca	College Lionel-Groulx	clionelgroulx.qc.ca
Cogeco Inc.	cogeco.com	College Militaire Royal de St-Jean	cmr.ca
Cogenec Inc.	cogenec.com		
Cogent Information Systems Inc.	cogentinfosys.com	College of Family Physicians Of Canada	cfpc.ca
Cogentex Inc.	cogentex.qc.ca	College of Geographic Sciences, The	cogs.ns.ca
Cogni-Case Inc.	cognicase.ca	College of New Caledonia	cnc.bc.ca
Cogni-Vision Inc.	infopig.com	College of Physicians & Surgeons of Ontario, The	cpso.on.ca
Cognologic Software Inc.	cogno.com		
Cognos Incorporated	cognos.com	College of Physicians and Surgeons, Province of Alberta	cpsa.ab.ca
Cognoscente Software International Inc.	cognoscente.com	College Printers	c-print.com
Cohn & Wells	belladvantage.com	College Universitaire de Saint-Boniface	ustboniface.mb.ca
Cohn & Wells	bellrealplus.com		
Cold Springs Farm Ltd.	coldsp.com	Collideascope Limited Partnership	collideascope.com
Coldwell Banker Coburn Realty	coburnrealty.com	Collie Rowland & Associates	worldtravelguide. com
Coldwell Banker Pinnacle Real Estate	coldwellpinnacle. com	Colliers	colliers-canada.com
Coles Book Stores, Limited	coles.ca	Colliers Damner Pike Inc.	colliers-usa.com
Colin Marsh	dl2000.com	Colliers Macaulay Nicolls Inc.	colliers-international.com
Collective Vision Inc.	collectivevision.com		
Collector's Exchange Ltd.	collex.com	Collingwood Appraisal	collingwood.com
College Boreal of Applied Arts and Technology	borealc.on.ca	Colortron Photo Services Ltd.	colortron.com
		Colorworks Reproduction & Design Inc	colorworks.com
College Charles Lemoyne	cclemoyne.edu	Colour Prints Corp.	colourprints.com

Name of Organization	Domain	Name of Organization	Domain
Columbia Redpoint Information Systems	redpoint.com	Commonwealth Association for Public Administration and Management	capam.org
Columbus Group Internet Marketing	columbus-group.com	Commonwealth Systems Group Ltd.	cmnwlth.com
Com-Cept Microsystems	theindex.net	Commtech Safety Ltd.	commtech-ca.com
Com-Cept Microsystems	ticonet.com	Commtech Safety Ltd.	cslcommtech.com
Com-Cept Microsystems Ltd.	comcept.ab.ca	Communaute Urbaine de Montreal (CUM)	cum.qc.ca
Com-West Radio System	com-west.com		
Comark Inc.	comark.ca	Communicaide Integrated Marketingservices Limited	communicaide.com
Combustion Dynamics Ltd	combdyn.com	Communicaide Marketing Services, Ltd.	cmsl.com
Combyne Data Inc.	combyne.qc.ca		
Comcept Canada Inc.	comcept.com	Communicare	communicare.com
Comcheq Services Ltd.	comcheq.ca	Communications Accessibles Montreal	cam.org
Comdev	comdev.ca		
Comdis	comdis.com	Communications Accessibles Montreal (Inc.)	cam.qc.ca
Comedy Bytes! BBS	comedy.com		
Comgate Engineering, Ltd.	comgate.com	Communications Babylonne	babylon.montreal.qc.ca
Cominco Ltd.	cominco.com		
Comite Canadien des Electrotechnologies (Cce)	cce.qc.ca	Communications Canada (The Federal Department of Communications)	doc.ca
Comlab Inc.	comlab.com		
Comm*Net Inc.	comm.qc.ca	Communications Design	cdesigns.com
Commercial Internet Services	cistor.com	Communications Evoluees Bell Inc.	ceb.qc.ca
Commercial Printers Ottawa, Ltd.	comprint.com	Communications Ganymede Inc	ganymede.com
Commission des Ecoles Protestantes du Grand Montreal (CEPGM) / Protestant School Board of Greater Montreal (PSBGM)	psbgm.qc.ca	Communications Mednet Inc.	mednet.qc.ca
		Communications MG Direct	geopages.net
		Communications MG Direct	mgdirect.com
		Communications Software, Inc	v-mail.com
Commission Scolaire Catholique de Sherbrooke	cscs.qc.ca	Communications, Energy and Paperworkers' Union of Canada	cep.ca
Commission Scolaire de Matane	csmatane.qc.ca	Communicators Credit Union Ltd.	comcu.mb.ca
Commission Scolaire des Cantons	cscantons.qc.ca	Communicopia Environmental Research & Communications	communicopia.bc.ca
Commission Scolaire des Draveurs	csdraveurs.qc.ca	Communicopia Environmental Research and Communications	actone.com
Commission Scolaire des Manoirs	csmanoirs.qc.ca	Communicopia Environmental Research and Communications	audience.com
Commit To A Healthier Brant	commit.org		

Name of Organization	Domain	Name of Organization	Domain
Communicopia Environmental Research and Communications	bchydro.com	Community Information Centres of Canada	ciac.org
Communicopia Environmental Research and Communications	ceia-bc.com	Community Real Estate Service	communityre.com
Communicopia Environmental Research and Communications	ceia.com	Community Skills Centres	csc.bc.ca
Communicopia Environmental Research and Communications	comcopia.com	Community Trust Company, Ltd.	comtrust.com
Communicopia Environmental Research and Communications	commando.com	Comnet Corporation	comnet.ca
Communicopia Environmental Research and Communications	commcopi.com	Comnetix Computer Systems	comnetix.com
Communicopia Environmental Research and Communications	delta-place.com	Comp-U-Call Computer Services	aetheronics.com
Communicopia Environmental Research and Communications	e-law.com	Compact Pipe Company	toke.com
Communicopia Environmental Research and Communications	ecotourism.com	Compcanada Technology Integration Inc.	compcanada.ab.ca
Communicopia Environmental Research and Communications	macblo.com	Compendium Design International, Inc.	abbcom.com
Communicopia Environmental Research and Communications	mediamon.com	Compeuphoria	euphoria.com
Communicopia Environmental Research and Communications	powersmart.com	Complete Integrations Inc.	cii.ab.ca
Communicopia Environmental Research and Communications	pro-vision.com	Compression Technologies Inc.	compression.com
Communicopia Environmental Research and Communications	provision.com	Compu Life	compulife.com
Communicopia Environmental Research and Communications	slocan.com	Compu-Clone Inc.	compu-clone.ns.ca
Communicopia Environmental Research and Communications	soulgate.com	Compu-Skills Internet Marketing	csim.com
Communicopia Environmental Research and Communications	sustainability.com	Compubbs	compubbs.com
Communicopia Environmental Research and Communications	tourism-bc.com	Compubbs	compubbs. edmundston.nb.ca
Communicopia Environmental Research and Communications	tourismbc.com	Compucentre	compucentre.com
Communicopia Environmental Research and Communications	wcenergy.com	Compucollege	compucollege.com
Communicopia Inc.	communicopia.com	Compucon	compucon.com
Communipomme Inc.	communipomme.com	Compudyn Systems Ltd.	compudyn.on.ca
Community Assets	assets.net	Compuexcel Consulting and Software, Inc.	compuexcel.com
Community Information Access Organization	ciao.trail.bc.ca	Compugard Services Inc.	compugard.com
		Compugen Systems	compug.com
		Compuphile Systems, Inc.	compuphile.ca
		Compuphone, Inc.	comp-u-phone.com
		Compuquest	compquest.com
		Compuquest 9015-9708 Quebec Inc.	compuquest.qc.ca
		Compuquest Inc.	compuquest.com
		Compusense, Inc.	compusense.com

Name of Organization	Domain	Name of Organization	Domain
Compusmart	compusmart.net	Computer Technology Network	ctn.on.ca
Compusmart Computers Ltd.	compusmart.bc.ca	Computer Telephony Solutions	ctsnet.com
Compusoft	compus.ca	Computer Tutor	computer-tutor.com
Compusoft Products Inc.	compusoft.com	Computer Wizards	comwiz.com
Compusolv Computer Systems Corporation	compusolv.com	Computer-Mate Technologies Limited	cmate.com
Compusult Limited	compusult.nf.ca	Computer-Mate Technologies Limited	webserver.com
Compusup Business Centre Inc.	compusup.com	Computeractive Inc.	computeractive.on.ca
Computability Inc.	computability.ns.ca	Computerhelp Resources, Inc.	computerhelp.ca
Computan Corporation	computan.on.ca	Computerized Portfolio Management Services Inc.	cpms.com
Computeach Systems	computeach.com	Computerized Solutions For Business	csb.com
Computer Action	c-action.com	Computerland	computerland.ca
Computer Advocacy, Inc.	road.com	Computerlink Online Inc.	cml.com
Computer And Business Integrators Inc.	cbi.bc.ca	Computerlink Online Inc.	compulink.com
Computer Business Centre, Inc.	cbcentre.com	Computerlink Online Inc.	game.org
Computer Catalyst, Inc.	compcat.com	Computerlink Online Inc.	idirect.com
Computer Communications Group	henry.net	Computers & More	compmore.net
Computer Concepts Ltd.	compcon.com	Computhotics Limited	computhotics.com
Computer Consulting Associates Intl.	ccai.com	Computime Computers & Software Ltd	computime.bc.ca
Computer Cowboys	cowboy.org	Computing Art Inc.	c-art.com
Computer Dynamics Online Service	compdyn.com	Computrad Inc.	computrad.com
Computer Ease	computer-ease.com	Computrends Systems	blade.com
Computer Information Services	cins.com	Compututor	vegan.com
Computer Insider	insider.com	Comquest Computer Services	accessable.com
Computer Media Inc.	netraders.com	Comspec Communications Inc.	comspec.com
Computer Methods International Corp.	cmic.ca	Comtec Multimedia Inc.	moneywise.com
Computer Modelling Group	cmgroup.com	Comtech Safety Ltd	comtech-ca.com
Computer Partners	compar.com	Comtel Plus Inc.	comtelplus.com
Computer People Resources, PClab	block-buster.com	Comunicaciones Globales	gua.net
Computer Post, The	cpost.mb.ca	Con-Fax Publishing Inc.	confax.com
Computer Resurrection Services	reaper.com	Conamara Technologies Ltd.	conamara.com
Computer Software Upgrades	csu.com	Conbrio Teamwork Inc.	conbrio.ca
		Concepts Zap	zap.qc.ca
		Conceptual Reality, Inc.	conceptualreality.com

Name of Organization	Domain	Name of Organization	Domain
Conceptual Technologies Inc.	conceptual.ca	Consensys Corp.	consensys.com
Concert Industries Ltd.	air-laid.com	Consolidated Access & Networks, Inc.	can.ca
Concord College	concordcollege.mb.ca	Consolidated Access & Networks, Inc.	can.net
Concord Pacific Communications	concordpacific.net	Consolidated Access and Networks	cyberrealm.com
Concord Pacific Developments Corp.	concordpacific.bc.ca	Consolidated Access and Networks	cybersphere.com
Concord Pacific Developments Corp.	concordpacific.com	Consolidated Access and Networks	cyberview.com
Concordia College	concordia.edmonton.ab.ca	Consolidated Access and Networks	eternity.net
Concordia University	concordia.ca	Consolidated Access and Networks	faeire.com
Concurrent Realities, Inc.	concur.com	Consolidated Access and Networks	faeire.net
Conestoga College	conestogac.on.ca	Consolidated Access and Networks	faerie.com
Conexions Ltd.	conexions.com	Consolidated Access and Networks	fairy.com
Confederation College	confederationc.on.ca	Consolidated Access and Networks	fairyland.com
Conference Board of Canada	conferenceboard.ca	Consolidated Access and Networks	rcw.com
Conference des Recteurs et des Principaux des Universites du Quebec	crepuq.qc.ca	Consolidated Access and Networks	webforce.com
Connaught Laboratories Limited	connaught.com	Consolidated Access and Networks	webgalaxy.com
Connect Tech, Inc.	connecttech.com	Consolidated Access and Networks	webverse.com
Connectalk Inc.	ctalk.com	Consolidated Access and Networks	webvillage.com
Connected World Technologies Inc.	cworld.com	Consolidated Access and Networks	webzoo.com
Connection Systems Inc.	asia-pacific.com	Consolidated Technologies Inc.	prefon.com
Connections Nova Scotia	connections.ns.ca	Consolidated Vector Systems Inc.	cvsi.com
Connectivity Technology Inc.	connectivity.com	Consortech Inc.	consortech.com
Connectric Systems Inc.	connectric.com	Consortia Systems International Ltd.	consortia.com
Connectware Solutions Inc.	cnctwr.ca	Consortium for Administration Systems Development	casd.bc.ca
Connelly Business Exhibitions Inc.	connelly.ca		
Conner's Brewery Inc.	conners.com		
Connexions	connex.ca		
Connor, Clark and Company Ltd.	connor-clark.com		
Connor, Clark and Company Ltd.	connor.com		
Consensys Computer Corporation	cnsnsys.com		

Name of Organization	Domain	Name of Organization	Domain
Consortium of College and University Media Centers	ccumc.org	Conwest Exploration Ltd.	conwest.com
		Conxsys Inc.	conxsys.on.ca
Conspiracy Records	conspiracy.com	Cook Roberts and Associates Ltd.	cookroberts.bc.ca
Constance Consultants, Ltd.	ccl.on.ca		
Construction Data	condata.mb.ca	Cooksmill Bookkeeping Services Ltd.	cooksmill.com
Construction Safety Association of Ontario, Inc.	constructsafety.on.ca	Cooper, Mlyneux & Makuz Chartered Accountants	cmm.com
Consulan Inc.	consulan.com		
Consulate of Mexico	consulmex.com	Cooperhead Brewing Co. Ltd.	copperhead-brewing.com
Consultronics Limited	consultronics.on.ca		
Consumer Net Services	consumer-net.com	Coopers & Lybrand	colybrand.ca
Consumers Distributing Inc / Distribution aux Consommateurs Inc	consumers.ca	Coopers & Lybrand	cooperslybrand.ca
		Coopnet	coopnet.org
		Coplanor Congres Inc.	coplanor.qc.ca
Consumers Distributing Inc / Distribution aux Consommateurs Inc	dac.ca	Coplanus Systems, Inc.	coplanus.com
		Cora Industries Ltd.	bikestorage.com
		Corcan	corcan.ca
Contact Canada	contactcan.com	Core Networking	eyeq.com
Contact Integration Inc.	contact.ca	Core Networking	unici2i.com
Contacts Target Marketing Inc.	contactsbc.com	Core*Lan	infoshare.net
Contax Inc.	contax.com	Core*Lan Inc.	corelan.com
Contech Electronics	scatmat.com	Core-Net Inc.	core-net.com
Continental Aviation (Canada) Ltd.	cont-aviation.com	Coreco Incorporated	coreco.com
		Coredev	coredev.com
Continental Healthcare Systems Canada Inc.	chs.mb.ca	Corel Corporation	corel.ca
		Corel Corporation	corel.com
Continental Insurance Management Ltd.	ciml.ca	Corenet Computer Services	corenet.com
		Cormark Communications Inc.	cormark.com
Continental PIR Communications	contcom.bc.ca	Cormex Research Inc.	cormex.on.ca
Continuing Legal Education Society of British Columbia, The	cle.bc.ca	Cornerstone Group	law-canada.com
		Cornflakes Fan Club	kelloggs.com
Contor Terminals Inc.	contor.com	Cornwallis Junior High School	cornwallis.halifax.ns.ca
Contour Microsystems Canada	contourmicrosystemscan.com		
		Corpomedia Inc.	branchez-vous.com
Contractors Network Corporation	cnccontracts.com	Corporate Infohub	corpinfohub.com
		Corporate Library, Canada Post Corporation	canpost.org
Contrad Technology Inc.	contrad.com		
Contraste Canada Inc.	contraste.ca	Corporate Software and Technologies Inc.	cst.ca
Control Systems Unlimited	sysu.com		
Controlled Environments Limited	conviron.mb.ca	Corporation of the City of Barrie, The	city.barrie.on.ca
Controltech Inc.	controltech.mb.ca		

Name of Organization	Domain	Name of Organization	Domain
Corporation of the City of Cambridge	city.cambridge.on.ca	Country 105 FM	ckry.com
		Country Day School, The	cds.on.ca
Corporation of the City of Cornwall, Ontario	city.cornwall.on.ca	County of Carleton Law Association	ccla.ottawa.on.ca
Corporation of the City of North Vancouver, The	city.north-van.bc.ca	County of Wellington	county.wellington.on.ca
Corporation of the City of North York, The	city.north-york.on.ca	Coup De Pouce Inc.	coupdepouce.com
Corporation of the City of Waterloo, The	city.waterloo.on.ca	Courdeau-Procinbec Inc.	procinbec.com
		Courex Communications	courex.com
Corporation of the District of North Vancouver	district.north-van.bc.ca	Couture Consulting	tfc.com
		Cows Inc.	cows.ca
Corporation of the Town of Fort Erie	town.fterie.on.ca	Coyote Communications Ltd.	coyote.ns.ca
		Coyote Marketing Group	coyote.ca
Corporation of the Town of Richmond Hill	gov.richmond-hill.on.ca	CP Limited	cp.ca
		CP Rail System	gaps.com
Corporation X Inc.	corpx.com	CP Rail Systems	cprs.com
Corriere Canadese, Inc.	corriere.com	CPAS Systems, Inc.	cpas.com
Cosburn Patterson Wardman Limited	cosburn.com	CPC Loyalty Communications	cpc-loyalty.com
Coscient Inc.	coscient.com	Cpused	cpused.com
Coska Information Service	coska.bc.ca	Crabtree Publishing Company	crabtree-pub.com
Cosmic Room Service Communications	crsland.com	Craig Dilks Computer Consulting Ltd.	cdccl.com
Cosmos Network Access & Service	cosmos.ab.ca	Crap Inc.	crap.com
		Crawford, Smith and Swallow	crawfordss.com
Cosmotek Interactive Technology Inc.	cosmotek.com	Crea ™, The Canadian Real Estate Association	crea.ca
Cossette Communications Marketing Inc.	cossette.com	Creations By Helen	florists.com
		Creative House	creativehouse.com
Cost Recovery Plan	crp.kingston.on.ca	Creative Information Solutions	creativeinfo.com
Cott Corporation	cott.com	Creative Online	creativity.com
Coty Division of Benckiser Inc.	coty.ca	Creative Research International Inc.	crii.com
Coull Consulting	coull.com		
Council International	council-intl.com	Creative Retirement Mantitoba, Inc.	crm.mb.ca
Council of Ministers of Education of Canada	cmec.ca	Credit Lyonnais Canada	credlyon.ca
Council of Ontario Universities	cou.on.ca	Credit Union Central of B.C.	cucbc.com
		Credit Union Central of Manitoba	cucm.mb.ca
Counsel Inc.	headhunt.com		
Counsel International	counsel-intl.com	Credit Union Insurance Services	cuis.com
Counsel International	counselintl.com		
Counsellor Training Institute	cti-van.com	Credit Valley Hospital	cvh.org

Name of Organization	Domain	Name of Organization	Domain
Creo Products Inc.	creo.bc.ca	Cumis Life Insurance Company	cumislife.com
Crimestoppers New Brunswick	crimestop.nb.ca	Current Services Inc.	currentservices.ns.ca
Crimson Dragon Fan Club	crim.org	Currie Maclean Inc.	curriemaclean.com
Crisp Management	crispinc.com	Custom House Currency Exchange	chce.com
Critics Choice	criticschoice.com		
Croda Canada, Ltd.	crodacan.com	Cyan Digital Media	cyancorp.com
Crohn's and Colitis Foundation of Canada	ccfc.ca	Cyanamid Canada Inc.	cyanamid.org
		Cyber Hotel	cyberhotel.com
Crone & Co.	financialserver.com	Cyber Miles	cybermiles.com
Crop Protection Institute of Canada	cropro.org	Cyber Pass, Inc.	cyber-pass.com
		Cyber Shopper The Online Supermall Ltd.	cyber-shopper.com
Crosfield Canada Inc.	crosfield.ca		
Cross Canada Resource	cscr.com	Cyber-Yonge	cyber-yonge.com
Cross Cultural Consulting Inc.	ccci.ca	Cyberangel	cyberangel.com
Cross Lake Education Authority	clea.mb.ca	Cyberart Inc.	cyberart.on.ca
Crossbridge Information Systems, Inc.	crossbridge.com	Cyberconcept Inc.	cyberconcept.com
		Cybercorp Inc.	veda.org
Crosskeys Systems Corporation	crosskeys.com	Cybercorp, Inc.	cybercorp.net
Crown Publications Ltd.	crownpub.com	Cyberdeals, Inc.	cyberdeals.com
Crowntek Business Centres	crowntek.ca	Cyberdine Systems BBS	csbbs.com
CRS Online Ltd.	crso.com	Cyberdyne Systems	cdyne.com
CRS Robotics Corporation	crsrobotics.com	Cyberealm	crealm.org
Cruiseship Centers	cruiseship.com	Cyberguard, A Division of Mae Ltd.	cyberguard.com
Cryptocard Corporation	cryptocard.com		
Crystal Controls Inc.	crystalcntrl.com	Cyberhigh	cyberhigh.org
Crystal Services	crystalinc.com	Cyberlink	clo.com
CSB Systems Ltd.	csbsys.com	Cyberlink Computers	cyberempire.com
CSR Information Network	opcyouth.org	Cyberlink Systems Corp.	cyberlink.bc.ca
CTFSystems Inc.	ctf.com	Cyberlinks Corp.	cyberlinks.com
CTH Industrial Control Ltd.	cth.ca	Cyberlist Real Estate Listings	cyberlist.com
CTI Datacom Inc.	ctidata.com	Cybermagic Designs	cybermagic.com
CTV Television Network Ltd	ctv.ca	Cybermall International	cyberemporium.com
Cubehouse Production	cubehouse.com	Cybermation Inc.	cybermation.com
CUC Broadcasting Ltd.	cuc.ca	Cybernet Communications Corp.	cybernet.ca
Cue Here BBS, Commodore Users of Edmonton	cuehere.edmonton.ab.ca		
		Cybernetic Control Incorporated	cybercon.nb.ca
Cultural Express	culturalexpress.com		
Culture Federations of Nova Scotia Inc.	culturefed.ns.ca	Cyberpace Business Services	alitalia.com
		Cyberpace Business Services	anna.com
Cumberland Computer Group Ltd	ccg.bc.ca	Cyberpace Business Services	brut.com

Name of Organization	Domain	Name of Organization	Domain
Cyberpace Business Services	casablanca.com	Cybertap	cybertap.com
Cyberpace Business Services	cathay-pacific.com	Cybertrends Inc.	trends.ca
Cyberpace Business Services	joico.com	Cyberus Online Inc.	cyberus.ca
Cyberpace Business Services	playtex.com	Cyberus Online, Inc.	cyberus.com
Cyberpace Business Services	rafuse.com	Cybervalley Productions Inc.	cybervalley.nb.ca
Cyberpace Business Services	vrdream.com	Cybervision Technologies	cybervision.com
Cyberpace Business Services	vrguitar.com	Cybervoice Services Ltd.	cybervoice.com
Cyberpage Internet Marketing	cyberpage.com	Cyberwave Technologies Inc.	cwave.com
Cyberpages International	cyberpages.com	Cyberworld Shopping Malls	cyworldmall.com
Cyberphuck Service Corporation, Ltd.	cyberphuck.com	Cyborg Communications Inc.	cyborg.ca
		Cycor Communications Inc.	cycor.ca
Cyberplex Interactive Media	cyberplex.com	Cygnus Technology Ltd.	cygnus.nb.ca
Cyberplex Issues Inc.	moneyissues.com	Cygnus Telecom Inc.	cygtel.com
Cyberplus Technologies Inc.	cyberplus.ca	Cyklone BBS	cyklone.com
Cyberplus Technologies Inc.	cyberplus.net	Cymbiont Inc.	cymbiont.ca
Cyberq Consortium Inc.	cyberq.net	Cymbolic Sciences International Inc.	cymbolic.com
Cybersecure, Inc.	cybersecure.com		
Cybershop	stamps.com	Cynical Computing	cynical.net
Cybersmith Inc.	csi.nb.ca	Cyprien Lomas	biggus-webus.com
Cybersmith Inc.	cybercast.com	Cyradis Technology Group	cyradis.com
Cybersmith Inc.	cybersmith.net	Cyranex Corporation	cyranex.com
Cybersmith Inc.	fredericton.com	D C Wilson Associates (Trade name of 507245 Alberta Ltd.)	dcwilson.ab.ca
Cybersmith Inc.	moncton.com		
Cybersmith Inc.	sabian.com	D'Arcy & Associates	darcy.com
Cybersmith Inc.	sackville.com	D'Arcy Cain Consulting	druid.com
Cybersmith Inc.	saintjohn.com	D'Arcy Warner	hrnetwork.com
Cybersouls Eternal Life Systems Inc.	cybersouls.com	D-Link Canada Inc.	d-linknetworks.com
		D.E.M. Allen & Associates Ltd.	dema.mb.ca
Cyberspace	cyberspc.mb.ca	D.E.M. Consulting	demconsulting.com
Cyberstage Productions	cyberstage.com	D.Flora Systems Inc.	dflora.com
Cyberstore Online Information Systems Inc.	cyberstore.ca	D.H. Kumka & Associates	dhka.bc.ca
		D.I.A.N.E.T.I.C.S. Inc.	dianetics.com
Cyberstore Systems, Inc.	cyberstore.com	D.M. Gow Communications Inc.	dmgow.com
Cyberstore Systems, Inc.	cyberstore.net		
Cyberstore Systems, Inc.	pole.com	D.P.I. Inc	provector.com
Cyberstream Inc.	cyberstream.net	D.R. Solutions	drsol.com
Cyberstream Inc.	nwd.com	D.S.D. Software	telecafe.com
Cyberstream Information Services	cyberstream.com	DAAC Systems	daacsys.com
		DAAC Systems	dcsnet.com
Cybersurf Inc.	cia.com		

Name of Organization	Domain	Name of Organization	Domain
Daemon Maxwell Group	ideafutures.com	Database Engineering	repository.com
Dairyworld Foods	dairyworld.com	Databits	databits.com
Daiseiko International	daiseiko.com	Databoat International Boat Plans	databoat.com
Daiwa (Canada) Limited	daiwa.com	Databridge Inc.	databridge.com
Dalar International	dalar.com	Databyte Consulting Corp.	databyte.com
Dale Intermediaries Limited	daleint.on.ca	Datacom Enr.	dcnet.com
Dalhousie University	dal.ca	Datacom Online Services Inc.	datacom.ca
Dallas Dutkel	inter-nexus.com	Datacorp Distributions	datacorp.montreal.qc.ca
Dalsa, Inc.	dalsa.com	Datafix Division	datafix.com
Dalton-Kessler Productions, Inc.	dalton-kessler.on.ca	Datalink Systems Corporation	datalink.net
Damar Communications	interaction.com	Datamax Research Corp.	iwinpak.com
Danara Software Systems Inc.	danara.ca	Datap Systems	datap.ca
Danaudio Inc.	danaudio.com	Datapad International	datapad.com
Danby Products Limited	danby.com	Datapanik Design	panik.vancouver.bc.ca
Daniels Committee	daniels.winnipeg.mb.ca	Datapanik Media Control	datapanik.com
Daniels Electronics Ltd.	danelec.com	Dataparc Communications Corporation	dataparc.com
Daniels Group, Inc., The	daniels.on.ca	Dataquest Incorporated	dqi.com
Danny Ho	compu-smart.com	Dataradio Inc.	dataradio.ca
Danny Larouche	danmedia.com	Dataradio Inc.	dataradio.com
Danville May Group, Inc.	dmginc.com	Datarev Information Technologies Inc.	datarev.com
DAR Systems	darsys.com	Datasoft Communications	datasoft.com
Darkzone Technologies Inc.	darkzone.mb.ca	Dataspace Insight Inc.	dataspace.ca
Darwin Open Systems	darwinsys.com	Datastore BBS	datastore.calgary.ab.ca
DAS Media	dasmedia.com	Datastore Inc.	datastore.com
Data Access Technologies Inc.	datech.com	Datatech Canada	datatech.org
Data Business Forms	databusiness.ca	Datatech Canada	dt-can.com
Data Courier On-Line	dco.org	Datatel	datatel-systems.com
Data Design Systems Inc.	datadesign.com	Dateline	datelineonline.com
Data Exchange	datex.com	Datrox Computer Technologies Inc.	datrox.ca
Data Integration Systems Company	disc-inc.com	Dave G. Watson	beneficial.net
Data Kinetics Ltd.	dkl.com	Dave G. Watson	waazubee.com
Data Link Canada West Ltd.	dlcwest.com	Dave Steeves and Associates Inc.	steeves.bc.ca
Data Perceptions	dataper.com	Dave Watson	utv.com
Data Pro Computer Services	homelineplus.com		
Data Recovery Labs	datarec.com		
Data Terminal Mart	dtm.bc.ca		
Data Wise	datawise.com		

Name of Organization	Domain	Name of Organization	Domain
Davgro Corporation	davgro.com	Dean Heights Florist	flowernet.com
David A Lumbers Consulting	lumott.com	Debug Computer Services	debug.ab.ca
David E. Cross & Associates Inc.	davidcross.mb.ca	Decus Canada, Digital Equipment Computer Users Society	decus.ca
David J. Wedge Computer Law	wedge.com	Deep Cove Online	deepcove.com
David Lowy and Associates	lowy.com	Dees Communications Eng. Ltd	dees.com
David Lowy Delivers	deliver.com	Dees Communications Ltd.	dees.ca
David T.C. Lin, MD, FRCSC, Inc.	lin.vancouver.bc.ca	Deeth Williams Wall	dww.com
David Wong	acompshop.com	Deforrest Ent BBS	defbbs.com
Davies Medical	daviesmed.com	Deftech	deftech.outremont.qc.ca
Davies Ward & Beck.	dwblaw.com		
Davis and Company	davis.ca	Deighton Associates Ltd	deighton.com
Davis Controls Limited	daviscontrols.on.ca	Delegation Inforoute (Division of 2740664 Canada Inc)	delegation.ca
Davis North America	davisna.com	Delgratia Mining Corp.	delgratia.com
Davro Integration Technologies	davro.ca	Delkiw Contracting Inc.	delkiw.com
Davro Integration Technologies	e-back.com	Deloitte & Touche Management Consultants	dtmc.ca
Davy International Canada Ltd.	davytor.com	Delorme Services Techniques Ltee.	dst.ca
Dawson College	dawsoncollege.qc.ca	Delphax Systems	delphax.com
Dawson Law Chambers	dawsonlaw.mb.ca	Delrina (Canada) Corporation	delrina.net
Daystorm Inc.	daystorm.com	Delrina Corporation	delrina.com
DB Enterprises	db.net	Delta Centre for Learning Technologies	delcen.com
DBA Communications System, Inc.	dba-tele.com	Delta Chamber of Commerce	deltachamber.org
DBA Curvet Information Systems	curvet.com	Delta Controls, Inc.	deltacontrols.com
DBA Victor Bonnah	wwwpage.com	Delta Cu Insurance	deltacu.com
DBCorp Information Systems Inv.	dbcorp.ab.ca	Delta Data Systems Ltd.	deltadata.com
		Delta Hotels & Resorts	deltahotels.com
DBM Reflex Entreprises Inc.	dbmreflex.qc.ca	Delta-C Technologies Inc.	delta-c.com
DBM Systems, Inc.	dbmsys.com	Deltastar Communications Ltd.	deltastar.nb.ca
DCP Research Corporation	datacompression.com	Deltaware Systems Inc.	deltaware.com
		Deluxe Entertainment, Inc.	deluxentinc.com
DCS Systems Ltd.	dcs-systems.com	Demand Side Solutions Ltd.	demandside.com
DDA Computer Consultants Ltd.	dda.ns.ca	Democratech Party of British Columbia	democratech.org
De Havilland Inc.	dehavilland.ca	Dempster's	dempster.com
Deacon Insurance Agencies Limited	deaconinsurance.ca	Dendron Resource Surveys, Inc.	dendron.com

Name of Organization	Domain	Name of Organization	Domain
Denfield Communications, Reg.	telegraph.com	Dexotek Canada Corp.	dexotek.ca
Denny's Restaurants Ltd.	dennys.ca	Dexter and Associates	dexter.com
Dental Database & Guide	dentaldata.com	DFC International	dfc.com
Dentofacial Software, Inc.	dentofacial.com	DFL Software Inc.	dfl.com
Department of Education and Culture Network	ednet.ns.ca	DGI The Development Group, Inc.	busdev.org
Department of Environment	doe.ca	DHD Postimage	postimage.com
Department of Fisheries and Oceans (Fisheries Canada)	dfo.ca	Diachem	diachem.com
		Diagnostic Chemicals Limited	dclchem.com
Department of National Defence	dnd.ca	Dial Computer Services	dialcomp.com
		Dial-A-File	daf.com
Department of National Defense	dnd.net	Diamed Lab Supplies, Inc.	diamedlab.com
Deposit Insurance Corp. of Ontario	dico.com	Diamond Aircraft Industries Ltd.	diamondair.ca
Descartes Systems Group, Inc.	descartes.com	Diane Francis	dianefrancis.com
Desert Penguin Communications	dp.org	Diazo Products (Windsor) Ltd	diazo.com
		Didatech Software Ltd.	didatech.com
Desert Rose Productions Inc.	desertrose.mb.ca	Diesel Marketing Inc	diesel-mktg.com
Design Choice	designchoice.com	Dieter Stalder	stdi.com
Design's on Paper & Media Matters	mediagrp.mb.ca	Digga Tech	digga.com
		Digi-Rule Inc.	digirule.com
Designed Information Systems Corp.	aurora-net.com	Digicom Inc.	digicom.qc.ca
Designed Information Systems Corp.	aurora.net	Digidyne Inc	digidyne.com
		Digidyne Inc.	digidyne.ca
Designed Information Systems Corporation	disc-net.com	Digiflex Information Systems Inc	digiflex.ca
Designs Incorporated	designsinc.com	Digigraphics Inc.	digigraphics.on.ca
Desjardins Ducharmes Stein Monast Avocats	ddsm.ca	Digimap Data Services	digimap.com
Desktop Training Centres	trainers.com	Digital Access BBS	digitalbbs.net
Desmarais Nyborg Lazar Technologies Inc.	dnl.com	Digital Alliance And Technology	webit.net
		Digital Broadcast Network Inc	dbn.ca
Deterministic Software Limited	deterministic.com	Digital Chameleon Ltd.	digicham.com
Detombe Habermel Communications	dhc.caledon.on.ca	Digital Design Networks	ddn.com
		Digital Development Corp	t-net.com
Develcon Electronics Ltd.	develcon.com	Digital Development Corporation	maxims.com
Development and Investment Management Services	canvest.com	Digital Directory Inc.	ddi.bc.ca
Developpement Purkinje Inc.	purkinje.ca	Digital Dreamland Bulletin Board System	digik.com
Devry Inc. Canada	devry.ca	Digital Equipment of Canada	digital.ca
Devtek Applied Electronics Inc.	devtek.ns.ca		

Name of Organization	Domain	Name of Organization	Domain
Digital Film Lab	digifilm.on.ca	Direct Technologies, Inc.	eprobe.com
Digital Fix Development	digifix.com	Direction Informatique, Plesman Publications Ltee	direction-informatique.qc.ca
Digital Fix Development	stepwise.com	Directional Technologies Canada	dtech.mb.ca
Digital Freedom BBS	df.org		
Digital Image F/X Ltd.	digital-fx.ca	Directions Canada Inc.	directions.ca
Digital Ink	internet-publishing.com	Directpc Internet Inc.	direct-pc.com
Digital Island	digitalisland.com	Directpc Internet Inc.	directpc.com
Digital Island	digitalisland.kingston.pe.ca	Directwest Publishers Ltd.	directwest.sk.ca
		Disability Information Services of Canada	disc.ca
Digital Island	redclayroad.com		
Digital Media	digimedia-bc.com	Disabled Peoples' International	dpi.org
Digital Media Network Inc.	the.com	Discover Communications Inc.	discover.bc.ca
Digital Objects	digiobj.com	Discovery Channel, The	discovery.ca
Digital Processing Systems	dpsys.com	Discovery Passage BBS	smorgasboard.org
Digital Rain Inc.	digital-rain.com	Discovery Technology	interarts.com
Digital Science Inc.	digsci.ab.ca	Discovery Training Network	dtn.bc.ca
Digital Systems Group, Inc.	dsg.sk.ca	Discreet Logic Inc	discreet.qc.ca
Digital Vellum Inc.	digivel.com	Discscribe	discribe.ca
Digital Video Systems	dvs.com	Disposable Sales Company	disposable.com
Digitalis Data Services	knotwork.com	DISST (Direction de l'Information sur la Sante et la Securite du Travail)	disst.qc.ca
Digitech Information Services	digitech.ab.ca		
Digizine Online Entertainment Magazine	digizinemag.com		
		Distican, Inc.	distican.com
Dilltech Systems	dilltech.vancouver.bc.ca	Distinct Micro Inc.	dmi.qc.ca
		Distributed Computing Experts Corp.	dcexpert.ab.ca
Dimension Labs Inc.	dli.com		
Dimensions Computer Automation Systems Limited	dcasl.com	Distribution Smartrain Internationnal Inc.	smartrain.com
Dimtrex Limited	dimtrex.on.ca	District of Chilliwack	gov.chilliwack.bc.ca
Dingo Software Systems Inc.	dingo.com	Distrivin Ltee	vinexpert.com
Dinmar Consulting Inc.	dinmar.com	Disturbed Zero Technology	dztech.com
Diocese of New Westminster Network	nwnet.org	Disus Division of Empirics Inc.	disus.com
		Disus Division of Empirics Inc.	disusdei.on.ca
Dipix	dipix.com	Ditek Software Corporation	ditek.com
Direct Answer	answerdir.com	Diva Travel & Adventure Co. Ltd.	divayyz.com
Direct Home Distributors	siesta.com		
Direct Marketing	wincash.com	Divemar	divemar.com
Direct Technologies, Inc.	direct-tech.com	DKG Display Technologies Inc.	pfnet.com
Direct Technologies, Inc.	earthprobe.com	DKW Systems Corporation	dkw.com
Direct Technologies, Inc.	edwards.com	DMC Ontario Networking	ontario.net

Name of Organization	Domain	Name of Organization	Domain
DMP Consultant	dmp.qc.ca	Doohwah Design Inc.	doowahdesign.com
DMP Digital Media Productions Inc.	hockeypool.com	Doppler Computer Superstore	dtv.com
		Dorfin Distribution Inc.	dorfin.ca
DMR Group	dmrgroup.com	Dorfmann Computer Service Incorporated	dorfmann.com
DMR Group Inc.	dmr.ca		
DNA Multimedia Corp.	dna.bc.ca	Doro Group	nextlevel.com
DNR Business Systems	dnrsystems.com	Double Exposure	doubleexposure.com
Docker Services Ltd.	docker.com		
Docusys Corporation	docusys.qc.ca	Double Trace Inc.	doubletrace.com
Docusystems Inc.	durham.net	Doughnut Appreciation Society	doughnut.com
Docuweb Information Services, Inc.	docuweb.ca	Douglas Ball Inc.	douglasballinc.qc.ca
Dofasco Inc.	dofasco.ca	Douglas College	douglas.bc.ca
Doin, Alexandre et Associes Inc.	daa.qc.ca	Dover Technology Ltd.	dovertec.ns.ca
		DPE Electronics	dpe.com
Dollar Mania	dollarmania.com	Dr Kazi Islam, Prof	psychocyber.com
Dollco Printing	dollco.com	Dr. Michel Bazinet	prostate.com
Dolmax World Distribution Inc.	dolmax.com	Dr. Murray Moffat	snore.com
		Dr. Robert Betzner	naturesvitamins.com
Dolphin (Flipper) Systems	flipper.com	Dream	fsex.com
Dolphin Communications Inc.	dolphincom.com	Dreamlan Network Consulting Ltd.	dreamlan.com
Dolphin House	hpiautodata.com		
Dolphin Systems, Inc.	dolphinsys.com	Dreams Online	toothfairy.com
Dome Productions Inc.	domeprod.ca	Dreamweaver Communications Inc.	dwc.com
Dome.FCB Ltd.	dome.ca		
Dominica Real Estate Services	dominica.com	Driver Design Labs, A Division of Clarendon Datex Ltd.	driver-design-labs.bc.ca
Dominion Communication Services	dcomm.com		
		Driver's Advocate	orient.com
Dominion Communication Services	dcomm.saskatoon.sk.ca	Drivers' Advocate	virtuacity.com
		Drog Inc.	drog.com
Dominion Communication Services	yourkingdom.com	DRPCS Systems	drpcs.com
		Drs Findlay, Samosh, Griesbrecht, and Hughes	oncniagara.com
Dominion Directory Company	dominion.bc.ca		
Dominion Textile Inc.	domtex.ca	Dryadeltee	dryad.com
Dominion Textile Inc.	domtex.com	DS&B	ds-b.com
Domtar Inc.	domtar.ca	DSH Incorporated	dsh-inc.com
Domtar Inc.	domtar.com	DSO Enterprises Reg'd	sssfff.com
Don Controls Investments Inc.	theprospector.com	DTEC Ltd.	dtec-canada.com
Doncar Systems, Inc.	doncarsys.mb.ca	Dtronix	dtronix.com
Donut Inc.	donut.com	Duford Graphics	dufordgraphics.com
Doodles Research Foundation	doodles.org	Dun & Bradstreet Canada, Ltd.	info-dnb.com

Name of Organization	Domain	Name of Organization	Domain
Duncan Mclaren Marketing Inc.	mclaren.com	Dynatec International Limited	dynatec.ca
Dunciad	dunciad.dorval.qc.ca	Dynatek Automation Systems Inc.	dynatek.ca
Dundurn Press, Ltd.	dundurn.com	Dynix Automated Library Systems Inc.	dynix.com
Dunn & Associates	dunn.com		
Duoject Inc.	duoject.com	Dyscreet Inc.	dyscreet.com
Durham College of Applied Arts and Technology	durhamc.on.ca	E-Commerce Inc.	e-commerce.ca
		E-Commerce Inc.	e-commerce.com
Durham Free-Net Inc.	durham.org	E-Concept	econcept.com
Durham Internet Services Inc.	dis.on.ca	E-Design Inc.	e-design.com
Durock Alfacing International	durock.com	E-Media	e-mediagroup.com
Duthie Books	duthiebooks.bc.ca	E-Search	e-search.com
Duthie Books Ltd.	literascape.net	E-Search, Inc.	compmall.com
Duthie's	duthiebooks.net	E.B. Eddy Forest Products, Ltd.	efpnet.com
Duthie's Book Services	duthie.com	E. Doucet Computer Services Inc.	edoucet.com
Duthie's Books	duthiebooks.com		
Duthie's Books Ltd.	literascape.com	E. M. Gorman Consulting	gorman.com
Duthie's Online Book Services	duthie.net	E. Sands & Associates Inc	sands-trustee.com
DVI Peripherals	dvip.com	E.B. Peerless Ltd	ebpeerlessltd.com
DVnet	dvnet.drayton-valley.ab.ca	E.B. System Limited	ebsys.mb.ca
		E.D.M. Bulletin Board Services Ltd.	edmbbs.com
Dweomer UNIX User's Group	dweomer.org		
Dy-4 Systems	dy4.com	E.H. Price Limited	ehprice.mb.ca
Dyad Digital Studios	dyad.com	E.MBA Net Corporation	embanet.com
Dyad Systems Inc.	dyadsys.ca	E.T.I.	eti-gaming.com
Dyadem International Ltd.	dyadem.com	E.T.I. (Montreal) Inc	etinet.com
Dye & Durham Co. Inc.	dyedurham.com	Eagle & Partners Inc	eagle-partners.com
Dylex Limited	dylex.com	Eagle & Partners Incorporated	eagle-partners.ca
Dymaxion Research Limited	dymaxion.ns.ca	Eagle Canada Inc.	eagle.ca
Dynamed Biomedical Services Inc.	dynamed.com	Eagle Eye Tours Inc	eagle-eye.com
		Earthquest Foods	earthquest.com
Dynamic Fund Management	dynamicfund.ca	Earthwork Communications Inc	earthwork.com
Dynamic Fund Management	dynamicfund.com		
Dynamic Fund Management Inc.	dynamic.ca	Earthworks Cooperative	ki.org
Dynamis Productivity Software Limited	dynamis.bc.ca	East Coast Music Awards Web Page	ecma.com
Dynamite Data Communications, Inc.	dynamite.com	East Kootenay Community College	ekcc.bc.ca
		Eastern Business Computer Institute	ebci.ca
Dynapro Systems Inc.	dsi.bc.ca		
Dynasty Components Inc.	dynasty.ca	Eastern College	eastcoll.nf.ca

Name of Organization	Domain	Name of Organization	Domain
Eastern Computing	eastern.org	Ed Tel Communications Inc.	edtel.com
Eastern Pentecostal Bible College	epbc.edu	Ed-Net Educational Electronic Information Service	ednet.bc.ca
Easton Sports Canada	easton-sports.com	EDA Instruments Inc	eda.com
Eastwood Management, Inc.	eastwood.bc.ca	EDAC Inc.	edac.net
Easy Internet Inc.	easyinternet.ca	Eddie's Hang Up Display Ltd.	eddies.com
Easy Sleep Co.	hardrockhotel.com	Edfor Information Consultants Inc.	edfor.com
Eaton's	eatons.com		
EBA Engineering Consultants Ltd.	eba-eng.com	Edgar Venture Management	edgar-g.com
EBA Engineering Consultants Ltd.	eba.ca	Edge Canadian Post-Secondary School Finder	edgeip.com
Ebco-Hamilton Partners	ebco-hamilton.com	Edge Interactive Publishing	schoolfinder.com
Eboard Inc.	eboard.ca	Edgewater Computer Systems, Inc.	edgewater.ca
Ecap Systems Inc.	ecap.ca	Edgeways! Infolink Online Services	edgeways.vancouver.bc.ca
Echidna Consulting, Inc.	echidna.com		
Echo Communications	echo.qc.ca	Edgewise Cafe Electrolit Centre	edgewisecafe.org
Eckhardt-Gramatte Foundation, The	egre.mb.ca	EDI Bridge, Inc.	edi-bridge.com
Eckler Partners, Ltd.	wm.com	EDI Council of Canada	edicc.ca
ECL Computing	telimax.com	EDI Integration	edi3.com
Eclair Inc.	eclair.ca	EDI Sirotic	woodworking.com
Eclectic Data	eclec.com	EDI World Institute - Institut Mondial Edi	ediwi.ca
Eclectic Enterprises Inc.	oxygen.com	Editions Beauchemin Ltd.	beauchemin.qc.ca
Ecodecision	ecodec.org	Editions Pandore Corp.	pandore.qc.ca
Ecodyne Limited	ecodyne.com	Ediwise	ontariowine.com
Ecole Commerciale du Cap	ecc.qc.ca	Ediwise, A Division of Abitibi Price	ediwise.com
Ecole de Technologie Superieure	etsmtl.ca		
Ecole des Hautes Etudes Commerciales de Montreal	hec.ca	Ediwise, A Division of Abitibi Price	toronto.net
Ecole Polytechnique de Montreal	polymtl.ca	Edmonton Catholic Schools	ecs.edmonton.ab.ca
		Edmonton Freenet	freenet.edmonton.ab.ca
Ecological Services for Planning Ltd.	gesp.com	Edmonton Power	edpower.com
Economic Development Edmonton Inc.	ede.edmonton.ab.ca	Edmonton Public Library	publib.edmonton.ab.ca
Economic Innovation and Technology Council	eitc.mb.ca	Edmonton Public School Board, District No. 7	epsb.edmonton.ab.ca
Econotech Services Ltd.	econotech.bc.ca	Edmonton Real Estate Board	realestatewkly.com
Ecstall Mining Corp	ecstall.com	Edmonton Remote Systems	ersys.edmonton.ab.ca
Ed Mock Enterprises	cinesphere.com	Edmonton Sun	edmsun.com

Name of Organization	Domain	Name of Organization	Domain
Edmonton Telephones	edtel.ab.ca	Electronic Graphics Interactive	canmail.net
Edmonton Telephones	eon.net	Electronic Graphics Interactive	prism1.net
Educating Networks Group (Ottawa) Inc.	ednet.on.ca	Electronic Library Network	eln.bc.ca
Education - Management Board Secretariat	edu.on.ca	Electronic Mail Pathways (1003662 Ontario Inc.)	empath.on.ca
Education Innovations Inc.	ei.ca	Electronic Media Creations Inc.	emci.com
Education Technology Centre of British Columbia	etc.bc.ca	Electronic Village	village.ca
Educational Technology Consulting	cortez.com	Electronics & Information Association of Manitoba Inc.	eiam.mb.ca
Educom Training Systems Inc.	educom.on.ca	Electronics Sales Professionals (ESP) Inc.	espinc.ca
Eduplus Management Group Inc.	eduplus.ca	Electrophysics Inc	electrophysics.on.ca
Edwards Marine Inc.	marinesupercentre.com	Elegant Communications Inc.	elegant.com
Eek-A-Geek	eek.org	Elgin and St. Thomas Community Center for Information Access	ccia.st-thomas.on.ca
Effem Foods Ltd.Div. Of Mars Incorporated	effemfoods.com	Elin Computer Resources, Inc.	elin.ca
Efos Canada, Inc.	efos.com	Elite Executive Services	elitexec.com
Egan Visual Inc.	egan.com	Elite Systems Inc.	elite-artwright.com
Eicon Technology Corp.	eicon.com	Elixir Technologies Corporation	elixir.com
Eicon Technology Corporation	eicon.qc.ca	Elizabeth Sutherland School	esutherland.halifax.ns.ca
Eidos Information Spaces Corp.	eidos.ca	Elizabeth Wong	canada-real-estate.com
Elastic BBS	elastic.org	Elle Quebec Inc.	ellequebec.com
Eldernet Project	eldernet.org	Ellinet	ellinet.com
Elections Manitoba	elections.mb.ca	Ellipse Enterprises, Ltd.	ellipsent.com
Electonic Partner	e-partner.com	Ellwood Turner Associates Inc.	ellwood.com
Electra Media Inc.	electramedia.com	Eloquent Systems Inc.	eloquent-systems.com
Electracity Cyberspace Development, Inc	electra-city.com	Elsag Bailey Canada Inc.	bailey.ca
Electric Playgroud	elecplay.com	Elsid Software Systems Ltd.	elsid.ca
Electric Vehicle Association of Canada	evac.ca	Eltek Electronics	eltek.com
Electro Source Inc	electro-source.com	Elty Publications Ltd. O/A Real Estate Weekly	rew.bc.ca
Electro Test Services	electrotest.com	Elysium Book Emporium	elysiumbooks.com
Electro-Byte Technologies	ebtech.net	Emailer Co.	emailer.com
Electro-Meters	electrometer.com	Emarket Inc	emarket.ca
Electrohome Electronics	electro.com	Emarketing Inc.	cyberblack.com
Electronic Circuit Repair & Technology Centre	electech.com	Emarketing Inc.	emarketing.com

Name of Organization	Domain	Name of Organization	Domain
Emco Distribution Group	emcodg.com	Enercana Corporate Finance Ltd. Consultants Ltd.	milkpowder.com
Emco Limited	emcoltd.com	Enercana Export Consultants Ltd.	cattlecom.com
Emcon Emanation Control Ltd.	emcon.com	Enercana Exports Consultants Ltd.	insemination.com
Emediac Inc.	emediac.com	Energia Systems Corporation	energia.ca
Emerald Sea Computing Inc.	esci.com	Energrated Systems Ltd.	energrated.bc.ca
Emergency Interact 88 Inc.	interactems.mb.ca	Energy Cost Management, Inc.	ecmi.com
Emgee Products International	emgee.on.ca	Enerlec Sales Ltd.	enerlec-van.com
EMI Music Canada	ritamcneil.com	Enermodal Engineering Limited	enermodal.com
EMI Music Canada	tomcochrane.com	Engenuity Corporation	engcorp.com
EMI Music Of Canada, Inc.	emimusic.ca	Enghouse Systems Ltd.	enghouse.com
Emily Carr Institute of Art and Design	eciad.bc.ca	Engineered Design Inc.	engdes.com
EMJ Data Ltd.	innorate.com	Engineered Mediums Group	emgee.com
EMJ Data Systems	emj.ca	Engineered Mediums Group	scottland.com
Empire Life Insurance Company, The	empire.ca	English Bay L.I.S.A.	englishbaylisa.org
Empire Media et Communications	empiremedia.com	Enhance Systems Inc	enhance.com
Empire Theatres Limited	empire-theatres.com	Enhance Systems Inc.	enhance.ca
Employment News	employmentnews.com	Enhanced Software Design Inc.	gwiz.com
Employment Referral & Counselling Service	ercs.com	Enhanced Systems Inc.	enhanced.ca
Employnet	employ-net.com	Enhansen Information Systems Ltd.	enhansen.ca
Empower Computerware, Inc.	empower.ca	Enigma	enigma.net
Empress Software Inc.	empress.com	Enne Inc.	enne.ca
EMS Inc.	ems.ca	Enterprise Bowlen Inc.	enterprise-bowlen.com
En Equilibre	boarder.com	Enterprise Information Systems Inc.	eis.ca
Encode Business Systems Inc.	encode.com	Enterprise Network Inc.	entnet.nf.ca
Encompass Information Technology	ncompass.com	Enterprise Online	ent.net
Enconair Ltd.	enconair.ca	Enterprise Online	enterprise.ca
End The Arms Race	peacewire.org	Enterprise Planning Systems Inc.	enterprise.on.ca
Endless Communications Inc.	endless.net	Enterprise Solutions, Ltd.	esol.com
Endlines	endlines.com	Entia Technology	entia.com
Enercana Capital Limited	chinacom.com	Entracte Inc.	entracte.qc.ca
Enercana Capital Limited	fastfood.com	Entrenet Systems	entrenet.com
Enercana Capital Limited	franchises.com	Entrepreneurial Strategic Planners (ESP) Inc.	esp.ca
Enercana Capital Limited	world-merchant-net.com		
Enercana Corporate Finance Ltd. Consultants Ltd.	art-russia.com		

Name of Organization	Domain	Name of Organization	Domain
Entreprise Twinmind	twinmind.qc.ca	ESC.Com	esc.net
Entreprises Julien Inc.	julien.ca	Escape Communications Corp.	escape.ca
Entrevision Inc.	entrevision.com	Escher Grad	escher.com
Entrevision Inc.	homespage.com	Escom Software Services Ltd.	escom.ca
Entropy Enterprises	halflife.com	ESDC — Engine System Development Center Inc.	esdc.com
Entrotec	entrotec.nf.ca	ESE Software	ese.com
Enviro Clean Ltd.	enviroclean.ca	Esker Inc.	esker.ca
Envirofit Consulting Inc	envirofit.mb.ca	Esna Technologies Inc.	esna.com
Enviromental Dynamics Inc	edynamics.com	Esnard Computer Consultants, Inc.	ecci.ca
Environics Research Group Limited	environics.ca	Espace Courbe	espacec.com
Environmental Services Association of Alberta	esaa.ab.ca	Espace Courbe	espacec.montreal.qc.ca
Envirosoft Technologies Inc.	envirosoft.org	ESSA Technologies Ltd.	essa.com
Envision Inc.	envision.ca	ESSA Technologies Ltd.	essatech.com
Envision, Inc.	envision-inc.net	Essema Communications Inc.	essemacom.ca
EPC Industries Ltd	epcind.ca	Essential Software Solutions, Inc	essoft.com
Epicad Inc.	epicad.com	ESSO Chemical Canada	esso.ca
Episet Corporation	episet.com	ESYS Corporation	esys.ca
EPS Essential Planning Systems Ltd.	eps.bc.ca	ETA Circuit Breakers	etacbe.com
Equifax Canada Inc.	equifax.ca	ETC Education Trans Canada Ltd.	spectr.com
Equinova Technology Inc.	equinova.com	Etcetera	etcetera.com
Equist Inc.	equist.com	Etherleap Communications	etherleap.com
Equitable Life of Canada, Inc.	equitable.ca	Ethnomedia Monitor Services Inc.	ethnomedia.on.ca
Equity Retirement Savings System	equity.ca	Etobicoke Board of Education	bdofed.etobicoke.on.ca
Erb and Erb Insurance Brokers Ltd.	erb-erb.com	Ets.Net	ets.net
Ergodesk	ergodesk.com	Ets.Net	exorcist.com
Eric Ansley & Associates Ltd	grx.com	Ets.Net	terror.com
Eric Woodward	neato.com	Euphony Online Publishing	euphony.com
Eric Woodward Inc.	grudges.com	Eureka Communication Inc.	eureka.qc.ca
Ericsson Canada Inc.	ericsson.ca	Eurocopter Canada Limited	eurocopter.com
Eridani Inc.	eridani.com	European University of Chinese Medicine	eucm.org
Erkware	erkware.com	Europlus Corp.	europlus.com
Ernst & Young	ey.ca	Evanic Perrault Robertson Management Consultants Inc.	epr.ca
Eros Marketing Inc.	erosex.com		
ERT West	ertwest.com		
ESC Computer Network Solutions Inc.	esc.on.ca		

Name of Organization	Domain
Evans Software	evanssoft.mb.ca
Event Horizon Technologies Inc.	blackhole.com
Eventwerx Software Inc.	eventwerx.com
Everest & Jennings Cdn., Ltd.	ejcdn.com
Evergreen Foundation	eagletree.com
Evergreen Foundation, The	evergreen.ca
Evergroup Development Enterprises Ltd	evergroup.com
Evert Communications Limited	evert.com
Evertz Microsystems, Ltd.	evertz.com
Everyware Development Corp.	everyware.com
Evolution Interactive, Inc.	evolution-inc.com
EXA Consulting Limited	exa.ca
Exacom Development Inc.	exacom.com
Excalibur Systems Limited	excalibur.com
Excel Computers Inc.	excel.ab.ca
Excelsior Software Systems	excelsior.com
Execulink Internet Services Corporation	execulink.com
Executive Accommodations	execacco.com
Executive Partners B.M. Inc	feelgood.com
Executive Promotions Inc	execprom.ca
Executive Promotions Inc	execprom.com
Executive Travel Appartment Suites, Inc.	etasuite.com
Exis, Inc.	exis.com
Exo-Info	exo-info.qc.ca
Exocom Systems Corporation	exocom.com
Exoterica Corporation	exoterica.com
Expert Systems Resources Inc.	esr.on.ca
Expert Systems Resources Inc.	expsys.com
Expert Systems Resources Inc.	jobsnet.com
Expert Technology Corporation	extec.mb.ca
Expert-Conseils Cogexel Inc.	cogexel.qc.ca
Expertiz 3D Inc.	expertiz.com
Experts-Conseils Cep Inc.	expcep.com
Exploranium G.S., Ltd.	exploranium.com
Explorer Inc.	explorer.ca
Explorer Net Inc.	explorer.net

Name of Organization	Domain
Explorer Software Inc.	explorer.bc.ca
Explorer Software, Inc.	explorer-software.com
Export Development Corporation	edc.ca
Express Lane Communications Corporation	xpresslane.ca
Express Magazines	expressmag.com
Expressvu Inc.	expressvu.ca
Expressvu Inc.	expressvu.com
Extend Communications, Inc.	extendcomm.com
External Services	harbour.com
Extra Bytes	extrabytes.com
Exwire Systems Inc.	exwire.com
Eye Research Institute of Canada	eric.on.ca
Eye Weekly	eye.net
Eye Weekly	eye.org
Eyepoint Inc.	eyepoint.com
Eyepoint Inc.	eyepoint.on.ca
Eyepoint Inc.	numerica.com
Eyeq Networking, Inc.	eyeq.net
Eyes Post Group	eyespost.com
EZ PC Computers Ltd.	ezpc.bc.ca
Ezenet Inc.	ezenet.ca
Ezmail	ezmail.net
Ezmail Inc	ezmail.com
F-Pro Canada (Freelance Professionals)	f-pro.ca
F-Word Communications	cyberbreak.com
F.C. O'Neill, Scriven and Associates Ltd.	oneillscriven.ns.ca
F.G. Commodity Electronics Inc.	chipexchange.com
F.M. Business Computing Services	fmbiz.com
F/X Studios Inc.	fxav.com
F1 Computer Corp.	f1digital.com
F1 Systems	peel-online.com
F1 Systems	safetynet.org
Fabco Data Inc.	fabcodata.com

Name of Organization	Domain	Name of Organization	Domain
Facet Decision Systems, Inc.	facet.com	Fat Dog Software	fatdog.com
Facs Record Centre	facs.mb.ca	Faulding Inc.	faulding.com
Fact Computers	factcomp.com	Faust Consultants	faust.com
Fact International Inc.	fact.com	Fax F/X Information Services Limited	faxfx.ca
Fairview College	fairviewc.ab.ca		
Fairview Technology Centre	ftcnet.com	Fax-Info-Base Corporation	faxinfobase.com
Fairway Business Club	fairway-club.com	Faximum Software Inc.	faximum.com
Falconbridge Limited	falconbridge.com	Faxon Canada Ltd.	faxon.ca
Faltec, Inc.	faltec.com	Faxtel Information Systems, Ltd.	marketfax.com
Famic Inc.	famic.ca	FCA International Ltd.	fcanet.com
Family Forum	efap.com	Federal Business Development Bank	fbdb.ca
Family Insurance Group	unity1.com		
Family Realty Corporation	familyrealty.com	Federal Business Development Bank	fbdb.com
Family Savings Credit Union Limited	fscu.com	Federated Insurance Company Of Canada	fed-ins.ca
Familyware	familyware.com	Federation des Cegeps	fedecegeps.qc.ca
Famous-Players Inc.	famous-players.com	Federation des Producteurs de Volailles du Quebec	volbec.qc.ca
Fanshawe College	fanshawec.on.ca		
Fantasia BBS, Enr.	fantasia.qc.ca	Fekete Associates Inc.	fekete.com
FAQ Inc.	faq.com	Feldspar Networks	feldspar.com
Faradyne Systems Inc.	faradyne.com	Fenders Leasing & Auto Leasing, Ltd.	fenders.com
Farano Green Barristers and Solicitors	fargreen.com		
		Ferguson Simek Clark	fsc.ca
Farnell Electronic Services	farnell.com	Feric (Institut Canadien de Recherches en Genie Forestier)	feric.ca
Farris, Vaughan, Wills and Murphy Barristers & Solicitors	farris.com		
		Fertility Inc.	fertility.ca
Farwest BBS	farwest.victoria.bc.ca	FG Commodity Electronics Inc.	fgcom.qc.ca
		Fiat Products, Ltd.	fiat.ca
Fasken Campbell Godfrey	fasken.com	Fidelity Investments Canada Ltd.	fidelity.ca
Fasstcom Computers Inc.	fasstnet.com		
Fast Doors BBS	fastdrs.com	Fidonet Net 250	net250.org
Fast Find Locators	fastfind.com	Fidonet Net 250	gryn.org
Fast Forward Technologies Inc.	fastfwd.com	Fidonet Net 250	tor250.org
Fastco Ltd.	fastco.com	Fieldstone Marketing and Public Relations Limited	fieldstone.ca
Fastforward Communications Inc.	ffwd.com		
		Fieldworker Products Ltd	fieldworker.com
Fastlane Technologies	fastlane.on.ca	Fifth Dimension Information Systems Inc.	fifthd.ca
Fastlane.Net Limited	fastlane.ca		
Fastman Software Systems, Inc.	fastman.ca	Figment Technologies, Inc.	figment.net
		Film Development Society of British Columbia	bcfilm.bc.ca
Fastron Computer, Inc.	globelnet.net		

Name of Organization	Domain	Name of Organization	Domain
Fim (Forum des Inforoutes et du Multimedia)	fim.org	Flecto Coatings Ltd.	flecto.com
		Fleet House	fleethouse.com
Fimetrics Systems Ltd.	fimetrics.com	Fleet House Electronic Publication	petnet.com
Financecycle	financecycle.com		
Financial Concept Group Securities Corporation	fcg.ca	Fleetrade International, Inc.	fleetrade.com
		Flemming System Corporation	4site.com
Financial Times of Canada	financialtimes.ca	Fletcher Challenge Canada Limited	fccl.com
Finders Keepers	lost-found.com		
Fine Kettle of Fish	redlobster.com	Fleximation Systems Inc.	flexnet.com
Fine Line Communications Ltd.	fineline.mb.ca	Flora St. Community Web	flora.ottawa.on.ca
Finite Systems Consulting	finite-systems.com	Florals Northwest Company	floralsnw.com
Finning Ltd.	finning.ca	FMG Timberjack Inc.	timberjack.com
Fireco Inc.	fireco.com	FMMO Publications Informatiques Inc.	fmmo.ca
Firestop Systems Inc.	firestop.com		
Firing Industries	firing.com	FMR Systems Inc.	fmrsystems.com
First Avenue Information Systems	firstavenue.com	Focam Technologies Inc.	focam.com
		Focus Automation Systems Inc.	focus-systems.on.ca
First Choice Haircutters Ltd.	firstchoice.com		
First Federal	firstlinedirect.com	Focus First Research Inc.	focusfirst.on.ca
First Impression Graphics	firstgraphics.com	Focus Technologies	focustech.com
First Marathon Securities Inc.	fmarathon.ca	Focus Technologies	ftn.net
First Marathon Securities, Inc.	fmarathon.com	Focus Technologies Networks	ftn.ca
First Nations Confederacy of Cultural Education Centers	fnccec.ca	Folio Design, Ltd.	foliodesign.com
		Folklorama™, Folk Arts Council Of Winnipeg, Inc.	folklorama.ca
First Nations Internet Service	first-nations.com		
First Nations Network Inc.	firstnations.ca	Folkstone Design Inc.	folkstone.bc.ca
First Performance Mortgage Company	mortgageselect.com	Fondation de l'Université de Lévis	ulevis.qc.ca
First Perspective, The	firstper.ca	Fonds Fcar	fcar.qc.ca
First Response Corporation	firstresponse.com	fonorola I*Internet Inc.	fonorola.net
First Web	firstweb.com	fonorola Inc.	fonorola.ca
Firstclass Systems Corp.	firstclass.ca	Food Institute of Canada	fic.ca
Firstcom Cato Johnson, Firstcom Marketing Inc.	firstcom.ca	Food Serv	grocery.com
		Foodservice and Hospitality Magazine, Inc.	foodservice.ca
Firstline Trust	firstline.com		
Fisheries Centre	fisheries.com	Foothills Provincial Hospital	fhhosp.ab.ca
Fizzle: A Virtual Washout	under21.com	Footmaxx International Inc.	sportmaxx.com
Flag Shop Inc., The	flagshop.ca	Footprint Software Inc.	footprint.com
Flakeboard Company Ltd.	flakeboard.ca	Footprint Software, Inc.	fsn.ca
Flare Magazine	flare.com	Footprints Software and Electronics	footprints.net
Flatland	flatland.mb.ca		

Name of Organization	Domain	Name of Organization	Domain
Ford Motor Company of Canada, Limited	ford.ca	Foxpacific	marina.net
		Francis, Brent	2tickets.com
Fording Coal Limited	fording.ab.ca	Francis, Brent	suite-300.com
Forefront Graphics	forefront.com	Francomedia	francom.org
Forefront Information Strategies Group, Inc.	forefront.ca	Frank Schaffer Publications, Inc.	frank-schaffer.com
Foreshore Technogies Inc	foreshore-tech.com	Frankel Enterprises	franenco.com
Foresite Creations	4creation.com	Frankfurt Money Strategist,	fmstrategist.com
Forest Alliance of BC	fabc.bc.ca	Fraser and Beatty	fraserbeatty.ca
Forest Engineering Research Institute of Canada	feric.bc.ca	Fraser Basin Management Program	fraserbasin.bc.ca
Forest Heights Collegiate Institute	fhci.kitchener.on.ca	Fraser Broadcaster Ltd.	areasite.com
Forest People International Search Ltd.	forestpeople.com	Fraser Broadcaster Ltd.	fraservalley.com
		Fraser Consulting	climb.com
Forestry Canada	forestry.ca	Fraser Institute, The	fraser.com
Foretell Technologies Limited	foretell.ca	Fraser Valley College	fvc.bc.ca
Forethought Systems Inc.	forethoughtsystems.com	Fraser Valley Information Society Dba Valleynet	valleynet.bc.ca
Foreword Demonstrations Inc.	foretelonline.com	Fraser Valley Real Estate Board	fvreb.bc.ca
Forintek Canada Corp.	forintek.ca	Fred J. Punko and Associates	fjp.com
Formal Systems Inc.	formalsys.ca	Fred Kay	wantok.com
Formats Business Services	formats-business.com	Fred Sawka	sawka.com
Forrest Films Incorporated	forrestfilms.com	Freed and Freed International Ltd.	freed.mb.ca
Forssman & Associates Consulting, Inc.	knowarch.com	Freedman Sharp and Associates Inc.	fsa.ca
Fort Erie Native Friendship Centre	native.fterie.on.ca	Freeman Rodgers Battaglia	frb.com
Fort Garry Industries Ltd.	fgiltd.ca	Freewheelin' Magazine Inc.	freewheelin.com
Fort Ignition Limited	fortignition.ca	Freewill Interactive	freewill.com
Fort Optical	eyewear.com	Freytag Consulting	freytag.com
Fort Whyte Centre	fortwhyte.mb.ca	Friden Neopost	friden.com
Fortier Design Group Inc.	fortierdesigngroupinc.on.ca	Friends of the Environment Fund	fef.ca
Fortis Inc.	fortis.ca	Friesen Tokar Architects	friesentokar.mb.ca
Forward Software	forsoft.com	Frisco Bay Industries, Ltd.	frisco-bay.ca
Four Seasons Hotels Ltd	fourseasons.ca	Frontier Computers	frontier-bc.com
Fox-Novator Systems, Inc.	novator.com	Frostzone BBS	frostzone.com
Foxnet Communications	moosenet.net	FSS Productivity Software Inc.	fssprod.com
Foxnet Communications A Division of Foxtec Computer Systems	foxnet.net	Fujitsu Canada, Inc.	fujitsu.ca
		Fulcrum Technologies Inc.	fultech.com

Name of Organization	Domain	Name of Organization	Domain
Fulton Research	eon.org	G3 Consulting Ltd.	g3consulting.com
Functionality Inc.	functionality.com	Gage Applied Sciences Inc.	gage-applied.com
Fundamental Investments Incorporated	bpeters.com	Gainbery Computer Products Inc.	gainbery.com
Fundamentals Group Ltd. Partnership, The	fun.mb.ca	Galafilm Inc.	galafilm.ca
Fundserv Inc.	fundserv.com	Galaxy Communications	galaxycom.com
Fundy Cable Ltd./Ltee.	fundycbl.com	Galaxy Online Services	galaxy.com
Fundy Cable Ltd/Ltee	fundycbl.ca	Galiano Venture Ltd	galiano.com
Fundy Computer Services Ltd.	fundycs.ca	Gallium Software Inc.	gallium.com
Fundy Perspectives	ashphalt.com	Gallium Software Inc.	prior.com
Fusion Communications	fusionweb.com	Galvan Plastics Inc.	galvanplastics.ca
Fusion Computer Services	viocomm.com	Game Ling BBS	gameling.com
Future Electronics Inc.	future.ca	Gamemaster / Le Maitre de Jeu (Enr.), The	gamemaster.qc.ca
Future Endeavors Inc.	endeavors.com	Gananoque Steel Forging Inc.	gsfi.on.ca
Future Linque	surfup.net	Gandalf Data Ltd.	gandalf.ca
Future Path Development Group Inc.	futpath.com	Gang-Nail Canada Inc.	gang-nail.com
Future Shop Ltd.	futureshop.com	Gapnet Technologies	gapnet.com
Future Simulations	futuresim.com	Garfield Fan Club	garfield.com
Future World Systems	fwsys.com	Garland Commercial Ranges	ventmaster.com
Futureskills	ibschool.com	Gastops Ltd.	gastops.com
Futuretron Software Services	futuretron.on.ca	Gastown Post	gastownpost.com
Futureworld BBS	futureworld.com	Gastown Webspace	gastown.com
FWJ Communications Ltd.	fwj.com	Gate West Communications	gatewest.mb.ca
FX Corporation	fxcorp.com	Gate West Communications	gatewest.net
G&A Telecom S.A.R.F.	ga-tel.com	Gateway BBS	gateway-bbs.com
G-Link Consulting	g-link.com	Gateway File Systems, A Division of Vsd Inc.	gwfs.bc.ca
G-Tek	g-tek.com	Gateway Freight Systems, Inc.	gatewayfrt.com
G. Henderson Manitoba Ltd.	hendersons.mb.ca	Gateway Publishing Co. Ltd.	gatepub.ca
G. Schipper & Assoc. Inc.	gsainc.com	Gathering Trading Cards	gathering.com
G. W. Loukes Consulting Services	gwl-consulting.com	Gaviller & Company, Chartered Accountants	gaviller.on.ca
G.C.O. Inc.	gco.qc.ca	Gay Menage BBS	gay.ca
G.F. Murray	gfmurray.com	Gay-Mart Enterprises Incorporated	gaymart.com
G.M. Systems	gmsys.com	Gaz Metropolitain	gazmet.com
G.T.M. Incorporated	gtm-inc.com	Gazette, A Division of Southam Inc., The	gazette.qc.ca
G.T.S.	gts.net		
G.T.S.	gts.org	GB Communications Inc	gbcomm.com
G.X.K. Ventures Inc.	gxk-ventures.com	GB Micro Electronics Inc.	gbmicro.com

Name of Organization	Domain	Name of Organization	Domain
GCI Communications	gcicanada.com	Geocare Association Of Canada	geocare.org
GCS Consulting	gerryt.com	Geocom Inc.	geocom.ca
GDT Softworks Inc.	gdt.com	Geodimeter Of Canada, Ltd.	geodimeter.com
GDT Softworks Inc.	infowave.net	Geodyssey Limited	geodyssey.com
Geac Computer Corporation	geac.com	Geoff's Inter-Networking Solutions Unlimited	ginsu.com
Gemcom Services Inc.	gemcom.bc.ca		
Gemini Fashions Of Canada Ltd.	gemfash.ca	Geofit Inc.	geofit.ca
		Geomatics International	geomatics.com
Gemini Learning Systems Inc.	gemini.com	Geomatics International Inc.	geomatics.on.ca
Gen-X Consulting Group	genx.mb.ca	Geomembrane Technologies Inc.	gti.ca
Genasys II, Inc.	genasys.bc.ca		
Genasys Inc.	genasys.qc.ca	Geophysical Micro Computer Applications	gmacalgary.com
Gendis Inc.	gendis.ca		
Gene Ware Inc.	geneware.com	Geopower Technologies Inc.	geopower.com
General Datacomm Ltd.	gdc.ca	Georef Systems Ltd.	georef.com
General Hospital Corporation, The	genhosp.nf.ca	George Brown College	gbrownc.on.ca
		George E. Mills Corporation	gemillscorp.com
General Telephone, Inc.	voice-mail.com	George Kelk Corporation	kelk.com
General Telephone, Inc.	voice-mail.net	George Mazurek	cmcautomated.com
Generation Net Services	furniturenet.com	George Weston Ltd.	weston.ca
Generation Net Services	infomontreal.net	Georgeopoulos & Co., Cga	geoco.com
Generation Net Services Inc.	generation.net	Georgeopoulos And Co., Cga	geoandco.com
Generation Seven	gen7.com	Georgian College	georcoll.on.ca
Genesis Architecture & Engineering Inc.	genesis.sk.ca	Geosoft Incorporated	geosoft.com
		Geoterrex Ltd.	geoterrex.ca
Genesis BBS	genesis.calgary.ab.ca	Geoware Software Design	geoware.com
		Gerald Fields & Associates	lawgroup.com
Genesis Media Inc.	genesismedia.com	Gescom Info:Communication Inc.	gescom.qc.ca
Genesis Microchip Incorporated	genesis-microchip.on.ca		
		Gespro Informatique Inc.	gespro.com
Genesys Design	geneart.com	Gestion DTR Inc.	dtr.qc.ca
Genetek Earth Research Corporation	genetek.com	Gestions Technologies Nouvelles Inc.	nebulae.com
Genetics Research Institute, Hospital For Sick Children	genet.org	GETC Software Inc.	getcsoftware.bc.ca
		Getwisdom	getwisdom.com
Geneva Holdings Inc.	legalmail.com	Getwise	getwise.com
Gennum Corporation	gennum.com	Getz Karby	getkar.com
Gentek Marketing Inc. / GVC Canada	gentek.com	Geybruce Inc.	greybruce.com
		GH Johnson's	gh-johnsons.com
Geo Graphics & Photography	geophoto.com	Giga Tron Associates Limited	gigatron.com
Geo. H. Young & Co. Ltd.	ghyoung.ca		

Name of Organization	Domain	Name of Organization	Domain
Gilbert Laustsen Jung Associates Ltd.	glja.com	Global Online, Inc.	go.net
Gilex, Inc.	gilex.com	Global Securities Corp.	globalsec.com
Ginn Photographic Inc.	ginnphoto.on.ca	Global Sourcing Network Inc.	gsnet.com
Girl Guides Of Canada	girlguides.ca	Global Strageties	gsc.com
Giro Enterprises Inc.	giro.ca	Global Strategy	globalstrat.com
Glacier BBS	glacerbbs.net	Global Television Network Inc.	globaltv.com
Glamis Gold, Ltd.	glamis.com	Global Travel Computer Services	global-travel.on.ca
Glegg Water Conditioning Inc.	glegg.com	Global Village Association	globalvillage.org
Glen-Net Communications, Inc.	glen-net.ca	Global Vision Consulting Ltd.	gvcl.com
Glenayre Electronics Ltd.	glenayre.com	Global Volunteers	globalvlntrs.org
Glengarry Biotech, Division of Flockton Analytical Management Inc.	gbt.ca	Global X Change	globalx.net
		Global-X-Change Communications Inc.	globalx.com
Glennie Stamnes Advertising Ltd.	gsstrategy.com	Global-X-Change Communications Inc.	globalx.on.ca
Glenrose Rehabilitation Hospital	grhosp.ab.ca	Global-X-Change Communications Inc.	tour-ottawa.org
Global Childnet	gcnet.org	Globalink Communications	glcom.com
Global Connexxions, Inc.	globalcon.com	Globalserve Communications Inc.	globalserve.net
Global Data Communications Inc.	global-data.com	Globalserve Communications Inc.	globalserve.on.ca
Global Data Communications Inc.	global-data.on.ca	Globe And Mail, The	globeandmail.ca
Global Dataflux Ltd.	dataflux.bc.ca	Globedirect Internet Inc.	globedirect.com
Global Edge Marketing Inc.	gem.ab.ca	Globelle Inc.	globelle.ca
Global Entrepreneurship Centre, Inc.	globalgec.com	Glotman Simpson Consulting Engineers	gsstructure.com
Global Expo Corp	globalexpo.com	GMI Communications Marketing	gmicom.com
Global Graphics	glogra.com	GMS Datalink	gmsdatalink.com
Global Helinet Inc.	heli-net.com	GN Navtel	gn.com
Global Hydroponics	hydroponics.com	GNA Consulting Group Ltd.	gnaconsult.com
Global Job Net Inc.	globaljobnet.com	Gnosis Software, Inc.	gnosis.com
Global Link On-Line Information Service	global-link.com	Go Direct Marketing	godirect.com
Global Marketing And Information Services	nettrader.net	Go Industries Inc.	hook.com
		Goal Electronics Inc.	goal.qc.ca
Global Monitor	globalmonitor.com	Goal Electronics Inc.	goal.waterloo.on.ca
Global Net Data Services Ltd.	global-net.com	Gobeil Financial Management Inc.	gobeil.ca
Global Online, Inc.	global-online.net	God Of Thunder Studios	thunder.mb.ca

Name of Organization	Domain	Name of Organization	Domain
Godin London Inc.	godin.on.ca	Gowling, Strathy & Henderson Barristers & Solicitors, Patent and Trademark Agents	gowlings.ca
Godin London Incorporated	godin.com		
Goede & Associates	internt.com		
Goede & Associates Inc.	goede.on.ca	Gowling, Strathy & Henderson Barristers & Solicitors, Patent and Trademark Agents	gowlings.com
Gold Coast Investments Inc.	gold-coast.com		
Gold Disk Inc	golddisk.com		
Golden Capital Securities Ltd	goldcompass.com	GPC Government Policy Consultants Inc.	gpc.ca
Golden Reach Consulting Inc.	goldenreach.com		
Golden Triangle BBS	golden.org	GPSnet	gpsnet.com
Golden Triangle Computer	events.org	Graffico	graffico.com
Golden Triangle Computer	golden.net	Graffoto	graffoto.com
Golden Triangle On Line	chym.com	Grafix Inc.	skicanada.com
Golden Triangle On Line	ckco.com	Grafix Inc.	skimag.com
Golden Triangle On Line	koolfm.com	Grafix Inc.	ubik.com
Goldstar Business Forms	gbf.com	Grafnetix Systems Inc.	grafnetix.com
Golem Consulting Services	golem.waterloo.on.ca	Grafnetix Systems Inc.	grafnetix.qc.ca
Golex Ltd.	golex.com	Graftek Inc.	labelview.com
Good Beefalo Enterprises	beefalo.com	Granary Enterprises Inc.	granary.com
Good Media Incorporated	goodmedia.com	Grand & Toy	grandtoy.ca
Goodfellow Consultants, Inc.	goodfell.com	Grand Yachts Inc.	grandyachts.com
Goodman Phillips & Vineberg	gpv.com	Grande Prairie Regional College	gprc.ab.ca
Goodway's Enterprises Computer Services	gecs.com		
		Grande Yellowhead Regional Division No.35	gyrd.ab.ca
Goodwill Industries of Toronto	goodwill.on.ca		
Googolplex Corporation	googolplex.com	Grandmaster Technology	grandmaster.bc.ca
Gord Reid and Family	ardan.com	Granny Galactica	grannyg.bc.ca
Gosee Internet Marketing	gosee.com	Grant Internet Communications	georgian.net
Gouvernement du Quebec Conseil du Tresor Services Gouvernementaux	gouv.qc.ca	Grant Internet Communications Inc.	grant.ca
		Grant Macewan Community College	gmcc.ab.ca
Government of Canada / Gouvernement du Canada	gc.ca		
		Grapes Canada Incorporated	grapes.ca
Government of Manitoba	gov.mb.ca	Graphic NRG Inc.	graphnrg.com
Government of Newfoundland And Labrador	gov.nf.ca	Graphics Syndicate	hotgraphics.com
		Graphor Inc.	graphor.qc.ca
Government of the Northwest Territories	gov.nt.ca	Grass Root Systems	grassys.bc.ca
		Grassroots Information Association	grassroots.ns.ca
Government of the Province of Ontario	gov.on.ca		
		Grassroutes Computer Services Ltd.	grassroutes.ns.ca
Government of Yukon	gov.yk.ca		

Name of Organization	Domain	Name of Organization	Domain
Graves and Associates	gravesassoc.com	Gregory Consulting Limited	gregcons.com
Gray Beverage Inc.	gray-beverage.ca	Grenada Real Estate Services	grenada.com
Gray Matter	graymatter.on.ca	Grenadines Real Estate Services	grenadines.com
Gray Research Group, The	gray.mb.ca		
Gray Sage Holdings, Ltd.	graysage.edmonton.ab.ca	Grey Advertising (Vancouver) Ltd.	grey-van.bc.ca
Graybar Electric (Ontario) Ltd.	graybar.on.ca	Grimmett Consulting	all-niter.org
Graystone Multimedia Design Group	graystone.com	Grind Business to Business Paper Inc., The	grind.mb.ca
Great Central Publishing Ltd	frankmag.com	Groupe Educalivres Inc.	educalivres.qc.ca
Great Lakes Pollution Prevention Centre	glppc.org	Grosvenor Square Business Capital Inc.	grosvenor-capital.com
Great Lakes Power Limited	glp.on.ca	Groundzero Production	groundzer0.com
Great Northern Satellite Company	gns.bracebridge.on.ca	Group Corallis	coralis.com
		Group Multimedia Network	gmn.com
Great Pacific News	gpnews.com	Group West Systems Ltd.	groupwest.ca
Great Plains Free-Net Inc	gpfn.sk.ca	Groupe Acces Communication	acces.com
Great Shots, Inc.	calm.com		
Great Western Computers	duncans.com	Groupe Cerveau Inc.	cerveau.ca
Great-West Life Assurance Company	gwl.ca	Groupe Conseil Sygertech Inc.	sygertech.com
		Groupe Cyr	cyr.com
Greater Hamilton BBS	ghbbs.com	Groupe Educalivres Inc.	educalivres.ca
Greater Toronto Home Builders' Association	newhomes.org	Groupe Environnement Shooner Inc.	shooner.qc.ca
Greater Vancouver Regional District	gvrd.bc.ca	Groupe Ist Inc.	istinc.ca
		Groupe Lactel	lactel.qc.ca
Greater Vancouver Regional Employees Union	gvrdeu.org	Groupe Mediom Inc.	mediom.qc.ca
		Groupe Morin Inc.	gmorin.qc.ca
Greater Vernon Chamber of Commerce	vernon.net	Groupe Quebecor Inc.	quebecor.ca
Greater Victoria Public Library	gvpl.victoria.bc.ca	Groupe Regean Dancause & Associes Inc.	dancause.qc.ca
Greater Victoria Savings Credit Union	gvscu.bc.ca	Groupe-Info Quatre Saisons	gi4s.qc.ca
		Grouptheory Systems Inc.	secura.com
Grebar Systems Inc.	grebar.mb.ca	Grower Direct	grower.com
Greenall Enterprises	ringworld.org	Growest Investment Services Inc	growest-ind-inc.com
Greenpark Holdings Inc.	greenparkhomes.com		
Greenpilot Technologies, Inc.	greenpilot.ca	Growth Ministries	growth.org
Greenware Environmental Systems Inc.	greenware.ca	GSA Consulting Group Inc.	gsalink.com
		GSA Consulting Group Inc.	peopletech.com
Greff Computers	greff.com	GSX Computing Corporation	alberta.com
Greg Misumi	misumi.com	GSX Computing Corporation	gsx.com

Name of Organization	Domain	Name of Organization	Domain
GT Net Works Inc.	gtnet.bc.ca	Hacksoft, Inc.	hack.com
GTC Transcontential Group	transc.com	Hagen's Travel	hagens.com
GTL Services Ltd.	gtl-securities.com	Haibeck Communications Inc.	haibeck.bc.ca
Guadeloupe Real Estate Services	guadeloupe.com	Haiti Real Estate Services	haiti.com
Guardian Hotels And Resorts Inc.	guardian.ca	Hakim Electronics Inc.	hakim.com
		Halco Software Systems Ltd.	halco.com
Guelph Freespace	freespace.net	Halhed Enterprises Inc. (HEI)	hei.ca
Guelph Police Services	police.guelph.on.ca	Halifax Economic Summit	summit.halifax.ns.ca
Guess Jeans	guesscanada.com	Halifax Grammar School, The	grammar.halifax.ns.ca
Guideline Digital Printing Service	guideline-dps.com	Halifax Herald Ltd	herald.ns.ca
Guideline Dynamic Sales Ltd.	guideline.com	Halifax Port Corporation Ltd.	hpc.ns.ca
Guild Consulting Ltd.	guild.bc.ca	Halifax Sun	halsun.com
Guild Edgeware Inc.	edgeware.com	Halifax-Dartmouth Real Estate Board	hdreb.ns.ca
Gulf Canada Resources Ltd.	gulf.ca	Hall Connectivity Service	hall.net
Gulf Islanders Assoc Of B.C.	islanders.com	Hallegenic Art Consulting	district.com
Gunther Mele Limited	gunthermele.ca	Hallegenic Art Consulting	indigena.com
Gutenberg Internet Services, Inc.	gutenberg.com	Hallux Consulting Inc.	hallux.on.ca
Gutter Press Inc.	gutter.ca	Halsall	halsall.com
Guy Larouche	guy-larouche.com	Halsall Associates Limited	buildingweb.com
Guysborough County District School Board	schoolboard.guysborough.ns.ca	Halton Board Of Education	haltonbe.on.ca
		Halton Hills Public Library	hhpl.on.ca
GVC Development, Inc.	glb.com	Ham Radio Ragchew BBS	hrr.com
GVC Technologies	gvc.com	Hamar Ventures, Ltd.	ventures-ltd.com
GWE Consulting Group	gwe.com	Hamilton Civic Hospitals	hamcivhos.on.ca
GWN Consultants	gwn.com	Hamilton Civic Hospitals	hch.org
GWN Systems Inc.	gwnsys.ca	Hamilton Telegraphics Inc.	htg.com
GWR Human Resource Services	gwresource.mb.ca	Hamilton-Wentworth Freenet	freenet.hamilton.on.ca
Gyra	gyra.com	Hammerson Canada Inc.	hammerson.com
Gyroscope Media	gyro.com	Hammon, Kennedy & Warnock	hkw.on.ca
H&H Technologies Inc.	vicnet.com	Hammond Manufacturing Company, Ltd.	hammond.ca
H&I Services	hiservices.com		
H. A. Simons Ltd.	hasimons.com	Hampson-Russell Software Services Ltd.	hampson-russell.com
H. L. Blachford	blachford.ca		
H.G. Engineering	hge.com	Hampton Power	hampton-power.com
H.S. Genesis Technologies	hsgenesis.com	Handmade Media	hand-made.com
H.Y. Louie	hylouie.com	Hanen Early Language Program	hanen.org
Hackers Unlimited	hackers-unlimited.com		

Name of Organization	Domain	Name of Organization	Domain
Hankook Tire Canadian Corp.	hankook.com	HCR Corporation	hcr.com
Hanscomb Consultants Inc.	hanscomb.com	HDM Digital	hdmdigital.com
Happy Day Inn Ltd.	happy-day-inn.com	Headed Reinforcement Corp.	hrci.com
Harbinger Solutions Co.	harbinger.bc.ca	Headgate Group of Companies Inc.	headgate.com
Hard Rock Cafe Canada Inc.	hardrockcafe.ca		
Hard Suits Inc.	hard-suits.com	Headquarter Entertainment	wen.com
Harder Software Ltd.	hardersoft.com	Headwaters Inc.	headwaters.com
Harding Enterprises	mdh.com	Headway Holdings Ltd.	headway.com
Hardsoft Systems Ltd.	bserv.com	Heal Society	heal.bc.ca
Hardware Canada Computing Inc.	hcc-unisol.com	Health Action Network Society	hans.org
		Health and Welfare, Canada	hwc.ca
Hardware Canada Computing, 697730 Ontario Incorporated	hcc.ca	Health Information Highway Committee	health.nb.ca
Harlequin Enterprises Ltd.	harlequinbooks.com	Health Net	hnet.bc.ca
Harley Street Software	harleystreet.com	Health Sciences Centre	hsc.mb.ca
Harris Adacom, Inc.	harrisadacom.ca	Healthcor Inc.	healthcor.com
Harris Computer Service	harriscs.on.ca	Healthscreen	healthscreen.com
Harrison, Young, Pesonen and Newell Inc.	hypn.com	Healthvision Corporation	healthvision.ca
		Healthware Technologies Inc.	healthware.on.ca
Harrison, Young, Pesonen and Newell Inc.	hypn.on.ca	Hearst Interactive Canada Inc.	hearst.ca
Harry Jarvlepp, Lawyer	jarvlepp.com	Heating, Refrigeration, and Air Conditioning Institute of Canada	hrai.ca
Hart&Lyne Limited	harte-lyne.ca		
Hartco Enterprises Inc.	cabtel.com	Heaven Sent Computer Services	heaven-sent.com
Hartco Enterprises Inc.	hartco.ca		
Hartco Enterprises Inc.	hartco.com	Hector Paz-Soldan	netcv.com
Hartco Networking Inc.	hartco.net	Helicon Systems Inc.	helicon.com
Hartlin Computer Systems Inc.	hartlin.on.ca	Helijet Airways	helijet.com
Hartman Technica	ht.org	Helikon Technologies, Inc.	helikon.com
Harvest International Venture Corp.	harvest-intl.com	Helios Graphic Design	heliozilla.com
		Helios Integrated Systems Inc.	heliosis.com
Hastings Park Raceway	hastingspark.com	Helix Internet	access-canada.com
Hatch & Associes Inc.	hatchcos.com	Helix Internet	biafra.org
Havergal College	havergal.on.ca	Helix Internet	canadiankids.com
Havers, Dillion & Associates Ltd	bailiffs.com	Helix Internet	geostamps.com
		Helix Internet	haqrz.com
Havi Echenberg & David Gero	havidave.com	Helix Internet	haxrz.com
Hawk Communications Inc.	hawk.nb.ca	Helix Internet	helix.net
Hayward Logic	haywardlogic.com	Helix Internet	kidsonly.com
Hazelton PC's	hazel.com	Helix Internet	minitronics.com
HCE Communications	hce.com		

Name of Organization	Domain	Name of Organization	Domain
Helix Internet	photosphere.com	Highland Logic Inc.	personals.org
Helix Internet	tarfu.com	Highspire Capital	highspire.com
Helix Internet	thincad.com	Highwave Boaterhomes Inc.	boaterhomes.com
Helix Internet	wargames.com	Highwire Information Inc.	highwire.com
Helix Internet Inc.	helix.bc.ca	Hilary Rowland	newfaces.com
Helix Investments (Canada) Inc.	helix.ca	Hilborn: The Newsletter Group, Inc.	hilborn.com
Helix Online	helix-online.com	Hill and Knowlton Corp.	hillknowlton.ca
Helmut Siepmann	helm.com	Hill and Knowlton Corp.	hillknowlton.com
Help Desk Technology Corp.	helpstar.com	Hillside Printing Ltd.	hillside.bc.ca
Hemmera Resource Consultants Ltd	hemmera.com	Hillside Systems	hillside.com
Hemp B.C.	hempbc.com	Hinz Consulting	hinz.com
Henrry Stephen & Associates	dispatches.com	Hip Communications	hip.com
Henry Armstrong	henry-armstrong.com	Hisc Ltd.	hisc.com
		HME Zymurgists Association	beer.org
Henry of Pelham	hopelham.com	HMT Internet Inc.	hmtnet.com
Herb A. Hill Consulting Inc.	northland.com	HMV Canada	hmv.com
Herbert Marshall McLuhan Foundation	mcluhan.ca	HMV Canada, A Division of Temi Canada Inc.	hmv.ca
Herbs in Blume Ltd	hersinblume.com	Hobitron Tech	hobit.com
Hero Communications Inc.	herocom.com	Hockey Hall of Fame	hhof.ca
Herrainco Design	herrainco.com	Hockey Hall of Fame	hhof.com
Herzig Somerville, Ltd.	herzig.com	Hoco Limited	fallswayhotel.com
Hewetson Repping Inc.	hewetson.com	Hogarth-Westmount Hospital	hwhosp.on.ca
Hexacom Info Services	hexacom.com	Holiday Inn by the Falls	holidayinn.com
Hexacom Info Services	hexacom.montreal.qc.ca	Holland College	hollandc.pe.ca
		Holland Marsh Management Group	hollandmarsh.com
Hexagon Computer Systems, Inc.	hexagon.ca	Hollinger Ltd.	hollinger.com
Hexonx Inc.	hexonx.com	Holloway & Schulz	recruiters.com
Hibitek	hibitek.on.ca	Holly Cole Trio	hollycole.com
Hickling Corporation Inc.	hickling.ca	Hollywood Toy & Poster Company	hollywdposter.mb.ca
Hicks Morley Hamilton Stewart Storie	hicks.com	Holmvall International Trading Ltd.	holmvall.markham.on.ca
Hidden Values, Inc.	hv.com	Holstein Association of Canada	holstein.ca
High Performance Concepts	hpcon.mb.ca	Holt Software Associates Inc.	hsa.on.ca
High Times Publications Limited	realestatead.com	Holy Cow Consulting	holycow.com
High-Point Rendel Canada Ltd	high-point-rendel.com	Holy Trinity School	hts.on.ca
High-Tech Direct	htd.com	Home and Garden Network	home-garden.com

Name of Organization	Domain	Name of Organization	Domain
Home Base BBS	homebase.com	HPC High Performance Computing Centre	hpc.com
Home Care Program for Metropolitan Toronto	homecare.toronto.on.ca	HR Solutions Ltd.	hrsolutions.com
Home Hardware Stores, Ltd.	homehardware.ca	HTS Engineering Limited	htseng.com
Home Hunters	homehunters.com	Hubert Un Architect Inc.	hubertun.com
Home Oil Company Limited	homeoil.com	Hudon Gendron Harris Thomas	hght.com
Home Ticket Network Ltd.	htn.com		
Home Trading Network	hometrader.com	Hudson's Bay Company	hbc.com
Homebase	homebase.net	Hughes Aircraft of Canada Ltd.	hac.ca
Homegrown	homegrown.com		
Homelife Benchmark Realty Corp.	homelife.com	Hughes, Amys	hughes-amys.on.ca
		Hugs International	hugs.com
Homenet ™, JEHC Computer Systems Consulting Ltd.	homenet.ca	Hugs International	hugsintl.com
		Hum Magazine Inc.	hum.com
Homepage Marketing	homepage.ca	Human Edge Consulting	humanedge.com
Homeroom ™, Mcnabb & Connolly Inc.	homeroom.on.ca	Human Rights Internet	hri.ca
		Humannet	human.net
Homes On Line	homesonline.com	Humansystems Incorporated	humansys.com
Hometax Information Systems	hometax.com	Humber College of Applied Arts and Technology	humberc.on.ca
Hometown Community Network	hometown.on.ca		
		Hummingbird Communications	hcl.com
Honeywell Limited	honeywell.ca	Hummingbird Communications Ltd.	hummingbird.com
Hong Kong Bank of Canada	hongkongbank.com		
Hookup Communication Corporation	hookup.ca	Humnet	hum.net
		Hunter and Associates	hunter-gis.com
Hookup Communications	hookup.net	Hunter Multimedia Inc.	hunter-mm.com
Hopital St-Francois d'Assise	hsfa.com	Huntington Resources	sportspro.com
Hopton-Scott Consulting	hopton-scott.com	Huron Telecommunication Cooperative Limited	hurontel.on.ca
Horizon Net Proprietorship	horizon.bc.ca		
Hort Inc.	hort.com	Husky Injection Molding Systems Ltd.	husky.on.ca
Hortus Botanicus BBS	hortus.bc.ca		
Hospital For Sick Children	sickkids.on.ca	Hustad Associates Consulting Ltd.	hustad.bc.ca
Hot N Juicy Condom-Mints Ltd.	hotandjuicy.com		
Hotel Jolivent Inc.	jvhotel.com	Hustad Associates Ltd.	hustad.com
Hothaus Technologies Inc.	hothaus.com	Hutchison Avenue Software Corporation	hasc.ca
House 'O Many People	house.org		
Houssennet Inc.	houssennet.nb.ca	HVW Technologies	hvwtech.com
How To Productions.	cybersurfer.com	Hycal Environmental Sciences	hycal.com
Howard Johnson	howardjohnson.com	Hyde Consulting Group	hyde.com
Howmet - Cercast	castit.com	Hydro-Quebec	hydro.qc.ca
		Hydromantis, Inc.	hydromantis.com

Name of Organization	Domain	Name of Organization	Domain
Hymarc, Ltd.	hymarc.com	IBM Canada, OS/2 Group	32bit.com
Hype! Inc.	hype.com	ICA Computer Ltd.	icacomp.com
Hypercomp, An Organization for High Performance Computing	hypercomp.ns.ca	ICAM Publishing Company	icam.com
		Icari Inc.	icari.qc.ca
Hypercube Inc.	hyper.com	Ice Computer Entertainment	iceonline.com
Hyperinfo Canada Inc.	hyperinfo.ca	Icefield Instruments Inc.	icefield.yk.ca
Hyperion Business Corporation	hyperion.bc.ca	Icesystems Limited	icesystems.com
ICI Forest Products	icisprc.com
Hypertech Initiatives Incorporated	hypertech.on.ca	ICI Services	ici-online.com
Hypertech North Inc.	hypertech.yk.ca	ICM International	hungarian.com
Hyprotech Ltd.	hyprotech.ab.ca	ICM International	justweb.com
Hyprotech Ltd.	hyprotech.com	ICM International	webmoney.com
Hystar Corporation	hystar.com	ICM International	wwwcard.com
I Hoffmann & Associates Inc.	h-plus-a.com	ICN Data Limited	icn.net
I&C Inc.	ic-net.com	Icom Internet Services	icom.ca
I&C Inc.	ic-net.net	Icom Ltd.	i-com.com
I*Internet Inc.	i-internet.ca	Icomos Canada Inc	icomos.net
I-Line Multimedia Inc.	iline.on.ca	Icomos Canada Inc	icomos.org
I-Site	i-site.on.ca	Icon Data Systems	icondata.com
I.C.E. Online Services	ice.bc.ca	Icon Internetworking Inc.	icon.bc.ca
I.D. Group Inc.	idgroup.ca	Iconode Inc.	iconode.ca
I.G.T. Inc.	igt.qc.ca	Iconode Inc.	iconode.com
I.Group Systems Inc.	igroupsystems.com	ICRG (Information And Communication Research Group)	icrg.com
I.R.G. Image Design	stocks2watch.com		
Ian Calvert and Associates, Inc.	calvert.org	ICT Systems Inc.	icts.com
Ian Fairlie	iffarch.com	Icynene, Inc.	icynene.on.ca
Ian Martin & Associates	coreenp.com	ID Biomedical Corporation	idbiomed.com
Ian Martin Limited	iml.com	Idea Corp.	ideacorp.nf.ca
Iatco Industries Inc.	iatco.com	Idea Resource Group Inc.	idearesource.com
Iatronet Communications Ltd.	iatronet.net	Ideal Freight, Ltd.	ideal-freight.com
IATSE Local 891	iatse.com	Idealogic Corporation	idealogic.com
IBA Microsystems Inc.	ibamicro.com	Ideas Online Business Net	ideasnet.com
IBC Computer Consulting	webworxx.com	Iders Inc.	iders.mb.ca
Ibertron Technologies Inc.	ibertron.com	Idon Corporation	idon.com
Ibex Technologies Inc.	ibex.ca	Idon Corporation	idon.ottawa.on.ca
Ibis Technology Corp.	charity-bingo.com	IGS, Inc.	igs-inc.com
Ibis Technology Corp.	tcc.net	IGW Canada Inc.	igw.ca
IBM Canada	ibm.ca	IHS Canada Ltd.	ihs.on.ca
		Ilink Communications	waterloo.net

Name of Organization	Domain	Name of Organization	Domain
Ilink Communications	watnet.com	Imediat Digital Creations Inc.	number.com
Illiad	illiad.com	Imediat Digital Creations Inc.	overseas.com
ILS Ltd	ils-ltd.com	Imediat Digital Creations Inc.	perfume.com
Image Color	imagecolor.com	Imediat Digital Creations Inc.	yen.com
Image House	imagehouse.com	IMI	montrealmall.com
Image House Digital Inc.	imagehouse.ns.ca	Immaculate Confection Ltd.	rockychoc.com
Image North Technologies, Inc.	inorth.com	Immad Broadcast Services	immad.com
Image Plus Laser Eye Centre Inc.	iplus.ca	Immedia Telematics Inc.	immedia.ca
		Immuno Canada Inc.	immuno.com
Image Works, The	imagewks.mb.ca	Impact 3000 Inc.	impact3000.com
Imageade Inc.	imageade.com	Impact Communications	impact.ca
Imagelynx Digital Trade Services	imagelynx.com	Imperial Benefit Plan Management Ltd.	kingofwheels.com
Imagen Communications Inc.	imagen.bc.ca	Imperial Flok Co. Ltd.	iflok.com
Imagen Communications Inc.	imagen.net	Imperial Oil Limited	iol.ca
Imagen Communications Inc.	realtimes.com	Imperial Tobacco Ltd.	itl.com
Imagen Communications Inc.	saltspring.com	IMS Canada: Intelligent Manufacturing Systems, Inc.	imscanada.ca
Imagen Communications Inc.	worldtimes.com	IMS Inter-Regional Secretariat	ims.org
Imagenation Media Inc	imagenation-media.com	In-Comm	incomm.com
Imagica S.E.N.C.	imagica.com	In-Line Computer Support Inc.	in-line.bc.ca
Imagination Media Company	imagine.ca	Inasec Incorporation	inasec.ca
Imagination Youth Marketing	iym.com	Incad Software Technologies Corporation	incad.com
Imaginative Computer Solutions, Inc.	ics.bc.ca	Incentive Technologies Inc.	res.com
Imagine That	imagine-that.com	Inch, Easterbrook & Shaker	inchlaw.com
Imagineer	imagineer.com	Inch, Easterbrook & Shaker	llds.com
Imagitek Network Graphic Design	imagitek.com	Inco Limited	inco.ca
		Inco Limited	incoltd.com
Iman Systems Ltd.	iman.com	Incognito Software Inc.	incognito.com
Imax Systems Corporation	imax.com	Incontext Corp.	incontext.ca
Imediat Digital Creations Inc.	call.com	Incontext Corporation	incontext.com
Imediat Digital Creations Inc.	cologne.com	Incremental	incremental.com
Imediat Digital Creations Inc.	communicate.com	Incross	incross.org
Imediat Digital Creations Inc.	digital-directory.com	Indas Limited	indas.on.ca
Imediat Digital Creations Inc.	doppler.com	Inde Electronics	inde.bc.ca
Imediat Digital Creations Inc.	imediat.com	Independent Jewellers Ltd.	independentjewellers.com
Imediat Digital Creations Inc.	importers.com		
Imediat Digital Creations Inc.	makeup.com	India Development Corporation	indevcorp.com
Imediat Digital Creations Inc.	normandie.com		

Name of Organization	Domain	Name of Organization	Domain
India Net	indohome.com	Info-Lynk Consulting Services Inc.	infolynk.on.ca
Indian and Northern Affairs Canada	inac.ca	Info-Pages	info-pages.com
Indian Claims Commission	indianclaims.ca	Info-Planet	info-planet.org
Indigo Information Services	sybernet.com	Info3000	info3000.com
Indigo Rose Software Design Corporation	indigorose.mb.ca	Infobahn Access Services Inc.	infobahn.mb.ca
Indimension	indimension.com	Infobahn Inc.	infobahn.ca
Indonesian Embassy to Canada	prica.org	Infobase Consultants Inc.	infobase.on.ca
Industrial Accident Prevention Association	iapa.on.ca	Infobase Technologies Inc.	ibtech.com
		Infobook	infobook.com
Industrial Research and Development Institute	irdi.on.ca	Infocomm Canada Inc.	infocomm.ca
		Infoconnections	infoconnections. mb.ca
Industry Science & Technology Canada	istc.ca	Infocorp Computer Solutions Ltd.	infocorp.mb.ca
Inetco Systems, Ltd.	inetco.com	Infodesign Corporation	idc.com
Inett	inett.com	Infodraf	infodraf.com
Inex Pharmaceuticals Corp.	inexpharm.com	Infoedge Inc.	infoedge.ca
Infac Corporation	infac.com	Infohighway Onramp Centre, Inc.	ramp.net
Inferno Enterprises	dante.com		
Infi-Net	infinet.mb.ca	Infokinetics Inc.	infokinetics.on.ca
Infiknit	infiknit.com	Infologic Systems	infologic.montreal. qc.ca
Infinite Global Networking	infini.com		
Infinitron International Inc.	infinitron.com	Infolytica Corporation	infolytica.qc.ca
Infinity Internet Communications Incorporated	infinity.ca	Infomagnetics Technologies Corporation	infomag.mb.ca
Infinity Online Services, Inc.	infinity-online.com	Infoman	infoman.mb.ca
Infinity Systems Design Group Ltd.	infinity.bc.ca	Infomaniac's Dial-A-File BBS	dafbbs.com
		Infomart Dialog Ltd.	infomart.com
Info Access (1988) Inc.	infoaccess.on.ca	Infomart Dialog, Ltd.	infomart.ca
Info Dock	infodock.net	Infomatch Communications Inc.	infomatch.com
Info Franchise News Inc.	infonews.com		
Info Media Ordinateurs Inc.	imo.qc.ca	Infomedia Centre Informatique Inc.	infomedia.qc.ca
Info Solution Group	ifsolution.com		
Info Technologies Management	infotech-mgmt.com	Infomedia International Inc.	infomedia.on.ca
		Infopacific	ipx.com
Info Ukraine Communications, Inc.	infoukraine.ca	Infopacific Development	infopac.com
		Infopacific Services	eastasia.com
Info-Data Technologies	markets-west.com	Infopacific Services	woodnet.com
Info-Doc Net Telematique Internationale Inc.	infodoc.ca	Infoplanete Inc.	iplanet.ca

Name of Organization	Domain	Name of Organization	Domain
Infopoint Information Technology Inc	infopt.com	Infostorm Technologies	infostorm.com
		Infostream Services Ltd.	infostream.ab.ca
Infopower International, Inc.	infopwr.com	Infoteck Inc.	infoteck.net
Infoquest PC Solutions	ipcs.com	Infoteck Inc.	infoteck.qc.ca
Inforamp Inc.	inforamp.com	Infotek, Ltd.	infotek.ca
Inforamp Inc.	inforamp.net	Infothink, Ltd.	infothink.com
Information Access Inc.	infoacc.com	Infovision Communications	infovision.net
Information Design Solutions	idscorp.com	Infoware Canada Inc	infoware.ca
Information London	info.london.on.ca	Infoweb Services	infoweb.ottawa. on.ca
Information Management & Economics	ime.com		
		Infoworks Inc.	infoworks.ca
Information Networking Consultants	informnet.com	Infrasoft Inc.	infrasoft.com
		Infrastructures For Information	i4i.org
Information Systems Architects, Inc.	prophecyisa.com	Infratec Systems Ltd.	infratec.com
		ING Corporation	ingcorp.com
Information Systems Incorporated.	cisl.com	Ingenious Systems Domain Inc.	in-sys.com
Information Systems Management (Alberta) Corporation	isma.com	Ingenious Systems Incorperated	dolcom.com
		Ingenious Systems Incorperated	e-fax.com
		Ingenious Systems Incorperated	franchise-sales.com
Information Systems Management Corporation	ism.ca	Ingenious Systems Incorperated	impark.com
		Ingenius Engineering	ingenius.on.ca
Information Technologies of Calgary Ltd.	info-tech.com	Ingram Micro Canada Inc.	imcan.com
Information Technology Association of Canada	itac.ca	Inline Communications Inc.	inline.ca
		Inline Communications Inc.	inline.net
Information Technology Group	itgroup.com	Inline Communications Inc.	inline.org
Information Technology Integration Inc.	iti.qc.ca	Inner Quest Communications Inc.	inner-quest.com
Information Technology Research Centre (ITRC)	itrc.on.ca	Inniskillin Wines	inniskillin.com
		Innovation and Development Corporation	idc.bc.ca
Informatique Multihexa Inc.	multihexa.ca		
Informatique Publiweb Inc.	publiweb.ca	Innovation Place	innovplace. saskatoon.sk.ca
Informatrix 2000 Inc.	informatrix.ca		
Informission Group Inc	grp-inform.ca	Innovation Technologique Intek Inc.	intek.qc.ca
Infosat - Information Via Satellites and Telecommunications	infosat.com		
		Innovative Computers Inc.	doppler.net
Infoserve Technologies Ltd.	infoserve.net	Innovative Edge Inc.	innovative-edge.on. ca
Infoshare Online, Inc.	infoshare.ca		
Infoskill Intelligent Solutions, Inc.	infoskill.com	Innovative Integration Inc.	innogration.com
		Innovative Online	iol.ns.ca.
Infospec Systems	infospec.com	Innovatron	inno.com

Name of Organization	Domain	Name of Organization	Domain
Innovatron	inno.org	Institute for Space and Terrestrial Science	ists.ca
Innovmetric Logiciels Inc.	imetric.qc.ca	Institute for Work and Health	iwh.on.ca
Innovus Inc.	innovus.com	Institute of Chartered Accountants of B.C.	ica.bc.ca
Innovus Inc.	innovus.on.ca		
Inquiry Management Systems Inc.	ims.ca	Institute of Chartered Accountants of Ontario, The	icao.on.ca
Insanely Interactive System Inc.	traveltravel.com	Institute of Electrical and Electronics Engineers of Canada	ieee.ca
Insanely Interactive Systems Inc.	bar.net		
Insanely Interactive Systems Inc.	fsight2.com	Institute of Marine Safety Auditors - IMSA (International)	imsa.com
Insanely Interactive Systems Inc.	iisys.com	Institute of Ocean Sciences	ios.bc.ca
INSI Integrated Systems Inc.	insi.mb.ca	Institute on Governance, Inc.	igvn.ca
Inside Net	insidenet.com	Instore Focus	instore.ca
Insideinfo BBS	insideinfo.com	Instrumar Limited	instrumar.nf.ca
Insight Canada Research Inc.	insight.ca	Insurance Bureau of Canada	ibc.ca
Insight Computer Solutions	icsnetwork.com	Insurance Canada Inc.	insurance-canada.ca
Insight Information	insightinfo.com		
Insight Information	insightinfo.on.ca	Insurance Corporation of British Columbia	icbc.bc.ca
Insight Marketing Communications Inc.	insightmc.com	Insurance Corporation of British Columbia	icbc.com
Insight News	insightnews.com	Insurance Warehouse	insuranceware.com
Insite Webzine Inc.	insitezine.com	Int'L Society for Orthomolecular Medicine	orthomolecular.com
Instant Access News	prepaid.com	Int'L Tasty Fry Inc.	inttastyfry.com
Instantiated Software, Inc.	instantiated.on.ca	Integain Corporation	integain.com
Instar Corporation	instar.com	Integral Investments Incorporated	integral.on.ca
Instep Mobile Communications Inc.	instep.bc.ca	Integrated Communication-Technology	icotec.com
Institut de Readaptation de Montreal Inc.	ireadapt.qc.ca	Integrated Engineering Software	integrated.mb.ca
Institut de Recherche d'Hydro-Quebec (IREQ)	ireq.ca	Integrated Management Resourcs Inc.	imr.on.ca
Institut de Recherche en Sante et en Securite du Travail du Quebec (IRSST) (Quebec Occupational Health and Safety Research Institute)	irsst.qc.ca	Integrated Mapping Technologies Inc.	intmaptech.com
		Integrated Messaging Inc.	imi.mb.ca
		Integrated Network Services Inc.	insinc.net
Institute for Clinical Evaluative Sciences, The	ices.on.ca	Integrated Open Systems Ltd.	iosl.ca
Institute for Computer Studies	icsca.com	Integrated Rural Delivery Network (IRDN) Alliance	irdn.nf.ca

Name of Organization	Domain	Name of Organization	Domain
Integrated Systems Applications Corporation	isac.ca	Interact Adv	interadv.com
Integrated Telecommunications Systems, Inc.	its.ca	Interactive Business Computers Inc.	ibcinc.on.ca
		Interactive Cafe	icafe.com
Integrate_Publishing	integrate-publishing.com	Interactive Client Services - Revenue Canada	icscan.com
Integration Informatique BDM Inc.	integration.qc.ca	Interactive Electronic Design	ied.com
Integrator Systems	itegrator.com	Interactive Image Technologies Ltd.	interactiv.com
Integrity Group Of Network Marketeers, Inc., The	integrity.ca	Interactive Media Inc.	itel.com
		Interactive Online Ltd.	ionline.net
Intek Inc.	soprin.com	Interactive Technical Services	itserv.com
Intelagent R & D Inc.	intelagent.qc.ca	Interactive Telecom Inc.	interactive.ns.ca
Intelatech Inc.	intelatech.com	Interactive Telecom Inc.	intertel.net
Intelecon Research & Consultancy Ltd.	intelecon.com	Interactivity Inc.	interactivity.com
Intelepath Internet Services	intelepath.sk.ca	Interautomation Inc.	iainc.com
Inteleq Inc.	inteleq.com	Interbec Inc.	interbec.com
Intelex Press	intelex.com	Intercime Inc.	intercime.qc.ca
Intella Digital Lists	idlnet.com	Intercom Management Resource Group	intercomplacement.com
Intellia Productions Inc.	intellia.com		
Intellibyte Inc.	intellibyte.com	Intercon Security Ltd.	intercon.ca
Intelligent Marketing Systems, Inc.	imsi.ab.ca	Interconnet	interconnet.com
		Interdata Enr.	interdata.qc.ca
Intelligent Microsystems, Ltd.	ims.on.ca	Interdoc	interdoc.com
Intelligent Touch Solutions Inc.	intouch.on.ca	Interdynamix Ltd.	interdynamix.com
Intellimedia Corporation	intmedia.com	Interexpo, Inc.	digitalmedia.com
Inter Find Locators	interfind.com	Interface Productions	it-online.com
Inter Pub Inc.	interpub.qc.ca	Interfacing Technologies Corp.	interfacing.com
Inter-Acces Communications	interax.net	Interhop Networking Services	interhop.net
Inter-Cable Internet Inc.	gig.net	Interlace Media	interlace.mb.ca
Inter-Com Information Services	icis.net	Interlan Consulting Inc.	interlan.ca
		Interlan Montreal Inc.	interlan.qc.ca
Inter-Com Information Services Ltd.	icis.on.ca	Interlink Inc.	interlink.net
		Interlink On-Line Services Inc.	interlink.bc.ca
Inter-Conn Telecomm	ictel.com	Interlinx Internet Inc.	interlinx.net
Intera Information Technologies	intera.ca	Interlinx Ltd.	interlinx.qc.ca
		Interlinx Support Services, Inc.	ilinx.com
Intera Tydac Technologies	tydac.com	Interlog Internet Services	interlog.com
Interaccess Technology Corp.	interaccess.ca	Intermagic, Inc.	intermagic.com
Interaccess Technology Corporation	iatech.com	Intermed ™, CHCA Inc.	intermed.ca

Name of Organization	Domain	Name of Organization	Domain
Intermed Canada	intermed-canada.com	International Forest Products Ltd.	interfor.bc.ca
Intermed Healthcare Systems	intermed.org	International Image Service Inc.	intl-image.com
Intermedia ™, Harris Media Systems Limited	intermedia.ca	International Institute for Sustainable Development	iisd.ca
Intermedia Association de Serveurs Telematique Inc.	intermedia.qc.ca	International Interactive Computing Society	iics.bc.ca
Intermedia Press Ltd.	impress.com	International Library Systems Corp.	ils.ca
Intermet	intermet.com	International Machinery	intl-mach.com
International Air Transport Association	iata.org	International Netmodels Agency	netmodels.com
International Association for Management of Technology	iamot.org	International Network Communications, Ltd.	korecom.com
International Association of Firefighters - Canadian Office	firefighters.ca	International Publishing & Development Inc	worldexport.com
International Association of Mathematical Geology	iamg.org	International Publishing & Development Inc.	cecd.com
International Aviation Development Corporation	iadc.com	International Publishing & Development Inc.	exporters.com
International Center for Agriculture Science and Technology	icast.sk.ca	International Publishing & Development, Inc	canexport.com
International Center for the Advancement of Community-Based Rehabilitation	icacbr.org	International Range Officers Association	iroa.com
International Civil Aviation Organization	icao.org	International Reliable Access Network, Inc	iran.com
International Comptech Engineering Services, Ltd.	canices.com	International Resource Centre	ircinc.com
		International Sea Search Inc.	seasearch.com
International Computer Group Inc.	digiverse.com	International Submarine Engineering Ltd.	ise.bc.ca
International Congress of Business Councils	icbc.org	International Systemap Corporation	ismcorp.com
International Council on Monuments And Sites	intcomos.com	International Systems Group Inc.	isgsys.com
International Data Corporation (Canada) Ltd.	idc.ca	International Tax Services Group Ltd.	tax-usa-can.com
International Data Corporation (Canada) Ltd.	idccanada.com	International Teletimes	teletimes.com
International Development Research Centre	idrc.ca	International Thermal Research	itrl.com
International Federation of Insititues for Advanced Studies	ifias.ca	International Thunderbird Gaming Corporation	internationaltbird.com
International Financial Centre	ifcvancouver.com	International Thunderbird Gaming Corporation	intltbird.com

Name of Organization	Domain	Name of Organization	Domain
International Travel Academy	sita.com	Internet Front Inc.	infront.on.ca
International Travel Holdings Limited	ith.ca	Internet Front Inc.	internetfront.com
International Verifact, Inc.	verifact.com	Internet Global Info-Access Inc.	global.ca
Internet - BBSI Inc.	bbsi.net	Internet Global Info-Access Inc.	globale.net
Internet Access	iax.com	Internet Group Inc., The	tig.ab.ca
Internet Access - Worldwide	iaw.com	Internet Innovations, Incorporated	in.on.ca
Internet Access Group	iag.com	Internet Kingston	kingston.net
Internet Access Inc.	intacc.ca	Internet Laurentides Inc.	intlaurentides.qc.ca
Internet Access Inc.	intacc.com	Internet Light & Power	ilap.com
Internet Access Inc.	intacc.net	Internet Light And Power	ilap.com
Internet Access Worldwide, Inc.	iaw.on.ca	Internet Lottery Corporation	lottery.net
Internet Advertising Inc.	classifieds.net	Internet Management Inc.	imi.net
Internet Advertising Inc.	whitepages.net	Internet Market Research	imar.com
Internet Advertising Inc.	yellowpages.net	Internet Media Solutions	internetmedia.com
Internet Aware Inc.	netaware.com	Internet Media Xm Inc.	intertower.com
Internet Canada Corporation	ican.ca	Internet Mont-Laurier, Enr.	imlaurier.qc.ca
Internet Coffee Club	coffeeclub.ns.ca	Internet Order House Ltd.	ioh.bc.ca
Internet Communications Inc.	intnet.bc.ca	Internet Outdoors	outdoorsman.com
Internet Communications Services Inc.	ics.mb.ca	Internet Pageworks	internetpagework.com
Internet Companion, The	tic.ab.ca	Internet Passport Services Inc.	ips.ca
Internet Connect	icnect.com	Internet Plus	internetplus.com
Internet Connect Niagara	vqa.com	Internet Portal Services	reinlink.com
Internet Connect Niagara	winecouncil.com	Internet Portal Services, Inc.	portal.ca
Internet Connect Niagara, Inc.	niagara.com	Internet Psychic's Network	psychics.net
Internet Connectivity Services Inc.	icons.net	Internet Publishing Corp.	corp.net
Internet Consultants	in.edmonton.ab.ca	Internet Publishing Inc.	interpub.com
Internet Consulting Group	icg.on.ca	Internet Publishing Inc.	personals.net
Internet Contact Lens Service	acuvue.com	Internet Publishing Inc.	wp.net
Internet Conversion, Inc.	conversion.com	Internet Publishing Inc.	yp.net
Internet Direct, Inc.	canada.net	Internet Resource Centre Inc	the-irc.com
Internet Direct, Inc.	direct.ca	Internet Saguenay Lac St-Jean Inc	saglac.qc.ca
Internet Direct, Inc.	netdirect.net	Internet Service Providers Consortium, Inc.	ispinc.com
Internet E-Mail Services, Inc.	emailme.com	Internet Services And Information Systems Inc.	isisnet.com
Internet Express	internetexpress.com	Internet Shop Inc., The	netshop.bc.ca
Internet Financial Network Inc.	ifinancial.com		

Name of Organization	Domain	Name of Organization	Domain
Internet Shop.Net Inc.	shop.net	Intertrends Communications	intertrends.com
Internet Software Develapment Corp	wiz.org	Intervac International	intervac.com
		Intervex Consulting	handbook.com
Internet Software Development Corp	wizywyg.com	Intervider Communication Inc.	intervider.net
		Intervider Communication Inc.	intervider.on.ca
Internet Software Technologies	ist.ca	Intervision Communications	intervision.com
Internet Solutions, Inc.	intersolve.com	Intervista, Inc.	intervista.ca
Internet Solutions, Inc.	solutions.net	Interweave Communication Group	iweave.mb.ca
Internet Solutions, Inc. (ISI)	solutions.mb.ca		
Internet Sports Pools Inc.	pool.com	Interweb Communications	web-o-rama.com
Internet Time	internettime.com	Interweb Internet Services	interweb.com
Internet Training Group Inc.	itgcan.com	Interweb Internet Services	interweb.net
Internet Trois-Rivieres Inc.	itr.qc.ca	Interweb Internet Services	tradeweb.com
Internet Victoriaville	intelagent.com	Interwood Marketing, Ltd.	interwood.com
Internet Victoriaville Ltd.	ivic.qc.ca	Interwork Software Inc.	interwork.com
Internet Voice Message, Inc.	ivm.com	INTI Communications	inti.com
Internetwork Solutions, Inc.	setup.net	Intranet Inc.	intranet.on.ca
Internetworking Systems Group	isginc.com	Intransnet Service Ltd.	intransnet.bc.ca
Internex Online Inc.	io.org	Intrawest Corporation	intrawest.com
Internode Networks	internode.net	Intrepid Information Systems Inc.	intrepid.on.ca
Internorth Construction Company Limited	iccl.on.ca	Intrinsix Design Media Ltd.	intrinsix.ca
Interpass Technologies, Inc.	interpass.com	Intunix Inc.	intunix.com
Interpath	interpath.barrie.on.ca	Inuit Gallery	inuit.com
		Invention Quebec Inc.	inventionquebec.qc.ca
Interpro Consultants Inc.	interpro.qc.ca		
Interprovincial Pipe and Steel Co. Inc.	ipsco.com	Investex Ltd	investex.com
		Investornet Inc.	investornet.com
Interprovincial Pipe Line Inc.	ipl.ca	Investorquest Communications Ltd.	investorquest.com
Intersketch International	intersketch.com		
Interspace Network Solutions	interspace.com	Investors Group	igroup.ca
Interspect Systems Consulting Corp.	interspect.com	Investors Network Ltd	investorsnetwork.com
Intertec Corporation	intertec.ca	Invisions Productions, Inc.	invisions.ca
Intertech Consultants Inc	intertech.qc.ca	Invitech Corporation	invitech.com
Intertech Systems Inc.	isi-can.com	Invoice Canine Equipment Inc.	caninequip.com
Intertech Systems Integrators, Inc.	isi.on.ca	Iograph Inc.	iograph.ca
Intertek Internet Technology Services Inc.	itsi.ca	Iona Appliance Inc./Fantom Technologies	fantom.com
Intertex Corp	intertex.com	Ionix Internet Educational Services	ionix.com

Name of Organization	Domain	Name of Organization	Domain
Iosat Incorporated	iosat.com	IWA Community Credit Union	iwaccu.com
Iosco	iosco.org	Iware Technology	iwaretech.com
Iotek Inc.	iotek.ns.ca	Iware Technology, Inc.	iware.on.ca
Ipfirewall Corporation	ipfirewall.com	Izaak Walton Killam Hospital for Children	iwkhosp.ns.ca
Ipts Inc.	iptsi.com	J Mode Marketing	jmode.com
Irenyx Data Group Inc.	ark.com	J-Squared Technologies	jsquared.com
Iris Systems Inc.	iris.mb.ca	J. Fichtner & Associates	fichtner.com
Irisco	irisco.com	J. J. Conklin Communications	jjconklin.mb.ca
Ironstone Technologies	ironstone.mb.ca	J. L. Ilsley High School	ilsley.halifax.ns.ca
Irwin Toy Ltd.	irwin-toy.com	J. O. R. Associates	jor.com
Island Internet Inc.	island.net	J. White & Associates, Inc.	jerrywhite.com
Island Internet Inc.	islandnet.bc.ca	J.A. Carroll Consulting	jacc.com
Island Net - AMT Solutions Group Inc.	duncan.net	J.B.'s Trophy and Award Mfg.	jbtrophy.mb.ca
Island Paper	islandpaper.com	J.C Kelly & Associates	jckelly.com
Island Services Network	isn.net	J.D. Mack Limited	jdmack.ns.ca
Island Services Network	pei.net	J.G. Noguera & Associates.	jgna.com
ISM Corporation, Sis Region	ismcan.com	J.J. Barnicke Limited	jjb.com
ISMBC	ismbc.com	Jacques Duranleau	lujac.com
Isolation Systems Ltd.	isolation.com	Jade Simulations International Corporation	jade.ab.ca
Isotro Network Management Inc.	isotro.ca	Jade Simulations International Corporation	jade.com
ISS Technologies Group	isscanada.com	Jag Computer Consultants	cyg.net
Isys Technology Inc.	isys.ca	Jag Lampshade Company	lampshade.com
IT Communications Canada	it.ca	Jagger Hims Ltd.	jhlstc.com
IT Multimedial Ltd.	itmultimedia.com	Jalsam Inc.	jalsam.com
IT Staffing	itstaff.com	Jambone Comics Inc.	jambone.com
IT/Net Consultants Inc.	itnet.ca	James G. Heller Consulting Inc.	jghcons.com
IT/Net Consultants Inc.	itnet.on.ca	James Glave	gyroscope.com
Itech Computer Products, Inc.	itech.on.ca	James Hoggan and Associates	jhapubrel.com
ITI Information Technology Institute Inc.	iti.ca	James Portman & Associates	jpa.com
ITI Logiciel Inc.	iti-logiciel.com	James R. Hay and Associates	haya.qc.ca
ITN Corporation	itncorp.ca	James Richard & Sons, Limited	jrsl.mb.ca
ITSI	itsi.net	Jamie Cooper Ltd	intsoc.com
ITV Ltd.	itv.ca	Jamm Infonet	jamm-infonet.com
Ivanhoe Inc.	ivanhoe.ca	Jammy's Amiga Gateway	jammys.net
IVR Interactive	ivr-interactive.com	Jamnan J. Law	janusis.com
Ivy Communications	ivy.com	Jana Publishing	jana.com
Ivy Realty Inc	ivy-realty-inc.com		

Name of Organization	Domain	Name of Organization	Domain
Janet Fortt	nasdaqstocks.com	Jetcom Communications	jetcom.com
Janna Systems, Inc.	janna.com	Jetform Corp.	jetform.com
Jannock Limited	jannock.com	Jetnet Systems Inc.	jetnet.ab.ca
Jannock Steel Fabrication Company	jsf.com	Jetwin Asia Canada Inc.	jetwin.ca
Janssen Pharmaceutical Inc.	janssen.ca	Jeunique International, Inc.	the1daydiet.com
Janssen-Ortho, Inc.	joi.ca	Jeunique Lifestyle Images	jeunique.com
Janus Technology Canada Inc.	janustech.com	Jitec Corporation	jitec.com
Japan Cultural Exchange Ltd.	jce.com	JKA Communications Ltd	jka.com
Japan Karate Association	jka.org	JKL Micro Distribution Inc.	jklmicro.com
Japan Travel Bureau	jtb.com	JKL Technologies Inc.	jkltech.com
Jarvis Business Center Inc.	jarviscentre.com	JM Design Ltd.	sober.com
Jasper BBS	bbs.jasper.ab.ca	JMG Compushoppe Ltd.	jmg.on.ca
Jay Winick Consulting	webhedz.com	Job Oriented Training Inc.	jot.nb.ca
Jazz Consulting	jazz.on.ca	Jobs Canada Incorporated	jci.ca
JC & Co.Ltd	jcco.com	Jobs Canada Incorporated	jobsinc.ca
JCC Networks	jcc.net	Jobs Canada Technologies Incorporated	jcitech.com
JCC Networks Enr.	jcc.qc.ca	John Coutts Library Services	coutts.on.ca
JCS Canada Inc.	jcs-canada.com	John Dafoe Photography	granville-island.com
JDP Computer Systems Inc.	worldsbest.com	John Forsyth Company	jforsyth.com
Jdp.Com	jdp.com	John Free Inc.	manitou.com
JDS Fitel Inc.	jdsfitel.com	John M. Fairley Consulting	jmfc.com
JDS Fitel, Inc.	fiberoptics.com	John Oram	oram.com
Jeep Jamboree Canada Corp.	jeepjamboree.ca	John Poyser Consulting	poyser.com
Jeff Voskamp	voskamp.waterloo.on.ca	John Richardson	prep.com
Jefferson Partners Capital Corporation	jefferson.com	John S. Koperwas	koperwas.org
		John Sherman Agency Ltd.	johnsherman.com
Jenera Inc.	jenera.com	John Sweeney Management Consultant Ltd	sweeney.com
Jenex Computer Systems Inc.	jenex.mb.ca	Johnson & Associates	bhm-boa.com
Jenkins Leaside Travel Ltd.	travel4u.com	Johnson's Furniture	johnsons-furniture.com
Jennel Enterprises	jennel.com	Jonathan Kean Design	jonk.com
Jeoffrey Chang & Com	bid-ask.com	Josaman Agencies Ltd.	josaman.mb.ca
Jeremy Hockenstein	hockenstein.com	Josef Mach	infohop.com
Jermey Wilson Consulting	jeremy.com	Jovial Communications	jovial.on.ca
Jerrwood	jerrwood.on.ca	Joya Consultants	joya.com
Jes Library Automation	jeslacs.bc.ca	Joymarmon Group Inc., The	joymrmn.on.ca
Jesco Automated Services Inc.	jesco.com	JPT Directories, Inc.	jptdir.com
Jesters BBS	jester.com	JR Group	jrgroup.com

Name of Organization	Domain	Name of Organization	Domain
JRV Informatique, Enr.	jrv.qc.ca	Karat Systems Inc.	karat.com
JS Radio Network	htzfm.com	Karhu Canada	karhu.ca
JTS Computer Systems Ltd.	jts.com	Karhu Canada	karhu.com
Judith Sams Enterprises Ltd.	borack.com	Karmax Heavy Stamping	karmax.com
Jumpstart Enterprises Ltd.	jel.com	Karo Design Resources, Inc.	karo.ab.ca
Jungle BBS, The	jungle.ottawa.on.ca	Kasten Chase Applied Research	kasten.on.ca
Junior Achievement Canada	jacan.org		
Junior Mine Services Ltd.	juniormine.on.ca	Katydid Information Systems Inc.	katydid.on.ca
Juniper Lumber Company Ltd.	juniperlumber.nb.ca	Kayaker	kayaker.ca
Junkyard BBS	jybbs.com	Kaydara Inc	kaydara.com
Jura Technologies	jura.com	Kazak Communications	corelnet.com
Justus Ottawa Consulting	ottawa.com	KB's BBS	kbsbbs.com
Juvenile Diabetes Foundation of Canada	jdfc.ca	KBS Technology Incorporated	kbs.com
Juxta Publishing	juxta.com	KC Computer Works	kccom.nf.ca
JVC Canada Inc.	jvc.ca	KCK Enterprises	kck-enterprises.com
JVMTECH Inc.	jvmtech.qc.ca	Kea Systems Ltd.	kea.bc.ca
JWI Ltd.	jwi.ca	Keating Technologies Inc	keating.com
K-12 Technology by Design Centre Ltd.	k12technology.bc.ca	Keewatin Community College	keewatincc.mb.ca
K-W Access-Ability	kwa.on.ca	Keith Medcalf & Associates	dessus.com
K.C. Chen Technology, Int'L. Ltd.	shentech.com	Kelman Seismic Processing Inc.	kelman.ab.ca
		Ken Haycock & Associates Inc	rockland.com
K.E.B. System 1 BBS	keb1.winnipeg.mb.ca	Ken Kittlitz	yeti.com
K.T.K. Communications Ltd.	ktk.com	Ken Roberts Computer Consltants Inc.	mirror.org
Kadak Products Ltd	kadak.com		
Kadis Computerized Services	kcstraining.com	Ken Schwabe	schwabe.winnipeg.mb.ca
Kagan & Kagan	kagan.on.ca	Kendall Systems	kensys.com
Kaitila Consulting	kaitila.com	Kenmount Motor Incorporated O/A City Honda	cityhonda.nf.ca
Kaizen Media Services	kmsi.com		
Kal Tire	kaltire.com	Kenonic Controls Ltd.	kenonic.com
Kalman Technologies Inc.	kalman.com	Keops Informatique Inc	keops.com
Kam-Ed Institute Inc.	kamed.bc.ca	Kerbel Communications, Inc.	kerbel.com
Kanatek Technologies	kanatek.ca	Kerr Controls Limited	kerrcon.ca
Kanatek Technologies	sofpak.com	Kerr Vayne Systems Ltd.	kvs.com
Kanotech Information Systems Ltd.	kanotech.ca	Key Research and Development	infoglobe.com
Kanservu Bureau	kanservu.com	Key Research and Development	infoglobe.net
Kao Infosystems Canada, Inc.	kaocanada.com	Keyano College	keyanoc.ab.ca
Karacters Design	karacters.com	Keystart	keystart.com

Name of Organization	Domain	Name of Organization	Domain
Keyword Office Technologies	keyword.com	KLR Consulting Inc.	klr.com
KFOC & Associates	kfoc.com	KMH Cardiology And Diagnostic Centres, Inc.	kmh.on.ca
Kidstuff	kidstuff.com		
Kilborn Engineers	kilborn.com	Kneehill Internet Services	kneehill.com
Kilreh Consulting	kilreh.toronto.on.ca	Knight Communication Systems	bintech.com
Kinesys Active Sportscare Inc.	kinesys.ca	Knightec BBS	knightec.com
Kinetic Inc.	kineticinc.com	Knossopolis	pearshaped.com
Kinetic Records Inc.	kinetic.ca	Knowledge Connection Corporation	kcc.ca
Kinetic Sciences Inc.	kinetic.bc.ca		
Kinetix Digital Animation and Design, Inc.	kinetix-da.com	Knowledge House Publishing Limited	khp.com
King's University	college,the	Knowledge Plus Multimedia Publishing	insports.com
Kings Edgehill School	kingsedge.windsor.ns.ca	Knowledge Plus Multimedia Publishing	kpp.com
Kingston College	kingston-college.com	Knowledge Plus Multimedia Publishing Ltd.	kplus.bc.ca
Kingston District Community Information Centre	info.kingston.on.ca	Knowledge-Space	knowledge-space.com
Kingston General Hospital	kgh.on.ca		
Kingston Online Services	kosone.com	Knowledgelink	knowledgelink.com
Kingsun Systems Inc.	kingsun.com	Kom Inc.	kom.org
Kingsway Computing Solutions	kingsway.com	Kom Inc.	kominc.com
Kintetsu International Express Canada	kiecan.com	Komex International Ltd	komex.com
		Kookooroo Restaurants	kookooroo.com
Kirk Computer Systems Ltd.	kirk.nt.ca	Kootenay Network Systems	kootenay.net
Kirstein, Neidig, & Vance,Ca	knv.com	Koreana Resources	krd.com
Kitchen Craft of Canada Ltd.	kitchencraft.ca	Korsa International	korsa.com
Kitchener-Waterloo Internet Cooperative	kwic.net	Kostuch Publications Limitedo/A Foodservice and Hospitality Magazine	kostuch.com
Kitchener-Waterloo Municipal Area Network	kw.net		
Kitchener-Waterloo Record	therecord.com	KPMG	kpmg.ca
		KR Data Communications Inc.	krdata.com
Kitco Minerals & Metals Inc.	kitco.com	Kraft General Foods Canada	kraft.ca
Kitsilano Network Research	kitsnet.vancouver.bc.ca	KRB Enterprises	vilgreen.com
		KRG	krg.com
Kitso Enterprises Ltd.	kitso.com	Krismic Consulting Inc.	krismic.com
Kiwi Consulting Inc.	kiwi.com	Kruger Inc.	kruger.com
KL Consulting	klconsulting.com	KT Global Enterprises	ktglobal.hamilton.on.ca
KL Group Inc.	klg.com		
Klohn Crippon	klohn.com	KT Industries Ltd.	ktindustries.mb.ca
Klondike Network Services	gold-rush.com	KTS Business Systems Inc.	kts.com
Klondike Network Services	klondike.com	Kubota Metal Corporation	kubotametal.com

Name of Organization	Domain	Name of Organization	Domain
Kuhn & Associates Ltd.	industrylink.com	Lacite College	lacitec.on.ca
Kumaran Systems, Inc.	kumaran.com	Lacure Corporate and Leisure, Inc.	lacure.com
Kvaerner Hymac Inc.	kvhymac.qc.ca	Ladner Downs Barristers and Solicitors	ladner.com
KW Net, A Division of Missing Link	kw-net.com	Lafarge Construction Materials	lafarge.com
KW Networks	kwnet.on.ca	Lafleur Brown S.E.N.C.	lafleurbrown.ca
Kwantlen College	kwantlen.bc.ca	Laidlaw Inc.	laidlaw.com
Kwanza Internet, Inc.	kwanza.com	Laidlaw Waste Systems, Canadian HQ	laidlawcan.com
Kylain Enterprises Inc.	kylain.ca		
Kyle Software	kyle.com	Laidlaw Waste Systems, Ltd.	laidlawbur.com
L & A Development (Canada) Ltd.	ladev.ca	Lake Harriet Sailing Club	nagle.com
L. G. Richings & Associates	lgrcne.com	Lakefield College School	lakefieldcs.lakefield.on.ca
L. Spark And Associates	lspark.com	Lakehead University	lakeheadu.ca
L.I. Business Solutions Inc.	li-business.ab.ca	Lakeland College	lakelandc.ab.ca
La Capitale, Cie d'Assurance Generale	capitale.qc.ca	Lakeshore Community Network	lakeshore.mb.ca
		Lakeway Associates Inc.	lakeway.com
La Capoterie	capoterie.com	Lambda Systems Ltd.	lamsys.com
La Chambre de Commerce de Saint-Laurent / The Saint-Laurent Chamber of Commerce	chambr.saint-laurent.qc.ca	Lambton College of Applied Arts & Technology	lambton.on.ca
La Division Scolaire Franco-Manitobaine Numero 49	dsfm.mb.ca	Lambton County Roman Catholic Separate School Board	lambtonrcssb.on.ca
La Musique Ready To Wear Music Inc.	ready2wear.ca	Lambur Scott Morris Architects Inc.	lsm-architects.com
La Presse Ltee.	lapresse.com	Lan Van, Inc.	lanvan.com
La Revue Quebec Science	quebecscience.qc.ca	Lanark Technologies Inc.	pythia.com
La Scala Ristorante Italiano Ltd.	northam.com	Lance Consulting Inc	sir-lancelot.com
		Lance Electronics Inc.	lance.ca
La Solidarite	solidarite.qc.ca	Lance Electronics Inc.	lance.net
Lab-Volt Quebec Ltee.	lab-volt.com	Land of the Darkside BBS, The	lotds.waterloo.on.ca
Labatt Breweries of Canada	labatt.com	Landa Incorporated	landa.com
Labatt Breweries of Canada, Ltd.	labatt.ca	Landcore Data Systems	landcore.com
		Landes Canada, Inc.	landes.com
Labatt Communication Inc.	lci.ca	Landmark Feeds Inc.	lmfeeds.mb.ca
Laboratory Proficiency Testing Program Inc.	lptp.on.ca	Lane Publishing	lane.on.ca
Laborie Surgical Enrg	laborie.com	Lang Mitchener	lmls.com
Labour.Net	labournet.com	Langara College	langara.bc.ca
Labrador College	labcoll.nf.ca	Langley Education Center	lec.langley.bc.ca
Labrecque Consulting Inc	labrecque.ca	Langtry Industries, Inc.	langtry.com
Labtronics Inc.	labtronics.com	Language Systems Design, Inc.	lossless.com

Name of Organization	Domain	Name of Organization	Domain
Lanhouse Communications Ltd.	lanhouse.com	Le Babillard Electronique du Quebec	beq.qc.ca
Lanius Corporation	lanius.com	Le BBS-I Enr.	bbsi.qc.ca
Lanser Wireless Inc	cellpac.com	Le Cafe Branche Ltd.	cafe.qc.ca
Lanser Wireless Inc	cellpac.net	Le Club Apple de Rimouski	car.qc.ca
Lanser Wireless Inc	lanser.net	Le Devoir	ledevoir.ca
Lanser Wireless Inc.	wirelessinc.ca	Le Groupe BCP Inc.	bcpmtl.com
Lansource Technologies	lansource.com	Le Groupe BDDS	bdds.com
Lanternette Inc	lanternette.com	Le Groupe Berclain Inc.	berclain.com
Lanworks Technologies Inc.	lanworks.com	Le Groupe Cogicom	cogicom.com
Lapointe Rosenstein S.E.N.C.	lapros.qc.ca	Le Groupe Comlink Inc.	clgroup.com
Larg-Net	larg-net.london.on.ca	Le Groupe Conseil Innovitech Inc.	innovitech.qc.ca
Largenet	large.net	Le Groupe Dessau	dessau.com
Larson Bryson Boulton	lbb.com	Le Groupe Dynavision	dynavision.com
Laser Expressions	laserx.com	Le Groupe Ex-S Info Inc.	exsinfo.com
Laserdata Information Systems	laserdata.com	Le Groupe Geagri Inc.	geagri.qc.ca
Lasersight International	lasersight.com	Le Groupe Informatique MEI Inc.	mei.ca
Lasmo Nova Scotia Limited	lasmo.ns.ca	Le Groupe Klanch Communication Inc.	klanch.com
Lasys Technologies Inc.	lasys.com	Le Groupe Koala Conseillers en Informatique Inc.	koala.qc.ca
Lateral Logic Inc	llogic.com		
Lateral Vision	latvis.com	Le Groupe Mallette Maheu	mallette.sherbrooke.qc.ca
Laughing Fan Club	gigglegiggle.com		
Launchpad Software	launchpad.ca	Le Groupe VDL2 Inc.	vdl2.ca
Laurels Pad Imprinting, Inc.	lrls.com	Le Groupe Videotron Ltee	videotron.ca
Laurentian University	laurentian.ca	Le Groupe Videotron Ltee	videotron.com
Laurentianchat	bahama.com	Le Groupe Videotron Ltee	videotron.net
Laurentianchat	laurentian.com	Le Jean Bleu	jeanbleu.com
Lavergne Information Services	lis.net	Le Relais BBS	relais.com
Lavy and Associates, Ltd.	lavy.mb.ca	Le Reseau Francomedia Inc.	francomedia.qc.ca
Law Society of Upper Canada	lsuc.on.ca	Leachim Enterprises Inc.	cyberx.net
Lawrence & Milley Consultants Inc.	lawmilcon.ca	Learning Tree International Inc.	ltree.ca
Lawson Lundell Lawson Mcintosh	lawsonlundell.com	Learnix Limited	learnix.com
		Learnix Ltd.	learnix.ca
Lawson Mardon Group	impana.com	Learnquest Training Centre Inc.	learnquest.ca
Lawtons Drug Stores Ltd.	lawtons.ca		
LCRnet Association	lcrnet.org	Lebrun Page et Associes	lebrunpage.com
LCS Software Consultants Inc.	lcs.on.ca	LECS Data Inc.	lecsdata.com
Le Babillard Electronique du Quebec	beq.com	Leder Belting Canada Ltd.	leder.ca

Name of Organization	Domain	Name of Organization	Domain
Lee Purvis	discoverysoft.com	Les Services et Solutions Logiscom, Inc.	logiscom.com
Legacy Computers Inc.	legacy-computer.com	Les Services Informatiques BRS Inc.	brs.qc.ca
Legacy Storage Systems Inc.	legacy.ca	Les Services Informatiques Silta Inc.	silta.ca
Legal Tech Solutions	mdclegal.com	Les Services Internet Dania	dania.com
Lehman Computer Group, Inc. O/A The Wollongong Group Canada	lehman.on.ca	Les Services NPK+ Inc.	npkservices.qc.ca
Lehmann Bookbinding, Ltd.	lehbook.com	Les Systemes Atrion (Systems) Inc.	atrion.ca
Leisure Activities Unlimited	leisureact.com	Les Systemes Informatiques Concepta Inc.	concepta.qc.ca
Leisureways Marketing Ltd.	legacy2000.com	Les Systemes Zenon Inc.	zenon.com
Leisureways Marketing Ltd.	leisureways.com	Les Telecommunications Axone TTI	canadainc.com
Leitch Video International, Inc.	leitch.com	Les Telecommunications Axone TTI Inc.	axone.net
Len Lidov New Media Consulting	invisible.com	Leslie Engineering Ltd.	lel.com
Leo Burnett Company, Ltd.	lbtoronto.com	Leslie Wiess	uhpdental.com
Lerner & Associates	lerner.on.ca	Lester B. Pearson Canadian Peace Keeping Training Centre	cdnpeacekeeping.ns.ca
Les Acci Systems Inc.	acci.qc.ca	Lethbridge Community College	lethbridgec.ab.ca
Les Conseillers Inro Consultants Inc.	inro.ca	Levine Architects	levinearch.com
Les Conseillers Kheops Technologies Inc.	kheops.qc.ca	Lewis Continental Inc.	lewcon.mb.ca
Les Consultants Androide Inc.	androide.qc.ca	Lexi-Tech Inc.	lexitech.ca
Les Consultants Genicom Inc.	safework.com	Lexicom Fry Consultants	lexcom.com
Les Consultants Mccubbin, Inc.	mccubbin.com	Lexicom Ltd.	lexicom.ab.ca
Les Disques Audiogram	audiogram.com	Leximage Inc.	leximage.com
Les Entreprises Commerciales	thebuyersclub.com	Lexspace ™, Marque d'Or Inc.	lexspace.ca
Les Entreprises Videoway Ltee	videoway.qc.ca	Lexus Technologies Inc.	lexus.com
Les Estampages ISE, Inc.	ise.qc.ca	LGL Ltd.	lgl.com
Les Lociciels Object Vision Inc. / Object Vision Software Inc.	ovs.com	LGS Group Inc.	lgs.ca
Les Logiciels Hypershell Inc.	hypershell.qc.ca	Li And Li Realty	lili.com
Les Logiciels Orchis Inc	orchis.com	Liberal Party of Canada / Federal Liberal Agency of Canada	liberal.ca
Les Logiciels Polysoft Inc.	polysoft.com	Liberty Health, A Division of the Liberty Mutual Insurance Group	bluecross.on.ca
Les Maitre Typographes Zibra	zibra.com		
Les Meubles Canadel Inc.	canadel.ca		
Les Produits de Marque Liberte Inc.	liberte.qc.ca	Liberty Mutual Insurance Group	lmig.ca
Les Publications Dacfo Inc.	dacfo.ca		
Les Reseaux Lan Cite Inc.	lancite.com		
Les Services d'Editique Graffiti Enr.	graffiti.qc.ca		

Name of Organization	Domain	Name of Organization	Domain
Liberty Software Corporation	liberty.bc.ca	Lipton ™, Thomas J. Lipton, A Division of U L Canada, Inc.	lipton.ca
Librairie Scolaire Canadienne Inc.	lsc.qc.ca	Liquid Image Corporation	liquidimage.ca
Libraxus Inc.	libraxus.com	Liquipure Systems Limited	liquipure.com
Life Guide	lifeguide.com	Lisa Roszel	lisa.com
Life Network Inc.	lifenet.ca	Liseco Inc.	dealersoft.com
Light Computer Centre, Lightning Solutions Inc.	light.on.ca	Lising Design	sleepyholo.com
Lighthouse Consulting	light-house.com	Litco Systems Inc.	litcosys.ca
Lighthouse International	homebiznet.com	Litco Systems Inc.	litcosys.on.ca
Lightning Communications Corp.	lightning.ca	Liteco Ltd.	lite.nb.ca
Ligue Nationale de Hockey	lnh.com	Lithotech Canada, Ltd.	lithotech.com
Limagrain Canada Seeds Inc.	limagrain.ca	Liverton Hotels International, Inc. O/A Metropolitan Hotels	metropolitan.ca
Lincoln County Public School Board	lincbd.on.ca	Living Wills Registry	livingwills.com
Lincoln County Roman Catholic Separate School Board	lincolnrc.on.ca	Livingston Group, Inc.	livgroup.com
Lindenwoods Child Care Center Inc.	linwoods.mb.ca	Lloyd Macilouham, Barrister & Solicitor	canimmlaw.com
Lindsay Kenney	lindsaykenney.bc.ca	LM Media Marketing Services Ltd.	lm-media.com
Line-Tap Computer Service	linetap.com	LMSOFT	lmsoft.ca
Linear Systems Ltd.	linsys.mb.ca	LMX Computer Servvices	lmx.com
Link Customs Services Limited	linkcustoms.on.ca	Loach Engineering Inc.	loacheng.on.ca
Link Data Communications	linkd.net	Loblaws Inc.	loblaws.com
Link Logistics, Inc.	linklogi.com	Locher Evers International, Inc.	lei.ca
Linkage Management Services Inc.	lincage.com	Lockheed Canada Inc.	lockheed.on.ca
Linkage Office Information Systems Inc.	linkage.com	Locus Systems Inc.	locus.on.ca
Linktek Corporation	freebalance.com	Loday Project Management International Ltd.	pmforum.org
Linktek Corporation	linktek.ca	Loday Systems Ltd.	loday.com
Linmor Information Systems Management, Inc	linmor.com	Loewen Windows, Ltd.	loewen.com
Linnet Geomatics International Inc.	linnet.ca	Log On Multimedia Designs, Ltd.	logon.on.ca
Linq Communciations	inforoute.net	Logi-Sports Inc.	logi-sports.qc.ca
Linq Communications	linq.com	Logibec Groupe Informatique, Ltee	logibec.com
Lintas Canada	lintasca.com	Logibro	logibro.com
Linuxworld	linuxworld.com	Logic Innovations	logic.on.ca
Lions Gate Media Works Ltd	lionsgate.com	Logical Conclusions Software Consulting Ltd.	locon.com
Lions Park Computers Ltd.	lions.com	Logical Solutions Inc.	logical.ca

Name of Organization	Domain	Name of Organization	Domain
Logical Solutions Inc.	logicnet.com	London Telecom Network	ltn.com
Logiciel Dr Tax Software Inc.	drtax.ca	Long & Cameron	patmark.com
Logiciel, Organisation & Bureautique Inc.	lob.com	Long Beach Model Forests Society	lbmf.bc.ca
Logiciels Auba, Division of Quebecor Multimedia Inc.	auba.com	Longhurst Consulting	longhurst.ab.ca
		Longview Solutions Inc.	longview.ca
Logiciels et Applications Scientifiques	las.com	Look Software Systems Ins	look.com
		Looking Glass Design	looking-glass.com
Logiciels et Applications Scientifiques Inc.	lasinc.qc.ca	Looking Glass Software Limited	looking.on.ca
Logiciels M.U. Inc.	lmu.qc.ca	Loomis Armored Car Service	loomis.com
Logicom Process Programming	logi.com	Loring Ward Investment Counsel Ltd.	loringward.ca
Logimens Inc.	logimens.com	Losers Inc.	losers.com
Login Informatique J-M.P.	login.net	Losers Inc.	ltd.com
Login Informatique J-M.P.	newmarket.com	Lotek Engineering Inc.	lotek.com
Login Informatique J-M.P.	safe.org	Lotek Engineering Inc.	lotek.on.ca
Login: Logiciel Interactif/ Interactive Software JMP/SDA Inc.	login.qc.ca	Loto-Quebec	loto-quebec.com
		Lotto Lotto International	lotto-lotto.com
		Lottonet	lotto.net
Loginius	loginius.com	Lotus Development Canada Ltd.	lotus.ca
Logisil Consulting Inc.	logisil.com	Louis Albert Associates, Inc.	laainc.com
Logistec Inc.	logistec.com	Lov'Lee Made Lingerie Inc.	lovleemade.com
Logistic Edge Inc.	logistic-edge.on.ca	Lovas Stanley / Paul Ray Berndtson	prbcan.com
Logon Services Corporation	logon.nf.ca		
Logres Inc.	logres.com	Lowe & Company	lowe-co.com
Lomas Data Management Inc.	dlomas.com	Lowe Sms	lowesms.com
Lomas Software Limited	thenetmall.com	Lower Canada College	lcc.ca
Lomas Software Ltd.	lomas.ab.ca	Lowland Care Concepts Inc.	careconcepts.com
London Drugs Insurance	ldinsurance.com	Loyalist College of Applied Arts and Technology	loyalistc.on.ca
London Free Net	lfn.com		
London Life Insurance Company	freedom55.com	Loyalty Management Group Limited	loyalty.com
London Life Insurance Company	londonlife.ca		
London Life Insurance Company	londonlife.com	LTX Software Inc.	ltxsi.ab.ca
London Life Insurance Company	performers.com	Lucie Payette Developpement de Logiciels	cyberpal.com
London Life Insurance Company	performeurs.com		
London Life, Vancouver Office	georgia-assoc.com	Lucky Lotto Corp.	lucky-lotto.com
London Place Eye Center	londonplace.com	Ludovic et Tina Celestin	lutina.quebec.qc.ca
London Police	police.london.on.ca	Lugroid Enterprises	lugroid.com
London Public Library	lpl.london.on.ca	Lunds Auctioneers & Appraisers Ltd.	lunds.com
London Reinsurance Group	lrg.com		

Name of Organization	Domain	Name of Organization	Domain
Lupine Entertainment Inc.	lupine.com	MacLawran Group Inc., The	maclawran.ca
Lura Group Inc.	lura.ca	Maclean Hunter Communications Inc.	maclean-hunter.ca
LV Software Canada Inc.	lvsoftware.ca	Maclean Hunter Communications Inc.	maclean-hunter.com
LVX, Inc.	lvx.com		
LXmail Mobile Gateway	lxmail.com	Maclean's Magazine	macleans.ca
Lynx Geosystems Inc.	lynxgeo.com	Maclean's Magazine	macleans.com
Lynx Internet	lynx.bc.ca	Maclibrary Partnership	maclibrary.com
M&M Meat Shops, Ltd.	mmms.ca	MacMillan Bloedel Ltd.	macblo.ca
M&PG Ltd.	mpgltd.com	Macneill Libraries	macneill.net
M.A.D.	fight.com	Macneill Library Service	macneill.com
M.K.Wong & Associates	mkw.com	Macneill Library Service Inc.	macneill.ca
M.S. Informatique Enr.	msinfo.com	Macsense	macsense.com
M.U.S.E	victoria.org	Macsys Inc.	macsys.com
M3D Communications	m3d.com	Mactech Distance Education Ltd.	mactech.ns.ca
M3I Systems Inc.	m3isystems.com		
M3I Systems Inc.	m3isystems.qc.ca	Macten Inc.	macten.net
M3Music	m3music.com	Made By Magik Productions Inc.	magik.bc.ca
Maas Biolabs	maas-biolabs.org		
Mac Station Technologies Corp.	macstation.com	Madokanet	kimagure.org
		Maestronet	maestronet.com
Maccosham Service Company	maccosham.ca	Maestronet	maestronet.org
		Mag-Net BBS	mag-net.com
Macdermott's Insurance Agency Ltd.	macdermott.com	Magellan Interactive Media	magellan.net
		Magi Data Consulting	can.org
Macdev Enr.	macdev.com	Magic Lantern Communications, Ltd.	magiclan.ca
Macdev Inc.	internetic.com		
MacDonald Dettwiler And Associates	mda.ca	Magic Online Services	envirolaw.com
		Magic Online Services	interhealthcan.com
Maceys Consulting	maceys.com	Magic Online Services Toronto	pennywise.com
Machina Sapiens Inc.	machinasapiens.qc.ca	Magic Online Services Toronto Inc.	magic.ca
Macinnis Engineering	maceng.com	Magic Online Services Winnipeg Inc.	magic.mb.ca
Macintosh Owners And Users Society Of Edmonton	mouse.edmonton.ab.ca		
		Magic Productions Inc.	magicinc.com
Mackay Center	mackayctr.org	Magic West Entertainment	magicwest.com
Mackenzie Financial Corporation	mfc.ca	Magna International Inc.	magnaint.com
		Magna-Tech	magnatech.com
Mackerel Interactive Media	mackeral.com	Magnet Corp.	mchannel.com
Mackerel Interactive Multimedia, Inc.	mackerel.ca	Magnet International	northernlife.com
Maclaren Mccann Advertising Canada, Inc.	maclaren.com	Magnet Internet Gateway Inc.	magnet.ca

Name of Organization	Domain	Name of Organization	Domain
Magnet Publishing	magnetmag.com	Malopan Advertising Inc.	minemart.com
Magnett Communications Ltd.	magnett.com	Malouin Designer Graphique Enr.	malouin.qc.ca
Magnett Ineractive Media	chom.com	Management Exchange Inc., The	manex.mb.ca
Magnett Internet Gateway, Inc.	deathstar.com		
Magnum Transport Inc.	magnum-transport.com	Management Systems Resources, Inc.	msrinc.on.ca
Magra Computer Product Inc.	magra.com	Managing Partner	partner.com
Magtech Computer Services Inc.	magtech.ab.ca	Manalta Coal Ltd.	manalta.com
Magus Communications Inc.	maguscom.on.ca	Manchester Plastics, Ltd.	manplast.com
Mahogany Row Management Consulting Inc.	mahogany.ca	Mandala Systems Limited	mandalas.com
		Mandel Scientific Co. Ltd	mansci.com
Mahogany Row Management Consulting Inc.	mgy.ca	Mandel Scientific Co.Ltd.	mansci.ca
		Mandrake Multimedia Inc.	mandrakemm.com
MAI Canada Ltd	mai.ca	Manglobe Virtual Corporation	manglobe.com
Mailing List Systems, Inc.	mlsi.com	Maniacom Inc.	maniacom.com
Maillink Communications	maillink.com	Manifest Communications Inc.	manifestcom.com
Mailtech	mailtech.com	Manitoba Association of Registered Nurses	marn.mb.ca
Main Street Jewellers	mainjewellers.com		
Mainland Information Systems Ltd.	mainland.ab.ca	Manitoba Association of Urban Municipalities	maum.mb.ca
Mainstay Communications	mainstay.on.ca	Manitoba Cancer Treatment And Research Foundation	mctrf.mb.ca
Makaera Vir Inc.	indiginet.com		
Makaera Vir Inc.	makaera.com	Manitoba Co-Operator	co-operator.mb.ca
Makaera Vir Inc.	montreal.com	Manitoba Education Research and Learning Information Network	merlin.mb.ca
Makaera Vir Inc.	powertrend.com		
Makaera Vir Inc.	vir.ca		
Makaera Vir Inc.	vir.com	Manitoba Go Association	goassoc.mb.ca
Makrocorp Inc.	makro.com	Manitoba Health Organizations	manhealthorg.mb.ca
Malahat Group	malahat.com		
Malaspina College	mala.bc.ca	Manitoba HVDC Research Centre	hvdc.ca
Malcolm Silver & Company	msco.com	Manitoba Hydro	hydro.mb.ca
Malcolm Weinstein Chartered Accountant	mwca.on.ca	Manitoba Institute of Management, Inc., The	maninstmgt.mb.ca
Malcom Construction Limited	malcom.mb.ca	Manitoba Lotteries Corporation	mlc.mb.ca
Malibu Computer Systems, Inc.	malcons.com	Manitoba Medical Association	medassoc.mb.ca
Malkin & Glaine Ltd.	mgltd.ab.ca	Manitoba Museum of Man and Nature	museummannature.mb.ca
Malofilm Distribution Inc.	malo.com		
Maloka BBS	maloka.com	Manitoba Nurses Union	nursesunion.mb.ca
Malopan Advertising Inc.	avirontech.com	Manitoba Organization of Faculty Associations	mofa.mb.ca
Malopan Advertising Inc.	malopan.com		

Name of Organization	Domain	Name of Organization	Domain
Manitoba Public Insurance Corporation	mpic.mb.ca	Marcom International Information Highwayinstitute	markom.com
Manitoba Regional Network (MBnet)	mbnet.mb.ca	Marcom Productions Inc.	mgrp.com
Manitoba Telephone System	mts.mb.ca	Marfeed Distributors, Ltd.	marfeed.com
Manitoba Telephone System	mts.net	Margaret Martyn	vse-hotstocks.com
Manitoba Television Network	mtn.ca	Mari-Tech Systems Inc.	audiowww.com
Manitoba Theatre Centre	mtc.mb.ca	Mari-Tech Systems Inc.	fanfare.com
Manitoba UNIX User Group	muug.mb.ca	Mari-Tech Systems Inc.	radiowww.com
Manitoba Women's Enterprise Centre	womentcen.mb.ca	Marine Frontiers	marine-frontiers.com
		Mariner Systems Services	mariner.com
Manitou Musique	manitou-music.com	Mariposa Communications Group	mcgroup.com
Manlab Resources Inc.	manlab.mb.ca	Maritime Information Technology Inc.	miti.nb.ca
Manor Wood Inc	manorwood.com	Maritime Information Tecnology Inc.	maritime.com
Manrex Limited	manrex.mb.ca	Maritime Information Tecnology Inc.	nbmit.com
Mantech Micro Innovations Ltd.	solutions-4u.com	Maritime Institute of Computer Technology Ltd.	mict.ns.ca
Mantis Computing	mantis.com	Maritime Internet Services Inc	cantel.com
Manufacturing Concepts Inc.	mfgcon.com	Maritime Internet Services Inc.	irving.com
Manufacturing Research Corp. of Ontario	mrco.org	Maritime Internet Services Inc.	mi.net
Manulife Financial	manulife.ca	Maritime Internet Services Inc.	sjport.com
Manulife Financial/Business Library	manulife.com	Maritime Internet Services, Inc	mis.nb.ca
Manvell & Associates	kmanvell-assoc.com	Maritime Marlin Travel Inc.	maritimemarlin.ca
Map Town	maptown.com	Maritime Provinces Higher Education Commission	mphec.ca
Mapart ™, Schwerdt Graphic Arts Ltd.	mapart.ca	Mark Helman	gateweb.com
Maple City BBS	maple-city.com	Mark Hodgson Inc	hodgson.com
Maple Creek Programming Ltd.	mcpl.com	Mark Swanson	mas.org
Maple Leaf Sightseeing	mapleleaf sightseeing.com	Mark Winter and Associates, Inc.	wintergroup.com
Maplewood Computing	maplewood.com	Marken Publishing & Sales Inc.	marken.com
Mar PC Inc.	marinfo.com	Markerry Electrical Equipment	markerry.com
Marathon Realty Company Limited	mrcl.com	Market Connections	sportsnet.com
Marathon Realty Company, Ltd.	mrthn.com	Market Connections	sportsrec.com
		Market Connections, Inc.	marketcon.mb.ca
Marc Staveley Consulting	staveley.com	Market Wise Realty	mkt-wise-realty.com
Marcam Canada, Inc.	zed.com	Marketaccess Communications	maracomm.com
Marclaire Communications	marclaire.com		

Name of Organization	Domain	Name of Organization	Domain
Marketdesk Inc.	marketdesk.com	Matrix Professional Video	matrixvideo.ca
Marketing Database Solutions Inc.	mdsi.com	Matrix Professional Video Systems Inc.	matrix.bc.ca
Marketing Solutions	marksol.com	Matrox Electronic Systems Ltd	giganet.com
Marketing Solutions	mktgsolutions.com	Matrox Electronic Systems Ltd.	matrox.com
Marnik Computer Systems	marnik.com	Matrox Electronics Systems Ltd.	matrox.qc.ca
Marquest Investment Counsel Inc.	marquest.ca	Mattew Wong	bcweb.com
Marr Consulting & Communications Ltd.	marrcc.mb.ca	Matthews Microcomputer Services Ltd.	matthewsmicro.ns.ca
Marsh & Mclennan Limited	mml.ca	Maurya Software Inc.	maurya.on.ca
Marshall Minerals Corp.	edenroc.com	Max Money	maxmoney.com
Marshall Research Corporation	marshallresearch.com	Maxam Rentals Ltd + 2809410 Manitoba Ltd + 2809428 Manitoba Ltd O/A Wyatt Rentals	wyattrentals.mb.ca
Marshall-Fenn Communications	marshall-fenn.com		
Martec Limited	martec.com	Maxi Poultry Co. Ltd.	maxi.com
Martin Marietta Canada Ltd.	mmcl.ca	Maxnet Services Inc.	maxnet.ca
Martineau Walker Advocates	martineau-walker.com	Maxon Services	maxon.ca
		Maxpage	maxpage.com
Martinique Real Estate Services	martinique.com	Maxwell Advance Systems	secworld.com
Mary Fote & Associates, Ltd.	fote.com	Maya Heat Transfer Technologies, Ltd	mayahtt.ca
Maska Internet	maska.net		
Massy-Forget Relations Publiques Limitee	massy-forget.qc.ca	Mayne Nickless Transport Inc. O/A Loomis Courier Service	loomis.ca
Master Flo Valve, Inc.	masterflo.com	Mayne Nickless, Inc.	maynenickless.com
Master School Of Bartending	bartending.com	MBnet UUCP User Group	bison.mb.ca
Master Works Video Productions	masterworks.bc.ca	MBS Program	mbs-program.com
		Mcauslan Brewery Inc.	mcauslan.com
Mastercom Consulting	mastercom.com	Mcavoy Brokers Ltd.	mcavoy.com
Masterquin Canada, Ltd.	xamayca.com	Mcbrain-Sharp Marketing and Communications	mcbrainsharp.com
Mastreo Trading	exportcanada.com		
Mat Tipping	cafe.net	MCC Inc.	mcc.qc.ca
Matchnet.Com	matchnet.com	MCC Systems	entry.com
Material Culture Management Inc.	mcmi.com	McCain Foods	mccain.com
		McCain Foods Ltd	mccain.ca
Matheson Giroux Inc	gcmg.com	McCaine Electric Ltd.	mccaine.mb.ca
Mathtrek Systems	mathtrek.com	McCarthy Tétrault	mccarthy.ca
Matrikon Consulting Inc	matrikon.ab.ca	Mcconnell Galloway Botteselle Porter Hetu	mgbph.com
Matrix Design	sixd.com		
Matrix Internet Directories, Inc.	directories.net	McCullough Computer Consulting	mcc.ab.ca

Name of Organization	Domain	Name of Organization	Domain
Mcdonald Systems Corporation	mcdsys.com	Medeasy Medical Office Systems Inc.	medeasy.mb.ca
Mcdonald's Restaurants Of Canada Limited	mcdonalds.ca	Medi-Trust Healthcare Services	hmo.com
McDougall Caron Inc.	mccaron.ca	Media Book Inc., The	mediabook.ca
McDougall Scientific Ltd.	mcd-sci.on.ca	Media Buying Services Limited	mbs.ca
McEachern Caissie	mc-law.com	Media Cannibals Ent. Inc.	cannibal.com
Mcfee Financial Management	mcfee.com	Media Fusion Inc.	mfusion.com
Mcgavin Foods Limited	mcgavin.com	Media FX	mediafx.com
McGill Management	mcgill.net	Media Renaissance Inc.	fivaonline.com
McGill Multimedia Inc.	mcgill.com	Media Spectrum	medspec.com
McGill University	mcgill.ca	Media Synergy Inc.	mediasyn.com
McGill University Internet	mcgill.edu	Media-FX Enr.	mediafx.qc.ca
Mcgovern, Hurley, Cunningham	mhc-ca.com	Media-Vox Montreal	mvox.com
Mcgrath Consulting/ Websmith Group	webg.com	Mediabox Communications	mediabox.com
McGraw-Hill Ryerson	mcgrawhill.ca	Mediacom Inc.	mediacom.ca
MCI Medical Clinics, Inc.	mcimed.com	Mediafactory Softworks, Inc.	mediafactory.com
Mcinnis Cooper & Robertson	mcrlaw.com	Mediafusion Inc.	mediafusion.ca
Mckeever's Software Wizardry Ltd.,	mswl.com	Mediagroup West	mediagroupwest.com
McKenna Information Technologies Inc.	mtech.com	Mediahouse Software Inc.	mediahost.com
Mckinnon Micro Distributing Ltd	mckinnon-micro.com	Medialinx Interactive Inc	medialinx.ca
Mclintock Technology	mclintock.com	Medialinx Interactive Inc.	infolinx.com
McMaster University	mcmaster.ca	Medialinx Interactive Inc.	medialinx.com
Mcnaught Pontiac Buick Cadillac Ltd.	mcnaughtmotors.ca	Medianet Communications Inc.	medianet.org
Mcwilliams	tdbank.com	Mediasaurus Ltd.	encyclomedia.com
MD Computer Consulting	mdcomp.toronto.on.ca	Mediasoft Interactive Distribution	mediamadam.com
MDR Telemanagement, Ltd.	mdr.com	Mediastats Inc.	mediastats.com
MDS Health Group	mdshealth.com	Mediatrix Peripherals Inc.	mediatrix.com
Measurex Devron	devronbc.com	Mediavation Inc.	mediavation.ca
Mechanical Contractors Association of B.C.	mcabc.com	Mediavision Inc.	mediavision.com
Med2020 Health Care Software Inc.	med2020.ca	Mediaweb	mediawb.com
Medcan Health Management, Inc.	medcan.on.ca	Mediaweb, Inc.	mediaweb.on.ca
Medchem Laboratories, Ltd.	medchem.com	Mediaworks Magazine	mediaworks.toronto.on.ca
		Medical Council of Canada Inc.	mcc.ca
		Medicine Hat College	mhc.ab.ca
		Medicor Inc.	medicor.com
		Medicore Inc.	medicore.com

Name of Organization	Domain	Name of Organization	Domain
Medicorp Inc.	medicorp.com	Meridian Communications	meridian-com.com
Medinet Systems Inc.	medi.net	Merisel Canada	merisel-ca.com
Medius Communications Inc.	medius.com	Merlin International Communications Inc.	sprintcanada.com
Mednet Canada	mednet-can.org	Merlin Systems Inc	merlin-systems.on.ca
Megagames Plus	megagames.com	Merlin Systems Inc	merlinsys.com
Megasys ™, Megasys Enterprises Ltd.	megasys.ca	Messa Computing, Inc.	messa.com
Megatoon Station Inc.	lastation.com	Met-Chem Canada Inc.	met-chem.com
Megatoon Station Inc.	megatoon.com	Met-Tec Installations Ltd.	met-tec.com
Megaweb Internet Network Inc.	megaweb.ca	Metadata Systems Software:	offline.com
		Metalex Investments Ltd.	metalex.com
Megaweb Internet Network Inc.	minet.ca	Metalink Communications Inc.	metalink.ca
		Metalogic Software	metalogic.bc.ca
Mehta, Koppes S.E.N.C.	mehta.qc.ca	Metamedia Research	metamedia.org
Meier Entertainment Group	meier.com	Metaware Technologies, Inc.	metaware.ca
Meighen Demers	meighen.com	Metcan Information Technologies Inc.	metcan.com
Meinzer for Mayor	for-mayor.com		
Melanie Carpenter Campaign Society	melcar.com	Metex Systems Inc.	metex.com
		Methanex Corporation	methanex.com
Melchior Management Systems Inc.	melchior.ca	Metocean Data Systems Limited	metocean.ns.ca
Membercare Financial Services, Ltd.	membercare.com	Metricom Inc. (Canada)	metricom.bc.ca
		Metrix Interlink Corp.	interlink.ca
Mementum	momentm.com	Metro Net - Metro Calgary Fiber Services Inc.	metronet.ab.ca
Memex Electronics	memx.com		
Memorial University of Newfoundland	mun.ca	Metro-Mcnair Clinical Laboratories	mmcl.com
Memory Access	memoryaccess.com	Metrocorp Capital	metrocorp.com
Memotec Communications Inc.	memotec.com	Metroland Newsmagazines	cityparent.com
Memra Software Inc.	memra.com	Metroline Wire Services	metroline.com
Mendelbaum Spergel Inc.	msg.ca	Metropolis Graphics Ltd.	metropolis.qc.ca
Mennonite Central Committee Canada	mennonitecc.ca	Metropolitain Internet Exchange	mix.ca
Mentor Engineering Ltd.	mentoreng.ca	Metropolitain Internet Exchange	mix.net
Mentor Networks, Inc.	mentor.ca		
Mer Systems Inc.	mers.com	Metropolitan Toronto Police	mtp.gov
Merak Projects Ltd.	merak.com	Metropolitan Toronto Reference Library	mtrl.toronto.on.ca
Merak Projects Pty.	merakau.com		
Mercedes-Benz Canada Inc.	mercedesbenz.ca	Metropolitian Media	mediacorp.com
Mercer Management Consulting Ltd.	mmc.on.ca	Metrowerks Inc.	metrowerks.ca
		Mexican Ministry of Tourism	mexico-tourism.com

Name of Organization	Domain	Name of Organization	Domain
Mexican Ministry of Tourism	mexico-travel.com	Micro Logic Sainte-Foy Ltee.	mlogic.qc.ca
Mexican Ministry of Tourism	tourism-mexico.com	Micro-C Systems Integration	micro-c.com
Mexican Ministry of Tourism	travel-mexico.com	Micro-Gazette Inc.	micro-gazette.com
MFP	mfp.org	Micro-Tech	micro-tech.com
MGI International Investments Ltd.	mgifunds.com	Microage Computer Center, Thunder Bay	microage-tb.com
MGL Systems Ltd.	mgl.ca	Microage Computer Centre	microswo.com
MGnet Ltd.	mgnet.ns.ca	Microage Computer Solutions	microage.ca
Mi-Com Technology	micomtech.com	Microcell 1-2-1 Inc.	microcell.ca
Miab Systems	miab.com	Microforum Inc.	microforum.com
Mica Management Resources	debono.com	Microforum Manufacturing	mf.com
Mica Management Resources, Inc.	mica.ca	Microlegend Inc.	mlegend.com
Michael Atlas Chartered Accountant	taxca.com	Micrologic Limited	micrologic.ab.ca
		Micromedia Ltd.	mmltd.com
Michael Boreskie Architect Inc.	boreskie.mb.ca	Micronav International Inc.	micronav.ca
Michael Caughey and Associates	canda.org	Microplacement Inc	microplacement.com
		Microplex Systems Inc	microplex.com
Michael Desjardins	beachcomber-spas.com	Microserv J.B.F. Inc.	microserv.ca
Michael J. Kolesar	kolesardesign.com	Microserve ™, #341234 BC Ltd DBA Microserve Business Computer Services Ltd.	microserve.ca
Michael Lister	trainingnet.com	Microset Systems, Inc.	msi.net
Michael Milne Associates Ltd.	mmilne.com	Microsoft Workgroup Canada	msworkgroup.bc.ca
Michael Nikolich Productions	nikolich.com	Microstar Software Ltd.	microstar.com
Michael's Inn	michaelsinn.com	Microstructure Inc.	microstr.mb.ca
Michal Hrushowy	meex.com	Microtech	microtech-service.com
Michel P Pare	barginfinder.com		
Michel Paradis	paradis.com	Microtel Pacific Research Ltd.	mpr.ca
Michener Institute Inc.	michener.on.ca	Microtrader Inc.	microtrader.ca
Micomputer, Division of 1028889 Ontario Ltd.	micomp.com	Microtrends	microtrends.com
		Microtronix Datacom Ltd.	microtronix.com
Micro Advice Inc.	manx.com	Microtronix Systems Ltd.	microtronix.ca
Micro Advice Inc.	microadvice.com	Microvar Inc.	microvar.com
Micro Automation, Inc.	microauto.com	Microworks	microworks.ca
Micro Centra	centra.com	Midland Walwyn Capital Inc.	midwal.ca
Micro Centra Inc.	centra.ca	Midnet Express	midxpress.com
Micro City Systems	mcstoon.com	Midnorth Utility	midnorth-util.com
Micro City Systems	microcity.com	Mighty Ducks International	mightyducks.com
Micro Computer Services Ltd.	mcsltd.com	Mighty Information Company, Inc.	mighty.ca
Micro Design	microdesign.com		
Micro Logic	mlogic.com		

Name of Organization	Domain	Name of Organization	Domain
Mili Computers Inc.	mili.com	Mindlab, Inc.	mindlab.com
Milkyway Networks Corporation	milkyway.ca	Minds Edge Productions Inc.	mep.com
Milkyway Networks Corporation	milkyway.com	Mindshare Ontario, Inc.	mshi.com
		Minerva Technology Inc.	minerva.ca
Millennia Net Inc.	millennia.com	Mingo Service Corp O/A Futurekids Western Canada	futurekids.ca
Millennia Net Inc.	millennia.net		
Millennia Net Inc.	mnis.com	Minicom Data Corp.	minicom.com
Millennium Structures	millenniumsc.com	Mining Association Of Canada	mining.ca
Miller Features Syndicate, Inc.	miller-features.on.ca	Minnam Racing Inc.	minnam.com
Miller Thomson	miltom.com	Mira Video Production Inc.	miravideo.com
Millican Marketing Communications	millican.com	Miracom, Inc.	miracom.com
		Miramay	miramay.com
Milliken Mills High School	milliken-mills.markham.on.ca	Mirus International Inc.	mirus.on.ca
		Missing Link Creative Computer Intelligence	mislink.com
Mills and Associates	redhead.com		
Mills Data Systems Group	mills.com	Missing Link Creative Computer Intelligence	mlink.ca
Mills Printing	millspns.com	Mission Consultants Inc.	missioninc.com
Milstein & Associ Inc.	milstein-assoc.com	Mississauga Library System	library.mississauga.on.ca
Milstein & Associates Inc.	milstein-assoc.qc.ca		
Milton Public Library	mpl.on.ca	Mistahia Regional Health Authority	mrha.ab.ca
Milton Systems	flewitt.com	Mitchell K. Wyatt, J.D.	lawoffice.com
Mimi Tong Selection & Search	mtselect.com	Mitel Corporation	mitel.ca
Mimosa Systems Inc.	mimosa.com	Mitel Corporation	mitel.com
Mind Computer Products	mind.mb.ca	Mitra Imaging Corporation	mitra.com
Mind Link!	mindlink.bc.ca	Mitra Imaging Corporation	mitra.on.ca
Mind Link! Communications Corp.	bcdining.com	Mitroflow International Inc.	mitroflow.com
Mind Link! Communications Corp.	goodfood.com	Mitsubishi Electric Sales Canada, Inc.	mesca.ca
Mind Link! Communications Corp.	mind.com	Mitsui & Co. (Canada) Ltd.	mitsui.bc.ca
		Mixed Media	mixed.com
Mind Link! Communications Corp.	mindlink.net	MKS Informatique	mksinfo.qc.ca
Mind Link! Communications Corp.	mlnet.com	MKS Informatique Inc.	mks.net
		MLA Systems Inc.	mlasys.com
Mindemoya Computing And Design	mcd.net	Mlink Inc.	mlink.net
		MMI Group Inc.	mmigroup.com
Mindemoya Computing And Design	mcd.on.ca	MMM (Montreal Mega Mall) Inc	mmm.qc.ca
Mindfarers Inc.	mindfarers.com	Mobile Computing Corporation	mobilecom.com
Mindflight Technologies	mindflight.com		

Name of Organization	Domain	Name of Organization	Domain
Mobile Data Solutions Inc.	mdsi.bc.ca	Moonfish Consulting	moonfish.bc.ca
Mobisoft Communications	bagit.com	Moore Business Forms & Systems	moore.ca
Mobius Technologies Corp.	mobtech.com		
Modatech Systems, Inc.	modatech.com	Moore Corporation Limited	moore.com
Mode Electric Inc.	mode-elec.com	Moore Resource Systems	moorers.com
Modem College Incorporated	modemu.com	Moovmento Design	moovmento.com
Modern Woman Magazine	modernwoman.com	Moran Dan Productions	morandan.com
Mohawk College Of Applied Arts And Technology	mohawkc.on.ca	More Delyte	moredelyte.com
		More Scope Data Searches	morescope.ab.ca
Moli Energy Ltd.	molienergy.bc.ca	Moreault Consulting	moreault.com
Molson Breweries	molson.com	Morg Inc.	micro.org
Molson Indy Vancouver	molsonindy-vcr.com	Morgan Newsletters & Publishing Ltd.	morgan-news.com
Momentum Software Corporation	momentum.ca		
		Morgan Stewart Ltd.	morganstewart.com
Momentun	momentum.org	Moriyama & Teshima Architects	mtarch.com
Monark Bodyguard	monbodyguard.com		
Monday Publications	monday.com	Morning Star Services	mornstar.com
Monde Virtuel Inc.	mondevirtuel.ca	Morphos Systems	morphos.com
Monenco Agra	agra.com	Morris Rose Ledgett	mrl.on.ca
Monenco Agra	monenco.ca	Mortice Kern Systems, Inc.	mks.com
Monitor ™, Monitor Magazine Inc.	monitor.ca	Mortimer Online	mortimer.net
Monkeyboy Computer Consulting	monkey-boy.com	Mosaid Technologies Incorporated	mosaid.com
		Mostly Harmless Book Club	harmless.com
Monro Multimedia	monrosynapse.com	Mother-Ease	mother-ease.com
Mont Tremblant Reservations Inc.	tremblant.com	Mothernode	mothernode.com
		Motive Magazine	motive.com
Montcrest School	montcrest.on.ca	Moto Models	moto.mb.ca
Montpetit Marketing Services	montpetit.com	Motor Coach Industries Ltd.	motorcoach.ca
Montpetit Marketing Services	montpetit.on.ca	Motorola Canada Limited	motorola.ca
Montreal Exchange	me.org	Motorsport News International	motorsport.com
Montreal Golfodrome Inc.	golfodrome.com		
Montreal Internet Inc.	montrealnet.ca	Mount Allison University	mta.ca
Montreal On-Line, Senc / Internexpert, Senc	mtlonline.com	Mount Royal College	mtroyal.ab.ca
		Mount Saint Vincent University	msvu.ca
Montreal Sun	monsun.com		
Montreal Trust	montrealtrust.com	Mount Sinai Hospital	mtsinai.on.ca
Montrusco et Associes Inc.	montrusco.com	Mountain Electronics	mountnet.com
Montserrat Real Estate Services	montserrat.com	Mountain Equipment Co-Op	mec.ca
Monument Manufacter Processing-Delivery	monsales.com	Mountain Lake Software Corporation	mtnlake.com

Name of Organization	Domain	Name of Organization	Domain
Mountain Park Lodges	mtn-park-lodges.com	Multiforce Informatique Inc.	multiforce.com
Mountainaire Information Exchange	minfox.com	Multimatic Technical Centre, Inc.	multiinc.com
Mountainview Consultants Inc.	mountainview.on.ca	Multimedia House	mmhouse.com
Mouse-Open-House	yelloweb.com	Multimedia House International Inc.	tomix.com
Mouvement des Caisses Populaires Desjardins	cpop.com	Multimedia Technologies Inc.	shipnet.com
Mpact Immedia Corporation	mpactimmedia.com	Multimedia User Support Enterprises	operashop.com
Mpact Immedia Inc.	mpact.ca	Multimeg Electronique Inc.	multimeg.com
MPB Technologies Inc.	mpbtech.qc.ca	Multinet Media Solutions	multinet.net
MPR Teltech	coecee.net	Multipath Business Systems	multipath.com
Mr. Bob Brown	talkpower.com	Multiple Retirement Services, Inc.	mrs.com
Mr. Jeff	mrjeff.com		
Mr2 Owners Club Of Victoria	mr2.com	Multiple Sclerosis Society of Canada	mssoc.ca
MRF Systems Inc.	mrf.com	Multiprocessor Toolsmiths Inc.	toolsmiths.on.ca
MRM Steel Ltd.	mrm.mb.ca	Multiserve Communications	multiserve.com
MRRM (Canada) Inc.	mrrm.ca	Municipal Associates	munassoc.com
Ms Thompson and Associates Holdings	msthompson-cnwl.com	Municipal Leasing	mflc.com
MSL Communications	midilink.org	Municipalite de la Baie-James	municipalite.baie-james.qc.ca
MT&T Limited	mtt.ca		
MT&T Limited	mtt.ns.ca	Municipality of Esquimalt	mun.esquimalt.bc.ca
Mt. Arrowsmith Community Network	macn.bc.ca	Municipality of Metropolitan Toronto	metrotor.on.ca
Mtlnet Inc.	mtlnet.org	Munro Engineering Inc.	worldmap.com
Muddy Waters Computer Society Inc.	mwcs.mb.ca	Munro Garrett Inc.	mgintl.com
		Munro Technolgy	hyundai.com
Mufon Canada	mufoncanada.com	Munro Technology	munro.com
Mujki Net Canada Ltd.	mujki.com	Murad	murad.com
Mulberry Hill Computers	mulberry.com	Murchies Pub	murchies.com
Mulberry Hill Computers	newsmulberry.com	Murphy Aircraft	murphyair.com
Mulberry Street BBS	mulb.com	Murray Axmith	murrayaxmith.com
Multi Mail Communications Inc.	multimail.com	Murray Axmith and Associates, Inc.	murrayaxmith.ca
Multi-Health Systems, Inc.	mhs.com	Murry Mcfadden, Md	prk.com
Multi-Medias Quebec Inc.	multi-medias.ca	Muse Corporation	musecorp.com
Multi-Serveur du Quebec Inc.	quebec.com	Music for Young Children	myc.com
Multi-Tech Computer Services	multi-tech.com	Music Manufacturing Services Inc.	mms.ca
Multiactive Corporation	multiactive.com		
Multiboard Communications Centre	mbcc.com	Musique Francais Fan Club	musique.org

Name of Organization	Domain	Name of Organization	Domain
Musique Plus Inc.	musiqueplus.com	National Bank of Canada	natbkcdn.ca
Muskoka.Com	cottage.net	National Book Service	nbs.com
Muskoka.Com	smellies.com	National Computer Products Ltd.	ncp.com
Muskoka.Com Inc.	musk.ca	National Energy Conservation Association	neca.ca
Mustang Survival	mustangsurvival.com		
Mutual Exchange Canada	mutualexchange.com	National Film Board of Canada / Office National du Film du Canada	nfb.ca
Mutual Exchange Of Canada	mutual.com		
Mutual Fund Clearing and Settlement, Inc.	mfcs.com	National Film Board of Canada / Office National du Film du Canada	onf.ca
Mutual of Omaha	mutualomaha.ca		
Mutual Un-Insurance Services Limited In Memory	muslim.com	National For Sale Phone	mrealestatecanada.com
Mutual/Hadwen Imaging Technologies Inc.	hadwen.com	National Grocers Company Limited	ngco.com
Mutuelle des Fonctionnaires du Quebec Corporation d'Assurance	mfq.qc.ca	National Grocers Company Ltd.	natgrocers.ca
MWG Music Group Inc.	musicwest.com	National Hockey League	nhl.ca
Myna Communications Inc.	myna.com	National Hockey League	nhl.com
Myra Systems Corp. Ltd	myra.com	National Hockey League Enterprises Incorporated	nhlec.ca
Myrias Computer Technologies	myrias.com		
Myrias Computer Technologies Incorporated	myrias.ab.ca	National Hockey League Players Association	nhlpa.com
Myrus Design	myrus.com	National Institute of Disability Management and Research	nidmar.ca
Myssiwyg*	myssiwyg.com	National Library of Canada	nlc-bnc.ca
Mythsion Communications	immacination.com	National Music Distributors	musicbooks.com
N	vigilante.com	National Optics Institute	ino.qc.ca
N E T S I G N Communications	netsign.com	National Research Council Canada	nrc.ca
N-Tech Enr.	ntech.qc.ca	National Round Table on the Environment and the Economy	nrtee-trnee.ca
N. Sanche Development	nsdev.edmonton.ab.ca		
		National Sea Products Limited	natsea.ca
N.C.B. Computer Services	ncb.mb.ca	National Speakers Bureau	nsb.com
N.O.D.E.	node.nf.ca	National Systems	cannat.com
Naftalink Inc.	naftalink.ca	National Systems	succeed.com
Nancy Maxwell & Associates	nama.com	National Taekwon-Do Federation	ntf.ca
Nancy & Robert's Shop	nabob.com		
Nanometrics, Inc.	nanometrics.on.ca	National Trust	ntrust.com
National Archives of Canada	archives.ca	National Trustco Inc.	nationaltrust.ca
National Association of Japanese Canadians	najc.ca	National-Com Internet Inc.	nationalnet.ca
		National-Com Internet Inc.	nationalnet.com

Name of Organization	Domain	Name of Organization	Domain
Native Clan Organization Inc.	nativeclan.mb.ca	Nelvana, Ltd.	nelvana.com
Native Education Centre	native-ed.bc.ca	Neocom Inc.	neocom.ca
Natratec	natratec.com	Neomedia, Groupe Conseil en Technologies de l'Informatique	neomedia.com
Natratec Inc	biocompatibles.com		
Natsumi Management Consulting Ltd	natsumi.com	Neotechnology Consultants Ltd.	neotec.com
Natural Designs for Tranquility Inc.	nat-designs.com	Neotext Sophtwear International, Inc.	neotext.ca
Natural Resources Canada (Formerly Dept. of Energy, Mines, and Resources)	emr.ca	Neoz Inc.	neoz.com
		Neptec Design Group	neptec.on.ca
Natural Sciences and Engineering Research Council	nserc.ca	Neptune Internet Services Inc.	neptune.on.ca
		Neray Marcom	nmarcom.com
Nature Conservancy of Canada, The	natureconservancy.ca	Neray Marcom	portfolios.com
		Neray Marcom	touristboard.com
Naturland Canada Inc.	naturland.com	Neray Marcom	touristboards.com
Nautical Data International, Inc.	ndi.nf.ca	Nesbitt Burns	nesbitt-burns.com
		Nesbitt Burns Inc.	nesbittburns.ca
NAV Communications, Inc.	nav.ca	Nesbitt Enterprises	nesbitt.mb.ca
Navatar, Ltd.	navatar.ca	Nestle Canada Inc.	nestle.ca
Navigators - The Electronic Book Corporation	navigate.com	Net Ads 'R' Us Classified	netadsrus.com
		Net App Systems Inc.	netapps.com
Navigo™, Worldlinx Telecommunications Inc.	navigo.ca	Net Direct Inc.	netdirect.ca
		Net Directories	netdirectories.com
Naviss Information Technologies	naviss.com	Net Income	netincome.com
Navitrak Inc.	navitrak.on.ca	Net Market Inc	maginet.com
Navtraxx Systems, Inc.	iplace.com	Net Miles	netmiles.com
Navy Street Bancorp Ltd.	navystreet.com	Net Presence Inc.	presencinc.com
NB*Net	nbnet.nb.ca	Net Results	results.net
NBS Technologies, Inc.	nbstech.com	Net Sport	netsport.com
NBtel Interactive 1994, Inc.	nbi.ca	Net Worth Consulting	ntiti.com
NCM Software Developers, Inc.	ncm-rubicon.com	Net-Innovation Inc.	netinov.ca
		Net-Mark Enterprises	net-mark.mb.ca
NCR Canada Limited	ncr.ca	Net-Tv Inc.	net-tv.com
ND Graphic Products Limited	ndgraphics.com	Net-Zone, Inc.	net-zone.com
Nebs Business Forms, Ltd.	nebs.ca	Net.Scandal, Inc.	scandal.com
Nebulus Network Control	nebulus.net	Net3 & Associates	net3.com
Necessary Illusions Productions Inc.	necessaryillusions.ca	Netaccess Systems Inc.	netaccess.on.ca
Need To Know	need-to-know.com	Netaxis	netaxis.qc.ca
Nelson Canada	nelson.com	Netbase Corp.	netbase.com
Nelson Chan	plutonium.com	Netcare Computing Inc.	ntcare.com

Name of Organization	Domain	Name of Organization	Domain
Netconnect Web Publishing	netprezence.com	Netwave Communications Inc.	netwave.ca
Netcore Professional Services	npsnet.com	Netwave Services	nwave.com
Netcore, Inc.	netcore.ca	Netwaves Corporation	netwaves.com
Netcorp Inc.	netcorp.qc.ca	Netway Computer Consulting Limited	netway.ab.ca
Netfitter	netfitter.com	Netwell Communications Inc.	netwell.com
Netinterior Computerlinks Ltd	netinterior.com	Netwide Marketing & Consulting Services	mabuhay.com
Netinterior Computerlinks, Ltd.	netinterior.bc.ca	Network Enterprise Technology, Inc.	netinc.ca
Netjobs Information Services	netjobs.com	Network Excellence	nxl.com
Netline 2000	nl2k.edmonton.ab.ca	Network North Communications Ltd.	netnorth.com
Netlink Communications Corporation	netlink.ca	Network North Communications Ltd.	nnc.nt.ca
Netlink Marketing Inc.	nl-marketing.com	Network Pathways Inc.	netpath.ns.ca
Netlink Online Information Services	netlink.on.ca	Network Resource Group of Manitoba Inc.	nrg.mb.ca
Netlink Technologies Ltd.	nlnet.com	Network Studios	netstudios.com
Netlinx	bajan.com	Network Support Inc.	nsupport.com
Netmedia Inc.	netmedia.qc.ca	Networks Control Logistics	netconlog.on.ca
Netmedia Productions	durham-info.com	Networks Inc.	bramnet.com
Netmedia Productions	netmediapro.com	Networks Tools	nwtools.com
Netnation Internet	netnation.com	Networkwide Applications	incorporated.com
Netnorth Consortium	netnorth.ca	Networkwide Applications Inc.	opportunity.com
Netpage Hunter-Dunn Business Services Ltd.	netpage.bc.ca	Networkwide Applications Incorporated	bdc.com
Netquest Communications	nq.com	Networkwide Applications Incorporated	networkwide.com
Netrade International Inc	ntrade.com	Networkwide Applications Incorporated	northwin.net
Netresults	nrzone.com	Networkwide Applications Incorporated	nwai.com
Netresults! Services	nresults.com	Networx Internet System	networx.on.ca
Netricom Inc.	netri.com	Networx Systems, Inc.	nwsystems.com
Netrix Incorporated	netrix.on.ca	Netx Systems Inc.	netxsys.com
Netron Inc.	netron.ca	Neuchatel Junior College	neuchatel.org
Netron, Inc.	netron.com	Neucomp Computers	neucomp.com
Netscapades Inc	netscapades.com	Neuma Technologies Corporation	neuma.com
Netsearch Communications	wwweb.net	Neumes Music Systems Ltd	neumes.com
Netsource Marketing	netsource-asia.com	Neural Storm	nstorm.com
Netstart Consulting	netstart.com		
Netsurf Inc.	netsurf.net		
Netsurf Technologies	netsurf.mb.ca		
Nettalk	nettalk.com		
Nettwerk Productions	nettwerk.com		
Netvision Inc.	netvis.com		

Name of Organization	Domain	Name of Organization	Domain
Neuromantics Canada	neuromantics.com	Newforce Communications Inc.	newforce.ca
Neutropenia Support Assoc. Inc.	neutropenia.ca	Newforce Communications Inc.	vidconf.com
Nevis Real Estate Services	nevis.com	Newforce Marketing Inc.	newforce.com
New Brunswick Community Colleges - Committee of Information Systems Managers	nbcc.nb.ca	Newfoundland and Labrador Computer Services	nlcs.nf.ca
New Brunswick Department of Education	nbed.nb.ca	Newfoundland and Labrador Institute of Fisheries and Marine Technology	ifmt.nf.ca
New Brunswick Provincial Government	gov.nb.ca	Newfoundland Capital Corp. Ltd.	ncc.ca
New Brunswick Publishing Company Ltd.	nbpub.nb.ca	Newfoundland Light & Power Co. Ltd.	nfpower.nf.ca
New Brunswick Telephone Co. Ltd.	nbtel.nb.ca	Newfoundland Regional Network	nlnet.nf.ca
New Democratic Party of Canada	ndp.ca	Newfoundland Telephone Company	ntc.nf.ca
New Democratic Party of Saskatchewan	ndp.sk.ca	Newlink Telecommunications	newlink.qc.ca
New Era Systems Limited	newera.ab.ca	Newman Consulting	newcon.com
New Faces Modelling & Talent Registry	newfacestalent.com	Newman Tools Inc.	newmantools.com
New Leaf Enterprises Inc.	newleaf.com	Newtco Realty Ltd	newtco.com
New North Media, Inc.	newnorthmedia.ca	Newtech Instruments Ltd.	newtech.nf.ca
New Paradigm Learning Corp.	nplc.com	Newtel Enterprises Ltd.	nel.nf.ca
New Westminster Public Library	nwpl.new-westminster.bc.ca	Newtel Enterprises Ltd.	newcomm.net
New World Commerce Ltd.	byte2eat.com	Newtel Information Solutions Ltd.	nisl.nf.ca
Newbook Productions, Inc.	newbook.com	Newtel Mobility Ltd.	mobility.nf.ca
Newbridge Networks Corporation	newbridge.com	Nexsys Corporation	nexsys.ca
Newcomm Inc.	newcomm.nf.ca	Next Generation Technologies, Inc.	nextgentech.com
Newcomp Solutions Inc.	newcomp.com	Next User Group Yukon Territory	nugyt.yk.ca
Newcourt Credit Group, Inc.	newcourt.com	Nextwork Desktop Technology Corp.	nextwork.com
Neweast Technologies, Inc.	neweast.ca	Nexus Computing, Inc.	nexus.ca
Newedge Technology Inc.	newedge.ca	Nexusweb	nexusweb.org
Newedge Technology Inc.	newedge.net	Nexxcorp Information Systems Inc.	nexxcorp.com
Newforce Communications Inc.	aylmer.com	NHC Communications Inc.	nhc.com
Newforce Communications Inc.	becool.com	Niagara College of Applied Arts and Technology	niagarac.on.ca
Newforce Communications Inc.	companions.com		

Name of Organization	Domain	Name of Organization	Domain
Niagara Composites Industries Inc.	nci.on.ca	Node 2001 BBS	node2001.com
		Node 2001 BBS	rhunebbs.com
Niagara Enterprise Agency	neai.com	Noesis Vision Inc	noesisvision.com
Niagara Falls Travel Agency	niagarafalls.com	Noma Industries Limited	noma.com
Niagara Grape & Wine Festival	foodland.com	Nomad (S.E.N.C.)	nomad.qc.ca
Niagara Internet Services	stkitts.com	Non Communications	non.com
Niagara Peninsula Industry Education Council	npiec.on.ca	Noram Inc.	noram-capital.com
		Noranda Inc.	noranda.com
Niagara Recycling	recycling.com	Noranet Inc.	noranet.com
Niagara Regional Police Service	nrps.com	Norcen Energy Resources Ltd.	norcen.com
		Norco Products Ltd.	norco.com
Niagara Television Ltd	chch.com	Nordicity Group Ltd.	ngl.com
Niagara-On-The-Lake Chamber Of Commerce	chamber.notl.on.ca	Norex Data	norex.com
		Norfolk Internet Services Inc.	nornet.on.ca
Niagra Grape & Wine Festival	wineland.com	Norham Radio Inc.	norham.com
Nias Inc.	nias.ca	Norlite Technology Inc.	norlite.com
Nibbles & Bytes	nibbles.com	Normont Industrial Hardware Canada Ltd.	normont.ca
Niche Technology Inc.	niche.mb.ca		
Nicholls-Associates	isdnwire.com	Norpac Controls	norpaccontrols.com
Nicholls-Radtke, Ltd.	nrl.com	Norpak Corporation Inc.	norpak.ca
Nichols Advanced Technology Inc.	nicholsinc.com	Norris-Whitney Communications Inc.	nor.com
Nidus Computers Inc.	nidus.on.ca	Norsat Inc.	cyberion.com
Nifco Synergy Ltd.	nifcosynergy.com	Norsat Inc.	norsat.com
Nightfall	nightfall.com	Norsat Inc.	rapidlink.com
Niho Land & Cattle Co.	niho.com	Norstan Canada, Inc.	norstan.ca
Nipissing University	unipissing.ca	Norsys Software Corp	norsys.com
Nirvcentre	web.net	Nortak Software, Ltd.	nortak.com
Nisa Online Systems	nisa.nanaimo.bc.ca	Nortek Computers Ltd.	nortek.on.ca
Nisa Online Systems	nisa.net	Nortek Electronics Ltd.	nortek.com
Nissei Sangyo	nsc-bc.com	North American Baptist College & Edmonton Baptist Seminary	nabcebs.ab.ca
Nissei Sangyo Canada, Inc.	nsctoronto.com		
Nite Out Entertainment	nite-out.com	North American Free Trade Initiative for Television	tvweb.net
Nixlab Inc.	nixlab.com		
Nlk Consultants Inc.	nlkeng.com	North American Media Engine	lunch.net
No Mo Money!	nomo.com	North American Media Engine	name.net
Nobis	nobis.ottawa.on.ca	North Island College	nic.bc.ca
Noble Lion Investments Corp.	noble.on.ca	North Norwich Telephones Ltd.	oxford.net
Noble, Jackson, & Associates Ltd.	nja.com		

Name of Organization	Domain	Name of Organization	Domain
North Okanagan Development Corp.	nocdc.bc.ca	Northern Micro, Inc.	nmicro.ca
		Northern Petrosearch	nps.com
North Okanagan Hospital Region	nohr.org	Northern Sales Co. Ltd.	northernsales.ca
		Northern Telecom Ltd.	nt.com
North Pole Beverages Co.	think-drink.com	Northern Telecom Magellan User Group	mug.com
North Pole Productions	northpole.net		
North West Company, The	northwest.ca	Northern Telephone Ltd.	nt.net
North West Dry Kilns Ltd.	nwdrykilns.com	Northern Telephone, Ltd.	nor-tel-ltd.com
North West Entertainment Group	orcabay.com	Northgate Information Systems	baritone.net
		Northnet Research Inc.	northnet.com
North West Entertainment Group	vancouver-canucks.com	Northridge Gas Marketing Inc.	northridge.com
North West Entertainment Group	vancouver-grizzlies.com	Northstar BBS	northstar.thompson.mb.ca
North West Homes Online	nwho.com	Northstar Software	falls.net
North West Realty	northwestgroup.com	Northstar Trade Finance, Inc.	northstar.ca
North York Board of Education	nybe.north-york.on.ca	Northwest Atlantic Fisheries Centre	nwafc.nf.ca
North York Branson Hospital	nybh.org	Northwest Community College	nwcc.bc.ca
North York Public Library	nypl.toronto.on.ca	Northwest Digital Ltd.	nwd.mb.ca
North*Star Communications	norcom.mb.ca	Northwest Entertainment Group	bearcountry.com
North/South Consultants Inc.	nscons.mb.ca		
Northart Galleries	northart.com	Northwest Entertainment Group	bigcountry.com
Northern Alberta Institute of Technology	nait.ab.ca	Northwest Hydraulic Consultants Inc.	nhc-van.com
Northern College of Applied Arts and Technology	northernc.on.ca	Northwest Imaging & FX	northwestfx.com
		Northwestern Health Services Region	nwhsr.ab.ca
Northern Computer	northern-computer.com	Northwestern Ontario Development Network	nodn.com
Northern Computer Inc.	ncikl.com		
Northern Computer Products Inc.	ncp.bc.ca	Northwood Pulp & Timber Ltd.	northwood.ca
		Nortran Pharmaceuticals	nortran.com
Northern Computer Systems, Inc.	ncs-rss.com	Nova Corporation Of Alberta	nova.ca
		Nova Magnetics Ltd.	novamag.ns.ca
Northern Concepts Inc.	norconcepts.com	Nova Scotia Advanced Technology Centre	nsatc.ns.ca
Northern Digital Inc.	ndigital.com		
Northern Electronics	digiterm.com	Nova Scotia Agricultural College	nsac.ns.ca
Northern Home Inspection Services	northernhome.com		
		Nova Scotia Association of Health Organizations	nsaho.ns.ca
Northern Lights BBS	nlights.com		
Northern Lights College	nlc.bc.ca	Nova Scotia College of Art and Design	nscad.ns.ca
Northern Lights Internet Solutions	lights.com		

Name of Organization	Domain	Name of Organization	Domain
Nova Scotia Community College	nscc.ns.ca	Nowsco Well Service Ltd.	nowsco.ca
		NR/NS Inc.	nrnsinc.on.ca
Nova Scotia Community College, Burridge Campus	burridgec.ns.ca	NRG Publishing	getnrg.com
		NRN Networks	netserv.net
Nova Scotia Department of Industry, Trade & Technology	ditt.ns.ca	NRN Networks	nrn.com
		NRS Block Brothers Ltd.	nrs.ca
Nova Scotia Development Group	scotia.com	NRZone Company Inc., The	nrzone.on.ca
		NS Basic Corp.	nsbasic.com
Nova Scotia Government	gov.ns.ca	NS Systems	ns-systems.com
Nova Scotia Innovation Corporation, The	innovacorp.ns.ca	NSG Network Software Group, Inc.	nsg.bc.ca
Nova Scotia Power Inc.	nspower.ns.ca	NSS Computer Systems Inc.	nss.ca
Nova Scotia Provincial Library System, The	library.ns.ca	NSTN Inc.	nstn.ca
		NSTN Inc.	nstn.net
Nova Scotia Research Foundation Corporation	nsrfc.ns.ca	NSTN Inc.	nstn.ns.ca
		NSTN Inc.	wwwshop.com
Nova Scotia Teacher's College	nstc.ns.ca	NSX Consulting	nsx.com
Nova Scotia Teachers Union	nstu.ns.ca	NT Secure Networks	entrust.com
Novacan Inc.	novacan.ns.ca	NTCS of Canada	ntcs.com
Novadata Information Systems Inc.	novadata.com	NTG International, Inc.	ntg-campus.com
Novalink Division of Optimum Computers Inc.	novalink.ca	NTN Bearing Corporation Of Canada Ltd.	ntn.ca
Novalink Inc.	nova.net	NTN Interactive Network	ntnc.com
Novamann Inc.	novamann.ca	NTnet Society	ntnet.nt.ca
Novamann Quebec Inc.	novamann.com	Nu Tech Solutions	tradelinks.com
Novanet Incorporated	novanet.ns.ca	Nu-Dawn Resources Inc.	nu-dawn.com
Novanor Inc.	novanor.qc.ca	Nuala Beck & Associates Inc.	neweconomy.com
Novasys Inc.	novasys.qc.ca	Nucap Investments Inc.	nucap.on.ca
Novatec Consultants Inc.	novatec-envirocorp.com	Nucleus Inc.	nucleus.com
Novatech Computer Careers	cyberschool.com	Nugraphix Communications Inc.	nu.net
Novatech Computer Careers	novatech.on.ca	Nugraphix Communications Inc.	nugraphix.com
Novatech Engineering Consultants Ltd.	novatech-eng.com	Nuke Laboratoire	nukelabs.com
Novatel Communications Limited	novatel.ca	Number Ten Architectural Group	ntag.mb.ca
Novaweb Inc.	novaweb.ca	Nunanet Worldwide Communications	nunanet.com
Novax Industries Corp.	novax.com		
Novix Inc.	novix.ns.ca	Nunavut Communications Ltd.	ncl.nt.ca
Now Communications Inc.	now.com	Nunavut Implementation Commission	nunavut.ca
Noweh Software	noweh.com		

Name of Organization	Domain	Name of Organization	Domain
Nunet Media Inc	nunation.com	Ocean Communications Inc.	oceanc.com
Nuratek Enterprises Incorporated	nuratek.nb.ca	Oceanside Communications Ltd.	oceanside.com
Nutat Technologies	nutat.com	Ocrinet Incorporated	ocrinet.ca
Nutat Technologies Inc.	nutat.ca	Odyssey Network Inc.	odyssey.on.ca
Nutri-Chem Inc.	nutrichem.com	Odyssey Research Associates Inc.	ora.on.ca
Nutrite Inc.	nutrite.com	Odyssey Travel Ltd.	odyssey-travel.com
Nuvo Network Management Inc.	nuvo.com	OE, A Division Of Canon Canada, Inc.	oecanon.ca
Nuvotech Ventures International Inc.	nvi.sk.ca	Oerlikon Aerospace Inc.	oerlikon.ca
NWT "Freenet" Public Access Group	freenet.nt.ca	Office National du Film du Canada	nfb-onf.ca
NWT Community Learning Network	learnnet.nt.ca	Offshore Systems Limited.	osl.com
O & Y Properties Inc.	oypi.com	Offworld Technologies Corporation	offworld.ca
O'Connor & Greespoon	oconnor-greenspoon. qc.ca	Ogden Facilities Services	ogden-canada.com
O'Connor Associates Environmental Inc.	oconnor.ca	OHK	olga.org
		OIC Confraternity	canada-immigrate. com
O'Neill Technologies Inc.	oneilltech.com	OJ Marketing	oj.com
O.E.M. Ribbons Inc.	oem-ribbons.mb.ca	Okanagan College	okanagan.bc.ca
Oakville Milton And District Real Estate Board	omdreb.on.ca	Okanagan Internet Junction	junction.net
Oakville Public Library	opl.on.ca	Okanagan Online Magazine	okanagan.com
Oakville Trafalgar Memorial Hospital	otmh.org	Okanagan Regional Library	orl.kelowna.bc.ca
		Okanagan Spring Brewery	okspring.com
Oasis Technology Ltd.	oasis.on.ca	Okanagan University College	ouc.bc.ca
Object People, The	objectpeople.on.ca	Okanagan Wine	okanaganwine.com
Object Systems Inc.	objects.com	Okidata	okicanada.com
Object Technology International Inc.	oti.com	Okiok Data Ltd.	okiok.com
		Old Town Craftworks	craftworks.com
Object Technology International Inc.	oti.on.ca	Olde Town Toronto Tours Limited	oldetown.toronto. on.ca
Objectario Inc	objectario.com	Olde Town Toronto Tours Limited	oldtowntoronto.com
Objectarts. Inc.	objectarts.com		
Objectime Limited	objectime.on.ca	Olde Town Toronto Tours Limited	torontotours.com
Objective Edge Inc.	objectiveedge.com		
Objectworks, Inc.	objectworks.com	Olds College	oldscollege.ab.ca
Obusforme	obusforme.com	Ole-Eh Mexican Imports	oleeh.com
Ocam Limited - The Giffels Group	giffels.com	Omega Network Services Inc.	omega.ca
		Omer Deserres Inc.	ods.ca

Name of Organization	Domain	Name of Organization	Domain
OMI Operational Management Inc	elefant.com	Online Telecommunications	onlinetel.com
OMMRI Corporations	ommri.org	Online Visions Ltd.	visions.com
Omni Media Productions Limited	omnimedia.com	Only Organic	only-organic.com
		Onramp Network Services Inc.	onramp.ca
Omni Ventures Inc.	omni.ca	Onstation Caving Software	onstation.com
Omnicom	omnicomtrans.com	Ontario Agricultural Training Institute	oati.com
Omnilogic Software Inc.	omnilogic.sk.ca	Ontario Association Of Radiation Technologists	oamrt.org
Omniplus Inc.	omniplus.com		
Omnitrans Inc.	omnitrans.com	Ontario Cancer Treatment And Research Foundation	octrf.on.ca
Omnitrans Inc.	omnitrans.qc.ca		
On Site Computer Training	on-site.com	Ontario Centre For Environmental Technology Advancement	oceta.on.ca
On Site Computer Training	osite.com		
On Track Computer Training	on-track.com	Ontario College Application Service	ocas.on.ca
On-Line Computer Services	on-line.net		
On-Line Ventures	ventures.ca	Ontario College of Art	oca.on.ca
One Globe Marketing	oneglobe.com	Ontario Community Newspapers Association	ocna.org
One Hour Motophoto	motophoto.com		
One Inc.	riotiym.com	Ontario Federation of Agriculture	ofa.on.ca
One Neo Eon	oneneoeon.org		
One World Artist Management Group Inc.	oneworld.ca	Ontario Financing Authority	ofina.on.ca
		Ontario Fish Net	fishnet.on.ca
Oneida Canada	ocl.com	Ontario Health Kare	olga.com
Onestop Internet Inc.	onestop.ca	Ontario Hydro	hydro.on.ca
Onet	onet.on.ca	Ontario Hydro Research Division	ohrd.com
Oneworld Online Nook	nook.com		
Online Business Systems	online.mb.ca	Ontario Hydro, Power System Planning Division	ohpspd.com
Online Computer Distribution	oncomdis.on.ca		
Online Construction and Exploration	oce.com	Ontario Inst. for Studies in Education	oise.on.ca
		Ontario Institute of Agrologists	oia.com
Online Corporation	bol.net		
Online Corporation	olcorp.com	Ontario Internet Consultants	oiconsult.com
Online Corporation	online.ab.ca	Ontario Investment Services	ois.on.ca
Online Data Corporation	onlinedata.com	Ontario Jockey Club, The	theojc.on.ca
Online Data Enterprises	torontoguide.com	Ontario Legislative Assembly	ola.org
Online Film Services Inc.	bcfilm.com	Ontario Library Association	ola.on.ca
Online Information Xchange	oix.com	Ontario Library Service - North	olsn.on.ca
Online Innovations	onlinein.com		
Online Now	oln.com	Ontario Library Services Centre	lsc.on.ca
Online Resource Group Ltd.	arqx.com	Ontario Library Services Centre	olsc.com

Name of Organization	Domain	Name of Organization	Domain
Ontario March of Dimes	omod.org	Oprel Technology, Inc.	oprel.com
Ontario Medical Association	oma.org	Optical Services Vancouver	optician.com
Ontario Milk Marketing Board	milk.org	Optim Corporation	optim.on.ca
Ontario Ministry of Agriculture, Food and Rural Affairs, Alfred College	alfred-college-rtt.com	Optima Facial Tone Inc.	optima.mb.ca
		Optimax Software Inc.	optimax.ns.ca
		Optimicro Technologies, Inc.	optimicro.com
Ontario Municipal Employee Retirement Board	omers.com	Optimil Machinery Inc.	optimil.com
Ontario New Home Warranty	newhome.on.ca	Optimum Communications, Inc.	optimum.nf.ca
Ontario Northland Transporation Commission, The	ontc.on.ca	Optimum Energy Products Limited.	specsoft.com
Ontario Northlands Telephone	onlink.net	Optimum Productions	optimumprod.com
Ontario Northlands Telephone	ontel.com	Optinet Telecommunications Inc.	optinet.ca
Ontario Place Corp.	ontarioplace.com	Options Software and Consulting Inc.	options.com
Ontario Prevention Clearinghouse	opc.on.ca	Opus Building Canada	obc.com
Ontario Science Centre	osc.on.ca	Opus Productions Ltd	opuspro.com
Ontario Secondary School Teacher's Federation	osstf.on.ca	Oracle Communications Inc.	oci.bc.ca
Ontario Society for Training and Development	ostd.ca	Orb Research and Development	orbonline.net
Ontario Swine Improvement Inc.	osi.org	Orbex Computer Systems Inc.	orbex.com
		Orbital Online	online.edmonton.ab.ca
Ontario Teachers' Pension Plan Board	otppb.com	Ordinox Network Inc.	ordinox.qc.ca
Ontario Universities' Application Centre	ouac.on.ca	Organization for Cooperation in Overseas Development	ocod.mb.ca
Onyx	onyx.victoria.bc.ca	Organization for Student Access and Development	hardrock.org
Onyx Computers Inc.	onyxcomputers.com	Organizers of Softworld'95	softworld.org
Opcom Solutions, Inc.	opcom.ca	Orientex Ind. Inc	orientex.ca
Open Learning Agency	ola.bc.ca	Origin International Inc.	origin.com
Open Storage Solutions	openstore.com	Origin International Inc.	originintl.com
Open Storage Solutions	ossq.com	Origo.Com Inc.	origo.com
Open Universal Software and Acom Computer Systems	universal.com	Orinoco Networks	orinoco.com
Openroad Communications Ltd.	oroad.com	Orion 2000 Technologies	orion2000.com
		Ornithologie Communication, Enr.	ornitho.com
Opensys Inc.	opensys.on.ca	Ortech International Inc	ortech.on.ca
OpenText Corporation	opentext.com	Ortho Active Appliances Ltd.	orthoactive.com
Opinion Search Inc.	opinionsearch.ca	Orthocom	orthocom.com
Opinion Search Inc.	opinionsearch.com	Oshawa General Hospital	hospital.oshawa.on.ca
Opinion Search Inc.	opinionsearch.on.ca		

Name of Organization	Domain	Name of Organization	Domain
Osiris (Software) Inc.	osiris.com	Ovation Electronic Publishers	boatshow.com
Ositech Communications Inc.	ositech.com	Over The Moon Chocolate Co. Ltd	over-the-moon.com
Osiware Inc.	osiware.bc.ca	Overseas Conatiner Forwarding	tradelanes.com
Osler, Hoskin & Harcourt	osler.com	Overture Marketing Ltd.	overture.com
Oster and Co.	oster.com	Owen D. Young, Barrister-At-Law	odylaw.com
OTG	ottawatelephony groupinc.	Owl Communications Inc.	owl.on.ca
Otis Systems	otis.net	Owltech Network Consulting	owltech.com
Otium Corporation	otium.com	Oyen Wiggs Green & Mutala	patentable.com
Ottawa Board of Education	obe.ottawa.on.ca	P-Squared Consulting	p-squared.com
Ottawa Business Interiors Ltd, Source FM Division	obi.on.ca	P.C. Smith	pcsmith.com
Ottawa Carleton Economic Development Corporation	ocedco.on.ca	P.D.N. Product Direct Network, Inc.	pdn.sk.ca
Ottawa Carleton Research Institute	ocri.ca	P.E.I. Farm Centre	farmctr.pe.ca
Ottawa Carleton Research Institute	ocri.on.ca	P.P.I. Financial Group, Ltd.	ppifinancial.ca
Ottawa Carleton Research Institute	tourottawa.org	Pacific Academy Private School	pacific-academy. surrey.bc.ca
Ottawa Carleton UNIX Group	ocunix.on.ca	Pacfor Equipment	pac4.com
Ottawa Citizen, The	thecitizen.ca	Pacicom, Ltd.	pacicom.com
Ottawa Civic Hospital	civich.ottawa.on.ca	Pacific Aids Resource Centre	parc.org
Ottawa Heart Institute	heartinst.on.ca	Pacific Cascade Corporation Ltd	pccltd.bc.ca
Ottawa Laser Copy Inc.	doculink.com	Pacific Coach Lines Ltd.	pacificcoach.com
Ottawa Sun	ottsun.com	Pacific Coast Credit Union	paccoast.bc.ca
Ottawa Systems Inc.	ottawa.net	Pacific Coast Feather Canada	downcomforters.com
Ottawa Valley Internet Industry Association	oviia.ca	Pacific Coast Net. Inc	pacificcoast.net
		Pacific Computers Ltd.	pacific-onramp.com
Ottawa-Carleton Board of Trade	ocbot.ottawa.on.ca	Pacific Food Resources	overwaitea.com
Otto Richter & Sons Equipment Ltd.	buynet.com	Pacific Geoscience Centre	pgc.bc.ca
		Pacific Information Exchange	pie.vancouver.bc.ca
Otto Richter and Sons Limited	herbs.com	Pacific Interconnect	pacific-interconnect. net
Otto Richter and Sons Limited	richter.com	Pacific International Mapping Corp.	pim.bc.ca
Our Computer Player Ltd.	computer-player.bc. ca	Pacific Internet Business Centre Inc.	pacnet.ca
Outernet Technology	outer-net.com	Pacific Music Industry Association	pmia.org
Outlandish Networks Inc.	outlandish.com		
Outrigger - Machelper	machelper.com	Pacific Northwest Business Exchange	bizness.com
Outside Music Inc.	outside.on.ca		
Ovalsys International Inc.	ovalsys.ca		

Name of Organization	Domain	Name of Organization	Domain
Pacific Northwest Business Exchange	pnwbe.com	Pangeo Communications	pangeo.com
Pacific Organization for Regional Networkers	porn.org	Panix Support Services	panix.surrey.bc.ca
		Panorama Resort	skipanorama.com
Pacific Paragon Financial Group Ltd.	pacificparagon.com	Panther Software Corp.	panther.ab.ca
		Panther Software Corp.	panthersoftware.com
Pacific Place Communications	pacificplace.net	Paprican	paprican.ca
Pacific Place Communications Ltd.	pacificplace.bc.ca	Paquette & Associes Inc.	paquette.qc.ca
		Par-Pak Ltd.	parpak.com
Pacific Place Communications Ltd.	pacificplace.com	Paradigm Consulting Group Inc.	paradigm.sk.ca
Pacific Potato Corp.	seedpotatoes.com	Paradigm Development Corporation	paradigm.bc.ca
Pacific Research Systems Ltd	prsystems.com		
Pacific Rim Communications Inc.	omegaweb.com	Paradon Computers	paradon.com
		Paradyme Interactive Communications	paradyme.com
Pacific Salmon Commission	psc.org		
Pacific Space Centre Society	pacific-space-centre. bc.ca	Paradynamics Inc.	paradynamics.com
		Paragon Computer Systems Ltd.	paragon.ab.ca
Pacific Web Publishing	cyber-web.com	Paragon Homes, Ltd.	paragonh.com
Pacific West Equities Limited	equity.bc.ca	Paragon Information Systems Inc.	paragon.nf.ca
Pacs	pacscan.com		
PAD Peripheral Advanced Design Inc.	pad.ca	Parallax Development Corp.	viewline.com
		Parallel Strategies Inc.	parallel.ca
Padd	padd.mb.ca	Parallel Strategies Inc.	parastrat.com
Padinox Inc.	chaudier.com	Paralogic Computers Inc.	paralogic.mb.ca
Padinox Inc.	padinox.ca	Park Medical Systems Inc.	parkmed.com
Padulo Integrated, Inc.	padulo.ca	Parkdale Community Server	pcs.org
Page Systems International, Inc.	pageint.com	Parkland Regional Library	parklandlibrary.mb. ca
Palliser Furniture	palliser.ca		
Palliser Furniture	palliser.com	Parkridge Computer Technology	parkridge.on.ca
Pallone Holdings Ltd.	pallone.com	Parks & Associates	parksassoc.mb.ca
Palmer Jarvis	pj.com	Parkview Education Centre	pvec.bridgewater. ns.ca
Paltron International Ltd.	handwel.com		
Paltron International Ltd.	paltron.com	Parkwood Hospital	parkwood.london. on.ca
Pan Graphia	pangraphia.mb.ca		
Pan Pacific Systems Corp.	panpacsys.com	Parry Sannes	palmtop.com
Pancanadian Petroleum Limited	pcp.ca	Parse Software Devices	parse.com
Pangaea Geographic Information Systems, Inc.	pangaeagis.com	Partium, Inc.	partium.com
		Partners Imaging, Inc.	partners-net.com
Pangaea Systems Inc.	pangaea.ca	Partsfinders Inc.	partsfinders.com
Pangea Corp.	pangea.ca	Pason Well Services Ltd	pason.com

Name of Organization	Domain	Name of Organization	Domain
Passport Online Corp	passport.ca	PC-Evolution Enr.	pcevolution.com
Passway Communications	passageway.com	PC-Magic Consulting Services	pcmagic.com
Patch Computers, Ltd.	patchvan.com	PC-Time Inc.	pctime.qc.ca
Paterson, Grant & Watson Ltd.	pgw.on.ca	PC/Media Inc.	pcmedia.qc.ca
Path International Inc.	pathint.com	PCB Informatique	pcbinfo.com
Path Technologies Inc.	pathinc.com	PCI Systems Inc.	pci.mb.ca
Pathfinder Learning Systems Corporation	plsc.com	PCI, Inc.	pci.on.ca
		PCP Hotels And Motels Inc.	motels.com
Pathway Communications	pathcom.com	PCS Wireless, Inc.	pcswire.com
Patrick White Communications	patwhite.com	PCsense	pcsense.com
Patriot Computer Corporation	patriot.com	Pcuisine	pcuisine.com
Patyrick Lengyel - Exploration and Mining Consultant	plengyel.mb.ca	PDE Publications Inc.	drivers.com
		PDN Product Direct Network, Inc.	pdn.ca
Paua Systems, Inc.	paua.com		
Paul F. Smith Realty, Ltd.	smithre.com	PE. W. Internet Gateway Corporation	intergate.bc.ca
Paul Gossen Counsulting Inc.	pgci.com		
Paul Lindros Design	lindros.com	Peac Inc.	peac.com
Paul S. Adler And Associates	psadler.com	Peace Region Internet Society	pris.bc.ca
Paul Sobey	lifepak.com	Peace River North School District	schdist60.bc.ca
Pawn Press	fpsmag.com		
Pax Services	pax.com	Peacock Public Relations Ltd.	peacock-pr.com
Payment Link Corporation	paylink.com	Pear Developments Inc.	pear.com
PB Marketing	bernardo.com	Pedagoguery Software	peda.com
PBN - Private Business Networks Inc.	pbn-inc.ns.ca	Peekaboo Inc.	peekaboo.com
		Peekay Chemicals Ltd.	chem-ice.com
PBSC Computer Training Centres	pbsctrain.ca	Peel Regional Police	peelpolice.gov
		Peel-Online	quality-leadship.org
PC 123 Corporation	autobahn.net	Peer Group Inc., The	peer.on.ca
PC 123 Corporation	compupartner.com	Pegasus Healthcare International, Inc.	pegasus.ca
PC Automation, Inc.	pcauto.com		
PC Dynamics Inc.	vi.net	Peguis Publishers Ltd.	peguis.mb.ca
PC Generation Computer Systems and Engineering Consultants Inc.	pcgeneration.mb.ca	PEI Crafts Council, Inc.	crafts-council.pe.ca
		PEInet Incorporated	peinet.pe.ca
		Pelican International Inc.	pelican.qc.ca
PC Milling Ltd.	pcmilling.bc.ca	Pelmorex Communications Inc.	pelmorex.ca
PC Outlet Inc.	pcoutlet.com		
PC Realm BBS	pc-realm. bridgewater.ns.ca	Peloton Computer Enterprise Ltd.	peloton.com
PC Resources	pc-resources.com	Pelyco Systems Inc.	pelyco.ca
PC Scavenger	pcscav.com	Pembina Cardium Renewal Consortium	pembina.ab.ca
PC Smart Company, Inc.	pcsmart.com		

Name of Organization	Domain	Name of Organization	Domain
Pembina Valley Development Corporation	pembinadc.mb.ca	PG Datanet Inc.	datanet.ab.ca
Pemnet Inc.	pemnet.on.ca	PG Music Inc.	pgmusic.com
Penmagic Software Inc.	penmagic.com	Phaedra V	phaedrav.on.ca
Penny Fuels Inc.	penny.com	Phalcon Skism	skism.org
Pentecostal Assemblies of Canada	paoc.org	Pharmacare	pharmacare.com
People and Computers	muskoka.com	Pharmaceutical Pricing Systems	pps.ca
People Power Inc.	peoplepower.com	Phil's Restaurants Ltd.	phils.ab.ca
Peoples Jewellwers Corporation	pjcorp.com	Philips Environmental	philips-env.com
Peoples Jewllers Corporation	peoplesj.com	Phillipe Cabanne	pacificboarder.com
Peoples Trust Company	peoplestrust.com	Phillips Consulting	repo.com
Pepsi Cola Canada Beverages, Division of Pepsi-Cola Canada Ltd.	pepsi.ca	Phillips Consulting Group	pcgbase.com
		Phillips, Hager and North	phnvan.com
Peregrine Graphics Systems	peregrin.com	Phillips-Fitel Inc.	pfiopgw.com
Perfect Electronics	perfect-elec.com	Phoenix (Mutual Funds Distributors) Ltd.	phoenixfunds.mb.ca
Perfect Timing Vancouver Ltd	perfecttiming.com	Phoenix Concert Theatre	phnxcon.com
Performance Engineering Inc.	performance.ca	Phoenix Data Trend	gestalt.com
Performx Inc.	performx.nb.ca	Phoenix Data Trend	steppingstone.com
Peripheral Express Inc.	pex.ca	Phoenix International Life Sciences Inc.	phoenix-life.com
Perlaw Limited (Perley-Robertson, Panet, Hill and Mcdougall)	perleys.ca	Phoenix International Life Sciences Inc.	pils.com
Perryscope Concert	perryscope.com	Phoenix Research and Trading Corporation	phnx.com
Persistence of Vision Multimedia Co-Op	pov.com	Phoenix Systems Synectics Inc.	phoenix.ca
Person Books	personbooks.com	Phone To Tone	phonetotone.com
Personal Computer Club of Toronto	pcct.org	Photo of U	photoofu.com
Personal Computer Club of Toronto	pcct.toronto.on.ca	Photon Systems Limited	photcan.com
		Physio-Net	physio.com
Personal Touch Computer Services, Ltd.	discountwld.com	Piccatas Restaurants	piccatas.com
Personatech Ltd.	personatech.ca	Pictorius Incorporated	pictorius.com
Personatech Ltd.	personatech.com	Pier Connection	pier.com
Perspective Technologies	pertech.com	Pika Technologies	pika.ca
Petcom Industries Ltd.	petcom.com	Pinetree Capital Inc.	pinecap.com
Petro-Canada	petro-canada.ca	Pinetree Instruments, Inc.	indigo.com
Petroff Partnership Architects	petroffarchitects.on.ca	Pinetree Instruments, Inc.	pinetree.on.ca
		Pipetronix Ltd.	pipetronix.com
		Pique Publishing Inc.	pique.com
PFW Systems Corporation	pfwsystems.ca	Pitney Bowes Leasing, Division of Pitney Bowes Canada Ltd.	pitney.ca

Name of Organization	Domain	Name of Organization	Domain
Pixel Productions	pixelprod.com	Plexus Real Estate Network Inc.	plexus-reni.com
Pixelmotion Images Inc.	pixelmotion.ns.ca	Plexxus Entertainment	cdcanada.com
Pixsoft Inc.	pixsoft.mb.ca	Plexxus Technologies, Inc.	plexxus.com
Pizza Nova Take Out, Ltd.	pizzapizza.com	PLM Direct	plmdirect.com
Pizza Pizza Limited	pizzapizza.ca	Pluralis Ltd.	pluralis.com
PJS Communications	pjs.com	Plus 8 Records	plus8.com
PKF Capital Corp.	pkf.com	Plus Computer Solutions, Inc.	accpac.com
PKTI - Infopol User Group	infopol.com	Plus Delta Communications Inc.	plusdelta.on.ca
Plaintree System Inc.	plaintree.on.ca	Plywood Pc BBS, The	plywoodbbs.victoria.bc.ca
Planet Communications & Computing Facility	earth.org		
Planet Communications And Computing Facility	planet.org	PMC-Sierra Inc.	pmc-sierra.bc.ca
		PMT Video Inc.	pmt.qc.ca
Planet Enr.	planet.qc.ca	Pnbreton Communications Enr.	pnbreton.com
Planet Genesis	norstarent.com	Point One	pointone.com
Planet Genesis	plnetgenesis.com	Point To Point Designs Inc.	point2point.com
Planet International	planet-int.net	Poirier Business Systems Limited	poirier.on.ca
Planet Internet	planete.com		
Planet Sun	planetsun.com	Polar Bear Heaven	polarbear.rankin-inlet.nt.ca
Planet X Clothing & Design	planetxclothing.com	Polar Bear Software Corp.	pbsc.com
Planete Quebec, Inc.	planete.qc.ca	Polar Interactive Inc.	polarint.com
Planex Facility Management Inc.	planex.com	Polar Symmetry Limited O/A Polarcompute	polar.on.ca
Planix, Inc.	planix.com	Polarix, Inc.	polarix.com
Planmatics Inc.	planmatics.com	Policy Research International, Inc.	pri.on.ca
Planon Telexpertise Inc.	planon.qc.ca		
Plant Genetic Systems (Canada) Inc.	plagensy.ca	Poly-Inter Communications Inc.	polyintc.qc.ca
		Popper & Associates	w4explore.com
Plant Productions Co. Ltd.	plantprod.com	Porcelain Toilets Online	toilet.com
Plastic Enginerring Ltd	presley.com	Port Moody Public Library	library.port-moody.bc.ca
Plastic Thought Inc.	plasticthought.com		
Plastic Thoughts Inc.	plasticthoughts.com	Portage Group, The	portage.on.ca
Platform Computing Corporation	platform.com	Portage New Media	prtg.com
		Portfolio Analytics Ltd.	pal.com
Platon Consulting	platon.com	POS Pilot Plant Corporation	pos.ca
Playbot Magazine	playbot.com	Positron Industries Inc.	positron.qc.ca
Playnet	playnet.net	Possum Enterprises	kill.com
PLC Powerlink Corporation	pl.com	Post Impressions Inc.	post.on.ca
Please Hold Canada Inc.	plsholdcan.com	Post Secondary Employers Association	psea.bc.ca
Pleiades Systems	pleiades.com		

Name of Organization	Domain
Post-Secondary Application Services	pas.bc.ca
Postal Workers Technology Support Group	postie.org
Postfax Inc.	postfax.com
Postscript	postscript.com
Potash Corporation Of Saskatchewan Inc.	pcsinc.ca
Poultrade, Inc.	poultrade.on.ca
Powell Equipment Ltd.	powell.ca
Powell River Chamber of Commerce	coc.powell-river.bc.ca
Power Plus	powerplus.com
Power Shift Computer Services Inc.	pshift.com
Power Smart Inc.	powersmart.ca
Power Up Computers & DTP	powerup.mb.ca
Powerland Computers Limited	powerland.mb.ca
Powerpaq Technologies Inc.	powerpaq.on.ca
Powerwindows Inc	powerwindows.ca
Poynton Vector Corporation	poynton.com
PPM Real Estate Limited	ppmcantor.com
Practical Approach Inc.	practical.on.ca
Praeda Management Systems Inc.	praeda.com
Prairie Bible Institute	pbi.ab.ca
Prairie Pride Enterprises	prairiepride.mb.ca
Prairie Research Associates	prairieresearch.mb.ca
Prairie Sky Books	prairiesky.mb.ca
Praline Internet Services	praline.net
Praxis Inc	praxis.ab.ca
Precarn Associates, Inc.	precarn.ca
Precise Software Technologies Inc.	psti.com
Precise Systems Corporation	precise.ab.ca
Precursor Systems	precursor.mb.ca
Predatron Corp.	predatron.ca
Premdor Canada Inc.	premdor.ca
Premier Inc.	premierehort.com
Premier Online Systems Inc.	nation.org

Name of Organization	Domain
Premier Technology Inc.	premieretech.com
Premiere Vision Inc.	premiere-vision.com
Premierhort Inc.	premierhort.com
Premiertech Inc.	premiertech.com
Prentice Hall Canada Inc.	prentice-hall.ca
Presentation Edge Inc.	presedge.com
Presse Ouest, Ltd.	presse-ouest.mb.ca
Presticom Inc.	presticom.ca
Preventative Maintenance Corp.	pmaint.com
Prihar Holdings Ltd.	prihar.com
Prima Telematic Inc.	prima.ca
Prime Restaurant Group Inc.	primerestaurants.com
Prime-Line Communications	primeline.net
Primelink Corporation	primelink.ab.ca
Primetech Electronics Inc.	primetech.ca
Primetech Institute	primetech.com
Primetime BBS	primetime.org
Primetime Gifts Limited	primetime-gifts.com
Primex Forest Products	primex.com
Prince Albert Comprehensive and Public Schools	paschools.pa.sk.ca
Prince Albert Network	panet.pa.sk.ca
Prince Edward Island Provincial Government	gov.pe.ca
Prince George Paradise BBS	doomtown.com
Prince of Wales Secondary School	pwss.vancouver.bc.ca
Princess Margaret Hospital, The	pmh.toronto.on.ca
Pringle Financial Services Inc.	termlife.com
Print and Paper Shoppe	printshop.com
Printex Inc.	printex.com
Printing House Inc., The	tph.ca
Prior Data Sciences	prior.ca
Priority One Computer Training Incorporated	ppi-priority-one.com
Prisco Tech Inc. (Division of Maska Internet)	prisco.net
Prism Communications Ltd.	prism.ca
Prism Courier	prism-courier.com
Prism Systems Inc.	prismsys.bc.ca

Name of Organization	Domain	Name of Organization	Domain
Prism Systems Inc.	prismsys.com	Progestic Inc.	progestic.com
Private Investors Management Inc.	pimi.com	Progestic Inc., Consultants in Management and Informatics	progestic.mb.ca
Private World Communications	shmooze.net	Progiciels Bourbeau-Pinard Inc.	progiciels-bpi.ca
Privy Council Office	pco-bcp.ca	Programmed Insurance Brokers	pib.com
Pro Engineering Inc.	proeng.com		
Pro Show Rentals Ltd.	proshow.bc.ca	Prograph International Incorporated	prograph.com
Pro-Eco Limited.	pro-eco.com	Progress Learning Inc.	progress.ca
Pro.Net Communications	pronet.net	Progressive Conservative Party of Manitoba, The	manpc.mb.ca
Pro.Net Communications Inc.	pro.net		
Pro.Net Communications Inc.	pronet.bc.ca	Progressive Conservative Party of New Brunswick	pcparty.nb.ca
Pro/Soft Technologies	prosoftech.com	Progressive Conservative Party of Ontario	ontariopc.on.ca
Proactive Information Services Inc.	proactive.mb.ca		
Procarry Systems International Inc.	procarry.com	Progressive Solutions Inc.	psi.bc.ca
		Project Cue	cue.bc.ca
Procom Professional Consultants Group Ltd.	pccg.com	Projex Inc.	projex.com
		Prolan Network Services Inc	prolan.com
Proctor & Redfern	pandr.com	Prologic Computer Corporation	prologic.ca
Prodata Corp.	pro-data.com		
Prodatel Communications Inc.	prodatel.com	Promacad	proma.com
Prodigy Technologies Corp.	prodigy.bc.ca	Promenade Properties	lakefrontproperty. com
Producers Hotline	producers.com		
Producers Optical Services Inc.	postport.com	Promis Systems Corporation	promis.com
		Pronet Internet & Computer Services	procom.net
Productions Jarnigoine Inc.	jarni.com		
Productions Video 30 Inc.	video30.com	Pronexus Inc.	pronexus.com
Produits Alba Inc.	alba.com	Propeller Heads United	prophead.org
Professional Communications Services Inc.	pcs.mb.ca	Propowr Nettwrk	propowr.com
		Proshred Security	proshred.com
Professional Engineers Ontario	peo.on.ca	Prosight Communications	prosight.com
Professional Institute of Public Service of Canada (PIPSC)	pipsc.ca	Prosoft Solutions Inc	prosoft.com
		Prospectus Hypernet Inc.	cec.org
Professional Publishing Associates Inc. O/A Today's Parent Group	todaysparent.ca	Prospectus Hypernet Inc.	hypernet.on.ca
		Prospectus Inc. - Hypernet	prospectus.com
Professional Team Solutions	prof.com	Protech Consulting, Inc.	protech.on.ca
Profil Credit Inc.	profilcredit.com	Protectair, Inc.	protectair.com
Profit Systems Inc.	profitsys.sk.ca	Proteus Group, Montreal Canada, The	proteus.qc.ca
Profitmaster Canada	profitmaster.mb.ca		
Progas Limited	progas.com	Proton Palace Professional BBS	proton.com

Name of Organization	Domain	Name of Organization	Domain
Protoware Corporation	protoware.com	Pulsion Design Inc.	pulsion.com
Prouse, Dash & Crouch	prousedash.ca	Pulsonic Technology Corporation	pulsonic.com
Provector	provector.net	Pulsus Group Publishing Inc.	pulsus.com
Proven Seed Ltd.	provenseed.com	Purchasemaster Science Inc.	purchasemaster.qc.ca
Proverbial	proverbial.com		
Providence College & Seminary	providence.mb.ca	Purdy's Wharf Development Limited	purdyswharf.com
Provigo Distribution Inc.	provigo.ca		
Proxima Online	proxsask.com	Purdy's Wharf Development Ltd.	purdys.ns.ca
Proxy Communications Corporation	proxy.com	Pure Data Ltd.	puredata.com
PSC Communications Group, Inc., The	pscinc.ca	Purolator Courier Ltd.	purolator.ca
		Purple Pages Inc.	purplepages.com
PSL Consulting Group	pslgroup.com	Purple Sky Inc.	purplesky.com
Psychometrics Canada Ltd.	psychometrics.com	Puzzle Solutions Inc.	puzzlesol.com
PTI Telecommunications Inc.	pti.on.ca	PWI Insurance Services Agency, Ltd.	pwi-insurance.ca
Ptolemy International	ptolemy.com		
Pubforum	pubforum.com	Q & P Semiconductor Technology Inc.	qpstech.ca
Public Affairs Services	eastern.com		
Public Image Communications, Inc.	paperless.com	Q Media Software Corporation	qmedia.com
Public Net	public.net	Q Music Productions	qmusic.com
Public Petroleum Data Model Associattion	ppdm.org	QCA Syatems Ltd.	qca-systems.com
		QCC Communications Corporation	qcc.sk.ca
Public Sector Systems	pssoft.com		
Public Service Alliance of Canada	psac.com	Qcislands Net	qcislands.bc.ca
		QL Systems Limited	quicklaw.com
Public Utilities Commission of the Corporation of The Town of Cochrane	puc.cochrane.on.ca	QL Systems, Ltd.	qlsys.ca
		Qnetix Computer Consultants Inc.	qnetix.ca
Public Works Canada	pwc-tpc.ca	QNX Software Systems	qnx.com
Publiclink BBS	publink.com	QNX Software Systems, Ltd.	qnx.ca
Publicmarket.Com Inc.	publicmarket.com	QP Enterprises & Rhema Systems	rhesys.mb.ca
Publiweb Inc.	publiweb.com		
Pubnix Montreal	pubnix.net	QR Group	qrg.com
Pubnix Montreal	pubnix.qc.ca	QSR Consulting	qsr.on.ca
Puckhead Webzine Inc.	puckhead.com	Qtech Hybrid Systems Inc.	qtech.ca
Pucnet Computer Connections	pucnet.com	Quadra Logic Technologies	qlt-pdt.com
Pulse & Digital	canlinks.com	Quadrant New Media	quadrant.net
Pulse Microsystems, Ltd.	pulsemicro.com	Quadratech Interactive Systems Inc.	quadra.com
Pulsearch Navigation Systems Inc.	pulsearch.ca		
		Quadravision Communications	quadravision.com

Name of Organization	Domain	Name of Organization	Domain
Quadrillion Corporation.	quadrillion.com	Quincunx Consulting	quincunx.com
Quadro Engineering, Inc.	quadro.com	R Lavender Consulting Inc.	rlcons.bc.ca
Quadrus Consulting and Development Services	quadrus.com	R-Node Public Access UNIX	hub.org
		R-Theta, Inc.	r-theta.on.ca
Quali-Tech	quali-tech.com	R. Caswell & Associates Inc.	caswell.com
Qualitran Professional Services	qualitran.com	R. Herbert Edgecomb	netwit.org
Quality Vending	quality.mb.ca	R. M. Developers	rmdev.com
Quant Analysis/People Research Laboratory (PEREL)	perel.com	R. Peter Singbeil	singbeil.com
		R.D. Nickel & Associates	rdn.com
Quanta Computers	sonetis.com	R.E. Schiedel Consulting, Ltd.	rescon.com
Quantext Information Systems	quantext.mb.ca	R.E. Taylor & Assoc., Ltd.	woodmrkts.com
Quantic Laboratories Inc.	quantic.mb.ca	R.U.R X. Comminications	rur.com
Quantum Leap BBS	qleap.com	R.V. Anderson Associates Limited	rvanderson.com
Quantum Leap Incorporated	qli.com		
Quarry Communications Group	quarry.com	Racal Canada Inc.	racalcanada.com
		Racca Scientific Consulting	racca-sc.com
Quayle-Tip Ears	q-tip.com	Radarsat International Inc.	rsi.ca
Quebec - Telephone	quebectel.com	Radical Computing	rcomp.com
Quebec - Telephone	quebectel.net	Radical Entertainment Ltd	radical.ca
Quebec Cartier Mining	qcmc.com	Radical Sheep Productions, Inc.	radsheep.com
Quebec Telephone	quetel.qc.ca		
Quebecfun	quebecfun.com	Radio Amateurs of Canada Inc.	rac.ca
Quebecmedia	qcmedia.com		
Quebecor Inc.	quebecor.com	Radio College of Canada	rcc.on.ca
Quebecor Multimedia	mediacor.com	Radio Free Nyongwa	nyongwa.montreal.qc.ca
Quebecor Multimedia Inc.	mediaccess.com		
Quebnet Inc.	quebnet.com	Radio One/GW Inc.	thechamp.com
Queen Elizabeth High School	qeh.halifax.ns.ca	Radio Quebec Inc.	rq.qc.ca
Queen Elizabeth II Hospital	qeiihosp.ab.ca	Radiomail Corporation	radiomail.ca
Queen's University at Kingston	queensu.ca	Raduis Retail Ltd.	rrna.com
Queensway Sleep Laboratory	sleeplab.com	Rage Pictures Inc.	outrage.com
Queenswood Consulting	qwc.com	Ragweed Press	gynergy.com
Quest for the Best Software / Hardware	qbs.com	Rainbow Consulting	raincon.com
		Rainforest Software Inc	rainforest.com
Quester Tangent Corporation	questercorp.com	Rainmaker Interactive	rain-maker.com
Queue Computer Systems, Inc.	omca.com	Raivac Corporation	raivac.com
		Rampart Partitions Inc.	rampart.ca
Queue Computer Systems, Inc.	queuecs.com	Rana Process Technologies Limited	rana.ca
Quiet Touch Computer Systems Inc.	quiettouch.com	Rand Technologies	rand.com

Name of Organization	Domain	Name of Organization	Domain
Randall International	randall-intl.com	Real Estate Board of Greater Vancouver	rebgv.bc.ca
Randcor Enterprises Ltd.	randcor.com	Real Time Communications	rtcent.com
Randles Photo Specialties	randles.com	Real Time Technologies Inc.	rtt.ab.ca
Randomlink Productions	randomlink.com	Realcase Software Research Corporation	realcase.com
Range & Bearing Envirnmental Resourse Mapping Corp.	range-bearing.com	Really Great Radio Productions	radiocontest.com
Ranmar Business Systems Ltd.	ranmar.qc.ca	Realm Communications Inc.	realm.ca
Rannie Printing and Publishing	rannie.com	Realnet Inc.	realnet.ca
Rant	rant.com	Realtime Consulting Ltd.	realtime.ab.ca
Rapport Communications	plainlanguage.com	Realtime's Live Concert Program	liveconcert.com
Rapport Communications	rapport.bc.ca	Realtor Net	realtornet.com
Raptor Telecommunications, Inc.	raptor.net	Realtor Web	realtorweb.com
Rare Indigo	rare-indigo.com	Realty Technologies International, Inc.	retech.com
Rareforms Design Group	rareforms.com	Realty World ™ - Canada, Realestate World Services Ltd.	realtyworld.ca
Rat Patrol Computer Accessories	ratpatrol.mb.ca	Recall Methods Training Corporation	recall.ca
Raven Information Systems	raven.net	Recherches Miranda Inc.	miranda.com
Raven Net	raven.bc.ca	Recherches Worldata Researches Corporation	worldata.ca
Raymah Design Inc.	raymah.com	Recochem Inc.	recochem.com
Raymond Aaron Group.	aaron.com	Recognition Canada	rec-can.com
Raymond Industrial Equipment	rie.com	Recognition Canada	recognition.ca
Raymond, Chabot, Martin, Pare	rcmp.com	Recon PVF Inc.	recon.ca
Raytheon Canada Limited	raytheon.ca	Recovery Resource Centre	rrc.org
RCAVE & Associates Engineering Ltd.	rcave.com	Recyclequip Inc.	recycle.net
RCO Consultants Inc.	rco.qc.ca	Red Deer Apple Users Group	reddaug.red-deer. ab.ca
RCS Netherwood	rcsn.nb.ca	Red Deer College	rdc.ab.ca
Re-Directions, Inc.	redirections.mb.ca	Red Deer Interchange	rdi.ab.ca
Re/Max	lethbridge.com	Red Deer Public School District #104	rdpsd104.red-deer. ab.ca
Re/Max Hallmark Realty	re-max.com	Red Electronics	red.ca
Re/Max Hallmark Realty Ltd.	remaxhallmark.com	Red Green BBS	rgreen.com
Re/Max Ontario-Atlantic Canada Inc.	remaxoa.ca	Red River Community College	rrcc.mb.ca
React Technologies, Inc.	reacttech.com	Red Wings Cricket Club	redwings.com
Reactor Art+Design, Ltd.	reactor.ca	Redeemer Reformed Christian College	redeemer.on.ca
Ready Kilowatt	readykilowatt.com		
Readysoft Incorporated	readysoft.com		

Name of Organization	Domain	Name of Organization	Domain
Redell Mining Corporation	redell.com	Renaissance Energy Ltd.	renergy.com
Redesign Resource Group Inc.	redesign.com	Renaissoft	renaissoft.com
Redhead, Inc.	red-head.com	Renaud, Brodeur Avocats	renaud-brodeur.com
Redlight Services	redlight.com	Renegade Capital Corporation	walmart.com
Redmond Technology Group Inc.	redmond.com	Renfrew Computer Club	renfrew.com
Redrock Solvers Incorporated	redrock.com	Rennie & Associates Reailty	rennie-realty.com
Reds Hair Design	reds.com	Rennie & Associates Reailty	rennie.com
Redtree Inc.	redtree.com	Rent Express Communications, Inc.	rentexpress.com
Redwing Computer Ltd.	redwing.on.ca	Repro Precisions Inc	repro.com
REF Retail Systems Corp	refretail.com	Repromax Impact Graphics	repromax.com
Reform Party Of Canada	reform.ca	Reptilian Research	reptiles.org
Regal Capital Group Inc.	regal.ca	Request Information Services Corp	requestinfo.com
Regency Court Of Canada, Inc	regencycourt.com	Res International Inc.	res.ca
Regent Park Realty	siu.com	Rescan Environmental Services Ltd.	rescan.com
Regie Inc.	regie.com	Rescom Ventures Inc.	rescom.ca
Regina Public Library	rpl.regina.sk.ca	Research In Motion Inc.	rim.net
Regina Sun	regsun.com	Research In Motion Inc.	rmotion.com
Region of Halton	region.halton.on.ca	Research In Motion Limited	rmotion.on.ca
Regional Municipality of Niagara, The	regional.niagara.on.ca	Research Planning Marketing, Ltd.	pricecheck.com
Regional Municipality of Waterloo	region.waterloo.on.ca	Research Planning Marketing, Ltd.	rpmltd.com
Registered Gardiner Roberts	gardiner-roberts.on.ca	Research, Development & Manufacturing Corp.	rdmcorp.com
Registered Nurses Association of British Columbia	rnabc.bc.ca	Reseau de Veille sur les Technologies de l'Information Inc.	rvti.qc.ca
Registered Psychiatric Nurses Association of Manitoba	psychiatricnurses.mb.ca	Reseau Electronique du Montreal Metropolitain Inc.	remm.montreal.qc.ca
Registrar of Imported Vehicles	riv.com	Reseau Electronique du Montreal Metropolitain Inc. (Free-Net Montreal)	free-net.montreal.qc.ca
Reid Crowther & Partner	reid-crowther.com		
Reid, Here & Associates, Ltd.	reidhere.com	Reseau Electronique du Montreal Metropolitain Inc. (Le Libertel de Montreal / Montreal's Free-Net)	libertel.montreal.qc.ca
Reid, Mcnaughton Barristers And Solicitors	reidlaw.com		
Reinhardt Residential Construction	reinhardt.com		
Reiter Software Inc.	rsoft.bc.ca	Reseau Equiglobe Network	tharsissia.com
Reliable Process Serving Co.	process-server.com	Reseau Interart ™, Richard Tetreault	reseau-interart.ca
Remcan Consulting, Inc.	remcan.ca		
Remuera Corp.	remuera.ca		

Name of Organization	Domain	Name of Organization	Domain
Reseau Internet Quebec Inc.	riq.qc.ca	Richard Downey	vanstar-bc.com
Reseau Interordinateurs Scienstifique Quebecois	risq.net	Richard Steel & Associates	personnel.org
Reseau Interordinateurs Scienstifique Quebecois	risq.qc.ca	Richardson Greenshields of Canada	richgreen.com
Reseau Plus Telematique a Valeure Ajoutee Quebec Inc	rplus.net	Richmond Public Library	rpl.richmond.bc.ca
Reseau Quebec-Concept	qc.com	Richmond Savings and Credit Union	rscu.com
Reseau Virtuel d'Ordinateur R.V.O. Inc.	rvo.qc.ca	Richter, Usher & Vineberg	richter.ca
Residential Technologies, Inc.	residential.com	Richters Inc.	richters.com
Resistance Records	resistance.com	Ridley College	ridley.on.ca
Resnet Inc.	resnet.ca	Rift Online Services	rift.com
Resonance Software Inc.	resonance.com	Rimrock	rimrock.com
Resource Connection BBS	resconbbs.com	Rinknet Marketing Inc.	rinknet.com
Resource Information Systems Inc	riscan.com	Rio Amarillo Mining Ltd.	rio-amarillo.com
Ressources Informatiques Migration	echomtl.com	Risc Systems	risc.com
Resudox	resudox.net	Ristorante Araxi	araxi.com
Results International Sales Automation Systems	risas.com	Ritchie-Bros-Auctioneers	ritchie.ca
Results International Sales Automation Systems, Inc.	results-online.com	River East School Division	resd.winnipeg. mb.ca
Retail Dynamics Inc.	rdynamics.com	Rivtow Marine Ltd	rivtow.com
Reuters Information Services (Canada) Ltd	ris.ca	RK Confertech	gasnet.com
Revelator Information Services	revelator.com	RMH Systems	rmh-sys.com
Revenue Canada Customs Excise and Taxation	revcan.ca	RMON Development Corporation	rmon.on.ca
Revere-Seton Inc.	seton.ca	RND Canada, Inc.	rnd.ca
Revolve Technologies Inc.	revolve.ab.ca	Roach Inc.	roach.org
Revtrack Inc.	revtrack.on.ca	Roach Software Inc.	roach.com
Rexcel Systems Inc.	rexcel.com	Road Radar Ltd.	rrl.com
Rezo I Media Inc.	rezo.ca	Robelle Consulting Ltd.	robelle.com
Rezonet Internet Services	rezonet.net	Robert A Heller	erss.com
RGB Computing Canada Ltd.	rgbcan.com	Robert Bell Canadian Gallery	bell-canada.com
RGB Technologies Inc.	rgbtech.com	Robert Harder Insurance Management Inc.	harder.com
RGD Communications	rgdc.ottawa.on.ca	Robert J. Metras	metras.com
Rheodatum Inc.	rheodatum.ca	Robert Noseworthy Consulting	noseworthy.com
Rhyzome Informatics Corporation	rhyzome.com	Robert Riker	dc-comics.com
		Robert's Sailboards Ltd	robertssailboard. com
		Robertson Info-Data	info-mine.com

Name of Organization	Domain	Name of Organization	Domain
Robertson Information Technologies	what.com	Ronald Smith & Associates Inc	forensicca.com
Robin Hood Multifoods Inc.	robinhood.ca	Ronneberger Computing, Incorporated	rci.ca
Robins Sharp Advertising	rsadvert.com	Rooney, Greig, Whitrod, Fillion & Associates	rgwf.com
Robinson Forgione Group, Inc.	rfgsales.com	Roots	roots.com
Robinson, Lott and Brohman Chartered Accountants Inc.	rlb.ca	Roots, Ltd.	roots.ca
		Rope Internet Services Ltd.	rope.ab.ca
Roblyn Marketing Inc.	roblyn.com	Rosborough Boats 234 7758 Nova Scotia Limited	rosboroughboats.ns.ca
Roche Ltee, Groupe-Conseil	roche.ca		
Rock Solid Manufacturing	arc-teryx.com	Roscan Imports	roscan.com
Rocket Internet Marketing	enviro.net	Rose Media	rose.com
Rocket Internet Marketing Ltd.	directlaw.com	Rose Systems Applications Ltd.	rosesys.com
Rocket Internet Marketing Ltd.	infolaw.com	Rose Technology Group Ltd.	rosetech.com
Rocket Internet Marketing Ltd.	priviteyes.com	Ross Video Ltd.	rossvideo.com
Rockingham School	rockingham.halifax.ns.ca	Rotting Grapes, Inc.	rott.com
		Routes, Inc.	routes.com
Rockstage	rockstage.com	Rowan, Williams, Davies & Irwin	rwdi.com
Rocky Mountain Bicycle Company, Ltd.	bikes.com		
		Roy & Lafortune	cognac.org
Rocky Mountain Infonet Society	rmin.net	Roy-Babin Multimedia Production	rbmulti.nb.ca
Rocky Mountain Infonet Society	rockymtn.bc.ca		
Rodents' Nest, The	rodents.montreal.qc.ca	Royal Alexandra Hospital	ra-hosp.ab.ca
		Royal Bank of Canada	royalbank.com
Rodeo Express Delivery Ltd	rodeoexp.com	Royal Canadian Mounted Police	rcmp-grc.ca
Rogers Communications Inc.	cablelink.net		
Rogers Data Services	rogers.com	Royal College of Physicians and Surgeons of Canada	rcpsc.edu
Rogers Shared Services	sunpub.com		
Rogidi Inc. O/A Canadian Commercenet	ccnet.ca	Royal Diamond Casino	rdc.com
		Royal Financial Transaction Corporation Limited	royal.net
Rogmar Enterprises	etches.com		
Rolf C. Hagen Inc.	rchagen.com	Royal LePage	lepage.com
Rolling Hills Software	tomqnx.com	Royal LePage Commercial Real Estate	officeleasing.com
Rolls Royce Canada Ltd.	rolls-royce.ca		
Rolls Royce Ltd.	rolls-royce.com	Royal Military Club 82	rmc82.com
Romel Corporation	romel.com	Royal Military College of Canada at Kingston	rmc.ca
Romware Canada	romware.com		
Romyr & Associates	romyr.com	Royal Ontario Museum	rom.on.ca
Ron & Ron Design & Photography	ronron.com	Royal Ottawa Health Care Group	rohcg.on.ca
		Royal Pacific Realty Ltd	royalpacific.com
Ron Proudfoot	mover.com	Royal Plastics Group	royplas.com

Name of Organization	Domain	Name of Organization	Domain
Royal Roads Military College	royalroads.ca	S-MOS Systems Vancouver Design Centre	smos.bc.ca
Royal Society of Canada	rsc.ca	S-S Technologies Inc.	sstech.on.ca
Royal Treatment Car Care Centre	royal.pe.ca	S-Tek	gai.com
Royal Victoria Yacht Club Ltd.	rvyc.bc.ca	S. Altner Associates	altnerassoc.mb.ca
Royes Music	royes.com	S. Paskal Inc.	paskal.ca
Royll	royll.com	S.M. Business Solutions	smsolutions.com
RP Schwenger & Associates	okkreatv.com	S.P.O.R.T.S. Inc.	sports-inc.ca
RPA Systems Farm, Inc	systemsfarm.com	S3 Regional Sports Television Network	s3.ca
RPM Desktop Publishing	rpmdp.com	Saber Consultants, Ltd.	saberedge.com
RRL Consulting Group	rrlgroup.ottawa.on.ca	Safariland Ltd	safariland.com
RRT Services	rrt.com	Safe Engineering Services & Technologies Ltd.	sestech.com
RTO Enterprises Inc.	rto.ca	Safe Software Inc.	safe.com
Rubbacan Manufacturing Inc.	rubbacan.on.ca	Safesoft Systems Inc.	safesoft.mb.ca
Rubber Brokers of Canada Inc.	rubber.com	Sage Foundation	sage.bc.ca
Rudd Inc.	sumtime.com	Sagegate Inc.	sagegate.com
Rumark Video Inc.	rumark.com	Sagit Investment Management	sagit.com
Rumours II Me	rumours.com	SAI Center of Ottawa Carlton	saibaba.com
Rush, Crane, Guenther & Adams	rcga.com	Sailoar Enterprises	sailoar.com
Russ Brown & Associates, Ltd.	userlab.com	Saint Francis Xavier University	stfx.ca
Russell Design, Inc.	rusdes.com	Saint Mary's University	stmarys.ca
Russo Inc.	adex.com	Saint Patrick's High School	stpats.halifax.ns.ca
Russo Inc.	russo.com	Salloum Doak	oklaw.com
Rutherforde Systems Group	rsg.on.ca	Salon Communications Inc.	beautynet.com
Rwam Insurance Administrators	rwam.com	Salon Communications Inc.	haircare.com
Ryan Milroy	kokanee.com	Salon Communications Inc.	salon.org
Rydex Industries Corporation	rydex.com	Salon Communications Inc.	salonline.com
Ryerson Centre for Tourism	geotourmatrix.com	Saltspring Software	saltspring.london.on.ca
Ryerson Centre for Tourism	hola-mexico.com	Salvation Army	sallynet.org
Ryerson Polytechnic University Centre For Tourism Studies	rpucts.com	Salvation Army Grace Maternity Hospital, The	gracehosp.ns.ca
Ryerson Polytechnical Institute	ryerson.ca	Sam's Kosher Meats	kosher.com
S & J Consulting Inc.	sjcon.ca	Samarqand Press	samarqand.com
S & MG Marketing, Ltd.	samg.com	Samco Software Inc.	samco.com
S & P Group Limited	sandp.on.ca	Samoth Capital Corporation	samoth.com
		Samplex Inc.	advantex.com
		Samtech Inc.	samtech.toronto.on.ca

Name of Organization	Domain	Name of Organization	Domain
Samtek International Inc.	boardwalkbbs.com	Saskatoon Free-Net Association Inc.	sfn.saskatoon.sk.ca
Samuel Lunenfeld Research Institute of Mt. Sinai Hospital	mshri.on.ca	Saskatoon Public Library	publib.saskatoon.sk.ca
Samurai Consulting	samurai.com	Saskatoon Real Estate Board	sreb.com
Sander Geophysics Ltd.	sgl.com	Saskenergy Inc.	saskenergy.sk.ca
Sandoz Canada Inc.	sandoz.ca	Sasktel	sasknet.com
Sandwell. Inc.	sandwell.com	Sasktel	sasktel-passport.com
Sanford Evans Communications Ltd.	sanfordevans.mb.ca	Sasktel	sasktel.com
Sangoma Technologies Inc.	sangoma.com	Sasquatch BBS	sasquat.com
Saniworld	saniworld.com	Satcorp Communications Inc.	satcorp.com
Sapience Inc.	sapience.ca	Satcorp Communications Inc.	satweb.com
Saratoga Systems, Ltd.	saratoga.com	Satellite Direct Communications	satdir.com
Sask#Net	sasknet.sk.ca	Satlantic Inc.	satlantic.com
Saskatchewan Crop Insurance Corporation	scic.sk.ca	Satsuma Enterprises Inc.	interindex.com
Saskatchewan Energy Conservation and Development Authority	secda.sk.ca	Sauder Industries Limited	sauderind.com
		Sault College of Applied Arts and Technology	saultc.on.ca
Saskatchewan Food Processors Association	sfpa.sk.ca	Saunders Book Company, A Division of Saunders Office and School Supplies Limited	saundersbook.ca
Saskatchewan Government	gov.sk.ca		
Saskatchewan Indian Federated College	sifc.sk.ca	Saved By Technology Inc.	savedbytech.com
		Savery Salmon Ltd.	sfn.com
Saskatchewan Institute of Applied Science and Technology	siast.sk.ca	Saville Systems	saville-systems.com
		Sayson Technologies Ltd	sayson.com
Saskatchewan Legislative Assembly	legassembly.sk.ca	Scalable Network Systems Ltd.	scalablenetwork.com
Saskatchewan Provincial Libraries	lib.sk.ca	Scarborough Board of Education (Computers in Education)	sbe.scarborough.on.ca
Saskatchewan Research Council	src.sk.ca	Scarborough Public Utilities Commission	spuc.org
Saskatchewan Telecommunications	sasktel.sk.ca	Scarborough/North York Mirrors, Etobicoke Guardian	metrodiv.com
Saskatchewan UNIX Users Group	suug.saskatoon.sk.ca	Scatliff & Associates Landscape Architects	scatliff.mb.ca
Saskatchewan Wheat Pool	swp.com	Scene II	scene2.com
Saskatoon Board of Education of the Saskatoon School Division No. 13 of Saskatchewan	sbe.saskatoon.sk.ca	Schaadnet	schaadnet.com
		Scheduled Solutions Inc.	scheduledsolutions.on.ca
Saskatoon District Health	sdh.sk.ca	Schema Technical Services	schema.sk.ca

Name of Organization	Domain	Name of Organization	Domain
Schenker of Canada Inc.	schenker.com	Scoopnet Inc.	scoopnet.ca
Schering Canada Inc.	schering.ca	Scotia-McLeod Inc.	scotia-mcleod.com
Schober & Company	schober.com	ScotiaMcLeod Inc.	rrsp.com
School District # 36 (Surrey)	sd36.surrey.bc.ca	Scott Construction Ltd	scott-constr.com
School District # 42 (Maple Ridge - Pitt Meadows)	schdist42.bc.ca	Scott Paper Ltd.	scottpaper.ca
School District # 42 (Maple Ridge - Pitt Meadows)	sd42.mapleridge.bc.ca	Scouten Mitchell Sigurdson & Associates Limited	smseng.mb.ca
School District # 43 (Coquitlam)	schdist43.bc.ca	Screaming Head Productions.	dope.com
School District #23 (Central Okanagan)	schdist23.bc.ca	Screencraft Printing, Ltd.	screencraft.com
School District #28 (Quesnel)	sd28.quesnel.bc.ca	SD Services	sar-net.com
School District #44 North Vancouver	schdist44.bc.ca	SDF Systems	sdf.com
		Sea Change Corporation	seachange.com
School District #57 (Prince George)	schdist57.bc.ca	Sea Change Corporation	seachg.com
School District #81 (Fort Nelson)	schdist81.bc.ca	Sea to Sky Freenet Association	sea-to-sky-freenet.bc.ca
School District No. 68 (Nanaimo)	sd68.nanaimo.bc.ca	Seaborne Information Technologies Ltd.	seaborne.ca
Schroeder Properties, Ltd.	schroederltd.com	Seac Software Engineering	seac.bc.ca
Schwerdt Graphic Arts Ltd.	mapart.com	Seacor Environmental Engineering Inc.	seacor.bc.ca
Scican, Division of Lux and Zwingenberger Ltd.	scican.com	Seadance Music	seadance.com
Science Group	sciencegroup.com	Seafirst Insurance Brokers	cfirst.com
Science Systems, Inc.	v-mail.net	Seagram Canada Inc	seagram-cdn.com
Science World Of British Columbia	scienceworld.bc.ca	Sean Mcshane & Associates	mcshane.com
Science-Tech Inc.	stech.ca	Seaparks Entertainment & Attractions Corporation	seaparks.com
Sciencetech Communications Inc	sciencetech.qc.ca	Seaport Consultants Canada	seaport.com
Sciencetech Communications Inc.	sciencetech.com	Search Group Inc.	search.com
Scientific Education Services	ses.org	Searden Freenet	freenet.sprague.mb.ca
Scientific Software-Intercomp	ssi.ab.ca	Seascape Access Ltd.	seascape.com
Sciex, A Division of MDS Health Group Ltd.	sciex.com	Seaspan International Ltd.	seaspan.ca
Scilink	scilink.org	Seatech Limited	seatech.ns.ca
Scinet Communications	scinet.com	Secret Service BBS	secretservice.com
Scinet Communications	scinet.net	Secrets of the Weird	weird.com
Scompitech Inc.	scompi.qc.ca	Secured Communications Incorporated	secured.on.ca
Scoop-A-Lot Inc.	scoop-a-lot.mb.ca	Secured Communiction Canada 93 Inc.	secured.com
		Securenet Information Services	securenet.net

Name of Organization	Domain	Name of Organization	Domain
Securiplex Technologies Inc.	spxtech.qc.ca	Servi-Litho et Copie Inc.	servi.com
Security Service International SSI Inc.	ssi.ca	Service d'Information Industrielle du Quebec Inc.	siiq.qc.ca
SED Systems, Inc.	sedsystems.ca	Service Internet NTIC Enrg.	ntic.qc.ca
See Magazine Inc.	see.ab.ca	Service Telematique Service Internet de Montreal Enr.	stsim.com
Seer Communications	seercom.com	Service Telematiques Rocler Inc.	rocler.qc.ca
Seize the Day Inc.	carpe-diem.com		
Selcom Industries Ltd	selcom.com	Services Informatiques R. Roy Enr.	sirr.qc.ca
Select a Disk Online	seladsk.com		
Self Management Resources Corp.	self-management.com	Services Internet Abacom Inc.	abacom.com
Selfhelp Crafts Canada	selfhelp.ca	Services Internet de L'Estuaire, Inc.	sie.qc.ca
Selkirk College	selkirk.bc.ca	Services Internet Montreal Inc.	sim.qc.ca
Selkirk Interlake Ruralnet	sirnet.mb.ca	Services Techniques Informatiques	hypo.com
Selwyn House Association	selwyn.ca		
Semex Canada	semex.com	Services Telemat	telemat.com
Semiconductor Insights Inc.	semiconductor.com	Services Telematiques Mtl	mtl.net
Semiodesign Inc	semiodesign.com	Services Univoc Inc	univoc.ca
Semo Co. Canada Ltd.	semo-canada.com	Serviceworks Distribution Inc.	serviceworks.ca
Seneca College of Applied Arts and Technology	senecac.on.ca	Servier Canada Inc.	servier.ca
Senes Consultants, Ltd.	senes.on.ca	Seven Oaks General Hospital	sogh.winnipeg.mb.ca
Senior University, Inc.	senioru.bc.ca	Sexe Virtuelle Enr.	sexe.com
Seniors Net Inc.	seniorsnet.com	Sexmall	sexmall.org
Sensors & Software Inc.	sensoft.on.ca	Sextau Inc.	sextau.com
Sentai Software Corporation	sentai.com	Sexual Disfunctions Inc.	erection.com
Sentex Communications Corporation	sentex.ca	SFG Technologies Inc.	sfg.com
		SGS Canada Inc.	sgs-can.com
Sentex Communications Corporation	sentex.net	SGS Canada, Inc.	sgsna.com
Sentient, Inc.	sentientinc.com	Shadowplay Communications & Design Inc.	shadowplay.net
Sentinel Alarm Co.	homesecurity.com	Shambhala International	shambhala.org
Sentinel Information Services	sentinel.ab.ca	Shana Corporation	shana.com
Sentinel Resources Ltd.	investment.com	Shapiro Cohen Andrews Finlayson	idealaw.com
Senton Incorporated	senton.com		
Sequel Microcomputers Inc.	sequelmicro.com	Sharecom Industries Ltd.	sharecom.ca
Sequiter Software Inc.	sequiter.com	Shared Computer Systems & Instruction	scsi.org
Serco Aviation Services Inc.	serco.ca		
Sertapak	sertapak.com	Shared Health Network Services, Ltd.	tool.com
Servacom America Inc.	servacom.ca	Shared Vision Magazine	shared-vision.com

Name of Organization	Domain	Name of Organization	Domain
Sharp Blackmore Partnerships	sbadvert.com	Sidney Electronics Ltd.	re-net.com
Sharp Is Consultants Inc.	siscon.on.ca	Sidoci Enr.	sidoci.qc.ca
Sharpe Metamedia Inc.	metamedia.bc.ca	Sidus Systems Inc.	sidus.ca
Shaw Communications Inc.	shaw.ca	Siemens Automotive Ltd.	namo.com
Shaw Festival	shawfest.com	Siemens Electric Ltd.	siemens-can.com
Shaw Industries Ltd.	shawind.ca	Siemens Electric Ltd.	siemens.ca
Sheldon Computer Services	sheldon.mb.ca	Siemens Electric, Siemens Nixdorf Division	gpo.com
Shell Canada Corporation	shell.ca		
Shellcast Foundries Inc.	shellcast.com	Siemens Nixdorf Information Systems Limited	sni.ca
Shelly Shapero	acgcan.com		
Shenstone Dynamics	shenstone.com	Sierra Semiconductor Canada Inc	sierracan.com
Sheraton Fallsview Hotel and Conference Centre	sheraton.com		
		Sierra Systems Consultants Inc.	sierrasys.com
Sheridan College	sheridanc.on.ca	Sierra Wireless Inc.	sierrawireless.ca
Sherritt Gordon Limited	sherritt.ca	Sierra Wireless Inc.	sierrawireless.com
Sherry Naso Start-Up Steps To Success Inc.	steps-to-success.com	Sietec Open Systems	sietec.com
		Sigil Communications Inc.	sigil.bc.ca
Shift Magazine, Inc.	shift.com	Sigma Computer Training Inc.	cjch.com
Shikatani Lacroix Design	sld.com	Sigma Computer Training Incorporated	scti.com
Shikatronics Inc.	shikatronics.ca		
Shinnova Management Ltd	shinnova.com	Sign Works Studios	sign.com
Ship to Shore Online Information System	ship.net	Signal Path Designs	signalpath.on.ca
		Signat (Special Interest Group For Network)	signat.org
Shipperbottom Scott Forbes	cgafeo.com		
Shoppers Drug Mart, National Office, Canada	shoppersdrugmart.ca	Signatel Ltd.	signatel.com
		Signature Brands Ltd.	sigbrand.com
Shopping Systems	rodeodrive.com	Silicon Valley	svcp.com
Shore International	shore-intl.com	Siltex Ltd.	siltex.ca
Shoreline Communications, Inc.	shoreline.ca	Silverado Mines Ltd	silverado.com
		Silverfoot	silverfoot.com
Showboat Inc.	showboat.com	Silverspar Minerals Inc.	silverspar.com
Showcase Television, Inc.	showcase.ca	Sim Canada	sim.ca
Showcom	showcom.com	Simard Hamel Communications Ltee	shc.ca
Showfest Productions Inc.	compfest.com		
Showvision Inc	showvision.com	Simbra Inc.	simbra.net
Shushwap School District #89	schdist89.bc.ca	Simmons Bolton Inc	simbol.com
Sico Inc.	sico.com	Simon Fraser University	sfu.ca
Sidbec-Dosco (Ispat) Inc.	sidispat.ca	Simon Treadwell + Company	stco.toronto.on.ca
Side Effects Software Inc	sidefx.com	Simon/Ross & Associates Inc.	simonross.com
Sidney Electronics	kcorp.com	Simple Solutions Ltd.	simple.on.ca
		Sims Snowboard Corp	simsnow.com

Name of Organization	Domain	Name of Organization	Domain
Simware, Inc.	simware.com	Slocan Forest Products Group Ltd.	sfp.bc.ca
Siprolab Inc.	sipro.com	Sloth	sloth.bc.ca
Sir Sandford Fleming College of Applied Arts and Technology	flemingc.on.ca	Sloth Industry	sloth.com
		Sly Industries Inc.	pacificablue.com
Sir Sanford Fleming College	fleming.edu	Smart Technologies Inc.	smarttech.com
Sirius Consulting Inc.	sirius.on.ca	Smartrisk Foundation	smartrisk.ca
Sirius Investments Ltd.	golfcanada.com	Smartspeaker Corporation	smartspeaker.com
Sirius Solutions Limited	sirius.ns.ca	Smartware Technologies	intertrek.com
Sisca Informatique Inc.	sisca.net	Smegheads, The Red Dwarf Appreciation Society	smegheads. montreal.qc.ca
Sisca Informatique Inc.	sisca.qc.ca	Smith Carter Architects and Engineers, Inc.	smithcarter.ca
Sisters of Charity of Ottawa Health Services	scohs.on.ca	Smith, Lyons, Torrance, Stevenson & Mayer	smithlyons.ca
Sit Inc.	sit.qc.ca		
Sitara International Travel	sitara.com	Smokenet Smoking Cessation Project	smokenet.org
SIV Data International Inc.	siv.com	Smoky River Coal Limited	smoky-river-coal.ab. ca
Sizzle Networking	sizzlenet.com		
Sizzle Products Inc.	sizzle.com	Smythe Ratcliffe	smythe-ratcliffe.com
Skeena Net Corporation	skeena.net	SNA International	snahoham.com
Ski Louise Ltd	skilouise.com	SNC-Lavalin Inc.	snc-lavalin.com
SKL Enterprises	skl.com	Snowboard Canada Magazine	snowboardcanada. com
Skydome Corporation	skydome.com		
Skyland Tours	skyland.com	Snowrama Inc	snowrama.com
Skylar Wireless Comunications	skylar.org	Snowshoe Inn (NWT) Limited	ssi.nt.ca
Skylark Tours & Travel Services Ltd.	skylark-tours.com	Snowy Mountain Software Ltd.	snowymtn.com
		So Exotic, Inc.	soexotic.com
Skylon Tower Corporation	skylon.on.ca	Soak In It!	palmolive.com
Skyservice Division of Sunquest	skyservice.com	Sobac Microcomputer Services	sobac.com
Skyservice FBO Incorporated	skyservice.ca	Sobeco Ernst & Young Inc.	sobeco.com
Slacker Software Systems	slacker.org	Sobeco Inc.	sobeco.ca
Slander Inc.	slander.com	Sobeys Inc.	sobeys.ca
Slater Steels	slater.com	SOCAN (Society of Composers, Authors and Music Publishers of Canada)	socan.ca
SLC Enterprises	nowhere.org		
Sleeptek Limited	sleeptek.ca		
SLG The Stocklogic Group, Inc.	stocklogic.com	SOCAN (Society of Composers, Authors and Musicians)	socan.org
SLM Software Inc.	slmsoft.ca		
SLM Software Inc.	slmsoft.com	Social Planning Council of Kitchener-Waterloo	spc-lamp.org
Sloan Media	freakout.com		

Name of Organization	Domain	Name of Organization	Domain
Social Science and Humanities Research Council	sshrc.ca	Softek Services Limited	softek.bc.ca
		Softel	softel.com
Societe de Marketing Universellia	universellia.com	Softfocus	softfocus.com
		Softfocus Inc.	softfocus.ca
Societe des Casinos du Quebec Inc.	casino.qc.ca	Softimage Inc.	softimage.com
		Softimage Inc.	softimage.qc.ca
Societe du Palais des Congres de Montreal	congresmtl.com	Softknowledge	softknowledge.com
Societe GRICS (Reseau Edupac)	edupac.qc.ca	Softline Systems	3rdparty.com
		Softnet Bulletin Board Services	softnet.com
Societe GRICS (Societe de Gestion du Reseau Informatique des Commissions Scolaires)	grics.qc.ca	Softouch Scheduling Services Inc.	softouch.bc.ca
		Softpulse Software	softpulse.com
Societe Progestacces	progesta.com	Softquad Inc.	fontweb.com
Societe Q.R.U. Inc.	soc-qru.qc.ca	Softquad Inc.	sq.com
Societe Radio Canada	src-mtl.com	Softquad Inc.	sqwest.bc.ca
Societe Radio Canada	src.ca	Softsource Computing Inc.	softoptions.com
Society for Educational Visits and Exchanges in Canada	sevec.org	Softvision	softvision.com
		Software 2000 Inc.	s2k.sk.ca
Society of Kabalarians of Canada	kabalarians.com	Software Alberta Society	sas.ab.ca
		Software Alternatives, Inc.	swalt.com
Société Cyberscol Inc.	cyberscol.qc.ca	Software Blackwares Incorporated	swbs.com
Société de Promotion Economique du Québec Métropolitain / Greater Québec Economic Development Corporation (SPEQM)	speqm.qc.ca	Software Dimensions Inc.	softdim.com
		Software Dynamics	borncanada.com
		Software Exoterica Corporation	xgml.com
Socom Technologies Inc.	socom.com	Software Experts Incorporated	softwareexperts.ns.ca
Soden Software Corporation	soden.toronto.on.ca	Software Human Resource Council, Inc.	shrc.ca
Sof2 Innova	s2i.com	Software Industry Association of Nova Scotia	sians.ns.ca
Sofpak Inc.	sofpak.ca		
Soft - C Computer Software	ringzero.com	Software Kinetics Ltd.	sofkin.ca
Soft Media Digital Photo Inc.	softmedia.qc.ca	Software Metrics Inc.	metrics.com
Soft Options / The Network Centre	softnc.com	Software Online, Inc.	softonline.com
		Software Productivity Center Ltd.	spc.ca
Softarc Inc.	softarc.ca	Software Technology Centre	softech.ca
Softarc Inc.	softarc.com	Softwarehouse (West) Inc./ Compusmart Edmonton	compusmart.ab.ca
Softbahn Inc.	softbahn.com		
Softbridge Technologies Corp.	softbridge.com		
Softcare Consulting Ltd.	softcare.com		
Softchoice Corporation	softchoice.com		
Softcop International, Inc.	softcop.com	Softwears	softwears.com

Name of Organization	Domain	Name of Organization	Domain
Softwords Research International	softwords.bc.ca	Sound and Vision	indie.com
Softworks Consulting Ltd.	softworks.bc.ca	Sound Dimensions	sound-dimensions.com
Softworks Consulting Ltd.	softworks.com	Sound Foundation	soundfound.ca
Softworld	softworld96.com	Sound Foundation	soundfound.com
Sogetra	sogetra.com	Sound Ideas	sound-ideas.com
Sointula Connection Inc.	alm.com	Sounds Virtual Inc.	sounds.com
Solar Communications Inc.	solarcom.qc.ca	Sourcer Media Services	microglobe.com
Solar Realms	srgames.com	Sources	sources.com
Solar Realms	srgames.org	Sources International	sourcesintl.com
Solcorp	solcorp.com	Sourceworks Consulting Inc	sourceworks.ca
Soldiers Memorial Hospital	soldiersmem.ns.ca	South West Bruce Internet	swbi.net
Solect Technology Group	solect.com	South Western Ontario UNIX Users Group	swouug.org
Solect Technology Group Limited	finnet.com	South Winnipeg Technical Centre	swtc.mb.ca
Solfina Information Systems Inc	solfina.com	Southam Construction Information Services	buildweb.com
Soliton Technologies	soliton.com	Southam Newspaper Group	southam.ca
Solucorp	solucorp.qc.ca	Southam, Inc.	southam.com
Solus Technologies Corp.	circon.com	Southbrook Farms Wine Advertising	southbrookfarms.com
Solution Quest Limited	solutionquest.com	Southern Alberta Institute of Technology	sait.ab.ca
Solution Tech Systems Inc.	solutiontech.com		
Solution Tree Corp.	soltree.com	Southern Ontario Library Service	sols.on.ca
Solutions Inc	winning.com	Southern Ontario Newspaper Guild	song.on.ca
Somerset Graphics	somrset.com		
Sonar Communications Group Inc	sonar.com	Southport Aerospace Centre Inc.	southaero.mb.ca
Sonata Software Systems Inc.	sonata.com	Southport Data Systems	southportdata.com
Sonetis	sonetis.org	Southport Technologies	everybody.com
Sonetis Corporation	sonetis.ca	Southport Technologies	nobody.com
Sonetis Internet Provider	sonetis.net	Southport Technologies	somebody.com
Sonic Drilling Ltd	sonicdrill.com	Southport Technologies Inc.	southport.com
Sonic Science	sonicscience.com	Southport Technologies Inc.	southport.on.ca
Sonie's Creations	sonies.com	Southside Digital Studios	zivot.com
Sony of Canada, Ltd.	sony.ca	Southwest Sun Inc.	southwestsun.com
Soonet Corporation	soonet.ca	Spaceport Canada Ltd.	spaceport.ca
Sooter Studios Ltd.	sooters.ca	Spantec Resources	spantec.com
Soquelec Ltd.	soquelec.com	Spar Aerospace Limited	spar.ca
Sorbus Canada Limited	sorbus.on.ca		
SOS Connection Ltd.	sos-connect.com		

Name of Organization	Domain	Name of Organization	Domain
Spar Construction Ltd.	sparconstruction.com	Spire Computing Services, Inc.	spire.on.ca
Spark Communications	spark-bc.com	Spirit Inc.	spirit.ca
Sparkice Asia Ltd.	sparkice.com	Spiritwalker Productions	spiritwalker.com
Sparkice Asia Ltd.	sparkice.on.ca	Splash Online	splash-online.com
Sparky Consulting Ltd.	sparky.ns.ca	Spockslogic	spocks-logic.com
Sparrow Arts Ltd.	sparrow.com	Spoon Worshippers Society	spoon.org
Speach Technology Research Ltd.	speechtech.com	Sport B.C.	sportbc.com
Specialized Communications Inc.	sci.bc.ca	Sport BC	sport.bc.ca
Specialty Installations Ltd.	specialty.ab.ca	Sport Information Resource Centre	sirc.ca
Spectra Computer Services Limited	spectra-online.com	Sports Network Inc., The	tsn.ca
Spectra Investment Systems, Inc.	spctra.com	Sportstrotter Publication	politicus.com
Spectra Investment Systems, Inc.	spctrm.com	Sportsworld Bulletin Board System Inc.	sportsworld.bc.ca
Spectracom Technologies Corporation	spectranomics.com	Spots Interconnect Inc.	spots.ab.ca
Spectranet Connections Inc.	spectranet.ca	Springfield International Real Estate Consultants Ltd.	springfieldintl.com
Spectrum Computing	spectrum-computers.com	Springhill Junior/Senior High School	school.springhill.ns.ca
Spectrum Informatics	spectrum.mb.ca	Sprint Canada Inc.	sprint.ca
Spectrum Internet Services	internet-investor.com	Sprung Instant Structures Ltd	sprung.com
Spectrum Investment Systems Inc.	spcinv.com	Sps Inc.	sps.ca
Spectrum Mutual Funds	spectrum.com	Sputnik Sound Design	sputnik-sound.com
Spectrum Mutual Funds	spectrumfund.ca	Spydernet Communications Systems Inc.	spydernet.com
Spectrum Signal Processing Inc	spectrumsignal.bc.ca	SQL Expert Systems Inc.	sqlx.com
Speedpro Ltd.	speedpro.com	Sqliaison Inc	sqliaison.com
Speedware Corp	speedware.com	Squirrel Systems	squirrel-rms.com
Spektra Multimedia Corp	spektra.com	SR Datascapes Ltd.	srdata.com
Spicer Corporation	spicer.com	SRG Software	srgsoft.com
Spider Works Design Canada	swdesign.com	SRW Software	srw.com
Spielo Gaming International	spielo.ca	SS.Org	ss.org
Spilltech Environment Clean-Up Inc.	spilltech.ca	SSMB Productions	ssmb.com
Spin Production Inc.,	spinpro.com	SST Systems Corporation	sstsystems.com
Spindrift Software Inc.	spindrift.qc.ca	St Michael's Hospital	smh.toronto.on.ca
Spinmaster.Inc.	spinmaster.com	St-Jean Internet Inc.	stjeannet.ca
Spinnaker Systems	spinnaker.com	St. Albert Protestant Schools	pschools.st-albert.ab.ca
		St. Andrew's College	sac.on.ca
		St. Catharines Chamber of Commerce	stc-chamber.com

Name of Organization	Domain	Name of Organization	Domain
St. Catharines Downtown Association	stcathdta.on.ca	Standards Council of Canada	scc.ca
St. Catharines General Hospital	scgh.com	Stanstead College	stansteadc.qc.ca
		Star Enterprises	grumpy.com
St. Catharines Parachute Club	skydiving.com	Star Paging (Canada) Inc.	castar.com
St. Catharines Public Library	scp.st-cath.on.ca	Star Trek Moo	stmoo.org
St. Clair College of Applied Arts and Technology	stclairc.on.ca	Star-Net Inc.	star-net.qc.ca
		Star-Net Inc.	starnet.qc.ca
St. Clement's School	scs.on.ca	Starboard Marketing Services Inc.	starboardinc.com
St. Croix Real Estate Services	stcroix.com		
St. Ives Laboratories	stivesswiss.com	Starbug Scifi Club	starbug.victoria.bc.ca
St. John Ambulance	sja.ca	Starfish Systems Inc.	starfish.ca
St. John's Infonet Association	infonet.st-johns.nf.ca	Stargarden Corp.	stargarden.com
St. Joseph's Health Centre	stjoe.on.ca	Stargate Network Design	thestargate.com
St. Joseph's Health Centre Hospital and Research Institution	stjosephs.london.on.ca	Starlight Incorporated	starlight.on.ca
		Starpoint Systems Inc.	starpoint.com
St. Joseph's Hospital	stjosham.on.ca	Starquote ™, Star Data Systems Inc.	starquote.ca
St. Joseph's Hospital & Health Centre	sjhhc.org	Starvision Systems Corporation	starvision.com
St. Lawrence Broadcasting	theriverrolls.com	Starwars Moo Role Playing Organization	starwars.org
St. Lawrence College	stlawrencec.on.ca	Stategic Leadership	strategic-lead.com
St. Lucia Real Estate Services	stlucia.com	Statistics Canada	statcan.ca
St. Michaels University School	smus.bc.ca	Statpower	statpower.com
St. Mildred's - Lightbourn School	smls.on.ca	STB Investor Software Inc.	stbinvestorsoftware.com
St. Paul's High School	stpaulshs.winnipeg.mb.ca	STC Laboratories Inc.	stclabs.mb.ca
		STD Systems	std.net
St. Paul's Hospital	stpaulshosp.bc.ca	STD Systems Inc.	std.ca
St. Paul's Roman Catholic Separate School Division	stpaulrcssd.saskatoon.sk.ca	STD Technology Inc.	stdgroup.com
		Steals Direct Computer Superstores	steals-direct.com
St. Peter's Hospital	sph.on.ca		
St. Pius X High School	spx.ottawa.on.ca	Steers Communication Associates Inc.	steers.com
St. Remy Press	stremy.com		
St. Thomas University	stthomasu.ca	Steers Communications Association Inc.	steers.on.ca
St. Vincent Real Estate Services	stvincent.com		
St. Vital School Division	stvital.winnipeg.mb.ca	Steffen Open Systems	huron.net
		Steffen Open Systems, Inc.	sos.on.ca
Stabilization Central Credit Union	stabil.com	Steinbach Bible College Incorporated	sbcollege.mb.ca
Stan Grist	explorenet.com		
Standard Aero Limited	standardaero.ca	Steinberg Inc.	steinberg.ca

Name of Organization	Domain	Name of Organization	Domain
Stelco Inc.	stelco.ca	Storm Technical Communications Inc.	stormtc.com
Stellar Systems Group	stellar.on.ca	Stormceptor Canada, Inc.	stormceptor.ca
Stellar Systems Group Inc.	stellar.bc.ca	Stormnet	stormnet.com
Stelwire, Ltd.	stelwire.com	Story Vision Network, Inc.	storyvision.ca
Stem-Net of Newfoundland And Labrador	stemnet.nf.ca	Straightline Replacement Services	pricehunter.com
Stemcell Technologies Inc.	stemcell.com	Strait Crossing Web Services	straitcrossing.com
Stem~Net - Newfoundland and Labrador K-12 Schools	k12.nf.ca	Strand Lighting Inc.	strand.ca
Stentor	stentor.ca	Strange Ink	strange.com
Stephen Kimber Associates	innovations.org	Strangelove Internet Enterprises, Inc.	strangelove.com
Sterling Group Design	sgd.com	Strata Software Limited	strataware.ca
Sterling Newspaper Ltd.	sterlingnews.com	Strata Software Limited	strataware.com
Sterling Pulp Chemicals, Ltd.	sterlingpulp.com	Stratacom Technologies Inc.	stratacom.bc.ca
Steve Dotto Enterprises	dotto.com	Stratalink Inc.	stratalink.com
Steve Macbeth	amber.com	Strategem Inc.	strategem.qc.ca
Steve's BBS	stevesbbs.org	Strategic Ampersand	stratamp.com
STI Inc.	stii.com	Strategic Communications	stratt.com
Stikeman Elliot	stikeman.ca	Strategic Focus	stratfocus.ottawa.on.ca
Stikeman Elliot	stikeman.com	Strategic Initiatives Group, Inc	sigroup.com
Still Current Canada Corporation	graphicintel.com	Strategic Microelectronics Consortium	smc.ca
Still Current Canada Corporation	weathermap.com	Strategic Objectives Inc.	strategic-objectives.com
Stimpy Fan Club	stimpy.com	Strategic Policy Group	spg.org
STO Inc.	sto.qc.ca	Strategic Resources Inc.	sri.bc.ca
Stock Deck Communications Inc.	stockdeck.com	Strategic UNIX Networks Corporation	strategic.victoria.bc.ca
Stockline Inc.	stockline.com	Strategy First Inc	strategy.qc.ca
Stocknet Industries	stocknet.com	Stratford Festival	stratford-festival.on.ca
Stockton Industries, Inc.	stockton.com	Strathcona Career Training Institute	scti.ab.ca
Stokes Seeds Ltd.	stokesseeds.com	Strathcona County	strathcona.ab.ca
Stoll Momentum Systems	fxfx.com	Stream-Flo Industries, Inc.	streamflo.com
Stone & Cox, Ltd.	stonecox.com	Stressgen Bio-Technologies	stressgen.com
Stone-Consolidated Corporation	stonecons.com	Stria Communications Inc.	stria.ca
Stonefield Systems Group Inc.	stonefield.com	Stria Communications Inc.	stria.com
Stonehenge Software Technology Inc.	stonehenge.bc.ca	Strive!	strive.com
Storkcraft Manufacturing Inc.	storkcraft.com		

Name of Organization	Domain	Name of Organization	Domain
Strive! Inc.	strive.ca	Superior Interactive Communications	sicem.com
STS Systems Ltd.	sts-systems.ca	Superior Network Software	snsi.com
Stucco Doctor Corp.	stucco-doctor.com	Superior Printing Ltd.	superiorprint.com
Studio Apropos	klco.com	Superior Weighing Systems Ltd.	supweigh.ca
Stuffers	stuffers.com		
Stylex Inc.	stylex.com	Supreme Court of Canada	supremect.ca
Stylus Inc.	stylus.ca	Suralform Inc.	suralform.com
Subud Canada	subud.ca	Sure Control Systems Inc.	sure.ca
Sumac Systems Inc.	sumac.com	Sure Foot Industries	ceramicsafety treatment.com
Summerland Marketting Int.	bc-alaska.com		
Summit 4WD Adventures Inc.	4wheeldrive.com	Sure Foot Industries	ceramicsaftey treatment.com
Sun Computer Systems Inc.	suncomp.ab.ca		
Sun Life Brokerage	slbrokerage.com	Surface Mount Technology Centre	smtc.com
Sun Life of Canada	slactuary.com		
Sun Microsystems of Canada, Inc.	sun.ca	Susan Mcwilliams	tdgreenline.com
		Sutherland Mark Somerville Bumstead	solicitors.com
Sun Systems Manitoba	sunsys-mb.com		
Sun Systems Manitoba	sunsystems.mb.ca	Sutherland Schultz Inc.	sutherland-schultz.com
Sunami	travelscene.com		
Sunbeam Rentals	sunbeam.com	Sutherland-Schultz, Ltd.	schultz.on.ca
Suncor Inc. (Resources Group)	suncor.com	Sutton Group	sutton.com
Sunlife of Canada	sunlife.com	Swabey Ogilvy Renault Inc	swabey.com
Sunni Micro Lab	sunni.com	SWI Systemware, Inc.	swi.com
Sunny Golf Company	sunnygolf.com	Swifton Holding Ltd.	swifton.nb.ca
Sunny Hill Health Centre for Children	sunnyhill.bc.ca	Swim Canada Magazine	swimnews.com
		Swinton And Company	answith.com
Sunoco, Inc.	sunoco.com	Switchview Inc.	switchview.com
Sunquest Vacations Limited	sunquest.ca	SY Systems	sy-systems.com
Sunservice Interational, Inc.	sunservice.ca	Sydney Steel Corporation	sysco.ns.ca
Sunset System Consulting	tgif.com	Sygmanet, A Value Added Network Service From	sygma.net
Sunshine Coast Community Network	sunshine.net		
		Sykora Technology Inc.	syk.com
Suntek Software Corporation	suntek.mb.ca	Sylvain Faust, Inc.	sfi-software.com
Super Service Tickets	scalper.com	Sylvis Environmental Services Inc.	sylvis.com
Super-Byte Computers Ltd.	superbyte.com		
Superb Entertainment	superb-e--hj.com	Symatix Software Ltd.	symatix.com
Supercom Associates Inc.	supercom.com	Symbolic Research Corp.	symbolic-research.com
Supercom of California Limited	supercom.ca		
		Symbols/923653 Ontario Inc.	symbols.com
Superior Data Services	superior.mb.ca	Symtech Canada Inc.	symtech.com

Name of Organization	Domain	Name of Organization	Domain
Symtrex Distribution, Inc.	symtrex.com	System Telly	telly.on.ca
Synamics Inc.	synamics.com	Systematic Computer Services	systematic.com
Synamics Inc.	synamics.on.ca	Systemax Informatique	systemax.com
Synapse Internet Solutions, A Division of Interactivity Inc.	synapse.ca	Systemcorp Inc.	systemcorp.com
Synaptic Communications Inc.	netbistro.com	Systeme, Consultation, Integration, et Recherche Ltd.	scir.ca
Synaptic Systems, Inc.	synapticsys.com	Systemes Beabien	beaubien.com
Synchronics Ltd.	synchronics.com	Systemes Informatiques Jovaco Inc.	jovaco.ca
Syncronys Systems Corporation	syncronys.com		
Syncros Applied Technologies	syncros.com	Systemetrix Corporation	systemetrix.ca
Syncrude Canada Ltd.	syncrude.com	Systemetrix Corporation	systemetrix.com
Syndesis Limited	syndesis.ca	Systemlogic Inc.	systemlogic.net
Syndesis Limited	syndesis.com	Systems Xcellence Ltd.	sx.com
Syndetic Systems Group	syndetic.com	Systemscope, Inc.	systemscope.com
Syndicat Professionnel des Scientifiques de l'IREQ	spsi.qc.ca	T J Paraczchych	handling.com
		T.E. Computing Incorporated	tec.ab.ca
Synectic Advice Inc.	synectic.on.ca	T.E.N. Private Cable Systems	aquarelle.com
Synectics Health Corporation	synectics.bc.ca	T.G. Hayton And Associates Inc.	tghacctg.mb.ca
Synergie les Specialistes du Documents Inc.	synergie1.com		
		T.L.C. Computers	tlc.mb.ca
Synergistics Consulting, Ltd.	synergistics.ca	T.W.E.	twe.com
Synergy Engineering	synergy-eng.com	Taarna System Inc.	taarna.qc.ca
Synergy Print and Copy Inc.	synergy.on.ca	Taaz Corporation	taaz.com
Synertech Systems Corporation Ltd.	synertech.bc.ca	Taiga Consulting	taiga.ca
		Taisbean Multimedia Productions	taisbean.com
Synervision Digital Productions Inc.	coolvision.com	Taisbean Multimedia Productions	taisbean.sydney.ns.ca
Synex Systems	synexsystems.com		
Synos Information Systems EDI Inc.	cancap.com	Take One BBS	takeone.com
		Talentweb	talentweb.com
Syntha-Voice Computers Inc.	synthavoice.on.ca	Talisman Software	talisoft.com
Sys-X	sys-x.com	Tall Sky Communications	tallsky.com
Sys.Sensato	sensato.com	Talon Consulting Inc.	talon.mb.ca
Syscom Consulting Inc.	sci-syscom.com	Talvest Fund Management	talvest.com
Sysgold Ltd.	sysgold.com	Talvest Fund Management	talvestfund.ca
Sysinct Inc.	sysinct.com	Tamago Development	webtech.com
Syspro Impact Software.	syspro.com	Tamarack Computers Corporation	tamarack.nt.ca
System Builders Inc.	systembuilders.com		
System Monitors Inc.	sysmon.mb.ca	Tamarack Creek Corporate Communications Inc.	tam-creek.ca
System Technology Development Inc	autoroute.net		
		Tamcan Corporation	fetishmall.com

Name of Organization	Domain	Name of Organization	Domain
Tanager Software Ltd.	tanager.com	TeamOS/2	teamos2.org
Tanda and Associates	tanda.on.ca	Tec Partners Canada Inc	tec.ca
Tanda Technologies	tantech.com	Tech Support Plus	tsplus.com
Tandem Capital	tandemcap.com	Tech'N Logos Systems Inc	technlogos.com
Tangent Thought Software	tthought.com	Techchoice	techchoice.com
Tangram Developments Ltd.	tangram-dev.com	Techcom Computer Systems, Ltd.	techcom.on.ca
Tanner Young Marketing Ltd.	tym.com	Techknowledge	north-pole.com
Tansen Company Ltd	tansen.com	Technet Information Systems Inc.	technetcom.com
Tantalus Communications	tantalus.com	Technical Consultants & Experts Group	autoinvest.com
Tantalus Technologies Inc.	mountain-inter.net	Technical Finance Adjusters	tfa.com
Tantus Electronics Corporation	tantus.com	Technical Magic	techmag.com
Tanzanian International Group	tigsite.org	Technical University of Nova Scotia	tuns.ca
Tarasoft	tarasoft.com	Technocap Inc.	technocap.com
Tarek Parallel Systems	tarek.com	Technocosm	technocosm.com
Target Marketing & Communications Inc.	targetmarketing.nf.ca	Technologies for Growth International	t4g.com
Target Surveys Inc.	quadrasurveys.com	Technologies Lyre Inc.	lyre.qc.ca
Targeted Communication Management	tcm.com	Technologies Sepia Inc.	sepia.com
Tartan Valley Monitoring Inc. O/A Tartan Cybernet Services	tartannet.ns.ca	Technologies Summit Inc.	summit.qc.ca
Taske Technology Inc.	taske.com	Technology Based Learning Network Canada	tbl.ca
Taxprep Info	taxprep.com	Technology Marketing	careersmidlyn.com
Taylor Mccaffrey, Barristers and Solicitors	taylormccaffrey.winnipeg.mb.ca	Technology Plus	techplus.com
Taylor/Wagner Inc.	taylorwagner.com	Technology Virtual Warehouse	tvw.com
Tazumi-Tech Business and Computer College (Canada) Inc.	tazumitech.ca	Technolust Corporation	technolust.com
TCB Corporation	tcb.com	Technovision Systems Ltd. DBA Uniserve Online	uniserve.bc.ca
TCC Communications	tcccallback.com	Techpro Electronics	igs.net
TCE Information Group Ltd.	tce.on.ca	Techpro Electronics, Inc.	techpro.com
TCI Trading Company Inc.	cimex.com	Techware Inc	techware.mb.ca
TCN Systems Group	tcn.net	Techwell Global Inc	global-online.com
TCP/IP Consultant Enr.	tcpip.qc.ca	Techzone	techzone.com
TCR	timecritical.com	Teck Corporation	teckcorp.ca
TCR Ltd.	tcrl.com	Tecnet Networking Ltd.	tecnet.ca
TDI Computer Systems Limited	tdi.org	Tecom Network, Inc.	tecom.com
TDK Consulting Services	tdkcs.waterloo.on.ca	Tecsult Inc.	tecsult.com
Teal Resources Inc.	tealcomm.com		
Team OS2	drifting.com		

Name of Organization	Domain	Name of Organization	Domain
Tecsys Inc.	tecsys.com	Telemedia Inc.	telem.com
Ted Y. Nitta & Associates	tyn.com	Telemedia Inc.	telemedia.org
Ted's Collision And Body Repair	teds.org	Telemedicine Canada	tmed.org
Teddy Bear Productions Ltd.	tbear.com	Telenium Division of CTI-Comtel Inc.	telenium.ca
Tee-Off Games	teeoff.com	Telepages Inc.	telepages.ca
Teenet Inc.	tee-net.com	Telephone Magic Inc.	telephonemagic.com
Teknekron Software Systems (Canada)	tss.ca	Teleport de Montreal Inc.	teleport.ca
Teknor Microsystemes Inc	teknor.com	Teleride Sage Ltd.	teleride.on.ca
Tekskil Industries Inc.	tekskil.com	Telesat Canada	telesat.ca
Tela Computer Consulting + Design	tela.bc.ca	Teleserve Canada Inc.	teleserve.ca
		Teleservice T Inc.	tst.qc.ca
Telarian Intenet Commerce Corporation	telarian.com	Telesis Systems, Inc.	telesis.on.ca
Telarian Internet Commerce Corporation	tradeshows.com	Telesystems SLW Inc.	telesystems.com
		Teletech Response	teletech-response.com
Telco Consulting	telco.on.ca	Televitesse Systems Inc	televitesse.com
Telco Consulting	telco.waterloo.on.ca	Televitesse Systems Inc	tvs.ca
Tele Fone Heaven	tfh.com	Televoice Communication	potp.com
Tele-Metropole Inc.	tele-metropole.com	Televolution Ltd.	televolution.on.ca
Telebec Inc.	telebec.com	Tellier Electronics Ltd.	tellier.mb.ca
Telebec Inc.	telebec.qc.ca	Telly Computing	telly.org
Telecommons Development Group Inc., The	tdg.ca	Telnet Canada Enterprises, Ltd.	tcel.com
Telecommunications Research Institute of Ontario, The	trio.ca	Telos Communications Inc.	amtex.com
		Telos Communications Inc.	telos.ca
Telecommunications Research Laboratories	trlabs.ca	Telos Communications Inc.	telos.org
		Telos Engineering Ltd	teloseng.com
Teleconsult Limited	teleconsult.com	Telpay Division of CTI-Comtel Inc.	telpay.ca
Teledigm Corporation	tdm.com	Telsoft Mobile Data Inc.	telsoft.com
Teledisc Systems Ltd.	teledisc.mb.ca	Telular Canada, Inc.	globaldata.com
Teleflex (Canada) Limited	teleflex.bc.ca	Telus Corporation.	telus.com
Teleglobe Canada	tgb.com	Tembec, Inc.	tembec.ca
Teleglobe Canada Inc.	teleglobe.ca	Templeton Management Ltd.	templeton.ca
Teleglobe Insurance Systems	tglobe.com	Templeton Management Ltd.	templeton.com
Telelearning Research Network	telelearn.ca	Tempo Marketing	tempo.mb.ca
Telelink Technologies Inc.	telelink.com	Temptation Fashion Design Inc.	temptation.com
Telematix Technologies Inc	telematix.com	Temtech	temtech.com
Telemedia Communications Inc.	telemedia.ca		

Name of Organization	Domain	Name of Organization	Domain
Tenderfoot Computer Consulting	tenderfoot.com	Thames Valley District Health Council	tvdhc.on.ca
Tenet Computer Group, Inc.	tenet.com	Thats the Ticket	tickets.com
Tequila Films Inc.	tequila.com	The 2111 Foundation	twentyone-11.org
Teranet Land Information Services Inc.	teranet.on.ca	The 71st Page Corporation	71st.com
Terminal Centre Corporation	terminalcentre.com	The Aaron Group	biga.com
Tern Solution Group Corporation	natscannet.com	The Abrazen Group of Companies	abrazen.com
Terra Surveys Limited	terrasurveys.com	The Acetech Academy for Chief Executives	acetech-ceo.com
Terra Venture Sales	plantpet.com	The Acetech Academy for Chief Executives	acetech.org
Terraffirmative	terranet.ab.ca	The Adoption Reunion Registry	directory.org
Terrafirma Research and Reports	terrafirma.com	The Adults at Play BBS	aaplay.org
Terrafirma Technologies Inc.	electron-ink.com	The Alcyone Network	alcyone.org
Terranet Technologies Inc.	terra-tech.nb.ca	The Alexandra Apt./Hotel	alexandra.com
Terraport Online Inc.	terraport.net	The Angling Edge Telecommunications Network	angling.com
Terraport Online Inc.	terraport.on.ca	The Anvil Group Inc.	tag001.com
Terrasat Television International	terrasat.com	The Aroga Group	aroga.com
Terratec Environmental, Ltd.	terratec.com	The Art of Investment	aofi.com
Terren Corporation	terren.com	The Autobank,A Division Of 1110897 Ontario Inc.	autobank.com
Terrix Consulting Inc.	terrix.bc.ca	The AWINC Network	awinc.net
Tertius Technologie Inc.	tertius.com	The B.A.S.P. Buy & Sell Press Ltd.	buysell.com
Tertius Technologie Inc.	tertius.nb.ca	The Babel Fish Corporation	babelfish.com
Teshmont Consultants Inc.	teshmont.mb.ca	The Bayshore Group of Companies	bayshoregrp.com
Tesma International, Inc.	tesma.on.ca	The Biographix Corporation	biographix.com
Tesseract Computers Ltd.	tesseract.bc.ca	The Board	directbbs.com
Testforce Systems Inc	testforce.com	The Body Shop	qbsc.com
Tesuji Software	tesuji.qc.ca	The Boucher Family	boucher.com
Tetres Consultants, Inc.	tetres.ca	The Braegen Group Inc.	braegen.com
Texar Software Corp.	texar.com	The Brughetti Corporation	brughetti.com
Texcan Cables Inc.	texcan.com	The Business Monitor	business-monitor.com
Textworks, Inc.	crossroads.com	The Bytown Group	bytowngroup.com
Texxen Consulting Limited	texxen.richmond.bc.ca	The Calgary Explorer	calexplorer.com
TFE Industries	justimagine.com	The Calling Station	assman.com
Thacker Network Technologies, Inc.	thacker.com		
Thales Corp.	geolink.com		

Name of Organization	Domain	Name of Organization	Domain
The Canadian Association for Management of Technology	canmot.org	The Cybersuite Experience	cybersuite.com
		The Decheudon BBS	decheudon.com
The Canadian Bar Association	cba.org	The Deev Group Computer Systems Inc.	deev.com
The Canadian Press	cpbn.com	The Devon Group Limited	devon.com
The Canadian Press and Broadcast News	broadnews.com	The Digital Victorian	dv.net
The Case For Advertising	webvisitmedia.com	The Do Duck Inn	do-duck-inn.com
The CD Press	cdpress.com	The Doctor's Network	doctor.net
The Cen-Ta Group	centa.com	The Donato Group	donato.com
The Centralized Equipment Pool Project	cepp.org	The Donwood Institute	donwood.org
The CEO Group	hitechcareer.com	The Duke of Edinburgh's Award Young Canadians Challenge	dukeofed.org
The Champlain Society	champlain.org	The Easter Seal Society	easterseals.org
The Chancellor Partners	chancellor-partners.com	The Eastwood Tourist Lodge	eastwood.com
The Coda Group	coda.com	The Edge of Reality	teor.com
The Colbert Group	colbert.com	The Electric Mail Company	electric.net
The Collosus Soo Resource Network	csrnet-bbs.com	The Eleet Group	eleet.org
The Colosseum BBS	colosseum.com	The Elm Street Computer Terminal	elmstreet.com
The Comic Book	superman.com	The Entrepreneurship Centre	entrepreneurship.com
The Commonwealth of Learning	col.org	The Era Banner	erabanner.net
The Communications Works	commworks.com	The Event Transportation System	etsys.com
The Comprehensive Consulting Group	ccg-chcl.com	The Exchange BBS	hbelec.com
The Computer Freelancer	freelancer.com	The Final Encyclopedia Project	final-e.com
The Computer Shoppe Inc.	imageport.com	The Financial Planning Group	tfpg.com
The Consortium of the Interchange of Museum Information	cimi.org	The Financial Post Company	finpost.com
		The Footmaxx Group Inc.	footmaxx.com
		The Forest Alliance of BC	forest.org
The Continuing Legal Education Society of B.C.	cle.com	The Forward Group Inc.	fwdgrp.com
		The Fund Library Inc.	fundlib.com
The Cookbook Store Ltd.	cook-book.com	The Funnel	thefunnel.com
The Council Of Forest Industries	cofi.org	The Future By Design Inc.	brenda.com
The Crimson Corporation	crimson-corp.com	The Giest Society	geist.com
The Cruise Mall	sea-cruise.com	The Global Exchange	tgx.com
The Cumis Group Ltd.	cumis.org	The Global Group	global-contract.com
The Cumis Group, Ltd.	cumisgroup.com	The Global Group	global-furniture.com
		The Global Group	global-group.com
		The Global Group	global-industries.com

Name of Organization	Domain	Name of Organization	Domain
The Global Group	global-upholstery.com	The Investor Relations Group	rgeist.com
The Global Group	teknion.com	The Ireland Fund Of Canada	irelandfunds.org
The Global Group	the-global-group.com	The James Gang Advertising, Inc.	jamesgang.com
The Global Sports Village	globalsports.com	The James Gang Advertising, Inc.	nerdheaven.com
The Great Canadian Computer Company	norlink.com	The Jungle BBS	thejungle.com
The Great Canadian Computer Company	swan.com	The K J Lee Group Inc.	kjlee.com
The Green Cart Magazine	greencart.com	The Kamda Systems	kamda.com
The Grizzlies Basketball Club	grizzlies.com	The Keg Restaurant	thekeg.com
The Grouse Association	grouse.com	The Kind Group	kindgroup.com
The Guild Mail Park	guild.org	The King's Center	tkc.com
The Guildnet BBS	guildnet.org	The Lan Shoppe, Inc.	lanshop.com
The Hard Rock Cafe	hard-rock.com	The Leadership Alliance Inc	tlainc.com
The Harvey Group	the-harvey-group.com	The Learning Curve	curve.com
The Hendrie Corporation	hendrie.com	The Learning Support Council of Canada	learn.org
The High Council of Gallifrey	tardis.org	The Legal Index Inc.	legalindex.com
The Hugh Group, Inc.	hughgroup.com	The Leningrad Carrot Conspiracy	yuggoth.org
The Humana Cortex Group Inc.	terramed.com	The Lisma Computer Corporation	lisma.com
The Information Atrium, Inc.	inforium.com	The Litigation Brief Inc.	litbrief.com
The Information Detective & Associates	rare-books.com	The Magellan Group	magellangroup.com
The International Programmers Guild (Canadian Chapter)	ipguild.org	The Market ICI World Network	iciworld.com
The International Tickets Network	ticket.net	The Martin Group	curlew-lake.com
The Internet Advertising Agency	tiaa.com	The Masonic Order of the Mango	mango.net
The Internet Carguide	carguide.com	The Media Book	mediabook.com
The Internet Conveyor, Ltd.	networkscon.com	The Medical Post's Outlook	mpoutlook.com
The Internet Galleria, Inc.	galleria.com	The Midwest Connection	midconn.com
The Internet Gothic Society	goth.org	The Millennium Foundation of Canada	millennia.org
The Internet Made Easy	time.net	The Mississauga News	mississauga.com
The Internet Shop Inc.	netshop.net	The Mississauga News	mississauganews.com
The Internet Store	net-store.com	The Monolit Group	monolit.com
The Internet Store	the-internet-store.com	The Musashi Fellowship	musashi.org
The Internet World Cafe	tiwc.com	The Natural Order	tno.com
The Investor Relations Group	invrel.com	The Network Centre	tnc.com

Name of Organization	Domain	Name of Organization	Domain
The New Home Buyers Network	homebuyers.com	The Software Group Limited	group.com
The Newland Group	newland.com	The Spectator	thespectator.com
The Newton Store	newtonstore.com	The Starlight Foundation	starlight.org
The Next City	nextcity.com	The Syndicate Organization	syndicate.org
The Observatory	blacksun.org	The System Works	tsw.com
The Original Fish Hotline	fishhotline.com	The T.E.A.M. Corporation	teamcorp.com
The Otis Index	otis-index.com	The Therapy Network	therapynet.com
The Party Palace BBS	ppalace.com	The Toronto Airway Management Foundation	medairway.org
The Peformax Sales & Marketing Group	performax.com	The Toronto Cabal	cabal.org
The Personnel Services Group	personnel.com	The Toronto Eaton Center	eaton-centre.com
The Pickering BBS	picbbs.com	The Toronto Municipal Area Networking Co-Operative	torman.net
The Pillar and Post	ppost.com	The Toronto Star	torstar.com
The Planet Internet Corporation	planetinternet.com	The Toronto Stock Exchange	tse.com
The Plant Software Inc.	egn.com	The Town Pump	pump.com
The Plant Software Inc.	notes.com	The Tracker Corporation	recovery.com
The Plant Software Inc.	theplant.com	The Tracker Corporation	tracker.com
The Pleasure Zone	pz.com	The Undiscovered Country BBS	undiscovered.com
The Positive Learning Centre	learningcentre.com	The United Church of Canada	unitedch.org
The Prep Store	prepstore.com	The Upallnite BBS	uan.com
The Printing House	printinghse.com	The Usual Suspects	suspects.com
The Proteus Group	tpg.org	The Vancouver Sun	vansun.com
The Providers Limited	canadamalls.com	The Vivid Group	vividgroup.com
The Province	theprovince.com	The Willcam Group, Ltd.	willcam.com
The Questor Project	questor.org	The Wire	the-wire.com
The Rapid Application Development Group Inc.	radgrp.com	The Wireless Group, Inc.	infopage.com
The Red Green Show	redgreen.com	The Wizard's Baud BBS	wizardbaud.com
The Renzland Trust	renzland.org	The WNDX Corporation	wndx.com
The Rubicon Organization	rubicon.org	The Women's Bank Society	womens-bank.com
The Saskatoon Fringe Festival	fringe.org	The Woodbridge Co. Ltd.	woodbridge.com
The Saunders Consulting Group	saunders.com	The Woodbridge Group	foam.com
The Science Group	science-group.com	The Wordwright Company	wordwright.com
The Second City	secondcity.com	The World Film Festival	ffm-montreal.org
The Sexton Clan	sexton.org	Thea Artworks	cyberbabe.com
The Sinai Group, Inc.	tsg.com	Themis Program Management & Consulting Ltd.	themis.bc.ca
The Society for the Message of God, Under Windows	godwin.org	Theoretix Electronics Ltd.	theoretix.com
		Thera-Ped Ltd	theraped.com
		Theratechnologies Inc.	theratech.com

Name of Organization	Domain	Name of Organization	Domain
Thermazone Informatics	reachit.com	Ticketmaster - Vancouver Ticket Centre Ltd.	ticketmaster.ca
Think+ Computer Resources Inc.	thinkplus.on.ca	Ticon Technology Inc.	ticon.com
Thinkage Ltd.	thinkage.com	Tictoc Corporation	tictoc.com
Thinkage Ltd.	thinkage.on.ca	Tie Communications Research	tcrtel.com
Thinker Toys	thinker.com	Tiger Media Inc.	tiger.ab.ca
Thinker Toys, Co.	thinker-toys.on.ca	Tilley Endurables Inc	tilley.com
Thinker Toys, Inc.	thinkertoys.com	Tim Horton Fanclub	timhortons.com
Thinking Cap Media	thinkcap.com	Tim Kutt	rocking.com
Thinknet Inc.	thinknet.com	Tim Louis and Company	timlouis.com
Thinkway Trading Corporation	thinkway.com	Timberline Data Services	timber.com
This Week	durhamnews.net	Timberline Forest Inventory Consultants	tfic.bc.ca
This Week In Bible Prophecy	twibp.com	Timeac Computer Systems Inc.	timeac.com
Thomas Cook Group	tcook.com	Timedancer Systems	timedancer.com
Thomas Cook Group	thomascook.com	Times Colonist	times-colonist.bc.ca
Thomas Haney Secondary	ths.mapleridge.bc.ca	Times-Mirror Professional Publishing, Ltd.	tmpp.ca
Thomas O'Bryan International Group	tobig.mb.ca	Timmins Area Bulletin Board System	tabb.com
Thomcom Canada Inc.	thomcom.ca	Tips Project Office	icsteam.org
Thomcom Canada Inc.	thomcom.com	Titan Computer Systems Ltd.	titancs.com
Thompson Public Library	publib.thompson.mb.ca	Titleworks Inc.	titleworks.com
Thompson-Nicola Regional District Library System	tnrdlib.bc.ca	Tivy Consulting	tivy.com
		TKM Software Limited	tkm.mb.ca
Thomson Healthcare Communications	mdnet.com	TLA Computexperts Inc.	computexperts.com
Thomson-CSF Systems Canada Inc.	thomson-csf.ca	TLC Executive	welcome-traveler.com
Thornhill Secondary School	thss.thornhill.on.ca	TLC Executives	apts4rent.com
Thought Link Systems	tls.com	TLD Computers	tld.com
Thought Technology Ltd.	thought.ca	TM Software Associates Inc.	tmsoftware.ca
Thrifty Auto Sales	car-sales.com	TMC Inc.	tmcadvisor.com
Thrifty Foods	thriftyfoods.com	TMR Telecommunications Management & Marketing Research Centre Inc.	tmres.org
Thunder Bay Public Library	tbpl.thunder-bay.on.ca		
Thunder Rd. Limited	thunderrd.on.ca	TNE Electronics Inc.	tne.ns.ca
Thunder Zone BBS	tzone.org	To-De Communications	to-de.com
Thunderbolt Software	tbsoftware.com	Toasted Media Inc.	toast.ca
Tiac Communications Ltd	tiaccom.com	Tobago Real Estate Services	tobago.com
Ticker	ticker.com	Todd Communications	toddcomm.com
		Toews Music&Sewing	toews.com

Name of Organization	Domain	Name of Organization	Domain
Tofino Expeditions Ltd.	tofino.com	Toronto School of Business	tsbsoo.com
Together Inc.	together.ca	Toronto School of Internet	gotsi.com
Toltec Systems, Inc.	toltec.com	Toronto Star ™, Toronto Star Newspapers Ltd.	torontostar.ca
Tonal Discord	tonal.com		
Tonto Mining	tonto.com	Toronto Star Newspapers Limited	tsnl.com
Toon Boom Technology Inc.	toonboom.com		
Top Tape & Label Limited	toptape.com	Toronto Sun	torsun.com
Topix Computer Graphics and Animation	topix.com	Toronto Twilight Communications.	ttcbbs.com
Topsystems Canada Inc.	topsys.com	Toronto-Dominion Bank	tdbank.ca
Tor Computerized Systems, Inc.	torcomp.com	Torque Systems	torque.net
Tordiff Communications Inc.	tordiff.com	Torrie Communication Services	torrie.org
Tordion Consulting Inc.	tordion.com	Torstar Corporation	torstar.ca
Toromont Industries, Ltd.	toromont.com	Tory Tory Deslauriers & Binnington	torytory.ca
Torontel Computers & Communications	torontel.com		
		Toshiba Canada Inc.	toshiba.ca
Toronto Argonauts Football Club	argonauts.on.ca	Toshiba of Canada Ltd	tcl.com
		Tosi Placement Services Inc.	tosi.com
Toronto Bar Network	bar.org	Total Access Inc	total.net
Toronto Blue Jays	bluejays.com	Total Client Services Inc.	totalclient.mb.ca
Toronto Blue Jays Baseball Club	bluejays.ca	Total Integration	totalint.mb.ca
		Total Vision System Inc.	total-vision.com
Toronto Consumer Information Directory Inc.	tcid.on.ca	Totem Building Supplies Ltd.	totem.ab.ca
		Totem Technologies Inc.	totem.com
Toronto Datacom & Cables Inc.	tdc.on.ca	Touch Communications Inc.	touch.com
Toronto Dominion Bank	tdhighway.com	Touch Tone Marketing	touchtone.com
Toronto East General Hospital	tegh.on.ca	Touchlink Communications Systems	touchlink.com
Toronto FM Communications Society	tfmcs.org		
		Touchnet Canada Inc	touchnet.ca
Toronto FM Communications Society Inc.	tfmcs.on.ca	Touchstone Real Estate Ltd.	touchstone-re.com
		Touchstone Technologies, Inc.	touchstone.com
Toronto Free-Net	torfree.net	Tour BC	visitbc.com
Toronto Free-Net Inc.	freenet.toronto.on.ca	Tour BC Inc.	bcsite.com
Toronto Hospital, The	torhosp.toronto.on.ca	Tour British Columbia	tourbc.com
Toronto Hydro	torhydro.toronto.on.ca	Touring.Ca	touring.ca
		Tourism Technology Virtual Warehouse	ttvw.com
Toronto Internet Co-Operative Inc.	tic.on.ca		
		Tourism Winnipeg	tourism.winnipeg.mb.ca
Toronto Life Ventures	tor-lifeline.com		
Toronto Linux Users Group	tlug.org	Tourlink Inc.	tourlink.com
Toronto Public Library	tpl.toronto.on.ca	Tower Travel	travel-escapes.com

Name of Organization	Domain	Name of Organization	Domain
Town of Niagara-On-The-Lake	town.notl.on.ca	Transgas Management Inc.	transgas.com
Townshend Computer Tools	tc.com	Transilient Business Systems, Inc.	transilient.com
Township of West Lincoln	twp.wlincoln.on.ca	Transition Partners	webpartners.com
Toxic Recovery Sciences International	trsi.com	Transkills Training Association Inc.	transkl.com
Toyota Canada Inc.	toyota.ca	Transportaion Action Now	trans-action.org
TP Communications	tpcom.com	Transylvania Press	transylvania.com
TPCI	tpci.com	Transys Networks Inc.	transysnet.com
Trac Insurance Services Ltd	trac.com	Transys Networks Inc.	transysnet.qc.ca
Traceamerica Inc.	traceamerica.com	Travel	prague.com
Tracknet Online Research	tracknet.com	Travel Exchange	travex.com
Tradart	tradart.ottawa.on.ca	Travel Underwriters	travelgold.com
Trade America Group	new-stuff.com	Travel-Net Communications	travel-net.com
Trade Wind Resources Ltd.	tradewindres.com	Travelink Network	tl.net
Tradenet	tradenet.com	Travelmatch Inc.	travelink.com
Tradesco Mold Limited	tradesco.com	Treasure-Will Technology, Ltd.	treasure-will.com
Tradex Import Export Inc.	interfair.com	Treasury Management Association of Canada	tmac.ca
Traductions Artra Translations	artra.vanier.on.ca	Tree of Death Books	mohammad.com
Trafalgar School for Girls	trafalgar.qc.ca	Treeline Planning Services Ltd.	treeline.nt.ca
Trajan Publishing Corp.	trajan.com	Trekka Sportswear Inc.	trekka.ca
Trance-Action Consultants	trance-action.com	Tremar Virtual	tremarvirtual.mb.ca
Tranquility Base Software Inc.	tranquility-base.com	Trent University	trentu.ca
Tranquility Base Software Inc.	tranquility.com	TRG Electronik	trgcorp.com
Trans Atlantic Dimensions	tad.com	Tri Transform Research, Inc.	transres.com
Trans Canada Options Inc.	tco.ca	Tri-University Meson Facility	triumf.ca
Trans Continental Printing Inc.	tcp-van.com	Triathlon Mapping Corp	tmc.bc.ca
Trans Mountain Pipe Line Co. Ltd.	tmpl.ca	Tribal Lands Consulting Group, Inc.	triballands.com
Trans Union of Canada Data Centre	tudc.com	Tribal Sportswear Inc.	tribal-inc.com
Transact Data Services, Inc.	tdsi.ca	Trident Information Systems Inc.	stnzebra.com
Transact Systems Inc	transys.com	Trigon Mapping Resources Limited	trigonmap.com
Transalta Utilities Corporation	transalta.ab.ca	Trigraph, Inc.	trigraph.on.ca
Transamerica Group Inc.	canada-law.com	Trillium Sound Research Inc.	trillium.ab.ca
Transcanada Pipelines	sbcwtcpl.com	Trilok Inc	trilok-inc.com
Transcanada Pipelines Limited	tcpl.ca	Trilok Inc	trilok.com
Transcom International Ltd.	transcom.mb.ca	Trimark Investment Management, Inc.	trimark.com
Transcorp Int.	transcorp.com	Trimax Retail Systems	trimax.com
Transdata Communications Inc.	transdata.ca		
Transfreight, Inc.	transfreight.com		

Name of Organization	Domain	Name of Organization	Domain
Trimension Inc.	trimension.com	TSB International Inc.	tsb.ca
Trimension Training and Consulting Group Inc.	trimension.ca	TSO Laboratory Inc.	tsolab.com
Trinidad Real Estate Services	trinidad.com	TSPN	tspn.com
Trinity College School	tcs.on.ca	TSQ Computer Services	milescorp.com
Trinity Western University	esli-twu.edu	TTS Meridian Systems Inc.	ttsmsi.com
Trinity Western University	twu.ca	Tube-E Communications	tube.com
Triolet Systems Inc.,	triolet.com	Tudhope & Company Limited	scribe.com
Trios Training Centres Ltd.	trios.ca	Tudhope Associates, Inc.	tudhope.com
Triple G Healthcare Systems Inc.	tripleg.com	Tug Enr.	tug.net
Triple R Community Futures Development Corporation	triplercfdc.mb.ca	Tundra Software, Inc.	tundra.com
Triple S Business Development Corporation	triplesbdc.mb.ca	Tunes & Treasures Limited	nettunes.com
		Tunix Ltd.	tunix.com
Tristar Global Media Inc.	tristarmedia.com	Turbomarine Limited	turbo.com
Triton Data Systems Limited	triton.nf.ca	Turks Caicos Real Estate Services	turks-caicos.com
Triton Enviormental Consultants Ltd.	triton-env.com	Turnpike BBS	trnpike.com
Triton Environmental Consultants Ltd.	soleil-enviro.com	Turnstone Press Limited	turnstonepress.mb.ca
		Tuttle and Associates	tanda.com
Trivalent Data Systems	trivalent.com	TV Hebdo Inc.	tv-hebdo.com
TRM Technologies Inc.	trm-technologies.on.ca	TV Ontario - On-Line Services	tvo.org
		TV5 OSBL Canada	tv5.ca
TRM Technologies, Inc.	trm.ca	TVA ™, Tele-Metropole Inc.	tva.ca
Trojan Technologies Inc.	trojanuv.com	TVC Enterprises	ham.com
Trom Electric Co. Ltd.	tromelectric.com	TVD Televector Enterprises Inc.	tvd.com
Trondata Systems	trondata.com	TVI Interactive Systems Inc.	tvinet.com
Tronica Computer Centre	tronica.mb.ca	TVL Inc.	tvl.com
Trooper Technologies	trooper.com	TVM Video-Monitor	tvm.com
Trov Data Systems Inc.	trov.com	TVOntario	tvo.on.ca
Trove Investment Corporation	trove.com	TWA Consulting Services Inc.	twa.on.ca
Trow Consulting Engineers Ltd.	trow.com	TWG The Westrheim Group	twg.bc.ca
Truck Loggers Association	trklogger.com	Twilight Exchange BBS	twilight-exchang.com
True Wind Corporation Ltd.	windsport.com	Twinax Connections	twinax.com
Truerisk Inc.	truerisk.com	Twinpak Inc.	twinpak.ca
Truger Technologies Inc.	truger.ca	Twl System	twlsys.com
Trunsduction Limited	maloca.com	Two Guys	twoguys.com
Tryllium Industries Inc.	tryllium.com	Two-T Services	two-t.com
Trytel Internet Inc.	trytel.com	Txbase Systems Inc.	txbase.com
Trytel Internet Inc.	trytel.on.ca	TXN Solution Integrators	txn.ca
TSB International Inc.	tsb-intl.ca	Tyax Heli Skiing Whistler	tyax.com

Name of Organization	Domain	Name of Organization	Domain
Tymeout BBS	tymeout.com	U.P.C. S.E.N.C.	upc.qc.ca
Typomage Inc.	typomage.com	Uniglobe Commercial Travel Services, Ltd.	unicomm.ca
U.S. Technologies Inc.	usxx.com	Uniglobe Instant Travel, Inc.	uniglobeinstant.on.ca
U.S. Virgin Islands Real Estate Services	usvirginislands.com	Uniglobe Intercontinental Travel, Inc.	uintercon.com
Uber Magazine	uber.com	Uniglobe Travel Inc.	uniglobe.ca
Ubitrex Corporation	ubitrex.mb.ca	Unilabs Research	unilabs.org
UFCW	ufcw.org	Unimer Inc.	unimer.com
Ugali International Corp.	ugali.com	Union Logic Software Publishing	unlogic.com
UGC Consulting Ltd.	ugc.ab.ca	Uniongas Ltd.	uniongas.com
Ukmail Network	ukmail.net	Unique Computer Systems	winacad.com
Ukrainian Canadian Consolidators	uccon.com	Unique Data Systems Inc.	unique.ca
Ultimate	wesleyme.com	Unis Lumin Inc.	unislumin.com
Ultraprint Inc.	ultraprint.com	Uniserve On Line	uniserve.com
Ultratech.Net Inc.	ultratech.net	Uniserve Systems	uniserve-systems.com
Ultratech.Net Inc.	ultratech.on.ca	Unisoft System, Inc.	unisoft-system.com
Ultratel Online Information	ultratel.com	Unisoft Wares Incorporated	uwi.bc.ca
Ultravision	ultravision.com	Unisol Inc.	unisol.net
Ulysses Systems	ulysses.bc.ca	Unisys Canada	iconix.com
Uma Engineering	umaeng.com	Unisys Canada	unisys.ca
Uma Group Ltd	umagroup.com	United Breeders, Inc.	ubi.com
Uma Systems, Inc.	umasystems.com	United Consultants	united-consultants.com
Under Foot Inc.	underfoot.com		
Under the Blue Cloud Society	ubc.org	United Farmers of Alberta Cooperative Ltd.	ufa.com
Uneclipse Software Systems Ltd.	uneclipse.com	United Financial Management Ltd.	unitedfml.ca
Unibase Telecom Ltd.	unibase.com		
Unibase Telecom Ltd.	unibase.sk.ca	United Fund Management	unitedfund.com
Unicad Canada Ltd.	unicad.com	United Grain Growers, Ltd.	unitedgrain.ca
Unicate Networks Inc.	unicate.com	United Nations Association in Canada	unac.org
Unicef Ontario Committee	unicef.ca		
Unicom Online	unicom.org	United Safety	unitedyc.com
Unicus Products, Inc.	unicus.com	United Systems Solutions	unitsys.com
Unifax Communiations Inc.	unifax.bc.ca	United Western Communications Ltd.	albertareport.com
Uniforce Informatique Inc.	unifor.com		
Uniforum Canada	uniforum.ca	Unitel Communications Inc	unitel.com
Uniforum Quebec	uniforum.qc.ca	Unitron Industries Ltd.	unitron.com
Unigiciel Inc.	unigiciel.com	Unity Computer Systems Inc.	bbear.com
Uniglobe Advance Travel	uniglobe-advance.com	Universal Computer Systems Ltd	ucs.on.ca

Name of Organization	Domain	Name of Organization	Domain
Universal Gateway Corporation	gateway.ca	University of Toronto	toronto.edu
Universal Gateway Corporation	ugc.net	University of Toronto	utoronto.ca
Universal Gateway Corporation	universal.net	University of Toronto Computing Services	ca.net
Universal Joint BBS, The	u-joint.kenora.on.ca	University of Toronto, Office of Student Affairs	utcampuslife.org
Universal Power Corporation	upc.ab.ca	University of Victoria	uvic.ca
Universal Systems Ltd. (USL)	universal.ca	University of Waterloo	uwaterloo.ca
Universal Teleresponse Corporation	utr.com	University of Western Ontario	uwo.ca
Universite de Moncton	umoncton.ca	University of Windsor	uwindsor.ca
Universite de Montreal	umontreal.ca	University of Winnipeg	uwinnipeg.ca
Universite de Sherbrooke	usherb.ca	Univirtuel	univirtuel.com
Universite du Quebec (C.S.C.Q.)	uquebec.ca	UNIXtech Integration Inc.	unixtech.com
Universite du Quebec a Montreal	uqam.ca	Unopsys Inc.	unopsys.com
Universite Laval	ulaval.ca	Uplink Communications	uplink.on.ca
Universite St. Anne	ustanne.ns.ca	Upper Canada College	ucc.on.ca
University College of Cape Breton	uccb.ns.ca	Upstairs	upstairs.com
University College of the Fraser Valley	ucfv.bc.ca	Uptowne BBS	uptowne.com
University Financial Services Inc.	nod.com	Urban Alliance on Race Relations	uarr.org
University Hospital	uh.london.on.ca	Urban Associates	urbanassoc.com
University of Alberta	ualberta.ca	Urban Development Institution	udi.org
University of British Columbia	ubc.ca	Urbandale Corp.	urbandale.com
University of Calgary	ucalgary.ca	Usana International	usana-intl.com
University of Guelph	uoguelph.ca	User First, Inc.	user-first.com
University of King's College	ukings.ns.ca	Usr/Group Edmonton	ugedm.ab.ca
University of Lethbridge	uleth.ca	Utech Electronics	utech.com
University of Manitoba	umanitoba.ca	Utex Scientific Instruments Inc.	utex.com
University of New Brunswick	unb.ca	Utlas International, Canada	utlas.ca
University of New Brunswick, Saint John Campus	unbsj.ca	Utopia Parkway Studios	utopia-pkwy.com
University of Northern British Columbia	unbc.edu	UUMH - UNIX Users of Medicine Hat	uumh.ab.ca
University of Ottawa	uofo.edu	UUNET Canada Inc.	mail.net
University of Ottawa	uottawa.ca	UUNET Canada Inc.	uunet.ca
University of Prince Edward Island	upei.ca	UUNET Canada Inc.	www.net
University of Regina	uregina.ca	UUNorth Incorporated	north.net
University of Saskatchewan	usask.ca	UUNorth Incorporated	uunorth.on.ca
		Uuserve&	uuserve.on.ca
		V Tape	vtape.org
		V-Com Computer Warehouse	vcom.ca

Name of Organization	Domain	Name of Organization	Domain
V.I.T. Voyages Intair Transit Inc.	travelcom.com	Vancouver Opera Association	vanopera.bc.ca
V.S. Cheng & Associates Inc.	vscheng.com	Vancouver Public Library	vpl.vancouver.bc.ca
V3 Corporation	vcubed.com	Vancouver Realty	vanrealty.com
Vacations International	vitravel.com	Vancouver Regional Freenet Association	freenet.vancouver.bc.ca
Valhalla Pure Outfitters	valhalla-pure.com		
Valiquet Lamothe Inc.	vli.ca	Vancouver Stock Exchange	vse.ca
Valley First Credit Union	valleyfirst.com	Vancouver Stock Exchange	vse.com
Value Added Computer Service Inc.	vacs.com	Vancouver Webpages	vancouver-webpages.com
Vamp Records	vamp.com	Vandenberg Systems Incorporated	vansys.com
Van Am Electronics	vanam.com		
Van Den Heede Computing	vdhcomp.on.ca	Vandergrif Holdings, Ltd. O/A Yhmtravel	yhmtravel.on.ca
Van Deren Consulting	godfra.com		
Van Dyck Properties	vandyck-property.com	Vansco Electronics Ltd.	vansco.mb.ca
		Vantage Digital Media Inc.	vantage.net
Van Kam Freightways Ltd.	trucking.com	Vantage Securities Inc.	vantage.ca
Van Waters & Rogers Inc.	vwr-ltd.com	Vari-Theatre Systems	vari-theatre.com
Van-Dazz	vandaaz.com	Varnet Information Systems Inc.	varnet.com
Vancouver City Savings Credit Union	vancity.com		
		Vasurelm Corporation	vasurelm.com
Vancouver Community College	vcc.bc.ca	Vaw Systems Ltd.	vawsystems.mb.ca
Vancouver Domain Park	vdp.org	Vaxxine Computer Systems Inc.	vaxxine.com
Vancouver Film School, Ltd.	vfs.com	VCDL Real Estate Services	vcdl.com
Vancouver Fire Department	firefit.com	VCI	vciglobal.com
Vancouver Free Press	straight.com	Vector Insurance Brokers Limited	vector.ca
Vancouver International Authority	yvr.org		
Vancouver International Film Festival	viff.org	Vela Information Management Consultants	vela.ca
		Velo Sportable Cycle	sportable.com
Vancouver Internet Pages Limited	vip.ca	Velo-Quebec Inc	velo.qc.ca
		Vendor Update Services	update.com
Vancouver Island Advanced Technology Center Inc.	viatec.bc.ca	Veneris	veneris.com
Vancouver Island Real Estate Board Ltd.	vireb.bc.ca	Vengrowth Capital Management Inc.	vengrowth.com
Vancouver Island Regional Library	virl.bc.ca	Ventures West Management Inc.	ventureswest.com
Vancouver Language College	vlc-canada.com	Veradon Information Systems	veradon.com
Vancouver Magazine	vanmag.com	Verg Inc.	verg.mb.ca
Vancouver Next Users Society	vnus.bc.ca	Veritas Seismic Ltd	vsl.com
		Vernon Rentals And Leasing	vernonrentals.ca
Vancouver Next Users Society	vnus.org	Versa Management Systems, Ltd.	versasys.com

Name of Organization	Domain	Name of Organization	Domain
Versatile Computer Products Ltd.	versatilecomputers. com	Viktor T. Toth Consulting	vttoth.com
Versus Informatique Inc.	versus.com	Ville de Brossard	ville.brossard.qc.ca
Versus Technologies	capitalworks.com	Ville de Gatineau	ville.gatineau.qc.ca
Versus Technologies Inc.	tradeit.com	Ville de Laval	ville.laval.qc.ca
Vertex Communications	worldweb.com	Ville de Montreal	ville.montreal.qc.ca
Vertical Addiction	vert.com	Ville de Sherbrooke	ville.sherbrooke.qc. ca
Vertigo Technology Inc.	vertigo.bc.ca	Vimi Laser Inc.	vimilaser.com
VFS Multimedia.	multimedia.edu	Vineland Estates Winery	vineland.com
VFX Video Inc	vfx.com	Vintage Consultants	vintage-net.com
VH Computer Systems	vhcs.com	Vinyls Cafe	vinyls.com
Via Rail Canada Inc.	via.ca	Viper Software Inc.	the-wave.com
Via Rail Canada Inc.	viarail.ca	Vircom Inc.	vircom.com
Vic's Hockey Schools	hockey-schools.com	Virgin Snow Productions	vsp.org
Viceroy Homes	viceroy.com	Viridae Clinical Sciences Inc.	viridae.com
Vickers & Benson Advertising	tpno.com	Virtek Vision Corporation	virtek.ca
Vicom Multimedia, Inc.	vicom.ca	Virtua Technologies Inc.	virtua.qc.ca
Victor Razanauskas Consulting	vpr.org	Virtual Adventures Camps Canada	internaut.org
Victoria Conference Centre	vcc.victoria.bc.ca	Virtual City Online	vconline.com
Victoria Digital	vonline.com	Virtual Connections Inc	vancouver-bc-ca. com
Victoria Digital Information Service	victoriadigital.bc.ca	Virtual Design Inc.	virtual.ca
Victoria Free-Net Association	freenet.victoria.bc.ca	Virtual Information Sevices	viramontes.com
Victoria General Hospital	victoriahosp. winnipeg.mb.ca	Virtual Marketing Inc.	virtualinx.com
		Virtual Marketing Inc.	virtualynx.com
Victoria Hospital	vichosp.london.on.ca	Virtual Media Inc.	virtualmedia.com
Victoria Online — Victoria Digital Information Service	victoriaonline.bc.ca	Virtual Noise	virtualnoise.com
		Virtual Prototypes Inc	virtualprototypes.ca
Victoria Order of Nurses	von.ca	Virtual Universe Corporation	vu.com
Victoria Real Estate Board Ltd.	vreb.bc.ca	Virtual Vancouver	vvan.com
Victoria Tours Ltd.	victoriatours.com	Virtual Voice	virtualvoice.com
Victoria Virtual Ventures	vvv.com	Virtuali	virtuali.com
Video Pool, Inc.	videopool.mb.ca	Virtueli	virtueli.com
Videoflicks Canada, Ltd.	videoflicks.com	Virtueli Inc.	virtueli.ca
Videotron Communications Ltd.	videotron.ab.ca	Viscount Comm. & Con. Systems	viscount.com
Videoway	videoway.com	Visible Decisions Inc.	vdi.com
Vigie Informatique 2000 Inc.	vigie.qc.ca	Visible Decisions Inc.	vizbiz.com
Vigilant Internet Services Ltd.	vigilant.bc.ca	Visible Genetics Inc.	visgen.com
Viglob Informatique Inc.	viglob.ca		

Name of Organization	Domain	Name of Organization	Domain
Visible Genetics, Inc.	genesoft.com	VMI Communications & Learning	vmicls.com
Visimage Corporation	visimage.ca	Voice Box Broadcasting	voicebox.com
Visinet ™, Invitech Corporation	visinet.ca	Voice Network Technologies, Inc.	voice.net
Vision Commerciale	visionmtl.com	Volante Distribution Ltd	volante.com
Vision Graphics	vgraphics.com	Volksware, Inc.	volksware.com
Vision TV - Canada's Faith Network	visiontv.ca	Volvic Inc.	volvic.ca
Visionary Solutions	ports-west.com	Volvo Trucks Of Calgary	volvotrx.com
Visionquest Web Services & Internet Consulting	vquest.com	Vortek Industries	vortek.com
Visiontech	visiontech.com	Voyages Aquanautes Inc	aquanautes.com
Vistar Telecommunications Inc.	vistar.ca	Voyageur Colonial Ltd.	voyageur.com
Vistel Communications Inc.	vistel.com	Voyageur.Net Inc.	voyageur.ca
Visuaide Inc.	visuaide.qc.ca	VPM Publishing Inc.	vpm.on.ca
Visual Applications Software, Inc.	fieldpro.com	VR Systems Inc	vrsystems.com
Visual Communications Corporation	viscom.bc.ca	VRX Commercial Services, Inc.	vrx.com
Visual Computing Group Inc.	visual.ca	VRX Cyberservices, Inc.	cyberservices.com
Visual Edge Software Ltd.	vedge.com	VRX Industries	null.net
Visual Net	storefront.net	VRX Network Services	cybercafe.com
Visual Net	visual.net	VRX Network Services Inc.	cybermall.net
Visual Systems Development Group	visual.com	VRX Network Services Inc.	vrx.net
Visual Wave Technologies Inc.	vwt.com	VRX Voicemail Services, Inc.	voicemail.com
Visualflex	visualflex.net	VRX Voicemail Services, Inc.	voicemail.net
Vita Health Co. (1985) Ltd.	vitahealth.ca	VSE Smallcap Stock Review	vse-stox.com
Vital Technologies Corporation	vitaltech.on.ca	Vsoft	vsoft.net
Vitaltech	vitaltech.com	Vtech Computer Systems Inc.	vtech.ca
Vitec Consultancy Service	vitec.on.ca	Vytalnet Inc.	vytalnet.com
Viteq, Vitrine Telematique du Quebec Inc.	viteq.qc.ca	W G Enterprises	watersedge.com
Vive Synergies Inc.	vive.ca	W. J. Cooke & Associates Ltd.	uncle.com
Vivid Graphics Ltd.	vividgraphics.com	W.B. Hamilton Shoes Ltd.	walkwel.com
VL Virtual Logistics Inc/VL Logistiques Virtuelle Inc.	virtlogic.ca	W3 Internet Services Ltd	eucanect.com
Vladimir Gretzky Hardware Store	gretzky.com	Wade Rowland Enterprises Inc.	canlit.com
VLSI Circuits Inc.	vlsi-pcb.com	Walkwell Shoes	walkwell.com
Vmark Software Canada	vmarkcan.com	Walmar (Eastern Canada) Limited	walmar.com
		Walsh Automation Inc.	walshaut.ca
		Walter Van Lieshout	opportunities.com
		Wanda Design	wanda.com
		Wandel & Goltermann, Inc.	wgcanada.com

Name of Organization	Domain	Name of Organization	Domain
Wang Canada Limited	wang.ca	Ways Magazine	waysmag.com
Ward Associates	ward-associates.com	Wealth-Wise Group Inc.	wealth-wise.com
Ward Consulting, Inc.	ward.com	Wearcheck Canada, Inc.	wearcheck.com
Wardop Engineering	wardrop.com	Weathertec Services Inc.	wxtec.mb.ca
Wardrop Engineering Inc.	wardrop.mb.ca	Weaver, Tanner & Miller	weaver.com
Warlight Industries Inc.	warlight.com	Weaver, Tanner & Miller - Kw	wtmkw.com
Warner Communications	radioshop.com	Weaver, Tanner & Miller - Ott	wtmott.com
Warner Music Canada Ltd.	warner-music.ca	Weaver, Tanner & Miller - Tor	wtmtor.com
Warringah Research	conveyor.com	Web Entertainment	web-e.com
Warrington Management Group, Inc.	wmgi.com	Web Links Consulting	global-commerce.com
Warwick Hamilton and Associates	warwickhamilton.com	Web Pool Inc	webpool.com
		Web Weaver Internet Services	webwis.com
Wascana Energy Inc. (Formerly Saskoil)	wei.sk.ca	Web-Server Communications	web-server.com
Wasserman & Partners	wasserman-partners.com	Webcon World Wide Web Consultants	webcon.net
Waste Bank Incorporated	fiberglass.com	Webgate Canada Communication Inc.	webgate.ca
Watcom	watcom.com	Webgate Internet Services Inc.	webgate.on.ca
Watcom International Corp.	watcom.on.ca	Webhead Inc.	webhead.ca
Water & Earth Science Associates, Ltd.	wesakw.com	Webhead Inc.	webhead.com
		Webmasters, Inc.	webmasters.com
Waterfront Regeneration Trust	wrtrust.com	Websmith Group Inc., The	websmith.ca
Waterloo Engineering Software	wes.on.ca	Webtroplolis	webtropolis.com
Waterloo Maple Software Inc.	maplesoft.on.ca	Webware International, Inc.	webware.net
Waterloo Maple Software Inc.	prescience.com	Webweavers	artworld.com
Waterloo Regional Domain Park	waterloo-rdp.on.ca	Webwerx Ltd.	zinerak.com
		Webwizardry Corp.	webwizardry.com
Waterous Securities Inc.	waterous.com	Webworks Worldwide Inc.	appleman.com
Waterstone Publishing	waterstone.com	Webworks Worldwide Inc.	sphere3.com
Watson Industrial Software	watson.com	Wedding Bells Magazine	weddingbells.com
Wave New Media Inc.	wave.com	Wednesday Web Press	wednesday.com
Waveform Digital Productions, Inc.	waveformdpi.com	Weenis Corp.	weenis.com
Wavelan Integration Services Inc.	wavelan.com	Weider Sports Equipment Co. Ltd.	weider.ca
Wax Tablet	waxtablet.com	Weidmuller Ltd.	weidmuller.ca
Waxworks Recording Studio, Inc.	waxworks.com	Weldwood of Canada Ltd.	canwel.com
		Weldwood of Canada Ltd.	cariboopulp.com
Way Insurance Services Inc., The	theway.ca	Weldwood of Canada Ltd.	weldwood.com

Name of Organization	Domain	Name of Organization	Domain
Wellesley Hospital Research Institute	whri.on.ca	WesTel Telecommunications, Ltd.	westel.com
Wellington Medical Systems Ltd.	wellmed.bc.ca	Westend Systems Corporation	westend.ca
Wellness Online	wellness.org	Western Business Machines Ltd	wbm.ca
Wescam Inc.	wescam.com	Western Computer Link Ltd.	link.ca
Weslink Datalink Corporation	weslink.ca	Western Electromed Holdings Ltd.	electromed.com
West Africa Technologies	westafrica.com	Western Explosives Ltd.	explosives.ca
West Carleton Amateur Radio Club	wcarc.on.ca	Western Glove Works	westernglove.mb.ca
West Coast Creations	dsoe.com	Western Inventory Services	wis.org
West Coast Creations	dsonline.com	Western Ontario Breeders, Inc.	wobi.com
West Coast Editorial Associates	wcea.org	Western Producer Publications	producer.ca
West Coast English Language Center	welc.com	Western Producer Publications	producer.com
West Coast Internet Express Corp.	express.ca	Western Profiles Limited	westprofiles.mb.ca
West Coast Title Search	mcts.com	Western Scale Co. Ltd.	wescale.com
West Coast Title Search	titlesearch.com	Western Shores	westernshores.com
West Coast Title Search	wcts.com	Western Theatre Ballet	westerntheatre.org
West Coast Write Word	ethics.com	Western Turbo and Fuel Injection Ltd.	westernturbo.mb.ca
West Edmonton Mall	westedmall.com	Western Works	westernworks.mb.ca
West Fraser	westfraser.com	Westgate Chev-Olds	westgatechev.com
West Fraser Timber Company Ltd.	westfrasertimber.ca	Westinghouse Canada, Inc.	wecan.com
West Vancouver Florists Ltd.	1flowers.com	Westlink Communications Ltd.	westlink.net
West-Net Consulting Services Ltd.	west-net.bc.ca	Westlink Systems Corp.	westlinksystems.com
Westbay Instruments Inc	westbay.com	Westminster International Computers Inc.	westminstr.com
Westcad Service Ltd	westcad.com	Westminster Savings Credit Union	wscu.com
Westcoast Energy Inc.	wei.ca	Weston Information Network	gwlwin.com
Westcoast Energy Ltd.	enersmart.com	Weston Woods Canada Ltd.	westonwoods.ca
Westcoast Interchange Enterprises Inc.	wie.com	Westonia Computer Systems of Canada	westonia.com
Westcoast Publishing Ltd.	west-coast.com	Westport Research, Inc.	westport.com
Westcom International Communications	westcom.com	Westroc Industries, Ltd.	westroc.com
Westcom International Communications	wic.ca	Westside Ski Inc.	westski.com
		Westsun International Inc.	westsun.ca
Westeel, A Div of Jannock Steel Fabricating Company	westeel.ca	Westviking College of Applied Arts, Technology and Continuing Education	westvikingc.nf.ca
		Wetlands for the Americas	wetlands.org

Name of Organization	Domain	Name of Organization	Domain
Wexl Inc.	wexl.com	Willowglen Systems Division of Datek Industries Inc.	willowglen.ab.ca
WGS Inc.	wgs.ca	Wils Ltd.	wils.org
What-A-Site Networks	whatasite.com	Wilson & Associates	implant.com
Where Magazines International	wheremags.com	Wilson King & Company	wilsonking.bc.ca
Wheretogo Database & Guide	wheretogo.com	Wilson's Fuel Company Ltd.	wilsons.ca
Whine Technologies	whine.com	Wimsey Associates	wimsey.bc.ca
Whistler Cable Ltd.	wctl.com	Wimsey Information Services Inc.	wimsey.ca
Whistler Networks	whistler.com	Wimsey Information Services Inc.	wimsey.com
Whistler Networks	whistler.net	Wimsey Information Services Inc.	wis.net
Whistler Networks	whistlernet.bc.ca		
Whitby Mental Health Centre	prenderp.com	Win-Com	wincom.net
White Oaks Tennis World Inc.	whiteoaks.on.ca	Win95 Fan Club	microserf.com
White Spot Ltd.	whitespotltd.ca	Winchester District Memorial Hospital	wdmh.on.ca
Whitehorse Free Internet Project	whfip.net	Windermere Real Estate	windermere-pac.com
Whitman Benn Group Inc.	whitmanbenn.ns.ca	Windhorse Productions	windhorse.com
Wholesale Heating Supplies	whs.com	Window Art	windowart.com
Whopnet Computers and Communications	whopnet.ab.ca	Windows Information Network	wininfonet.mb.ca
Whycocomagh Consolidated School	whycocomagh.ns.ca	Windsock Communications	windsock.org
Wi-Lan Inc.	wi-lan.com	Windsor Regional Cancer Center	wrcc.on.ca
Widecom Inc.	widecom.com	Windstar Corporation	windstar.com
Widman Consulting Ltd.	widman.com	Windswept Ltd	windswept.com
Wightman Communications Limited	wcl.on.ca	Winexpert Inc.	winexpert.com
Wigmar Construction Ltd.	wigmar.bc.ca	Wing Wing Co. Ltd.	wing-wing.com
Wild Strawberries	strawberries.com	Wingham Online	wingham.com
Wildlife Habitat Canada	whc.org	Winning Spirit Stores	winningspirit.com
Wilfrid Laurier University	wlu.ca	Winnipeg Art Gallery	wag.mb.ca
Wilkor Computing Services	wilkor.ab.ca	Winnipeg Convention Centre	wpgconvctr.mb.ca
William E Coutts Co Ltd O/A Hallmark Cards Canada	hallmark.ca	Winnipeg Free Press	freepress.mb.ca
William F. White Limited	whites.com	Winnipeg International Airport	ywg.com
William M. Mercer Limited	mercer.ca	Winnipeg PC User Group	wpcusrgrp.org
William R. Waters, Ltd.	wrw.com	Winnipeg PC User Group, Inc.	wpcusrgrp.mb.ca
William Shackleton	diversity.org	Winnipeg School Division No. 1, The	wsd1.winnipeg.mb.ca
William Switzer Associates Ltd.	finefurniture.com		
Willow Information Systems Inc.	willow.on.ca	Winnipeg Sun	winsun.com

Name of Organization	Domain	Name of Organization	Domain
Winsome Computer Consulting	winsome.com	Workers' Compensation Board of the NWT	wcb.nt.ca
Winvest BBS	winvest.com	Working Opportunities Fund	wofund.com
Wiresong Publishing	wiresong.com	Working Ventures Canadian Fund, Inc.	workingventures.ca
Wise Communications	wisepr.com		
Wittmad	wittmad.com	Worknet	worknet.net
Wiz Zone Computers For Kids Inc.	wizzone.com	Workplace Health & Safety Agency	whsa.on.ca
Wiz Zone Computers For Kids Incorporated	wizzone.vancouver.bc.ca	Workplace Strategies Inc.	wplstrat.bc.ca
Wizard Solutions	intoronto.com	Worksmart Computer Training Inc.	worksmart.com
WJK Desktop Design	wjk.on.ca	World Access BBS	wa-bbs.com
Wm. De Jong Enterprises Inc.	dejong.com	World Access Net Inc.	canadas.net
Wmb Publishing Inc.	project-manager.com	World Chat	wchat.on.ca
Woldring and Company Ltd	woldring.com	World Connect	worldconnect.com
Wolf Creek Regional Division No. 32	wolfcreek.ab.ca	World Hospitality Online	who.net
Wolf Den BBS	wolfden.com	World of Computer Supplies	wocs.com
Wolf Manufacturing Inc.	wolf-mfg.on.ca	World Online	worldonline.com
Wollongong Group Canada, Inc., The	twg.on.ca	World Online Inc.	worldonline.ca
		World Online Organization	worldonline.org
Woloshyn Mattison	wolmat.sk.ca	World Radio Transcripts	wrt.com
Wolverton Securities Ltd	wolverton.com	World Tel	canimmigration.com
Women's Television Network	wtn.ca	World Tel	canolaoil.com
Wonder Computers Inc.	wonder.ca	World Tel	chamberofcommerce.com
Wood Gundy Analytic Trading Group	wgatg.com	World Tel	chinafranchise.com
Wood Lake Books	woodlake.com	World Tel	citic.com
Wood's Research	woodresearch.com	World Tel	commoditiescom.com
Wor-Ker Window Technology Inc.	wor-ker.ca	World Tel	commoditiesworld.com
Wordcraft Systems Corporation	wcraft.bc.ca	World Tel	constructioncom.com
		World Tel	consultantsworld.com
Worddancer Systems Inc.	worddancer.ca		
Wordlink Internet Services Inc.	wordlink.net	World Tel	corpfinance.com
Wordn Systems	wordn.com	World Tel	edibleoils.com
Wordplay Bookstore	wordplay.com	World Tel	electronicgoods.com
Wordsurf Inc.	wordsurf.com	World Tel	engineeringcom.com
Wordwrap Associates Inc.	wordwrap.com	World Tel	fishlips.com
Workers Compensation Board of Manitoba	workerscomp.mb.ca	World Tel	forrent.com
		World Tel	goldcom.com
Workers' Compensation Board of British Columbia	wcb.bc.ca	World Tel	goldseal.com

Name of Organization	Domain	Name of Organization	Domain
World Tel	imasters.com	World Tel	worldtel.com
World Tel	importexport.com	World Tel	worldtelfax.com
World Tel	indonesiacom.com	World Tel	yellowebpages.com
World Tel	intercomm-95.com	World Tel Clients	environmentlaw.com
World Tel	japancom.com	World Tel Clients	internationalaw.com
World Tel	jobmarket.com	World Tel Clients	taxationlaw.com
World Tel	lawcenter.com	World Vision Canada	world-vision.org
World Tel	londondrugs.com	World Vision Canada	worldvision.ca
World Tel	lumbercom.com	World Web Technologies Inc.	discoveralberta.com
World Tel	matrimonialworld.com	World Web Technologies Inc.	discovercalgary.com
World Tel	merchantbank.com	World Web Technologies Inc.	discoveredmonton.com
World Tel	nannyhelp.com	World Web Technologies Inc.	discoveryplace.com
World Tel	netidea.com	World Web Technologies Inc.	dob.com
World Tel	oil-gas.com	World Web Technologies Inc.	interalia.com
World Tel	okanagan-online.com	World Web Technologies Inc.	mck.com
World Tel	pacrim-law.com	World Wide Better Business Bureau Inc.	wwbbb.com
World Tel	personnelworld.com	World Wide Language Institute	wwli.com
World Tel	phillipinescom.com	World Wide Publishers	publishers.net
World Tel	pilipinas.com	World's Biggest Bookstore	wbb.com
World Tel	raptors.com	Worldchat Internet Services.	worldchat.com
World Tel	riceworld.com	Worldgate	worldgate.edmonton.ab.ca
World Tel	schools-english.com	Worldgate Inc.	worldgate.net
World Tel	schools-private.com	Worldlink Internet Services Inc.	worldlink.ca
World Tel	se-asiacom.com	Worldlinx	dauphin.com
World Tel	skihills.com	Worldlinx	navigo.com
World Tel	smokedsalmon.com	Worldlinx Telecommunications Inc.	autolinx.com
World Tel	soyaworld.com	Worldlinx Telecommunications, Inc.	worldlinx.com
World Tel	stockbroker.com	Worldnet Online Corp.	worldnet.ca
World Tel	stratexport.com	Worldwide Data Communications Inc.	onlinesys.com
World Tel	tradeglobal.com	Worldwide Data Communications Inc.	wwdc.com
World Tel	tradeinternational.com	Worldwide Health Web Inc.	healthweb.ca
World Tel	translations.com	Wrapmation Inc	wrapmation.com
World Tel	webcash.com		
World Tel	worldconventions.com		
World Tel	worldpersonnel.com		
World Tel	worldtel-nelson.com		

Name of Organization	Domain	Name of Organization	Domain
Wright Mogg and Associates, Ltd.	wright-mogg.com	Xyberlynx	xyberlynx.net
Writedoc	writedoc.com	Xylaur Enterprises Limited	xylaur.nb.ca
WSI Worldwide Systems Integration Inc.	wsi.ca	Xypex Chemical Corporation	xypex.com
Wuerz Publishing Ltd.	wuerzpubl.mb.ca	XYZ Publishing, Ltd.	xyzpress.com
Wyeth-Ayerst Canada Inc.	waci.com	Yaletown Club	yaletown.com
Wysiwyi Technologies, Inc.	wysiwyi.com	Yamatech Connectivity Solutions	ycs.net
X*Cite Technology	xcite.com	Yankee Ingenuity Computing	yank.kitchener.on.ca
X-Cal Resources Ltd.	x-cal.com	Yarmouth Consolidated Memorial High School	ycmhs.yarmouth.ns.ca
X2 Communication	x2com.com	Yellow Pages ™, Teledirect (Publications) Inc.	yellowpages.ca
Xabyte Technologies Corporation	xabyte.ca	Yellowhead Computer Services Inc.	ycs.ab.ca
Xana Network Systems Ltd.	xana.bc.ca	Yes Canada - B.C.	yescanadabc.org
Xavante Systems	xavante.com	Yes Canada-BC	yes-canada.org
Xbase Technologes Corp.	xbase.com	Yes Enterprise Systems	yes.net
XBR Communications Inc.	xbrcom.qc.ca	Yetmans Ltd.	yetmans.mb.ca
Xcan Grain Pool Ltd	xcan.com	Yevshan Communications Inc.	yevshan.com
Xceedx Technologies	xceedx.com	Yield Consulting	yield.com
XCG Environmental Services Inc.	xcg.com	YMCA Canada	ymca.ca
Xenitec Consulting Services	xenitec.on.ca	Yolles Partnership Inc.	yolles.com
Xenon Electronic Mail Network	xemail.net	York Region Board Of Education	yrbe.on.ca
Xenon Laboratories	xe.net	York Regional Network	york.net
Xenon Laboratories Incorporated	xe.com	York Regional Police	police.york.on.ca
Xentel	xentel.com	York School, The	tys.on.ca
Xerox Canada Ltd.	xerox.ca	York University	yorku.ca
Xersys Technologies	xersys.com	Yorkland Investments Corp.	yorkland.com
Xfactor Financial Resources Inc.	xfactor.com	Yorkton Securities Inc.	yorkton.com
XI	xi.org	Yorkville Sound	yorkville.com
Xinex Labs	xinex.com	Yorkville Travel Ltd.	traveldeals.com
Xinu Enterprises Inc.	xinu.com	You're A Nation Inc.	pee.com
Xiris, Inc.	xiris.com	Young Monkey Studios	youngmonkey.ca
XON Digital Communications Ltd.	xondigital.ns.ca	Your Investment Shoppers Incorporated	yis.ca
XON/XOFF	xonxoff.com	YouTV Inc.	youtv.ca
Xpress Softnet Technology Inc.	xpress.ab.ca	YTV	ytv.com
XSM Systems Inc.	xsm.com	YTV Canada Inc.	ytv.ca
Xyberlinx	xyberlinx.net	Yu, Eva	estca.com
		Yukon Housing Corporation	housing.yk.ca

Name of Organization	Domain	Name of Organization	Domain
Yukon Systems	yukonsys.com	Zentra Computer Technologies Inc.	zentra.com
YukonNet Operating Society	yknet.yk.ca	Zentronics	zentronics.ca
Yukyuks Comedy Club	yukyuks.com	Zephyr Enterprises	zephyr-ent.com
Yyz	yyz.org	Zeppelin Design	zeppelin.com
Yzrnur Consulting	yzrnur.com	Zeus Enterprises Inc.	mailboxesetc-42.com
Z.I. Probes Incorporated	ziprobes.com	Zhang Information Services	zhang.com
Z95.3FM	z95.com	Zhang Yingchun Information Services	zy.com
Zadall Systems Group, Inc.	zadall.com		
Zebra Group	zebragroup.com	Ziebmef Public Access UNIX	mef.org
ZED Data Systems	zed.ca	Ziftech Computer Systems Inc.	ziftech.on.ca
Zeifman Management Corporation	zeifman.ca	Zivilcourage Media	zivilcourage.com
Zelkova International (Canada) Inc.	zelkova.ca	Zone Internet Inc.	zone.ca
		Zooid	zooid.org
Zelkova International (Canada) Inc.	zelkova.com	Zoomit Corporation	zoomit.com
		Zoonet Inc.	zoo.net
Zellers Inc.	zellers.com	Zoonet Inc.	zoonet.qc.ca
Zeneca Bio Products	zenecanatc.com	Zounds	zounds.com
Zeneca Seeds (Canada)	zenecaseed.ca	Zuniq Corporation	zuniq.com
Zener Online Inc.	zener.com	Zurich Canadian Holdings Limited	zurichcan.ca
Zenox Communications Corp.	marketingthemedium.com		
Zenox Communications Corporation	zenox.com		

Canadian Government Subdomains

As discussed in Chapter 5, there is now a Canadian Government Domain Registrar (gc.ca Domain Registrar) that is responsible for allocating domain names to federal government departments and agencies in Canada. This appendix presents a list of Canadian government subdomains and the names of the government bodies to which they were issued. A current list of government subdomains will be available on the World Wide Web at **http://www.gc.ca**.

Subdomain	Government Body	Subdomain	Government Body
crtc.gc.ca	Canadian Radio-television and Telecommunications Commission	epc.gc.ca	Emergency Preparedness Canada
hrdc-drhc.gc.ca	Human Resources Development Canada	nspd.gc.ca	Network Planning and Support Division
prfa.gc.ca	Prairie Farm Rehabilitation Administration	parl.gc.ca	Parliament of Canada
gtis.gc.ca	Government Telecommunication and Informatics Services	fin.gc.ca	Finance Canada
parksnet.gc.ca	Parks Canada (Canadian Heritage)	tbs-cts.gc.ca	Treasury Board Secretariat
inalib.gc.ca	Indian and Northern Affairs Library	psc-cfp.gc.ca	Public Service Commission
hrdbli.gc.ca	Human Resources Development Library	ci.gc.ca	Citizenship and Immigration Canada
acdi-cida.gc.ca	Canadian International Development Agency	cmhc-schl.gc.ca	Canadian Mortgage & Housing Corporation
tc.gc.ca	Transport Canada	pch.gc.ca	Canadian Heritage
nrcan.gc.ca	Natural Resources Canada	x400.gc.ca	X.400 Gateway Service

pco.gc.ca	Privy Council Office of Canada	hc-sc.gc.ca	Health Canada
csc-scc.gc.ca	Correctional Services Canada	swc-cfc.gc.ca	Status of Women Canada
justice.gc.ca	Department of Justice, Canada	sgc.gc.ca	Solicitor General Secretariat Canada
ic.gc.ca	Industry Canada	ceaa.gc.ca	Canadian Environmental Assessment Agency
polarcom.gc.ca	Canadian Polar Commission	space.gc.ca	Canadian Space Agency
cci-icc.gc.ca	Canadian Conservation Institute	saskvision.gc.ca	Saskatchewan Region – Human Resources
chin.gc.ca	Canadian Heritage Information Network	bfdrq-fordq.gc.ca	Federal Office of Regional Development (Québec)
cac.gc.ca	Consulting Audit Canada	rcmp-grc.gc.ca	Royal Canadian Mounted Police
pwgsc.gc.ca	Public Works and Government Services Canada	refcda.gc.ca	Reference Canada
dfait-maeci.gc.ca	Department of Foreign Affairs & International Trade	osfi-bsif.gc.ca	Office of the Superintendent of Financial Institutions Canada
oag-bvg.gc.ca	Office of the Auditor General of Canada	citt.gc.ca	Canadian International Trade Tribunal
irb-cisr.gc.ca	Immigration and Refugee Board	www.gc.ca	Gift Information Finder Technology

Places to Start Surfing on the World Wide Web

This Appendix contains a list of places to start surfing the Net if you are not sure where to begin or if you are looking for something in particular. We have organized our list into three sections. The first section contains a list of directories on the World Wide Web that can you browse through, and sometimes search. The second section contains a list of search engines on the Web. Search engines are searchable databases of Internet resources. The third section contains a few additional suggestions. Have fun!

Directories of World Wide Web Sites

Canada-Specific Directories

Central Index of Canadian World Wide Web Sites

World Wide Web: http://www.csr.ists.ca/w3can/Welcome.html

This index contains the Internet's most comprehensive directory of Canadian World Wide Web sites. Entries can be viewed by scope or geographical location. Categories include associations, businesses, colleges, universities, government, and schools.

Manitoba Internet Resources Page

World Wide Web: http://www.kwanza.com/alice manitoba.html

A directory of Internet resources in Manitoba. Categories include universities and colleges, K-12 education, community networks, computer user groups, sports, travel and tourism, and government and politics. The directory is maintained by Ryan Schultz of Manitoba.

Alberta World Wide Web Server Index

World Wide Web: http://www.tcel.com/albertawww/index.html

This site provides a list of Internet resources in Alberta.

Links to Newfoundland and Labrador

World Wide Web: http://mirror.det.mun.ca/~triche/NFlinks.html

Tina Riche of Newfoundland has assembled this great collection of World Wide Web sites in Newfoundland and Labrador.

British Columbia Web Servers

World Wide Web: http://www.freenet.vancouver.bc.ca/bc-pages/

A set of pointers to Web sites in British Columbia, maintained by the Vancouver Regional FreeNet Association. Categories include non-profit organizations, educational institutions, and government agencies.

British Columbian Home Pages

World Wide Web: http://www.freenet.victoria.bc.ca/bcw3list.html

A large collection of Web sites in British Columbia, maintained by the Victoria Free-Net.

NETLiNkS! Canadian Links Page

World Wide Web: http://www.interlog.com/~csteele/canada.html

Categories include education, media, music, natural resources, transportation, sports, and tourism.

Canadiana — The Canadian Resource Page

World Wide Web: http://www.cs.cmu.edu/afs/cs.cmu.edu/user/clamen/misc/Canadiana

A great compilation of Canadian Internet resources from Stuart Clamen at Carnegie Mellon University. Categories include news and information, travel and tourism, government services and information, politics and history, science and education, technology and commerce, and culture and entertainment.

Open Government Project

World Wide Web: http://www.ic.gc.ca/opengov

This Industry Canada project provides links to Canadian federal and provincial government resources on the Internet. Check here to see if your favorite ministry is on-line!

Canadian Government Information on the Internet

World Wide Web: http://library.uwaterloo.ca/discipline/Government/CanGuide/index.html

Anita Cannon of the University of Waterloo has prepared this excellent guide to Canadian government sites on the Internet. It covers all three levels of government in Canada (federal, provincial, and municipal).

New Brunswick Internet Exchange

World Wide Web: http://www.discribe.ca/newbie

The New Brunswick Internet Exchange is an index to World Wide Web sites in New Brunswick. Categories include culture, education, entertainment, government, people, and recreation and leisure.

Nova Scotia Links

World Wide Web: http://www.mfusion.com/kellock/nslinks

A listing of World Wide Web sites in Nova Scotia. Categories include travel and tourism, universities and schools, restaurants, recreation, business, and music.

Non-Canada-Specific Directories

Yahoo

World Wide Web: **http://www.yahoo.com**

Located at Stanford University, Yahoo is probably the closest thing that the Internet has to a "yellow pages." It is one of the most comprehensive and up-to-date subject-oriented World Wide Web indices on the network. Yahoo is useful because of its index structure. For example, you can quickly narrow in on specific topics such as astronomy or board games. Yahoo includes an extensive list of Canadian resources.

City.Net

World Wide Web: **http://www.city.net**

City.Net provides an excellent geographic index to information on the Internet. It provides pointers to information resources on cities, towns, and countries around the world. There are many links to Canadian villages, towns, and cities with sites on the Web.

ElNet Galaxy

World Wide Web: **http://galaxy.einet.net**

A searchable, subject-oriented directory of Internet resources. Categories include arts and humanities, business and commerce, government, leisure and recreation, medicine, and science. There are lots of Canadian resources buried in this directory.

NCSA's What's New Index

World Wide Web: **http://gnn.com/gnn/wn/ whats-new.html**

The What's New Index is the Internet's most popular directory of new World Wide Web sites. Several hundred new Web sites are announced on this site every week. Entries are organized alphabetically by week and the archives are searchable.

Open Market's Commercial Sites Index

World Wide Web: **http://www.directory.net**

The Commercial Sites Index is one of the best places to look for the World Wide Web sites of commercial organizations. Thousands of organizations are listed, with hundreds of new organizations added every week.

Whole Internet Catalog

World Wide Web: **http://gnn.com/wic**

The Whole Internet Catalog lists hundreds of World Wide Web resources by subject category. Categories include arts and entertainment, business and finance, computers, education, government, health and medicine, recreation, science and technology, the social sciences, and travel.

World Wide Web Virtual Library

World Wide Web: **http://info.cern.ch/hypertext/ DataSources/bySubject/Overview.html**

The World Wide Web Virtual Library contains dozens of subject-specific Web directories, covering everything from aboriginal studies to medieval studies to whale watching.

Clearinghouse for Subject-Oriented Internet Resource Guides

World Wide Web: **http://asa.ugl.lib.umich.edu/ chhome.html**

Provides subject-specific guides to Internet resources. Over 70 guides are available, covering such subjects as agriculture, business, cancer, economics, film, history, journalism, and telecommunications. The clearing house is sponsored by the University of Michigan's University Library and School of Information and Library Studies.

World Wide Web Search Engines

Canada-Specific Search Engines

Champlain: Canadian Information Explorer

World Wide Web: **http://Info.IC.GC.CA/champlain/champlain.html**

Champlain is a searchable database of Canadian federal, provincial, and municipal information on the Internet.

Non-Canada-Specific Search Engines:

SavvySearch

World Wide Web: **http://www.cs.colostate.edu/~dreiling/smartform.html**

SavvySearch lets you query multiple Internet search engines simultaneously. Try it out! Search for your favorite sport or hobby to see how it works.

WebCrawler

World Wide Web: **http://www.webcrawler.com**

WebCrawler is a search tool operated by America Online. The database is searchable by key word (e.g., Manitoba).

OpenText

World Wide Web: **http://www.opentext.com**

OpenText is a powerful search engine from Open Text Corporation. You can search its database of Web pages for a particular word, phrase, or combination of words and phrases.

Lycos

World Wide Web: **http://www.lycos.com**

Lycos calls itself "the catalog of the Internet." It is hosted by Carnegie Mellon University.

Other Places to Start Surfing

Cool Site of the Day

World Wide Web: **http://www.infi.net/cool.html**

Each day, this site recognizes a World Wide Web resource as "cool." Web sites are chosen based on their content, style/presentation, innovation, and/or graphics.

Point Communications Top Sites of the Web

World Wide Web: **http://www.pointcom.com**

This site reviews and rates thousands of sites on the World Wide Web. Categories include arts and humanities, business and finance, computers and the Internet, education, entertainment, government, health and medicine, leisure activities, and science and technology.

Netsurf

World Wide Web: **http://www.netsurf.com**

Netsurf is an upbeat, interesting newsletter that summarizes recent Internet news and profiles new World Wide Web sites established on the Internet. Each issue contains dozens of new surfing sites.

Canadian USENET Newsgroups

This is a directory of major Canadian USENET newsgroups (USENET was discussed in Chapter 8). Not all Internet access providers in Canada will carry every one of these newsgroups. Most Canadian Internet providers are willing to carry additional newsgroups on request, so if you see a newsgroup below that you like, ask your provider to carry it.

This Appendix is divided into three sections. The first section lists Canadian USENET newsgroups in the Canadian USENET hierarchies; the second section lists Canadian-related discussion groups in the mainstream USENET hierarchies; and the third section lists Canadian-related newsgroups in the ClariNet hierarchies.

Canadian Hierarchies

NAME OF NEWSGROUP	DESCRIPTION
ab.general	General discussion for people in Alberta
ab.jobs	Job/Employment discussions in Alberta
ab.politics	Discussion about politics in Alberta
bc.bicycling	Discussion about bicycling in British Columbia
bc.general	General discussion for people in British Columbia
bc.jobs	Job/Employment discussions in British Columbia
bc.politics	Discussion about politics in British Columbia
brocku.forsale	Items for sale—Brock University, St. Catharines, Ontario
brocku.general	General discussion at Brock University, St. Catharines, Ontario

Newsgroup	Description
calgary.announce	Announcements in Calgary, Alberta
can.atlantic.general	General discussion about the Altantic Provinces
can.community.military	General discussion about the military in Canada
can.config	General discussion about new newsgroup proposals in the can.* hierarchy
can.domain	New Canadian domain registrations and discussion about the Canadian domain name system
can.english	General discussion about English-language issues in Canada
can.forsale	Items for sale in Canada
can.francais	General discussion about francophone issues in Canada
can.general	General discussion for Canadians
can.gov.announce	Canadian government announcements
can.gov.general	General discussion about government in Canada
can.infohighway	General discussion about Canada's information highway
can.jobs	Job/Employment openings in Canada
can.legal	General discussion about Canadian law
can.motss	General discussion about gay/lesbian/bisexual issues in Canada
can.newprod	General discussion about new products in Canada
can.politics	General discussion about Canadian politics
can.schoolnet.biomed.jr	General discussion about biology and medicine for elementary school students participating in SchoolNet
can.schoolnet.biomed.sr	General discussion about biology and medicine for secondary school students participating in SchoolNet
can.schoolnet.chat.students.jr	General discussion for elementary school students participating in SchoolNet
can.schoolnet.chat.students.sr	General discussion for secondary school students participating in SchoolNet
can.schoolnet.chat.teachers	General discussion for teachers participating in SchoolNet
can.schoolnet.chem.jr	General discussion about chemistry for elementary school students participating in SchoolNet
can.schoolnet.chem.sr	General discussion about chemistry for secondary school students participating in SchoolNet
can.schoolnet.comp.jr	General discussion about computer science for elementary school students participating in SchoolNet
can.schoolnet.comp.sr	General discussion about computer science for secondary school students participating in SchoolNet
can.schoolnet.earth.jr	General discussion about the earth sciences for elementary school students participating in SchoolNet

can.schoolnet.earth.sr	General discussion about the earth sciences for secondary school students participating in SchoolNet
can.schoolnet.elecsys.jr	General discussion about electrical/systems engineering for elementary school students participating in SchoolNet
can.schoolnet.elecsys.sr	General discussion about electrical/systems engineering for secondary school students participating in SchoolNet
can.schoolnet.eng.jr	General discussion about engineering for elementary school students participating in SchoolNet
can.schoolnet.eng.sr	General discussion about engineering for secondary school students participating in SchoolNet
can.schoolnet.english	General discussion about English curriculum for SchoolNet participants
can.schoolnet.firefighters	General discussion about firefighting and fire safety issues for SchoolNet participants
can.schoolnet.history	General discussion about history for SchoolNet participants
can.schoolnet.math.jr	General discussion about math for elementary school students participating in SchoolNet
can.schoolnet.math.sr	General discussion about math for secondary school students participating in SchoolNet
can.schoolnet.phys.jr	General discussion about physics for elementary school students participating in SchoolNet
can.schoolnet.phys.sr	General discussion about physics for secondary school students participating in SchoolNet
can.schoolnet.physed	General discussion about physical education for SchoolNet participants
can.schoolnet.problems	General discussion about SchoolNet problems
can.schoolnet.projects.calls	SchoolNet requests for proposals
can.schoolnet.projects.discuss	General discussion about SchoolNet projects
can.schoolnet.school.improvement	General discussion about improving Canada's schools
can.schoolnet.socsci.jr	General discussion about the social sciences for elementary school students participating in SchoolNet
can.schoolnet.socsci.sr	General discussion about the social sciences for secondary school students participating in SchoolNet
can.schoolnet.space.jr	General discussion about space sciences for elementary school students participating in SchoolNet
can.schoolnet.space.sr	General discussion about space sciences for secondary school students participating in SchoolNet
can.schoolnet.staff.development	General discussion about staff development issues in Canada's schools
can.scout-guide	General discussion about scouting in Canada
can.talk.bilingualism	General discussion about bilingualism in Canada
can.talk.guns	General discussion about guns and gun control in Canada

can.talk.smoking	General discussion about smoking issues in Canada
can.taxes	General discussion about Canadian tax matters
carleton.general	General discussion at Carleton University, Ottawa, Ontario
concordia.announce	Announcements at Concordia University, Montreal, Quebec
concordia.general	General discussion at Concordia University, Montreal, Quebec
dal.general	General discussion at Dalhousie University, Halifax, Nova Scotia
edm.general	General discussion for people in Edmonton, Alberta
edm.politics	General discussion about politics in Edmonton, Alberta
hfx.general	General discussion for people in Halifax, Nova Scotia
kingston.events	Events in Kingston, Ontario
kingston.forsale	Items for sale in Kingston, Ontario
kingston.general	General discussion for people in Kingston, Ontario
kw.forsale	Items for sale in Kitchener/Waterloo, Ontario
kw.general	General discussion for people in Kitchener/Waterloo, Ontario
kw.housing	Discussions about accommodation/housing in Kitchener/Waterloo, Ontario
kw.jobs	Job/Employment discussions in Kitchener/Waterloo, Ontario
man.politics	General discussion about politics in Manitoba
man.general	General discussion for people in Manitoba
mcgill.general	General discussion at McGill University, Montreal, Quebec
mtl.general	General discussion for people in Montreal, Quebec
mtl.vendre-forsale	Items for sale—Montreal, Quebec
mun.general	General discussion at the Memorial University of Newfoundland, St. John's
mun.wanted	Items wanted—Memorial University of Newfoundland, St. John's
nb.biz	Commercial postings in New Brunswick
nb.forsale	Items for sale in New Brunswick
nb.general	General discussion for people in New Brunswick
nbgov.info.highway	General discussion about the information highway in New Brunswick
nbgov.investment.newbrunswick	General discussion about investment in New Brunswick
nf.birds	General discussion about birding in Newfoundland
nf.computing	General discussion about computing in Newfoundland
nf.general	General discussion for people in Newfoundland
nf.wanted	Items wanted in Newfoundland

nf.women	General discussion about women's issues in Newfoundland
ns.forsale	Items for sale in Nova Scotia
ns.general	General discussion for people in Nova Scotia
nwt.general	General discussion for people in the Northwest Territories
ont.archives	General discussion about archival issues in Ontario
ont.bicycle	General discussion about bicycling in Ontario
ont.general	General discussion for people in Ontario
ott.events	Events in Ottawa, Ontario
ott.forsale	Items for sale in Ottawa, Ontario
ott.general	General discussion for people in Ottawa, Ontario
ott.housing	Discussions about accommodation/housing in Ottawa, Ontario
ott.jobs	Job/Employment discussions in Ottawa, Ontario
ott.online	General discussion about the on-line world in Ottawa, Ontario
qc.general	General discussion for people in Quebec
qc.jobs	Jobs in Quebec
qc.jobs.wanted	Jobs wanted in Quebec
qc.politique	Discussion about politics in Quebec
queens.events	Announcements of events—Queen's University, Kingston, Ontario
queens.forsale	Items for sale—Queen's University, Kingston, Ontario
queens.general	General discussion at Queen's University, Kingston, Ontario
rye.general	General discussion at Ryerson Polytechnic University, Toronto
sfu.general	General discussion at Simon Fraser University, Vancouver
sj.general	General discussion for people in St. John's, Newfoundland
sk.announce	Announcements in Saskatchewan
sk.forsale	Items for sale in Saskatchewan
sk.general	General discussion for people in Saskatchewan
sk.internet	General discussion about the Internet in Saskatchewan
sk.jobs	Job/Employment discussions in Saskatchewan
sk.politics	General discussion about politics in Saskatchewan
sk.sports	General discussion about sports in Saskatchewan
stemnet.announce	Announcements at STEM~Net, St. John's Newfoundland
stemnet.general	General discussion at STEM~Net, St. John's, Newfoundland
tor.arts	General discussion about the arts in Toronto, Ontario
tor.eats	General discussion about restaurants and eating in Toronto, Ontario

tor.events	Event listings in Toronto
tor.forsale	Items for sale in Toronto, Ontario
tor.housing	General discussion about housing in Toronto
tor.jobs	Job/Employment discussions in Toronto, Ontario
trentu.general	General discussion at Trent University, Peterborough, Ontario
ualberta.general	General discussion at the University of Alberta, Edmonton
ubc.events	Events at the University of British Columbia, Vancouver
ubc.general	General discussion at the University of British Columbia, Vancouver
umoncton.annonces	Announcements at the University of Moncton, New Brunswick
umontreal.general	General discussion at the University of Montreal
uqam.general	General discussion at the University of Quebec (Montreal)
usask.general	General discussion at the University of Saskatchewan
ut.general	General discussion at the University of Toronto
ut.jobs	Job/Employment discussions—University of Toronto
uvic.forsale	Items for sale—University of Victoria, British Columbia
uvic.general	General discussion at the University of Victoria, British Columbia
uvic.jobs	Job/Employment discussions—University of Victoria
uw.forsale	Items for sale—University of Waterloo, Ontario
uw.general	General discussion at the University of Waterloo, Ontario
uwo.events	Events at the University of Western Ontario, London
uwo.forsale	Items for sale—University of Western Ontario, London
uwo.general	General discussion at the University of Western Ontario, London
van.general	General discussion for people in Vancouver, British Columbia
wpg.forsale	Items for sale—Winnipeg, Manitoba
wpg.general	General discussion for people in Winnipeg, Manitoba
yk.general	General discussion for people in the Yukon
york.announce	Announcements at York University, Toronto
york.general	General discussion at York University, Toronto

Mainstream Hierarchies

NAME OF NEWSGROUP	DESCRIPTION
alt.music.canada	Discussion about Canadian music

alt.radio.networks.cbc	Discussion about CBC Radio
alt.tv.networks.cbc	Discussion about CBC Television
alt.tv.discovery.canada	Discussion about Canada's Discovery Channel
alt.sports.baseball.montreal-expos	Discussion about the Montreal Expos
alt.sports.baseball.tor-bluejays	Discussion about the Toronto Blue Jays
alt.sports.hockey.nhl.clgry-flames	Discussion about the Calgary Flames
alt.sports.hockey.nhl.mtl-canadiens	Discussion about the Montreal Canadiens
alt.sports.hockey.nhl.tor-mapleleafs	Discussion about the Toronto Maple Leafs
alt.sports.hockey.nhl.vanc-canucks	Discussion about the Vancouver Canucks
alt.sports.hockey.nhl.winnipeg-jets	Discussion about the Winnipeg Jets
misc.immigration.canada	Discussion about Canadian immigration issues
misc.invest.canada	Discussion about Canadian investments
rec.sport.football.canadian	Discussion about Canadian football
rec.travel.canada-usa	Travel discussion for Canada/U.S.A.
soc.culture.canada	Discussion about Canadian culture
soc.culture.quebec	Discussion about Quebec culture

ClariNet Hierarchies

NAME OF NEWSGROUP	DESCRIPTION
clari.world.americas.canada	General Canadian news (moderated)
clari.world.americas.canada.business	Canadian business news (moderated)
clari.world.americas.canada.review	Review of Canadian news (moderated)

Community Networking Organizations in Canada

This is a directory of Canadian communities that had operational community computer systems in September 1995. Many community computer networks are known as Free-Nets. The Free-Net movement started in 1986 with the establishment of the Cleveland Free-Net in Cleveland, Ohio. Soon thereafter, the National Public Telecomputing Network was established in the United States as a coordinating body for the many Free-Net organizations that began to spring up in the United States and abroad. A legal dispute over ownership rights to the name Free-Net led many Canadian community networks to change their names in 1995. For example, the Chebucto Free-Net changed its name to the Chebucto Community Net. Regardless of what they are called, most community computer networks in Canada have similar principles and objectives.

What Is a Community Computer Network?

Most community computer networks are not-for-profit organizations, run primarily by volunteers within the community. Community computer networks provide a wide spectrum of on-line information services to the local communities they serve. These services include on-line access to local information resources, (limited) Internet access, and local discussion areas. Many community networks in Canada are modelled on the same principle as public libraries and provide their information and services at no charge to the end user. However, not all community networks are free. Due to high operating and administration costs, several community networks in Canada charge a mandatory membership fee. Other community networks have made the registration fee optional. In all cases donations are always welcome.

A key element of the community network concept is the participation of "information providers", organizations from all sectors of the community that provide information on the system. Information providers are responsible for maintaining and updating their information on the network.

How Can You Help Your Local Community Network?

Volunteer

Since volunteers are the lifeblood of most community networks, community networks are always seeking new volunteers. If you have experience in fund-raising, training, technical writing, public/media relations, computer networking, or volunteer management, or you just want to help out, check the directory below and contact a community network near you. Experience is not required to volunteer. Most community networks are more than happy to train new volunteers.

Sponsor Your Local Community Network

Community networks rely on government, corporate, and user support for funding. In return, sponsors receive on-line recognition of their support and contribute to the development of an important community resource. In addition to making monetary contributions, organizations can assist community networks by donating expertise, services, and/or equipment. Contact your local community network to find out how you or your organization can help.

Become an Information Provider

Community networks feature a wide array of information on topics such as community events, medical and health care, education, law, science and technology, social services, government, entertainment, travel and tourism, and employment. If you work for an organization that has community-related information to distribute, contact your local community network to find out how you can make your information available on their system.

Where Can I Find Out More?

If you would like to keep abreast of the community networking movement in Canada, we suggest that you join the **can-freenet** mailing list, which has been established for the discussion of Canadian community networking initiatives. To subscribe to the list, send a message to the following Internet address: **listserv@cunews.carleton.ca** and place the following command on the first line of the body of the message: **subscribe can-freenet <FIRSTNAME> <LASTNAME>**; for example, **subscribe can-freenet Joe Smith**.

Telecommunities Canada is a national umbrella organization for community networks in Canada.

Telecommunities Canada mission statement:

1. To ensure that all Canadians are able to participate in community-based communications and electronic information services by promoting and supporting local community network initiatives.

2. To represent and promote Canadian community networking movement at the national and international level.

Telecommunities Canada has a World Wide Web site that contains general information about the organization and highlights from past Canadian community networking conferences.

Telecommunities Canada:

708 Oakenwald Avenue

Winnipeg Manitoba R3T 1M7

e-mail: **michaelg@freenet.mb.ca** (Michael Gillespie, President)

Telecommunities Canada home page:

http://www.freenet.mb.ca/tc/index.html

Peter Scott at the University of Saskatchewan has assembled a useful collection of pointers to Free-Nets and community networks in Canada and around the world.

Peter Scott's Free-Nets and community networks home Page:

http://www.usask.ca/~scottp/free.html

The National Public Telecomputing Network (NPTN) maintains a list of Free-Nets and organizing committees on its World Wide Web site.

NPTN home page:

http://www.nptn.org

BRITISH COLUMBIA

Community Information Access Organization (CIAO!)

Trail, British Columbia

Contact:

CIAO! Free-Net
Box 166
Trail, British Columbia V1R 4L5

Voice: (604) 368-2244
e-mail: info@ciao.trail.bc.ca

How to Access:

Internet:
Telnet: **ciao.trail.bc.ca**
Login: **guest**

Modem:
(604) 368-5764; 14,400 bps
Login: **guest**

World Wide Web:
http://www.ciao.trail.bc.ca

Membership:
$25.00 per year ($24.00 registration and $1.00 for membership)

Mission/Mandate:
To develop cost-effective access to the internet for all citizens within the CIAO! area.

Prince George Free-Net

Prince George, British Columbia

Contact:

210 North Quinn St.
Prince George, British Columbia V2M 3J5

Voice: (604) 562-9281
Fax :   (604) 562-8463
e-mail: **support@freenet.unbc.edu**

How to Access:

Internet:
Telnet: freenet.unbc.edu
Login: **guest**

Modem:
(604) 563-3977; 14,400 bps
Login: **guest**

Membership:
Free. Donations are encouraged.

Mission/Mandate:
The mission of the Prince George Free-Net is to raise telecomputing literacy in the region, develop local content, and provide basic Internet access in the form of electronic mail, USENET forums, and access to public information sites. The Prince George Free-Net invites local businesses to function as information providers in the interest of assisting them to gain experience with this electronic medium.

Rocky Mountain Information Network

Operated by the Rocky Mountain Infonet Society
Sparwood, British Columbia

Contact:

Box 471
Sparwood, British Columbia V0B 2G0

Voice: (604) 425-2605
Fax: (604) 425-7130
e-mail: **info@rmin.net**

How to Access:

Modem:
(604) 425-7805; 14,400 bps
Login: **guest**

Membership:
e-mail and USENET newsgroup access fee: $50.00/year/adult; $35.00/year/student or senior; $100/year/family.

Mission/Mandate:
The mission of the Rocky Mountain InfoNet is to act as a community information resource for southeast British Columbia

Sea to Sky Free-Net

Squamish, British Columbia

Contact:

Box 2539
Squamish, British Columbia V0N 3G0

Voice: (604) 892-5531
Fax: (604) 892-5227
e-mail: **admin@sea-to-sky-freenet.bc.ca**

How to Access:

Internet:
Telnet: **sea-to-sky-freenet.bc.ca**
Login: **guest**

Modem:
(604) 892-3500; 14,400 bps
Login: **guest**

World Wide Web:
http://www.mountain-inter.net:80/~freenet

Membership:
Free. Donations are encouraged.

Mission/Mandate:
The mission of the Sea-to-Sky Free-Net is to establish a community information computer system for the sea-to-sky corridor communities, which will enable members of the community to have access to information resources and electronic mail at no charge to end-users.

Vancouver Regional FreeNet Association

Vancouver, British Columbia

Contact:

Second Floor
411 Dunsmuir Street
Vancouver, British Columbia V6B 1X4

Voice: (604) 257-3811
e-mail: **info@freenet.vancouver.bc.ca**

How to Access:

Internet:
Telnet: **freenet.vancouver.bc.ca**
Login: **guest**

Modem:
(604) 257-8778; 14,400 bps
Login: **guest**

World Wide Web:
http://www.freenet.vancouver.bc.ca

Membership:
Free. Donations are encouraged.

Mission/Mandate:
The eight goals of the Vancouver Community Network are

◆ to establish, operate, and own a free, publicly accessible, community computer utility in the Lower Mainland of British Columbia, providing the broadest possible range of information and possibilities for the exchange of experience, ideas, and wisdom;

◆ to encourage the development of a wide range of electronic community information resources;

◆ to encourage the broadest possible participation of information providers in making their information available on the network;

◆ to work toward the widest possible public access to government and other information through community computer networks and other non-profit organizations, such as libraries;

◆ to work toward building a network of similar services in cities and towns internationally;

◆ to work with other Canadian community computer networks to create a Canadian community computer network;

◆ to educate and to encourage the public in the use of computer telecommunications and information retrieval systems;

◆ to research ways of improving and expanding public access to, and use of, electronic information resources and facilities.

Victoria Free-Net

Victoria, British Columbia

Contact:
Victoria Free-Net Association
4252 Commerce Circle
Victoria, British Columbia V8Z 4M2

Voice: (604) 727-7057
e-mail: **vifa@freenet.victoria.bc.ca**

How to Access:

Internet:
Telnet: **freenet.victoria.bc.ca**
Login: **guest**

Modem:
(604) 479-6500; 14,400 bps
Login: **guest**

World Wide Web:
http://www.freenet.victoria.bc.ca/vifa.html

Membership:
Free. Donations are encouraged.

Mission/Mandate:
The Victoria Free-Net is a community-based computer network available at no cost to residents and visitors of the Greater Victoria region. Modelled on the highly successful Cleveland Free-Net, the service goals of the Victoria Free-Net include

◆ computer-mediated communications among Victoria Free-Net users and community members;

◆ easy access to information posted by community organizations, individuals, businesses, and government;

◆ worldwide electronic mail;

◆ access to selected on-line public access resources throughout the world;

◆ alternative news services.

The Victoria Free-Net is run by a core of dedicated volunteers belonging to the Victoria Free-Net Association, a registered non-profit society formed on June 17, 1992. The Victoria Free-Net began operating on November 17, 1992.

ALBERTA

Calgary Free-Net

Calgary, Alberta

Contact:

Calgary Free-Net Association
#810, 400-3rd Ave. S.W.
Calgary, Alberta T2P 4H2

Voice: (403) 264-9535
Fax: (403) 269-4776
e-mail: **manager@freenet.calgary.ab.ca**

How to Access:

Internet:
Telnet: **freenet.calgary.ab.ca**
Login: **guest**

Modem:
(403) 282-4075; 14,400 bps
Login: **guest**
(403) 282-3707, 14,400 bps
Login: **guest**

World Wide Web:
http://freenet.calgary.ab.ca

Membership:
There is no cost to use Calgary Free-Net, but membership in the association is encouraged. The fee for individuals is $50/year. Members have voting rights at the annual general meeting. In addition, several local businesses and organizations provide discounts to Calgary Free-Net Association members.

Mission/Mandate:
The Calgary Free-Net Association was established to promote awareness of and increase the knowledge and understanding of computers, computer networks, and the benefits of having access to electronic information. The association is responsible to its members in accomplishing its objectives by

- establishing and maintaining a computer system that provides free access to community information stored on that system, computer databases networked with that system, and the global computer network, the Internet;

- offering information providers access to the Free-Net computer system in order to allow them to disseminate their electronic information to users of the Calgary Free-Net computer system;

- producing and disseminating information regarding the use of the Calgary Free-Net computer system and other computer networks;

- collaborating and participating in projects with universities, colleges, technical institutions, and other organizations to develop a better understanding of and promote the use of computers, computer networks, and electronic information;

- providing presentations and classes regarding the use of computers, computer networks, and gaining access to electronic information.

Edmonton FreeNet

Edmonton, Alberta

Contact:

Keith Gross, Executive Director
Edmonton FreeNet
First Edmonton Place
405, 10665 Jasper Ave.
Edmonton, Alberta T5J 3S9

Voice: (403) 421-1745
Fax: (403) 421-7159
e-mail: **postmaster@freenet.edmonton.ab.c**a

Membership:
$15.00/year. Members have access to the following services: electronic mail, over 200 local information providers, local and global USENET discussion groups, and text access to the World Wide Web. Limited support is available for FTP, Telnet and Gopher services.

Mission/Mandate:

The Edmonton FreeNet is a community-based, electronic network offering access to local community resources and the Internet. Its mission is to enable people in the greater Edmonton region

◆ to list and to retrieve information about, or of interest to, themselves;

◆ to prepare themselves to function effectively in an information society;

◆ to communicate with public and private members of the local and global community.

SASKATCHEWAN

Great Plains Free-Net Inc.

Regina, Saskatchewan

Contact:

55 Cowburn Crescent
Regina, Saskatchewan S4S 5R9

Voice: (306) 565-6046 or (306) 584-9615
Fax: (306) 565-6046
e-mail: **suggittm@gpfn.sk.ca**
         rhg@gpfn.sk.ca
         info@gpfn.sk.ca

How to Access:

World Wide Web:
http://www.gpfn.sk.ca

Mission/Mandate:

The mandate of the Great Plains Free-Net is to provide the Saskatchewan community with a broad range of local and relevant information services and to promote local-call access in rural areas. If you are interested in following the progress of the Great Plains Free-Net, you can join the Great Plains Free-Net mailing list. Send the message: **subscribe gpfn-l <Your Name>** (e.g., subscribe gpfn-l Joe Smith) to the following Internet address: **listserv@max.cc.uregina.ca.**

Saskatoon Free-Net

Saskatoon, Saskatchewan

Contact:

Saskatoon Free-Net Association
Box 339
RPO University
Saskatoon, Saskatchewan S7N 4J8
Voice: (306) 374-8288
e-mail: **helpdesk@freenet.sfn.saskatoon.sk.ca**

How to Access:

Internet:
Telnet: **freenet.sfn.saskatoon.sk.ca**
Login: **guest**

Modem:
(306) 956-3700; 14,400 bps
Login: **guest**

World Wide Web:
http://www.sfn.saskatoon.sk.ca

Membership:
Free. Donations are encouraged.

Mission/Mandate:

The Saskatoon Free-Net is a computer network operating as a community-based, community information service for Saskatoon and the surrounding area.

MANITOBA

Blue Sky Community Networks of Manitoba Inc.

Winnipeg, Manitoba

Contact:

P.O. Box 1441
Winnipeg, Manitoba R3C 2Z4
Voice: (204) 992-HELP
e-mail: **info@freenet.mb.ca**

How to Access:

Internet:
Telnet: **winnie.freenet.mb.ca**
Login: **guest**

Modem:
(204) 987-1234; 14,400 bps
Login: **guest**

World Wide Web:
http://www.freenet.mb.ca

Membership:
No charge. Donations encouraged.

Mission/Mandate:
Blue Sky Community Networks of Manitoba is a community network serving the province of Manitoba, Canada. It is a provincially incorporated not-for-profit umbrella organization established to facilitate the creation and operation of community networks throughout the province. The mission statement of Blue Sky Community Networks is "to bring free, public access, community-based electronic information services to Manitoba, Canada; to provide community organizations with the means to disseminate information; and to encourage public discussion and education." The stated objectives of Blue Sky Community Networks are

◆ to bring free, public access, computer-based information services to the citizens of Manitoba;

◆ to partner with government and industry to gain equal cost access to FreeNet information, by eliminating user telecommunications charges or providing alternate access;

◆ to create connections with other computer-based networks to allow the free, interactive flow of information between different community groups;

◆ to establish complementary relationships with existing free and fee for service computer-based information services in the Manitoba community;

◆ to provide education and training to the community in the access of computer-based community information.

ONTARIO

Durham Free-Net

Durham Region, Ontario (Ajax, Pickering, Whitby, Oshawa, Clarington, Port Perry, Uxbridge, and Brock Townships)

How to Access:

Modem:

Oshawa: (905) 725-0544; 14,400 bps
Ajax-Pickering: (905) 619-1666; 14,400 bps
Port Perry: (905) 985-9536; 14,400 bps

Off-line mail readers only:
Ajax-Pickering: (905) 619-2007; 14,400 bps
Oshawa: (905) 725-9525; 14,400 bps
Port Perry: (905) 985-9915; 14,400 bps
Login: **guest**

World Wide Web:
http://www.freenet.durham.org

Membership:
Free. Donations are encouraged.

Mission/Mandate:
The purpose of the Durham Free-Net is to provide all members of the community with free and equal computer access to public information and the ability to communicate interactively with all participating organizations on the network, on a local, national, and international level.

Halton Community Network (Halton Net)

Halton Region, Ontario

Contact:

Halton Community Network
Sheridan College
1430 Trafalgar Road
Oakville, Ontario L6H 2L1

Voice: (905) 815-4010 (help/information line)
e-mail: **hcn@sheridanc.on.ca**

How to Access:

Internet:
Telnet: **halinet.sheridanc.on.ca**
Login: **guest**

Modem:
(905) 845-0057; 14,400 bps
Login: **guest**

Membership:
Free. Donations are encouraged.

Mission/Mandate:
To empower the residents and businesses of Halton Region by providing access to electronic communications and information facilities, and by so doing, strengthen the community and enable the residents to function effectively in the automated, informational society. All Halton-area libraries are interconnected with each other and with the Boards of Education and Sheridan College into a network called Halinet. The Halton Community Network is building on the Halinet infrastructure and providing a front door for the community to those resources and beyond.

Hamilton–Wentworth FreeNet

Hamilton, Ontario

Contact:

Hamilton–Wentworth FreeNet
Jackson Square
2 King Street West
Hamilton, Ontario L8P 1A1

Voice: (905) 528-HWFN (4936)
Help desk: (905) 528-9334
Fax: (905) 528-7578
e-mail: **office@freenet.hamilton.on.ca**

How to Access:

Internet:
Telnet: **freenet.hamilton.on.ca**
Login: **guest**

Modem:
(905) 540-5000; 28,800 bps
Login: **guest**

World Wide Web:
http://www.freenet.hamilton.on.ca

Membership:
Basic membership is free (includes e-mail, text-based World Wide Web, 0.5 MB storage space for files, 1 hour/log-on, 2 hours maximum /day, 14 hours maximum /week). Enhanced membership is $20/year (includes e-mail with a personalized alias, text-based World Wide Web, 0.5 MB storage space for files, hour/log-on, 3 hours maximum/day, 14 hours maximum/week. Voting privileges at FreeNet general meetings.

Premium membership is $50/year (includes e-mail with a personalized alias, World Wide Web, 2.0 MB storage space for files, 2 hours/log-on, 4 hours maximum/day, 21 hours maximum/week, voting privileges at FreeNet general meetings. Access to a separate modem pool with a lower caller-to-line density.

Mission/Mandate:
The mandate of the Hamilton–Wentworth FreeNet is to develop and to implement a world-class electronic information network in the community, to access and to share local and global knowledge, and to assist businesses in competitiveness. Our vision is to bring the community together and to increase knowledge by electronic means. This will be achieved by offering the people of Hamilton–Wentworth access, and the opportunity to exchange information through a FreeNet. The motto of the Hamilton–Wentworth FreeNet is "Connecting the Community."

HOMEtown Community Network

London, Ontario

Contact:

HOMEtown Community Network
11 St. John's Drive
Arva, Ontario N0M 1C0
Telephone: (519) 522-0020

Fax: (519) 522-0025
e-mail: **ht325@hometown.on.ca**
          (Larry Dillon, Executive Director)

How to Access:

Internet:
Telnet: forest.hometown.on.ca
Login: **guest**
Password: **hometown** (must be lowercase)

Modem:
London:
(519) 679-3909; 28,800 bps
Login: **guest**
Password: **hometown** (must be lowercase)
St. Marys:
(519) 284-0787; 28,800 bps
Woodstock: (519) 421-1895; 28,800 bps
Exeter: (519) 235-4589; 28,800 bps
Clinton: (519) 482-1393; 28,800 bps
Login: **guest**
Password: **hometown** (must be lowercase)

World Wide Web:
http://www.hometown.on.ca

Membership:
$60.00/year plus GST.

Mission/Mandate:
To develop and to provide universal and affordable access to a comprehensive communication service across five counties. HOMEtown will serve the counties of Huron, Oxford, Middlesex, Elgin, and Perth, and the cities of London, St. Thomas, and Stratford.

National Capital FreeNet

Ottawa, Ontario

Contact:

National Capital FreeNet
Carleton University
1125 Colonel By Drive
Ottawa, Ontario K1S 5B6

Voice: (613) 788-3947
e-mail: **info-request@freenet.carleton.ca**
          ncf@freenet.carleton.ca
          office@freenet.carleton.ca

How to Access:

Internet:
Telnet: freenet.carleton.ca
           freenet2.carleton.ca
           freenet3.carleton.ca
Login: **guest**

Modem:
(613) 564-3600; 2,400 bps
Login: **guest**
(613) 564-0808; 14,400 bps
Login: **guest**

World Wide Web:
http://www.ncf.carleton.ca

Membership:
Free. Donations are encouraged.

Mission/Mandate:
The National Capital FreeNet is a free, computer-based information sharing network. It links the people and organizations of this region, provides useful information, and enables an open exchange of ideas with the world. Community involvement makes FreeNet an important and accessible meeting place and prepares people for full participation in a rapidly changing communications environment.

Niagara Peninsula Free-Net

Region of Niagara – St.Catharines, Ontario

Contact:

Niagara Peninsula Free-Net
Niagara Peninsula Industry Education Council
(N.P.I.E.C.)
3340 Schmon Parkway, Unit 2
Thorold, Ontario L2V 4Y6

Voice: (905) 684-7200
Fax: (905) 684-4230
e-mail: **npfstaff@freenet.npiec.on.ca**

How to Access:

Internet:
Telnet: **freenet.npiec.on.ca**
Login: **guest**

Modem:
(905) 684-6736; 14,400 bps
Login: **guest**

Membership:
Free. Donations are encouraged.

Mission/Mandate
The Niagara Peninsula Free-Net's mission is to create a computer-based network that will

◆ help meet the personal, professional, and educational needs of people in the Niagara community;

◆ foster communication between individuals and the institutions that serve them;

◆ support community groups in their efforts at professional development, outreach, and community service;

◆ enhance opportunities for sustainable, community-based economic development;

◆ create a favorable environment for business and employment growth;

◆ allow cooperation with other groups to support the development and linking of community networks in Canada and the world.

Toronto Free-Net

Toronto, ON

Contact:

Toronto Free-Net Inc.
c/o Ryerson Polytechnic University Library
350 Victoria Street
Toronto, Ontario M5B 2K3

Voice: (416) 979-9224
e-mail: info@freenet.toronto.on.ca

How to Access:

Internet:
Telnet: freenet.toronto.on.ca
Login: **guest**

Modem:
(416) 780-2010; 14,400 bps
Login: **guest**

Membership:
Free. Donations are encouraged.

Mission/Mandate:
The mandate of the Toronto Free-Net is to provide the residents of Metropolitan Toronto with free, electronic access to community-related information, while giving information providers a means of disseminating their information as widely and as economically as possible.

QUEBEC

Libertel Montreal

Montreal, Quebec
1030, rue Beaubien Est, Suite 201
Montreal, Quebec H2S 1T4

Voice: (514) 990-REMM
Fax: (514) 278-1498
e-mail: **info@libertel.montreal.qc.ca**

How to Access:

Internet:
Telnet: **libertel.montreal.qc.ca**
Login: **guest**

World Wide Web:
http://www.libertel.montreal.qc.ca

Membership:
Free. Donations are encouraged.

Mission/Mandate:
Libertel Montreal is a volunteer-run, non-profit organization whose mission is to enhance community life and educate its users by providing people and organizations in the metropolitan Montreal region with access to a computerized information clearinghouse and messaging service. Libertel Montreal's services are free and are offered in both French and English. Free-Net Montreal will be the first

community network to be fully accessible in both French and English.

NOVA SCOTIA

Cape Breton Community Network

Sydney, Nova Scotia

Contact:

Cape Breton Community Network
P.O. Box 1191
Sydney, Nova Scotia B1A 6G9

Voice: (902)-567-3842
Fax: (902) 562-3480
e-mail: **policy@highlander.cbnet.ns.ca**

How to Access:

Internet:
Telnet: **highlander.cbnet.ns.ca**
Login: **guest**

Modem:
(902) 562-7695; 14,400 bps
Login: **guest**

World Wide Web:
http://highlander.cbnet.ns.ca

Membership:
$96.00 for one year; $30.00 for a three-month trial.

Mission/Mandate:
The Cape Breton Community Network is a non-profit, public information computing network. Modelled upon successful systems already in operation, it is designed to supplement and enhance existing community resources. Information provided by citizens and for citizens will help individuals and communities meet their economic, cultural, recreational, and educational needs. Based on principles of partnership and cooperation, this system will

- establish Cape Breton firmly within the global web of information networks

- provide users with a comprehensive and easily accessible listing of community resources;

- provide individuals of all ages with the opportunity for distance education and lifelong learning;

- by locating computer terminals in libraries, schools, and other community outlets, help the general public become more familiar with the electronic highways that are redefining our concepts of communication.

Chebucto Community Net

Halifax, Nova Scotia

Contact:

Chebucto Community Net
c/o Dept. of Mathematics, Statistics & Computing Science
Dalhousie University
Halifax, Nova Scotia B3H 3J5

Voice: (902) 494-2449
e-mail: **cfn@cfn.cs.dal.ca**

How to Access:

Internet:
Telnet: **ccn.cs.dal.ca**
Login: **guest**

Modem:
(902) 494-8006; 14,400 bps
Login: **guest**

World Wide Web:
http://www.ccn.cs.dal.ca

Membership:
Access to the system is free to all registered users. The Chebucto Community Net is run by the Metro Community Access Network (Metro*CAN) Society. Membership in the Metro*CAN Society provides voting privileges and a say in how the Chebucto Community Net is run. Membership is $20.00 for adults, $40.00 for families, $12.00 for youths under the age of 18, $12.00 for unwaged individuals, and $200.00 for institutions. Donations are encouraged.

Mission/Mandate:

The vision of the Chebucto Free-Net is for every Nova Scotian to have free access to a community access network, as part of a province-wide electronic network linked to the world-wide Internet.

Mission statement:

To achieve our vision, the Metro Community Access Network Society will establish a community access network for the Halifax–Dartmouth Metro area, which will

- ◆ help meet personal and professional information needs of people;

- ◆ foster communication between individuals and the institutions that serve them;

- ◆ support community groups in their efforts at professional development, outreach, and community service;

- ◆ enhance opportunities for sustainable, community-based economic development;

- ◆ create a favorable environment for business and employment growth;

- ◆ cooperate with other groups to foster and support the development and linking of community access networks in other parts of Nova Scotia, Atlantic Canada, the rest of Canada, and the world.

The Chebucto FreeNet is an HTTP server using Lynx as a browser.

NEWFOUNDLAND

St. John's InfoNET

St. John's, Newfoundland

Contact:

P.O. Box 23222
Churchill Square Post Ofice
St. John's, Newfoundland A1B 4J9

Principal contacts:

Randy Dodge	Louise McGillis
Voice: (709) 737-4595	(709) 737-7427
Fax: (709) 737-3514	(709) 737-2153

e-mail: randy@kean,ucs.mun.ca
           mcgillis@morgan.ucs.mun.ca

How to Access:

Internet:

Telnet: infonet.st-johns.nf.ca
Login: **guest**
Password: Press **<Enter>**

Modem

(709) 737-3301; 2,400 bps
(709) 737-3461; 2,400 bps
(709) 737-3425; 14,400 bps
(709) 737-3426; 14,400 bps
Login: **guest**
Password: Press **<Enter>**

World Wide Web:

http://www.InfoNET.st-johns.nf.ca

Membership:

Access to the system is free to all registered users. Membership in the St. John's InfoNET Association is $10/year and allows you to attend meetings and to vote on InfoNET issues. Donations are encouraged.

Mission/Mandate:

To support and stimulate the growth of community networking in St. John's and to facilitate the growth of similar organizations throughout Newfoundland and Labrador.

Objectives:

- ◆ to ensure that all people in the community have access to public information;

- ◆ to empower people by developing a more information and computer-literate citizenry;

- ◆ to improve access to community and government information;

- ◆ to enhance residents' understanding of community issues and encourage their active participation;

- ◆ to make community and government organizations more effective in serving people;

- ◆ to provide public access through the public library system.

Staying Current

Keeping up with the Internet can be a daunting task. There are some excellent print publications available that will help you keep abreast of new Internet trends, technologies, and services. For beginners and experienced users alike, these magazines and newsletters can offer a wealth of helpful advice and information. In this appendix, we present some of our favourite Internet publications. You should also consider joining a local Internet organization or club if one exists. Several Canadian Internet organizations are listed below.

Print Publications

GENERAL INTEREST INTERNET PUBLICATIONS

Internet World Magazine

c/o Mecklermedia Corporation
20 Ketchum Street
Westport, CT
06880

Editorial: Tel: (203) 226-6967
Subscriptions Only: 1-800-573-3062
Fax: (203) 454-5840
Home Page: http://www.iw.com/mags/
iw/iwhome.htm

You can pick up Internet World at most newsstands in Canada or purchase a mail subsciption. It is published monthly. The single issue price is $5.95

Online Access

900 North Franklin Street
Suite 700
Chicago, IL
60610

Tel: (312) 573-1700
Subscriptions Only: 1-800-366-6336
                                (708) 656-8259
Fax: (312) 573-0520
E-Mail: 74514,3363@compuserve.com
                                (Subscription Inquiries)
Home Page: http://www.oamag.com/online/
                                access.html

You can pick up Online Access at most newsstands in Canada or purchase a mail subscription. It is published monthly. The single issue price is $5.95.

NetGuide

600 Community Drive
Manhasset, New York
11030
U.S.A.

Tel: (516) 562-5000
Subscriptions Only: 1-800-829-0421
Fax: (516) 562-7406
E-Mail: netmail@netguide.cmp.com
Home Page: http://techweb.cmp.com/
                                techweb/ng/current

You can pick up NetGuide at most newsstands in Canada or purchase a mail subscription. It is published monthly. The single issue price is $3.95.

The Computer Paper

Suite #8
3661 West 4th Avenue
Vancouver, B.C.
V6R 1P2

Tel: (604) 733-5596 (Vancouver)
               (403) 228-3355 (Calgary)
               (416) 588-1580 (Toronto)
               (613) 789-6431 (Ottawa)
               (514) 843-4770 (Montreal)
E-Mail: editorial@tcp.mindlink.bc.ca
               (Editorial Correspondence Only)
Home Page: http://tcp.ca

The Computer Paper is published monthly, and is available for free in computer stores and computer book stores across Canada. If you are in a remote part of the country or you simply wish to receive it by mail, you can purchase a subscription for $24.95 a year. The Computer Paper covers computers in general, but most issues have good coverage of the Internet

BUSINESS-ORIENTED INTERNET PUBLICATIONS

Internet Week

1201 Seven Locks Road
Potomac, MD 20854-2931
U.S.A.

Voice: (301) 340-1520
Fax: (301) 424-4297
Home Page: http://www.phillips.com/pbi/iw

Internet Week is published weekly both in print and on the World Wide Web. A one-year print and Web subscription is U.S.$569.00.

CommunicationsWeek/Interactive Age

600 Community Drive	Tel:	(516) 562-5000
Manhasset, New York	Home Page:	http://techweb.cmp.com/
11030		techweb/ia/current
U.S.A.		

CommunicationsWeek/Interactive Age is available on the Internet or by mail subscription. Subscription is free.

Membership Organizations

British Columbia Internet Association

P.O. Box 8024	Voice:	(604) 479-5666
Victoria, British Columbia	E-Mail:	execdir@bcia.bc.ca
V8W 3R7		(Ed Oscapella, Executive Director)
		commdir@bcia.bc.ca (Clyde Forrest, Communications Director)
	Home Page:	http://www.bcia.bc.ca/bcia

The purposes of the British Columbia Internet Association are:

(1) to support the development of a knowledge-based communications infrastructure in British Columbia

(2) to promote the development of reliable, stable and evolving Internet service throughout British Columbia with equitable access for all residents

(3) to provide a forum for discussion among providers, developers, operators and carriers associated with Internet services in British Columbia

(4) to provide advice and guidance to the government on the development and implementation of Internet services in British Columbia

(5) to promote public awareness and education about Internet services available in British Columbia to individuals, small businesses, non-profit, corporations and government

(6) to provide assistance and support to groups involved in the use, operation and evolution of Internet services in British Columbia.

(7) to monitor, research and share information to members and the general public about current developments on the Information Highway

(8) to carry on activities conducive to the achievement of the foregoing purposes

(9) to raise funds and other resources to carry out the foregoing purposes

Membership Rates:

Commercial Network Providers, TYPE I (more than 5 employees)
$1000 for one year, $500 for six months.

Commercial Internet Network Providers, TYPE II (five employees or less)
$500 for one year, $250 for six months.

Public Sector Internet Providers
$1000 for one year.

BC Government Branch/Offices
$500 for one year.

Internet Professionals (Includes people involved in Internet-enabled services like training, consulting, interface design, publishing, customer service, etc.)
$100 for one year.

Bulletin Board Operators (Non-Internet)
$100 for one year.

Non-Profit Organizations
$100 for one year.

Businesses
$100 for one year.

Internet-Using Individuals
$50 for one year.

Internet Association of Manitoba

c/o 1026 London Street
Winnipeg, Manitoba
R2K 3Y7

E-Mail: info@iweave.mb.ca
Fax: (204) 275-5806
Home Page: http://www.mbnet.mb.ca/
iweave/IAM

The Internet Association of Manitoba (IAM) is a non-profit organization formed to provide a forum for on-line users to increase their Internet knowledge and improve their Internet abilities.

Mission: The Internet Association of Manitoba exists to serve existing Internet users by providing forums where they can learn to apply emerging on-line technology to benefit themselves personally and professionally. While novice participation is welcomed, the emphasis in IAM presentations will be to extend the on-line abilities of those who already are on-line.

1995-1996 IAM Executive:

- President: gerard@solutions.net (Gerard Masse)
- Vice-President: infoman@infoman.mb.ca (Roger Rempel)
- Treasurer: gdikkema@mbnet.mb.ca (Gary Dikkema)
- Software: pickell@cyberspc.mb.ca (Stu Pickell)
- Liaison: gunter@cyberspc.mb.ca (Gunter Wenzel)
- Consultant: smythe@mbnet.mb.ca (Terry Smythe)
- Consultant: ffoidart@ustboniface.mb.ca (Firmin Foidart)
- Consultant: flegace@gatewest.net (Fred Legace)
- Webmaster: apowell@iweave.mb.ca (Adrian Powell)

Membership
$5.00 per meeting.

Calgary Internet Users Group

300 5 Ave S.W.	Voice:	(403) 261-9909
Suite 1810	E-Mail:	calpres@cadvision.com
Calgary, Alberta T2P 3C4	Home Page:	http://www.worldweb.com/Calgary/CalNet

The Calgary Internet Users Group is a nonprofit service organization dedicated to "Encouraging the use and understanding of the Internet." They meet the 3rd Thursday of every month at 7:00 PM. The location is the main auditorium of the Alberta Vocational College 332-6 Ave S.E. in downtown Calgary. Meetings are comprised primarily of presentations on Internet-related subjects with speakers drawn from the ranks of the Calgary Internet Users Group, Internet Service Providers, and industry experts. Admission to meetings is free for members, and $5 for nonmembers.

Membership Rates
The annual personal membership fee is $25.00.

The Internet Society

Internet Society	Voice:	(703) 648-9888
12020 Sunrise Valley Drive	Fax:	(703) 648-9887
Suite 210	General information:	info@isoc.org
Reston, VA 22091	Individual Membership information:	membership@isoc.org
U.S.A.	Organizational membership information:	org-membership@isoc.org
	Home Page:	http://www.isoc.org

The Internet Society is a non-profit organization with members in over 110 countries. It sponsors an annual Internet conference and publishes a bimonthly print publication called OnTheInternet. The Society's specific goals and purposes include:

- ◆ development, maintenance, evolution, and dissemination of standards for the Internet and its internetworking technologies and applications;

- ◆ growth and evolution of the Internet architecture;

- ◆ maintenance and evolution of effective administrative processes necessary for operation of the global Internet;

- ◆ education and research related to the Internet and internetworking;

- ◆ harmonization of actions and activities at international levels to facilitate the development and availability of the Internet;

- ◆ collection and dissemination of information related to the Internet and internetworking, including histories and archives;

- ◆ assisting technologically developing countries, areas, and peoples in implementing and evolving their Internet infrastructure and use;

- ◆ liaison with other organizations, governments, and the general public for coordination, collaboration, and education in effecting the above purposes.

Membership
Individual
$35 U.S. for one year.
Student
$25 U.S. for one year.
Membership includes a free subscription to OnTheInternet.

APPENDIX I

Identifying Countries on the Internet

As discussed in Chapter 5, at the extreme right of every Internet address is either a two-letter country code or a three-letter descriptive zone name. In Canada and the United States both types of addressing are used. In Canada, for example, you will see many Internet addresses that end in **.ca** (the two-letter country code for Canada). You will also see many Canadian Internet addresses that end in **.com, .org, .net,** or **.edu**. Similarly, in the United States many Internet addresses end in **.us** (the two-letter country code for the United States). You will also see many American Internet addresses that end in **.com, .org, .net, .gov, .mil,** and **.edu** (.mil and .gov are not used in Canada with one exception, **mtp.gov** belongs to the Metropolitan Toronto Police Department).

While the three-letter descriptive zone names are common in North America, most countries and territories/dependencies on other continents use two-letter country codes that have been assigned by the International Organization for Standardization in Switzerland. To help you identify Internet addresses and their countries of origin, this Appendix lists two-letter country codes that have been assigned by the International Organization for Standardization. For example, suppose you are surfing the Internet and you come across a World Wide Web site with an address like this:

http://www.simi.is

Notice that the two-letter country code in this address is **is.** To determine what country this address is from, look up the country code in the table below. You will find that **is** is the country code for Iceland.

Here is another example. Suppose you are reading a USENET newsgroup and you see an e-mail address that looks like this:

johns@tidco.co.tt

According to the list of country codes below, **tt** is the country code for Trinidad and Tobago. Therefore, you know that this e-mail address belongs to someone in Trinidad and Tobago. In the list below the code is followed by the name of the country or geographical region.

It's that easy. Have fun!

AD	Andorra
AE	United Arab Emirates
AF	Afghanistan
AG	Antigua and Barbuda
AI	Anguilla
AL	Albania
AM	Armenia
AN	Netherlands Antilles
AO	Angola
AQ	Antarctica
AR	Argentina
AS	American Samoa
AT	Austria
AU	Australia
AW	Aruba
AZ	Azerbaijan
BA	Bosnia–Herzegovina
BB	Barbados
BD	Bangladesh
BE	Belgium
BF	Burkina Faso
BG	Bulgaria
BH	Bahrain
BI	Burundi
BJ	Benin
BM	Bermuda
BN	Brunei Darussalam
BO	Bolivia
BR	Brazil
BS	Bahamas
BT	Bhutan
BV	Bouvet Island
BW	Botswana
BY	Belarus
BZ	Belize
CA	Canada

CC	Cocos (Keeling) Islands
CF	Central African Republic
CG	Congo
CH	Switzerland
CI	Ivory Coast/Côte d'Ivoire
CK	Cook Islands
CL	Chile
CM	Cameroon
CN	China
CO	Colombia
CR	Costa Rica
CU	Cuba
CV	Cape Verde
CX	Christmas Island
CY	Cyprus
CZ	Czech Republic
DE	Germany
DJ	Djibouti
DK	Denmark
DM	Dominica
DO	Dominican Republic
DZ	Algeria
EC	Ecuador
EE	Estonia
EG	Egypt
EH	Western Sahara
ER	Eritrea
ES	Spain
ET	Ethiopia
FI	Finland
FJ	Fiji
FK	Falkland Islands
FM	Micronesia
FO	Faroe Islands
FR	France
GA	Gabon

GB	United Kingdom (generally uses UK)
GD	Grenada
GE	Georgia
GF	French Guiana
GH	Ghana
GI	Gibraltar
GL	Greenland
GM	Gambia
GN	Guinea
GP	Guadeloupe
GQ	Equatorial Guinea
GR	Greece
GT	Guatemala
GU	Guam
GW	Guinea–Bissau
GY	Guyana
HK	Hong Kong
HM	Heard and McDonald Islands
HN	Honduras
HR	Croatia
HT	Haiti
HU	Hungary
ID	Indonesia
IE	Ireland
IL	Israel
IN	India
IO	British Indian Ocean Territory
IQ	Iraq
IR	Iran
IS	Iceland
IT	Italy
JM	Jamaica
JO	Jordan
JP	Japan
KE	Kenya

KG	Kyrgyz Republic
KH	Cambodia
KI	Kiribati
KM	Comoros
KN	St. Kitts and Nevis
KP	North Korea
KR	South Korea
KW	Kuwait
KY	Cayman Islands
KZ	Kazakhstan
LA	Laos
LB	Lebanon
LC	Saint Lucia
LI	Liechtenstein
LK	Sri Lanka
LR	Liberia
LS	Lesotho
LT	Lithuania
LU	Luxembourg
LV	Latvia
LY	Libya
MA	Morocco
MC	Monaco
MD	Moldova
MG	Madagascar
MH	Marshall Islands
MK	Macedonia
ML	Mali
MM	Myanmar
MN	Mongolia
MO	Macau
MP	Northern Mariana Islands
MQ	Martinique
MR	Mauritania
MS	Montserrat
MT	Malta

MU	Mauritius	RU	Russian Federation	
MV	Maldives	RW	Rwanda	
MW	Malawi	SA	Saudi Arabia	
MX	Mexico	SB	Solomon Islands	
MY	Malaysia	SC	Seychelles	
MZ	Mozambique	SD	Sudan	
NA	Namibia	SE	Sweden	
NC	New Caledonia	SG	Singapore	
NE	Niger	SH	St. Helena	
NF	Norfolk Island	SI	Slovenia	
NG	Nigeria	SJ	Svalbard and Jan Mayen Islands	
NI	Nicaragua	SK	Slovakia	
NL	Netherlands	SL	Sierra Leone	
NO	Norway	SM	San Marino	
NP	Nepal	SN	Senegal	
NR	Nauru	SO	Somalia	
NT	Neutral Zone	SR	Suriname	
NU	Niue	ST	Sao Tome and Principe	
NZ	New Zealand	SU	Soviet Union	
OM	Oman	SV	El Salvador	
PA	Panama	SY	Syria	
PE	Peru	SZ	Swaziland	
PF	French Polynesia	TC	Turks and Caicos Islands	
PG	Papua New Guinea	TD	Chad	
PH	Philippines	TF	French Southern Territories	
PK	Pakistan	TG	Togo	
PL	Poland	TH	Thailand	
PM	St. Pierre and Miquelon	TJ	Tajikistan	
PN	Pitcairn	TK	Tokelau	
PR	Puerto Rico	TM	Turkmenistan	
PT	Portugal	TN	Tunisia	
PW	Palau	TO	Tonga	
PY	Paraguay	TP	East Timor	
QA	Qatar	TR	Turkey	
RE	Reunion	TT	Trinidad and Tobago	
RO	Romania	TV	Tuvalu	

TW	Taiwan
TZ	Tanzania
UA	Ukraine
UG	Uganda
UM	U.S. Minor Outlying Islands
US	United States
UY	Uruguay
UZ	Uzbekistan
VA	Vatican City State
VC	Saint Vincent and the Grenadines
VE	Venezuela
VG	British Virgin Islands

VI	U.S. Virgin Islands
VN	Vietnam
VU	Vanuatu
WF	Wallis and Futuna Islands
WS	Samoa
YE	Yemen
YT	Mayotte
YU	Yugoslavia
ZA	South Africa
ZM	Zambia
ZR	Zaire
ZW	Zimbabwe

Canadian Internet Relay Chat Servers

This appendix contains a handy list of Canadian IRC servers that you can connect to if you are using a SLIP or PPP IRC client. You should connect to the server that is closest to you. If your closest server refuses your connection, ask your Internet access provider for advice or try one of the U.S. servers listed below. You can also seek help on the Canadian IRC Users mailing list [see below for details]. Canadian IRC servers come and go. For the most up-to-date list of operational IRC servers in Canada, consult the list maintained by Christopher Oates <oates@cs.mun.ca>. It is available on the World Wide Web:

> Christopher Oates' Canadian IRC Servers List
>
> **http://www.cs.mun.ca/irc/ca-servers.html**

Be aware that most of the IRC servers listed in the table below restrict access to Internet sites in their area. For example, the IRC server at the Memorial University of Newfoundland [**irc.cs.mun.ca**] is only available to Internet users in Newfoundland and Prince Edward Island.

Canadian IRC Servers

SERVER ADDRESS	AREA SERVED (RESTRICTIONS MAY APPLY)
irc.magic.mb.ca (Winnipeg)	Manitoba/Western Canada
irc.pangea.ca (Winnipeg)	Manitoba/Western Canada
irc.mbnet.mb.ca (Winnipeg)	Manitoba/Western Canada

SERVER ADDRESS	AREA SERVED (RESTRICTIONS MAY APPLY)
irc.io.org (Toronto)	Ontario
green.ariel.cs.yorku.ca (Toronto)	Ontario
irc.polymtl.ca (Montréal)	Québec
irc.mcgill.ca (Montréal)	Québec
irc.unb.ca (Fredericton)	New Brunswick
elk.nstn.ca (Dartmouth)	Nova Scotia
irc.cs.mun.ca (St. John's)	Newfoundland and PEI
vancouver.bc.ca.undernet.org (Vancouver)	Western Canada [Undernet Network][*]

[*] Undernet is an IRC Network that operates independently of the other IRC servers listed in this table.

U.S. IRC Servers

SERVER ADDRESS	AREAS SERVED (RESTRICTIONS MAY APPLY)
irc.eskimo.com [Seattle, Washington]	Western Canada/U.S.
cs-pub.bu.edu [Boston, Massachusetts]	Eastern Canada/U.S.
irc-2.mit.edu [Cambridge, Massachusetts]	Eastern Canada/U.S.
irc.apk.net [Cleveland, Ohio]	Eastern Canada/U.S.
irc.colorado.edu [Boulder, Colorado]	Central/Western Canada/U.S.

Canadian IRC Users Mailing List

A mailing list exists for the discussion of Internet Relay Chat in Canada. To join, send an e-mail message to **listserv@sifon.cc.mcgill.ca** and place the following command on the first line of the body of the message:
subscribe ircusers <Your First Name> <Your Last Name>
for example, **subscribe ircusers John Smith**. To remove yourself from this mailing list, send the message **unsubscribe ircusers** to **listserv@sifon.cc.mcgill.ca**.

Additional Help

For help in learning how to use IRC, check out the following sources of information:

Internet Relay Chat frequently asked questions:

http://www.kei.com/irc.html

The Internet Relay Chat Primer:

http://www.kei.com/irc/IRCprimer1.1.txt

Internet Relay Chat USENET Newsgroups:

alt.irc and **alt.irc.questions**

Internet forms

This appendix contains four forms:

◆ the application form for a subdomain from the CA Domain Registrar
   Use this when you want to apply for a subdomain under the **.ca** domain.
   This form is available at **ftp://ftp.cdnnet.ca/ca-domain/application-form**

◆ the application form for a domain from the InterNIC
   Use this when you want to apply for a **.com**, **.org**, **.edu**, or **.net** domain.
   This form is available at **ftp://rs.internic.net/templates/domain-template.txt**

◆ the application form for a Class C Network Number in Canada
   Use this when you want to apply for an IP number for your computer network. Organizations that are establishing permanent, dedicated connections to the Internet will need one or more IP numbers. When applying, you must establish a specific need for the IP number.
   This form is available at **ftp://ftp.canet.ca/canet/templates/ip-req.txt**

◆ the GC.CA Subdomain Application Form
   Use this form if you are with a federal government department.
   This form is available at **http://www.gc.ca**

Completion of these forms requires some technical knowledge. Most commercial Internet service providers will fill out and/or submit these forms for you. These forms are provided for reference purposes only. You can obtain the most recent versions of these forms on the Internet at the URLs included above.

CA Subdomain Application Form

CA Subdomain Application Instructions (Updated 1995 September 9)

This document describes the CA subdomain application form. To apply for a subdomain, please fill out an application form and submit it to the appropriate liaison from the list below. It is recommended that you edit the sample form included below and change the information as appropriate for your organization.

Your liaison may charge a fee for the registration service, and may also require further information. Organizations applying directly to the CA Registrar may be charged a fee. Currently, the registrar cannot accept telephone requests.

Please note that your application is being made on behalf of your entire organization. It is particularly important that the person in charge of your organization's corporate image approve the choice of subdomain name.

A given organization may register at most one CA subdomain, with two exceptions. The first is an allowance for a temporary overlap interval while changing from one CA subdomain name to another. This may happen, for example, when a provincial or territorial organization becomes federally incorporated and wishes to change from a third-level to a second-level subdomain name. The second exception is for an organization whose legal name has both an English form and a French form, and which wishes to apply for one CA subdomain corresponding to each form.

See below for instructions on how to obtain more information on the CA domain, such as an introduction to the domain and a list of current subdomain registrations. Consulting the list before applying will allow you to choose a subdomain name which cannot easily be confused with an existing name.

Here is a description of each field of the application form:

Subdomain:

The name of the subdomain applied for. Since the CA domain is structured according to Canadian political geography, this will be of the form "yourorg.CA", or "yourorg.province-or-territory.CA", or "yourorg.locality.province-or-territory.CA".

"province-or-territory" is one of the following provincial and territorial abbreviations, as recommended by the Department of the Secretary of State: AB, BC, MB, NB, NF, NS, NT, ON, PE, QC, SK, and YK. "locality" is the full name of a city, town, or village. Hyphens are used to replace spaces, e.g., Niagara-Falls, New-Westminster. In some situations — in particular when the locality name is very long — it may be appropriate to use the abbreviation approved by a responsible official of the government of the locality. Either the full locality name or its approved abbreviation may be used; however, it is very desirable that any particular locality should have just one subdomain name.

Here are requirements and guidelines to help determine the appropriate level of subdomain name for your organization:

(1)   second (national) level — To qualify for a second level domain, your organization must have offices or other points of presence (such as computer hosts or dial-up facilities wholly owned by your organization) in more than one province or territory, or be incorporated or chartered nationally, or own a trademark which is registered with the Canadian Registrar of Trade Marks and which is being put forward in full as the organizational part of the subdomain name.

(2)   third (provincial or territorial) level — To qualify for a third level domain, your organization must have offices or other points of presence (such as computer hosts or dial-up facilities) in more than one locality, or be incorporated or registered provincially or territorially. Provincial and terri-

torial governments, referral hospitals, and post-secondary degree- or certificate- granting educational institutions such as universities and colleges should have third level subdomain names.

(3) fourth (municipal) level — Small organizations, such as companies which do most of their business in one locality, and bulletin board systems should apply for a fourth level or municipal subdomain name, as should organizations such as local hospitals, libraries, municipal governments, and schools.

When applying for anything other than a fourth level subdomain name, please provide supporting information such as your incorporation number, office locations, etc.

"yourorg" is a string that encodes the proper name of your organization, or is your registered trademark in full. Determining the string is a matter of establishing the "corporate electronic identity" of your organization for years to come. This is something you should discuss with the individual in your organization whose authority includes the "corporate image." If the appropriate string is not immediately obvious to this person, then we suggest that you use the following steps to determine the string for which you are applying.

(1) Start with the full proper name by which your organization conducts its business. (e.g.: "AB Systems Incorporated", "University of Waterloo")

(2) Remove all the blanks. (e.g.: "ABSystemsIncorporated", "UniversityofWaterloo")

(3) Remove truly extraneous components, if there are any. (e.g.: "ABSystems", "UniversityWaterloo")

(4) If it is excessively long, abbreviate by trimming the parts whose removal will result in the least loss of recognizability outside the sphere in which your organization is already well known. (e.g.: "ABSystems", "UWaterloo")

(5) Please choose a descriptive abbreviation of your organization's name, and try to avoid a cryptic abbreviation that defeats the objective of step (4) above. To repeat, it is essential that your choice be approved by the person in charge of your organization's corporate image. If you are in doubt about your choice, ask your CA Domain Committee member to offer an opinion before you submit the application.

It is your responsibility to ensure that you have the right to use the name you have chosen. Registering a domain name does not confer any legal rights to that name; you should consider registering a trademark if you have not already done so. Any disputes between parties over the rights to use a particular name are to be settled between the contending parties using normal legal methods.

Obscene names are not permitted.

Geographical place names, such as municipality and province names, are reserved.

Legal characters are letters, digits, and the hyphen. You may mix upper and lower case, or use all upper or all lower case. Software will ignore case, and users can type in whatever case they like. You should capitalize your subdomain name as you wish it to appear in machine-generated lists, such as the return address generated in your outgoing electronic mail. Hyphens may be used to separate words if necessary or consistent with normal references to the proper name of your organization.

The CA domain registrar is the final authority on all matters relating to registration and subsequent use of your subdomain name. Your subdomain name must be approved by the CA domain registrar before it is used in network communications. If you devise further subdomains of your domain name, then you in turn will have final authority on matters relating to the use of those subdomains.

Since the CA domain was first created, the requirements and guidelines have been modified from time to time. Although all existing registrations remain in effect, some registered subdomain names might not be permitted if applied for today. New applications and voluntary applications for re-registration will be considered using the current guidelines.

Examples:

MegaCo.CA	National company.
WidgetCo.PE.CA	Provincial Company.
CityAutoLtd.Melville.SK.CA	Small business.
AlphaBetaU.MB.CA	University.

Organization:

The full name of your organization. For a for-profit corporation, the full name includes its legal element, e.g. Limited, limitée, Incorporated, incorporée, Corporation, or Société par actions de régime fédéral, or an abbreviation such as Ltd, ltée, Inc, Corp, or S.A.R.F. For a non-profit organization, depending on where it is incorporated, the name may be required to include one of the legal elements specified above, or a word such as Society, Association, or Club.

If a trademark is being proposed as the organizational part of the subdomain name, please include both the trademark and the full organization name in the Organization field as shown in this example for the subdomain coke.ca:

Organization: Coke™, Coca Cola Ltd.

You may register just one CA subdomain name, so please be very careful when proposing to use a trademark which does not cover all of your organization's activities.

Type:

Type of organization. Here are some suggested types: For-Profit Corporation

Federally Incorporated For-Profit Corporation
Provincially Incorporated For-Profit Corporation
Territorially Incorporated Non-Profit Corporation
Federally Incorporated Non-Profit Corporation
Provincially Incorporated Non-Profit Corporation
Territorially Incorporated Registered Proprietorship Proprietorship Registered For-Profit Partnership
    For-Profit Partnership
Degree granting university
Degree granting College
High School
School Provincial Government
Municipal Government
Chartered Bank
Credit Union
Hospital Referral Hospital

Description:

A short paragraph describing your organization. Please include any appropriate justification for your choice of subdomain level. For example, please state whether your corporation is federally or provincially incorporated, and whether your corporation has offices in more than one province.

    Admin-Name:
    Admin-Title:
    Admin-Postal:
    Admin-Phone:
    Admin-Fax:
    Admin-Mailbox:

The name, title, full mailing address, phone number, facsimile number, and electronic address of an administrative contact for the organization. This person is within the subdomain's organization and is the contact point for administrative and policy questions about the subdomain. This person is responsible for this application and for any future changes. We recommend that you choose a person who is expected to be around and in a position of authority for many years, and that you use a properly maintained generic electronic address.

If this person is not obviously in charge of the organization's corporate image, please include a note stating the name and position of a responsible person in the organization who has approved the choice of subdomain name.

For example:

Admin-Name:	John Smith
Admin-Title:	Administrative Assistant
Admin-Postal:	Alpha Beta University
	Dept. of Computer Science
	1234 Main St.
	Hoople, Manitoba
	M1B 2C3
Admin-Phone:	+1 (204) 555 1511
Admin-Fax:	+1 (204) 555 9095
Admin-Mailbox:	admin@AlphaBetaU.MB.CA

Tech-Name:
Tech-Title:
Tech-Postal:
Tech-Phone:
Tech-Fax:
Tech-Mailbox:

The name, title, full mailing address, telephone number, facsimile number, and electronic address of two or more technical contacts. This is the contact point for problems with the subdomain and for updating information about the subdomain. The registrar will verify changes by sending the current registration information back to the submitter and to the administrative contact. We recommend that you use a properly maintained generic electronic address.

Don't list people who hate to get electronic mail. One or more of the contacts must read their mail often enough to respond quickly, should a problem arise. For very small organizations, it is permissible to have only one technical contact. It is appropriate to have at least one contact corresponding to each of the forwarders within the organization. Forwarders are described below.

For example:

Tech-Name:	Jean Smith
Tech-Title:	Researcher
Tech-Postal:	Alpha Beta University
	Dept. of Computer Science
	1234 Main St.
	Hoople, Manitoba
	M1B 2C3
Tech-Phone:	+1 (204) 555 1512
Tech-Name:	Fred Rogers
Tech-Title:	Computing Staff
Tech-Postal:	Alpha Beta University
	Dept. of Computer Science
	1234 Main St.
	Hoople, Manitoba
	M1B 2C3

Tech-Phone:	+1 (204) 555 1513
Tech-Fax:	+1 (204) 555 9099
Tech-Mailbox:	tech@AlphaBetaU.MB.CA

Location:

The latitude and longitude of the subdomain. (This can be taken as the location of the main organizational machine, or the headquarters, or the contact persons; usually the machine is used.) Give as much precision as you know; if you can determine the location only to the nearest minute, or the nearest few minutes, that's satisfactory. Include "city" only if you are using the location of your city center, for which information is often available in an atlas, at a library, City Hall, or a nearby airport. At a minimum, please provide the location of your city center. This field is used to draw maps.

For example:

52 04 05 N / 97 37 46 W

or

52 04 N / 97 37 W city

Net-Provider:

The name of your primary network provider. Your network provider is the organization which provides your IP connectivity to the Internet. Here is a list of network providers:

ARnet
auroraNET
BC Systems
BCnet
DREnet
fONOROLA
Global-X-Change
HookUp
Information Gateway Services
MBnet
Metrix Interlink
NB*net
NLnet
NSTN
NTnet
ONet
Pacific InterConnect
PEInet
RISQ
SASK#net
UUNet Canada
westel
Wimsey

If you have no IP connectivity to the Internet but do have UUCP connectivity, specify "UUCP" as your provider. If you have no connectivity but wish to apply for a subdomain name anyway, specify "none" as your provider.

The list above will be expanded as needed. If your network provider is not on the list, have them retrieve the "net-provider" document available as described below.

Forwarder:

The forwarder fields describe how your organization can be reached FROM specified networks. This information is used to guide tasks such as the routing of electronic mail to your organization. (They do not describe how your organization sends traffic TO any network.) For the purposes of your application, there are two kinds of forwarders:

Organization-Internal Forwarder. Your organization has one or more computing systems that have direct Internet or UUCP connections. Also, all computing systems within your organization are internally connected. Please see the examples below for what to do in the case of a forwarder that cannot reach all recipients within your organization.

Organization-External Forwarder. Your organization is directly connected to network A; another organization is directly connected to both networks A and B, and has agreed to provide a forwarder that will accept mail from network B and forward it to your organization-internal forwarder in network A.

Within the application form, each forwarder specification appears as follows:

Forwarder: networkname: "forwarder_address(comment)<reference_address>";

or

Forwarder: networkname: "none";

or:

Forwarder: Internet: "DNS";

Where "networkname" is the name of the network, "forwarder_address" is the network-specific electronic address of the forwarder, "(comment)" is optional explanatory text, and "reference_address" is the electronic address of an individual to whom questions regarding the use of that forwarder may be sent. For an organization-internal forwarder, the reference will be some entity within your organization subdomain; for an organization-external forwarder, it will be the entity external to your organization that has authorized your organization to use that forwarder.

Specify forwarder fields for both the Internet and UUCP, even if you do not have access to both. For historical reasons, existing registrations may have forwarder fields for CDNnet and NetNorth.

Example 1 — Internet and UUCP connections

In this case, the organization can be reached directly from both networks.

Forwarder: Internet: "DNS";

Forwarder: UUCP: "**abunix<rob@AlphaBetaU.MB.CA>**";

When DNS (Domain Name System) is specified, please provide as supplementary information the subdomain names and IP addresses of at least two nameserver hosts (one primary and at least one secondary) for the new subdomain. See the sample application form below for an example.

Example 2 — Internet only

Here are the forwarder specifications for an organization which is directly connected to the Internet, but which has no direct UUCP connection.

Forwarder: Internet: "DNS";

Forwarder: UUCP: "none";

Example 3 — External Internet forwarder

Forwarder: Internet: "**relay.otherorg.ca<joe@otherorg.ca>**";

Forwarder: UUCP: **abunix <rob@AlphaBetaU.MB.CA>**;

Here the organization does not have direct Internet connectivity, but joe@otherorg.ca (whose organization is on the Internet) has agreed to forward mail from the Internet to the organization. In this case the CA nameserver administrator will put the appropriate MX records into the CA nameservers to make this work.

Example 4 — UUCP-only

Here is an example of the forwarder specification for an organization with a direct UUCP connection, but with no access to the Internet.

Forwarder: Internet: "none";

Forwarder: UUCP: "**abunix<rob@AlphaBetaU.MB.CA>**";

Note that in this case, your organization will not be directly addressable from the Internet. That is, your subdomain name will not appear in the DNS.

Example 5 — No connectivity

When applying for a subdomain name for your organization's future use, specify "none" for the forwarders.

Forwarder: Internet: "none';

Forwarder: UUCP: "none";

Once you establish forwarders, resubmit the application with the updated information.

Notes:

(1) In the case of direct connection to a network but lack of full organization-internal connectivity, please do not omit the forwarder specification. If you can arrange full connectivity with the help of an external organization, specify the forwarder as above. Otherwise, specify:

Forwarder: networkname: "none";

(2) Each network -administration body may have specific regulations covering the valid uses of its network. The acceptance of an application for a CA subdomain in no way alters or eliminates your obligations to adhere to the regulations for the uses of those networks.

Applications and updates may be submitted to the following contacts:

UUCP sites and unaffiliated organizations:
> Ed Hew
> CA Registry
> c/o XeniTec Consulting Services
> 199 Silver Aspen Court
> Kitchener, ON
> N2N 1H5
> E-mail: **registry@cs.utoronto.ca**, **registry@utai.uucp**, ...**!utai!registry**

UUNet Canada:
> Lynda Fincham
> UUNet Canada Inc.
> 1 Yonge Street, Suite 1400
> Toronto, ON
> M5E 1J9
> E-mail: **support@uunet.ca**

BCnet and British Columbia:
> Jason Halm
> BCnet

515 West Hastings Street, Suite 134
Vancouver, BC
V6B 5K3
E-mail: **Jason.Halm@BC.net**

ARnet and Alberta:
Geoffrey Holan
University of Alberta
Computing and Network Services
103-H General Services Building
Edmonton, AB
T6G 2H1
E-mail: **geoffrey@dc-next.ucs.ualberta.ca**
Fax: +1 (403) 492 1729
Phone: +1 (403) 492 9320

MBnet and Manitoba:
Gary Mills
Networking Group, Computer Services
Room 603, Engineering Building
University of Manitoba
Winnipeg, MB
R3T 2N2
E-mail: **mills@ccu.umanitoba.ca**

ONet:
ONet Networking
Membership Technical Support
4 Bancroft Avenue, Room 101
Toronto, ON
M5S 1A1
E-mail: **support@onet.on.ca**

RISQ and Quebec:
François Robitaille
Centre de recherche informatique de Montréal (CRIM)
1801, McGill College Avenue, Suite 800
Montreal PQ
H3A 2N4
E-mail: **f_robita@crim.ca**

NBnet and New Brunswick:
Brian Kaye
Computing Services
University of New Brunswick
P.O. Box 4400
Fredericton, NB
E3B 5A3
E-mail: **nic@unb.ca**

NSTN and Nova Scotia
Daniel MacKay
Communications Services
Dalhousie University
Halifax, NS
B3H 4H8
E-mail: **daniel@nstn.ca**

fONOROLA:

    Joseph Ghaby

    fONOROLA

    250 Albert Street, Suite 205

    Ottawa, ON

    K1P 6M1

    E-mail: **josephg@fonorola.net**

    Fax: +1 (613) 232 4329

    Phone: +1 (613) 235 3666

    Affiliation: fONOROLA

British Columbia Systems Corporation:

    Russ Forster

    Interconnect Services

    British Columbia Systems Corporation

    4000 Seymour Place

    Victoria, BC

    V8X 4S8

    E-Mail: **RForster@Galaxy.GOV.BC.CA**

    Fax: +1 (604) 389-3412

    Phone: +1 (604) 389-3186

HookUp Communications:

    Murray S. Kucherawy

    HookUp Communications

    1075 North Service Road West, Suite 207

    Oakville, ON

    L6M 2G2

    E-mail: **mskucher@hookup.net**

    Fax: +1 905 847 8420

    Phone: +1 905 847 8000 x348

SASK#net and Saskatchewan:

    Derek Andrew

    Room 35, Education Building

    University of Saskatchewan

    Saskatoon, SK

    S7N 0W0

    E-mail: **andrew@duke.usask.ca**

Other organizations:

    CA Domain Registrar

    c/o John Demco

    Department of Computer Science

    University of British Columbia

    Vancouver, BC

    V6T 1Z4

    E-mail: **ca-registrar@CDNnet.CA**

Information about the CA domain is available via electronic mail, anonymous FTP, and gopher.

To retrieve CA domain information via electronic mail, specify a line of the following form:

"index ca-domain"

or

send "ca-domain<filename>[<filename> ...]"

in the subject line or body of an electronic mail message to the CDNnet archive server. Send this message to:

archive-server@relay.CDNnet.CA

Example:

To: **archive-server@relay.CDNnet.CA**

Subject: send ca-domain Introduction Application-form

To retrieve CA domain information via anonymous FTP or gopher, use these URLs:

ftp://ftp.cdnnet.ca/ca-domain
gopher://owl.nstn.ns.ca/11/White%20Pages
gopher://gopher.fonorola.net/11/ca-domain

Here is a sample application form:

Subdomain:	AlphaBetaU.MB.CA
Organization:	Alpha Beta University
Type:	Ph.D.-granting university
Description:	Alpha Beta University is a degree-granting academic organization widely known for its program in Greek studies.
Admin-Name:	Jean Smith
Admin-Title:	Network Manager
Admin-Postal:	Alpha Beta University
	Computing Services
	1234 Main St.
	Hoople, Manitoba
	M1B 2C3
Admin-Phone:	+1 (204) 555 1511
Admin-Fax:	+1 (204) 555 9095
Admin-Mailbox:	**admin@AlphaBetaU.MB.CA**
Tech-Name:	John Smith
Tech-Title:	Systems Manager
Tech-Postal:	Alpha Beta University
	Dept. of Computer Science
	1234 Main St.
	Hoople, Manitoba
	M1B 2C3
Tech-Phone:	+1 (204) 555 1512
Tech-Fax:	+1 (204) 555 9099
Location:	52 04 05 N / 97 37 46 W
Net-Provider:	MBnet
Forwarder:	Internet: DNS;
Forwarder:	**UUCP: abunix <rob@AlphaBetaU.MB.CA>;**
Nameserver information:	hub.alphabetau.mb.ca 199.3.2.1
	relay.otherorg.ca 200.1.2.3

Robin Leblanc, Vice-President for External Affairs at Alpha Beta University, has approved the choice of subdomain name.

Application Form for a Domain from the InterNIC

[**URL ftp://rs.internic.net/templates/domain-template.txt**] [09/95]

******************** Please DO NOT REMOVE Version Number ********************

Domain Version Number: 2.0

**************** Please see attached detailed instructions ****************

******** Only for registrations under ROOT, COM, ORG, NET, EDU, GOV ********

0. (N)ew (M)odify (D)elete:
1. Purpose/Description:
2. Complete Domain Name:

Organization Using Domain Name

3a. Organization Name:
3b. Street Address:
3c. City:
3d. State.:
3e. Postal Code:
3f. Country.:

Administrative Contact

4a. NIC Handle (if known):
4b. Name (Last, First):
4c. Organization Name.:
4d. Street Address:
4e. City:
4f. State:
4g. Postal Code:
4h. Country:
4i. Phone Number:
4j. E-Mailbox:

Technical Contact

5a. NIC Handle (if known):
5b. Name (Last, First):
5c. Organization Name:
5d. Street Address:
5e. City:
5f. State:
5g. Postal Code:
5h. Country:
5i. Phone Number:
5j. E-Mailbox:

Billing Contact

6a. NIC Handle (if known):
6b. Name (Last, First):
6c. Organization Name:
6d. Street Address:

6e. City:
6f. State:
6g. Postal Code.:
6h. Country:
6i. Phone Number:
6j. E-Mailbox:

Primary Name Server

7a. Primary Server Hostname:
7b. Primary Server Netaddress:

Secondary Name Server(s)

8a. Secondary Server Hostname:
8b. Secondary Server Netaddress:

Invoice Delivery

9. (E)mail (P)ostal:

A domain name registration fee of US $100.00 is applicable. This charge will cover the $50.00 maintenance fee for two (2) years. After the two-year period, an invoice will be sent on an annual basis.

The party requesting registration of this name certifies that, to her/his knowledge, the use of this name does not violate trademark or other statutes.

Registering a domain name does not confer any legal rights to that name and any disputes between parties over the rights to use a particular name are to be settled between the contending parties using normal legal methods (see RFC 1591).

By applying for the domain name and through the use or continued use of the domain name, the applicant agrees to be bound by the terms of NSI's then current domain name policy (the "'Policy Statement'") which is available at **ftp://rs.internic.net/policy/internic/internic-domain-1.txt.**

(If this application is made through an agent, such as an Internet Service Provider, that agent accepts the responsibility to notify the applicant of the conditions on the registration of the domain name and to provide the applicant a copy of the current version of the Policy Statement, if so requested by the applicant.) The applicant acknowledges and agrees that NSI may change the terms and conditions of the Policy Statement from time to time as provided in the Policy Statement.

The applicant agrees that if the use of the domain name is challenged by any third party, or if any dispute arises under this Registration Agreement, as amended, the applicant will abide by the procedures specified in the Policy Statement.

This Registration Agreement shall be governed in all respects by and construed in accordance with the laws of the United States of America and of the State of California, without respect to its conflict of law rules. This Registration Agreement is the complete and exclusive agreement of the applicant and NSI ("parties") regarding domain names. It supersedes, and its terms govern, all prior proposals, agreements, or other communications between the parties. This Registration Agreement may only be amended as provided in the Policy Statement.

[Full instructions on completing the InterNIC application form are available at **ftp://rs.internic.net/templates/domain-template.txt.**]

Application Form for a Class C Network Number

Canadian Internet Protocal Network Number Application
for
Class C Network Number(s)
Template[8/23/93/hck]

This template is to be used to obtain a TCP/-IP number from CA*net. It supercedes Form [1/3/tjm] which should no longer be used.

This template is in two parts. The first part is a sample template and the second part is the template itself, which should be filled out carefully, using the guidelines in the sample template, and returned as indicated below.

Please fill in the template in EXACTLY the same format as shown in the sample. This information is scanned by software and any errors WILL result in delays in the issuance of the number(s) to you. In this situation, EXACTLY means EXACTLY as shown, line by line, item by item, field by field. The NIC software designed to parse the application can accept no other format. Please do not change this format in any way. Do not combine fields that are on different lines and separate them with a semi-colon; the NIC software will not handle this. Please, in this case, EXACTLY really does mean EXACTLY.

Please note that the network name is not the domain name of the network. The network name may contain dashes but no other special characters and must be less then or equal to twelve characters. This name is used as an identifier for the network in the Network Information Center (NIC) "Whois" database and will be changed by the Network Registrar if the name is already in use.

Applications may be sent by e-mail or by fax to:

CA*Net IP Registry
Email: **ipregist@canet.ca**
Fax: (416) 978 6620

If possible, send your request by e-mail. E-mail submissions allow us to automatically process the application and will therefore result in the request being processed in a shorter time than if the request is submitted by fax.

Please do not send requests to the NIC in the USA. They will be forwarded by the NIC to the Canadian IP Registry office who will then process the number. You will lose a considerable amount of time if you send your request to the NIC.

Replies will be via e-mail if the request was received through e-mail and via telephone if the request was received by fax.

In the following, the "Type of Organization" should be either "government," "educational," or "commercial" while the fifth item deals with the actual number of networks being requested. In the case of Class C addresses, IP numbers are assigned in blocks to CA*net and then reassigned to specific organizations through this template. Enter the number of Class C addresses you desire here. If you wish a Class B address, contact the IP registrar BEFORE submitting this form.

Item 6 is required for installations that are currently connected to or planning to be connected to one of the provincial networks such as MBnet, ARCnet, etc. It is used strictly to gather statistical information for CA*net and is not used for routing or any other technical purpose whatsoever. As this form is to be used by any organization in Canada to obtain an IP number or numbers, it should be left blank by those organizations not planning to join a regional network.

Thus, in the following example, the Pooh Software Company is requesting two Class C networks and planning to connect to ONet.

-------------------Sample Template----------------------------

1a. Technical Contact Name (Lastname, Firstname): Smith, John
1b. Technical Contact Title: Sr. Programmer
1c. Mail Address:
    1230 Main Street
    Toronto, Ontario; M5S 1A1
    Canada
1d. Phone: +1 (604) 432-8711
1e. Net Mailbox: smith@pooh.on.ca
 2. Network Name: pooh.on.ca
3a. Postal Address for Main/Headquarters Network Site:
    1230 Main Street
    Toronto, Ontario; M5S 1A1
    Canada
3b. Name of Organization: Pooh Software Company
 4. Type of Organization: Commercial
 5. Quantity of Network Numbers Being Requested: 2
 6. Regional Network Affiliation: ONet

Please fill out the following carefully using the above as as a guide line.

++

-------------Application Template--------------------------

1a. Technical Contact Name (Lastname, Firstname):
1b. Technical Contact Title:
1c. Mail Address:
1d. Phone:
1e. Net Mailbox:
 2. Network Name:
3a. Postal Address for Main/Headquarters Network Site:
3b. Name of Organization:
 4. Type of Organization:
 5. Quantity of Networks Being Requested:
 6. Regional Network Affiliation:

GC.CA Subdomain Application Form

GC.CA DNS Subdomain Application Instructions

(Updated June 1, 1995)

This document describes the Government of Canada (GC) Domain Name System (DNS) subdomain application form. To apply for a subdomain, please fill out an application form and submit it to the appropriate liaison (i.e. your intended Internet access service provider from the list below). If submitting an application by electronic mail, we recommend that you edit the sample form included and add the information as appropriate for your organization. If you cannot submit a completed form by e-mail, complete the application form that was forwarded to you with this application guide, and return it by mail or fax.

Your liaison may charge a fee for the registration service, and may also require further information. Unaffiliated organizations (i.e. organizations not intending to connect to the Internet, at least at this time) wishing to reserve a name for future or internal use may register directly with the GC Registrar.

Please note that your application is being made on behalf of your entire organization. As such, it is important that you are authorized to speak for your entire organization in this matter and that you obtain the agreement of all interested parties within your organization prior to submission.

Here is a description of each field of the application form:

Subdomain:

The name of the subdomain applied for. Since the GC domain is structured according to federal government organizational divisions, this will be of the form "yourorg.GC.CA".

In order to qualify as a GC subdomain, your organization should be an independent federal government organization. This includes departments, but may also include separately identifiable portions of departments with distinct and well differentiated mission statements, usually reporting to the most senior level of departmental management (i.e. the deputy minister). Examples include special operating agencies (e.g. GTIS), independent commissions (e.g. CRTC), and boards.

The GC domain does not include Crown corporations (e.g. Post Office, Air Canada, CBC) or other government organizations that report directly to Parliament.

Once a subdomain name has been allocated, the name space may be further sub-divided by your organization as deemed necessary for administrative purposes.

"yourorg" is a string that encodes the proper name of your organization. Determining the string is a matter of establishing the "corporate electronic identity" of your organization for years to come. It is best to chose a string that most readily identifies you in the mind of other government organizations, companies and the segment(s) of the public with which your organization most often deals with. In addition to the "significance" of the string, another consideration is the length of the string. The electronic names resulting from the use of your domain name may need to be printed on business cards, and may need to be typed for each instance of communication initiated by some users in other organizations wishing to communicate with your organization. The selection of this string may be something you should discuss with the individual in your organization whose authority includes the "corporate image."

In some cases, your organization's officially recognized acronym (e.g. RCMP) will serve this function very well.

If the acronym is not bilingual (e.g. RCMP), there are two possible alternatives:

(1)   Apply for your subdomain with your preferred name, French or English, (e.g. RCMP.GC.CA) and have the second language acronym as your alias name (e.g. GRC.GC.CA). This will require duplicate entries to be maintained in your DNS for each host.

(2) Apply for your subdomain including both the French and English version of the acronym separated by a hyphen (e.g. RCMP-GRC.GC.CA or GRC-RCMP.GC.CA).

If your organizational acronym is considered too cryptic to adequately identify your organization to its full intended audience, the following guidelines may be used to assist in your selection:

(1) Start with the full proper name by which your organization conducts its business.

(2) Remove all the blanks.

(3) Remove truly extraneous components, if there are any.

(4) If it is excessively long, abbreviate by trimming the parts whose removal will result in the least loss of recognizability outside the sphere in which your organization is already well known.

It is your responsibility to ensure that you have the right to use the name you have chosen. The GC registrar will not issue a subdomain name to your organization that is in conflict with an officially recognized title (including the acronym) of another federal government organization.

The following additional general rules apply:

(1) Obscene names are not permitted.

(2) Legal characters are letters, digits, and the hyphen. You may mix upper and lower case, or use all upper or all lower case. Software will ignore case, and users can type in whatever case they like. You should capitalize your subdomain name as you wish it to appear in machine-generated lists, such as the return address generated in your outgoing electronic mail. Hyphens may be used to separate words if necessary or consistent with normal references to the proper name of your organization.

The GC domain registrar is the final authority on all matters relating to registration and subsequent use of your subdomain name. Your subdomain name must be approved by the GC domain registrar before it is used in network communications. If you devise further subdomains of your domain name, then you in turn will have final authority on matters relating to the use of those subdomains.

Prior to the creation of the GC domain, many federal organizations registered directly under the CA domain. Voluntary applications for re-registration under the GC domain will be considered and coordinated with the CA domain registrar.

Alias (if required):

Refer to alternative #(1) for handing non-bilingual acronyms (above, under Subdomain).

Organization:

The full name of your organization.

Type:

Type of organization.
For example:
Department
Special Operating Agency
Commission
Board

Description:

A short paragraph describing your organization. For organizations other than federal government departments, this paragraph should also describe the department with which your organization is affiliated, and an indication of why your organization is considered independent of the department for the purposes of the allocation of GC subdomains.

Admin-Name:

The name, title, full mailing address, phone number, facsimile number, and electronic address of the administrative contact for the organization. This person is within the subdomain's organization and is the contact point for administrative and policy questions about the subdomain. This person is responsible for this application and for any future changes. This person should occupy a position of considerable responsibility within your organization, and should typically be the person responsible for all telecommunications and informatics matters within your organization. Note that this information must be kept current and that any changes should be submitted to the GC Registrar.

For example:

```
Admin-Name:      Joan Smith
Admin-Title:     Director General, Information Technology
Admin-Postal:    Education Canada
                 1234 Main St.
                 Ottawa, Ontario
                 M1B 2C3
Admin-Phone:     +1 (613) 990 1511
Admin-Fax:       +1 (613) 990 9095
Admin-Mailbox:   jsmith@Edu.GC.CA
```

Tech-Name:

The names, titles, full mailing addresses, telephone numbers, facsimile numbers, and electronic addresses of two or more technical contacts. These are the contact points for problems with the subdomain and for updating information about the subdomain. The registrar will verify changes by sending the current registration information back to the submitter and to the administrative contact. We recommend that you use a properly maintained generic electronic address. Note that this information must be kept current and that any changes should be submitted to the GC Registrar.

Don't list people who hate to get electronic mail. One or more of the contacts must read their mail often enough to respond quickly, should a problem arise. For very small organizations, it is permissible to have only one technical contact.

For example:

```
Tech-Name:       John Smith
Tech-Title:      Network Administrator
Tech-Postal:     Education Canada
                 Network Operations
                 1234 Main St.
                 Ottawa, Ontario
                 M1B 2C3
Tech-Phone:      +1 (613) 990 1512
Tech-Fax:        +1 (613) 990 9097
Tech-Mailbox:    admin@Edu.GC.CA
Tech-Name:       Fred Rogers
Tech-Title:      Network Analyst
Tech-Postal:     Education Canada
                 Network Engineering
                 1234 Main St.
                 Ottawa, Ontario
                 M1B 2C3
Tech-Phone:      +1 (613) 990 1513
Tech-Fax:        +1 (613) 990 9099
Tech-Mailbox:    frogers@Edu.GC.CA
```

Net-Provider:

The name of your primary network provider. Your network provider is the organization which provides, or will provide, your IP connectivity to the Internet. Here is a sample list of network providers for Internet connectivity:

ARnet	NB*net
BC Systems	NLnet
BCnet	NSTN
DREnet	ONet
fONOROLA	PEInet
GTIS (GENet)	RISQ
HookUp	SASK#net
MBnet	UUNet Canada

If you have no IP connectivity to the Internet but do have UUCP connectivity, specify "UUCP" as your provider.

If you have no connectivity but wish to apply for a subdomain name anyway, specify "none" as your provider. No further information would be required at this time but the application must be updated when connectivity is needed.

If you have connectivity, the balance of the application must be completed showing nameserver or MX record information and IN-ADDR.ARPA instructions.

Nameserver Information:

The hostname and IP address of your primary and secondary name servers must be provided for pointers to be set in the GC.CA DNS server for passing delegation of authority. The CPUType/OpSys information is required for completing the IN-ADDR.ARPA form. GTIS can provide a secondary nameserver if requested.

For example:

Primary: (Hostname) onet.on.ca (IP Address) 128.100.102.112 (CPUType/OpSys) SUN 4/75 / SUN OS 4.1.1

Secondary: (Hostname) relay.srv.gc.ca (IP Address) 192.197.83.1 (CPUType/OpSys) DEC/ALPHA OSF1

MX Record:

If you are not directly connected to the Internet, you may still require an MX (Mail Exchanger) record to be entered in the GC.CA DNS server.

For example:

MX Record : acme.gc.ca. IN MX 10 sentinel.synapse.net. IN MX 20 nic.fonorola.net.

*.acme.gc.ca. IN MX 10 sentinel.synapse.net. IN MX 20 nic.fonorola.net.

IN-ADDR.ARPA Registration:

Your network numbers should be registered in the IN-ADDR.ARPA domain. This is to provide a guaranteed method to perform Host Address to Host Name mapping. A template application can be obtained from **hostmaster@nic.ddn.mil** or from the GC.CA DNS Registrar. GTIS will process this application if requested by the client.

For example:

IN-ADDR.ARPA Registration: (Select one)

A. Client to forward application

B. GTIS to forward application for client — non-GENet applicants MUST provide their IP network numbers to be registered:

_____

Applications and updates may be submitted to

GC.CA Domain Registrar
Government Telecommunications and Informatics Services
365 Laurier Avenue West
Ottawa, Ontario
K1A 0C8
Phone: +1 (613) 998-5563
FAX: +1 (613) 990-4120
E-mail: **registry@gc.ca**

Mailing List Software Commands

Discussion Lists: Mail Server Commands
Version 1.26
July 1, 1995
James Milles
Saint Louis University Law Library
millesjg@sluvca.slu.edu

1. E-mail discussion lists constitute one of the most popular methods of group communication on the Internet. Discussion lists support group communication by providing, at minimum, two basic functions: (1) the ability to distribute a message to a group of people by sending it to a single, central address, and (2) the ability to quietly join and leave the list at any time.

1.1. In order to provide these separate functions, an e-mail discussion list typically has two addresses associated with it: (1) a "listname address," the address to which you send any messages that you intend to be read by the list subscribers; and (2) an "administrative address," the address to which you send any commands or requests that affect your subscription to the list. It is easy to remember this distinction by thinking of your local newspaper: the first address is somewhat analogous to sending a "letter to the editor," while the second is like sending a letter to the newspaper's subscription office.

1.2. With most discussion lists, the "administrative address" is a computer program that allows the subscriber to subscribe and unsubscribe automatically, without external intervention. There are at least five popular mail server programs used to manage Internet discussion lists: REVISED LISTSERV (also called BITNET LISTSERV), UNIX ListProcessor (or Listproc), Mailbase, Mailserv, and Majordomo. The commands for subscribing and unsubscribing under most of these programs are the same; however, other useful commands differ greatly from one program to another, and some programs support features that others do not.

1.3. This document does not describe all the features supported by any of these programs, only those most commonly used. For more information on any of these programs, send a message containing only the word "help" to the appropriate mail server. Additional programs and commands will be added in future revisions of this document.

1.4. This document also does not deal with discussion lists to which one subscribes by sending a message to "[listname]-request," sometimes referred to as "Internet lists." There are a great many discussion lists of this type; some are distribution lists maintained manually by the listowner, while others use some form of mailer software ranging from a simple script to a fairly sophisticated mailing list program. Some require that subscription requests be placed in the message text; others require them to be included in the ((Subject:)) line. Because of the variety of methods of maintaining these lists, it is impossible to generalize about their command features. However, as a rule, assume that any discussion list with an administrative address of "[listname]-request" is maintained manually by a human being. Accordingly, you should subscribe by sending a friendly message in plain English to "[listname]-request." If a program responds with instructions for subscribing, follow the instructions.

1.5. The latest version of this document is available by e-mail and by anonymous ftp:

E-mail: Send a message containing only the line

GET MAILSER CMD NETTRAIN F=MAIL
to **LISTSERV@UBVM.cc.buffalo.edu**.

FTP: Anonymous ftp to **ubvm.cc.buffalo.edu**
cd /nettrain
get mailser.cmd

or

anonymous ftp to **sluaxa.slu.edu**
cd /pub/millesjg
get mailser.cmd
Web:**http://lawlib.slu.edu/home.htm**

2. When you subscribe to a list, you will typically receive a "welcome" message describing the purpose of the list and telling you how to unsubscribe. Save this message! It tells you which program the discussion list is run under and how to get further help.

2.1. Mail servers can be confusing. Many people use the term "listserv" generically, to refer to any list mail server program. To make things worse, the UNIX ListProcessor (listproc) program was originally called "listserv," just like REVISED LISTSERV. Many listproc hosts are still configured with the name "listserv" and will accept commands addressed to "listserv@[host]" as well as to the correct name, "listproc@[host]."

2.2. Usually — but not always — you can find out which program a discussion list is run under by examining the message headers. For instance, listproc lists should include a line saying "UNIX ListProcessor." However, the best practice is to save any "welcome" message you receive when you subscribe and to note at that time which set of commands is applicable.

3. Remember to send all commands to the "administrative address" — [mailserver]@[host] — not to the "listname address." [Mailserver] is the program that maintains the list (either Listproc, LISTSERV, mailbase, mailserv or majordomo); [host] is the address of the host computer (for example, **ucdavis.edu** or **cleo.murdoch.edu.au**).

3.1. Be sure to leave the ((Subject:)) line blank and to delete any signature file if your mailer allows you to do so.

3.2. Always include the name of the list in the message to (([mailserver]@[host].)) Most mailserver sites maintain many different discussion lists, and it is essential that you tell the mail server which list you are talking about.

3.3. For instance, to join the discussion list **law-lib@ucdavis.edu**, send an e-mail message containing only the command

SUBSCRIBE LAW-LIB John Doe
to **listproc@ucdavis.edu**.

The other examples used below are
INT-LAW@UMINN1.BITNET (REVISED LISTSERV),
law-europe@mailbase.ac.uk (Mailbase),
envirolaw@oregon.uoregon.edu (Mailserv), and
elaw-j@cleo.murdoch.edu.au (Majordomo).

4. For information on how to obtain and install these discussion list packages and many others, see the FAQ "Mail Archive Server Software List: A Summary of Available Mail Archive Server Software" by Piero Serini, available by anonymous ftp from **rtfm.mit.edu**, directory **/pub/usenet/news.answers/mail/archive-servers, file faq**.

Join a list:

Listproc:	SUBSCRIBE [listname] Firstname Lastname
	(e.g., SUBSCRIBE LAW-LIB John Doe)
LISTSERV:	SUBSCRIBE [listname] Firstname Lastname
	(e.g., SUBSCRIBE INT-LAW John Doe)
Mailbase:	JOIN [listname] Firstname Lastname
	(e.g., JOIN LAW-EUROPE John Doe)
Mailserv:	SUBSCRIBE [listname] Firstname Lastname
	(e.g., SUBSCRIBE ENVIROLAW John Doe)
	Optionally, include the e-mail address at which you wish to receive list mail:
	SUBSCRIBE [listname] Firstname Lastname [address]
Majordomo:	SUBSCRIBE [listname]
	(e.g., SUBSCRIBE ELAW-J)
	Optionally, include the e-mail address at which you wish to receive list mail:
	SUBSCRIBE [listname] [address]

Leave a list:

Listproc:	UNSUBSCRIBE [listname]
LISTSERV:	SIGNOFF [listname]
	or
	UNSUBSCRIBE [listname]
Mailbase:	LEAVE [listname]
Mailserv:	UNSUBSCRIBE [listname]
	(UNSUBSCRIBE [listname] [address] if you subscribed under a different e-mail address.)
Majordomo:	UNSUBSCRIBE [listname]
	(UNSUBSCRIBE [listname] [address] if you subscribed under a different e-mail address.)

Receive the list in digest format (multiple messages compiled into a single mailing, usually daily or weekly):

Listproc:	SET [listname] MAIL DIGEST
LISTSERV:	SET [listname] DIGEST
Mailbase:	Not supported.
Mailserv:	Not supported.
Majordomo:	SUBSCRIBE [listname]-DIGEST
	In the same message, unsubscribe from the undigested version:
	UNSUBSCRIBE [listname]

(Note: with those programs that support the digest option, whether or not to offer the digest format is within the discretion of the listowner; consequently, not all lists offer digests.)

Cancel digest format; receive the list as separate mailings:

Listproc:	SET [listname] MAIL ACK
LISTSERV:	SET [listname] MAIL
Mailbase:	Not supported.
Mailserv:	Not supported.
Majordomo:	UNSUBSCRIBE [listname]-DIGEST
	In the same message, subscribe to the undigested version:
	SUBSCRIBE [listname]

Suspend mail temporarily (without unsubscribing):

Listproc:	SET [listname] MAIL POSTPONE
LISTSERV:	SET [listname] NOMAIL
Mailbase:	SUSPEND MAIL [listname]
Mailserv:	Not supported.
Majordomo:	Not supported.

Resume receipt of messages:

Listproc:	SET [listname] MAIL ACK
	or
	SET [listname] MAIL NOACK
	or
	SET [listname] MAIL DIGEST
LISTSERV:	SET [listname] MAIL
	or
	SET [listname] DIGEST

Mailbase:	RESUME MAIL [listname]
Mailserv:	Not supported.
Majordomo:	Not supported.

Receive copies of your own messages:

Listproc:	SET [listname] MAIL ACK
LISTSERV:	SET [listname] REPRO
	(to simply receive an automatic acknowledgement that your message has been sent to the list, use:)
	SET [listname] ACK
Mailbase:	Standard feature; you always receive your own messages.
Mailserv:	Same as mailbase.
Majordomo:	Same as mailbase.

Do not receive copies of your own messages:

Listproc:	SET [listname] MAIL NOACK
LISTSERV:	SET [listname] NOREPRO
Mailbase:	Not supported.
Mailserv:	Not supported.
Majordomo:	Not supported.

Obtain a list of subscribers:

Listproc:	RECIPIENTS [listname]
LISTSERV:	REVIEW [listname] F=MAIL
	Can also be sorted by name or by country:
	REVIEW [listname] BY NAME F=MAIL
	or
	REVIEW [listname] BY COUNTRY F=MAIL
Mailbase:	REVIEW [listname]
Mailserv:	SEND/LIST [listname]
Majordomo:	WHO [listname]

Hide your address, so that it does not appear on the list of subscribers:

Listproc:	SET [listname] CONCEAL YES
	To reverse this command, use:
	SET [listname] CONCEAL NO
LISTSERV:	SET [listname] CONCEAL
	To reverse this command, use:
	SET [listname] NOCONCEAL
Mailbase:	Not supported.
Mailserv:	Not supported.
Majordomo:	Not supported.

Obtain a list of lists maintained by this mail server:

Listproc:	LISTS
LISTSERV:	LISTS

To obtain a list of all known LISTSERV lists, send the command
LISTS GLOBAL;
to search for LISTSERV lists with a given keyword or character string in the description, send the command
LISTS GLOBAL /[keyword],
e.g., LISTS GLOBAL /LAW.

Mailbase:	LISTS
Mailserv:	DIRECTORY/LIST
Majordomo:	LISTS

Obtain a listing of archive files for a particular list:

Listproc:	INDEX [listname]
LISTSERV:	INDEX [listname]
Mailbase:	INDEX [listname]
Mailserv:	INDEX [listname]
Majordomo:	INDEX [listname]

Retrieve an archive file:

Listproc:	GET [listname] [filename]
	(e.g., GET LAW-LIB feb94)
LISTSERV:	GET [filename] [filetype] [listname] F=MAIL
	(e.g., GET INT-LAW LOG9406 INT-LAW F=MAIL)
Mailbase:	SEND [listname] [filename]
	(e.g., SEND LAW-EUROPE 05-1994)
Mailserv:	SEND [listname] [filename]
	(e.g., SEND ENVIROLAW smith.txt)
Majordomo:	GET [listname] [filename]
	(e.g., GET ELAW-J BOYLE.TXT)

Search the archives for keywords (where available—some lists do not keep archives):

Listproc:	SEARCH [listname] "[keywords]"

Boolean searches are possible using the symbols "&" (and), "|" (or), and "~" (not). For example, to search for "mead" or "mdc" in law-lib, use the command SEARCH LAW-LIB "mead | mdc"

LISTSERV: LISTSERV uses a sophisticated and powerful search engine that does lots of neat things like finding "sounds like" matches; however, it uses a difficult, batch-coded search language to construct queries. I find it useful to keep a "template" file in my Internet account and then edit the file as appropriate when I need to do a search. Here is the search file:

// JOB Echo=No
Database Search DD=Rules
//Rules DD*
Search nafta in int-law since 93/6/1
Index
/*

To run a search, send this file in an e-mail message to ((LISTSERV@[host].)) The Search line can be modified as needed. The date is optional; Boolean combinations, nesting with parentheses, and a great number of other capabilities are supported. For a full

description of LISTSERV search functions, send the command
GET LISTDB MEMO F=MAIL to
LISTSERV@UMINN1.BITNET.
Once you have received a list of messages matching your query, send another message to
LISTSERV@[host]
to retrieve the specific messages you want:
// JOB Echo=No
Database Search DD=Rules
//Rules DD *
Search nafta in int-law since 93/6/1
Print all of 636 637 640
/*

Mailbase:	Archives of Mailbase lists are searchable through the Mailbase Gopher (**gopher mail-base.ac.uk**). Mailbase does not support batch searching by e-mail request.
Mailserv:	Not supported.
Majordomo:	Not supported.

Using Windows 95 With An Existing Internet Service Provider

The instructions that follow are provided to give you an idea of what is involved in getting Windows 95 to work with an Internet service provider other than Microsoft. These instructions are specific to InfoRamp and will not work with your own ISP, since the domain address, domain name server, and other details will be different. We provide these instructions here to give you an idea of what is involved.

This information has been reprinted with the kind permission of InfoRamp.

InfoRamp

134 Adelaide Street East, Suite 207, Toronto, Ontario M5C 1K9

Voice: (416) 363-9100 Fax: (416) 363-3551 Support/Sales: **staff@inforamp.net**

Configuring Windows 95 for InfoRamp

PRE-INSTALL: Have your WIN95 install disks 11 to 13 or WIN95 CD ROM ready.

Setting up the Network

I. Installing the Network

    A.   Click on the **Start** button.

    B.   Select **Settings**.

    C.   Select **Control Panel**.

    D.   Double click on the **Network** icon.

You should now see a new window labeled **Network** and three tabs labeled **Configuration**, **Identification**, and **Access Control**. Just below that you should see a white window labeled **The Following Network Components are Installed**: and a list of components.

◈InfoRamp

The following components must be listed before we can proceed:

A. Dial-Up Adapter
B. TIC-IP (if you are on a local area network, then this line should read Dial-Up Adapter -> TCP/IP)

If you are missing any of the two above, then you need to install them.

A. Single click the **Add** button.
B. Double click on **Adapter**.
C. Select **Microsoft** from the list of manufacturers on the left.
D. Select **Dial-Up Adapter** from the list of Network Adapters on the right.
E. Click on **OK**. Windows will be busy for 5–10 seconds; be patient.

A. Single click on the **Add** button.
B. Double click on **Protocol**.
C. Select **Microsoft** from the list of manufacturers on the left.
D. Select **TCP/IP** from the list of network protocols on the right.
E. Click on **OK**. Windows will be busy for 5–10 seconds; be patient.

II. You should now be back at the **Network** window.

A. Double click on **Dial-Up Adapter**.
B. Select **Bindings** from the pull tabs at the top of the window.
C. Make sure that *only* **TCP/IP** has a check mark beside it. If there are any other entries present, ensure they are "unchecked."
D. Click on **OK** at the bottom right corner of the screen.

III. You should now be back at the **Network** window. Double click on **TCP/IP** or **Dial up Adapter->TCP/IP**, whichever one is listed.

IV. You should see a new window labeled **TCP/IP Properties** and six pull tabs at the top of the screen.

A. Click on the **IP Address** top pull tab. Ensure that "Obtain an IP address automatically" is selected.
B. Click on the **WINS Configuration** top pull tab. Ensure that **Disable WINS Resolution** is selected (the top choice).

C. Click on the **Gateway** top pull tab. Enter **198.53.144.1** under **New Gateway**, and then single click on the **Add** button. You should now see **198.53.144.1** in the **Installed Gateways** box.

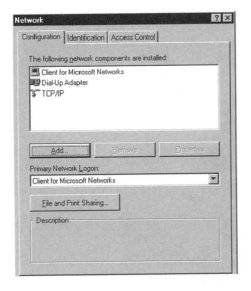

D. Click on the **DNS Configuration** top pull tab. Ensure that the **Enable DNS** check box is selected. Under the **Host**: field, type **PC**. Under the **Domain**: field, type **inforamp.net**. Enter **198.53.144.2** under **Server Search Order**, then single click on **Add**. Enter **198.53.144.3** under **Server Search Order**, then single click on **Add**. You will now have two numbers in the **Server Search Order** box.

E. Under the **Domain Suffix Search Order** list, key **inforamp.net**, and click on **Add**. You will now have **inforamp.net** in the **Domain Search Order** box.

F. Click on the **Bindings** top pull tab. Ensure that **Client for Microsoft Networks** is selected with a check mark.

G. Click on the **Advanced** top pull tab. Ensure that **Set this protocol to be the default protocol** is selected with a check mark.

H. Single click on **OK** at the bottom of the screen. You should now be back at the **Network** window.

I. Single click on **OK** once again, to close the **Network Setup**.

J. Windows 95 will not prompt you for your install disks/CD ROM. It will then copy some files from the install disks.

K. You will then be prompted with a window that says that you must restart your computer before the new settings will take effect. Restart your computer by clicking on **YES**.

Setting up Dial-Up-Networking

I. Ensure Dial-Up Networking is installed:

    A. Click on the **Start** button, then **Programs**, then **Accessories**, and then select **Dial-Up Networking**. If you cannot find it, then you will need to install it.

    B. What follows are instructions on how to install it from the Windows 95 install disks/CD ROM. You can skip the following if you already have Dial-Up Networking installed.

        1. Single click on the **Start** button, then **Settings**, then **Control Panel**.

        2. Double click on **Add/Remove Programs**.

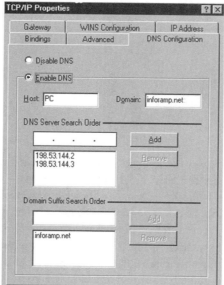

        3. Select the **Windows Setup** top pull tab.

        4. Single click on **Communications** in the list of components. Single click on the button. Ensure that **Dial-Up Networking** is checked. Click **OK**, then **OK** once more. You will then be prompted for your WIN95 install disks or your WIN95 CD ROM.

II. Click on **Start** button, then click on **Programs**, then **Accessories,** and then select **Dial-Up Networking**. Note: If Windows 95 asks you to install a modem, follow the instructions on your screen to install your modem. If you have any troubles with this, please give us a call before continuing.

III. This is assuming that you already have a modem installed on your PC.

    A. Double click on **Make New Connection**.

    B. Enter **inforamp** as the name of the computer you are dialing.

    C. Choose your modem from the **Select a Modem** list, and click on **Next**.

D. If you are calling from the 905 area code *and* you are using a local 10-digit number to call Inforamp, then enter **905** in the **Area Code** box. Otherwise, enter **416** in the **Area Code** box.

E. In the phone number slot, enter either **363-2815** (if you are calling from the 416 area code) or **416-363-2815** (if you are calling from outside the 416 area code).

F. Click on **Next**, then **Finish**. You should now be back at the **Dial-Up Networking** window.

G. Single click on the **InfoRamp** connection icon.

H. Select **File** from the pull down menu, and click on **Properties**.

I. Click on **Configure**.

J. Select the **Connection** pull tab.

K. Ensure **Disconnect a call if idle for more than 30 mins** is checked.

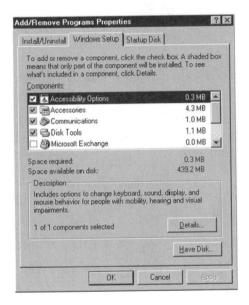

L. Select the **Options** pull tab. Select **Bring up terminal window **AFTER** dialing**. Ensure you selected **AFTER** dialing. Click on **OK**. You should now be at the **Inforamp** window.

M. Click on **Server Type**. Uncheck (take off the check mark) for **Log on to Network**.

N. Uncheck **NetBEUI** and **IPX/SPX Compatible**.

O. Click **OK**, and then **OK** once more.

IV. You are now ready to try out your connection! Double click on the **Inforamp** connection icon.

V. Now you should see a window that says **Connect to**. The **Username** and **Password** fields within this window are not used for your connection to InfoRamp; ignore them. Just click on **Connect**.

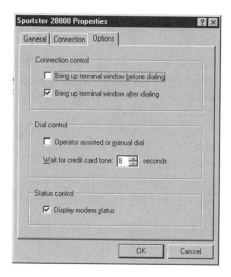

VI. You should now hear your modem dial the phone. Hit **Enter** a few times until a **Username**: prompt appears.

VII. Type in your username, and hit **Enter**. Remember, your username does not include the **@inforamp.net** at the end — this is your mail address. So if your username is **win95**, your e-mail address is **win95@inforamp.net**, and you log in with **win95**. Ensure that your username and password are in lowercase.

VIII. You will then be prompted for your password. Key it in, and hit **Enter**. For security reasons, you will not see your password as it is keyed in.

IX. You will then see a prompt similar to **ts3>**. It may be **ts4**, **ts10**, or whatever. It does not matter.

X. Key in **ppp default** and hit **Enter**. Then click **Continue**. Please note that just before you click on **Continue** you may see some "garbage" on the screen; do not worry about this; it is just Inforamp's computer speaking the "PPP language" to your computer.

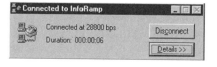

Within a few moments, you will see a message saying that you are connected. You will also see a timer, incrementing, showing your connection length. You are now on the Internet. Minimize that window (two buttons to the left of the **X** at the top right of the current window) and click on any of the InfoRamp icons. Welcome to the Internet and happy surfing!

If you run into any trouble, feel free to call us at (416) 363-9100.

Automating Your Log-on Further

In the instructions, InfoRamp requires you to enter the user ID and password separately. You can completely automate this process by setting up a "script" that will automatically have Windows 95 provide your user ID, password, and any special log-in instructions to your ISP. You should only do this if you are familiar with the concept of "scripting" or have some programming experience. You might also seek guidance from your ISP to see if they have a script available to you, so that you do not have to set one up on your own.

The script interacts, in our case, with the ISP InfoRamp as soon as Windows 95 connects, in order to provide the user ID, password, and other information necessary to establish the PPP connection. To set up this script, do the following:

◆ *Turn off the option "Bring up terminal window after dialing" as found in step III above.*

◆ *In your notepad, prepare a file that contains the following. Note that the following is prepared specifically for InfoRamp, and you will likely have to change it for the specific prompts used by your ISP.*

```
proc main
integer nTries = 3
string szLogin = "sername:"
integer nLoginTimeout = 3
string szPW = "assword:"
integer nPWTimeout = 3
string szPrompt = ">"
integer nPromptTimeout = 3
string szConnect = "ppp default"
boolean bUseSlip = TRUE
delay 2
transmit "^M^M"
while 0 < nTries do
waitfor szLogin then DoLogin
until nLoginTimeout
TryAgain:
transmit "^M" ; ping
nTries = nTries — 1
endwhile
goto BailOut
DoLogin:
transmit $USERID, raw
transmit "^M"
waitfor szPW until nPWTimeout
if FALSE == $SUCCESS then
goto TryAgain
endif
transmit $PASSWORD, raw
transmit "^M"
```

```
waitfor szPrompt
transmit szConnect, raw
transmit "^M"
if bUseSlip then
set ipaddr getip
endif
goto Done
BailOut:
set screen keyboard on
halt
Done:
endproc
```

◆ *Save the file above into the **\Program Files\Accessories** directory under the name **Inforamp.scp**.*

The next time you use Windows 95, you will find that all you have to do is click one button to link into the Internet via your ISP.

Glossary

.ab.ca Organizations located in Alberta and registered under the Alberta subdomain.

.bc.ca Organizations located in British Columbia and registered under the British Columbia subdomain.

.ca Organizations registered in the Canadian domain; usually organizations that are national in scope or are federally incorporated.

.com Organizations registered in the commercial domain.

.edu Organizations registered in the educational domain.

.gc.ca Organizations registered in the Canadian government domain.

.gov Organizations registered in the government domain.

.int Organizations registered in the international organizations domain.

.mb.ca Organizations located in Manitoba and registered under the Manitoba subdomain.

.mil Organizations registered in the U.S. military domain.

.nb.ca Organizations located in New Brunswick and registered under the New Brunswick subdomain.

.net Organizations registered in the network domain; often the domain in which Internet service providers register.

.ns.ca Organizations located in Nova Scotia and registered under the Nova Scotia subdomain.

.nt.ca Organizations located in the Northwest Territories and registered under the Northwest Territories subdomain.

.nu.ca Organizations located in Nunavut and registered under the Nunavut subdomain.

.on.ca Organizations located in Ontario and registered under the Ontario subdomain.

.org Organizations registered in the "other" domain, primarily not-for-profit groups.

.pe.ca Organizations located in Prince Edward Island and registered under the Prince Edward Island subdomain.

.qc.ca Organizations located in Quebec and registered under the Quebec subdomain.

.sk.ca Organizations located in Saskatchewan and registered under the Saskatchewan subdomain.

.yk.ca Organizations located in Yukon and registered under the Yukon subdomain.

Archie A program that permits you to search, by computer file name, computer file archives around the Internet.

ATM Asynchronous transfer mode, an emerging technology now being deployed by telephone companies that permits extremely fast data communication speeds.

AUP Acceptable use policies, policies that were in place as recently as two years ago on parts of the Internet, and that restricted use of the network to research and education purposes only. AUPs restricting business on the Internet are now pretty well extinct, but ISPs now put in place AUPs that pre-scribe acceptable network behavior.

bandwidth A term used to describe the amount of information that we can get through our communication networks.

baud A term used to measure the speed at which a modem can transmit and receive information.

BBS Bulletin board system, a computer-based system that permits people to exchange e-mail, discuss topics within discussion groups, or download computer files or software. There are thousands of BBSs across Canada, many of which permit you to send and to receive Internet e-mail as well as information from selected USENET newsgroups.

binary enclosure or file A program, document, spreadsheet, or other type of computer file that has been included in an e-mail message in either binhex, MIME, or uuencoded format.

binhex A program used to convert a binary enclosure or computer file into a special text format so that the binary enclosure or file can be sent through e-mail. Many e-mail programs support binhex capability.

BITNET A global network separate from the Internet that links academic institutions and research organizations worldwide. A system that emerged in the 1980s, BITNET's role is rapidly decreasing with the growth of the Internet.

bookmark A feature found in Gopher and Web client software that permits you to keep track easily of sites to which you wish to return.

bps Bits per second, a measure of speed of transmission.

browser software A client software that you can use to travel through the World Wide Web; also known **as** Web browsers, the most popular of which are Netscape and Mosaic.

caching A feature found with many Web browsers that keeps a copy, on your hard disk, of Web pages that you have previously visited. The next time you visit the site, the page is retrieved from your computer rather than through the Internet. This speeds up your use of the Web dramatically.

CD-ROM Compact disc-read only memory, small discs like compact discs, that hold up to 600+ megabytes of information.

client/server A type of computing in which a client computer runs a program that acts on behalf of a user to access data located on a server computer. Client/server computing is the cornerstone of the Internet, so that you can use one client (i.e., a Web browser) to access many servers (i.e., Web sites) around the globe.

closed list An electronic mailing list that requires you to meet some type of qualification in order to join.

computer protocol An agreed-upon definition on how a particular piece of computer hardware and software should work. Protocols are either agreed upon formally by various organizations or are informal in nature.

crossposting Posting to several USENET newsgroups at one time.

CRTC Canadian Radio-television and Telecommunications Commission.

dedicated access A full-time connection to the Internet through your corporate network.

dedicated ISDN See ISDN

dial-up access Casual or temporary access to the Internet using a modem.

dial-up ISDN See ISDN

DNS Domain Name Service, a large, globally distributed database found throughout the Internet that provides a route to each organization on the Internet.

Domain Name System Permits each computer on the Internet to be reached by a simple name rather than just by an IP address.

domain registration The process of registering a domain name on the Internet.

e-mail address The term used to describe the address you input to reach someone through e-mail on the Internet.

e-mail filter A program that presorts your e-mail based on parameters you have established. E-mail filters are a very convenient way of dealing with large quantities of e-mail.

electronic mailing list A collection of e-mail addresses. Members use the mailing list as a quick method of distributing information or to ask a question of other mailing list members.

encoded An enclosure or computer file that is to be included in an e-mail message is "encoded" so that it can be sent through e-mail.

encryption Encryption is the capability of turning information into a special encoded format that can only be read by providing a special "key." Information on the Internet is sometimes encrypted in order to ensure the security of that information as it is sent through the network.

Error 404 A common message found on the Web. Information previously found at a specific address is no longer there, or some type of error has occurred in accessing that particular Web page.

FAQs Frequently asked questions, a document summarizing questions that are asked frequently. FAQs on a variety of topics can be found in USENET newsgroups and in many other areas of the Internet.

Finger A program used to find out the status of particular users of the Internet. It is also used on occasion to permit you to find out information from particular computers on the network.

firewall If you have linked your corporate network directly to the Internet, you put in place a firewall, a system that protects your network from unauthorized access by people on the Internet.

flaming The tendency for someone to quickly key an e-mail or USENET message in anger without thinking the message through.

frame relay An emerging communications technology that provides higher-speed access to the Internet.

FTP File transfer protocol, a program used to retrieve files and information from FTP sites available throughout the Internet.

GB Gigabyte, a measure of information on a computer, 1024 megabytes.

Gopher An older information retrieval system found on the Internet that permits access to a wide variety of information resources. Gopher is generally falling into disfavor with the massive growth of the World Wide Web.

GUI Graphical user interface, a term used to describe the interface found on Macintosh computers and in Microsoft Windows.

home page Introductory page of a Web site, that is the first page you see when you access a particular Web site.

host A computer connected to the Internet that "hosts" or holds information for a particular company or organization.

HTML Hypertext markup language, the language that is used to create documents that will be accessed through the World Wide Web.

HTTP Hypertext transfer protocol, the protocol that supports communications between a Web server and a Web client (browser).

HTTPS Secure transactions using the hypertext transfer protocol.

hypertext The term used to describe pages of information that are "interlinked" to many other pages of information.

Hytelnet A search tool found on the Internet.

IAB Internet Architecture Board, an organization involved in dealing with evolving standards concerning the global Internet.

Internet access provider An organization that sells, or provides at no charge, access to various Internet services. We use the more general term, Internet service providers, of which there are two types: Internet access providers and Internet presence providers.

Internet Explorer World Wide Web browser software made available by Microsoft as part of its Windows 95 program.

Internet presence providers Companies or organizations that assist others in gaining a presence on the Internet, particularly the World Wide Web.

InterNIC Internet Network Information Center, an organization based in the United States that processes domain name requests under the **.com**, **.org**, and other domain hierarchies.

IP address The "phone" number of a specific computer on the Internet.

IP Registry The organization responsible for allocating and managing IP addresses on a global basis.

IPng IP addresses "next generation," a newly emerging protocol that solves the potential problems that exist due to an upper limit in the number of possible IP addresses.

IRC Internet Relay Chat, a program that allows you to participate in on-line "discussions" in real time with other Internet users through your keyboard.

ISDN Integrated services digital network, a method of obtaining high-speed access to the Internet through the telephone network. ISDN access is available from many Internet service providers in Canada.

ISP Internet service provider, a company or organization that will provide you with an account with which you can dial into the Internet, or that will provide your organization with a link to the network through some type of permanent connection.

KB Kilobyte, a measure of information on a computer, 1024 bytes of information.

Kbps Kilobits per second, a measure of networking speed.

killfiles Also known as bozo filters. Killfiles automatically delete USENET postings or e-mail sent to you containing certain subjects or sent from certain people. Killfiles thus help you to screen out particular messages.

knowledge networking The ability to harness on-line information, either by regularly tracking information on a particular topic with USENET or by seeking information or answers to questions by discussing a topic with others on-line.

LAN Local area network, the term used to describe computers that have been linked together within an organization.

leased line One method of establishing a dedicated connection to the Internet.

listserv Also known as a list manager, a specialized piece of software that manages an electronic mailing list and processes your request to be added to or deleted from a mailing list.

mail robot A program that runs on an Internet server, and that takes apart incoming messages sent to the "robot" and mails back some type of response automatically.

mailing lists Another method where people on different computer systems can discuss particular topics or share information concerning specific issues. Similar to USENET.

MB Megabyte, a measure of information on a computer, 1024 kilobytes.

Mbps Megabits per second, a measure of networking speed.

MIME Multipurpose Internet multimedia extensions, a program used to convert a binary enclosure or file into a special format of text so that the binary enclosure or file can be sent through e-mail. Allows the binary enclosure or file to be transferred between different computer systems and platforms. MIME is emerging as the preferred form of sending files through the Internet and is replacing older methods such as binhex and uuencode.

modem A computing device that lets your PC "talk" to another computer.

moderated list A special type of electronic mailing list in which all messages are first sent to a moderator, who then determines if the message should be posted to the rest of the list, thus helping to ensure that the list stays on topic.

moderated newsgroup Similar to a moderated list in that a volunteer prereads all the postings to the specific newsgroup. Only those postings that fit the spirit of that particular newsgroup are then posted.

Mosaic World Wide Web browser software. Originally the "hottest" Web software, it has now been largely overtaken by Netscape, which has 70% of the browser software marketplace.

MSN Microsoft Network.

NCSA U.S. National Center for SuperComputing, the location where the original design and programming of Mosaic occurred.

netiquette Network etiquette. Term used to describe the unique on-line culture that exists within USENET and other areas of the Internet.

Netscape World Wide Web browser software from Netscape Communications Inc.

Netsurfers Those who surf the Internet.

newsgroups Topics within USENET.

newsreader software A program used to read information posted to USENET newsgroups and to post messages to those USENET newsgroups.

NNTP Network news transfer protocol, the program in use by Internet service providers that permits the global exchange of information through USENET.

Pegasus A public domain/shareware e-mail program.

postmaster A person who manages the link to Internet e-mail at an organization. In some cases, you can contact this individual if you are trying to locate a particular person's e-mail address at that organization.

PPP Point to point protocol, the computer protocol that manages a connection between your computer and the Internet. Usually used by those who access the Internet through a dial-up modem. PPP provides you with a "direct connection" to the Internet, so that you can use many of the more sophisticated client software programs that are available.

public domain programs Similar to shareware.

ROT-13 A very simple method of changing characters in a message so that politically incorrect or offensive information is not automatically seen within USENET.

router A computing device found throughout the Internet that "routes" information through the Internet based on TCP/IP addressing and domain names.

shareware Software that is available throughout the Internet. You can usually try out such software for free, and if you plan to use it, pay a fee in order to properly licence it.

shell account An account that leaves you at a UNIX prompt, once you have identified yourself with a user ID and password. Because you are not "directly connected" to the Internet, shell accounts are more difficult to use than SLIP/PPP accounts.

site A location on the Web that contains information in the form of text, images, sound, or video.

SLIP Serial line interface protocol. Similar to PPP, SLIP accounts are generally falling into disfavor as more ISPs begin to support PPP.

smileys Also called emoticons. Symbols that, when turned on their side, represent some type of character that expresses emotion. Used often within e-mail and USENET. Here is a smiley: :-)

SMTP Simple mail transfer protocol, the software that defines how messages should be sent between different computers on the Internet.

sound card A device in your computer that allows you to listen to computer sound files, such as those you might retrieve through the Internet.

sound player A program that plays a sound file.

spiders A computer program that "travels" throughout the World Wide Web on a regular basis and discovers information, sites, topics, etc. The spider then builds an index that you can query. A good example of such a "spider" and index is found with OpenText, which provides a Web index at **http://www.opentext.com**.

surfing Traveling from site to site on the World Wide Web.

TCP/IP Transmission control protocol/Internet protocol, the protocol at the heart of the global Internet. All computers directly linked to the Internet "talk" TCP/IP and hence can link to all other computers linked to the Internet around the world.

Telnet An "older" Internet application used to access other computers on the Internet. Today, it is the primary method of accessing library catalogues on the Internet. Otherwise, Telnet is not often used due to the explosive growth of the World Wide Web.

UNIX A powerful, "multitasking" system that permits one computer to do many things at once. The operating system found on many servers throughout the global Internet.

unmoderated list An electronic mailing list in which any message sent to the mailing list is automatically sent to all members of the list.

unmoderated newsgroup Anyone can post information to these newsgroups on the USENET as long as they stick to the specified topic.

URL Uniform resource locator, the common method now used to describe the address for Web sites, gopher sites, FTP sites, and other information sites on the Internet; for example, the URL of the Web site for the *Canadian Internet Handbook* is **http://www.csi.nb.ca/handbook/**.

USENET A global system found within the Internet which is used for the exchange of information on thousands of topics.

UUCP UNIX to UNIX copy protocol, a store and forward file transfer utility found within most UNIX systems and used by some individuals to retrieve and send their electronic mail and USENET news.

uuencoded A program used to convert a binary enclosure or file into a special format of text so that the binary enclosure or file can be sent through e-mail. Allows the binary enclosure or file to be transferred between different computer systems and platforms. Falling into disfavor with the increased usage of MIME.

viewer A program that is used with the World Wide Web in order to "view" special information types, such as video, specialized images, or sound and audio files.

VRML Virtual reality modeling language, an emerging technology that permits people to browse through three-dimensional Web sites.

Web server A computer running the HTTP protocol, which can be accessed by Web clients.

Web site A location on the Internet containing information in HTML format, so that it can be accessed using a program such as Netscape or Mosaic.

WHOIS server A simple program that lets you query the name of an organization or individual somewhere on the Internet.

World Wide Web Also known as the Web. A database or server application that contains information that can be accessed with special browser software such as Netscape. A WWW server can include text, sound, images, voice, and even video.

Yahoo One of the largest indexes to information found on the World Wide Web; it can be found at **http://www.yahoo.com**.

Index

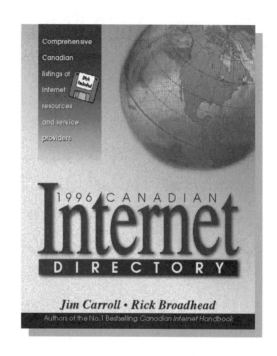

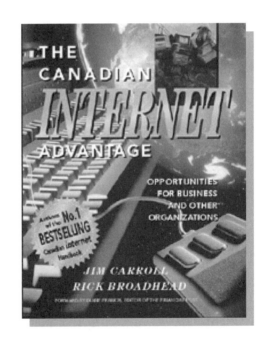

Jim Carroll ... In Person

Learn more about the INTERNET...
the opportunities and strategies

Jim Carroll, co-author of the *Canadian Internet Advantage*, the *Canadian Internet Directory* and the bestselling *Canadian Internet Handbook*, is a popular speaker and seminar leader, in high demand by people and companies seeking advice and strategies concerning the Internet and the global information highway. Jim provides seminars and keynote speeches throughout North America, and provides consulting services to companies and organizations wishing to take strategic advantage of the Internet.

He has provided high-profile speeches on the topic of the Internet to groups as diverse as the Young Presidents Organization, the Canadian Society of Magazine Editors, the Canadian Society of Association Executives, the Ontario Science Centre, the Treasury Management Association of Canada, Hewlett Packard, Ernst & Young, the British Columbia Ministry of Small Business, Tourism and Culture, the Toronto Board of Trade, the Canadian Institute of Chartered Accountants, IBM Canada, the Alberta Library Association, the Ontario Hospital Association, and the Propane Gas Association of Canada.

For more information concerning personal appearances by Jim Carroll, call:

THE NATIONAL SPEAKERS BUREAU

IN CANADA 1-800-661-4110

INTERNATIONAL AND USA 1-604-224-2384

FAX 1-604-224-8906

INTERNET
Theresa Gill (**tgill@nsb.com**), Cathy Worrall (**cworrall@nsb.com**), or
Michael Downes (**mdownes@nsb.com**)

Full details concerning speeches by Jim Carroll are also available on the
World Wide Web at **http://www.e-commerce.com/jacc.html**

To reach Mr. Carroll, call 905-855-2950
or fax 905-855-0269

*Internet Presentations
By Rick Broadhead*

Rick Broadhead, co-author of the *Canadian Internet Advantage,* the *Canadian Internet Directory* and the national bestseller *Canadian Internet Handbook*, provides Internet seminars and Internet consulting to organizations across Canada. He has been a speaker at conferences and seminars across the country, and has made presentations on the Internet for a wide range of government organizations, not-for-profit organizations, professional associations, and businesses in Canada. Rick has also taught a course on Internet business strategy at York University's Downtown Management Centre in Toronto.

He has addressed organizations such as the Canadian Football League, the Design Exchange, the Financial Management Institute of Canada, the Ontario Ministry of Economic Development and Trade, the Municipal Information Systems Association, Credit Union Central of Canada (Canadian Conference for Credit Union Executives), the International Association of Business Communicators, the Ontario Society for Training and Development, the City of North Bay, the City of Kanata, the Instrument Society of America, the University of Alberta, and the Canadian Information Processing Society.

In 1995, Rick was commissioned by VISA International to prepare an article on the strategic implications of the Internet for financial institutions worldwide. Rick is a contributing author to a nationally syndicated newspaper column on the Internet and is an authority on the Internet in Canada.

For further information about an Internet presentation for your organization or conference, please contact Rick Broadhead using any of the methods below:

TELEPHONE: 416-487-5220
FAX: 416-440-0175
E-MAIL: rickb@inforamp.net